delirium
delusional disorder
mood disorder
organic mental disorder NOS
Sedative, hypnotic, or anxiolytic
intoxication
Uncomplicated sedative, hypnotic, or anxiolytic
withdrawal
withdrawal delirium
amnestic disorder
Other or unspecified psychoactive substance
intoxication
withdrawal
delirium
dementia
amnestic disorder
delusional disorder
hallucinosis
mood disorder
anxiety disorder
personality disorder
organic mental disorder NOS

Organic Mental Disorders associated with Axis III
physical disorders or conditions, or whose etiology
is unknown.
Delirium
Dementia
Amnestic disorder
Organic delusional disorder
Organic hallucinosis
Organic mood disorder
Organic anxiety disorder
Organic personality disorder
Organic mental disorder

PSYCHOACTIVE SUBSTANCE USE DISORDERS

Alcohol
dependence
abuse
Amphetamine or similarly acting sympathomimetic
dependence
abuse
Cannabis
dependence
abuse
Cocaine
dependence
abuse
Hallucinogen
dependence
abuse

Inhalant
dependence
abuse
Nicotine
dependence
Opioid
dependence
abuse
Phencyclidine (PCP) or similarly acting arylcyclohexylamine
dependence
abuse
Sedative, hypnotic, or anxiolytic
dependence
abuse
Polysubstance dependence
Psychoactive substance dependence NOS
Psychoactive substance abuse NOS

SCHIZOPHRENIA

Types: catatonic
disorganized
paranoid
undifferentiated
residual

DELUSIONAL (PARANOID) DISORDER

Delusional (Paranoid) disorder
Types: erotomanic
grandiose
jealous
persecutory
somatic
unspecified

PSYCHOTIC DISORDERS NOT ELSEWHERE CLASSIFIED

Brief reactive psychosis
Schizophreniform disorder
Schizoaffective disorder
Induced psychotic disorder
Psychotic disorder NOS (Atypical psychosis)

MOOD DISORDERS

Bipolar Disorders
Bipolar disorder
Cyclothymia
Bipolar disorder NOS

Depressive Disorders
Major Depression
Dysthymia (or Depressive neurosis)
Depressive disorder NOS

ABNORMAL PSYCHOLOGY

Spencer A. Rathus
Jeffrey S. Nevid

St. John's University

Prentice Hall, Englewood Cliffs, New Jersey 07632

Library of Congress Cataloging-in-Publication Data

Rathus, Spencer A.
    Abnormal psychology / Spencer A. Rathus, Jeffrey S. Nevid.
        p.   cm.
    Includes bibliographical references and index.
    ISBN 0–13–005216–7 (student text)   —ISBN 0–13–005224–8
(instructor's edition)
    1. Psychology, Pathological.   2. Psychiatry.   I. Nevid, Jeffrey
S.   II. Title.
    [DNLM: 1. Mental Disorders.   2. Psychopathology.   WM 100 R235]
RC454.R35   1991
616.89—dc20
DNLM/DLC
for Library of Congress   90–7909
                                                              CIP

Editorial/production supervision: Virginia L. McCarthy
Interior and cover design: Meryl Poweski
Page layout: Meryl Poweski
Acquisition editor: Susan Finnemore
Photo editor: Lorinda Morris-Nantz
Photo researcher: June Whitworth
Cover photo researcher: Lois Fichner-Rathus
Cover art: Photograph of French sculptor
   Jacques Villon's studio by Alexander
   Liberman, 1954. © Alexander Liberman.
Prepress buyer: Debbie Kesar
Manufacturing buyer: Mary Ann Gloriande

This book is dedicated to
Judith Wolf-Nevid
          &
Lois Fichner-Rathus

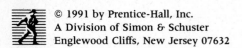

© 1991 by Prentice-Hall, Inc.
A Division of Simon & Schuster
Englewood Cliffs, New Jersey 07632

Printed in the United States of America
10   9   8   7   6   5   4   3   2

ISBN 0-13-005216-7 (Student Text)
ISBN 0-13-005224-8 (Instructor's Edition)

Prentice-Hall International (UK) Limited, *London*
Prentice-Hall of Australia Pty. Limited, *Sydney*
Prentice-Hall Canada Inc., *Toronto*
Prentice-Hall Hispanoamericana, S.A., *Mexico*
Prentice-Hall of India Private Limited, *New Delhi*
Prentice-Hall of Japan, Inc., *Tokyo*
Simon & Schuster Asia Pte. Ltd., *Singapore*
Editora Prentice-Hall do Brasil, Ltda., *Rio de Janeiro*

Contents

4

Stress-Related Disorders   118

5

Psychological Factors and Health   150

6

Anxiety Disorders   190

7

Dissociative and Somatoform
Disorders   224

8

Mood Disorders and Suicide   248

9

Disorders of Personality and Impulse
Control   290

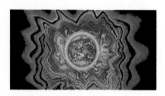

10

Substance Abuse and Dependence   328

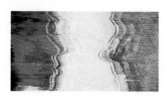

11

Sexual Disorders and Variations in Sexual Behavior   372

12

Schizophrenia and Delusional (Paranoid) Disorder   412

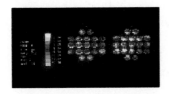

13

Organic Disorders and Abnormal
Behavior   454

14

Developmental Disorders   482

15

Methods of Therapy and Treatment   524

16

Contemporary and Legal Issues   560

Preface

The field of abnormal psychology is a moving target. At any moment, new scientific findings are being reported, new assessment techniques are being devised, and innovative methods of treatment are emerging. Just in recent years, for example,

Advances in brain imaging techniques have enabled researchers to probe the structures and functioning of the brain with greater precision than ever before, revealing new evidence of brain abnormalities in schizophrenia (see Chapter 12).

Developments in the use of cognitive techniques of assessment have allowed researchers to more clearly distinguish the thinking patterns of depressed and nondepressed groups and differentiate between the automatic thought patterns of depressed and anxious people (see Chapters 3 and 8).

Research findings have sparked new controversies, including whether or not post-partum depression is a distinct form of depression (see Chapter 8) and whether or not Type A behavior pattern increases CHD risk (see Chapter 5).

The importance of psychological factors in physical health has given impetus to the development of psychoneuroimmunology, with exciting advances being reported almost daily in the relationships between stress and immunological functioning (see Chapter 5).

All in all, the authors of textbooks in abnormal psychology face an enormous challenge in keeping up with the literature and integrating the many important research findings that shape our present understandings of abnormal behavior patterns and their treatment. When we undertook the task of writing this text, it was with the recognition that users of the book would expect us to present material that reflects the "state of the art" and not a rehashing of material gleaned from our earlier teaching experiences. Toward this end, we have incorporated more than 1000 references to scientific findings from the literature since 1985. But a textbook is more than a compendium of recent developments in a field of study. It is a repository of accumulated knowledge and thinking that has defined and shaped the field of study over the years.

Perhaps more than anything else, a textbook is a teaching device—a means of presenting material to students in a way that best encourages understanding and critical thinking. We approach this task by adopting a style of writing that speaks to the reader in a clear expository style, explaining complex material in understandable terms and providing ample examples that assist comprehension. We also go further toward encouraging interest and student involvement in the material by incorporating certain pedagological features (such as a listing of learning objectives and "Truth-or-Fiction" statements in each chapter) and student-oriented features, such as questionnaires, thought-provoking boxed inserts, and resource materials that highlight special concerns and applications (e.g., "Rape Prevention," "How to Handle Menstrual Discomfort," "Suicide Prevention," "Ways of Decreasing Type A Behavior," and "Coping with a Panic Attack").

Because the publication of articles and books lags behind their completion, a textbook on abnormal psychology chances being out of date the moment it is published. Yet our motives for writing a new textbook in this already overcrowded field were compelling:

1. **The significance of the field.** The problems discussed in this book are of immense importance. They address personal, social, financial, and political crises and challenges, many of which are painful, frightening, and confusing. They include problems that are all-too pervasive, such as headaches, sexual dysfunctions, obesity, and alcohol and substance abuse; problems that are relatively infrequent but have profound impact, such as schizophrenia and bipolar disorder; and problems that are exotic and challenge present understandings, such as multiple personality disorder and Münchausen syndrome. Embarking upon this project we felt that many contemporary issues were left largely unexplored in existing texts, such as the outcomes of deinstitutionalization, the related issue of the plight of the psychiatric homeless population, and the psychological aspects of AIDS and the role of psychologists in meeting the challenge of the AIDS epidemic. We also include special attention to the problem of post-traumatic stress disorder and the Vietnam veteran.

2. **The pervasiveness of abnormal behaviors.** Abnormal behaviors are not the problem of a few.

They affect all of us, or nearly all of us, each day of our lives. The majority of us will experience one or more of the problems discussed in this book at some time or another, or will have a friend or loved one who will. And even if these problems were to lie completely outside our personal ken, we would still be touched by society's response—or lack of response—to them.

3. **The need for a fresh look at the boundaries between normal and abnormal behaviors.** We wished to take a critical look at standard views on the demarcations between normal and abnormal behaviors. As with hyperactivity and adjustment problems, the borders are sometimes blurry. As pointed out in Chapter 4, if students are having difficulty concentrating on schoolwork because of the break-up of a recent romance, they may be diagnosed as suffering from a "mental disorder," according to the Diagnostic and Statistical Manual of Mental Disorders (DSM-III-R) of the American Psychiatric Association. We address questions of boundaries between normal and abnormal behavior by helping students recognize the criteria and judgments that are involved in determining abnormality, and the controversies that have ensued concerning the labeling of certain behavioral patterns (like "Late Luteal Phase Dysphoric Disorder") as mental disorders.

4. **The need for a psychological perspective.** We felt strongly that a textbook with an unbiased and empirical *psychological* perspective was needed—one that embraced the broad spectrum of "abnormal behaviors" and their "features" or "characteristics," not with "mental illnesses" and their "symptoms." While we do not wish to war with conventional medical terminology, neither do we use it pervasively and uncritically. (If we wish to encourage students to separate descriptions from inferences, as we suggest in Chapter 1, it seems unsuitable to automatically use terms like "illness" and "symptom" to refer to abnormal behavior patterns). While we highlight the importance of research findings concerning possible roles of biological factors in many patterns of abnormal behavior, we do not wish to suggest uncritical acceptance of the medical model by adopting its terminology. Moreover, we recognize that understandings of phenomena as complex as abnormal behavior patterns must take into account interactive, multiple causes that involve psychological, social, and biological factors.

5. **The need for a textbook whose coverage extends beyond the DSM.** We believe that the issues that concern the psychology of abnormal behaviors are much broader than those touched upon by the DSM-III-R. Although our coverage of the diagnostic categories described in the DSM-III-R is comprehensive, we are not contained by them. We also focus on the psychological factors that are involved in personal and social issues such as AIDS, rape, premenstrual syndrome, pornography, obesity, incest, and battered women, although these pressing human concerns find little or no representation in the DSM-III-R.

6. **Need for coverage of types of research methods and ways of appraising the validity of research.** We felt that students should not only be exposed to the different methods of research, but should also be provided with a way of appraising the validity of experimental studies. In Chapter 1, we introduce students to the concepts of internal, external, and construct validity with illustrations that suggest how an uncritical reading of research findings can lead to spurious conclusions. In Chapter 3, we cover issues relating to the reliability and validity of techniques of assessment. Later in the text (Chapter 15), we highlight issues involved in conducting research on psychotherapy effectiveness and expose students to the findings that derive from several of the major meta-analyses in the field.

FEATURES OF THE TEXTBOOK

Textbooks walk balance beams, as it were, and they can fall off in three directions, not just two. Textbooks, that is, must do justice to their subject matter while they also meet the needs of instructors and students. In subject matter, this textbook is comprehensive, providing depth and breadth. It contains full coverage of the history of societal responses to abnormal behaviors, historic and contemporary models of abnormal behaviors, methods of assessment, psychological and biological models of treatment, contemporary issues, the comprehensive range of problem behaviors set forth in the DSM-III-R, and a number of other behavioral problems that entail psychological factors—most notably in the interfaces between psychology and health.

This book also contains a number of features that are intended to keep it "on the beam" as a vehicle for instruction and learning:

The Sixteen-Chapter Format

Although the coverage is comprehensive, the material is organized into a sixteen-chapter format so that instructors will be able to teach approximately a chapter a week.

Truth-or-Fiction? Items

Each chapter begins with a number of "Truth-or-Fiction?" items that are intended to whet students' appetites for the subject matter within the chapter. We have used such items in our other textbooks for many years, and instructors and students have repeatedly reported that they are effective ways of stimulating and challenging students. Some of the items are intended to be generally motivating ("Innocent people were drowned in medieval times as a way of certifying that they were not possessed by the Devil") or to highlight interesting research findings ("Cycles of dieting and regaining lost weight make it progressively more difficult to take off extra pounds"). Others are specifically written to encourage students to take a scientific look at the subject matter by questioning folklore and preconceptions ("People can recognize when their blood pressure is high," and "There is a thin line between creativity and insanity.").

Learning Objectives

Following the "Truth-or-Fiction?" items is a double-duty list of learning objectives. Why "double-duty"? First, these objectives are organized according to the major headings within the chapter, so they provide a means of organizing the chapter according to major headings. Second, they provide students with concrete educational goals for each chapter.

Truth-or-Fiction-Revisited Sections

The "Truth-or-Fiction?" items are revisited in these sections at the points in the text where the topics are discussed. Students are thus given rapid feedback concerning the accuracy of their preconceptions in the light of the material being addressed.

"A Closer Look" Inserts

These sections include applications, focused discussions on controversial issues (e.g., "AIDS and the Duty to Warn," "Why Do Women Stay in Abusive Relationships?," "Late-Luteal Phase Disorder?"), and information on "state of the art" techniques of assessment (e.g., advances in brain imaging techniques, biological markers for depression, and measurement of sexual arousal).

Self-Scoring Questionnaires

Self-scoring questionnaires ranging from the "Locus of Control Scale" to the "Fear of Fat Scale" involve students in the discussion at hand and permit them to evaluate their own behavior. We have not included questionnaires whose results might be particularly upsetting to students. We have screened the questionnaires to ensure that they will provide students with useful information to reflect upon as well as serve as a springboard for class discussion.

Chapter Summaries

Chapter summaries are organized according to the major headings within the chapters. Students who use the SQ3R method may be advised by their instructors to read them before the chapters as a way of surveying the material and helping form questions to guide their reading.

Glossary

Key terms are boldfaced in the text and defined in a comprehensive glossary. Note that the origins of key terms are often discussed. By learning to attend to commonly found Greek and Latin word origins, students can acquire skills that will help them decipher the meanings of new words. These decoding skills are a valuable objective for general education as well as a specific asset for the study of abnormal psychology.

ANCILLARIES

No matter how comprehensive a textbook is, today's instructors and students require a complete teaching package to advance teaching and comprehension. *Abnormal Psychology* is accompanied by the following ancillaries:

Instructor's Edition—Designed to provide you with maximal assistance in preparing your class, each chapter of the Instructor's Edition includes: film and video descriptions, a research list of film and video distributors, abstracts of recent research articles to keep your lectures on the cutting edge of the field, activities and discussion topics, suggested further readings, chapter summary, and key terms.

Test Item File—The Test Item File contains over 1600 questions—both conceptual and applied—with page references to the text. Our multiple choice, true-false, and essay questions range in level of difficulty, so you have a wide variety to choose from.

Prentice Hall DataManager—Unmatched by any other computerized testing software, Prentice Hall DataManager is a state-of-the-art classroom management system. It contains three key components that will help you efficiently organize vital information: Test Manager, Grade Manager, and Study Manager. All components are easy to learn and use.

Telephone Test Preparation Service—Select up to 200 questions from the Test Item File and call us toll free at (800) 842-2958. Prentice Hall prepares the test (and an alternate version if requested) on bond paper or a ditto master within 48 hours and mails it together with a separate answer key directly to the instructor.

MicroTest III, Macintosh Version—MicroTest III is designed to streamline the test design process and offer greater flexibility in the actual test generation. Incorporating questions taken directly from the text or from your own files, MicroTest III enables you to create, refine, update, store, and print a variety of tests.

Study Guide and Workbook—Each chapter includes a chapter review, learning objectives, key concepts/terms with definitions, self-tests including multiple choice and true-false questions, and activities to aid the student.

Handouts and Transparency Masters—Involve your students and stimulate classroom discussion! These versatile questionnaires and activities can be handed out in class or turned into overhead transparencies.

Prentice Hall Transparencies for Abnormal Psychology, Series I—To support material covered in the book and augment in-class discussions, we offer 30 full color transparencies exploring topics such as ''Symptoms of Depression,'' ''Reactions to Stress,'' ''Sex Differences in Personality Disorders,'' ''Varying Degrees of Paranoid Thinking,'' and many more.

Video Offer—We are pleased to offer a wide selection of videos on psychology for dynamic classroom viewing. The videocassettes, which are free to keep, are available to any school which orders over 100 copies or more of Rathus and Nevid's **Abnormal Psychology.**

Film and Video Guide—Here in one compact source are valuable suggestions for films and videos appropriate for classroom viewing. This guide provides summaries, discussion questions, and rental sources for each film recommended.

A Contemporary View: Abnormal Psychology—A collection of recent articles from *The New York Times*, provided directly to your students. See the end of this preface for details.

ACKNOWLEDGMENTS

We noted that the field of abnormal psychology is a moving target. We are deeply indebted to a number of talented individuals who helped us hold our camera steady, focus in on the salient features of our subject matter, and develop our snapshots through prose.

First, our professional colleagues, who reviewed our manuscript at various stages in its development and made invaluable suggestions that helped us further refine and strengthen the material:

Bernard S. Gorman, Ph.D.
Nassau Community College
and Hofstra University Doctoral Programs
William G. Iacono
University of Minnesota
Robert Lavallee, Ph.D.
St. Michael's College
Robin J. Lewis, Ph.D.
Old Dominion University
Robert J. McMahon, Ph.D.
University of Washington
Caton F. Roberts, Ph.D.
State University of New York, Buffalo
Jerome Small, Ph.D.
Youngstown State University
Robert M. Tipton, Ph.D.
Virginia Commonwealth University

Second, but by no means second-rate, are the publishing professionals at Prentice Hall. Susan Finnemore, psychology editor, acquired the project for Prentice Hall (and for us) and was a source of inspiration, encouragement, and support since its conception. Leslie Carr, developmental editor, helped organize and distill the suggestions of our colleagues into a well-organized and cohesive structure. Betty Gatewood is also to be credited for her role in the developmental process. She did an admirable job of placing herself in the roles of instructor and student in helping us examine our coverage more critically and fine-tune our wording to meet the needs of both instructors and students. Virginia McCarthy, the project manager, carried out all the tasks necessary to transform typed pages into a bound book and she did so within an extraordinarily collapsed time frame. Meryl Poweski designed the book and is thus responsible for the physical appearance of the work you are now holding in your hands. Lori Morris-Nantz researched the photos within the textbook, but Lois Fichner-Rathus researched the cover photograph. We also wish to thank our editor in chief, Charlyce Jones Owen, for her support in this project. Charlyce was involved with our first textbook, so it seems fitting that she is playing a role in the production and marketing of this—our finest collaborative effort.

Third, we wish to thank Dr. Rafael Javier of St. John's University for his review of several passages relating to psychodynamic theory.

Fourth, we wish to thank Vincent Tsushima, Pat Adams, and Barrie Franklin for their assistance with the library research that helped make this book as comprehensive in its coverage of recent scientific findings as possible.

Finally, we especially wish to thank the two people without whose inspiration and support this effort would never have materialized or been carried through to completion, Judith Wolf-Nevid and Lois Fichner-Rathus.

Both authors made major primary contributions to this project. The order of their names was decided at random.

J.S.N.
New York, New York

S.A.R.
Summit, New Jersey

ABOUT THE AUTHORS

Spencer A. Rathus received his Ph.D. from the State University of New York at Albany in 1972. He is on the psychology faculty at St. John's University. His areas of interest include psychological assessment, cognitive behavior therapy, and deviant behavior. Dr. Rathus is the author of the Rathus Assertiveness Schedule as well as several books, including PSYCHOLOGY, BEHAVIOR THERAPY, and PSYCHOLOGY AND THE CHALLENGES OF LIFE. The latter two titles were co-authored by Dr. Jeffrey Nevid.

Jeffrey S. Nevid is a professor of psychology at St. John's University, where he directs the Doctoral Program in Clinical Psychology. He received his Ph.D. in clinical psychology from the State University of New York at Albany, and he has published numerous articles in the areas of clinical and community psychology and health psychology, as well as training models in clinical psychology and methodological issues in clinical research. He has earned a Diplomate in Clinical Psychology from the American Board of Professional Psychology and has served on the editorial board of the *Journal of Consulting and Clinical Psychology*.

THE NEW YORK TIMES and PRENTICE HALL are sponsoring A CONTEMPORARY VIEW: ABNORMAL PSYCHOLOGY, a program designed to enhance student access to current information of relevance in the classroom.

Through this program, the core subject matter provided in the text is supplemented by a collection of time-sensitive articles from one of the world's most distinguished newspapers, THE NEW YORK TIMES. These articles demonstrate the vital, ongoing connection between what is learned in the classroom and what is happening in the world around us. To enjoy the wealth of information in THE NEW YORK TIMES daily, a reduced subscription rate is available. For information, call toll-free: 1-800-631-1222.

PRENTICE HALL and THE NEW YORK TIMES are proud to co-sponsor A CONTEMPORARY VIEW. We hope it will make the reading of both textbooks and newspapers a more dynamic, involving process.

1 What Is Abnormal Psychology?

- ■ ____ Abnormal behavior affects virtually everyone.
- ■ ____ Unusual behavior is abnormal.
- ■ ____ Behavior that is normal in one culture may be regarded as abnormal in another.
- ■ ____ Innocent people were drowned in medieval times as a way of certifying that they were not possessed by the Devil.
- ■ ____ Many of the nation's homeless people are discharged mental patients.
- ■ ____ In order to carry out valid research, it may be necessary at times to keep people unaware of the treatments they receive.
- ■ ____ Surveys of several million Americans may not represent the general population.
- ■ ____ Case studies have been conducted on people who have been dead for hundreds of years.

LEARNING OBJECTIVES

When you have completed your study of Chapter 1, you should be able to:

WHAT IS ABNORMAL BEHAVIOR? (pp. 2–5)

1. Discuss six criteria that are used to define abnormal behavior.

HISTORY OF CONCEPTS OF ABNORMAL BEHAVIOR (pp. 5–18)

2. Recount the history of the demonological approach to abnormal behavior, referring to ancient and medieval times.

3. Describe the contributions of Hippocrates, Galen, Weyer, Pasteur, Griesinger, and Kraepelin to the development of medical science and thinking.

4. Describe the development of treatment centers for abnormal behavior from asylums through the mental hospital.

5. Discuss the reform movement and the use of moral therapy, focusing on the roles of Pussin, Pinel, Rush, and Dix.

6. Discuss the factors associated with the current exodus from mental hospitals in the United States.

7. Discuss various contemporary concepts or models of abnormal behavior.

RESEARCH METHODS IN ABNORMAL PSYCHOLOGY (pp. 18–30)

8. Discuss the objectives of a scientific approach to abnormal behavior.

9. Describe the steps involved in the scientific method.

10. Discuss the value and limitations of the naturalistic-observation method.

11. Discuss the importance of drawing representative samples from target populations.

12. Discuss the value and limitations of correlational research.

13. Discuss longitudinal research.

14. Describe the purpose and features of the experimental method.

15. Explain ways in which experimenters control for subjects' and researchers' expectations.

16. Describe three types of experimental validity.

17. Discuss the value and limitations of quasi-experiments.

18. Discuss the value of, and sources of error in, the epidemiological method.

19. Discuss the value and limitations of the case-study method.

20. Provide examples of single-case experimental designs and explain how they help researchers overcome some of the limitations of the case-study method.

A bnormal behavior might seem the concern of a few. After all, only a minority of the population will ever be admitted to a psychiatric hospital. Most people never seek the help of a **psychologist** or **psychiatrist.** Only a few people plead not guilty to crimes on the grounds of insanity. Many of us have an "eccentric" relative, but few of us have relatives we would consider truly bizarre.

Yet the belief that abnormal behavior is a problem affecting only a few is incorrect. The truth of the matter is that abnormal behavior affects everyone in one way or another. If we confine our definition of abnormal behavior to traditional mental disorders—anxiety, depression, schizophrenia, abuse of alcohol and other drugs, and the like—perhaps one in three of us have been affected at one time or another (Robins et al., 1984). If we include sexual dysfunctions and difficulties adjusting to the demands of adulthood or life stress, many more are added. If we extend our definitions to include maladaptive or self-defeating behavior patterns like compulsive gambling and nicotine dependence in the form of habitual smoking, a clear majority of us are affected. We shall see that contemporary views of mental disorders include these and other categories that broaden the traditional definitions of abnormal behavior. And if we expand the meaning of "being affected" by these problems to the family members, friends, and fellow workers of those who are afflicted, and to those who foot the bill for mental health services in the form of taxes and health insurance premiums, virtually none of us remain uninvolved.

> **?** It is true that virtually everyone is affected by abnormal behavior, even if only a minority display traditional disorders such as anxiety, depression, and schizophrenia.

Abnormal psychology is the branch of the science of psychology that addresses the description, causes, and treatment of patterns of abnormal behavior.

In this chapter we first struggle with the challenging task of delineating just what is meant by abnormal behavior. We see that abnormal behavior is defined by several criteria and that throughout the course of history, and prehistory, abnormal behavior has been viewed from several different perspectives, or models. We follow the historic development of concepts of abnormal behavior and its treatment; we see that "treatment" too often meant what was done *to* people with abnormal behavior rather than *for* them. Finally, we review the ways in which psychologists and other scholars study abnormal behavior today.

WHAT IS ABNORMAL BEHAVIOR?

There are diverse patterns of abnormal behavior. Some are typified by anxiety or depression, but most of us become anxious or depressed from time to time, and our behavior is not deemed abnormal. It is normal to become anxious in anticipation of an important job interview or a final examination. It is appropriate to feel depressed when you've lost someone close to you or when you have failed at a test or on the job.

So when are emotions like anxiety and depression judged abnormal? One answer is that these feelings may be appraised as abnormal when they are not appropriate to the situation. It is normal, as noted, to feel down because of failure on a test, but not when one's grades are good or excellent. It is normal to feel anxious during an interview for graduate or professional school, but not whenever one enters a department store or boards a crowded elevator. Abnormal behavior may also be suggested by the magnitude of the problem. Although some anxiety is normal enough before a job interview, the feeling that one's heart is hammering away so relentlessly that it might leap from one's chest— and consequently cancelling the interview—is not. Nor

(a)

(b)

Negative emotions such as anxiety are considered abnormal when they are judged to be inappropriate to the situation. Anxiety is generally considered normal when it is experienced during a job interview (photo a) but abnormal if it is experienced whenever one boards a crowded elevator (photo b).

is it normal to feel so anxious in this situation that your clothing becomes soaked with perspiration.

Psychologists generally concur that behavior may be deemed abnormal when it meets some combination of these criteria:

1. *Behavior is unusual.* Behavior that is unusual is often considered abnormal. Only a few of us report seeing or hearing things that are not really there; "seeing things" and "hearing things" are almost always considered abnormal except, perhaps, in cases of religious experience (see Chapter 12). Becoming overcome with feelings of panic when entering a department store or when standing in a crowded elevator is also uncommon and considered abnormal. But uncommon behavior is not in itself abnormal. Only one person can hold the

record for swimming or running the fastest hundred meters. The record-holding athlete differs from you and us but, again, is not considered abnormal.

> **?** Unusual or statistically deviant behavior is not necessarily abnormal. Excellent behavior, for example, also deviates from the norm.

Thus, rarity or statistical deviance is not a sufficient basis for labeling behavior to be abnormal; nevertheless, it is one yardstick often used to judge abnormality.

2. *Behavior is socially unacceptable or violates social norms.* All societies have standards or norms that define the kinds of behaviors that are acceptable in given contexts. In our society, standing on a soapbox in a park and repeatedly shouting "Kill!" to passersby would be labeled abnormal; shouting "Kill!" in the grandstands at an important football game is usually within normal bounds, however tasteless it may seem. While the use of norms remains one of the important standards for defining abnormal behavior, we should be aware of some shortcomings of this definition.

One problem in basing the definition of abnormal behavior on social norms is that norms reflect relative standards, not universal truths. What is normal in one culture may be abnormal in another. For example, Americans who assume that strangers are devious and try to take advantage are usually regarded as distrustful, perhaps even **paranoid.** But such suspicions were justified among the Mundugumor, a tribe of cannibals studied by anthropologist Margaret Mead (1935). Within that culture, male strangers, even the male members of one's own family, *were* typically malevolent toward others.

> **?** Thus behavior that is deemed normal in one culture may be viewed as abnormal in another.

Clinicians need to weigh cultural differences in determining what is normal and abnormal. In the case of the Mundugumor, this need is more or less obvious. Sometimes, however, differences are more subtle. For example, what is seen as healthful, outspoken behavior by most American women might be interpreted as brazen behavior within Hispanic-American subcultures. Although many clinicians appear to consider clients' culture in evaluating abnormal behavior, little research has been conducted into the relationships between cultural factors and clinical judgments (Lopez & Hernandez, 1986).

Moreover, what strikes one generation as abnormal may be ordinary to another. Living together without

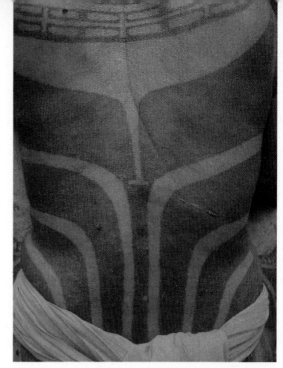

Behavior which is considered normal in one culture may be labeled abnormal in another. While full-body tatooing is an acceptable custom on the Pacific island of Yap, it may be labeled abnormal in Western cultures. But even in Western cultures, such practices may be common in certain subcultures.

being married (cohabitation) was nearly unheard of as recently as the 1950s but has become commonplace today. Many people today argue that contemporary societal norms should include homosexuality as a normal variation in behavior.

Another concern with basing normality on compliance with social norms is the tendency to brand nonconformists as mentally disturbed. Behavior we do not like or understand may come to be regarded as "sick."

3. *Perception or interpretation of reality is faulty.* Normally speaking, our sensory systems and cognitive processes permit us to form accurate mental representations of the environment. But seeing things and hearing voices that are not present are considered **hallucinations,** which are often signs of mental disorder. Similarly, holding unfounded ideas or **delusions,** such as **ideas of persecution** that the CIA, the mafia, or the communists are "out to get" one may be regarded as signs of mental disturbance—unless, of course, they *are.* (A former Secretary of State is credited with having remarked that he might, indeed, be paranoid; his paranoia, however, did not mean that he was without enemies.)

It is normal in American society to say that one "talks" to God through prayer; however, if a person claims to have literally seen God or heard the voice of God—as opposed to, say, being divinely inspired—he or she may be regarded as mentally disturbed.

3

4.   *The person is in severe personal distress.* States of personal distress caused by troublesome emotions, such as anxiety, fear, or depression, may be considered abnormal. As noted earlier, however, anxiety and depression are sometimes appropriate responses to one's situation. Real threats and losses occur from time to time, and *lack* of emotional response to them would be regarded as abnormal. Appropriate feelings of distress are not considered abnormal unless they become prolonged or persist long after the source of anguish has been removed (after most people would have adjusted) or if they are so intense that they impair the individual's ability to function.

5.   *Behavior is maladaptive or self-defeating.* Behavior that leads to unhappiness rather than self-fulfillment can be regarded as abnormal. Behavior that limits our ability to function in expected roles, or to adapt to our environments, may also be considered abnormal. According to these criteria, persistent alcohol consumption that impairs one's health or social and occupational functioning may be viewed as abnormal.

Agoraphobic behavior, characterized by intense fear of venturing into public places, is abnormal in that it is uncommon. But people who show such behavior may also be unable to fulfill their work and family responsibilities; so agoraphobia is maladaptive as well. People with faulty perceptions of reality may also be unable to meet day-to-day responsibilities to their employers and families. Hallucinations or delusions may preoccupy or confuse them when they should be focusing on the job.

6.   *Behavior is dangerous.* Behavior that is dangerous to oneself or other people may be considered abnormal. Here, too, the social context is crucial. In wartime, people who sacrifice themselves or charge the enemy with little apparent concern for their own safety may be characterized as courageous, heroic, and patriotic. But people who threaten or attempt suicide because of the

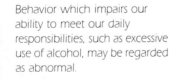

Behavior which impairs our ability to meet our daily responsibilities, such as excessive use of alcohol, may be regarded as abnormal.

pressures of civilian life are usually considered abnormal.

Football and hockey players, even adolescent boys who occasionally get into altercations, may be normal enough. Given the cultural demands of the sports, unaggressive football and hockey players would not last in the college or professional ranks. But individuals who are involved in frequent unsanctioned fights may be regarded as abnormal. Physically aggressive behavior is most often maladaptive in modern life. Moreover, outside the contexts of sports and warfare, physical aggression is discouraged as a way of resolving interpersonal conflicts—although it is by no means uncommon.

Abnormal behavior thus has multiple definitions. In most cases, a combination of these criteria is used to define abnormality. Some criteria may be weighed more heavily than others, depending on the situation. Let us consider some **cases** and see how they can advance our understanding of the kinds of behaviors that are considered abnormal:

■ It was about 2:00 A.M. when the police brought Margaret to the Emergency Room. She looked to be about 45, her hair was matted and uncombed, her clothing disheveled. Her face was expressionless, fixed in a blank stare. She clutched a clove of garlic in her right hand. She did not respond to the interviewer's questions: "Do you know where you are? Can you tell me your name? Can you tell me if anything is bothering you?"

The police officers filled in the details. Margaret had been found meandering along the painted line that divided the main street through town, apparently oblivious to the cars which swerved around her. She was waving the clove of garlic in front of her. She said nothing to the officers when they arrived on the scene, but she offered no resistance.

Margaret was admitted to the hospital and brought to the psychiatric ward. The next morning, she was brought before the day staff, still clutching the clove of garlic, and interviewed by the chief psychiatrist. She said little but her intentions could be pieced together from mumbled fragments. Margaret said something about "devils" who were trying to "rob" her mind. The garlic was meant to protect her. She had decided that the only way to rid the town of the "devils" that hounded her was to walk down the main street, waving the garlic in front of her.

Margaret would become well known to the hospital. This was but one of a series of **psychotic** episodes.

The Authors' Files ■

Margaret's behavior met several of the criteria for abnormality: For one thing, it is statistically deviant—rare!—for a person to be ambling along the divider in a busy main street, sweeping the area of supernatural forces. Margaret's behavior was socially unacceptable or deviant, and indeed unlawful. It was also maladaptive—dangerous to herself and to those who swerved to avoid her. Moreover, she showed faulty perception of reality. It is normal within various religious perspectives to believe that a Devil may be waging a cosmic conflict with God—with humankind in the middle. But it is abnormal to believe that one is personally besieged by devils. Moreover, her thoughts were jumbled and confused, impairing her ability to sift through and evaluate the welter of frightening beliefs and perceptions. Margaret came to be diagnosed as schizophrenic (see Chapter 12).

Phil, unlike Margaret, was not out of touch with reality. Still, his behavior may be considered abnormal:

■ Phil was 42, a police photographer. It was his job to take pictures at crime scenes. "Pretty grisly stuff," he admitted, "corpses and all." Phil was married and had two teenage sons. He sought a psychological consultation because he was bothered by fears of being confined in enclosed spaces—**claustrophobia.** Many situations evoked his fears. He was terrified of becoming trapped in an elevator and took the stairs whenever possible. He felt uncomfortable sitting in the back seat of a car. He had lately become fearful of flying, although in the past he had worked as a news cameraperson and would often fly to scenes of news events at a moment's notice—usually by helicopter.

"I guess I was younger then and more daring," he related. "Sometimes I would hang out of the helicopter to shoot pictures with no fear at all. But now, just thinking about flying makes my heart race. It's not that I'm afraid the plane will crash. I just start trembling when I think of them closing that door, trapping us inside. I can't tell you why."

The Authors' Files ■

Phil recognized that his fears exceeded a realistic appraisal of danger in the situations that evoked his fears. While he was not hampered by faulty perceptions of reality, his behavior could be considered abnormal on the basis of several other criteria listed earlier. Of primary concern were Phil's feelings of personal distress—his fear of enclosed spaces and the resulting limitations on his behavior. His fears also impaired his ability to carry out his occupational and familial responsibilities. The criterion of statistical infrequency might also be employed. Most people are not so fearful of confinement that they avoid flying or taking elevators.

Jessica, a 20-year-old communications major, engaged in a pattern of maladaptive, self-defeating behavior:

■ Jessica was engaged to be married in three months. There was one problem, she told the psychologist, "I have to stop bingeing and throwing up."

Jessica had kept a personal secret for the past three years. "I would go on binges, and then throw it all up. It made me feel like I was in control, but really I wasn't." To conceal her secret, she would lock herself in the

bathroom, run the water in the sink to mask the sounds, and induce vomiting. She would then clean up after herself and spray an air deodorant to mask any tell-tale odors.

"The only one who suspects," she said with embarrassment, "is my dentist. He said my teeth were beginning to decay from stomach acid."

Jessica was diagnosed as showing **bulimia nervosa,** an eating disorder characterized by recurrent cycles of bingeing and purging. Jessica decided that she wanted to overcome her problem before her marriage. "I don't want Ken [her fiancé] to find out," she explained. "I don't want to bring this into the marriage."

The Authors' Files ■

Jessica, like Phil, was personally distressed about her behavior. Her behavior was also self-defeating and physically harmful or dangerous: it was decaying her teeth and may have led to other, more serious health consequences (see Chapter 14). She also anticipated that her cycles of bingeing and purging would impair her forthcoming marriage.

So several criteria lead professionals to label behavior as abnormal. It is one thing to recognize and label behavior as abnormal; it is another to understand and explain it. Philosophers, physicians, natural scientists, and psychologists have used various approaches or **models** in the effort to explain abnormal behavior. Some approaches have been based on superstition; others have invoked religious explanations. Some current views are predominantly biological; others, psychological. Let us consider various historical and contemporary approaches to understanding abnormal behavior.

HISTORY OF CONCEPTS OF ABNORMAL BEHAVIOR

Throughout the history of Western culture, concepts of abnormal behavior have been shaped, to some degree, by the prevailing **world view** of the time. Throughout much of history, beliefs in supernatural forces, demons, and evil spirits held sway. Abnormal behavior was often taken as a sign of **possession.** In more modern times, the predominant—but by no means universal!—world view has shifted toward beliefs in science and reason. Abnormal behavior has come to be viewed as the product of physical and psychosocial factors, not demonic possession.

The Demonological Model

Let us begin our journey with an example from prehistory. Archaeologists have unearthed human skeletons from the Stone Age with egg-sized cavities in the skull. One interpretation of these holes is that our prehistoric

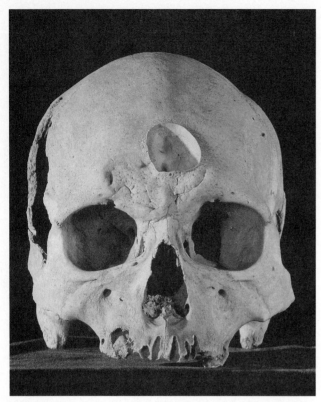

Trephining refers to a practice in some prehistoric cultures of chipping a hole into a person's skull. Some authorities speculate that the practice represented an ancient form of surgery. But it is also possible that it was intended to release demons that were believed responsible for aberrant behavior.

ancestors believed that abnormal behavior reflected the invasion of evil spirits. Perhaps they used the harsh method—called **trephining**—of creating a pathway through the skull to provide an outlet for those irascible spirits. Fresh bone growth indicates that some people managed to survive the ordeal.

Most of the time, however, trephining put an end to the person as well as any disturbing behavior. Threat of trephining may have persuaded people to comply with group or tribal norms to the best of their abilities. But since no written records or accounts of the purposes of trephination exist, other explanations are possible. For example, it's been recently suggested that trephination may have been used only for the purpose of surgically removing shattered pieces of bone or blood clots that resulted from traumas or blows to the head (Maher & Maher, 1985).

Explanation of abnormal behavior in terms of supernatural or divine causes is termed the **demonological model.** In ancient times, natural forces were explained in terms of divine will and spirits. The ancient Babylonians believed that the movements of the stars and the planets were fashioned by the adventures and conflicts of the gods (Boorstin, 1983). The ancient Greeks believed that their gods toyed with humans; when aroused to wrath, they could unleash forces of nature to wreak havoc on disrespectful or arrogant humans, even cloud their minds with madness. In the time of Homer (ca. 800 B.C.), author of the epics *The Iliad* and *The Odyssey*, it was widely believed that strange or bizarre behavior signified punishment of insolent humans by the gods.

In ancient Greece, people who behaved abnormally were often sent to temples dedicated to Asclepius, the god of healing. Priests believed that Asclepius would visit the afflicted persons while they slept in the temple and offer them restorative advice through dreams. Rest, a nutritious diet, and exercise were also believed to contribute to treatment. Incurables might be driven from the temple by stoning.

Origins of the Medical Model: In "Ill Humor"

Not all ancient Greeks believed in the demonological model. Hippocrates (ca. 460–377 B.C.), the celebrated physician of the Golden Age of Greece, attempted to challenge the prevailing beliefs of his time by arguing that illnesses of the body and mind were the result of natural causes, not possession by supernatural spirits. Hippocrates believed that the health of the body and mind depended on the balance of **humors** or vital fluids in the body: phlegm, black bile, blood, and yellow bile. An imbalance of humors, he thought, accounted for abnormal behavior. A lethargic or sluggish person was believed to have an excess of phlegm, from which we derive the word **phlegmatic.** An overabundance of black bile was believed to cause depression, or **melancholia.** An excess of blood created a **sanguine** disposition: cheerful, confident, and optimistic. An excess of yellow bile made people "bilious" and **choleric**—quick-tempered, that is.

Hippocrates' concept of humors attained much currency. The adjectives *phlegmatic, melancholy, sanguine,* and *choleric* have remained in use over the millennia. Two thousand years later, Shakespeare wrote of the brooding Hamlet as that "melancholy Dane." Today Hippocrates' view is known to be without physiological merit, but it was of historic importance because of its break from demonology.

Hippocrates' view that abnormal behavior could result from biological imbalances formed the basis of the modern **medical model.** Also called the *disease model,* the medical model seeks to explain abnormal behavior as rooted in underlying biological or biochemical abnormalities. Hippocrates made many contributions to modern thought and, indeed, to modern medical practice. Medical schools continue to pay homage to Hippocrates by having new physicians swear the Hippocratic oath.

Hippocrates' belief in natural causes also led to some strange turns. **Hysteria** refers to a pattern of

A CLOSER LOOK
A Sexist Thing Happened on the Way to the Forum

In *A Funny Thing Happened on the Way to the Forum*, a play of the 1960s, an excitable character is named Hysterium—the masculine rendition of the word "hysteria." It was once believed that hysteria was essentially a "woman's problem," which is one reason that the name *Hysterium* drew laughs.

"Hysterical," you see, derives from the Greek *hystera*, meaning uterus or womb. Like many of his fellow Greeks, Hippocrates believed that hysteria was exclusively a female complaint that was attributed to the effects of a wandering uterus. It was thought that the uterus was not anchored in place and was free to roam about the body. As the uterus roamed, it would cause pains and odd sensations in different organs. It was further believed, by the way, that pregnancy anchored the uterus and ended these complaints. So what did Greek physicians prescribe to put an end to monthly aches and pains? Good guess.

Men would never complain of these mysterious maladies, naturally. Of course, Hippocrates and his fellow Greeks never encountered male pilots who suffered from "hysterical" night blindness during World War II. In Chapter 7 we discuss the modern-day counterpart to hysteria, which is called *conversion disorder*.

---

behavior characterized by a dramatic display of physical complaints that have no identifiable biological basis. As noted in the nearby *A Closer Look* section, Hippocrates attributed hysteria to a wandering uterus that, among other things, had the effect of branding such behavior a "woman's disorder." (We discuss the modern counterparts of hysteria in Chapter 7.)

There were other physicians in ancient times who adopted and expanded upon the teachings of Hippocrates. One was Galen (ca A.D. 130–200), a Greek who attended the Roman emperor-philosopher Marcus Aurelius. Among Galen's contributions was the discovery that arteries carried blood, not air, as had been formerly believed.

So the seeds of naturalistic explanations of abnormal behavior were sown by Hippocrates and developed by other physicians, especially Galen. Hippocrates had even begun to classify abnormal behavior patterns, using three main categories: *melancholia* to characterize excessive depression, *mania* to refer to exceptional excitement, and *phrenitis* (from the Greek meaning "inflammation of the brain") to characterize the bizarre kinds of behavior that might typify **schizophrenia,** a severe type of mental disorder that is characterized by bizarre behavior, strange thoughts, and auditory or visual **hallucinations** (that is, "hearing voices" or seeing things that are not present).

Medieval Times

The Middle Ages, or medieval times, cover the millennium of European history from about A.D. 476 through 1450. The Middle Ages are also sometimes referred to as the Dark Ages because some historians view them as a time of intellectual and cultural decline and stagnation.

After the passing of Galen, belief in supernatural causes, especially the doctrine of possession, increased in influence and eventually dominated medieval thought. The doctrine of possession held that abnormal behaviors were a sign of possession by evil spirits of the Devil. This belief was embodied within the teachings of the Christian Church, which became the unifying force in Western Europe following the decline of the Roman Empire. Although belief in possession antedated the Christian Church and is found in ancient Egyptian and Greek writings, the Church revitalized it. The treatment of choice for abnormal behavior was **exorcism.** Exorcists were employed to persuade evil spirits that the bodies of their intended victims were basically uninhabitable. Methods included prayer, waving a cross at the victim, beating and flogging, even starving the victim. If the victim still displayed unseemly behavior, there were yet more powerful remedies, such as the rack, a device of torture. It seems clear that recipients of these "remedies" would be motivated to conform their behavior to social expectations as best they could.

The Renaissance—the great European revival in learning, art, and literature—began in Italy in the 1400s and spread gradually throughout Europe. The Renaissance is considered the transition from the medieval world to the modern. Therefore, it is ironic that fear of witches also reached its height during the Renaissance.

A medieval woodcut representing the practice of exorcism.

Witchcraft

The late fifteenth through the late seventeenth centuries were especially dangerous times to be unpopular with your neighbors. These were times of massive persecutions of people, particularly women, who were accused of witchcraft. Church officials believed that witches made pacts with the Devil, practiced satanic rituals, and committed heinous acts, such as eating babies and poisoning crops. In 1484 Pope Innocent VIII decreed that witches be executed. Two Dominican priests compiled a manual for witch-hunting, called the *Malleus Maleficarum* ("The Witches' Hammer"), to help inquisitors identify suspected witches. One hundred thousand or more accused witches were killed over the next two centuries.

There were also creative "diagnostic" tests for detecting possession and witchcraft. One was a water-float test. It was based on the principle that pure metals settle to the bottom during smelting, whereas impurities bob up to the surface. Suspects who sank and were drowned were ruled pure. Suspects who were able to keep their heads above water were regarded as being in league with the Devil. Then they were in "real" trouble. This trial is the fount of the phrase, "Damned if you do and damned if you don't."

 Innocent people were in fact drowned in medieval times as a way of certifying that they were not possessed by the Devil.

Modern scholars once believed that the "witches" of the Middle Ages and the Renaissance were actually people with mental disorders. They were believed to be persecuted because their abnormal behavior was taken as evidence that they were in league with the Devil. It is true that many suspected witches confessed to impossible behaviors, such as flying or engaging in sexual intercourse with the Devil. At face value such confessions might suggest disturbances in thinking and perception that are consistent with a modern diagnosis of mental disorders, such as schizophrenia. Most of these confessions can be discounted, however, because they were extracted under torture by inquisitors who were bent on finding evidence to support accusations of witchcraft (Spanos, 1978). In other cases, the threat of torture and other forms of intimidation were sufficient to extract false confessions. Although some of those who were persecuted as witches probably did show abnormal behavior patterns, most did not (Schoenman, 1984). Rather, accusations of witchcraft appeared to be a convenient means of disposing of social nuisances and political rivals, of seizing property, and of suppressing heresy (Spanos, 1978). In English villages, many

The "water-float" test was one of the ways in which medieval authorities sought to detect possession and witchcraft. Managing to stay above the water line was taken as a sign of impurity. In the lower right-hand corner, you can perhaps see the bound hands and feet of one poor unfortunate who failed to remain afloat, but whose drowning would have cleared any suspicions of possession.

of the accused were poor, unmarried elderly women who were forced to beg their neighbors for food. If misfortune befell people who declined to help, the beggar might be accused of causing the misery by casting a curse on the uncharitable family (Spanos, 1978). If the woman was generally unpopular, accusations of witchcraft were more likely to be followed up.

Although demons were believed to play roles both in abnormal behavior and witchcraft, there was a difference between the two. Victims of possession might have been afflicted as retribution for wrongdoing, but it was allowed that some people who showed abnormal behavior might be totally innocent victims of demonic possession. Witches, on the other hand, were believed

A CLOSER LOOK
The Devilish Sect—Victims of Possession or Food Poisoning?

The year was 1374. The Black Death—the name given the bubonic plague—had killed hundreds of thousands in Europe a generation earlier. Now there were epidemics of frenzied dancing—the so-called dancing mania. The dancers were labeled the devilish sect because their crazed, sexually provocative gestures were believed to signify possession. Many dancers were dragged to churches for exorcism. "Get thee hence, unclean spirit!" a priest might admonish, while restraining the agitated dancer. Some dancers went on till they literally dropped. Some died from exhaustion. Some scholars (Backman, 1952) suggest that the children of the village of Hamelin, who—according to legend—followed the Pied Piper out of town and disappeared, were also smitten by the dancing mania.

The dancing mania is usually presented as an example of so-called *mass hysteria*—in which one person expresses an unusual idea or engages in bizarre behavior, and it spreads through the community like a plague bacillus. We have apparently had some instances of mass hysteria in modern times, such as communal screeching and fainting at rock concerts.

It's possible that the dancing mania might actually have been caused by food poisoning of grains such as rye, oats, and wheat (Backman, 1952). Food poisoning often comes on the heels of drought and famine—the circumstances that succeeded the Black Death. Food poisoning could have plunged the blood pressure, causing feelings of suffocation and agitation. Frenetic dancing might have elevated the blood pressure and brought temporary relief. The poisoning and the "cure" might also have produced abdominal and thoracic pains that could have been relieved by binding of the abdomen—a frequent practice of the dancing sect.

Some dancers died, apparently either from food poisoning or physical activity, but for most, the "mania" endured for about ten days, then passed. The people assumed that the Devil had done his work and then went on to debauch purer pastures.

A painting by Kate Greenaway from the original 1879 edition of Robert Browning's *The Pied Piper of Hamelin*. Some historians speculate that the children in the fable of the Pied Piper had actually been afflicted with the "dancing mania."

1978). Most explanations involved natural causes for unusual behavior, such as illness or trauma to the head. In England, in fact, some disturbed people were kept in hospitals until they were restored to sanity (Allderidge, 1979).

The Renaissance Belgian physician Johann Weyer (1515–1588) also took up the cause of Hippocrates and Galen by arguing that abnormal behavior and thought patterns were caused by physical problems.

to have voluntarily entered into a pact with the Devil and renounced God. Witches were generally seen as more deserving of torture and execution (Spanos, 1978).

Historic trends do not follow straight lines. Although the demonological model held sway during the Middle Ages and much of the Renaissance, it did not universally supplant belief in naturalistic causes (Schoenman, 1984). In Medieval England, for example, demonic possession was only rarely invoked as the cause of abnormal behavior in cases in which a person was held to be insane by legal authorities (Neugebauer,

■ Asylums   By the late fifteenth and early sixteenth centuries, **asylums** or "madhouses" began to crop up throughout Europe. Many were former leprosariums, which were no longer needed because of a decline in leprosy that occurred during the late Middle Ages. Asylums often gave refuge to beggars as well as the disturbed, and conditions were generally appalling. Residents were often chained to their beds and left to die in their own waste or wander about unassisted. Some asylums became public spectacles. In one asylum in London, Bethlehem Hospital—from which the word "bedlam" is derived—the public could buy tickets to observe the bizarre antics of the inmates, much as they would visit a sideshow in a circus or animals at a zoo.

The bizarre antics of the patients at Bethlehem Hospital in London in the 18th century were a source of entertainment and amusement for the well-heeled gentry of the town.

Patients in Bethlehem Hospital and in other early asylums were often subject to cruel and barbaric mistreatment, such as being chained to their beds.

The Rise of Modern Thought

By the late seventeenth century, now called the Age of Reason, and the eighteenth century, the Age of Enlightenment, society at large began to turn from religious dogma to reason and science to explain natural phenomena and human behavior. The nascent sciences of biology, chemistry, physics, and astronomy offered promise that knowledge could be derived from scientific methods of observation and experimentation.

■ **Advances in Medicine**   The eighteenth and nineteenth centuries witnessed rapid developments in medical science. Scientific discoveries uncovered the microbial causes of some kinds of diseases and gave rise to preventive measures. In 1796, the smallpox vaccine was developed by the English physician Edward Jenner. By 1864, Frenchman Louis Pasteur devised the process of pasteurization. In 1865, an English surgeon, Joseph Lister, performed the first antiseptic surgery, using carbolic acid on a wound. In the same year, Gregor Mendel published his theory of genetics. By 1871, the bacillus that causes leprosy was discovered by G. A. Hansen. Robert Koch discovered the bacillus that causes anthrax in 1876 and he developed a vaccine for the disease in 1883.

Against this backdrop the German physician Wilhelm Griesinger (1817–1868) asserted that abnormal behavior was rooted in diseases of the brain. Griesinger's views influenced another German physician, Emil Kraepelin (1856–1926), who wrote an influential textbook on psychiatry in 1883 in which he likened mental disorders to physical diseases. Griesinger and

Kraepelin paved the way for the development of the modern **medical model,** which attempts to explain abnormal behavior on the basis of underlying biological defects or abnormalities, not evil spirits. According to the medical model, people behaving abnormally suffer from mental illnesses or disorders that can be classified, like physical illnesses, according to their distinctive causes and **syndromes,** or sets of symptoms. While not all those who adopt the medical model believe that all forms of abnormal behavior are products of defective biology, they maintain that abnormal behavior patterns can be likened to physical illnesses in the sense that their features can be conceptualized as "symptoms" of underlying disorders.

■ **Emil Kraepelin**   Kraepelin specified two main groups of mental disorders or diseases: **dementia praecox** (from roots meaning "precocious [premature] insanity"), which we now call schizophrenia, and manic-depressive psychosis, which is now labeled **bipolar disorder.** Kraepelin believed that dementia praecox was caused by a biochemical imbalance and manic-depressive psychosis by an abnormality in body metabolism. But his major contribution was the development of a classification system that forms the cornerstone for current diagnostic systems.

The medical model was supported by evidence that a form of derangement called **general paresis** represented an advanced stage of syphilis in which the syphilis bacterium directly invaded brain tissue. Scientists grew optimistic that other biological causes and, as important, treatments would soon be discovered for other so-called mental disorders. But this early optimism has remained largely unfulfilled, since the causes of most abnormal behavior patterns, biological or otherwise, remain obscure.

The Reform Movement and Moral Therapy

The modern era of treatment can be traced to the efforts of individuals like the Frenchmen Jean-Baptiste Pussin and Phillipe Pinel in the late eighteenth and early nineteenth centuries. They argued that people who behaved abnormally suffered from disease and should be treated humanely. This was not a popular view at the time. The public regarded deranged people as threats to society, not as sick people in need of treatment.

From 1784 to 1802, Pussin, a layman, was placed in charge of a ward for people considered "incurably insane" at La Bicêtre, a large mental hospital in Paris. Although Pinel is often given credit for freeing the inmates of La Bicêtre from their chains, it was actually Pussin who first succeeded in unchaining a group of the "incurably insane." These unfortunates had been considered too dangerous and unpredictable to be left unchained. But Pussin believed that if they were treated with kindness, there would be no need for chains. As

he predicted, most of the shut-ins became manageable and calm when their chains were removed and they could walk the hospital grounds and take in fresh air. Pussin also forbade the staff from treating the residents harshly, and he discharged employees who disregarded his directives.

Pinel (1745–1826) became medical director for the incurables' ward at La Bicêtre in 1793 and continued the humane treatment that Pussin had begun. He stopped harsh practices, such as bleeding and purging, and moved patients from darkened dungeons to well-ventilated, sunny rooms. Pinel also spent hours talking to inmates, in the belief that understanding and concern would help restore them to normal functioning.

The philosophy of treatment that emerged from these efforts was labeled **moral therapy,** since it was based on the belief that functioning could be restored by providing humane treatment in a relaxed and decent environment. Similar reforms were instituted at about this time in England by William Tuke and later in the United States by the reformer Dorothea Dix. Another influential figure was the American physician Benjamin Rush (1745–1813)—also a signatory to the Declaration of Independence. Rush, considered the "father of American Psychiatry," penned the first American textbook on psychiatry in 1812: *Medical Inquiries and Observations upon the Diseases of the Mind.* Rush believed that madness was caused by engorgement of the blood vessels of the brain. To relieve pressure, he recommended bloodletting and other harsh treatments like purging and ice-cold baths. But he also advanced humane treatment by encouraging the staff of his Philadelphia Hospital to treat patients with kindness and understanding. His hospital became the first in the United States to admit patients for mental disorders.

Dorothea Dix (1802–1887), a Boston schoolteacher, traveled about the country decrying the deplorable conditions in the jails and almshouses where deranged people were often placed. As a direct result of

The 18th-century reformer Philippe Pinel directing that the chains be removed from an inmate of La Bicêtre.

her efforts, 32 mental hospitals were established throughout the United States.

■ A Step Backward

In the latter half of the nineteenth century, however, the belief that patterns of abnormal behavior could be successfully treated or cured by moral therapy fell into disfavor, and a period of apathy ensued in which these behavior patterns were regarded as incurable (Grob, 1983). American mental institutions grew in size and came to provide little more than custodial care. Conditions deteriorated. Mental hospitals became frightening places. It was not uncommon to find residents "wallowing in their own excrements," in the words of a New York State official of the time (Grob, 1983). Straitjackets, handcuffs, cribs, straps, and other devices were used to restrain excitable or violent patients.

Deplorable hospital conditions remained commonplace through the middle of the twentieth century, when public attention began to focus on revamping the mental-health system. By the mid-1950s, the population in mental hospitals had risen to half a million patients. Although some good state hospitals provided decent and humane care (Grob, 1983), many were described as little more than *human snakepits*, with residents crowded into wards that lacked even rudimentary sanitation. Inhabitants were literally locked up for indefinite stays and received little more than custodial care. By the mid-twentieth century, the appalling conditions that many mental patients were forced to endure led to increasing calls for reforms of the mental-health system in the United States.

■ The Contemporary Exodus from State Hospitals

Two major factors led to a mass exodus from mental hospitals in the post-World War II era: the advent of a new class of drugs—the *phenothiazines*—and the community mental-health centers act of 1963. The 1950s ushered in the **phenothiazines**—a group of "major tranquilizers" that quelled the most flagrant behavior patterns associated with schizophrenia. Phenothiazines reduced the need for indefinite hospital stays and permitted the release of large numbers of schizophrenics to less restrictive living quarters in the community, such as halfway houses, group homes, even independent living.

In response to the growing call for reform of the mental-health system, Congress established in 1963 a nationwide system of community mental-health centers that was intended to offer continuing support and care to former hospital residents. It was hoped that these centers would help patients return to their communities and assume more independent and fulfilling lives. The ensuing **deinstitutionalization** led to a steady decline in the mental-hospital census. The mental-hospital population across the United States declined from about

560,000 in 1955 to 125,000 in 1981 (Kiesler & Sibulkin, 1987). By 1983 it was estimated that 93 percent of those who would otherwise be hospitalized were living in the community (Goldman et al., 1983).

Many critics now contend that the exodus from state hospitals abandoned tens of thousands of marginally functioning people to communities that lack adequate housing and other forms of support. Many of the homeless people we see wandering city streets and sleeping in bus terminals and train stations are discharged mental patients.

 Many of the nation's homeless are in fact former residents of mental hospitals who have been discharged to the community.

In Chapter 15 we shall examine whether deinstitutionalization is a failed policy or a promise unfulfilled. In Chapter 16 we shall focus on the challenges faced by mental-health professionals to meet the needs of homeless people with mental disorders.

While deplorable conditions may continue to persist in some institutions, most mental hospitals today are better managed and provide more humane care than those of the nineteenth and early twentieth centuries. The daily life of today's mental hospital is more treatment oriented and focused on preparing residents to return to community living. For younger and intensely disturbed people, the hospital stay is usually brief, lasting only until their condition allows them to reenter society. To elderly chronic clients, however, the mental hospital may be the only stable home they have known as adults. They find themselves unprepared to handle the most rudimentary tasks of independent life—shopping, cooking, and cleaning.

Contemporary Concepts of Abnormal Behavior

Today many scholars of abnormal behavior adhere to the medical model, although research into the biological and biochemical correlates of abnormal behavior is by no means limited to medical personnel. Psychologists, biologists, and others are also intensely involved in this investigation. A number of psychological models of abnormal behavior have also attained prominence, including psychodynamic, learning, cognitive, and existential-humanistic perspectives.

■ The Medical Model and Biological Perspectives

The medical model, inspired by physicians from Hippocrates through Kraepelin, remains a powerful force in contemporary psychology. In fact, much of the terminology in current use reflects the pervasive influence of the medical model. It is because of the medical model that many professionals and lay people speak of those who show abnormal behavior as mentally *ill* or mentally *disordered*. It is because of the medical model that so many speak of the *symptoms* of abnormal behavior, rather than the features or characteristics of abnormal behavior. Some of the other terms spawned by the medical model include *mental health, syndrome, diagnosis, patient, mental patient, mental hospital, prognosis, treatment, therapy, cure, relapse,* and *remission.*[1]

The medical model certainly represents a major advance over demonology. It inspired the idea that abnormal behavior should be treated by learned professionals and not punished. Compassion supplanted hatred, fear, and persecution.

But the medical model has its shortcomings. For one, as noted, biological causes for most forms of abnormal behavior have not yet been unearthed. Also the model implies that people with "mental illnesses," like those with physical illnesses, are not responsible for their difficulties. In the past, this belief often led to hospitalization and suspension of occupational and family responsibilities among people with abnormal behavior problems. Removed from the real world, their abilities to function often showed further decline rather than return to normal. Today, however, even most devotees of the medical model recognize the value of encouraging sufferers to remain in the community and maintain whatever responsibility they can. Within the medical model, treatment of abnormal behavior involves the application by medical personnel of biological therapies that seek to control or correct the assumed underlying biological or biochemical abnormalities. We shall discuss biological treatment approaches more fully in Chapter 15 and elsewhere in the text. But, as we shall see, treatments derived from other models have also been shown to be of help with various patterns of abnormal behavior.

The medical model represents a biological perspective on abnormal behavior. We prefer to use the term biological perspectives, rather than medical model, to refer to approaches that emphasize the role of biological processes in explaining abnormal behavior and that use drugs and other biologically based treatments to help change abnormal behavior patterns. In this way,

we can speak of biological perspectives without adopting the tenets of the medical model, which treat abnormal behavior patterns as *disorders* and their features as *symptoms*. For example, certain behavior patterns (shyness or a lack of musical ability) may reflect biological factors, such as genetics, but not be considered "symptoms" of underlying "disorders."

While it has not been shown that biological factors play an important role in all patterns of abnormal behavior, there are diverse sources of evidence to support biological perspectives of abnormal behavior. For example, genetics may play a prominent role in the transmission of many abnormal behavior patterns that tend to run in families. Researchers have also found links between certain abnormal behavior patterns, like severe depression and schizophrenia, and chemical imbalances in the brain. In addition, biological treatments, such as drug therapies, have been effective in treating various forms of abnormal behavior.

■ *Psychodynamic Perspectives* While the medical model was gaining influence in the nineteenth century, there were those who believed that organic factors alone could not explain the many forms of abnormal behavior. The contributions of a French neurologist, Jean Martin Charcot (1825–1893), and a Viennese physician, Joseph Breuer (1842–1925), were to excite the interest of a young physician, Sigmund Freud (1856–1939), who would go on to develop the first major psychological theory of abnormal behavior. But first let us set the stage.

Earlier, the Austrian physician Friedrich Mesmer (1734–1815), from whose name the term "mesmerism" is derived (we still sometimes speak of people being "mesmerized" by things), had become quite a controversial figure on the basis of his experiments into "animal magnetism." Mesmer focused on so-called **hysterics,** or people with hysteria, who have physical complaints without any identifiable physical cause. Hysterical complaints may involve feelings of numbness or pain, paralysis of the arms or limbs, even blindness. Mesmer believed that hysteria was caused by an underlying imbalance in the distribution of a magnetic fluid in the body. To effect a cure, Mesmer would have persons with hysterical complaints sit around a covered tub that held bottles of chemicals and protrusions of metal rods. The lights were dimmed, and Mesmer made his entrance with much flourish and fanfare. Then he prodded afflicted parts of clients' bodies with his hands and the rods. Mesmer maintained that the rods transmitted animal magnetism to clients' bodies, correcting the distribution of magnetic fluid and curing afflictions. A scientific commission dismissed Mesmer's claims for animal magnetism as charlatanism, but the astonishing aspect of his treatment—recognized even by the commission—was that it often produced relief. Today, Mes-

---

[1] Because the medical model is not the only way of viewing abnormal behavior patterns, we adopt a more neutral language in this text in describing abnormal behavior patterns. For example, we will often refer to "features" or "characteristics" of abnormal behavior patterns, rather than "symptoms." But our adoption of nonmedical jargon is not an absolute rule. In some cases, there may be no handy substitutes for certain terms that derive from the medical model, like the term "remission" or like referring to patients in mental hospitals as "mental patients." In other cases we may use terms like "disorder," "therapy," and "treatment," because they are so commonly used by both medical practitioners and by nonmedical personnel, such as psychologists, who "treat" mental "disorders" with psychological "therapies."

A teaching clinic held by the Parisian neurologist Jean Martin Charcot. Here, Charcot presents a woman patient who exhibits the highly dramatic behavior associated with hysteria, such as becoming faint at a moment's notice. Charcot was an important influence on the young Sigmund Freud.

mer's "cures" are largely attributed to the power of suggestion. Today, Mesmer's technique is recognized as perhaps the first medical use of the technique we now call **hypnosis.**

Although Mesmer's views were debunked, interest in hypnosis began to grow in the latter part of the nineteenth century, especially in France. A highly respected Parisian neurologist, Jean Martin Charcot, experimented with the hypnotic induction of hysterical symptoms in normal people. Charcot had once discounted the importance of psychological factors in explaining states of abnormal behavior, like hysteria. But experiments with hypnosis eventually persuaded him otherwise. Charcot demonstrated that hysterical behaviors, like paralysis or numbness in the arms, could be induced in normal subjects under hypnosis through use of suggestions. Hypnotically induced hysterical behavior was indistinguishable from "genuine" hysterical behavior. Even more startling, Charcot and others who experimented with hypnosis demonstrated that hysterical behavior could often be eliminated by suggesting to hypnotized clients that their "symptoms" would vanish when they awoke.

Among the young physicians who observed Charcot's work was Sigmund Freud. Charcot's work with hypnosis had a profound impact on Freud, for it demonstrated that hysterical behavior—which could be treated or abolished by the suggestion of "ideas"—was psychological in origin (Jones, 1953). Freud was also influenced by his association with Joseph Breuer, a prominent Viennese physician, 14 years Freud's senior. Breuer too had used hypnosis to treat a woman—"Anna O"—with hysterical complaints. The case of "Anna O" figured prominently in Freud's eventual development of **psychoanalysis** (Spitzer et al., 1989). For this reason we'll take a closer look at the case.

Sigmund Freud at about 30 years of age.

The Case of Anna O. When Anna was 21, she assumed the responsibilities of night nurse for her father, who lay dying with tuberculosis. Anna was very much attached to her father and sat with him every night, watching him gradually deteriorate in pain. Soon she began to be troubled by problems with no apparent physical basis—"hysterical symptoms." She complained of paralysis in her limbs, numbness, and distur-

Bertha Pappenheim (1859–1936), more widely known as "Anna O."

bances of vision and hearing (Jones, 1953). A "paralyzed" muscle in her neck prevented her from turning her head. Immobilization of the fingers of her left hand made it all but impossible for her to feed herself. Breuer believed there was a strong psychological component to the symptoms. He treated her by encouraging her to talk about them, sometimes under hypnosis. Recalling and talking about events connected with the appearance of the symptoms—especially events that evoked feelings of fear, anxiety, or guilt—appeared to provide relief of symptoms.

The hysterical symptoms apparently represented the transformation of these blocked-up emotions, forgotten but not lost, into physical complaints. In Anna's case, the symptoms seemed to disappear once the emotions were brought to the surface and "discharged." Breuer labeled the therapeutic effect **catharsis,** a Greek term meaning purgation or purification of feelings. Anna referred to the treatment as the "talking cure" or, when joking, as "chimney sweeping." After 18 months of treatment, she seemed well enough that Breuer told her she no longer needed to see him. But that very night Breuer was summoned to Anna's house, where he found her thrashing about in her bed, as if delivering a child, and insisting that the baby was his. Breuer managed to calm Anna with hypnosis, but he left the house in a cold sweat and never saw her again.

Breuer and Freud published the case of Anna O. in their classic *Studies in Hysteria.* Cases of hysteria, like that of Anna O., seemed to have been a common occurrence in the later Victorian period, but are relatively rare today (Spitzer et al., 1989). After Breuer's

departure from her life, Anna had intermittent episodes for several years and spent considerable lengths of time in a sanatorium. She completely recovered by the age of 30, however, and went on to become the first social worker in Germany and an early feminist leader. Anna, whose real name was Bertha Pappenheim, became a popular speaker and apparently had no recurrences of hysteria. She developed very negative attitudes toward "the talking cure," however, and at one point refused to allow one of the residents of a home she ran for "wayward girls" to be psychoanalyzed. In 1936, at the age of 77, she died of abdominal cancer (Spitzer et al., 1989).

His own case experiences led Freud to the belief that psychological problems, such as hysteria, are derived from unconscious conflicts of childhood origin. Such conflicts involved the opposition of primitive sexual and aggressive drives and the effort to keep these drives from being expressed in direct action. According to **psychoanalytic theory,** which Freud developed, abnormal behavior patterns reflect the dynamic struggle within the mind between opposing psychic forces. Freud viewed abnormal behavior patterns as "symptoms" of these conflicts. In the case of hysteria, the "symptom" represented the *conversion* of an unconscious psychological conflict into a physical problem.

Freud's psychoanalytic theory represents a **psychodynamic model** or perspective of abnormal behavior. But psychodynamic perspectives also incorporate the views of Freud's followers who differed with Freud in some respects but still retained the central belief that unconscious dynamic processes or conflicts are at the root of abnormal behavior patterns. Psychodynamic theorists believe that psychological disorders require resolution of the unconscious conflicts that underlie them. Freud initially followed Breuer's example and experimented with hypnosis as a means of unearthing conflicts. He eventually became disillusioned with the technique, however, because not every client could be hypnotized and the "cures" so attained were impermanent (Brill, 1938). Freud came to believe that many of the beneficial effects of hypnosis were fleeting because they largely represented the client's attempt to please the hypnotist (Jones, 1953). Once the hypnotist was gone, the symptoms might return. Freud developed the method of **psychoanalysis** to replace hypnosis. Psychoanalysis uses techniques like **free association** and dream analysis (see Chapter 15).

■ **Learning Perspectives** Psychodynamic models of Freud and his followers were the first major psychological theories of abnormal behavior, but other relevant psychologies were also taking shape early in the twentieth century. Among the most important was the behavioral perspective, which is identified with contributions

John B. Watson, the founder of American behaviorism.

their learning histories, that is, might differ from most people's. For example, stern reproof for early exploratory behavior, such as childhood sexual exploration, might give rise to adult anxieties over autonomy or sexuality. Inconsistent discipline, as shown in haphazard rewards for good behavior and capricious punishment of misconduct, might give rise to antisocial behavior. Then, too, children with abusive or neglectful parents might learn to pay more attention to inner fantasies than the world outside, giving rise, at worst, to difficulty in separating reality from fantasy.

Watson and other behaviorists, such as Harvard University psychologist B. F. Skinner, believed that human behavior is basically the product of genetic endowment and environmental or situational influences. The behavioral perspective has given rise to a treatment approach called **behavior therapy,** which applies principles of learning to help people overcome psychological problems and develop more effective behaviors (see Chapter 15).

In Chapter 2 we shall see that other learning theorists have called for an expanded model, called **social learning theory,** which focuses on the roles that our personal values, expectancies, and observations of others play in explaining the development and maintenance of behavior.

by the Russian physiologist Ivan Pavlov, the discoverer of the conditioned reflex, and the American psychologist John B. Watson, the father of **behaviorism.** The behavioral perspective focuses on the role of learning in explaining both normal and abnormal behavior. From the behavioral perspective, abnormal behavior represents the learning of inappropriate, maladaptive behaviors.

From the medical and psychodynamic perspectives, abnormal behavior is *symptomatic*, respectively, of underlying biological or psychological problems. From the behavioral perspective, however, abnormal behavior need not be symptomatic of anything. The abnormal behavior itself is the problem. Abnormal behavior is regarded as learned in much the same way as normal behavior. Why, then, do some people behave abnormally? One reason is found in situational factors:

■ **Humanistic-Existential Perspectives** A "third force" in modern psychology emerged during the mid twentieth century—humanistic psychology. Humanistic theorists such as American psychologists Carl Rogers and Abraham Maslow believed that human behavior was neither a product of unconscious conflicts nor conditioning. Rejecting the determinism implicit in these theories, they saw people as *actors* in the drama of life, not *reactors* to instinctual or environmental pressures. Humanistic psychology is closely linked with the school of European philosophy called *existentialism*. The existentialists, notably the philosophers Martin Heidegger

(a)

(b)

Carl Rogers (a) and Abraham Maslow (b), two of the principal forces in humanistic psychology.

(1889–1976) and Jean-Paul Sartre (1905–1980) focused on the roles of meaningfulness and choice in human existence. Existentialists believe that our humanness makes us responsible for the directions that our lives will take.

The humanists maintain that people have an inborn tendency toward *self-actualization*—to strive to become all that they are capable of being. Each of us possesses a singular cluster of traits and talents that gives rise to an individual set of feelings and needs and grants us a unique perspective on life. Despite the finality of death, we can each imbue our lives with meaning and purpose if we recognize and accept our genuine needs and feelings. By being true to ourselves, we live *authentically*. We may not decide to act out on every wish and fancy, but self-awareness of authentic feelings and subjective experiences can help us to make more meaningful choices.

To understand abnormal behavior, in the humanist's view, we need to understand the roadblocks that people encounter in striving for self-actualization and authenticity. To accomplish this, psychologists must learn to view the world from clients' own perspectives, since their views of their world lead them to interpret and evaluate their experiences in self-enhancing or self-defeating ways. The humanistic-existential viewpoint is sometimes called the *phenomenological* perspective, because it involves the attempt to understand the subjective or phenomenological experience of others.

■ **Cognitive Perspectives**   The word *cognitive* derives from the Latin *cognitio*, meaning "knowledge." Cognitive theorists study the cognitions—the thoughts, expectations, and attitudes—that attend and may underlie abnormal behavior.

Philosophers have debated how "purely" our perceptions and mental images represent the world outside for many millennia. In recent years, however, many clinically oriented psychologists have also focused on how reality is colored by our expectations, attitudes, and so forth, and how inaccurate or biased processing of information about the world—and our places within it—can give rise to abnormal behavior. Researchers have learned that the cognitions we hold about ourselves and the world around us are important aspects of our behavioral and emotional adjustment.

One cognitive approach to explaining abnormal behavior has been strongly influenced by computer science, or information processing. Information-processing theorists relate the functions of the mind to those of the computer and describe human cognition on the basis of cycles of sensory input, storage, retrieval, manipulation, and output of information. They perceive abnormal thought processes as disturbances in the cycle. Such disturbance might reflect the distortion or blocking of input, or the faulty storage, retrieval, or manipulation of information. These may lead, in turn, to impoverished output (lack of behavior) or distorted output (that is, outlandish behavior). As we'll see in Chapter 12, schizophrenic people, for example, often jump from topic to topic in a chaotic manner, which information-processing theorists may explain in terms of problems in manipulating stored information.

Other cognitive theorists focus on the effects of self-defeating beliefs and attitudes. Albert Ellis (1977, 1987), for example, views excessive anxiety as frequently stemming from irrational, overwhelming desires for social approval and perfectionism. Psychiatrist Aaron Beck suggests that depression may result from "cognitive errors" such as judging oneself entirely on the basis of one's flaws or failures, and interpreting events in a negative light (sort of wearing blue-colored glasses) (Beck et al., 1979). Many behavior therapists today identify with an expanded model of therapy, *cognitive* behavior therapy, which focuses on modifying self-defeating beliefs in addition to overt behaviors.

■ **Sociocultural Perspectives**   Does abnormal behavior arise from forces within the person as the psychodynamic theorists propose, or from the learning of maladaptive behaviors, as the learning theorists suggest? To the sociocultural theorists, abnormal behavior is not the product of conflicts within the person or of faulty learning. Sociocultural theorists look for the causes of abnormal behavior in the failures of society, rather than in the person. Within this view, abnormal behavior is rooted in societal ills, such as poverty, urban decay, discrimination and lack of opportunity. Some of the more radical psychosocial theorists even deny the existence of mental illness, believing that abnormal behavior is merely a label that society attaches to people who act differently in order to stigmatize and subjugate them. The sociocultural theorists have focused much needed attention on the social stressors that may lead to abnormal behavior. As we shall see in Chapter 2, evidence shows that people from lower socioeconomic levels are more likely to be institutionalized for abnormal behavior. But does this suggest that abnormal behavior is caused by poverty and other social ills, or that it is merely a convenient label used by the establishment to discredit the behavior of people of lesser means and social power whose behavior violates social norms? Or might there be other explanations linking abnormal behavior and social class?

■ **Eclectic Models**   Many researchers and clinicians are **eclectic.** They refer to multiple models to explain and treat abnormal behavior. Many social-learning theorists, for example, regard some abnormal behavior problems as arising from biochemical factors or the interaction of biochemistry and experience. They are willing to use a combination of drugs and behavior therapy to deal with problems like bipolar disorder and schizophrenia. Or they might borrow psychodynamic concepts to help explain the development of long-standing personality problems.

Clinicians trained in psychodynamic approaches may also be eclectic. They may believe that extreme fears or phobias symbolize unconscious childhood conflicts that carry over into adulthood. Still, they may employ behavior therapy techniques to help clients overcome their fears directly, even as they attempt more probing analysis of the childhood roots of the fears in long-term therapy.

Models of abnormal behavior not only provide perspectives for understanding and treatment but they also suggest various kinds of research into abnormal behavior. The medical model, for example, fosters inquiry into genetic and biochemical research. Learning models encourage inquiries into the situational determinants of abnormal behavior. In the following section we consider the types of research conducted by investigators of abnormal behavior.

RESEARCH METHODS IN ABNORMAL PSYCHOLOGY

Imagine that you are a brand-new graduate student in psychology and are sitting in your research methods course on the first day of the term. The professor, a distinguished woman of about 50, enters the class. She is carrying a small wire-mesh cage with a white rat. She smiles and sets the cage on her desk.

The professor removes the rat from the cage and places it on the desk. She asks the class to observe its behavior. As a serious student, you attend closely. The animal moves to the edge of the desk, pauses, peers over the edge, and seems to jiggle its whiskers at the floor below. It maneuvers along the edge of the desk, tracking the perimeter. Now and then it pauses and vibrates its whiskers downward in the direction of the floor.

The professor picks up the rat and returns it to the cage. She asks the class to describe the animal's behavior.

A student responds, "The rat seems to be looking for a way to escape."

Another student: "It is reconnoitering its environment, examining it." Reconnoitering? you think. That student has seen too many war movies.

The professor writes each response on the blackboard. Another student raises her hand. "The rat is making a visual search of the environment," she says. "Maybe it's looking for food."

The professor prompts other students for their descriptions.

"It's looking around," says one.

"Trying to escape," says another.

Your turn arrives. Trying to be scientific, you say, "We can't say what its motivation might be. All we know is that it's scanning its environment."

"How so?" the professor asks.

"Visually," you reply, confidently.

The professor then turns to the class, shaking her head. "Each of you observed the rat," she said, "but none of you described its *behavior*. Each of you made certain *inferences*, that the rat was 'looking for a way down' or 'scanning its environment' or 'looking for food' and the like. These are not unreasonable inferences, but they are inferences, not descriptions. They also happen to be wrong. You see, the rat is blind. It's been blind since birth. It couldn't possibly be looking around, at least not in a visual sense."

Description, Explanation, Prediction, and Control: The Objectives of Science

Description is one of the primary objectives of science. To understand abnormal behavior, we must first learn to describe it. Description allows us to recognize abnormal behavior and provides the basis for explaining it.

Descriptions should be clear, unbiased, and based on careful observation. Our anecdote about the blind rat illustrates the point that our observations and our attempts to describe them can be influenced by our expectations, or biased. Our expectations include our models of behavior, and they may incline us to perceive events—such as the rat's movements and other people's behavior—in certain ways. Describing the rat in the classroom as "scanning" and "looking" for something is *inferential* and is based on our models of how animals explore their environments. It would be more descriptive to simply chart its movements around the desk, measuring how far in each direction it moves, how long it pauses, how it bobs its head from side to side, and so on.

Inference is also important in science, however. Inference allows us to jump from the particular to the general—to suggest laws and principles of behavior that can be woven into models and *theories* of behavior, such as psychodynamic and learning models. Without a way of organizing our descriptions of phenomena in terms of models and theories, we'd be left with a buzzing confusion of unconnected observations. The crucial issue is to distinguish between description and inference—to recognize when one jumps from a description of events to an inference based on an interpretation of events. For example, one does not *describe* a person's behavior as "schizophrenic," but rather one *interprets* behavior as schizophrenic on the basis of one's model of schizophrenia. To do otherwise, we would affix ourselves to a given label or model and lose the intellectual flexibility that is needed to revise our inferences in the light of new evidence or ways of conceptualizing information.

Theories help scientists explain puzzling behavior and predict future behavior. Prediction entails the discovery of factors that anticipate the occurrence of events. Geology, for example, seeks clues in the forces that affect the earth that can forecast natural events such as earthquakes and volcanic eruptions. Scientists who study abnormal behavior seek clues in overt behavior, biological processes, family interactions, and so forth that predict the development of abnormal behaviors as well as factors that might predict response to various treatments. It is not sufficient for theoretical models such as psychodynamic or learning models to help us explain or make sense of events or behaviors that have already occurred. Useful theories must allow us to make predictions. So one test of psychodynamic and learning models is whether or not they lead us to predict the occurrence of particular behaviors.

The idea of controlling human behavior—especially the behavior of people with serious problems—is controversial. The history of societal response to abnormal behaviors—including abuses such as exorcism and cruel forms of physical restraint—render the idea particularly distressing. Within science, however, the word *control* need not imply that people are coerced into doing the bidding of others—like puppets dangling on strings. Psychologists, for example, are committed to the dignity of the individual, and the concept of human dignity requires that people be free to make decisions and exercise choices. Within this context, *controlling behavior* means using scientific knowledge to help people shape their own goals and more efficiently use their resources to accomplish them. Today, in the United States, even when helping professionals restrain people who are violently disturbed, their goal is to assist them to overcome their agitation and regain the ability to exercise meaningful choices in their lives.[2] Ethical standards prohibit the use of injurious techniques in research or practice.

Psychologists and other scientists use the *scientific method* to advance the description, explanation, prediction, and control of abnormal behavior.

The Scientific Method

The scientific method is an approach to testing theoretical assumptions through empirical research. It has four basic steps:

1. *Formulating a research question.* Scientists derive research questions from their observations and theories of events and behavior. For instance, observations of dietary habits or theories about nutrition–behavior relationships might motivate psychologists to conduct research into whether or not the ingestion of sugar exacerbates **hyperactivity** among hyperactive children.

2. *Framing the research question in the form of a hypothesis.* A **hypothesis** is a precise prediction about behavior that is examined through research. The specific hypothesis regarding sugar and hyperactivity might be that the administration of so many ounces of a sugar-sweetened drink in the morning would produce greater disruption of behavior among hyperactive children than a sweet-tasting drink flavored with a sugar substitute.

Or consider this hypothesis about depression: Depressed people hold more negative thoughts about themselves and their lives than do normal people. (Research along these lines is described in Chapter 8.) Or one might hypothesize that **antisocial personality disorder,** which is characterized by social conflict and disregard of the rights of other people, is transmitted genetically. (See Chapter 9.)

3. *Testing the hypothesis.* Scientists test hypotheses through carefully controlled observation and experimentation. The hypothesis about sugar and hyperactivity might be tested by randomly assigning hyperactive children to experimental conditions in which they consume either (a) a sugared drink or (b) a drink containing an artificial sweetener for several mornings. After ingesting these beverages, the children would be carefully observed at school or at play by trained observers for evidence of disturbed behavior.

The hypothesis concerning attitudinal differences between depressed and nondepressed people might be tested by the administration of attitude questionnaires that focus on negative beliefs. The hypothesis about genetic contributions to antisocial personality disorder might be tested by sorting out genetic and environmental influences on behavior, as described more fully in Chapter 2.

4. *Drawing conclusions about the hypothesis.* In the final step, scientists draw conclusions from their findings about the correctness of their hypotheses. Psychologists use statistical methods to determine the likelihood that differences between groups are **significant** as opposed to chance fluctuations. Psychologists are reasonably confident that group differences are significant—that is, not due to chance—when the probability that chance alone can explain the difference is less than 5 percent. When well-designed research findings fail to bear out hypotheses, scientists can modify the theories from which the hypotheses are derived. Research findings often lead to modifications in theory, new hypotheses and, in turn, subsequent research.

The findings regarding depression confirm that depressed people hold more negative attitudes. However, a question remains as to whether negative beliefs lead to depression or are a result of depression. Research

---

[2] Here we are talking about violently confused and disordered behavior, not criminal behavior. Criminals and disturbed people may both be dangerous to others, but with criminals the intention of restraint is usually limited to protecting society.

has not confirmed a consistent relationship between sugar and hyperactivity (see Chapter 14). The findings regarding genetic contributions to antisocial behavior are more complex, as we shall see in Chapter 9, but they suggest that there are genetic and environmental contributions to antisocial personality disorder.

Let us now consider the major research methods used by psychologists: the naturalistic-observation, correlational, experimental, quasi-experimental, epidemiological, and case-study methods.

The Naturalistic-Observation Method

The **naturalistic-observation method** is used to observe behavior "in the field," where it happens. Anthropologists have lived among primitive tribes throughout the world in order to study human diversity. Sociologists have followed the activities of adolescent gangs in inner cities. Psychologists have spent weeks observing the behavior of the homeless in city train stations and bus terminals. They have even observed the eating habits of slender and overweight people in fast-food restaurants, searching for clues to obesity. They have observed whether overweight people eating their burgers and fries take larger mouthfuls, chew less frequently, and finish eating more quickly than normal-weight people. As we note in Chapter 5, research evidence does confirm these differences.

Scientists take every precaution to ensure that their naturalistic observation is **unobtrusive,** to prevent any interference with the behavior they observe. Otherwise, the presence of the observer may distort the behavior that is observed. Over the years naturalistic observers have sometimes found themselves in controversial situations. For example, they have allowed sick or injured apes to die when medicine could have saved them. Observers of substance abuse and deviant sexual behavior have allowed illicit behavior to go unreported to authorities. In such cases, the ethical trade-off is that unobtrusive observation can yield information that will be of benefit to all.

There may also be some unexpected dangers in observing others without their knowledge. Your second author once dispatched undergraduate research students to measure differences in eating behavior (duration of eating, number of bites, etc.) between obese and normal-weight patrons of a fast-food restaurant. With stopwatches and hand-counters at the ready, the students positioned themselves so as not to draw the attention of patrons. There was one hitch: The escort of a female "subject" took offense when he noticed that two male observers were watching her while she ate. It took more than a little gentle persuasion to convince him that the observers were in pursuit of science, not his girlfriend.

■ **Samples and Populations**   The subjects or individuals who are observed or who participate in the research are said to comprise a research **sample.** A sample is a segment or part of a **population** of interest, and researchers need to ensure that the subjects in the research sample *represent* the target population. For example, the population of interest might be the student population of your college or university. Selecting your research sample from one particular dormitory or class is unlikely to constitute a representative sample unless the dormitory or class in question was truly representative of the student body at large.

Naturalistic observation provides a good deal of

Using the naturalistic-observation method, researchers attempt to unobtrusively observe and record behavior as it occurs in real-life settings such as cafeterias or fast-food restaurants. Psychologists have recorded the eating behavior of patrons of fast-food restaurants to see if obese people eat faster and take larger bites than do normal weight people.

information as to how subjects behave, but it does not necessarily reveal why they do so. Men who frequent bars and drink, for example, are more likely to get into fights than men who do not. But such observations do not show that alcohol *causes* aggression, however. As we'll see in the following pages, questions of cause and effect are best approached by means of controlled experiments.

Correlational Research

Correlation is a statistical measure of the relationships between two factors or **variables.** In the naturalistic-observation study that occurred in the fast-food restaurant, eating behaviors were related—or correlated—to patrons' weights. They were not directly manipulated. In other words, the investigators did not manipulate the weights or eating rates of their subjects, but merely measured the two variables in some fashion and examined whether they were statistically related to each other. When one variable (weight level) increases as the second variable (rate of eating) increases, there is a **positive correlation** between them. If one variable decreases (for example, incidence of heart disease) as the other variable increases (level of physical activity), however, the correlation between the variables is said to be **negative.** In Chapter 5 we shall see that the correlation between activity levels and incidence of heart disease is generally negative, but somewhat more complex.

Although correlational research reveals whether or not there are connections between variables, it does not show cause and effect relationships. Consider the research which links cigarette smoking with cardiovascular disorders and cancer. In Chapter 5 we shall report correlational evidence that shows that people who smoke run higher risks of heart attacks and certain kinds of cancer, such as lung cancer. But correlation does not, in itself, rule out rival hypotheses concerning causation. Rather than smoking causing disease, people who experience more stress in their lives may be more likely to turn to smoking to help them cope as well as eventually becoming physically ill as the result of prolonged stress. But more direct experimental evidence exists that supports the causal link between cigarette smoking and health problems.

Causal connections sometimes work in unexpected directions, and sometimes there is no causal connection between variables that are correlated. There are correlations between depression and negative attitudes, and it may seem logical that depression is caused by such attitudes. However, it is also possible that feelings of depression give rise to negative thoughts. More-over, depression and negative thinking may both reflect a common causative factor, such as stress, and not be causally related to each other at all.

Although correlational research does not reveal cause and effect, it can be used to serve the scientific objective of prediction. When two variables are correlated, we can use one to predict the other. In other words, we can predict that smokers are more likely than nonsmokers to incur various kinds of diseases, even if questions remain concerning causality. Knowledge of correlations between alcoholism, family history, and attitudes toward drinking helps us predict which adolescents are at great risk of developing problems with alcohol, although causal connections are complex and somewhat nebulous. But knowing which factors predict future problems may help us direct prevention efforts toward these high-risk groups to help prevent these problems from developing.

Although correlational research does not in itself demonstrate cause and effect, it can be an early step in a research program that leads to controlled experiments that more directly address cause and effect. Experiments do a better job of ruling out rival hypotheses, for the variables in controlled experiments are directly manipulated.

■ **The Longitudinal Study**   One type of correlational study is the *longitudinal study*, in which subjects are studied at periodic intervals over protracted periods, perhaps for decades. By studying people over time, researchers can investigate the events that are associated with the onset of abnormal behavior and, perhaps, learn to identify factors that predict the development of such behavior. However, such research is time-consuming and costly. It requires a commitment that may literally outlive the original investigators. Therefore, long-term longitudinal studies are relatively rare.

Perhaps the best-known example of longitudinal research in abnormal psychology is the work of Sarnoff Mednick and his colleagues. Since 1962 they have been following 207 offspring of Danish schizophrenic mothers. When the study began, the children averaged about 15 years of age and were matched with a reference group of children of normal mothers. In 1967, when the children were about 20, they were examined closely (Mednick & Schulsinger, 1968). The researchers found that the schizophrenic mothers of offspring who developed abnormal behavior—though not necessarily schizophrenic behavior—had experienced a relatively high rate of complications during pregnancy or childbirth. Schizophrenic mothers of children who had not developed abnormal behavior had had easier pregnancies and deliveries. These findings raised the possibility that a combination of genetic factors and complications in birth or pregnancy play a causal role in the development of severe forms of abnormal behavior. Again, however, causal interpretations must be tempered by the fact that the longitudinal data were correlated and not necessarily causally connected. One rival hypothesis would be that complications of pregnancy or childbirth and eventual abnormal behaviors are both effects of genetic defects in the fetus. If that were so, then the pregnancy and birth complications would play no direct role in the development of abnormal behavior. Still, longitudinal research provides clues to possible causal factors. We shall discuss the longitudinal research into schizophrenia at greater length in Chapter 12.

So a combination of genetic factors and pregnancy or birth complications helps us *predict* the later occurrence of abnormal behavior in the offspring, even though causal connections remain open to rival hypotheses. Prediction is based on the *correlation* between events or factors that are separated in time. But we must be careful not to infer *causation* from *prediction*. A **causal relationship** between two events involves a time-ordered relationship in which the second event is the direct result of the first. We need to meet two strict conditions to posit a causal relationship between two factors:

1. The effect must follow the cause in a time-ordered sequence of events.
2. Other plausible causes of the observed effects (rival hypotheses) must be eliminated.

In the experimental method, scientists seek to demonstrate causal relationships by first manipulating the causal factor and then measuring its effects under controlled conditions that minimize the risk of possible rival hypotheses.

The Experimental Method

The term *experiment* can cause some confusion. Broadly speaking, an "experiment" is a trial or test of a hypothesis. From this vantage point, any method that actually seeks to test a hypothesis could be considered "experimental"—including naturalistic observation and correlational studies. But investigators usually limit the use of the term **experimental method** to refer to studies in which researchers seek to uncover cause-and-effect relationships by directly manipulating possible causal factors. By using an experimental manipulation, sometimes called a *treatment*, researchers can come closer to answering questions such as whether or not alcohol causes aggression, cigarette smoking causes cancer, or psychotherapy relieves anxiety.

The factors or variables that are hypothesized to play a causal role are manipulated or controlled by

TABLE 1.1: Examples of Independent and Dependent Variables in Experimental Research

Independent Variables	Dependent Variables
Type of Treatment: for example, comparisons between different types of drug treatments or psychological treatments	Behavioral variables: for example, measures of adjustment, activity levels, eating behavior, smoking behavior
Treatment Factors: for example, comparisons between brief and long-term treatment, or between inpatient and outpatient treatment	Physiological variables: for example, measures of physiological responses such as heart rate, blood pressure, and brain-wave activity
	Self-report variables: for example, measures of anxiety, mood, or marital or life satisfaction

the investigator in experimental research. These are called the **independent variables.** The observed effects are labeled **dependent variables,** since changes in them are believed to depend upon the independent or manipulated variable. Dependent variables are observed and measured, not manipulated, by the experimenter. Examples of independent and dependent variables of interest to investigators of abnormal behavior are shown in Table 1.1.

In an experiment, subjects receive a *treatment or independent variable*; for example, drinking an alcoholic beverage in a laboratory setting. They are then observed or examined to determine whether the treatment makes a difference in their behavior, or, more precisely, whether the independent variable affected the dependent variable—in this case, whether they behave more aggressively.

■ **Experimental and Control Subjects** Model experiments assign subjects to experimental and control groups at random. **Experimental subjects** are given the experimental treatment. **Control subjects** are not. Care is taken to hold other conditions constant for each group. By using random assignment and holding other conditions constant, experimenters can be reasonably confident that the independent variable (experimental treatment), and not uncontrolled factors such as room temperature or differences between the types of subjects in the experimental and control groups, brought about the outcome.

■ **Random Assignment** Why should experimenters assign subjects to experimental and control groups at random? Consider a study intended to investigate the effects of alcohol on behavior. If we allowed subjects to decide whether or not they wanted to be in a group that drank alcohol, a **selection factor,** rather than the independent variable, might be responsible for the results. In this example, subjects who chose to drink might differ in important ways from those who preferred not to drink. One of their differences might lie in their aggressiveness. Therefore, we would not know whether the experimental manipulation (giving them or not giving them alcohol) or the selection factor was ultimately responsible for observed differences in behavior. Moreover, knowledge of which treatment they were receiving might also affect the experimental outcome—in this case by shaping subjects' expectations.

■ **Controlling for Subjects' Expectations** Apparent treatment effects may stem from subjects' expectations regarding their effects rather than from treatments themselves. Thus, researchers also try to control for subjects' expectations about the treatments. In order to do so, they may have to render subjects "blind" as to what treatment they are receiving.

We can illustrate the concept of keeping subjects blind as to whether or not they have received an experimental treatment by referring to research into the effects of alcohol on sexual and aggressive behaviors. These studies will be elaborated on in Chapter 10, but here let us note that these studies attempt to sort out the effects of alcohol itself from the effects of subjects' expectations about drinking alcohol. Assume, for example, that college men are more likely to act aggressively after they have been drinking. Do they do so because of the effects of alcohol or because they believe that alcohol causes or excuses aggression? Giving an experimental group some liquor—say, vodka—and then observing the group's behavior would not answer this question because the subjects would *know* they had had a drink. In order to control subjects' expectations about the effects of alcohol, subjects would have to be unaware of—or blind to—whether or not they had drunk alcohol. How can researchers run studies in which people are kept blind to whether or not they have drunk alcohol?

Such "blindness" is made possible by the fact that the taste of vodka cannot be detected when vodka is mixed with tonic water in certain amounts. In a typical study, as described in Figure 1.1, some subjects are given highballs containing vodka; others are given tonic water alone. Moreover, half of the subjects in each group are deceived as to the actual content of their drinks. Half of those who actually drink vodka are misled to believe that they are drinking tonic water only. Half of those who drink tonic water only were misinformed that they are drinking highballs with vodka. Thus the effects of actually drinking alcohol (vodka) can be sorted out from the effects of *believing* that one is drinking alcohol.

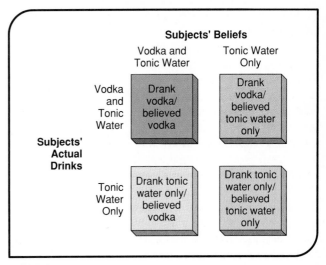

FIGURE 1.1
The experimental conditions in the vodka-and-tonic-water study that separate the effects of subjects' beliefs or expectancies from the effects of the alcohol.

■ **Placebo-Control Studies** Drug-treatment studies are often designed to control for subjects' expectations by keeping subjects in the dark as to whether they are receiving the experimental drug or an *inert placebo* control. The term **placebo** derives from the Latin meaning "I shall please," referring to the fact that belief in the effectiveness of a treatment (its pleasing qualities) may inspire hopeful expectations that help people mobilize themselves to overcome their problems—regardless of whether the substance they receive is chemically active or inert. In medical research on chemotherapy, a placebo—also referred to as a "sugar pill"—is an inert substance that physically resembles an active drug. By comparing the effects of the active drug with those of the placebo, the experimenter can determine whether or not the drug has specific effects beyond those accounted for by expectations.

In a *single-blind placebo-control study*, subjects are randomly assigned to treatment conditions in which they receive an active drug (experimental condition) or a placebo (placebo-control condition), but they are kept blind or uninformed about which drug they are receiving. It is also helpful to keep the dispensing researchers blind as to which substances the subjects are receiving, lest the researchers' expectations come to affect the results. So in the case of a *double-blind placebo design*, neither the researcher not the subject is told whether an active drug or a placebo is being administered. Of course, this approach assumes that the subjects and the experimenters cannot "see through" the blind. In some cases, however, tell-tale side effects or obvious drug effects may break the blind. Still, the double-blind placebo control is among the strongest and most popular experimental designs, especially in drug-treatment research.

Placebo-control groups have also been used in psychotherapy research in order to control for subject expectancies. Assume that you were to study the effects of therapy method A on mood. It would be inadequate to randomly assign the experimental group to therapy A and the control group to a no-treatment waiting list. The experimental group might show improvement because of group participation, not because of therapy method A. Participation might raise expectations of success, and these expectations might be sufficient to engender improvement. Changes in control subjects placed on the "waiting list" would help to account for effects that were due to the passage of time, but they would not account for placebo effects, such as the benefits of therapy that result from instilling a sense of hope.

An *attention-placebo* control group is often used to separate the effects of a particular form of psychotherapy from placebo effects. In an attention-placebo group, subjects are exposed to a believable or credible treatment that contains the nonspecific factors that therapies share—such as the attention and emotional support of a therapist—but not the specific ingredients of therapy represented in the active treatment. Attention-placebo treatments commonly substitute general discussions of participants' problems for the specific ingredients of therapy that are contained in the experimental treatment. Unfortunately, although attention-placebo subjects may be kept blind as to whether or not they are receiving the experimental treatment, the therapists themselves are generally aware of which treatment is being administered. Therefore, the attention-placebo method may not control for therapists' expectations.

? In order to carry out experimental research, it may in fact be necessary to keep participants blind as to whether or not they are receiving the experimental treatment or a placebo. Otherwise, we may not be able to control for the effects of expectations.

■ Experimental Validity Experimental studies are judged as to whether or not they are valid, or sound. The concept of experimental validity has multiple meanings and we shall consider three of them: *internal validity*, *external validity*, and *construct validity*.

Experiments are said to have **internal validity** when the observed changes in the dependent variable(s) can be causally related to the independent or treatment variable. Assume that a group of depressed subjects is treated with a new antidepressant medication (the independent variable), and changes in their mood and behavior (the dependent variables) are tracked over time. After several weeks of treatment, the researcher finds

that most subjects have improved and claims that the new drug is an effective treatment for depression. "Not so fast," you think to yourself, "how does the experimenter know that the independent variable and not some other factor was causally responsible for the improvement? Perhaps the subjects improved naturally as time passed, or perhaps they were exposed to other events that were responsible for their improvement." Experiments lack internal validity to the extent that they fail to control for other factors (called *confounds*, or threats to validity) that might pose rival hypotheses for the results.

We've noted that experimenters randomly assign subjects to treatment and control groups to help control for such rival hypotheses. Random assignment helps ensure that subjects' attributes—intelligence, motivation, age, race, and so on—and life events are randomly distributed across the groups and are not likely to favor one group over the other. Through the random assignment to groups, researchers can be reasonably confident that significant differences between the treatment and control groups reflect the effects of independent (treatment) variables and not confounding selection factors.

External validity refers to the generalizability or applicability of the results of an experimental study to other subjects, settings, and at other times. In most cases, researchers are interested in generalizing the results of a specific study (for example, effects of a new antidepressant medication on a sample of depressed subjects) to a larger population (depressives in general). The external validity of a study is strengthened to the degree that the sample is representative of the target population. In studying the problems of the urban homeless, it is essential to make the effort to recruit a representative sample of the homeless population, rather than focusing on a few homeless people who happen to be available. One way of obtaining a representative sample is by means of random sampling. In a **random sample,** every member of the target population has an equal chance of being selected.

Researchers may seek to extend the results of a particular study by replication, which refers to the process of repeating the experiment in other settings, with samples drawn from other populations, or at other times. A treatment for hyperactivity may be helpful with economically deprived children in an inner-city classroom but not with children in affluent suburbs or rural areas. The external validity of the treatment may be limited since its effects do not generalize to other settings. That does not mean that the treatment is less effective, but that its range of effectiveness is limited to certain populations or situations.

Analogue Studies One method of research that gives rise to many questions of external validity is the **analogue study.** Analogue studies usually take place in laboratory settings that are designed to simulate **in vivo** (real life) behaviors or events. In the laboratory, however, the experimenter has the ability to investigate the behavior of interest under more tightly controlled conditions. In Chapter 6 we shall see that subjects with panic disorders who receive infusions of certain substances in the laboratory are more likely than normal people to report feelings of panic. It may not be feasible to monitor panic attacks in the natural setting, and by inducing panicky sensations under laboratory conditions, researchers may be better able to determine the causal mechanisms that give rise to attacks in the natural environment. But the external validity of such experimental analogues has been challenged. Abnormal behaviors (in this case, "panicky" feelings) that are induced in the laboratory are not necessarily the same as naturally occurring behaviors.

Researchers have also conducted analogue experiments on animals on the effects of smoking. For example, rodents and other animals have been randomly assigned to smoking and nonsmoking conditions in which the amount of smoke that is introduced into their environments is precisely controlled in order to investigate the long-term effects of inhaling cigarette smoke. Such studies, for obvious ethical reasons, could not be conducted with humans.

To the extent that experimental arrangements for analogue studies are reasonable counterparts of natural settings, we can have confidence in their applicability to "real-life" settings. To the extent that we share physiological processes with other species, animal experiments may have much to teach us about ourselves. We have learned much from animal studies about the relationships between stress and development of physical disorders or diseases such as ulcers and cancer, and about the harmful effects of cigarette smoke on health. Animal experiments may also inform us about kinds of learning that are shared by humans and animals. We should be careful, however, in conjecturing about whether or not animals can become "depressed" or "anxious" or suffer loss of problem-solving ability in ways that mirror these experiences among humans.

Construct (pronounced CON-struct) **validity** represents a conceptually higher level of validity—the degree to which treatment effects can be accounted for by the theoretical mechanisms or constructs that are represented in the independent variables. A drug, for example, may have predictable effects but not for the theoretical reasons assumed by the researchers.

Consider a hypothetical experimental study of a new antidepressant medication. The research may have internal validity in the form of solid controls and external validity in the form of generalizability to most seriously depressed people. However, it may lack construct validity if the drug does not work for the reasons proposed by the researchers. Perhaps the researchers assumed that the drug would work by raising the levels of certain chemicals in the nervous system, whereas the drug actually works by increasing the sensitivity of receptors for those chemicals. So what? you may think. After all, the drug still works. True enough—in terms of immediate clinical applications. However, a better understanding of why the drug works can advance theoretical knowledge of depression and give rise to the development of yet more effective treatments.

We can never be certain about the construct validity of research. Scientists recognize that current theories may eventually be toppled by theories that better account for research findings.

Quasi-Experimental Methods

The major features of true experiments are random assignment of subjects to experimental and control groups and manipulation of the independent variables. However, randomization is not always possible or ethically responsible. It would be irresponsible, for example, to assign people in crisis to a group-discussion placebo control at random in an effort to determine the benefits of a crisis-intervention technique. Or we may be interested in whether or not children who watch the television show *Sesame Street* are better prepared for school than those who don't, but may not be able to control experimentally which preschoolers watch the show at home.

So-called **quasi-experiments** (*Quasi* is a Latin word meaning "as if") contain some but not all of the features of a true experiment. When experimenters cannot directly assign subjects randomly to treatment or control conditions, quasi-experiments may yet offer valuable information about the relationship between the independent and dependent variables. Unlike correlational studies, quasi-experiments are concerned with investigating the causal effects of the independent variable on the dependent variables of interest. However, they do not provide the degree of confidence we associate with true experiments. Having noted this drawback, some quasi-experiments are nearly as powerful as true experiments in controlling for possible confounds (Campbell & Stanley, 1963; Cook & Campbell, 1979).

The basic problem with quasi-experimental designs is the lack of random assignment of subjects to experimental conditions. Lacking random assignment, the researcher may be unable to account for the possible differences in the types of subjects that make up the experimental and control groups. Thus, differences in outcomes between treatment and control groups may have more to do with differences in the types of people making up the groups than to the treatment itself. While experimenters may be able to control for certain subject characteristics, such as by ensuring that both treatment and control groups have equal numbers of males and females, only random assignment is likely to balance the groups on the many characteristics that the experimenter was unable to control.

Constraints on the use of random assignment in conducting research in various field settings challenges researchers to design quasi-experiments that provide a reasonable degree of confidence in the results. Consider a quasi-experiment on the effectiveness of inpatient versus outpatient behavioral treatment for **obsessive-compulsive disorder** (van den Hout et al., 1988). Obsessive-compulsive people are bothered by nagging thoughts (obsessions) and by urges to repeat certain behaviors (compulsions), such as repeated hand-washing or checking that appliances are turned off. In this particular study, the researchers could not control which subjects received inpatient treatment and which received outpatient care. The study found significant decreases in obsessive-compulsive behavior among subjects in both treatment settings but no significant differences between the two settings. However, the finding of no difference does not show that both treatment settings were equally effective because subjects admitted to the hospital setting might have had greater problems. That is, a selection factor could have masked *true* differences in treatment effectiveness. Still, the value of this study is that it suggests that outpatient treatment may yield similar benefits as the much more costly inpatient form of treatment. But more definitive conclusions must await experiments in which subjects are randomly assigned to inpatient or outpatient treatment settings.

Epidemiological Method

The **epidemiological method** studies the rates of occurrence of abnormal behavior in various settings or population groups. One type of epidemiological study is the **survey** method, which relies on interviews or questionnaires. Survey methods, for example, have shown that rates of alcoholism vary among diverse ethnic groups (see Chapter 10), in part because ethnic groups have different attitudes toward alcohol and regulate alcohol consumption in different ways.

Like other samples used in research, survey samples need to reflect accurately the population they are intended to represent. A researcher who sets out to study smoking rates in a local community by interviewing people drinking coffee in late-night cafes will probably overestimate its true prevalence.

We've noted that one method of obtaining a representative sample is random sampling. A random sample is drawn in such a way that each member of the population of interest has an equal probability of selection. Researchers also use **stratified random samples,** which are drawn so that known subgroups in the population are randomly selected in proportion to their numbers. For example, blacks constitute about 12 percent of the population in the United States. Thus, a racially stratified sample of the United States would be approximately 12 percent black. Practically speaking, large randomly selected samples show reasonably proportionate stratification. Scientists use randomly drawn nationwide samples of about 1,500 people to gain an accurate picture of the voting patterns of the general U.S. population. But a sample of several million that was haphazardly drawn might not provide an accurate picture.

In one famous example of this error, *Literary Digest* magazine polled millions of readers in 1936 and predicted that Alf Landon, the Republican candidate for President, would defeat the incumbent Franklin D. Roosevelt in a landslide. Actually, the landslide victory went in the opposite direction. The *Literary Digest* readership, you see, contained a higher proportion of conservative voters than the nation at large.

 It is true that a sample of several million people might not represent the population of the United States. A large sample size does not guarantee that members of the target population have an equal chance of being selected.

The epidemiologist must also determine whether people who participate in a study differ in important ways from those who refuse to participate, or else the conclusions might only represent the types of people who are willing to participate rather than the general population. This can be a vital issue in population surveys of the prevalence of abnormal behavior. For one thing, persons who show abnormal behavior are to some degree stigmatized by society, and may thus be reluctant to come forth. For another, people with some patterns of abnormal behavior shun social contacts and for that reason may be unwilling to participate.

Epidemiologists also rely on public health records and records of hospital admissions to track prevalences of disorders. But the survey method may be the only means of measuring certain behaviors that are not included in public records, such as rates of self-initiated smoking cessation.

Epidemiological studies may point to potential causal factors in illness and disorders, even though they lack the power of experiments. By finding that illnesses or disorders "cluster" in certain groups or locations, researchers may be able to identify underlying causal factors that place these groups or regions at higher risk. For example, the Japanese who live in Japan eat low-fat diets and have low rates of colorectal cancer. However, Americans of Japanese descent eat higher-fat diets and have relatively higher rates of colorectal cancer, suggesting that the ingestion of fats is connected with the development of this kind of cancer. Of course, such epidemiological studies cannot control for selection factors—that is, they cannot rule out rival hypotheses concerning other differences between Japanese and Japanese-Americans that may play a causal role. Therefore, they must be considered suggestive of possible causal influences that must be further tested in experimental studies.

The Case-Study Method

Case studies have been important influences in the development of theories and treatment of abnormal behavior. Psychodynamic theory, originated by Sigmund Freud, was developed primarily on the basis of case studies, such as that of Anna O. Although learning theories focus more on laboratory research, learning theorists have also compiled a number of model cases, such as that of Little Albert (see Chapter 2).

■ **Types of Case Studies** There are many kinds of case studies. Generally speaking, **case studies** are carefully sketched biographies of the lives of individuals. Some case studies are basically historical and aim to divulge the factors that cause or contribute to abnormal behavior patterns. These case studies may be based on clinical interviews with subjects, interviews with persons who were close to the subjects, or writing by or about the subjects. Freud, for example, carried out such a case study on the Renaissance artist and inventor Leonardo da Vinci.

 Case studies have in fact been conducted on people who have been dead for hundreds of years, such as Freud's study of Leonardo. Such studies rely on historic records rather than interviews with subjects and their contemporaries.

Other case studies reflect an in-depth analysis of an individual's course of treatment. Such case studies typically include detailed histories of the subject's background and response to treatment. The therapist attempts to glean information from a particular client's experience in therapy that may be of help to other therapists treating similar clients.

Despite the richness of clinical material that case studies can provide, they are much less rigorous as research designs than experiments. There are bound to be gaps in memory when people discuss historic events, especially those of their childhoods. Many of

us have the impression that we have vivid recollections of events from the first two or three years of life, but studies that attempt to verify these memories through interviews with older, independent witnesses show that they are riddled with inaccuracies (Sheingold & Tenney, 1982). Freud himself was aware of this problem and labeled it *childhood amnesia.*[3] Moreover, again as noted by Freud, people may distort their pasts, even to themselves, in the effort to avoid painful memories. Then, too, some clients purposefully color events in such a way as to make a favorable impression on the interviewer; others aim to shock the interviewer with exaggerated or fabricated recollections.

Interviewers themselves may unintentionally encourage subjects to slant their histories in ways that are compatible with their theoretical perspectives. Psychoanalysts have been reproached, for example, for directing clients into viewing their personal histories from the psychodynamic perspective (see, for example, Bandura, 1986). But clinicians and interviewers who hold other theoretical perspectives also run the risk of subtly guiding subjects into uttering what they expect to hear. Then, too, clinicians and interviewers may unintentionally slant subjects' reports when they jot them down—again, subtly shaping them in ways that are more consistent with their own outlooks. And, in his case study of Leonardo, Freud had never met the subject. (Freud was also aware of this limitation.)

So the remembrance of things past, as recounted in case studies, is subject to many distortions. Case reports of treatment effectiveness also have certain problems. When clinicians try out a treatment with a client in the course of practice, they are manipulating treatment as the independent variable. However, they are doing so with one or a small number of people who are hardly representative of the general population. For example, they have sought (or been placed in) professional treatment. Another weakness of the treatment-oriented case study is the lack of a control group. There is usually one client ("subject"), and he or she receives the treatment. In the absence of a control group, it is difficult to tell whether beneficial changes in behavior that are observed over the course of treatment are due to:

1. Specific treatment techniques,
2. Nonspecific therapeutic factors such as raising clients' expectations or giving them time to talk about their problems with a supportive therapist,

---

[3] Freud attributed childhood amnesia to the repression of primitive sexual and aggressive impulses, but contemporary theorists note that the status of neurological and language development during the first few years provides a more likely explanation (Rathus, 1990).

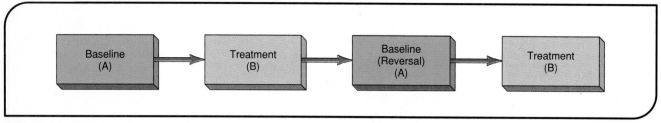

FIGURE 1.2 Diagram of an A-B-A-B reversal design.

3. Naturally occurring ("spontaneous") improvement over time, or

4. External factors such as advice from loved ones, winning the lottery, and so forth.

Like many of us, therapists sometimes engage in self-serving explanations of therapy outcomes: They tend to accept credit for treatment successes but to blame treatment failures on other factors, such as lack of full cooperation on the part of the client.

■ **The Single-Case Experimental Design** The limitations of traditional treatment-oriented case studies have led researchers to develop more sophisticated methods, called **single-case experimental designs,** in which subjects are used as their own controls. One of the most common forms of the single-case experimental design is the A-B-A-B or so-called *reversal design* (see Figure 1.2). The reversal design consists of the repeated measurement of clients' behavior across four successive phases:

1. *A baseline phase* (A). The baseline phase occurs prior to the inception of treatment and is characterized by repeated measurements of the target problem behaviors at periodic intervals. This measurement allows the experimenter to establish a **baseline** rate for the behavior before treatment begins;

2. *A treatment phase* (B). Now the target behaviors are measured as the client undergoes treatment;

3. *A second baseline phase* (A, again). Treatment is now temporarily withdrawn or suspended. This is the reversal in the reversal design, and it is expected that the positive effects of treatment should now be reversed since the treatment has been withdrawn; and

4. *A second treatment phase* (B, again). Treatment is reinstated and the target behaviors are assessed yet again.

Clients' target behaviors or response patterns are compared from one phase to the next in order to determine the effects of treatment. The experimenter looks for evidence of a correspondence between the subject's behavior and the particular phase of the design to determine whether or not the independent variable (that is, the treatment) has produced the intended effects. If the behavior improves whenever treatment is introduced (during the first and second treatment phases) but returns (or is reversed) to baseline levels during the reversal phase, the experimenter can be reasonably confident that the treatment had the intended effect.

The method is illustrated by a case in which Azrin and Peterson (1989) used a controlled blinking treatment to eliminate a severe eye tic—a form of squinting—in which a 9-year-old girl's eyes shut tightly for a fraction of a second. The tic occurred about 20 times a minute when the girl was at home. In the clinic, the rate of eye tics or squinting was measured for 5 minutes during a baseline period (A). Then the girl was prompted to blink her eyes softly every 5 seconds (B). The experimenters reasoned that voluntary "soft" blinking would activate motor (muscle) responses that were incompatible with those producing the tic, thereby suppressing the tic. As you can see in the Figure 1.3, the tic was virtually eliminated in but a few minutes of practicing the incompatible, or competing, response ("soft" blinking) but returned to near baseline levels during the reversal phase (A) when the competing response was withdrawn. The positive effects were quickly reinstated during the second treatment period (B). The child was also taught to practice the blinking response at home during scheduled 3-minute practice periods and whenever the tic occurred or she felt an urge to squint. The tic was completely eliminated during the first six weeks of the treatment program and remained absent at a follow-up evaluation two years later.

Although reversal designs offer better controls than traditional treatment case studies, it is not always possible or ethical to reverse certain behaviors or treatment effects. Clients in programs aimed at quitting smoking, for example, may reduce their rate of smoking during treatment but not revert to baseline rates when treatment is temporarily withdrawn. Such "failure to reverse" can have various explanations. One possibility is simply that the treatment had a desired *and lasting*

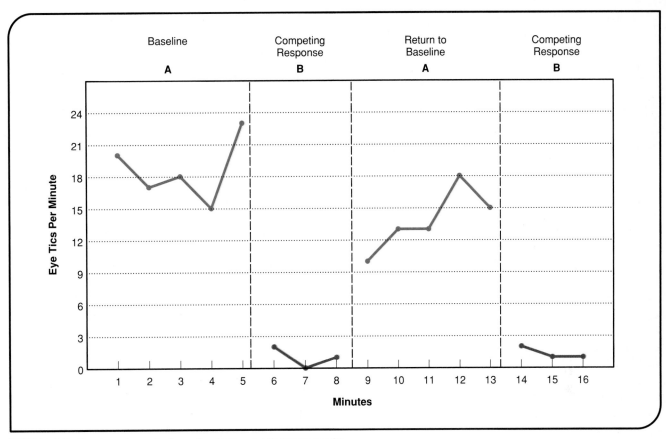

FIGURE 1.3 Treatment results from the Azrin and Peterson study.

Notice how the target response, eye tics per minute, decreased when the competing response was introduced in the first "B" phase, increased to near baseline levels when the competing response was withdrawn during the second "A" phase, and decreased again when the competing response was reinstated in the second "B" phase.

positive effect. Or perhaps such clients learn that they can cut down their cigarette consumption and are not about to return to baseline levels when treatment is suspended.

It may also be unethical to withdraw a treatment program, even briefly, merely to demonstrate that the treatment was effective in maintaining the improvement. We would hardly encourage withdrawing a treatment which appears to be controlling repetitive head-banging in a disturbed child simply to meet the requirements of a more scientific approach to the case study. Nor would a school psychologist who helps a teacher develop a treatment strategy to control a student's unruly behavior in the classroom be willing to reverse treatment in order to demonstrate that the student's behavior during "reversal" will return to baseline levels. (Or if the psychologist were willing to do so, the classroom teacher might decide to become "unruly" and "reverse" the behavior of the psychologist.) Nor are most therapists pleased at the thought of attempting to restore clients' behaviors to baseline levels once improvement has been achieved. Thus, the utility of the

reversal design is generally limited to situations in which behavior can be readily reversed without undesirable consequences.

The *multiple-baseline design* is a type of single-case experimental design that does not require a reversal phase. In a multiple-baseline design *across behaviors*, treatment is applied, in turn, to two or more behaviors following a baseline period. A treatment effect would be inferred if changes in each of these behaviors corresponded to the time at which each was subjected to treatment. Since no reversal phase is required, many of the ethical and practical problems associated with reversal designs are avoided.

A multiple-baseline design was used to evaluate the effects of a social-skills training program in the treatment of the case of a shy, unassertive, 7-year-old girl named Jane (Bornstein et al., 1977). The program taught Jane to maintain eye contact, speak more loudly, and make requests of other people through **modeling** (therapist demonstration of the target behavior), **rehearsal** (practice), and therapist **feedback** regarding the effectiveness of practice. However, the behaviors were taught sequentially, not simultaneously. Measurement of each behavior, and an overall rating of assertiveness, were obtained during a baseline period from observations of Jane's role-playing of social situations with other children, such as playing social games at school and conversing in class. As shown in Figure 1.4, Jane's performance of each behavior improved following treatment. The rating of overall assertiveness showed more gradual improvement as the number of behaviors included in the program increased. Treatment gains were generally maintained at a follow-up evaluation.

To show a clear-cut treatment effect, changes in target behaviors should occur only when they are subjected to treatment. In some cases, however, changes in the treated behaviors may lead to changes in the yet-untreated behaviors, apparently because of generalization. Multiple-baseline designs may not be too useful in situations in which generalization occurs, since it may be unclear whether the changes that occur in either the treated or untreated behaviors were due to the treatment itself or to some external factor. Fortunately, though, generalization effects have tended to be the exception, rather than the rule, in experimental research (Kazdin, 1984).

No matter how tightly controlled the design, or how impressive the results, single-case designs suffer from weak external validity because they do not show whether a treatment that is effective for one person is effective for others. Replication with other individuals can help strengthen external validity. Encouraging results in replication studies may also lead to controlled experiments.

Scientists are generally agreed that experiments are the research designs of choice. Other forms of research are generally conducted in order to pave the way for controlled experiments, or because such experiments would be impractical or unethical.

In this chapter we have defined abnormal behavior and considered historic and contemporary ways of conceptualizing abnormal behavior. We have also reviewed methods of research that investigators use to learn more about the causes of abnormal behavior and to determine effective treatments. In the following chapter we expand upon contemporary models of abnormal behavior.

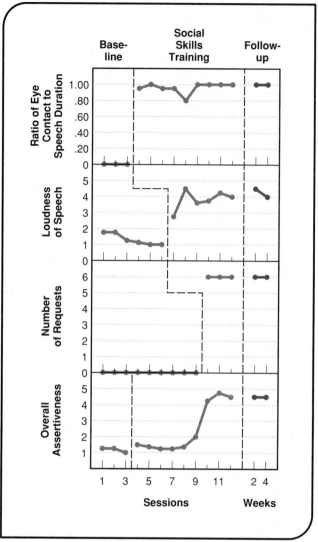

FIGURE 1.4 Treatment results from the Bornstein et al. study. The dotted line resembling the step ladder shows the point at which social skills training was applied to each of the targeted behaviors in turn. Here we see that the targeted behaviors (eye contact, loudness of speech, number of requests) improved only when they were subject to the treatment approach (social skills training), which provides supportive evidence that the treatment—and not some other factor—accounted for the results. The bottom graph shows the ratings of Jane's overall level of assertiveness across the treatment program.

SUMMARY

What Is Abnormal Behavior?

Various criteria are used to define abnormal behavior. Psychologists generally consider behavior abnormal when it meets some combination of the following criteria: (1) unusual or statistically infrequent; (2) socially unacceptable or in violation of social norms; (3) fraught with misperceptions or misinterpretations of reality; (4) associated with states of severe personal distress; (5) maladaptive or self-defeating; or (6) dangerous.

History of Concepts of Abnormal Behavior

Ancient societies attributed abnormal behavior to divine or supernatural forces. Prehistoric peoples may have practiced trephining as a form of treatment, although recent evidence suggests that this practice may represent an ancient form of surgery. In ancient Greece, people who behaved abnormally were sometimes sent to special temples where divine intervention was sought to effect a cure. In medieval times, belief in possession held sway, and exorcists were used to rid people who behaved abnormally of the evil spirits believed to possess them.

There were some authorities in ancient times, like the Greek physician Hippocrates, who believed that abnormal behavior reflected natural causes, specifically imbalances in bodily fluids or humors. Different concentrations of these humors resulted in different types of abnormal behavior. Galen, a Greek physician who attended the Roman Emperor Marcus Aurelius, adopted Hippocrates' teachings and is credited with discovering that arteries carried blood, not air, as was formerly believed. Johann Weyer, a Belgian physician during the Renaissance, took up the cause of Hippocrates and Galen by arguing that abnormal behavior and thought patterns were caused by physical problems. Modern scholars discount the view that people accused of witchcraft in the Middle Ages and the Renaissance were mentally disturbed.

Louis Pasteur was among the many scientists of the eighteenth and nineteenth centuries who helped spearhead the development of medical science. He is credited with the discovery of pasteurization in 1864. The nineteenth-century German physician Wilhelm Griesinger argued that abnormal behavior was caused by diseases of the brain. He and another German physician who followed him, Emil Kraepelin, were influential in the development of the modern medical model, which likens abnormal behavior patterns to physical illnesses. Kraepelin's categorization of mental disorders set the stage for the development of modern systems of classification.

Asylums or "madhouses" began to crop up throughout Europe in the late fifteenth and early sixteenth centuries, often on the site of former leprosariums. Conditions in these asylums were dreadful and for some, such as Bethlehem Hospital in England, a circus atmosphere prevailed. With the rise of moral therapy in the nineteenth century, largely spearheaded by the Frenchmen Jean-Baptiste Pussin and Phillipe Pinel, conditions in mental hospitals improved. Proponents of moral therapy believed that mental patients could be restored to functioning if they were treated with dignity and understanding. The cause of humane treatment was advanced in the United States by such figures as Benjamin Rush, the "Father of American Psychiatry," and the schoolteacher Dorothea Dix. But Rush also used certain harsh treatments, which are now discredited, such as purging and ice-cold baths. Dix, who traveled widely throughout the United States advocating more humane treatment for people with mental disorders, was credited with the establishment of some 32 mental hospitals across the country. The decline of moral therapy in the latter part of the nineteenth century led to a period of apathy and to the belief that the "insane" could not be successfully treated. Conditions in mental hospitals deteriorated, and they offered little more than custodial care.

Not until the middle of the twentieth century did public outrage and concern about the plight of mental patients mobilize legislative efforts toward the development of community mental health centers as alternatives to long-term hospitalization. This movement toward deinstitutionalization was spurred by the introduction of psychoactive drugs, called phenothiazines, which curbed the more flagrant features of schizophrenia. The mental hospital census was cut by more than half by the early 1980s. But critics have charged that deinstitutionalization has resulted in "dumping" large numbers of mental patients in communities without the support services and continuing care they require to adjust successfully to community life.

Abnormal behavior may be viewed from various contemporary perspectives. The medical model conceptualizes abnormal behavior patterns, like physical diseases, in terms of clusters of symptoms, called *syndromes*, which have distinctive causes that are presumed to be biological in nature. Biological perspectives incorporate the medical model but refer more broadly to approaches which relate abnormal behavior to biological processes and which apply biologically based treatments. Psychodynamic perspectives reflect the views of Freud and his followers, who believed that abnormal behavior stemmed from psychological causes involving underlying psychic forces. After abandoning hypnosis as a form of treatment, Freud developed psychoanalysis as a means of uncovering the unconscious conflicts dating back to childhood that he believed were at the root of mental disorders such as hysteria. Also arising in the early twentieth century were learning perspectives that flowered from the work of the physiologist Ivan Pavlov and the contributions of behaviorists like John Watson and B. F. Skinner. Learning theorists posit that the principles of learning can be used to explain both abnormal and normal behavior. Behavior therapy is an outgrowth of the learning model. Humanistic-existential perspectives reject the determinism of psychodynamic theory and behaviorism. Humanistic and existential theorists believe that it is important to understand the obstacles that people encounter as they strive toward self-actualization and authenticity. Cognitive theorists focus on the role of distorted and self-defeating thinking in explaining abnormal behavior. Some adopt an information-processing model to explain abnormal behavior. Sociocultural perspectives believe that abnormal behavior is rooted in social ills, such as poverty, not in the individual. Eclectic models attempt to integrate the contributions of various models.

Research Methods in Abnormal Psychology

The scientific approach focuses on four general objectives: description, explanation, prediction, and control. Description involves careful observation and reporting of abnormal behavior patterns. Scientists develop theories that help to explain abnormal behavior and predict future behavior. Scientists use their knowledge to help people control their behavior more effectively.

There are four basic steps to the scientific method. The first step involves formulating a research question on the basis of observations and theories of behavior. Step two involves framing the research question in the form of a hypothesis, which is a specific prediction about behavior that can be tested in research. The third step involves testing the hypothesis through carefully controlled observation and experimentation. The final step involves drawing conclusions about the correctness of the hypotheses, based upon statistical analysis of the data generated in the research.

Research samples need to be representative of the target population, or else measures of their behavior may not reflect the behavior of the population of interest. Understanding of abnormal behavior is approached from various types of research strategies or designs. The naturalistic-observation method allows scientists to measure behavior under naturally occurring conditions. The method may be limited by the need to ensure unobtrusive measures and by unexpected dangers that may arise in observing people without their knowledge. In addition, the method does not necessarily reveal why people behave the way they do. Correlational research explores the relationship between variables, which may help predict future behavior and suggest possible underlying causes of behavior. But correlational research does not directly test cause-and-effect relationships. Longitudinal research is a type of correlational design that involves the study of selected subjects at periodic intervals over long periods of time, sometimes spanning decades. The advantage is that the development of abnormal behavior can be carefully monitored over time. But the costs and length of time involved in such studies severely limit their usage.

In the experimental method, the investigator directly controls or manipulates the treatment or independent variable under controlled conditions in order to demonstrate cause-and-effect relationships. Experiments use random assignment as the basis for determining which subjects (called experimental subjects) receive the experimental treatment or independent variable, and which others (called control subjects) do not. By using random assignment and holding other conditions constant, experimenters can be reasonably confident that the independent variable (experimental treatment), and not uncontrolled factors or differences between the types of subjects in the experimental and control groups, was causally related to the outcome.

Researchers use various methods to attempt to control for subjects' and researchers' expectations. In a *single-blind placebo-control study*, subjects are randomly assigned to treatment conditions in which they receive an active drug (experimental condition) or a placebo (placebo-control condition), but they are kept blind or uninformed about which drug they are receiving. *Double-blind placebo designs* seek to control both subjects' and researchers' expectancies by keeping both researchers and subjects uninformed about whether an active drug or a placebo is being administered. *Attention-placebo* control groups are sometimes used in psychotherapy research to control for expectancy effects.

Experiments are evaluated in terms of their experimental validity. *Internal validity* refers to the ability of an experimental study to justify a cause-and-effect relationship between the independent or treatment variable and the dependent variable. Internally valid studies control for possible confounds or rival hypotheses. *External validity* refers to the degree to which experimental results can be generalized to other subjects, settings, and at other times. *Construct validity* refers to the degree to which treatment effects can be accounted for by the theoretical mechanisms or constructs that are represented by the independent variables.

Quasi-experiments are sometimes used when random assignment to treatment or control conditions is not possible. However, the lack of direct control over the types of people who compose the treatment and control groups places serious limitations on the ability to justify cause-and-effect relationships between the independent and dependent variables (that is, internal validity).

The epidemiological method examines the rates of occurrence of abnormal behavior in various population groups or settings. Evidence of how disorders cluster in certain groups or geographic areas may reveal underlying causes. But nonrepresentativeness of survey samples, volunteer biases, and selection factors represent possible sources of error.

Case-study methods can provide a richness of clinical material, but they are limited by difficulties of obtaining accurate and unbiased client histories, by possible therapist biases, and by the lack of control groups. Single-case experimental designs are intended to help researchers overcome some of the limitations of the case-study method. The two most common types of single-case experimental designs are reversal designs and multiple baseline designs. By systematically introducing and withdrawing treatment (reversal design) or by staggering the introduction of treatment across target behaviors (multiple baseline design), investigators are better able to tell whether the observed effects are due to treatment or to other factors, such as the mere passage of time.

2 Theoretical Perspectives

- ___ According to psychodynamic theory, the mind is analogous to an immense iceberg: only the tip of it emerges into awareness.
- ___ Fingernail biting and cigarette smoking as an adult are signs of early childhood conflict.
- ___ A woman was expelled from the New York Psychoanalytic Institute for arguing that little girls are not envious of boys' penises.
- ___ Researchers conditioned a young boy to fear rats by clanging steel bars behind his head while he played with a rat.
- ___ Punishment does not work.
- ___ People are more motivated to tackle arduous tasks if they believe that they will succeed at them.
- ___ People make themselves miserable by the ways in which they interpret events.
- ___ Abnormal behavior is connected with chemical imbalances in the brain.
- ___ Anxiety can give you indigestion.
- ___ Abnormal behavior runs in families.

LEARNING OBJECTIVES

When you have completed your study of Chapter 2, you should be able to:

PSYCHODYNAMIC PERSPECTIVES (pp. 36–46)
1. Describe the basic tenets of Sigmund Freud's psychoanalytic theory.
2. Describe more recent psychodynamic theories, comparing and contrasting them to Freud's views.
3. Critically evaluate psychodynamic theories.

LEARNING PERSPECTIVES (pp. 46–55)
4. Describe behaviorism and the principles of conditioning.
5. Describe social-learning theory and the situation and person variables that influence behavior.
6. Critically evaluate learning theories.

COGNITIVE PERSPECTIVES (pp. 55–58)
7. Discuss the information-processing approach, and the theoretical contributions of George Kelly, Albert Ellis, and Aaron Beck.
8. Critically evaluate cognitive theories.

HUMANISTIC-EXISTENTIAL PERSPECTIVES (pp. 58–63)
9. Outline some tenets of humanistic and existential philosophies.

10. Describe the views of Viktor Frankl, Abraham Maslow, and Carl Rogers.
11. Critically evaluate humanistic-existential theories.

SOCIOCULTURAL PERSPECTIVES (pp. 63–65)
12. Discuss the sociocultural views of abnormal behavior.
13. Critically evaluate the sociocultural perspectives.

BIOLOGICAL PERSPECTIVES (pp. 65–74)
14. Describe the structure and functions of the nervous system and explain how neurons communicate with each other.
15. Describe the structures of the brain and their functions.
16. Describe the functions of the endocrine system and explain how hormones are implicated in human behavior.
17. Explain how various kinds of kinship studies suggests roles for genetics in abnormal behavior.
18. Critically evaluate theories concerning the relationships between biological structures and processes and abnormal behavior.

Since earliest times humans have sought explanations for strange or deviant behavior. In ancient times and through the Middle Ages, beliefs about abnormal behavior centered on the role of demons and other supernatural forces. But even in ancient times, as you recall from Chapter 1, there were some scholars, such as Hippocrates and Galen, who sought explanations of abnormal behavior in terms of natural processes. In contemporary times, the understanding of abnormal behavior has been largely approached from psychological, sociocultural, and biological perspectives.

While models of abnormal behavior can be traced back to earliest times, the scientific study of abnormal psychology is still relatively young. We are only beginning to understand many disorders, and as we do, our earlier beliefs are modified or replaced by new ones. In this chapter we explore the various contemporary perspectives on abnormal behavior. Each perspective has led to the development of theories about why we behave normally, and why we do not. Each has something to offer to our understanding of abnormal behavior, but none have been accepted by everybody. This is not surprising given the complexity and range of human behavior in general, and abnormal behavior in particular. Some perspectives have more to offer our understanding of certain abnormal behavior patterns than they do of others. We will return to these theoretical perspectives at many points in the text as we review in coming chapters the specific patterns of abnormal behavior. For now, let us turn our attention to some of the principles and viewpoints of each of the major perspectives.

PSYCHODYNAMIC PERSPECTIVES

As you'll recall from Chapter 1, psychodynamic theory is based on the contributions of Sigmund Freud and his followers. While there are differences among psychodynamic theorists, they have a number of things in common. Each endorses the principle of **psychic determinism,** the view that our behavior—normal and abnormal—is determined by the outcome of dynamic processes and conflicts within the mind. Our inner drives such as sex and aggression, in this view, come into conflict with social rules and moral codes. The social rules and moral codes become internalized as parts of ourselves. And so the dynamic struggle becomes a conflict of opposing *inner* forces. At a given moment our observable behaviors, as well as our thoughts and emotions, represent the outcome of these inner clashes.

Psychodynamic theories also agree that many of the motivating forces within us are fully or partially unconscious. We do not fully recognize them, even when they are powerful determinants of our behavior. These theories also focus on the importance of early childhood experience. In this view, the seeds of psychological disorders are planted during our early, "formative" years.

Each psychodynamic theory owes its origin to the psychoanalytic theory of Sigmund Freud, and so our coverage begins with his contributions.

Sigmund Freud's Theory of Psychosexual Development

The year was 1856. In a small Czechoslovakian village, an elderly woman prophesized that a newborn child would become a great man. The child, Sigmund Freud (1856–1939), was reared with great expectations. As a man, Freud himself would be skeptical of this belief. Soothsayers, after all, earn larger favors by forecasting good news than bad. But the revelation about Freud proved prescient. Few have had such an enormous impact on our contemplations of human nature.

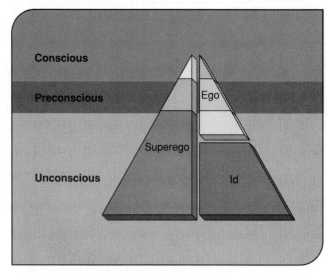

FIGURE 2.1 The "human iceberg."
According to psychodynamic theory, only a small part of the mind rises to conscious awareness at any moment in time. While material in the preconscious may be brought into consciousness if we focus our attention on it, the impulses and ideas in the unconscious tend to remain veiled in mystery.

Trained as a physician, Freud was intrigued early in his career by the fact that some of his patients appeared to suffer the loss of feeling in parts of their bodies or paralysis of their arms or legs without any medical disorder that could explain their symptoms. These symptoms, which were taken as signs of hysteria, often disappeared once the patients, under hypnosis, recalled and discussed upsetting events and feelings of anxiety and guilt that appeared to be connected with the symptoms. These feelings and experiences had remained hidden beneath the level of awareness for great lengths of time. Even so, they appeared to influence present behavior.

This clinical evidence led Freud to conclude that the mind was like an iceberg (Figure 2.1). Only the tip of an iceberg is visible above the surface of the water. The great mass of the iceberg lies below the surface, darkening the deep. Freud came to believe that people, similarly, were only aware of a small number of the ideas, wishes, and impulses that dwelled within their minds and contributed to or motivated their behavior. Freud held that the larger part of the mind, which includes our deepest wishes, fears, and urges, remained below the surface of consciousness.

Freud's psychodynamic theory does consider the mind as analogous to an immense iceberg, with only the tip rising into conscious awareness.

■ **Conscious, Preconscious, Unconscious: The Geography of the Mind** Freud labeled the region that corresponds to one's present awareness the **conscious** part of the mind. The regions that lay beneath the surface of awareness were labeled the *preconscious* and the *unconscious*.

In the **preconscious** mind are the memories of experience that are not presently in awareness, but which can be brought to the level of awareness by simply focusing on them. Your telephone number, for example, remains in the preconscious until you focus on bringing it into consciousness. But the **unconscious** mind, the largest part of the mind, remains shrouded in mystery. Its contents can only be brought to awareness with great difficulty, if at all. Freud believed that the unconscious was the repository of biologically based drives or instincts such as sex and aggression. He posited that there exist **defense mechanisms,** such as **repression,** that protect us from recognizing wishes or impulses that would be inconsistent with our moral values and social responsibilities. Repression, or motivated forgetting, involves the automatic process by which anxiety-evoking ideas and desires are pushed down into the unconscious and kept out of awareness. With repression, the person can remain outwardly calm and controlled, but inwardly harbor murderous or lustful impulses of which he or she is unaware.

■ **The Structure of Personality** Freud also developed the **structural hypothesis,** according to which the clashing forces of personality could be divided into three mental or **psychic** structures. Psychic structures could not be seen or directly measured, but their presence was reflected in our observable behavior, thoughts, and emotions. There is a tendency to think of these psychic structures as separate people who reside in the personality and oppose each other in pitched battle. But Freud treated these structures as metaphors to describe the strong motivational forces within the personality, not as distinct entities or persons. Freud posited the existence of three psychic structures: the *id, ego,* and *superego.*

The **id** is the only psychic structure that is present at birth. The id represents the biological drives and is completely unconscious. It is, in Freud's view, "a chaos, a cauldron of seething excitations" (1964, p. 73). The id follows what Freud termed the **pleasure principle.** It demands instant gratification of instincts without consideration of social custom or the needs of others. One way of achieving rapid gratification is by **primary process thinking,** or the conjuring up of mental images of the objects of desire. The id, that is, operates in a world of desire and fantasy.

During the first year of life, the child discovers that its every demand is not instantly gratified. It must learn to cope with delay of gratification. The **ego** devel-ops during this first year to organize reasonable ways of coping with frustration. Standing for "reason and good sense" (Freud, 1964, p. 76), the ego seeks to curb the demands of the id and direct behavior that is in keeping with social customs and expectations, so that gratification can be achieved, but not at the expense of the disapproval of others. The id prompts you to realize that you are hungry. Were it to have its way, the id might prompt you to stuff your face with any food at hand or even to swipe the food off someone else's plate. But ego creates the thought of walking to the refrigerator, making yourself a sandwich and pouring a glass of milk.

The ego is governed by the **reality principle.** It takes into account that which is practical and possible, as well as the urgings of the id. It is the ego that brings into being the conscious sense of self. The ego engages in **secondary process thinking,** or the remembering, planning, and weighing of circumstances that permit us to mediate between the fantasies of the id and the realities of the outer world.

During middle childhood, the moral standards and values of the child's parents and other important people in its life become internalized in the form of the **superego** through a process called **identification.** The superego operates according to the **moral principle,** the governing rule that demands adherence to moral standards. In part the superego represents the moral values of an ideal self, called the **ego ideal.** But it also serves as a conscience, or internal moral guardian, monitoring the ego and passing judgment on right and wrong. It metes out punishment in the form of guilt and shame when it finds that ego has failed to adhere to superego's moral standards. Ego stands between the id and the superego. It endeavors to satisfy the cravings of the id without offending the moral standards of the superego. An overly powerful superego can create excessive feelings of guilt and lead to depression. An underdeveloped superego is believed to play a role in explaining antisocial behavior tendencies (discussed in Chapter 9) of people who intentionally hurt others without feelings of guilt.

■ **Defense Mechanisms**

Happiness is good health and a bad memory. (Ingrid Bergman)

People use thought only to justify their wrongdoings, and speech only to conceal their thoughts. (Voltaire, *Dialogue xiv. Le Chapon et la Poularde*)

While part of the ego rises to consciousness, some of its activity is carried out unconsciously. In the unconscious, the ego serves as a kind of watchdog or censor that screens the impulses that arise from the id. The ego makes use of psychological defenses to prevent socially unacceptable impulses from rising into consciousness. If it were not for these defenses, or **defense mechanisms,** the darkest sins of our childhoods, the primitive demands of our ids, and the censures of our superegos would overwhelm our capacity to adjust and psychologically disable us. Repression is considered the most basic of the defense mechanisms. A listing of some of the defense mechanisms are contained in Table 2.1.

So a dynamic struggle takes place in the unconscious between id and ego, one that pits biological drives that strive for expression, the id, against the embodiment of social acceptability, the ego, which seeks to restrain or channel them into more acceptable outlets in ways that do not incur the condemnation of the superego. The resultant conflict can give rise to various psychological disorders and behavioral problems. Since

TABLE 2.1 Some Defense Mechanisms of the Ego, According to Psychodynamic Theory

Defense Mechanism	Definition	Theoretical Examples of Defense Mechanisms in Normal Behavior	Theoretical Examples of Defense Mechanisms in Abnormal Behavior
Repression	The ejection of anxiety-evoking ideas from awareness.	A client in psychoanalysis forgets an appointment at a time when anxiety-evoking material is about to be brought up.	A person who has hurt people close to him cannot recall his identity or the facts concerning his personal life.
Regression	The return, under conditions of stress, of a behavioral pattern that was characteristic of an earlier stage of development.	An adolescent cries when denied the opportunity to travel abroad. An adult becomes dependent on his parents following the dissolution of his marriage.	Under extreme stress a person regresses to the first months of life, where she is ruled by impulses and cannot distinguish between fantasy and reality.
Rationalization	The use of justifications for unacceptable behavior as a form of self-deception.	A student who is caught cheating blames her teacher for leaving the room during the exam. A man explains his continued smoking by saying, "Cancer doesn't run in my family."	A man justifies raping a woman by claiming that she was dressing provocatively.
Displacement	The transfer of impulses or wishes toward threatening objects onto safer or less threatening objects.	An employee who is sharply criticized by her boss starts a fight with her roommate when returning home from work.	A man who is frustrated at work kills his family.
Projection	The attribution to others of one's own unacceptable impulses.	A hostile, argumentative person perceives others as having problems controlling their tempers. A sexually inhibited person interprets innocent glances from others as sexual advances.	A hostile person develops delusions that others are attempting to destroy him.
Reaction formation	The adoption of behavior that is opposite in nature to one's genuine impulses in order to keep such impulses repressed.	A person who deeply resents a relative goes out of his way to be nice toward the relative.	A conservative woman who cannot accept her own sexual desires goes on a compulsive crusade to ban pornography.
Denial	Refusal to accept the reality of a threat.	A college student in academic difficulty refuses to accept the possibility of failure.	A person with a heart condition denies the seriousness of recurring symptoms, placing himself at greater risk by refusing to seek medical attention.
Sublimation	The channeling of unacceptable impulses into positive, constructive pursuits.	A person becomes devoted to artistic pursuits. A hostile person directs aggressive energies into competitive sports.	(Sublimation is not usually associated with abnormal behavior.)

Source: *Adapted from Rathus, 1990, p. 396.*

According to psychodynamic theory, denial is a defense mechanism in which the ego fends off anxiety by preventing the recognition of the true nature of a threat. Failing to take seriously the warnings of health risks from cigarette smoking is a form of denial.

we cannot view the unconscious mind directly, Freud first experimented with but ultimately rejected the technique of hypnosis as a means of probing the unconscious. In its place, he developed a method of mental detective work called **psychoanalysis.** In psychoanalysis clients are encouraged to talk about anything that comes to mind, a process called **free association.** People may eventually achieve **self-insight** into their unconscious motivation through this process of pursuing the thoughts that "pop" into awareness. But the defense mechanisms may not permit full disclosure of unsettling or threatening material. The same defense mechanism of repression that serves to block unacceptable thoughts from consciousness also prompts **resistance,** or the blocking of ideas or thoughts whose awareness would produce anxiety. Overcoming such resistances can make psychoanalysis a process that can take years.

According to psychodynamic theory, the use of defense mechanisms to cope with feelings like anxiety, guilt, and shame is perfectly normal. The mechanisms

"This is where Herbert works out his aggressions."

Drawing by B. Tobey; © 1983 The New Yorker Magazine, Inc.

enable all of us to keep a lid on impulses from the id as we go about our daily business. In his book *The Psychopathology of Everyday Life*, Freud noted how slips of the tongue and forgetfulness represented hidden motives or ways of keeping them repressed. If a friend means to say "I hear what you're saying," but it comes out "I hate what you're saying," are her real unconscious feelings revealed? If a lover storms out in anger but forgets his umbrella, is it because he's unconsciously looking for an excuse to return?

Psychological defenses may also give rise to abnormal behavior patterns. For example, Freud hypothesized that hysterical symptoms represent a defense against unbearable memories or wishes. A hysterical symptom, like the paralysis of an arm that remains immobile despite the absence of any organic problem, may represent a defense against acting out unconscious aggressive wishes to harm others. Since the arm will not move, it cannot be used to act upon these wishes. The symptom symbolizes or represents the unconscious dynamic struggle taking place, beneath the surface of awareness, between the unacceptable or threatening urges or impulses seeking expression and the counter-forces or defenses, organized by the ego, that seek to restrain them or rechannel them into more acceptable outlets. This hypothesis developed into the theory of psychoanalysis, with which Freud hoped to explain all of human behavior, normal and abnormal, not just hysteria.

When the ego is too weak, we are in danger of being overwhelmed by the forces of the id. In Freud's theory, **neuroses** develop as ways of trying to stem the leakage of unacceptable impulses from the id. Neuroses refer to maladaptive behavior patterns, such as hysteria or **phobia,** which Freud believed represented or symbolized these inner conflicts. **Neurotic anxiety** occurs when the ego senses that unacceptable impulses might break through to consciousness. Neurotic anxiety, then, is a fear of one's own forbidden impulses or impulses, in contrast to **reality anxiety,** which represents fear of external dangers or threats (for example, feeling afraid if you were awakened at night by sounds of an intruder). Neurotic symptoms such as hysterical paralysis or phobias are believed to serve a purpose of shielding the self from awareness of these unconscious promptings. The person remains aware of the symptom, but not of the underlying conflict it represents. The symptom may also serve to prevent the expression of the threatening impulse, as noted with respect to hysterical paralysis. So, too, the person with **acrophobia,** an excessive fear of heights, might harbor unconscious self-destructive tendencies that are kept in check by avoiding situations, such as high balconies, in which he or she might be unable to control deep-seated urges to jump. The neurotic person is generally able to function but is impaired in some respects by the neurotic symptom. People with a phobia of heights, for example, may be able to function quite normally, as long as they avoid situations involving heights.

Freud believed that the underlying conflicts in neuroses had childhood origins that were buried in the depths of the unconscious. Through psychoanalysis, he sought to help people uncover and "work through" these underlying conflicts to free themselves of the need to maintain the overt symptom. We'll take a closer look at the traditional categories of neuroses in Chapters 6 and 7. We'll also take a closer look at the technique of psychoanalysis in Chapter 15.

When the id breaks through completely, a person's behavior becomes **psychotic** or detached from reality. Primary process thinking and bizarre behavior rule the day. Psychoses are characterized, in general, by more severe disturbances of functioning than neuroses, by the appearance of bizarre behavior and thoughts, and by faulty perceptions of reality, such as **hallucinations** ("hearing voices" or seeing things that are not present). The most prominent form of psychosis is **schizophrenia,** which is discussed in Chapter 12.

■ **Stages of Psychosexual Development** Freud aroused heated controversy in the medical establishment of his time by arguing that sexual drives were dominant factors in the development of personality, even among children. Freud believed that the child's basic relationship to the world in its first several years of life was organized in terms of its pursuit of bodily pleasures. (In Freud's view, all activities that were physically pleasurable, such as eating or moving one's bowels, were in essence sexual.)

The drive for sexual pleasure represented, in Freud's view, the expression of a major life instinct, which he called **Eros**—the basic drive to preserve and perpetuate life. The energy contained in Eros that allows it to fulfill its function was termed **libido,** or sexual energy. Freud believed that libidinal energy is expressed

In the so-called oral stage, many of the child's encounters with the world are experienced through the mouth.

through sexual pleasure in different body parts, called **erogenous zones,** as the child progressed through development. In Freud's view, the stages of human development were **psychosexual** in nature since they correspond to the transfer of libidinal energy from one erogenous zone to another. Freud proposed that there were five psychosexual stages of development: oral, anal, phallic, latency, and genital. Let us briefly review these stages.

During its first year, the child's encounters with the world are mostly experienced through its mouth. Anything that fits into the mouth, goes into the mouth. Freud labeled this period the **oral stage** and argued that oral stimulation, in the form of sucking and biting, is a source of both sexual gratification and nourishment.

One of Freud's central beliefs is that the child may encounter conflict during each of the psychosexual stages of development. Conflict during the oral stage centers around the issue of whether or not the infant receives adequate oral gratification. Too much gratification could lead the infant to expect that everything in life is given with little or no effort on its part. In contrast, early **weaning** might lead to frustration. Too little or too much gratification at any stage could lead to **fixation** in that stage, which leads to the development of personality traits characteristic of that stage. Oral fixations could include an exaggerated desire for "oral activities," which could become expressed in later life in smoking, alcohol abuse. overeating, and nail biting. Like the infant who is dependent on the mother's breast for survival and gratification of oral pleasure, orally fixated adults may also become clinging and dependent in their interpersonal relationships.

 Within psychodynamic theory, fingernail biting and cigarette smoking as an adult may be considered signs of early childhood conflict.

While fixations are not insurmountable, they frequently are very resistant to change. Freud himself showed signs of such stubbornly fixated oral behaviors. He never gave up his habit of smoking cigars, despite the fact that it may have contributed to the development of cancer of the jaw and mouth, which not only required many operations but also eventually led to his death in 1939.

During the **anal stage** of psychosexual development, the child experiences sexual gratification through contraction and relaxation of the sphincter muscles that control elimination of bodily waste. While elimination had been controlled reflexively during much of the first year of life, the child now learns that he or she is able, though perhaps not reliably at first, to exercise voluntary muscular control over elimination.

Now the child begins to learn that it can delay gratification of the need to eliminate when it feels the urge. During toilet training, parental demands for self-control may lead to conflict between parents and child. **Anal fixations** that derive from this conflict are associated with two sets of traits. Harsh toilet training may lead to the development of **anal-retentive** traits, which involve excessive needs for self-control. These include perfectionism and extreme needs for orderliness, cleanliness, and neatness. By contrast, excessive gratification during the anal period might lead to **anal-expulsive** traits, which include carelessness and messiness.

The next stage of psychosexual development, the **phallic stage,** generally begins during the third year of life. The major erogenous zone during the stage is the phallic region (the penis in boys, the clitoris in girls). Conflict between parent and child may occur over masturbation—the rubbing of the phallic areas for sexual pleasure—which parents may react to with threats and punishments. Perhaps the most controversial of Freud's beliefs was his suggestion that phallic-stage children develop incestuous wishes for the parent of the opposite sex and begin to view the parent of the same sex as a rival for the affections of the parent they wish to possess.

■ **The Oedipus and Electra Complexes**   Conflict at the phallic stage is believed to have far-reaching consequences in determining later development and assumption of **sex roles.** Freud believed that **castration anxiety** played an important role in resolving the conflict for boys. Adults sometimes threaten boys with castration to try to get them to stop touching themselves. Freud documented such castration threats from parents or nurses in several case studies. At some point boys discover that girls are different from themselves by not having penises. Freud conjectured that boys might imagine that girls had lost their penises as a form of punishment. Going further, Freud hypothesized that boys develop **castration anxiety,** based on the fantasy that their rivals for their mother's affections, namely their fathers, would seek to punish them for their incestuous wishes by removing the organ that has become connected with sexual pleasure. To prevent castration, Freud argued, boys repress their incestuous wishes for their mothers and identify with their fathers. Keep in mind that Freudian theory posits that these developments are quite normal, and ordinarily lead to the boy's development of the aggressive, independent characteristics associated with the traditional masculine sex role. The conflict in boys was labeled the **Oedipus complex,** after Oedipus the King, the legendary Greek monarch who unwittingly slew his father and married his mother.

The female counterpart to the Oedipal conflict has sometimes been called the **Electra complex,** after the character of Electra, who, according to Greek legend, avenged the death of her father, king Agamemnon, by slaying her father's murderers—her own mother

Childhood sexuality? Freud's belief that even young children have sexual impulses shocked the medical establishment of his time. But many of his own followers believed that Freud had placed too much importance on sexual motivation.

and her mother's lover. The Electra complex is like a mirror image of the Oedipus complex in boys. When resolved successfully, in Freud's view, it leads girls to identify with their mothers and acquire the more passive, dependent characteristics traditionally associated with the feminine sex role. Freud believed that little girls become envious of boy's penises. This jealousy leads them to become resentful toward their mothers, whom they blame for their lack of a penis. Girls then desire to possess the father, in a way substituting the father's penis for their own missing ones. But the rivalry with the mother for the father's affection places them in peril of losing the love and protection of the mother.

The crisis resolves with girls forsaking their incestuous desires for their fathers and identifying with their mothers. Eventually the wish for a penis is transformed into the desire to marry a man and bear children, which represents the ultimate adjustment of surrendering the wish "to be a man" by accepting a baby as a form of penis substitute. Freud hypothesized that, in adulthood, women who retain the wish for a penis of their own ("to be a man") can become maladjusted and develop masculine-typed characteristics such as competitiveness, dominance, and even female homosexuality.

Freud's views of female psychosexual development have been roundly attacked by women and by

Karen Horney

modern-day psychoanalysts. One of the most prominent critics, the psychoanalyst Karen Horney (1885–1952), for example, argued that evidence of penis envy was not confirmed by observations of children and that Freud's view reflected the cultural prejudice in Western society against women. To Horney, cultural expectations played a great role in shaping women's self-images, not penis envy. Interestingly, Horney's outspoken opposition to the manner in which the psychoanalytic establishment of her time conceptualized and treated women led to her expulsion from the staid New York Psychoanalytic Institute (Quinn, 1987).

> **?** A woman was indeed expelled from the New York Psychoanalytic Institute for arguing that traditional psychodynamic views of personality development—such as the penis-envy hypothesis—were degrading to females. Her name was Karen Horney.

We should also note that Freud's psychodynamic theory was a product of its day. While there are still people today who believe that women should be passive and dependent on men, the oppression of women was far greater in Freud's day than it is today. Back then, motherhood and family life were, by and large, the only socially proper avenues of fulfillment for women. Women who pursued careers rather than motherhood were rare and often deemed abnormal. Today, the choices available to women are more varied, and normality is not conceived in terms of rigidly defined sex roles.

The Oedipus and Electra complexes come to a point of resolution by about the time the child is 5 or 6 with the repression of incestuous wishes for the parent of the opposite sex and the identification with the parent of the same sex. From this identification comes the internalization of parental values in the form of the

superego. Children then enter the **latency stage** of psychosexual development, a period of late childhood during which sexual impulses remain in a latent state. Interests become directed toward school and play activities. But sexual drives are once again aroused with the **genital stage,** beginning with puberty, which reaches fruition in mature sexuality, marriage, and the bearing of children. The sexual feelings toward the opposite-sex parent that had remained repressed during the latency period emerge during adolescence, but are displaced, or transferred, onto socially appropriate members of the opposite sex. But boys might still look for girls "just like the girl that married dear old Dad." And girls might still be attracted to boys who resemble their "dear old Dads."

In Freud's view, successful adjustment during the genital stage involves the attainment of sexual gratification through intercourse with someone of the opposite sex. Other forms of sexual expression, such as oral or anal stimulation, masturbation, and homosexual activity, are considered **pregenital** fixations, or immature forms of sexual conduct.

Other Psychodynamic Theorists

Freud left a rich intellectual legacy that has stimulated the thinking of many theorists. Psychodynamic theory has been shaped over the years by the contributions of psychodynamic theorists who shared certain central tenets in common with Freud, such as the belief that behavior reflects unconscious motivation, inner conflict, and the operation of defensive responses to anxiety (Wachtel, 1982). But they tended to de-emphasize the roles of basic instincts such as sex and aggression, and to place greater emphasis on conscious choice, self-direction, and creativity. These theorists also differ from each other in various ways.

One of the most prominent of the early psychodynamic theorists was Carl Jung (1875–1961), a Swiss psychiatrist who was formerly a member of Freud's inner circle. His break with Freud came when he developed his own psychodynamic theory, which he called **analytical psychology.** Like Freud, Jung believed that unconscious processes were important in explaining behavior. Jung believed that an understanding of human behavior must incorporate the facts of self-awareness and self-direction as well as the impulses of the id and the mechanisms of defense. He believed that not only do we have a *personal* unconscious, a repository of repressed memories and impulses, but we also inherit a **collective unconscious.** To Jung, the collective unconscious represented the accumulated experience of humankind, which he believed was passed down genetically through the generations. The collective unconscious was believed to contain primitive images, or **ar-**

Carl Gustav Jung

chetypes, which reflect upon the history of our species, including vague, mysterious mythical images like the All-Powerful God, the fertile and nurturing mother, the young hero, the wise old man, and themes of rebirth or resurrection. While archetypes remain unconscious, in Jung's view, they influence our thoughts, dreams, and emotions.

Alfred Adler (1870–1937), like Jung, had held a place in Freud's inner circle, but broke away as he developed his own beliefs that people were basically driven by an **inferiority complex,** not by the sexual instinct as Freud had maintained. For some people, feelings of inferiority are based on physical problems and the resulting need to compensate for them. But all of us, because of our small size and helplessness during childhood, encounter feelings of inferiority to some degree. These feelings lead to a powerful **drive for superiority,** which motivates us to achieve prominence and social dominance. In the healthy personality, however, strivings for dominance are tempered by devotion to helping other people.

Adler, like Jung, believed that self-direction and self-awareness play major roles in the development of personality. Adler spoke of a **creative self,** a self-aware aspect of personality that strives to overcome obstacles and develop the individual's potential. The creative self develops within a social context, so that our social circumstances and relationships play formative roles in our personality development. With the hypothesis of the creative self, Adler shifted the emphasis of psychodynamic theory from the id to the ego. Because we all have unique potentials, Adler's theory has been termed **individual psychology.**

There are many other psychodynamic models that have arisen with the work of Freud's followers, who are sometimes referred to collectively as **neo-Freudians.** Some psychodynamic theorists, such as Karen Horney and Harry Stack Sullivan (1892–1949), focused on the social context of psychological problems and stressed the importance of child-parent relationships in determining the nature of later interpersonal relationships. Sullivan, for example, maintained that children of rejecting parents tend to become self-doubting and anxious. These personality features persist and impede the development of close relationships in adult life.

More recent psychodynamic models also place a greater emphasis on the self or the ego, and less emphasis on the sexual instinct, than did Freud. Today, most psychoanalysts see people as motivated on two tiers: by the growth-oriented, conscious pursuits of the ego as well as by the more primitive, conflict-ridden drives of the id. Heinz Hartmann (1894–1970) was one of the originators of **ego psychology,** which posits that the ego has energy and motives of its own. Freud, remember, believed that ego functions were fueled by the id, were largely defensive, and were perpetually threatened by the irrational. Hartmann and other ego analysts find Freud's views of the ego—and of people in general—too pessimistic and ignoble. Hartmann argued that the cognitive functions of the ego could be independent and free of conflict. The choices to seek an education, dedicate oneself to art and poetry, and further humanity were not defensive forms of sublimation, as Freud had seen them.

Another ego analyst, Erik Erikson (1902–   ), attributed more importance to children's social relationships than to unconscious processes. Whereas Freud viewed development as psychosexual, Erikson saw it as **psychosocial.** Erikson posited eight stages of psychosocial development, as seen in Table 2.2. Each stage is named according to the possible outcomes, which are polar opposites.

Whereas Freud's psychosexual stages of development end with the genital stage, beginning in early adolescence, Erikson focuses on continued development processes throughout adulthood. The goal of adolescence, in Erikson's view, is not genital sexuality, but rather the attainment of **ego identity.** Adolescents who achieve ego identity develop a clearly defined and firm sense of who they are and what they believe in. Adolescents who drift without purpose or clarity of self remain in a state of **role diffusion** and are especially subject to negative peer influences.

One popular contemporary psychodynamic approach is termed **object-relations theory,** which focuses on how children come to develop symbolic representations of important others in their lives, especially their parents. (An "object," in psychodynamic terms, is generally a parent or other person to whom one becomes attached.) One of the major contributors to object-relations theory was Margaret Mahler (1897–1985), who saw the process of separating from the mother during the first three years of life as crucial to personality development. According to psychodynamic

TABLE 2.2 Erik Erikson's Stages of Development

Time Period	Life Crisis	The Developmental Task
Infancy (0–1)	Trust versus mistrust	Developing trust in the mother and the environment
Early childhood (2–3)	Autonomy versus shame and doubt	Developing the desire to make choices and the self-control to follow through on choices
Preschool years (4–5)	Initiative versus guilt	Adding planning to choice; becoming active
Grammar school years (6–12)	Industry versus inferiority	Becoming absorbed in tasks and productive pursuits
Adolescence	Identity versus role diffusion	Connecting skills and interests to the formation of career objectives
Young adulthood	Intimacy versus isolation	Committing oneself to another in an intimate relationship
Middle adulthood	Generativity versus stagnation	Needing to be needed; guiding the younger generation; striving to be creative
Late adulthood	Integrity versus despair	Accepting one's place in the life cycle; achieving wisdom and dignity

Source: *Erikson, 1963, pp. 247–269.*

theory, we **introject,** or incorporate into our own personalities, elements of major figures in our lives. Introjection is more powerful when we fear losing others to death or having them disapprove of us. Thus, we might be particularly apt to incorporate elements of people who *disapprove* of us or who see things differently.

In Mahler's view, these symbolic representations, which are formed from images and memories of others, come to influence our perceptions and behavior. We experience internal conflict as the attitudes of introjected people battle with our own. Some of our perceptions may be distorted or seem unreal to us. Some of our impulses and behavior may seem unlike us, as if they come out of the blue. With such conflict, we may not be able to tell where the influences of other people end and our "real selves" begin. The aim of Mahler's therapeutic approach was to help clients separate their own ideas and feelings from those of the introjected objects so that they could develop as individuals—as their own persons.

Psychodynamic Perspectives on Normality and Abnormality

Psychodynamic theorists account for abnormal behavior in various ways. According to Freud, there is a thin line between the normal and the abnormal. Normal as well as abnormal people are motivated or driven by the irrational drives of the id. The difference between normal and abnormal people may be largely a matter of degree.

■ **The Continuum of Normality, Neurosis, and Psychosis**   Normality is a matter of the balance of energy among the psychic structures of id, ego, and superego. Freud believed that we may all be capable of becoming neurotic or even psychotic when these mental structures become unbalanced. Among normal people, the ego has the strength to control the instincts of the id and to withstand the condemnation of the superego. The presence of acceptable outlets for the expression of some primitive impulses, such as the expression of mature sexuality in marriage, decreases the pressures within the id, and, at the same time, lessens the burdens of the ego in repressing the remaining impulses. Being reared by reasonably tolerant parents might prevent the superego from becoming overly harsh and condemnatory.

Among neurotic and psychotic people, the balance of energy is lopsided. Neurotic people spend a great deal of energy attempting to keep threatening impulses tamped down. As a result, they may feel weak, drained of energy. Yet some impulses may "leak," producing anxiety, or lead to the development of neurotic behavior patterns, or symptoms, such as hysteria and phobias. Or the superego may come crashing down, flooding the person with feelings of guilt, shame, and fears of being alone in the world.

Perpetual vigilance and defense takes its toll. The ego can weaken and, in extreme cases, lose the ability to keep a lid on the id. Psychosis results when the urges of the id spill forth, untempered by an ego that has either been weakened or is underdeveloped. In such cases, the ego is overrun and the person loses the ability to distinguish between fantasy and reality.

Inner thoughts are perceived as originating outside. Speech may become incoherent and there may be bizarre posturing and gestures.

■ The Abilities to Love and to Work

Freud equated psychological health with the abilities to love and to work. The normal person can care deeply for other people, find sexual gratification in an intimate relationship, and engage in productive work. To accomplish these ends, there must be an opportunity for sexual impulses to be expressed in a relationship with an opposite-sex partner. Other impulses must be channeled or sublimated into socially productive pursuits, such as work, enjoyment of art or music, or creative expression. When some impulses are expressed directly and others are sublimated, the ego has a relatively easy time of it repressing those that remain in the boiling cauldron.

■ Differentiation of the Self

For Jung and Adler, normality depends, in part, on the differentiation of a self—the unifying force that directs behavior and helps a person develop to his or her potential. For Mahler, similarly, abnormal behavior derives from failure to separate ourselves from those we have psychologically brought within us. Belief in a guiding self creates bridges between psychodynamic theories and other theories, such as humanistic-existential theories (which also considers the role of the self in the fulfillment of inner potential) and social-learning theory (which speaks in terms of self-regulatory processes). We'll consider these theoretical models later in the chapter.

■ Compensation for Feelings of Inferiority

None of us can expect to be "good at everything." In Adler's view, normal people compensate for feelings of inferiority by striving to excel in other arenas of human endeavor. So choosing how best to apply ourselves, by examining our abilities and developing our talents, constitutes healthful behavior.

■ Erikson's Positive Outcomes

Positive outcomes in Erikson's psychosocial stages contribute to the development of a healthy personality. For example, it is healthful to establish a basic sense of trust in the environment during infancy, to become industrious during the grammar school years, to develop occupational plans or goals during adolescence, to form intimate relationships during the period of young adulthood, to be productive and contribute to the development of the younger generation during middle adulthood, and so on.

Evaluating Psychodynamic Perspectives

In evaluating psychodynamic theory, we must first note its pervasive influence. Psychodynamic theory has changed the Western world. It has focused attention on our inner lives—our dreams, our fantasies, our hidden motives. People unschooled in Freud per se nevertheless look for the symbolic meanings of each other's slips of the tongue and assume that abnormalities can be traced to early childhood. Terms like "ego" and "repression" have become commonplace, although their everyday meanings do not fully overlap with those intended by Freud.

Psychodynamic theories are popular in part because they are "rich" theories. They incorporate many concepts in attempting to explain the diverse varieties of human behavior, both normal and abnormal. People who wish to explore the hidden recesses of themselves will often turn to psychoanalysis.

One of the major contributions of the psychodynamic model was the increased awareness that people may be motivated by hidden drives and impulses of a sexual or aggressive nature. For centuries, human beings had placed themselves on a pedestal, believing that they, unlike other species, were motivated by pure reason and thought and were capable of consciously controlling their baser drives. Freud had us take a fuller accounting of ourselves as both intelligent and animalistic. With Freud, we come to see that we may not be as aware of our deeper motives as perhaps we would like to believe.

Freud's beliefs about childhood sexuality were both illuminating and controversial. Before Freud, children were perceived as *pure innocents*, free of any sexual desires. That is why they were so often depicted in paintings of the Renaissance period without any clothing. Without lust, there was no need for shame. But Freud recognized that young children, even infants, are motivated to seek pleasure in ways relating to the stimulation of the oral and anal cavities and the phallic region. But his beliefs that these primitive drives universally lead to incestuous desires and to jealous rivalries and conflicts, together with his beliefs in castration anxiety and penis envy, remain sources of controversy, even within psychodynamic circles. The stages of psychosexual development have also been subject to criticism. Many observers have noted that children may begin to masturbate in their first year, not in the "phallic stage." And masturbation may continue through the so-called latency period when sexual drives are believed to remain dormant. But still, one of the strengths of the psychodynamic model is its attention to the importance of childhood experiences in shaping personality development and abnormal behavior patterns.

Another major contribution was the recognition that defensive processes may distort people's perceptions of their feelings, needs, and desires. The listing of defense mechanisms has become much a part of everyday parlance. Whether or not we attribute these cognitive distortions to unconscious processes, it seems that our thinking processes can become distorted by our attempts to defend ourselves against anxiety and guilt.

Despite their richness, psychodynamic theories have met with extensive criticism. Many critics, including some of Freud's own followers, believe that he placed too much emphasis on sexual and aggressive impulses in explaining personality and abnormal behavior and underemphasized social relationships. Critics have also argued that the psychic structures—the id, ego, and superego—may be little more than convenient fictions, poetic ways to represent inner conflict. Along these lines, Sir Karl Popper (1985) argued that Freud's psychic structures fail to meet the standards of scientific concepts since they cannot be directly observed or tested. Therapists can speculate, for example, that a client "forgot" about a scheduled appointment because he or she "unconsciously" did not want to attend the session. But there may be no way of verifying this unconscious motivation.

Popper also argued that scientific propositions must be subject to tests that can show them to be false. Popper held that Freud's propositions about mental structures are unscientific because there are no imaginable types of evidence that can disprove them. That is, any behavior (for example, showing up or not showing up for an appointment) can be explained in terms of the interactions of these hypothesized (but unobservable) mental structures. As another example, note that belief in God is theological and not scientific because it is impossible to prove scientifically the *nonexistence* of God. But the belief, say, that stress suppresses the functioning of the immune system is capable of being falsified. That is, we can experimentally expose organisms to stressful stimuli and measure the functioning of the immune system, as you will see in Chapter 5. In science, we speak of disproving theories, not proving them. Theories are not truth in themselves. Rather, they approximate truth, and scientists should stand ready to revise or discard even their favored theories when disconfirming evidence comes along. But Freudian concepts may not lend themselves to such possible disconfirmation through scientific tests.

Freud formulated his views on normal development on the basis of case studies of troubled people in Victorian Vienna. Persons seeking therapy may not represent the general population and are likely to have more problems than the population at large. Freud carried out his work in an era of culturally repressed sexuality and concluded that all people undergo similar sexual conflicts. He based his views of childhood on the recollections of his clients, not direct observation. Most of his clients were upper-middle-class women between the ages of 20 and 44 (Fisher & Greenberg, 1977). In sum, Freud used a very narrow sample for the making of generalizations about our species. Also, as the philosopher Adolph Grünbaum (1985) took note, Freud's

approach to gathering evidence from the therapy session may be suspect. Therapists may influence their clients in subtle ways to produce material that they expect to find. Therapists may also be negligent in separating the information reported by their clients from their own interpretations.

LEARNING PERSPECTIVES

The existence of abnormal behavior provided the wellsprings of psychodynamic theory. Without psychological problems, and troubled clients, there would have been no psychodynamic theory. Learning theory would exist even in the absence of abnormal behavior. It focuses largely on the normal processes of learning from experience. Learning theorists have also attempted to explain abnormal behavior. Broadly speaking, learning theorists assume that the principles of learning that account for normal (adaptive) behavior also account for many kinds of abnormal (maladaptive) behavior. In one sense, their views overlap with Freud's: They are largely committed to the idea that abnormal behavior results from experience. In other ways, their views differ markedly: Psychodynamic theorists look to the importance of certain pivotal early learning experiences and see abnormal behavior as symbolic of unconscious conflicts. Learning theorists do not posit specific stages of learning or experience that determine later adjustment. Nor do learning theorists see behavior, normal or abnormal, as resulting from, or symbolic of, unconscious forces.

In this section we focus on two broad learning perspectives: behaviorism and social-learning theory.

Behaviorism

> Give me a dozen healthy infants, well-formed, and my own specified world to bring them up in and I'll guarantee to take any one at random and train him to become any type of specialist I might suggest—doctor, lawyer, merchant-chief and, yes, even beggar-man and thief, regardless of his talents, penchants, tendencies, abilities, vocations, and the race of his ancestors. (John B. Watson, 1924, p. 82)

Thus did Johns Hopkins University psychologist John B. Watson sound the battle cry of the **behaviorist** movement. Watson argued that environmental influences—not spirits, demons, or intrapsychic forces—shape our behavior. For psychology to be accepted as a science, unseen mental structures would have to be rejected in favor of behavior that could be detected and measured by scientific instruments—behaviors such as pressing a lever; turning left or right; eating and mating; or even involuntary body functions such as heart rate, dilation of the pupils of the eyes, blood pressure, or emission of brain waves. All these behaviors are public because they can be measured by observation or laboratory instruments. Even brain waves are made public by scientific instruments, and separate observers readily agree about their reality and qualities. In the 1930s, Watson's hue and cry was taken up by B. F. Skinner, who suggested that we focus on the impact that reinforcers have upon behavior.

Like Freud, Watson and Skinner reject concepts of personal freedom, free choice, and self-direction. But whereas Freud saw us as driven by irrational inner forces, behaviorists see us as products of environmental influences that shape and manipulate our behavior. To Watson and Skinner, even the belief that we have free will is determined by our environment just as surely as our learning to raise our hands in class before speaking.

Behaviorists focus on two basic types of learning: classical conditioning and operant conditioning.

■ Classical Conditioning   **Classical conditioning**
was discovered by chance. The Russian physiologist Ivan Pavlov (1849–1936) was exploring the biological pathways of dogs' salivation glands, but the animals fouled up his results by apparently arbitrary salivation. Upon inquiry, Pavlov noted that the animals were in fact salivating in response to his assistants' coming into the lab or the accidental clanging of metal upon metal. So Pavlov undertook a clever experimental program to show that the dogs salivated to these events because the events were *associated* with feeding.

When you put meat on a dog's tongue, the dog salivates. Salivation in response to meat is a reflex—a simple kind of unlearned behavior. People also have many reflexes, such as blinking the eye in response to a puff of air and jerking the knee in response to a tap beneath. Dilation of the pupils of the eyes and orgasm are other reflexes.

A change in the environment, like putting meat on a dog's tongue or tapping beneath the knee, is referred to as a **stimulus.** A reflex is one type of **response** to a stimulus. Reflexes are not learned, but they can be *conditioned* to, or associated with, various stimuli.

To demonstrate the power of classical conditioning, Pavlov (1927) strapped dogs into harnesses (see Figure 2.2). He then placed meat powder on their tongues, and they salivated. He repeated the procedure a number of times, with one difference. He rang a bell before presenting the meat. After numerous pairings of the bell and the food, Pavlov rang the bell but did not follow it with the meat. The dogs salivated anyway. They had learned to salivate when the bell was rung because the bell had been repeatedly presented just prior to the meat.

In this classic demonstration, meat is an **unconditioned stimulus** (US). Salivation in response to the presentation of the meat powder is termed an **unconditioned response** (UR). ''Unconditioned'' means unlearned. Originally, the bell is a neutral or meaningless stimulus. But after being associated repeatedly with the US (meat), the bell becomes a learned or **condi-**

FIGURE 2.2

Pavlov used an apparatus such as this to demonstrate the conditioned response. To the left is a two-way mirror, behind which the researcher would ring a bell and then place the meat powder on the dog's tongue. With successive pairings of the bell and the meat powder, the dog learns to salivate to the bell alone. The saliva passes through the tube to a vial. The quantity of saliva in response to the bell alone is taken as a measure of the strength of the conditioned response.
Source: Morris, *Psychology: An Introduction*, 7th ed. Englewood Cliffs, NJ: Prentice Hall, 1990, p. 179.

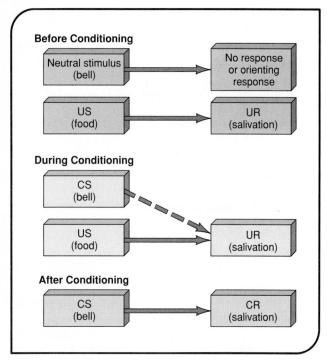

FIGURE 2.3 Illustration of classical conditioning.
Preceding conditioning, the placement of food on the animal's tongue elicits salivation (UR). A neutral stimulus, a bell in this case, elicits either an orienting response or no response. During conditioning, the bell is rung just before the food is placed on the animal's tongue. After several repetitions of the pairing of the bell and the food, the bell, now a CS, comes to elicit salivation, the conditioned response or CR.

tioned stimulus (CS). The bell is then capable of eliciting salivation. Salivation in response to the bell is termed a learned or **conditioned response** (CR).

Can you recognize classical conditioning in your life? Do you flinch in the waiting room at the sound of the dentist's drill? The drill sounds may be conditioned stimuli for conditioned responses of fear and muscle tension. John Watson and Rosalie Rayner (1920) showed how fears could be conditioned, by demonstrating the acquisition of a fear of a white rat in a laboratory experiment with an eleven-month-old boy known in the psychological literature as "Little Albert." The boy was first shown a rat and then an iron bar was banged behind his head as he reached

for the rat. Before conditioning, Albert had shown no fear of laboratory rats and had even played with them. After numerous pairings of the rat and the clanging, however, Albert cried when the rat was brought in and tried to avoid it. Through classical conditioning we come to associate stimuli, so that a response elicited by one is then elicited by the other. With Little Albert, jarring clanging was associated with a rat, so that the rodent came to evoke the fear elicited by the noise.

 Researchers did condition a young boy to fear rats by clanging steel bars behind his head while he played with a rat. His name was "Little Albert" and the researchers were John B. Watson and Rosalie Rayner.

From the behaviorist perspective, normal behavior involves responding adaptively to stimuli—including conditioned stimuli. After all, if we do not learn to be afraid of touching a hot stove after one or two pairings of the sight of the crimson burner and pain, we shall suffer unnecessary burns. If we do not learn to abstain from eating food that nauseates us, we may become poisoned. On the other hand, acquiring inappropriate and maladaptive fears may cripple our efforts to function in the world. We will see, in Chapter 4, that conditioning may help to explain certain stress-related psychological disorders, such as **post-traumatic stress disorder,** an abnormal pattern of behavior that follows exposure to traumatic experiences. In our discussion of disorders relating to anxiety in Chapter 6, we will see how the principles of conditioning may help to explain the development of phobias.

■ **Extinction and Spontaneous Recovery**   Researchers **extinguish** conditioned responses (CRs) by presenting conditioned stimuli (CSs) repeatedly in the absence of the unconditioned stimuli (USs). Pavlov found that salivation to the bell could be extinguished by presenting the bell (CS) repeatedly and not following with the meat (US). Extinction can be adaptive. If your dentist becomes more adroit or uses an effectual painkiller, why then should the sound of the drill persist in making you cringe? If you acquire solid social skills, why should you persist in experiencing anxiety at the

Ivan Pavlov (center with beard) demonstrating the apparatus for classical conditioning to his students.

B. F. Skinner

prospect of meeting people or asking them out on dates?

Extinguished responses may recur simply as a function of the passage of time. Such recurrence is termed **spontaneous recovery.** After Pavlov had extinguished salivation in response to a bell, his dogs would salivate again if the bell were presented a few days later. You might cower again in your dentist's office if a year has passed between checkups, even though you remained calm throughout your last (painless) procedure. If you haven't dated for several months, the thought of asking someone out might again elicit anxiety, even if your most recent efforts were successful.

■ Operant Conditioning   Classical conditioning is also referred to as *respondent* conditioning, because organisms learn responses which are largely *elicited* by certain stimuli. In **operant conditioning,** organisms learn to *emit* learned behaviors because of the behavior's effects. Operant behavior is so-called because it operates upon, or manipulates, the environment to produce certain effects.

Operant conditioning can occur mechanically with lower animals. Skinner (1938) showed that food-deprived pigeons will learn to peck buttons when food pellets drop into their cages as a result. It takes a while for the birds to happen on the first peck, but after a few repetitions of the button-pecking–food association, pecking becomes fast and furious until the pigeons have had their fill. Food-deprived rats similarly learn to press levers to obtain food.

In operant conditioning, organisms acquire responses or develop skills that lead to **reinforcement.** Reinforcers are changes in the environment (stimuli) that increase the frequency of the preceding behavior.

A **reward** is a *pleasant* stimulus that increases the frequency of behavior, and so it is a type of reinforcer. But Skinner found the concept of reinforcement to be preferable to that of reward because it is defined in terms of relationships between observed behaviors and environmental effects. In contrast to *reward*, the meaning of reinforcement does not depend on "mentalistic" conjectures about what is pleasant to another person or lower animal. Many psychologists use the words *reinforcement* and *reward* interchangeably, however.

Psychologists talk about various types of reinforcers, and we need to be able to differentiate them as well. **Positive reinforcers** boost the frequency of behavior when they are presented. Food, money, social approval, and the opportunity to mate are examples of positive reinforcers. **Negative reinforcers** increase the frequency of behavior when they are removed. Fear, pain, and social disapproval are examples of negative reinforcers. We usually learn to do what leads to the removal or abatement of fear, pain, or the censure of others.

Adaptive, normal behavior involves learning responses or skills that permit us to obtain positive reinforcers and avoid or avert negative reinforcers. In the preceding examples, adaptive behavior means procuring skills that permit us to obtain money, food, and social approval, and to avoid fear, pain, and social condemnation. But if our early learning environments do not provide opportunities for learning new skills, we might be hampered in our efforts to obtain reinforcers.

We can also differentiate primary and secondary, or conditioned, reinforcers. **Primary reinforcers** influence behavior because they satisfy basic physical needs. We do not learn to respond to these basic reinforcers; we are born with that capacity. Food, water, sexual stimulation, and escape from pain are examples of primary reinforcers. **Secondary reinforcers** influence behavior through their association with established reinforcers. Thus, we learn to respond to secondary reinforcers. People learn to seek money—a secondary reinforcer—because it can be exchanged for primary reinforcers like food and heat (or air conditioning).

■ Punishment **Punishments** are painful, aversive events that decrease or suppress the frequency of the preceding behavior. Negative reinforcers, by contrast, increase the frequency of the preceding behavior by their removal.

Punishment can suppress unsuitable behavior rapidly. So its use may be appropriate in emergencies, such as when a child is trying to run into the street. Many learning theorists, however, discourage use of punishment, particularly in rearing children. They point out that punishment does not in itself suggest alternate, permissible kinds of behavior. For punishment to be effective, the recipient must have skills available to execute alternate behaviors. Punishment only suppresses unwanted behavior in circumstances in which it is used reliably, but does not eliminate the behavior. It may also encourage people to withdraw from such learning situations. Punished children may cut classes, drop out of school, or run away. Punishment may generate anger and hostility, rather than constructive learning. Finally, since people also learn by observation, punishment may become imitated as a means for solving interpersonal problems.

So rewarding desirable behavior is generally preferable to punishing misbehavior. But rewarding good behavior requires paying attention to it, not just to misbehavior. Some children who develop behavioral problems can only gain the attention of other people by misbehaving. They learn that by "acting out," other people will pay attention to them. To them punishment may actually serve as a positive reinforcer, increasing the rate of response of the behavior it follows. Learning theorists point out that it is not sufficient to "expect" good conduct from children. Instead, adults need to teach children proper behavior and regularly reinforce them.

Classical and operant conditioning stress the importance of environmental factors, which are also called *situation variables*, in explaining behavior. Let us now consider a contemporary model of learning, called social learning theory, which broadens the focus of traditional learning theory by considering how both situation and person variables affect human behavior.

Social-Learning Theory

Social-learning theory represents the contributions of learning theorists such as Albert Bandura, Julian B. Rotter and Walter Mischel. Social-learning theorists emphasize the roles of cognitive activity and learning by observation in human behavior. Social-learning theorists view people as impacting upon their environments, just as the environment impacts upon them. Social-learning theorists concur with more traditional

Social learning theorists believe that modeling is an important influence on behavior.

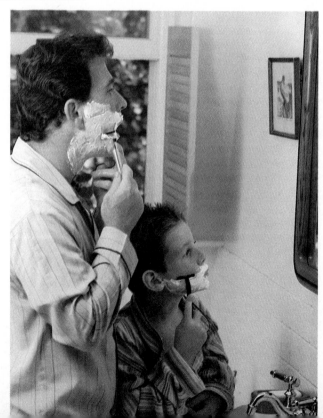

> **?** Actually, punishment *does* work. That is, severe enough punishment suppresses the behavior it follows. However, many psychologists advise against punishing children because of various problems associated with the use of punishment.

behaviorists that theories of human behavior should be tied to observable responses. They also assert, however, that factors *within* the person—**person variables**—must be considered in explaining human behavior.

Social-learning theorists see people as self-aware and purposeful learners who seek information about their environments, not just respond automatically to the stimuli that impinge upon them. Rotter (1972) argues that behavior cannot be predicted from situational factors alone. Whether or not people behave in certain ways also depends on their **expectancies** about the outcomes of their behavior and the **subjective values** of those outcomes.

■ Observational Learning

Observational learning, or learning through **modeling,** refers to the process of acquiring new behaviors and knowledge by observing others. Operant conditioning occurs when an organism (1) engages in a response and (2) that response is reinforced. But observational learning takes place even when the observer does not engage in the behavior or is not directly reinforced. Observational learning can occur while observing the behaviors of others firsthand or by observing models in films or television, or by reading about others. Both normal and abnormal behavior patterns can be acquired vicariously, by observation. For example, Albert Bandura and his colleagues (1963) showed in a classic study that children will imitate aggressive models they observe in films, whether the film models are real people or cartoons. In Chapter 11 we'll review evidence that suggests that men who observe sexual violence against women in films become more aggressive themselves when later interacting with women.

■ Person Variables

Social-learning theorists believe that behavior stems from a fluid, continuous interaction between person and **situation variables.** Situation variables refer to the external determinants of behavior, such as rewards and punishments. **Person variables** incorporate such characteristics of the person as competencies, encoding strategies, expectancies, subjective values, and self-regulatory systems and plans (Mischel, 1986; see Figure 2.4). We focused on the role of situation variables in learning in the context of classical and operant conditioning. Now let us consider such person variables as competencies, encoding strategies,

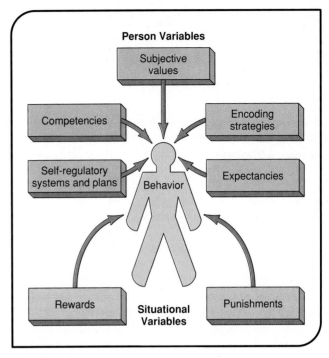

FIGURE 2.4

Social learning theorists believe that the determinants of behavior include both person and situational variables.

expectancies, subjective values, and self-regulatory systems.

Competencies **Competencies** are skills and knowledge that have been acquired from past learning. These include academic skills such as reading, writing, and arithmetic; athletic skills such as hitting a tennis serve or tossing a football properly; and social skills such as knowing what to say or how to dress on a job interview or how to ask someone out on a date. Our capacity to use information to plan behavior depends on our competencies.

Encoding Strategies **Encoding** refers to the process of symbolizing or representing stimuli. People may encode the same stimuli in different ways. Some people encode a tennis game as an opportunity to relax and have some fun. Others encode the game as a demand to prove their mettle or perfect their serves and volleys. Some people encode unsuccessful dates as signs of their social ineptitude. Others encode failed dates as evidence that people sometimes are not ''meant for each other.'' Encoding strategies may help to explain why some people become depressed and withdrawn following setbacks and disappointments, while others shrug them off and remain unperturbed. In Chapter 8 we shall see that ways in which people interpret or *encode* events may play an important role in determining their proneness toward depression.

Expectancies

> . . . if one advances confidently in the direction of his dreams, and endeavors to live the life which he has imagined, he will meet with a success unexpected in common hours. (Henry David Thoreau, *Walden*)

Expectancies are personal predictions about the outcomes (or potential for reinforcement) of engaging in particular responses. Expectancies can be represented as "if-then" statements: If I do "A" then I expect "B" to follow. Bandura (1982) distinguishes between two types of expectations: outcome and efficacy expectations. Outcome expectations are anticipations that certain behavior patterns will have certain effects. For example, you may expect that by diligently studying the material in the textbook, you are more likely to do well on the course examinations. (Outcome expectations may or may not prove true, of course). **Self-efficacy expectations** concern beliefs that one will be able to execute behavior successfully. Taking the example further, believing that you can acquire the information in the textbook if you put your mind to it would represent high self-efficacy. Believing that you couldn't possibly learn this material despite your best efforts would be an example of low self-efficacy. Efficacy expectancies are based in part on our competencies and on our own experiences in similar situations. Compe-

> **?** People are in fact more likely to tackle arduous tasks if they believe that they will succeed at them. Positive self-efficacy expectancies foster striving and persistence.

tencies affect expectancies, and expectancies, in turn, affect motivation to perform. People who think that they are competent are more likely to attempt arduous tasks than those who doubt that they can master them.

Bandura suggests that one of the common beneficial features of psychotherapy is the changing of clients' self-efficacy expectations from "I can't" to "I can." For this reason, clients are inspired to attempt new, more adaptive, patterns of behavior.

Subjective Values   The same events or stimuli tend to be valued differently by different people. What frightens one person may allure another. What interests one may repel another. Social-learning theorists, in contrast to behaviorists, do not see us as controlled by external events and stimuli. Rather, we imbue events with meaning and value and the meanings we give them affect our behavior. If your grades have little value to you, then your mood is unlikely to be affected if you do poorly in your courses. You will also be little motivated to apply yourself to obtain good grades. By contrast, if your grades are very important to you, then

We are more likely to attempt challenging tasks that we judge ourselves capable of performing successfully. With a strong sense of self-efficacy, we are more likely to approach tasks with vigor and sustained effort.

Social learning theorists believe that the value of a reward depends on the meaning that we attach to it. This young man places great reward value on his automobile. What is rewarding to you?

QUESTIONNAIRE
The Expectancy for Success Scale

What do you do when faced with an arduous challenge? Do you rise to the occasion, or do you back off?

Social-learning theorists note that our outcome and efficacy expectancies influence our behavior. When we think that we can realize great achievements through our own endeavors, we marshall our resources and dedicate ourselves. When we believe that our exertion will pay off, we are likely to persevere.

The following scale, developed by Fibel and Hale (1978), offers insight as to whether or not you expect that your efforts will be successful. Compare your expectancies to those of other undergraduates taking psychology courses by filling out the questionnaire and referring to the answer key at the end of the chapter.

Directions: Indicate the degree to which each item applies to you by circling the appropriate number, according to this key:

1 = highly improbable
2 = improbable
3 = equally improbable and probable, not sure
4 = probable
5 = highly probable

In the Future I Expect That I Will:

1. Find that people don't seem to understand what I'm trying to say   1 2 3 4 5
2. Be discouraged about my ability to gain the respect of others   1 2 3 4 5
3. Be a good parent   1 2 3 4 5
4. Be unable to accomplish my goals   1 2 3 4 5
5. Have a stressful marital relationship   1 2 3 4 5
6. Deal poorly with emergency situations   1 2 3 4 5
7. Find my efforts to change situations I don't like are ineffective   1 2 3 4 5
8. Not be very good at learning new skills   1 2 3 4 5
9. Carry through my responsibilities successfully   1 2 3 4 5
10. Discover that the good in life outweighs the bad   1 2 3 4 5
11. Handle unexpected problems successfully   1 2 3 4 5
12. Get the promotions I deserve   1 2 3 4 5
13. Succeed in the projects I undertake   1 2 3 4 5
14. Not make any significant contributions to society   1 2 3 4 5
15. Discover that my life is not getting much better   1 2 3 4 5
16. Be listened to when I speak   1 2 3 4 5
17. Discover that my plans don't work out too well   1 2 3 4 5
18. Find that no matter how hard I try, things just don't turn out the way I would like   1 2 3 4 5
19. Handle myself well in whatever situation I'm in   1 2 3 4 5
20. Be able to solve my own problems   1 2 3 4 5
21. Succeed at most things I try   1 2 3 4 5
22. Be successful in my endeavors in the long run   1 2 3 4 5
23. Be very successful working out my personal life   1 2 3 4 5
24. Experience many failures in my life   1 2 3 4 5
25. Make a good first impression on people I meet for the first time   1 2 3 4 5
26. Attain the career goals I have set for myself   1 2 3 4 5
27. Have difficulty dealing with my superiors   1 2 3 4 5
28. Have problems working with others   1 2 3 4 5
29. Be a good judge of what it takes to get ahead   1 2 3 4 5
30. Achieve recognition in my profession   1 2 3 4 5

Source: *Fibel and Hale, 1978, p. 931.*

---

you are more likely to work harder and your emotional responses are more likely to reflect the outcomes.

Self-Regulatory Systems and Plans Social-learning theorists note that people regulate their own behavior, even when observers and external constraints are not present. People set their own goals and standards, make plans for attaining them, and applaud or reprimand themselves, according to their progress. In fact, social-learning theorists see self-rewards ("Hey, I'm doing fine!") and self-punishments ("I'm such a jerk! I'll never get this right.") as equally potent to or more potent than external rewards and punishments.

Learning Perspectives on Abnormal Behavior

Learning theorists focus on the role of learning in explaining both normal and abnormal behavior. As noted earlier, they largely see abnormal behavior patterns as learned according to the same principles, such as conditioning and observational learning, that govern normal behavior. While behaviorists may admit that genetic inheritance also plays a part in determining behavior, they submit that our behavior is largely a function of how we learn to adapt to our environment. Let us focus on a few of the ways in which learning models account for abnormal behavior.

■ **Acquisition of Abnormal Behavior Patterns**   Some abnormal behavior patterns, such as phobias, may be learned on the basis of conditioning. The conditioning explanation of phobias suggests that a previously neutral stimulus may become a phobic stimulus by virtue of its pairing or association with a painful or aversive stimulus. So, for example, an individual may develop a fear or phobia of riding on elevators following a traumatic or painful experience or experiences while riding on elevators in the past. We'll look closer at conditioning explanations of phobias in Chapter 6. Social-learning theorists suggest that such fears may also be learned vicariously, by observing the phobic reactions of others or even by observing models in movies and television suffer traumatic experiences while interacting with phobic stimuli. **Behavior therapy** represents the application of learning principles to help people overcome problem behaviors, like phobias, and learn more adaptive behaviors. Throughout the text we will refer to specific techniques that behavior therapists have developed to foster adaptive behavioral changes.

■ **Lack of Competencies**   Abnormal behavior may reflect a lack of adequate knowledge and skills—for example, social skills. Lack of social skills can reduce the opportunities for reinforcements from others, especially when the person withdraws from social situations. Therapeutic approaches that seek to teach people more effective social skills have been applied to a wide range of abnormal behavior patterns, including depression, social anxiety, and even schizophrenia.

■ **Inappropriate or Inadequate Reinforcement**   Most people are positively reinforced by the praise of their family members, teachers, and employers. Children with conduct disorders, on the other hand, may find teacher *disapproval* positively reinforcing. Inadequate levels of reinforcement may also be involved in explaining abnormal behavior patterns. In Chapter 8 we will explore learning models that relate changes in the level of reinforcement to the development and maintenance of depression.

■ *Self-Defeating Expectancies, Encoding, and Self-Regulatory Systems*   People who believe that their efforts will meet with failure may develop feelings of helplessness and hopelessness and become depressed. But positive self-efficacy expectancies increase our motivation and persistence in tackling difficult challenges.

Some people become socially withdrawn and depressed because they encode one or two social failures as emblematic of their worthlessness and of the utter futility of social interaction. Some people become hostile and engage in violent behavior because they encode social provocations as injuries that must be avenged, not as social problems that need to be solved. Still other people fail to develop or apply self-regulatory systems that enable them to reinforce themselves for achieving small steps toward desired goals.

Evaluating the Learning Perspectives

There is little doubt that learning theorists have made substantial contributions to the understanding of normal and abnormal behavior. One of the principal values of learning models is their emphasis on observable behavior and environmental stimuli. Psychodynamic theorists focus on hypothesized internal variables that may not be available to scientific study, like psychic structures and unconscious conflicts. Learning theorists emphasize the significance of environmental or situational variables, such as rewards and punishments, which can be systematically varied and their effects on behavior carefully measured. Social-learning theorists have broadened the scope of conditioning models of learning by taking into account how both person and situation variables affect human behavior and learning.

Learning theories have had a broad impact on psychology. They deal with issues ranging from learning to animal behavior, motivation, child development, abnormal behavior, therapy methods, even attitude formation and change. Learning models have spawned the development of **behavior therapy,** which has become a prominent method of treatment for a wide variety of abnormal behavior patterns.

Critics contend that learning models, especially behaviorism, cannot explain the richness of human behavior and that human experience cannot be reduced to observable responses. Many learning theorists, too—especially social-learning theorists—have been dissatisfied with the behavioristic view that environmental conditions mechanically force responses upon organisms, including humans. Humans experience thoughts and dreams, formulate goals and aspirations, and behaviorism seems not to address much of what it means to be human. Behaviorism also seems at a loss to explain how many people will strive, despite hardships, to realize remote inner visions. If people only repeat reinforced behaviors, how do they struggle—without external reinforcers—to invent new ideas and works? How do composers and mathematicians sit still for hours, then all at once pen new concertos and equations? As we shall see, humanistic and existential theorists propose that the human capacity for self-expression and growth cannot be explained by environmental influences.

In contrast to traditional behaviorism, social-learning theorists see human beings as active seekers of information, not as passive reactors to environmental stimuli. Social-learning theory has evolved so far from its behaviorist forebears that its overlap with cognitive theories and models is striking indeed. Critics of social-learning theory do not accuse it of denying the value or role of cognitive activity. They might contend, however, that social-learning theory has not developed satisfying statements about the formation of personality traits or accounted for self-awareness. In addition, social-learning theory—like its intellectual progenitor, behaviorism—does not always pay adequate attention to genetic factors in explaining individual differences in behavior or in accounting for abnormal behavior patterns.

Now let us turn our attention to cognitive perspectives, which focus on processes of thinking and cognition in explaining human behavior.

COGNITIVE PERSPECTIVES

Psychological perspectives continue to evolve. They draw on the philosophies and technologies of the day. Sigmund Freud was impressed by the internal combustion engine. Perhaps this suggested to him a way of viewing people as containing seething inner energies—as needing to vent some of their "steam" (by verbalizing feelings and finding acceptable ways of partially gratifying impulses) if they were to avert an explosion in the personality. One of the great technologies of the modern day is computer science, or information processing. So it is not surprising that many cognitive psychologists conceptualize human behavior and **cognition** in terms of information-processing models. Others, such as George Kelly, Albert Ellis, and Aaron Beck, focus on how people interpret events that they experience, and how these interpretations affect their moods and behavior.

Information Processing

Many cognitive psychologists are influenced by concepts of computer science. Computers process information which they are fed in the form of input. Once input, information is placed in *memory* while it is manipulated. You can also place the information permanently in *storage*, as on a floppy disk or a hard disk. So information-processing theorists think in terms like the input (based on perception), storage, retrieval, manipulation, and output of information. They view psychological disorders as disturbances in these processes. Disturbances might be caused by the blocking or distortion of input or by faulty storage, retrieval, or manipulation of information. Any of these can lead to lack of output or distorted output (bizarre behavior). Schizophrenics, for example, frequently jump from topic to topic in a disorganized fashion, which may reflect problems in retrieving and manipulating information. They also seem to have difficulty focusing their attention and "filtering out" extraneous stimuli, like distracting noises.

This may represent problems relating to initial processing of input from their senses (discussed in Chapter 12).

Some theorists focus on the ways in which social information is encoded. It has been found, for example, that aggressive boys and adolescents are likely to incorrectly encode other people's behavior as threatening (Dodge, 1985; Lochman, 1987). They assume that other people intend them ill when they do not (Dodge & Frame, 1982; Jurkovic, 1980). Similarly, some rapists, particularly date rapists, misread women's expressed wishes. They assume, for example, that dates who say "no" mean yes and are playing male-female games (Lipton et al., 1987).

George Kelly

According to George Kelly (1955, 1958), people function much like scientists, in that people strive to understand, anticipate, and control the events in their own lives. To understand people, we must discern the ways in which they categorize and interpret experience—the ways in which they *construe* events. People construe similar events in diverse ways. Consider an example offered by Walter Mischel:

> A boy drops his mother's favorite vase. What does it mean? The event is simply that the vase has been broken. Yet ask the child's psychoanalyst and he may point to the boy's unconscious hostility. Ask the mother and she tells you how "mean" he is. His father says he is "spoiled." The child's teacher may see the event as evidence of the child's "laziness" and chronic "clumsiness." Grandmother calls it just an "accident." And the child himself may construe the event as reflecting his "stupidity" (1986, pp. 207–208).

George Kelly

According to Kelly, people try to understand the world around them by employing **personal constructs** that allow them to anticipate events. Personal constructs are psychological dimensions according to which we categorize ourselves, others, and the events we experience. For example, people may appraise certain experiences by employing such constructs as "good–bad," "dull–stimulating," and "safe–dangerous." For example, a certain event, like swimming in deep water, may be construed by some as "good" and also "stimulating" and "safe." But an inexperienced swimmer might construe the same event as "bad," "dangerous," but also "stimulating." Kelly reminds us that these qualities are not intrinsic properties of the events themselves but are imposed on the events by the person who construes them. People come to predict or anticipate events by means of these personal constructions. The inexperienced swimmer, for example, will come to predict that swimming in deep water is dangerous and is to be avoided. The experienced swimmer may predict that it's fun.

Various ways of construing an event—alternate constructions of an event—give rise to different emotional responses and, perhaps, different courses of action. The boy construed the event in terms of a smart–stupid construct, in such a way that might engender self-loathing. Over time, such patterns of negative self-appraisal might lead to depression. Kelly argued that there may be no absolutely true way of construing events. Instead, when our constructions of events make us anxious or depressed and prevent adaptive behavior, we might be better off by changing how we construe events. His approach to therapy focused on helping people develop more adjustive constructions of events.

Kelly was optimistic about human behavior. He saw people as capable of continuous change, of enacting different roles and forming different constructions in life. If our life roles and patterns of construing events are making us miserable, we can make broad, sweeping changes in our constructions of experience and our day-to-day behavior.

Albert Ellis

Psychologist Albert Ellis (1977a, 1985, 1987), the developer of **rational-emotive therapy,** also focuses on the ways in which people process information or encode experience. Ellis points out that people's beliefs about events can make them miserable and foster maladaptive behavior. Consider an example in which someone loses a job and is anxious and despondent about it. It may seem that being fired is the cause of the person's misery, but the misery actually stems from the person's beliefs about the loss, and not the loss itself.

Ellis uses an "A-B-C approach" to explain the causes of the misery. Being fired is an *activating event*

(A). The ultimate outcome, or *consequence* (C), is distress. But the activating event (A) and the consequences (C) are mediated by various *beliefs* (B). Some of these beliefs might include: "That job was the major thing in my life," "What a useless washout I am," "My family will go hungry," "I'll never be able to find another job as good," "I can't do a thing about it." Beliefs like these compound depression, nurture helplessness, and distract us from evaluating what to do. For instance, the belief that "I can't do a thing about it" promotes helplessness. The belief "What a useless washout I am" internalizes blame and is an exaggeration that is, perhaps, based on perfectionism. The belief that "My family will go hungry" may also be an exaggeration.

The situation can be diagrammed like this:

Activating events → Beliefs → Consequences

Ellis points out that apprehension about the future and feelings of disappointment are perfectly normal when people face losses. However, the adoption of irrational beliefs can **catastrophize** the magnitude of losses and contribute to profound distress and depression. By intensifying emotional responses and nurturing feelings of helplessness, such beliefs impair coping ability. Such beliefs also lower self-efficacy expectations and distract people from trying to solve their problems. Rational-

Cognitive theorists believe that the ways in which we interpret events play an important role in shaping our emotional responses and behavior. To this young woman, a failure on a course examination was interpreted as evidence that she was incapable of succeeding in college. Cognitive theorists believe that such self-appraisals can set the stage for depression.

emotive therapists help clients dispute these irrational beliefs and substitute more rational ones.

Ellis submits that irrational beliefs, such as those listed below, are obstacles to happiness in themselves and may intensify the impact of negative events.

1. You must have love and approval nearly all the time from people who are important to you.

2. You must be completely competent in all your endeavors. Or you must have real expertise or talent in something important.

3. Life must go the way you want it to. Things are awful when you don't get your first choices.

4. Other people should treat everyone fairly. When people are unfair or unethical, they are horrible and rotten and are to be punished or avoided.

5. People and things should turn out better than they do turn out. It's awful and terrible when quick solutions to life's hassles are not forthcoming.

6. Your past is a strong influence on your behavior and must continue to affect you and determine your behavior.

7. You can find happiness by inertia, inactivity, or passivity.

Ellis notes that the desire for others' approval is understandable, but it is irrational to assume that you cannot survive without it. It would be marvelous to excel in everything we do, but it's absurd to demand it. Sure, in tennis it would be great to play like a pro, but most people haven't the leisure or talent to perfect the game. Insisting on perfection deters people from playing simply for fun.

Ellis admits that childhood experiences are involved in the origins of irrational beliefs, but cognitive appraisal—the here and now—causes people misery. For most people who are anxious and depressed, the ticket to greater happiness does not lie in discovering and liberating deep-seated conflicts, but in recognizing and modifying irrational self-demands.

Aaron Beck

Psychiatrist Aaron Beck (Beck, 1976; Beck et al., 1979; Beck et al., 1985) also focuses on how cognitive distortions contribute to misery. He encourages therapy clients to see the irrationality of their thought patterns. For example, minimizing accomplishments and assuming that the worst will come to pass intensifies feelings of despondency. Cognitive errors or distortions—such as minimization and pessimism—can occur so quickly and routinely that they are difficult for the person to detect. Beck's approach to therapy, called **cognitive therapy,** helps clients identify these cognitive errors and correct them.

Aaron T. Beck

Beck stresses the pervasive roles of four basic types of cognitive errors that contribute to emotional distress:

1. *Selective abstraction.* People may *selectively abstract* the parts of their experiences that reflect upon their flaws and ignore evidence of their competencies.

2. *Overgeneralization.* People may *overgeneralize* from a few isolated experiences. For example, they may see their futures as hopeless because they were laid off or believe that they will never marry because they were rejected by their dating partners.

3. *Magnification.* People may blow out of proportion, or *magnify*, the importance of unfortunate events. Students may catastrophize a bad test grade by jumping to the conclusion that they will flunk out of college and their lives will be ruined.

4. *Absolutist thinking.* Absolutist thinking is seeing the world in black and white terms, rather than in shades of gray. Absolutist thinkers may assume that any grade less than a perfect "A," or a work evaluation less than a rave, is a total failure.

 People can make themselves miserable by the ways in which they interpret events.

Evaluating the Cognitive Perspectives

Cognitive perspectives have had an enormous impact in the development of contemporary therapeutic approaches. We will note these many contributions of cognitive therapists to the treatment of various emotional disorders throughout the course of this text. The cognitive approaches to therapy, like the behavioral, focus on making changes in the *here and now*, rather than probe the distant past in great depth, like therapists who adopt a traditional psychodynamic approach. The overlap between the behavioral and cognitive approaches is best represented by the emergence of cognitive-behavior therapy, a form of therapy that integrates behavioral and cognitive techniques. While cognitive behavior therapy will be explored in more depth in Chapter 15, suffice it to say that cognitive-behavior therapists employ a variety of treatment techniques which foster adaptive behavioral and cognitive changes.

The contributions of cognitive theorists have also had a major impact on theories of emotional disorders. Cognitive theorists believe that the ways in which we construe our failures and shortcomings are linked to our emotional responses. We will examine how cognitive theories have been applied to various emotional disorders and evaluate the research evidence that supports the role of cognitive factors.

A major issue concerning cognitive perspectives is their range of applicability. Cognitive therapists have largely focused on emotional disorders relating to anxiety and depression, but have had less impact on the development of treatment approaches, or conceptual models, of schizophrenia. Moreover, in the case of depression, it remains unclear whether distorted thinking patterns are causes of depression or merely effects of depression, as we shall see in Chapter 8. We next turn our attention to humanistic-existential perspectives, which, like the cognitive perspective, focuses on the importance of conscious experience.

HUMANISTIC-EXISTENTIAL PERSPECTIVES

> My experience in therapy and in groups makes it impossible for me to deny the reality and significance of human choice. To me it is not an illusion that man is to some degree the architect of himself. (Carl Rogers, 1974, p. 119)

> Man . . . is the particular being who has to be aware of himself, be responsible for himself, if he is to become himself. He also is that particular being who knows that at some future moment he will not be; he is the being who is always in a dialectical relation with non-being, death. And he not only knows he will sometime not be, but he can, in his own choices, slough off and forfeit his being. (Rollo May, 1958, p. 42)

Technology, science, automation, artificial intelligence—these are some of the artifacts of twentieth-century life. World war and genocide are others. In the midst of modern upheaval, humanists and existentialists have chosen to dwell on the ultimate meaning of life. Intensely aware of their own consciousness, of their transient existence on the third planet out from Sol, personal awareness of being in the world becomes the focus of the humanist-existentialist quest for meaning.

The term *humanism* has existed for hundreds of years and has had different meanings. Humanism emerged as a third force in American psychology in the 1950s and 1960s, in part as a reaction to the prevailing psychodynamic and behavioral models. But humanistic thought was also in part a reaction to the increasing industrialization and automation of modern society. Terms like "rat race" were current, and humanists contested the placement of people on the treadmills of industry. "Alienation" became a buzz word. People complained of feeling alienated in a society that was becoming increasingly technological and divorced from inner sources of meaning. It was against this backdrop that humanistic theories of psychologists Abraham Maslow and Carl Rogers gained prominence.

Existentialism is a school of philosophy that has roots in the contributions of such modern European philosophers as Søren Kierkegaard (1813–1855), Edmund Husserl (1859–1938), Martin Heidegger (1889–1976), and Jean-Paul Sartre (1905–1980). This philosophy is termed *existentialism* because it concerns the larger questions of existence that confront us as we come to terms with our mortality and our experience of being in the world.

The twentieth century existentialist philosophers Jean-Paul Sartre (in France) and Martin Heidegger (in Germany) saw human existence as meaningless within the grand scheme of things, and they wrote about our consequent feelings of alienation. The Swiss psychiatrists Ludwig Binswanger and Medard Boss translated these philosophical views into the more personal world of psychology. They argued that this world view could give rise to abnormal behavior patterns related to philosophical alienation—withdrawal and apathy, for example. To them, salvation is personal and psychological, when it occurs at all, and is based on making personal choices that reflect the personal meanings we implant on things. In other words, if life is essentially meaningless, it is our own task to make it meaningful. Although there is pain in life—in our being in the world—and life ends ultimately in death, we are at least capable of seeing the world as it is and of making real, **authentic** choices. It is the role of psychotherapy to respond to clients' feelings of alienation and help them make the choices that may imbue their lives with some meaning.

Freud's psychoanalytic theory argued, in contrast, that unconscious irrational motives and defensive distortions of reality prevent us from even perceiving the world as it is, much less making free choices. Behaviorists like Watson and Skinner saw freedom as an illusion that is determined from without just as our wants and fears are. If behaviorists saw a "meaning" in life, it was whatever "meaning" people were conditioned to believe in and talk about. Even social-learning theorists focus on the combination of situation and person vari-

person-centered therapists aim to provide a therapeutic environment in which clients can manage the anxiety that attends focusing on the disowned parts of the self.

Rogers also believes that people have mental images of what they are capable of becoming, or **self-ideals.** People strive to reduce the discrepancy between their self-concepts and their self-ideals. But as they actualize themselves, their self-ideals may grow more intricate. Their aspirations may change in magnitude or quality. The self-ideal is akin to the carrot suspended from the stick strapped to the burro's head. The burro labors to grasp the carrot without appreciating that its own advancement causes the carrot to move ahead. Progress creates more distant goals. People may be happiest when their goals seem within grasp and they are striving confidently toward them. People may never be fully satisfied with their achievements, but, according to Rogers, the act of striving to achieve meaningful goals—the good struggle—makes for happiness.

Evaluating Humanistic-Existential Perspectives

Humanistic perspectives have also had an enormous impact on society at large. They were responsible in part for the Human Potential Movement of the 1960s and 1970s. They have underscored ways in which technological advances threaten to leave humanity behind. Humanistic thought has spawned popular slogans, such as "doing your own thing," as well as the common assumption that we should trust ourselves: "If it feels right, go with it." Certainly the notion of free will—and the debate over it—has been with humankind for millennia. The humanistic-existential movement put concepts of free choice, inherent goodness, responsibility, and authenticity back on center stage and brought them into a psychology that had been dominated by psychodynamic and behavioral perspectives earlier in the century.

The strengths of humanistic-existential perspectives to the understanding of abnormal behavior lie largely in their focus on conscious experience and their innovation of therapy methods that assist people along pathways of self-discovery and self-acceptance. As individuals, we treasure our conscious experiences (our "selves"). For lower organisms (or so we presume), life means movement, food processing, exchanging oxygen and carbon dioxide, and reproduction. For people, life also means conscious experience—the bittersweet sense of the self progressing through space and time. Humanistic-existential perspectives capture these aspects of life through their blending of philosophy and psychology.

Unlike the psychodynamic and behavioral theorists, the humanistic-existential theorists see us as being free to make authentic choices that give meaning to our lives. Psychodynamic theorists and behaviorists suspect that the sense of freedom may be an illusion. For humanistic-existential psychologists, genuine personal freedom is axiomatic. Many of the theorists we have discussed have made important innovations in the practice of psychotherapy, especially Carl Rogers, as we shall explore further in Chapter 15.

Ironically, the primary strength of the humanistic-existential approaches—their focus on conscious experience—may also be their primary weakness. Conscious experience is private. Therefore, the validity of formulating theories in terms of consciousness has been questioned. How can psychologists be certain that they are accurately perceiving the world through the eyes of their clients?

Nor can the concept of self-actualization—which is so basic to Maslow and Rogers—be proved or disproved. Like a psychic structure, a self-actualizing force is not directly measurable or observable. It is inferred from its supposed effects. Self-actualization also yields circular explanations for behavior. When someone is observed engaging in striving, what do we learn by attributing striving to a self-actualizing tendency? The source of the tendency remains a mystery. And when someone is observed not to be striving, what do we gain by attributing the lack of endeavor to a blocked or frustrated self-actualizing tendency? We must still determine the source of frustration or blockage.

SOCIOCULTURAL PERSPECTIVES

Sociocultural theorists are philosophically related in some ways to humanists and existentialists. They, too, speak of feelings of alienation. However, whereas existentialists think in terms of humanity's relationship to the universe and mortality, proponents of the **sociocultural perspective** focus on the relationship of the individual to social and cultural codes and expectations.

Sociocultural theorists propose that the causes of abnormal behavior are not found in the individual but rather in society itself. People develop psychological problems when they are subjected to extreme stress brought on by poverty, social decay, discrimination, and lack of opportunity. According to the more radical sociocultural theorists, such as the psychiatrist Thomas Szasz (1961), mental illness is no more than a myth—a concept used to stigmatize and subjugate people whose behavior is socially deviant. Szasz argued that so-called mental illnesses were really "problems in living," not diseases in the sense that influenza, hypertension, and cancer are diseases. Szasz argued that people who offend others or engage in socially deviant behavior are perceived as threats by the establishment. Labeling them as sick allows others to deny the validity of their problems and put them away.

R. D. Laing

Sociocultural theorists maintain that once the label of "mental illness" is applied, it becomes very difficult to remove. The label also affects how others respond to the person labeled "mentally ill," in ways that lead to stigmatization and social degradation. Job opportunities may be denied, friendships may dissolve, and the "mentally ill" person becomes increasingly alienated from society. Szasz argues that treating people as "mentally ill" strips them of their human dignity, for it denies them responsibility for their own behavior and choices. Thus, people who have problems coping with societal demands and are labeled "mentally ill" become even more alienated from society. Instead, Szasz argues, troubled people should be encouraged to take more responsibility for managing their lives and solving their problems.

Another prominent contributor to the sociocultural perspective is the British psychiatrist R. D. Laing (1979). Laing shares with the humanists a concern for various social ills in contemporary society. But, generally speaking, he takes a more critical stance, accusing society of being basically unjust, striving to keep the underclasses in "their place." Laing also critically eyes modern communication, especially family patterns of communication. Children are given double messages, such as "Stop being such a child!" and "What do you mean, you want to drive the car?" Or, "You've got to go out there and beat the other guys!" and "Why can't you be more sharing?" Double messages and confused social mores provide conflicting, meaningless goals and urge us to suppress authentic behavior. By adulthood, believes Laing, we are cut off from our true selves. We develop, instead, false selves that interface

with the social world. Even those of us who do not develop obviously disturbed patterns of behavior feel alienated within.

Evaluating Sociocultural Perspectives

Some evidence for the sociocultural perspective is found in studies of social class and mental illness. Classic research in New Haven, Connecticut, showed that people from the lower socioeconomic classes are more likely to be institutionalized for abnormal behavior (Hollingshead & Redlich, 1958; Myers & Bean, 1968). For one thing, they have less access to private, outpatient care. For another, their problems are more likely to be expressed through aggressive behavior. Lower-class people were more likely to be labeled antisocial and psychotic and confined to a mental institution. Upper-class people, who were more likely to express "deviance" in terms of withdrawal and self-disapproval, were more often labeled neurotic and encouraged to seek outpatient therapy.

There are competing explanations as to why people of lower socioeconomic status may have more severe behavior problems, however. For example, problem behaviors, such as excessive drinking, can lead people to drift downward in social status. Genetic factors may also be associated both with lowered socioeconomic status and the incidence of various kinds of abnormal behavior patterns. We will return to consider the sociocultural perspective in our discussion of the research on schizophrenia in Chapter 12.

Certainly it is valuable for sociocultural theorists to focus on the social stressors that may contribute to abnormal behavior. Certainly it is desirable for social critics like Szasz to rivet our attention to the political implications of our responses to deviance. The views of Szasz and other critics of the mental health establishment have been influential in the past thirty years in bringing much needed changes to better protect the rights of mental patients in institutions. In Chapter 16 we take a closer look at these issues of patient rights and the practice of **psychiatric commitment.** But let's also recognize that most of the writings of Szasz, Laing, and other sociocultural theorists focused on mental health practices in the 1950s through the 1970s. As you'll recall from Chapter 1, deinstitutionalization has shifted the priorities of mental health treatment toward community-based care and shorter-term hospitalizations. Patients in mental hospitals are increasingly encouraged to assume more active, independent roles that will better prepare them for return to the community. But critics have charged that many mental patients have been "dumped" into the community without the

sympathetic and the **parasympathetic.** These branches have mostly opposing effects. Many organs and glands are served by both branches of the ANS. The sympathetic division is most involved in processes that draw body energy from stored reserves, which helps prepare the person to fend off threats or dangers (see Chapter 4). The parasympathetic division becomes more active during processes that replenish energy reserves, like eating. When we are afraid or anxious, the sympathetic branch of the ANS accelerates the heart rate. When we relax, the parasympathetic branch decelerates the heart rate. The parasympathetic branch incites digestion, but the sympathetic branch constrains digestive activity. Since the sympathetic branch dominates when we are fearful or anxious, fear or anxiety can cause indigestion.

 Sure, anxiety can give you indigestion. A threat heightens activity of the sympathetic branch of the ANS, giving rise to biological aspects of anxiety and, at the same time, interfering with parasympathetic activities like digestion.

■ **The Cerebral Cortex**   The key human activities of thought and language involve the two hemispheres of the cerebrum. Each hemisphere is divided into four parts or lobes, as shown in Figure 2.9.

When light stimulates the retinas of the eyes, neurons in the occipital lobe are activated, creating the sense of sight. The auditory area of the cortex is in the temporal lobe. Sounds induce structures in the ear to vibrate, which relay messages to the auditory area. When activated, neurons in this area produce our experience of sound or hearing. The **sensory cortex** receives messages from skin senses all over the body. When neurons in the **motor cortex** are active, we move certain parts of our bodies. If a surgeon were to electrically stimulate a certain part of the left hemisphere of the motor cortex, you would lift your right arm. The movement would be detected in the sensory cortex, and you might not be sure whether you had "meant" to raise the arm.

So-called association areas of the cerebral cortex are involved in learning, thought, memory, and language. In many ways the hemispheres duplicate each other's functions, but they are not fully equal. For 96 percent of right-handed people, the left hemisphere contains language functions and is dominant (Rasmussen & Milner, 1975). The left hemisphere also has language functions and is dominant in about 70 percent of left-handed people. The right hemisphere has language functions in about 15 percent of left-handed people. The remaining 15 percent of left-handed people have language functions in both hemispheres.

The Endocrine System

The body has two kinds of glands: glands that carry their secretions to specific locations by means of ducts, and ductless glands that pour their secretions into the bloodstream. Saliva, tears, and sweat reach their destinations by ducts. Psychologists are particularly interested in the chemicals secreted by ductless glands because of their behavioral effects. The ductless glands make up the **endocrine system,** and they secrete chemicals called **hormones.**

Hormones, like neurotransmitters, have specific receptor sites. Although they are discharged into the bloodstream and circulate throughout the body, they act on receptors in specific locations. Certain hormones released by the hypothalamus influence the pituitary gland, for example. Some hormones secreted by the pituitary affect the adrenal cortex, others the testes and ovaries, and so on. Some endocrine glands are shown in Figure 2.10.

The hypothalamus produces various releasing hormones, or "factors," that induce the pituitary gland to release corresponding hormones. The pituitary gland is so vital that it has been referred to as the "master gland." The anterior (front) and posterior (back) lobes of the pituitary secrete many hormones. Growth hormone regulates development of muscles, bones, and glands. Excessive growth hormone can cause *acromegaly*, a biological disorder in which people can grow two to three feet above normal size. Many professional athletes inject growth hormone along with anabolic steroids to enlarge their muscle mass. Prolactin regulates maternal behavior in lower mammals, like rats, and stimulates milk production in women. Adrenocorticotrophic hormone (ACTH) causes the adrenal cortex to release several steroids (cortisol is one) that help the body manage stress by countering inflammation and allergic reactions.

The pancreas regulates the blood sugar level through the hormones insulin and glucagon. Diabetes mellitus is characterized by excess levels of sugar in the blood (hyperglycemia) and urine; it can cause coma and death. Diabetes is caused by deficient secretion or utilization of insulin. The biological disorder **hypoglycemia** is characterized by a deficient blood sugar level. Symptoms of hypoglycemia include shakiness, lack of energy, and dizziness—a syndrome easily mistaken for anxiety. Many people seek help for anxiety and learn by means of blood tests that they actually have hypoglycemia. Hypoglycemia is usually controlled by diet.

The thyroid gland produces **thyroxin,** which affects the metabolic rate. Thyroxin deficiency can cause **cretinism** in children, a disorder characterized by mental retardation and stunted growth. Adults deficient in thyroxin are said to have **hypothyroidism.** They may

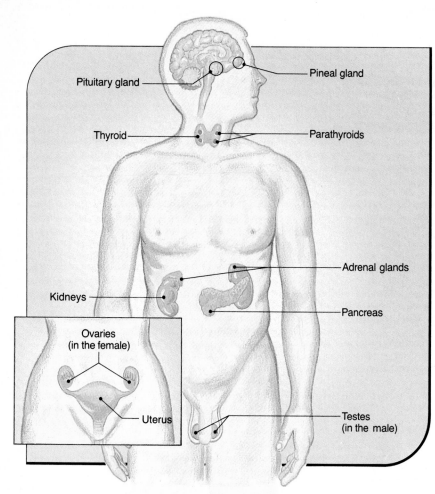

FIGURE 2.10 *The location of the major glands of the endocrine system.*
Source: Morris, *Psychology: An Introduction*, 7th ed. Englewood Cliffs, NJ: Prentice Hall, 1990, p. 59.

feel sluggish and put on weight. Excess thyroxin can cause **hyperthyroidism,** which is characterized by excitability, insomnia, and weight loss. We will return to these disorders in the course of our discussion on organic disorders and abnormal behavior in Chapter 13.

The adrenal glands, situated above the kidneys, have an exterior layer, or cortex, and an interior core, or medulla. The cortex is regulated by ACTH. The cortex secretes many **corticosteroids,** or cortical **steroids.** Cortical steroids boost resistance to stress, foster muscle development, and induce the liver to release sugar, providing energy for emergencies. Anabolic steroids (synthetic forms of the male sex hormone testosterone) are sometimes used to enhance athletic prowess. Anabolic steroids, which are illegal in many states for athletic use, have been implicated in cardiovascular problems and have certain psychological effects. They may bolster self-esteem, stimulate the sex drive, and increase one's energy level. However, they may lead to sleep disorders and be connected with apathy and depression when they are discontinued.

The **catecholamines** adrenalin and noradrenalin are released by the adrenal medulla. **Adrenalin** (also

called epinephrine) is secreted solely by the adrenal glands. Noradrenalin (norepinephrine), however, is also manufactured elsewhere in the body. In Chapter 4 we shall see that under stress, the sympathetic branch of the ANS prompts the adrenal medulla to secrete a mixture of adrenalin and norepinephrine that prepares the body to cope. Norepinephrine raises the blood pressure. In the nervous system, it functions as a neurotransmitter.

The male sex hormone **testosterone** is produced by the testes. A few weeks following conception, it prompts prenatal development of male sex organs. During puberty it fosters growth of muscle and bone and the ripening of **primary** and **secondary sex characteristics.** Primary sex characteristics differentiate the sexes and are directly involved in reproduction. The sex organs are prime examples. Secondary sex characteristics, such as deepening of the voice and growth of the beard, also differentiate the sexes but are not directly involved in reproduction. Testosterone levels vary somewhat with stress and time of day, but are kept at fairly even levels by the hypothalamus, pituitary gland, and testes.

The ovaries secrete **estrogen** and **progesterone.**

Estrogen is a collective name for numerous female sex hormones that spur development of female reproductive capacity and secondary sex characteristics. They account for accumulation of fatty deposits in the breasts and hips. Progesterone also has many functions. It induces growth of the female reproductive organs and preserves pregnancy.

In Chapter 5 we shall discuss evidence of the roles of female sex hormones in menstrual disorders. In Chapter 11 we shall examine the roles of sex hormones in sexual disorders and variations of sexual behavior.

Genetics and Behavior Genetics

Heredity plays an important role in the determination of our traits. The structures we inherit make our behavior possible (humans can walk and run) as well as place limits on us (humans cannot fly without artificial equipment) (Kimble, 1989). The branch of biology that studies heredity is called **genetics.** *Behavior genetics* bridges the sciences of biology and psychology. It is concerned with how heredity affects behavior.

Genetics is fundamental in the transmission of physical traits such as height, race, and the color of the eyes. Genetics also appears to be a factor in the origins of psychological traits like intelligence (Plomin, 1989), **extraversion** and **neuroticism** (Loehlin et al., 1982; Martin & Jardine, 1986; Pedersen et al., 1988; Scarr et al., 1981; Tellegen et al., 1988), shyness (Kagan, 1984; Plomin, 1989), social dominance, and aggressiveness (Goldsmith, 1983).

Genetic influences are also implicated in abnormal behavior patterns such as schizophrenia (Gottesman & Shields, 1982), bipolar (manic-depression) disorder (Vandenberg et al., 1986), and alcoholism and antisocial personality (Mednick et al., 1987). In the coming chapters we will examine more closely the evidence regarding genetic contributions to these and other patterns of abnormal behavior.

Now let us review the biological mechanisms of heredity.

■ **Genes and Chromosomes** **Genes** are the basic units of heredity and are found on the chromosomes in every cell in the body. **Chromosomes** are the rod-shaped genetic structures that reside in the nuclei of cells, each consisting of more than a thousand genes. A human cell normally contains 46 chromosomes, which are organized into 23 pairs.

There are about 100,000 genes in every cell in our bodies. Chromosomes are made up of large, complex molecules of deoxyribonucleic acid, or DNA for short. Genes occupy various segments along the length

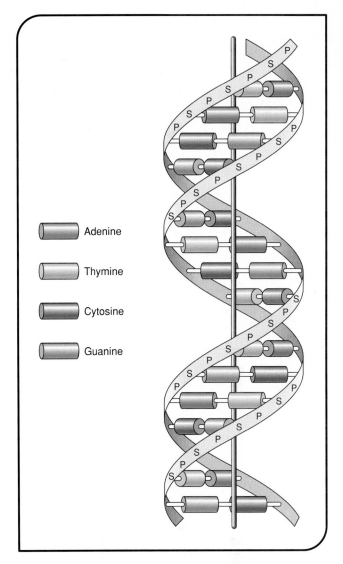

Adenine

Thymine

Cytosine

Guanine

FIGURE 2.11 *The double-helix structure of DNA.*

of chromosomes. The form or structure of DNA was first shown by James Watson and Francis Crick (1958). In all living things, DNA is in the form of a double helix, which resembles a twisting ladder (see Figure 2.11). The sequence of our genes is referred to as our genetic codes.

The combination of traits that are specified by our genetic codes are called our **genotypes.** But our traits are also influenced by environmental factors such as learning, nutrition, exercise, and, unfortunately, accident and illness. Our actual traits are our **phenotypes.** That is, our expressed traits represent the interaction of our genes and our environment. A genetic propensity toward, say, shyness might be increased or even reversed by powerful social influences. So, too, with abnormal behavior patterns. In the view of behavior geneticists, we may not develop certain forms of abnormal

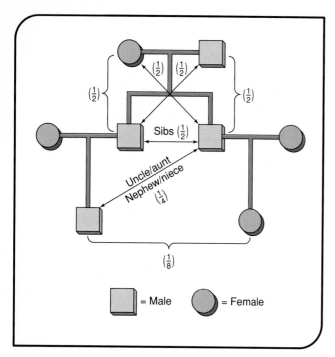

FIGURE 2.12 A family tree showing the proportion of shared inheritance among relatives.

The biological perspective seeks evidence of genetic transmission in abnormal behavior patterns through various types of studies, such as kinship studies, including twin studies and adoptee studies.

■ **Kinship Studies** The more closely people are related, the more genes they have in common. Children receive half their genes from each parent, so there is said to be a 50 percent overlap in genetic heritage between parents and their offspring. Siblings (brothers and sisters) similarly share half their genetic heritage. Aunts and uncles who are related by blood to their nephews and nieces have a 25 percent overlap; first cousins, a 12.5 percent overlap.

In order to determine whether a pattern of abnormal behavior has a genetic basis, researchers locate one case and then study how the disorder is distributed among family members. The case first diagnosed is referred to as the *index case*, or *proband*. If the distribution of the disorder among family members approximates their degree of kinship, there may be genetic involvement. However, the closer their kinship, the more likely people also are to share environmental backgrounds. For this reason, adoption studies are of particular value, as we shall see below.

■ **Twin Studies** Sometimes a fertilized egg cell (or zygote) divides into two cells that separate, so that each develops into a person. In such cases, there is a 100 percent overlap in genetic makeup, and the couple are known as identical twins, or **monozygotic (MZ) twins.** Sometimes a woman releases two egg cells, or ova, in the same month, and they are both fertilized. In such cases, the zygotes develop into fraternal twins, or **dizygotic (DZ) twins.** DZ twins overlap 50 percent in their genetic heritage, just as other siblings do.

Identical, or MZ, twins are important in the study of the relative influences of heredity and environment because differences between MZ twins are the result of environmental influences. MZ twins look alike and are closer in height than DZ twins. In twin studies, researchers identify disordered people who are MZ or DZ twins and then study the other twins. A role for genetic factors is suggested when MZ twins are significantly more likely than DZ twins to share a disorder. In later chapters, we will examine the differences in the rates of **concordance** for MZ versus DZ twins for particular forms of abnormal behavior, such as schizophrenia and mood disorders. Even among MZ twins, though, environmental influences cannot be ruled out. Parents and teachers, for example, often encourage MZ twins to behave in similar ways. Put it another way: If one twin does X, everyone expects the other to do X also. Expectations have a way of influencing behavior and making for self-fulfilling prophecies.

behavior, such as depression or schizophrenia, unless we possess a particular genotype and are exposed to certain stressful environmental influences (birth complications, family conflict, loss of loved ones, etc.) that leads to the emergence of the particular pattern of abnormal behavior. In the parlance of behavior geneticists, individuals who possess such genotypes for particular forms of abnormal behavior are said to have a *genetic predisposition* that makes them more likely to develop the abnormal behavior pattern in response to stress.

The interaction between genetics and environment in determining the development of abnormal behavior patterns is expressed in a model that is often referred to as the **diathesis–stress** hypothesis. According to this approach, the genotype provides a vulnerability (or diathesis) within the person that interacts with stress to produce the disorder (which is part of the phenotype). Not all susceptible offspring develop the disorder. Many environmental, behavioral, and psychological factors may also be involved, ranging from situational stresses to learning from parents to ways of encoding experience and mentally representing the world. But in some cases, the diathesis (the biological predisposition, or vulnerability) may be so potent that the person will develop the disorder even in the most benign of environments. The diathesis–stress hypothesis may apply to a number of disorders, especially schizophrenia, as we will consider further in Chapter 12.

Identical (MZ) twins may share a lot more in common than identical genes. They may also be reared in similar ways—treated alike, dressed alike, etc. A greater concordance rate on certain traits between MZ twins than between DZ twins suggest a genetic influence on the traits in question, but environmental (rearing) factors that may distinguish the MZ twins need also to be considered.

■ **Adoption Studies** Adoption studies can provide powerful arguments for or against genetic factors in the appearance of psychological traits and behavior patterns, including abnormal behavior patterns. Assume that children are reared by adoptive parents from a very early age—perhaps from birth. The children share environmental backgrounds with their adoptive parents, but not their genetic heritages. Then assume that we compare the traits and behavior patterns of these children to those of their natural biological parents and their adoptive parents. If the children show a greater similarity to their natural parents than their adoptive parents on certain traits or disorders, we have strong evidence indeed for genetic factors in these traits and disorders. Evidence is particularly powerful when MZ twins are separated at birth and reared quite differently, yet their traits and behavior patterns strongly overlap.

> **?** Yes, many abnormal behavior patterns run in families. However, unless we examine adoption studies, we may not be able to distinguish between the effects of heredity and of the environment.

Unfortunately for science, but fortunately for the children involved, MZ twins are rarely separated at early ages. Moreover, when they are separated, the confidentiality of adoption records can make them difficult to trace. Still, a sprinkling of such cases has enriched the scientific literature.

In later chapters we shall explore the role that adoptee and other kinship studies play in ferreting out genetic and environmental influences in many patterns of abnormal behavior.

Evaluating Biological Perspectives

The biological perspective has had much to offer to our understanding of abnormal behavior. Biological research is replete with current successes and future promise. Drugs for some disorders are synthesized on the basis of knowledge of the actions of neurotransmitters and hormones. Drugs have been developed that quell the more flagrant features of schizophrenia but cannot effect a "cure." As we shall see in Chapter 12, such drugs also carry potentially dangerous side effects. Nor can drugs alone prepare the institutionalized patients for reentry into society. As the sociocultural theorists remind us, hospitalized patients may become socialized within a dependent "sick role" in institutional settings. Learning the skills that would prepare them for participating in more independent *citizenry* roles in the community requires psychosocial or psychoeducational training approaches. Drugs are used in the treatment of a wide variety of other abnormal behavior patterns, including disorders relating to anxiety and disturbances of mood. In some cases, researchers are finding that the combination of psychological and **chemotherapy** approaches may be more effective than either approach alone. In other cases, one or the other approach may be more effective. We will evaluate the role of drugs in the treatment of various patterns of abnormal behavior in later chapters.

Genetic engineering remains a future promise that may someday be realized. Perhaps in the future a number of disorders that are connected with certain genetic defects may be corrected in the womb or by direct manipulation of parental sperm and egg cells.

There is also no question that biological structures and processes are involved in many patterns of abnormal behavior. In some cases, as in Alzheimer's disease, biological processes play the primary causative role. But even then, the precise causes remain to be discovered. In other cases, such as with schizophrenia, biological factors, especially genetics, appear to interact with stressful environmental factors in the development of the disorder.

At this time, no one theoretical perspective can fully account for all kinds of abnormal behavior or offer the final word in treatment. As rounded human beings, we can extract that which is of value from each of them. Even the most controversial sociocultural ideas at least remind us to keep an eye on the political aspects of our assumptions. In many ways the main theories overlap, as in the nearly universal concept of a self and the nearly universal notion that our interpretations of events influence our emotional and behavioral reactions. Nor would any scientist deny that mental experience is dependent on the brain. As we learn more about people and about abnormal behavior, our theories will probably focus on subtler and more complex interactions.

SUMMARY

Psychodynamic Perspectives

The psychodynamic perspectives include the contributions of Freud and his followers. While there are differences among psychodynamic theorists, they all share certain tenets in common, such as beliefs in psychic determinism, unconscious motivation, and the importance of childhood experiences in shaping personality and behavior.

Freud believed that the mind is composed of three regions, the conscious, the preconscious, and the unconscious. The conscious refers to mental experiences in current awareness. Mental contents which are not presently in awareness but which can be easily brought into consciousness reside in the preconscious. The unconscious, the largest part of the mind, is the repository of basic instincts such as sex and aggression. Its contents can only be brought to awareness with great difficulty. Freud posited the existence of three mental or psychic structures, the id, the ego, and the superego. The only mental structure present at birth, the id represents the basic biological drives and resides in the unconscious. Id follows the pleasure principle and seeks immediate gratification. The ego stands for reason and follows the reality principle, seeking to find socially acceptable ways of gratifying the urgings of the id. The superego, which is formed through a process of identification in middle childhood, represents the embodiment of moral values and operates according to the moral principle. Defense mechanisms, such as repression, protect the ego from anxiety by keeping unacceptable impulses out of awareness. While the use of defense mechanisms is quite normal, it can lead to abnormal behavior patterns.

Abnormal behavior patterns occur from imbalances among the mental structures. Neurotic anxiety occurs when the ego senses that unacceptable impulses may break through to consciousness. Neuroses are means of stemming the leakage of these impulses and are characterized by maladaptive behavior patterns that represent or symbolize the inner conflict. In contrast, reality anxiety represents a fear of external danger. In psychoses, such as schizophrenia, the id completely breaks through and primary process thinking and bizarre behavior become dominant.

Freud charted five stages of psychosexual development that correspond to changes in the transfer of sexual energy, or libido, from one erogenous zone to another. The stages are oral, anal, phallic, latency, and genital. Undergratification or overgratification at particular stages can lead to fixation, which is characterized by the development of traits associated with the particular stage.

Freud highlighted the importance of the Oedipus and Electra complexes, which he believed occur during the phallic stage. These conflicts are characterized by incestuous wishes to possess the parent of the opposite sex and resentment of the same-sex parent. Normally, these conflicts are resolved through repression of the incestuous wishes and identification with the parent of the same sex. Sexual drives then remain dormant during the so-called latency stage, and are again aroused, in the genital stage. Mature psychosexual development involves the displacement of the previously repressed incestuous wishes onto more appropriate partners of the opposite sex in the context of marital (genital) sex and reproduction. Freud was criticized, even among his followers, for his beliefs concerning female psychosexual development, especially for his concept of penis envy in girls.

Other psychodynamic theorists placed lesser importance on primitive drives, such as sex and aggression, and greater importance on the functions of the ego, especially the development of concepts of the self. Psychodynamic perspectives have had profound impact on Western culture and the understanding of human behavior. But many of its propositions remain speculative, since they may not be testable by scientific means.

Learning Perspectives

Learning theorists attempt to account for both normal and abnormal behavior on the basis of principles of learning, rather than on unconscious mental processes. Behaviorists such as John Watson and B. F. Skinner rejected concepts of mind and personality altogether. Behaviorists focus on classical and operant conditioning, in which learning is believed to be shaped by the environment. In classical conditioning, a response that occurs naturally to a certain stimuli (the unconditioned stimulus or UCS) becomes elicited by a previously neutral stimuli (the conditioned stimulus or CS) through repeated pairings of these stimuli. Extinction involves the weakening of such conditioned responses (CRs) through exposure to the CS without the UCS. After the passage of time, though, the conditioned response may recur, a process labeled spontaneous recovery.

In operant conditioning, behavior is acquired on the basis of reinforcement. Reinforcers increase the frequency of occurrence of the behavior they follow. Positive reinforcers increase behavior by means of their introduction; negative reinforcers increase behavior by means of their removal. Primary reinforcers, such as food and water, exert their influence naturally, while secondary reinforcers influence behavior through their prior association with previously established reinforcers. Punishments are painful or aversive stimuli that decrease or suppress the behavior they follow. But punishments have their drawbacks, and psychologists generally favor the use of positive reinforcers.

Social learning theorists focus on the importance of cognitive variables in learning and learning by observation. They believe that situational variables, like rewards and punishments, are not sufficient to account for learning and behavior and believe that person variables need to be considered. Person variables include competencies, encoding strategies, expectancies such as outcome expectancies and self-efficacy expectations, subjective values, and self-regulatory systems and plans.

Learning theorists see abnormal behavior as largely learned by means of the same principles of learning as normal behavior. Behavior therapy represents the application of principles of learning to help people overcome abnormal behavior patterns and develop more adjusted behaviors.

In contrast to psychodynamic perspectives, learning perspectives emphasize observable behavior and environmental stimuli that are more available to scientific study. However, learning models have been criticized for not paying adequate attention to genetic factors in explaining normal and abnormal behavior and for failing to account for the richness of human experience. Social learning theorists have broadened the traditional behavioral model by focusing on human beings as active seekers of information, not just as passive reactors to environmental stimuli. They share much in common with the cognitive theorists.

Cognitive Perspectives

Cognitive theorists focus on the roles of thinking and information processing in explaining human behavior. Information processing models liken the human organism to the computer in terms of processes relating to input, storage, retrieval, manipulation, and output of information.

Kelly viewed people as personal scientists who seek to understand and predict events through the use of personal constructs, or dimensions for categorizing events. To understand people, we need to understand how they construe events. Kelly's approach to therapy focused on helping people make more adjustive constructions of events.

Ellis believes that people endure emotional misery because of the ways they interpret events, rather than from the events themselves. By exaggerating the importance of negative events, people can turn disappointment into despair. He proposed an A—B—C model for analyzing the relationships between activating events (A's), intervening beliefs (B's), and emotional consequences (C's). Ellis' rational-emotive therapy attempts to help clients dispute their irrational beliefs and substitute more rational alternative beliefs.

Beck also focuses on tendencies of people to exaggerate negative consequences of upsetting events, which he calls cognitive distortions or errors in thinking. Beck's approach to therapy, namely cognitive therapy, focuses on helping clients identify and correct such cognitive errors as selective abstraction, overgeneralization, magnification, and absolutist thinking.

Cognitive theorists focus on how maladaptive thoughts or cognitions may lead to emotional problems. Cognitive theorists have helped spawn the development of cognitive behavior therapy, a model of treatment that integrates behavioral and cognitive techniques, as well as developing their own particular methods of therapy. But cognitive theorists have had less impact on our understanding or treatment of certain disorders, like schizophrenia, and questions remain about whether distorted cognitions cause emotional problems like depression or merely result from these problems.

Humanistic-Existential Perspectives

Humanistic and existential theorists focus on the importance of conscious awareness and the uniqueness of the individual. They also believe in free choice and personal responsibility for one's actions. Humanists emphasize self-actualization, the inner tendency to strive toward one's potential. Existentialists focus on the importance of authenticity, living according to the dictates of one's own values and goals.

Frankl focused on the person's pursuit of meaning in life, and he developed a model of therapy, called logotherapy, that helps people find meaningful ways of talking about and organizing their lives.

Maslow believed that there is a hierarchy of needs that traverse the basic biological needs to the highest levels of self-actualization.

Rogers developed self-theory, which views the self, the center of experience, as the innate, organized and consistent basis by which people relate to others and to the world. The self strives to develop its unique potential but may be fettered by conditional positive regard, which leads to denial or disownment of parts of the self that meet with rebuke from others. Rogers' approach to therapy, called person-centered therapy, provides a therapeutic environment that fosters self-awareness and self-acceptance.

The humanistic-existential theorists have also had profound influence on modern society and concepts of human nature. Their focus on conscious experience and innovations in therapy, especially those of Rogers, have assisted people in their pursuit of self-discovery and self-awareness. But behaviorists claim that the sense of freedom may be an illusion. Critics contend that conscious experience is private and cannot be validated by scientific tests.

Sociocultural Perspectives

The sociocultural theorists look for causes of abnormal behavior in society rather than the individual. People become disturbed when they are subjected to extreme social pressures, such as poverty, prolonged unemployment, discrimination, and social decay. The more radical psychosocial theorists, such as Szasz, dispute the existence of mental illness, believing that mental illness is merely a label that society uses to stigmatize people whose behavior is socially deviant.

While some studies show that people of lower social classes are at greater risks of institutionalization, the causal connections between social class and abnormal behavior remain unclear. Sociocultural theorists have identified abuses in mental institutions and have focused much needed attention on the social factors that may contribute to abnormal behavior. But many mental hospitals today focus on preparing patients for release, not long-term institutionalization.

Biological Perspectives

Biological perspectives focus on the roles of biological structures and processes. In some cases, most notably Alzheimer's disease, biological factors are implicated as direct causes. Other cases reflect more of an interaction of biological and psychological causes.

The nervous system is composed of neurons that communicate with one another through means of chemical messengers, called neurotransmitters, which transmit nervous impulses across the gaps, or synapses, between neurons. The balance of neurotransmitters in the brain is believed to play an important role in various mental disorders, but the precise role is not yet determined.

Various parts of the brain have specialized functions involving control of vital life functions like breathing and heart rate and higher functions like attention, thinking, and perceiving. The brain is connected to the outer world by way of the peripheral nervous system, which consists of two divisions, the somatic nervous system and the autonomic nervous system. The biological aspects of anxiety involve the activity of the autonomic nervous system, especially the sympathetic branch of the system.

The endocrine system consists of glands that release various hormones involved in regulating different bodily functions, such as growth and reproduction, as well as helping the body manage stress by countering inflammation and allergic reactions.

Behavior geneticists use various types of studies, including kinship studies, twin studies, and adoption studies, to explore the influence of genetics on abnormal behavior patterns.

Biological perspectives have had an important influence on conceptions and treatment of abnormal behavior. Abnormal behavior may reflect, in many cases, the interaction of biological and psychological factors. A prominent model, the diathesis—stress hypothesis, posits a role in the development of abnormal behavior patterns for both genetic vulnerability (or diathesis) and stress. This model has been especially influential in guiding present understandings of schizophrenia.

SCORING KEY FOR THE EXPECTANCY FOR SUCCESS SCALE

To calculate your total score on the Expectancy for Success Scale, first reverse your scores on the following items: 1, 2, 4, 6, 7, 8, 14, 15, 17, 18, 24, 27, and 28. This means that a 1 becomes a 5, a 2 becomes a 4, a 3 stays the same, a 4 becomes a 2, and a 5 becomes a 1. Then sum all the scores.

The highest possible score is 150; the lowest, 30. The higher your total score, the greater your expectancies of future success. Social learning theory suggests that the more positive your expectancies, the more motivated you will be to pursue your goals and strive to overcome challenges. Fibel and Hale administered the scale to undergraduate students in psychology courses. The women's scores ranged from 65 to 143, with a mean (average) score of 112.32. The men's scores ranged from 81 to 138, with a nearly identical mean (average) score of 112.15.

3 Classification and Assessment of Abnormal Behavior

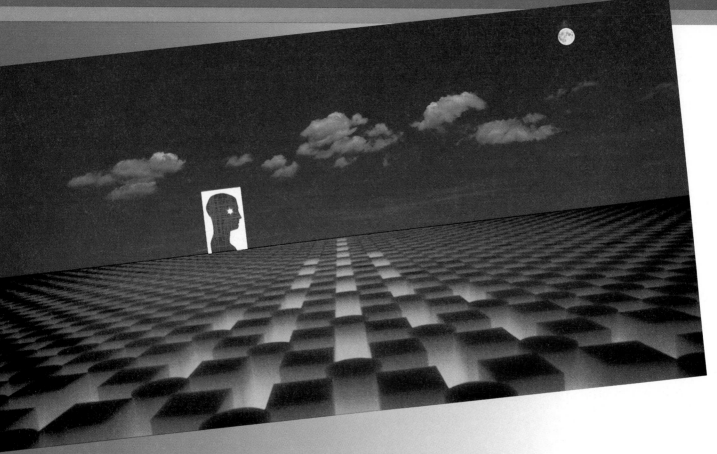

LEARNING OBJECTIVES

When you have completed your study of Chapter 3, you should be able to:

CLASSIFICATION OF ABNORMAL BEHAVIOR (pp. 79–86)

1. Discuss historical origins of modern diagnostic systems.
2. Define the concept of "mental disorders" in the DSM–III–R system and show how the diagnostic system adheres to the medical model.
3. Describe the features of the DSM–III–R system.
4. Explain the multiaxial feature of the DSM–III–R system.
5. Describe the strengths and weaknesses of the DSM–III–R.

CHARACTERISTICS OF METHODS OF ASSESSMENT (pp. 86–88)

6. Explain three approaches to demonstrating the reliability of methods of assessment.
7. Explain three approaches to demonstrating the validity of methods of assessment.

THE CLINICAL INTERVIEW (pp. 88–93)

8. Describe what is meant by a structured interview.
9. Describe the elements of the mental status examination.
10. Describe various aspects of effective interviewing.
11. Describe the use of standardized interview techniques.

PSYCHOLOGICAL TESTS (pp. 93–95)

12. Discuss the nature and value of psychological tests.

INTELLIGENCE TESTS (pp. 95–97)

13. Discuss the history and features of the Stanford-Binet Intelligence Scale.

14. Discuss the features of the Wechsler scales.

PERSONALITY TESTS (pp. 97–104)

15. Distinguish between self-report and projective personality assessment techniques.
16. Discuss the history, features, reliability, and validity of personality tests, focusing on the MMPI, the Rorschach, and the TAT.

NEUROPSYCHOLOGICAL ASSESSMENT (pp. 104–106)

17. Describe the use of psychological tests in the assessment of neuropsychological functioning.

BEHAVIORAL ASSESSMENT (pp. 106–110)

18. Discuss the advantages and limitations of behavioral assessment.
19. Describe the following techniques: the behavioral interview, self-monitoring, use of contrived measures, direct observation, and behavioral rating scales.

COGNITIVE ASSESSMENT (pp. 110–111)

20. Discuss the use of thought diaries and questionnaires that assess automatic thoughts and dysfunctional attitudes.

PHYSIOLOGICAL MEASUREMENT (pp. 111–114)

21. Explain the relationships between emotional states and physiological measurement.
22. Describe contemporary brain imaging techniques.

Systems of classification of abnormal behavior date back to ancient times. Hippocrates, for example, classified abnormal behaviors on the basis of his theory of humors. While his theory proved to be flawed, he nonetheless arrived at some diagnostic categories that generally correspond to those in modern diagnostic systems. His description of melancholia, for example, is similar to present conceptions of depression, while his description of "mania" resembles what is now called a manic episode. Hippocrates' conception of phrenitis describes behaviors that today would roughly correspond to schizophrenia.

It is true that the most widely used contemporary system for the classification of abnormal behaviors can trace some of its roots to a system of classification proposed more than 2,000 years ago. Hippocrates, the physician of the Golden Age of Greece, proposed a number of categories that have since been revised but remain in use.

During the Middle Ages, some "authorities" classified abnormal behaviors according to those that represented possession and those that represented natural causes. The nineteenth-century German psychiatrist Emil Kraepelin is generally considered the first modern theorist to develop a comprehensive model of classification based on the distinctive features or "symptoms" associated with abnormal behavior patterns. The most commonly used classification system today is largely an outgrowth and extension of Kraepelin's work: the *Diagnostic and Statistical Manual of Mental Disorders* (DSM), which is published by the American Psychiatric Association. In the DSM system, abnormal behavior patterns are classified as mental disorders on the basis of specified diagnostic criteria.

In this chapter we review the classification and assessment of abnormal behavior. First we review the DSM system of classification. Why is it important to classify abnormal behavior patterns? One reason is that important decisions are made on the basis of how abnormal behavior patterns are classified. For example, treatment techniques vary according to the kinds of problems shown by clients. A clinician might know that a certain abnormal behavior pattern responds better to one form of therapy or another, or to one type of drug or another. Classification may also help clinicians predict future behavior. Some patterns of abnormal behavior, such as schizophrenia, tend to follow more or less predictable courses of development. Classification is also extremely important to researchers, for it helps them identify populations with similar patterns of abnormal behavior. By classifying groups of people as depressed, for example, researchers might be able to identify common features in their backgrounds or their psychological functioning that might help to explain the origins of depression. Nor could a researcher test the effectiveness of a new drug for depression unless there existed a group of people who were classified as depressed, and unless there were clear criteria for classifying them as such.

Following the discussion of the DSM system, we explore the methods of assessment that psychologists and other mental health professionals use to classify patterns of abnormal behavior. We first review the basic requirements for methods of assessment—that they be reliable and valid. Then we consider the methods of assessment that help clinicians arrive at diagnostic impressions, including interviews, psychological testing, self-report questionnaires, behavioral measures, and physiological measures. The role of assessment, however, goes further than classification. A carefully conducted assessment provides a wealth of information about the client's personality and cognitive functioning. This information helps clinicians reach a broader understanding of their clients' problems and make appropriate recommendations for treatment.

THE DSM SYSTEM

The DSM was introduced in 1952 and has been revised several times. The current edition is a revision of the third edition, published in 1987—the DSM–III–R. Another common system of classification is used mainly for compiling statistics on the occurrence of disorders in various countries: the *International Classification of Diseases, Ninth Revision* (ICD–9), which is published by the World Health Organization. The DSM–III–R was designed to be compatible with the ICD–9; DSM–III–R diagnoses can be easily coded in the ICD–9 system as well.

We make use of the DSM–III–R because of its widespread adoption by mental health professionals. However, psychologists and others have criticized the DSM–III–R on several grounds, such as relying too strongly on the medical model. So view our focus on the DSM–III–R as recognition of its widespread use, not an endorsement.

In the DSM–III–R, people are regarded as showing abnormal behaviors—or, in the medical jargon of the manual, as having "mental disorders"—if they experience emotional distress or show impairment in functioning. Impaired functioning includes difficulties in meeting responsibilities at work or in family and societal roles. It includes behavior that places people at risk for personal suffering, pain, or death, or that prevents them from meeting their responsibilities.

Diagnosis of abnormal behavior also requires that the behavioral pattern not represent an expected response to a stressful event, such as the loss of a loved one. People who shows signs of bereavement or grief following the death of loved ones are not considered disordered, even if their behavior is significantly impaired—for a time. If their behavior remains significantly impaired for an extended period of time, however, a diagnosis of an abnormal behavior pattern and not normal grief or bereavement might be appropriate.

The DSM–III–R and Models of Abnormal Behavior

In a sense, the DSM–III–R system adheres to the medical model. It treats abnormal behaviors as signs or symptoms of underlying disorders or pathologies. However, unlike the strictest form of the medical model, the manual does not assume that abnormal behaviors necessarily reflect biological causes or defects. It recognizes that the causes of most abnormal behaviors remain uncertain: Some disorders may be found to have biological causes; others, psychological causes. Still other abnormal behaviors might reflect the interaction of psychological, biological, and social factors.

Nor does the DSM–III–R subscribe to a particular theory of abnormal behavior. With the introduction of the DSM–III in 1980, terms linked to specific theories (such as **neurosis,** traditionally a psychoanalytic term) have been de-emphasized in favor of atheoretical descriptive terms like ''anxiety disorders'' and ''mood disorders.'' Disorders are now classified on the basis of their clinical features and behavior patterns, not on the basis of inferences about underlying theoretical mechanisms. Since the DSM–III–R does not endorse particular theoretical models, unless evidence of causal factors for certain disorders seems overwhelming, it can be used by practitioners of diverse theoretical persuasions. This means that clinicians and researchers from different theoretical persuasions can all agree on what constitutes anxiety disorders, mood disorders, and schizophrenic disorders, even if they disagree on the causes and most appropriate treatments of these conditions.

Features of the DSM–III–R

The DSM–III–R is descriptive, not explanatory. It describes the diagnostic features—or, in medical terms, symptoms—of abnormal behaviors rather than attempting to explain their origins. Let us consider a number of features of the DSM–III–R classification system:

Specific diagnostic criteria are used. The clinician is helped to arrive at a diagnosis by matching clients' behaviors with the diagnostic criteria that define particular patterns of abnormal behavior or ''mental disorders.'' Diagnostic categories are described in terms of *essential features* (criteria that must be present for the diagnosis to be made) and *associated features* (criteria that are usually but not always present). An example of diagnostic criteria for a particular disorder, Conduct Disorder in Childhood, is shown in Table 3.1.

Abnormal behaviors that share common clinical features are grouped together. Abnormal behaviors are categorized according to their shared clinical features, not theoretical speculation as to their causes. For example, abnormal behavior patterns that are chiefly characterized by anxiety are classified as anxiety disorders. Behaviors chiefly characterized by disruptions in mood are categorized as mood disorders.

A multiaxial system is used. The DSM–III–R employs a multiaxial or multidimensional system of assessment that provides a broad range of information about the individual's functioning, not merely a diagnosis. The

TABLE 3.1 Diagnostic Criteria for Conduct Disorder in Childhood

A. A pattern of disturbed conduct, lasting for at least 6 months, which is characterized by at least three of the following behaviors:

   (1) stealing property on more than one occasion, but without actually confronting the victim
   (2) running away from home overnight on at least two occasions (or once without returning) while residing in parent's home or in a parental surrogate's home
   (3) frequent lying (except when attempting to avoid physical or sexual abuse)
   (4) deliberate fire-setting
   (5) truancy from school (or if older, absent from work)
   (6) breaking into someone else's home, building or car
   (7) deliberately destroying other people's property (except by fire-setting)
   (8) showing physical cruelty to animals
   (9) forcing another person into sexual activity with him or herself
   (10) using a weapon in a fight on more than one occasion
   (11) starting physical fights
   (12) stealing with confrontation of the victim, as in a mugging, purse-snatching, armed robbery, or extortion
   (13) engaging in physical cruelty toward other people

B. If age 18 or older, person does not meet diagnostic criteria for Antisocial Personality Disorder.

Source: Adapted from DSM–III–R, p. 55.

multiaxial system consists of the following five ''axes'' or dimensions of functioning:

1. *Axis I, the Clinical Syndromes,* includes a wide range of diagnostic classes, such as anxiety disorders, mood disorders, schizophrenia, and some disorders of childhood.

2. *Axis II, Developmental Disorders and Personality Disorders,* includes the more enduring or chronic patterns of maladaptive behavior that generally originate in childhood or adolescence and persist into adulthood. Disorders classified on Axis II include such developmental disorders as **autism** and **mental retardation** and personality disorders such as **antisocial personality disorder.**

Separating the diagnostic categories into Axes I and II provides the clinician with greater flexibility in reaching diagnostic impressions. People may be diagnosed with either Axis I or Axis II diagnoses, or a combination of the two when both apply. When evaluating adults, the clinician can code the diagnosis that corresponds to the primary presenting complaint—generally an Axis I diagnosis—as well as any enduring personality disorders or continuing developmental problems from childhood (Axis II) which may co-exist with the Axis I diagnosis. For example, a person may receive a diagnosis of a particular anxiety disorder (Axis I) and a second

TABLE 3.2 Psychosocial Stressors Often Coded on Axis IV

Types of Stressors	Examples
Marital and nonmarital	Engagement or marriage, marital discord, separation, or the death of a spouse
Parenting	Becoming a parent, conflict with child, or illness of child
Other types of interpersonal problems	Problems with friends, neighbors, employers, or associates
Occupational	Work- or school-related problems, problems managing a household, or unemployment
Living circumstances	Moving or changing one's residence, experiencing threats to one's personal safety
Financial	Financial hardships or setbacks
Legal	Arrest or imprisonment, or becoming involved in a lawsuit or trial
Developmental	Making transitions at various phases of the life cycle, such as puberty, early adulthood, or menopause
Physical illness or injury	Illnesses, accidents, surgery, abortion, etc. The diagnostic manual allows that a physical illness (coded on Axis III) may also represent a source of psychological stress.
Other psychosocial factors	Natural or manmade disasters, persecution, out-of-wedlock birth, rape, or unwanted pregnancy
Family stressors affecting children and adolescents	Conflicts between parents; abuse or neglect of child, physical or mental illness in parent or family member; lack of guidance from parents; severely harsh or inconsistent parental control; inadequate, inconsistent, or excessive levels of stimulation in home and social environment; inconsistent or disruptive patterns of parental custody or arrangements for visitation; inadequate living situation in institutional or foster care settings.

Note: Clinicians code the presence and severity of psychosocial stressors, such as those listed above. The rating is also given which indicates whether the stressor(s) are *predominantly acute events* (less than 6 months in duration, such as beginning a new job, or suffering the death of a loved one), or *predominantly enduring circumstances* (greater than 6 months in duration, such as chronic marital discord, or continuing patterns of harsh parental discipline or abuse).
Source: Adapted from DSM–III–R, pp. 19–20.

diagnosis of a particular personality disorder (Axis II) if the diagnostic criteria for both are met. When multiple diagnoses are given, the *principal diagnosis* is the condition that apparently precipitated the evaluation. Clients may also have multiple diagnoses within axes. For example, they may be given Axis I diagnoses for a substance abuse disorder and a mood disorder, if both apply. When evaluating children, the separation between the two axes allows the clinician to distinguish between disorders involving difficulties in developing social, cognitive, and motor skills (Axis II) and those involving other developmental problems (Axis I).

3. *Axis III, Physical Disorders and Conditions*, lists physical illnesses that may affect clients' functioning or response to treatment.

4. *Axis IV, Severity of Psychosocial Stressors*, rates the severity of stressful events, such as those listed in Table 3.2, in the year preceding evaluation that may have initiated the disorder, exacerbated an existing disorder, or brought on the recurrence of an earlier disorder.

5. *Axis V, Global Assessment of Functioning*, refers to clinician's overall judgment of clients' psychological, social, and occupational functioning. Based on the Global Assessment of Functioning Scale (GAF) (see Table 3.3), the clinician rates clients' current functioning and highest level of functioning achieved for a period of two months during

The assessment of functioning takes into account the ability to manage the responsibilities of daily living, such as personal hygiene. This young retarded man is able to meet the responsibilities of living in a group home for retarded men.

TABLE 3.3 Global Assessment to Functioning Scale (GAF)

Code	Severity of Symptoms	Examples
81–90	Absent or minimal symptoms, no more than everyday problems or concerns	Mild anxiety before exams Occasional argument with family members
71–80	Transient and predictable reactions to stressful events, *or* no more than slight impairment in functioning	Difficulty concentrating after argument with family Temporarily falls behind in schoolwork
61–70	Some mild symptoms, *or* some difficulty in social, occupational, or school functioning, but functioning pretty well	Feels down, mild insomnia Occasional truancy or theft within household
51–60	Moderate symptoms, *or* moderate difficulties in social, occupational, or school functioning	Occasional panic attacks Few friends, conflicts with co-workers
41–50	Serious symptoms, *or* any serious difficulty in social, occupational, or school functioning	Suicidal thoughts, frequent shoplifting Unable to hold job, has no friends
31–40	Some difficulty in reality testing or communication, *or* major impairment in several areas	Speech illogical Depressed man unable to work, neglects family, and avoids friends
21–30	Strong influence on behavior of delusions or hallucinations, *or* serious difficulties in communication or judgment, *or* inability to function in almost all areas	Grossly inappropriate behavior, speech sometimes incoherent Stays in bed all day, has no job, home, or friends
11–20	Some danger of harming self or others, *or* occasionally fails to maintain personal hygiene, *or* gross impairment in communication	Suicidal gestures, frequently violent Smears feces Largely incoherent or mute
1–10	Persistent danger of severely harming self or others, *or* persistent inability to maintain even minimal personal hygiene, *or* serious suicidal act	Serious suicidal attempt, recurrent violence

Source: Adapted from DSM–III–R, p. 12.

the preceding year. The level of current functioning is taken to indicate the current need for treatment or intensity of care. The level of highest functioning is suggestive of the level of functioning that might be restored.

An overview of the DSM–III–R multiaxial system is shown in Table 3.4. Table 3.5 offers an example of the diagnoses and other codes that may be applied to an individual.

Evaluation of the DSM–III–R System

Two of the basic criteria used in evaluating the value of a diagnostic system such as the DSM–III–R are its reliability and validity. A diagnostic system may be considered **reliable,** or consistent, if diverse diagnosticians using the system are likely to arrive at the same diagnoses when they evaluate the same cases. Versions of the DSM system that preceded the 1980 introduction of the DSM–III generally suffered from poor reliability. Skilled diagnosticians often disagreed on the correct diagnoses for clients, largely because the diagnostic criteria were often fuzzy or ambiguous.

The DSM–III, which was based on more specific, tighter diagnostic criteria than the DSM–II, showed greater interrater reliability (that is, agreement among diagnosticians) than its predecessor in its early trials. Axis I and Axis V showed generally adequate interrater reliability, but Axes II and IV were generally weaker in reliability (Spitzer et al., 1979; Spitzer & Forman, 1979). The DSM–III showed particularly weak reliability in the diagnosis of the Axis II personality disorders (Drake & Vaillant, 1985). It is too early to tell whether the 1987 revision of the DSM–III—the DSM–III–R—will buttress the reliability of personality disorders.

The issue of **validity,** or accuracy of diagnostic categories, is more complex. How are we to know whether a diagnosis is valid or accurate? A physician may seek to confirm the validity of a *medical* diagnosis by means of a laboratory test. If blood samples are taken and the suspected microbe is found, the diagnosis may be confirmed. No such laboratory tests exist for abnormal behaviors, at least not yet (but see Chapter 8 for a discussion of a possible biological test for depression).

The discovery of **biological markers** for abnormal behaviors would bolster the disease model of abnormal behavior. But today the most appropriate test of the validity of the diagnostic system is based on observations of behavior, not on biochemical analysis. Re-

TABLE 3.4 The Multiaxial Classification System of DSM–III–R

Axis	Type of Information	Brief Description
Axis I	Clinical Syndromes	The patterns of abnormal behavior ("mental disorders") that impair functioning and are stressful to the individual
	"V Codes"	Conditions that are not attributable to a mental disorder but are nonetheless a focus of attention or treatment, such as academic, vocational, or social problems.
Axis II	Developmental Disorders	Disorders that generally begin in childhood or adolescence and persist in stable form into adult life, such as mental retardation, autism, and specific developmental disorders in academic skills, language and speech, or motor skills
	Personality Disorders	Deeply ingrained, maladaptive ways of perceiving others and behavior that are stressful to the individual or those who relate to the individual. Notable personality traits can be listed here, even when no personality disorder per se is diagnosed.
Axis III	Physical Disorders and Conditions	Chronic and acute illnesses, injuries, allergies, and so on that affect functioning and treatment, such as cardiovascular disorders, athletic injuries, and allergies to medication
Axis IV	Severity of Psychosocial Stressors	Stressors that occurred during the past year that may have contributed to the development of a new mental disorder or the recurrence of a prior disorder or that may have exacerbated an existing disorder, such as divorce occurring during a depressive episode. Stressors can be marital, parental, occupational, financial, legal, developmental, physical, and so on.
Axis V	Global Assessment of Functioning	Overall judgment of current functioning and the highest level of functioning in the past year according to psychological, social, and occupational criteria

Source: S. A. Rathus (1990). *Psychology*, 4th edition, p. 482. Ft. Worth, Tx: Holt, Rinehart and Winston. Based on DSM–III–R, pp. 3–21.

TABLE 3.5 Example of DSM–III–R Diagnosis in Multiaxial System

Axis I	Generalized Anxiety Disorder
Axis II	Dependent Personality Disorder
Axis III	Hypertension
Axis IV	Psychosocial stressors: New marriage
	Severity: 3—Moderate (acute event)
Axis V	Current GAF: 65
	Highest GAF past year: 75

searchers generally approach the question of validity in terms of whether or not the behavior of people who are given particular diagnostic labels differs in predictable ways from that of people given different diagnoses. Certain DSM–III–R classes, such as anxiety disorders, appear to have generally good validity in terms of grouping people with similar behaviors (Turner et al., 1986). The validity of other diagnostic classes remains to be investigated by similar means.

The predictive validity of the DSM system may be tested by determining whether or not it is useful in *predicting* the course the disorder is likely to follow or the response to treatment. Evidence is accumulating that persons classified in certain categories respond better to certain types of medication. Persons with bipolar disorder, for example, respond reasonably well to lithium (see Chapter 8). Specific forms of psychological treatment may also be more effective with certain diagnostic groupings. For example, persons who are classified as *simple phobics* are generally highly responsive to behavioral techniques for reducing fears (see Chapter 6).

Another yardstick by which a diagnostic system is evaluated is its degree of coverage, or its ability to place cases of abnormal behavior into appropriate categories (Blashfield & Draguns, 1976). A system with low coverage would be one that essentially "dumps" or sweeps aside a large number of cases that don't precisely fit existing categories into a catchall or so-called wastebasket category like "unspecified disorder." But attempts to increase the coverage of the system may occur at the expense of reducing the "purity" of the diagnostic categories. Think of it this way: The more cases with slightly varying patterns one tries to "squeeze" into a given category, the less similar the cases assigned to the particular category are likely to be.

The DSM–III contained tighter diagnostic criteria than its predecessors, thereby increasing the diagnostic purity of the categories but at the expense of reduced coverage. The pendulum may have swung back with the 1987 introduction of the revised version, the DSM–III–R. One of the purposes of the revised DSM–III–R system was to increase coverage so that fewer cases would fall between the cracks of the existing categories and be placed in the catchall categories labeled "atypical" or "disorder not otherwise specified." It appears that coverage of Axis II personality disorders increased with the revised criteria (that is, there are fewer unspecified cases), but at the expense of increasing the number of cases that seem to fit two or more diagnostic categories, which reduces purity (Morey, 1988). And so it goes.

Advantages and Disadvantages of the DSM–III–R System

Many consider the major advantage of the DSM–III–R to be its designation of specific diagnostic criteria. With the DSM–III–R, the clinician can quickly match up the client's presenting complaints and associated clinical features with the criteria listed in the manual to see which diagnostic category best fits the particular case. The multiaxial system helps clinicians form a comprehensive picture of clients by integrating information concerning abnormal behaviors, stress, and level of functioning (Rey et al., 1988). The possibility of making multiple diagnoses prompts clinicians to consider presenting problems (Axis I) and relatively long-standing personality problems (Axis II) that may contribute to the presenting problems.

Criticisms have also been leveled against the DSM–III–R system. We already noted that questions remain about the system's reliability (especially when diagnosing Axis II disorders) and its validity. Other challenges have been posed as well.

The DSM–III–R system is based on a medical approach to classification: Problem behaviors are viewed as symptoms of underlying syndromes or disorders, in much the same way that physical symptoms might be classified as signs of underlying diseases or illnesses. The very use of the term *diagnosis* presumes that the medical model is an appropriate basis for classifying abnormal behaviors. Some clinicians feel that behavior, abnormal or otherwise, is too complex and meaningful to be treated merely as symptomatic. They assert that the medical model focuses too much on what may happen within the individual and not enough on external influences on behavior, such as societal and familial pressures.

Another concern is that the medical model focuses on categorizing people rather than on describing their behavioral strengths and weaknesses. The DSM–III–R aims to determine what "disorders" people "have"—not what they can "do" in particular situations. Later we shall see that an alternative model of assessment, the behavioral model, focuses more on behaviors than on underlying processes—more on what people "do" than on what they "are" or "have." Of course, behaviorists and behavior therapists also use the DSM–III–R, in part because mental-health centers and health-insurance carriers require the use of a diagnostic code, in part because they want to communicate in a common language with practitioners of other theoretical persuasions. Many behavior therapists view the DSM–III–R diagnostic code as a convenient means of labeling patterns of abnormal behavior, a kind of shorthand for a more extensive behavioral analysis of the problem.

The DSM–III–R aims to be atheoretical, but the very act of designating certain behaviors as normal or abnormal is carried out within certain cultural and professional contexts. You may think it is normal to eat raw fish when others consider uncooked fish appropriate for bait. You may find it normal to spend your evenings watching game shows or to dress formally at home for dinner. But the behaviors that were included as diagnostic criteria in the DSM–III–R were determined by the consensus of 200 or so mental-health experts, mostly American-trained psychiatrists, psychologists, and social workers. Had the American Psychiatric Association invited 200 practitioners of Zen Buddhism to develop their diagnostic manual, the definitions of abnormal behaviors might have looked somewhat different.

Some critics argue that the DSM–III–R has gone too far in removing certain conceptualizations of abnormal behavior that are derived from particular theories, such as the concept of neurosis. Some would like to see a return to a diagnostic system that focuses more on the causes of abnormal behaviors. It is one thing to describe abnormal behaviors, critics claim, but quite another to explain them. Many critics likewise claim that the DSM–III–R focuses too much on current behaviors and not enough on prior history or childhood experiences.

The DSM system, despite its critics, has become part and parcel of the everyday practice of the vast majority of American mental-health professionals. It may be the one professional book that is found on the bookshelves of nearly all practicing psychologists and psychiatrists and well-worn from repeated use. Perhaps the DSM is best considered a working document, not a final product. We expect that new editions will be published to correct for deficiencies in the present version. In the meantime, the DSM–III–R provides researchers and clinicians a common basis for investigating and communicating about abnormal behaviors.

Now let us consider various ways of assessing abnormal behavior. We begin with a discussion of the characteristics of useful methods of assessment: reliability and validity.

CHARACTERISTICS OF METHODS OF ASSESSMENT

Important decisions are made on the basis of psychological classification and assessment. For example, treatment techniques vary according to the kinds of problems shown by clients. Moreover, the labels we assign clients help shape our expectations for future behavior. Therefore, methods of assessment, like diagnostic categories, must be *reliable* and *valid*.

Reliability

The reliability of a method of assessment, like that of a diagnostic system, is its consistency. A gauge of height would be unreliable if people looked taller or shorter at every measurement. A reliable measure of abnormal behavior, like a reliable yardstick, must yield similar results on various occasions. Also, different people should be able to check the yardstick and agree on the measured height of the subject. A yardstick that shrinks and expands markedly with the slightest change in temperature will be unreliable. So will one that is difficult to read.

There are three main approaches for demonstrating the reliability of assessment techniques.

■ **Internal Consistency**   Correlational techniques are used to show whether the different parts or items of a test yield results that are consistent with one another and with the technique or test as a whole. **Internal consistency** is crucial for tests that are intended to measure single traits or construct dimensions. When the individual items or parts of a test are highly correlated with each other, we can assume that they are measuring some trait or construct dimension in common. For example, a self-administered depression inventory may contain various items measuring different aspects of depression. If the responses to these items are not highly correlated with each other, then there is no basis for assuming that the test as a whole measures a single dimension or construct that is labeled depression.

One commonly used method of assessing internal consistency, called **coefficient alpha,** is based on a statistical computation of the average intercorrelations (interrelationships) of all the items making up the particular test. The higher the coefficient alpha, the greater the internal consistency of the test.

■ **Temporal Stability**   Reliable methods of assessment have **temporal stability.** That is, they yield similar results on separate occasions. We would not trust the reliability of a bathroom scale that yielded different results each time we weighed ourselves—unless we had stuffed or starved ourselves between weighings. The same principle applies to psychological tests. In the case of tests, temporal stability is measured by means of **test–retest reliability.** Correlational methods compare scores obtained on different testing occasions. The higher the correlation, the greater the temporal stability or test–retest reliability of the test.

Assessment of test–retest reliability is most important in the measurement of traits that are assumed to remain stable over time, such as intelligence and aptitude. Interestingly, measures of test–retest reliability of tests of intelligence and aptitude can be compromised because of improved scores that are due to familiarity with the items and the testing technique.

■ **Interrater Reliability**   **Interrater reliability**—also referred to as **interjudge reliability**—is usually of greatest importance in making diagnostic decisions and for measures requiring ratings of behavior. You'll recall that a diagnostic system is not reliable unless expert raters (psychologists, psychiatrists, and the like) agree as to their diagnoses on the basis of the system. Two teachers might also be asked to use a behavioral rating scale to evaluate a child according to behaviors suggestive of aggressiveness, hyperactivity, and sociability. The level of agreement between the raters would be used as an index of the reliability of the rating scale.

Validity

The validity of assessment techniques or measures refers to the degree to which the instruments in question measure what they are intended to measure. There are various kinds of validity, such as *content, construct,* and *criterion validity.*

■ **Content Validity**   The **content validity** of an assessment technique is determined by analyzing the degree to which its content covers a representative sample of the behaviors associated with the construct dimension or trait in question. For example, depression includes features such as sadness and lack of interest in previously enjoyed activities. Thus, in order to have content validity, techniques that assess depression should have features or items that directly address these two areas, among others. One type of content validity, called **face validity,** refers to the degree to which the interview questions or test items bear an apparent relationship to the constructs or traits they purport to measure. An example of a face-valid item on a test of assertiveness might be, ''I have little difficulty standing up for my rights." In contrast, an item that might be found lacking in face validity would be, "I usually subscribe to magazines that contain features about world events."

The limitation of face or content validity is its reliance on subjective judgments in determining whether or not the test measures what it is supposed to measure. The apparent or face validity of a test or scale is not sufficient to establish its scientific value.

■ Criterion Validity

The **criterion validity** of an assessment technique is the degree to which responses correlate with an independent, external criterion (standard) of what the technique is intended to assess. There are two general types of criterion validity: concurrent validity and predictive validity.

Concurrent validity refers to the degree to which test responses predict scores on criterion measures taken at about the same point in time. Most psychologists presume that intelligence is in part responsible for academic success. Thus the concurrent validity of intelligence test scores is frequently studied by correlating test scores with criteria such as school grades and teacher ratings of cognitive abilities. A self-report scale of depression might be validated against judgments of experts based on concurrent clinical interviews.

Predictive validity is the ability of a diagnostic technique or test to predict future behavior. A test of academic aptitude may be validated in terms of its ability to predict school performance in that particular area. General intelligence tests taken during childhood have predictive validity in terms of occupational status as an adult. In one longitudinal study, intelligence test scores obtained beyond the age of 7 correlated moderately positively with occupational status (McCall, 1977). We should note, though, that motivation to succeed and level of adjustment also influence school performance and eventual occupational status (Anastasi, 1983; Hrncir et al., 1985; Scarr, 1981).

■ Construct Validity

Construct validity involves the degree to which a test or assessment technique corresponds to the theoretical model of the underlying construct or trait it purports to measure. Consider problems in determining the construct validity of a test that purports to measure anxiety. Anxiety is not a concrete object or phenomenon that can be measured directly by counting it, weighing it, or holding it in your hands to examine it. Anxiety is a theoretical construct that helps to explain phenomena like a pounding heart or sudden inability to speak when you ask an attractive person out on a date. Anxiety may be measured by various means, including self-report measures (rating one's own level of anxiety in various situations) and physiological measures (measuring, for example, the changes in electrical conductivity on the palms of one's hands).

The construct validity of a test or measure of anxiety requires that the test response be correlated with other aspects of behavior that are theoretically associated with the construct of anxiety. Let's say your theoretical model leads you to predict that highly anxious college students should experience greater difficulties speaking clearly and coherently when asking a member of the opposite sex for a date than do low-anxious students, but that no differences between the groups would be expected under low-anxiety conditions when they are merely rehearsing their speech in private. The degree to which the speech behavior of high and low scorers on a test of anxiety fit these predicted patterns would provide a measure of the construct validity of the test in question.

Assessment techniques can be highly reliable but invalid. Nineteenth-century **phrenologists** believed that they could gauge people's personalities by measuring the bumps on their heads. Their calipers provided reasonably reliable measures of their subjects' bumps and protrusions; the measurements, however, did not provide valid estimates of personality characteristics.

Phrenology. In the 19th-century some subscribed to the belief that mental faculties and abilities were based in certain areas in the brain and could be measured by means of gauging the bumps and indentations of the skull.

The phrenologists were bumping in the dark, so to speak. A test of musical aptitude might have excellent reliability but be invalid as a measure of general intelligence.

> **?** A psychological test can indeed have excellent reliability yet also be invalid. A test of musical aptitude may have superb reliability but be invalid as a measure of general intelligence or of height.

THE CLINICAL INTERVIEW

The interview is the most widely used means of assessment because it is employed by psychologists, psychiatrists, social workers, other helping professionals and even paraprofessionals. The interview, moreover, is usually the client's first face-to-face contact with a clinician.

The interview is usually initiated by a phone call made by a client or someone who is concerned about the client's behavior—perhaps a family member, a member of the clergy, or a social service agency. A brief screening might be conducted over the phone to determine whether it seems appropriate to schedule the client for a person-to-person interview, or whether the individual might better be referred to an agency better suited to evaluate the apparent problem.

A client who would apparently profit from the services offered by the clinic or agency is scheduled for an **intake interview**—a process that provides the clinician an initial opportunity to learn more about the client's **presenting problem** and history. On the basis of this information, the interviewer may arrive at an initial diagnostic impression and recommend further evaluation or appropriate treatment.

The primary means of obtaining clinically useful information is a **structured interview.** The interviewer asks a fairly standard series of questions to gather information about the client's presenting complaints or problems, mental state, life circumstances, and psychosocial or developmental history. The interview may cover a wide range of topics and vary in structure from client to client, but they usually follow a plan and are designed to gather certain forms of essential information. Most interviewers are reasonably flexible, however, since no two clients are alike. Some clients are cooperative; others are stubborn or reticent. Some are insightful; others offer little insight. Some need immediate reassurances; others show little interest in their problems or the proceedings.

Clinicians often begin by asking clients to describe the presenting complaint in their own words. They may say something like "Can you describe to me the problems you've been having lately?" (Therapists learn not

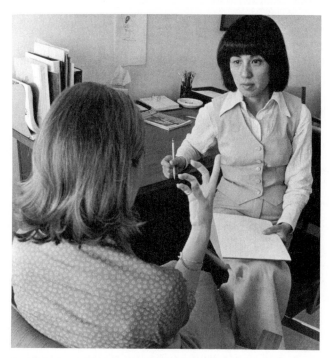

An intake interview allows the clinician to learn about the client's problems and background.

to ask "What brings you here?" to avoid receiving answers like, "A car," "A bus," or "My social worker.") The clinician will then usually probe aspects of the presenting complaint, such as behavioral abnormalities and feelings of discomfort, the circumstances regarding the onset of the problem, history of past episodes, and how the problem affects the client's daily functioning. The clinician may explore possible precipitating events, such as changes in life circumstances, especially changes in social relationships, employment, or schooling.

The interviewer encourages the client to describe the problem in his or her own words so as to understand the presenting problem from the client's point of view. If the client is a child, the parent usually describes the problem and its history. The therapist still often interviews the child to ascertain how the child views the problem.

The course of the interview is also influenced by the interviewer's theoretical framework. A behaviorally oriented interviewer might seek detailed information about the events that precede and follow the occurrence of the problem behavior—searching for stimuli or antecedents that might act as conditioned stimuli or cues that trigger the problem behavior, and for social and other reinforcements that serve to maintain the behavior.

Consider the case of Pamela:

■ A young woman of 19, Pamela, is seen for an initial evaluation. She complains of fear of driving her car across a bridge on a route that she must take to attend college.

She reports that she fears "freezing up" at the wheel and causing an accident if she were to drive across the bridge. Upon interview, she reports that the problem began six months earlier, shortly after she experienced intense anxiety driving across a different bridge. It nearly caused her to lose control of the car. Now she takes three buses to make the trip, increasing her commutation by more than an hour each way. But she has heard that the bus company may close her route, so she would have to take another local bus to make connections, adding another half hour or more to the trip. She wonders whether she should transfer to a community college near her home, even though it doesn't offer the program of studies which interests her.

The Authors' Files ■

Pamela's behavioral interviewer might try to determine the stimulus cues that evoke a fear response. For example, is the fear greater or lesser depending on the height of the bridge? The depth of the ground or water below? The steepness of the incline? The narrowing of the road? Can the client rank-order the fear she encounters at the inclines, overpasses, and bridges in the roadways she uses? Such information might help the therapist map out a strategy of gradual exposure to these stimuli (discussed in Chapter 6).

The psychodynamically oriented interviewer might focus on issues relating to Pamela's early childhood experiences or developmental history, seeking clues as to how her fear of driving over bridges may symbolize underlying conflicts. Might the crossing of a bridge symbolically represent separation from her parents and signify conflict concerning issues of independence and separation? Did Pamela experience separation anxiety as a child that might be reactivated in her current travel? Does her travel phobia protect her from facing adult challenges that require more independence and self-confidence than she can muster—such as attending a college outside her immediate community and pursuing the more demanding career opportunities that the college offers?

Whatever the theoretical orientation of the interviewer, interviewing skills and techniques have some features in common. Psychologists and other professionals are trained to establish **rapport** and feelings of trust with the client. These feelings help put the client at ease and encourage candid communication. Effective interviewers usually do not pressure clients to disclose information that makes them feel uncomfortable. Nevertheless, clients are generally more willing to disclose their personal feelings and experiences to someone who shows concern and understanding, someone they feel they can trust. When the interviewer is skillful, clients are less likely to fear that they will be criticized or judged for revealing personal information.

Although the format of the intake process may

vary from clinician to clinician, most interviews cover topics such as these:

1. *Identifying Data.* Information regarding the client's sociodemographic characteristics: address and telephone number, marital status, age, gender, racial/ethnic characteristics, religion, employment, family composition, and so on.

2. *Description of the Presenting Problem(s).* How does the client perceive the problem? What troubling behaviors, thoughts, or feelings are reported? How do they affect the client's functioning? When did they begin? Have they occurred in the past?

3. *Psychosocial History.* Information describing the client's developmental history: educational, social, and occupational history; early family relationships.

4. *Medical/Psychiatric History.* History of medical and psychiatric hospitalizations and mental health treatment. Is the present problem a recurrent episode of a previously existing problem? How was the problem handled in the past? Was treatment successful? Why or why not?

5. *Medical Problems/Medication.* Description of present medical complaints and present treatment or use of medication. The clinician is alert to ways in which medical problems may affect the presenting psychological problem; for example, drugs for certain medical conditions can have effects on mood and the body's general level of arousal.

In the course of the interview, the clinician may also conduct a formal assessment of the client's cognitive functioning through what the psychiatric community usually refers to as a **mental status examination.** A diagnostic impression is usually based on the client's presenting problems, history, and apparent cognitive functioning.

Mental Status Examination

The mental status examination is based upon observation of the client's behavior and questioning of various aspects of cognitive functioning and self-presentation. The specifics of the mental status exam may vary from clinician to clinician; however, the general categories of the mental status exam include the following (Maloney & Ward, 1976):

1. *Appearance.* A description of the appropriateness of the client's general appearance, grooming style, and manner of dress or attire.

2. *Behavioral Observations.* The examiner notes signs of psychological disturbance in the client's verbal and

nonverbal behavior. Does the client maintain eye contact? (Avoidance can indicate simple shyness, depression, or other serious problems.) Are indications of underlying emotional states expressed through facial expressions or general posture? What is the client's manner of relating to the interviewer—cooperative and friendly, or hostile and evasive? Are there signs of more serious disturbance, such as bizarre behavior, inappropriate laughter, or giggling? Is the client's manner of speech pressured and rapid or controlled and hesitant?

3. *Orientation*. Normally speaking, we know who we and our relations are, where we are, and what time it is—although your authors are usually off by a day or two. The clinician notes whether the client shows lapses in *orientation* and, if there is any doubt, questions the client as to who he or she is, who others are, where they are (where the interview is taking place), and what time it is (year, day, time of day). An elderly woman with organic impairment told the authors that her hospital room was "some kind of spaceship" and that "Nixon" was president (at the time, Ronald Reagan was president). Disorientation may be associated with problems such as degeneration of the brain, drug intoxication, or schizophrenia.

4. *Memory*. Is the client's memory intact for recent events and remote events? Can the client recall last night's dinner (recent memory) or when and where he or she was married (remote memory)? In some conditions associated with advanced age, people can recall events 30 years in the past but have difficulty forming new memories. As a result, they may not be able to recall whether they have taken their medication or the name of a new grandchild.

5. *Sensorium*. **Sensorium** derives from the Latin *sensus*, meaning "sense," and *-ium*, a suffix used to form the names of biological structures. The term *sensorium* is defined as the individual's entire sensory apparatus and is used by clinicians to refer to the client's focusing of attention, capacity for concentration, and level of awareness of the world. Clients whose attention or concentration drifts in and out during the interview, or who are generally unresponsive, may have difficulties processing information from the external world, perhaps due to organic impairment. Clinicians may write that the client's "sensorium is clear" to indicate apparently accurate sensing of the external world.

6. *Perceptual Processes*. Perception is a psychological process by which people interpret the information provided by the senses. Sometimes, as in the case of hallucinations, perceptions may occur in the absence of external sensory input, and the client may not be able to distinguish them from reality. The clinician notes whether or not the client appears to be responding to hallucinations, such as attending to voices or seeing things that are not there. In the case of schizophrenia, the senses may be flooded with false perceptions (hallucinations).

7. *Mood and Affect*. These terms are often used interchangeably, but have a slightly different meaning. The noun **affect** (pronounced AFF-ect) refers to the emotions or feelings that the client attaches to objects or ideas. The central issue is whether or not the affect is *appropriate* to the client's life situation and the ideas being expressed. Inappropriateness of affect (such as laughing while discussing tragic events), or impoverished emotional reactivity (described as blunted or flat affect) is often connected with severe problems such as schizophrenia. **Mood** refers to the prevailing emotions displayed during the interview, such as sadness, anxiety, or anger.

8. *Intelligence*. The clinician usually judges the client's general level of intellectual functioning on the basis of the client's speech (level of vocabulary and ability to formulate and express ideas clearly), apparent level of sophistication (general knowledge), and achieved socioeconomic status (educational and employment history). If questions arise as to the client's cognitive abilities, the interviewer may direct questions that test the client's ability to interpret proverbs, to name officeholders like the local mayor or governor, or to compute simple arithmetic tasks—questions that assess the client's capacities for acquiring and manipulating information.

9. *Thought Processes*. This category refers both to the form and content of thought. Concerning the form of thought, the clinician notes whether or not the client's thought processes appear logical and coherent. Or is there a loosening of associations—an apparent stringing together of loosely connected or disconnected thoughts or ideas that is suggestive of disordered thinking processes that often occur in schizophrenia? Is there evidence of thought blocking—a gap or pause in the client's speech when a troubling topic is touched upon? Is there evidence of flight of ideas—a tendency to jump from topic to topic that may prevent the examiner from following the connections, as might occur during manic episodes? Does the client speak very little, perhaps because of impoverishment of thought? Description of the client's thought content touches upon any evidence of troubling belief patterns such as delusional beliefs (false ideas) or obsessions (nagging, repetitious thoughts).

10. *Insight*. Does the client recognize that the problem exists, as is usually the case in anxiety and depression? Has the client developed a reasonable understanding of the factors that might account for the problem? Does the client deny the existence of the problem or blame others for it, as may occur in personality disorders?

11. *Judgment*. Does the client apply sound and reasonable judgments in making life decisions? Does the client approach problem situations thoughtfully and rationally? Or does the client act in a rash or impulsive manner, failing to consider the consequences of his or her actions, as may happen, for example, in manic episodes, personality disorders, or substance abuse?

Aspects of Effective Interviewing

Clinical interviewing requires a number of fundamental skills that help establish rapport and trust. These skills are of use during the intake process and subsequent treatment sessions. One is the skill of conveying empathy, or accurate understanding of what the client is experiencing. The clinician conveys empathy verbally and nonverbally (Cormier & Cormier, 1985). Verbally, the interviewer shows empathy by (1) demonstrating a genuine desire to understand the client's point of view or perspective, (2) focusing in on what is truly important to the client, (3) reflecting the client's feelings by naming or labeling them, and (4) showing comprehension of the client's innermost feelings and thoughts, which may lie below the client's level of awareness. Nonverbally, the interviewer shows empathy by (1) looking directly at the client, (2) establishing eye contact, and (3) leaning forward in his or her seat in an expression of interest in the client.

The skillful interviewer is an active, attentive listener. Listening to a client is not a passive activity. The attentive listener attends fully to the client's verbal and nonverbal behaviors and processes information in a way that promotes accurate understanding. The attentive listener makes use of the visual and auditory senses. The interviewer uses vision to recognize visual cues that might reveal underlying emotions, such as gestures, facial expressions, and body posture. The interviewer uses hearing not only to record the client's words but also the emotional connotations of inflections or nonverbal utterances like sighs or coughs. Cormier and Cormier (1985) describe various listening techniques that encourage understanding. Consider the following examples:

1.   *Clarification.* Clarification is a form of questioning that leads the client to explain and elaborate what he or she is saying. Through clarification, the interviewer attempts to confirm the accuracy of his or her understanding of the client's message. Clarification also helps prevent the interviewer from jumping to conclusions.

CLIENT: Sometimes I just don't feel like getting up. What's the point of it? Nothing seems to work out for me.

INTERVIEWER: Let me see if I understand what you're saying. Do you mean that things just seem so hopeless at times that there's no point in even getting out of bed?

CLIENT: Yea, I just get this feeling of hopelessness. Like anything you try is just like banging your head against the wall.

In this example, the interviewer had correctly understood the client. But when the interviewer does not initially comprehend the message, clarification can help bring it into focus:

CLIENT: Sometimes I just don't feel like getting up. What's the point of it? Nothing seems to work out for me.

INTERVIEWER: Do you mean that you feel that things will never work out for you, that they're completely hopeless?

CLIENT: No, I wouldn't say that. Not completely hopeless.

INTERVIEWER: So let me see if I understand. Does it seem that while things may seem hopeless now, they might not always be this way?

CLIENT: Yes, it's just right now things seem so hopeless. I mean I'm not giving up on myself.

2.   *Paraphrasing.* The interviewer rephrases or recasts the *content* of the client's message to show understanding and check his or her interpretation. Paraphrasing does not merely parrot or mimic the client. Rather, it expresses understanding in a way that helps the client get his or her own thoughts into perspective and encourages further exploration.

Consider the following dialogue with the same client:

CLIENT: You know it's like I was out with my girlfriend the other night, and she didn't want to sit close to me in the car. I kept motioning to her to move closer, but she just sat on her side. I just felt like she didn't care. Like I was nothing to her.

INTERVIEWER: I sense that when your girlfriend wouldn't move closer to you, you took that as a sign of rejection, that she didn't care about you. Is that about right?

CLIENT: Yea, it was like I wasn't even there.

3.   *Reflection.* The interviewer paraphrases or reflects the *emotional components* of the client's message. Reflection heightens client awareness of his or her emotional reactions and encourages further elaboration of feelings.

CLIENT: When we got to her parent's house, I leaned over to kiss her goodnight and she just let me kiss her. Maybe it's no big thing, but it didn't feel like she was kissing me back. I didn't say anything, but I just felt that she didn't care.

INTERVIEWER: So it felt like she didn't care enough to kiss you back. It sounds like you were *feeling rejected.*

CLIENT: Yea, it just kind of brought me down. Maybe I shouldn't have taken it as a rejection, but that's how it felt.

4. *Summarization.* The interviewer ties together several paraphrases to summarize the key issues or themes that the client has expressed. Summarization provides feedback to the client by extracting the important issues that might become the focus for therapy. In the following example, the interviewer summarizes several of the client's messages by combining reflection of feeling and paraphrasing of content:

CLIENT: I guess the way I'm looking at things, other people seem to get their lives together, and I'm just banging my head against the wall. I just think about losing her and how this happens to me again and again. I just don't think it will ever change.

INTERVIEWER: Let me see if I have a sense of what you're saying. I can understand that you're fearful that your girlfriend might leave you and that you wouldn't be able to handle it. You seem to be saying that since you've experienced rejection in the past, then it's bound to happen again and again, as if your fate is already cast.

CLIENT: I guess I've just been thinking the worst is going to happen. I'm afraid I won't be able to handle it, like this rejection would be too much to cope with.

■ **Interpretation of Nonverbal Behavior** The interviewer is also sensitive to the client's nonverbal behavior. The client's body movement and posture, facial expressions, and gestures are clues to the client's emotions. The interviewer looks for subtle changes in the client's nonverbal behavior throughout the interview, connecting nonverbal cues that accompany expression of particular topics to become better aware of the emotions that these issues may evoke. Because clients are generally more aware of their verbal behavior than their nonverbal behavior, directing clients' attention to these nonverbal cues helps broaden their understanding of their feelings and their overt behavior (Cormier & Cormier, 1985).

Nonverbal cues can provide a great deal of information. A client who squirms in the seat may be experiencing anxiety or backache. The interpretation of nonverbal cues considers the particular client and the context in which they occur. The client whose jaws are clenched and who grimaces throughout the interview may be expressing generalized discomfort or anxiety, but if these behaviors occur only in response to questions about his wife, they may reflect more specific feelings toward her.

The tone of voice and style of speech are also important sources of information. Pressured or rapid speech may suggest stress or a manic episode. Slow, halting speech is more characteristic of depression or of organic impairment.

Clinicians are alert to apparent discrepancies between verbal and nonverbal behavior. Nonverbal cues may be more accurate reflections of emotional state than verbal reports. Clients may deny anger toward their parents but raise their voices when they discuss them. Clients may deny problems at work but tightly grasp the arms of their chairs when they talk about work. Clients may not be fully aware of their anger and frustrations or may be trying to conceal information about their feelings. The interviewer may note the apparent contradiction for later reference or direct clients' attention to such contradictions in ways that encourage exploration rather than place clients on the defensive. Consider this example: "On the one hand, I hear that these problems at work don't affect you very much. But on the other hand, I notice that your hands appear to be grasping the arms of your chair rather tightly. I wonder what your hands might be saying about your feelings?"

Standardized Interview Techniques

One problem with the clinical interview as an assessment device is its lack of standardization. Different interviewers might ask different sets of questions or evaluate information in different ways. Lack of standardization in interviewing may thus reduce the consistency or **reliability** of diagnostic judgments based upon interviewing. A **standardized interview** may be of considerable value to the clinician in determining the most appropriate diagnostic classification. In recent years, standardized interview techniques based on the DSM system and other diagnostic schemes have been developed to enable clinicians to pose similar sets of questions. These include the National Institute of Mental Health's Diagnostic Interview Schedule (DIS; Robins et al., 1981), the Schedule for Affective Disorders and Schizophrenia (SADS; Endicott & Spitzer, 1978), and the Structured Clinical Interview for the DSM–III (SCID; Spitzer & Williams, 1984).

The DIS uses a prearranged set of questions that can be administered by a clinician or a lay interviewer (see Table 3.6). The interview responses are fed into a computer that determines the most appropriate diagnostic category. In addition to specifying the behaviors shown and reported by the client, the DIS outlines the recent and long-term history of these problems and the life experiences and events associated with them.

The clinician or layperson must be well trained in administering the interview. The DIS, for example, requires a one- to two-week training course. The DIS shows high interjudge reliability; its use produces high rates of agreement in diagnostic judgments among professional clinicians (Helzer et al., 1985). Evidence is mixed concerning the reliability of information attained

---

TABLE 3.6 A Section of the DIS Relevant to Panic Disorder

61. Have you ever considered yourself a nervous person?
62. Have you ever had a spell or attack when all of a sudden you felt frightened, anxious, or very uneasy in situations when most people would not be afraid?

For those answering yes to Q. 62, the following questions would be asked. If the answer is no, the interviewer skips to the next series of questions.

A. During one of your worst spells of suddenly feeling frightened or anxious or uneasy, did you ever notice that you had any of the following problems?

During this spell—
(1) were you short of breath—having trouble catching your breath?
(2) did your heart pound?
(3) were you dizzy or light-headed?
(4) did your fingers or face tingle?
(5) did you have tightness or pain in your chest?
(6) did you feel like you were choking or smothering?
(7) did you feel faint?
(8) did you sweat?
(9) did you tremble or shake?
(10) did you feel hot or cold flashes?
(11) did things around you seem unreal?
(12) were you afraid either that you might die or that you might act in a crazy way?

B. How old were you the first time you had one of these sudden spells of feeling frightened or anxious? Age _____

Whole Life = code 02
If Don't know and age under 40, code 01
If Don't know and age 40 or more, ask: "Would you say it was before or after you were 40?"

C. Have you ever had 3 spells like this close together—say within a 3-week period?

D. Have spells like this occurred during a least 6 different weeks of your life?

E. Have you had a spell like this within the last two weeks?

Note: A panic disorder (discussed in Chapter 6) is a type of anxiety disorder characterized by recurrent panic attacks.

---

by nonprofessional interviewers, however, even when they are well trained (Erdman et al., 1987).

The SADS is intended to be used in conjunction with specific diagnostic criteria, called Research Diagnostic Criteria (RDC), which help the clinician use interview information to reach a more definitive diagnosis. However, the SADS was developed before the DSM–III and does not help the clinician formulate diagnoses within the DSM–III system. The SADS led to the development of the Structured Clinical Interview for DSM–III, or SCID, which was designed to assist the clinician in making DSM–III diagnoses.

Although the DIS provides information that a computer can analyze to make DSM–III diagnoses, it more closely resembles a symptom checklist or questionnaire than an interview, which is why it can be administered by a lay interviewer. The SCID, on the other hand, is designed for use by a professional who is experienced in interviewing and familiar with the DSM–III system. The SCID includes **closed-ended questions** to determine the presence of behavior patterns that suggest specific diagnostic categories and **open-ended questions** that allow clients to elaborate their problems and feelings. The line of questioning tests various diagnostic impressions as the interview progresses, arriving at a definitive diagnostic impression by the end of the interview. Recent research supports the reliability of the SCID (Riskind et al., 1987).

Several standard interview schedules, such as the SADS and the SCID, caution the interviewer to consider clients' cultural backgrounds when they are assessing the deviance of their beliefs or perceptual experiences (Lopez & Nunez, 1987). An experience that may be foreign to the interviewer, such as an hallucination occurring in the context of a religious rite, may not be deviant for some cultural groups.

PSYCHOLOGICAL TESTS

Psychological tests are structured methods of assessment that are used to evaluate reasonably stable traits such as intelligence and personality. Tests are usually standardized on large numbers of subjects, providing norms that show how clients' scores deviate from the average. Comparison of the test responses of normal and abnormal populations suggests ways of responding that reveal patterns of abnormal behavior.

Tests have yet greater structure than structured interviews. The instructions are precise. Even when tests are administered orally, the examiner is instructed to follow strict procedures. The structure of tests allows them to be interpreted more objectively than most structured interviews. Moreover, test responses can be readily quantified, facilitating assessment of their relia-

A CLOSER LOOK
Would You Tell Your Problems to a Computer?

Picture yourself seated before a computer screen in the not-too-distant future. The message on the screen asks you to type in your name and press the return key. Not wanting to offend, you comply. This message then comes on the screen: "Hello, my name is Sigmund. I'm programmed to ask you a set of questions to learn more about you. May I begin?" You shake your head yes, momentarily forgetting that the computer can only "perceive" key strokes. You type "yes" and the interview begins.

The future, as the saying goes, is now. Computerized clinical interviews have been used for more than 20 years. Computers offer some advantages over us traditional human interviewers (Farrell et al., 1987):

1. Computers can be programmed to ask a specific set of questions in a predetermined order, whereas human beings, by virtue of their lack of training, biases, or forgetfulness, may omit critical items or steer the interview toward less important topics,

2. The client may be less embarrassed about relating personal matters to the computer since computers, unlike human interviewers, do not show emotional responses to clients' responses,

3. Computerized interviews can free clinicians to spend more time at providing direct clinical services, such as case conferences and therapy.

Consider a computerized interview system named CASPER, which includes interview and update functions. The interview component takes about 30 minutes and contains 127 questions that cover 62 target problems. The questions cover a wide range of topics, such as demographic information, family relations, social activities, sex, life satisfaction, and behavioral problems related to physical and mental disorders. The interview questions and response options, such as the following, are presented on the screen:

"About how many days in the past month did you have difficulty falling asleep, staying asleep, or waking too early (include sleep disturbed by bad dreams)?"

"During the past month, how have you been getting along with your spouse/partner? 1. Very satisfactory; (2) Mostly satisfactory; (3) Sometimes satisfactory, sometimes unsatisfactory; (4) Mostly unsatisfactory; (5) Very unsatisfactory." (From: Farrell et al., 1987, p. 692)

The subject presses a numeric key that corresponds to the response to each item. CASPER is a branching program that follows up on problems suggested by clients' responses. For example, if the client indicates difficulty in falling or remaining asleep, CASPER asks whether or not sleep has become a major problem—"something causing you great personal distress or interfering with your daily functioning" (p. 693). If the client indicates yes, the computer will return to the problem after other items have been presented and ask the client to rate the duration and intensity of the complaint during the past week on a scale of 1 to 10. Clients may also add or drop complaints—change their minds, that is. The computer record of the

Would you be more or less likely to tell your problems to a computer than to a person? Computerized clinical interviews have been used for more than 20 years, and some research suggests that the computer may be highly effective in teasing out problems.

interview includes a complete listing of the client's responses to the interview items, as well as a listing of specific target complaints, along with the ratings of intensity and duration.

CASPER sounds useful enough, and Farrell and his colleagues have found some empirical support for its utility (McCullough & Farrell, 1983; McCullough et al., 1986). More research is needed to establish the reliability and validity of computerized interviews, however.

In one study, 103 outpatient clients compared the results of an interview "by CASPER" with those obtained by means of a clinical interview and a self-report symptom checklist. The results were supportive of use of the computer as a means of assessing complaints. Clients were generally able to complete the computer interview with little difficulty, and most rated the procedure favorably. Tendencies to report target complaints did not appear to reflect underlying response biases to make a favorable or unfavorable impression. However, it appeared that clients reported a greater number of target problems to CASPER than to a flesh-and-blood clinician, paralleling other findings (Angle et al., 1979). Because the problem lists obtained by computers and humans may differ, the researchers suggest that clinicians should compare both sources of data in reaching a diagnostic impression. The computer interview may be especially helpful in identifying problems that the client is embarrassed or unwilling to report to a human. At the risk of putting ourselves out of business, however, we must note that it is also possible that the tendency to report more problems to a computer reflects greater "sensitivity" on the part of the computer interviewer in ferreting out complaints. Perhaps the computer just seems more willing to take the time to note all the complaints.

Research shows that clients are generally more willing to admit to problems when interviewed by computers than by humans. Perhaps people are less concerned about being "judged" by computers.

bility and validity. Tests used in clinical settings include tests of intelligence, personality, and neuropsychological functioning.

INTELLIGENCE TESTS

Assessments of abnormal behavior often include tests of intelligence for several reasons. For one, formal tests of intelligence are used to help diagnose mental retardation (discussed in Chapter 14). They are also used to assess intellectual impairment that may be due to other mental disorders, such as organic mental disorders (discussed in Chapter 13). Moreover, intelligence tests may be used as a measure of intellectual strengths and weaknesses in order to develop a treatment plan that is best suited to the individual's level of competence. But **intelligence** is a controversial concept in psychology. Even attempts at definition stir debate. David Wechsler, the originator of a widely used series of intelligence tests, defined intelligence as "capacity . . . to understand the world . . . and . . . resourcefulness to cope with its challenges" (1975). From his perspective, intelligence has to do with the ways in which we (1) mentally represent the world and (2) adapt to its demands. There are various intelligence tests, including group tests and those that are administered individually, such as the Stanford-Binet and Wechsler scales. Individual tests allow examiners to observe the behavior of the respondent as well as record answers. Thus examiners can develop hypotheses as to whether factors like testing conditions, language problems, illness, or level of motivation contribute to a given test performance.

The Stanford-Binet Intelligence Scale

The Stanford-Binet Intelligence Scale (SBIS) was originated by two Frenchmen, Alfred Binet and Theodore Simon, in 1905 in response to the French public school system's quest for a test that could identify children who might profit from special education. The Binet-Simon scale yielded a score called a **mental age,** or MA, which represents the child's overall level of intellectual functioning. The child who receives an MA of 8 is functioning like the typical 8-year-old. Children received "months" of credit for correct answers, and their MA's were determined by simple summation. Binet assumed that intelligence grew as children developed. Therefore, older children would obtain more correct answers. Hence, his questions were age-graded, as in Table 3.7, and arranged according to difficulty.

Louis Terman of Stanford University adapted the Binet-Simon test for American children in 1916, which is why it is now called the *Stanford*-Binet Intelligence

TABLE 3.7 Items Similar to Those on the Stanford-Binet Intelligence Scale

Level (Years)	Item
2 years	1. Children show knowledge of basic vocabulary words by identifying parts of a doll such as the mouth, ears, and hair.
	2. Children show counting and spatial skills along with visual-motor coordination by building a tower of four blocks to match a model.
4 years	1. Children show word fluency and categorical thinking by filling in the missing words when they are asked questions such as: "Father is a man; mother is a _____?" "Hamburgers are hot; ice cream is _____?"
	2. Children show comprehension by answering correctly when they are asked questions such as: "Why do people have automobiles?" "Why do people have medicine?"
9 years	1. Children can point out verbal absurdities, as in this question: "In an old cemetery, scientists unearthed a skull which they think was that of George Washington when he was only five years of age. What is silly about that?"
	2. Children show fluency with words, as shown by answering the questions: "Can you tell me a number that rhymes with snore?" Can you tell me a color that rhymes with glue?"
Adult	1. Adults show knowledge of the meanings of words and conceptual thinking by correctly explaining the differences between word pairs like "sickness and misery," "house and home," and "integrity and prestige."
	2. Adults show spatial skills by correctly answering questions like: "If a car turned to the right to head north, in what direction was it heading before it turned?"

Source: S. A. Rathus. (1990). *Psychology*, 4th edition, p. 289. Ft. Worth, TX: Holt, Rinehart & Winston.

Scale (SBIS). The SBIS also yielded an **intelligence quotient (IQ),** not an MA, which reflected the relationship between a child's MA and chronological age (CA), according to this formula:

$$IQ = \frac{MA}{CA} \times 100$$

Examination of this formula will show that children who received identical mental-age scores might differ markedly in IQ, with the younger child attaining the higher IQ.

Today the SBIS is used with children and adults, and test-takers' IQ scores are based on their deviation from the norms of their age group. A score of 100 is defined as the mean. People who answer more items

It is true that children who answer intelligence test items identically may differ markedly in intelligence. The younger child (that is, the child with the lower *CA*) will receive the higher IQ score.

correctly than the average obtain IQ scores above 100; those who answer fewer items correctly obtain scores of less than 100.

The so-called **deviation IQ** was developed by psychologist David Wechsler, who also originated various intelligence tests of his own.

The Wechsler Scales

Wechsler developed several intelligence scales for children and adults. The Wechsler scales group questions into subtests like those shown in Table 3.8, each of which measures a different intellectual task. The Wechsler scales are thus designed to offer insight into respondents' relative strengths and weaknesses, and not simply yield an overall score.

TABLE 3.8 Subtests from the Wechsler Adult Intelligence Scale–Revised (WAIS-R)

Verbal Subtests	Performance Subtests
1. *Information*: "What is the capital of the United States?"	7. *Digit Symbol*: Learning and drawing meaningless figures that are associated with numbers.
2. *Comprehension*: "Why do we have Zip codes?" "What does 'A stitch in time saves 9' mean?"	8. *Picture Completion*: Pointing to the missing part of a picture.
3. *Arithmetic*: "If 3 candy bars cost 25 cents, how much will 18 candy bars cost?"	9. *Block Design*: Copying pictures of geometric designs using multicolored blocks.
4. *Similarities*: "How are good and bad alike?" "How are peanut butter and jelly alike?"	10. *Picture Arrangement*: Arranging cartoon pictures in sequence so that they tell a meaningful story.
5. *Digit Span*: Repeating a series of numbers forward and backward.	11. *Object Assembly*: Putting pieces of a puzzle together so that they form a meaningful object.
6. *Vocabulary*: "What does canal mean?	

Source: S. A. Rathus. (1990). *Psychology*, 4th edition, p. 288. Ft. Worth, TX: Holt, Rinehart & Winston.

Items for verbal subtests 1, 2, 3, 4, and 6 are similar but not identical to actual test items.

Wechsler's scales describe so-called *verbal* and *performance* subtests. Verbal subtests generally require knowledge of verbal concepts; performance subtests are largely based on spatial-relations skills. (Figure 3.1 shows items like those on performance scales of the Wechsler scales.) Wechsler's scales allow for computation of verbal and performance IQs.

Wechsler's concept of the deviation IQ based IQ scores on how respondents' answers deviated from those attained by their age-mates. The mean whole test score at any age was defined as 100. Wechsler distributed IQ scores so that 50 percent of the scores of the population lie within a "broad average" range of 90 to 110.

Most IQ scores cluster around the mean (see Figure 3.2). Just 5 percent of them are above 130 or below 70. Wechsler labeled people who attained scores of 130 or above as "very superior"; those with scores below 70 as "intellectually deficient." In Chapter 14 we shall see that IQ scores below 70 are one of the criteria that are used in diagnosing individuals as mentally retarded.

Social-Class, Racial, and Ethnic Differences in Intelligence

Research has shown that persons from various social, racial, and ethnic groups score differently on intelligence tests. Lower-class American children attain IQ scores 10 to 15 points beneath scores of middle- and upper-class children. Black children typically attain scores some 15 to 20 points lower than white children (Hall & Kaye, 1980; Loehlin et al., 1975). Hispanic American and Native American children also tend to attain lower scores than whites. Many studies of IQ have confounded social class with race because disproportionate numbers of blacks, Hispanic Americans, and Native Americans are of lower socioeconomic status. Even when we confine our observations to certain racial groups, however, there remains an effect for social class. Middle-class blacks, Hispanic Americans, and Native Americans outscore lower-class members of their own race.

Japanese people residing in Japan obtain higher IQ scores than white Britishers or Americans. The mean Japanese IQ is 111, one point above the top of the high-average range in the United States (Lynn, 1977, 1982). Children in Japan and Taiwan also attain higher achievement-test scores in reading and math than U.S. children (Stevenson et al., 1985, 1986). But questions remain as to whether racial differences in IQ scores reflect real differences in underlying competence or differences in cultural values, life experiences, and opportunities.

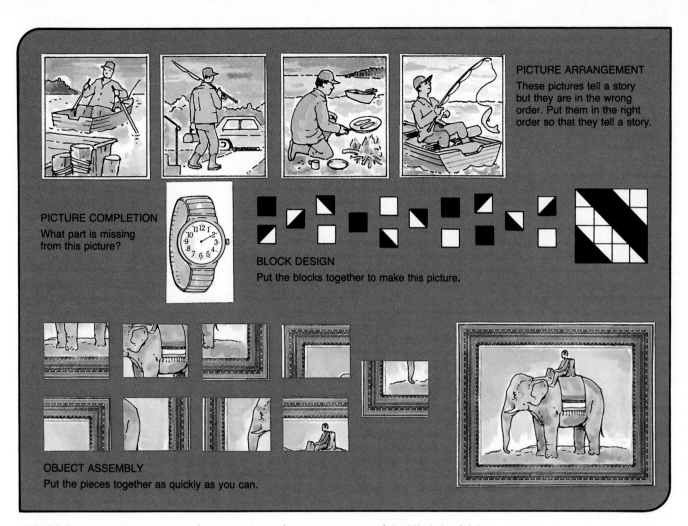

PICTURE COMPLETION
What part is missing from this picture?

BLOCK DESIGN
Put the blocks together to make this picture.

OBJECT ASSEMBLY
Put the pieces together as quickly as you can.

FIGURE 3.1 Items similar to those found on the performance subtests of the Wechsler Adult Intelligence Scale.

FIGURE 3.2 The distribution of IQ scores approximates a *normal curve.*
Weschler defined the deviation IQ in such a way that 50% of the scores fall within the broad average range of 90–110.

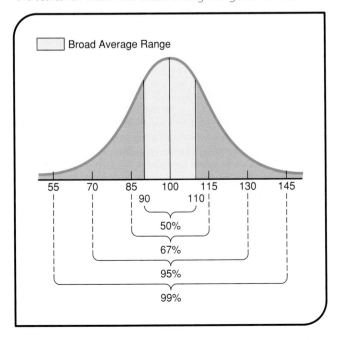

PERSONALITY TESTS

Clinicians use various formal tests to assess an individual's personality. We shall consider two prominent types of personality tests: *self-report* and *projective* tests.

Self-Report Personality Inventories

Do you like automobile magazines? Are you easily startled by noises in the night? Are you bothered by periods of anxiety or shakiness? Self-report inventories use structured items, similar to these, to measure personality traits like anxiety, depression, emotionality, hysteria, masculinity–femininity, and introversion. Comparison of clients' responses on scales measuring these characteristics to those of a normative sample reveal their relative standing according to these traits.

Self-report personality inventories are also called **objective tests.** They are objective in that the range of possible responses to items is limited and also empirical objective standards—rather than psychological theory—are used as the basis for construction of test items.

Tests might ask respondents to check adjectives that apply to them, to mark statements as true or false for them, to select preferred activities from groups of three or more, or to rate the relevance of items for them according to codes such as "always," "sometimes," or "never." Tests with **forced-choice formats** require respondents to mark which of two statements is truer for them or which activity they prefer of a group of three. They cannot answer "none of the above." Forced-choice formats are commonly used in interest inventories, as in this item:

I WOULD RATHER

a.   be a forester.

b.   work in an office setting.

c.   play in a band.

In some tests, as with the most popular and most widely researched self-report inventory, the Minnesota Multiphasic Personality Inventory (MMPI), items were selected empirically—according to whether or not they differentiated clinical diagnostic groups from normal people.

■ Minnesota Multiphasic Personality Inventory (MMPI)   The MMPI contains several hundred true–false statements that assess interest patterns, habits, family relationships, somatic complaints, attitudes, beliefs, and behaviors characteristic of psychological disorders. Although it is also used widely in personality research (Costa et al., 1985), the MMPI was basically intended to help diagnose abnormal behavior.

The MMPI has been administered to thousands of people over the past several decades, permitting psychologists to compare the response patterns of clients to those of people with diagnosed problems. A similar pattern of responses to the test is suggestive of comparable problems. Psychologists can send completed test records to computerized scoring agencies or score them with on-site computers. Computers can generate MMPI reports either by interpreting responses according to certain rules or by comparing them to test records held in memory (Fowler, 1985).

In the 1930s, the developers of the MMPI—Starke Hathaway, a psychologist, and Charles McKinley, a psychiatrist—constructed the MMPI scales on the basis of clinical data. This was an innovation, for most personality tests at the time were based upon a rational or theoretical approach, by which the developer derived test items according to his or her theoretical belief that the item measured a particular psychological attribute (Graham, 1987). For example, the meaning given to responses to the Rorschach inkblot test, as we'll see later, is based on psychodynamic theory, not on empiri-

cal data. Items were assigned to MMPI scales, however, according to the way different clinical groups and normal groups answered them.

Consider a hypothetical item: "I often read detective novels." If depressive groups were demonstrated to answer the item in a direction different from normal groups, the item would be placed on the depression scale—regardless of whether or not the item has face validity. Many items that discriminate normal people from clinical groups are transparent in meaning, such as "I feel down much of the time." But some items are more subtle in meaning or bear no manifest relationship to the measured trait.

Test items can be used to measure traits even when they bear no apparent relationship to the trait. Such items may lack face validity, but they are of use if they are shown to have criterion validity.

Derivation of scales on the basis of their ability to distinguish the response patterns of target comparison groups is called the **contrasted groups approach.** The contrasted groups technique establishes concurrent validity; group membership is the criterion by which the validity of the test is measured.

The MMPI was standardized by comparing the responses of normal groups, composed primarily of relatives and visitors of patients in the University of Minnesota hospitals, to those of carefully selected diagnostic groups, such as depressives, schizophrenics, and paranoids. Eight clinical scales were derived through the contrasted groups approach. Two additional clinical scales were developed by using nonclinical comparison groups: a scale measuring maculinine–feminine interest patterns and another measuring social introversion. The clinical scales are described in Table 3.9.

Validity scales that assess tendencies to distort test responses in a favorable ("faking good") or unfavorable ("faking bad") direction were also constructed. Many items on objective tests like the MMPI are obvious testimony of disturbed thoughts and feelings, as in items of the type, "I frequently hear things that are not there." The transparency of these items makes them fertile ground for faking. The MMPI has several validity scales, including the L (Lie) scale, the F scale (for *Frequency*), and the K (correction) scale. The L scale contains items that refer to minor foibles or flaws in character that nearly all of us possess and admit to readily. An example of a similar item would be, "I sometimes do not answer the phone in a cheerful manner." People who disavow these foibles may also deny items with more serious clinical implications. The F scale contains items that were endorsed by less than 10 percent of the normal

TABLE 3.9 Clinical Scales of the MMPI

Scale No.	Scale Label	Items Similar to Those Found on MMPI Scale	Sample Traits of High Scorers
1	Hypochondriasis	My stomach frequently bothers me. At times, my body seems to ache all over.	Many physical complaints, cynical defeatist attitudes, often perceived as whiny, demanding
2	Depression	Nothing seems to interest me anymore. My sleep is often disturbed by worrisome thoughts.	Depressed mood; pessimistic, worrisome, despondent, lethargic
3	Hysteria	I sometimes become flushed for no apparent reason. I tend to take people at their word when they're trying to be nice to me.	Naive, egocentric, little insight into problems, immature; develops physical complaints in response to stress
4	Psychopathic Deviate	My parents often disliked my friends. My behavior sometimes got me into trouble at school.	Difficulties incorporating values of society; rebellious, impulsive, antisocial tendencies; strained family relationships; poor work and school history
5	Masculinity-Femininity	I like reading about electronics. (M) I would like to have worked in the theater. (F)	Males endorsing feminine attributes: has cultural and artistic interest, effeminate, sensitive, passive Females endorsing male interests: Aggressive, masculine, self-confident, active, assertive, vigorous
6	Paranoia	I would have been more successful in life but people didn't give me a fair break. It's not safe to trust anyone these days.	Suspicious, guarded, blames others, resentful, aloof, may have paranoid delusions
7	Psychasthenia	I'm one of those people who has to have something to worry about. I seem to have more fears than most people I know.	Anxious, fearful, tense, worried, insecure, difficulties concentrating, obsessional, self-doubting
8	Schizophrenia	Things seem unreal to me at times. I sometimes hear things that other people can't hear.	Confused and illogical thinking, feels alienated and misunderstood, socially isolated or withdrawn, may have blatant psychotic symptoms such as hallucinations or delusional beliefs, or may lead detached, schizoid lifestyle
9	Hypomania	I sometimes take on more tasks than I can possibly get done. People have noticed that my speech is sometimes pressured or rushed.	Energetic, possibly manic, impulsive, optimistic, sociable, active, flighty, irritable, may have overly inflated or grandiose self-image or unrealistic plans
0	Social introversion	I don't like loud parties. I was not very active in school activities.	Shy, inhibited, withdrawn, introverted, lacks self-confidence, reserved, anxious in social situations

sample. A high F score may suggest random or careless responding, difficulty in reading or comprehending the test items, or an effort to "fake bad" or exaggerate complaints. An irony that clouds interpretation of the MMPI is that abnormal validity scale scores do *not* in-validate the test for highly disturbed respondents. Schizophrenics, for example, would be expected to answer large numbers of items in unusual ways. The K scale measures a more subtle form of distortion, called psychological defensiveness or guardedness—respondents' tendency to conceal genuine feelings about sensitive issues in order to create a favorable impression. The K scale is used as a correction factor; scores on clinical scales that may be biased by tendencies to cover up are augmented (corrected) by a quantity based on the K scale score. The questionnaire below concerns another kind of response set that results in denial of certain aspects of being human.

The MMPI may be scored by computer or by hand. The respondent's raw score for each scale is simply the number of items scored in a clinical direction. Raw scores are converted into **standard scores** with a mean of 50 and a standard deviation of 10. A standard score of 65 or more on a particular scale places an individual at approximately the 92nd percentile or higher of the revised normative sample, and is considered to be clinically significant.

MMPI scales are regarded as reflecting continua of personality traits associated with the diagnostic categories represented by the test. For example, a high score on psychopathic deviation suggests that the respondent holds a higher-than-average number of nonconformist beliefs and may be rebellious, but it does not establish a diagnosis of psychopathic deviation or antisocial per-

---

QUESTIONNAIRE
The Social-Desirability Scale

Do you tell people what is on your mind, or do you misstate your ideas and opinions to earn social approval? Do you respond to questions frankly, or do you tell people what you think they want to hear?

Telling other people what we presume they want us to say is a type of response set referred to as *social desirability*. This response set prompts us to falsify our ideas and experiences during interviews and on psychological tests. The following scale devised by Crowne and Marlowe (1960) may suggest whether or not you tend to manufacture socially desirable answers.

Directions: Read each item and decide whether it is true (T) or false (F) for you. Try to work rapidly and answer each question by circling the T or the F. Then consult the scoring key at the end of the chapter.

T F   1.   Before voting I thoroughly investigate the qualifications of all the candidates.
T F   2.   I never hesitate to go out of my way to help someone in trouble.
T F   3.   It is sometimes hard for me to go on with my work if I am not encouraged.
T F   4.   I have never intensely disliked anyone.
T F   5.   On occasions I have had doubts about my ability to succeed in life.
T F   6.   I sometimes feel resentful when I don't get my way.
T F   7.   I am always careful about my manner of dress.
T F   8.   My table manners at home are as good as when I eat out in a restaurant.
T F   9.   If I could get into a movie without paying and be sure I was not seen I would probably do it.
T F 10.   On a few occasions, I have given up something because I thought too little of my ability.
T F 11.   I like to gossip at times.
T F 12.   There have been times when I felt like rebelling against people in authority even though I knew they were right.

T F 13.   No matter who I'm talking to, I'm always a good listener.
T F 14.   I can remember "playing sick" to get out of something.
T F 15.   There have been occasions when I have taken advantage of someone.
T F 16.   I'm always willing to admit it when I make a mistake.
T F 17.   I always try to practice what I preach.
T F 18.   I don't find it particularly difficult to get along with loudmouthed, obnoxious people.
T F 19.   I sometimes try to get even rather than forgive and forget.
T F 20.   When I don't know something I don't mind at all admitting it.
T F 21.   I am always courteous, even to people who are disagreeable.
T F 22.   At times I have really insisted on having things my own way.
T F 23.   There have been occasions when I felt like smashing things.
T F 24.   I would never think of letting someone else be punished for my wrong-doings.
T F 25.   I never resent being asked to return a favor.
T F 26.   I have never been irked when people expressed ideas very different from my own.
T F 27.   I never make a long trip without checking the safety of my car.
T F 28.   There have been times when I was quite jealous of the good fortune of others.
T F 29.   I have almost never felt the urge to tell someone off.
T F 30.   I am sometimes irritated by people who ask favors of me.
T F 31.   I have never felt that I was punished without cause.
T F 32.   I sometimes think when people have a misfortune they only got what they deserved.
T F 33.   I have never deliberately said something that hurt someone's feelings.

sonality. Tests are interpreted according to individual scale elevations and interrelationships among scales. For example, a "2–7 profile," which is commonly found among people seeking therapy, refers to a test pattern in which scores for scales 2 (Depression) and 7 (Psychasthenia) are clinically elevated. Various "atlases" or descriptions of people who usually attain the 2–7 profile and others are available to the clinician.

While the MMPI was originally intended as a diagnostic instrument, it has frequently been criticized for its failure to diagnose respondents accurately. One reason for its diagnostic shortcomings is that the clinical scales are not pure measures of the diagnostic categories; respondents may score high on several scales since many of them are interrelated (Graham, 1987). Intercorrelations among the scales stem in part from the fact that many of them share items. It is difficult for the clinician to use the test to pinpoint a diagnosis when a respondent attains several high-scale scores. In addition, clients with clinically diagnosable disorders may score within the normal range on the test and normals may score in the elevated range (Graham, 1987).

Perhaps it is unfair to expect that the MMPI, which was developed under a largely outmoded diagnostic system, should provide diagnostic judgments that are consistent with the DSM–III–R. Even so, MMPI profiles suggest possible diagnoses that can be considered in the light of other sources of evidence. Moreover, many clinicians use the MMPI to gain general information about respondents' personality traits and attributes rather than a diagnosis per se.

The MMPI has recently undergone a major revision and restandardization on the basis of a nationwide sample of approximately 2,600 normal adults (Butcher et al., 1989; Graham, 1990), including a proportionate representation of blacks (the original normative group was composed of all whites). The revised version, called the MMPI–2, contains all of the original scales and some new scales measuring such content dimensions as anxiety, anger, family problems, and low self-esteem. The wording of a number of items has been updated to reflect more modern usage, and some items in the original test have been dropped that referred to customs in the 1930s that are all but unknown today, such as "dropping the handkerchief" (P.S. Ask your grandparents). There is also a new adolescent version available.

■ **The Millon Clinical Multiaxial Inventory (MCMI)** The MCMI (Millon, 1982) was developed to help the clinician make diagnostic judgments within the DSM–III system, especially in the personality disorders found on Axis II. The MCMI consists of 175 true–false items that yield scores for 20 clinical scales that are associated with DSM–III categories. The MCMI is the only objective personality test that focuses on personality style

and disorders (Antoni et al., 1986). The MMPI, in contrast, focuses on personality patterns associated with Axis I diagnoses, such as mood disorders, anxiety disorders, and schizophrenic disorders. Combining the MCMI and the MMPI may help the clinician make more subtle diagnostic distinctions than would be possible with either test alone since these tests assess different patterns of psychopathology (Antoni et al., 1985, 1986).

Self-Report Symptom Questionnaires

Some self-report inventories are more symptom-oriented than either the MMPI and MCMI. Examples include the Hopkins Symptom Checklist (HSCL) (Derogatis et al., 1974) and the Beck Depression Inventory (BDI) (Beck et al., 1961).

■ **The Hopkins Symptom Checklist (HSCL)** The HSCL is a 58-item questionnaire that assesses complaints usually made by outpatients. A **factor analysis** defined five complaint or "symptom" dimensions in the HSCL: somatization (physical or bodily complaints), depression, anxiety, obsessive-compulsiveness, and interpersonal sensitivity (that is, complaints regarding interpersonal conflicts). Clients use a four-point scale ranging from "not at all" to "extremely" to indicate how much they have been bothered by these complaints in the preceding week. Scores on these dimensions are compared to normative data obtained from 2,500 subjects—1,800 psychiatric outpatients and 700 normal people.

■ **The Beck Depression Inventory (BDI)** Some inventories assess a single trait or dimension, such as the Beck Depression Inventory (BDI). The BDI was developed by Aaron Beck, who is known for his cognitive approach to treatment of depression, and his colleagues (Beck et al., 1961). The 21 BDI items measure various features of depression, such as downcast mood and changes in appetite and sleeping patterns. Each presents four response options that vary in level of severity. Subjects select the response that represents their feelings during the preceding week. The items are summed to yield a total score, which can range between 0 and 63. The higher the score, the more severe the depression. A score of 10 or more is considered to indicate at least mild depression. The BDI has been used extensively in research on depression and as a clinical measure of outcome in the treatment of depression. It correlates highly with clinician ratings of depression (Bumberry et al., 1978; Metcalfe & Goldman, 1965; Schwab et al., 1967), which is a common way of assessing the validity of such scales.

■ **Evaluation of Self-Report Inventories** Self-report tests have the benefits of relative ease and economy of administration. Since the tests permit limited response options, such as marking items either true or false, they can be scored with high interrater reliability. Moreover, the accumulation of research findings on respondents provides a quantified basis for interpreting test responses.

A disadvantage of self-rating tests is that they rely upon clients as the source of data. Test responses may therefore reflect underlying response biases rather than accurate self-perceptions. Even the validity scales found in some tests, like the MMPI, may be biased in some situations by underlying response sets (McGovern & Nevid, 1986).

Tests are also only as valid as the criteria that were used to validate them. The MMPI developed in the 1930s was limited in its role as a diagnostic instrument by virtue of the obsolete diagnostic categories that were used to classify the clinical groups. Moreover, if a test does nothing more than identify people who are likely to belong to a particular diagnostic category, its utility is usurped by more economical means of arriving at diagnoses, such as by the structured clinical interview. We expect more from personality tests than diagnostic classification, and the MMPI has shown its value in generating research into the relationships between personality characteristics and response patterns. Psychodynamically oriented critics suggest that self-report instruments tell us little about possible unconscious processes. The use of such tests may also be limited to relatively high-functioning individuals who can read well, respond to verbal material, and focus on a potentially tedious task. Clients who are disorganized, unstable, or confused may not be able to complete such tests.

Projective Personality Tests

Projective tests, unlike objective tests, offer no clear, specified answers. Clients are presented with ambiguous stimuli, such as vague drawings or inkblots, and are usually asked to describe what the stimuli look like or to relate stories about them. The tests are called projective because they were derived from the psychodynamic projective hypothesis—the belief that people impose or "project" their psychological needs, drives, and motives, much of which may lie in the unconscious, onto their interpretations of ambiguous or unstructured stimuli. Ambiguous stimuli can be interpreted in diverse ways, and people are free to draw upon their own psychological processes as well as stimulus cues in determining their responses.

We noted in Chapter 2 that the psychodynamic model holds that potentially disturbing impulses and wishes, often of a sexual or aggressive nature, are often hidden from consciousness by psychological defense mechanisms, principally repression. Defense mechanisms may thwart direct probing of threatening material. Indirect methods of assessment, however, such as projective tests, may offer clues to unconscious processes that the trained clinician can interpret. More behaviorally oriented critics contend, however, that the interpretation of projective tests is based more on clinicians' subjective impressions of the meaning of the test responses than on empirical evidence.

The two most prominent projective techniques are the Rorschach inkblot test and the Thematic Apperception Test (TAT).

■ **Rorschach Inkblot Test** The Renaissance artist and inventor Leonardo da Vinci, suggested that individual differences could be studied by means of people's interpretations of cloud formations. A century later, Hamlet—the hero of the Shakespearean play of the same name—toyed with Polonius by suggesting alternately that a cloud formation resembled a camel, a hunched weasel, or a whale. Polonius showed more political savvy than integrity because he agreed with each suggestion. Hamlet saw through him, of course.

Hermann Rorschach (1884–1922), the Swiss psychiatrist, also believed that ambiguous figures could be used to help clinicians "see through"—or better understand—people with psychological problems. But Rorschach turned to inkblots, not clouds. As a child, Rorschach was intrigued by the game of dripping ink on paper and folding the paper to make symmetrical figures. He noted that people saw different things in the same blot, and he believed that their "percepts" reflected their personalities as well as the stimulus cues provided by the blot. In high school his fellows gave him the nickname *Klecks*, which means "inkblot" in German. As a psychiatrist, Rorschach experimented with hundreds of blots to identify those that could help in the diagnosis of psychological problems. He finally found a group of 15 inkblots that seemed to do the job and could be administered in a single session. Ten blots are used today because Rorschach's publisher did not have the funds to reproduce all 15 blots in the first edition of the text on the subject. Rorschach never had the opportunity to learn how popular and influential his inkblot test would become. The year following its publication, at the age of 38, he died of complications from a ruptured appendix.

  Some clinicians do use psychological tests made up of inkblots to help them arrive at diagnostic impressions. The most widely used of these is the Rorschach inkblot test.

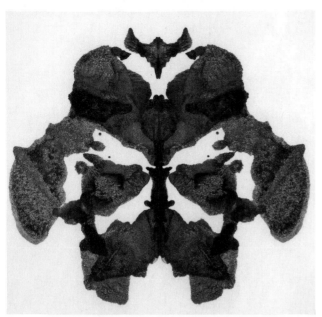

A figure similar to those on the Rorschach inkblot test. The Rorschach test is based on the belief that responses to inkblots represent projections of clients' needs, drives, and motives.

Five of the inkblots are black and white—like that shown above, and the other five have color. Each inkblot is printed on a separate card, which is handed to subjects in sequence. Subjects are asked to tell the examiner what the blot might be or what it reminds them of. The following instructions are typical:

> People see all sort of things in these inkblot pictures. Now tell me what you see, what it might be for you, what it makes you think of. (Klopfer & Davidson, 1962, p. 28)

There are various systems for scoring responses, but most refer to the *location, determinants, content,* and *form level* of responses. After the subject has responded to all cards, the examiner conducts an **inquiry** to clarify which aspects of the blot gave rise to the responses. If the subject says that a card looks like "two dancing bears," the examiner might ask, "What was it about the card that reminded you of dancing bears?" The examiner does *not* say, "Was it the shape of these areas or their shagginess that led you to see bears?" That would be leading the "witness."

The location is the area of the blot selected—the whole card or a prominent or minor detail. **Determinants** include properties of the blot such as form, shading, texture, or color that inspire the response, and features of the percept that the respondent imposes upon, or reads into, the blot, such as **movement**—perceiving figures as animated, as running, dancing, or flying. The content is the *what* of the percept, for instance a winged creature, a jack-o'-lantern, or a torso.

Form level signifies (1) the consistency of a response with the shape of the blot and (2) the complexity of the response. The Rorschach test is asserted to provide information about a subject's intelligence, interests, cultural background, anxiety level, reality testing, degree of introversion or extraversion, and many other factors.

Clinicians who use the Rorschach tend to interpret responses in the following ways. Clients who use the entire blot in their responses show ability to perceive part–whole relationships and integrate events in meaningful ways. People whose responses are based solely on minor details may have obsessive–compulsive tendencies that, in psychodynamic theory, protect them from having to cope with the larger issues in their lives. The determinants are suggestive of emotional response (Klopfer & Davidson, 1962). Relationships between form and color as determinants are suggestive of clients' capacity to control impulses. When responses integrate color but are guided by the form of the blots, clients are believed capable of feeling deeply but also of holding their feelings in check. When color predominates—as in perceiving any reddened area as "blood"—clients may not be able to exercise control over impulses. A response that is consistent with the form or contours of the blot is suggestive of adequate **reality testing.** Movement responses may imply intelligence and creativity. Content analysis may shed light on underlying psychological conflicts. For example, adult clients who see animals but no people may have problems relating to other people. Clients who appear confused about whether or not percepts of people are male or female may, according to psychodynamic theory, be in conflict over their own gender.

Evaluation of the Rorschach   The validity of the Rorschach test has been the subject of extensive debate. One problem with the Rorschach is that the interpretation of clients' responses is not objective; it depends to some degree on the subjective judgment of the examiner. Two examiners may interpret the same Rorschach response differently depending upon their own subjective judgments. Another problem is lack of a standard scoring procedure. There are several scoring systems, and even within systems, the scoring of responses has met with questionable interrater reliability. Recent attempts to develop a comprehensive scoring approach, such as the Exner system (Exner, 1978; Exner & Weiner, 1982), have advanced the effort to standardize scoring of responses.

Even if a Rorschach response can be scored reliably, the interpretation of the response—what it means—remains an open question. Critics and some proponents of the Rorschach technique (Hertz, 1986) suggest that there is a lack of empirical research to support the interpretation of particular responses. On the whole, though, the test may have adequate reliability and validity, as judged by a recent review of research studies conducted between 1971 and 1980 (Parker et al., 1988).

Although these recent results are encouraging for Rorschach proponents, more carefully conceived Rorschach research needs to be carried out. It should also be noted that many psychologists view the Rorschach not only as a diagnostic technique but also as an experimental means of discovering how people construct meaning from unstructured or ambiguous situations (Blatt, 1986). The Rorschach test may yet contribute to our understanding of how the individual comes to perceive the world and develop a meaningful construction of reality.

■ **The Thematic Apperception Test (TAT)**   The Thematic Apperception Test (TAT) was developed by psychologist Henry Murray (1943) at Harvard University in the 1930s. *Apperception* is a French word that can be translated as "interpreting (new ideas or impressions) on the basis of existing ideas (cognitive structures) and past experience." The TAT consists of a series of cards, like that shown in Figure 3.3, each of which depicts an ambiguous scene. Respondents are asked to make up stories about the cards, and it is assumed that their tales will reflect their experiences and outlooks on life—and, perhaps, also shed light on deep-seated needs and conflicts.

Respondents are asked to describe what is happening in each scene, what led up to it, what the characters are thinking and feeling, and what will happen next. Psychodynamically oriented clinicians assume that respondents identify with the protagonists in their stories and project their psychological needs and conflicts into the events that they *apperceive*. On a more superficial level, the stories also suggest how respondents might interpret or behave in similar situations that occur in

their own lives. TAT results are also suggestive of clients' attitudes toward others, particularly family members and lovers.

The TAT has been used extensively in research on motivation as well as in clinical practice. For example, psychologist David McClelland (1958, 1982), also of Harvard, helped pioneer the TAT assessment of social motives such as the needs for achievement and power. The rationales for this research are that we are likely to be somewhat preoccupied with our needs, and that our needs are projected into our reactions to ambiguous stimuli and situations.

Evaluation of the TAT   One criticism of the TAT is that the stimulus properties of some of the cards, such as cues depicting sadness or anger, may exert too strong a "stimulus pull" on the subject (Goldfried & Zax, 1965). If so, clients' responses may represent reactions to the stimulus cues rather than projections of features of their personalities. The TAT, like the Rorschach, is open to criticism that both the scoring and the interpretation of responses are largely dependent on the clinician's subjective impressions. The validity of the TAT in eliciting deep-seated responses is also yet to be demonstrated.

Proponents of projective testing argue that in skilled hands tests like the TAT and the Rorschach can yield meaningful information that might not be revealed in interviews or by self-rating inventories. Moreover, allowing subjects freedom of expression as through projective testing reduces the tendency of individuals to offer socially desirable responses. Despite the lack of evidence for the projective hypothesis, the appeal of projective tests among clinicians remains high (Lubin et al., 1984; Lubin et al., 1985).

NEUROPSYCHOLOGICAL ASSESSMENT

Various methods of **neuropsychological** assessment help researchers and clinicians evaluate whether or not behavioral problems reflect underlying organic conditions or brain damage.

When neurological impairment is suspected, a neurological evaluation may be requested from a *neurologist*, a medical doctor who specializes in disorders of the nervous system, to ascertain whether there is any medical evidence of neurological impairment. A clinical **neuropsychologist** might also be consulted to administer a battery of neuropsychological tests. Neuropsychologists use techniques of observation and psychological testing to reveal underlying organic impairment. Neuropsychological tests not only suggest whether or not clients are suffering from organic impairment, but also indicate which parts of the brain might be involved.

FIGURE 3.3 A drawing similar to those on the TAT. *What is happening in the scene? What led up to it? How will it turn out? How might your responses reveal aspects of your own personality?*

Neurologists and neuropsychologists often work closely together to determine organic impairment.

The Bender Visual Motor Gestalt Test

One of the first tests devised to measure organic impairment by psychological testing is the Bender Visual Motor Gestalt test (Bender, 1938). The Bender consists of geometric figures that illustrate various gestalt principles of perception and remains in use today.

The client is asked to reproduce nine geometric designs on a piece of paper, each of which is printed on a separate card (see below). Signs of possible brain damage include rotation of the reproduction of figures, distortions in shape, and sizing the figures incorrectly in relation to one another. Then the examiner asks the client to reproduce the designs from memory, since neurological damage can impair memory functioning.

Although the Bender remains a convenient and economical means of uncovering possible organic impairment, it has been criticized for producing too many **false negatives**—that is, persons with neurological impairment who make satisfactory drawings (Bigler & Erhenfirst, 1981). In recent years, more sophisticated composite test batteries have been developed.

The Halstead-Reitan Neuropsychological Battery

The Halstead-Reitan may be the most widely used neuropsychological battery. Psychologist Ralph Reitan developed the battery by adapting tests used by his mentor, Ward Halstead, an experimental psychologist, to study brain–behavior relationships among organically impaired individuals. The battery contains tests that measure perceptual, intellectual, and motor skills and performance. A battery of tests permits the psychologist to observe patterns of results, and various patterns of performance deficits are suggestive of certain kinds of organic defects. The tests in the battery include:

1. *The Category Test.* This test measures abstract thinking ability, as indicated by the individual's proficiency at forming principles or categories that relate different stimuli to one another. A series of groups of stimuli that vary in shape, size, location, color, and other characteristics are flashed on a screen. The subject's task is to discern the principle that links the stimuli, such as shape or size, and to indicate which stimuli in each group represent the correct category by pressing a key. A correct response is signalled by a bell, an incorrect choice by a buzzer. By analyzing the patterns of correct

In the Bender Visual Motor Gestalt Test, the subject is asked to copy the geometric figures shown in part A. Part B was drawn by a person suffering from organic brain damage.

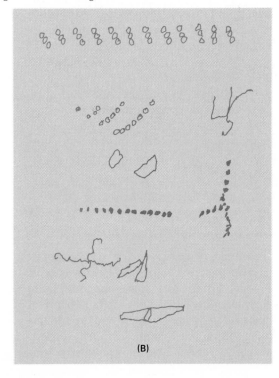

and incorrect choices, the subject normally learns to identify the principles or rules that determine the correct choice. Performance on the test is believed to reflect functioning in the frontal lobe of the brain.

2. *The Rhythm Test*. This is a test of concentration and attention. The subject listens to 30 pairs of tape-recorded rhythmic beats and indicates whether the beats in each pair are the same or different. Performance deficits are associated with damage to the right temporal area of the brain.

3. *The Tactual Performance Test*. This test requires the blindfolded subject to fit wooden blocks of different shapes into corresponding depressions on a form board. Afterward, the subject draws the board from memory as a measure of visual memory.

The Luria Nebraska Test Battery

The Luria Nebraska Test Battery is based on the work of the Russian neuropsychologist A. R. Luria, and it was developed by psychologists at the University of Nebraska (Golden et al., 1980). Like the Halstead-Reitan, the Luria Nebraska reveals patterns of skill deficits that are suggestive of sites of organic brain damage. The Luria Nebraska is more efficiently administered than the Halstead-Reitan, requiring about one-third of the time to complete.

A wide range of skills is assessed. Tests measure tactile, kinesthethic, and spatial skills; complex motor skills; auditory skills at detection of rhythms and pitches; receptive and expressive speech skills; reading, writing, and arithmetic skills; and general intelligence and memory functioning. Although the Luria Nebraska is promising, early research has questioned its reliability (Adams, 1984; Stanbrook, 1983).

Neuropsychological tests hold the promise of revealing brain dysfunctions without surgical procedures that may carry the risk of injury and death. Later in the chapter we examine other contemporary techniques that figuratively and literally allow us to see inside the brain without surgery.

BEHAVIORAL ASSESSMENT

The traditional model of assessment, or **psychometric approach,** holds that psychological tests reveal *signs* of reasonably stable traits or dispositions that largely determine the individual's behavior. The psychometric approach aims to classify people in terms of personality types according to traits such as anxiety, introversion–extraversion, obsessiveness, hostility, impulsivity, and

aggressiveness. This model inspired development of trait-based tests such as the Rorschach, TAT, and the MMPI.

An alternative model of assessment, **behavioral assessment,** treats test results as samples of behavior that occur in specific situations rather than signs of underlying personality types or traits (Goldfried & Kent, 1972). According to the behavioral approach, behavior is primarily determined by environmental or situational factors, such as stimulus cues, rewards, and punishments.

The behavioral model has inspired the development of techniques that aim to sample an individual's behavior in situations that maximize the relationship between the testing situation and the criterion: the real-life situation. Behavioral assessment might focus on measuring observable behavior in such settings as the individual's home, school, or work environment. The examiner might also try to simulate situations in the clinic or laboratory that serve as **analogues** of the problems that the individual confronts in daily life.

The examiner might also conduct a **functional analysis** of the problem behavior—relating it to the *antecedents*, or stimulus cues that trigger it, and the *consequences*, or reinforcements, that maintain it. Knowledge of the environmental conditions in which a problem behavior occurs may help the therapist work with the client and the family to change the conditions that trigger and maintain the behavior.

Consider the case of Kerry:

■ A 7-year-old boy, Kerry, is brought by his parents for evaluation. His mother describes him as a "royal terror." His father complains that he won't listen to anyone. Kerry throws temper tantrums in the supermarket, screaming and stomping his feet if his parents refuse to buy him what he wants. At home, he breaks his toys by throwing them against the wall and demands new ones. Sometimes, though, he appears sullen and won't talk to anyone for hours. At school he appears inhibited and has difficulty concentrating. His progress at school is slow and he has difficulty reading. His teachers complain that he has a limited attention span and doesn't seem motivated.

The Authors' Files ■

The psychologist might use direct observation, preferably in the home, to assess the pattern of interactions between Kerry and his parents. Alternately, the psychologist might observe Kerry's interactions with his parents in a clinic observation room by means of a one-way mirror. These observations may suggest interactions that help explain the child's noncompliance. For example, Kerry's noncompliance may follow parental requests that are vague (for example, a parent says, "Play nicely now," and Kerry responds by throwing toys) or inconsistent (a parent says, "Go play with your toys but don't make a mess," to which Kerry responds by scattering the toys). Observation may suggest ways in which Kerry's parents can improve communication and cue and reinforce desirable behaviors.

Children's behavior may also be assessed in the school setting. Clinicians may directly observe children's behavior in the classroom or ask teachers to complete behavior rating scales that highlight problem behaviors that can be targeted for treatment. Clinicians can also observe children performing school tasks, such as math problems, in the clinic to evaluate their approach to problem solving and possible deficits in attention or concentration.

Behavioral clinicians may supplement behavioral observations with traditional forms of assessment, such as the MMPI, even with projective tests, such as the Rorschach or TAT. However, they are likely to interpret test data as samples of the clients' behavior at a particular point in time, and not as signs of relatively fixed aspects of their personalities. Traditional, trait-oriented clinicians may similarly employ behavioral assessment techniques to learn how personality "traits" are "revealed" in different settings and to see how particular traits affect clients' daily functioning.

Let us consider some of the techniques of behavioral assessment and the issues that they raise.

The Behavioral Interview

In a **behavioral interview,** the clinician asks a series of questions to learn more about the problem behavior in terms of its history and its relationship to situational factors. Establishment of rapport is important to the behavioral interview as to other forms of clinical interviewing. Rapport helps put the client at ease and encourages open discussion of personal feelings, thoughts, and experiences. The behavioral interviewer also observes clients' nonverbal behaviors, seeking discrepancies between verbal and nonverbal behaviors, and noting movements, gestures, or facial expressions that may reflect emotional reactions to topics that are raised.

The behavioral interview more so than the general clinical interview focuses on the situational factors that relate to the problem behavior. If a client seeks help for feelings of panic, the behavioral interviewer might begin by asking how the client experiences these panic attacks—when, where, how often, under what circumstances. The interviewer looks for precipitating cues, such as thought patterns (for example, thoughts of dying or losing control) or situational factors (such as entering a department store) that provoke an attack. The interviewer seeks information about reinforcers that may maintain the panic. Does the client leave the situation when an attack occurs? Is such escape reinforced by relief from anxiety? Has the client learned to lessen anticipatory anxiety by avoiding exposure to situations

in which attacks have occurred? How have other aspects of the client's life been affected by the problem behavior? Do family members relate differently to the client because of the problem? For example, have family members assumed added responsibilities to relieve the stress on the client, thereby reinforcing dependent behaviors? Does the client possess behavioral competencies or skills—such as self-relaxation skills—that might foster successful coping with the problem? Or are there skill deficits that might impede progress in coping, such as deficiencies in communication or social skills?

The behavioral interviewer may also assess cognitive factors that might affect the problem behavior. The interviewer may ask the client to relate any thoughts that he or she can associate with an attack. The interviewer might probe the client's attitudes and beliefs to ascertain whether distorted beliefs (such as mislabeling a minor bodily sensation as a sign of an impending heart attack) are present in the chain of events that lead to a panic attack.

Self-Monitoring

A direct method of relating problem behavior to the settings in which it occurs is to train clients to record or monitor the problem behavior in their daily lives. In **self-monitoring,** clients assume the primary responsibility for assessing the problem behavior.

An early example of self-monitoring was described by Benjamin Franklin. He kept records of the daily frequency of 13 "virtues" that he attempted to increase:

> I made a book, in which I allotted a page for each of the virtues. I ruled each page with red ink, so as to have seven columns, one for each day of the week, marking each column with a letter for the day. I crossed these columns with thirteen red lines, marking the beginning of each line with the first letter of one of the virtues, on which line, and in its proper column, I might mark by a little black spot every fault I found upon examination to have been committed respecting that virtue upon that day. (Cited in Thoresen & Mahoney, 1974, p. 41)

Franklin's diary is comparable to the present-day self-monitoring of "nonvirtuous" behaviors such as cigarette smoking or overeating. Self-monitoring permits direct measurement of the problem behavior whenever and wherever it occurs. Behaviors that can be easily counted, such as food intake, cigarette smoking, nail-biting, hair pulling, studying times, dating, or other social interactions, are well-suited for self-monitoring. In most cases, clients are the only ones in a position to know the frequency of these behaviors and their situational contexts. Self-monitoring can also produce highly accurate measurement since the behavior is recorded as it occurs, and not reconstructed from memory.

Various devices exist for keeping track of the targeted behavior. A behavioral diary or log, like Franklin's, is a handy way to record calories taken in or cigarettes smoked. Such logs are organized in columns and rows to track the frequency of occurrence of the problem behavior and the situations in which it occurs (time, setting, feeling state, etc.) A record of eating may include entries for the type of food eaten, the number of calories, the location in which the eating occurred, the feeling states associated with eating, and the consequences of eating (for example, how the client felt afterward). In reviewing an eating diary with the clinician, a client can identify problematic eating patterns, such as eating when feeling bored or in response to TV food commercials, and devise better ways of handling emotional and external stimuli.

Behavioral diaries can also help clients increase desirable but low-frequency behaviors, such as self-assertive or dating behaviors. For example, an unassertive client might track occasions that seem to warrant an assertive response and jot down their actual response to each occasion. Afterward, client and clinician review the log to highlight problematic situations and rehearse assertive responses. A date-anxious client might record the frequency of social contacts with the opposite sex.

Another popular device for counting troubling behaviors, like nail-biting, that occur frequently throughout the day is the wrist or golf counter. In one case, a boy who was treated for **trichotillomania** (hair pulling) was instructed to make a record of every hair pull by means of a wrist counter (Anthony, 1978).

Self-monitoring, though, is not without its disadvantages. Some clients are unreliable and do not keep accurate records of the targeted behavior. They become forgetful or sloppy, or they underreport undesirable behaviors, such as overeating or smoking, because of embarrassment or fear of criticism. To offset these biases, clinicians may, with clients' consent, corroborate the accuracy of self-monitoring by gathering information from another party, such as clients' spouses. Some behaviors, however, cannot be corroborated in this way, such as eating or smoking in private. Sometimes other means of corroboration, such as physiological measures, are available. For example, biochemical analysis of the carbon monoxide in clients' breath samples can be used to corroborate reports of abstinence from smoking. In order to measure the effects of treatment, clinicians may encourage clients to engage in a **baseline** period of self-monitoring before treatment is begun.

Another issue in self-monitoring is *reactivity*, or changes in measured behavior that stem from the very act of measurement. Some clients may change their undesirable behaviors simply as a consequence of focusing on recording them. When it leads to more adaptive

One form of behavioral assessment of phobia is the measurement of the degree to which the person can approach, or interact with, the phobic stimulus. In this photo, a snake-phobic woman is tentatively reaching out to touch the phobic object.

behavior, reactivity renders the measurement process an effective therapeutic tool in itself. In actual practice, however, self-monitoring itself tends to have only modest effects on lasting changes in behavior.

Analogue or Contrived Measures

Analogue or contrived measures are carried out in laboratory or controlled settings that are intended to simulate the setting in which the behavior naturally takes place. Role-playing exercises are common analogue measures. Consider the assessment of assertiveness in clients who have difficulty expressing dissatisfaction, especially to authority figures. Clinicians cannot follow them throughout the day, and self-monitoring may raise questions of accuracy. Instead, the clinician may rely on role-playing exercises, such as having the client enact challenging an apparently unfair grade. A scene might be described to the client as follows: "You've worked very hard on a term paper and received a very poor grade, say a D or an F. You approach the professor, who asks, 'Is there some problem?' What do you do now?" The client's enactment of the scene may reveal deficits in self-expression that can be addressed in therapy or assertiveness training.

Perhaps the most popular example of an analogue measure is the Behavioral Approach Task, or BAT (Lang & Lazovik, 1963), which measures the approach behavior of a phobic person to a feared object, such as a snake. The approach behavior is broken down into a number of levels of response, such as looking in the

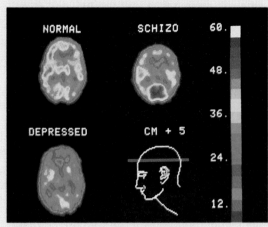

PET scan recordings showing differences in metabolic processes of the brains of a normal person, a schizophrenic, and a depressed person. The levels of metabolic activity of various parts of the brain are shown in hues that range from blue (low activity) to red (high activity).

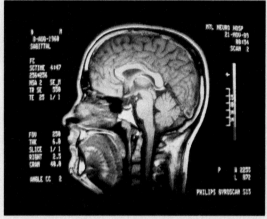

An image of the brain produced by Nuclear Magnetic Resonance (also called *Magnetic Resonance Imaging* (MRI).

A third imaging technique is **nuclear magnetic resonance** (NMR). In NMR, the person is placed in a donut-shaped tunnel that generates a strong magnetic field. Radio waves of certain frequencies are then directed at the person. As a result, parts of the brain emit signals that are measured from several angles. As with the CAT scan, the signals are integrated into an image of the brain.

Brain electrical activity mapping (BEAM) uses the computer to analyze brain wave patterns to reveal areas of relative activity and inactivity from moment to moment. Twenty or more electrodes are attached to the scalp and simultaneously feed information about brain activity to a computer. The computer analyzes the signals and displays the pattern of brain activity on a color monitor, providing a colorful image of the electrical activity of the brain at work. BEAM technology has been helpful in identifying cases of brain tumors (Duffy, 1982), epilepsy (Lombroso & Duffy, 1982), and dyslexia (Duffy et al., 1980), and—as noted in Chapter 12—for examining differences in brain activity between schizophrenics and nonschizophrenics (Morisa et al., 1983).

> **?** Modern imaging techniques such as the CAT scan, the PET scan, NMR, and BEAM do allow us to form inner images of the brain without surgery.

In later chapters we shall see how modern imaging techniques are furthering our understanding of various patterns of abnormal behavior.

(a)

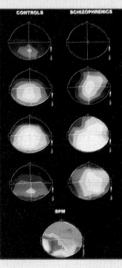

(b)

Brain Electrical Activity Mapping (BEAM) uses electrodes attached to different parts of the scalp (photo a) to measure the electrical activity of regions of the brain. The left column of photo (b) shows the average level of electrical activity of the brains of 10 normal control subjects at four time intervals. The column to the right shows the average level of activity of 10 schizophrenic subjects. Lower levels of activity are represented by darker colors. Higher activity levels are depicted in increasing order by yellows, reds, and whites. The bottom center diagram shows the differences in activity levels between the brains of the normals and schizophrenics. Areas of the brain depicted in blue show small differences between the groups, while areas shown in white reflect larger differences.

ical responses can also be measured through sensors or probes that are connected to various parts of the body. For example, the EEG measures brain wave patterns by means of electrodes that are attached to the scalp (refer to the nearby *A Closer Look* section).

Changes in muscle tension are also often associated with states of anxiety or tension, and they can be detected through the **electromyograph** (EMG), which monitors muscle tension by means of sensors placed over selected muscle groups. (*Myo-* derives from the Greek *mys*, meaning "mouse" or "muscle." The Greeks observed that muscles moved mouselike beneath the skin.) Placement of EMG probes on the forehead, for example, can indicate muscle tension associated with tension headaches. Other types of electrical probes may be used to assess sexual arousal (see Chapter 11).

Ambulatory blood pressure devices allow clinicians to monitor clients' blood pressure at scheduled intervals throughout the day. Clients may log their corresponding activities or feeling states to reveal how changes in blood pressure relate to stressful experiences.

> **?** Clients can be fitted with equipment that allows psychologists to measure *physiological markers* of their emotional responses as they go about their daily lives.

■ **Response Systems**   Lang (1968) has suggested that fear or anxiety consists of three different response systems—behavioral, physiological, and verbal. The behavioral response is avoidance behavior of fear-inducing objects or situations. The physiological response can be measured in terms of changes in heart rate,

GSR, or other response systems during exposure. The verbal system involves the measurement of subjective experience of anxiety. These response systems may act independently, however, so that changes in one may not be generalized to another (Rachman & Hodgson, 1974). For example, people may report that they feel progressively less anxious when they confront a fearful situation, but their hearts may continue to pound. Or people may be able to approach a phobic situation—such as having blood tests or undergoing surgery—even though they report lingering anxiety or fear. Because response systems can be independent, most researchers recommend that investigations include multiple measures of anxiety or fear (Holden & Barlow, 1986), including self-report of subjective feelings, behavioral approach measures, and physiological measurement.

And so people's psychological problems, which are no less complex than people themselves, are assessed in many different ways. Clients are generally asked to explain their problems as best they can, and sometimes a computer does the asking. Psychologists can also draw upon batteries of tests that assess intelligence, personality, and neuropsychological integrity. When possible, many psychologists prefer to observe people's behavior directly, and sometimes the observations are recorded by devices that assess physiological markers of emotional states. The methods of assessment selected by clinicians reflect the problems of their clients, the clinicians' theoretical orientations, and the clinicians' mastery of specialized technologies.

As we survey abnormal behavior patterns in the following chapters, we shall see that our expanding ability to assess people's problems has led to new insights and raised a host of new questions.

SUMMARY

Classification of Abnormal Behavior

The early seeds of the modern diagnostic system may be traced to Hippocrates, who classified such disorders as melancholia, mania, and phrenitis, which generally correspond to several modern diagnostic categories. But the modern era of diagnosis of mental disorders was ushered in by Kraepelin in the late nineteenth century. His classification system influenced the development of the DSM system, the most widely accepted diagnostic system today.

The DSM–III–R categorizes abnormal behavior patterns that produce emotional distress or impairment in functioning as mental disorders. Like the medical model, it treats abnormal behaviors as signs or symp-

toms of underlying disorders or pathologies. However, unlike the strictest form of the medical model, it does not assume that abnormal behaviors necessarily reflect biological causes or defects.

The features of the DSM–III–R include the use of specific diagnostic criteria, grouping patterns of abnormal behaviors together that share common clinical features, and the use of a multiaxial or multidimensional system of evaluation. Multiple axes or dimensions are used to encompass a broader range of psychological functioning. Axis I consists of the major clinical syndromes. Axis II includes personality disorders and developmental disorders that originate in childhood and usually continue in some stable form into adulthood. Axis III lists physical disorders and conditions. Axis

IV codes psychosocial stressors in terms of their occurrence and severity. Axis V requires a global rating of the client's overall level of functioning.

Some of the major strengths of the DSM–III–R system include its use of specified diagnostic criteria and the adoption of a multiaxial system to provide a more comprehensive picture of the person's functioning. Weaknesses noted by some critics include nagging questions about reliability and uncertain validity; the adoption of a medical model framework, which may focus too little attention on environmental influences; too great a focus on classification rather than on determining an individual's behavioral strengths and weaknesses; too much attention focused on present behavior rather than past history or childhood experiences; and too little attention paid to conceptualizations of abnormal behavior derived from particular theoretical models.

Characteristics of Methods of Assessment

To be scientifically useful, methods of assessment, like diagnostic categories, must be reliable and valid. Reliability of assessment techniques is shown in various ways, including internal consistency, temporal stability, and interrater reliability. Internal consistency refers to the degree to which the various parts or items on a test or assessment technique are correlated with each other. Temporal stability refers to correlation of test scores at two different points in time, or test-retest reliability. Interrater reliability refers to the level of agreement between two or more raters of the same behavior.

Validity is measured in diverse ways. Content validity refers to the degree to which a test or assessment device samples or represents the various aspects of a trait or construct of interest. Criterion validity refers to the degree to which the scores on a test or assessment technique relate to an independent criterion or standard. Criterion validity includes concurrent validity (correlation between the test and criterion at the same point of time) and predictive validity (correlation between the test and a criterion measure of future behavior). Construct validity, a higher conceptual level of validity, involves the degree to which a test or assessment technique relates to the theoretical model of the underlying construct or trait it purports to measure.

The Clinical Interview

The most widely used method of assessment, the clinical interview involves the use of a set of questions designed to elicit relevant information from people seeking treatment. Clinicians generally use a structured interview, which consists of a fairly standard series of questions to gather a wide range of information concerning presenting problems or complaints, present circumstances, and past history. The range of questions asked also tends to reflect the interviewer's theoretical framework. Effective interviewers establish rapport and feelings of trust with clients.

While the specific format of the interview may vary, clinical interviews usually cover such topics as the following: (a) identifying data, (b) description of the presenting problem, (c) psychosocial history, (d) medical/psychiatric history, and (e) medical problems/medication use. Interviewers may also conduct a mental status examination, which is a more formal assessment of such features of the client's cognitive functioning and self-presentation as appearance, behavioral observations, orientation, memory, sensorium, perceptual processes, mood and affect, intelligence, thought processes, insight, and judgment.

Effective interviewers are able to convey empathy, or accurate understanding of what the client is experiencing, through both verbal and nonverbal means. They also are attentive listeners who are able to process cues from the client's verbal and nonverbal behavior that help promote accurate understanding. Effective interviewers use such skills as clarification, paraphrasing, reflection, and summarization to help capture what the client is experiencing and feeling. They also attend to the client's nonverbal behavior and are sensitive to discrepancies between the client's verbal and nonverbal behavior as signs of emotions that the client may not fully apprehend or is trying to conceal.

The standardized interview involves the use of a prearranged set of questions to guide the interviewer to reach the most appropriate diagnostic impression. Examples of standardized interview protocols that have been developed in recent years include the DIS, the SADS, and the SCID. Computerized clinical interviews, such as CASPER, have been developed in which the client is asked by computer a series of questions in a prearranged order. Some research suggests that people may be more likely to tell their problems to the computer than to a human interviewer.

Psychological Tests

Psychological tests are structured methods of assessment that are used to evaluate reasonably stable traits such as intelligence and personality.

Intelligence Tests

Tests of intelligence, like the Stanford-Binet and the Wechsler scales, are used for various purposes in clinical assessment, including determining evidence of mental retardation or cognitive impairment, and assessing strengths and weaknesses. Intelligence is expressed in the form of an intelligence quotient (IQ), which is computed on the basis of the deviation of the person's score from a norm. Wechsler scales allow computation of both performance and verbal IQs.

Personality Tests

Self-report personality inventories, like the MMPI, use structured items to measure various personality traits, such as anxiety, depression, and masculinity–femininity. These tests are considered *objective* in the sense that they make use of a limited range of possible responses to items and use an empirical or objective method of test construction. The Millon Clinical Multiaxial Inventory (MCMI) is a self-report personality test that is intended to assist the clinician in making diagnostic judgments. It is the only personality test that specifically focuses on personality disorders. Other self-report inventory focus more on symptom complaints, such as the Hopkins Symptom Checklist, while some, like the Beck Depression Inventory, are focused on a single trait or dimension, such as depression, rather than on multiple dimensions like the MMPI.

Projective personality tests ask subjects to interpret ambiguous stimuli in the belief that their answers may shed light on their unconscious processes. In the Rorschach inkblot test, subjects are presented with ten inkblots and are asked to say what the inkblots look like to them and how they formed their responses. The responses are scored for such characteristics as location, determinants, content, and form level. While the validity of the Rorschach remains subject to debate, recent attempts have been made to develop more standardized scoring systems, such as the Exner system. In the Thematic Apperception Test (TAT), the subject is presented with a series of cards that depict ambiguous scenes. The subject is asked to make up a story that describes what is happening in the scene, what led up to it, and what is likely to happen next. It is believed that subjects identify with the protagonist in their stories and project their needs and conflicts into the stories they tell. But evidence that TAT responses undercover deeply laden conflicts remains to be demonstrated.

Neuropsychological Assessment

Methods of neuropsychological assessment help determine organic bases for impaired behavior and psychological functioning. Neuropsychologists make use of various tests to reveal underlying organic impairment. The Bender Visual Motor Gestalt Test requires subjects to reproduce nine geometric designs on a piece of paper.

Poor performance may indicate possible brain damage, but the test has been criticized for producing too many false negatives—people who score well but have demonstrated brain damage. The Halstead-Reitan Neuropsychological Battery is a more sophisticated battery of tests measuring various perceptual, intellectual, and motor skills and performance. The subject's specific pattern of responses are suggestive of certain types of brain damage. The Luria Nebraska Test Battery also assesses a wide range of skills, but some have questioned its reliability.

Behavioral Assessment

In behavioral assessment, test responses are taken as samples of behavior rather than as signs of underlying traits or dispositions. The behavioral examiner may conduct a functional assessment, which relates the problem behavior to its antecedents and consequents. Methods of behavioral assessment include behavioral interviewing, self-monitoring, use of analogue or contrived measures, direct observation, and behavioral rating scales.

Cognitive Assessment

Cognitive assessment focuses on the measurement of thoughts, beliefs, and attitudes in order to help identify distorted thinking patterns. Specific methods of assessment include the use of a thought record or diary, the use of rating scales such as the Automatic Thoughts Questionnaire (ATQ) and the Dysfunctional Attitudes Scale (DAS).

Physiological Measurement

Physiological measurement involves the use of physiological measures of emotional states such as anxiety. Measures of physiological function include heart rate, blood pressure, galvanic skin response (GSR), muscle tension, and brain wave activity. Researchers have determined that different response systems (behavioral, physiological, verbal) may act independently, so that change in one may not generalize to changes in the others.

Researchers and clinicians use sophisticated brain-imaging techniques to probe the workings of the brain. The electroencephalograph (EEG) records electrical activity of the brain. Computerized axial tomography or CAT scan assesses brain structures for evidence of tumors and lesions by means of a sophisticated X-ray technique. In positron emission tomography, or PET scan, a radioactive compound is tracked as it makes its way through the brain, revealing areas of relative activity or inactivity—the brain at work. In nuclear magnetic resonance, or NMR, a magnetic field in which the person is suspended is used to reveal an image of the brain. In brain electrical activity mapping (BEAM), a computer analyzes brain wave patterns from multiple electrodes placed on the scalp to reveal areas of relative activity and inactivity from moment to moment.

SCORING KEY FOR THE SOCIAL-DESIRABILITY SCALE

Place a check mark in the appropriate blank space each time your answer agrees with the one shown in the scoring key. Add the check marks and write the total number on the line marked "Total Score."

1. T ____	12. F ____	23. F ____
2. T ____	13. T ____	24. T ____
3. F ____	14. F ____	25. T ____
4. T ____	15. F ____	26. T ____
5. F ____	16. T ____	27. T ____
6. F ____	17. T ____	28. F ____
7. T ____	18. T ____	29. T ____
8. T ____	19. F ____	30. F ____
9. F ____	20. T ____	31. T ____
10. F ____	21. T ____	32. F ____
11. F ____	22. F ____	33. T ____

TOTAL SCORE ____

Interpreting Your Score

■ **Low Scorers (0–8)** One respondent in six attains a score of 0 to 8. These individuals have answered in the socially *undesirable* direction most of the time. They may be more willing than most people to answer test items candidly, even when their responses meet with social disapproval.

■ **Average Scorers (9–19)** Two respondents in three attain scores between 9 and 19. They show average concern over the social desirability of their answers. Their actual behavior may represent an average degree of compliance with social rules and conventions.

■ **High Scorers (20–33)** One respondent in six attains a score of 20 to 33. These respondents are apparently highly concerned about social approval and answer test items in a manner that allows them to avoid disapproval from people who know of their responses. Their actual behavior may display strict compliance with social rules and conventions.

4 Stress-Related Disorders

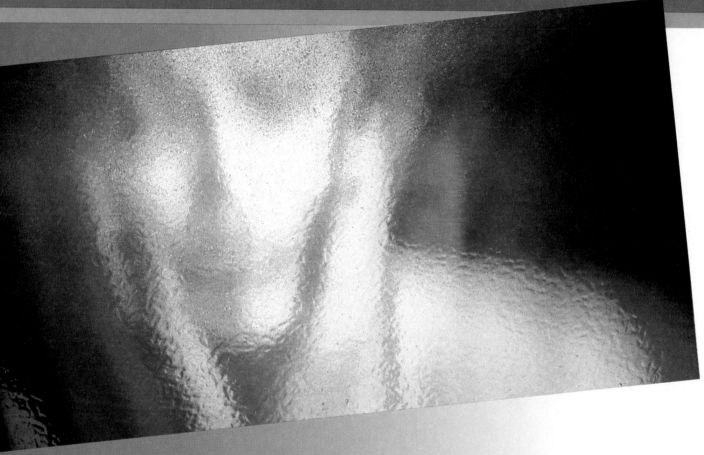

LEARNING OBJECTIVES

When you have completed your study of Chapter 4, you should be able to:

STRESS (p. 120)

1. Define stress.

SOURCES OF STRESS (pp. 120–129)

2. Enumerate the sources of stress.
3. Discuss research concerning the links among daily hassles, life events, and illness.

RESPONSES TO STRESS (pp. 129–131)

4. Describe the general adaptation syndrome (GAS).
5. Explain the involvements of the endocrine system and the autonomic nervous system in the GAS.
6. Discuss emotional responses to stress.
7. Discuss psychological methods for lowering arousal.

PSYCHOLOGICAL MODERATORS OF THE IMPACT OF STRESS (pp. 131–140)

8. Explain how each of the following may moderate the effects of the stress: self-efficacy expectancies, psychological hardiness, humor, whether one is in a goal-directed or playful mode, predictability, and social support.

9. Explain the relationships among social support, life expectancy, and the stress of natural and technological disasters.

ADJUSTMENT DISORDERS (pp. 140–141)

10. Describe the features of adjustment disorders.
11. Explain why labeling an adjustment disorder as a "mental disorder" blurs the line between what is normal and what is abnormal.

POST-TRAUMATIC STRESS DISORDER (pp. 141–145)

12. Describe the features of PTSD.
13. Explain why the Vietnam conflict may have been more likely than others to induce PTSD.
14. Describe the conditioning model of PTSD.

TREATMENT OF STRESS-RELATED DISORDERS (pp. 145–147)

15. Describe various approaches to treatment of stress-related disorders.

I n this chapter we explore various sources of stress and people's reactions to stress. But people respond to stress in diverse ways. We will see that psychological moderators, which are believed to temper the person's response to stress, may explain why some people are better able to cope with stress. We also explore active coping skills for handling stress, such as self-relaxation and meditation, which can be used to lower states of physiological arousal. We will also examine several disorders that are associated with difficulties in coping with stress.

STRESS

In physics, stress is a pressure exerted on a body. Sources of physical stress are found in tons of rock crushing the earth, in cars smashing into one another, in stretching rubber bands. Psychological stresses also "press," "push," and "pull." People can feel "crushed" by the need to make an immense decision. They can feel "smashed" by disaster, or "stretched" to the brink of "splitting."

In psychology, stress can be defined as a demand on an organism to adjust, to cope, to adapt. We usually think of stress in negative terms, as demands or pressures placed upon us by others, or as annoyances or hassles that we are forced to cope with in our everyday lives—like traffic jams and demands from our employers that we work late some nights. Unfortunate events, such as the loss of a loved one or a job can become extremely stressful and tax our abilities to cope to the limit. But positive events can also be stressful. Going off to college, or starting a new job, can be both exciting and joyful, but also require us to cope with new responsibilities or adjust to new living environments. The birth of a child can bring great happiness to its parents, but also raise the level of stress in their lives. The Canadian researcher Hans Selye (1980) pointed out that small or moderate amounts of stress can even be good for us by keeping us alert and occupied. Some stress, in other words, can be healthful and desirable. Selye referred to "good stress" as *eustress*, from the Greek *eu*, meaning "good" or "well." However, intense, enduring stress can diminish our capacity for adjustment, dampen our dispositions (Eckenrode, 1984; Stone & Neale, 1984), and apparently have detrimental effects on the body.

 A certain amount of stress does appear to be healthful.

SOURCES OF STRESS

There are various sources of stress that researchers have enumerated, such as daily hassles, life changes, pain and physical discomfort, frustration and conflict, and environmental stressors such as natural and technological disasters.

Daily Hassles

Common **daily hassles** are sources of stress that seem to be unavoidable features of everyday life. These are

"Stress!"

Drawing by Frascino; © 1982 The New Yorker Magazine, Inc.

conspicuous daily nuisances and incidents that threaten or harm people's well-being (Lazarus, 1984). Researchers have found that daily hassles could be clustered as follows (Lazarus et al., 1985):

1. *Household hassles*: These include making meals, shopping, and keeping the home in order.

2. *Health hassles*: These include physical sickness, concern about medical care, and the side effects of medicines.

3. *Time-pressure hassles*: These include having too many things to get done, too many obligations, and not enough time.

4. *Inner-concern hassles*: These include feelings of loneliness, fears of social confrontations, concerns about the meaning of one's daily activities.

5. *Environmental hassles*: These include air pollution, traffic congestion, traffic noise, neighborhood deterioration, and crime.

6. *Financial-responsibility hassles*: These include concerns about debts, such as mortgage loan installments; concerns about sending the children to college.

7. *Work hassles*: These include dissatisfaction on the job, problems with supervisors and co-workers, and not liking one's work duties.

8. *Future-security hassles*: These include concerns about job security, property investments, taxes, vacillations in the stock market, getting by in retirement.

Lazarus and his colleagues (1985) found the frequency of these hassles was generally associated with such negative features as nervousness, worrying, lack of energy, sadness, and feelings of isolation. But not everyone reacts to daily hassles in the same way. Some people use active coping skills that diminish the impact of these minor annoyances, such as focusing on pleasant mental imagery when faced with a traffic jam, or planning more realistic time schedules to avoid imposing impossible demands on themselves.

Daily hassles, such as commuting to work in congested traffic, challenge our ability to adjust. Can you think of coping responses that you can use to lessen the impact of common annoyances?

Life Changes

You may have heard the saying, the last straw will break the camel's back. Similarly, stresses can accumulate until we can no longer cope with them. Stress researchers Thomas Holmes and Richard Rahe (1967) focused on the impact of life changes as sources of stress. Life changes contrast with daily hassles in two major ways: (1) Some life changes are beneficial and enticing, whereas hassles, by definition, are disagreeable. (2) Daily hassles occur routinely in our daily lives. Life changes, however, are relatively more isolated—for example, a significant change in financial status or a relocation to a new dwelling.

Holmes and Rahe assembled a scale to gauge the effect of life changes. They calibrated the scale by assigning marriage a weight of 50 "life-change units." Then, using marriage as a reference point, subjects from various walks of life assigned units to additional life changes. Most changes were considered less stressful than marriage. A few, however, were rated as more stressful, including death of a spouse (100 units) and divorce (73 units). Other items are listed in Table 4.1. Desirable changes like a striking personal achievement and vacation made the list as well.

It seems self-evident that hassles and life changes—especially disagreeable ones—affect us psychologically by causing worry and dampening our moods. But another question is whether or not hassles and life changes (even seemingly beneficial changes) can increase the risk of physical illness. Holmes and Rahe (1967) reported that about 80 percent of the people who chalked up 300 or more life-change units during a year developed medical problems. By contrast, only about 30 percent of those who "earned" fewer

TABLE 4.1 Scale of Life-Change Units

Life Event	Life-Change Units
Death of one's spouse	100
Divorce	73
Marital separation	65
Jail term	63
Death of a close family member	63
Personal injury or illness	53
Marriage	50
Being fired at work	47
Marital reconciliation	45
Retirement	45
Change in the health of a family member	44
Pregnancy	40
Sex difficulties	39
Gain of a new family member	39
Business readjustment	39
Change in one's financial state	38
Death of a close friend	37
Change to a different line of work	36
Change in number of arguments with one's spouse	35
Mortgage over $10,000*	31
Foreclosure of a mortgage or loan	30
Change in responsibilities at work	29
Son or daughter leaving home	29
Trouble with in-laws	29
Outstanding personal achievement	28
Wife beginning or stopping work	26
Beginning or ending school	26
Change in living conditions	25
Revision of personal habits	24
Trouble with one's boss	23
Change in work hours or conditions	20
Change in residence	20
Change in schools	20
Change in recreation	19
Change in church activities	19
Change in social activities	18
Mortgage or loan of less than $10,000	17
Change in sleeping habits	16
Change in number of family get-togethers	15
Change in eating habits	15
Vacation	13
Christmas	12
Minor violations of the law	11

*This figure seemed appropriate in 1967, when the scale was constructed. Today, inflation and advances in real estate prices probably balloon this figure to at least $100,000.

Source: Holmes and Rahe (1967).

QUESTIONNAIRE
Social Readjustment Rating Scale

Life changes can be stressful. How many changes have you gone through during the last year? To compare the quantity of change-related pressure you have faced with that encountered by other students, fill out the questionnaire below.

Directions: *Mark how often ("frequency") you have undergone the following events throughout the past 12* months. *Next, multiply the frequency (the maximum frequency for any event is limited to 5) by the number of life-change units (or "value") connected with each event. Enter the product in the "total" column. Next, add all the points to arrive at a total score. To interpret the meaning of your total, see the answer key at the end of the chapter.*

EVENT	VALUE	FREQUENCY	TOTAL
1. Death of a spouse, lover, or child	94		
2. Death of a parent or sibling	88		
3. Beginning formal higher education	84		
4. Death of a close friend	83		
5. Miscarriage or stillbirth of pregnancy of self, spouse, or lover	83		
6. Jail sentence	82		
7. Divorce or marital separation	82		
8. Unwanted pregnancy of self, spouse, or lover	80		
9. Abortion of unwanted pregnancy of self, spouse, or lover	80		
10. Detention in jail or other institution	79		
11. Change in dating activity	79		
12. Death of a close relative	79		
13. Change in marital situation other than divorce or separation	78		
14. Separation from significant other whom you like very much	77		
15. Change in health status or behavior of spouse or lover	77		
16. Academic failure	77		
17. Major violation of the law and subsequent arrest	76		
18. Marrying or living with lover against parents' wishes	75		
19. Change in love relationship or important friendship	74		
20. Change in health status or behavior of a parent or sibling	73		
21. Change in feelings of loneliness, insecurity, anxiety, boredom	73		
22. Change in marital status of parents	73		
23. Acquiring a visible deformity	72		
24. Change in ability to communicate with a significant other whom you like very much	71		
25. Hospitalization of a parent or sibling	70		
26. Reconciliation of marital or love relationship	68		
27. Release from jail or other institution	68		
28. Graduation from college	68		
29. Major personal injury or illness	68		
30. Wanted pregnancy of self, spouse, or lover	67		
31. Change in number of type of arguments with spouse or lover	67		
32. Marrying or living with lover with parents' approval	66		
33. Gaining a new family member through birth or adoption	65		
34. Preparing for an important exam or writing a major paper	65		
35. Major financial difficulties	65		
36. Change in the health status or behavior of a close relative or close friend	65		
37. Change in academic status	64		
38. Change in amount and nature of interpersonal conflicts	63		
39. Change in relationship with members of your immediate family	62		
40. Change in own personality	62		
41. Hospitalization of yourself or a close relative	61		
42. Change in course of study, major field, vocational goals, or work status	60		
43. Change in own financial status	59		
44. Change in status of divorced or widowed parent	59		
45. Change in number of type of arguments between parents	59		
46. Change in acceptance by peers, identification with peers, or social pressure by peers	58		
47. Change in general outlook on life	57		
48. Beginning or ceasing service in the armed forces	57		

EVENT	VALUE	FREQUENCY	TOTAL
49. Change in attitudes toward friends	56	————	————
50. Change in living arrangements, conditions, or environment	55	————	————
51. Change in frequency or nature of sexual experiences	55	————	————
52. Change in parents' financial status	55	————	————
53. Change in amount or nature of pressure from parents	55	————	————
54. Change in degree of interest in college or attitudes toward education	55	————	————
55. Change in the number of personal or social relationships you've formed or dissolved	55	————	————
56. Change in relationship with siblings	54	————	————
57. Change in mobility or reliability of transportation	54	————	————
58. Academic success	54	————	————
59. Change to a new college or university	54	————	————
60. Change in feelings of self-reliance, independence, or amount of self-discipline	53	————	————
61. Change in number or type of arguments with roommate	52	————	————
62. Spouse or lover beginning or ceasing work outside the home	52	————	————
63. Change in frequency of use of amounts of drugs other than alcohol, tobacco, or marijuana	51	————	————
64. Change in sexual morality, beliefs, or attitudes	50	————	————
65. Change in responsibility at work	50	————	————
66. Change in amount or nature of social activities	50	————	————
67. Change in dependencies on parents	50	————	————
68. Change from academic work to practical fieldwork experience or internship	50	————	————
69. Change in amount of material possessions and concomitant responsibilities	50	————	————
70. Change in routine at college or work	49	————	————
71. Change in amount of leisure time	49	————	————
72. Change in amount of in-law trouble	49	————	————
73. Outstanding personal achievement	49	————	————
74. Change in family structure other than parental divorce or separation	48	————	————
75. Change in attitude toward drugs	48	————	————
76. Change in amount and nature of competition with same sex	48	————	————
77. Improvement of own health	47	————	————
78. Change in responsibilities at home	47	————	————
79. Change in study habits	46	————	————
80. Change in number or type of arguments or conflicts with close relatives	46	————	————
81. Change in sleeping habits	46	————	————
82. Change in frequency of use or amounts of alcohol	45	————	————
83. Change in social status	45	————	————
84. Change in frequency of use or amounts of tobacco	45	————	————
85. Change in awareness of activities in external world	45	————	————
86. Change in religious affiliation	44	————	————
87. Change in type of gratifying activities	43	————	————
88. Change in amount or nature of physical activities	43	————	————
89. Change in address or residence	43	————	————
90. Change in amount or nature of recreational activities	43	————	————
91. Change in frequency of use or amounts of marijuana	43	————	————
92. Change in social demands or responsibilities due to your age	43	————	————
93. Court appearance for legal violation	40	————	————
94. Change in weight or eating habits	39	————	————
95. Change in religious activities	37	————	————
96. Change in political views or affiliations	34	————	————
97. Change in driving pattern or conditions	33	————	————
98. Minor violation of the law	31	————	————
99. Vacation or travel	30	————	————
100. Change in number of family get-togethers	30	————	————

Source: *Peggy Blake, Robert Fry, and Michael Pesjack,* Self-assessment and behavior change manual (*New York: Random House, 1984), pp. 43–47. Reprinted by permission of Random House, Inc.*

Many life changes, both positive and negative, are perceived as stressful. The most stressful life change identified by Holmes and Rahe is the death of one's spouse.

than 150 units within a year developed medical difficulties. Other investigators have also reported a link between hassles and physical illness (for example, Kanner et al., 1981). Still others found that marital disruption in the form of separation or divorce was linked to higher rates of physical illnesses such as cancer and emotional problems (Somers, 1979; Ernster et al., 1979). High numbers of life-change units amassed within a year have also been linked to problems ranging from heart

Although we tend to link stress with daily annoyances and negative life changes, a positive life change, such as a new marriage, may also be stressful because it too requires adjustment. But positive life changes seem to cause less distress than do daily hassles and negative life changes.

disease to accidents, school failure, and relapses among persons with schizophrenia (Lloyd et al., 1980; Perkins, 1982; Rabkin, 1980; Thoits, 1983).

■ **Links Among Daily Hassles, Life Changes, and Physical Illness: A Critique**   Research supports the existence of connections among daily hassles, life changes, and physical illness. However, we need to be cautious in our interpretations. For one thing, the links are correlational and not experimental (Dohrenwend et al., 1982; Monroe, 1982). On the surface, it may seem logical that hassles and life changes cause physical illness; however, the hassles and changes were not manipulated experimentally. In other words, researchers did not (and would not!) assign subjects to conditions in which they would be exposed to either high or low levels of hassles and life changes to see what effects these conditions might have on the subjects' health over time. Rather, the existing data are based on observations of relationships between hassles and life changes, on the one hand, and psychological and physical problems on the other. These relationships are open to other interpretations. It could be that people who are predisposed to physical or psychological difficulties face more hassles and garner more life-change units. For example, physical illness may contribute to more life disruptions that take the form of hassles and life changes, such as quarrels with one's family, changes in housing and sleeping patterns, and so forth. Hence, in many cases the causal direction may be reversed: Physical and psychological problems may give rise to rather than stem from daily hassles and life changes (Dohrenwend et al., 1984; Dohrenwend & Shrout, 1985; Monroe, 1983).

The life-change–illness connection is based on the view that positive life changes, like negative life changes, are stressful because they require adjustment. Positive life changes seem to be less disruptive than daily hassles and negative life changes, however, even when they are major changes in terms of life-change units (Lefcourt et al., 1981; Perkins, 1982; Thoits, 1983). In other words, a major improvement in the well-being of a member of the immediate family tends to be less stressful than a relapse. Or to put it another way: A change for the better may be a change, but it is less of a hassle.

Personality differences also temper the findings of Holmes and Rahe. As mentioned, people respond to stress in diverse ways. Later in the chapter, for example, we shall see that psychologically hardy people may be better able to manage stress than their ''frail'' counterparts. Other factors like self-confidence and support from one's family also seem to moderate the effects of stress (Holahan & Moos, 1985).

The amount of stress connected with an event also reflects the event's meaning to the individual. For example, whether pregnancy is a positive or negative

Life changes may be negative or positive depending on the meaning of the event to the individual. Whether a pregnancy is a positive or negative life change depends on such factors as the couple's desire for a baby and their ability to provide. This couple views the pregnancy as a positive life change.

Pain is a sign of a bodily problem. Pain is adaptive in that it prompts us to find the source and do something about it. But for some people, pain persists beyond the point that it serves as a useful signal, sapping vitality and the enjoyment of daily life. Let us take a closer look at the origins of pain from injury.

Pain signals originate at the site of injury, as with a stubbed toe. Several chemicals are released at the site, including **prostaglandins.** Neurons transmit the pain message to the central nervous system. Prostaglandins expedite transmission of the message to the brain and increase circulation to the injured area, resulting in the redness and swelling termed *inflammation.* Inflammation attracts infection-fighting white blood cells to the affected area to protect against invading microbes. **Analgesic** drugs such as aspirin and ibuprofen inhibit production of prostaglandins and thus decrease fever, inflammation, and pain.

When the brain receives pain signals, it triggers release of **endorphins,** a kind of neurotransmitter. The term *endorphin* is a contraction of *endogenous morphine. Endogenous* derives from Greek roots meaning "developing from within." Endorphins are similar in function to the narcotic morphine, and they are found in the brain and the bloodstream. Endorphins "lock into" the receptor sites for substances that convey pain messages to the brain. After the endorphin "key" has fit in, pain-causing substances are locked out and cannot deliver their messages. In cases of chronic or persistent pain, however, these natural painkillers are of little avail.

 Our bodies do have natural painkillers that are chemically similar to the narcotic morphine. They are called endorphins.

The primary treatment of pain involves medical intervention to determine and treat the underlying pathology and provide symptomatic relief of the pain by means of analgesic drugs. But drugs do not always work to relieve pain and the physical cause of pain cannot always be determined and treated successfully. People can also develop tolerance for certain narcotic painkillers like morphine and Demerol. When they do, larger doses are needed to realize the same results. Pain and discomfort may also be secondary to medications and medical interventions that are used to treat various diseases. Because of problems like these, psychological and psychosocial techniques have been offered to help people manage and cope more effectively with pain. These approaches include the following:

1.   *Providing accurate information.* A basic psychological technique of pain management is providing sufferers accurate and complete information. Many people try

life change depends on a couple's desire for a child and their readiness to care for a child. In social-learning theory terms, the stress of pregnancy is moderated by the subjective value of children in a couple's eyes and their self-efficacy expectancies concerning child-rearing. We cognitively evaluate hassles and life changes (Lazarus et al., 1985). The same event is less taxing for people who appraise it as meaningful and believe they can cope with it.

In any case, hassles and life changes do demand adjustment. Let us consider some of the other chief sources of stress.

Pain and Discomfort

Pain and discomfort from physical illness or impairment are sources of stress that may impair our capacity to adjust. The emotional stress of enduring chronic or persistent pain can lead to withdrawal, depression, or even suicide.

to avoid thinking about symptoms (and their significance) early in an illness. In the administration of discomforting treatments, like chemotherapy for cancer, information about the details of therapy, including its duration and intensity, can help patients cope—especially patients who like to have information that helps them maintain a sense of control over their situations (Martelli et al., 1987). Accurate information is even helpful to small children who must cope with painful procedures (Jay et al., 1983).

2.   *Distraction and fantasy.* Psychologists have also explored ways of minimizing discomfort once medical procedures are under way. Several methods include use of distraction or fantasy. Patients can distract themselves from discomfort by centering on details of their surroundings—as in counting the hairs on the back of their hands or the ceiling tiles, or by cataloguing the clothing worn by medical staff and passersby (Kanfer & Goldfoot, 1966; McCaul & Haugvedt, 1982). Trying to recall lists of meaningless words also lowers sensitivity to pain (Farthing et al., 1984; Spanos et al., 1984). Children from nine to their teens have been helped to handle the side effects of cancer chemotherapy by playing video games (Kolko & Rickard-Figueroa, 1985; Redd et al., 1987).

 Video games have been shown to help children cancer patients manage the side effects of chemotherapy. For one thing, the games distract them from the side effects.

3.   *Hypnosis.* Hypnosis is used regularly to help patients manage pain in childbirth, dentistry, even some types of surgery. Hypnosis often, but not always, makes significant reductions in pain (Barber, 1982; Turk et al., 1983; Turner & Chapman, 1982b). **Hypnosis** is defined as an altered state of consciousness induced by focusing on repetitive stimuli, like the hypnotist's voice, and by following suggestions—for example, suggestions that your arms and legs are growing warmer and heavier, and that they are "going to sleep." Hypnosis is not sleep, but people translate these directions as a request to become yielding, to follow instructions, and assume a passive what-happens-happens attitude. It was once believed that hypnotism induces a special state referred to as a "trance." Contemporary psychologists downplay this idea, however. Ernest Hilgard (1978), for example, ascribes the pain-relieving effects of hypnosis to relaxation, narrowing of attention, and suggestibility. Theodore X. Barber (1982) ascribes much of the value of hypnosis to suggestions of peace and well-being that are made by a reputable authority figure like a psychologist or physician. Suggestions that limbs are growing warmer and heavier also have relaxing effects: They foster the supply of blood to the body's periphery and reduce the activity of the sympathetic division of the ANS (Pennebaker & Skelton, 1981).

4.   *Relaxation training.* It is possible to attain similar benefits to hypnosis by simply inducing some of the bodily changes associated with hypnosis. **Relaxation training** refers to various psychological methods for relaxing muscles and lowering sympathetic arousal. Later in the chapter we shall see that some relaxation methods center on relaxing muscle groups. Others rely on breathing exercises. Still others center on guided imagery, and may, like hypnosis, include suggestions that limbs are growing warmer and heavier. Relaxation-training methods are about as effective as hypnosis in helping people manage pain (Moore & Chaney, 1985; Turner & Chapman, 1982a).

5.   *Coping with irrational beliefs.* Irrational beliefs about pain intensify pain. For example, in a study that correlated knee pain with beliefs about pain it was found that thoughts that pain is unbearable and will never cease heighten discomfort (Keefe et al., 1987). So cognitive techniques aimed at modifying irrational belief systems about pain also hold some promise.

6.   *Social support.* Later in the chapter we shall see that supportive social networks moderate the effects of stress and, in this way, help people cope with discomfort. Thus, visiting patients and encouraging them to return to health is good psychology as well as folklore (Rook & Dooley, 1985).

Frustration and Conflict

Frustration and conflict can also be sources of stress. We feel frustrated when our goals or needs are thwarted. Many sources of frustration are evident. We may feel frustrated when we are passed over for promotions at work. Or we may feel frustrated when there is too little time in the day to attend to our personal needs as well as meet our family and work responsibilities. Or we can frustrate ourselves by setting goals that are too high, or by making excessive self-demands. We are likely to feel frustrated, as Albert Ellis (1977, 1987) notes, if we believe we cannot survive without the approval of others or if we insist on being perfect in all of our endeavors.

Conflict is a source of frustration in which an opposing motive acts as a barrier. People in conflict may feel "damned if they do and damned if they don't." The emotional barriers of anxiety and fear may thwart our efforts to meet our goals and place us in conflict. A high-school senior who wants to go away to college may be frustrated by apprehensions about leaving home. An adult may want to ask a co-worker out on a date but hesitates for fear of rejection. Psychologists often classify conflicts into four types:

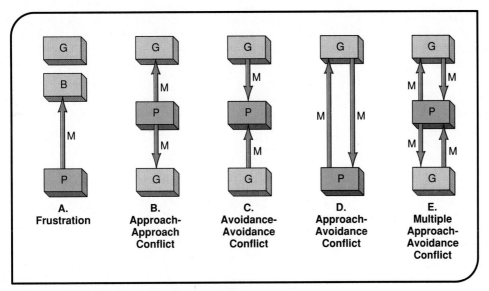

FIGURE 4.1 *Models for frustration and conflict*

Frustration (Part A) results when a person (P) with a motive (M) to reach a certain goal (G) is thwarted by a barrier (B). Part B illustrates an approach-approach conflict, in which a person is attracted to two positive goals but cannot pursue both of them simultaneously. Part C represents an avoidance-avoidance conflict, in which the avoidance of one undesirable goal requires the approach of another. Part D depicts an approach-avoidance conflict, in which the same goal has both desirable and undesirable features. Part E is a representation of a multiple approach-avoidance conflict, in which two goals or more each have positive and negative features.

■ **Approach-Approach Conflict** An **approach-approach conflict** (Figure 4.1, Part B) is considered the least stressful type of conflict. Each of two goals in an approach-approach conflict is positive and within reach. You may decide you want to date Tom or Dick next Saturday night, and have to decide between the two. Or you may be torn between spending your vacation in Maine or in Cape Cod. While such conflicts are generally resolved by deciding one way or the other, people in a state of conflict may **vacillate** until they reach a decision, and may experience regrets afterwards if their choice falls short of their expectations.

■ **Avoidance-Avoidance Conflict** In an **avoidance-avoidance conflict** (Figure 4.1, Part C), the person seeks to avoid each of two negative goals. This is considered a more stressful form of conflict, because avoiding one goal requires approaching the other. You may want to avoid a dental visit, but you also want to avoid losing your teeth. Both goals are negative; hence, the conflict is termed avoidance-avoidance. If the conflict is highly stressful, and there is no clear resolution in sight, the person may avoid dealing with the conflict by focusing attention on other concerns or, in the extreme, by virtually becoming immobilized. Some people who are highly conflicted may have difficulty even getting out of bed in the morning or completing their routine responsibilities.

■ **Approach-Avoidance Conflict** In the **approach-avoidance** (Figure 4.1, Part D) form of conflict, the same goal elicits both approach and avoidance motives. There are "pros and cons," good points and bad points, to both goals. You may want to pursue a master's or doctoral degree but dread the expense and commitment of time involved. A social phobic (see Chapter 6) may want to ask someone on a date but feel immobilized by fear of rejection.

■ **Multiple Approach-Avoidance Conflict** The **multiple approach-avoidance conflict** is considered the most complex form of conflict because it involves choosing among several different courses of action that each have their own positive and negative aspects (Figure 4.1, Part E). Each alternative has its good and bad points. Many undergraduates experience conflict over whether they should enter the work force or seek advanced training on graduation. If they elect to work, cash will soon jingle in their pockets. Later on, however, they may wonder whether they would have gone further by continuing their education. By continuing their education, on the other hand, they delay the emancipation and satisfaction that are provided by becoming a breadwinner.

Conflict involves motives that point in contrary directions. When one motive is decidedly more powerful than another, it should not be too stressful to express the stronger motive. For example, when you are "starved," and only mildly concerned about your figure, you will probably eat without too much conflict. But when both motives exert strong pressures in opposite directions, you may experience high levels of stress and have difficulty deciding what to do. When each conflicting motive is powerful and there is no clearly correct choice, you may encounter high levels of stress and confusion about the proper course of action.

Disasters

Some say the world will end in fire,
Some say in ice.

Robert Frost

Hurricanes, blizzards, monsoons, floods, tornadoes, wind storms, ice storms, earthquakes, avalanches, mud-slides, and volcanic eruptions provide a sampling of the natural disasters humankind has faced. Sometimes we are warned of natural disasters. We may be aware of living in earthquake- or flood-prone areas. When warned, we may be able to evade or avert personal disaster. Otherwise, we are dazed by the abruptness of a disaster and left numb.

Natural disasters are dangerous at the time and may subsequently cause life changes to pile atop one another. They can take the lives of our loved ones, destroy our property, and disrupt our communities. Thus, they are among the most stressful types of experiences. Electric power, water, and other services that had been taken for granted may be disrupted. Homes and businesses may be devastated, forcing people to rebuild or relocate (Fisher et al., 1984).

We owe our dominion over nature to technological advances, but technology sometimes fails or back-fires. Examples include the leakage of poisonous gas at Bhopal, India in 1984; the collapse of a bridge along the Connecticut Turnpike in 1983; the nuclear accident at Three Mile Island in 1979; the Buffalo Creek dam collapse in 1976; the fire at the Beverly Hills Supper Club in 1977 (Green et al., 1983); blackouts, airplane disasters, and the leakage of toxic wastes—these are but a sample of the human-made disasters that befall us.

After the Buffalo Creek dam collapse, thousands of tons of water inundated the town of Saunders, West Virginia. The flood lasted 15 minutes but killed 125 people and left over 5,000 homeless. Reactions included anxiety, withdrawal or numbness, depression, physical symptoms, unfocused feelings of anger (Hargreaves, 1980), regression among children, and sleep distur-bances, including nightmares (Gleser et al., 1981). Many victims experienced **survivor guilt** that they had been spared the deluge while family members and friends had drowned (Titchener & Kapp, 1976).

During the nuclear accident at Pennsylvania's Three Mile Island, radioactive gases and liquids leaked into the atmosphere. A nuclear explosion, meltdown, or massive release of radiation was feared. Evacuation was advised, after a delay, further contributing to peo-ple's fears that they had already been contaminated. Local inhabitants endured the greatest stress (Bromet, 1980; Houts et al., 1980). The psychological effects (anxiety and depression) and physical symptoms (head-aches, backaches) lingered 15 to 22 months after the accident (Baum et al., 1982, 1983; Schaeffer & Baum, 1982).

When disasters occur, we lose our sense of control over things, which has the effect of compounding stress (Davidson et al., 1982). There may be some panic at the time, but survivors usually show relative calm. But a solid minority of survivors—perhaps 25 to 30 per-cent—report what the DSM–III–R labels *adjustment dis-orders* with anxiety and depression for several months (Logue et al., 1979). People who lose more tend to show more distress (Parker, 1977). Adverse reactions to physical traumas may also linger or occur at later periods of time, and significantly impact daily function-ing, such as in the case of *post-traumatic stress disorders* (PTSD, for short), which we will return to later in the chapter.

Disasters and other traumatic experiences also have aftermaths that are predictable from humanistic-existential theories. For example, they shatter victims' senses of living in an orderly, understandable, meaning-ful world (Silver & Wortman, 1980). This "loss of faith" may generate a search for different kinds of meanings. Some people seek meaning or purpose in the tragedy itself, perhaps as a way of denying recognition of under-lying chaos. Some go on a quest for the proverbial "silver linings."

Technological disasters differ from natural disas-ters in that in the former there is someone to blame

Natural or technological disasters tax our coping abilities. Here we see the remains of an apartment complex in the Marina area of San Francisco in the aftermath of the 1989 earthquake.

(Baum, 1988). As a consequence, there may be legal suits. Lawsuits tend to go on for years, providing a continuing source of stress to the victims and to those identified as responsible for the disaster.

 Technological disasters do seem to be more stressful than comparable natural disasters. In the former case there is someone to blame, and the stress of the disaster itself may be compounded by protracted lawsuits.

RESPONSES TO STRESS

There are many sources of stress. Similarly, people have many kinds of responses to stress and different people respond to stress in different ways. In this section we consider the range of physiological, emotional, and behavioral responses to stress. In a later section we will focus on the psychological factors that are believed to moderate individual differences in response to stress.

Physiological Responses

Although the empirical connections among hassles, life changes, and physical illness remain unsettled, there are also theoretical links. In this section we explore our general physiological responses to stress. In Chapter 5 we shall explore the role of stress and psychological factors in various physical disorders.

■ **General Adaptation Syndrome** Stress researcher Hans Selye (1976) coined the term **general adaptation syndrome** (GAS) to describe a common biological response pattern to prolonged or excessive stress shown by all of us. Selye pointed out that our bodies respond similarly to many kinds of stressors, whether the source of stress is an invasion of microscopic disease organisms, a divorce, or the aftermath of a flood. The GAS model suggests our bodies, under stress, are like clocks with alarm systems that do not shut off until their energy is perilously depleted.

The GAS includes three stages: the alarm reaction, the resistance stage, and the exhaustion stage. Perception of an immediate stressor triggers the **alarm reaction.** The alarm reaction mobilizes the body for defense. It is initiated by the brain and regulated by the endocrine system and the sympathetic branch of the autonomic nervous system (ANS). In 1929 Harvard University physiologist Walter Cannon called the initial mobilization of the body's defenses the **fight-or-flight reaction.**

Stress has a domino effect on the endocrine system. First, the hypothalamus secretes corticotrophin-releasing hormone (CRH), which causes the pituitary gland to secrete adrenocorticotrophic hormone (ACTH). ACTH, in turn, stimulates the adrenal cortex to release cortisol and other corticosteroids (discussed in Chapter 2). Corticosteroids help defend the body by fighting allergic reactions (like difficulty breathing) and inflammation.

The sympathetic branch of the ANS activates the adrenal medulla, causing the release of a mixture of the catecholamines—epinephrine (adrenalin) and norepinephrine (noradrenalin) (also discussed in Chapter 2). The mixture mobilizes the body by accelerating the heart rate and stimulating the liver to release stored glucose (sugar), making more energy available where it can be of use.

 Under stress, our bodies do produce natural chemicals that mobilize us to fight or flee from enemies. These include epinephrine and norepinephrine.

A summary of the bodily changes that occur during the alarm reaction is given in Table 4.2.

In one study of the relationships between stress and hormone levels, 18 men monitored their levels of stress on the Daily Stress Inventory (DSI), a measure of daily hassles constructed by Phillip Brantley and his colleagues (1987). Urine specimens were also collected daily. The specimens were analyzed for presence of cortisol and for metabolic by-products of the catecholamines, epinephrine and norepinephrine. As shown in Figure 4.2, these chemical measures were about twice as high during high-stress periods as during low-stress

---

TABLE 4.2 Components of the Alarm Reaction

Corticosteroids are released	Muscles tense
Epinephrine is released	Blood shifts from the internal organs to the skeletal muscles
Norepinephrine is released	Digestion is inhibited
Respiration rate escalates	Sugar is released by the liver
Heart rate escalates	Blood coagulability elevates
Blood pressure escalates	

Stress triggers the alarm reaction. The reaction is defined by secretion of corticosteroids, catecholamines, and activity of the sympathetic branch of the ANS. The alarm reaction mobilizes the body for combat or flight.

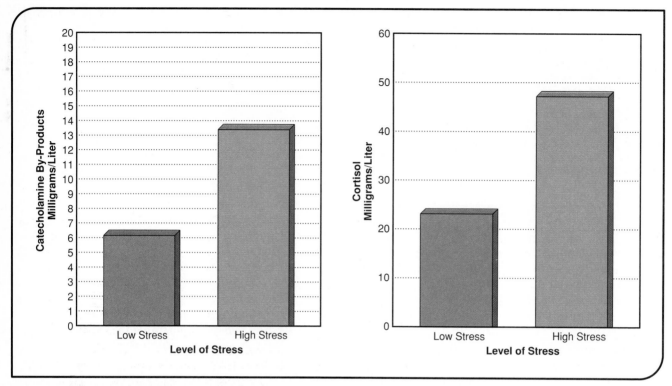

FIGURE 4.2 Urine levels of metabolic by-products of the catecholamines (left) and of cortisol (right) during low-stress and high-stress periods.
Cortisol is a corticosteroid (cortical steroid) produced by the adrenal cortex that helps the body cope with stress by fighting allergic reactions and reducing inflammation. The metabolic by-products of the catecholamines and of cortisol increase during times of stress.
Source: Based on data from Brantley et al. (1988)

periods (Brantley et al., 1988). Such evidence supports the use of cortisol and catecholamines as objective measures of stress.

We inherit the fight-or-flight reaction from our early ancestors, who faced times when many stressors threatened their lives. The reaction was provoked by sight of a predator or by rustling in the undergrowth. But our ancestors usually did not experience prolonged activation of the alarm reaction. Once a threat is eliminated, the body reinstates a lower level of arousal. Our ancestors fought or they fled quickly; if not, they failed to contribute their genes to the genetic pools of their groups. Put it more briefly: They died. Sensitive alarm reactions bestowed survival.

Do touchy alarm reactions remain an advantage? Our ancestors did not invest years in the academic grind. Nor did they carry 30-year, adjustable mortgages. Modern pressures can excite our alarm systems for hours, days, or weeks at a time. So exceptionally sensitive alarm systems may be a handicap today.

If the alarm reaction is aroused and the stressor persists, we progress to the **resistance stage,** or adaptation stage, of the GAS. Endocrine and sympathetic activities remain at high levels, but not so high as during the alarm reaction. During this stage the body tries to renew spent energy and repair damage. When stressors continue to persist, we may advance to the final or **exhaustion stage** of the GAS. Although there are individual differences in capacity to resist stress, all of us will eventually become exhausted. Our cardiovascular systems and muscles will grow fatigued. We will deplete our bodies of the resources required to combat stress. Exhaustion is characterized by dominance of the parasympathetic branch of the ANS. Consequently, our heart and respiration rates decelerate. Other signs of sympathetic activity are reversed; if we had been wide-eyed with fear (if our pupils had dilated), now our pupils constrict. Do we profit from the respite? Not necessarily. The source of stress is persisting. Moreover, stress during the exhaustion stage may induce what Selye terms "diseases of adaptation." Such diseases range from allergic reactions to ulcers and coronary heart disease—and, at times, to death.

Although the GAS occurs in response to most stressors, the patterns of bodily arousal also differ somewhat from stressor to stressor, as we shall see in our discussion of emotional responses to stress.

Emotional Responses

Emotions give color to life. We speak of being green with envy, blue with sorrow, and red with anger. Positive emotions like love and joy fill our days, but negative emotions, like those brought on by stress, can make each day a dreadful chore. Different stressors evoke different emotional responses. No two people share the exact same emotional responses, but some generalizations are possible. We shall consider three major emotional responses to stress: anxiety, anger, and depression.

■ **Anxiety** **Anxiety** is a generalized sense of fear or apprehension. On a physiological level, anxiety involves predominantly sympathetic activity, as characterized, for example, by rapid heart and respiration rates, sweating, and muscle tension. Anxiety is a perfectly normal response to stressful or threatening events, such as a final exam, a big date, an interview for a job, or a dental visit. But when anxiety persists when the stressor is removed, or when it impairs the person's ability to function, or causes significant personal distress, it may represent a type of anxiety disorder (see Chapter 6). Moderate levels of anxiety may have value, however. For example, anxiety about failing a forthcoming test may help motivate us to be better prepared.

■ **Anger** Anger is a typical response to stressors like frustration and social provocation. Hostility is an enduring form of anger that many researchers believe places people at risk for cardiovascular disorders, as we shall see in Chapter 5. Physiologically, anger may involve a combination of sympathetic and parasympathetic activity (Funkenstein, 1955). Anger also induces diverse changes in heart rate, blood pressure, and muscle tension (Ax, 1953; Schwartz, et al., 1981).

■ **Depression** Depression may occur in response to many kinds of stressors, such as the loss of a loved one or a personal failure or defeat, or to protracted stress from any source. Depression is typified by parasympathetic dominance, which also characterizes the exhaustion stage of the GAS. Depression and other mood disorders are discussed in Chapter 8.

■ **Emotions and Behavior** Emotions motivate behavior. Negative emotions like anxiety, anger, and depression can activate maladaptive behavior. Anxiety tends to encourage escape or avoidance behavior; anger, belligerent behavior; and depression, withdrawal.

High levels of arousal that accompany emotional responses to stress may impair cognitive activity and diminish the capacity to solve problems. Instead of trying to find adaptive ways of responding to danger and social provocations, for example, excessive fear or anger may lead us toward more primitive fleeing or fighting responses, respectively, when we are highly aroused. High arousal can also impair cognitive functioning by distracting us from the problems to be solved. That is, we may focus on our bodily responses and cognitions that we are in danger—not on the problems at hand.

PSYCHOLOGICAL MODERATORS OF THE IMPACT OF STRESS

While the general adaptation syndrome suggests that there may be common features in people's response to different types of stress, the effects of stress vary among people. Different individuals are affected by stress in different ways. Genetic factors apparently account for some of the variability. In subsequent chapters we shall see that people may inherit predispositions toward certain disorders in which stress is believed to play a part, such as mood disorders and schizophrenia. Current psychological factors also have a role, however. Just as self-defeating cognitions can heighten the impact of stress, adaptive psychological factors can *moderate*, or temper, the impact of stress.

Let us consider various psychological moderators of stress: self-efficacy expectancies, psychological hardiness, humor, goal-directedness versus playfulness, predictability, and social support

Self-Efficacy Expectancies

One potential psychological moderator of the effects of stress is termed self-efficacy expectancies, which refer to one's perceived ability to cope, to perform certain behaviors, or to effect change (Bandura, 1982, 1986; Bandura et al., 1985). We may be better able to manage stress if we feel confident in our ability to cope effectively with the stressors we face. Recent research by Bandura and his colleagues (Bandura et al., 1985) showed that spider-phobic women who doubted their ability to cope with tasks that required them to interact with spiders, such as letting a spider crawl on their lap, showed high levels of the catecholamines epinephrine and norepinephrine in the bloodstream. But as their confidence or self-efficacy expectancies for coping with these tasks increased, the levels of catecholamines declined. The catecholamines, as noted in Chapter 2, are secreted by the adrenal glands when we encounter stress. They arouse the body by way of the sympathetic branch of the ANS. As a consequence, we are likely to feel shaky, to have "butterflies in the stomach" and general feelings of nervousness. Since high self-efficacy expectancies appear to be associated with lower secretion of catecholamines, people who believe that they can cope

A CLOSER LOOK
Methods for Lowering Arousal

Once people realize that stressors are impacting on them, and are working on plans for coping, it no longer helps—and it can hurt—to have blood pounding fiercely through their arteries. Exposure to prolonged stress may prevent our bodily alarm systems from switching off, impairing our ability to function optimally and possibly increasing the risk of illness. Psychologists and other professionals have developed a number of methods for helping people lower excessive arousal. In this section we consider two widely used methods of lowering arousal, meditation and progressive relaxation.

Meditation Meditation comprises several ways of narrowing consciousness to moderate the stresses of the outer world. Yogis study the design on a vase or a mandala. The ancient Egyptians riveted their attention on an oil-burning lamp, which is the inspiration for the tale of Aladdin's lamp. Islamic mystics of Turkey, so-called whirling dervishes, fix on their movements and the cadences of their breathing.

There are many meditation methods, but they share the common thread of narrowing one's attention by focusing on repetitive stimuli. Through passive observation, the regular person–environment connection is transformed. Problem-solving, worry, planning, and routine concerns are suspended, and, consequently, levels of sympathetic arousal are reduced.

Thousands of Americans regularly practice **transcendental meditation** (TM), a simplified kind of Indian meditation brought to the United States in 1959 by Maharishi Mahesh Yogi. Practitioners of TM repeat **mantras**—relaxing sounds like *ieng* and *om*.

Benson (1975) studied TM practitioners aged 17 to 41—students, business people, artists. His subjects included relative novices and veterans of nine years of practice. Benson found that TM yields a so-called relaxation response in many people. The relaxation response decreases the metabolic rate, as gauged by oxygen consumption, and the blood pressure of people with high blood pressure (hypertension). Regular meditators showed normalized blood pressure through the day (Benson et al., 1973). Meditators also produced more alpha waves, that is, brain waves that are connected with relaxation.

Other researchers concur that meditation lowers arousal but contend that similar effects can be attained by other relaxing activities (West, 1985), or simply by resting silently for an equal amount of time (Holmes et al., 1983; Holmes, 1984, 1985). The Holmes group (1983) reported no differences between veteran meditators and subjects who simply sat quietly, in heart or respiration rate, blood pressure, and galvanic skin response (GSR), which is a gauge of the amount of sweat in the palms of the hands. Critics of meditation do not hold that meditation is without value; they suggest, instead, that meditation may have no distinct effects when compared to a restful break from a stressful routine.

Meditation is a popular method of managing stress by reducing states of bodily arousal. This woman practices yoga, a form of meditation. Contrast her meditative state with the apparent stress of the man behind her.

While differences exist among meditative techniques, the following suggestions illustrate some general guidelines:

1. Try meditation once or twice a day for 10 to 20 minutes at a time.

2. Keep in mind that when you're meditating, what you *don't* do is more important than what you do. So embrace a passive attitude: Tell yourself, "What happens, happens." In meditation, you take what you get. You don't *strive* for more. Striving of any kind hinders meditation.

3. Devise a hushed, calming environment. For example, don't face a light directly.

4. Avoid eating for an hour before you meditate. Avoid caffeine (found in coffee, tea, many soft drinks, and chocolate) for at least two hours.

5. Get into a relaxed position. Modify it as needed. You can scratch or yawn if you feel the urge.

6. For a focusing device, you can concentrate on your

breathing or sit in front of a serene object like a plant or incense. Benson suggests "perceiving" (not "mentally saying") the word *one* each time you breathe out. That is, think the word, but "less actively" than you normally would. Other researchers suggest thinking the word *in* as you breathe in and *out* or *ah-h-h*, as you breathe out. They also suggest mantras like *ah-nam*, *rah-mah*, and *shi-rim*.

7. When preparing for meditation, repeat your mantra aloud many times—if you're using a mantra. Enjoy it. Then say it progressively more softly. Close your eyes. Focus on the mantra. Allow thinking the mantra to become more and more "passive" so that you "perceive" rather than think it. Again, embrace your "what happens, happens" attitude. Keep on focusing on the mantra. It may become softer or louder, or fade and then reappear.

8. If unsettling thoughts drift while you're meditating, allow them to sort of "pass through." Don't worry about squelching them, or you may become tense.

9. Remember to take what comes. Meditation and relaxation cannot be forced. You cannot force the relaxing effects of meditation. Like sleep, you can only set the stage for it and then permit it to happen.

10. Let yourself drift. (You won't get lost.) What happens, happens.

Progressive Relaxation Progressive relaxation was originated by University of Chicago physician Edmund Jacobson in 1938. Jacobson noticed that people tense their muscles under stress, intensifying their uneasiness. They tend to be unaware of these contractions, however. Jacobson reasoned that if muscle contractions contributed to tension, muscle relaxation might reduce tension. But clients who were asked to focus on relaxing muscles often had no idea as to what to do.

Jacobson's method of progressive relaxation teaches people how to monitor muscle tension and relaxation. With this method, people first tense, then relax, muscle groups in the arms; facial area; the chest, stomach, and lower back muscles; the hips, thighs, and calves; and so on. The sequence heightens awareness of muscle tensions and helps people differentiate feelings of tension from relaxation. The method is "progressive" in that people progress from one group of muscles to another in practicing the technique. Since the 1930s, progressive relaxation has been developed by a number of behavior therapists. Joseph Wolpe and Arnold Lazarus (1966) are two of them.

The following instructions from Wolpe and Lazarus (1966, pp. 177–178) illustrate how the technique is applied to relaxing the arms. Relaxation should be practiced in a favorable setting. Settle back on a recliner, couch, or a bed with a pillow. Select a place and time when you're unlikely to be disturbed. Make the room warm and comfortable. Dim sources of light. Loosen tight clothing.

Tighten muscles about two-thirds as hard as you could if you were trying your hardest. If you sense that a muscle could have a spasm, you are tightening too much. After tensing, let go of tensions completely.

You can memorize instructions (small variations from the text won't do any harm), tape-record them, or have a friend read them aloud.

Relaxation of Arms (time: 4–5 minutes). Settle back as comfortably as you can. Let yourself relax to the best of your ability. . . . Now, as you relax like that, clench your right fist, just clench your fist tighter and tighter, and study the tension as you do so. Keep it clenched and feel the tension in your right fist, hand, forearm . . . and now relax. Let the fingers of your right hand become loose, and observe the contrast in your feelings. . . . Now, let yourself go and try to become more relaxed all over. . . . Once more, clench your right fist really tight . . . hold it, and notice the tension again. . . . Now let go, relax; your fingers straighten out, and you notice the difference once more. . . . Now repeat that with your left fist. Clench your left fist while the rest of your body relaxes; clench that fist tighter and feel the tension . . . and now relax. Again enjoy the contrast. . . . Repeat that once more, clench the left fist, tight and tense. . . . Now do the opposite of tension—relax and feel the difference. Continue relaxing like that for a while. . . . Clench both fists tighter and together, both fists tense, forearms tense, study the sensations . . . and relax; straighten out your fingers and feel that relaxation. Continue relaxing your hands and forearms more and more. . . . Now bend your elbows and tense your biceps, tense them harder and study the tension feelings . . . all right, straighten out your arms, let them relax and feel that difference again. Let the relaxation develop. . . . Once more, tense your biceps; hold the tension and observe it carefully. . . . Straighten the arms and relax; relax to the best of your ability. . . . Each time, pay close attention to your feelings when you tense up and when you relax. Now straighten your arms, straighten them so that you feel most tension in the triceps muscles along the back of your arms; stretch your arms and feel that tension. . . . And now relax. Get your arms back into a comfortable position. Let the relaxation proceed on its own. The arms should feel comfortably heavy as you allow them to relax. . . . Straighten the arms once more so that you feel the tension in the triceps muscles; straighten them. Feel that tension . . . and relax. Now let's concentrate on pure relaxation in the arms without any tension. Get your arms comfortable and let them relax further and further. Continue relaxing your arms even further. Even when your arms seem fully relaxed, try to go that extra bit further; try to achieve deeper and deeper levels of relaxation.

with their problems may be less likely to feel nervous. Interestingly, subjects in the Bandura study who said they could not handle a performance task with the phobic object and then refused to attempt it showed sudden drops in catecholamine levels. In other words, avoiding a frightening task was reinforced by immediate reductions in fear arousal. This finding has important implications for our discussion of anxiety disorders in Chapter 6.

 The expectation that we can manage stress may be connected with lesser amounts of epinephrine (and norepinephrine) in the bloodstream. As a result, we may feel less jumpy or nervous when we believe that we can manage.

People with higher self-efficacy expectancies show less emotional arousal as they complete performance tasks; so their performance is less hindered by distracting arousal. When ability is held constant, people with higher self-efficacy expectancies appear to regulate problem-solving behavior more competently and to bounce back more easily from failure. Life's challenges seem less stressful to them.

People who quit smoking or lose weight also face stresses in their everyday lives that can lead to relapse. But research has shown that people with higher self-efficacy expectancies for handling stressful situations without relapsing are less likely to return to overeating or smoking once they have lost weight or quit smoking cigarettes (Condiotte & Lichtenstein, 1981; Marlatt & Gordon, 1980). Perhaps their beliefs that they can cope with stress without cigarettes or overeating helps prevent relapse. During childbirth, women with higher self-efficacy expectancies are more likely to waive pain-killing medication (Manning & Wright, 1983).

The connection between perceived self-efficacy and performance is apparently a two-way street. Not only do self-efficacy expectancies contribute to success, but Feltz (1982) found that enhanced performance (in women divers) also boosts self-efficacy expectancies. This is one reason that "success experiences" are so important to children and to people who doubt themselves.

Psychological Hardiness

Psychological hardiness refers to a cluster of traits that may help people manage stress. Research on the subject is largely indebted to Suzanne Kobasa (1979) and her colleagues who investigated business executives who resisted illness despite heavy burdens of stress. Three key traits distinguished the psychologically hardy executives (Kobasa et al., 1982, pp. 169–170):

1.   The hardy executives were high in *commitment*.

Rather than feeling alienated from their tasks and situations, they involved themselves fully. That is, they believed in what they were doing. (Recall Frankl's view, noted in Chapter 2, that people can better endure hardships when they find meaning in what they are doing.)

2.   The hardy executives were high in *challenge*. They believed that change was the normal state of things, not sterile sameness or stability for the sake of stability. They encoded change as an engrossing incentive for personal development, and not as imperilling their security.

3.   The hardy executives were also high in perceived *control* over their lives. They believed and acted as though they were effectual rather than powerless in facing the rewards and punishments of life. In terms suggested by social-learning theorist Julian Rotter (1966), psychologically hardy individuals have an internal **locus of control.**

Research evidence has shown relationships between proneness to illness and psychological hardiness in people with behavior patterns that may place them at risk of cardiovascular illness, such as the Type A behavior pattern (discussed in Chapter 5). Psychologically hardy Type A people have been shown to be more resistant to coronary heart disease than were Type A people who did not show psychological hardiness (Booth-Kewley & Friedman, 1987; Friedman & Booth-Kewley, 1987; Kobasa et al., 1983; Rhodewalt & Agustsdottir, 1984). Kobasa suggests that hardy people are better able to handle stress because they perceive themselves as *choosing* their stress-creating situations. They encode stress as rendering life interesting, not as intensifying the pressures on them. Activation of control helps them regulate the amount of stress they face (Maddi & Kobasa, 1984). Of the three factors in psychological hardiness listed above, Hull and his associates (1987) maintain that commitment and control help people manage stress most effectively.

 Some people are psychologically hardier than others. They may be more capable of resisting illness when they are under stress.

A sense of control appears to be a key factor in psychological hardiness. You can fill out the locus-of-control questionnaire that follows to learn whether or not you see yourself as in command of your life.

Humor: Does "A Merry Heart Doeth Good Like a Medicine?"

The notion that humor eases the burdens of the day has been with humankind for millennia (Lefcourt &

Martin, 1986). Ponder the biblical adage, "A merry heart doeth good like a medicine" (Proverbs 17:22). It may be that we can cope more effectively when we are able to maintain a sense of humor in the face of stress.

Sigmund Freud considered humor "the highest of [the] defensive processes" (1960, p. 233). Freud wrote, "The essence of humor is that one spares oneself the [emotional responses] to which the situation would naturally give rise and overrides with a jest the possibility of such an emotional display" (1959, p. 216). Rollo May, the humanistic-existential psychologist, proposed that humor played the role of "preserving the sense of self. [Humor] is the healthy way of feeling a distance between one's self and the problem, a way of standing off and looking at one's problem with perspective" (1953, p. 61).

Until recently, the stress-moderating benefits of humor were conjectural and anecdotal. But a recent study by Canadian psychologists Rod Martin and Herbert Lefcourt (1983) suggests that humor may indeed play a stress-buffering role. The investigators administered a measure of mood disturbance and a negative-life-events checklist to college subjects. The mood-disturbance measure also provided a stress score. Moreover, students filled out scales about their sense of humor, and behavioral measures of their capacity to produce humor under stress were taken. Overall, there was a significant correlation between life events and stress scores; high numbers of negative life events were linked to high levels of stress. But the negative life events had less of an impact on students with senses of humor and students who could produce humor in adversity. Humor may play a stress-buffering role, but we should be careful about drawing causal inferences from such correlational relationships. Persons with the better-developed sense of humor may also possess other qualities that buffer the impact of stress.

 A sense of humor may buffer or moderate the impact of stress, but more research would need to be done to determine whether it plays a causal role.

Goal-Directedness versus Playfulness

The same levels of arousal that may distress us at work may be encoded as enjoyable on the weekend, and vice versa! The question seems to be whether or not we are in a playful or goal-directed frame of mind. When we are striving to achieve goals, we also tend to be sober-minded and avoidant of high levels of arousal. Moderate and high levels of arousal are encoded as detrimental to goal attainment and are experienced as stressful in goal-directed situations (Martin et al., 1987). But when we are in playful moods, we

The level of arousal we find stressful may depend on whether we are in a playful or goal-directed frame of mind. Like these young people at a rock concert, you may seek higher levels of stimulation when you are in a playful mood than when you are trying to concentrate on your work.

are more spontaneous and seek higher levels of arousal. People who consider moderate levels of arousal stressful when they are goal-directed may ironically consider low levels of arousal stressful when they are in a playful mode.

Predictability

When we can predict the onset and intensity of stressors, they seem to bother us less. Predictability permits us to brace ourselves for the unavoidable and may also allow us to generate ways of coping. For example, people with accurate knowledge of the effects of medical procedures tend to cope with them more effectively than people who remain in the dark (Shipley et al., 1978; Staub et al., 1971). There is a relationship, however, between personality factors, such as desire to take charge of one's situation, and the value of information about forthcoming stressors (Lazarus & Folkman, 1984). Predictability may be of greater value to people with an internal, rather than an external, locus of control.

■ **Animal Research** Research with animals supports the idea that there are benefits to predictability, particularly when predictability allows one to control a stressor (Weinberg & Levine 1980). In a classic study with laboratory rats, Weiss (1972) showed that providing subjects with a signal that a stressor was on the way apparently buffered its impact.

Weiss matched three groups of rats according to age and weight and placed them in individual sound-

QUESTIONNAIRE
Locus of Control Scale

Men at some time are masters of their fates:
The fault, dear Brutus, is not in our stars,
But in ourselves, that we are underlings.

Shakespeare, *Julius Caesar*, I, ii.

It matters not how strait the gate,
How charged with punishments the scroll,
I am the master of my fate:
I am the captain of my soul.

William Henley, *Echoes*, iv.

Psychologically hardy people have internal loci of control. They see themselves as in charge of their own lives. Non-hardy people tend to have an external locus of control; they see their fates as being out of their hands.

Are you more "internal" or "external"? To gather insight into this question, place a check mark in the Yes or No column for each item. When you have filled out the questionnaire, see the key at the end of the chapter.

		YES	NO
1.	Do you believe that most problems will solve themselves if you just don't fool with them?	___	___
2.	Do you believe that you can stop yourself from catching a cold?	___	___
3.	Are some people just born lucky?	___	___
4.	Most of the time do you feel that getting good grades meant a great deal to you?	___	___
5.	Are you often blamed for things that just aren't your fault?	___	___
6.	Do you believe that if somebody studies hard enough he or she can pass any subject?	___	___
7.	Do you feel that most of the time it doesn't pay to try hard because things never turn out right anyway?	___	___
8.	Do you feel that if	___	___

		YES	NO
	things start out well in the morning it's going to be a good day no matter what you do?		
9.	Do you feel that most of the time parents listen to what their children have to say?	___	___
10.	Do you believe that wishing can make good things happen?	___	___
11.	When you get punished does it usually seem it's for no good reason at all?	___	___
12.	Most of the time do you find it hard to change a friend's opinion?	___	___
13.	Do you think cheering more than luck helps a team win?	___	___
14.	Did you feel that it was nearly impossible to change your parents' minds about anything?	___	___
15.	Do you believe that parents should allow children to make most of their own decisions?	___	___
16.	Do you feel that when you do something wrong there's very little you can do to make it right?	___	___
17.	Do you believe that most people are just born good at sports?	___	___
18.	Are most other people your age stronger than you are?	___	___
19.	Do you feel that one of the best ways to handle most problems is just not to think about them?	___	___

	YES	NO			YES	NO
20. Do you feel that you have a lot of choice in deciding who your friends are?	_____	_____		31. Most of the time do you find it useless to try to get your own way at home?	_____	_____
21. If you find a four-leaf clover, do you believe that it might bring you good luck?	_____	_____		32. Do you feel that when good things happen they happen because of hard work?	_____	_____
22. Did you often feel that whether or not you did your homework had much to do with what kind of grades you got?	_____	_____		33. Do you feel that when somebody your age wants to be your enemy there's little you can do to change matters?	_____	_____
23. Do you feel that when a person your age is angry with you, there's little you can do to stop him or her?	_____	_____		34. Do you feel that it's easy to get friends to do what you want them to do?	_____	_____
24. Have you ever had a good-luck charm?	_____	_____		35. Do you usually feel that you have little to say about what you get to eat at home?	_____	_____
25. Do you believe that whether or not people like you depends on how you act?	_____	_____		36. Do you feel that when someone doesn't like you there's little you can do about it?	_____	_____
26. Did your parents usually help you if you asked them to?	_____	_____		37. Did you usually feel it was almost useless to try in school because most other children were just plain smarter than you were?	_____	_____
27. Have you ever felt that when people were angry with you it was usually for no reason at all?	_____	_____		38. Are you the kind of person who believes that planning ahead makes things turn out better?	_____	_____
28. Most of the time, do you feel that you can change what might happen tomorrow by what you did today?	_____	_____		39. Most of the time, do you feel that you have little to say about what your family decides to do?	_____	_____
29. Do you believe that when bad things are going to happen they are just going to happen no matter what you try to do to stop them?	_____	_____		40. Do you think it's better to be smart than to be lucky?	_____	_____
30. Do you think that people can get their own way if they just keep trying?	_____	_____				

Developed by Nowicki and Strickland (1973).

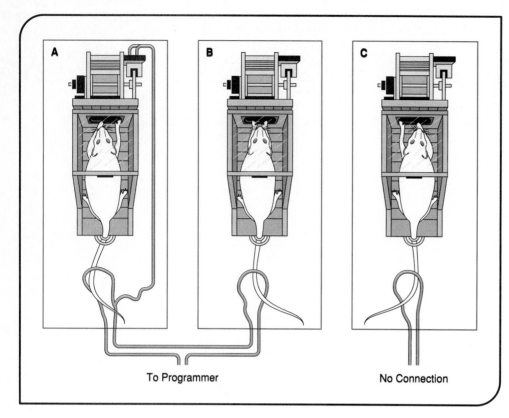

FIGURE 4.3 Diagram of the Weiss study
The rat on the left (A) received a signal prior to the delivery of an electric shock and could terminate the shock by turning the wheel. The rat in the middle (B) received the same shock as the rat on the left, but was not signaled prior to the delivery of the shock. Nor could it terminate the shock. The rat on the right (C) received neither signals nor shocks.

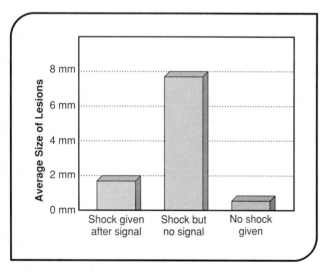

FIGURE 4.4 The results of the Weiss study
Rats who could not predict or control shock showed greatest ulceration.

proofed cages, like those in Figure 4.3. The rat in the cage to the left was shocked with electricity following a signal. The rat could then bring the shock to an end by turning the wheel. The rat in the center cage received shock in tandem with the first rat, but it had no warning signal and could not do anything to terminate the shock. The rat in the cage to the right was given no signal and no shock. It was placed in identical apparatus,

however—even with electrodes connected to its tail—to control for the effects of this eccentric environment.

As shown in Figure 4.4, shock caused the rats to develop ulcers. The rats in the cage to the right, who were given no signal and no shock, had barely any ulceration. Rats who received shock unwarned developed the largest ulcers. Rats who were warned and could terminate the shock also developed ulcers, but less than the helpless rats.

The Weiss experiment suggests that inevitable stressors may be less detrimental to our health when they are foreseeable and we can do something about them. Predictability and capacity to exercise control buffer stressors' impacts. Whether or not a stressor is predictable is, in part, a function of the situation. If we try to learn what we can about the sources of stress in our lives, however, so that we can attempt adaptive responses, we may buffer their impact—and perhaps live longer. Even if we cannot terminate stressors, perhaps we can brace ourselves for them and—as the humanistic-existential theorists suggest—choose our own attitudes.

Social Support

Social support also seems to buffer the impact of stress (Cohen & Wills, 1985; Pagel & Becker, 1987; Rook &

Dooley, 1985). Social support does depend on the availability of supportive others, but, under stress, we can choose whether we shall draw upon our relationships or retreat into shells. Interestingly, there are some children who thrive despite developing in harsh environments. These resilient children show a remarkable knack for attaining support from adults—even before their fourth birthdays (Farber & Egeland, 1987). Social support, in turn, assists children to be more resilient.

There are various kinds of social support, including the following:

1. *Emotional concern.* Emotional concern entails listening attentively to other people's problems and expressing understanding, sympathy, caring, and reassurance.

2. *Instrumental aid.* Instrumental aid entails material assistance and services that support adaptive behavior. Following a disaster, the government may make low-interest loans available so survivors can rebuild. Food, medicine, temporary living quarters are additional examples.

3. *Information.* This is cognitive guidance and advice that enhances people's capacity to cope. Seeking information about how to manage stress is, of course, a key motive for going into psychotherapy or talking with religious advisors.

4. *Appraisal.* Appraisal is the furnishing of feedback from other people as to how well one is managing. Appraisal entails helping people encode, or "make sense of," their tragedies in useful ways. As suggested by George Kelly (see Chapter 2), there can be alternate ways of construing events, and some ways may be more adaptive than others.

5. *Socializing.* Benefit is also derived from social interaction itself, even if the expressed goal has nothing to do with solving problems or managing stress (Fiore, 1980). Examples include "aimless" conversation, leisure activities, or just shopping with another person. (*Source*: Adapted from House [1981, 1984] and Fiore [1980]).

Social support moderates the effects of stress in situations from crowding to problems at work to large-scale disasters. It is helpful for people under stress to collect to talk about their thoughts and feelings. Consider an experiment on sex differences in the effects of crowding. Studies on crowding are frequently carried out by having subjects "wait" in crowded rooms to participate in experiments. Actually, they are already participating while they are waiting; their responses to the conditions in the waiting room are the dependent variables under study. Women typically find being crowded less aversive than men do. One study concluded that women fare better because they feel freer than men to talk to each other and share their feelings

Social support may help buffer the effects of stress. One form of social support is emotional concern, which involves listening attentively to another person's problems and expressing understanding, sympathy, caring, and reassurance.

of discomfort (Karlin et al., 1976). Men who adhere to the tough, independent male stereotype are more likely to keep a "stiff upper lip." So women are more likely to form supportive social networks that help them manage stress.

Also consider the nuclear accident at Three Mile Island. Area residents with solid networks of social support—friends and relatives with whom they could share the ordeal—reported less stress than did residents who had to go it alone (Fleming et al., 1982). People with social support may even live longer, as suggested by studies of Alameda County, California (Berkman & Syme, 1979; Berkman & Breslow, 1983), and Tecumseh, Michigan (House, Robbins, & Metzner, 1982). The Tecumseh study followed 2,754 adults from 1967 through 1979. Throughout the 12 years, the mortality rate was significantly lower for men who were married, who attended meetings of voluntary associations regularly, and who participated frequently in social leisure activities. Women who had lower mortality rates were more frequent churchgoers and watched *less television* than did their shorter-lived peers! It may be tempting to conclude that marriage saves lives and television is lethal, but keep in mind that these findings are correlational. Men who get married may also be generally more stable or more apt to take care of themselves.

 Actually, married men tend to live longer than single men.

In the same way, women "addicted" to "the tube" may be more sedentary than others; and activity and

139

exercise have health benefits, as we shall see in Chapter 5. Now, what about church-going? Does church attendance per se extend women's lives? Do factors that contribute to regular attendance (personal stability and social interactions may be two) tack on the years? What hypotheses can you generate?

A variety of factors appear to moderate the effects of stress. Let us now consider some of the disorders that can occur when people are less able to mitigate the impact of stress. While the DSM–III–R maintains no specific category for stress-related disorders, there are several diagnostic categories in which stress plays a clearly prominent role, such as adjustment disorders and post-traumatic stress disorder. While our focus in this chapter is attendant to these disorders, we recognize that stress has been implicated in playing a role in a wide variety of other disorders. In Chapter 5, we examine the role of stress in relation to physical disorders and conditions. In Chapter 8, we explore the role of stress in relation to the mood disorders. In Chapter 12, we shall see how stress is believed to play a role in the development and course of schizophrenia.

ADJUSTMENT DISORDERS

Adjustment disorders are the first mental disorders we discuss in this book, and they are among the mildest. According to the DSM–III–R, an **adjustment disorder** is a maladaptive reaction to an identified stressor or stressors. It is characterized either by impairment in occupational (or school) functioning or in social activities or relationships, or by features that are considered to be in excess of what would normally be considered an expected reaction to the particular stressor. The maladaptive reaction occurs within three months following the stressor(s). The disturbance may be resolved if the stressor is removed or the individual learns to adapt to it successfully. Adjustment disorders are temporary by definition. If the maladaptive reaction continues beyond six months' time, the diagnosis is changed to another mental disorder.

If a meaningful relationship came to an end and you haven't been able to keep your mind on schoolwork, you may fit the bill for "adjustment disorder with academic inhibition." That label is more official-sounding than "not being able to get one's homework done," but it encompasses the same behavioral difficulties. If your uncle has been feeling low and has moped around ever since his divorce from Aunt Jane three months ago, he may qualify for "adjustment disorder with depressed mood." If, since the breakup, your cousin Billy has been cutting classes and painting dirty words on the school walls with a spray can, he may qualify for "adjustment disorder with disturbance of conduct." The adjustment disorders listed in the DSM–III–R are listed in Table 4.3.

The concept of "adjustment disorder" as a *mental disorder* highlights some of the difficulties in attempting to define what is normal and what is not. When something important goes wrong in life, we should feel bad about it. If there is a crisis in business, if we are victimized by a crime, if there is a flood or a devastating hurricane, it is understandable that we might become

TABLE 4.3 Types of Adjustment Disorders

Disorder	Brief Description
Adjustment Disorder with Anxious Mood	The chief features are worrying, nervousness, and jitters.
Adjustment Disorder with Depressed Mood	The chief features are sadness, crying, and feelings of hopelessness.
Adjustment Disorder with Disturbance of Conduct	The chief feature is violation of the rights of others or violation of social norms appropriate for one's age. Sample behaviors: vandalism, truancy, fighting, reckless driving, defaulting on legal obligations (for example, stopping alimony payments).
Adjustment Disorder with Mixed Disturbance of Emotions and Conduct	There is a combination of emotional features and disturbance of conduct.
Adjustment Disorder with Mixed Emotional Features	There is a combination of emotional reactions. DSM–III–R provides the example of an adolescent who has moved away from home and reacts with mixed feelings, including anger, anxiety, depression, and increased dependence.
Adjustment Disorder with Physical Complaints	The chief feature is physical symptoms like headaches, backaches, or fatigue.
Adjustment Disorder with Withdrawal	The chief feature is social withdrawal.
Adjustment Disorder with Work (or Academic) Inhibition	The chief feature is inability to carry out one's work or academic obligations, often associated with anxiety and depression. The diagnosis is made only when one's previous work performance was adequate.

Source: *Adapted from the DSM–III–R, p. 331.*

An adjustment disorder involves a maladaptive reaction to a stressful event. It may take the form of impaired functioning at school or at work, such as having difficulties keeping one's mind on one's studies.

anxious or depressed. There might, in fact, be something more seriously wrong with us if we did not react in a "maladaptive" way—at least temporarily.

Consider the example of a student who leaves home to attend college for the first time—an identified stressor. Brief reactions such as loneliness and a mildly depressed mood following separation from family and friends, or anxiety over meeting new people or completing academic assignments, may represent a normal adjustment to the stressor. The clinician must gauge whether or not the individual's emotional complaints exceed an expectable level, or whether or not the individual's ability to function is impaired. In the example, an adjustment disorder might involve evidence of impaired functioning (for example, avoidance of social interactions, difficulty getting out of bed or attending classes) or by emotional features such as anxious or depressed mood that the clinician considers excessive under the circumstances. But this is a matter of judgment on the part of clinician. There are no clear criteria to establish where the boundaries should be drawn between an "expectable reaction" and an "adjustment disorder."

> **?** If you are having trouble concentrating on your schoolwork because of the breakup of a recent romance, you may have a mild form of "mental disorder" called an *adjustment disorder*.

In some cases of adjustment disorder, the stressor is severe enough to occasion significant distress in most people. The diagnosis of adjustment disorder may still apply, if the subjective distress—anxiety and/or depression—impairs the ability to function in occupational or social roles. In the following case, for example, a diagnosis of adjustment disorder can be justified by evidence of impaired occupational functioning, despite the fact that the stressor involved, being told that one is infected with the HIV or AIDS virus, is so severe that it would likely produce emotional distress in most people:

■ Marvin was a 35-year-old journalist who tested positive for the HIV virus in his system, but was presently in good health, except for some bothersome allergies which produced sore throat and other physical symptoms. He worries that his symptoms might represent the first signs of AIDS, and has been bothered by frequent and intrusive thoughts about dying and recurrent fantasies of becoming seriously ill and dependent on others. His anxiety has become so severe that he finds it difficult to concentrate at work and is worried that exposure to job-related stress may weaken his body's immune system, leaving him more vulnerable to the disease. He is considering quitting his job and retiring to a country home, where he could lead a simpler life. His anxiety was heightened in the past week in hearing that two acquaintances were diagnosed as having AIDS. He now avoids reading anything about AIDS in the newspaper or attending social situations in which AIDS may be discussed. Marvin had never contacted a mental health professional before and always regarded himself, until now, as a happy person who was fulfilled in his work and personal relationships.

Adapted from Spitzer et al., 1989, pp. 5–7 ■

POST-TRAUMATIC STRESS DISORDER

In the adjustment disorders, the distressing event is usually within the range of normal human experience—business or marital problems, chronic illness, bereavement over a loss. In **post-traumatic stress disorder (PTSD),** the distressing event is beyond the range of common experience and would be notably disturbing to nearly anyone. Events giving rise to PTSD include physical threats to oneself or one's family, rape, destruction of one's community, or observing the violent death of another person. At the time, the event is experienced with intense fear and feelings of helplessness. The basic features of PTSD are reexperiencing of the event, avoidance of stimuli connected with the event, a numbing of general responsiveness (for example, a loss of ability to have loving feelings), and heightened bodily arousal. PTSD has disturbed many veterans of the Vietnam War, rape victims, and people who have witnessed the destruction of their homes and communities by natural disasters like floods or tornadoes, or technological disasters like railroad or airplane crashes. The diagnosis is not made unless the disturbance is endured for at least one month. Sometimes the symptoms do not begin until six months or more after the trauma.

The traumatic event is reexperienced in various ways. There can be intrusive memories, recurrent dis-

Victims of post-traumatic stress disorder may in fact develop symptoms years after their disturbing experiences.

turbing dreams, and the feeling that the event is indeed recurring (as in "flashbacks" to the event). The DSM–III–R states that sufferers can go for days during which they believe that they are reliving the event.

Exposure to events that resemble the traumatic experience can cause intense psychological distress. People with PTSD tend persistently to avoid stimuli associated with the event. For example, they may not be able to handle a television account of it or a friend's wish to talk about it. People with PTSD often report feelings of detachment or estrangement from other people. They may show less responsiveness to the external world after the traumatic occurrence, losing the ability to enjoy previously pursued activities or to express intimate feelings.

Have you ever been awakened by a nightmare and been loath to return to sleep for fear of reentering the orb of the dream? Nightmares involving the reexperiencing of the traumatic event frequently awaken people with PTSD during the night and prevent them from returning to sleep—because of fear and because nightmares also elevate levels of arousal. Other features of heightened arousal in PTSD include difficulties falling asleep, "hypervigilance" (being continuously on guard), and an exaggerated startle response (jumping in response to sudden noises or other stimuli).

Diagnostic criteria as outlined in the DSM–III–R are shown in Table 4.4. Because of the intense fear encountered by the PTSD sufferer, PTSD is classified as an anxiety disorder in the DSM–III–R. It differs from other anxiety disorders, however, because it involves a stress-related disorder that follows exposure to a certain traumatic experience.

Combat-Induced Disorders

Exposure to combat has always been associated with psychological distress (Solomon et al., 1987). Soldiers (and local civilians) can face numerous brushes with death. Civilians witness the annihilation of their neighborhoods and way of life. Soldiers typically confront cold, rain, and filth along with the threat of death. Even if they escape personal harm, their fellows may be killed and wounded. If they succeed in their missions, they must come to terms with the devastation that they unleash on others in the course of war. Perhaps the one saving grace is that "everyone is in it together." But when buddies are lost, the sudden withdrawal of social support compounds the individual's ability to cope with the stressful trauma of combat.

Although PTSD entered the popular vocabulary

TABLE 4.4 Diagnostic Criteria for Post-Traumatic Stress Disorder

A. The individual has faced an unusual traumatic experience such as a serious physical threat to oneself or family; destruction of his or her home or community; or witnessing the serious injury or death of another person.

B. The individual persistently reexperiences the event in one or more of the following ways:
  1. Intrusive, recurrent memories of the event
  2. Recurrent disturbing dreams about the event
  3. Sudden feelings that the event is recurring (or behaving as though it is recurring)
  4. Intense distress when exposed to stimuli that are similar to or symbolize the event, such as anniversaries of the event

C. The individual persistently avoids stimuli connected with the traumatic experience, or there is "numbing" of general responsiveness, as shown in three or more of the following ways:
  1. Attempts to avoid ideas or feelings connected with the event
  2. Attempts to avoid activities or circumstances that kindle memories of the event
  3. Inability to remember an important feature of the event ("psychogenic amnesia")*
  4. Notably lessened interest in normally engrossing activities
  5. Feelings of detachment or estrangement from other people
  6. Restricted range of emotional response, such as inability to experience feelings of love
  7. A sense that life has reached its climax; anticipations about family life, a career, and life itself are foreshortened

D. The individual has persistent signs of heightened arousal, as shown by two or more of the following:
  1. Insomnia
  2. Irritability or angry outbursts
  3. Difficulty in concentration
  4. Hypervigilance (excessive alertness and wariness)
  5. Exaggerated startle response
  6. Physical reactivity to events that are similar to or symbolize the traumatic experience (DSM–III–R provides the example of a rape victim who breaks out into a sweat when she enters an elevator)

E. The disorder has persisted for at least one month.

Source: *Table adapted from DSM–III–R, pp. 250–251.*
* *Psychogenic amnesia is discussed in Chapter 7. The term means psychologically caused inability to remember.*

after the Vietnam conflict, World War II and Korean veterans are estimated to account for some 30 percent of the total number of combat-related cases (Gelman, 1988). Some aging veterans of Korea and the battlefields of World War II continue to complain of recurrent dreams of battlefield dismemberments and deaths through the course of 40 or more years. But it remains unclear why some soldiers are affected by the disorder and others are not (Gelman, 1988). A study of 188 World War II POWs were evaluated for 40 years following their return home to evaluate the lifetime prevalence of PTSD among this group (Kluznik et al., 1986). Two out of three of the men (67 percent) showed evidence of having suffered PTSD at some point following their

LEARNING OBJECTIVES

When you have completed your study of Chapter 5, you should be able to:

PSYCHOLOGICAL FACTORS AFFECTING PHYSICAL CONDITION (pp. 152–153)

1. Explain ways in which psychological factors affect our physical condition.

THE IMMUNE SYSTEM (pp. 153–156)

2. Explain the functions of the immune system.
3. Explain the effects of stress on the immune system.

HEADACHES (pp. 156–157)

4. Differentiate between tension headaches and migraine headaches.
5. Describe research concerning the origins of various kinds of headaches.
6. Describe biological and psychological ways of treating headaches.

MENSTRUAL PROBLEMS (pp. 157–160)

7. Describe various kinds of menstrual problems.
8. Describe theory and research concerning the origins of menstrual problems.

HYPERTENSION (pp. 160–161)

9. Describe theory and research concerning the origins of essential hypertension.
10. Describe biological and psychological approaches to managing hypertension.

CARDIOVASCULAR DISORDERS (pp. 161–169)

11. Describe the risk factors for coronary heart disease (CHD).
12. Summarize research concerning the connections between the Type A behavior pattern and coronary heart disease.
13. Describe ways in which modifying behavior can reduce exposure to the risk factors for coronary heart disease.

GASTROINTESTINAL DISORDERS (pp. 169–172)

14. Discuss the theoretical perspectives on ulcers.

ASTHMA (pp. 172–173)

15. Discuss the theoretical perspectives on asthma.

CANCER (pp. 173–175)

16. Describe the risk factors for cancer.
17. Discuss research findings investigating psychological factors in the course and treatment of cancer.

ACQUIRED IMMUNE DEFICIENCY SYNDROME (AIDS) (pp. 175–178)

18. Discuss the biological and psychological effects of AIDS.
19. Discuss roles for psychologists in the prevention of AIDS and treatment of AIDS victims.

OBESITY (pp. 178–186)

20. Discuss theoretical perspectives on obesity.
21. Summarize research concerning treatments of obesity.

Norman Cousins, the editor of the *Saturday Review*, was hospitalized in 1964 for a rare and painful collagen disorder that is somewhat akin to arthritis. Cousins did not accept the role of "good patient." From the outset he griped about hospital routines, like the low-calorie, flavorless diet; the slapdash taking of X-rays, and the heavy prescription of drugs, including analgesics (painkillers) and tranquilizers.

Even with this cornucopia of procedures, his doctors gave him but a slim chance of a complete recovery. So Cousins decided to take his health into his own hands, as he describes in his 1979 book, *Anatomy of an Illness*. First, Cousins left the hospital setting—which fosters passive compliance with the patient role—and moved to a nearby hotel room. Second, he swapped the immense dosages of painkillers and other drugs for laughter and vitamins. He viewed Marx Brothers films and his favorite television comedy shows. He was determined to maintain a positive attitude. To his doctors' astonishment, Cousins made a substantial recovery from his malady.

Several years later, at the age of 65, Cousins suffered a heart attack. He was taken to the hospital by ambulance. Again, he was an awful patient. His first transgression was taking charge of the ride. He declined the painkiller morphine because he wanted to experience his problem and remain fully lucid. He asked the ambulance driver not to turn on the siren and to stay within the speed limit. He said that he would take full responsibility for any resultant problems. He refused the endless routine medical tests and returned home within a few days, before his doctors were comfortable releasing him. As Cousins explained in his 1983 book, *The Healing Heart*: *Antidote to Panic and Helplessness*, he employed dietary measures, exercise, and a positive attitude—not medicine—to recuperate.

The manner in which Norman Cousins managed his sickness is heartening to people who have taken exception to hospital practices or been annoyed by inflexible behavior in physicians. The approach taken by Cousins does not seem to have hurt him. Indeed, it may have abetted his recovery from his illnesses. Keep in mind, however, that we have no proof that the path to recovery is paved with rebellion. Cousins' experiences provide a fascinating, but scientifically uncontrolled, case study. But Cousins' ways of handling his ordeals highlight some of the connections between psychological factors (such as assuming control, keeping a positive attitude, choosing one's diet, and exercising) and physical disorders. Cousins' narratives also seem consonant with popular conceptions that suggest that we should maintain a "fighting spirit" and not "give in" to illness.

Cousins' writings provide one more chapter in the age-old debate concerning the relationships between the mind and the body. We know that the existence of mind is dependent on the brain. But since the workings of the mind differ in quality from biological processes, there is continuing temptation to regard them separately. Despite the apparent separateness of body and mind, many people have realized that bodily states can have effects on mental functioning. We will see in later chapters how mental disorders are believed to be affected by biological factors. But we've come to see that causality can also work in the other direction—that the mind might influence the functioning and welfare of the body. In this chapter we focus on psychological factors that are believed to affect physical disorders.

Mind and body have increasingly come to be seen as highly interrelated. The field of psychosomatic medicine was developed as a means of exploring the possible health-related connections between the mind and the body. The term *psychosomatic* is derived from the Greek roots *psyche*, meaning "soul" or "intellect," and *soma*, which means "body." Today these relationships are under intense study by medical researchers and psychologists, particularly **health psychologists.** Psychosomatic or *psychophysiological* disorders are physical disorders or conditions involving actual organic or tissue damage in which psychological factors are believed to play a causal role. In this chapter we consider the interface between mind and body by examining the influence of psychosocial factors in physical illness and by exploring how psychological treatments may help improve physical health and assist people with physical disorders to cope more successfully with illness. Researchers are also coming to see that styles of coping with serious illness may affect not only one's ability to adjust but also one's very survival.

Many of the physical disorders discussed in this chapter are believed to be influenced by heightened or prolonged states of stress or physiological arousal. In Chapter 4 we saw how stress can lead to impaired functioning and to difficulties in adjustment. We also saw how traumatic forms of stress can lead to serious disturbances associated with the post-traumatic stress disorder. In this chapter we consider how stress can affect such physical disorders as headaches, cancer, cardiovascular disease, ulcers, and asthma. While stress is implicated in the development of many physical disorders, the precise role that it plays remains subject to debate.

PSYCHOLOGICAL FACTORS AFFECTING PHYSICAL CONDITION

The DSM–III–R has a category for *psychological factors affecting physical condition*, which describes many disorders that were previously labeled psychosomatic or psychophysiological. The physical condition itself is recorded on Axis III. In order for a disorder (or a single symptom, like vomiting) to be diagnosed in this manner, it must be shown that psychological factors are involved in initiating or exacerbating the physical condition. The DSM–III–R lists the disorders shown in Table 5.1 as common examples that may be appropriate for this category.

Psychological factors may be involved in the course of most if not all illnesses, and the treatment of physically ill people has both psychological and medical importance. In the course of this chapter we will consider the role of stress and psychological factors in several of the disorders listed in Table 5.1—for example, headaches, hypertension, cardiovascular disorders, ulcers, asthma, and obesity. We also include a discussion of psychological factors relating to menstrual disorders such as premenstrual syndrome (PMS), although in

TABLE 5.1 Physical Conditions that Are Initiated or Exacerbated by Psychological Factors

Obesity	Gastric (stomach) ulcer
Tension headache	Duodenal (intestinal) ulcer
Migraine headache	Cardiospasm (sudden contractions of the heart muscle)
Angina pectoris (recurrent pain in the chest and the left arm, caused by sudden decrease in the blood supply to the heart)	Pylorospasm (spasms of the muscular tissue leading from the stomach into the small intestine)
Painful menstruation	Nausea and vomiting
Sacroiliac (lower back) pain	Regional enteritis (inflammation of the intestine, especially the small intestine)
Neurodermatitis (skin inflammations, such as hives)	
Acne	Ulcerative colitis (inflammation and open sores of the colon, or large intestine)
Rheumatoid arthritis (painful inflammation of the joints)	
Asthma	Frequency of micturition (frequent urination)
Tachycardia (rapid heart beat)	
Arrhythmia (irregularity in the rhythm of the heart)	

Source: DSM–III–R, p. 333.

PMS, perhaps too much emphasis has been placed on the possible psychological aspects of causality—perhaps to the disparagement of women. Our coverage of physical conditions that may be affected by psychological factors also includes a discussion of cancer, because of evidence suggesting that stress may influence the course of the disease. Moreover, many psychological issues attend cancer prevention and the treatment of cancer victims. We include acquired immune deficiency syndrome (AIDS) in our discussion for similar reasons: Stress may affect the course of AIDS, and psychological issues attend AIDS prevention and the treatment of AIDS victims.

The relationship between stress and physical illness poses questions, such as these, which we will explore in the course of our discussion of various physical disorders:

1. Why is it that certain people, under stress, are afflicted by one type of disorder, whereas other people are beset by another? According to the **diathesis–stress** model, stress in combination with some *predisposition* or diathesis within the person accounts for the form of the disorder. How have these predispositions or diatheses been conceptualized?

2. Can stress-management techniques lead to improvement of various physical disorders like headaches and hypertension? How might psychological treatments help people reduce the identified risk factors for cardiovascular disease? What role might psychological interventions play in the treatment of diseases like cancer and AIDS?

One of the ways in which stress may affect the courses of physical illnesses is by suppressing the immune system. Thus, we now examine the functioning of the immune system and then consider the psychological factors involved in illnesses and physical conditions ranging from headaches to obesity.

THE IMMUNE SYSTEM

Given the intricacies of the human body and the rapid advance of scientific knowledge, we tend to consider ourselves dependent on highly trained specialists to contend with illness. Actually we cope with most diseases by ourselves, through the functioning of our **immune system.**

The immune system combats disease in a number of ways. The immune system produces white blood cells that systematically envelop and kill **pathogens** like bacteria, viruses, and fungi; worn out body cells; and cells that have become cancerous. White blood cells are referred to as **leukocytes.** Leukocytes sustain microscopic warfare. They undertake search-and-destroy missions; they identify and eradicate foreign agents and infirm cells.

A second role of the immune system is recognizing foreign agents to enhance the efficiency of future combat. Foreign agents that are identified and annihilated

White blood cells attacking and engulfing pathogens.

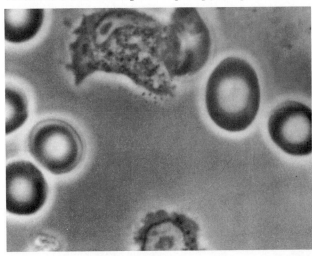

by leukocytes are termed **antigens.** Some leukocytes terminate the antigens, but others produce **antibodies,** kinds of specialized proteins, that attach to their antigens and mark them for destruction. (Infection by the AIDS virus may be determined by examining the blood for the presence of AIDS antibodies.).

Special "memory lymphocytes" (lymphocytes are a type of leukocyte) are held in reserve, rather than marking antigens for destruction or going to war against them. They can remain in the bloodstream, sometimes for several years, and they form the basis for a quick immune response to an invader the second time around.*

A third function of the immune system is **inflammation.** When injury befalls, blood vessels in the region initially contract to check bleeding; then they dilate. Dilation expands blood flow to the injured region, causing the redness and warmth that identify inflammation. The elevated blood supply also brings in an army of leukocytes to combat invading microscopic life forms, like bacteria, that would otherwise use the local injury as a beachhead into the body.

> **?** It is true that millions of microscopic warriors in your body are engaged in search-and-destroy missions against invading microbes as you read this page. They are leukocytes and they form the basis for the body's immune response.

Effects of Stress on the Immune System

Psychologists and medical researchers have recently opened a new field of study that concerns relationships between psychological factors and the immune response: **psychoneuroimmunology** (Schindler, 1985). One of the chief concerns of psychoneuroimmunology lies in the effects of stress on the immune system.

In Chapter 4 it was noted that persistent stressors eventually exhaust our capacities to cope. One reason for this is that stress incites the production of steroids. Steroids, in turn, suppress the activity of the immune system. Steroids have negligible effects when they are intermittently produced. Continuous secretion, however, decreases inflammation and disrupts the generation of antibodies. As a result, we grow more vulnerable to various diseases.

■ Empirical Findings in Psychoneuroimmunology
Research demonstrates the hypothesized stress–im-

mune system connection. Research also highlights the moderating effects of psychological factors like locus of control and social support in our responses to stress.

A study in which rats were shocked mirrors the Weiss (1972) experiment, as described in Chapter 4. This time, however, the dependent variable was immune system activity, not formation of ulcers (Laudenslager et al., 1983). The rats received unavoidable electric shocks, but, as in the Weiss study, one experimental group could exert control and end the shock. Other rats who could *not* do anything to terminate the shock showed decreased immune response, defined as lower levels of antibodies in their blood. But the rats who could terminate the shock exhibited no deficiency.

One study with humans recruited dental students (Jemmott et al., 1983). Saliva levels of immunoglobulin A, an antibody that combats a kind of bacteria that causes respiratory infection and dental cavities, were measured during stressful school periods and right after relaxing vacations. The students showed a weaker immune response, in terms of immunoglobulin A levels, during stressful school periods.

> **?** Stress can contribute to dental cavities by suppressing levels of antibodies that fight the bacteria that cause cavities.

Medical students, similarly, show poorer immune functioning during exam time than they do a month before exams, when their lives are generally less stressful (Glaser et al., 1985, 1986, 1987). Medical and dental students with fewer numbers of friends show a poorer immune response than students with more friends (Jemmott et al., 1983; Kiecolt-Glaser et al., 1984). Social support, it seems, buffers the stresses of school life as well as other stresses (McClelland, 1989). In one study, undergraduates were encouraged to think about selfless love by watching a film in which Mother Teresa of Calcutta cared for abandoned babies and sick people. The students showed significantly higher immunoglobulin A levels after viewing the film (McClelland & Kirshnit, 1988), but these levels returned to normal in about an hour. In a follow-up study, however, students were able to maintain enhanced immune system functioning, as assessed by immunoglobulin A levels, by thinking about loving experiences. McClelland (1989) speculates that people "who chronically think a lot about loving . . . might develop higher stable levels" of immunoglobulin A (1989, p. 678).

Another study with college students found that the stress produced by examinations suppressed the immune response to the Epstein-Barr virus, a nonlethal pathogen that causes fatigue and related problems (Kiecolt-Glaser et al., 1984). Consistent with the previously described study, lonely students showed greater

---

* Vaccination is the placement of a weakened form of an antigen in the body, which activates the creation of antibodies and memory lymphocytes. Smallpox has been annihilated by vaccination, and researchers are trying to develop a vaccine against the virus that causes AIDS.

Students show lower immunological response at times of high stress, such as during exams, than at times of low stress, such as immediately following relaxing vacations. Thus, we may be more susceptible to illness when we are under stress.

suppression of the immune response than did students with greater social support. In Chapter 4 we noted that major "life events" are stressful. It turns out that people who undergo more such life events also show lower antibody levels (Irwin et al., 1987). Newly separated and divorced people also show suppressed immune response, especially those who remain more attached to their ex-partners (Kiecolt-Glaser et al., 1987, 1988).

Research in the field of psychoneuroimmunology remains mostly correlational. Most studies have examined immunological functioning in relation to certain sources or times of stress, such as loneliness or examination periods, and among certain groups of people who may be subject to particular stresses, such as bereaved

widows or widowers, and newly divorced or separated men and women. Correlational research, as you will recall from Chapter 1, helps researchers understand the relationships between variables, some of which may be causally explained. But correlation does not prove causation. Preparing for a medical examination may be stressful and stress may depress immunological functioning, but we can't say whether it is the stress of the examination or some other factor that **co-varies** with stress that is causally responsible for the lowered immunological response. Perhaps students preparing for examination sleep less than they usually do, or eat irregularly. Changes in sleep or eating patterns might be causally responsible for immunological changes, not the stress itself of preparing for the examination. Bereavement may be causally related to immunological changes, but it's possible that a third (co-varying) factor is the causal influence and explains the relationship between bereavement and immunological response. Perhaps bereaved widows or widowers, like college students preparing for an exam, sleep or eat irregularly. We would need to account for these other factors to establish a causal connection between the variables of interest. But even if we were to account for these likely co-varying factors, it's possible we may have overlooked some other factor that may in fact be the causal agent. That is why correlational research needs to be followed by carefully designed experiments that isolate the variables of interest under controlled conditions.

Some controlled research has demonstrated that specific forms of psychological treatment can enhance immunological functioning. One experiment with elderly people demonstrated that a combination of relaxation training and training in coping skills *enhanced* the functioning of the immune-system (Kiecolt-Glaser et al., 1985). Immunological functioning is known to decline with age, so efforts to help improve immune function in the elderly could conceivably increase their resistance to disease and even prolong their lives. Other controlled research has shown that writing about traumatic events that one has experienced in the past led to improved immunological functioning (Pennebaker et al., 1988). The process of holding back or inhibiting thoughts or feelings about traumatic events may place a stressful burden on the autonomic nervous system, leading over time to the development of stress-related disorders. Confronting the trauma by talking or writing about it may free the individual from the need to inhibit or hold back these thoughts and feelings. However, we note that the validity of the study by Pennebaker and his colleagues has been challenged on statistical grounds (Neil, 1988). Research in this area is still in an early stage of development and we await the findings of additional research to see how behavioral treatment may affect immunological functioning.

Research has also begun to see if immunological

response among individuals infected with the HIV (AIDS) virus might be enhanced by interventions that focus on increasing the individual's personal and social resources for handling stress. We will have more to say later in the chapter about the challenge to psychology and other health professionals posed by the AIDS epidemic.

HEADACHES

Headaches are symptomatic of many medical disorders. When they occur in the absence of other symptoms, however, they are often assumed to be stress-related. Severe headaches are one of the more widespread stress-related physical disorders, affecting as many as 45 million Americans (Bonica, 1980).

The muscle-tension headache is the most frequently reported kind of headache. Persistent stress can lead us to persistently contract the muscles of the face, scalp, neck, and shoulders, leading to muscle-tension headaches. Such headaches develop gradually, and are generally characterized by a dull, steady pain on both halves of the head and by feelings of pressure or tightness.

Most other types of headaches, including migraine headaches, are thought to involve changes in the blood supply to the brain. Migraine headaches affect perhaps as many as 18 million Americans (Brody, 1988). Typical migraines affect one side of the brain, lasting for hours, even for days. They may occur as often as daily or as seldom as every other month. Piercing or throbbing sensations may become so intense that they seem intolerable. Sleep, mood, and thinking processes may be affected as the individual's mental state becomes dominated by the misery of a brutal migraine.

In the so-called classic migraine, an aura, or cluster of warning sensations, precedes the attack of about one migraine sufferer in five. Auras are typified by perceptual distortions, such as flashing lights, bizarre images, or blind spots. These sensations are apparently connected with fluctuations of the serotonin and norepinephrine available to the brain. The so-called common migraine is characterized by sudden onset and sensations of throbbing on but one side of the head. Migraine attacks are frequently accompanied by exquisite sensitivity to light; nausea and vomiting; loss of appetite; sensory disturbances; loss of balance; and mood changes.

that people may respond to the same stressor in idiosyncratic ways. Differences in response may reflect a combination of genetic influences, histories of learning, and ways of encoding experience. In classic research reported more than 40 years ago, Malmo and Shagass (1949) used the same pain-inducing stimulus with patients with muscular complaints (in this case, backaches) and patients with hypertension. The hypertensive patients responded to the stimulus with larger changes in the heart rate, whereas the backache group showed greater muscle contractions. Thus, tension-headache sufferers may be more likely to respond to stress by tensing the muscles of the forehead, shoulders, and neck.

According to the vascular model formulated by Harold Wolff in 1938, migraine attacks reflect stress-related changes in the blood vessels supplying the head. Under stress, the blood vessels in some parts of the brain become constricted while the blood vessels in other parts of the brain dilate. These contrasting effects produce throbbing, piercing sensations. Today, many theorists have replaced the vascular theory with the belief that individuals who are prone to migraine attacks may have a genetically caused dysfunction in the brain mechanisms responsible for regulating the amount of serotonin in the brain (Brady, 1988). Disregulation of other neurotransmitters, such as norepinephrine, may also be involved in causing the symptoms associated with migraine attacks. From this perspective, the constriction or dilation of blood vessels may be just another effect of serotonin disregulation, rather than the direct cause of the migraine headache. The drugs that are most helpful against migraine attacks, such as ergotamine, appear to affect the levels of serotonin in the brain (Brody, 1988), lending further support to the disregulation theory. Further research is necessary to clarify the relationships between neurotransmitter disregulation, the blood supply to the head, and migraine headaches.

Given a genetic predisposition to migraines (the diathesis), many situational factors (sources of stress) are implicated in attacks. These include stress itself; stimuli like bright lights; barometric pressure; pollen; certain drugs; the chemical monosodium glutamate (MSG), which is often used to enhance the flavor of food; and red wine. Hormonal changes of the sort that affect women prior to and during menstruation can also trigger attacks, and the incidence of migraines among women is about twice that among men.

Theoretical Perspectives

Why, under stress, do some people develop tension headaches? One possible answer is found in the principle of **individual response specificity,** which holds

Treatment

Aspirin and ibuprofen (brand names Medipren, Nuprin, Advil, etc.) often relieve pain, such as headache pain, by inhibiting the production of hormones (prostaglan-

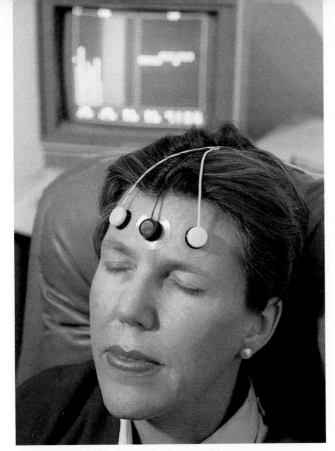

Psychological techniques such as biofeedback and relaxation training have been shown to help headache sufferers. The woman pictured here suffers from tension headaches and is receiving biofeedback training to help her learn to relax muscle tension in her forehead.

dins) that are involved in the transmission of pain messages to the brain. Ergotamine, as noted, helps many migraine sufferers, possibly by regulating serotonin levels in the brain.

The behavioral methods of relaxation training and biofeedback are also of help. Progressive relaxation, which focuses on reducing muscle tension, is particularly helpful in relieving tension headache pain (Blanchard et al., 1985, 1987; Teders et al., 1984). Relaxation training with biofeedback has also been shown to be effective.

Biofeedback training (BFT) helps people gain control over various physiological functions, such as muscle tension or brain wave patterns, by providing them with information or *feedback* about these functions in the form of an auditory signal (a ''bleep'') or visual display. The person learns to attend to ways of making the signal change in the desired direction.

Electromyographic (EMG) biofeedback relays information about muscle tension in the forehead by means of an electromyograph or EMG. EMG biofeedback can help people become better aware of their muscle tension and how to reduce it. Blanchard and his colleagues (1985, 1987) have successfully treated between 50 to 60 percent of tension-headache sufferers with relaxation training, or with relaxation and EMG

biofeedback when relaxation alone does not do the job. Tension-headache patients treated with biofeedback and relaxation generally maintained initial reductions of headache pain for four years following treatment (Blanchard et al., 1987).

Thermal biofeedback training for migraine headaches alters the blood supply to the head and is thus connected with the vascular model (Blanchard et al., 1985; 1987). One way of providing thermal feedback is by attaching a **thermistor** to a finger. A console ''bleeps'' more slowly* as the temperature rises. The temperature rises because more blood is flowing into the limb—away from the head. The client can imagine the finger growing warmer to facilitate the change in the body's distribution of blood. In one study, relaxation training combined with thermal biofeedback led to improvement in 52 percent of migraine and combined migraine/tension headache subjects (Blanchard et al., 1985). Migraine sufferers showed slight but not significant reductions in treatment gains through the course of a four-year follow-up period (Blanchard et al., 1987).

? Some people have in fact relieved migraine headaches by raising the temperature in a finger. This biofeedback technique modifies patterns of blood flow throughout the body.

As we learn more about the relationships among neurotransmitters, vascular factors, and pain, headache treatments are bound to become more effective.

MENSTRUAL PROBLEMS

Women, the old argument goes, are eternally subject to the whims and wherefores of their biological clocks. Their raging hormonal cycles make them emotionally unstable and intellectually unreliable. If women have second-class status, we are told, it is because they cannot control the implacable demands of that bouncing estrogen. (Karen Paige, 1973, p. 41)

Many women have menstrual discomfort. Painful menstruation is believed to affect nearly 75 percent of women (Wildman & White, 1986). Kinds of menstrual symptoms reflect the nature of the research samples. Women who have been pregnant may experience a lower incidence of menstrual pain but a higher incidence of premenstrual symptoms and menstrual discomfort (Wildman & White, 1986).

As pointed out by psychologist Karen Paige, the

---

* Or more rapidly. The choice of direction is decided by the therapist or therapist and client.

stereotype of women has been that "raging hormones" doom them to irritability and poor judgment at this time of the month. Because of this view, many women have been denied opportunities to take on responsible positions in society. Research reports during the 1960s and 1970s were not helpful to women either. The British investigator Katharina Dalton reported that the grades of English schoolgirls decline during the eight days prior to and including menstruation. Later, Dalton (1972, 1980) reported that women are more likely to commit suicide or crimes, call in sick at work, and develop physical and emotional problems before or during menstruation. We will see that Dalton's reports exaggerate menstrual problems.

There are several types of menstrual problems. The term *dysmenorrhea* refers in general to menstrual pain or discomfort. In some cases, the dysmenorrhea is *secondary*, or caused by, organic problems. Endometriosis, pelvic inflammatory disease, and ovarian cysts are just a few of the organic disorders that give rise to secondary dysmenorrhea. In *primary dysmenorrhea*, there is no apparent organic pathology that explains the menstrual discomfort. But research evidence is accumulating that so-called primary dysmenorrhea may actually be *secondary*, in many cases, to hormonal changes, even though the exact relationships have not been defined.

A recent survey of 420 female undergraduate psychology students aged 17 to 25 found that menstrual complaints in these women, all of whom were believed to be free of any organic causes of menstrual discomfort, could be broken down into three clusters of symptoms: menstrual pain; physiological discomfort during menstruation; and premenstrual symptoms, or **premenstrual syndrome (PMS),** which is usually confined to a four-day interval prior to menstruation (Wildman & White, 1986). PMS is characterized by psychological and physiological symptoms—including irritability and depression, weight gain (from buildup of fluids), and abdominal discomfort.

About three in four women experience premenstrual physical or emotional changes, according to survey results, with most complaints falling in the mild or moderate range of severity (Brody, 1989). Only about 10 percent of women report symptoms severe enough to impair their social, academic, or occupational functioning. Despite Dalton's claims, only a small percentage miss work because of them. Fewer than 1 percent of the employed women in another recent survey reported missing work because of menstrual problems (Gruber & Wildman, 1987). Despite Dalton's reports to the effect that menstruation hurt the grades of schoolgirls, there is no reliable evidence of decline in academic performance at this time of the month (Walsh et al., 1981). The accompanying "A Closer Look" section examines a proposed diagnostic category that focuses on the small

---

A CLOSER LOOK
Late Luteal Phase Disorder?

The DSM–III–R includes a diagnosis of late luteal phase (premenstrual) dysphoric disorder (LLPD) as a proposed diagnostic category that requires further study. LLPD would apply to the minority of women whose premenstrual discomfort is persistent and intense enough to markedly affect their ability to function in their social and occupational roles. But several difficulties with the proposed diagnosis have been identified (Gallant, 1988).

The LLPD diagnosis may prove difficult to study because of the vagueness of diagnostic criteria and because of reliance on self-reports of complaints. Concern has also been raised that the diagnostic category may stigmatize women with severe PMS by labeling them with a psychiatric diagnosis. The diagnosis may also abet tendencies to blame the victim by attributing her pain and suffering to a mental, rather than a physical, condition. There are also legal implications to the diagnosis, since it could possibly be used as a basis for an insanity plea in cases in which women are accused of violent crimes. Women so diagnosed may also encounter prejudice in the workplace from employers who expect them to fall short in their work performance or attendance on a monthly basis. For reasons such as these, it's been suggested that alternatives to the LLPD diagnosis should be explored (Gallant, 1988)

---

percentage of women whose menstrual distress seriously disrupts their lives.

Theoretical Perspectives

There is growing evidence showing a link between hormone levels and mood in women. Judith Bardwick (Bardwick, 1971; Ivey & Bardwick, 1968) found women's moods to be most positive during ovulation, when estrogen levels peak. Karen Paige (1971) studied women whose hormone levels were kept rather even by birth-control pills and others whose hormone levels varied naturally throughout the cycle. She found that women whose hormone levels fluctuated appeared to show somewhat greater anxiety and hostility prior to and during menstruation. However, they did not exhibit extreme behaviors, commit crimes, or wind up in mental hospitals.

It has been suggested that PMS may reflect unusually high levels of estradiol (an estrogen) and progesterone, or an imbalance in levels between the two (Rubinow & Roy-Byrne, 1984). One well-controlled study tracked the hormone levels of women with and without PMS through a complete menstrual cycle (Trunnel et al., 1988). Women without PMS showed little change in emotional or physical symptoms throughout their cycles. Women with PMS, however, suffered more de-

A CLOSER LOOK
How to Handle Menstrual Discomfort

The majority of women have some menstrual discomfort. Most of them remind themselves that it is normal and then focus their attention elsewhere. But the minority of women who encounter more severe pain may profit from some of the following suggestions:

1. Don't blame yourself! Menstrual problems were once erroneously attributed to women's "hysterical" nature. This is nonsense. Menstrual problems in large part reflect hormonal variations during the menstrual cycle. Researchers have not yet fully identified all the causal elements and patterns, but their lack of knowledge does not make sufferers hysterical.

2. Keep a menstrual calendar so that you can anticipate your worst days. Develop strategies for dealing with these days that enhance the pleasure you receive or reduce the stress affecting you on those days. Distract yourself. Go see a movie or get into that novel you've been meaning to read.

3. Ask yourself whether you harbor self-defeating attitudes toward menstruation that might be compounding distress. Do any family members see menstruation as an illness, a time of "pollution," or as a dirty thing? Have you adopted any of these attitudes—if not verbally, then in your behavior?

4. See a doctor about your concerns. Severe menstrual symptoms are often secondary to medical disorders like endometriosis and pelvic inflammatory disease (PID). Check it out.

5. Develop nutritious eating habits—throughout the entire cycle (that means always). Consider limiting intake of alcohol, caffeine, fats, salt, and sweets, especially during the days preceding menstruation.

6. Spirited exercise may be helpful, including jogging, swimming, bicycling, fast walking, dancing, skating, even jumprope. Exercise is associated with changes in hormones and neurotransmitters. Moreover, the woman who exercises is not taking dysmenorrhea "lying down"! She remains active, the master of her physical fate. By the way, develop regular exercise habits—don't seek to become a premenstrual athlete.

Regular vigorous exercise may help reduce menstrual discomfort.

7. Diuretics may lessen bloating and weight gain, although they do not affect emotional changes. Ask your doctor.

8. Check with your doctor about vitamin and mineral supplements (such as calcium and magnesium). Vitamin B-6 appears to have helped some women.

9. Ibuprofen (brand names Medipren, Advil, Motrin [Motrin is prescription strength], etc.) may be helpful with cramping. But check first with your doctor before taking any medication, even those sold over the counter. Other medications prescribed by your doctor may also be helpful.

10. Remind yourself that menstrual problems are time-limited. Don't worry about getting through "life" or a career. Focus on just getting through the next couple of days.

pression and physical symptoms, but only during the luteal phase of their menstrual cycles. So PMS appears to be phase-specific; women who suffer from PMS are not otherwise psychological or physically impaired. On the other hand, results concerning hormone-level differences between the groups were inconclusive. In sum, though most researchers believe that PMS reflects changes in estrogen and progesterone, they have not yet clearly identified differences in levels or actions of these hormones between women with severe symptoms and those with milder symptoms or no symptoms (Brody, 1989).

Prostaglandins, which as you'll recall from Chapter 4 are involved in transmission of pain messages, may also play a role in menstrual distress. Prostaglandins are hormones secreted by the uterus that cause muscle fibers in the uterine wall to contract, as during labor. Most contractions go unnoticed, but strong, unrelieved contractions are uncomfortable in themselves and may temporarily deprive the uterus of oxygen, another source of pain (American College of Obstetricians and Gynecologists, 1985). The painful cramping reported by many women prior to and during menstruation appears related to copious secretion of prostaglandins. In such cases prostaglandin-inhibiting drugs such as ibuprofen and indomethacin help many women (Owen, 1984).

Psychological factors also appear to play a role in menstrual problems. In a survey by Gruber and Wildman (1987), for example, perception of menstruation as debilitating was actually a more powerful predictor of absenteeism from work than was discomfort itself. Some women respond to negative cultural attitudes toward menstruation as well as to menstrual symptoms (Brooks-Gunn & Ruble, 1980; Sherif, 1980). In some societies, menstruating women have even been consigned to special living quarters because of expectations of foul temper (Paige, 1977). The historical view of menstruation as a time of pollution (Fisher, 1980; Paige, 1978) may make women highly sensitive to internal sensations at certain times of the month, as well as make them concerned about discreet disposal of the menstrual flow. Women who do not share highly traditional cultural attitudes—including attitudes about the debilitating nature of menstruation—are less likely to show mood changes throughout the different phases of the menstrual cycle (Paige, 1973).

HYPERTENSION

Ten to 30 percent of Americans are reported to have **hypertension,** or high blood pressure (Seer, 1979). Every contraction (or beat) of the heart expels blood from the heart and through blood vessels, causing them to dilate. The blood vessels also dilate and constrict according to internal biological factors and external factors, like stress. Your blood pressure (BP) is the pressure that blood exerts on the walls of your blood vessels. Blood pressure varies according to the degree of constriction of the blood vessels. The more constricted the vessels, the harder it is for the blood to squeeze through, and the higher the BP. In most people, when the BP rises beyond normal limits, so-called baroreceptors (*baro* derives from the Greek *baros*, meaning "weight" or "pressure") signal the brain, which, in turn, relaxes the walls of the blood vessels.

In hypertensive people the system works inadequately, leaving the vessel walls constricted. In a minority of cases, the vessel walls remain constricted and the BP remains high because of known organic problems, such as kidney malfunction (Shapiro & Goldstein, 1982). When high BP has no identifiable organic cause,

it is termed *essential hypertension.* Hypertension predisposes people to cardiovascular disorders like **arteriosclerosis** (thickening of the walls of the arteries), heart attacks, and strokes (Berkman et al., 1983). Since elevated blood pressure can damage the cardiovascular system for years without producing any noticeable symptoms, it is crucial to have your BP checked periodically.

 People actually tend *not* to recognize high blood pressure.

Theoretical Perspectives

Stressors like high levels of noise can raise the blood pressure (Cohen et al., 1979). In an industrial setting, workers over age 55 who had suffered hearing loss, presumably from prolonged exposure to workplace noise, showed significantly higher BP than age-mates who had not suffered hearing loss (Talbott et al., 1985). Blood pressure also becomes elevated in situations requiring continuous vigilance, whether people are in combat, in the workplace, at home, or stuck in traffic. Commuting on congested highways is connected with elevated BP, increases in heart rate, and reports of chest pains (Stokols & Novaco, 1981). However, some people may also be predisposed to hypertension, and develop it while the rest of us do not. Most research into the predisposition, or diathesis, has been conducted from the psychodynamic and biological perspectives.

The prevailing psychodynamic perspective has

Job-related stressors, such as noise and demand for continuous vigilance, may increase the blood pressure. The commodities traders pictured here are exposed to high levels of job-related stress throughout the workday.

been that hypertensive people have difficulty expressing pent-up feelings of anger (Alexander, 1939). According to traditional psychodynamic theory, people's psychological functioning is akin to a steam engine. The buildup of emotions creates pressures that must be vented, if the system is to avert disaster. In hypertension, pent-up feelings press against a biological barrier—the walls of blood vessels, threatening to rupture, as in a stroke. Some supportive evidence has been found by Diamond (1982): normal (nonhypertensive) people show elevated BP when they are angered. Their BP remains elevated as long as they suppress their feelings, but returns to normal if they vent them.

From the biological perspective, essential hypertension may reflect overresponsiveness of the cardiovascular system to stress (Steptoe et al., 1984). So-called **hot reactors,** for example, respond to stress with quickened heart rate and constriction of blood vessels in peripheral areas of the body, whereas others do not (Eliot & Buell, 1983). Evidence that cardiovascular responsiveness to stress—the diathesis—might have genetic origins is found in the fact that blacks are more likely to suffer hypertension than whites (Diamond, 1982; Harburg et al., 1973).

Treatment

High BP is frequently controlled by medicine. Unfortunately, because of lack of symptoms, many hypertensive patients fail to take their medication reliably, if at all, because they don't "feel sick." Dietary components, especially sodium (salt), can elevate the BP. Dietary restrictions are therefore part of the usual treatment program for hypertensives.

One study underscored the potential of dietary behavior modification in the treatment of hypertension. The subjects were 496 hypertension patients whose BP had been maintained within normal limits by medication for five years (Langford et al., 1985). Medication was discontinued and patients were assigned to a general weight-loss diet or to a sodium-restricted diet. Both dietary approaches worked for the majority of patients: 72 percent of the weight-loss group and 78 percent of the sodium-restricted group maintained normal BP without medication.

Behavioral methods like relaxation training and meditation show promise in treating high BP (Agras et al., 1983; Benson et al., 1983.) In one study, hypertensive patients received training in progressive relaxation. Some supplemented clinic training with home practice. Both relaxation training groups significantly reduced their BP by comparison with a control group placed on a waiting list (Hoelscher et al., 1987).

Many hypertensive patients require two drugs to normalize their BP, which boosts costs and the potential for side effects. Some two-drug patients may be able to substitute behavioral methods for at least one of them, however. A study by Blanchard and his colleagues (1986) compared the effectiveness of two behavioral treatments—thermal biofeedback and relaxation training. Nearly two out of three patients (65 percent) receiving thermal biofeedback were successfully withdrawn from the second medication for at least two months. By comparison, only 27 percent of the relaxation-training patients could successfully discontinue the second drug. At one year follow-up, about one-third of the biofeedback patients (35 percent) maintained normalized BP on a single drug. The modest long-term results of the study indicate that more work needs to be done to see if the overall rate of effectiveness of combining behavioral treatment with a single-drug approach can be increased. Nevertheless, the study suggests that psychological methods have a place in supplementing the medical armamentarium for hypertension.

CARDIOVASCULAR DISORDERS

Cardiovascular disorders account for nearly half the deaths in the United States (U.S. Department of Health and Human Services, 1984). They include heart disease and disorders of the circulatory system, the most common of which is stroke.

Coronary heart disease (CHD), also called arteriosclerotic heart disease, accounts for more than 1.5 million deaths per year. About 700,000 people are hospitalized for heart attacks each year (Kaplan, 1988). The American Heart Association estimates that more than 4,000 Americans suffer a heart attack each day (Blumenthal & Emery, 1988). CHD is the leading cause of death among men over the age of 40 and women over the age of 70. But there is some good news: There has been a 20 percent decline in age-adjusted deaths in the past 20 years (Rosenberg et al., 1979).

The disease process in CHD is arteriosclerosis, or thickening of the walls of the blood vessels, which impedes the passage of blood. A major cause of arteriosclerosis is **atherosclerosis,** or buildup of fatty deposits in the blood vessels, thickening them and causing them to lose their elasticity. The deposits clog the blood vessels serving the heart, gradually decreasing their diameter and eventually obstructing the flow of blood to the heart. Obstruction leads to the destruction of muscular tissue of the heart—causing a **myocardial infarction,** or heart attack (Blumenthal & Emery, 1988).

Risk Factors

There are several risk factors for CHD that researchers have identified:

1. *Age.* The risk of CHD increases sharply with age from about 40 upward. For men, the rate of increase is steady. For women, it is slow until menopause and then increases rapidly (Jenkins, 1988).

2. *Sex.* Men are victimized by CHD twice as frequently as women. The mortality rate among women approximates that of men 15 years younger. A 65-year-old woman has about the same risk of dying from a heart attack as a man of 50 (Jenkins, 1988). It has been hypothesized that men are at greater risk because they possess a disproportionate number of other risk factors like smoking, Type A behavior, and pressure at work (Waldron, 1976).

3. *Family history.* People with family histories of cardiovascular disease are more likely to develop cardiovascular disease themselves (Feist & Brannon, 1988). It was surprising when running enthusiast James Fixx died a few years ago because he had been running ten six-minute miles a day. However, his family history of CHD was against him, and his running might have staved off death for many years.

4. *Socioeconomic status* (SES). Persons of low SES are at greater risk for CHD than persons higher in SES. Persons of lower SES are more likely to smoke, less likely to watch their diets, and more likely to encounter various kinds of stresses and strains (Jenkins, 1988).

5. *Physiological conditions.* Such conditions include obesity, hypertension, and high levels of **serum cholesterol**.

6. *Patterns of consumption.* Such patterns include heavy drinking, smoking, overeating and/or eating high cholesterol foods (Epstein & Perkins, 1988; Jeffery, 1988; Jenkins, 1988; Stamler et al., 1986).

How many risk factors for cardiovascular disease can you identify in this photograph?

7. *Type A behavior.* Evidence implicating the Type A behavior pattern as a risk factor for CHD remains unclear. Still, it is a possible risk factor.

8. *Work overload.* Overtime work, assembly-line labor, and exposure to conflicting demands all make their contributions (Jenkins, 1988).

9. *Chronic fatigue and emotional strain.*

10. *A physically inactive life-style.*

Notice something about the first three risk factors: You can't do anything about them. Notice something about the last six: You can do something about these. Let us consider some of the risk factors we can alter, beginning with obesity.

■ **Obesity**   Obesity is a major risk factor for CHD (Hubert et al., 1983; Jenkins, 1988). Obesity may do its harm through the accumulation of body fat, the heightening of cholesterol levels, or elevating the blood pressure (Jenkins, 1988).

One frequently cited study of the obesity–CHD relationship followed 2,252 men and 2,818 women in Framingham, Massachusetts (Blumenthal et al., 1978; Dawber, 1980; Haynes et al., 1980, 1983; Zyzanski, et al., 1976). Participants were first assessed between 1948 and 1950, then reexamined every two years for a period of 26 years. Initial levels of obesity predicted CHD throughout the duration of the study. Later weight gains were also linked to CHD. The incidence of CHD might have been reduced by 25 percent if everyone had maintained an optimal weight. Later in the chapter we shall learn more about obesity and discuss methods of weight control.

■ **Cholesterol**   Although much attention has been paid to the role of serum cholesterol as a risk factor in CHD, we have recently grown aware of the distinction between so-called bad cholesterol (low-density lipoprotein, or LDL) and good cholesterol (high-density lipoprotein, or HDL). LDL is believed to increase risk for CHD, whereas HDL is actually thought to lower the risk of CHD (Jenkins, 1988). LDL is found in animal fats (including the fat in whole milk). The body also converts so-called saturated fats to cholesterol, so even vegetable matter that does not contain cholesterol may be dangerous if it is high in saturated fats. Coconut and palm oils and cashew nuts are examples of plant foods high in saturated fats. Regular exercise also appears to lower the level of harmful (LDL) cholesterol in the blood.

■ **Alcohol**   High levels of alcohol are harmful to the heart, but low to moderate levels (for example, a drink a day) may actually reduce the risk of CHD and certain kinds of strokes by lowering the level of LDL in the blood (Jenkins, 1988; Stampfer & Hennekens, 1988).

We shall pursue this issue at greater length in Chapter 10. Let us note here, however, that no researchers suggest that abstainers purposefully begin imbibing in order to reduce their risks of CHD.

■ **Smoking**   As compared to nonsmokers, smokers stand about twice the chance of developing or dying from CHD (USDHHS, 1983). The level of risk is directly related to the daily number of cigarettes smoked and to the percentage of tar and nicotine in the cigarettes (Jenkins, 1988; Pettite & Friedman, 1985). On the other hand, people who quit smoking before the age of 65 can reduce the risk of CHD by as much as 50 percent (Kannel et al., 1984). The longer an ex-smoker remains abstinent, the lower the risk of CHD (USDHHS, 1983). Smoking may intensify the effects of stress on the cardiovascular system, thereby increasing the risk of CHD to a greater extent than either factor would in itself (Epstein & Perkins, 1988).

■ **Type A Behavior**   The next risk factor we discuss is the Type A behavior pattern (TABP). But before proceeding, we invite you to complete the following questionnaire.

The Type A behavior pattern (TABP) is usually assessed by a structured interview or by a self-rating scale similar to the one you filled out—the Jenkins Activity Survey.

QUESTIONNAIRE
Are You Type A or Type B?

Place a check mark under Yes if the behavior pattern described is typical of you. Place one under No if it is not. Work rapidly and answer all items. Then check the scoring key at the end of the chapter.

DO YOU: Yes   No

1. Strongly emphasize important words in your ordinary speech?
2. Walk briskly from place to place or meeting to meeting?
3. Think that life is by nature dog-eat-dog?
4. Get fidgety when you see someone complete a job slowly?
5. Urge others to complete what they're trying to express?
6. Find it exceptionally annoying to get stuck in line?
7. Envision all the things you have to do even when someone is talking to you?
8. Eat while you're getting dressed, or jot down notes while you're driving?
9. Catch up on work during vacations?
10. Direct the conversation to things that interest you?
11. Feel as if things are going to pot because you're relaxing for a few minutes?
12. Get so wrapped up in your work that you fail to notice beautiful scenery passing by?
13. Get so wrapped up in money, promotions, and awards that you neglect expressing your creativity?
14. Schedule appointments and meetings back to back?
15. Arrive early for appointments and meetings?
16. Make fists or clench your jaws to drill home your views?
17. Think that you have achieved what you have because of your ability to work fast?
18. Have the feeling that uncompleted work must be done *now* and quickly?
19. Try to find more efficient ways to get things done?
20. Struggle always to win games instead of having fun?
21. Interrupt people who are talking?
22. Lose patience with people who are late for appointments and meetings?
23. Get back to work right after lunch?
24. Find that there's never enough time?
25. Believe that you're getting too little done, even when other people tell you that you're doing fine?

Type A personalities approach their work with great intensity and feel pressured to get things done rapidly.

Type A people are impatient, competitve, and aggressive (Matthews et al., 1982; Holmes & Will, 1985). They feel rushed, under pressure; they keep one eye glued to the clock. They are prompt and often early for appointments (Strahan, 1981). They walk, talk, and eat rapidly. They grow restless when others work slowly (Musante et al., 1983). They try to dominate group discussions (Yarnold et al., 1985). Type A people do not easily relinquish control or share power (Miller et al., 1985; Strube & Werner, 1985). They are loath to delegate power in the workplace, and consequently expand their own work loads. They also "accentuate the negative": Type A people are ruthless in self-reproach when they fall short on an assignment (Brunson & Matthews, 1981). Moreover, they hunt out their shortcomings to improve themselves (Cooney & Zeichner, 1985).

Type A people don't just jaunt out on the tennis court to bat the ball around. They scrutinize their form, polish their strokes, and demand consistent self-improvement. They guide their lives by the irrational belief that they must excel at everything they undertake.

Type B people, by contrast, relax readily and can focus on the quality of life. Type B's are less ambitious and less irritable; they pace themselves. Type A's perceive time to pass more swiftly than do Type B's and work more briskly (Yarnold & Grimm, 1982). Type A's tend to earn more money and better grades than do Type B's who are equal in intelligence (Glass, 1977). Type A's also pursue more challenging tasks than do

Type B's (Ortega & Pipal, 1984). Sad to say, Type A's tend to respond to challenge with higher blood pressure (Holmes et al., 1984).

■ Type A Behavior and CHD: Conflicting Evidence

Many studies have found that the Type A behavior pattern (TABP) places people at greater risk for CHD than the Type B behavior pattern (for example, Bernardo et al., 1985; Cohen & Reed, 1985; DeBacker et al., 1983; French-Belgian Collaborative Group, 1982; Weiss & Richter-Heinrich, 1985).

One of the primary studies that supported the Type A–CHD connection was the Western Collaborative Group Study. The study followed 3,200 initially healthy men for eight and one-half years. TABP men in the study showed twice the incidence of CHD and five times the incidence of recurrent heart attacks throughout the period (Rosenman et al., 1975). Eight- and ten-year longitudinal studies in Framingham, Massachusetts, found that Type A men and women were about twice as likely as Type B men and women to develop CHD (Haynes et al., 1980, 1983). The Type A effect was more pronounced among men: The incidence of CHD was nearly three times as high among male Type A white-collar workers as among male Type B white-collar workers. The TABP was also connected with development of atherosclerosis among men referred for cardiovascular evaluation (Blumenthal et al., 1978; Zyzanski, et al., 1976). Young Type A women were at greater risk than Type B women by a factor of about 2.5, but for women, the Type A–Type B difference in risk decreased with age.

But just when it seemed accepted that Type A behavior predisposed people to cardiovascular disease, a fascinating reversal of findings occurred in the TABP literature. During the first 20 years of investigation, TABP was consistently associated with increased incidence of CHD (Jenkins, 1988). Since 1980, however, the research pendulum has swung in the opposite direction. Large-scale surveys, such as the Multiple Risk Factor Intervention Trial (MRFIT), which studied 12,700 men from 1973 to 1982, and the Aspirin Myocardial Infarction Study (Shekelle et al., 1985) have failed to confirm the TABP–CHD connection. Other studies have failed to demonstrate a relationship between TABP and development of atherosclerosis (Dimsdale et al., 1978; Krantz et al., 1981), or between TABP and recurrent heart attacks among male cardiac patients (Case et al., 1985).

In a study published in the *New England Journal of Medicine*, Ragland and Brand (1988) found that the TABP actually placed men at *lower risk* for recurrent heart attacks than the Type B behavior pattern. The researchers followed 257 heart attack victims for a dozen years. The death rate for the 160 Type A patients was 19.1 per thousand person-years. (A person-year is defined as the number of patients times the number of years of survival.) The death rate for the 71 Type B patients was 31.7 per thousand person-years. In other words, five Type B patients died for every three Type A patients who died.

Explaining the discrepancies in studies of the TABP—CHD connection is no easy matter. Different studies used different measures of the Type A construct—some an interview measure and some a self-report activity survey—so perhaps the various definitions of the TABP account for part of the discrepancy (Leon et al., 1988). Meyer Friedman, one of the originators of the Type A concept, claims that the assignment of subjects to Type A and Type B categories in the MRFIT study was based on substandard interviewing techniques (Fischman, 1987). Krantz and his colleagues (1988) note that the studies that find no TABP—CHD link or find TABP associated with positive outcomes were based on samples of CHD patients or men at high risk, rather than the general population. Perhaps the TABP is not as sensitive a predictor of negative outcomes among CHD patients or high-risk individuals because it is so common among these groups. This interpretation is tempered, however, by studies that show that reducing the TABP through cognitive-behavioral techniques lowers the risk of recurrent heart attacks for CHD patients. Perhaps the clinical effectiveness of these treatments is due to a lessening of general levels of stress, or increased social support, rather than changes in the TABP per se.

> **?** Research actually is unclear as to whether or not Type A people are at greater risk for heart attacks.

Because the TABP—CHD connection remains uncertain, some investigators are focusing on the cardiovascular risks of various components of the TABP. Some researchers suggest that the proneness-to-hostility component predicts atherosclerosis and other aspects of CHD (Barefoot et al., 1983; Chesney & Rosenman, 1985; Friedman et al., 1985; Shekelle et al., 1983; Wright, 1988). Proneness to hostility is characterized by a tendency to react to frustrating situations with feelings of anger; hostility; irritation over petty annoyances, like waiting in line; and contempt for others (MacDougall; Dembroski, Dimsdale & Hacket, 1985; Mathews et al., 1977). However, some researchers have failed to confirm a relationship between hostility and later mortality and CHD (McCranie et al., 1980; Leon et al., 1988). Other researchers suggest that a factor related to hostility—expecting the worst from people, or cynicism—is the culprit. Still other researchers point

to the possible consequences of holding in rather than expressing anger—not only for hypertension, but also for CHD (see Dembroski et al., 1985; Spielberger et al., 1985).

It seems that there is no one-to-one relationship between any behavior pattern and CHD (Jenkins, 1988; Krantz et al., 1988). According to the principle of individual response specificity, different people's cardiovascular systems react to stress differently. And some people, including some Type A people, moderate the effects of stress successfully through psychological means of the kind discussed in Chapter 4. For example, Type A people who are psychologically hardy appear to be more resistant to illness, including CHD, than are Type A's who are not hardy (Booth-Kewley & Friedman, 1987; Friedman & Booth-Kewley, 1987; Kobasa et al., 1983; Rhodewalt & Agustsdottir, 1984).

Treatment of Type A Behavior Although the TABP—CHD association has been questioned, reducing the TABP, at least among people who have suffered heart attacks, appears to reduce the risk of future attacks.

Psychologists and other health care professionals have investigated ways to help people modify their Type A behaviors, through anxiety reduction techniques, cognitive behavior therapy techniques (Haaga, 1987), or rational-emotive therapy (Thurman, 1985a, 1985b). Successful interventions have been found to reduce Type A behavior patterns on self-administered inventories and directly observed behaviors (Roskie et al., 1986; Blumenthal, et al., 1987). Cardiac patients in such programs have shown favorable changes in blood pressure, serum cholesterol, perceptions of time urgency (Roskies et al., 1979), and physiological reactivity to stress (Razin et al., 1986). However, open questions remain about whether or not modifying Type A behavior reduces

Some researchers believe that proneness to hostility may be the most harmful feature of the TABP. However, the relationship between hostility and coronary heart disease remains unsettled. Still, it may be prudent for people to make behavioral changes that lessen their hostility.

health risks (Haaga, 1987). Methodological concerns have been expressed about such issues as the lack of consistency in the measurement of Type A behavior in TABP reduction programs, the lack of no-treatment control groups in a number of studies, and a need for replication of findings (Blumenthal & Emery, 1988).

The largest and best-controlled study in changing the TABP is the Recurrent Coronary Prevention Program (RCPP). RCPP focused on men who had suffered a heart attack in hope of preventing recurrence. Ninety-eight percent of the 868 men who participated were classified as Type A. Each had suffered a heart attack at least six months earlier and was under 65 years of age. The study used a controlled comparison of two types of treatment and a waiting list control group (Friedman et al., 1984; Powell et al., 1984). Subjects were divided into three groups:

1.   a health information condition that provided exercise, diet, and medical information

2.   a multimodal (comprehensive) treatment condition that combined health information with cognitive-behavioral treatment techniques, and

3.   a no-treatment condition.

The multimodal treatment incorporated training in relaxation and lifestyle changes designed to change the pace of daily life and reduce the sense of time urgency. Men who participated in multimodal therapy showed greater reductions in Type A behavior than did men in the health information condition. The rate of recurrence of cardiac events (defined as heart attacks and other cardiovascular incidents) among the men who received the multimodal treatment was significantly lower than among men in the other two groups (see Figure 5.1).

After three years, subjects in the multimodal group had only one-third as many recurrent heart attacks as did subjects in the control group (Friedman & Ulmer, 1984; Friedman et al., 1986). As promising as the RCPP is, there were so many facets to the multimodal treatment that it may be impossible to ferret out which were most beneficial.

■ **Physical Inactivity**   The heart is built of muscle tissue. Exercise has a healthful effect on the heart, as it does on other muscles. The sedentary life, in contrast, weakens the capacity of the heart, just as it saps the power of the large skeletal muscles.

Many health professionals recommend **aerobic** exercise as part of the overall treatment plan for people who are at risk for CHD and for people who have had a heart attack. Aerobic exercise requires a sustained increase in the consumption of oxygen. Aerobic exercises include running and jogging, brisk walking, aerobic dancing, jump rope, bicycle riding, basketball, swim-

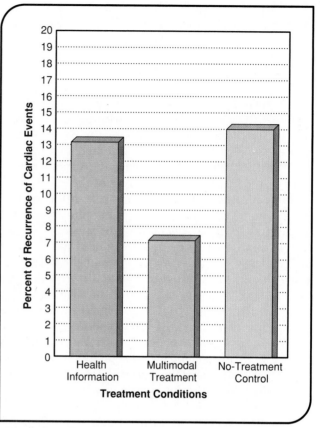

FIGURE 5.1 Results of the Recurrent Coronary Prevention Program (RCPP).
Men who received multimodal treatment were less likely to experience a recurrent cardiac event than were men who received health information only or were placed in a no-treatment control condition.

ming, racquetball, and cross-country skiing. Health professionals usually provide warm-up and cool-down periods, in addition to intervals of vigorous exercise. **Anaerobic exercises,** by contrast, involve short bursts of muscle activity, as in weight-training sports like baseball, in which there are infrequent bursts of strenuous activity. The cardiovascular benefits of exercise are obtained from aerobic exercise.

Aerobic exercise fosters cardiovascular *fitness*, or "condition." Fit people process larger quantities of oxygen during spirited activity and pump more blood per heartbeat (Pollock, et al., 1978). Since conditioned athletes pump more blood per beat, they have slower pulse rates—or fewer beats per minute. While they are exercising, however, they may double or even triple their resting heart rates for minutes at a time.

Aerobic activity also apparently reduces the risk of cardiovascular disorders in terms of incidence of heart attacks and overall mortality rates. An English study correlated the incidence of cardiovascular disease and physical exertion among transportation and postal workers (Morris et al., 1953). Conductors aboard London's double-decker buses, who continually moved

A CLOSER LOOK
Ways of Decreasing Type A Behavior

Cardiologist Meyer Friedman, an originator of the Type A concept, and Diane Ulmer reported some results of the San Francisco Recurrent Coronary Prevention Project (RCPP) in 1984. The RCPP was designed to help Type A heart-attack victims modify their behavior in an effort to avert future attacks.

Readers will find a thorough description of the treatment program in Friedman and Ulmer's *Treating Type A Behavior and Your Heart* (1984). Here we note broad guidelines and some specifics of the program. The three broad guidelines were alleviating men's sense of time urgency, hostility, and such self-destructive tendencies as gorging on high-fat foods, drinking heavily, smoking, and working excessively. The buffering effects of humor were noted also. Some specific suggestions follow; they were offered for helping participants alleviate the sense of time urgency and reduce hostility.

Alleviating the Sense of Time Urgency For Type A people, the day begins urgently and never lets up. The initial step in handling time urgency is to confront and alter the self-defeating beliefs that support it, such as "I can't do anything about it" (Friedman & Ulmer, 1984, p. 182) or "My sense of time urgency has helped me gain social and economic success" (p. 179).

Friedman and Ulmer counter that maladaptive habits can be changed even in later adulthood and that impatience and irritation do not contribute to success. They also offer the following suggestions to reduce the sense of time urgency:

1. Increase social activity with family and friends.
2. Each day, spend a few minutes recalling distant events. Peruse photos of family and old friends.
3. Read books—biographies, literature, drama, politics, nature, science, science fiction. (Books on business and on climbing the corporate ladder are not recommended!)
4. Visit art galleries and museums. Consider works for their aesthetic value, not their prices.
5. Go to the movies, theater, concerts, ballet.
6. Write letters to family and old friends.
7. Take an art course; begin violin or piano lessons.
8. Keep in mind that life is by nature unfinished. You needn't have all your projects finished by a certain date.
9. Ask family members what they did during the day. *Listen* to the answer.

Alleviating Hostility Some researchers believe that hostility is the most harmful feature of the TABP. Friedman and Ulmer (1984) write that hostility (like time urgency) is supported by irrational beliefs. It is helpful to recognize maladaptive, irrational beliefs and substitute adaptive beliefs. Some of the irrational beliefs they identified that support hostility include, "I need a certain amount of hostility to get ahead in the world" (p. 222), "Giving and receiving love is a sign of weakness" (p. 228), and "I can't do anything about my hostility" (p. 222). Countering beliefs include the recognition that instant irritation,

There are many ways in which people can reduce the sense of time urgency in their lives, including enjoyment of nature and family-oriented activities.

aggravation, and anger do not contribute to success, that giving and receiving love is not a sign of weakness, and, as above, behavior change can occur at any age.

In addition to challenging irrational ideas, Friedman and Ulmer (1984) offer suggestions like these for alleviating hostility:

1. Tell your family that you love them.
2. Make new friends.
3. Let friends know that you are available to help them.
4. Get a pet and care for it.
5. Don't get involved in discussions that you know lead to pointless arguments.
6. When others do things that disappoint you, consider situational factors like education and cultural background that affect their behavior. Don't jump to the conclusion that they intend to get you upset.
7. Focus on the beauty and pleasure in things.
8. Don't curse as much.
9. Express appreciation to people for their support and assistance.
10. Play to lose, at least occasionally.
11. Say "Good morning" cheerfully.
12. Check out your face in the mirror from time to time. Look for signs of anger and aggravation; ask yourself if you really need to look like that.

about collecting fares, had approximately half the heart attacks of the more inactive drivers. Among postal workers, mail carriers had fewer heart attacks than did clerks in the same stations.

Two decades later, Ralph Paffenbarger (1972) and his associates surveyed 3,700 San Francisco longshoremen. Longshoremen who handled cargo continuously suffered about 60 percent as many heart attacks as those engaged in less-exhausting activity. The Paffenbarger group (1978, 1984, 1986) has been tracking 17,000 Harvard University alumni through university records and questionnaires and correlated incidence of heart attacks with physical activity levels. The incidence of heart attacks decreases as activity levels increase to a level of exertion equivalent to "burning" about 2,000 calories per week (see Figure 5.2). This is the exercise equivalent of running about 20 miles a week. Above

2,000 calories a week, however, the incidence of heart attacks gradually climbs again, but not steeply. Inactive alumni incur the greatest risks of heart attacks. Alumni who burn up at least 2,000 calories per week through exercise live an average of two years longer than less-active alumni.

The Morris and Paffenbarger studies are limited in that they are correlational and not experimental. Persons who are already in better health may elect, and enjoy, higher activity levels. Thus, better health would account for both higher rates of physical activity and a lower incidence of heart attacks.

It remains unclear whether exercise can reduce the risk of recurrent heart attacks. A review of the evidence, however, suggests that exercise does prolong lives among CHD patients, with an overall reduction of about 19 percent in the mortality rate (Blumenthal & Emery, 1988). Later in the chapter we shall explore the value of exercise in weight-reduction programs.

FIGURE 5.2 The frequencies of heart attacks among Harvard University alumni as a function of level of physical exercise. The probability of heart attacks declines as the physical activity level increases up to about 2,000 calories expended per week. Then the frequency of heart attacks increases gradually with further increases in physical activity. You can expend about 2,000 calories a week by jogging about three miles a day or walking for approximately an hour a day.

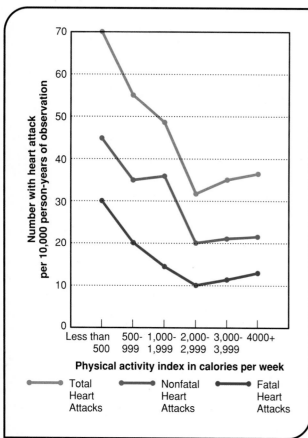

■ **Environmental Stress** Environmental stress also appears to heighten the risk of CHD (Krantz, 1988). However, the stress–CHD connection is not straightforward. For example, the effects of demanding occupations are apparently moderated by factors such as psychological hardiness and whether or not people find their work meaningful (Krantz,1988; Cohen et al., 1986). People who can exercise control over their own productivity find their jobs less stressful (Glass & Singer, 1972; Wells, 1985).

One model relates the demands of an occupation to the degree of control afforded the individual worker. For example, as suggested by Figure 5.3, waiters and waitresses, store managers, and firefighters have highly demanding jobs. Architects, scientists, physicians, and some others have occupations in which they exert enormous control over their own job-related activity. So-called **high-strain** jobs are high in demand and low in the amount of personal control they afford. High-strain jobs apparently place workers at highest risk for CHD (Karasek et al., 1981, 1982; Krantz et al., 1988). Workers in high-strain occupations were found to have about one and one-half times the risk of CHD as workers in low-strain occupations (LaCroix & Haynes, 1987). Working women in general have not been found to incur a greater risk of CHD as compared to housewives and to men. However, women are at greater risk for CHD when they hold clerical (low-control) jobs, when they have nonsupportive bosses (high stress), and when they have children and incur high family demands (Haynes & Feinleib, 1980; Krantz et al., 1988).

We finish this section with encouraging news. Various risk factors for cardiovascular disorders, especially smoking and high-fat diets, have been known for 25 years or more. The American public has appar-

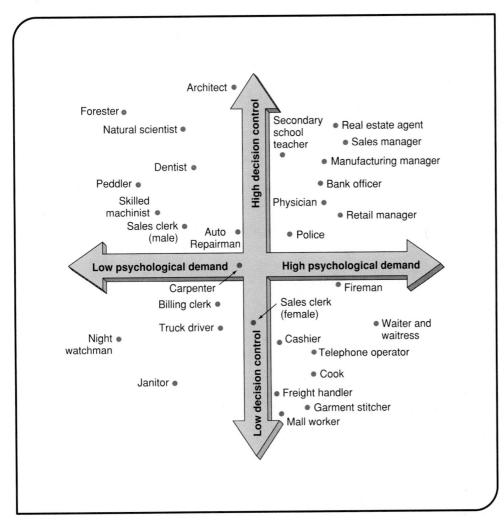

FIGURE 5.3

The job strain model shows the relationship of various occupations to dimensions of job strain ("decision control" and "psychological demand"). Occupations characterized by both *low* control and *high* demand (the lower right quadrant) are associated with greater risk of cardiovascular disease.

Source: "Bosses Face Less Risk Than the Bossed," April 3, 1983, The New York Times. Copyright 1983 by the New York Times Company. Reprinted by permission.

ently responded to this knowledge by making changes in their lifestyles, so that the incidence of CHD has declined (Pell & Fayerweather, 1985; Stamler, 1985a, 1985b). Stamler also found that better-educated people are more likely to modify unhealthful behavior patterns and reap the benefits of change. Is there a message in Stamler's findings for you?

GASTROINTESTINAL DISORDERS

Gastrointestinal disorders are problems of the digestive system. (*Gastro* derives from the Greek *gaster*, meaning "stomach.") There are some clear connections that link stress, emotional response, and gastrointestinal problems. Diarrhea, for example, is a nearly universal feature of anxiety and can beset people before important job interviews, during examinations, or before delivering a speech. Acid stomach and indigestion are also related to stress. The symptoms of indigestion can be so severe that people believe that they are experiencing a heart attack. Whereas diarrhea and acid stomach can come and go according to whether or not we experience anxiety, ulcers are a more enduring gastrointestinal disorder.

Ulcers

Ulcers are believed to afflict about one person in ten and cause perhaps as many as 10,000 deaths annually in the United States (Whitehead & Bosmajian, 1982). Ulcers are open sores on the lining of the stomach or the small intestine. So-called peptic ulcers are related to, or caused by, *pepsin*, an enzyme found in gastric juices that helps break down proteins into digestive form. Persons with ulcers tend to have high levels of pepsinogen, a gastric secretion that is converted into pepsin by hydrochloric acid. People who develop ulcers under conditions of stress frequently have higher levels of pepsinogen than those who do not (Weiner et al., 1957).

There are two kinds of peptic ulcers, determined by their location. Gastric ulcers develop in the stomach, and duodenal ulcers develop in the duodenum, the

A CLOSER LOOK
Styles of Coping with Illness

What do you do when faced with a serious problem? Do you pretend that it does not exist? Like Scarlett O'Hara in *Gone with the Wind*, do you say to yourself, "I'll think about it tomorrow" and then banish it from your mind? Or do you take charge and confront it squarely?

Pretending that problems do not exist is a form of denial. Denial is an example of **emotion-focused coping** (Lazarus & Folkman, 1984). In emotion-focused coping, people take measures that immediately reduce the impact of the stressor, such as denying its existence or withdrawing from the situation. Emotion-focused coping, however, does not eliminate the stressor or help the individual develop better ways of managing the stressor. In **problem-focused coping,** by contrast, people examine the stressors they face and do what they can to change them or modify their own reactions to render stressors less harmful. These basic styles of coping—emotion-focused and problem-focused—have been applied to ways in which people respond to illness.

Emotion-Focused Coping: Reducing Awareness of Physical Trauma Denial is one of the principal ways of passively coping with illness. It can take various forms, including:

1.   Failure to recognize the seriousness of the illness
2.   Minimization of the emotional distress that the illness causes
3.   Misattribution of symptoms to other causes (for example, assuming that the appearance of blood in the stool represents nothing more than a local abrasion), and
4.   Ignoring of threatening information about the illness (Levine et al., 1987).

It has been speculated, interestingly, that denial may actually improve the chances of surviving a heart attack—at least on a short-term basis (Hackett et al., 1968). The idea is that the use of denial protects the heart by shielding it from the physiological effects of anxiety or heightened arousal (Byrne et al., 1981). Research, however, has failed to confirm that the chances of recovery from a heart attack are improved by the use of denial (Krantz, 1980). Regardless of whether or not denial offers short-term benefits in the acute phase of an illness, denial is connected with poorer recovery over the long haul (Krantz, 1980; Mullen & Suls, 1982). Persistent denial apparently impedes compliance with appropriate medical treatment (Levine, 1987).

Another form of emotion-focused coping, the use of wish-fulfillment fantasies, has also been linked to poorer adjustment in coping with serious illness. Examples of wish-fulfillment fantasies include ruminating about what might have been had the illness not occurred and longing for better times. Wish-fulfillment fantasy offers the patient no means of coping with life's difficulties other than an imaginary escape (Felton & Revenson, 1984).

Does this mean that people are invariably better off when they face their illness squarely? Not necessarily. Whether or not you will be better off handling the facts of an illness may depend on your preferred style of coping. A mismatch between the individual's style of coping and the amount of information provided may hamper recovery. In one study, cardiac patients with a repressive style of coping (relying on denial) who received information about their condition showed a higher incidence of medical complications than repressors who were kept in the dark (Shaw et al., 1985). Sometimes ignorance helps people manage stress—at least temporarily.

Imparting medical information when patients cannot make use of it can be an empty and possibly harmful gesture. In one study, patients were either given high or low amounts of information about their conditions and were or were not provided with ways of controlling certain aspects of their treatment (Cromwell et al., 1977). Patients in the high information/high control condition were found to have shorter stays in the hospital. But the provision of information in the absence of ways of exercising control was associated with prolonged stays.

Problem-Focused Coping: Confronting the Trauma of Serious Illness Problem-focused coping involves strategies to deal directly with the source of stress, as by seeking information about the illness through self-

---

first part of the small intestine (the part that first receives food products and gastric juices as they leave the stomach).

■ **Theoretical Perspectives**   Concepts of *stimulus specificity* and *individual response specificity* may help to explain the development of ulcers. That is, certain stimulus situations involving stress (stimulus specificity) may be connected with vulnerability to ulcers. Also, certain people (individual response specificity) may be at greater risk to the effects of stress by virtue of their characteristic response patterns.

High levels of stress are often implicated in the development of ulcers, as we can see in the following case example:

■ Mr. M was a 30-year-old electronics engineer in an aerospace company who designed supersonic aircraft. He was given the enormous responsibility of preparing designs to be submitted to the government in an effort to attain government contracts. He appeared to delight in the challenge and saw it as a major opportunity for career advancement. The first symptom of gastric problems was burning, gnawing sensations following a dinner. The sensations returned periodically after eating

One form of active coping with physical illness is to seek information about one's medical condition. Information-seeking may help people who face serious illness maintain a more hopeful outlook in the belief that the information will be of benefit to them.

study and medical consultation. Information-seeking may help the individual maintain a more optimistic frame of mind by creating an expectancy that the information will prove to be useful, an approach that has been shown to be adaptive among cancer patients (Weisman & Worden, 1976).

The ways in which we come to terms with serious illness affect our emotional adjustment and, perhaps, our survival. Finding a silver lining in a dark cloud is apparently healthful. One study interviewed heart-attack victims seven weeks after they were stricken. Victims who were able to cite benefits of their attacks were less likely to suffer recurrent attacks and were more likely to have survived at an eight-year follow-up than patients who were unable to recognize benefits associated with the attack (Affleck et al., 1987). The types of benefits connected with subsequent health are shown in Table 5.2. Blaming others for the initial heart attacks and attributing them to stress responses (for example, excessive worrying or anxiety) were associated with increased mortality at the eight-year follow-up. Patients who saw their heart attacks as caused by factors they could control, like diet and smoking, more often followed-through on behavioral programs that modified these risk behaviors.

TABLE 5.2 Examples of Perceived Benefits Following Heart Attack Associated with Increased Rates of Survival

Type of Perceived Benefit	Life Changes Associated with Perceived Benefits
Helped victim recognize the benefits of preventative health behaviors	Smoking cessation Regular exercise Proper diet
Helped lead or expected it would lead to positive life changes	Taking life easier Taking more vacations Slowing down the pace of daily life
Helped produce changes in "philosophy of life," personal values, and religious views.	Becoming more content with accepting one's lot in life. Taking each day as it comes Valuing home life more Renewing religious faith

Source: Adapted from Affleck et al., 1987.

and were diagnosed as revealing a peptic ulcer.

M had been hard-working and independent since adolescence. M was the oldest child in a large family. He worked during high school because his parents had turned their attention to his younger siblings. College was a great burden, but M saw it through. He married and had a family. He moved from firm to firm in an effort to attain more responsible and remunerative positions. His family lived on a careful budget so that they could take advantage of property investments that came along from time to time. Just before being assigned the government project, M was subjected to multiple decision-making pressures: decisions as to whether or not to buy a new

house, to move his oldest son to a new school, to go on a long vacation, and to sell an investment property.

The ulcer was controlled by diet and life-style changes that reduced the pressures assailing him. He retained the government project but was counseled to declare a moratorium on making the other decisions. He took up some recreational activities and worked on ways of reducing family and occupational pressures. Ulcer pain lessened within a few months.

(Adapted from Suinn, 1975, p. 360) ■

The view that the body responds to different stimuli, or different sources of stress, in different ways has been supported by some fascinating historic case histories. Consider the case of "Tom," a man who underwent major gastrointestinal surgery in 1947 (Wolf & Wolff, 1947). A plastic window was installed over his stomach, making it possible to observe its operation. It turned out that Tom's flow of gastric juices decreased when he was exposed to anxiety-evoking stimuli—a sign of sympathetic activity, which inhibits digestion. The juices increased when he was provoked by anger-inducing stimuli—a sign of parasympathetic activity. Now, when copious quantities of digestive juices are secreted and there is no food matter to digest, the gastrointestinal tract may begin to devour itself. This is one reason that a link may exist between ulcers and long-term exposure to sources of stress (stimuli) that provoke anger.

Other stimulus factors have also been implicated in the development of ulcers. For example, a number of adolescents with high pepsinogen levels have developed ulcers following separation from or loss of loved ones (Ackerman et al., 1981).

People may also differ in their characteristic response patterns to stress. Some individuals may be "gastric reactors," in the sense of secreting greater levels of pepsinogen under conditions of stress. In social-learning theory terms, the situational variables (exposure to stressful, anger-provoking stimuli) and person variables (differences in individual response patterns) interact to create conditions that may foster the development of ulcers. But why might some individuals be more prone to produce gastric secretions under conditions of stress?

The psychodynamic approach speculates that an individual's physiological response to stress can reflect disturbances in psychosexual development. The somatic expression of the conflict (for example, increased secretion of gastric juices such as pepsinogen) would be symbolic of the character of the underlying conflict (Alexander, 1950). For example, since food may symbolize parental love, adults with unfulfilled but repressed wishes for parental love may experience a persistent "hunger" that leads to overactivation of the stomach. The stomach, in effect, continuously prepares itself for food, the symbolic equivalent of love. Evidence of the psychodynamic perspective is drawn largely from case studies of clients whose histories appear to be consistent with the theory (Fann et al., 1982). But uncontrolled case studies may be open to other interpretations.

According to the biological perspective, heredity largely determines levels of pepsinogen (Mirsky, 1958). There are numerous kinship studies in which pepsinogen levels, and incidence of ulcers, appear to follow genetic patterns. In one of them, the concordance rate for ulcers among 34 pairs of monozygotic twins was 50 percent, as compared to 14 percent among 78 pairs of dizygotic twins (Eberhard, 1968). These results are consistent with a genetic explanation, since monozy-gotic twins share 100 percent genetic similarity, compared to 50 percent genetic overlap between dizygotic twins. Still, while genetic endowment may create a predisposition (or diathesis) for the development of ulcers, other factors, such as the level of stress and the individual's reactions to stress, may determine whether or not ulcers actually develop.

ASTHMA

Asthma is a respiratory disorder that can stem from allergic reaction which contract the main tubes of the windpipe—the bronchi. As a result, people wheeze, cough, and find it difficult to breathe in enough air. Sufferers can feel as though they are suffocating and will die. Asthma afflicts about 3 percent of the American population, and about one-third of the sufferers are children below the age of 16. Attacks can last from a few minutes to several hours and vary notably in intensity. Series of attacks can harm the bronchial system, causing mucus to collect and muscles to lose their elasticity. Sometimes the bronchial system is weakened to the point where a subsequent attack is lethal. Few sufferers die from asthma, however.

Theoretical Perspectives

Asthma has been linked to stress, but the causal connection remains unclear. In one study, for example, efforts were made to induce asthma attacks by subjecting asthma sufferers to stress. The outcome was a slightly decreased air flow, but not an actual attack (Weiss et al., 1976). Other evidence, however, suggests that asthma sufferers can experience attacks in response to the suggestion that their air flow will become constricted (Luparello et al. , 1971). This research and numerous case examples suggest that fear of impending attack, unfortunately, is the type of stressor that sometimes does bring one on.

The diathesis, or predisposition, that is connected with asthma is also less clear. Some researchers suggest that there are two kinds of asthma: allergic and nonallergic. Allergic individuals may have attacks in response to pollen, mold spores, and animal dander. Nonallergic types could stem from a variety of causes, including respiratory infections such as bronchitis and pneumonia. In most cases, the initial attack does follow on the heels of a respiratory infection (Alexander, 1981). In some cases, there is no apparent organic cause. On the other hand, regardless of the original cause, it does seem that stress can heighten the frequency and severity of attack. Asthma, moreover, has psychological consequences. Some sufferers avoid all strenuous activity, for example, for fear of increasing their demand for

mashed in butter—all seem inextricably interwoven with American values and agricultural abundance.

Yet many Americans are paying the price of plenty—**obesity:**

> Forty percent of Americans label themselves overweight (Burros, 1988).
>
> Thirty-five percent want to take off 15 pounds or more (Toufexis et al., 1986).
>
> At least 20 percent of American adults are obese (weigh more than 20 percent above their recommended weight (Wallis, 1985).
>
> Eleven million American adults exceed their desirable body weight by 40 percent or more (Wallis, 1985).
>
> Americans consume 815 billion calories of food each day, which is 200 billion calories more than necessary to maintain their weight at moderate levels of activity (Jenkins, 1988). These extra calories are enough to feed a country of 80 million people (Jenkins, 1988).
>
> Some 65 million Americans diet each year, using some 30,000 different dietary approaches (Blumenthal, 1988).
>
> Within a few years, two-thirds of "successful" dieters have regained all the weight they have lost—and even more (Toufexis et al., 1986).
>
> Despite the fact that food can be expensive, the incidence of obesity is highest among people of lower socioeconomic status (Brownell, 1982).

The United States idealizes slender heroes and heroines. For those of us who more than "measure up" to media idols, food seems to have replaced sex as a major source of guilt.

Why is obesity included in an abnormal psychology textbook? There are at least four reasons:

1. Various psychological factors contribute to obesity or impair dieting efforts. These include negative emotions like depression (Baucom & Aiken, 1981; Ruderman, 1985) and anxiety (Herman et al., 1987).
2. Obesity is a risk factor for various stress-related illnesses, including hypertension, CHD, respiratory illnesses, diabetes, gallbladder disease, gout, and certain kinds of cancer (Bary, 1986; Feist & Brannon, 1988; Sorlie et al., 1980).
3. Obesity is associated with negative psychological consequences, such as low self-esteem (Rosen et al., 1987; Smith & Fremouw, 1987).
4. Psychological approaches have been shown to help obese people take off pounds and keep them off (Kaplan, 1988; Perri et al., 1988).

It must be noted that extreme thinness is at least as unhealthful as obesity, and extreme thinness has become fairly common, especially among young women. In Chapter 14 we shall discuss the eating disorders of anorexia nervosa and bulimia nervosa, each of which involves maladaptive methods of keeping weight down.

Theoretical Perspectives

Why are so many people overweight? Is obesity a biological problem, a psychological problem, or a combination of the two? Research suggests that both biological and psychological factors play roles in obesity.

■ **Heredity** It is generally accepted that obesity runs in families. The question is *why*? It was once assumed that obese parents simply encouraged their children to become heavy by keeping high calorie foods in the house and setting a poor example. But a study of Scandinavian adoptees by psychiatrist Albert J. Stunkard and his colleagues (1986) revealed that children's weight is more closely related to the weight of their biological parents than to that of their adoptive parents. Heredity, then, may play a stronger role in determining weight than environmental influences.

One way in which heredity influences physique is through transmission of tendencies toward various **metabolic rates,** or rates of processing food (Ravussin et al., 1988). Metabolic rates tend to run in families and, in a prospective study of 126 southwestern American Indians, predicted weight gains four years into the future (Ravussin et al., 1988).

Although a diathesis toward obesity may be genetically transmitted, we shall see that environmental factors also play a role. Since we are "stuck" with our heredity, that is good news. We *can* exercise influence over the environmental factors that affect us.

■ **Fat Cells** The efforts of heavy people to keep a slender profile may be sabotaged by cells within their own bodies termed **fat cells.** No, fat cells are not corpulent

Obesity does tend to run in families. The question is, Why?

cells. They are adipose tissue—cells that store fat. Hunger is related to the quantity of stored fat. As time passes after eating, the blood sugar level declines, drawing fat from these cells to supply more nourishment. At some point—termed the **set point**—the hypothalamus is signalled of the depletion of fat in these cells. The hypothalamus, in turn, signals the cerebral cortex, triggering the hunger drive.

People with higher levels of adipose tissue send more signals of depletion to the brain than do people equal in weight but with fewer fat cells. As a result, they feel food-deprived sooner. Obese individuals, and *formerly* obese individuals, usually have more fatty tissue than people of normal weight (Braitman et al., 1985). (Sad to say, dieters do not expel fat cells; instead, they sort of shrivel them up.) So many dieters, even successful dieters, complain that they are constantly hungry as they struggle to maintain normal weight levels.

How is the number of fat cells in our bodies determined? Unfortunately, heredity seems to play a major role. Early dietary habits may also have an influence, however.

■ Adipose Tissue and Metabolism   People with high levels of adipose tissue are doubly beset because adipose tissue metabolizes food more sluggishly than does muscle. People with high fat-to-muscle ratios metabolize food more slowly than do people of the same weight with lower fat-to-muscle ratios. In other words, people of the same weight metabolize food at different paces, according to their bodies' apportionment of muscle and fat.

The standard distribution of adipose tissue is "sexist." The average man is composed of 40 percent muscle and 15 percent fat. The average woman is composed of 23 percent muscle and 25 percent fat. These differences may account for much of the "sex appeal" of the opposite sex; however, if men and women with typical distributions of fat and muscle are equal in weight, the woman—with relatively more adipose tissue—will have to take in fewer calories to maintain the same weight. So women have a metabolic advantage over men in times of famine. In times of abundance, women may be at a disadvantage; the number of dieting women in the United States significantly exceeds the number of dieting men (Toufexis et al., 1986), although cultural factors, which impose greater social pressures on thinness in women, may better account for sex differences in dieting.

■ Compensating Metabolic Forces That Affect Dieters   The body is a wondrous thing. It adjusts to all sorts of conditions, including deprivation. Sad to say, this capacity for adjustment can backfire on dieters. Dieters and people who have lost notable amounts of weight usually do not take in enough calories to satisfy the set points of their hypothalamuses (Keesey, 1986). As a result, the body sets compensating metabolic forces in motion; that is, the body burns fewer calories.

■ The Yo-Yo Syndrome   Repeated cycles of crash dieting and regaining weight—the "yo-yo syndrome"—may be especially traumatic to the body's set point. These cycles apparently "teach" the body that it will be episodically deprived of food. As a result, body metabolism may slow down (Brownell, 1986; Blumenthal, 1988). For this reason, formerly overweight people who have repeatedly lost and regained weight in the past must usually take in fewer calories than people of equal weight who were always thin, if they wish to maintain a slender profile.

As highlighted by the case of Christine, Brownell (1988) notes a second effect of yo-yo dieting that frustrates repeat dieters:

> Christine . . . drops from 140 pounds down to 120 pounds. She might lose 15 pounds of fat and 5 pounds of muscle. If she regains the 20 pounds, will she replace all 5 pounds of muscle? [Animal studies] suggest that she won't, so Christine may replace 18 pounds of fat and only 2 pounds of muscle. She may be the same weight before and after this cycle, but her metabolic rate would be lower after the cycle because she has more fat, which is less metabolically active than muscle. (Brownell, 1988, p. 22)

In other words, it is harder for Christine just to maintain her 140 pounds the second time around. In fact, if she takes in as many calories as she had when she was previously 140 pounds, her weight will rise above 140. And now that she has increased her fat-to-muscle ratio, her body is overall "less metabolically active." So it will be more difficult for her to lose the same 20 pounds again.

 Cycles of dieting and regaining lost weight (the yo-yo syndrome) do make it progressively more difficult to take off extra pounds. During each cycle, some muscle tissue is replaced by adipose tissue, which metabolizes food more slowly.

Christine's plight apparently affects high-school wrestlers who routinely go on crash diets to fit desired weight categories. One study compared such wrestlers to wrestlers whose weights remained stable throughout the wrestling season (Kolata, 1988). Body metabolism rates in the subsequent off-season were 14 percent lower among the crash dieters, even though both groups maintained similar weight.

In addition to sabotaging future dieting efforts, yo-yo dieting may also have injurious effects to the heart. For example, a study of 21,000 middle-aged men carried out by the University of Texas School of Public Health found a higher rate of death due to CHD among men whose weights fluctuated markedly (Blumenthal, 1988).

In any event, one way to prevent a slowdown in metabolism due to repeated dieting may be to take weight off slowly and gradually (Blumenthal, 1988). Another, as we shall see, is regular exercise.

■ Internal and External Eaters: Is Out of Sight Out of Mouth?

During the 11:00 o'clock news, as your authors are settling in for sleep, fast-food pizza ads assault them from the television set. Visions of melted cheese and drippy sauce threaten our self-control. Our stomach growlings provide evidence that hunger can be precipitated by external stimuli, like the sight of food, as well as by blood-sugar levels and signals to and from the hypothalamus.

People who become hungry chiefly in response to internal stimuli are termed **internal eaters.** People who become hungry predominantly in response to external stimuli, such as fast-food commercials or aromas from the kitchen, are labeled **external eaters.**

Several studies have suggested that obese people are more apt than normal-weight people to be external eaters (Schachter & Gross, 1968; Stunkard, 1959). Why might heavy people be relatively more responsive to external stimulation? In "weighing" this question, Schachter (1971) drew parallels between the eating behaviors of obese people and **hyperphagic** rats—animals who go on eating binges because of the destruction of the "stop-eating centers" in their hypothalamuses. Many heavy people, like hyperphagic rats, are fussy eaters; that is, they are highly sensitive to the taste of food (Schachter, 1971; Schachter & Rodin, 1974). Obese people and hyperphagic rats eat relatively more of sweet foods, like vanilla milk shakes, and less of bitter foods. Obese people, like hyperphagic rats, take large mouthfuls, chew less frequently, and finish their food more quickly than do their normal-weight counterparts (LeBow et al., 1977; Marston et al., 1977). For reasons like these, Schachter surmised that the hunger drives of overweight people may be afflicted by faulty neural regulation in the hypothalamus.

The faulty-neural-mechanism hypothesis is not universally accepted as a cause of obesity in people, however. Judith Rodin (1980), for example, found that some people in all weight categories, and not just obese people, are external eaters. Rodin also found that moderately overweight individuals (who are 15 to 25 percent overweight) are apt to be external eaters, whereas exceedingly obese people (who are at least 50 percent above their ideal weights) are relatively less affected by external cues than moderately obese people. So the connection between obesity and susceptibility to external cues is not as strong as had once been thought.

■ Other Psychological Factors

According to psychodynamic theory (and, in this case, by definition), eating is an oral activity. Psychoanalysts generally assume that people fixated in the oral stage by conflicts concerning dependence and independence are likely to regress to

It may seem that we are constantly bombarded by food cues in the environment. People who are more responsive to external stimuli, such as environmental cues or aromas from the kitchen, are called *external eaters.* People whose eating behavior is largely governed by internal stimuli, such as hunger pangs, are termed *internal eaters.* Some research suggests that people with moderate obesity are more likely to be external eaters than are those with excessive obesity.

oral activities, such as eating, when they are under stress.

Additional psychological factors that are connected with overeating and obesity involve low self-esteem, lack of self-efficacy expectancies, conflicts with parents and spouses, and troubling emotions. While the connections between these factors and obesity affect both sexes, women most frequently seek assistance from professionals and diet centers, largely because of the pressures brought upon them by society to adhere to expectations of thinness. Consider the cases of Joan and Terry:

■ Joan was trapped in the yo-yo syndrome, repeatedly dropping 20 pounds and regaining it. Whenever Joan got stuck at a certain weight plateau, or started to regain weight, her thoughts became dominated by perceptions of poor self-esteem. She'd hear herself muttering "Who am I kidding? I'm not worthy of being thin. I should just accept being fat."

She related an incident with her mother that revealed how her negative thinking was often triggered. Joan had lost 24 pounds from an original weight of 174 and was beginning to feel good about herself. Most other people reinforced her by complimenting her on her weight loss. She called her mother, who lived in another state, to share the good news. Instead of jumping on the bandwagon, her mother cautioned her not to expect too much from her success. After all, her mother pointed out, she had been repeatedly disappointed in the past. The message came through loud and clear: Don't get your hopes up because you will only be more disappointed in the end. Joan's mother may have meant well in trying to protect Joan from eventual disappointment, but the message she conveyed reinforced the negative view that Joan held of herself: You're a loser. Don't expect too much of yourself. Accept your reality. Don't try to change. You're a hopeless case.

As soon as she hung up the receiver, Joan rushed to the pantry. Without hesitation she grabbed three packages of Famous Amos Chocolate Chip Cookies, devouring them in a frenzied binge as she sat alone on the stairway. The next day she explained to her psychologist how this binge had reactivated memories of childhood binging on Oreo cookies while hiding under the stairwell.

■ For years Terry's husband had scrutinized every morsel she consumed. "Haven't you had enough?" he would ask derisively. The more he harped on her weight, the more angry she felt, although she did not express her feelings directly. The criticism did not apply only to her weight. She heard "You're not smart enough. . . . Why don't you take better care of yourself? . . . How come you're not sexy?" After years of assault on her self-esteem, Terry petitioned for divorce, convinced that the single life could be no worse than her marriage.

While separated and awaiting the final divorce decree, Terry felt free to be herself for the first time in her adult life. However, she had not expected the effect that her sense of freedom would have on her weight. She ballooned from 155 pounds to 186 pounds within a few months.

She identified left-over resentment from her marriage as the driving factor in her weight gain. "There's no one to make me diet anymore," she said. Her overeating was like saying, "See, I can eat if I want to." With her husband absent, she could express her anger and outrage toward him by eating to excess. Unfortunately, her mode of expressing anger was self-defeating. Terry's anger and past hurts encouraged her to act spitefully rather than constructively.

The Authors' Files ■

In some cases, people who seek help in losing weight may profit from counseling to the effect that they may not be as heavy as they think. Women, all in all, appear to be burdened by nearly impossible standards—so much so that the "normal" (that is, typical) eating pattern for American women today *is* dieting (Polivy & Herman, 1987)! Dieters also need to be made aware of the perils of yo-yo dieting. And when losing weight appears to be a losing battle, health professionals may consider helping the client develop an improved self-concept and adopt a generally healthful lifestyle, rather than focusing all efforts on weight loss per se (Smith & Fremouw, 1987).

 Dieting has indeed become the "normal" way of eating for American women. The majority of women go on weight-loss diets at some time in their lives.

Methods of Weight Control

Literally thousands of methods of weight control have been proffered in recent years. Some, like surgery and diet pills, involve biological interventions. Others, like modifying eating habits and exercising, involve changes in behavior. Still other methods combine biological and behavioral approaches. Because our attitudes and expectations—including self-efficacy expectancies—also influence our adherence to weight-loss regimens, behavioral programs usually have significant cognitive components.

■ **Very Low Calorie Diet (VLCD) Programs** Very low calorie diet (VLCD) programs have increased in popularity in recent years and have shown some early encouraging results. These diet programs replace the individual's regular foods with a liquid protein mixture that provides between 300 and 600 calories per day. The liquid protein diet used today is based on dairy protein and is nutritionally balanced with respect to vital amino acids and nutrients. VLCD programs provide 70 to 100 grams of protein daily to spare the loss of lean body mass. They are associated with very rapid weight losses, on the average about 45 pounds in a 12-week period, and appear to be safe when medically

A CLOSER LOOK
On Emotions, Dietary Restraints, and Overeating

Imagine that you have a big test tomorrow and you're plugging away at the books. At this point your grades are borderline, and you want desperately to pull the course out. Now and then you feel sweat forming on your brow. Nervously you tap the floor until your roommate politely requests that you cut it out. Suddenly it's dinnertime. You drag yourself to the dining hall and load up your tray as usual, but your thoughts remain on that test. Then you sit down and look at the food in front of you. Are you likely to inhale it and go back for seconds, or are you likely to toy with a few mouthfuls and then pass it up? The answer may very well depend on whether you are on a diet.

Consider a study on the effects of anxiety on eating among dieters and nondieters (Herman et al., 1987). The study was set up like this: Subjects were told that they would be participating in a taste test for a brand new gourmet ice cream. Subjects then fasted for several hours before the study to induce hunger. Half of the subjects were then given a milk shake prior to the taste test in order to reduce hunger. The remaining subjects had nothing to eat. Subjects also received one of two sets of expectations to induce different levels of anxiety, as shown in Figure 5.4: In the low-anxiety condition, subjects were led to expect that they would be asked, after the taste test, to discuss the features of the ice cream that they thought might best be used in advertising the product. In the high-anxiety condition, subjects were told that they would be asked to compose a jingle describing the product and be videotaped performing it. Subjects were allowed to eat as much ice cream as they wished to gather their taste impression.

The researchers were actually interested in how much ice cream subjects ate during the "taste-test," not whether or not subjects liked the taste. The results showed that anxiety had contrary effects for dieters and nondieters, but only when the subjects were initially hungry. Among nondieters, anxiety suppressed hunger among the hungry subjects (those who did not receive a milk shake "preload"). Anxiety had no effect on nondieters who had been given the milk shake, and presumably were less hungry. Among dieters, however, anxiety increased eating among hungry subjects and had no effects on subjects who were

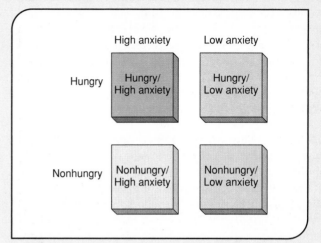

FIGURE 5.4 Conditions in the study on effects of anxiety on dieters and nondieters.

given the prior milk shake. It appears that hungry dieters are disinhibited (freed of dietary restraints) when they experience states of negative arousal, like anxiety. By regularly limiting their food intake, dieters are likely to feel hungry much of the time. But when anxiety or another negative emotion intrudes, dieters' abilities to maintain dietary constraints may be impaired, prompting excessive eating. The dieters who were asked to down milk shakes, however, and thus to violate their self-imposed constraints, were probably already disinhibited. Anxiety, therefore, had no additional effect on them.

Nondieters react to emotional cues in converse fashion. When they feel calm, nondieters respond to physiological hunger cues by eating. But these physiological cues may be overridden by negative emotional cues that suppress their desire to eat. Consider nonhungry dieters. Their desire to eat is already suppressed by an absence of physiological hunger cues, so anxiety does not affect their eating. So if you are a normal eater, or a nondieter, you may feel less like eating on the evening of a job interview or a big exam. But if you are a strict dieter, watch out for binge-eating on the evening of the big day that lies ahead.

supervised and limited to this period of time (Brownell & Wadden, 1986). In contrast, liquid protein formulas that were sold over the counter in the 1970s were often nutritionally inadequate and not properly supervised. A number of deaths were reported that were associated with their use. Today, liquid protein diets are dispensed only by a physician, and the patient's health is closely monitored from week to week. Most VLCD programs involve a 12-week liquid protein diet followed by gradual refeeding. The typical program is

combined with behavior modification to help the individual learn to correct problem eating habits. One of the most popular of the liquid protein diets, the Optifast program, has been administered to 300,000 or more individuals in about 450 different centers in the country (Blumenthal, 1988). To be eligible for the program, the individual must be either 50 pounds overweight or be 30 percent or more above their ideal body weight (Blumenthal, 1988). While liquid protein diets are associated with rapid and large weight losses in the initial stages, the question remains whether the participants are able to maintain these weight losses once they resume eating regular food. Present findings, however, are not encouraging. Three years following a combined treatment of a very low calorie diet and behavior therapy program, subjects in one research study had regained about 31 pounds, on the average, of their original weight losses of about 42 pounds, on the average (Wadden et al., 1988). Only about one in five (19%) subjects maintained weight losses within 2.2 kg (about 4.4 pounds) of their end-of-treatment weights.

■ **Surgery**   New forms of surgical treatment have revolutionized the medical treatment of the morbidly obese—that is, persons who are at least twice as heavy as their ideal weights (Stunkard et al., 1986). Morbid obesity is considered to pose serious health threats and to be resistant to more conservative forms of treatment. Among the surgical techniques being used to produce large weight losses are intestinal bypass, gastric restriction, vagotomy, jaw wiring, and intragastric balloon surgery.

More common is the cosmetic surgery technique of liposuction, in which adipose tissue is removed from areas of the body, such as the hips, that may remain undesirably plump despite dietary restrictions and exercise. However, the safety of surgical treatments of obesity has been questioned, and these methods continue to receive careful scrutiny from the medical community and lay critics (Ernsberger, 1987; Stunkard et al., 1987).

■ **Behavioral Approaches**   Successful behavioral approaches do not involve fad diets like fasting, eliminating carbohydrates, or eating excessive amounts of grapefruit or rice (Brownell, 1988). Instead, (Epstein et al., 1985; Israel et al., 1985; Stalonas & Kirschenbaum, 1985) they often involve changes in lifestyle that include enhancing nutritional knowledge, lessening calorie intake, exercise, and behavior modification.

Because taking in fewer calories is the chief method of decreasing weight, dieters need nutritional knowledge. Knowledge helps ensure that dieters do not deprive themselves of basic food elements and suggests strategies for losing pounds without feeling overly deprived. Ingesting fewer calories does not only mean taking smaller portions. It also means switching to some lower-calorie, nutritious foods, such as fresh, unsweetened fruits and vegetables (apples, not apple pie); lean meats; poultry and fish; and skim milk and cheeses. Generally speaking, the same foods that help control weight are also high in vitamins and fiber and low in fats. Thus, they may lower the risk of CHD, cancer, and other diseases as well as the numbers on the bathroom scale.

There is little doubt that exercise fosters weight loss (Stern & Lowney, 1986). In one study, obese women who walked 30 minutes or longer a day lost about 20 pounds in one year, whereas women who walked less than 30 minutes failed to lose a significant amount of weight (Gwinup, 1975). Unfortunately, 20 to 80 percent of the obese people who start an exercise program drop out within a few months (Stunkard & Brownell, 1979). People are more likely to adhere to exercise programs when they are convenient, not overly stressful, and conducted in a group setting (Stern & Lowney, 1986). The support of one's spouse is also helpful.

Dieting combined with exercise is more effectual than dieting alone (Epstein et al., 1984a; Stern & Lowney, 1986). When people restrict calories, their metabolic rates compensate by decreasing (Apfelbaum, 1978; Polivy & Herman, 1985). Exercise burns calories in itself and also increases the metabolic rate throughout the day, even when people restrict calories (Donahoe et al., 1984).

Behavior modification tends to focus on the "ABCs" of eating. The A's are the *antecedents* of eating—cues or stimuli that may "trigger" eating responses. These include stimuli in the environment, such as the sight and aromas of food, and internal stimuli, such as sensations of hunger, or emotional states like anxiety, fatigue, anger, depression, even boredom. Controlling the A's of eating involves redesigning the environment so that people are not continuously bombarded by food-related cues.

The B's of eating refer to eating *behaviors* themselves. As noted, for example, overweight people usually eat more quickly than do thin people. In so doing, they prevent their brains from "catching up" to their stomachs, since it takes about 15 minutes or so for feelings of satiety to register in the brain after food reaches the stomach. The B's of eating extend to preparatory behaviors like shopping patterns, food storage habits, and so on.

The C's of eating are the *consequences*. Too often the immediate positive consequences of overeating—the sensory pleasure and the allaying of feelings of hunger—overshadow the long-term negative consequences of obesity and risk to health. Food is also connected to other reward systems. Food can become a substitute friend or lover. When people feel depressed, they can lift their spirits with food, if only temporarily. Because food activates the parasympathetic branch of the autonomic nervous system (through digestive processes), food also acts as a natural sedative or tranquilizer, quelling feelings of anxiety or tension, helping people relax or get to sleep. In helping people cope with the C's of eating, psychologists make the long-term benefits of sensible eating more immediate. Methods commonly used to address the ABCs of eating are shown in Table 5.3.

In a review of 105 studies of self-control behav-

TABLE 5.3 Some Behavioral Techniques of Modifying the ABCs of Eating to Foster Weight Loss

Changing the A's of Overeating

Changing the Environmental A's	Avoid settings that trigger overeating. (Eat at The Celery Stalk, not The Chocolate Gourmet.)
	Don't leave tempting treats around the house.
	Serve food on smaller plates. Use a lunch plate rather than a dinner plate.
	Don't leave seconds on the table.
	Serve preplanned portions. Do not leave open casseroles on the table.
	Immediately freeze leftovers. Don't keep them warm on the stove.
	Avoid the kitchen as much as possible.
	Disconnect eating from other stimuli, such as watching television, talking on the telephone, or reading.
	Establish food-free zones in your home.
	Imagine there is a barrier at the entrance to your bedroom which prevents the passage of food.
Controlling the Internal A's	Don't bury disturbing feelings in a box of cookies or a carton of mocha delight ice cream.
	Relabel feelings of hunger as signals that you're burning calories. Say to yourself, "It's okay to feel hungry. It doesn't mean I'm going to die or pass out. Each minute I delay eating, more calories are burned."

Changing the B's of Overeating

Slow Down the Pace of Eating	Put down utensils between bites.
	Take smaller bites.
	Chew thoroughly.
	Savor each bite. Don't bite down to make room for the next.
	Take a break during the meal. Put down your utensils and converse with your family or guests for a few minutes. (Give your rising blood sugar level a chance to signal your brain.)
	When you resume eating, ask yourself whether you need to finish every bite.
	Leave something over to be thrown away or enjoyed later.
Modify Shopping Behavior	Shop from a list. Don't browse through the supermarket.
	Shop quickly. Don't make shopping the high point of your day.
	Treat the supermarket like enemy territory. Avoid the aisles containing junk food and snacks. If you must walk down these aisles, put on mental blinders and look straight ahead.
	Never shop when hungry. Shop after meals, not before.
Practice Competing Responses	Substitute nonfood activities for food-related activities. When tempted to overeat, leave the house, take a bath, walk the dog, call a friend, or walk around the block.
	Substitute low-calorie foods for high-calorie foods. Keep lettuce, celery, or carrots in the middle of the refrigerator so that they are available when you want a snack.
	Fill spare time with nonfood-related activities: volunteer at the local hospital, play golf or tennis, join exercise groups, read in the library (rather than the kitchen), take long walks.
Chain Breaking	Stretch the overeating chain. Before allowing yourself to snack, wait 10 minutes. Next time wait 15 minutes, etc.
	Break the eating chain at its weakest link. It's easier to interrupt the eating chain by taking a route home that bypasses the bakery than to exercise self-control when you're placing your order.

Changing the C's of Overeating

Reward Yourself for Meeting Calorie/ Diet Goals	One pound of body weight is equivalent to 3,500 calories. To lose one pound of weight per week, you need to cut 3,500 calories per week, or 500 calories per day, from your typical calorie intake level, assuming your weight has been stable. Reward yourself for meeting weekly goals. Reward yourself with gifts that you would not otherwise purchase for yourself, such as a special gift for yourself, like a cashmere sweater or tickets to a show. Repeat the reward program from week to week. If during some weeks you miss your calorie goals, don't lose heart. Get back on track next week.
Use Self-Punishment	Charge yourself for deviating from your diet program. Send one dollar to a political candidate you despise, or to a hated cause, each time the chocolate cake wins.

ioral treatment of obesity, the mean post-treatment weight loss (among 6,121 subjects) was about 12 pounds, and the mean follow-up loss for 5,453 subjects was only slightly less than 12 pounds (11.86 pounds) (Bennett, 1986). Generally speaking, the longer the treatment and the greater number of therapy hours, the greater the weight loss. Regular exercise and adhering to a rigorous diet were connected with greater weight losses.

Appetite-suppressing drugs may be connected with greater initial weight loss, but negatively associated with maintenance of weight losses over time. In one study, the use of an appetite suppressant (fenfluramine hydrochloride), either alone or in combination with behavior therapy, initially led to more rapid weight losses (32 and 34 pounds, respectively) than behavior therapy alone (24 pounds) (Craighead et al., 1981). However, at a one-year follow-up, subjects treated with the drug alone had regained 18 pounds, and those treated with both the drug and behavior therapy had regained 24 pounds. In sharp contrast, subjects treated with behavior therapy alone had regained an average of only 4 pounds. The point seems to be that teaching coping skills has more enduring effects than handing out pills. Combining behavioral treatments with pharmacological approaches, such as the use of appetite suppressants, may increase recidivism since the clients may attribute their initial successes to the drug rather than to their own efforts (Craighead, 1984). At the present time, pharmacotherapy does not appear to increase the effectiveness of behavior therapy and may actually diminish its utility (Brownell & Wadden, 1986).

In sum, while most behavior therapy programs can help mildly to moderately obese individuals lose a moderate amount of weight (Kaplan, 1988), maintaining weight loss is a more difficult proposition. Structured attempts at maintaining initial weight loss seem helpful. In one study, participants placed in a one-year weight-loss maintenance program kept off about 83 percent of the weight they had lost, or an average of about 23.5 pounds (Perri et al., 1988). Participants who received behavior therapy without the maintenance program kept off only about one-third of the weight they had lost.

In this chapter we have focused on the relationships between psychological factors and physical disorders and conditions. Psychology has much to offer our understanding of the causes and treatments of physical illness. We have seen how stress may play a role in various physical illnesses and how psychological factors may be involved in moderating the effects of stress. We have also seen that psychological approaches to treatment may be helpful in the treatment of such physical disorders as headaches and hypertension, and in reducing the risk of recurrent cardiac incidents among men with prior heart attacks. Psychologists can also help people reduce high-risk behaviors and cope more effectively with serious illness, such as cancer and AIDS. But this is only the beginning. New emerging disciplines like psychoneuroimmunology may well lead to a better understanding of the intricate relationships between mind and body.

SUMMARY

Psychological Factors Affecting Physical Condition

A number of physical disorders or conditions are believed to be affected by psychological factors. Physical disorders or conditions in which psychological factors are believed to play a causal role are called psychosomatic or psychophysiological disorders. The DSM–III–R uses the category *psychological factors affecting physical condition* to refer to many physical disorders and conditions that previously had been labeled as psychosomatic or psychophysiological. But most if not all illnesses may have psychological components, and treatment of physically ill people involves psychological factors. Many physical disorders discussed in the chapter are

believed to be influenced by the heightened levels of physiological arousal that occur during prolonged or extreme stress.

The Immune System

The immune system is involved in combating disease in several ways. White blood cells, or leukocytes, directly attack pathogens, like bacteria, or mark them with antibodies for later destruction. Some leukocytes, the memory leukocytes, can remain in the bloodstream for years, preparing the body for quick defense against a second invasion of the antigens in the future. Memory leukocytes are formed in the process of vaccination.

A third function of the immune system, inflammation, involves expanding the flow of blood to an injured area, carrying with it an army of leukocytes to prevent infection at the site of the injury.

The growing field of psychoneuroimmunology looks for relationships between psychological factors, such as exposure to stress, and immune response. Stress activates the secretion of steroids, which suppresses immune activity. With continuous secretions, vulnerability to disease may increase. Animal research has shown that rats exposed to the stress of unavoidable electric shock exhibited a lower immune response. Correlational research with humans has provided additional links between stress and lowered immune functioning. Some recent research suggests that forms of psychological treatment involving training in relaxation and coping skills, and writing about traumatic events, may actually increase immune response.

Headaches

There are several types of headaches. The most frequent type, the muscle-tension headache, involves muscle contractions in the shoulders, neck, forehead, and scalp. Other headaches, such as migraines, appear to involve changes in the blood supply to the head. Migraines tend to affect one side of the brain and to last for hours or even days, occurring perhaps daily, or perhaps as seldom as once every other month. Pain can be so intense as to be intolerable, and other mental processes may be affected, such as mood, sleep, and thinking.

The principle of individual response specificity suggests that different people may respond to stress in different ways. Some may respond to stress with muscle contractions that lead to tension headaches, whereas others may respond with vascular changes that are associated with migraine attacks. Researchers today believe that disregulation of certain neurotransmitters, such as serotonin and norepinephrine, may play a causal role in migraines, but further research is needed. The diathesis-stress model posits an interaction between the diathesis (a genetic predisposition) and situational sources of stress in explaining migraines. While various drugs decrease headache pain, behavioral methods such as relaxation training and biofeedback, have been shown to be of benefit.

Menstrual Problems

There are several kinds of menstrual problems. Dysmenorrhea, or menstrual pain or discomfort, may be either secondary to organic problems, or primary, if no organic cause is determined. But even primary dysmenorrhea may actually be secondary to underlying hormonal changes, although the precise relationships have not been determined. A recent study of college women categorized menstrual problems into three types: menstrual pain; physiological discomfort during menstruation; and premenstrual symptoms, or premenstrual syndrome (PMS). PMS, which generally occurs during the four days preceding menses, involves both psychological and physiological symptoms, such as increased irritability and depression, weight gain, and abdominal discomfort.

While survey results suggest that most (perhaps three in four) women experience premenstrual changes, most complaints fall in the mild or moderate range, and only about 10 percent experienced impaired functioning and even fewer (< 1%) report missing work because of menstrual problems. There is also no reliable evidence of menstrual-related academic impairment. Late luteal phase dysphoric disorder (LLPD) has been proposed as a possible diagnostic category that is intended to apply to the small minority of women whose premenstrual discomfort is so severe that it significantly affects their ability to function. But further study is required before LLPD could be officially accepted in the diagnostic manual and various difficulties with the diagnosis have been identified.

PMS may be related to the levels of estrogen and progesterone, or to their relative balance, but research evidence remains unclear. But psychological factors also appear to play an important role, as women who do not view menstruation as debilitating are generally less likely to show mood changes related to the menstrual cycle.

Hypertension

Hypertension, or high blood pressure, affects perhaps 10 to 30 percent of Americans. High BP with no identifiable organic cause is termed essential hypertension. Hypertension places people at greater risk of various cardiovascular disorders. Various stressful factors may increase blood pressures, such as noise, situations requiring continuous alertness, and driving in congested traffic.

In the traditional psychodynamic view, people with hypertension are believed to have difficulty expressing pent-up anger. The pent-up feelings are believed to press against the blood vessel walls, leading to hypertension. But biological models favor the view that essential hypertension may reflect overresponsiveness of the cardiovascular system to stress. People with essential hypertension may inherit such a genetic predisposition.

Hypertension is frequently controlled by drugs and dietary management (avoiding salt, for example). Behavioral methods, such as relaxation training and meditation, have also shown promise in helping hypertensive individuals lower their blood pressure.

Cardiovascular Disorders

Coronary heart disease (CHD) is the leading cause of death for men over the age of 40 and women over the age of 70. Various risk factors for CHD have been identified, including increased age; male sex; family history of CHD; low socioeconomic status; various physiological conditions, such as hypertension, obesity, and high levels of serum cholesterol; various patterns of consumption, such as heavy drinking, smoking, overeating, and eating food high in cholesterol or saturated fats; Type A behavior; work overload; chronic fatigue and emotional strain; and a physically inactive lifestyle.

Controversy remains about the role of the Type A behavior pattern (TABP) and risk of CHD. However, treatment studies that focus on reducing Type A behavior among cardiac patients have shown promising results in reducing the risk of recurrent heart attacks and other cardiovascular incidents.

Physical inactivity may play a role in CHD. Aerobic activity apparently reduces the risk of cardiovascular disorders, although the evidence is based on correlational, not experimental, research. Environmental stress may also heighten the risk of CHD, although the stress–CHD connection may be moderated by such psychological factors as psychological hardiness and attitudes toward one's work, such as perceptions of meaningfulness and control.

Different styles of coping may play a role in psychological adjustment to serious illness, or even mortality. Emotion-focused coping are ways of reducing the emotional impact of the stressor, as in denial or withdrawing from the situation. Problem-focused coping refer to attempts to render stressors less harmful by changing them or by modifying one's reactions to them. Emotion-focused coping, such as denial, may reduce emotional responsiveness following a stressful event, like a heart attack, but is likely to impair chances of long-term recovery due to noncompliance with medical interventions. But finding hidden benefits in a serious illness may help us survive.

Gastrointestinal Disorders

The development of ulcers may be related to both stimulus specificity and individual response specificity. People who are exposed to certain stressors (stimulus specificity) may be at greater risk for developing ulcers. People with certain characteristic response patterns (individual response specificity) to stress may also be at greater risk. While psychodynamic theorists have postulated that physiological response to stress may reflect disturbances in psychosexual development, the evidence in support of the theory is largely drawn from uncontrolled case studies. Biological perspectives focus on the role of heredity.

Asthma

Asthma has also been linked to stress, but the causal relationships remain unclear. Children with psychological disturbances may be at greater risk of dying from asthma, but caution must be taken in drawing causal inferences.

Cancer

Heredity and such behavior patterns as smoking, use of alcohol, and sunbathing increase the risk of cancer. Diet is also believed related to the risk of cancer, with some dietary practices believed to increase cancer risks while others may actually reduce the risk of some forms of cancer. Controversy remains about whether or not psychological factors pose a risk for cancer. Some research suggests that high levels of stress, especially stress from the loss of significant others, may increase the risks of cancer. But these studies have been criticized as relying on retrospective reports of cancer victims and causal relationships remain unclear. Experimental studies with rats suggest that stress may influence the course of cancer in at-risk animals, but not affect the eventual outcome.

Acquired Immune Deficiency Syndrome

While stress does not directly cause AIDS or cancer, stress may affect the course of AIDS in much the same way that stress is suspected to affect the course of cancer. Psychologists have also become involved in work with AIDS because certain behavior patterns are clearly associated with increased risk of infection. Psychologists and others are working to develop effective behavior change assistance approaches to help reduce the frequency of risky behaviors among high-risk groups. Psychologists, too, work with AIDS victims in counseling and support groups, providing psychological assistance to help them cope more effectively with the devastating impact of the disease.

Obesity

Various psychological factors contribute to obesity, such as negative emotions like depression and anxiety. Obesity is a risk factor for other stress-related disorders and often has negative emotional consequences. Psychological techniques, such as behavior modification, are often used in the treatment of obesity. While a diathesis toward obesity may be genetically transmitted, environment also plays an important role.

Various methods have been used to help people lose weight and keep it off, including biological interventions like diet pills and surgery, and behavioral techniques that focus on modifying eating habits and exercising. Very low calorie diet (VLCD) programs have shown initial rapid weight losses, but recent research suggests that much of the weight is eventually regained. Surgical techniques for the morbidly obese may produce large weight losses but some techniques remain controversial on grounds of safety. Behavioral methods are generally associated with moderate amounts of weight loss, but maintaining weight losses remains a nagging problem. The use of appetite-suppressing drugs has not increased the effectiveness of behavioral methods and may actually decrease their long-term efficacy.

KEY FOR TYPE A QUESTIONNAIRE

"Yes" responses are suggestive of a Type A behavior pattern, which is characterized by a sense of time urgency and hard-driving ambition. The scale was adapted from descriptions of the Type A behavior pattern by Matthews et al. (1982), Musante et al. (1983) and Friedman and Ulmer (1984). Do not be concerned with adding up your total score, since we have no normative data to compare it with. But, as noted by Friedman and Rosenham (1984, p. 85), you should have little difficulty determining whether or not you are a "hardcore" Type A personality or are "moderately afflicted." That assumes, of course, that you've been honest with yourself in answering the items.

6

Anxiety Disorders

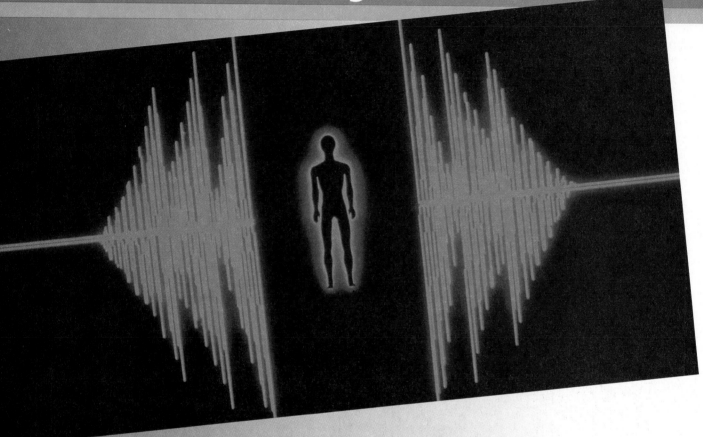

- ___ Some people are suddenly overtaken by feelings of panic, even though there is no external threat.
- ___ Some people live in dread of receiving injections even though the potential pain doesn't bother them a bit.
- ___ Some people feel compelled to check and recheck that they have locked the doors and windows, so that they are delayed in leaving the house for an hour or more.
- ___ Some people may bring on panic attacks because of fear of anxiety.
- ___ Relaxing in a recliner and fantasizing can be an effective way of reducing fears.

LEARNING OBJECTIVES

When you have completed your study of Chapter 6, you should be able to:

ANXIETY DISORDERS (pp. 191–192)
1. Describe the chief features of anxiety and define the term anxiety disorder.

HISTORICAL PERSPECTIVES ON ANXIETY DISORDERS (pp. 192–194)
2. Discuss the historical changes in the classification of anxiety disorders.

PANIC DISORDER (pp. 194–195)
3. Define and describe panic disorder and explain the differences between panic attacks and other forms of anxiety.

GENERALIZED ANXIETY DISORDER (pp. 195–196)
4. Define and describe generalized anxiety disorder.

PHOBIC DISORDERS (pp. 197–202)
5. Define and describe simple phobia, social phobia, and agoraphobia.

OBSESSIVE-COMPULSIVE DISORDER (pp. 202–203)
6. Define and describe obsessive-compulsive disorder.

THEORETICAL VIEWS OF ANXIETY DISORDERS (pp. 203–213)
7. Describe various theoretical perspectives on the anxiety disorders.

TREATMENT OF ANXIETY DISORDERS (pp. 213–220)
8. Describe various methods for treating anxiety disorders.
9. Recount research concerning the efficacy of various treatment approaches.

Anxiety is a generalized state of apprehension or fear about what may happen. There is much to be anxious about—health, social relationships, examinations, careers, international relations, and the environment are but a few. It is normal, even desirable and adaptive, to be somewhat anxious about these aspects of life. Anxiety serves us well when it prompts us to seek regular medical check-ups or when it motivates us to study harder for tests. Anxiety is an appropriate response to threatening situations, but anxiety can be abnormal when its level is out of proportion to the threat, or when it seems to "come out of the blue"— that is, when its occurrence is not in response to environmental changes. In extreme forms, anxiety can impair our ability to function in meeting our daily responsibilities, like commuting to work. Consider the case of Dick:

■ Slowly the trains snake their way through the maze of tunnels that lie beneath the city, carrying the Dashing Dans and Danielles on their way to work each morning. Most commuters pass the time by reading the morning newspapers, sipping their coffee, or catching a few last winks of sleep. For Dick, the morning commute became an experience of sheer terror on one rather ordinary day in July. At first, Dick noticed the perspiration clinging to his shirt. The air conditioning seemed to be working fine, for a change. No reason, he thought, to account for the perspiration that clung to his shirt, under his charcoal gray suit and yellow "power tie." As the train entered the tunnel and darkness covered the windows, Dick was gripped by a feeling of sheer terror. He sensed his heart beating faster, the muscles in his neck tightening. A sickening feeling of queasiness filled his stomach. He felt like he might pass out at any moment. The other commuters, engrossed in their morning papers or their own private thoughts, paid no heed to Dick, nor did they seem concerned about the darkness that enveloped the train.

Dick had known these feelings all too well before. But now the feelings of terror seemed worse. Other days he could bear it. But this time, it seemed to start earlier than usual, even before the train entered the darkened tunnel. He thought to himself that perhaps it would pass. "Just don't think about it," he said to himself, hoping it would pass. "I must think of something to distract myself," he thought. He tried humming a song, but the panic only grew worse. He tried calming himself down, telling himself that it would be all right, that any moment the train would enter the station and the doors would open. Not this day, however. On this day, the train came to a screeching halt; the conductor announced a signalling problem. Dick tried to talk calmly to himself, "It's only a short delay. We'll be moving soon." But the train did not start moving soon. More apologies were announced by the conductor. A train had broken down farther ahead in the tunnel. Dick realized it could be a long delay, maybe even hours. Suddenly he felt an urgent desire to escape. But how, he thought. Barely enough room for a crawl space outside the train. That's if you could break the window and crawl out of the train, if worse came to worse.

He felt like he was losing control. Sudden wild imaginings entered his mind. He saw himself running wildly down the aisles in a desperate attempt to escape, knocking people over, trying unsuccessfully to pry the doors open. He was filled with a sense of impending doom. Something terrible was about to happen to him. "Was this the first sign of a heart attack?" he wondered anxiously. By now the perspiration had soaked through his clothes. His once neatly tightened tie was loosened awkwardly. He felt his breathing becoming heavy and forced, drawing attention from other passengers. "What do they think of me?" he thought. "Would they help me if I needed them?"

But suddenly, the train starting moving again. Suddenly he realized he would soon be free. "I'm going to be okay," he told himself, "the feelings will pass. I'm going to be myself again." The train slowly pulled into the station, twenty minutes late. The doors opened and the

passengers hurried to their jobs. Leaving the train, Dick tightened his tie and readied himself to start the day. He felt like he'd been through a war. Nothing that his boss could dish out could hold a candle to what he'd been through on the 7:30 train.

Dick had suffered a panic attack, one of many such attacks he'd experienced in a period of several months before seeking treatment. The attacks varied in frequency, sometimes occurring daily, sometimes once a week or so. He would never know whether an attack would occur on any particular day. He knew, however, that he couldn't go on living like this. He imagined that one day he would suffer a heart attack on the train. He pictured some of his fellow passengers trying vainly to revive him, while others just stared at him in the way that people are drawn to stare at traffic accidents. He pictured the emergency workers rushing to the train, bearing him on a stretcher through the darkened tunnels to a waiting ambulance.

For a while he considered changing jobs, accepting a lower-paying job closer to home that would free him of the need to take the train to work. At first he thought of driving to work, but realized that the roads were too heavily clogged with traffic. No choice, he figured; either commute by train or change jobs. His wife, Jill, was unaware of his panic attacks. She did wonder about why his shirts were so heavily stained by perspiration and why Dick began to talk about changing jobs. She worried whether the family would be able to make ends meet on a lower income. But she had no idea that it was the train ride, and not the job itself, which Dick so desperately sought to avoid.

The Authors' Files ■

Panic attacks, like the one suffered by Dick in the case example, are a feature of **panic disorder,** a severe type of **anxiety disorder.** During a panic attack, the level of anxiety rises to the point of sheer terror.

A host of anxiety-related physical features, cognitions, and behaviors are shown in Table 6.1. While anxiety is not often experienced with the full range of features shown in the table, it is easy to see why anxiety is a major form of emotional distress.

HISTORICAL PERSPECTIVES ON ANXIETY DISORDERS

The anxiety disorders, along with the dissociative disorders and somatoform disorders (discussed in Chapter 7), have been classified as **neuroses** throughout most of the past century. The term *neurosis* derives from roots meaning "an abnormal or diseased condition of the nervous system." It was coined by the Scottish physician William Cullen in the eighteenth century. As the derivation implies, it was assumed that the behavior patterns included by the term had biological origins—some sort of affliction of the nervous system that produced a number of unusual behavior patterns.

TABLE 6.1 Some Features of Anxiety

Physical Features of Anxiety	Jumpiness, jitteriness	Cognitive Features of Anxiety	Worrying about something
	Trembling or shaking of the hands or limbs		A nagging sense of dread or apprehension about the future
	Sensations of a tight band around the forehead		Belief that something dreadful is going to happen, with no clear cause
	Tightness in the pit of the stomach or chest		Preoccupation with bodily sensations
	Heavy perspiration		Keen awareness of bodily sensations
	Sweaty palms		Feeling threatened by people or events that are normally of little or no concern
	Light-headedness or faintness		Fear of losing control
	Dryness in the mouth or throat		Fear of inability to cope with one's problems
	Difficulty talking		Thinking that one's world is caving in
	Difficulty catching one's breath		
	Shortness of breath or shallow breathing		Thinking that things are getting out of hand
	Heart pounding or racing		Thinking that things are swimming by too rapidly to take charge of them
	Tremulousness in one's voice		
	Cold fingers or limbs		Worrying about every little thing
	Dizziness		Thinking the same disturbing thought over and over
	Weakness or numbness		
	Difficulty swallowing		Thinking that one must flee crowded places or else pass out
	A "lump in the throat"		
	Stiffness of the neck or back		Finding one's thoughts jumbled or confused
	Choking or smothering sensations		
	Cold, clammy hands		Not being able to shake off nagging thoughts
	Upset stomach or nausea		
	Hot or cold spells		Thinking that one is going to die, even when one's doctor finds nothing medically wrong
	Frequent urination		
	Feeling flushed		
	Diarrhea		Worrying that one is going to be left alone
	Feeling irritable or "on edge"		
Behavioral Features of Anxiety	Avoidance behavior		Difficulty concentrating or focusing one's thoughts
	Clinging, dependent behavior		
	Agitated behavior		

At the beginning of our own century, Cullen's organic assumptions became largely replaced by Sigmund Freud's psychodynamic view that neurotic behavior stems from the threatened emergence of unacceptable, anxiety-evoking ideas into conscious awareness. The various neurotic behavior patterns—anxiety disorders, somatoform disorders, and dissociative disorders—might look quite different from each other in terms of observable behavior, but according to Freud, they all represented various ways in which the ego attempts to protect itself from anxiety. This **etiological** assumption, in other words, united the disorders as neuroses. Freud's concepts were so widely accepted earlier in the century that they formed the basis for the classification systems found in the first two editions of the *Diagnostic and Statistical Manual of Mental Disorders*.

You will recall from Chapter 3 that the classification system of the third edition of the DSM—that is, the DSM–III (1980) and the DSM–III–R (1987)—no longer contains a category called "neuroses." The present diagnostic system is based on similarities in observable behavior and distinctive features rather than theoretical assumptions of causation—whether from the psychodynamic or from other theoretical traditions. But it is important to recognize that many clinicians continue to use the terms *neurosis* and *neurotic* in the manner in which Freud described them. In addition, many clinicians retain use of the term "neuroses" as a convenient means of grouping milder forms of behavioral disturbances in which contact with reality is relatively well maintained, in contrast to **"psychoses,"** such as schizophrenia, which are generally more severe and involve loss of touch with reality in the form of such features as bizarre behavior, beliefs, and hallucinations. It also needs to be said that anxiety—or anxiety-related behaviors—are not limited to the categories considered "neuroses." People with adjustment problems, depression, and even psychotic behavior patterns can encounter anxiety.

In this chapter we review the various types of anxiety disorders. The anxiety disorders we consider in this chapter include panic, phobias such as simple phobia, social phobia, and agoraphobia, generalized anxiety, and obsessive-compulsive disorder.* The anxiety disorders are not mutually exclusive. People may, and frequently do, meet diagnostic criteria for more than one anxiety disorder (Turner & Beidel, 1989). A social phobic may also be agoraphobic; a person with a simple phobia may also show evidence of obsessive compulsive disorder.

PANIC DISORDER

According to the DSM–III–R, the essential feature of a **panic disorder** is the recurrent experience of panic attacks. Panic attacks are intense anxiety reactions that include such features as rapid heart rate and respiration, shortness of breath or difficulty breathing, heavy perspiration, and weakness or dizziness. There is a stronger physical component to panic attacks than to other forms of anxiety, suggesting that panic attacks may be qualitatively different from other forms of anxiety as well as more intense (Barlow et al., 1985; Rapee, 1987). These symptoms are often accompanied by a feeling of sheer terror and fears of losing control, going crazy, or even dying. The attacks usually last for several minutes, but can extend to a few hours. Initially the panic attacks are not triggered by a specific object or situation. They seem to occur unexpectedly or "out of the blue."

The causes of panic attacks are not clear. Some suggest that panic attacks reflect biological causes (Klein, 1980; Sheehan, 1982) while others have proposed explanations based on the interaction of cognitive and biological factors (Rapee, 1987). Victims feel exhausted afterward, as if they have survived a truly traumatic experience. The following case highlights the terror of such attacks:

■ I was inside a very busy shopping precinct and all of a sudden it happened; in a matter of seconds I was like

This man was walking to his car when he was suddenly overcome by a panic attack that was accompanied by physical features such as shortness of breath and dizziness. Panic attacks have stronger physical components than other types of anxiety reactions, which suggests that they are qualitatively different than other forms of anxiety, not merely more intense.

a mad woman. It was like a nightmare, only I was awake; everything went black and sweat poured out of me—my body, my hands, and even my hair got wet through. All of the blood seemed to drain out of me; I went white as a ghost. I felt as if I was going to collapse; it was as if I had no control over my limbs; my back and legs were very weak and I felt as though it were impossible to move. It was as if I had been taken over by some stronger force. I saw all of the people looking at me—just faces, no bodies; all merged into one. My heart started pounding in my head and my ears; I thought that my heart was going to stop. I could see black and yellow lights. I could hear the voices of the people but from a long way off. I could not think of anything except the way that I was feeling and that how I had to get out and run quickly or I would die. I must escape and get into fresh air. Outside it subsided a little but I felt limp and weak; my legs were like jelly as though I had run a race and lost; I had a lump in my throat like a golf ball. The incident seemed to me to have lasted hours. I was absolutely drained when I got home and I just broke down and cried; it took until the next day to feel normal again.

Hawkrigg, 1975, pp. 1280–1282. ■

People often describe panic attacks as the worst experiences they have ever had. Their coping abilities are completely overwhelmed. The behavioral response is a tendency to flee, or when flight seems useless, they may freeze. There is often a tendency to seek help from others, to cling to them for support. Some people

---

* The DSM–III–R also includes post-traumatic stress disorder as an anxiety disorder. We discussed PTSD in relation to stress-related disorders in Chapter 4.

with a history of panic attacks fear going anywhere without a trusted companion.

While panic-disorder sufferers usually first experience spontaneous or unexpected panic attacks, they may later come to experience panic attacks that are cued by certain situations, such as driving a car, being in a confined space, or riding aboard a train—like in the case of Dick. Panic-attack sufferers whose attacks seem to occur out of the blue tend to report more severe distress than those whose attacks seem more predictable (Barlow et al., 1985). Unpredictable panic may involve different biological processes than situationally cued attacks. However, the distinction between predictable and unpredictable panic may not be so clearly drawn at times. Panic sufferers may be unaware of more subtle cues that precipitate attacks, such as cues relating to decision making, even making such small decisions as filling out a grocery list. Panics may also be triggered by subtle physiological changes that lie outside the person's awareness, that are brought about by stress, sexual arousal, vigorous exercise, or even sudden temperature changes (Barlow et al., 1985). The panic may be perceived as unpredictable because the cues are so subtle they are not easily detected by the individual (Barlow et al., 1985). If panic sufferers are unable to identify these triggering factors, they may be more likely to attribute their sensations to threatening events, such as experiencing a heart attack or "going crazy." In a later part of the chapter we shall see that the cognitive appraisal of one's own bodily sensations may play an important role in panic disorder.

Some people who suffer from panic disorder are in fact suddenly overtaken by feelings of panic in the absence of an external threat. Other panic sufferers are aware of certain situations that heighten the probability of an attack.

In order for people to be diagnosed as having panic disorder, according to the DSM–III–R, they must suffer four "unexpected" attacks in a month or have at least one attack followed by persistent fear of a subsequent attack for a period of at least a month. The DSM–III–R also requires that individuals show at least four of the 13 physical and cognitive indications shown in Table 6.2 in at least one of their panic attacks.

Persons with panic attacks may be at risk for cardiovascular disorders. A study of 35 patients undergoing evaluation for heart transplants found that 29 had a history of panic disorder (Kahn et al., 1987). It is conceivable that repeated panic attacks weaken the cardiovascular system, but it is perhaps more likely that cardiovascular irregularities are implicated in both panic disorder and heart problems. For example, a chronic increased heart rate and high levels of circulating **catecholamines** may contribute to sensations of panic, inflammation of the muscle tissue of the heart (myocar-

TABLE 6.2 Physical and Cognitive Features of Panic Attacks

1. Shortness of breath or smothering sensations	8. Feelings of depersonalization or derealization (discussed in Chapter 7)
2. Dizziness, unsteadiness, or faintness	9. Numbness or tingling
3. Heart palpitations or tachycardia	10. Hot flashes or chills
4. Trembling or shaking	11. Chest pains or discomfort
5. Sweating	12. Fear of dying
6. Choking	13. Fear of going crazy or losing control
7. Nausea or other abdominal distress	

Source: *Adapted from DSM–III–R, p. 238.*

ditis), and other heart problems. The DSM–III–R notes that malfunctions of the tubing within the heart (mitral valve prolapse) can contribute to panicky sensations. So can high levels of amphetamines and caffeine, as well as the endocrine disorder, **hyperthyroidism.**

In many cases, panic sufferers limit their activities, avoiding places in which they fear attacks may occur or where they are cut off from their usual supports. Panic disorder is thus often associated with agoraphobia, the fear of being out in public places. We will have more to say about agoraphobia later in the chapter.

The onset of panic disorder is usually in late adolescence or early adulthood. Occasional episodes of panicky sensations afflict from one-third to one-half of the general population (Norton & Rhodes, 1983; Norton et al., 1985) and five out of six people who are diagnosed as having other anxiety disorders (Barlow et al., 1985). But only between 1 to 2 percent of the general population in community surveys of several metropolitan areas were found to meet diagnostic criteria for panic disorder (Robins et al., 1984). Women are about twice as likely as men to experience panic attacks (Barlow et al., 1985).

GENERALIZED ANXIETY DISORDER

Generalized anxiety disorder is characterized by persistent anxiety of at least six months' duration. The anxiety is not attributed to a specific object, situation, or activity, but rather seems to be what Freud labeled "free-floating." The DSM–III–R makes the diagnosis when people are excessively apprehensive about two or more life circumstances, such as finances, the well-being of children, or social relationships. Children with the disorder are more likely to be worried about academics, athletics, and other social aspects of school life. The DSM–III–R also requires that six of a listing of 18 features be present, broken down according to motor tension (shakiness, inability to relax, furrowed brow, fidgeting, etc.); autonomic overarousal (sweating, dry mouth, racing heart, light-headedness, frequent urina-

FREE-FLOATING ANXIETY
(MAGNIFIED 200,000,000 TIMES)

Drawing by M. Stevens; © 1982 The New Yorker Magazine, Inc.

tion, nausea, diarrhea, etc.); and "vigilance and scanning" that can impair cognitive functioning (for example, feeling on edge, showing an exaggerated startle response, distractibility, insomnia, and irritability). Generalized anxiety is about equally common in males and females and tends to come on in young adulthood (in one's 20s and 30s).

Although panic and generalized anxiety are both considered anxiety disorders, they are quite different in quality. Generalized anxiety is more diffuse and generally not as impairing. The physical aspects of panic are much more potent, as in the pounding of the heart and the heaviness of the sweating that accompanies panic. Thus, it may be that the biological correlates of the disorders differ in quality as well as intensity. People with generalized anxiety are also often depressed. Sometimes the anxiety follows a depressive episode, but chronic anxiety can also become depressing in its own right.

The diagnosis of generalized anxiety is applied only when other possible sources of anxiety—such as anxieties over physical problems, over leaving the house, or anxiety over possible panic attacks—are ruled out. A sizable percentage of individuals with other anxiety disorders, such as agoraphobia and obsessive-compulsive disorder, also meet the diagnostic criteria for generalized anxiety disorder (Barlow et al., 1986), which raises the question as to whether or not generalized anxiety disorder is indeed a distinct diagnostic category.

In the following case example we find a number of features of generalized anxiety disorder that are associated with a significant level of impairment.

■ Earl was a 52-year-old supervisor at the automobile plant. His hands trembled as he spoke. His cheeks were pale. His face was somewhat boyish, making his hair seem grayed with worry.

He was reasonably successful in his work, although he noted that he was not a "star." His marriage of nearly three decades was in "reasonably good shape," although sexual relations were "less than exciting—I shake so much that it isn't easy to get involved." The mortgage on the house was not a burden and would be paid off within 5 years, but "I don't know what it is; I think about money all the time." The three children were doing well, one employed, one in college, and one in high school, but "With everything going on these days, how can you help worrying about them? I'm up for hours worrying about them."

"But it's the strangest thing," Earl shook his head. "I swear I'll find myself worrying when there's nothing in my head. I don't know how to describe it. It's like I'm worrying first and then there's something in my head to worry about. It's not like I start thinking about this or that and I see it's bad and then I worry. And then the shakes come, and then, of course, I'm worrying about worrying, if you know what I mean. I want to run away; I don't want anyone to see me. You can't direct workers when you're shaking."

Going to work had become a major chore. "I can't stand the noises of the assembly lines. I just feel jumpy all the time. It's like I expect something awful to happen. When it gets bad like that I'll be out of work for a day or two with shakes."

Earl had been worked up "for everything; my doctor took blood, saliva, urine, you name it. He listened to everything, he put things inside me. He had other people look at me. He told me to stay away from coffee and alcohol. Then from tea. Then from chocolate and Coca-Cola, because there's a little bit of caffeine [in them]. He gave me Valium and I thought I was in heaven for a while. Then it stopped working, and he switched me to something else. Then that stopped working, and he switched me back. Then he said he was 'out of chemical miracles' and I better see a shrink or something. Maybe it was something from my childhood."

The Authors' Files ■

Anxiety is an unpleasant emotional state characterized by heightened physiological arousal, feelings of tension, and a sense of foreboding about the future.

PHOBIAS

The word *phobia* derives from the Greek *phobos*, meaning "fear." The concepts of fear and anxiety are closely related. **Fear** is the feeling of anxiety and agitation in response to a threat. Phobic disorders are persistent fears of objects or situations that are disproportional to the threat posed by them. The experience of gripping fear when one's car is about to go out of control is normal, for there is objective jeopardy in the situation. In phobic disorders, however, the fear exceeds any reasonable appraisal of danger. A person with a phobia for cars, for example, might become fearful even when the vehicle is traveling well below the speed limit on a sunny, uncrowded highway. Or be so afraid that he or she wouldn't drive, or even ride in a car. Phobic disorders include a behavioral component—avoidance behavior—in addition to the physical and cognitive features of anxiety. Phobic people strive to avoid the stimuli that unsettle them. Phobias may also interfere with people's normal routines, possibly impairing their occupational or social functioning. People afflicted by phobias generally realize that their fears are excessive or unreasonable. Their cognitive functioning is not distorted to the point where they are out of touch with reality. Put it this way: A person with a phobia for elevators may refuse to enter one at all costs, but he or she realizes that the fear exceeds the objective danger.

Phobias usually involve fears of the ordinary events in life, not the extraordinary. Phobics become fearful of ordinary experiences that most people take for granted, such as riding on an elevator or driving on a highway. Phobias become disabling when they interfere with daily tasks like taking buses, planes, or trains; driving; shopping; or leaving the house.

Phobias are quite common. Surveys of several metropolitan communities in the United States have reported rates of prevalence in the general community of between 7.8 to 23.3 percent (Robins et al., 1984). Different kinds of phobias tend to appear at different ages, as noted in Table 6.3. The various ages of onset appear to reflect factors such as cognitive development and the nature of life experiences. Animals are commonly found in children's fantasies, for example. The

kinds of experiences that may be related to reluctance to leave the house (as in agoraphobia), however, may accumulate over several years of adult life.

The DSM–III–R identifies three types of phobic disorders: *simple phobia, social phobia,* and *agoraphobia.*

The woman in photo (a) has a simple phobia involving an intense fear of injections. The young man sitting by himself in photo (b) is a social phobic. He would like to form relationships with his peers, but keeps largely to himself because of fears of social criticism and rejection. In photo (c) we see a woman with such severe agoraphobia that she resists leaving her house even when accompanied by her daughter.

(a)

(b)

(c)

TABLE 6.3 Typical Age of Onset for Various Phobias

	N	Mean Age of Onset
Animal phobia	50	7
Blood phobia	40	9
Dental phobia	60	12
Social phobia	80	16
Claustrophobia	40	20
Agoraphobia	100	28

Source: *Ost* (1987).

QUESTIONNAIRE
The Temple Fear Survey Inventory

Thunder? Cars? Being alone? Tests? Blood? Needles and knives? Illness? High or tight places? Making a speech? Creepy-crawlies? What objects or situations do you fear? What stimuli do you strive to avoid?

To compare your fears with those of undergraduate students at Temple University, use this code to signify the amount of fear you encounter when faced with each of the stimuli given below:

1 = None
2 = Some
3 = Much
4 = Very Much
5 = Terror

Then check the answer key at the end of the chapter.

_____ 1. Noise of vacuum cleaners
_____ 2. Being cut
_____ 3. Being alone
_____ 4. Speaking before a group
_____ 5. Dead bodies
_____ 6. Loud noises
_____ 7. Being a passenger in a car
_____ 8. Driving a car
_____ 9. Auto accidents
_____ 10. People with deformities
_____ 11. Being in a strange place
_____ 12. Riding a roller coaster
_____ 13. Being in closed places
_____ 14. Thunder
_____ 15. Falling down
_____ 16. One person bullying another
_____ 17. Being bullied by someone
_____ 18. Loud sirens
_____ 19. Doctors
_____ 20. High places
_____ 21. Being teased
_____ 22. Dentists
_____ 23. Cemeteries
_____ 24. Strangers
_____ 25. Being physically assaulted
_____ 26. Failing a test
_____ 27. Not being a success
_____ 28. Losing a job
_____ 29. Making mistakes
_____ 30. Sharp objects (knives, razor blades, scissors)
_____ 31. Death
_____ 32. Death of a loved one
_____ 33. Worms
_____ 34. Imaginary creatures
_____ 35. Dark places
_____ 36. Strange dogs
_____ 37. Receiving injections
_____ 38. Seeing other people injected
_____ 39. Illness
_____ 40. Angry people
_____ 41. Mice and rats
_____ 42. Fire
_____ 43. Ugly people
_____ 44. Snakes
_____ 45. Lightning

Simple Phobias

Simple phobias are persistent, excessive fears of specific objects or situations. The fears of simple phobics produce powerful avoidance motives (Lang, 1985). When they imagine the fear-inducing stimuli, simple phobics tend to show greater arousal, as measured by changes in heart rate and skin conductance, than social or agoraphobics (Cook et al., 1988). Unpleasant arousal helps mobilize the individual to escape or avoid the feared stimulus (Cook et al., 1988). While a simple phobic who fears white mice can probably avoid or escape a confrontation with the feared object, a social phobic whose fear is evoked by talking to a group of people or conversing with strangers may not be able to just simply walk away from the situation.

One simple phobia is fear of elevators. Some phobics will not enter elevators despite hardships such as walking six or more flights of stairs. True, the cable _could_ break. Yes, the ventilation _could_ fail. One _could_ get caught in midair waiting for repairs. But these calamities are uncommon, and most would agree that it is unreasonable to walk many flights of stairs simply to avoid them, or to reject an attractive job offer because the company is located on a high floor. In the same way, persons with simple phobias for hypodermic syringes may refuse injections, even when their health suffers as a result. Injections are sometimes painful, but most phobics would accept equally painful pinches in the arm if these would improve their health.

 Some people do live in dread of receiving injections, although they are not bothered by the pain. They have a phobia for injections.

_____ 46. Sudden noises

_____ 47. Swimming alone

_____ 48. Witnessing surgical operations

_____ 49. Prospects of a surgical operation

_____ 50. Deep water

_____ 51. Dead animals

_____ 52. Blood

_____ 53. Seeing a fight

_____ 54. Being in a fight

_____ 55. Being criticized

_____ 56. Suffocating

_____ 57. Looking foolish

_____ 58. Being a passenger in an airplane

_____ 59. Arguing with parents

_____ 60. Meeting someone for the first time

_____ 61. Being misunderstood

_____ 62. Crowded places

_____ 63. Being a leader

_____ 64. Losing control

_____ 65. Being with drunks

_____ 66. Being self-conscious

_____ 67. People in authority

_____ 68. People who seem insane

_____ 69. Boating

_____ 70. God

_____ 71. Being with a member of the opposite sex

_____ 72. Stinging insects

_____ 73. Crawling insects

_____ 74. Flying insects

_____ 75. Crossing streets

_____ 76. Entering a room where other people are already seated

_____ 77. Bats

_____ 78. Journeys by train

_____ 79. Journeys by bus

_____ 80. Feeling angry

_____ 81. Dull weather

_____ 82. Large open spaces

_____ 83. Cuts

_____ 84. Tough-looking people

_____ 85. Birds

_____ 86. Being watched while working

_____ 87. Guns

_____ 88. Dirt

_____ 89. Being in an elevator

_____ 90. Parting from friends

_____ 91. Feeling rejected by others

_____ 92. Odors

_____ 93. Feeling disapproved of

_____ 94. Being ignored

_____ 95. Premature heart beats

_____ 96. Nude men

_____ 97. Nude women

_____ 98. Unclean silverware in restaurants

_____ 99. Dirty restrooms

_____ 100. Becoming mentally ill

Fear survey inventory reprinted from P. R. Braun & D. J. Reynolds (1969). A factor analysis of a 100-item fear survey inventory. Behaviour Research and Therapy, _399–402, 7._

Consider the intense fear of a 28-year-old high school teacher of English:

■ "This will sound crazy, but I wouldn't get married because I couldn't stand the idea of getting the blood test. [Blood tests for syphilis were required at the time.] I finally worked up the courage to ask my doctor if he would put me out with ether or barbiturates—taken by pills—so that I could have the blood test. At first he was incredulous. Then he became sort of sympathetic but said that he couldn't risk putting me under any kind of general anesthesia just to draw some blood. I asked him if he would consider faking the report, but he said that 'administrative procedures' made that impossible.

"Then he got me really going. He said that getting tested for marriage was likely to be one of my small life problems. He told me about minor medical problems that could arise and make it necessary for blood to be drawn, or to have an IV in my arm, so his message was I should

try to come to grips with my fear. I nearly fainted while he was talking about these things, so he gave it up.

"The story has half a happy ending. We finally got married in [a state] where we found out they no longer insisted on blood tests. But if I develop one of those problems the doctor was talking about, or if I need a blood test for some other reason, even if it's life-threatening, I really don't know what I'll do. But maybe if I faint when they're going to [draw blood], I won't know about it anyway, right? . . .

"People have me wrong, you know. They think I'm scared of the pain. I don't like pain—I'm not a masochist—but pain has nothing to do with it. You could pinch my arm till I turned black and blue and I'd tolerate it. I wouldn't like it, but I wouldn't start shaking and sweating and faint on you. But even if I didn't feel the needle at all—just the knowledge that it was in me is what I couldn't take."

The Authors' Files ■

Other examples of simple phobias include **claustrophobia** (fear of enclosed places), **acrophobia** (fear of heights), and fears of snakes, mice, and various other "creepy-crawlies."

Social Phobia

Many of us suffer from mild fears of social situations, such as dating, parties, and social gatherings. A **social phobia,** however, is an intense fear of being judged negatively by others. Social phobics have persistent fears of doing something that will be humiliating or embarrassing. They tend to depreciate their own performance, fear negative evaluations by other people, and experience physiological overarousal in social interactions (Turner et al., 1986). Social phobics may feel as if a thousand observing eyes are pinned on them, scrutinizing them for any flaw. They become preoccupied with the impressions they are making, and they may assume that they are negative. They tend to avoid the social situations that evoke their fears, but in so doing they prevent themselves from learning to overcome them. Stage fright and speech anxiety are examples of common social phobias.

Social phobics may find excuses for declining social invitations and may take lunch at their desks to avoid socializing with their co-workers. Or they may encounter social situations and make a quick escape for the exit at the first sign of anxiety. Escape behavior is reinforced by the relief from anxiety that it produces, but at the cost of not enabling the individual to learn to cope with socially fearful situations more adaptively. Leaving the scene before the anxiety dissipates only serves to strengthen the association between the social situation and anxiety.

Some anxiety in unfamiliar social situations is perfectly normal and adaptive in that it prompts us to pay some attention to what we wear, say, and do. Simple shyness also occurs frequently enough. The psychologist Albert Bandura has noted that many people with complaints of shyness and social anxiety seem to be well skilled in handling themselves in social situations, but suffer from setting unrealistically high expectations of themselves, judging themselves harshly in comparison to extraordinarily skillful models. Although shy people and people with social phobias both share features such as fear of criticism, social phobia generally involves impairment in daily functioning whereas shyness may not (Turner & Beidel, 1989).

Social phobias often affect various areas of life functioning, producing significant emotional distress and impairing social and vocational functioning (Turner et al., 1986). Social phobias may prevent people from completing educational goals, advancing in their careers, or even holding a job (Liebowitz et al., 1985). Social phobics often try to "medicate" themselves with alcohol or turn to tranquilizers (see Figure 6.1). In some extreme cases, social phobics may become so fearful of interacting with others that they become virtually housebound (Turner & Beidel, 1989).

Social phobias may be expressed in different ways. Some social phobics are unable to order food in a restaurant for fear that the waiter or their companions might

FIGURE 6.1

Percentages of social phobics reporting specific difficulties associated with their fears of social situations.
Source: Adapted from Turner & Beidel, 1989

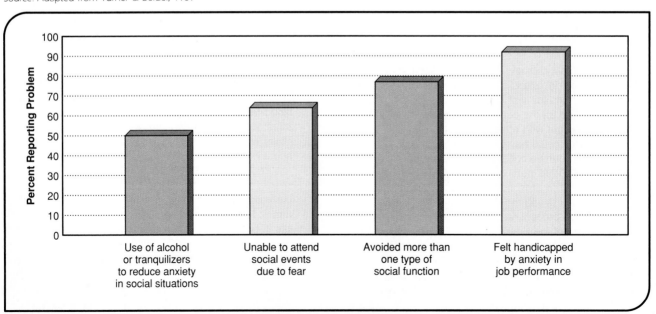

make jest of the foods they order or how they pronounce them. Others fear meeting new people and dating. Still others cannot sign their signatures in public, as in this case:

> ■ Estelle was a signature phobic. She was literally terrified of signing her name in public. She had structured her life to avoid situations requiring a signature. She paid cash rather than by credit card. She filed documents by mail rather than in person. She even registered her car in her husband's name so that he would be responsible for signing the motor vehicle forms. Like many phobics, Estelle was clever at restructuring her life so that she could avoid exposing herself to these fearful situations. She had even kept her phobia from her husband for 15 years.
>
> Estelle's phobia was maintained by an underlying fear of social embarrassment. She feared ridicule for an illegible or sloppy signature, or that authority figures like bank officers or motor vehicle officials would think that her signature was phony or a forgery. Estelle knew that she could prove her identity by other means than her signature and also recognized that no one really cared whether or not her signature was legible. Estelle had created a vicious cycle of anxiety: She felt she must prevent her hands from shaking so that she could write legibly. But her anxiety was so strong that she began to shake whenever her signature was required. The more she tried to fend off the anxiety, the stronger it became. Her anxiety confirmed her belief that her signature would be ridiculed.
>
> The Authors' Files ■

Social phobia is believed to have an earlier age of onset than most other anxiety disorders (Turner & Beidel, 1989), generally beginning in adolescence (Liebowitz et al., 1985; Turner & Beidel, 1989). Social phobias tend to follow a chronic and persistent course (Liebowitz et al., 1985).

Agoraphobia

The word agoraphobia is derived from Greek words meaning "fear of the marketplace," or fear of being out in open, busy areas. Because a person with agoraphobia may be literally afraid of leaving the house, this can be the most incapacitating type of phobia. Agoraphobia involves fears of places and situations from which it might be difficult or embarrassing to escape; or of places and situations where help might not be handy in case of anxiety symptoms or a panic attack. Agoraphobics may fear shopping in crowded stores or walking through crowded streets, eating in restaurants, or traveling. Agoraphobics may become literally housebound. Agoraphobics typically structure their lives to avoid exposing themselves to the situations that evoke their fear. Agoraphobia is more common in women than men and frequently begins in the late teens or early 20s, although it can occur later in life.

The DSM–III–R recognizes two different types of agoraphobia: agoraphobia that occurs as part of a panic disorder and agoraphobia that occurs without a history of panic disorder. In panic disorder with agoraphobia, the experience of one or more panic attacks leads to a fear (agoraphobia) of being in places in which panic attacks might again occur and escape might be difficult or embarrassing or help unavailable. Panic attacks may be so terrifying that victims live in fear of recurrent attacks. They may then avoid situations in which panic attacks have occurred or in which they fear an attack may occur (Franklin, 1987). Because panic attacks can descend from nowhere, some panic sufferers stay home most of the time or severely restrict their activities away from home, for fear of making public spectacles of themselves or finding themselves without help. Or they may only venture outside the home with a companion or somehow manage to endure the intense anxiety evoked by phobic situations. The following case illustates panic disorder with agoraphobia:

> ■ A 30-year-old accountant experienced recurrent panic attacks through a six-month period. The attacks occurred unexpectedly several times a week in a variety of situations, which led him to avoid driving by himself or shopping in department stores, lest he suffer an attack in such situations in which help might not be immediately available. He persuaded his wife to accompany him on errands and eventually became so fearful of leaving the house that he took a medical leave from work.
>
> Adapted from Spitzer et al., 1989, pp. 213–214 ■

A study of 60 agoraphobics who had a history of panic attacks found that many had other diagnosable disorders, such as depression, alcohol abuse, and other anxiety disorders (Breier et al., 1986). The panic attacks appeared to precede the development of agoraphobia in most cases, a finding that is consistent with the view that agoraphobics learn to avoid situations in which they fear the recurrence of a panic attack. In three out of four cases, agoraphobia developed within a year of the initial panic attack.

Panic attacks have also been associated with other anxiety disorders, such as simple phobia and social phobia (Barlow et al., 1985). However, people with panic disorder or panic disorder with agoraphobia reported that their panic attacks included a greater number of distressing symptoms, especially symptoms such as dizziness and fears of losing control or "going crazy" associated with their attacks, than did simple phobics or social phobics who experienced panic attacks (Barlow et al., 1985).

Agoraphobics without a history of panic disorder experience anticipatory anxiety of a wide range of public situations in which escape would be difficult or embarrassing, or help unavailable in the event that distressing or embarrassing symptoms occurred, such as dizziness, feelings of strangeness, or loss of bladder or bowel control. They too may become dependent on nonphobic companions. The following case of agoraphobia without a history of panic disorder illustrates the dependence of agoraphobics:

■ A 32-year-old housewife complains that she is terrified of leaving home for fear of losing her balance and falling or fainting, although she has never fallen or fainted. She began having problems shortly after she and her family moved further away from her mother. Before the move she was able to walk to her mother's and sister's homes, but afterwards the greater distance between them prevented them from immediately coming over if she felt that she needed them. In addition, her husband started his own business, keeping him away from home for much of the time. While at first she avoided leaving her home, she eventually was able to shop on her own in the neighborhood stores when they were not crowded. But then a friend of hers, a 41-year-old man, died of a brain cyst. She then became continually anxious, was unable to leave the house, and only felt comfortable at home when her husband was with her. While no history of panic attacks is reported, the woman did experience similar agoraphobic symptoms 12 years earlier, immediately following her marriage, another point of separation from her family on whom she was dependent.

Adapted from Spitzer et al., 1989, pp. 134–135 ■

OBSESSIVE-COMPULSIVE DISORDER

An **obsession** is a recurrent idea that creates anxiety and seems beyond the person's ability to control. Obsessions can be potent and persistent enough to interfere with daily life. They include doubts, impulses, and mental images. For example, one may doubt repeatedly whether or not one has locked the doors and turned off the gas jets. One may be obsessed with the impulse to do away with his or her spouse. Some people complain that they cannot get the lyrics to songs

One type of obsession involves recurrent, intrusive images of a calamity occurring as the result of some act of carelessness, such as the image that one's house has caught fire due to an overheated appliance that one had failed to turn off.

"out of my head," but most of the time the lyrics "pass through" and do not reach obsessional proportions.

The line between obsessions and the firmly held, but patently false beliefs called **delusions,** which are found in schizophrenia, is sometimes less than clear. The DSM–III–R states that obsessions, such as the belief that one is contaminating other people, can, like delusions, become "almost unshakable" (p. 246). However, people with obsessions can usually concede that their beliefs may be groundless "after considerable discussion," whereas true delusions "cannot be shaken" (p. 246).

A **compulsion** is an apparently irresistible, repetitious urge to perform a certain act, such as repeatedly checking to see that the door locks are secure. The impulse can occur frequently and forcefully enough to interfere with daily life. A compulsive hand-washer, Corrinne, engaged in elaborate hand-washing rituals. She spent several hours daily at the sink and later complained, "My hands look like lobster claws." Some people literally take hours before leaving home to check and recheck that all the appliances are off (Goleman, 1988).

 Some obsessive-compulsive people are in fact delayed in leaving the house for an hour or more as they carry out their checking rituals.

Most compulsions fall into two categories: checking rituals and cleaning rituals (Rachman & Hodgson, 1980). Although the rituals can be annoying, they apparently reduce anxieties that would occur if they were prevented. These rituals can become the focal point of life. Checking rituals, like repeatedly checking that the gas jets are turned off or that the doors are securely locked whenever one leaves the house, can cause unnecessary delays and annoy one's companions; cleaning can occupy several hours a day. Some relatively common obsessions and compulsions are listed in Table 6.4.

The DSM–III–R diagnoses **obsessive-compulsive disorder** when people are troubled by recurrent obsessions, compulsions, or a combination of the two to the point where they cause marked distress, occupy more than an hour a day, or significantly interfere with normal routines and functioning. Compulsions appear to partially relieve the anxiety that is created by obsessive thinking (Steketee & Foa, 1985).

Surveys of several metropolitan communities in the United States have shown that obsessive-compulsive disorder affects between 1 and 3 percent of the population at one time or another (Robins et al., 1984). A recent national survey of 18,572 Americans suggested

TABLE 6.4 Examples of Obsessive Thoughts and Compulsive Behaviors

Obsessive Thought Patterns	Compulsive Behavior Patterns
Thinking that one's hands remain dirty despite repeated washing.	Rechecking one's work time and time again.
Difficulty shaking the thought that a loved one has been hurt or killed.	Rechecking the doors or gas jets before leaving home.
Repeatedly thinking that one has left the door to the house unlocked.	Retyping an entire page if one small error is made.
Worrying constantly that the gas jets in the house were not turned off.	Performing a certain behavior in the same, exact way every time.
Repeatedly thinking that one has done terrible things to loved ones.	Constantly washing one's hands to keep them clean and germ-free.

an overall incidence of about 2.5 percent (Goleman, 1988). The disorder seems to afflict both sexes in equal numbers.

The case of Jack illustrates a checking compulsion:

■ Jack, a successful chemical engineer, was urged by his wife, Mary, a pharmacist, to seek help for "his little behavioral quirks," which she had found increasingly annoying. Jack was a compulsive checker. When they left the apartment, he would insist on returning to recheck that the lights or gas jets were off, or that the refrigerator doors were shut. Sometimes he would apologize at the elevator and return to the apartment to carry out his rituals. Sometimes the compulsion to check struck him in the garage. He would return to the apartment, leaving Mary fuming. Going on vacation was especially difficult for Jack. The rituals occupied the better part of the morning of their departure. Even then, he remained plagued by doubts.

Mary had also tried to adjust to Jack's nightly routine of bolting out of bed to recheck the doors and windows. Her patience was running thin. Jack realized that his behavior was impairing their relationship as well as causing himself distress. Yet he was reluctant to enter treatment. He gave lip service to wanting to be rid of his compulsions. However, he feared that surrendering his compulsions would leave him defenseless against the anxieties they helped assuage.

The Authors' Files ■

THEORETICAL PERSPECTIVES

The anxiety disorders offer something of a theoretical laboratory. Many theories of abnormal behavior were developed with these disorders in mind. Classic case studies and experiments have been carried out to affirm or disprove various points of view. In Chapter 2 we explored humanistic-existential hypotheses concerning the meaning and origins of anxiety. In this section we examine anxiety disorders from psychodynamic, learning, cognitive, and biological perspectives.

Psychodynamic Perspectives

From the psychodynamic perspective, anxiety disorders are viewed as neuroses. The anxiety experienced in neuroses reflects (1) the efforts of unacceptable, repressed impulses to break into consciousness and (2) fear as to what might happen if they do. Feelings of anxiety represent danger signals that threatening impulses are nearing the level of awareness. To fend off these threatening impulses, the ego tries to stem or divert the tide through defense mechanisms. Let us illustrate how the theory explains the development of phobias.

Phobias develop through the employment of **displacement** and **projection.** A phobic reaction may represent a projection of the person's own threatening impulses onto the phobic object. For instance, people who are excessively fearful of knives and other sharp instruments may harbor unconscious desires to use these implements on themselves or others. Similarly, acrophobic people may have unconscious wishes to jump that are controlled by avoiding heights. Freud believed that phobias serve an important function—they help contain threatening impulses and keep them out of conscious awareness by motivating the person to stay a safe distance away from the phobic object or situation. The phobic object or situation symbolizes or represents unconscious wishes or desires. The person is aware of the phobia, but not of the unconscious impulses which it symbolizes.

Freud believed that most of our motives are unconscious and that we repress socially unacceptable ideas. This way we can ignore their existence and need not fear punishment or self-condemnation. Impulses seek expression, however, and are often expressed by symbols. These conflicts are believed to have childhood origins. Take the case of "Little Hans," for example, a 5-year-old boy who feared that he would be bitten by a horse if he left his house. In Freud's (1909) case study of the boy's phobia, he wrote it was not horses that Hans really feared—it was what the animals sym-

Psychodynamic theorists suggest that phobias represent the operation of unconscious defense mechanisms like projection and displacement. In their view, a fear of heights, or acrophobia, may represent the ego's attempt to defend itself against the emergence of threatening self-destructive impulses, such as an impulse to jump from a dangerous height. By avoiding heights, the person can maintain a safe distance from such threatening impulses. Since this process occurs unconsciously, the person may only be aware of the phobia, not of the unconscious impulses that it symbolizes.

bolized to him. Hans's fear of horses was held to symbolize an unconscious fear of his father, a form of displacement in which the fear of horses came to substitute for his real (and more threatening) fear of his father. Recall that Freud's conception of the Oedipal conflict holds that, unconsciously, the young boy incestuously desires to possess his mother and fears retribution from his father as a rival for his mother's affection. The horse, then, is believed to symbolize Hans's father. Fear of being bitten may symbolize fear of castration. This unconscious drama is enacted through these symbols.

Hence, according to psychodynamic theory, phobias—such as Hans's horse phobia—symbolize unconscious conflicts. If phobias are to be overcome, the unconscious conflict must be worked through. In Vienna, in the spring of 1922, Freud happened to meet Little Hans, but no longer was he little. He was a "strapping"

young man of 19. Now Hans suffered from no inhibitions about horses or other large animals. The early childhood events were lost to memory. Hans had apparently overcome his phobia naturally. The ancient inner conflict had become resolved by time and maturity. It no longer required symbolic expression. It remains the position of many of those who work in the Freudian tradition that successful elimination of many fears requires resolution of the inner conflicts they are thought to represent.

Learning theorists view Hans's childhood fears as a case in classical conditioning (Bandura, 1969; Wolpe & Rachman, 1960). They argue that Hans's fear had been learned from an experience of being frightened by an accident involving a horse and a transport vehicle, which generalized to fears of horses. The story of Little Hans is one of the great cases in the psychoanalytic literature. The interpretation of the case has sparked a fascinating debate.

Let us consider how the various types of anxiety disorders may be conceptualized within the psychodynamic model. In people with generalized anxiety disorder, unconscious conflicts remain hidden, but anxiety leaks through to the level of awareness. The person is unable to account for the anxiety because its source remains shrouded in unconsciousness, however. In panic disorder, sexual or aggressive impulses approach the boundaries of consciousness and the ego strives desperately to repress them, generating high levels of conflict and producing the attack. Panic then dissipates when the impulse has been safely repressed. Psychoanalysts view obsessions in terms of the leakage of unconscious impulses. Compulsions are acts that allow people to keep such impulses partly repressed. Cleanliness rituals, for example, are thought to reflect the mechanisms of fixation and reaction formation—the ego's defense against the emergence of infantile urges to soil and play with the feces. Soiling may also be an infantile way of punishing harsh or neglectful parents.

People who become obsessed with thoughts of harming the people they love may harbor unconscious aggressive impulses that intrude into consciousness. The aggressive impulses may be clearly expressed, as in the case of a man who becomes obsessed with thoughts of killing his wife. The aggressive impulses may also be indirectly expressed, in the form of obsessions or repeated fantasies of one's children or spouse being struck by a car or involved in a terrible accident. Consider, for example, the case of Bonnie:

■ Bonnie was an extremely attractive 29-year-old who complained of being obsessed by fantasies that her 8- and 11-year-old children were run over on their way home from school. It was April and the fantasies had begun in September, gradually occupying more time during the day.

"I'm usually all right for most of the morning," she explained. "But after lunch the pictures come back to me. There's nothing I can do about it. The pictures are in my head. I see them walking home and crossing the street, and I know what's going to happen and I think 'Why can't I do something to stop it?' but I can't. They're walking into the street and a car is coming along speeding, or a truck, and then it happens again, and they're lying there, and it's a horrible mess.'' She broke into tears. "And I can't function. I can't do anything. I can't get it out of my head."

"Then sometimes it bothers me at night and [my husband] says 'What's wrong?' He says I'm shaking and white as a ghost and 'What's wrong?' I can't tell him what's going on because he'll think I'm crazy. And then I'm in and out of [the children's] bedrooms, checking that they're all right, tucking them in, kissing them, making sure I can see that they're breathing. And sometimes I wake [the 11-year-old] up with my kissing and he says 'Mommy' and I start crying as soon as I get out of the room."

Through discussions with the psychologist, it appeared that Bonnie was generally dissatisfied with her life. She had gotten married at a young age because she had become pregnant and she had remained in the home. Her daytime companion was her television set. Her husband was generally good to her, but he did not understand why Bonnie might be unhappy, "especially when so many women have to work these days to make ends meet." Within a few weeks Bonnie came to the conclusion that it was "all right" for her to feel resentments toward being "thrown" into the role of mother at an early age. Her resentment at never having made decisions about the course her life would take did not mean that she was a bad mother. Open discussion of her frustrations was connected with a marked decrease in her report of obsessive thoughts.

The Authors' Files ∎

The case of Bonnie provides the type of case account that may lend support to psychodynamic views. It suggests that obsessions and other kinds of anxious behavior patterns sometimes reflect hostilities that we sweep under the rug or do not think about (that is, no "good mother" should have hostile feelings toward her children). On the other hand, it can be argued that Bonnie's case does not offer direct evidence of the existence of such unconscious impulses or conflicts.

Learning Perspectives

From the behavioral perspective, anxiety disorders are acquired through conditioning. According to O. Hobart Mowrer's (1948) **two-factor model,** both classical and operant conditioning are involved in phobias. Phobias are assumed to be acquired by means of classical conditioning. As with Little Albert, the boy who was conditioned to fear rats by John Watson and Rosalie Rayner (1920), it is assumed that neutral objects and situations gain the capacity to produce a fear response by being paired with aversive stimuli. A child who is

frightened by a dog's loud barking may acquire a phobia for dogs. A child who receives a particularly painful injection may develop a phobia for hypodermic syringes. Once acquired, phobias are maintained by means of operant conditioning. Avoiding fear-inducing stimuli is negatively reinforced by relief from anxiety.

From the behavioral perspective, generalized anxiety is precisely that: a product of stimulus generalization. People who are concerned about broad life themes, such as finances, health, and family matters, are likely to experience their apprehensions in a variety of settings. Anxiety would thus become connected with almost any environment or situation. Agoraphobia would similarly be a kind of generalized anxiety, in which anxiety becomes associated with a wide range of social or vocational situations away from home in which the individual is expected to perform in independent roles, such as shopping, traveling, or going to work. In both cases clinicians are encouraged to help clients pinpoint the anxiety-evoking stimuli so that clients can overcome their fears by methods such as gradual exposure (discussed later in the chapter) or learning how to manage the situations that distress them. Some learning theorists also assume that the panic that descends "out of nowhere" actually has specific triggers that remain unidentified.

There are many challenges to these behaviorist notions. For example, many phobic individuals argue that they cannot recall painful exposures to the dreaded stimuli. Behaviorists may counter that since many phobias are acquired in early childhood, it would be understandable for their origins to be beyond memory. But many phobias, such as social phobias and agoraphobia, develop at later ages and appear to involve cognitive processes relating to the appraisal of threat in social situations (fear of embarrassment or criticism) or public places (perceptions of helplessness or fears of panic attacks). We shall explore cognitive factors in anxiety disorders later in the chapter.

∎ The "Value" of Avoiding Fear-Evoking Stimuli
There is strong evidence for the idea that avoiding phobic stimuli brings fast relief from anxiety. In the experiment by Bandura and his colleagues reported in Chapter 4, women who feared spiders were given tasks like allowing a spider to crawl on them. While the women confronted the spiders, blood samples were collected and analyzed for concentrations of the catecholamines—epinephrine and norepinephrine. Catecholamines arouse the body by way of the sympathetic branch of the ANS. As a result, we feel shaky, have "butterflies in the stomach," and other signs of anxiety. In the study, women who said they could not manage facing the spider *and who then refused to try to do so* showed sudden drops in catecholamine levels. That is, *avoidance of a fear-inducing stimulus was reinforced by*

immediate reductions in arousal associated with fear. So the Bandura study adds to the body of evidence suggesting that people learn to avoid fear-evoking stimuli because of reduction of anxiety.

On the other hand, Bandura (1982), a social-learning theorist, points out that there is no mechanical, one-to-one relationship between one's anxiety level and willingness to confront fear-evoking stimuli. Beliefs as to whether or not one can manage fear-inducing stimuli—that is, self-efficacy expectancies—can be more powerful predictors of behavior than anxiety level. For example, many women tackled the spiders when they believed they could manage them, regardless of their catecholamine levels (Bandura et al., 1985). Social-learning and cognitive theorists suggest that anxiety can be maintained by thinking that one is in a terrible situation and cannot manage it.

There may be immediate benefits to avoiding feared stimuli, but there is a long-term price. Avoidance of fearful stimuli may prevent the individual from extinguishing fear of them. We will see, later on, that behavioral methods involving gradual exposure to fear-inducing stimuli have been used with success in helping people overcome phobias.

■ **Reinforcement of Obsessive-Compulsive Behavior** From the learning perspective, compulsive behaviors are operant responses that are reinforced by relieving the anxiety engendered by obsessive thinking. If a person has obsessive thoughts that other people's hands are contaminated by dirt or foreign bodies, ordinary acts like shaking hands or turning a door knob may evoke powerful anxiety. The compulsive ritual of hand washing following exposure to a possible contaminant provides some relief from this anxiety. Thus people become more likely to repeat the obsessive-compulsive cycle the next time they are exposed to anxiety-evoking cues, such as shaking hands or touching door knobs.

Of course, the question remains as to why some people develop obsessive thoughts while others do not. Some theorists look for an interaction of learning and biological factors for possible answers. For example, perhaps people who develop obsessive-compulsive disorder are physiologically sensitized to overreact to minor cues of danger (Steketee & Foa, 1985). The concept of *prepared conditioning* also assumes an interaction between learning and biological factors.

■ **Prepared Conditioning** Seligman and Rosenhan (1984) suggest that people are genetically *prepared* to acquire phobic responses to certain classes of stimuli. For this reason, this model is referred to as **prepared conditioning.** The model suggests that evolutionary forces would have favored the survival of human ancestors who were genetically predisposed to acquire fears of large animals or snakes, or of heights, entrapment, sharp objects, and even strangers (McNally, 1987). Humans who were not so genetically endowed and didn't readily acquire these fears would have been less likely to survive and to pass along their genetic stock. Therefore, people today may have inherited a tendency to develop certain kinds of phobias that had survival value in the past, but not necessarily so in the present.

Subjects in laboratory experiments have received electric shock while being shown photographs of a wide range of stimuli (Hugdahl & Ohman, 1977; Ohman et al., 1976). The subjects acquired fear reactions to some stimuli (for example, spiders and snakes) much more readily than others (say, flowers and houses), as measured by galvanic skin response to later exposure to these stimuli. People are also relatively more resistant to attempts to extinguish fears of snakes and spiders (McNally, 1987). All in all, subjects seem more *prepared* to acquire fear responses to stimuli like snakes and spiders. These experiments do not demonstrate that the subjects are *genetically* prepared to develop their fear responses, however. (Keep in mind that subjects were reared in a society in which many people react negatively to these "creepy crawlies.") People might therefore be culturally and cognitively prepared—not genetically prepared—to acquire fear responses to snakes, spiders, and other stimuli generally perceived as repugnant in our society.

According to the prepared conditioning model, we may inherit tendencies that prepare us to more readily acquire phobic responses to certain types of stimuli that may have threatened the survival of our early ancestors, such as reptilian creatures and large animals. Perhaps that's why exaggerated forms of such creatures have been favored by producers of monster movies.

■ **Observational Learning of Fears** Learning theorists have also noted a role of observational learning in acquiring fears. As described by Mowrer (1960), newborn chicks are indifferent to chicken hawks. But when their elders see the shadow of a swooping hawk on the ground, they frenziedly flap and clatter and squawk around the yard. After a few repetitions, the chicks squawk it up on their own when an ominous shadow appears.

In a classic study with human subjects, Bandura and Rosenthal (1966) hooked up a confederate to a frightening-looking display of electrical equipment. A buzzer was sounded, and the confederate's arm shot up as though he had been shocked intensely. He also yowled and grimaced convincingly, but no shock was actually given. The true subjects in the study watched the confederate while their own physiological responses were being monitored. After a few repetitions, the subjects showed higher autonomic reactivity when the buzzer was sounded, even though they were in no danger of receiving shock.

Similarly, if parents squirm or shudder at the sight of mice, blood, or even dirt on the kitchen floor, their children might encode these stimuli as threatening or awful and show high autonomic reactivity and avoidance in response to them. Thus, fears may be learned by observing other people's fearful reactions to particular stimuli, even without any direct aversive exposure to these stimuli.

Cognitive Perspectives

Cognitive theorists and researchers have identified various patterns of thinking, or cognitive factors, which are associated with anxiety disorders, including overprediction of fear, irrational beliefs, oversensitivity to threats, low self-efficacy expectancies, self-defeating thoughts, and attributional styles.

■ **Overprediction of Fear** Anxious people tend to overpredict the fear they will experience when they encounter a fear-evoking object or situation (Rachman & Bichard, 1988). In one study, subjects who had a phobia about snakes overpredicted the fear that would be induced by exposure to snakes (Rachman & Lopatka, 1986). In another, three out of four panic sufferers overestimated the fear they would encounter when exposed to fear-inducing situations (Rachman et al., 1988).

Overprediction of fear may have survival value as an internal warning system that encourages people to keep their distance from fear-evoking situations (Rachman & Bichard, 1988). But from the cognitive perspective, avoidance of fear-inducing situations prevents people from gaining experience that can promote a more benign reappraisal of the stimuli. Research has shown that fearful subjects do become more accurate in predicting their level of fear following exposure to the fearful situation (Rachman & Bichard, 1988). A clinical implication is that with repeated exposure, phobic clients may become more accurate in predicting their responses to fear-inducing stimuli. It can be pointed out to clients that anticipated fear often exceeds the actual fear, and that exposure can therefore reduce expectancies of fear.

■ **Irrational Beliefs** Phobics have been found to hold more irrational beliefs than nonfearful people, especially beliefs centering around exaggerated needs to be approved of by everyone they meet in order to feel good about themselves and to avoid any situation in which problems might occur (Mizes et al., 1987). Consider these beliefs: "I couldn't stand it if people saw me having an attack. What would they think of me? They might think I was crazy. I couldn't stand it if they looked at me that way." Such beliefs encourage people to avoid situations in which attacks may occur for fear of embarrassment or social disapproval. So it should not be surprising that 65 percent of the anxious subjects in one study endorsed the belief that one must be loved by, and earn the approval of, practically everyone—as compared to only 2 percent of nonanxious subjects (Newmark et al., 1973). Results of another study may hit closer to home: College men who believe that it is awful to be turned down when requesting a date show more social anxiety than men who are less likely to catastrophize rejection (Gormally et al., 1981).

Cognitive theorists relate obsessive-compulsive disorder to tendencies to exaggerate the risk of negative outcomes and to adopt irrational beliefs, especially perfectionistic beliefs (Stekette & Foa, 1985). Because they expect bad things to happen, obsessive-compulsive people engage in compulsive rituals that they believe may prevent those things from happening. An accountant who imagines terrible consequences for making slight mistakes may feel compelled to recheck his or her work again and again. The perfectionist exaggerates the consequences of turning in anything less than perfect, and may feel compelled to redo his or her efforts until every detail is flawless.

■ **Oversensitivity to Threats** Phobic people may harbor cognitions that prompt them to perceive danger in situations that most people consider safe. These cognitions may involve exaggerated perceptions of external dangers (as in, "The bridge might collapse," or "The elevator cables may break"). They may refer to internal cues that function as signs of danger (as in "I think I'm going to fall apart," or "I feel like I'm about to lose control"). Sometimes the cognitions involve themes of social embarrassment or rejection (as in

"What if they think I'm stupid? That would be awful," or "I'm afraid of making a scene"). Phobic people may dwell on various combinations of self-defeating cognitions. Fear of flying may involve perceptions of the plane as unsafe ("What's that vibration? It feels like the plane is about to come apart"), perceptions of personal vulnerability ("What if I have an anxiety attack? There's no escape at 35,000 feet!") and threats of social embarrassment ("Everybody will notice that I'm shaking. They'll think I'm a fool").

Some recent research supports the view that phobics are overly sensitive to perceptions of threat. In comparison to normal people, agoraphobics more often perceive ambiguous physical stimuli and internal states of arousal as threatening (McNally & Foa, 1987).

■ Low Self-Efficacy Expectancies   Another cognitive factor associated with anxiety is low self-efficacy. You'll recall that self-efficacy expectations refer to the individual's belief in being able to perform a certain behavior or task. You might, for example, be confident in your ability to play a Beethoven sonata on the piano. Others, most notably the authors of your textbook, would have very low perceived self-efficacy for performing such a task. When you feel capable of performing a certain task—playing the piano, giving a speech in public, riding on a train without panicking, or touching a small rodent or insect—you are less likely to be troubled by anxiety or fear than if you had little or no confidence in your

abilities. Beliefs that we shall not be able to manage a threat (low self-efficacy expectancies) tend to heighten anxiety (Bandura, 1982; Bandura et al., 1985). On the other hand, beliefs that we are in control (positive self-efficacy expectancies) may lessen anxiety (Miller, 1980).

When people rivet their attention on perceived incapacities, they may fail to search for personal resources that might be used to cope with stressful situations, as we see in the case of Brenda:

■ Brenda, a 19-year-old sophomore, was plagued by anxiety almost from the moment she began her college studies. She had enrolled in a college several hundred miles away from home. While she had been away from home before—at sleep-away camp and on a teen tour through Europe—college life presented various challenges and stresses which she felt a lack of ability to handle. She seemed to be most anxious when meeting new friends and when sitting in class, especially the small seminar classes in which she expected to be called on by the professor. She found herself becoming tongue-tied and dripping with perspiration whenever she confronted these situations. What was more surprising and perplexing to her was that she had never had any trouble before either making new friends or talking in class.

In both situations, Brenda lost confidence in her ability to express herself. The ideas she wished to express were blocked by anxiety, which impaired her ability to think and speak clearly. The anxiety was maintained by a perception of herself, however erroneous, that she was incapable of saying the right thing when called upon in class or when meeting new people. Brenda reported that she hadn't had any problems in high school either speaking up in class or making new friends. College, however, was a different experience. At college there were people she hadn't grown up with, and there were professors who had no tolerance, or so she believed, for any student who wasn't a budding genius. Her whole mental set had shifted into a defensive attitude in which self-doubts replaced self-confidence.

Brenda's past history of social and academic success couldn't shield her from the nagging self-doubts she began to experience as she confronted the more demanding stresses of college life. Brenda was not any less capable of coping with these challenges in college than she was in high school. She didn't suddenly lose her wits or her social skills when she entered college. What was different was that she began to perceive herself as unable to cope with the demands of a new environment that seemed both unsupportive and threatening. Appraising herself this way, it was little wonder that she experienced anxiety in class and social situations, which impaired her efforts to speak clearly. She then interpreted her speech difficulties as evidence of her inadequacies, feeding the vicious circle of anxiety in which self-doubt leads to anxiety, which hampers performance, which occasions more self-doubts and anxiety, and so on.

The Authors' Files ■

According to the self-efficacy model, we are likely to feel more anxious in situations in which we doubt our ability to perform competently. Even accomplished athletes may be seized with anxiety in pressure situations, especially if they begin to doubt their abilities. Anxiety may hamper their performance, making it more difficult for them to perform successfully.

Self-doubts about the capacity to handle challenges or stressors place people in a pattern of thinking that cognitive theorist Aaron Beck and his colleagues (Beck et al., 1985) labels the **vulnerability mode.** The vulnerability mode is associated with a pattern of distorted thinking that results in processing information in terms of perceived weaknesses rather than strengths.

Consider the example of the task-oriented surgeon who is able to become completely immersed in work. The surgeon's hands move naturally, as if guided by a wisdom and confidence of their own. Yet if the surgeon begins to doubt his or her skills and enters the vulnerability mode, anxiety creates internal obstacles or inhibitions that hamper performance. The surgeon's mind may go blank or his or her hands freeze up. Such inhibitory mechanisms can be activated even by slight threats to self-confidence, such as a negative look from a colleague. A track record of success is no guarantee that the vulnerability mode cannot be activated by self-doubts.

■ Self-Defeating Thoughts   Note the ways in which self-defeating thoughts can heighten and perpetuate anxiety and phobic disorders. When faced with fear-evoking stimuli, many people have thoughts such as "I've got to get out of here," or "My heart is going to leap out of my chest" (Meichenbaum & Jaemko, 1983). Thoughts like these intensify autonomic arousal, disrupt planning, magnify the aversiveness of stimuli, prompt avoidance behavior, and decrease self-efficacy expectancies concerning capacity to control the situation. Schwartz and Michelson (1987) found that agoraphobics tend to produce self-defeating thoughts prior to treatment and more adaptive thoughts during and immediately following treatment. Those who show the most improvement with treatment showed the greatest shifts from self-defeating to adaptive thoughts.

■ Attributions for Panic Attacks   Cognitive models of panic disorders generally assume that panic attacks involve catastrophic misinterpretations of bodily sensations (Clark, 1986). Unless people are psychologically and biologically sophisticated, they are likely to misread the sensations of a panic attack. Victims are likely to attribute the sensations to threatening events, such as an impending heart attack or "going crazy." People who suffer from other kinds of anxiety, which are less physically traumatic, tend to recognize their sensations for what they are and not to confuse them with physical illness (Rapee, 1985). Clark (1986) offers these examples of the misinterpretations of panic sufferers:

1.   A physically healthy person perceives heart palpitations or accelerated heart rate as evidence of impending heart attack.

2.   A physically healthy person perceives slight breathlessness and dizziness as evidence of impending cessation of breathing and death.

3.   The person perceives a shaky feeling as evidence of impending loss of control or insanity.

The triggering stimuli for panic attacks may be external—such as entering a supermarket in which a previous attack has occurred. More often, however, the precipitating stimuli involve internal cues like minor changes in physical sensations, thoughts, and images. If these internal cues are perceived as threatening, mild anxiety or apprehension may develop, which compounds the bodily sensations. When these secondary anxiety signals are "blown out of proportion" or catastrophized, anxiety is exacerbated and this further intensifies bodily sensations. This can further increase one's fear, leading to a vicious circle that may culminate in a full-blown panic attack (see Figure 6.2).

FIGURE 6.2

A model of panic disorder that involves the interaction of cognitive and physiological factors. In panic-prone people, perceptions of threat from internal or external cues lead to feelings of apprehension or anxiety, which lead to changes in body sensations (for example, cardiovascular symptoms), which in turn lead to catastrophic interpretations of these body sensations, thereby intensifying the perception of threat, which further heightens anxiety, and so on in a vicious circle that may culminate in a full-blown panic attack.
Source: Adapted from Clark, 1986.

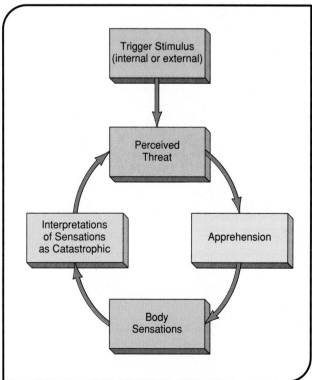

Some people may have such a *fear of anxiety* that they encode sensations of anxiety as awful and thereby heighten them, setting the stage for this vicious circle of panic. Fears of anxiety may arise from various factors, such as biological predispositions, personality characteristics such as the need to avoid embarrassment and maintain control at all times, and a history of frightening anxiety attacks that may have sensitized the individual to anxiety cues (Reiss et al., 1987).

Several recent studies shed light on some of these cognitive factors. In one, agoraphobics with panic were asked to describe their thoughts about their first panic attacks (Breier et al., 1986). Most attributed the attack to grave origins such as a heart attack, stroke, brain tumor, or to "going crazy." Those who perceived their first attacks as life-threatening were more likely to de-velop agoraphobia than those who attributed them to anxiety. Also, people whose initial attacks seemed spontaneous or "out of the blue" were more likely to progress to agoraphobia than people whose attacks seemed connected with specific stimuli. Spontaneous attacks may instill the belief that outside activities must be avoided since attacks might occur during them. People who receive accurate information following their initial panic attacks may be less likely to develop agoraphobia.

 Such factors as catastrophic misinterpretations of anxiety cues, and fear of anxiety, apparently can set a vicious circle into motion that brings on panic attacks in some people.

FIGURE 6.3

Measures of subjective arousal (reported anxiety and excitement), heart rate, galvanic skin response, and blood pressure (systolic and diastolic) of persons with panic disorder and normal controls at baseline and under conditions of true and false feedback (FB). People with panic disorder showed changes in the direction of increased subjective and physiological arousal following false feedback, while normal controls showed decreased physiological arousal and no significant changes in subjective arousal.
Source: Adapted from Ehlers et al., 1988.

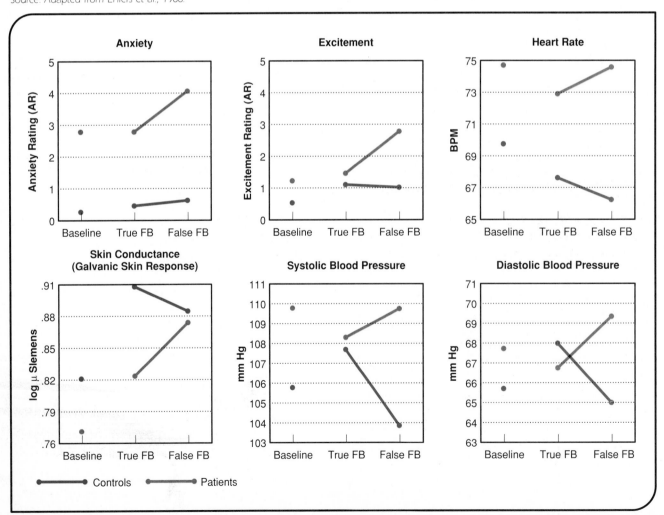

LEARNING OBJECTIVES

When you have completed your study of Chapter 7, you should be able to:

DISSOCIATIVE AND SOMATOFORM DISORDERS

1. Distinguish the dissociative and somatoform disorders from the anxiety disorders in terms of the theorized role of anxiety.
2. Describe the historical changes in the classification of these diagnostic classes.

THE DISSOCIATIVE DISORDERS (pp. 226–238)

3. Describe the chief features of the dissociative disorders.
4. Describe multiple personality disorder.
5. Describe psychogenic amnesia and explain how it differs from other types of amnesia.
6. Describe psychogenic fugue.
7. Describe depersonalization disorder.
8. Explain why inclusion of depersonalization disorder as a dissociative disorder generates controversy.

9. Recount various theoretical perspectives on the dissociative disorders.
10. Explain the theoretical significance of the Spanos study that was inspired by the Hillside Strangler.
11. Describe various methods for treating dissociative disorders.

SOMATOFORM DISORDERS (pp. 238–244)

12. Describe the features of conversion disorder, hypochondriasis, and somatization disorder.
13. Discuss theoretical perspectives on somatoform disorders.
14. Distinguish somatoform disorders from malingering.
15. Describe the features and theoretical accounts of Münchausen syndrome.

I n this chapter we explore a number of intriguing but perplexing diagnostic categories that are related—or have been theorized to be related—to anxiety in various ways. In Chapter 6 we reviewed the category of anxiety disorders, in which various features of anxiety were directly expressed in the form of generalized anxiety, phobias, panic, and obsessive-compulsive behavior. In generalized anxiety disorder and panic disorder, anxiety is usually the principal complaint. In phobic disorders, anxiety is experienced in the presence of the feared object or stimulus. In obsessive-compulsive disorder, anxiety is often directly experienced if the individual attempts to resist the obsessive thoughts or compulsive urges.

In this chapter we focus on two classes of disorders, the dissociative and somatoform disorders, in which the role of anxiety is inferred rather than directly expressed in behavior. Persons with *dissociative disorders* may show no signs of overt anxiety but manifest other psychological difficulties, such as loss of memory or changes in identity, that are theorized within the psychodynamic model to serve a purpose of keeping underlying sources of anxiety out of direct awareness. Persons with *somatoform disorders* experience physical symptoms that have no apparent organic basis. They often manifest a queer sense of indifference to physical ailments that would cause most of us extreme concern. Here, too, it is theorized that the symptoms mask underlying sources of anxiety that remain outside of awareness. This strange sense of indifference to their physical problems has suggested to theorists that their symptoms may play an important role in preventing anxiety from intruding into consciousness.

We noted in Chapter 6 that dissociative and somatoform disorders—along with anxiety disorders—were all classified within the general category of neurosis in the first and second editions of the DSM and conceptualized according to the psychodynamic model. The writers of these earlier editions of the DSM system were greatly influenced by psychodynamic formulations in their conceptualizations and categorization of mental disorders. The chief characteristic of neurosis, according to the DSM–II, was anxiety, in either its direct or inferred forms. As you no doubt recall, the present diagnostic manual, the DSM–III–R, adopts a system of classification based more on descriptive criteria and observable patterns of behavior, rather than on particular theoretical formulations. Thus the DSM–III–R separates the anxiety disorders from the other categories of neuroses with which they were historically linked. But, as also noted in Chapter 6, many practitioners continue to use the broad conceptualization of neuroses as a useful framework for classifying these disorders.

DISSOCIATIVE DISORDERS

The key feature of the **dissociative disorders** is a change or disturbance in the usually "integrative functions of identity, memory, or consciousness" (DSM–III–R, p. 269). Normally speaking, we know who we are. Perhaps we are not certain of ourselves in the existential, philosophical sense, but at least we know our names, where we live, and what we do for a living. We also tend to remember the salient events of our lives. We may not recall every detail, and we may confuse what we ate for dinner on Tuesday with what we had on Monday, but we generally recall what we have been doing for the past several days, weeks, and years. Normally speaking, we possess a unified consciousness that provides a sense of self. We perceive

Billy Milligan.

our selves as progressing through space and time. But in the dissociative disorders, one or more of these aspects of daily living is disturbed—sometimes bizarrely so.

The DSM–III–R lists four major dissociative disorders: *multiple personality*, *psychogenic amnesia*, *psychogenic fugue*, and *depersonalization disorder*. In each disorder there is a disruption of the normal functions of memory, consciousness, or identity that normally make us whole.

Multiple Personality Disorder

■ The Ohio State campus dwelled in terror through the long fall of 1978. Four college women were seized, coerced to cash checks or get money from automatic teller machines, then raped. A cryptic phone call led to the capture of Billy Milligan, a 23-year-old drifter who had been dishonorably discharged from the Navy.

Billy wasn't quite the boy next door.

He tried twice to commit suicide while he was awaiting trial, so his lawyers requested a psychiatric evaluation. The psychologists and psychiatrists who examined Billy deduced that ten personalities dwelled inside of him. Eight were male and two were female. Billy's personality had been fractured by a brutal childhood. The personalities displayed diverse facial expressions, memories, and vocal patterns. They performed in dissimilar ways on personality and intelligence tests.

Arthur, a sensible but phlegmatic personality, conversed with a British accent. Danny, 14, was a painter of still lifes. Christopher, 13, was normal enough, but somewhat anxious. A 3-year-old English girl went by the name of Christine. Tommy, a 16-year-old, was an antisocial personality and escape artist. It was Tommy who had joined the Navy. Allen was an 18-year-old con artist. Allen also smoked. Adelena was a 19-year-old introverted lesbian. It was she who had committed the rapes. It was probably David who had placed the mysterious phone call. David was an anxious 9-year-old who wore the anguish of early childhood trauma on his sleeve. After his second suicide attempt, Billy had been placed in a straitjacket. When the guards checked his cell, however, he was sleeping with the straitjacket as a pillow. Tommy later explained that he had effected Billy's escape.

The defense argued that Billy was afflicted with multiple personality disorder. Several alternate personalities resided within him. The alternate personalities knew about Billy, but Billy was unaware of them. Billy, the core or dominant personality, had learned as a child that he could sleep as a way of avoiding the sexual and physical abuse of his father. A psychiatrist claimed that Billy had likewise been "asleep"—in a sort of "psychological coma"—when the crimes were committed. Therefore, Billy should be judged innocent by reason of insanity.

On December 4, 1978, Billy was decreed not guilty by reason of insanity. He was committed to a mental institution. In the institution, 14 additional personalities emerged. Thirteen were rebellious. The fourteenth was the "Teacher," who was competent and supposedly represented the integration of all the other personalities. Billy was finally released in 1984.

Adapted from Keyes, 1982 ∎

Billy was adjudged to be suffering from multiple personality disorder (MPD). In MPD, which is sometimes referred to as "split personality," two or more personalities—each with well-defined traits and memories—"occupy" one person. They may or may not be aware of one another. Various personalities may even require different eyeglass prescriptions, according to the DSM–III–R.

Braun (1988) reports cases in which different personalities display different allergic reactions. In one person, a personality called Timmy was not susceptible to orange juice. But when other personalities took control and drank orange juice, they would erupt in hives. Hives would also break out when Timmy drank orange juice if another personality appeared as the juice was being digested. Moreover, if Timmy reemerged when the allergic reaction was in full sway, the hives at once would cease to itch, and the blisters—filled with water—would begin to recede. In other cases, different personalities in the same person show different responses to the same medicine. Or one personality is color blind, whereas others have sound color vision (Braun, 1988). If fascinating cases such as these stand up to further scientific scrutiny, they may offer a remarkable illustration of the diversity of perceptions and behavior patterns that are possible for people with an identical biological makeup.

> **?** People with multiple personality disorder (MPD) are considered to have several personalities, and some evidence suggests that each personality may in fact have its own set of allergies and eyeglass prescription.

Celebrated MPD cases have been depicted in the popular media. One became the subject of the movie *The Three Faces of Eve*. In this film, Eve White is a timid housewife who harbors two other personalities: Eve Black, a libidinous antisocial personality; and Jane, a balanced, developing personality who could accept her primitive urges but still engage in socially appropriate behavior. The three faces eventually merged into one—Jane, providing a "happy ending." In real life, however, Eve is named Chris Sizemore. After Sizemore's personality was apparently integrated, it reportedly split into 22 subsequent personalities. A second well-known case is that of Sybil. Sybil was played by Sally Field in the film of the same name and she reportedly had 16 personalities.

There are many variations in MPD. Sometimes two personalities vie for control of the person. Sometimes there is one dominant or core personality and several subordinate personalities. Some of the more common alternate personalities include an affectionate child aged 4 to 6; an angry child whose emotions were shaped by parental abuse; an older prepubertal child; an asexual early adolescent of the opposite sex; an older woman, often a prostitute; and a homosexual

In the film The Three Faces of Eve, *Joanne Woodward portrayed three distinct personalities in the same woman: the timid and inhibited housewife, Eve White (a); the promiscuous and antisocial Eve Black (b); and Jane (c), an integrated personality who was able to accept her sexual and aggressive urges.*

(a)

(b)

(c)

personality. Some of these personalities may appear psychotic. All in all, the clusters of personalities serve as something of a microcosm of conflicting urges and cultural themes. Themes of sexual ambivalence and ambiguity are particularly common. It is as if conflicting internal impulses cannot coexist or achieve dominance. As a result, each is expressed as the cardinal or steering trait of an alternate personality. The clinician can sometimes elicit alternate personalities by inviting them to make themselves known, as in asking, "Is there another part of you that wants to say something to me?"

The case of Margaret illustrates the emergence of an alternate personality:

■ [Margaret explained that] she often "heard a voice telling her to say things and do things." It was, she said, "a terrible voice" that sometimes threatened to "take over completely." When it was finally suggested to [Margaret] that she let the voice "take over," she closed her eyes, clenched her fists, and grimaced for a few moments during which she was out of contact with those around her. Suddenly she opened her eyes and one was in the presence of another person. Her name, she said, was "Harriet." Whereas Margaret had been paralyzed, and complained of fatigue, headache and backache, Harriet felt well, and she at once proceeded to walk unaided around the interviewing room. She spoke scornfully of Margaret's religiousness, her invalidism and her puritanical life, professing that she herself liked to drink and "go partying" but that Margaret was always going to church and reading the Bible. "But," she said impishly and proudly, "I make her miserable—I make her say and do things she doesn't want to." At length, at the interviewer's suggestion, Harriet reluctantly agreed to "bring Margaret back," and after more grimacing and fist clenching, Margaret reappeared, paralyzed, complaining of her headache and backache, and completely amnesic for the brief period of Harriet's release from prison.

Nemiah, 1978, pp. 179–180. ■

As with Billy Milligan, Chris Sizemore, and Margaret, the dominant personality is often unaware of the existence of the alternate personalities, so that it seems that the mechanism of dissociation is controlled by unconscious processes. Although the dominant personality lacks insight into the existence of the other personalities, he or she may vaguely sense that something is wrong. There may even be a history of "interpersonality rivalry" in which one personality aspires to do away with another, usually in blissful ignorance of the fact that conferring the *coup de grace* on an alternate would result in the death of all. The diagnostic criteria for MPD are listed in Table 7.1

Although MPD is generally considered to be rare, the prevalence of the disorder is a topic of debate. It's difficult for professionals to acquire reliable information about how frequently the disorder occurs. Few psychologists have ever encountered a case of MPD. The first

TABLE 7.1 Diagnostic Features of Multiple Personality Disorder

1. At least two distinct personalities exist within the person, with each having a relatively enduring and distinct pattern of perceiving, thinking about, and relating to the environment and the self.
2. Two or more of these personalities repeatedly take complete control of the individual's behavior.

Source: *Adapted from DSM–III–R, p. 272.*

case was reported in 1817, and since that time fewer than 200 cases have been described in the scientific literature (Boor, 1982). Four or five women are diagnosed with MPD for every man (Kluft, 1984; Schafer, 1986). The DSM–III–R offers the illuminating comment that "Recent reports suggest that this disorder is not nearly so rare as it has commonly been thought to be" (p. 271). Some practitioners have also suggested that the disorder is more common than is generally believed (Bliss & Jeppsen, 1985; Schafer, 1986). But others believe that the research evidence does not clearly demonstrate increased prevalence (Ludolph, 1985). One problem with determining the prevalence of multiple personality disorder is that estimates are often obtained from clinicians who specialize in treating the disorder and who may see more cases of multiple personality than other clinicians do (Ludolph, 1985). Increased public attention paid to the disorder in recent years may also account for the perception that it has increased in frequency, rather than any actual change in prevalence.

Multiple personality disorder, which is often called "split personality" by laypersons, should not be confused with schizophrenia. As we shall see in Chapter 12, schizophrenia (literally meaning "split brain") occurs much more commonly than multiple personality disorder and involves the "splitting" of cognition, affect, and behavior, so that there may be little agreement between the thoughts and the emotions, or between the individual's perception of reality and what is truly happening. The schizophrenic, for example, may become giddy when told of disturbing events, or may experience hallucinations or delusions. In multiple personality disorder, the personality apparently divides into two or more personalities, but each of them usually shows more integrated functioning on cognitive, affective, and behavioral levels than is true of people with schizophrenia.

Clouding the issue of diagnosis, however, is the finding that some persons who receive a MPD diagnosis also show behaviors associated with schizophrenia, such as auditory and visual hallucinations (Kluft, 1987). The dominant personalities of people with MPD may report hearing two voices arguing about themselves. One of the voices may be threatening and the other protective. Another common auditory hallucination involves voices that provide a running commentary on the dominant personality's behavior, often derogatory. (The subordinate personalities typically comment on the dominant personality.) In sum, people considered to have MPD frequently show behaviors associated with psychoses like schizophrenia. However, MPD is not considered a form of schizophrenia, because the personalities within the individual can think and act in a coherent fashion, although quite variably and perhaps in conflict with one another.

The DSM criteria for MPD are somewhat open to interpretation. The DSM–III–R notes, for example, that some people with the disorder complain of being "possessed" but are actually experiencing the influence of an alternate personality. Many clinicians, however, are likely to take a client's claim of being possessed as a type of schizophrenic delusion. It has been suggested that more MPD cases might be diagnosed if the competing diagnosis of schizophrenia were not so common (Putnam et al., 1986). Clinicians may also be reluctant to use the MPD diagnosis out of concern that others might believe that they had been duped by clients who had faked their symptoms. Some clinicians have been accused of being in collusion with their clients to protect them from, say, criminal charges, by providing them with a basis for a pleading of "not guilty by reason of insanity." So knowledge of the "true" prevalence of the disorder remains cloudy.

Perhaps because MPD is considered rare and its features sometimes overlap with other diagnoses, clinicians may be reluctant to render an MPD diagnosis. People with MPD may go unrecognized or alternatively diagnosed for years after their initial evaluations (Schafer, 1986). In a study of 100 people with MPD diagnoses, the mean length of time between initial assessment and ultimate diagnosis was 6.8 years (Putnam et al., 1986). These people averaged 3.6 alternative diagnoses in the process. These alternative diagnoses may also reflect the finding that individuals with MPD display a wide range of abnormal behaviors, including physical complaints with no known organic basis; a history of amnesia; depression and suicidal behavior; anxiety and panic attacks; and other disturbances in states of consciousness, such as depersonalization and **derealization** (Bliss, 1984).

Several features may alert the clinician to the possible presence of MPD:

1. Amnesic periods (that is, "blackouts") in the dominant personality (Schafer, 1986).

2. Severe physical or sexual abuse in childhood (Greaves, 1980).

3. A stormy or turbulent history of psychiatric or psychological treatment (Schafer, 1986).

4. A nickname that doesn't seem to fit the individual's dominant personality. Perhaps an alternate

personality is known by that name to others (Schafer, 1986).

5. High hypnotizability (Bliss, 1984). Braun (1986) suggests that hypnotizability may be used as a diagnostic criterion when it is necessary to distinguish between various diagnostic possibilities.

Some individuals diagnosed as having MPD lead surprisingly accomplished lives, in fact. Three such cases, two physicians and a research scientist, were recently reported (Kluft, 1986). High-functioning multiple personalities often elude diagnosis because clinicians are not likely to probe for evidence of MPD among clients who seem to be functioning reasonably well. Accomplished people with MPD may also have developed elaborate strategies to cloak their alternate personalities—sometimes with the cooperation of the alternate personalities themselves, who, for one reason or another, cooperate by remaining out of the limelight. The careers of such individuals are stabilizing influences, and they may maintain a veneer of normality for fear of losing their careers.

We next consider a form of dissociative disorder, *psychogenic amnesia*, in which losses of memory are believed to serve the function of protecting the individual from recalling past traumatic experiences.

Psychogenic Amnesia

Amnesia derives from the Greek roots *a-*, meaning "not," and *mnasthai*, meaning "to remember." **Psychogenic amnesia,** is characterized by a sudden loss of ability to recall important personal information. Such memory losses cannot be attributed to physical problems, such as head trauma or alcoholic intoxication. Thus, it is *psychogenic*, or psychological in origin. We will consider amnesia that arises from organic causes in Chapter 13. Psychogenic amnesia may pesist for hours or even years. Termination of amnesia tends to occur suddenly and spontaneously.

There are four types of psychogenic amnesia: localized, selective, generalized, and continuous:

1. **Localized amnesia.** In this most commonly occurring type, all events that took place during a specific time period are lost to memory. For example, the person cannot remember anything that happened for hours after a traumatic incident, as in warfare or as in the case of a survivor of an accident who escapes without physical injury. The medical corpsman described in Chapter 4 (see pp. 143–144) could not recall the events that occurred on a Pacific island after a rifle was thrust into his hands.

2. **Selective amnesia.** In this form of amnesia, people forget only the disturbing particulars that took place during a certain time period. A person may recall the period of life during which he conducted an extramarital affair, but not the guilt-arousing affair itself. The soldier may recall most of the battle, but not the death of his buddy.

3. **Generalized amnesia.** In generalized amnesia, people forget their entire lives—who they are, what they do, where they live, whom they live with. This form of amnesia is rare, but it is the one most likely to be depicted in daytime soap operas and other fictional accounts. Individuals with generalized amnesia cannot recall personal information, but they tend to retain their habits, tastes, and skills. If you had generalized amnesia, you would still know how to read, although you would not recall your elementary school teachers. You would still prefer French fries to baked potatoes—or vice versa.

4. **Continuous amnesia.** In this form of amnesia, people forget all events that take place after the problem begins. Everything from that time through to the present is lost and, of course, the present keeps moving ahead. If you had continuous amnesia since the time you began college, all of your college experiences would be lost to you. You would not be able to recall what you are reading; all new information would "go in one ear and out the other." In Chapter 13 we shall see that certain kinds of *organic* damage can prevent the formation of new memories. Continuous amnesia is a rare form of *psychogenic* amnesia, however.

Although only one type of psychogenic amnesia is labeled selective, most instances of amnesia are selective. That is, people usually forget events or periods of life that were traumatic—that generated strong, negative emotions such as horror or guilt. Consider the case of Rutger:

■ He was brought to the emergency room of a hospital by a stranger. He was dazed and claimed not to know who he was or where he lived, and the stranger had found him wandering in the streets. Despite his confusion, it did not appear that he had been drinking or abusing drugs or that his amnesia could be attributed to physical trauma. After staying in the hospital for a few days, he awoke in distress. His memory had returned. His name was Rutger and he had urgent business to attend to. He wanted to know why he had been hospitalized and demanded to leave. At time of admission, Rutger appeared to be suffering from general amnesia: He could not recall his identity or the personal events of his life. But now that he was requesting discharge, Rutger showed localized amnesia for the period between entering the emergency

room and the morning he regained his memory for prior events.

Rutger provided information about the events prior to his hospitalization that was confirmed by the police. On the day when his amnesia began, Rutger had killed a pedestrian with his automobile. There had been witnesses, and the police had voiced the opinion that Rutger—although emotionally devastated—was blameless in the incident. Rutger was instructed, however, to fill out an accident report and to appear at the inquest. Still nonplussed, Rutger filled out the form at a friend's home. He accidentally left his wallet and his identification there. After placing the form in a mailbox, Rutger became dazed and he lost his memory.

Although Rutger was not responsible for the accident, he felt awful about the pedestrian's death. His amnesia was probably connected with feelings of guilt, the stress of the accident, and concerns about the inquest.

Adapted from Cameron, 1963, pp. 355–356 ■

Amnesic people seem less concerned about their memory problems than do their family, friends, and the people who are trying to help them. This relative lack of concern has inspired hypotheses that the memory loss serves the adaptive function of relieving anxiety or some other kind of psychological pain associated with past trauma. Sometimes the painful circumstances can be recalled under hypnosis.

People sometimes report that they cannot recall certain events of their lives: engaging in socially unacceptable behavior, making promises, and so forth. Falsely claiming amnesia as a way of escaping responsibility is a form of **malingering,** which represents the conscious attempt to fabricate symptoms or make false claims for personal gain. Current research methods cannot guarantee that we can distinguish all malingerers from people suffering from dissociative disorders. We shall have more to say about malingering later in the chapter.

 Experienced clinicians *cannot* invariably differentiate the true amnesiac from the malingerer.

But experienced clinicians can make reasonably well-educated guesses.

Psychogenic Fugue

Fugue derives from the Latin *fugere*, meaning "flight." The word *fugitive* has the same origin. Fugue is amnesia "on the run." In **psychogenic fugue,** as defined in the DSM–III–R, the person experiences loss of memory for past events, travels suddenly away from home or from one's place of work, and takes on a new identity. The person may either not think about the past, or may fill in the past with bogus memories that are not recognized as untrue.

Whereas people with amnesia appear to wander aimlessly, people in a fugue state act more purposefully. Some people in a fugue state stick close to home. They spend the afternoon in the park or in a theater, or they spend the night at a hotel under another name, usually having little if any contact with others during the fugue state. But the new identity is incomplete and fleeting and the individual's former sense of self soon returns in a matter of hours or a few days. More uncommon is a pattern in which the fugue state would last for months or years, involving travel to distant cities or even to foreign lands. These individuals may create whole new identities and pasts for themselves, assuming an identity that is usually more uninhibited and sociable than their former selves, which were typically rather "quiet" and "ordinary." They may establish new families and successful businesses that are maintained for many years. Although these events may sound rather bizarre, the fugue state is not considered psychotic because people with the disorder can think and behave quite normally—in their new lives, that is. Then one day, quite suddenly, their awareness of their past identity returns to them, and they are flooded with the memories of the past they had dissociated. Now they typically do not recall the events that happened during the fugue state; the new identity, the new life—including all its involvements and responsibilities—vanish from memory.

Fugue, like amnesia, is rare. As noted in the DSM–III–R it is most likely to occur in wartime or in the wake of another kind of disaster. So the underlying notion is that the dissociation in the fugue state serves to protect the indivdual from traumatic memories or some other source of psychological pain.

The DSM–III–R notes that fugue can also be difficult to distinguish from malingering. That is, a number of persons who were dissatisfied with their former lives could claim to be amnesic when they are uncovered in their new locations and new identities. The DSM–III–R suggests that the truth of the matter can sometimes be brought out by "careful questioning under hypnosis or during an amobarbital [one type of "truth serum"] interview" (p. 273), but admits that there are no guarantees.

Consider, for example, the following case, in which the evidence supports a diagnosis of psychogenic fugue (Spitzer et al., 1989). There is the inability to recall one's past, the sudden and unexpected travel to a distant location, and the assumption of a new identity—the characteristics that define the disorder, according to the DSM–III–R.

■ The man told the police that his name was Burt Tate. "Burt," a 42-year-old white male, had gotten into a fight at the diner where he worked. When the police arrived, they found that he carried no identification. He told them he had drifted into town a few weeks earlier, but could not recall where he had lived or worked before arriving in town. While no charges were pressed against him, the police prevailed upon him to come to the ER for evaluation. "Burt" knew the town he was in and the current date, and recognized that it was somewhat unusual that he couldn't remember his past, but didn't seem to be concerned about it. There was no evidence of any physical injuries or head trauma, or of drug or alcohol abuse. The police made some inquiries and discovered that "Burt" fit the profile of a missing person, Gene Saunders, who had disappeared a month earlier from a city some 2,000 miles away. Mrs. Saunders was called in and confirmed that "Burt" was indeed her husband. She reported that her husband, who had worked in middle-level management in a manufacturing company, had been having difficulty at work before his disappearance. He was passed over for promotion and his supervisor was highly critical of his work. The job stress apparently affected his behavior at home. Once easygoing and sociable, he withdrew into himself and began to criticize his wife and children. Then, just before his disappearance, he had a violent argument with his 18-year-old son. His son called him a "failure" and stormed out the door. Two days later, the man disappeared. When he came face to face with his wife again, he claimed he didn't recognize her, but appeared visibly nervous.

Adapted from Spitzer et al., 1989, pp. 215–216 ■

While the presenting evidence would support a diagnostic impression of psychogenic fugue, the clinician must be careful to distinguish between true amnesia and amnesia that is faked for the purpose of giving oneself a new start on life. The few clinicians who encounter such a case must exercise their best judgment in reaching the most appropriate diagnostic impression.

Depersonalization Disorder

Depersonalization is a feeling of detachment from oneself. In a state of depersonalization, people may feel detached from their minds or bodies. They may have the sense of not being able to believe that they are where they are or that they are doing what they are doing; so they may feel as though they are observing themselves or their thought processes from outside. They may feel like robots, as though they are operating on automatic pilot. They may feel as if their movements are impaired, as they might be in walking underwater or in a dream.

Derealization—strange changes in perception of surroundings, or in the sense of the passage of time—may also be present. People and objects may seem to change in size or shape; they may sound different. All these feelings can be associated with feelings of anxiety,

Episodes of depersonalization are characterized by feelings of detachment from oneself. It may feel as if one is walking in a dream or outside one's body.

including dizziness and fears of going insane, or with depression.

Although these sensations are very strange, people with depersonalization maintain contact with reality. They can distinguish reality from unreality, even during the depersonalization episode. In contrast with amnesia and fugue, they know who they are and where they are. Their memories are intact and they know where they are—even if they do not like their present state. Feelings of depersonalization usually come on suddenly but fade gradually.

What is even more unusual about all this is that we have only described normal *feelings of depersonalization. According to the DSM–III–R, single, brief episodes of depersonalization are experienced by as many as 70 percent of young adults!*

> According to the DSM–III–R, the majority of young adults will at some time encounter the feeling that they are detached from their own bodies or mental processes.

Consider Richie's experience:

■ "We went to Orlando with the children after school let out. I had also been driving myself hard, and it was time to let go. We spent three days 'doing' Disneyworld, and it got to the point where we were all wearing shirts with mice and ducks on them and singing Disney songs like 'Yo ho, yo ho, a pirate's life for me.' On the third day I began to feel unreal and ill at ease while we were watching these middle-American Ivory-soap teenagers singing and dancing in front of Cinderella's Castle. The day was finally cooling down, but I broke into a sweat. I became shaky and dizzy and sat down on the cement next to the 4-year-old's stroller without giving [my wife] an explanation. There were strollers and kids and [adults'] legs all around me, and for some strange reason I became fixated on the pieces of popcorn strewn on the ground. All of a sudden it was like the people around me were all silly mechanical creatures, like the dolls in the 'It's a Small World' [exhibit] or the animals on the 'Jungle Cruise.' Things sort of seemed to slow down, the way they do when you've smoked marijuana, and there was this invisible wall of cotton between me and everyone else.

"Then the concert was over and my wife was like 'What's the matter?' and did I want to stay for the Electrical Parade and the fireworks or was I sick? Now I was beginning to wonder if I was going crazy and I said I was sick, that my wife would have to take me by the hand and drive us back to the Sonesta Village [motel]. Somehow we got back to the monorail and turned in the strollers. I waited in the herd [of people] at the station like a dead person, my eyes glazed over, looking out over kids with Mickey Mouse ears and Mickey Mouse balloons. The mechanical voice on the monorail almost did me in and I got really shaky.

"I refused to go back to the Magic Kingdom. I went with the family to Sea World, and on another day I dropped [my wife] and the kids off at the Magic Kingdom and picked them up that night. My wife thought I was goldbricking or something, and we had a helluva fight about it, but we had a life to get back to and my sanity had to come first."

The Authors' Files ■

Richie's depersonalization experience was limited to the one episode and would not qualify for a diagnosis of **depersonalization disorder.** The DSM–III–R diagnoses depersonalization disorder only when episodes are persistent or recurrent and they cause marked dis-

TABLE 7.2 Diagnostic Criteria for Depersonalization Disorder

1. Experiences of depersonalization must be recurrent or persistent, and noted by either of the following:

    a. an experience in which one feels detached from one's mental processes or body, as if one were an outside observer.

    b. an experience in which one feels like an "automaton" or as if one is dreaming

2. The individual is able to maintain reality testing (that is, distinguish reality from unreality) during the depersonalization state

3. The depersonalization experiences are sufficiently persistent and severe to cause marked distress

4. Depersonalization experiences are the predominant complaints and cannot be attributed to other disorders

Source: *Adapted from DSM–III–R, pp. 276–277.*

tress, as seen in Table 7.2, and in the following case example:

■ A 20-year-old college student feared that he was going insane. For two years he had increasingly frequent experiences of feeling "outside" himself. During these episodes, he experienced a sense of "deadness" in his body, and felt wobbly, frequently bumping into furniture. He was more apt to lose his balance during episodes which occurred when he was out in public, especially when he was feeling anxious. During these episodes, his thoughts seemed "foggy," reminding him of his state of mind when he was given shots of a pain-killing drug for an appendectomy five years earlier. He tried to fight off these episodes when they occurred, by saying "stop" to himself and by shaking his head. This would temporarily clear his head, but the feeling of being outside himself and the sense of deadness would shortly return. The disturbing feelings would gradually fade away over a period of hours. By the time he sought treatment, he was experiencing these episodes about twice a week, each one lasting from three to four hours. His grades remained unimpaired, and had even improved in the past several months, since he was spending more time studying. However, his girlfriend, in whom he had confided his problem, felt that he had become totally absorbed in himself and threatened to break off their relationship if he didn't change. She had also begun to date other men.

Adapted from Spitzer, et al., 1989, pp. 234–235 ■

The DSM–III–R notes that inclusion of depersonalization disorder as a dissociative disorder is controversial, because in contrast to the other three major dissociative disorders, there is no disturbance in memory. We should like to note another important difference: In MPD, amnesia, and fugue, the dissociative process seems to *protect* the individual from anxiety. In depersonalization, however, the process of dissociation—and the resultant sense that things are unreal—frequently *generates* anxiety. Note, too, that depersonalization in-

volves some cardiovascular sensations (for example, dizziness) that can be misinterpreted as serious and generate further cycles of anxiety. Richie, for example, was motivated to avoid another visit to the Magic Kingdom at Disneyworld. In fact, he also managed to be elsewhere when the children watched the Disney Channel on the TV cable.

Depersonalization, in short, may be more closely related to disorders such as phobias and panic than to dissociative disorders. Depersonalization can motivate avoidance behavior, and our reactions to the sensations of depersonalization can generate cycles of anxiety.

Theoretical Perspectives

The major theoretical accounts of the dissociative disorders are drawn from the psychodynamic and cognitive-behavioral models, and it is these perspectives to which we now turn.

■ **Psychodynamic Perspectives** According to the psychodynamic model, dissociation represents a means of psychological defense that allows people to block out troubling memories and unacceptable impulses. There has been increasing documentation of a connection between MPD and childhood trauma in many cases, particularly severe child abuse (Wilbur, 1986). This lends support to the view that dissociative disorders, such as MPD, may serve a protective role of blocking out painful memories. Some children who are severely abused may learn to dissociate parts of themselves and retreat into these alternate personalities as a means of psychologically "escaping" from their suffering. In the face of repeated abuse, these alternate personalities may become stabilized to the point that the individual is unable to maintain an integrated personality. Certainly only a few children who suffer extreme abuse develop multiple personalities. Multiple personality is, after all, very rare. In adulthood, people with MPD may continue to block out traumatic childhood memories and their emotional reactions to them—sort of wiping the slate clean and beginning life anew in the guise of alternate personalities (Schafer, 1986).

Children with more active and creative imaginations and richer fantasy lives, who also tend to be more hypnotizable, may be prone to construct alternate personalities as a defense against unbearable abuse. As children, people with MPD showed evidence of a rich fantasy life, inventing imaginary playmates and frequently enacting games of make-believe (Spanos et al., 1985). Cornelia Wilbur (1986) notes, with Bliss (1984), that adults with MPD are also highly hypnotizable, which suggests to her that they possess a knack of

A CLOSER LOOK
Types of Dissociative Experiences

We have noted that many of us experience brief dissociative experiences from time to time, such as transient feelings of depersonalization. Dissociative disorders, by comparison, involve the occurrence of more persistent and severe dissociative experiences. Researchers have recently developed a measure, the Dissociative Experiences Scale (DES) (Bernstein & Putnam, 1986) to offer clinicians a means of measuring dissociative experiences that occur among both normal and abnormal populations. Normals tend to report fewer, and less varied, dissociative experiences than do people with dissociative disorders, such as multiple personalities, but they still often report some such experiences. Below is a listing of some of the types of dissociative experiences drawn from the Dissociative Experiences Scale. Bear in mind that transient experiences such as these tend to be reported by both normal and abnormal populations in varying frequencies.

HOW OFTEN HAVE YOU EXPERIENCED THE FOLLOWING?

1. Suddenly realizing, when you are driving the car, that you don't remember what has happened during all or part of the trip.
2. Suddenly realizing, when you are listening to someone talk, that you did not hear part or all of what the person said.
3. Finding yourself in a place and having no idea how you got there.
4. Finding yourself dressed in clothes that you don't remember putting on.
5. Being approached by other people you do not know who call you by another name and insist that they know you.
6. Experiencing a feeling that seemed as if you were standing next to yourself or watching yourself do something and actually seeing yourself as if you were looking at another person.
7. Losing the memories of important events in your life, such as your wedding or graduation.
8. Looking in a mirror and not recognizing yourself.
9. Feeling sometimes that other people, objects, and the world around you are not real.
10. Feeling sometimes that your body does not seem to belong to you.
11. Remembering a past event so vividly that it seems like you are reliving it in the present.
12. Having the experience of being in a familiar place but finding it strange and unfamiliar.
13. Becoming so absorbed in watching television or a movie that you are unaware of other events happening around you.
14. Becoming so absorbed in a fantasy or daydream that it feels as though it were really happening to you.
15. Talking out loud to yourself when you are alone.
16. Finding that you act so differently in a particular situation compared with another that it feels almost as if you were two different people.
17. Finding that you cannot remember whether or not you have just done something or perhaps had just thought about doing it (for example, not knowing whether you have just mailed a letter or have just thought about mailing it).
18. Feeling sometimes as if you were looking at the world through a fog such that people and objects appeared far away or unclear.

dissociating various aspects of consciousness from others. There may also be a link between self-hypnosis and multiple personality. Multiple personalities may actually be hypnotizing themselves into trance-like states in which they enact their alternate personalities (Bliss, 1984).

Dissociative disorders are theorized to involve the massive use of repression to avert recognition of unacceptable impulses. In psychogenic amnesia and in fugue, the ego protects itself from becoming flooded with anxiety by blotting out memory or dissociating profoundly disturbing impulses. In multiple personality, people may express unacceptable impulses through the enactment of alternate personalities. In depersonalization, people stand outside themselves—safely distanced from the turmoil within.

Despite its rarity, much theoretical attention has been paid to MPD—partly because the disorder is fascinating, partly because it serves as a sort of inspiration to theorists of various persuasions. Early theoretical work by Janet (1889) and Prince (1906) outlined psychological mechanisms believed responsible for splitting the personality and connected the fracturing of consciousness with childhood trauma.

Because of their dissociative capacities, persons who develop MPD may handle that intense anger and hatred that is generated by cruel acts by forming alternate personalities that are capable of expressing their negative feelings. The core or dominant personality thus finds it easier to keep such feelings repressed, easing the censoring chores of the ego. Wilbur notes that sometimes during therapy, an angry, violent subordinate personality may emerge who threatens or attacks the analyst. Persons with MPD may also have phobic reactions to stimuli that may be associated with their early traumatic experiences. Alternate personalities may emerge that are specifically capable of confronting and managing these phobic objects and situations.

It is normal for children to have imaginary playmates. In the case of children who become multiple personalities, however, games of "make believe" and the invention of imaginary playmates may be used as psychological defenses against abuse.

■ **Learning and Cognitive Perspectives** Learning and cognitive theorists generally view dissociative disorders as behaviors which people have learned to help them avoid thinking about disturbing acts or thoughts that would evoke unpleasant feelings of anxiety, guilt, or shame. So, *not thinking about these matters* is negatively reinforced by anxiety relief, or by removal of feelings of guilt or shame.

Social-learning and cognitive theorists also suggest that people can learn to enact the role of a multiple personality by means of observational learning and reinforcement. This is not quite the same as pretending or malingering; people can honestly come to organize their behavior patterns according to particular roles that they have observed. They might also become so absorbed in role-playing that they "forget" that they are enacting a role. Many reinforcers may become contingent on the enactment of MPD roles—receiving attention from others and evading accountability for unacceptable behavior are two (Spanos et al., 1985; Thigpen & Cleckley, 1984). According to Nicholas Spanos and his colleagues (1985), films and television shows like *The Three Faces of Eve* and *Sybil* have provided the public with detailed examples of the behaviors that characterize MPD. That is, people may learn how to enact the role of individuals with MPD by watching others enacting the role on TV and in the movies.

Perhaps most of us can divide our consciousness so that we become unaware of—at least temporarily—those events that we normally focus on. Perhaps most of us can thrust the unpleasant from our minds and enact various roles—parent, child, lover, business person, soldier—that help us meet the requirements of our situations. Perhaps the wonder is *not* that attention can be splintered, but that human consciousness is normally integrated into a meaningful whole.

Treatment of Dissociative Disorders

Psychogenic amnesia and fugue are usually transient and terminate abruptly. Episodes of depersonalization can be recurrent and persistent, and as noted in the DSM–III–R, they are most likely to occur when people are undergoing periods of mild anxiety or depression. In such cases, clinicians usually focus on managing the anxiety or the depression.

Theorists and clinicians have developed some interesting approaches to treatment of MPD, which are the focus of this section.

■ **Psychodynamic Approaches** Traditional psychoanalysis is relevant in the treatment of MPD because it aims to help clients uncover and learn to cope with early childhood traumas. Wilbur (1986) offers some variations on the theme in her discussion of the psychoanalytic treatment of MPD.

First, Wilbur points out that the analyst can work with whatever personality is in ascendance during the therapy session. Any and all personalities can be asked to talk about their memories as best they can. Any and all personalities can be assured that the therapist will help them make sense of their anxieties and to safely "relive" traumatic experiences so that they can be made conscious and free the psychic energy that is trapped by them. Wilbur enjoins therapists to keep in mind that anxiety experienced during a therapy session may lead to a switch in personalities, since alternate personalities were presumably developed as a means of coping with intense anxiety. Eventually, however, sufficient early experience may be brought to light such that reintegration of the personality becomes possible.

Wilbur describes the formation of another treatment goal in the case of a woman with MPD:

A CLOSER LOOK
Did Clinicians Create Personalities for the Hillside Strangler?

"Part, are you the same thing as Ken or are you different?" Although this question may seem more fitting of an exorcism from the Middle Ages, the questioner was actually a police psychiatrist in modern-day Los Angeles. The interviewee was Kenneth Bianchi—known to the press as the "Hillside Strangler." The Hillside Strangler had terrorized Los Angeles, leaving prostitutes dead in the hills overlooking the city.

Under hypnosis, Bianchi claimed that a hidden personality named "Steve" had committed the murders. "Ken"—his dominant identity—knew nothing of them. Was this a "true" MPD case, or was Bianchi's performance staged to evade responsibility for his behavior? Perhaps the so-called true cases of MPD can also be explained as a form of role-playing behavior.

Psychologist Nicholas Spanos and his colleagues (Spanos et al., 1985) argue that MPD can indeed be explained through a social psychological model of role-playing behavior. People learn to enact the MPD role by picking up on cues from therapists and other people that guide their performance. Perhaps the interrogation methods used with Bianchi had cued him to enact the role of a person with MPD.

In order to determine whether certain interviewing techniques could give rise to enactment of MPD-related behaviors, Spanos and his colleagues performed an experiment with college students that was modeled after the Bianchi interrogation. They asked normal college students to enact the role of an accused murderer in an interview with an experimenter playing the part of a police psychiatrist. There were three conditions:

1. *The Bianchi Condition.* This group of "accused murderers" was exposed to cues that paralleled the Bianchi interrogation. They were told that hypnosis would be used to uncover hidden aspects of their personalities, and perhaps another part of themselves would want to talk to a psychiatrist. These "Bianchi" subjects were then hypnotized and the "other part"

Kenneth Bianchi, the so-called "Hillside Strangler."

was encouraged to reveal itself to the interviewer by reporting its name. The precise question that had been asked of Bianchi under hypnosis was put to the hypnotized students: "Part, are you the same thing as [student's name] or are you different?"

2. *The Hidden-Part Condition.* Another group of "accused murderers," a "hidden-part" group, was also told that hypnosis would be used to help the psychiatrist talk to a hidden part of themselves. They were not asked the question posed to Bianchi and to students in the Bianchi condition, however.

3. *The Control Group.* The third group of "accused murderers" was neither hypnotized during the interview nor told that the psychiatrist would ask to talk to a hidden part of themselves.

■ A 45-year-old woman had suffered from MPD throughout her life. Her dominant personality was timid and self-conscious, rather reticent about herself. But soon after she entered treatment, a group of "little ones" emerged, who cried profusely. The therapist asked to speak with someone in the personality system who could clarify the personalities that were present. It turned out that they included several children, all of whom were under 9 years of age and had suffered severe, painful sexual abuse at the hands of an uncle, a great-aunt, and a grandmother. The great-aunt was a lesbian with several voyeuristic lesbian friends. They would watch the sexual abuse, generating fear, pain, rage, humiliation, and shame.

It was essential in therapy for the "children" to come

to understand that they should not feel ashamed because they had been helpless to resist the abuse.

Adapted from Wilbur, 1986, pp. 138–139 ■

By and large, reports of the effectiveness of psychoanalytic psychotherapy rely on case studies. The relative infrequency of the disorder has hampered efforts to conduct controlled experiments which compare different forms of treatment with each other and with control groups. In one of the few reports of multiple case studies, Coons (1986) followed 20 persons with MPD aged from 14 to 47 at time of intake for an average of $3\frac{1}{4}$ years. They were treated primarily by means of

It turned out that 81 percent of the students in the Bianchi condition revealed a second name during the interview, compared to 31 percent of the hidden-part subjects and none of the control subjects. After they were "awakened" from their "trances," the majority (63%) of the Bianchi and hidden-part subjects claimed amnesia for the events that took place under hypnosis, denying knowledge of the alternate personality they had enacted. The control group stood firm in denying guilt for the crimes of which they were accused. The Bianchi and hidden-part subjects were more likely to admit guilt, but to ascribe it to the alternate personality.

> **?** When appropriately cued in a laboratory experiment, college students did in fact enact a multiple personality role and have the alternate personality take the blame for a murder that they were accused of committing.

With the proper cues, it was a relatively simple matter for students to enact the MPD role. The student "multiples" readily picked up the cues that encouraged the enactment of a "hidden part" in their personalities. The hidden part had its own name and showed a unique pattern of psychological test responses. The hidden part, moreover, could be assigned the blame for wrongdoing; the core personality could safely claim ignorance of the alternate personality and of the alternate's crimes.

The Spanos experiment is only a laboratory simulation of a Bianchi-type interrogation. It did not study persons diagnosed as having MPD. Nevertheless, it prompts consideration of whether or not normal people can be induced to enact the multiple-personality role when they are tipped off as to how to do so and given the right incentives. Perhaps the manner in which the Bianchi interrogation was conducted had cued Bianchi to enact the role of a multiple personality.

Relatively few MPD cases involve criminal behavior, in which enactment of the MPD role may be connected with clear expectations of gain. But even in more typical cases, there may be subtle incentives for enacting the MPD role. Such incentives include the therapist's expression of interest and excitement at the possibility of discovering a multiple personality. People who seek help for problems may be ready to accept their clinicians' interpretations of their distressing behavior patterns—even when unusual possibilities such as MPD are raised. People with MPD, as noted, were often highly imaginative during childhood. Accustomed to playing games of make-believe, such people may readily adopt alternate identities if adequate informational cues are present to direct them in ways of enacting the role and there are external sources of validation—such as a clinician's interest and concern. This is not to suggest that multiple personalities are "faking" any more than it would be to suggest that you are faking your behavior when you perform many customary roles in your daily life, such as the roles of student, spouse, or worker. You may enact the role of a student (for example, sitting attentively in class, raising your hand when you wish to talk, etc.) because you've learned to organize your behavior according to the nature of the role and because you've been rewarded for your role enactments by teachers and others. So, too, multiple personalities may have learned to identify with the MPD role through cueing and repeated reinforcement to such an extent that they no longer realize that they are merely "playing a role."

The social reinforcement model may help to explain why some clinicians seem to "discover" many more multiple personalities in their case experiences than others. Clinicians who are "MPD-magnets" may unknowingly convey cues to clients that steer enactment of the MPD role and reinforce the performance with extra attention and concern. With the right set of cues, certain clients may adopt an MPD role to please their clinicians by giving them what they think they want. But it remains to be seen how many MPD cases can be accounted for by role-playing.

psychoanalytically oriented psychotherapy and hypnosis. Only five of the subjects showed a complete reintegration of their personalities. Therapy was reportedly hampered by continuation of mechanisms of repression and denial and the use of secrecy—a pattern that had begun during childhood. Reflecting the difficulties in working therapeutically with such clients, therapists often reported feelings of anger, emotional exhaustion, and exasperation.

■ **Biological Approaches** No drugs have yet been developed for treating MPD directly by bringing about integration of the alternate personalities. However, persons with MPD frequently suffer from depression, anxiety, and other problems that may be treated with drugs such as antidepressants and anti-anxiety agents. Drugs tend to be most readily prescribed when the different personalities "agree" in the problems they present—whether anxiety, depression, or other problems (Barkin et al., 1986). However, more research is needed to investigate biological approaches that may help clinicians foster integration of the various personalities.

■ **Behavioral Approaches** Learning-theory–derived techniques have been applied to the treatment of MPD. But here as well, we are limited to the isolated case study. Kohlenberg (1973), for example, reported a case in which token reinforcers (poker chips that could be exchanged for tangible rewards) were used to increase the frequency of response of the best adjusted of three alternate personalities in a 51-year-old institutionalized person. Any time the preferred personality emitted a response, the subject earned a token and a pat on the hand. During reinforced trials, the preferred personality "appeared" significantly more often. During extinction trials, however, when reinforcement was withheld, the preferred personality dropped to a response level below the original baseline, and alternate personalities spent more time out in the open.

Kohlenberg concluded that MPD is a learned response pattern whose performance is connected with reinforcement contingencies. In the case of MPD, as noted by Spanos and his colleagues (1985), reinforcement can take the form of extra attention from therapists who consider MPD to be glamorous and exotic. It is too early to say whether other MPD cases will respond to selective reinforcement of the most adaptive personality—remember, there are relatively few MPD cases. This form of therapy also raises the ethical issue as to whether or not therapists have the right to determine which personality should be selectively reinforced.

SOMATOFORM DISORDERS

The word *somatoform* derives from the Greek *soma*, meaning "body." In the **somatoform disorders,** people show or complain of physical symptoms suggestive of physical disorders, but no organic abnormalities can be found. Moreover, there is evidence, or some reason to believe, that the symptoms reflect psychological factors or conflict. Some people complain of problems in breathing or swallowing, or of a "lump in the throat." Problems such as these can reflect overactivity of the sympathetic branch of the autonomic nervous system (dryness in the mouth that is related to anxiety can impair swallowing). Sometimes the symptoms take more unusual forms, as in a "paralysis" of a hand or leg that is inconsistent with the workings of the nervous system. In yet other cases, people are preoccupied with the belief that they are seriously ill, yet no evidence of a physical disorder can be found. We will consider several forms of somatoform disorders, including *conversion disorder*, *hypochondriasis*, and *somatization disorder*. We will also consider the puzzling disorder known as *Münchausen syndrome*, a form of feigned illness or **factitious disorder,** which seems to be knowingly motivated by the desire to be hospitalized and treated for phony illnesses.

Conversion Disorder

Conversion disorder involves a major change or loss of physical function, although there is no medical evidence to account for the disorder. The symptoms are not faked or intentionally produced, and they usually come on suddenly in stressful situations. A soldier's hand may become "paralyzed" during intense combat, for example.

Conversion disorder was so-named because of the psychodynamic belief that it represented the channelling or *conversion* of repressed sexual or aggressive energies into physical symptoms. Conversion disorder was formerly called *hysteria* or *hysterical neurosis*. Investigations of cases of hysterical neurosis played a prominent role in the development of psychoanalysis. In Chapter 1 we introduced you to one of the classic cases in the annals of abnormal behavior, the case of Anna O., a young woman who complained of numerous physical problems that fit the pattern of hysteria (now, conversion disorder). As noted in our discussion of the case, hysterical or conversion disorders seem to have been common in Freud's day but are relatively rare today.

According to the DSM–III–R, the most "classic" conversion symptoms mimic neurological disorders: paralysis, epilepsy, problems in coordination, blindness and tunnel vision, loss of the sense of hearing or of smell, or loss of feeling in a limb (anesthesia). Symptoms may also involve the autonomic nervous system, as in vomiting, or the endocrine system, as in false pregnancy ("pseudocyesis"), which is characterized by suspension of menstruation, nausea, and other pregnancy-related symptoms, such as abdominal distention.

The bodily symptoms found in conversion disorders often do not fully match the medical conditions they suggest. For example, conversion epileptics, unlike true epileptic patients, may maintain control over their bladders during attack. People whose vision is supposedly impaired may wend their ways through the physician's office without bumping into the furniture. People who become "incapable" of standing or walking may nevertheless perform other leg movements normally.

If you suddenly lost your vision, or if your legs no longer supported your weight, you would probably show understandable concern. But some people with conversion disorders, like those with psychogenic amnesia, show a remarkable indifference to their symptoms, a phenomenon termed **la belle indifférence** ("beautiful indifference"). The DSM–III–R warns against relying on indifference to symptoms in making a diagnosis, however, because many people cope with real physical disorders by denying their pain or concern about their illness, which provides the semblance of indifference and relieves anxieties—at least temporarily. (See Table 7.3.)

TABLE 7.3 Diagnostic Features of Conversion Disorder

1. Loss or alteration in physical functioning that suggests the presence of a physical disorder.
2. Psychological factors are judged to be causative factors because the onset or exacerbation of the physical symptom is linked to the occurrence of a psychosocial stressor that appears to be related to an underlying psychological conflict or need.
3. The person is not aware of consciously producing the physical symptom.
4. The symptom cannot be explained as a cultural ritual or response pattern, nor can it be explained by any known physical disorder on the basis of appropriate testing.
5. The sympton is not restricted to complaints of pain or problems in sexual functioning.

Source: *Adapted from DSM–III–R, p. 259.*

We should caution that labels of hysteria or conversion disorder are now and then erroneously applied to people with underlying medical conditions that go unrecognized and untreated, as in the case of Gladys:

■ Gladys was a 57-year-old housewife who complained to her physician of a "lump in the throat." The physician found no organic basis for the complaint and referred her to a psychiatrist who informed her that her symptom was a common neurotic symptom and probably reflected her unwillingness to "swallow" her lot in life, now that the children were grown and she sat alone in the house much of the day. Several months later, the symptom persisted and Gladys visited a psychologist at a community mental-health center. Before treating the "hysterical symptom," the psychologist referred her to medical specialists in Boston so that an organic basis for the disorder could be ruled out. Throat cancer was diagnosed, but the cancer had metastasized and it was too late to save Gladys's life.

The Authors' Files ■

Gladys's case is not unique. One study compared the subsequent medical histories of 56 psychiatric clients who had been diagnosed as having conversion disorder with those of 56 clients who had been diagnosed as suffering from anxiety or depression. Thirty-five (62.5%) of the clients diagnosed with conversion disorder later developed organic brain disorders as compared with only 3 (5.3%) of those diagnosed as having disorders of anxiety or depression (Whitlock, 1967). Another study took a very different approach and examined 30 consecutively admitted patients to a hospital neurology unit, each of which had documented neurological damage. Most patients showed varying degrees of "hysterical features" that are generally associated with conversion disorder, such as *la belle indifférence* and sensory losses that were not consistent with recognized organic patterns of pathology (Gould et al., 1986). In the opin-

ion of these researchers, certain classes of people, including women and homosexual men, are at greater risk of being misdiagnosed as hysterical because of commonly held beliefs among clinicians that they are more prone toward such disorders. Perhaps as many as 80 percent of individuals given the diagnoses of conversion disorder have real neurological problems that may go undiagnosed (Gould et al., 1986).

 Persons with conversion disorder do lose sensory and motor functions without evidence of organic pathology. (However, some people who are assumed to have conversion disorders have organic involvements that go undiagnosed.)

Hypochondriasis

The term **hypochondriasis** is derived from the Greek *hypochondrion*, which refers to the abdomen, the soft part of the body below (*hypo*) the cartilage (*chondrion*) of the breastbone. This area of the body is the site of many—but not all—of the physical complaints of the hypochondriac. Based on their interpretation of bodily signs (for example, sores) or sensations (for example, "heaviness in the chest"), hypochondriacs are preoccupied with the fear of having, or the belief that they have, a grave disease. No organic basis can be found for the complaints, however. Fear of serious illness persists despite medical reassurance. Hypochondriacs are not faking their symptoms; they truly believe they suffer from a serious disease and they truly experience their reported pains and discomfort. Unlike conversion disorder, hypochondriasis does not involve the loss or distortion of physical function, according to the DSM–III–R. And unlike the attitude of indifference toward one's symptoms that are sometimes found in conversion disorders, hypochondriacs tend to express great concern and apprehension about their symptoms.

In order to be diagnosed as hypochondriacal, the problem must persist for at least six months. According to the DSM–III–R, the disorder is about equally common in men and women and most often begins between the ages of 20 and 30, although it can begin at any age. The DSM–III–R also notes the alternate term *hypochondriacal neurosis*, reflecting reliance on the Freudian assumption that hypochondriacal symptoms may be rooted in unresolved, unconscious conflicts.

Hypochondriacs may focus on slight changes in heart beat and minor aches and pains. Anxiety about one's physical status produces its own physical sensations, however—for example, heavy sweating, dizziness, even fainting. Hypochondriacs may be incredulous and resentful when the doctor explains how their own

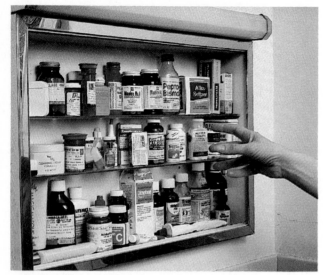

Hypochondriacs are preoccupied with fear that they are seriously ill. They frequently medicate themselves with over-the-counter drugs and find little if any reassurance in doctors' assertions that they are healthy.

TABLE 7.4 Diagnostic Features of Hypochondriasis

1. The person is preoccupied with a fear of having a serious illness, or with the belief that one has a serious illness. The person interprets bodily sensations or physical signs as evidence of physical illness.
2. No organic basis can be determined to explain the physical sensations or signs. Nor can these complaints be considered features of a panic attack.
3. Fears of physical illness, or beliefs of having a physical illness, persist despite medical reassurances.
4. The disturbance has persisted for six months or longer.
5. The person recognizes the possibility that his or her fear of having, or belief in having, a serious disease may be unfounded.

Source: *Adapted from DSM–III–R, p. 261.*

fears may be plaguing them. They frequently go "doctor-shopping" in the hope that some competent and sympathetic physician will heed them before it is too late. Physicians, too, can be hypochondriacs, as we see in the following case example:

■ A 38-year-old radiologist has just returned from a ten-day stay at a famous diagnostic center where he has undergone extensive testing of his entire gastrointestinal tract. The evaluation proved negative for any significant physical illness, but rather than feel relieved, the radiologist appeared resentful and disappointed with the findings. The radiologist has been bothered for several months with various physical symptoms, which he describes as symptoms of mild abdominal pain, feelings of "fullness," "bowel rumblings" and a feeling of a "firm abdominal mass." He has become convinced that his symptoms are due to colon cancer and has become accustomed to testing his stool for blood on a weekly basis and carefully palpating his abdomen for "masses" while lying in bed every several days. He has also secretly performed X-ray studies on himself after regular hours. There is a history of a heart murmur that was detected when he was 13 and his younger brother died of congenital heart disease in early childhood. When the evaluation of his murmur proved to be benign, he nonetheless began to worry that something might have been overlooked. He developed a fear that something was actually wrong with his heart, and while the fear eventually subsided, it has never entirely left him. In medical school he worried that he had the diseases that he learned about in pathology. Since graduating, he has repeatedly experienced concerns about his health that follow a typical pattern: noticing certain symptoms, becoming preoccupied with what the symptoms might mean, and undergoing physical evaluations that proved negative. His decision to seek a psychiatric consultation was prompted by an incident with his nine-year-old son. His son accidentally walked in on him while he was palpating his abdomen and asked, "What do you think it is this time, Dad?" He becomes tearful as he relates this incident, describing his feelings of shame and anger—mostly at himself.
            Adapted from Spitzer et al., 1989, pp. 16–18 ■

Hypochondriasis is generally considered to be more common among elderly people. But as noted by Paul Costa and Robert McCrae (1985) of the National Institute on Aging, authentic age-related health changes do occur, and most "hypochondriacal" complaints probably reflect the changing health status of older people. (See Table 7.4.)

Somatization Disorder

Somatization disorder, formerly known as Briquet's syndrome, is characterized by multiple and recurrent somatic complaints that began prior to the age of 30 (but usually during the teen years) and have persisted for many years. There are usually a large number of complaints involving many different organ systems (Spitzer et al., 1989). There is seldom a year that passes without some physical complaint that prompts a trip to the doctor. As with conversion disorder and hypochondriasis, the complaints cannot be explained by any apparent physical causes. Complaints tend to have a vague or exaggerated quality, and the individual frequently receives medical care from a number of physicians, sometimes at the same time. The DSM–III–R provides a list of 35 symptoms and specifies that in order to be diagnosed as having somatization disorder, the individual must complain of at least 13 of them from among six groups. The groups of symptoms are categorized as gastrointestinal (for example, vomiting or diarrhea), pain, cardiopulmonary (shortness of breath, dizziness), conversion (difficulty swallowing, blurry vision, paralysis, or weakness), sexual, and female-reproductive (dysmenorrhea, for example).

The essential feature of hypochondriasis is fear of disease, of what bodily symptoms might portend. Persons with somatization disorder, by contrast, are pestered by the symptoms themselves. But both diagnoses may be given to the same individual if the diagnostic criteria for both disorders are met. Somatization disorder is rarely diagnosed in males, whereas hypochondriasis, as noted, is believed to affect both sexes about equally.

Though the diagnostic category of somatization disorder originated with the DSM–III in 1980, the psychiatrist Emil Kraepelin, who was one of the fathers of modern psychiatry, presented a case in the nineteenth century that closely parallels somatization disorder (Spitzer et al., 1989). The case account describes that of a 30-year-old woman who complained of many physical problems that dated back to her adolescence for which no physical cause could be determined, including seizures, difficulty walking, muscle weakness, abdominal pain, diarrhea, menstrual problems, chest pain, and urinary problems, among others. Like many others with the disorder, the woman also presented genuine physical problems, but her physical condition could not account for the wide range of physical complaints. Every type of treatment available at the time was tried, but with only temporary benefits or none at all, including various types of therapeutic baths, periods of rest in the Riviera and in the country, and even the use of mild electric currents.

Theoretical Perspectives

Theoretical accounts of the somatoform disorders, like those of the dissociative disorders, have most often sprung from psychodynamic and learning theory perspectives. But before turning our attention to these modern theoretical perspectives, you might recall from Chapter 1 that conversion disorder, or "hysteria," was known to Hippocrates, who attributed the strange bodily symptoms to a wandering uterus, which created internal chaos. As you will also recall from Chapter 1, the term *hysterical* derives from the Greek *hystera*, meaning "uterus." Hippocrates noticed that these complaints were less common among married women. He prescribed marriage as a "cure" on the basis of these observations, and also on the theoretical assumption that pregnancy would satisfy uterine needs and fix it in place. Pregnancy fosters hormonal and structural changes that are of benefit to some women with menstrual complaints, but Hippocrates' beliefs in the "wandering uterus" has contributed to degrading interpretations of complaints by women of physical problems throughout the centuries. Despite Hippocrates' beliefs that hysteria (now conversion disorder) was exclusively a female concern, it is known to occur in both sexes. Hysterical disorders provide an arena for some of the debate between the psychological and biological theories of the nineteenth century. The alleviation—albeit often temporary—of hysterical symptoms through hypnosis by Charcot, Breuer, and Freud contributed to the belief that hysteria was rooted in psychological, rather than physical, causes and led Freud to the development of the theory of the unconscious mind. In Chapter 2 we mentioned that Freud held that the ego manages to control unacceptable or threatening impulses from the id, which are sexual or aggressive in nature, by means of various defense mechanisms, such as repression. The control of these impulses prevents the outbreak of anxiety that would occur if the individual were to become aware of these underlying conflicts. In some cases, the left-over emotion or energy that is "strangulated" or cut-off from the unacceptable or threatening impulses becomes *converted* into a physical symptom, like hysterical paralysis or blindness.

According to psychodynamic theory, hysterical symptoms are functional: They allow the person to achieve **primary gains** and **secondary gains.** The primary gains consist of allowing the individual to keep internal conflicts out of awareness—repressed. The person is aware of the physical symptom, but not of the inner conflict it represents. In such cases, the "symptom" is symbolic of, and provides a partial solution of, the underlying conflict. For example, hysterical paralysis may symbolize but also prevent the individual from acting out unacceptable sexual (for example, masturbatory) or aggressive (murderous) impulses that the ego has kept repressed in the unconscious. This process occurs unconsciously, so that the individual remains unaware of the underlying conflicts. The secondary gains may allow the person to avoid burdensome responsibilities and to gain the support—rather than the condemnation—of those around them. For example, soldiers sometimes experience sudden "paralysis" of their hands, which prevents them from firing their weapons in battle. They may then be sent to recuperate at a hospital rather than face the enemy fire. But the symptoms are not believed to be consciously faked or contrived, as would be the case in malingering. A number of bomber pilots during World War II suffered hysterical "night blindness" that prevented them from carrying out dangerous nighttime missions. In the psychodynamic view, their "blindness" may have achieved a primary gain of shielding them from guilt associated with dropping bombs on civilian areas. It might also have achieved a secondary purpose of helping them avoid dangerous combat missions. *La belle*

B-29 bombers during a bombing mission on Japan during WWII. Some pilots were reported to have suffered from hysterical night blindness, which prevented them from carrying out dangerous nighttime missions. Their night blindness may have shielded them from guilt over dropping bombs on civilian areas—a type of primary gain. It may also have served the secondary purpose of helping them avoid danger.

indifférence, first noted by Charcot, occurs because the physical symptoms help relieve, rather than cause anxiety. So the psychodynamic view is that conversion disorders, like dissociative disorders, serve a purpose.

Although the early psychodynamic formulation of hysteria is still widely held, empirical evidence has been lacking (Miller, 1987). One problem with the Freudian view is that it does not explain how energies left over from unconscious conflicts become transformed into physical symptoms (Miller, 1987). Because of these limitations, learning theories have recently gained some favor. Before exploring the learning perspectives, however, let us consider a classic case reported by the influential learning theorists John Dollard and Neal E. Miller in 1950. It permits a variety of interpretations:

■ Mrs. C was a 35-year-old married woman whose legs were "paralyzed." Mrs. C was reared by a stern mother who "belted" her repeatedly so that she would remain a "good" girl. As a girl, Mrs. C swore that she would never get married, and her resolve changed only later in life. Marriage was apparently a means for escaping the punishment of home life. Ignorant of sex and conception, Mrs. C reported that she "felt nausea every time my husband touched me."

During 15 years of marriage, Mrs. C became pregnant four times and had three surviving children. Her sexual aversion became stronger after her most recent, painful pregnancy. She allowed her husband to engage in intercourse only once or twice a month, and only after extensive pleading. She gave in only because of "pity."

After the fourth pregnancy, Mrs. C developed a morbid fear of pregnancy. She connected the fear to feelings of "doom" related to the fact that a paternal aunt had been hospitalized for a mental disorder. The fear was not sufficient to put off her husband, and Mrs. C next developed symptoms in her legs, which felt "weak, wobbly and trembled." Soon afterward she was brought to the hospital,

unable to flex her knees, walk, or stand. Although her symptoms might reflect serious pathology, her anxiety level was low, which was attributed to *la belle indifférence*.

Physicians showed that the symptoms were not organic. Organic signs of paralysis were lacking, and Mrs. C's legs were freely movable under the influence of sodium pentothal—a barbiturate that relieves anxiety and alters one's state of consciousness. (It has also been referred to as "truth serum.") Mrs. C was unwilling to try psychotherapy, so the doctors resorted to forcing Mrs. C to try walking. They helped her stand and used pressure to bend her knees. In short, they proved to her that she could stand and walk. Rather than showing relief and gratitude that her disorder was not severe, Mrs. C became enraged, expressing her hostility toward the doctors and nurses.

Upon returning home, Mrs. C contemplated divorce and spent some time living with a sister. Conflict with the sister's family forced a return home. Mrs. C refused intercourse with her husband, heightening the conflict between them. Eventually she received contraceptive advice, but she did not use it, apparently because her aversion to sex extended beyond fears of pregnancy. There was no happy ending.

Adapted from Dollard & Miller, 1950, pp. 168–170 ■

Mrs. C's weakness in the legs seemed to have clear primary and secondary gains. They relieved her of having to deal more directly with her deep-seated aversion to sex and pregnancy. Her symptom also provided her with perhaps more than a "partial solution" to her problem: With weak, wobbly legs, she could not be expected to take care of her family or engage in intercourse with her husband. On the other hand, there was no evidence that Mrs. C's complaint was the symbolic expression of unconscious conflicts involving the banishment of unacceptable impulses to the unconscious. Within a learning-theory perspective, then, conversion symptoms may serve the purpose of helping the individual avoid or escape from stressful situations without confronting them directly.

Dollard and Miller explained the "gains" associated with Mrs. C's complaints in learning-theory terms. They suggested that a passing weakness in the legs might have prompted the passing thought, "This will prevent intercourse" (1950, p. 169). The thought would relieve anxiety over sex and thus reinforce the symptom. Dollard and Miller do not suggest that Mrs. C consciously seized her opportunity by purposefully faking the symptom, but rather that the reinforcer of anxiety relief heightened the probability of its occurrence. Dollard and Miller explain Mrs. C's indifference to her symptom as evidence of the anxiety-relieving role it played. They interpret her rage at being deprived of her symptom as further evidence of its anxiety-relieving role.

Psychodynamic theory and learning theory concur that the symptoms in conversion disorders relieve anxiety. Psychodynamic theorists, however, seek the causes of anxiety in unconscious conflicts. Learning theorists focus on the more direct reinforcing properties of the symptom.

From the learning perspective, the symptoms in conversion and other somatoform disorders may also carry the benefits of, or reinforcing properties of, the "sick role" (Kendell, 1983). Persons with conversion disorders may be relieved of chores and responsibilities like going to work or performing household tasks (Miller, 1987). As noted earlier, being "physically ill" also usually earns sympathy and support from other people. People who received such reinforcers during past illnesses are especially likely to learn to adopt a sick role even when they are not ill (Kendell, 1983). Differences in learning experiences may explain why conversion disorders were historically more often reported among women. It may be that women in our culture have been socialized, more so than men, to react to stress by enacting a sick role (Miller, 1987). We are not suggesting that people with conversion disorders are fakers; we are merely pointing out that people may learn to adopt roles that lead to reinforcing consequences, regardless of whether or not they deliberately seek to enact these roles.

Most theorists, in fact, distinguish between **malingering,** or consciously making false claims to achieve various gains, and conversion disorder, in which the symptoms are not seen as being consciously directed (Miller, 1987). Malingerers fake or exaggerate physical or psychological symptoms in order to obtain external rewards or incentives, such as avoiding military service or obtaining better living conditions. If people with conversion disorders fake their symptoms, they do not appear to be consciously aware of it. One might even say that they are deceiving *themselves* as well as others about the legitimacy of their physical complaints.

Some learning theorists see the hypochondriac's pattern of repeatedly seeking medical consultations and reassurance as a form of obsessive-compulsive behavior (Salvoskis & Warwick, 1986). You will recall that obsessive-compulsive behavior involves a pattern of persistent, disturbing thoughts, called obsessions, which are followed by urges to perform certain behaviors, which are called compulsions. Both the obsessional thoughts and compulsions are experienced as being beyond the individual's ability to control. Hypochrondiacs are bothered by obsessive, anxiety-inducing thoughts that something terrible is wrong with their health. The urge to run from doctor to doctor may be seen as a type of compulsion which is reinforced by the temporary but partial relief from anxiety they experience when reassured by their doctors that their fears are unwarranted. But the troublesome thoughts eventually return, prompting repeated visits to the physician. The cycle may then repeat itself time and time again.

Cognitive theorists have speculated that some hypochondriacs may use their complaints as a type of self-handicapping strategy (Smith et al., 1983). That is, they may complain of physical symptoms in situations in which sickness can serve as a reasonable excuse for poor performance. In other cases, diverting attention to physical complaints can serve as a means of avoiding thinking about other life problems.

Treatment of Somatoform Disorders

The treatment approach pioneered by Freud, psychoanalysis, began with the treatment of cases of hysteria, or what is now termed conversion disorder. Psychoanalysis seeks to uncover and bring to the level of awareness unconscious conflicts of childhood origins. Once the conflict is aired and worked-through in psychoanalysis, the symptom should disappear since it is no longer needed as a "partial solution" to the conflict. The psychoanalytic method is supported by case studies, some reported by Freud and others by his followers. However, the infrequency of conversion disorders in contemporary times has made it difficult to mount controlled studies of the psychoanalytic technique.

The behavioral approach to treating conversion disorders, and other somatoform disorders, may focus on removing sources of secondary reinforcement (or secondary gain), which may become connected to physical complaints. Individuals with somatization disorder, for example, are often perceived by family members and others as sickly and infirmed and incapable of carrying out normal responsibilities. Family members and others may be unaware of how they may be reinforcing dependent and complaining behaviors on the part of the person with somatoform complaints, such as reinforcing excessive bedrest and relieving the person of household responsibilities. The behavior therapist may work with family members to help them reward attempts by the individual to assume more responsibility and withdraw attention for nagging, complaining behaviors. The behavior therapist may also work more directly with the person with a somatoform disorder, helping the individual learn more adaptive ways of handling stressful or anxiety-arousing situations, such as by the use of relaxation techniques and cognitive restructuring. Here again, the absence of controlled studies in the treatment of somatoform disorders prevents a fair assessment of the relative efficacy of different approaches.

In this chapter we have focused on disorders that have traditionally been categorized as neuroses but that now stand as diagnostic classes on their own. The dissociative and somatoform disorders are among the most intriguing and least understood patterns of abnormal behavior.

A CLOSER LOOK
Münchausen Syndrome

A woman staggered into the emergency room of a New York City hospital bleeding from the mouth, clutching her stomach, and wailing with pain. It was some entrance. Even in that setting, forever serving bleeders and clutchers and wailers, there was something about her, some terrible star quality that held stage center. Her pain was larger than life.

She told a harrowing story: A man had seduced her, then tied her up, beat her, forced her to surrender money and jewelry on threat of death. She had severe pain in her lower left side, and an unbearable headache.

She was admitted, and exhaustively tested. Nothing could be found; no reason for the bleeding or the pain; the specialists were left scratching their heads.

Then, one day, a hospital aide came upon these items in her bedside table: a needle, syringe, and a blood thinner called heparin. Eureka. Inject yourself with enough blood thinner and you, too, can take stage center in an emergency room.

Confronted, she denied all charges. The stuff was not hers; someone was trying to frame her; if nobody believed her, she would check out of the place and find doctors who really cared. And off she went. Later, it was learned that she had recently been in two other hospitals: The same story, same symptom and same sequence of events. Diagnosis: Münchausen syndrome.

Source: Lear, 1988, p. 21. Copyright © 1988 by The New York Times Company. Reprinted by permission.

Münchausen syndrome was named after Baron Karl von Münchausen, one of history's great fibbers. The good Baron, an eighteenth-century German army officer, entertained friends with tales of outrageous adventures. In the vernacular, *Münchausenism* describes tellers of "tall tales." But in abnormal psychology, **Münchausen syndrome** refers to patients who tell "tall tales" or outrageous lies to their doctors. The Baron was a jolly man, but patients who carry his name for their particular condition usually

Baron Münchausen, who regaled his friends with tales of his incredible feats. In one of his "tall tales," depicted here, he had fallen asleep inside a cannon and was inadvertently shot across the Thames River.

suffer deep anguish as they bounce from hospital to hospital and subject themselves to unnecessary, painful, and sometimes risky medical treatments (Schoenfeld et al., 1987).

Although there may be gains in having physical symptoms, individuals with somatoform disorders do not purposefully produce them. Even if there is no medical basis to their symptoms, they do not set out to deceive others. Münchausen syndrome, thus, is not a somatoform disorder. Rather, it is a kind of **factitious disorder.** Factitious disorders involve the deliberate fabrication of physical and/or psychological complaints. Münchausen syndrome, in particular, refers to a chronic pattern of deliberate fabrication of seemingly plausible physical complaints.

In factitious disorders, as with malingering (faking), physical or psychological symptoms are consciously and deliberately produced. The malingerer does consciously invent a complaint, but does so for obvious gain. Perhaps the malingerer wishes to be relieved of military service or jury duty, wants to take a day off from work or school, or would like to avoid some other distasteful activity. Because malingering is motivated by such external incentives, it is not considered a mental disorder, according to the DSM–III–R. In factitious disorders, by contrast, there is

SUMMARY

Dissociative and Somatoform Disorders

The dissociative and somatoform disorders were historically linked with the anxiety disorders as forms of neuroses. The various forms of neurosis were theorized to be related to anxiety in different ways. Anxiety is expressed directly in different forms in the anxiety disorders, but its role in the dissociative and somatoform disorders is inferred.

Dissociative Disorders

Dissociative disorders involve changes or disturbance in identity, memory, or consciousness that affect the ability to maintain an integrated sense of self. The DSM–III–R lists four major dissociative disorders: multiple personality, psychogenic amnesia, psychogenic fugue, and depersonalization disorder.

In multiple personality disorder (MPD), two or

nothing obviously to be gained by producing the symptoms. The absence of external incentives suggests that factitious disorder serves a psychological need; hence, it is judged a mental disorder by the DSM–III–R. Factitious disorders are maladaptive. Persons with factitious disorders seem compelled to feign illness even though their fakery may subject them to painful or dangerous medical procedures (Schretlen, 1988).

Persons with Münchausen syndrome may travel widely, visiting emergency rooms in one city after another, where they present themselves as suffering from acute, dramatic symptoms.

> **?** People with Münchausen syndrome may in fact show up repeatedly at emergency rooms, feigning illness and demanding treatment. Their motives remain a mystery.

Persons with Münchausen syndrome deliberately weave tales of illness for no apparent reason other than to gain admission to the hospital. The syndrome may be seen as a form of compulsive behavior, perhaps even a form of "addiction" to hospitals, in which people crave the sick role (Lear, 1988). They may go to great lengths to seek a confirmatory diagnosis, such as agreeing to exploratory surgery to assist their physicians in making a diagnosis. They may acquire sophisticated medical knowledge to feign complaints or manufacture plausible medical symptoms. For example, they may inject themselves with certain drugs to produce skin rashes. When confronted with evidence of their deception, they may turn nasty and stick to their guns. Unlike malingerers, persons with Münchausen disorder are often unaware of their underlying motivation for their behavior (Schoenfeld et al., 1987).

The psychological needs served by Münchausen syndrome are somewhat conjectural. It has been suggested that persons with Münchausen disorder may be trying to expunge guilt for felt misdeeds by subjecting themselves to painful medical procedures. Perhaps they hold grudges against doctors or hospitals for perceived injustices at the

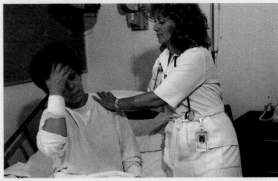

Münchausen syndrome is characterized by the fabrication of medical complaints for no apparent purpose other than to gain admission to hospitals. Some people may produce life-threatening symptoms in their attempts to deceive doctors.

hands of the medical establishment (Lear, 1988) and they delight in their ability to "put one over on the doctors." The person's methods of inducing physical symptoms can be dangerous in themselves and have sometimes been interpreted as a suicidal wish (Schoenfeld et al., 1987).

Some conjectures focus on the early childhood of Münchausen patients. Perhaps they learned to garner attention from parents in childhood by "playing sick," and this childhood pattern is reactivated when they need attention in adult life (Lear, 1988). Their childhoods were often characterized by parental rejection or deprivation, family instability and placement in foster homes, parental illness, or childhood hospitalizations (Schoenfeld et al., 1987). Somehow they learn about what being sick means. Perhaps enacting the sick role in the protected hospital environment provides a sense of security that was lacking in childhood. Perhaps the hospital becomes a stage on which they can act out resentments against doctors and parents that have been brewing since childhood. Perhaps they are trying to identify with a parent who was often sick. Speculations about possible motives abound, but researchers are only now beginning to explore this puzzling and disturbing disorder.

more distinct personalities, each possessing well-defined traits and memories, exist within the person and repeatedly take control of the person's behavior. Two alternate personalities may vie for control. Or there may be a dominant or core personality and several subordinate personalities. The core personality is often unaware of the existence of the alternates. While the disorder is generally considered to be rare, some authorities believe that its incidence may be increasing, but research evidence of its prevalence remains unclear. Multiple personality, which is sometimes called "split personality," should not be confused with schizophre-

nia. But the diagnosis may be clouded in cases of people who have features of both MPD and show behaviors associated with schizophrenia, such as hallucinations. People with features of MPD often receive several other diagnoses before an MPD diagnosis is given.

Psychogenic amnesia involves loss of memory for personal information. The condition is not due to organic factors. There are four types of psychogenic amnesia: localized, selective, generalized, and continuous. Localized amnesia is the most common type. The lack of concern shown by people with psychogenic amnesia has led theorists to suggest that the memory loss serves the adaptive function of relieving anxiety or other forms of psychological pain associated with past trauma. Psychogenic amnesia, as with other dissociative disorders, should be distinguished from malingering, the conscious attempt to fabricate symptoms or make false claims for personal gain. But clinicians cannot always identify malingerers.

In psychogenic fugue, the person shows a loss of memory for the past, travels suddenly away from home or place of work, and takes on a new identity. Fugue states are usually fleeting, but can last for years. Like psychogenic amnesia, fugue is believed to occur most often during warfare or following other kinds of extreme trauma or disaster. This buttresses the belief that dissociative states like fugue protect the person from psychological pain or traumatic memories.

Depersonalization involves experiences of feeling that one is detached from oneself. During such experiences, people may feel detached from their minds or bodies, or they may feel like they are dreaming or are robots. Depersonalization disorders involve persistent or recurrent episodes of depersonalization that are of sufficient severity to cause significant distress. Still, the person can distinguish reality from unreality during these depersonalization experiences. Transient depersonalization experiences are actually quite common among normal people. Unlike other dissociative states, there is no loss of memory. Also, depersonalization episodes are often anxiety-inducing, whereas other forms of dissociative behavior seem to protect the self from anxiety.

Psychodynamic theorists view dissociative experiences as a form of psychological defense by which the ego defends itself against troubling memories and unacceptable impulses by blotting them out of consciousness. There is increasing documentation of a link between dissociative disorders, especially MPD, and early childhood trauma, which lends support to the view that dissociation may serve to protect the self from troubling memories. Children with more fertile imaginations may be more likely to invent alternate personalities as a means of psychologically escaping from their suffering. In MPD, people may also express unacceptable impulses through alternate personalities. Repression is believed to play a role in blotting out painful memories or dissociating threatening impulses in psychogenic amnesia and in fugue states. Depersonalization is believed to allow people to stand outside of themselves and remain detached from the threatening impulses or painful memories that lie within.

To the learning and cognitive theorists, dissociative experiences involve ways of learning not to think about certain troubling behaviors or thoughts that might lead to feelings of guilt or shame. Relief from anxiety negatively reinforces this pattern of dissociation. Social-learning theorists and cognitive theorists suggest that multiple personality may represent a form of role-playing behavior. Multiple personalities may have learned to enact the role by observing models of multiple personality in films and television shows or perhaps by responding to cues. Therapists and others who respond to multiple personality role enactments with interest and concern may inadvertently reinforce the enactment of the role. A recent study by Spanos and his colleagues showed that normal college volunteers enacted various components of the multiple personality role when they were appropriately cued in a laboratory experiment.

Some dissociative states, like psychogenic amnesia and fugue, are often transient and terminate abruptly. More persistent dissociative disorders, like depersonalization disorder, may occur more frequently during periods of anxiety or depression. In such cases, treatment may be directed at managing anxiety or depression. Treatment of MPD is approached from several theoretical perspectives. Psychodynamic approaches help the individual uncover and cope with dissociated painful experiences from childhood. Biological approaches focus on the use of drugs to treat the anxiety and depression often associated with MPD, but drugs have not been able to bring about reintegration of the personality. Learning perspectives focus on the use of behavioral methods of reinforcement of the most well-adjusted personality. The rarity of MPD has limited any analysis of behavioral and psychodynamic approaches to the occasional case study or to multiple case studies.

Somatoform Disorders

In somatoform disorders, there are physical complaints for which no organic basis can be found. Thus, the symptoms are theorized to reflect psychological rather than organic factors. Three types of somatoform disorders are considered: conversion disorder, hypochondriasis, and somatization disorder.

In conversion disorder, there is an apparent major change or loss of physical function in the absence of any medical basis for the condition. Conversion disorder, which was formerly called hysteria or hysterical neurosis, derives its present name from the psychodynamic belief that it represents the channelling or conversion of repressed sexual or aggressive energies into physical symptoms. In some cases, people with conversion disorders show a remarkable lack of concern about their symptoms, which has been labeled *la belle indifférence*. In some (but not all) cases a diagnosis of conversion disorder may mask an actual organic problem that has gone unrecognized and untreated.

Hypochondriasis is a preoccupation with the fear of having, or the belief that one has, a serious medical illness, but no medical basis for the complaints can be found and fears of illness persist despite medical reassurances. Like people with conversion disorders, hypochondriacs are not consciously faking their symptoms. But unlike conversion disorder, there is no loss of physical function.

Formerly known as Briquet's syndrome, somatization disorder involves multiple and recurrent complaints of physical symptoms that have persisted for many years and which began prior to the age of 30, but most typically during adolescence. Like other somatoform disorders, no physical basis can be found that would account for the person's many complaints. People with somatization disorder tend to be bothered more by the complaints themselves, whereas hypochondriacs tend to be more concerned that their symptoms may be signs of a dreaded disease.

Freud's belief that hysterical complaints (now called conversion disorders) were rooted in psychological, rather than physical, causes led to his development of a theory of the unconscious mind. The psychodynamic view holds that conversion disorders represent the conversion into physical symptoms of the leftover emotion or energy that is "strangulated" or cut off from unacceptable or threatening impulses that the ego has prevented from reaching awareness. The symptom is functional, allowing the person to achieve both primary and secondary gains. Primary gains shield the person from recognition of the inner conflict. The person is aware of the symptom but not the conflict it represents or symbolizes. The symptom also provides a partial solution to the conflict by preventing the expression of the unacceptable impulse. Secondary gains are achieved by avoiding burdensome or dangerous situations and eliciting support and sympathy from others. Attitudes of indifference that are sometimes found in conversion disorders support the view that the physical symptoms serve a hidden psychological purpose.

Learning theorists also focus on the secondary gains or reinforcements that are associated with conversion disorders. They focus on the anxiety-relieving role of such symptoms, but they do not posit that anxiety is rooted in unconscious conflicts. Learning theorists also focus on the reinforcing effects of adopting a "sick role." A recent learning theory view likens hypochondriasis to obsessive-compulsive behavior. Cognitive theorists propose that hypochondriacal complaints may represent a type of self-handicapping strategy.

Münchausen syndrome is a form of factitious disorder involving the conscious fabrication of medical complaints for no apparent cause other than to gain admission to a hospital. Malingering, by contrast, involves the fabrication of physical or psychological symptoms for obvious external gain. Münchausen syndrome is not well understood, but it may represent a type of compulsion in which the person feels compelled to gain admission to a hospital in order to occupy a "sick role."

Traditional psychoanalysis began with the treatment of cases of hysteria (now conversion disorders). Psychoanalysis seeks to uncover and bring to the level of awareness the unconscious conflicts, originating in childhood, that are believed to be at the root of the problem. Once the conflict is uncovered and worked-through, the hysterical symptom should disappear since it is no longer needed as a partial solution to the underlying conflict. Behavioral approaches focus on removing sources of secondary reinforcement that may be maintaining the abnormal behavior pattern. Behavioral therapists may also work more directly to help people with somatoform disorders learn to handle stressful or anxiety-arousing situations more effectively. Finally, despite the history of treatment of somatoform disorders, there is an absence of controlled studies examining the effectiveness of different treatment approaches.

8 Mood Disorders and Suicide

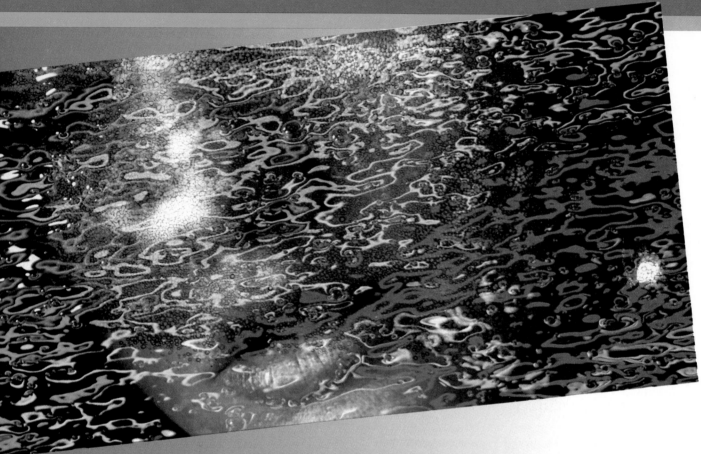

LEARNING OBJECTIVES

When you have completed your study of Chapter 8, you should be able to:

MOOD DISORDERS (p. 250)

1. Define the term *mood disorder*.

MAJOR DEPRESSION (pp. 250–257)

2. Distinguish between normal and abnormal depressed mood.
3. Describe the features of major depression.
4. Describe the course of major depression.
5. Discuss the incidence of major depression and the role of stress in depression.
6. Discuss seasonal affective disorder.
7. Differentiate between reactive and endogenous depression.
8. Discuss postpartum depression.

DYSTHYMIA (p. 257)

9. Describe the features of dysthymia and differentiate between dysthymia and major depression.

BIPOLAR DISORDER (pp. 257–259)

10. Describe the features of bipolar disorder.
11. Describe the features of a manic episode.

CYCLOTHYMIA (p. 259)

12. Differentiate between bipolar disorder and cyclothymia.

THEORETICAL PERSPECTIVES (pp. 260–274)

13. Discuss psychodynamic perspectives on the mood disorders.
14. Discuss behavioral perspectives, focusing on relationships between reinforcement and depression.

15. Discuss cognitive perspectives on depression, focusing on Beck's cognitive theory and the reformulated helplessness (attributional) theory.
16. Discuss genetic factors in the mood disorders.
17. Discuss biochemical factors in the mood disorders, focusing on the catecholamine hypothesis.
18. Discuss the dexamethasone suppression test as a procedure for detecting depression.
19. Discuss the relationships between creative genius and mood disorders.

TREATMENT (pp. 274–281)

20. Discuss psychodynamic approaches to treating the mood disorders.
21. Discuss behavioral approaches to treating the mood disorders, focusing on Lewinsohn's *Coping with Depression Course*.
22. Discuss cognitive approaches to treating the mood disorders, focusing on Beck's cognitive therapy methods.
23. Discuss the use of antidepressant drugs, focusing on the actions of tricyclics and MAO inhibitors.
24. Discuss the use of lithium for treating bipolar disorder.
25. Discuss the controversy surrounding use of ECT in treatment of depression.

SUICIDE (pp. 281–286)

26. Discuss the incidence of suicide.
27. Discuss theoretical perspectives on the causes of suicide.
28. Discuss suicide prevention.

L ife has its ups and downs. Most of us feel elated when we have received high grades, earned the affections of Mr. or Ms. Right, or received a big promotion. Most of us feel down or depressed when we are rejected by a prospective date, fail an important test, or suffer financial reverses. It is normal and appropriate to be elated by uplifting events. It is just as normal, just as appropriate, to feel depressed by dismal events. It might very well be "abnormal" if one were *not* depressed by life's miseries.

? Feeling depressed is *not* abnormal when we have encountered depressing events or circumstances.

Personal ups and downs—these emotional poles—can be quite normal when they occur in response to the ups and downs of daily living. Some people, however, experience emotional extremes of elation, depression, or both, which seem partly or completely divorced from what is happening to them at the time or which are more prolonged or profound than usual. In some cases illness or the loss of a loved one triggers a depressive response that comes to seem abnormal because of its extent and duration. Other people become severely depressed when things appear to be going reasonably well, or when they experience mildly upsetting events that most others would take in stride. Still other people experience polar mood swings, going from the heights of elation to the depths of depression, and back, without any apparent reference to outside events at all. Some people, that is, ride an emotional roller coaster with dizzying heights and abysmal depths when the world around them remains largely on an even keel.

While changes in mood in response to the ups and downs of everyday life are normal, persistent or severe changes in mood, or cycles of extreme elation and depression, suggest the presence of a mood disorder.

MOOD DISORDERS

Our **moods** are enduring states of feeling that color our psychological lives. When we are in a "good mood," many of the insults of daily life roll off our backs. When our moods are depressed, however, even the happiest of happenstances does little to cheer us. According to the DSM–III–R **mood disorders** are characterized by disturbances in mood that are serious enough to impair daily functioning. In this chapter we focus on two kinds of depressive disorders, major depression and dysthymia, and two kinds of disorders that involve mood swings, bipolar disorder and cyclothymia (see Table 8.1). The depressive disorders are considered **unipolar,** because the disturbance in mood concerns one emotional direction or pole. The disorders that involve mood swings are considered **bipolar,** because they involve excesses both of depression and elation.

Depression has been referred to as the "common cold" of psychological problems (Seligman, 1973) and is often the most frequent complaint prompting outpatient psychiatric visits (Woodruff et al., 1975). Depressive disorders are characterized by features such as those shown in Table 8.2. People who are depressed commonly show difficulties that involve changes in emotional states, motivation. functioning and motor behavior, and cognition. We first consider the depressive disorders of major depression and dysthymia. Then we turn our attention to the mood swing (or bipolar) disorders, one of which is labeled bipolar disorder and the other cyclothymia.

MAJOR DEPRESSION

Many if not most of us experience feelings of sadness or depressed mood from time to time. We may feel "down in the dumps" or complain of a loss of interest in usually pleasurable activities or in socializing with others, a loss of self-esteem, difficulty concentrating, periods of crying, pessimistic thoughts, or even occasional thoughts of suicide. But for most of us, these changes in mood pass quickly and do not significantly affect our ability to function. Among people with **major depression,** however, changes in mood tend to be more severe and to affect daily functioning. People with major depression may also have a poor appetite and lose substantial weight, and they may be physically agitated, or—at the other extreme—show a slowing down of physical activity. They may lose interest in most of their usual activities and pursuits, have difficulty concentrating and making decisions, display indifference, and have recurrent thoughts about death or attempt suicide.

Persons with major depression may have faulty perceptions of reality. In this case, depression may have

TABLE 8.1 Types of Mood Disorders

Depressive Disorders (Unipolar Disorders)

Major Depression	Occurrence of one or more major depressive episodes with no history of manic or hypomanic episodes. May be typed as major depression, single episode, if only one episode has occurred, or major depression, recurrent, if two or more discrete episodes have occurred that were separated by a return to more or less normal functioning for at least two months. May be specified as seasonal if the major depressive episode occurs during particular seasons.
Dysthymia	A pattern of chronic disturbance of mood involving depressed mood (but perhaps an irritable mood in children or adolescents) that occurs in more days than not, for most of the day, for a period of at least two years in adults and at least one year in children and adolescents.

Bipolar Disorders

Bipolar Disorder	Disorders with one or more manic episodes (episodes of inflated mood and hyperactivity in which judgment and behavior are often impaired). In bipolar disorder, manic episodes are usually accompanied by one or more major depressive episodes.
Cyclothymia	A chronic mood disturbance involving numerous hypomanic episodes (episodes with manic features of a lesser degree of severity than manic episodes) and numerous periods of depressed mood that are not of the severity to meet the criteria of major depressive episodes.

Source: *Adapted from the DSM–III–R, pp. 226–233.*

TABLE 8.2 Common Features of Depression

Changes in Emotional States	Changes in mood (persistent periods of feeling down, depressed, sad or blue). Tearfulness or crying, feeling guilty or remorseful about past misdeeds. Increased irritability, jumpiness, or loss of temper.
Changes in Motivation	Feeling unmotivated, or having difficulty getting out of bed in the morning. Reduced level of social participation or interest in social activities. Loss of enjoyment or interest in pleasurable activities. Reduced interest in sex. Failure to respond to praise or rewards.
Changes in Functioning and Motor Behavior	Moving about or talking or moving about more slowly than usual. Changes in sleep habits (sleeping too much or too little, awakening earlier than usual, and having trouble getting back to sleep in early morning hours—so-called early morning awakening). Changes in appetite (eating too much or too little). Changes in weight (gaining or losing weight). Functioning less effectively than usual at work or school.
Cognitive Changes	Difficulty concentrating or thinking clearly. Thinking negatively about oneself and one's future. Lack of self-esteem or feelings of inadequacy. Thinking about death or suicide.

psychotic features. Psychotic features include delusions of unworthiness, misplaced guilt for assumed immense wrongdoings, even thoughts that one's body is rotting away from physical illness. Severely depressed people may also experience hallucinations, as in hearing condemning voices or of experiencing peculiar sensations in the body.

The most prominent feature of depression is a downcast mood. Depressed people also may be unable to find pleasure in activities and events enjoyed by others (Miller, 1987). An ebbing capacity for pleasure discourages depressed individuals from participating in normally pleasant activities, such as family barbecues or sporting events.

Major depression is diagnosed on the basis of one or more major depressive episodes in the absence of a history of **manic** episodes. This is why major depression is considered a unipolar disorder rather than a bipolar (or manic-depressive) disorder. A major depressive episode is diagnosed upon the occurrence of five or more of the features listed in Table 8.3. Either depressed mood or loss of interest or pleasure must be present if the diagnosis is to be made. Although psychotic features—hallucinations and delusions—can occur during a major depressive episode, they do not occur for prolonged periods in the absence of the mood disturbance. When psychotic features do persist in the absence of disturbance in mood, they are more likely to reflect other disorders, such as schizophrenia. The disturbance cannot be due to organic factors, such as a tumor or other physical illness, for the diagnosis to be made. Nor can it represent a normal grief reaction to the death of a loved one, which is termed **bereavement.**

The following case of major depression, complicated by sleep difficulties, illustrates the wide range of features associated with major depression:

Major depression should be distinguished from a normal grief reaction to the death of a loved one, which is termed bereavement. But major depression may occur in people whose bereavement becomes prolonged and interferes with a return to normal functioning.

TABLE 8.3 *Diagnostic Features of a Major Depressive Episode*

1. Depressed mood during most of the day, nearly every day. Can be irritable mood in children or adolescents.
2. Greatly reduced sense of pleasure or interest in all or almost all activities, nearly every day for most of the day.
3. A significant loss or gain of weight (more than 5 percent of body weight in a month) without any attempt to diet, or an increase or decrease in appetite.
4. Daily (or nearly daily) insomnia or hypersomnia.
5. Excessive agitation or slowing down of movement responses nearly every day.
6. Feelings of fatigue or loss of energy nearly every day.
7. Feelings of worthlessness or misplaced or excessive guilt nearly every day.
8. Reduced ability to concentrate or think clearly or make decisions nearly every day.
9. Recurrent thoughts of death or suicide without a specific plan, or occurrence of a suicidal attempt or specific plan for committing suicide.

Source: *Adapted from DSM–III–R, pp. 222–223.*

■ A 38-year-old female clerical worker has suffered from recurrent bouts of depression since she was about 13 years of age. Most recently, she has been troubled by crying spells at work, sometimes occurring so suddenly she wouldn't have enough time to run to the ladies' room to hide her tears from others. She has difficulty concentrating at work and feels a lack of enjoyment from work she used to enjoy. She harbors severe pessimistic and angry feelings, which have been more severe lately since she has been recently putting on weight and has been neglectful in taking care of her diabetes. She feels guilty that she may be slowly killing herself by not taking better care of her health. She sometimes feels that she deserves to be dead. She has been bothered by excessive sleepiness for the past year and a half, and her driving license has been suspended due to an incident the previous month in which she fell asleep while driving, causing her car to lose control and hit a telephone pole. She wakes up most days feeling groggy and just "out of it," and remains sleepy throughout the day. She has never had a steady boyfriend, and lives quietly at home with her mother, with no close friends outside of her family. During the interview, she cried frequently and answered questions in a low monotone, staring downward continuously.

Adapted from Spitzer et al., 1989, pp. 59–62 ■

The course of major depression is variable. As noted in the DSM–III–R some people experience but a single episode of major depression, with a full restoration to earlier levels of functioning. Other people have repeated episodes, with only partial restoration of earlier functioning between episodes. More than half of those who suffer a major depressive episode will apparently have another. However, the longer a person who overcomes an episode remains functioning normally, the lower the likelihood of recurrence (Belsher & Costello, 1988). Most recurrences occur within a year of the first episode. The recurrence rate then tapers off. About 40 percent of those who have had a major depressive episode will have another by the end of the first year; the overall incidence of recurrence increases to 50 percent two years afterward (Belsher & Costello, 1988).

Who Gets Depressed?

Major depression seems to affect about twice as many women as men (Nolen-Hoeksema, 1987). According to the DSM–III–R, depression has a lifetime prevalance of 9 to 26 percent of the female population and 5 to 12 percent of the male population. Surveys of community residents in several metropolitan areas in the United States showed that major depression affected 1.3 to 2.2 percent of the men and 2.2 to 3.5% of the women in the six-month period preceding the survey (Myers et al., 1984).

The reasons why women are more likely than men to encounter major depressive episodes remain unclear, although biological sex differences may be involved. Nolen-Hoeksema (1987) proposed a psychological explanation for the sex difference. Men, according to this hypothesis, are more likely to engage in distracting behaviors when they are depressed, whereas women are more likely to amplify depression by ruminating about their feelings and their possible causes. Regardless of whether or not the initial precipitants of depression are biological or psychological, one's responses may be able to exacerbate or reduce the severity and duration of depressive episodes.

While the initial onset of depression can occur in childhood (see Chapter 14), the risks are very low through age 14 (Lewinsohn et al., 1986). The risks of first developing depression then increase in late adolescence and early adulthood, eventually peaking in the middle-age range (ages 45–55). The likelihood of initial onset of depression then falls off sharply with advancing age. People over the age of 70, for example, who have never experienced a depressive episode are relatively unlikely to become depressed at that advanced age. Still, depression can occur or recur at any age—among children, young adults, middle-aged adults, and elderly people.

A review of studies reported between 1978 and 1987 showed that major depression may have decreased in frequency among the elderly during this period, but increased among segments of the population born since the end of World War II—among so-called baby boomers (Klerman et al., 1989). Researchers speculate that baby boomers may be more susceptible to depression because of factors such as unfulfilled economic expectations, increased urbanization, increased relocation from town to town (destroying networks for social support), and the pressures of adjusting to changing roles for men and women in the home, the marketplace, and society at large (Klerman et al., 1989).

Stress and Depression

In Chapters 4 and 5 it was noted that stress is related to vulnerability to various emotional and physical disorders. Stressors such as the loss of a loved one, physical illness, marital discord, failure, or increased pressure at work can all contribute to the onset or maintenance of depression (Coyne et al., 1987; Eckenrode, 1984; Lewinsohn & Amenson, 1978; Stone & Neale, 1984). We may be most likely to feel depressed when we assume responsibility for undesirable events, such as school-related problems, financial difficulties, unwanted pregnancy, interpersonal problems, and problems with the law (Hammen & DeMayo, 1982).

Depressed persons tend to report a greater number of stressful life events, including family difficulties, physical disorders, and work-related problems, than do nondepressed people (Billings et al., 1983). A recent study showed that mothers of handicapped children, who tend to be exposed to high levels of stress in their daily lives, suffered a greater number of major depressive episodes than did a comparison group of mothers of nonhandicapped children (Breslau & Davis, 1986). People who have experienced a great number of stressful events within a brief period (and those with a family history of depression) are especially vulnerable to depression (Weissman, 1987). Other groups who are exposed to chronic stress, such as people living in poverty and the chronically unemployed, are also more likely to suffer depression. People with more depressive features have also been shown to report a greater number of hostile stressful encounters than do people with fewer signs of depression—another indication that stress may increase vulnerability to depression (Folkman & Lazarus, 1986).

The demonstrated links between stress and depression are correlational rather than experimental. Researchers are prohibited by ethical considerations from experimentally inducing stress in human subjects and observing whether or not subjects become depressed. Because of the cloudy connections between cause and effect, rival hypotheses in explaining the stress–depression connection must also be considered. One possibility is that people with prior psychopathology are more likely to encounter stress (Dohrenwend, et al., 1984). Perhaps people who are prone to depression are more likely to be fired from a job or to fail to get a promotion because of difficulties in motivation and concentration. In such cases, depression may precede rather than follow life changes.

The stress of unemployment, like other sources of stress, may precipitate or prolong a depressive episode.

(Menaghan & Lieberman, 1986). In another study that similarly considered the initial level of depression, wives who rated their husbands as more supportive were less likely to be depressed a year later than wives who reported less marital support (Monroe et al., 1986).

■ **Coping with Stress** Depression-proneness may also be related to the person's style of coping with stress. In addition to having fewer supportive relationships, depressed people are less likely than nondepressed persons to use active problem-solving strategies to alleviate stress (Asarnow et al., 1987; Billings et al., 1983; Nezu & Ronan, 1985). Differences in coping styles between depressed and nondepressed persons have not been consistently replicated in the research literature, however (Barnett & Gotlib, 1988). The role of coping styles in depression requires further study.

Although the direction of causality between stress and depression remains open to debate, some research shows that exposure to significant life stress often does come before, rather than after, the onset of depression (Paykel, 1979). This is consistent with the view that life stress can trigger depression. It also appears that persistent stress may make it more difficult to overcome a depressive episode (Billings & Moos, 1985).

As noted in Chapter 4, some people seem better able to withstand stress or recover from losses better than others. Researchers have found that the relationships between stress and depression may be moderated by such psychosocial factors as social support and coping styles.

■ **Social Support** People who are divorced or separated have the highest rates of depression; married people have the lowest. Divorce and separation are often stressful in themselves but are often compounded by the fact that the remaining spouse may have to go it alone in coping with stress. Marital support may help reduce vulnerability to depression, perhaps because the spouse helps to buffer the effects of stress on the partner. Other research has shown that people with a low level of "social integration"—defined in terms of lack of important relationships and low levels of participation in social activities—are more likely to suffer depression (Barnett & Gotlib, 1988).

Other evidence supports the role of social support as a buffer against stress. For example, the lack of a successful intimate relationship may make one more vulnerable to depression in the face of stressful events (Brown & Harris, 1978). In one study, people with more negative marital relationships reported more signs of depression when evaluated four years later than people with more positive relationships, even when the initial level of depression was taken into consideration

Reactive vs. Endogenous Depression

Some depressive episodes seem to be associated with life events or stresses, such as the loss of a loved one or failure to achieve a desired professional goal. Changes that affect intimate relationships figure prominently among stressors connected with depression, especially "exit events," which involve the departure or loss of significant others through death, divorce, or academic or military obligations (Paykel, 1979).

It is normal for a person to feel or look depressed following the loss of a loved one. A pattern of normal or "uncomplicated" bereavement or grief is distinguished from major depression following a loss in that the latter persists beyond what is considered a normal time period or involves more pervasive features than "simple grief." In contrast to uncomplicated bereavement, major depression may entail feelings of worthlessness, suicidal thinking, significant impairment in ability to function, or a slowing down of psychological activity and physical or motor responses (**psychomotor retardation**).

Depressive episodes linked to stressful events are often called reactive depressions because it is believed that they are activated by these precipitating events. But many depressive episodes seem to occur in the absence of any clear stressful precipitating events or life changes. These depressive episodes are often labeled **endogenous,** which derives from Greek roots meaning "born from within." Such episodes seem to occur from within, that is, rather than in response to external events. Endogenous depression is often seen as biologically based since its occurrence is presumably linked to internal causes rather than to psychological stresses or negative life events (Heiby et al., 1987). In contrast, reactive depressions (also referred to as *non*endogenous

A CLOSER LOOK
Seasonal Affective Disorder

Do you ever feel gloomy on overcast days? Do you find it hard to keep yourself going during those long winter months? Do you tend to feel more cheerful on bright sunny days?

Many people report that their moods vary with the weather, especially with the amount of direct sunlight. Some people, in fact, experience major depressive episodes during the fall and winter months and bounce back during the spring and summer months. Seasonal affective (or mood) disorder (SAD) is a type of major depression that affects people who suffer from a repeated pattern of severe winter/fall depressions and spring/summer elevations in mood (Rosenthal et al., 1984).

 The changing of the seasons apparently does produce a depressive disorder in some people.

Some people complain of a pattern of depression during the fall and winter seasons, then bounce back during the spring and summer. This pattern of depression has been called seasonal affective disorder, or SAD, and is associated with changes in climate, especially seasonal changes in the amount of sunlight.

The features of SAD include fatigue, excessive sleeping, carbohydrate craving, and weight gain (Jacobsen et al., 1987). These depressions tend to lift with the early buds of spring. SAD affects women more often than men, and it is most common among young adults, with many sufferers, nearly half, reporting that their episodes began during childhood or adolescence (Murray, 1989b).

Although the causes of SAD remain unknown, the disorder has been treated successfully with the use of bright artificial light for several hours (generally 2 to 3 hours) a day during the winter season, which apparently serves as a replacement for the missing sunlight (Jacobsen et al., 1987; Lewy, 1987; Rosenthal et al., 1984, 1985). People with SAD may sit with their eyes open at a comfortably close distance from the light source and eat their meals, or read and write during the treatment periods (Murray, 1989b). Phototherapy directed at the eyes tends to produce greater effects than direct exposure to the skin (Wehr et al., 1987), perhaps because the pathway by which light

is normally absorbed by the body is mediated by the eye. While improvement generally occurs within several days of phototherapy, the therapeutic effects depend upon continued treatment until the season changes (Murray, 1989b). Recurrence of depression generally appears several days after light is withdrawn (Rosenthal et al., 1984). Although different theories have emerged to explain the effectiveness of phototherapy, the mechanisms of therapeutic action remain unclear (Murray, 1989b). However, subjects' expectations of improvement with phototherapy may predict their responsiveness, suggesting a possible role for expectations in response to light therapy (Wehr et al., 1987). Because phototherapy appears to help some but not all SAD sufferers, research is needed to fine-tune the factors that will optimize the method's effectiveness (Murray, 1989b).

---

depressions) have generally been thought to reflect psychological causes (Zimmerman & Coryell, 1986).

Problems arise in distinguishing reactive from endogenous depressions on the basis of precipitating factors, however. For one, people who are depressed may suffer impaired memory or confusion and be unable to recall life events or stressors that might have played a role in precipitating their depression. Their friends and loved ones may also be unaware of the stressors to which they were exposed. Depressed people may also report negative life events that actually occurred coincidentally with the onset of the depressive episode but did not play a precipitating role. Our clinical experience has suggested that it is nearly always possible to

find some apparent precipitant of a depressive episode, even when things are apparently going well in general. It is useful to remain cautious in labeling events as precipitants of depression, just as it is useful to remain cautious in any endeavor that attempts to ferret out cause and effect.

The distinction between reactive and endogenous depressions today rests more on the type of reported features than on the presence or absence of potential precipitants. Endogenous depression is characterized by the "vegetative" or physical features of depression, such as loss of weight or appetite, early morning awakenings (awakening two or more hours before one's usual time and having difficulty falling back to sleep),

A CLOSER LOOK
Postpartum Depression

Many, perhaps most, new mothers experience mood changes, periods of tearfulness, and irritability in the days or weeks following the birth of their children. These mood changes, which affect perhaps 50 to 80 percent of new mothers (Harding, 1989), are commonly called the "maternity blues," the "postpartum blues," or, more in the vernacular, the "baby blues." They usually last about 48 hours and are believed to be a normal response to hormonal changes that attend childbirth (Harding, 1989; Yalom et al., 1968).

Some mothers, however, undergo more persistent, severe mood changes, called **postpartum depression** (PPD), which may last for a year or more. *Postpartum* derives from the Latin roots *post*, meaning "after," and *papere*, meaning "to bring forth." PPD is often accompanied by disturbances in appetite and sleep, low self-esteem, and difficulties in maintaining concentration or attention. Between 8 and 15 percent of mothers have been found in recent research to have a diagnosable depressive disorder of moderate severity in the months following childbirth (Gitlin et al., 1989). But questions remain about whether these rates of diagnosable depression are greater among women following childbirth than they are among women of the same age and social background (Gitlin et al., 1989). If not—and the evidence is not yet clear—it would call into question whether PPD, as a specific form of depression linked to the period following childbirth, even exists (Gitlin et al., 1989).

Although PPD may also involve biological factors, psychological considerations, such as stress, a troubled marriage, previous depressions, or an unwanted or sick baby, all increase a woman's vulnerability to the disorder (Mansnerus, 1988; Gitlin et al., 1989). Mothers who appear to be most at risk include first-time mothers, single mothers, and mothers who lack social support from their partners or other family members (Mansnerus, 1988; Gitlin et al., 1989).

A prospective study of 124 women carrying their first-borns showed that PPD could be predicted on the basis of factors such as depressed mood and marital stress during pregnancy (Whiffen, 1988). PPD was also related to the mother's perceptions of the infant as temperamentally difficult and as crying excessively (crying often and over prolonged periods). Caring for a difficult, temperamental infant heightens the mother's level of stress and can contribute to feelings of maternal inadequacy, which may, in turn, contribute to depression. Ironically, PPD was more likely among women who were more optimistic about their babies during pregnancy. Perhaps overly rosy expectations lead to depression when the realities of caring for an infant, especially a more difficult infant, contradict these expectations.

Although great expectations about one's baby may sometimes be counterproductive, it may be that general optimism is helpful. In one study, 75 women in the third trimester of pregnancy were tested for signs of optimism

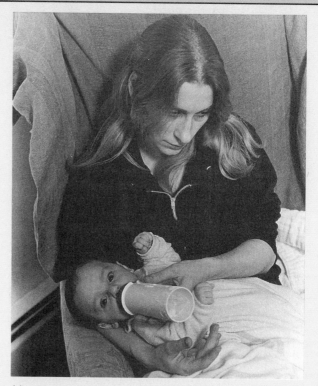

Many new mothers experience transient changes in mood in the weeks following childbirth. However, so-called postpartum depression is characterized by more persistent or severe mood changes. It affects 8 to 15 percent of new mothers and can last a year or more.

and depressive mood (Carver & Gaines, 1987). The depressive mood measure was then readministered three weeks after delivery. PPD was inversely related to optimism; that is, the more positive the mood in late pregnancy, the less depression was encountered following childbirth. It is tempting to suggest that maintaining an optimistic frame of mind during pregnancy may help to ward off PPD, but it is also possible that outside factors account both for the optimism and the superior adjustment postpartum. High self-efficacy expectancies, for example, could generate optimism prior to childbirth and coping behavior afterward.

Another form of postpartum psychiatric disturbance, **postpartum psychosis,** is estimated to occur in perhaps 2 in 1,000 women following childbirth (Harding, 1989). Postpartum psychosis usually involves manic features, which may be accompanied by a break with reality involving auditory hallucinations and delusions (Harding, 1989; Mansnerus, 1988). Past evidence of a psychotic disorder and a family history of psychosis appear to be the best predictors of risk (Mansnerus, 1988). Perhaps as many as 1 in 5 women with a previous psychosis experience a recurrent psychotic episode following childbirth (Mansnerus, 1988).

indifference to most or all activities, and psychomotor retardation. These physical features appear to be less prominent in reactive depressions.

The DSM–III–R labels major depressive episodes that fit the endogenous pattern as the "melancholic type." The melancholic type is also characterized by a history of favorable response to biological treatments such as antidepressant medication or electroconvulsive therapy (ECT) and by an absence of personality disturbance before the onset of the first major depressive episode. The physical features and the response to biological treatments in the melancholic type of major depression support the belief that biological factors are directly involved. However, research evidence does not yet demonstrate that different causal mechanisms account for endogenous and reactive depressions.

DYSTHYMIA

Major depression is usually quite severe and marked by a relatively abrupt change from the preexisting state. There is a milder form of depression that seems to follow a chronic course of development that often begins in childhood or adolescence (Klein et al., 1988). Earlier diagnostic formulations had characterized this type of depression as "neurotic" or as a "depressive neurosis." It was so labeled in an effort to account for several features that are traditionally connected with neurosis, such as early childhood origins and milder levels of severity of the disorder. The DSM–III–R labels this form of depression **dysthymia,** which derives from the Greek roots *dys-*, meaning "bad" or "hard," and *thymos,* meaning "spirit."

Persons with dysthymia do feel "bad-spirited" or "down in the dumps" most of the time, but they are not so severely depressed as those with major depression. To meet the DSM–III–R diagnostic criteria for the disorder, the disturbance of mood must be present during most of the day, on more days than not, for a period of at least two years for adults, or one year or more for children and adolescents. Some cases of dysthymia develop during childhood or adolescence, whereas others develop in adulthood. While major depression tends to occur in discrete or time-limited episodes marked by a dramatic decline in functioning, dysthymia tends to persist more or less continuously in a milder but nagging form for many years. Major depression is also more likely than dysthymia to be associated with suicidal thoughts and loss of appetite (Steer et al., 1987).

In dysthymia, complaints of depression may become such a fixture of people's lives that it seems to be intertwined with their personality structures (Klein et al., 1988). The persistence of these depressive complaints may lead others to perceive dysthymics as excessively whining and complaining (Akiskal, 1983). Although dysthymia is less severe than major depression, the persistent feelings of depressed mood and low self-esteem often affect the person's occupational and social functioning, as we see in the following case:

■ The woman, a 28-year-old junior executive, complained of chronic feelings of depression since the age of 16 or 17. Despite doing well in college, she brooded about how other people were "genuinely intelligent." She felt she could never pursue a man she might be interested in dating because she felt inferior and intimidated. While she had extensive therapy through college and graduate school, she could never recall a time during those years when she did not feel somewhat depressed. She got married shortly after college graduation to the man she was dating at the time, although she didn't think that he was anything "special." She just felt she needed to have a husband for companionship and he was available. But they soon began to quarrel and she's lately begun to feel that marrying him was a mistake. She has had difficulties at work, turning in "slipshod" work and never seeking anything more than what is basically required of her, showing no initiative. While she dreams of acquiring status and money, she doesn't expect that she or her husband will rise in their professions because they lack "connections." Her social life is dominated by her husband's friends and their spouses and she doesn't think that other women would find her interesting or impressive. She lacks interest in life in general and expresses dissatisfaction with all facets of her life—her marriage, her job, her social life.

Adapted from Spitzer et al., 1989, pp. 37–39 ■

Dysthymia may occur concurrently with a major depressive episode (Klein et al., 1988). Clinicians have begun to use the term **double depression** to describe people who have a major depressive episode superimposed upon a more persistent dysthymia (Miller et al., 1986). Major depressive episodes tend to occur more frequently and to be longer in duration among these so-called double depressives than among "pure" major depressives (Miller et al., 1986).

BIPOLAR DISORDER

Most of us, as noted earlier, have our ups and downs, but people with bipolar disorder have severe mood swings from extreme elation and hyperactivity (mania) to major depression. The initial episode is usually manic, although some bipolar disorders begin with a depressive episode. Manic episodes are usually shorter in duration and end more abruptly than do depressive episodes. Some people with bipolar disorder attempt suicide "on the way down" from the manic phase of the disorder.

They relate that they would do almost anything to escape from the depths of depression that they see ahead of them.

According to the DSM–III–R, bipolar disorders are estimated to affect 0.4 to 1.2 percent of the adult population. Unlike major (unipolar) depression, bipolar disorder tends to affect men and women about equally. The essential feature of bipolar disorder is the occurrence of one or more manic episodes, which are usually but not always followed by a major depressive episode. In a small number of cases, episodes of mania may occur without intervening episodes of depression (Goodwin & Jamison, 1987). But such cases are also labeled bipolar since they occur rarely and because it is thought that depression will eventually appear or has been previously overlooked. In a few cases of bipolar disorder, called the mixed type, features of mania and depression may occur together. More frequently, though, elated and depressed mood states alternate with intervening periods of normal mood. Sometimes there are periods of "rapid cycling" in which the individual experiences two or more full cycles of mania and depression within a year without intervening normal periods. Rapid cycling is relatively rare, however.

Manic Episode

Bipolar disorders are recognized by the presence of **manic episodes,** or periods of mania. According to the DSM–III–R, manic episodes typically begin in one's early twenties but may first occur as late as the age of 50 or older. Such episodes typically begin abruptly, gathering force within a matter of days, and they tend to last from a few days to a few months.

The manic person experiences a sudden elevation or expansion of mood and feels unusually cheerful, euphoric, or optimistic. In stark contrast to the depressed state, people in a manic phase have seemingly boundless energy, are likely to be hyperactive, and are extremely sociable, although they tend to become demanding and overbearing toward others. Their friends and loved ones tend to recognize this sudden shift in mood as excessive and unjustified in light of the individual's circumstances. It is one thing to feel elated if one has just won the state lottery. It is quite another to feel euphoric because it happens to be Wednesday.

People in a manic episode tend to be overly excited and may strike others as acting silly, by carrying jokes too far, for example. They tend to show poor judgment and to become argumentative with others, sometimes going as far as destroying property (Depue et al., 1981). Roommates may find them annoying or abrasive and seek to avoid them. People in a manic phase often speak very rapidly (showing **pressured speech**) and

their thinking and speech may jump from topic to topic, displaying **rapid flight of ideas.** Others may find it almost impossible to "get a word in edgewise." People in a manic state may be extremely generous, as in making large contributions to charity or dispensing expensive possessions. They may not be capable of sitting still or of sleeping restfully. They almost always experience a decreased need for sleep and tend to awaken several hours earlier than usual, feeling well rested and full of energy. Manics may sometimes go for days without sleep and yet not feel tired. Although persons in a manic episode may have abundant stores of energy, they seem unable to organize their efforts constructively. Their excesses in mood and self-image typically disrupt their ability to function and maintain normal relationships.

People in a manic episode generally experience an inflated sense of self-esteem, which may range from excessive self-confidence to outright delusions of grandeur. They may feel capable of solving the world's problems or of composing symphonies, despite a lack of special knowledge or talent. Manic persons may spout off about matters on which they know little, such as how to solve world hunger or develop an effective nuclear defense. It soon becomes clear that their thoughts and behavior are disorganized and that they are incapable of completing their projects. They become highly distractible and their attention is easily diverted by such irrelevant stimuli as the sound of a ticking clock or of people talking in the next room. They also tend to take on multiple tasks, biting off much more than they can chew. Manic persons may suddenly quit a regular job in order to enroll in law school during the day, wait tables at night, and organize charity drives on the weekends, while also attempting to write the great American novel in their spare time. Individuals in manic states tend to exercise poor judgment and fail to weigh the consequences of their actions, which tends to get them into trouble as a result of lavish spending, reckless driving, or sexual escapades. In severe cases, manics may experience disorders of thinking similar to those of schizophrenics. They may also experience hallucinations or become grossly delusional, believing, for example, that they have some special relationship to God.

 Some people do ride an emotional roller coaster, swinging from the heights of elation to the depths of depression without external cause. They are said to have bipolar disorder.

The following case provides a firsthand account of what a manic episode feels like. Notice how the early stages of the manic episode are dominated by feelings of euphoria, increased energy, lessened need for sleep, and an inflated sense of self. But as the mania intensifies, the individual may become unable to separate reality from fantasy. Thoughts become chaotic and confused:

■ When I start going into a high, I no longer feel like an ordinary housewife. Instead I feel organized and accomplished and I begin to feel I am my most creative self. I can write poetry easily. I can compose melodies without effort. I can paint. My mind feels facile and absorbs everything. I have countless ideas about improving the conditions of mentally retarded children, of how a hospital for these children should be run, what they should have around them to keep them happy and calm and unafraid. I see myself as being able to accomplish a great deal for the good of people. I have countless ideas about how the environment problem could inspire a crusade for the health and betterment of everyone. I feel able to accomplish a great deal for the good of my family and others. I feel pleasure, a sense of euphoria or elation. I want it to last forever. I don't seem to need much sleep. I've lost weight and feel healthy and I like myself. I've just bought six new dresses, in fact, and they look quite good on me. I feel sexy and men stare at me. Maybe I'll have an affair, or perhaps several. I feel capable of speaking and doing good in politics. I would like to help people with problems similar to mine so they won't feel hopeless.

It's wonderful when you feel like this. . . . The feeling of exhilaration—the high mood—makes me feel light and full of the joy of living. However, when I go beyond this stage, I become manic, and the creativeness becomes so magnified I begin to see things in my mind that aren't real. For instance, one night I created an entire movie, complete with cast, that I still think would be terrific. I saw the people as clearly as if watching them in real life. I also experienced complete terror, as if it were actually happening, when I knew that an assassination scene was about to take place. I cowered under the covers and became a complete shaking wreck. As you know, I went into a manic psychosis at that point. My screams awakened my husband, who tried to reassure me that we were in our bedroom and everything was the same. There was nothing to be afraid of. Nevertheless, I was admitted to the hospital the next day.

From Fieve, 1975, pp. 27–28 ■

CYCLOTHYMIA

Cyclothymia is derived from the Greek *kyklos*, which means "circle," and *thymos*, which, as we have noted, means "spirit." The notion of a circular-moving spirit is an apt description, because this disorder involves a chronic, cyclical pattern of mood disturbance characterized by mild mood swings of at least two year's duration.

Cyclothymia usually begins in late adolescence or early adulthood and usually continues for years. Few, if any, periods of normal mood last for more than a month or two. The periods of elevated or depressed mood are not severe enough to warrant a diagnosis of bipolar disorder, however.

The periods of elevated mood are called **hypomanic episodes,** from the Greek prefix *hypo-*, meaning "under" or "less than." *Hypo*manic episodes are less severe than manic episodes; however, they are more restless and irritable than normal. Hypomanic episodes also occur without the marked difficulties in social or occupational functioning that are typical of full-blown manic episodes. In the hypomanic phase, cyclothymic persons may feel unusually charged with energy and mentally alert. They may be capable of working long hours with little fatigue or need for sleep. But their work projects may be left unfinished when their mood swings in the opposite direction. Then they enter a period of mildly depressed mood, finding it difficult to summon the energy or the interest to persevere. They tend to feel lethargic and depressed, but not to the extent that is typical of a major depressive episode.

Relationships with others may become strained by these shifting moods. Social invitations, eagerly sought during hypomanic periods, may be declined during depressed periods. Phone calls may not be returned as the mood state shifts to depression. Sexual interest waxes and wanes. Social and occupational functioning may be impaired during these depressed phases, but again not to the extent associated with major depressive episodes. Still, the boundaries between bipolar disorder and cyclothymia are not yet clearly established. According to the DSM–III–R, cyclothymia may actually represent a milder form of bipolar disorder. Although cyclothymia is a chronic disorder that can last for a lifetime, it also frequently progresses to bipolar disorder.

The following case presents an example of the mild mood swings that typify cyclothymia:

■ The man, a 29-year-old car salesman, reports that since the age of 14 he has experienced alternating periods of "good times and bad times." During his "bad" periods, which generally last between 4 and 7 days, he sleeps excessively and feels a lack of confidence, energy and motivation, as if he were "just vegetating." Then his moods abruptly shift for a period of three or four days, usually upon awakening in the morning, and he feels aflush with confidence and sharpened mental ability. During these "good periods" he engages in promiscuous sex and uses alcohol, in part to enhance his good feelings and in part to help him sleep at night. The good periods may last upwards of 7–10 days at times, before shifting back into the "bad periods," generally following a hostile or irritable outburst.

Adapted from Spitzer et al., 1989, pp. 96–97 ■

THEORETICAL PERSPECTIVES

Major psychological and biochemical theories of abnormal behavior have focused on the problem of depression. The causes and treatment of bipolar disorders have been largely approached on the basis of the biological perspective.

Psychodynamic Perspectives

Psychodynamic theorists suggest a number of possible explanations for mood disorders, all of which involve inner, frequently unconscious sources. In this section we consider classic psychodynamic theory and then turn to a more recent model that bridges psychodynamic and cognitive perspectives.

■ **Classic Psychodynamic Theory**   The classic psychodynamic theory of depression of Freud (1917) and his followers (for example, Abraham, 1916) holds that depression represents anger directed inward rather than against others. Anger may become directed against the self following the actual or *threatened* loss of supportive others.

Freud believed that **mourning,** or normal bereavement, was a healthful process by which one eventually came to separate from a person who was lost. Pathological mourning, however, did not promote separation and could prompt feelings of lingering depression. Pathological mourning was likely to occur in people who held powerful **ambivalent** feelings—strongly positive (love) and negative (anger, hostility)—toward the person who is lost to them due to death, divorce, or separation, or whose loss is threatened or feared. The depressed person's feelings of anger toward the loved one turn to rage when faced with loss. Even if the person does nothing to harm the other, rage triggers conscious and unconscious imagery of harm, producing guilt. Guilt, in turn, prevents the person from venting anger directly at the lost object.

In an effort to preserve the lost object, the person **introjects,** or brings inward, his or her mental representation of the other person, incorporating the other into the self. Now anger is further turned inward, against the part of the self that represents the inward representation of the lost person, producing self-loathing and associated feelings of depression.

From the psychodynamic viewpoint, bipolar disorder is seen in terms of the shifting dominance of the individual's personality by the ego and superego. In the depressive phase, the superego is dominant, producing exaggerated notions of wrongdoing and flooding the individual with feelings of guilt and worthlessness. After a time, the ego rebounds and asserts supremacy, producing feelings of elation and self-confidence that

According to psychodynamic theorists, one's reactions to loss play an important role in depression.

come to characterize the manic phase. But the excessive display of ego leads eventually to a return of guilt, once again plunging the individual into a state of depression.

More recent psychodynamic models of depression have focused on the effects of loss on the individual's sense of self-worth or self-esteem. According to the self-focusing model, for example, depression may occur when an individual pursues love objects or goals when it would be more adaptive to surrender them (Pyszczynski & Greenberg, 1987). The self-focusing model considers how people allocate their attentional processes after the loss. Thus it can be viewed as a type of psychodynamic-cognitive model. The self-focusing model shares with the traditional psychodynamic model an emphasis on the depressed individual's reaction to loss. But the emphasis in this model is more on how the loss of an important person (or object) or occupational goal can lead to lowered self-worth and self-esteem, rather than on ways in which internal representations of others are incorporated within the individual's self-identity and become the objects of self-loathing.

The self-focusing model explains depression in terms of people's response to stressful life events. When depression-prone people experience stressors such as major losses or disappointments, like the termination of an intimate relationship or failure to attain an occupational goal, they undergo a period of intense self-examination or self-focus in which they try to reconcile the discrepancy between what they have and what they want. They become overly self-absorbed following failure because of inability to surrender hope of regaining the lost object or goal. Fruitless focus on restoring the lost object or goal gives rise to self-blame, diminishing their self-images and depressing their moods. Present disappointments may rekindle self-criticism for previous disappointments, such as failed relationships, which compounds negative feelings and further diminishes self-esteem. They become so trapped in negative self-focusing that they may be unable to integrate success experiences to redefine their self-concepts, and they tend to focus attention away from themselves following success experiences. They attribute negative events to personal shortcomings, but they explain away positive events as "good fortune." They come to expect the worst in relationships, an expectation that may become a self-fulfilling prophecy.

Consider a person who must cope with the termination of a failed romantic relationship. It may be clear to all concerned that the relationship is beyond hope of revival. The self-focusing model proposes, however, that the depression-prone individual persists in focusing his or her attention on ways of restoring the relationship, rather than recognizing the futility of the effort and getting on with life. Moreover, the self-focusing model proposes that the lost partner provided emotional support that helped the depression-prone individual maintain feelings of self-esteem. Following the loss, the depression-prone individual feels stripped of all hope and optimism since all hope and optimism had been placed in the other person, the lost object. The loss of feelings of self-esteem and security, not the loss of the relationship per se, precipitates the depression in such people. Or if depression-prone individuals peg their self-worth on attaining a specific occupational goal, such as achieving success in a new business, they would be at increased risk of depression by virtue of their negative self-focusing style following their failure to achieve their goal. Only by surrendering the object or lost goal and fostering alternate sources of identity and self-worth can the cycle be broken.

■ **Research Evidence** Psychodynamic theorists have focused on the importance of loss in explaining depression. Research does show that the losses of significant others (through death or divorce, for example) are often associated with the onset of depression (Paykel, 1982), but such losses may also lead to other psychological disorders. There is a lack of research evidence to support another component of Freud's theory—that repressed anger toward the departed loved one is turned inward in depression. More recent psychodynamic formulations, such as the self-focusing model, also focus on the importance of loss in depression but shift the emphasis from unresolved anger toward the departed object toward the role that the lost object had played in helping the person maintain a sense of self-esteem. Modern psychodynamic approaches favor greater emphasis on the development of the self, but there is insufficient data to evaluate fully the validity of such approaches.

Some early research on the self-focusing model is supportive, however. This research has shown that depressed people engage in higher levels of self-focusing than do normal people following failures, and engage in relatively lower levels of self-focusing following successes (Pyszczynski & Greenberg, 1985, 1986).

Humanistic-Existential Perspective

In the humanistic-existential perspective, depressed people find the world drab and meaningless because they are unable to infuse their existence with meaning by living according to their values and exercising choices that lead to self-fulfillment. Human beings' search for meaning gives color and substance to their lives. Guilt may arise in the recognition that one has failed to live up to his or her potential and make meaningful choices. Humanistic psychologists challenge us to take a long, hard look at our lives. Are our lives meaningful and enriching? Or are they drab and routine? If the latter, it may be that we have frustrated our needs for self-actualization. We may be settling, coasting through life, but feeling an inner sense of dreariness that becomes expressed in depressive behavior—lethargy, sullen mood, and withdrawal.

Like the psychodynamic theorists, humanistic theorists also focus on the loss of self-esteem that can arise when people lose friends or family members, or suffer occupational setbacks or losses. We tend to connect our personal identity and sense of self-worth with the roles we play in life, as parent, spouse, student,

According to the humanistic-existential perspective, depression may result from inability to find meaning and purpose in life.

or worker. But when these role identities are lost, through the death of a spouse, the departure of children to college, or loss of a job, our sense of our purpose in life and self-worth can be shattered. We can be left feeling empty, purposeless, worthless. Depression is a frequent consequence of such losses. This is especially true when we base our self-esteem on our occupational role or success. The loss of a job, a demotion, or even a failure to achieve a desired promotion are frequent precipitants of depression, especially when we are raised to value ourselves on the basis of our work and the success that we achieve.

Learning Perspectives

Whereas psychodynamic perspectives focus on inner, often unconscious, determinants of mood disorders, learning perspectives dwell more on situational contributors, such as the loss of positive reinforcement. When levels of reinforcement are satisfactory, people experience a balance between effort and reward. But changes in either the frequency or effectiveness of reinforcement can shift the balance so that life begins to feel unrewarding, which can sap motivation and induce feelings of depression.

■ Level of Positive Reinforcement and Depression

According to University of Oregon psychologist Peter Lewinsohn (1974), depression may result when a person's behavior receives too little reinforcement from the environment. With too little reinforcement, the individual may become unmotivated to strive to obtain positive reinforcements, leading to inactivity and feelings of depression. A vicious circle may ensue in which inactivity and social withdrawal lead to fewer opportunities for reinforcement; lessened opportunity engenders more withdrawal and less reinforcement, and so on. The low rate of activity that is typical of depression may also be a source of secondary gain or secondary reinforcement. That is, depression can lead to sympathy from family members or release from ordinary responsibilities. Rather than helping the depressed individual regain a normal level of instrumental behavior, sympathy may backfire by serving to maintain depressed behavior.

A reduction in the level of reinforcement can occur for several reasons. A person who is recuperating from a long illness may find little to do at home that is reinforcing. Loss of rewards can also result from the death or departure of people who had provided social reinforcement. The person who suffers a social loss may lack the social skills necessary to form new reinforcing relationships. First-year college students sometimes find that they lack the skills necessary to form rewarding friendships and relationships away from home. Widows

and widowers who were able to maintain a marriage may be at a loss in asking someone for a date or starting a new relationship. Consequently, they may become socially withdrawn and depressed.

Changes in life circumstances may also alter the balance of effort and reinforcement. A prolonged layoff can reduce financial reinforcements, which may in turn force painful cutbacks in lifestyle. A disability or an extended illness can also impair ability to ensure a steady flow of reinforcements.

■ Interactional Theory

The interactions between depressed persons and important others may help to explain the shortfall in positive reinforcement that contributes to depression (Coyne, 1976). The interactional theory, developed by University of Michigan psychologist James Coyne, proposes that the adjustment to living with a depressed person can become so stressful that the partner or family member becomes progressively less reinforcing toward the depressed person.

Interactional theory is based on the concept of reciprocal interaction—that people's behavior influences and is influenced by the behavior of others. The theory holds that depression-prone people react to stressful events by demanding greater support and reassurance from others. At first the depressed person may succeed in garnering support. Over time, however, the depressed person's demands and depressed behavior begin to elicit more aversive reactions and feelings of anger or annoyance. Loved ones may keep negative feelings to themselves, so as not to upset the depressed person further. But negative feelings may surface in subtle ways that amount to rejection of the depressed person and withdrawal of social reinforcement. The depressed person may then react to rejection by becoming even more depressed and demanding, which causes further rejection and withdrawal of reinforcement in a vicious circle.

Family members apparently find living with a depressed person stressful and distressing. They may find it especially stressful to adjust to a depressed person's troubling behavior patterns, in particular the person's withdrawal, lack of energy, interminable worrying, and expressions of hopelessness. In one study, 40 percent of family members of currently depressed people showed signs of emotional distress that seemed significant enough to warrant psychological intervention, a significantly higher number than among family members of formerly depressed people (Coyne et al., 1987). In another study, spouses whose partners were formerly depressed were often as distressed as spouses whose partners remained depressed, suggesting that some distress lingers even as the partner's depression lifts (Krantz & Moos, 1987). Depressed people may react to signs of distress in their family members by feeling even worse about themselves. So people who are depressed may affect and be affected by their interactions with their loved ones.

■ **Research Evidence** Lewinsohn's model, which has received the most research attention among the behavioral theories, is supported by findings that associate depression with a low level of positive reinforcement. For example, Lewinsohn and Libet (1972) noted a correspondence between depressed moods and lower rates of participation in potentially reinforcing activities. People with depressive disorders were found to report fewer pleasant activities than did nondepressed people (Mac-Phillamy & Lewinsohn, 1974). It remains unclear, however, whether depression antecedes or follows a decline in the level of reinforcement (Williams, 1984). Depressed people may lose interest in pleasant activities or withdraw from potentially reinforcing social interactions, rather than lack of activity causing the depression. Nor has it been determined that there are specific patterns of social skills deficits that predispose people to depression by making it more difficult for them to secure reinforcers from others, as might be expected from Lewinsohn's theory (Williams, 1984).

Interactional theory is supported by some evidence of increased marital strain among couples in which one of the partners is depressed (Haas et al., 1985). But the research evidence is less clear in determining whether or not interacting with a depressed person leads one to become depressed or more rejecting toward the depressed person (King & Heller, 1984; Boswell & Murray, 1981). One study (McNiel et al., 1987) failed to find evidence that an initial face-to-face contact with a depressed person, involving a 15-minute "getting-to-know-you" conversation, led to feelings of negative mood and rejection of the depressed person. But Coyne's interactional model may have greater relevance for sustained, intimate relationships.

In sum, reinforcement patterns appear to be linked to depression. It is unclear, however, whether changes in reinforcement patterns precede or follow depression, or if there is a causal connection between the two. But treatment approaches formulated on the basis of learning principles may help depressed people overcome depression, as we shall see, by assisting them in increasing their level of pleasant activity and by training them in social skills that they can use to better obtain reinforcements from others.

Cognitive Perspectives

Cognitive theorists relate the origin and maintenance of depression to ways in which people perceive themselves and the world. In the cognitive view, our moods mirror the way we see ourselves and the things that happen to us.

■ **Aaron Beck's Cognitive Theory** One of the most influential cognitive theorists, psychiatrist Aaron Beck (Beck, 1976; Beck et al., 1979; Beck & Young, 1986) describes depression in terms of the adoption of an habitual style of negative thinking, called the **cognitive triad of depression** (see Table 8.4). This triad involves the adoption of negative beliefs about oneself (for example, "I'm no good"), the environment or the world at large ("This school is awful"), and the future ("Nothing will ever turn out right for me"). Such negative concepts or *schemas* are believed to be largely acquired in childhood and are later activated by negative events such as losing a job or getting a poor grade. The child's early learning experiences are believed to play a major role in shaping these negative attitudes. For example, negative attitudes may be learned when children find that nothing they do is ever good enough to please their parents or teachers. As a result, they may come to think of themselves as basically incompetent and perceive their future prospects as dim. These concepts may sensitize them in later life to interpret any failure or disappointment as a crushing blow or a total defeat, which then leads to depression. So minor disappointments or personal flaws become magnified in importance or blown out of proportion—specific errors in thinking that are labeled cognitive distortions.

These cognitive distortions were summarized by psychiatrist David Burns (1979):

1. *All or Nothing Thinking.* The tendency to see events only in black or white terms, as either all good or all bad. For example, one may perceive a relationship that ended in disappointment as a totally negative experi-

TABLE 8.4 The Cognitive Triad of Depression

Negative view of oneself	Perceiving oneself as worthless, deficient, inadequate, unlovable, and as lacking the skills necessary to achieve happiness.
Negative view of the environment	Perceiving the environment as imposing excessive demands and/or presenting obstacles that are impossible to overcome, leading continually to failure and loss.
Negative view of the future	Perceiving the future as hopeless and believing that one is powerless to change things for the better. All that one expects of the future is continuing failure and unrelenting misery and hardship.

According to Aaron Beck, depression involves the adoption of an habitual style of negative thinking—the so-called cognitive triad of depression.
Source: *Adapted from Beck & Young, 1986; and Beck et al., 1979.*

QUESTIONNAIRE
The Pleasant Events Schedule

Peter Lewinsohn has suggested that depression results from a low rate of positively reinforced behavior. To keep our moods on an even keel, we need feedback from our environment that our efforts are reinforced. We need to engage in reward-producing activities, or—as Lewinsohn labels them—pleasant events that grant opportunities for our efforts to be rewarded.

Lewinsohn and his colleagues have developed a number of Pleasant Events Schedules that list various pleasurable activities, from observing a sports event to taking a long, hot bath. Which of the activities listed in the questionnaire below do you find enjoyable?

You can run a personal "experiment" in the relationship between your moods and your activities. Track your daily moods by use of a scale from 1 to 10 (1 = "severely depressed . . . down in the dumps"; 10 = best possible mood . . . feel wonderful"). Rate your mood at the same time each day (before going to bed, for example). Each week select and engage in several events you find pleasurable. Average your daily mood ratings for each week and see whether or not your average daily mood is related to the number or kinds of pleasant activities you engaged in that week.

1. Being in the country
2. Wearing expensive or formal clothes
3. Making contributions to religious, charitable, or political groups
4. Talking about sports
5. Meeting someone new
6. Going to a rock concert
7. Playing baseball, softball, football, or basketball
8. Planning trips or vacations
9. Buying things for yourself
10. Being at the beach
11. Doing art work (painting, sculpture, drawing, moviemaking, etc.)
12. Rock climbing or mountaineering
13. Reading the Scriptures
14. Playing golf
15. Rearranging or redecorating your room or house
16. Going naked
17. Going to a sports event
18. Going to the races
19. Reading stories, novels, poems, plays, magazines, newspapers
20. Going to a bar, tavern, club
21. Going to lectures or talks
22. Creating or arranging songs or music
23. Boating
24. Restoring antiques, refinishing furniture
25. Watching television or listening to the radio
26. Camping
27. Working in politics
28. Working on machines (cars, bikes, radios, TV sets)
29. Playing cards or board games
30. Doing puzzles or math games
31. Having lunch with friends or associates
32. Playing tennis
33. Driving long distances
34. Woodworking, carpentry
35. Writing stories, novels, poems, plays, articles
36. Being with animals
37. Riding in an airplane
38. Exploring (hiking away from known routes, spelunking, etc.)
39. Singing
40. Going to a party
41. Going to church functions
42. Playing a musical instrument
43. Snow skiing, ice skating
44. Wearing informal clothes, "dressing down"
45. Acting
46. Being in the city, downtown
47. Taking a long, hot bath
48. Playing pool or billiards
49. Bowling
50. Watching wild animals
51. Gardening, landscaping
52. Wearing new clothes
53. Dancing
54. Sitting or lying in the sun
55. Riding a motorcycle
56. Just sitting and thinking
57. Going to a fair, carnival, circus, zoo, amusement park
58. Talking about philosophy or religion
59. Gambling
60. Listening to sounds of nature
61. Dating, courting
62. Having friends come to visit
63. Going out to visit friends
64. Giving gifts
65. Getting massages or back rubs
66. Photography
67. Collecting stamps, coins, rocks, etc.
68. Seeing beautiful scenery
69. Eating good meals
70. Improving your health (having teeth fixed, changing diet, having a checkup, etc.)
71. Wrestling or boxing
72. Fishing
73. Going to a health club, sauna
74. Horseback riding
75. Protesting social, political, or environmental conditions
76. Going to the movies
77. Cooking meals
78. Washing your hair
79. Going to a restaurant
80. Using cologne, perfume
81. Getting up early in the morning

According to psychologist Peter Lewinsohn, reinforcing activities, such as pleasant events, help keep our moods on an even keel.

_____ 82. Writing a diary
_____ 83. Giving massages or back rubs
_____ 84. Meditating or doing yoga
_____ 85. Doing heavy outdoor work
_____ 86. Snowmobiling, dune buggying
_____ 87. Being in a body-awareness, encounter, or "rap" group
_____ 88. Swimming
_____ 89. Running, jogging
_____ 90. Walking barefoot
_____ 91. Playing Frisbee or catch
_____ 92. Doing housework or laundry, cleaning things
_____ 93. Listening to music
_____ 94. Knitting, crocheting
_____ 95. Making love
_____ 96. Petting, necking
_____ 97. Going to a barber or beautician

_____ 98. Being with someone you love
_____ 99. Going to the library
_____ 100. Shopping
_____ 101. Preparing a new or special dish
_____ 102. Watching people
_____ 103. Bicycling
_____ 104. Writing letters, cards, or notes
_____ 105. Talking about politics or public affairs
_____ 106. Watching attractive women or men
_____ 107. Caring for houseplants
_____ 108. Having coffee, tea, or Coke, etc., with friends
_____ 109. Beachcombing
_____ 110. Going to auctions, garage sales, etc.
_____ 111. Water skiing, surfing, diving
_____ 112. Traveling
_____ 113. Attending the opera, ballet, or a play
_____ 114. Looking at the stars or the moon

Source: _Adapted from MacPhillamy & Lewinsohn, 1982._

ence, despite any positive feelings or experiences that may have occurred. Perfectionism is a type of all or nothing thinking in which one judges any outcome that is less than a total success to be a total failure. Thinking this way, any grade lower than a perfect A may be taken as a mark of failure, even an A−. Even an A may seem like a failure if it is not the highest A. Or, one may come to feel like an abject failure when one falls but a few dollars short of the sales quota or when one receives a positive but not overly glowing job performance evaluation.

2. *Overgeneralization.* The tendency to believe that if one negative event occurred in a particular situation, it is likely to recur in other situations that are even slightly similar. Thinking this way, one tends to see a single negative event as if it foreshadowed a seemingly never-ending series of negative events in the future. For example, one receives a letter of rejection from a potential employer and automatically expects that every other job application will be rejected.

3. *Mental Filter.* The tendency to focus one's attention only on negative details of events, thereby excluding from awareness any positive features of one's experiences. Like a droplet of ink that spreads to discolor an entire beaker of water, focusing only on a single negative detail can darken one's entire vision of reality. Beck called this cognitive distortion **selective abstraction,** meaning that the individual tends to selectively abstract only the negative details from events and ignore any positive features. Thinking this way, one measures one's self-esteem only on the basis of perceived weaknesses and failures, blotting out awareness of positive features or accomplishments. For example, one receives a job evaluation that contains positive and negative comments but focuses only on the negative.

4. *Disqualifying the Positive.* The tendency to convert neutral or positive events into negative events. An example is to dismiss the congratulations of others for a job well done by saying, "Oh, it's no big deal. Anyone could have done it." By disqualifying the positives, one manages to snatch defeat from the jaws of victory.

5. *Jumping to Conclusions.* The tendency to form a negative interpretation of events, despite a lack of evidence to support one's conclusion. Two examples of this style of thinking are "Mind Reading" and "The Fortune Teller Error." In Mind Reading, one arbitrarily jumps to the conclusion that others don't like or respect one, as in interpreting a friend's not calling for a while as a rejection. The Fortune Teller Error is the prediction that something bad is always about to happen, which one takes as factual in the absence of evidence. For example, one concludes that pain in the chest can only mean an impending heart attack—despite evidence that might lead to other conclusions.

6. *Magnification and Minimization.* Magnification, or

catastrophizing, refers to the tendency to make mountains out of molehills, or exaggerate the importance of negative events and of personal flaws, fears, or mistakes. Minimization involves the opposite type of cognitive distortion—minimizing or underestimating one's good points.

7. *Emotional Reasoning.* This error of thinking involves basing reasoning on emotions—thinking, for example, "If I feel guilty, it must be because I've done something really wrong." Thinking this way, one judges reality on the basis of emotions rather than evaluating situations realistically.

8. *Should Statements.* The tendency to think in terms of personal imperatives or self-commandments, in the form of "shoulds" or "musts," such as, "I *should* be a better student!". . or, "I *must* do better in this course!" **Musterbation**—the label given this form of thinking by psychologist Albert Ellis—leads one to feel depressed when one falls short of these highly unrealistic expectations.

9. *Labeling and Mislabeling.* The tendency to explain behavior by attaching negative labels to oneself and others. Thinking this way, one is likely to explain a poor grade on a test by thinking that one is "lazy" or "stupid," not simply unprepared or, perhaps, ill. Labeling other people can engender hostility when one criticizes their behavior as a sign of their "stupidity" or "insensitivity." Mislabeling involves applying labels that are highly emotionally laden and inaccurate, such as calling oneself a "pig" because one ate a forbidden food while dieting.

10. *Personalization.* The tendency to believe one is responsible for other people's problems and behavior, or that others' feelings somewhat relate to oneself, while others' feelings and problems actually have little or nothing to do with oneself. For example, one may see one's spouse crying and assume that he or she is crying because of something one has done.

Consider the errors in thinking illustrated by the following case example:

■ Christie was a 33-year-old real estate sales agent who suffered from frequent episodes of depression. Whenever a deal fell through, she would blame herself, "If only I had worked harder . . . negotiated better . . . talked more persuasively . . . the deal would have been set." After several successive disappointments, each one followed by self-recriminations, she felt like quitting altogether. Her thinking became increasingly dominated by negative thoughts, which further depressed her mood and lowered her self-esteem: "I'm a loser. . . . I'll never succeed. . . . It's all my fault. . . . I'm no good and I'm never going to succeed at anything."

Christie's thinking included cognitive errors such as the following: (1) *personalization* (believing herself to be the sole cause of negative events), (2) *labeling and mislabeling* (thinking of herself as a "nothing"); (3) *overgeneralization* (predicting a dismal future on the basis of a present disappointment); and (4) *mental filter* (judging her entire personality on the basis of her disappointments). In therapy, Christie was helped to think more realistically about events and not to jump to conclusions that she was automatically at fault whenever a deal fell through, or to judge her whole personality on the basis of disappointments or perceived flaws within herself. In place of this self-defeating style of thinking, she began to think more realistically when disappointments occurred, as in telling herself, "Okay, I'm disappointed. I'm frustrated. I feel lousy. So what? It doesn't mean I'll never succeed. Let me discover what went wrong and try to correct it the next time. I have to look ahead, not dwell on disappointments in the past."

The Authors' Files ■

This football player missed a crucial tackle and is rehashing it. He is putting himself down and telling himself that he can do nothing to improve his performance. Cognitive theorists believe that distorted interpretations of negative events can set the stage for depression.

Distorted thinking tends to be experienced as occurring automatically, as if the thoughts had popped into one's head from "out of the blue." So-called **automatic thoughts** are likely to be accepted at face value, as if they were statements of fact and not as either habitual ways of interpreting events or as expressions of opinion. The nearby Inventory of Negative Thoughts may help alert you to cognitive distortions and negative automatic thoughts that "pop" into your mind.

Beck (1976) formulated a **cognitive-specificity hypothesis** that proposes that different types of disorders, anxiety disorders and depressive disorders in particular, are characterized by different types of automatic thoughts—thoughts that seem to "pop into the person's

QUESTIONNAIRE

Inventory of Negative Thoughts Cognitive theorists believe that people can make themselves depressed by thinking negative thoughts. The following inventory includes many negative thoughts that are commonly linked to depression. How many of them have you experienced in recent months? Do they strike you as accurate and appropriate to your situation? Or are you giving in to cognitive distortions that can lead to feelings of depression?

Directions: Using the code below, write in a number from 1 to 4 to indicate how frequently you have the thoughts contained in the list that follows. Pay particular attention to the content of the thought rather than the specific wording.

1. Never
2. Seldom
3. Often
4. Very often

____ 1. It seems such an effort to do anything.
____ 2. I feel pessimistic about the future.
____ 3. I have too many bad things in my life.
____ 4. I have very little to look forward to.
____ 5. I'm drained of energy, worn out.
____ 6. I'm not as successful as other people.
____ 7. Everything seems futile and pointless.
____ 8. I just want to curl up and go to sleep.
____ 9. There are things about me that I don't like.
____ 10. It's too much effort even to move.

____ 11. I'm absolutely exhausted.
____ 12. The future seems just one string of problems.
____ 13. My thoughts keep drifting away.
____ 14. I get no satisfaction from the things I do.
____ 15. I've made so many mistakes in the past.
____ 16. I've got to really concentrate just to keep my eyes open.
____ 17. Everything I do turns out badly.
____ 18. My whole body has slowed down.
____ 19. I regret some of the things I've done.
____ 20. I can't make the effort to liven up myself.
____ 21. I feel depressed with the way things are going.
____ 22. I haven't any real friends anymore.
____ 23. I do have a number of problems.
____ 24. There's no one I can feel really close to.
____ 25. I wish I were someone else.
____ 26. I'm annoyed at myself for being bad at making decisions.
____ 27. I don't make a good impression on other people.
____ 28. The future looks hopeless.
____ 29. I don't get the same satisfaction out of things these days.
____ 30. I wish something would happen to make me feel better.

Source: *Reprinted with permission of The Free Press, a Division of Macmillan, Inc. from* The Psychological Treatment of Depression: A Guide to the Theory and Practice of Cognitive-Behavior Therapy *by J. Mark G. Williams. Copyright © 1984 by J. Mark G. Williams.*

TABLE 8.5 Automatic Thoughts Associated with Depression and Anxiety

Some Common Automatic Thoughts Associated with Depression:

1. I'm worthless.
2. I'm not worthy of other people's attention or affection.
3. I'll never be as good as other people are.
4. I'm a social failure.
5. I don't deserve to be loved.
6. People don't respect me anymore.
7. I will never overcome my problems.
8. I've lost the only friends I've had.
9. Life isn't worth living.
10. I'm worse off than they are.
11. There's no one left to help me.
12. No one cares whether I live or die.
13. Nothing ever works out for me anymore.
14. I have become physically unattractive.

Some Common Automatic Thoughts Associated with Anxiety:

1. What if I get sick and become an invalid?
2. I am going to be injured.
3. What if no one reaches me in time to help?
4. I might be trapped.
5. I am not a healthy person.
6. I'm going to have an accident.
7. Something will happen that will ruin my appearance.
8. I am going to have a heart attack.
9. Something awful is going to happen.
10. Something will happen to someone I care about.
11. I'm losing my mind.

Source: *Adapted from Beck et al., 1987.*

head'' without any effort to summon them up. The results of a recent study (Beck et al., 1987) showed some interesting differences in types of automatic thoughts that people with depressive and anxiety disorders reported (see Table 8.5). Depressed people more often reported automatic thoughts that were focused on themes of loss, self-deprecation, and negative attitudes about the future and the past. Typical depressive thoughts included "I'm worthless" and "I don't deserve to be loved." Anxious people more often reported cognitions concerning danger and overestimating the potential for harm. People with anxiety disorders were more likely to report thoughts such as, "What if I get sick and become an invalid?", or "What if no one reaches me in time to help?"

Differences in the content of automatic thoughts between anxious and depressed people support the content-specificity hypothesis. They are also consistent with the belief of cognitive therapists that the cognitions of people with anxiety disorders are generally characterized by perceptions of vulnerability to harm, whereas the thought patterns of depressed people tend to focus on negative attitudes toward themselves and the future.

■ **Research Evidence** Evidence has accumulated that depressed people tend to think more negatively than do other people. For example, groups of depressed college students (Michael & Funabiki, 1985; Dobson & Breiter, 1983; Gotlib, 1984) and depressed clients at clinics (Eaves & Rush, 1984) show greater incidence of distorted, negative cognitions than do nondepressed reference groups. Students with more distorted thoughts tend to be more depressed and also to perceive greater amounts of stress in their lives (Olinger, et al., 1987). They also become more depressed in response to negative life events such as illness, relocation, or death of loved ones than other students with more productive outlooks (Wise & Barnes, 1986). Distorted, negative thinking also appears to make it more difficult to overcome a depressive episode (Dent & Teasdale, 1988; Kovacs & Beck, 1978).

Is the presence of any negative thinking destructive? Not necessarily. Research using a thought-counting method has found that psychologically functional people produce approximately 1.7 positive thoughts for each negative thought (Schwartz, 1986). Mildly dysfunctional people, by contrast, produce positive and negative thoughts in about equal numbers. Some negative thoughts may not be harmful, as long as they are balanced or "outweighed" by positive thoughts.

Depressed people accentuate the negative. They seem to act like their own worst enemies by minimizing their accomplishments and by exaggerating the importance of even minor failures. In one study, depressed college students exaggerated the importance of a personality trait when informed that they had done poorly on a test purported to measure the trait in question (see Figure 8.1). Nondepressed students, by contrast, tended to inflate the importance of a trait only when they received feedback that they had high levels of the trait (Wenzlaff & Grozier, 1988). This finding is consistent with Beck's view that depressed people magnify failures and view the traits on which they judge themselves to be lacking as more important. In contrast, people who are not depressed tend to be more self-enhancing; they emphasize the importance of qualities they are judged to possess.

Beck's cognitive model proposes that people whose cognitions are distorted negatively are more vulnerable to depression in the face of stressful life events. Although negative thinking is more common among depressed people, it is not yet clear whether distorted thinking leads to depression or whether depression leads to cognitive distortions. Some research suggests that distorted cognitions accompany rather than precede the onset of depression, in which case cognitive distortions would be a consequence rather than a cause of depression (Lewinsohn et al., 1981). More research is needed to tease out the intricacies of possible cause–effect relationships.

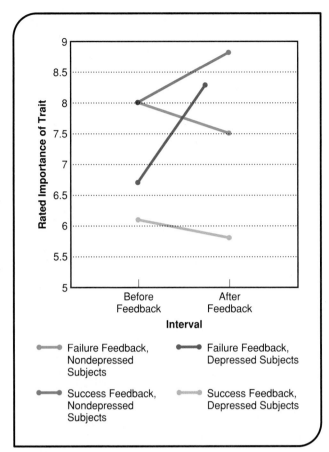

FIGURE 8.1 Ratings of importance of a trait following success and failure feedback.

Depressed students rated the importance of a personality trait (social perceptiveness) higher after receiving feedback that they had done poorly on a test measuring the trait (failure feedback). In contrast, nondepressed students rated the trait higher in importance after learning that they had succeeded on the test (success feedback).

Source: Adapted from Wenzlaff & Grozier (1988)

Even if distorted cognitions do not directly cause depression, they may play important roles in maintaining a depressed state or in increasing vulnerability to recurrence. The presence of negative cognitive distortions following improvement from a depressive episode does seem to predict recurrence of depressive complaints (Rush et al., 1986). If this is so, formerly depressed people would be well-advised to explore the accuracy of their attitudes toward themselves and the future.

Some critics have contended that research has not supported the crucial hypothesis that depressed people think more negatively because their thinking is unrealistic or distorted (Beidel & Turner, 1986). Instead, depressed people may be more pessimistic and less hopeful about the future because they have faced more distressing life circumstances. A review of research on the relationship between stress and depression con-

cluded that depressed people experience a greater number of stressful life events, have fewer intimate relationships, and have more troubled relationships than do nondepressed people (Krantz, 1985). Depressed people also tend to have poorer social skills, which makes it more difficult for them to establish and maintain relationships. The stress of coping with depressed behavior itself—such as tendencies toward staying in bed and crying—represents an additional burden that can weaken positive beliefs and strengthen negative ones. Thus, some depressed people with negative attitudes may be accurately sizing up their frustrations and their possibilities and not distorting events in a negative direction (Hammen, 1978). Perhaps there are subgroups of depressed people: those who experience a relatively low number of negative life events but respond to stress with negative, distorted thinking, and those who think clearly but experience a greater number of stressful life events (Hammen, 1978).

This line of research suggests that cognitively oriented therapists should work not only to change disordered thinking but also to help clients develop skills to help them achieve more meaningful sources of reinforcement (Krantz, 1985). Unless the disappointing life circumstances that many depressed people face are changed, improvements brought about by cognitive approaches to therapy may not be lasting (Michael & Funabiki, 1985). Although depressives may fail to see that every "cloud has a silver lining," it may also be true that depressives "have more clouds in their horizons than do nondepressives" (Krantz, 1985, pp. 607–608).

■ **Learned Helplessness (Attributional) Theory**   The **learned helplessness** model teaches that people may become depressed when they learn to view themselves as helpless to control the reinforcements in their environment or to change their lives for the better. The originator of the learned helplessness concept, University of Pennsylvania psychologist Martin Seligman (1974, 1975), believes that people learn to perceive themselves as helpless because of their experiences. Thus the learned helplessness model straddles the behavioral and the cognitive: Situational factors prompt the development of attitudes that tend to foster feelings of depression.

The learned helplessness model was originally based on laboratory studies of animals by Seligman and his colleagues. In an early study, Overmier and Seligman (1967) discovered that dogs exposed to an inescapable electric shock later failed to learn avoidance or escape responses when the shock was made escapable. Helplessness could apparently be learned by exposure to uncontrollable shock. Another experiment showed that it was not the exposure to the shock itself, but rather its uncontrollability, that produced the learned helplessness effect (Seligman & Maier, 1967). Animals who developed the helplessness effect through exposure to uncontrollable shock showed a wide range of deficits, including lethargy, lack of motivation, and difficulties in learning new behaviors (Maier & Seligman, 1976). In many ways, they appeared to resemble depressed people.

Seligman (1975) proposed that some forms of depression in humans could be explained in terms of learned helplessness. Depression, like learned helplessness, might result from exposure to apparently uncontrollable situations. The issue was whether or not the experiences instilled the expectation that future reinforcements were beyond the individual's control. Seligman's work suggests that a particularly cruel vicious circle may operate with many depressed people. Exposure to a few unavoidable failures may produce feelings of helplessness and expectations of further failure. Perhaps you know of people who have failed certain subjects, such as mathematics. They may come to believe themselves incapable of succeeding in math. As a consequence, they may decide that studying for the quantitative section of the Graduate Record Exam is a waste of time. Then they do poorly, completing the self-fulfilling prophecy by confirming their expectations.

Although it stimulated much interest, Seligman's model failed to account for the low self-esteem that is typical of depressed people. Nor did it explain variations in the persistence of depression. Seligman and his colleagues (Abramson et al., 1978) offered a reformulation of the theory to meet such shortcomings. The revised theory held that perception of a lack of control over reinforcement alone did not explain the persistence and severity of depression. It was also necessary to consider cognitive factors—particularly the ways in which people explain the origins of events, especially failures and disappointments.

Seligman and his colleagues borrowed the concept of **attributional style** from social psychology in recasting helplessness theory. An attributional style is a personal style of explanation. Seligman and his colleagues believe that when disappointments or failures occur, we may explain them in various characteristic ways. We may blame ourselves or circumstances, we may see bad experiences as typical or as isolated events, and we may see them as evidence for broader problems or simply as evidence of specific shortcomings. In terms of the revised helplessness theory, our attributions may be *internal* or *external, stable* or *unstable,* and *global* or *specific.* The revised theory, called the reformulated helplessness theory, held that people who explain the causes of negative events (like failure in work, school, or romantic relationships) in terms of three types of attributions are most vulnerable to depression:

1. **Internal factors** (beliefs that helplessness is due

to their own personal inadequacies) rather than **external factors** (beliefs that helplessness is due to environmental factors);

2. **Global factors** (beliefs that helplessness reflects sweeping deficiencies in their personality) rather than **specific factors** (beliefs that helplessness is limited to specific areas of functioning); and

3. **Stable factors** (beliefs that helplessness is based on fixed personality factors) rather than **unstable factors** (beliefs that helplessness is changeable).

Let us illustrate these attributional styles with the example of a first-year student who goes on a disastrous date. Afterward he shakes his head in wonder and tries to make sense of his experience. An internal attribution for the calamity would involve self-blame, as in "I really messed it up." An external attribution, by contrast, would place the blame elsewhere, as in "Some couples just don't hit it off," or, "She must have been in a bad mood." A stable attribution would suggest a problem that cannot be eliminated, as in "It's my personality." An unstable attribution, on the other hand, would suggest a transient condition, as in "It was probably the head cold." A global attribution for failure magnifies the extent of the problem, as in "I really have no idea what I'm doing when I'm with people." A specific attribution, in contrast, chops the problem down to more manageable size, as in "My problem is how to make small talk to get a relationship going."

The revised theory held that each attributional dimension plays a specific role in determining variations in helplessness effects. Internal attributions are linked to diminished self-esteem. Stable attributions help explain the persistence—or, in medical terms, the chronicity—of signs of depression. Global attributions are associated with the generality or pervasiveness of feelings of helplessness following negative events.

Research is generally but not completely supportive of the reformulated helplessness (attributional) model. It has been shown, for example, that many depressed people overgeneralize the importance of a single failure (Carver & Ganellen, 1983; Carver et al., 1985), thereby increasing its apparent relationship to internal, stable, and global factors. Depressed people have been shown in some research to be more likely than nondepressed people to attribute the causes of failures to internal, stable, and global factors (Blumberg & Izard, 1985; Heimberg et al., 1987; Miller et al., 1982; Peterson et al., 1981; Pyszczynski & Greenberg, 1985; Raps et al., 1982; Rizley, 1978; Seligman et al., 1979, 1984). Moreover, people who view themselves as better able to control events (as less helpless) react more adaptively in stressful social situations (Sacks & Bugental, 1987): They speak more often; they are more affable and less contentious toward unresponsive conversants. For these reasons, they are less likely to flounder in their social interactions and less likely to become depressed by them. Depressed people appear to exaggerate the blame due them and to see their problems as nearly impossible to eliminate.

A review of 12 studies of depressives treated in psychiatric centers found the predicted relationships between attributional style and depressive features (Sweeney, 1986). Despite the weight of all these studies, some researchers have not found the predicted relationships between depression and attributional style (for example, Devins et al., 1981; Hammen & de Mayo, 1982). This inconsistency has not been clearly explained (Peterson et al., 1985). It also remains to be seen whether attributional style is a cause or an effect of depression (Beidel & Turnel, 1986).

Biological Perspectives

Although various psychological factors have been linked to mood disorders, biological factors also appear involved. In fact, most researchers suspect that biological factors are largely responsible for some mood disorders, like bipolar disorder (Klein & Depue, 1985). Biological factors may also play a role in other types of mood disorder.

■ **Genetic Factors**   Mood disorders tend to run in families. According to the DSM–III–R, for example, first-degree biological relatives (parents and siblings) of people with major depression stand 1.5 to 3 times the risk of suffering a major depression as does the general population. Families, however, share environmental similarities as well as genetic similarities. Family members may share blue eyes (an inherited attribute) but also a common religion (a cultural attribute). Evidence from twin and adoptee studies sheds more light on the possible genetic contribution.

A higher concordance rate among monozygotic (MZ) twins than dizygotic (DZ) twins is taken as evidence of genetic factors, since both types of twins share common environments but MZ twins share 100 percent genetic similarity as compared to 50 percent genetic similarity among DZ twins. Allen (1976) reviewed differences in rates of concordance for mood disorders between MZ and DZ twins. Overall, the rate of concordance for depressive (unipolar) disorders was 40 percent for the MZ twins but only 11 percent for the DZ twins. These differences were generally confirmed in a large-scale Danish study that found concordance rates for depressive disorders of 43 percent of MZ twins versus 18 percent for DZ twins (Bertelsen et al., 1977). There is also a higher concordance rate for bipolar disorder among MZ than among DZ twins (Bertelsen et al., 1977; Klein et al., 1985; Smith & Winokur, 1983). Researchers report an overall concordance rate of 72 percent among MZ twins for bipolar disorder, as compared to only 14 percent among DZ twins (Allen, 1976).

Evidence from adoptee studies is sparse and should be interpreted cautiously. Some research has failed to show that either the biological or adoptive parents of depressed adoptees had higher rates of mood disorders than did the parents of nondepressed adoptees (von Knorring et al., 1983). In more than 90 percent of these depressed adoptees, there was no history that either biological parent had even been treated for depression. Adoptee studies provide relatively stronger evidence of genetic transmission in bipolar disorders, however. In one study of 29 adoptees who had bipolar disorder, researchers found more than double the rate of mood disorders (all types) in their biological parents than in their adoptive parents, 28 versus 12 percent, respectively (Mendlewicz & Rainer, 1977). A recent estimate suggests that perhaps 80 percent of the risk of developing bipolar disorder may be accounted for by genetic factors (McGuffin & Katz, 1986). However, the mode of genetic transmission in bipolar disorder remains unclear (Blehar et al., 1988).

In a study of the Amish community in Pennsylvania, Janice Egeland and her colleagues (1987) traced the distribution of bipolar disorder in one large (81 member) extended family which has a high incidence of the disorder. The researchers isolated a specific gene on chromosome 11 that was associated with the presence of bipolar disorder. But a reevaluation of the data raised serious doubts about whether bipolar disorder is linked to this particular chromosome (Kelsoe et al., 1989).

In sum, genetics appears to play a limited role in explaining mood disorders. Genetics is believed to play a greater role in explaining endogenous rather than reactive types of depression, and in explaining bipolar than unipolar mood disorders (McGuffin & Katz, 1986). It appears at present that while genetic factors are likely to account for a predisposition for bipolar disorder, they do not, in and of themselves, determine its appearance. Increased levels of stress may also be involved in triggering bipolar disorder (Hirschfeld & Cross, 1982).

■ **Biochemical Factors in Depression**   If there is a genetic component to mood disorders, what exactly is inherited? Perhaps the genetic vulnerability expresses itself in abnormalities in neurotransmitter actions. The dominant biological model of depression during the past 25 years—the **catecholamine hypothesis** (Schildkraut, 1965)—has focused on the role of norepinephrine in explaining depression. Catecholamines are a class of hormones that includes the neurotransmitters norepinephrine (noradrenalin), epinephrine (adrenalin), and dopamine. Research shows that rats whose levels of norepinephrine are experimentally lowered exhibit behavior patterns similar to those of depressed humans (Ellison, 1977). They are less belligerent than their colony-mates and appear withdrawn and apa-

A CLOSER LOOK
In Search of Biological Markers of Depression

Imagine this. You're feeling down and moody and consult your doctor to see if you're depressed or perhaps physically run-down. After a brief examination, your doctor asks you, "Please roll up your sleeves. I want to test you for depression. We'll take a sample of blood and see whether or not you're depressed." Sound far-fetched? After all, depression concerns *feelings,* and feelings are psychological events. So what can be revealed by studying a sample of blood?

Quite a bit, perhaps. Researchers have been searching for a *biological marker* of depression that might be revealed by a simple laboratory test—such as a blood test. Although it remains experimental, one such test already exists: the dexamethasone suppression test, or DST. The DST has already become the most extensively studied biological test in psychiatry (American Psychiatric Association, 1987b), although questions remain about its validity.

The dexamethasone suppression test involves the oral administration of a synthetic steroid, dexamethasone, which in normal people suppresses the release of the hormone cortisol from the adrenal gland for a period of about 24 hours. Low levels of cortisol in the blood following the administration of dexamethasone are indicative of a normal (nondepressed) response. High levels of cortisol represent nonsuppression, which is thought to indicate the presence of clinical depression. For the test to be valid, it must demonstrate high levels of sensitivity (as measured by the percentage of actual cases that are detected by the test) and specificity (as measured by the percentage of normal subjects who yield negative test results). Research to date shows that the sensitivity of the DST procedure is only modest at best, about 40 to 50 percent. This means that the test is able to detect less than half (about 45 percent overall) of people with depression (Belsher & Costello, 1988). But the sensitivity of the test may be lower still. In one recent study, the DST was able to detect depression in only one third of a sample of 45 people with major depression (Heiby et al., 1987). However, sensitivity appears to be higher in more severe cases of depression, between 60 and 70 percent (American Psychiatric Association, 1987b). Thus, the DST may be a marker for some but not all cases of depression.

Specificity of the test appears to be higher, with over 90 percent of normals showing negative (nondepressed) test results. This means that the test is relatively unlikely to suggest that you are depressed if you are not. Hence, it seems that a positive DST might help confirm a diagnosis of a depressive disorder, but a negative test result would not necessarily contraindicate the presence of depression (American Psychiatric Association, 1987b).

Other evidence challenges the validity of the DST on the grounds that positive test results in actual depressives may be confounded by various factors, such as the

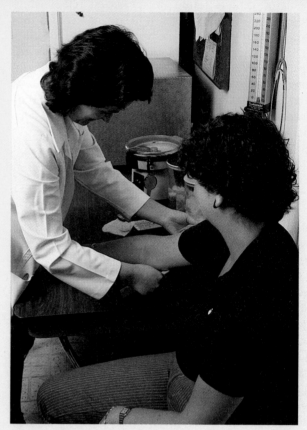

Is there a blood test for depression? The dexamethasone test (DST) has been proposed as a possible biological measure of depression, but its validity remains questionable.

use of psychotropic medications, by chemical effects of drug withdrawal, and by concomitant use of other drugs such as caffeine (Krauss & Brown, 1988). It may be that a positive (nonsuppression) result is actually picking up the effects of these other drugs and is not sensitive to depression itself. Until research is conducted that better controls for these confounding factors, the routine use of the test as a diagnostic indicator of depression does not seem to be justified.

Another limitation of the test is that it has not been able to predict the likelihood of response to antidepressant medications. But the test may help researchers predict the course of depression. Some research suggests that failure to convert to normal suppression of cortisol with apparent remission may suggest an increased risk of recurrence of depression (Arana et al., 1985; Braddock, 1986). However, determination of the utility of the test as a prognostic indicator also requires further study (American Psychiatric Association, 1987b).

It is true that there is a blood test for the diagnosis of depression (the DST). However, the validity of the DST has been closely questioned.

thetic. They lie around lethargically in their burrows. Their appetites wane and they lose weight.

The catecholamine theory proposes that depression results from deficiencies in norepinephrine, whereas excessive levels of norepinephrine produce manic behavior. Other researchers believe that the neurotransmitter serotonin, which belongs to the indoleamine class, also plays an important role in mood disorders (see Berger, 1978). Neurotransmitters of both the catecholamine and indoleamine class are monoamines—organic compounds that have nitrogen in one amino acid group. Still other researchers argue for roles for acetylcholine deficiencies (Nadi et al., 1984) or for excessive production of thyroid hormones (Whybrow & Prange, 1981) in mood disorders.

Evidence for the role of neurotransmitters was first found in the 1950s on the basis of two lines of research. One line of research focused on the findings that hypertensive patients who were taking the drug reserpine often reported feelings of depression. Reserpine is known to reduce the supplies of various neurotransmitters in the brain, including norepinephrine and serotonin. The second line of research focused on the discovery of antidepressant effects of two classes of drugs that act to increase the supply of norepinephrine and serotonin in the brains of laboratory animals and that help relieve depression in humans. These drugs, called the antidepressants, consisted of **tricyclics,** such as imipramine (trade name Tofranil) and amitriptyline (trade name Elavil), and **monoamine oxidase** (MAO) **inhibitors,** such as phenelzine (trade name Nardil). And so the apparent actions of antidepressant drugs suggest further evidence of a role for neurotransmitters in depression.

More recent research, however, has raised doubts about the direct role of neurotransmitters in depression. Research has not consistently demonstrated reduced levels of norepinephrine or serotonin in the brains of depressed people, based on examination of biological fluids (such as urine or blood serum) or upon autopsies (Deakin & Crow, 1986; Cooper et al., 1986). Nor is it known whether the changes in neurotransmitter levels in the brains of laboratory animals who are given antidepressant drugs have therapeutic significance for explaining changes in depression in humans (Green & Goodwin, 1986). Another problem with the catecholamine hypothesis is that antidepressant drugs increase the availability of neurotransmitters in the brain within hours of treatment, but the therapeutic effects of the drugs in relieving depression take two to three weeks to develop (Katona et al., 1986). Therefore, it is unlikely

that the mechanism of therapeutic action is simply due to an increased supply of neurotransmitters. Perhaps the heightened presence of these neurotransmitters gradually increases the sensitivity of the receptor sites on the neurons which they stimulate. It should also be noted that some research has failed to show a relationship (which the catecholamine hypothesis would predict) between the ability of antidepressants to increase the supply of neurotransmitters on the one hand, and their therapeutic effects on the other (Ghose & Coppen, 1977; Wood, 1986). All in all, antidepressant drugs appear to have more complex effects on the brain than was originally thought (Deakin & Crow, 1986).

In sum, most researchers believe that neurotransmitter imbalances play some role in explaining depression. However, the causal linkages between neurotransmitters and depression and the therapeutic mechanisms that explain the effects of antidepressant drugs remain unclear (Cooper et al., 1986; Deakin & Crow, 1986).

Depression is a complex phenomenon that appears to involve psychological and biological factors. Biological factors (levels of neurotransmitters) may interact with psychological factors (such as cognitive distortions or learned helplessness) to exacerbate feelings of depression. For example, researchers have found that experimentally induced helplessness in dogs was associated with a reduction in the amounts of norepinephrine available to their brains (Seligman, 1975; Weiss, 1982). Thus, helplessness and inactivity—two common features of depression—appear to be linked to lower norepinephrine levels in other mammals. We can speculate that this relationship, among humans, might involve a vicious circle: Exposure to a highly aversive stressor that appears inescapable (say, loss of one's job) may decrease the availability of norepinephrine in the brain, especially among people with a genetic predisposition for depression. Changes in the actions of neurotransmitters might, in turn, intensify depressive mood and behavior, making it more difficult for the individual to cope effectively, which could further heighten stress, and so on.

TREATMENT

In this section we review both psychological and biological approaches in the treatment of mood disorders.

Psychodynamic Approaches

Traditional psychoanalysis focuses on helping depressed people uncover their ambivalent feelings toward the lost object. By learning to recognize and work through their feelings of anger toward the lost object, anger can be turned outward—as through appropriate verbal expression of feelings—and not left to fester and then turn inward.

Traditional psychoanalysis is a lengthy process that can continue for years in the effort to uncover and work through unconscious conflicts. Modern psychoanalytic approaches also focus on unconscious conflicts. But they tend to be more direct and briefer and to focus more on exploring conflicted relationships in the present. Consistent with the self-focusing model, for example, clients would be encouraged to surrender pursuit of the lost object or disappointing experience and to achieve a sense of self-worth through the development of new goals and relationships. Some psychodynamic therapists who are more eclectic in their approach may also utilize behavioral methods for helping their clients develop a broader social network and acquire social skills that facilitate the process.

Humanistic-Existential Approaches

Humanistic and existential therapists focus on helping clients expand their awareness of their authentic feelings and needs for self-actualization and personal fulfillment. They help clients recognize that authenticity involves living one's life according to one's own values and choices, not submerging one's needs to the will of others. But authentic living does not mean that we expect that our lives be filled at all times with wonder and merriment. Both self-satisfaction and self-worth come from being true to ourselves and instilling life with meaning and purpose. We may experience genuine reactions to upsetting events by feeling saddened and depressed. But then we go on to find renewed meaning in life.

Abraham Maslow, one of the foremost humanistic theorists, focused on the importance of finding pathways to meaning through the pursuit of self-actualization. Maslow (1963) described his treatment approach in the case of a woman who complained of various features related to depression, such as boredom, lack of interest in life, and insomnia, among other physical complaints. The woman had been a brilliant psychology student who was forced to leave graduate school for economic reasons during the Great Depression of the 1930s and take a job working as a personnel officer in a factory. Maslow writes:

> Half-consciously then she saw a whole lifetime of greyness stretching out ahead of her. I suggested that she

A CLOSER LOOK
Is There a Thin Line Between Creativity and Insanity?

Ah, the indignities of mediocrity. Antonio Salieri, the court composer of eighteenth-century Vienna, was represented in the play and film *Amadeus* as having received the adulation of the Emperor and others at court that was denied Mozart. Yet Salieri knew that he was no Mozart, no genius. No matter how hard Salieri worked and reworked his compositions, they never sounded as pure, as angelic, as truly inspired as those of Mozart. Mozart, it seemed, merely had to transcribe the notes that filled his head, as if the voice of God were speaking through him.

We come away from the play with the recognition that we must come to terms with our own mediocrities, however it pains us. We must recognize that while we may be able to hit a few 18-foot jump shots (okay, make that 10-foot shots), the Lakers won't be beating down our doors to sign us to multimillion-dollar contracts nor will our writing style ever be compared to Shakespeare. Those of us, like Salieri, who ply our trade without the benefit of creative genius, may take some small comfort in the popular belief that there is a thin line between creative genius and insanity. Creative genius, if you allow us the pun, may not be what it's cracked up to be. Some recent research, however, suggests a different interpretation.

Although it is widely believed that genius and insanity (in the form of schizophrenia) are related to each other, perhaps because of the sometimes wild imaginings that occur in both, the startling number of creative writers who have taken their own lives—including luminaries like Sylvia Plath, Virginia Woolf, and Ernest Hemingway—suggests that creativity may actually be more closely linked to depression and suicide than to schizophrenia (Andreasen, 1987). Nancy Andreasen compared differences in the rates of mental disorder among a group of 30 creative writers, a group of 30 control subjects matched on sex, age, and educational level, and a group consisting of the immediate (first-degree) relatives of both groups. The writers were selected during a period of 15 years from among the visiting faculty members (27 males and 3 females) of the University of Iowa Writer's Workshop. The results of the study showed no evidence of schizophrenia in either the writers or the controls, which was consistent with the view that creativity, if not genius per se, is not related to insanity. However, there was a greater prevalence of other mental disorders, especially depression and bipolar disorder, among the creative writers and their family members than among the controls or their relatives. Four of every five writers reported experiencing at least one depressive episode in their lives, compared to only 30 percent of the controls. Forty-three percent of the writers, versus

might be feeling profoundly frustrated and angry simply because she was not being her own very intelligent self, that she was not using her intelligence and her talent for psychology and that this might well be a major reason for her boredom with life and her body's boredom with the normal pleasures of life. Any talent, any capacity, I thought, was also a motivation, a need, an impulse. With this she agreed, and I suggested that she could continue her graduate studies at night after her work. In brief, she was able to arrange this and it worked well. She became more alive, more happy, and zestful, and most of her physical symptoms had disappeared at my last contact with her. (Maslow, 1963, pp. 43–44)

Behavioral Approaches

Behavioral or learning-theory approaches to treatment are based on the assumption that depressive behaviors like social withdrawal and negative thinking are learned and can be unlearned. Behavior therapists focus on modifying depressive behaviors directly rather than on helping clients grow aware of possible unconscious causes of these behaviors.

Lewinsohn and his colleagues (Lewinsohn et al., 1984) have designed a group-treatment approach for

depression that is presented in the form of a 12-session, 8-week course—the *Coping with Depression Course*. The course helps depressed clients acquire relaxation skills, increase their participation in pleasant activities, and acquire social skills that enhance their ability to obtain reinforcements from others. Participants learn to generate a self-change plan, think more adaptively and less negatively, and develop a lifetime plan to help maintain treatment gains and prevent future depressive episodes. The therapist is considered a teacher; the client, a student; the session, a class. No one is considered sick or "crazy." Each participant is treated as a responsible adult who is capable of learning. The structure is one of lectures, activities, and homework. Each session has a lesson plan that begins with a review of homework and continues with a presentation of a new topic. Assertiveness skills such as learning how to ask friends to join in activities and how to accept compliments are taught to help participants raise the frequency and quality of their social interactions.

The following case illustrates how this multifaceted course helped one participant:

■ Liz Foster, a 27-year old woman diagnosed as suffering from major depression, participated in an eight-member Coping with Depression Course. Prior to therapy, Liz had been feeling depressed for two months, eating poorly,

 There may be a "thin line" (connection) between creative genius and mental disorders (in the form of mood disorders) for samples of creative writers and other artists in that severe depression, suicide, and some other mood-related problems are more common among creative artists. However, many questions remain about the nature of the link.

10 percent of the controls, had experienced a bipolar disorder at some point in their lives. Rates of alcoholism were also significantly higher among the writers, 30 percent vs. 7 percent. The immediate family members of the writers also showed greater rates of mental disorders, especially mood disorders, as compared to the relatives of controls. A higher rate of creativity was also found among the writers' relatives than among the relatives of control subjects. Interestingly, creativity and mental disorder in the families of the writers frequently occurred together, suggesting an intertwining of these traits that suggest that both may be genetically transmitted in part.

Now we caution that these results are limited to a single small-scale study. And the subjects were creative writers, not necessarily creative geniuses. Nor were other

creative people studied—painters, composers, choreographers, etc. But the results do suggest a possible connection between creativity and mood disorders. The writers reported that their greatest periods of creative productivity were not during periods of low or high mood, but rather during periods of normal moods. Although the connections between creativity and mental disorder need to be further explored, we may consider several possible relationships between creativity and mood disorders. Perhaps depressive episodes become a source of inspiration for creative people, providing them with an opportunity, however painful, to peer into the depths of their own despair and find something of meaning that they can use creatively in their work. Or perhaps creative people are more likely to become depressed because they think too deeply about certain troubling issues relating to life and death that the rest of us are able blissfully to ignore. Or perhaps creativity and mental disorders are not related to each other in a logical, psychological sense, but rather share a common genetic link, like blue eyes and blond hair. Whatever the connection, we can hope that new advances in the treatment of depression may help prevent the premature loss of creative people like Sylvia Plath and others to suicide.

sleeping excessively, and experiencing suicidal thoughts. She had had similar bouts of depression during the previous eight years. When she was depressed, she would spend most of her time alone at home—watching TV, reading, or just sitting. She engaged in a low rate of pleasant activities.

Liz had been laid off from work eleven months earlier and had few social contacts other than her boyfriend. She rarely saw her family, and two of her closest friends had moved away. Her remaining friends rarely visited, and she made no effort to see them.

With the eight other women in her class, Liz learned to focus on behaviors that she could change to increase her level of pleasant activities. At first she complained, "I don't feel like doing anything." The group instructors acknowledged that it would be hard, at first, to select desired reinforcers. Group members were encouraged to try out activities they had formerly enjoyed to see if they still found pleasure in them. Group members were instructed to identify stressful situations or hassles that increased their level of daily stress and were trained in relaxation techniques that they could use to cope with these stresses. They were given Pleasant Events Schedules to complete and encouraged to increase their frequency of pleasant activities.

Liz and the other group members plotted on a graph their level of pleasant activities from week to week and rated their mood levels on a daily basis. Most group members, including Liz, noticed a relationship between their moods and pleasant activities. Liz, whose initial rate of pleasant activities was about 8 per day, decided to increase her rate to 15–20 activities a day, and devised a plan to reinforce herself with rewards of 25 cents for each activity she completed over 13, pooling her rewards until she had earned $8.00, which she then used to buy a record album. Liz was able to increase her rate to 20 and noticed that her mood had improved.

The course also exposed participants to various techniques for controlling their thoughts. Liz selected the technique of self-reward/self-punishment: she rewarded herself with money for positive thoughts and charged herself (a nickel a thought) for negative thoughts. In tracking her thoughts, Liz found that she was able to increase her daily average of positive thoughts from 6 to 11 and decrease her negative thoughts from 7 to 2. By the eighth session, Liz was reporting that she was no longer depressed and felt more in control of her thoughts and feelings.

In later class sessions, group members learned assertive techniques for handling conflicts, such as dealing with aggressive salespeople, and for starting conversations with strangers. In later sessions, group members prepared life plans which they could use to deal with major life events and maintain the progress they had made. Liz recognized that she needed to maintain her frequency of pleasant activities at a high level, and she continued to monitor these activities to ensure that the frequency remained above a critical level. At a class-reunion six months following the course, she reported

that she continued to use the techniques she had learned. Follow-up evaluations through a period of one and one half years showed that Liz maintained her gains.

Adapted from Lewinsohn et al., 1983, pp. 94–101 ∎

Cognitive Approaches

Cognitive theorists attribute depression to distortions in thinking and suggest that treatment of depression should focus on helping the individual change these distorted patterns. Aaron Beck and his colleagues have developed a multicomponent treatment approach to depression, called **cognitive therapy,** that centers on helping depressed clients identify distorted, self-defeating thoughts and beliefs and substitute more rational ones. When people feel depressed, they tend to focus on their feelings of fatigue, lethargy, sadness, hopelessness, despair, and discouragement, rather than on the thoughts that may give rise to these feelings. That is, depressed people are usually more aware of how bad they feel than of the thoughts that may be maintaining their feelings.

Like behavior therapy, cognitive therapy entails a brief therapy format, frequently 15 to 20 weekly sessions. The therapy uses both behavioral and cognitive techniques to help clients change underlying thoughts and beliefs and develop more adaptive behaviors.

Clients are instructed to monitor their automatic negative thoughts by using a thought diary or daily record. They note when and where the thoughts occur and how they feel at the time. In this way, clients can make connections between disruptive thoughts and negative moods. Once disruptive thoughts are identified, the therapist helps the client engage in a process of reality-testing by challenging the validity of these thoughts. For example, a depressed person might react to the termination of a relationship by thinking, "I'll never find anyone to love." The therapist might probe for evidence of the validity of this thought by asking the client to consider whether or not there was once a time when he or she was not dating but had held a more positive attitude. Or the therapist might ask whether there is a logical basis for believing that the future can be predicted with such certainty. Through this process, the client may begin to doubt the validity of these disruptive thoughts or to rate them with a lower degree of certainty, even if the thoughts are not completely rejected. Homework assignments are often given as part of the process of reality-testing to help the client evaluate preconceived (and often false) ideas.

The following case shows how a cognitive therapist uses logic to dispute the validity of the cognitive distortion called *selective abstraction*—the tendency to judge oneself entirely on the basis of specific weaknesses or flaws in character. In this case, the client judged herself to be completely lacking in self-control because she ate a piece of candy while she was on a diet.

CLIENT: I don't have any self-control at all.

THERAPIST: On what basis do you say that?

C: Somebody offered me candy and I couldn't refuse it.

T: Were you eating candy every day?

C: No, I just ate it this once.

T: Did you do anything constructive during the past week to adhere to your diet?

C: Well, I didn't give in to the temptation to buy candy every time I saw it at the store. . . . Also, I did not eat any candy except that one time when it was offered to me and I felt I couldn't refuse it.

T: If you counted up the number of times you controlled yourself versus the number of times you gave in, what ratio would you get?

C: About 100 to 1.

T: So if you controlled yourself 100 times and did not control yourself just once, would that be a sign that you are weak through and through?

C: I guess not—not *through* and *through* (smiles).

Source: Beck et al. (1979), p. 68.

Or consider the case of Cliff, a 22-year-old stock clerk employed in an auto parts store:

■ Cliff became depressed in the course of a romantic relationship that followed a seesaw pattern of breakups and brief reconciliations. Most of the time a breakup would follow an incident in which Cliff had reacted excessively and angrily when he perceived—or rather misperceived—his girlfriend as acting distant or aloof, even in trivial matters such as how far away from him she sat in the front seat of the car. Cliff needed constant reassurance of love and was acutely sensitive to verbal criticism and nonverbal cues of emotional distance. His girlfriend would say to him, "You must really want this relationship, since you're always badgering me to tell you that I love you."

Cliff's thinking was patterned by a set of underlying beliefs that helped undermine his relationships. These beliefs included musterbation ("This relationship must work out . . . or else"), personalizing ("If she's in a bad mood it's because she doesn't really love me"), and catastrophizing ("I won't be able to survive if this relationship breaks up"). In therapy, Cliff began to see that his way of viewing himself and the world limited

possibilities for growth. Cliff was a quick study and readily learned to monitor his thoughts and replace self-defeating thoughts with rational alternatives. Instead of responding automatically to a perception that his girlfriend was rejecting him, he stopped and asked himself, "Where's the evidence for that? Might there be another explanation for her behavior?" When she wasn't available to see him on a particular night, he was able to attribute it to her feeling fatigued rather than misconstrue it as a sign of rejection. When problems arose in the relationship, Cliff learned to feel disappointed but not depressed. He began to ease his expectations, seeing the relationship less as a "do or die" situation and more as a growth experience.

The Authors' Files ■

Biological Approaches

The most common biological approaches to the treatment of mood disorders involve antidepressant drugs and electroconvulsive therapy for depression, and lithium for bipolar disorder.

■ **Antidepressant Drugs** Drugs used to treat depression include tricyclics and monoamine oxidase (MAO) inhibitors, both of which affect the levels and, perhaps, the actions of neurotransmitters in the brain. These two classes of drugs appear to increase the availability of neurotransmitters in different ways (see Figure 8.2). The tricyclics, which are so-named because of their three-ringed molecular structure, are believed to interfere with the reuptake (the return to the storage vesicles) of norepinephrine and serotonin. As a result, the concentration of these chemical messengers at the synapse is increased, thereby enhancing the sensitivity of the postsynaptic cell to continue firing neural impulses. The MAO-inhibitors increase the availability of neurotransmitters by inhibiting the action of monoamine oxidase, an enzyme that normally breaks down or degrades neurotransmitters in the synaptic cleft.

Among the most frequently prescribed antidepressants are the tricyclics, which include imipramine (Tofranil), amitriptyline (Elavil), desipramine (Norpramin), and doxepin (Sinequan). Approximately 60 to 70 percent of depressed people respond positively to tricyclic drugs (Georgotas & McCue, 1986). Their effectiveness has been clearly established on the basis of controlled comparisons with placebos (Paykel & Hale, 1986). A review of 93 studies conducted between 1958 and 1972 showed that 62 (about two-thirds) showed superior effects for the tricyclic drugs as compared with placebos, whereas 31 failed to show significant drug effects (Morris & Beck, 1974).

It is commonly believed that endogenous depressions respond better than reactive depressions to tri-

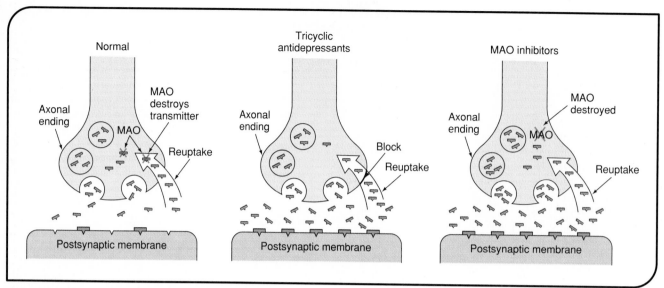

FIGURE 8.2 *The actions of tricyclic antidepressants and MAO inhibitors at the synapse.*
MAO inhibitors increase the availability of neurotransmitters by inhibiting the action of MAO.
Tricyclics increase the availability of neurotransmitters by blocking the reuptake of these chemicals
by the presynaptic neuron.
Source: Schneider & Tarshis (1986), p. 173.

cyclic antidepressants, but the evidence is not clear-cut (Paykel & Hale, 1979), perhaps because of two reasons: (1) some reactive depressions also respond to antidepressant therapy, and (2) some severe endogenous depressions associated with psychotic features may respond poorly to drug treatment (Paykel & Hale, 1979). There is also some evidence that antidepressant medication (imipramine) is more effective than a placebo control in treating dysthymic disorder (Kocis et al., 1988). While new antidepressants have been brought to clinical practice in recent years, such as fluoxetine hydrochloride (trade name Prozac), their long-term effectiveness remains to be studied, as discussed further in Chapter 15. It also remains to be seen whether any of the newer antidepressants are any more effective over the long term than the earlier tricyclics (Georgotas & McCue, 1986).

The side effects of tricyclics can include psychomotor retardation, dry mouth, constipation, blurred vision, and, less frequently, urinary retention, paralytic ileus (a paralysis of the intestines that impairs the passage of intestinal contents), confusion, delirium, and cardiovascular complications, such as reduced blood pressure.

Another problem associated with the use of tricyclics is the delayed onset of therapeutic effects. Amelioration of depression may require up to three weeks of treatment, if it occurs at all. Tricyclics are highly toxic, raising the prospect of suicidal overdoses prior to taking effect if the drugs are used without close supervision.

MAO inhibitors were used in the treatment of depression prior to the advent of the tricyclics; however, they play a smaller role in treatment of depression be-

cause of potentially serious interactions with other substances and doubts regarding their effectiveness (Paykel & Hale, 1986). Some of the more common MAO inhibitors include isocarboxazid (Marplan), tranylcypromine (Parnate), and phenelzine (Nardil).

Drug–placebo comparisons have failed to demonstrate consistently the efficacy of MAO inhibitors (Paykel & Hale, 1986). The most serious side effect of MAO inhibitors is a sudden, potentially life-threatening rise in blood pressure that can occur when a user consumes foods that contain tyramine. Tyramine is found in common foods like cheeses and chocolate, and also in beer and red wines. Therefore, people taking MAO inhibitors must closely monitor their diets.

Other drugs have also been introduced as possible treatments for mood disorders. Carbamazepine, a tricyclic drug used to treat epilepsy, is believed also to be effective in treating severe unipolar depressions (Post & Uhde, 1983) and bipolar disorders, especially those characterized by rapid mood shifts or cycling between highs and lows (Paykel & Hale, 1986).

One problem with antidepressant medication is the potential for recurrence of depression following suspension of usage. A recent review of drug-withdrawal studies showed relapse rates of up to 69 percent when antidepressants were terminated within two months of a treatment response. This is at least double the rate among depressives who were continued on the medication for periods of six months to one year (Paykel & Hale, 1986). It remains unclear, however, whether or not recurrence of depression would become less likely with longer periods of use.

A CLOSER LOOK
Correcting Cognitive Distortions with Rational Alternatives

Cognitive theorists suggest that distortions in thinking can lead to depression if they are left to rummage around in the individual's mind unchallenged. Consequently, cognitive therapists help their clients to recognize the cognitive distortions in their thinking and to replace them with more rational alternative thoughts.

Table 8.6 lists some common examples of automatic thoughts, the types of cognitive distortions they represent, and some rational alternative responses.

TABLE 8.6 Cognitive Distortions and Rational Responses

Automatic Thought	Kind of Cognitive Distortion	Rational Response
I'm all alone in the world.	All or Nothing Thinking	It may feel like I'm all alone, but there are some people who care about me.
I keep screwing-up. Nothing will ever work out for me.	Overgeneralization	No one can look into the future. Concentrate on the present.
My looks are hopeless.	Magnification	I may not be perfect-looking, but I'm far from hopeless.
I guess I'm just a born loser.	Labeling and Mislabeling	Nobody is destined to be a loser. Stop talking yourself down.
I've only lost eight pounds on this diet. I should just forget it. I can't succeed.	Mental Filter/Minimization/ Disqualifying the Positives/ Jumping to Conclusions/All or Nothing Thinking	Eight pounds is a good start. I didn't gain all this weight overnight, and I have to expect that it will take time to lose it.
I know things must really be bad for me to feel this awful.	Emotional Reasoning	Feeling something doesn't make it so. If I'm not seeing things clearly, my emotions will be distorted too.
I know I'm going to flunk this course.	Fortune Teller Error	Give me a break! Just focus your thoughts on getting through this course, not on jumping to negative conclusions.
I know John's problems are really my fault.	Personalization	Stop blaming yourself for everyone else's problems. There are many reasons why John has these problems that have nothing to do with me.
Someone my age should be doing better than I am.	Should Statements	Stop comparing yourself to others. All anyone can be expected to do is their best. What good does it do to compare myself to others? It only leads me to get down on myself, rather than get motivated.
I just don't have the brains for college.	Labeling and Mislabeling	Stop calling yourself names like stupid. I can accomplish a lot more than I give myself credit for.
It would be awful if Sue turns me down.	Magnification	It might be upsetting. But it needn't be awful unless I make it so.
If something doesn't get better soon, I'll go crazy.	Jumping to Conclusions/ Magnification	I've dealt with these problems this long without falling apart. I just have to hang in there. Things are not as bad as they seem.
I can't believe I got another pimple on my face. This is going to ruin my whole weekend.	Mental Filter/Jumping to Conclusions	Take it easy. A pimple is not the end of the world. It doesn't have to spoil my whole weekend. Other people get pimples and seem to have a good time.

■ **Lithium**   Bipolar disorder is most commonly treated with the metal lithium, an element similar to potassium and sodium (Crammer et al., 1982). It could be said that the ancient Greeks and Romans were among the first to use lithium as a form of chemotherapy. They prescribed mineral water that contained lithium for people with turbulent mood swings.

> **?**   The ancient Greeks and Romans did use a contemporary form of chemotherapy to treat turbulent mood swings. That chemical is lithium.

Lithium has been found to be effective in treating both the manic and depressive phases of the disorder, and has **prophylactive** value when taken regularly in reducing both the frequency and severity of subsequent recurrences (Janicak & Boshes, 1987; Johnson, 1975; Prien, 1977). People with bipolar disorder may need to use lithium indefinitely to control their mood swings, just as individuals with diabetes need to continue to use insulin to control their illness. Lithium is given orally in the form of a natural mineral salt, lithium carbonate. Lithium appears to be most effective in treating manic episodes, with success rates reported of about 67 percent (Janicak & Boshes, 1987). Some cases of unipolar depression also seem to respond to lithium, especially in people with no personal history of manic episodes but with a family history of bipolar disorder (Fieve, 1977).

Lithium treatment must be closely monitored because of the possibility of toxic effects if blood levels of the drug exceed certain limits. There are also a number of reported side effects of lithium treatment, such as impaired memory and diminished motor speed (Shaw et al., 1987). Lithium seems to slow people down. Memory impairment is the primary reason that people who are prescribed preventive regimens of lithium discontinue the drug (Jamison & Akiskal, 1983).

Although lithium is widely prescribed for bipolar disorders, its biochemical mode of action remains unclear (Crammer et al., 1982).

■ **Electroconvulsive Therapy**   Electroconvulsive therapy (ECT) is used to treat major depression and involves the administration of an electrical current to the head. A current of between 70 to 130 volts is used to induce a convulsion similar to a grand-mal type of epileptic seizure. ECT, or "shock therapy" as it is more commonly known, is usually administered in a series of 6 to 12 treatments over a period of several weeks. In the past, the individual receiving ECT was usually awake during the procedure until the seizure was induced. The force of the shock produced such strong muscular spasms, or convulsions, that people sometimes suffered broken bones. The image of the individual convulsing wildly was a sight most frightening to onlookers and not easily forgotten. Nowadays, ECT is administered under a brief-acting anesthetic in combination with a muscle relaxant to prevent the individual from convulsing wildly and suffering injury. The spasms may be barely perceptible to onlookers. The individual awakens a few minutes after the procedure and generally remembers nothing.

Although ECT often leads to dramatic relief from severe depression, no one really knows how ECT works. ECT produces such mammoth chemical and electrical changes in the body that it is difficult to pinpoint the mechanism of therapeutic action, although it is sus-

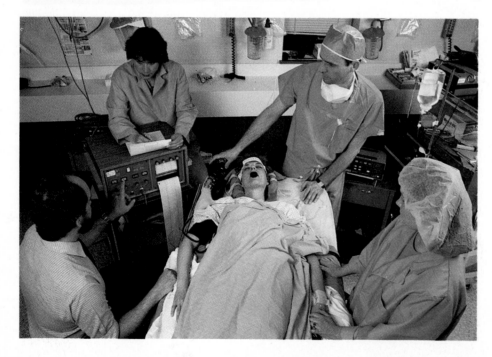

In ECT, an electric current is passed through the head to induce a seizure, uplifting the mood in many cases of severe depression. Many professionals regard ECT as a safe and effective form of treatment for severe depression. Yet controversy persists concerning its long-term effectiveness and side effects.

pected that ECT may help correct imbalances in neuro-transmitter levels in the brain.

The effectiveness of ECT remains a matter of debate. ECT is regarded by many mental-health professionals as an effective form of treatment for depression, especially for more severe or endogenous forms of depression (NIMH, 1985; Paykel, 1979; Paykel & Hale, 1986; Scovern & Kilmann, 1980). But critics have questioned whether ECT is more effective than alternative forms of treatment (Breggin, 1979). An averaging of results from various studies comparing real ECT treatment to simulated or sham ECT treatment (that is, treatment which follows the same procedure as ECT but does not deliver actual shock) showed clear evidence of superiority of the real treatment, with overall improvement rates of 72 percent for real ECT vs. 40 percent for sham ECT (Janicak et al. 1985). We must be cautious in interpreting these results because it appears that four of the six studies included in the averaged results were at least 20 years old. Newer, more methodologically sound studies were not included in the analysis (Uebersax, 1987). These newer studies failed to show that ECT produced superior *long-term* effects over simulated ECT. Moreover, the relative effectiveness of ECT as compared to antidepressant medications is less clear: Some studies showed superior results for ECT while others showed no differences (Janicak et al., 1985).

ECT may be administered either to both sides of the head (*bilateral ECT*) or to one side of the head (*unilateral ECT*). Unilateral ECT is applied to the nondominant hemisphere of the brain, which, for most people, is the right side. There is disagreement in the research literature concerning the relative effectiveness of these approaches. Some studies show clear advantages for bilateral ECT (Abrams et al., 1983), whereas others show only marginal superiority for bilateral treatment (D'Elia & Raotma, 1975). A recent review of the research suggested that bilateral and unilateral ECT are about equal in effectiveness (Janicak et al., 1985).

Memory loss is a frequent side effect of ECT, especially for events preceding administration. Although memory functioning appears about normal for most people a few months following treatment, some individuals appear to suffer more lasting memory impairment (Roueche, 1980). It is possible, however, that more profound memory losses that are apparently associated with ECT may be due to severe depression itself rather than the treatment (Squire & Slater, 1983). It is clear that unilateral ECT is associated with less memory loss than bilateral ECT (American Psychiatric Association, 1978; Janicak et al., 1985; Squire, 1982; Squire & Zouzounis, 1986). Since it may reduce memory loss, unilateral ECT is often tried first, followed by bilateral ECT only in people who fail to respond (Abrams & Fink, 1984; Paykel & Hale, 1986).

Some research suggests that briefer pulses of electricity than are typically applied in ECT may produce therapeutic effect about equal to those of conventional administration but with less interference with memory (Weiner, et al., 1984). However, these findings have not been consistent (Squire & Zouzounis, 1986). In sum, questions remain about the origins, extent, and duration of memory losses associated with ECT. For reasons such as these, many professionals view ECT as a treatment of last resort, to be used only after other treatment approaches have failed.

■ **Who Gets ECT?**   After the introduction of major tranquilizers for the treatment of schizophrenia, use of ECT became generally limited to the treatment of major depression. The advent of antidepressants has limited the application of ECT even more—to depressives who fail to respond to drug treatment. But even as a treatment of last resort, about 60,000 to 100,000 people in the United States each year receive ECT (Sackheim, 1985).

Although the debate over ECT continues, its use may be declining. Data from the National Institute of Mental Health show that the use of ECT declined by 46 percent between 1975 and 1980. Only a small percentage of persons (2.4%) who were hospitalized in psychiatric facilities in 1980 received ECT (Thompson & Blaine, 1987). Most people who received ECT in 1975 and 1980 were diagnosed as having mood disorders (72.8 and 69.8%, respectively), but relatively few people with mood disorders received ECT in 1975 (13%) and fewer still in 1980 (6.2%). Women were more likely to receive ECT than were men, even within the same diagnostic categories. Whites were more likely to receive ECT than were blacks. ECT was most often used (about two-thirds of cases) in private general hospitals. The prototype of the individual most likely to receive ECT is a white woman over the age of 40 who is diagnosed as suffering from a mood disorder and is treated in a voluntary, private general hospital.

SUICIDE

Suicidal thoughts are common enough. Many if not most people have contemplated suicide at time of great stress. However, the great majority of people who entertain such thoughts never act on them. But nearly one-quarter of a million Americans attempt suicide each year (Blumenthal, 1985). About 30,000 of them succeed (U.S. Bureau of the Census, 1989).

■ **Who Commits Suicide?**   Who is most likely to commit suicide? As you can see in Figure 8.3, more whites commit suicide than blacks. While more women in the United States attempt suicide, more men "succeed."

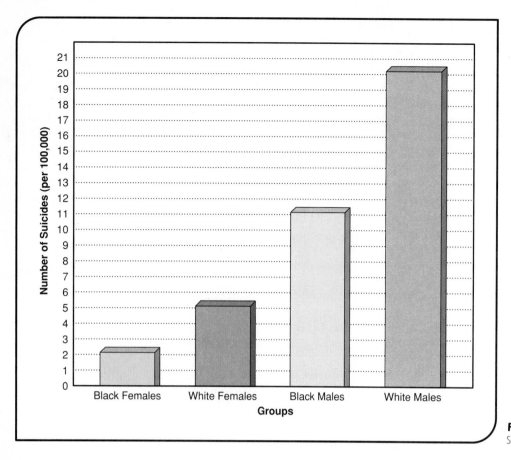

FIGURE 8.3 Suicide rate by sex and race.
Source: U.S. Bureau of the Census (1989)

FIGURE 8.4 Suicide rate by age.
Source: U.S. Bureau of the Census (1989)

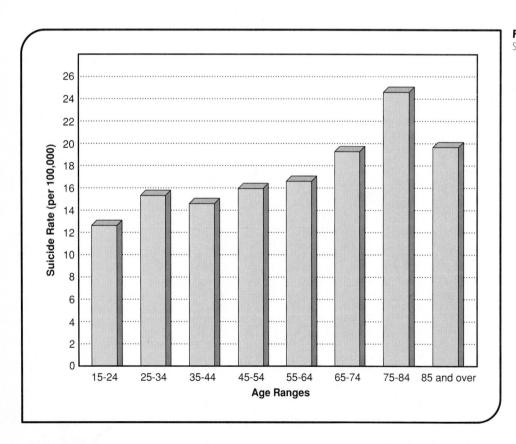

Men actually commit between 2.5 and 4 times as many suicides as women (Rich et al., 1988; National Center for Health Statistics, 1967; Centers for Disease Control, 1985). It appears that more males succeed in committing suicide because they tend to choose quicker-acting and more lethal means (Carlson & Miller, 1981). A study of 204 San Diego County suicides that took place in the early 1980s found that males who committed suicide were more likely to use guns (60% of the males vs. 28% of the females) (Rich et al., 1988). Females who committed suicide more often used drugs or poisons (44% of the females vs. 11% of the males).

Although teenage suicides tend to receive the media spotlight, government statistics show that the elderly are much more likely to commit suicide (see Figure 8.4). The suicide rate among the elderly is 21.6 cases per 100,000 people, nearly twice the national rate of 12.8 cases (Tolchin, 1989). The rate of suicide among older people increased in the 1980s, reversing the trend of a half-century of decline (Tolchin, 1989). This increase is somewhat surprising because the rate of major depression among the elderly appears to have declined in recent years (Klerman et al., 1989). Government statistics showed a 25 percent increase in the suicide rate among people 65 years of age and older during the period between 1981 and 1986. No other age group has shown a comparable increase. In fact, teenage suicides reached a peak in 1977 and has since declined (McIntosh & Osgood, 1986).

Today's elderly are generally healthier and more financially secure than in earlier years, which leaves professionals perplexed about their suicide rate. Several possible causes have been suggested for the high suicide rate among those aged 65 and above (Tolchin, 1989). With longer life, older people are more susceptible to diseases such as Alzheimer's (see Chapter 13), which can leave them feeling helpless. Thus, some suicides may stem from fear of impending helplessness. Or perhaps society's increased tolerance of suicide as a means of "solving" problems makes it a more attractive alternative. Despite life-extending advances in medical care, some elderly people may find that the quality of their lives is less than satisfactory. Many elderly people also suffer a mounting accumulation of losses as time progresses. The loss of a spouse, loss of friends and family members, loss of good health and a responsible role in the community may erode the will to live. Whatever the causes, suicide has become an increased risk for elderly people. Perhaps society should focus its attention as much on the quality of life that is afforded our elderly and not simply on providing them the medical care that helps make longer life possible.

Why Do People Commit Suicide?

Why do people commit suicide? To many lay observers, suicide seems so extreme an act that they believe that only "insane" people (meaning people who are out of touch with reality) would commit suicide. However, suicidologist Edwin Schneidman of the UCLA Neuropsychiatric Institute explains that suicidal thinking does not necessarily suggest the presence of psychosis, neurosis, or even personality disorder. The contemplation of suicide, instead, generally reflects a narrowing of the range of options people think are available to them (Cordes, 1985). That is, they are discouraged by their problems and see no other way out.

It is *not true* that suicide is a sign of insanity.

The majority of suicides are apparently connected with depression (Leonard, 1977; Schotte & Clum, 1982), which is why we include the topic in this chapter. It has been estimated that as many as 15 percent of people diagnosed as having depressive disorders eventually take their own lives (Fawcett et al., 1987). Although most people who try to take their lives show signs of hopelessness and despair, they do not appear psychotic or out of touch with reality (Leonard, 1974). Although suicide is most closely linked to the mood disorders, many people who take their lives are alcoholics or schizophrenics (Fawcett et al., 1987).

Stress also appears to play an important role in many suicides. Suicide attempts occur more frequently following exposure to highly stressful life events, especially "exit events" such as the death of a spouse, close friend, or relative; divorce or separation; a family member's leaving home; or the loss of a close friend (Slater & Depue, 1981). People who considered taking their lives in response to stressful events have been found to have poorer problem-solving skills than those who did not consider suicide (Schotte & Clum, 1987). It appears that people who consider suicide in times of stress may be less able to find alternative ways of coping with the stressors they face. The risks of suicide may be lessened by teaching suicidal people problem-solving and assertiveness skills to help them cope more effectively with stress in their relationships with others (Linehan et al., 1987).

Theoretical Perspectives on Suicide

Recall that the classic psychodynamic model held that depression involves the turning inward of anger against the internal representation or *introjection* of the lost love object that has been incorporated into the self. Psychodynamic theorists believe that suicide represents anger turned inward against the self, which reaches a level of murderous rage. Suicidal people, then, do not seek to destroy themselves, but rather to vent their murderous rage against the representation of the love object that they have internalized within themselves. But in so doing, they destroy themselves as well. In his later writings, Freud speculated that suicide may be motivated by the "death instinct"—a tendency to return to the state of nothingness that preceded birth in which there was an absence of any tension.

Existential and humanistic theorists relate suicide to the perception that life has become meaningless and lacking in purpose and hope. Suicidal people report that they find life duller, emptier, and more boring than do nonsuicidal people. Suicidal people also feel more anxious, excitable, angry, guilt-ridden, helpless, submissive, and inadequate than other people (Mehrabian & Weinstein, 1985; Neuringer, 1982). According to Shneidman (1985), people who attempt suicide are usually experiencing unbearable psychological pain and are trying to terminate awareness of their suffering.

In the last century, social thinker Emile Durkheim (1958) noted that people who experienced *anomie*—who felt lost, without identity, rootless—were more likely to commit suicide. Sociocultural theorists likewise believe that alienation in present-day society may play a role in suicide. In today's modern, mobile society, people frequently move hundreds or thousands of miles for the sake of education and employment. It is not uncommon for executives and their families to be relocated every two years or so. Military personnel and their families may be shifted about yet more rapidly. So many people may feel socially isolated or cut off from their support groups. Moreover, city dwellers tend to limit or discourage informal social contacts because of crowding, overstimulation, and fear of crime. So it is not surprising that many people find few sources of support in times of crisis.

Moreover, the availability of a "close" family is no guarantee that this will be helpful. In a Boston University study, college women who had attempted suicide were more likely than nonsuicidal peers to implicate their parents as a source of their troubles (Cantor, 1976). The suicidal students were also less likely to feel able to ask their parents or others for help when they were in crisis. "Close" relations are sometimes perceived as part of the problem, not part of the solution.

Learning theorists point to the reinforcing effects of prior suicide threats and attempts, and to the effects of stress, especially when combined with a lack of available coping or problem-solving resources. People who threaten or attempt suicide may receive sympathy and support from loved ones and others, perhaps making future—and more lethal—attempts more likely. This is not to suggest that suicide attempts or gestures should be ignored. The majority (70 to 80%) of people who commit suicide give clear clues concerning their intentions beforehand (Cordes, 1985; Leonard, 1977). More-

over, 75 percent of those who commit suicide have made prior attempts (Cohen et al., 1966).

 It is *not* true that people who threaten to commit suicide are only seeking attention. Many people who commit suicide have informed others of their intentions.

Social-learning and cognitive theorists recognize that suicide may be motivated by positive outcome expectancies—that one will be missed or eulogized by others after death, or that others will be punished with guilt for past mistreatments. Suicidal psychiatric patients have been shown to hold more positive expectancies concerning suicide than did nonsuicidal psychiatric samples. They more often expressed the belief that suicide would solve their problems, for example (Linehan et al., 1987). Suicide may represent a desperate attempt to solve one's problems by wiping the slate clean in "one fell swoop," rather than attempting to solve them one by one (Appelbaum, 1963).

Social-learning theory also focuses on the potential modeling effects of observing suicidal behavior in others, especially among teenagers who feel overwhelmed by academic and social stressors. A *social contagion*, or spreading of suicide in a community, may occur in the wake of suicides that receive widespread publicity. Teenagers, who seem to be especially vulnerable to these modeling effects, may even romanticize the suicidal act as one of heroic courage. A recent study showed that the incidence of suicide among teenagers rose markedly in the week following a broadcast of a news report about suicide (Phillips & Carstensen, 1986).

Predicting Suicide

"I don't believe it. I just saw him last week and he looked fine."

"She sat here just the other day, laughing with the rest of us. How were we to know what was going on inside her?"

"I knew he was depressed, but I never thought he'd do something like this. I didn't have a clue."

"Why didn't she just call me?"

Friends and family members often respond to news of a suicide with disbelief, or with guilt that they failed to pick up any signs of the impending act. Yet even trained professionals find it difficult to predict who is likely to commit suicide.

A CLOSER LOOK
Suicide Prevention

Imagine yourself having an intimate conversation with a close campus friend, Chris. You know that things have not been good. Chris's grandfather died six weeks ago, and the two were very close. Chris's grades have been going downhill, and Chris's romantic relationship also seems to be coming apart at the seams. Still, you are unprepared when Chris says very deliberately, "I just can't take it anymore. Life is just too painful. I don't feel like I want to live anymore. I've decided that the only thing I can do is to kill myself!"

When somebody discloses that he or she is contemplating suicide, you may feel bewildered and frightened, as if a great burden has been placed on your shoulders. It has. If someone confides suicidal thoughts in you, your goal should be to persuade him or her to see a professional mental-health worker, or to get the advice of a professional yourself as soon as you can. But if the suicidal person declines to talk to another person and you sense that you can't break away for such a consultation, there are some things you can do:

1. Draw the person out. Shneidman advises framing questions like, "What's going on?" "Where do you hurt?" "What would you like to see happen?" (1985, p. 11). Such questions may prompt people to verbalize thwarted psychological needs, providing some relief. They also grant you the time to appraise the risk and contemplate your next move.

2. Be sympathetic. Show that you fathom how troubled the person is. Don't say something like, "You're just being silly."

3. Suggest that means other than suicide can be discov-

ered to work out the person's problems even if they are not apparent at the time. Shneidman (1985) notes that suicidal people can usually see only two solutions to their predicaments—either suicide or some kind of magical resolution. Professionals try to broaden the available alternatives of people who are suicidal.

4. Inquire as to *how* the person expects to commit suicide. People with explicit methods who also possess the means (for example, a gun or drugs) are at greater risk. Ask if you may hold onto the gun, drugs, or whatever for a while. Sometimes the person assents.

5. Propose that the person accompany you to consult a professional right *now*. Many campuses have "hot lines" that you or the suicidal individual can call. Many towns and cities have such hot lines that can be called anonymously. Other possibilities include the emergency room of a general hospital, a campus health center or counseling center, or the campus or local police. If you are unable to maintain contact with the suicidal person, get professional assistance as soon as you separate.

6. Don't say something like "You're talking crazy." Such comments are degrading and injurious to the individual's self-esteem. Don't press the suicidal person to contact specific people, such as parents or a spouse. Conflict with them may have given rise to the suicidal thoughts.

Above all, keep in mind that your primary goal is to confer with a helping professional. Don't "go it alone" any longer than you have to.

Suicide hot-lines have been established in many communities.

Most people who commit suicide do give prior signals of their intentions. Many specifically warn of suicide. Others, though, attempt to cover up their intentions. But still there may be clues in their behavior that might reveal their suicidal intent. People contemplating suicide, for example, may develop a sudden interest in sorting out their affairs, as in drafting a will or making arrangements for a cemetery plot. Suicidal people may purchase guns despite lack of prior interest in keeping firearms. A sense of peacefulness may suffuse a previously troubled person following the decision to commit suicide, reflecting a sense of relief that he or she will not have to contend with life problems for much longer. This sudden calm may be misinterpreted by others as a hopeful sign. We should be alert to such clues in people who are severely depressed or appear to be without hope of solving their problems. But we should understand that suicide is a private act and if the individual truly doesn't want others to know—or to attempt to prevent the act—then we shouldn't berate ourselves needlessly for failing to recognize an impending suicide.

Some specific features of persons with mental disorders may be helpful in appraising suicidal risk. A four-year study of 954 people with major mood disorders examined the factors that distinguished those who later committed suicide (25 in total) from the 929 who did not (Fawcett et al., 1987). Features were assessed shortly following admission to treatment. The features that emerged as significant predictors of later suicide included a sense of hopelessness, loss of pleasure or interest in pleasant activities, fewer prior episodes of mood disorder, a loss of reactivity to external events, fewer friendships in adolescence, and the occurrence

TABLE 8.7 *Some Predictors of Suicidal Risk Among People with Mood Disorders*

Hopelessness
Loss of pleasure or interest
Fewer prior episodes of mood disorder
Loss of reactivity
Fewer friendships during adolescence
Presence of mood swings

Source: *Adapted from Fawcett et al., 1987.*

of mood swings (from depressive to manic phases, or vice versa) during the treatment episode (see Table 8.7). Let us example these relationships more closely.

Relationships between depression and hopelessness have become well established in the clinical literature (Fawcett et al., 1987). The loss of reactivity and the capacity to experience pleasure is associated with more severe types of depression that may make life seem unrewarding. The finding that suicide was more likely among those persons with fewer episodes of mood disorder in the past may suggest that people with more prior episodes have been able to come to terms with their disorder or make necessary accommodations. The occurrence of fewer friendships in adolescence among the suicide victims suggests that these people may lack social skills and be less able to obtain reinforcements from others. These different features suggest there may be different pathways to suicide among persons with mood disorders. The clinician needs to be alert to these various features in appraising the potential risk of suicide among people so diagnosed.

SUMMARY

Mood Disorders

Mood disorders are disturbances in mood that are serious enough to impair daily functioning. There are various kinds of mood disorders, including depressive (unipolar) disorders such as major depression and dysthymia, and disorders involving mood swings, such as bipolar disorder and cyclothymia.

Major Depression

People with major depression experience profound changes in mood that impair their ability to function.

There are many associated features of major depression, including depressed mood, changes in appetite, difficulty sleeping, reduced sense of pleasure in formerly enjoyable activities, feelings of fatigue or loss of energy, sense of worthlessness, excessive or misplaced guilt, difficulties concentrating, thinking clearly or making decisions, repeated thoughts of death or suicide, attempts at suicide, or even psychotic behaviors (hallucinations and delusions).

The course of major depression is variable, with some people experiencing but one episode, while others have recurrent episodes. About twice as many women as men seem to be affected by major depression, but the reasons for this sex difference remain unclear. De-

LEARNING OBJECTIVES

When you have completed your study of Chapter 9, you should be able to:

TYPES OF PERSONALITY DISORDERS (p. 292)
1. Define the common features of personality disorders.
2. Describe the different clusters of personality disorders.

PERSONALITY DISORDERS CHARACTERIZED BY ODD OR ECCENTRIC BEHAVIOR (pp. 292–294)
3. Describe the features of paranoid, schizoid, and schizotypal personality disorders.

PERSONALITY DISORDERS CHARACTERIZED BY DRAMATIC, EMOTIONAL, OR ERRATIC BEHAVIOR (pp. 294–302)
4. Describe the features of antisocial, borderline, histrionic, and narcissistic personality disorders.

PERSONALITY DISORDERS CHARACTERIZED BY ANXIOUS OR FEARFUL BEHAVIOR (pp. 302–305)
5. Describe the features of avoidant, dependent, and obsessive-compulsive personality disorders.

PROPOSED PERSONALITY DISORDERS "NEEDING FURTHER STUDY" (p. 306)
6. Describe the features of sadistic and self-defeating personality disorders and discuss the controversies involved in proposing these disorders.

7. Discuss the reasons why researchers believe that women who remain in abusive relationships should be perceived as trauma survivors, not masochists.

PROBLEMS WITH CLASSIFICATION OF PERSONALITY DISORDERS (pp. 306–310)
8. Discuss controversies in classifying personality disorders.

THEORETICAL PERSPECTIVES (pp. 310–317)
9. Discuss theoretical perspectives on the personality disorders.

TREATMENT (pp. 317–320)
10. Discuss the approaches to treatment of personality disorders and the difficulties faced by therapists in treating people with these disorders.

IMPULSE DISORDERS (pp. 320–324)
11. Define the common features of impulse disorders.
12. Discuss the features and treatments of pathological gambling.
13. Discuss the features of kleptomania.

In most of us by the age of thirty, the character has set like plaster, and will never soften again.

William James

A ll of us have particular styles of behavior and ways of relating to others. Some of us are very orderly, others rather sloppy. Some of us prefer solitary pursuits, others are more socially oriented. Some of us are followers; others, leaders. Some of us seem immune to rejection by others, whereas others avoid taking social initiatives for fear of getting "shot down." Only when these behavior patterns or personality traits become so inflexible or maladaptive that they cause significant personal distress or they impair the person's social or occupational functioning is a diagnosis of a personality disorder considered to be appropriate (DSM–III–R, p. 335).

Personality disorders are excessively rigid patterns of behaviors, or ways of relating to others, that ultimately become self-defeating because their rigidity prevents the person from adjusting to the demands of external events. These personality traits usually become evident by adolescence or early adulthood and continue through much of adult life, becoming so deeply ingrained that they are highly resistant to change.

Despite the self-defeating consequences of their behavior, people with personality disorders do not generally perceive a need to change themselves. Using psychodynamic terminology, the DSM–III–R notes that people with personality disorders tend to perceive their traits as **ego-syntonic**—as natural parts of themselves. As a result, people with personality disorders are more likely to be brought to the attention of mental-health professionals by others than to seek services themselves. In contrast, people with anxiety disorders or mood disorders tend to view their disturbed behaviors as **ego-dystonic.** They do not see their behaviors as parts of their self-identities and are thus more likely to seek help to relieve the distress caused by them.

As noted in Chapter 3, the DSM–III–R groups clinical syndromes on Axis I and personality disorders on Axis II. Thus, both clinical syndromes and personality disorders may be diagnosed in clients whose behavior meets the criteria for both classes of disorders. For example, a person may have an Axis I mood disorder, like major depression, and also show the characteristics associated with an Axis II personality disorder.

Types of Personality Disorders

The DSM–III–R lists eleven diagnosable personality disorders. They are divided into three clusters:

Cluster A: People who are perceived as odd or eccentric. This cluster includes paranoid, schizoid, and schizotypal personality disorders.
Cluster B: People whose behavior is overly dramatic, emotional, or erratic. This grouping consists of antisocial, borderline, histrionic, and narcissistic personality disorders.
Cluster C: People who often appear anxious or fearful in their behavior. This cluster includes avoidant, dependent, obsessive-compulsive, and passive-aggressive personality disorders.

In this chapter we consider each of these personality disorders, organized according to "cluster." We then discuss two personality disorders "proposed" in the DSM–III–R, but also characterized by the manual as "needing further study": sadistic personality disorder and self-defeating (masochistic) personality disorder. The provisional nature of these diagnoses reflects their

controversy and the need for additional evidence of their validity. Finally, we discuss disorders of impulse control which, like personality disorders, represent maladaptive and often self-defeating patterns of behavior.

PERSONALITY DISORDERS CHARACTERIZED BY ODD OR ECCENTRIC BEHAVIOR

This group of personality disorders includes paranoid, schizoid, and schizotypal disorders. The behaviors associated with these disorders are often perceived by others as odd or eccentric. People with these disorders often have difficulty relating to others, or they may have little or no interest in developing social relationships.

Paranoid Personality Disorder

The defining trait of the **paranoid personality disorder** is pervasive suspiciousness—the tendency to interpret other people's behavior as deliberately threatening or demeaning. People with the disorder are mistrustful of others, and their relationships suffer for it. They may be suspicious of co-workers and supervisors but can generally hold onto jobs.

The following case illustrates the unwarranted suspicion and reluctance to reveal or confide in others that typifies people with paranoid personalities:

■ An 85-year-old retired businessman was interviewed by a social worker to determine the health-care needs for himself and his wife. The man had no history of treatment for a mental disorder. He appeared to be in good health and mentally alert. He and his wife had been married for 60 years, and it appeared that his wife was the only person he's ever really trusted. He had always been suspicious of others. He would not reveal personal information to anyone but his wife, believing that others were out to take advantage of him. He had refused offers of help from acquaintances because he suspected their motives. When called on the telephone, he would refuse to give out his name until he determined the nature of the caller's business. He'd always involved himself in "useful work" to occupy his time, even during the 20 years of his retirement. He spends a good deal to time monitoring his investments and has had altercations with his stock broker when errors on his monthly statement prompted suspicion that his broker was attempting to cover up fraudulent transactions.

Adapted from Spitzer et al., 1989, pp. 163–164 ■

Paranoid personalities tend to be overly sensitive to criticism, whether real or imagined, and take offense at the smallest slight. They become quickly angered and hold grudges when they think they have been mistreated. They are unlikely to confide in others be-

differences. The DSM–III–R system places a greater emphasis on specific undesirable behaviors, such as a history of lying, cheating, or criminal behavior; or inability to maintain steady employment or meet family or financial responsibilities. Although he recognized specific antisocial behaviors as part of his overall profile, Cleckley also emphasized interpersonal and subjective aspects of the antisocial personality, such as superficial charm and lack of capacity for love, along with inability to profit from experience. By focusing more clearly on specific behaviors, the DSM–III–R may help improve reliability of diagnostic judgments of antisocial personality. Cleckley's clinical profile, however, provides researchers and clinicians a richer understanding of its psychological features:

1. *Superficial charm and intelligence.* The antisocial personality may be superficially charming, even while committing cruel or murderous actions. The antisocial personality may appear friendly and easy to talk to, giving no impression of being fraudulent or manipulative.

2. *Absence of anxiety in stressful situations.* The antisocial personality may be well-poised and cool under pressure, not displaying nervousness in stressful situations that might cause others to feel embarrassed or anxious.

3. *Insincerity and lack of truthfulness.* The antisocial personality is able to speak convincingly of feelings toward loved ones and appears to be sensitive to the needs of others, even while taking advantage of them.

4. *Lack of remorse and shame.* The antisocial personality feels no pangs of guilt or remorse, no feelings of shame for misdeeds and injurious behavior.

 Antisocial personalities can intentionally injure others without experiencing feelings of guilt or remorse.

5. *Inability to experience love or genuine emotion.* Although the antisocial personality may profess feelings of love, often convincingly so, the feelings are not genuine. The antisocial personality is egocentric, lacking the capacity to love and often hurting the purported objects of love. Lack of empathy and deep feelings may facilitate the callous mistreatment of "loved ones."

6. *Unreliability and irresponsibility.* Antisocial personalities lack senses of obligation, duty, or responsibility. They may walk away from jobs or desert their families, leaving behind a pile of unpaid bills.

7. *Impulsivity and disregard for socially acceptable behavior.* Antisocial personalities tend to act on the spur of the moment, drifting from place to place without concrete goals or destinations in mind. They may commit impulsive antisocial acts with little or no planning, such as stealing a car because they "felt like it," using illicit drugs, or passing bad checks when money runs out. The aimlessness with which they break the law separates them from committed criminals whose crimes are planned and rehearsed. Antisocial personalities seem unable to tolerate frustration or delay gratification. They demand to have (or take) what they want when they want it, even if it means stealing or otherwise breaking the law.

8. *Absence of delusions or irrational thinking.* Antisocial personalities seem to be clear-headed. Others may per-

---

A CLOSER LOOK
The Pause That Reflects

People with antisocial personalities are notoriously undeterred by punishment. They may repeatedly engage in self-defeating patterns of behavior, such as gambling and coming in late for work, despite the negative consequences of their behavior. Perhaps one reason that sociopaths fail to profit from experience is their difficulty in switching gears (changing their behavior) in the face of changing reinforcement contingencies. They may once have won at gambling or been able to sneak into work late without getting caught. But gambling losses eventually exceed winnings, and latenesses eventually put them on the unemployment line. Nonetheless, antisocial personalities are apparently stuck in maladaptive patterns of behavior—a response deficit that psychologists label **perseveration.**

Perserveration (and what might be done about it) was demonstrated in a recent card-playing experiment with antisocial personalities and normal control subjects (Newman et al., 1987). Subjects could win or lose money by playing repeated hands of cards. The odds of winning were "stacked," however, so that subjects were likely to win in the early rounds and lose in the later rounds. Both groups of subjects, people with antisocial personality disorders and normals, were free to stop at any time. Normals tended to play as long as they were winning and to quit when they started to lose as frequently as they won. They apparently recognized that the odds had turned against them and chose to take their winnings and leave. Antisocial personalities, however, tended to play on when their "luck" changed until they lost all their money or were out of cards.

However, in another condition, a forced delay of a few seconds was introduced between rounds. The antisocial personalities who had to pause terminated their playing when the odds changed just as did the normal control subjects. Giving antisocial personalities time to think about punishment apparently disrupted their perseveration and helped them to benefit from experience. Perhaps antisocial personalities would benefit from other treatments that focus on teaching them to stop and think about the consequences of their behavior before they act.

ceive them as holding firm, rational convictions and being capable of warm responses toward their families and loved ones.

9. *Inability to profit from experience.* Antisocial personalities may commit the same misdeeds repeatedly, despite a history of punishment. Punishment has little effect on their behavior; despite promises to "go straight," they eventually return to impulsive, antisocial behavior.

10. *Lack of insight.* Antisocial personalities are unable to see themselves as others do. They are more likely to blame others for their difficulties than to recognize that they have brought their problems on themselves.

Borderline Personality Disorder

People with borderline personality disorder have apparently failed to develop a stable or coherent self-image. They are uncertain about their goals, values, loyalties, careers, choice of friends, perhaps even their sexual orientations. This instability in self-image or identity leaves them with perpetual feelings of inner emptiness and boredom. They cannot tolerate being alone and will make desperate efforts to avoid feelings of abandonment, even when abandonment is only imaginary. Fear of abandonment by people they depend on renders them clinging and demanding, but their clutching may actually push people away. They may become enraged by signs of rejection, placing further strain on their relationships. Consequently, their feelings toward others are intense and unstable, alternating between extremes of adoration (when their needs are met) and hatred (when they are not). They tend to view other people as being all good or all bad, shifting abruptly in their attitudes from one extreme to the other. As a result, they tend to move from partner to partner in a series of brief and stormy relationships. People whom they had idealized are treated with contempt when these relationships end (Gunderson & Singer, 1986).

The label of borderline personality has been applied to people as diverse as Marilyn Monroe, Lawrence of Arabia, Adolf Hitler, and the philosopher Sören Kierkegaard (Sass, 1982). According to the DSM–III–R, the primary feature of **borderline personality disorder** is instability in self-image, relationships, and mood. Borderline personality disorder was first recognized as a diagnostic category in 1980 with the publication of the DSM–III. It is estimated to occur in perhaps 3 to 5 percent of the general population and has become one of the most commonly applied diagnoses in mental-health settings, with about 20 percent of psychiatric patients having received the diagnosis (Frances & Widiger, 1986). Some theorists believe that we live in highly fragmented and alienating times that give rise to the difficulties in establishing a cohesive identity and forming stable relationships that tend to characterize borderline problems (Sass, 1982). "Living on the edge," or border, can even be seen as a metaphor for an unstable society (Sass, 1982).

The term *borderline personality* was originally used to refer to people whose behavior appeared "on the border" between neuroses and psychoses. They appeared more severely impaired than most neurotics but not quite as dysfunctional as psychotics. It now seems, however, that borderline personality is perhaps closest to the mood disorders. Some researchers have found that nearly half of those diagnosed as borderline personalities also met the diagnostic criteria for either major depression or bipolar disorder (Pope et al, 1983). Many also met the criteria for other personality disorders, such as histrionic, narcissistic, and antisocial personality disorders. All in all, it remains unclear whether or not borderline personality disorder represents a distinct category. According to the DSM–III–R, borderline personalities generally maintain better contact with reality

A number of famous people, such as Marilyn Monroe and Lawrence of Arabia, have been described as having personality characteristics associated with borderline personality disorder.

than do psychotic people, although they may show transient psychotic behaviors during times of extreme stress.

Instability of moods is another characteristic of borderline personality disorder. Moods run the gamut from anger and irritability to depression and anxiety, with each lasting from a few hours to a few days. Borderline personalities have difficulty controlling anger and are prone to fights or smashing things. They often act on impulse, for example, running off and getting married to someone they have just met. This impulsive and unpredictable behavior is often self-destructive, involving spending sprees, drug abuse, sexual promiscuity, reckless driving, binge eating, or shoplifting. Suicidal threats or gestures and acts of self-mutilation, such as scratching their wrists or burning cigarettes on their arms, are seen in some extreme cases:

CLIENT: I've got such repressed anger in me; what happens is . . . I can't *feel* it; I get anxiety attacks. I get very nervous, smoke too many cigarettes. So what happens to me is I tend to *explode*. Into tears or hurting myself or whatever . . . because I don't know how to contend with all those mixed up feelings.

INTERVIEWER: What was the more recent example of such an "explosion"?

CLIENT: I was alone at home a few months ago; I was frightened! I was trying to get in touch with my boyfriend and I couldn't. . . . He was nowhere to be found. All my friends seemed to be busy that night and I had no one to talk to. . . . I just got more and more nervous and more and more agitated. Finally, *bang!*—I took out a cigarette and lit it and stuck it into my forearm. I don't know why I did it because I didn't really care for him all that much. I guess I felt I had to do something dramatic. . . ."

Adapted from Stone, 1980, p. 400 ∎

Sometimes self-mutilation is carried out in anger, or as a means of manipulating others. It's possible that such acts may sometimes be intended to counteract self-reported feelings of "numbness," particularly in times of stress.

Borderline personalities are difficult to work with in psychotherapy. They demand a great deal of support from therapists, calling them at all hours or acting suicidally to induce the therapist to help them. The outlook for therapy is poor, except for people who have a coexisting mood disorder that is more amenable to treatment (Pope et al., 1983). Their feelings toward therapists, as toward other people, undergo rapid alterations

between idealization and outrage. These abrupt shifts in feelings are interpreted by psychoanalysts as signs of "splitting," or the inability to reconcile the positive and negative aspects of one's experience of oneself and others, resulting in sudden shifts from moment to moment between both extremes. From the modern psychodynamic perspective, borderline people cannot synthesize positive and negative elements of personality into complete wholes; therefore, they fail to achieve fixed self-identities or images of others. Rather than viewing important figures in their lives as sometimes loving and as sometimes rejecting, borderline personalities shift back and forth between viewing them as all-good or all-bad (Abend et al., 1983), between idealization and abhorrence. The psychoanalyst Otto Kernberg, a leading authority on borderline personality, tells of a woman in her 30s whose attitude toward him vacillated in such a way:

> In one session, the patient may experience me as the most helpful, loving, understanding human being and may feel totally relieved and happy, and all the problems are solved. Three sessions later, she may berate me as the most ruthless, indifferent, manipulative person she has ever met. Total unhappiness about the treatment, ready to drop it and never come back. (Cited in Sass, 1982, p. 15. Copyright © 1982 by The New York Times Company. Reprinted by permission.)

Borderline personality disorder remains a perplexing and frustrating problem.

Histrionic Personality Disorder

Formerly called *hysterical* personality, **histrionic personality disorder** refers to people who show an excessive need to be the center of attention and who seek constant reassurance, praise, and approval from others. Derived from the Latin, *histrio*, which means "actor," people with histrionic personality disorder tend to be highly dramatic and emotional, but their emotions appear shallow, exaggerated, and rapidly shifting. The supplanting of *hysterical* with *histrionic* and the associated exchange of the roots *hystera* (meaning "uterus") and *histrio* allow professionals to distance themselves from the notion that the disorder is intricately bound up with being female. However, the DSM–III–R notes that the disorder is diagnosed more frequently in women than in men (1987, p. 349). Whether this gender discrepancy reflects the actual prevalence of the disorder, prejudices among diagnosticians, or other factors remains something of an open question.

People with histrionic personalities may become unusually upset by news of a sad event and cancel plans for the evening, inconveniencing their friends. They may exude exaggerated delight in meeting someone or become enraged when someone fails to notice their hair style. They may faint at the sight of blood or blush at the slightest faux pax. They tend to demand that others meet their needs for praise and attention and play the "victim" role when others fall short of their expectations. If they feel a touch of fever, they may insist that friends or family drop everything to rush them to the doctor. They tend to be self-centered and intolerant of delays of gratification; they want what they want when they want it. They grow quickly restless with routine and crave novelty, stimulation, and excitement. They are drawn to "fads." Others may see them as putting on airs or play acting, although they may evince a certain charm. They may enter a room with a flourish. They embellish their experiences with dramatic flair. But when pressed for details, they fail to paint in the specifics of their colorful tales. They tend to be flirtatious and seductive but are too wrapped up in themselves to develop intimate relationships or have deep feelings toward others. They are overly concerned with their physical appearance; glitter takes precedence over substance. In their relationships, they are frequently egocentric and inconsiderate of partners' needs. As a result, their relationships tend to be stormy and ultimately ungratifying.

People with histrionic personalities may be attracted to professions like modeling or acting, where they can be the center of attention. Despite outward successes, they may lack self-esteem and strive to impress others as a way of boosting feelings of self-worth. But if they suffer setbacks or lose their place in the limelight, their inner doubts may become exposed and result in depression.

The case of Marcella shows some of these features:

■ Marcella was a 36-year-old, attractive, but overly made up woman who was dressed in tight pants and high heels. Her hair was in a bird's nest of the type that had been popular when she was a teenager. Her social life seemed to bounce from relationship to relationship, from crisis to crisis. Marcella sought help from the psychologist at this time because her 17-year-old daughter, Nancy, had just been hospitalized for cutting her wrists. Nancy lived with Marcella and Marcella's current boyfriend, Morris, and there were constant arguments in the apartment. Marcella recounted the disputes that took place with high drama, waving her hands about, clanging the bangles that hung from her bracelets, and then clutching her breast. It was difficult having Nancy live at home, because Nancy had expensive tastes, was "always looking for attention," and flirted with Morris as a way of "flaunting her youth." Marcella saw herself as a doting mother and denied any possibility that she was in competition with her daughter.

Marcella came for a handful of sessions during which she basically ventilated her feelings and was encouraged to make decisions that might lead to a reduction of some of the pressures on her and her daughter. At the end of each session she said, "I feel so much better" and thanked the psychologist profusely. At termination of "therapy," she took the psychologist's hand and squeezed it endearingly. "Thank you so much, doctor," she said and made her exit.

The Authors' Files ■

Marcella also showed a number of features of narcissism, which we discuss next.

Narcissistic Personality Disorder

Narkissos was a handsome youth who, according to Greek myth, fell in love with his reflection in a spring. Because of his excessive self-love, in one version of

TABLE 9.2 Features of Normal Self-Interest as Compared to Self-Defeating Narcissism

Normal Self-Interest	Self-Defeating Narcissism
Appreciating acclaim, but not requiring it in order to maintain self-esteem.	Craving adoration insatiably; requiring acclaim in order to feel momentarily good about oneself.
Being temporarily wounded by criticism.	Being inflamed or crushed by criticism and brooding about it extensively.
Feeling unhappy but not worthless following failure.	Having enduring feelings of mortification and worthlessness triggered by failure.
Feeling "special" or uncommonly talented in some way.	Feeling incomparably better than other people, and insisting upon acknowledgment of that preeminence.
Feeling good about oneself, even when other people are being critical.	Needing constant support from other people in order to maintain one's feelings of well-being.
Being reasonably accepting of life's setbacks, even though they can be painful and temporarily destabilizing.	Responding to life's wounds with depression or fury.
Maintaining self-esteem in the face of disapproval or denigration.	Responding to disapproval or denigration with loss of self-esteem.
Maintaining emotional equilibrium despite lack of special treatment.	Feeling entitled to special treatment and becoming terribly upset when one is treated in an ordinary manner.
Being empathic and caring about the feelings of others.	Being insensitive to other people's needs and feelings; exploiting others until they become fed up.

Source: Adapted from Goleman, 1988a, p. C1.

The mythic character, Narkissos, who, according to one version of the myth, fell into a spring and drowned while admiring his reflection and was transformed by the gods into a flower.

Narcissistic personalities are often preoccupied with fantasies of success and power, ideal love, or recognition for their brilliance or beauty. They may pursue careers which provide opportunities for public recognition and adulation, such as acting, modeling, or politics. They may be deeply wounded by the slightest hint that they are not as special as they believe themselves to be.

the myth he was transformed by the gods into the flower we know as the narcissus. People with **narcissistic personality disorder** have inflated or grandiose senses of themselves. They brag about their accomplishments and expect others to shower them with praise. They are keenly sensitive to criticism and may be wounded by any hint that they are not as special as they fancy themselves to be. They expect others to notice their special qualities, even when their accomplishments are ordinary, and they enjoy basking in the light of adulation. They are self-absorbed and lack empathy for others. They demand to be the center of attention and show interest in others only when they are the focus of discussion. Although they share certain features with histrionic personalities, such as demanding to be the center of attention, they have a much more inflated view of themselves and are less melodramatic than histrionic personalities. Sometimes they are confused with borderline personalities. But narcissists are generally able to organize their thoughts and actions better than borderline personalities. They tend to be more successful in their careers and more capable of rising to positions of status and power. Relationships with people with borderline personalities tend to be somewhat less stable and more intense.

A certain amount of narcissism or self-aggrandizement may represent a healthful adjustment to insecurity, a shield from the effects of criticism and failure, or a motive for achievement (Goleman, 1988a). But an excess of narcissistic qualities can become unhealthful, especially when the cravings for reassurance and adulation become insatiable.

Table 9.2 compares what we refer to as normal self-interest with the self-defeating extremes of narcissism. Up to a point, self-interest helps us become successful and happy, but in more extreme cases, as with narcissism, it can cause serious problems in relationships and careers.

Narcissistic personalities tend to be preoccupied with fantasies of success and power, ideal love, or recognition for their brilliance or beauty. Narcissistic personalities, like histrionic personalities, may gravitate toward careers in which they can receive adulation, such as modeling, acting, or politics. Although they tend to exaggerate their accomplishments and abilities, many narcissistic personalities are vocationally successful. But they envy those who achieve yet greater success. Driven by an insatiable ambition, they may tirelessly devote themselves to work. They are driven to succeed, not for the pleasure of success, but for the adulation that comes with success. Because they need constant reassurance, narcissistic personalities are especially vulnerable to impaired self-esteem or what therapists call narcissistic injuries in response to criticism or rejection.

But interpersonal relationships are invariably strained by narcissists' interpersonal demands and by their lack of empathy and concern for other people. Narcissistic personalities seek the company of sycophants who lavish them with unconditional praise. Narcissistic personalities are often superficially charming and friendly, drawing people to them. But their interest in people is one-sided: They only want people who will serve their interests and nourish their feelings of self-importance (Goleman, 1988a). Narcissistic personalities have feelings of entitlement that lead them to exploit others. They treat sex partners as devices to be used for their own pleasure or to bolster their self-esteem.

The case of Bill illustrates several features of the narcissistic personality:

■ Most people agreed that Bill, a 35-year-old investment banker, had a certain charm. He was bright, articulate, and attractive. He possessed a keen sense of humor that drew people to him at social gatherings. He would always position himself in the middle of the room, where he could be the center of attention. The topics of conversation invariably focused on his "deals," the "rich and famous" people he had met, and his outmaneuvering of opponents. His next project was always bigger and more daring than the last. Bill loved an audience. His face would light up when others responded to him with praise or admiration for his business successes, which were always inflated beyond their true measure. But when the conversation shifted to other people, he would lose interest and excuse himself to make a drink or to call his answering machine. When hosting a party, he would urge guests to stay late and feel hurt if they had to leave early; he showed no sensitivity to, or awareness of, the needs of his friends.

The few friends he had maintained over the years had come to accept Bill on his own terms. They recognized that he needed to have his ego fed or that he would become cool and detached.

Bill had also had a series of romantic relationships with women who were willing to play the adoring admirer and make the sacrifices that he demanded—for a time. But they inevitably tired of the one-sided relationship or grew frustrated by Bill's inability to make a commitment or feel deeply toward them. Lacking empathy, Bill was unable to recognize other people's feelings and needs. His demands for constant attention from willing admirers did not derive from selfishness, but from a need to ward off underlying feelings of inadequacy and diminished self-esteem. It was sad, his friends thought, that Bill needed so much attention and adulation from others and that his many achievements were never enough to calm his inner doubts.

The Authors' Files ■

PERSONALITY DISORDERS CHARACTERIZED BY ANXIOUS OR FEARFUL BEHAVIOR

This cluster of personality disorders includes the avoidant, dependent, obsessive-compulsive, and passive-aggressive types. While the behaviors associated with these disorders are varied, they share in common a component of fear or anxiety.

Avoidant Personality Disorder

People with **avoidant personality disorder** are so terrified of rejection and criticism that they are generally unwilling to enter relationships without ardent reassurances of acceptance. As a result, they may have few close relationships outside their immediate families. They also tend to avoid group occupational or recreational activities for fear of rejection. They prefer to lunch alone at their desks. They shun company picnics and parties, unless they feel completely assured of being accepted.

Unlike schizoid personalities, with whom they share the feature of social withdrawal, avoidant personalities have interest in, and feelings of warmth toward, other people. However, fear of rejection prevents them from striving to meet their needs for affection and acceptance. In social situations, they tend to hug the walls and avoid conversing with others. They fear public embarrassment—the thought that others might see them blush, cry, or act nervously. They tend to stick to their routines and exaggerate the risks or effort involved in trying something new. For example, they may refuse to attend a party that is an hour away on the pretext that the late drive home would be too taxing.

The case of Harold illustrates several of the features of the avoidant personality:

■ Harold, a 24-year-old accounting clerk, had dated but a few women, and he had met them through family introductions. He never felt confident enough to approach a woman on his own. Perhaps it was his shyness that first attracted Stacy. Stacy, a 22-year-old secretary,

Avoidant personalities often keep to themselves because of fears of rejection.

worked alongside Harold and asked him if he would like to get together sometime after work. At first Harold declined, claiming some excuse, but when Stacy asked again a week later, Harold agreed, thinking that she must really like him if she were willing to pursue him. The relationship developed quickly, and soon they were dating virtually every night. The relationship was strained, however. Harold interpreted any slight hesitation in her voice as a lack of interest. He repeatedly requested reassurance that she cared about him and evaluated every word and gesture for evidence of her feelings. He was alert to the slightest cues of rejection—a change in her tone of voice, an embrace or a kiss that seemed perfunctory. After several months, Stacy decided she could no longer accept Harold's nagging, and the relationship ended. Harold assumed that Stacy had never truly cared for him.

The Authors' Files ■

Avoidant personality disorder looks similar to social phobia in that both problems involve fear of criticism or rejection and avoidance of threatening social situations. But according to the DSM–III–R, in social phobia, specific situations like parties or public speaking are avoided; people with avoidant personalities generally dodge interpersonal relationships. People with avoidant personalities may be unable to form and maintain relationships because of lack of social skills (Marks, 1985), whereas social phobics may be socially skillful but handicapped by anxiety in particular social situations, such as dating or giving a speech. In one laboratory study, social phobics were judged to be more socially skillful than were avoidant personalities, as measured, for example, by eye contact and appropriateness of tone of voice, in interacting with others and giving an impromptu speech (see Figure 9.1) (Turner et al., 1986). Despite differences such as these, the disorders can, and do, co-exist in many people.

Dependent Personality Disorder

Dependent personality disorder describes people who are overly dependent on others; they find it extremely difficult to do things on their own. People with dependent personality disorder may seek advice in making the smallest decision. Children or adolescents with the problem may look to their parents to select their clothes, their diets, their schools or colleges, even their friends. Adults with the disorder allow others to make important decisions for them. Sometimes they even permit others to make marital decisions, as in the case of Matthew:

■ Matthew, a 34-year-old single accountant who lives with his mother, sought treatment when his relationship with his girlfriend came to an end. His mother had objected to the marriage because his girlfriend was of a different religion, and—because "blood is thicker than water"—Matthew acceded to his mother's wishes and ended the relationship. Yet he is angry with himself and at his mother because he feels that she is too possessive to ever grant him permission to get married. He describes his mother

FIGURE 9.1

Ratings of social skills of social phobics and avoidant personalities when interacting with same-sex and opposite-sex persons, and when giving an impromptu speech.
Source: Turner, Beidel, Dancu, & Keyes (1986).

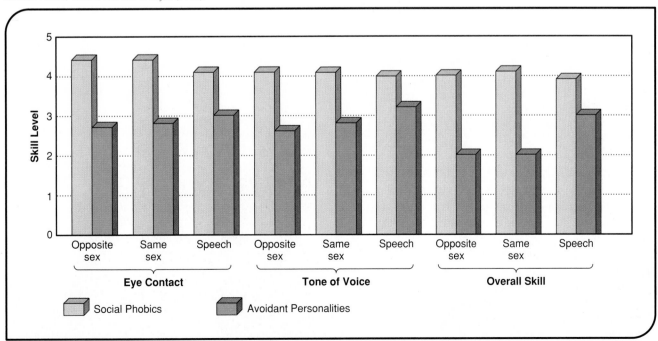

as a domineering woman who "wears the pants" in the family and is accustomed to having things her way. Matthew alternates between resenting his mother and thinking that perhaps she knows what's best for him.

Matthew's position at work is several levels below what would be expected of someone of his talent and educational level. Several times he has declined promotions in order to avoid increased responsibilities that would require him to supervise others and make independent decisions. He has maintained close relationships with two friends since early childhood and has lunch with one of them on every working day. On days his friend calls in sick, Matthew feels lost. Matthew has lived his whole life at home, except for one year away at college. He returned home because of homesickness.

Adapted from Spitzer et al., 1989, pp. 123–125 ∎

After marriage, dependent personalities may rely on spouses for decisions such as where they should live, which neighbors they should cultivate, how they should discipline the children, what jobs they should take, how they should budget money, and where they should go on vacations. Like Matthew, people with dependent personality disorder avoid positions of responsibility. They turn down challenges and promotions, and they work beneath their potentials. They tend to be overly sensitive to criticism and are preoccupied with fears of rejection and abandonment. They may be devastated by the end of a close relationship or by the prospect of living on their own, feeling inadequate to manage their lives. Because of fear of rejection, they often subordinate their wants and needs to those of others; they may agree with incorrect statements and do degrading things to ingratiate themselves.

The DSM–III–R notes that dependent personality is diagnosed more frequently in women. The diagnosis is often applied to women who, for fear of abandonment, tolerate husbands who openly cheat on them, physically abuse them, or gamble away the family's resources. Underlying feelings of inadequacy and helplessness discourage them from taking effective action, and, in a vicious circle, their passivity encourages further abuse, leading them to feel yet more inadequate and helpless.

Dependent personality disorder has been linked to a number of physical problems such as hypertension, cancer, and gastrointestinal disorders like ulcers and colitis (Greenberg & Bornstein, 1988a). There also appears to be a link between dependent personality and what psychodynamic theorists refer to as "oral" behavior problems, such as smoking, eating disorders, and alcoholism (Greenberg & Bornstein, 1988b). Psychodynamic writers trace dependent behaviors to the utter dependence of the newborn baby and the baby's seeking of nourishment through oral means (suckling). From infancy, they suggest, people associate provision of food with love. Food may come to symbolize feelings of love, and people with dependent personalities may overeat as a symbolic way of expressing their needs for love.

Research does show that dependent personalities are less self-reliant and more reliant on others for support and guidance as compared to nondependent people (Greenberg & Bornstein, 1988a). Dependent personalities often attribute their problems to physical rather than emotional causes and seek support and advice from medical doctors rather than psychologists or mental health counselors (Greenberg & Bornstein, 1988b).

Obsessive-Compulsive Personality Disorder

The defining features of **obsessive-compulsive personality disorder** include such traits as orderliness, perfectionism, rigidity, difficulty coping with ambiguity, difficulties expressing feelings, and a tendency to be overly meticulous in work habits. But unlike obsessive-compulsive (anxiety) disorder, there are no true obsessions or compulsions. It is possible, however, for someone with an obsessive-compulsive anxiety disorder to also possess the inflexible and maladaptive characteristics associated with the personality disorder. In such cases, both diagnoses would be appropriate.

People with obsessive-compulsive personality disorder are so preoccupied with achieving perfection that they literally find themselves unable to get things done on time. Their efforts inevitably fall short of their expectations and they force themselves to redo their work. Or they may ruminate about how to prioritize their assignments rather than get started. They focus on details that others perceive as trivial and, as the saying goes, they often fail to see the forest for the trees. Their rigidity impairs their social relationships; they insist on doing things their way rather than compromising, and their zeal for work prevents them from participating in normal social and leisure activities. They also find

Obsessive-compulsive personalities often have excessive needs for orderliness in their environment.

it difficult to make decisions; they postpone or avoid decisions for fear of making the wrong choice. They tend to be overly rigid about morality and ethics because of inflexibility in their personality rather than because of deep-seated religious or moral convictions. They tend to be overly formal in their relationships and find it difficult to express feelings or give time or money to others. It is hard for them to relax and enjoy pleasant activities; they worry about what their diversions are costing in terms of money and time.

Consider the case of Jerry:

■ Jerry, a 34-year-old systems analyst, was perfectionistic, overly concerned with details, and rigid in his behavior. Jerry was married to Marcia, a graphics artist. He insisted on scheduling their free time hour by hour and became unnerved when they deviated from his agenda. He would circle a parking lot repeatedly in search of just the right parking spot to ensure that his car would not be scraped by another. He refused to have the apartment painted for over a year because he couldn't decide on the color. He had arranged all the books in their bookshelf alphabetically and insisted that every book be placed in its proper position.

Jerry never seemed to be able to relax. Even on vacation, he was bothered by thoughts of work that he had left behind and by fears that he might lose his job. He couldn't understand how people could lie on the beach and let all their worries evaporate in the summer air. "Something can always go wrong," he figured, "so how can people let themselves go?"

The Authors' File ■

Passive-Aggressive Personality Disorder

The defining attribute of **passive-aggressive person-ality disorder** is the tendency to communicate hostile feelings through passive means rather than openly or directly. Passive-aggressive personalities are not "hot-headed" or blatantly aggressive; in fact, they are quite the contrary. They express their resentments through procrastination, dawdling, sulking, work slowdowns, intentional errors, convenient "forgetting," or other ob-structive tactics. Consider the case of a 34-year-old psy-chiatrist:

■ The psychiatrist had recently been asked to resign his clinic job, for such reasons as repeated lateness in arriving at work and at meetings, missed appointments, forgotten assignments, failure to comply with instructions, lateness in filing statistics, and lack of motivation. The psychiatrist felt that he had been treated unfairly and that his supervisor was excessively demanding and obsessive. But he also reported a long history of similar difficulties with authority figures. During childhood, he was insubordinate and oppositional with his mother and teachers and was sent to an all-boys preparatory school where the male teachers made him "toe the line." But he continued to resent taking direction from teachers and stubbornly wanted to have things his way. Although he was a brilliant student, his performance was erratic; he worked only hard enough to please himself and he "punished" the teachers he resented by refusing to carry out assignments.

Unhappily married, the psychiatrist sees his wife as "nitpicking." He generally refuses to assume household responsibilities and often leaves the few tasks he does take on incomplete. Though he has a charming side to his personality, his friends become annoyed with him when he fails to go along with group decisions concerning choice of activities and restaurants. He expresses his objections by sulking all night long or by "forgetting" to bring his wallet.

Adapted from Spitzer et al., 1989, pp. 107–109. ■

As we see in this case, even helping professionals are not "immune" to personality problems that impair social and occupational functioning (Spitzer et al., 1989). In another example, a husband who resents his wife's request to help out with the dishes may not state his resistance openly but react by doing a poor job or "accidentally" breaking a dish. "Look," he can protest, "I tried to do a good job. Could I help it if I'm clumsy?" A reluctant employee who is given a rush job for a meeting may jam the copy machine so that the job cannot be completed in time. The employee maintains a veil of innocence and can say, "I would have finished the work if the copy machine didn't go on the blink when I needed it."

Passive-aggressive people tend to be complainers. They protest to co-workers that supervisors are taking advantage of them by giving them an unreasonable amount of work. They resist any suggestion that their work loads are reasonable or that they can be more productive. When asked to do something they prefer not to do, they may sulk or become so argumentative that the person making the request feels that it may not be worth the effort.

Passive-aggressive people are often lacking in self-confidence and become dependent on others. But their passive-aggressive behavior ultimately proves self-de-feating. The passive-aggressive employee may be passed over for promotion or fired. At home, passive-aggressive behavior may give rise to marital troubles. Passive-ag-gressive people usually show little insight into how they bring about their own problems.

Note, however, that not all passive-aggressive be-havior is evidence of passive-aggressive personality dis-order. In some situations direct assertive behavior may be discouraged or punished, as by the police or the military. The diagnostic category applies only to people whose passive-aggressive behavior is persistent, long-standing, and widespread—cutting across many situa-tions in which more direct means of expressing dissatis-faction are available.

PROPOSED PERSONALITY DISORDERS "NEEDING FURTHER STUDY"

The DSM–III–R recognizes that some proposed personality disorders require further study before they might be officially included in the diagnostic manual. The two diagnoses proposed for further study are **sadistic personality disorder** and **self-defeating (masochistic) personality disorder.** The tentative nature of these diagnoses reflects their controversy and the need for further documentation of their validity.

Sadistic Personality Disorder

Sadism usually becomes evident in early adulthood. The sadistic personality is intentionally cruel and enjoys making other people suffer. Cruelty may take the form of physical violence or humiliation. Sadists pick their targets strategically; they treat family members or subordinates with cruelty but show respect toward people of higher status or in authority. Acts of physical violence or cruelty are intended to establish social dominance, not merely to facilitate crimes in which money is the goal. Sadists lack empathy and respect for others and may purposely humiliate them in public or subject them to harsh punishment.

The DSM–III–R provides examples of a father who severely punishes his child for a minor breach of table manners and of a teacher who forces a student to spend hours in detention following a minor infraction of the rules. Sadists seek to control others, sometimes through threatening glances, sometimes through threats or acts of violence. Only rarely do people with sadistic personality disorder seek treatment. They are usually seen by therapists when they are remanded by the courts following arrest for a crime or in the course of an investigation of a charge of child or spouse abuse.

There is no question about the existence of sadistic behavior. The controversy involves its inclusion in the DSM as a "mental disorder." If sadistic people can be "diagnosed" as having "mental illnesses," they may then claim that they are not criminally responsible for their misconduct by reason of "mental disease or defect."

 It has not been demonstrated that sadistic people are suffering from mental disorders. In fact, inclusion of sadistic personality disorder as a "proposed" disorder in the DSM stirs controversy because of the possibility that some people who receive the label may try to evade criminal responsibility for misconduct by reason of "mental disease or defect."

Self-Defeating Personality Disorder

Self-defeating personality disorder refers to a pattern of self-defeating behavior, generally beginning by early adulthood, which is revealed in a variety of life contexts. People with self-defeating personality disorder are drawn to others who mistreat them or make them suffer and may resist efforts of others to help them. They tend to avoid or reject sexual partners who are caring and loving. They may avoid any opportunities for pleasure, including vacations and social outings. The label self-defeating personality disorder was proposed to supplant an earlier label of **masochistic personality** to avoid the implication that people who show self-defeating behavior derive pleasure from pain and suffering.

One objection to this diagnosis has been that it seems to blame the victims in abusive relationships, such as victims of wife beating, by portraying them as having "mental disorders" that might prompt them to taunt their mates. Instead, the perpetrators of abuse—for example, wife beaters—should be perceived as violent criminals. The DSM–III–R argues that the diagnosis is intended to be used in cases of spouse abuse only when the abuse is part of a persistent pattern of involvement in self-defeating situations and relationships when better behavioral options are available. Still, the diagnosis requires further study to ensure that it is not applied in a way that further victimizes the victims of abuse. In addition, a recent research study failed to show that the proposed diagnosis added any significant information concerning clinical features that are not already provided by existing diagnoses (Reich, 1987). So its clinical utility remains in doubt.

Problems with the Classification of Personality Disorders

Various problems in the classification of personality disorders have raised concern among researchers and clinicians. Nagging questions remain about the reliability and validity of the diagnoses of personality disorders. Another concern is that there may be too much overlap among the categories to justify so many discrete categories of personality disorders. Another is that the present classification seems to blur the distinctions between normal and abnormal variations in personality. Yet another is that some categories of personality disorder may have underlying sexist biases. Finally, there is concern that the diagnoses may confuse labels with explanations.

■ **Undetermined Reliability and Validity**   In Chapter 3 we mentioned that the present DSM system sought to clarify the ambiguities in the diagnostic criteria of earlier versions by providing descriptive criteria that more tightly define particular disorders. But evidence remains to be determined as to the reliability and validity of the new definitions. Early indications were that reliability of Axis II personality disorder diagnoses (in DSM–III) were not as strong as desired (Drake & Vaillant, 1985). It remains to be seen whether the revised version, the DSM–III–R, or future versions, will increase the reliability of these diagnoses.

■ **Overlap Among Disorders**   A second problem is a high degree of overlap among the descriptions of the personality disorders. Overlap undermines the DSM's conceptual clarity or purity by increasing the number of cases that seem to fit two or more diagnostic categories (Livesley et al., 1986; Livesley, 1985; Morey, 1988). While some of the personality disorders have quite distinct features, many appear to share numerous traits. For example, the same person may have traits suggestive of dependent personality disorder (inability to make decisions or initiate activities independently) and of avoidant personality disorder (extreme social anxiety and heightened sensitivity to criticism). The DSM–III–R deals with this problem by directing the clinician to diagnose two or more personality disorders when the criteria for more than one type are met. However, given the degree of overlap that exists, it may be argued that the DSM–III–R class of personality disorders is divided into too many categories (Livesley et al., 1985). One recent study found that as many as 25 percent of diagnosed schizoid personality disorders could also be diagnosed as avoidant personality disorders, for example (Reich & Noyes, 1986). Thus, some "disorders" may actually represent different aspects of the same disorder, not distinct diagnostic categories. It has been argued, for example, that the schizoid, avoidant, and schizotypal personality disorders should be regarded as different aspects of a schizoid personality (Livesley et al., 1985).

■ **Difficulty in Making the Distinction Between Variations in Normal Behavior and Abnormal Behavior**
Another problem with the diagnosis of personality disorders is that they involve traits which, in lesser degrees, describe the behavior of most normal individuals. Feeling suspicious now and then does not mean that you have a paranoid personality disorder. Nor does the tendency to exaggerate your own importance mean that you are narcissistic. Most of us now and then express anger in indirect ways, but this behavior pattern does not render us passive-aggressive personalities. We may avoid social interactions for fear of embarrassment or rejection without having an avoidant personality disorder, and we may be especially conscientious in our work without having an obsessive-compulsive personality disorder. Because the defining attributes of these disorders are commonly occurring personality

traits, clinicians should only apply these diagnostic labels when the patterns are so pervasive that they interfere with the individual's functioning or cause significant personal distress.

It can be difficult indeed to draw the line between normal variations in behavior and personality disorders.

Sexist Biases   Another problem is that certain types of personality disorders may represent subtle forms of sexism. The concept of the histrionic or hysterical personality, for example, seems to be drawn as a parody of the traditional stereotype of the feminine personality: flighty, emotional, shallow, attention-seeking. After all, if the feminine stereotype corresponds to a mental disorder, what of the masculine stereotype of the "macho male"? It may be possible to show that overly masculinized traits are associated with significant distress or impairment in social or occupational functioning in certain males; after all, highly masculinized males often get into many fights and experience difficulties working for female bosses. But there is no present diagnosis that categorizes "macho males" as personality disordered. The diagnosis of dependent personality disorder may also unfairly stigmatize women who have been socialized into dependent roles as showing a "mental disorder." Women may be at greater risk of receiving diagnoses of histrionic or dependent personality disorders because clinicians perceive these patterns as existing more commonly among women or because women are more likely than men to be socialized into these behavior patterns.

The concepts of histrionic and dependent personality disorders may be sexist. It could be argued that the descriptions of these disorders are parodies of the traditional feminine sex-role stereotype.

■ **Confusion of Labels with Explanations**   It may seem obvious that we should not confuse diagnostic labels with explanations, but in practice the distinction is sometimes clouded. If we confuse labeling with explanation, we may fall into the trap of circular reasoning. For example, what is wrong with the logic of the following statements?

1.   John's behavior is antisocial.
2.   Therefore, John has an antisocial personality disorder.
3.   John's behavior is antisocial because he has an antisocial personality disorder.

A CLOSER LOOK
Why Do Women Stay in Abusive Relationships?

Approximately 1.8 million American women are beaten by their husbands each year, and about 1,700 die as a result of these attacks. Yet about half of the abused women who seek professional assistance return to their abusive husbands or partners (Strube, 1988).

Why do women remain in abusive relationships or take back abusive partners after a separation? Are they driven by unconscious, masochistic needs to punish themselves? This traditional explanation essentially blames the victim for her lot, yet research does not support the view that abused women are masochistic.

> **?** Women who remain in abusive relationships have not been shown to be masochistic. The concept of masochism has the unfortunate effect of blaming the victim for her troubles.

According to Strube (1988), victims of spouse abuse may be better understood as survivors of trauma than as masochists. Their reactions as survivors may have much in common with those of other survivors, such as former hostages or kidnap victims. In all these cases, exposure to abuse may impair the victims' ability to think clearly enough to develop effective problem-solving strategies and plans. In many cases, battered wives have no economic means of support for themselves or their children and so may fear becoming destitute if they leave the batterer.

Viewing the victim as a survivor also shifts blame away from her onto the perpetrator. A recent review of the literature focuses on some of the factors that may help to explain how the trauma of spouse abuse may affect the battered woman's ability to cope effectively (Follingstad et al., 1988):

1. *Shattering the myth of personal invulnerability.* Most people maintain a belief that they are personally invulnerable to traumas or tragic events (Janoff-Bulman & Frieze, 1983). They maintain the illusion that although bad things (like crippling traffic accidents, rapes, and cancers) may happen to other people, they are immune. This illusion is believed to help people function by creating a sense of security (Frieze, 1979). But this sense of invulnerability may be broken in women exposed to the trauma of abuse. If women can be brutalized by men in whom they had placed their trust, other bad things can also happen. The shield of invulnerability cracks. The senses of safety and security that women felt in their own homes are also destroyed.

    The toll of victimization on the battered woman may be greater than that experienced by victims of other traumas, because the agent of abuse was trusted and loved. Betrayal of trust may intensify women's emotional reactions and further impair ability to cope with trauma.

2. *Reduced problem-solving ability.* Trauma may hamper women's abilities to weigh alternative solutions to their problems. Victims may become so preoccupied with the immediate problem of preventing recurrent beatings that they cannot focus on ways of making life changes that will extricate them and their children from the marriages. Women may even come to believe that they cannot take control of events

Viewing abused women as survivors, rather than as masochists, may help encourage the development of programs which provide supportive services to victims of domestic violence, like the one pictured here.

TABLE 9.3: Rationalizations That Serve to Justify Spouse Abuse

Type of Rationalization	Examples
Denial of the injury	Refusing to recognize the harm done by the batterer ("He didn't really mean it").
Redirecting blame from the batterer to external factors beyond his control	Blaming the battering on alcoholism and other problems. The battered woman may come to think that the answer to the problem lies in helping the batterer to control his drinking, rather than seeking to help herself.
Denial of victimization	Tending to blame herself for the abuse.
Denial of options	Refusing to recognize that other solutions are possible.
Appeal to the salvation ethic	Focusing on helping the husband solve his problems but in the meantime accepting continued abuse.
Appeal to higher loyalties	Accepting abuse as a measure of duty to a higher ethic, such as a religious or marital obligation, or "keeping the family together."
Legitimizing violence as normal behavior	Perceiving violence as a normal aspect of family life.

and that submission is the only realistic way of preventing further abuse (Cooper, 1976).

3. *Stress-related reactions.* Battered women may also experience a form of post-traumatic stress disorder (PTSD) that further impairs coping ability. As with soldiers who have had traumatic combat experiences, battered women may reexperience beatings in the form of nightmares, flashbacks, and intrusive images of abuse; become numbed to the environment; have sleep disturbances; feel anxious in the presence of cues or reminders of beatings; and avoid situations or stimuli that are connected with beatings. Anxiety and feelings of dread may lead battered women to withdraw from the outside world and cut off support from other people. Feelings of pessimism, anger, guilt, and depression are common, along with suicidal thoughts and attempts. Battered women may also develop alcohol or drug abuse (Finn, 1985) that further impairs their functioning.

4. *Thought conversion.* The effects of chronic victimization have been well chronicled in reports of other victims of chronic trauma, such as hostages or kidnap victims. Hostages and kidnap victims sometimes experience a conversion in attitude and come to regard their captors with positive or sympathetic feelings (see Ochberg, 1966), at the same time developing negative feelings toward potential rescuers. Battered women may similarly come to view their tormenters in more sympathetic terms.

5. *Finding meaning in the abuse.* According to existential psychiatrist Viktor Frankl (1963), people have a basic psychological need to find meaning in their experiences, even in brutal victimization. Some battered women may try to find meaning in, or justify, their situations through **rationalization.** As shown in Table 9.3, Farraro and Johnson (1983) have chronicled some of the more common rationalizations that may serve to justify abuse.

6. *Learned helplessness.* According to the learned helplessness model, people who undergo persistent, uncontrollable traumas may develop a sense of helplessness that saps motivation to overcome the trauma. Helplessness may develop as the abused woman finds that her repeated attempts to make changes in the relationship fail or when her requests for external help are met with frustrating "run-arounds" or lack of concern from criminal-justice or mental-health personnel.

7. *Difficulties handling troubling emotions.* Battered women may have difficulty handling their anger toward the abuser, perhaps because they have learned, from his example, that anger is a dangerous or uncontrollable emotion (Carmen, 1984). Unexpressed anger may become redirected inward, filling victims with self-blame and self-loathing, which, in turn, lead to resignation, depression, and self-destructive behaviors ranging from substance abuse to suicide attempts (Carmen et al., 1984; Hibelman & Fouts, 1978). Depression may further hamper women's abilities to change their lives.

When we see battered women as victims and survivors, not as masochists, we supplant blaming the victims with efforts to understand the psychological factors that lead them to feel trapped in their relationships. Such understanding may facilitate the development of programs that help abused women make hard decisions and counteract tendencies toward rationalization, self-hatred, and denial.

The statements are circular in reasoning because they (1) use behavior to make a diagnosis and then (2) use the diagnosis as an explanation for the behavior. We may be guilty of circular reasoning in our everyday speech. Consider: "John never gets his work in on time; therefore, he is lazy. John doesn't get his work in because he's lazy." The label allows for general conversation, but lacks scientific rigor. In order for a construct such as laziness to have scientific rigor, we need to understand the causes of laziness and the factors that help to maintain it, and not fall into the mistake of confusing the label we attach to the behavior with the cause of the behavior itself.

Personality disorders are convenient labels for identifying common patterns of ineffective and ultimately self-defeating behavior, but labels do not explain their causes. Still, the development of an accurate descriptive system is an important step toward scientific explanation. The establishment of reliable diagnostic categories sets the stage for valid research into causation and treatment.

THEORETICAL PERSPECTIVES

In this section we consider various theoretical perspectives on the personality disorders. Many of the theoretical accounts of disturbed personality derive from the psychodynamic model, and so we begin by reviewing both traditional Freudian and more recent psychodynamic models.

Psychodynamic Perspectives

Traditional Freudian theory focused on Oedipal problems as the foundation for many abnormal behaviors, including personality disorders such as antisocial personality. Freud's theory of psychosexual development recounts processes by which children come to control their primitive impulses and develop concern for others. A particularly salient event in the process is the Oedipus complex. Freud believed that the moral conscience, or superego, represented the proper resolution of the Oedipus complex. Children normally resolve the Oedipus complex by forsaking incestuous wishes for the opposite-sex parent and identifying with the same-sex parent. As a result, they incorporate the parent's moral principles in the form of a personality structure called the superego. Many factors may interfere with appropriate identification, however, such as a weak or absent father or an antisocial parent. When such interferences sidetrack the normal developmental process, children fail to develop the moral constraints that prevent antisocial behavior and are also free from feelings of guilt or remorse that normally follow behavior that is hurtful to others. Freud's account of moral development fo-

cused mainly on the development of males. Freud has been criticized for failing to account for the moral development of females.

More recent psychodynamic theories have generally focused on the earlier, pre-Oedipal period of about 18 months to 3 years, during which infants are theorized to begin to develop a sense of separateness or an identity apart from their parents. These recent advances in psychodynamic theory focus on the development of the sense of self in explaining such disorders as narcissistic and borderline personality disorders, as we see next.

■ **Hans Kohut**   One of the principal shapers of modern psychodynamic concepts is Hans Kohut, whose views are labeled **self-psychology.** Kohut focused much of his attention on the development of the narcissistic personality.

Kohut (1966) believed that a self-image riddled with insecurity lay beneath the inflated veneers of people with narcissistic personality disorders. The narcissist's self-esteem is like a reservoir that needs to be constantly replenished lest it run dry. A steady flow of praise and attention by others prevents the narcissist from being withered by feelings of inadequacy and insecurity. A sense of grandiosity helps narcissistic personalities mask their feelings of worthlessness. Failures or disappointments threaten to expose these feelings and to drive the narcissist into a state of depression. Narcissistic personalities may defend themselves from despair by diminishing the importance of disappointments or failures. They may become enraged by people who fail to protect them from disappointment or who decline to bathe them in reassurance, praise, and admiration. They may become infuriated by slight criticism, no matter how well intentioned; or they may mask feelings of rage and humiliation by adopting a facade of cool indifference. Narcissistic personalities can make difficult psychotherapy clients, for they may become enraged when therapists puncture their inflated self-images in order to help them develop more realistic self-concepts.

Kohut believed that early childhood is characterized by a normal stage of "healthy narcissism." Infants feel powerful, as though the world revolves around them. Infants also normally perceive older people, especially parents, as idealized towers of strength and wish to be one with them in order to share this power. Empathic parents reflect their children's inflated perceptions, making children feel that anything is possible and thereby nourishing children's self-esteem. Even empathic parents are critical from time to time, however; they puncture their children's grandiose senses of self or else fail to measure up to the children's grandiose views of them. Gradually, unrealistic expectations begin to dissolve and are replaced by more realistic appraisals. Normal childhood narcissism sets the stage for subsequent ego development. Earlier grandiose self-images form the basis for assertiveness later in childhood and set the stage for ambitious striving in adulthood. In adolescence, childhood idealization is transformed into realistic admiration for parents, teachers, and friends. In adulthood, these ideas develop into a set of internal ideals, values, and goals.

Lack of parental empathy and support, however, may set the stage for pathological narcissism in adulthood. Children who are not prized by parents may fail to develop a sturdy sense of self-esteem and be unable to tolerate even slight blows to their self-worth. Such children develop damaged self-concepts and feel incapable of being loved and admired because of personal inadequacies or flaws. Pathological narcissistic personalities construct grandiose facades as a way of avoiding facing their perceived inadequacies; they fail to shape realistic self-images and images of others that incorporate imperfections. But the facade of self-perfection is shaky and fails to provide a secure sense of self-worth. Narcissistic personalities need constant reassurances to maintain their inflated veneers of self-esteem and are vulnerable to painful self-depreciation if they fail to achieve their goals or suffer rejection.

Kohut's approach to therapy provides narcissistic clients an initial opportunity to express their grandiose self-images and to idealize the therapist. Over time, however, the therapist helps clients explore the childhood roots of their narcissism and gently points out imperfections in both clients and themselves to encourage clients to form more realistic images of themselves and others.

■ **Otto Kernberg** Modern psychodynamic views of the borderline personality also trace the disorder to difficulties in self-development in early childhood. Otto Kernberg (1967), a leading psychodynamic theorist, views borderline personality in terms of a pre-Oedipal failure to develop a sense of constancy and unity in one's image of the self and others. Kernberg proposes that childhood failure to synthesize contradictory images of good and bad results in **identity diffusion** and tendencies toward **splitting**—shifting back and forth between viewing oneself and other people as "all good" or "all bad."

In Kernberg's view, parents, even excellent parents, invariably fail to meet all their children's needs. Infants therefore face the early developmental challenge of reconciling images of the nurturing, comforting "good mother" with those of the withholding, frustrating "bad mother." Failure to reconcile these opposing images into a realistic unified and stable parental image may fixate children in the pre-Oedipal period. As adults, then, they may retain the rapidly shifting attitudes that borderline personalities experience toward their therapists and others.

■ **Margaret Mahler** Mahler, another influential modern psychodynamic theorist, explained borderline personality disorder in terms of childhood separation from the mother figure. Mahler and her colleagues (Mahler et al., 1975; Mahler & Kaplan, 1977) believe that during the first year the infant develops a **symbiotic** attachment to its mother. *Symbiosis* is a biological term that derives from Greek roots meaning "to live together" and describes life patterns in which two species lead interdependent lives. In psychology, symbiosis is likened to a state of oneness in which the child's identity is fused with the mother's. Normally, children gradually differentiate their own identities or senses of self from their mothers'; the process is called **separation-individuation.** Separation is development of a separate psychological and biological identity from the mother. Individuation is recognition of the personal characteristics that define one's self-identity. Separation-individuation may be a stormy process. Children may vacillate between seeking greater independence and moving closer to, or "shadowing," the mother, which is seen as a wish for reunion. The mother may disrupt normal separation-individuation by refusing to let go of the child or by too quickly pushing the child toward independence. The tendencies of the borderline personality to react to others with ambivalence, to alternate between love and hate, is suggestive to Mahler of earlier ambivalences toward the separation-individuation process. Thus, borderline personality disorder may arise from failure to master this developmental challenge successfully.

Psychodynamic theories of the personality disorders remain controversial. All in all, psychodynamic theory provides a rich theoretical mine for the understanding of the development of several personality disorders. But some critics contend that theories of such disorders as borderline personality disorder and narcissistic personality disorder are based largely on inferences drawn from the behavior and retrospective accounts of adults, and not on observations of children (Sass, 1982). Mahler's theory has also been challenged by evidence that even infants show a certain degree of psychological differentiation from others (Klein, 1981). We may also question whether direct comparisons should be made between normal childhood experiences and abnormal behaviors in adulthood. For example, the ambivalences that characterize the adult borderline personality may bear only a superficial relationship to children's vacillations between closeness and separation with maternal figures during separation-individuation.

Learning Perspectives

Learning theorists tend to focus more on the acquisition of behaviors than on the notion of enduring personality traits. Similarly, they think more in terms of maladaptive behaviors than of disorders of "personality." Personality traits are theorized to steer behavior—to provide consistent behavior in diverse situations. Many critics, however, like Walter Mischel (1979), argue that behavior is actually not as consistent across situations as trait theorists would suggest. Behavior may depend more on the situational demands than on inherent traits. For example, we may describe a person as lazy and unmotivated. But is such a person always lazy and unmotivated? Or are there some situations in which the person may be energetic and ambitious? What differences in these situations might explain these differences in behavior? Learning theorists are generally interested in defining the learning histories and circumstances that give rise to maladaptive behaviors and the reinforcers that maintain them.

Learning theorists suggest that many salient experiences that contribute to maladaptive habits (personality disorders) occur in childhood. Repeated punishment or lack of reward or encouragement of childhood assertiveness and exploratory behavior may result in dependent behaviors, or a dependent personality, for example. Obsessive-compulsive personality disorder may be connected with excessive parental discipline or overcontrol in childhood. Social-learning theorist Theodore Millon (1981) suggests that children whose behavior is rigidly controlled and punished by parents, even for slight transgressions, may develop inflexible, perfectionistic standards for their behavior. As such children mature, they may strive to develop an area in which they excel, such as schoolwork or athletics, as a way of avoiding parental criticism or punishment. Overattention to a single area of development may prevent them from becoming well-rounded so that they squelch spontaneity and avoid new challenges or risks, and so develop behaviors associated with the obsessive-compulsive personality pattern.

Millon suggests that histrionic personality disorder may be rooted in childhood experiences that connect reinforcers, such as parental attention, with physical appearance and performances for others, especially when reinforcers are dispensed inconsistently. Inconsistent attention teaches children not to take approval for granted and to strive for it constantly. People with histrionic personalities may also have identified with parents who are dramatic, emotional, and attention-seeking. Extreme sibling rivalry would further heighten motivation to perform.

Social-learning theories emphasize the role of reinforcement in explaining the origins of antisocial behaviors. Leonard Ullmann and Leonard Krasner (1975) proposed, for example, that antisocial personalities fail to respond to other people as potential reinforcers. Most children learn to treat others, especially parents, as reinforcing agents because others reinforce them with praise when they behave appropriately and punish them for misbehavior. Reinforcement and punishment provide feedback (information about social expectations) that helps children modify their behavior to maximize the chances of future rewards and minimize the risks of future punishment. As a consequence children become socialized; they become sensitive to the demands of powerful others, usually parents and teachers, and learn to modify their behavior accordingly. Thus they adapt to social living. They learn what to do and what to say, how to dress, and how to act to attain reinforcers.

Antisocial personalities, by contrast, may not become socialized because early learning experiences lack the consistency and predictability that help other children connect their behavior with rewards and punishments. Perhaps they were sometimes rewarded for doing the "right thing," but just as often not. They may have suffered harsh, physical punishments that depended more on parental whims than on their own conduct. As adults they may not place much value in what other people expect since there was no clear connection between their own behavior and reinforcement in childhood. Snyder (1977) found that children with conduct disorders also tend to have punitive parents. Moreover, parental reinforcements are generally arbitrary—not contingent on prosocial behavior. Children may thus learn that they can do little to prevent punishment and lack the motivation to try. Although Ullmann and Krasner's view may account for some features of antisocial personality disorder, it may not adequately address the charming antisocial person who is apparently skillful at reading social cues produced by other people and using them for personal advantage (Smith, 1978).

Social-learning theorist Albert Bandura has studied the role of observational learning in aggressive behavior, which is one of the common components of antisocial behavior. He and his colleagues (see Bandura et al., 1963) have shown that children acquire skills, including aggressive skills, by observing the behavior of others. Bandura (1973, 1986) does not believe that children and adults display aggressive behaviors in a mechanical way; in fact, people usually do not imitate aggressive behaviors unless they are provoked and believe that they are more likely to be rewarded than punished for it. Media violence and living people may all provide children with aggressive models (Bandura, 1973). When models "get away" with misconduct, or are rewarded for misbehavior, imitative behavior in children may follow. Children may also acquire antisocial behaviors like cheating, bullying, or lying by direct reinforcement if they find that such behaviors successfully help them avoid blame or manipulate others.

All in all, learning approaches to personality disorders, like psychodynamic approaches, have their limitations. They are grounded in theory rather than in observations of children and family interactions that presage development of personality disorders. Research remains to be conducted to determine whether or not the backgrounds hypothesized by learning and psychodynamic theorists do characterize people with particular personality disorders.

Family Perspectives

Many theorists have argued that disturbances in family relationships may help account for the development of antisocial personality disorder. Some have noted that antisocial personalities more frequently experience parental loss than do normal or neurotic people (Greer, 1964), a finding that has implications for psychodynamic and learning theories. Others have pointed to parental rejection or neglect as contributing causes to antisocial behavior (McCord & McCord, 1964).

The McCords cite a German legend that tells of a cruel experiment conducted by the Emperor Frederick II in the 1400s. Frederick ordered that a group of infants be raised at court with their every wish and fancy gratified but for one—their need to be loved. As a result, all the children died. Even if this tale were accurate, the Emperor's experiment would have been uncontrolled, such that illness in the court might also have occasioned the dire outcome. While this fable suggests that the lack of love may lead to death, the McCords believe that emotional deprivation in childhood, in the form of parental rejection and neglect, creates the conditions leading to the development of antisocial behavior in adulthood.

The McCords suggest that children normally learn to associate parental approval with conformity to parental practices and values, and disapproval with disobedience. When tempted to transgress, children then feel anxious for fear of loss of parental love. Anxiety serves as a signal that encourages the child to inhibit antisocial behavior. Eventually, the child identifies with parents and internalizes these social controls as a conscience. But when parents do not show love for their children, identification and the development of a moral conscience does not occur. Children do not fear loss of love because they have not had love, and the anxiety that might have served to restrain antisocial and criminal behavior is also absent.

Parental rejection and neglect may also leave children unable to empathize with others. Children who are rebuffed by their parents may not develop warm feelings of attachment. Future antisocial personalities may develop indifference toward others. Some may wish to develop loving relationships but lack the ability to experience genuine feelings.

The McCords cite their own research that shows a strong connection between early childhood emotional deprivation and subsequent delinquency. They write that frequent, harsh physical punishments may temporarily coerce youngsters into obedience but that when the threat of punishment is removed, children who are emotionally deprived lack inner restraints or "residues of conscience" to inhibit antisocial behavior. Although lack of parental love does not invariably cause antisocial behavior, the more severe the parental rejection, the more likely the child will become aggressive and lack the capacity for guilt or remorse. In the McCords' view, less severe forms of parental rejection may also interact with other factors to give rise to antisocial behavior, such as modeling effects provided by an antisocial parent.

The McCords' views may apply to some children, but certainly not to all. Although family factors may be implicated in some cases of antisocial personality disorder, many neglected children do not later show antisocial or any other abnormal behaviors. We are left to develop other explanations to predict which deprived children will develop antisocial personalities or other abnormal behaviors, and which will not.

Cognitive Perspectives

We noted that there is some question as to just how stable personality traits and behaviors tend to be. It has been shown that people who are high in a cognitive factor labeled **private self-consciousness**—who carefully monitor their own behavior—are more likely to show consistent behavior from situation to situation than are people who are low in private self-consciousness (Fenigstein et al., 1975; Scheier et al., 1978; Underwood & Moore, 1981). The role of self-monitoring would seem to call for a view of behavior as more flexible than suggested by the psychodynamic and, as we will see, the biological perspectives.

Cognitively oriented psychologists have also shown that the ways in which antisocial adolescents encode social information may influence their behavior. As noted in Chapter 2, they have found that antisocial adolescents tend to erroneously encode other people's behavior as threatening (Dodge, 1985; Lochman, 1987). Perhaps because of their family and community experiences, they tend to presume that others intend them ill when they do not (Dodge & Frame, 1982; Jurkovic, 1980). In a promising cognitive therapy method based on such findings, **problem-solving therapy,** antisocial adolescents have been encouraged to reconceptualize their social interactions as problems to be solved rather than as threats to their "manhood" (Lochman et al., 1984). They then generate nonviolent solutions to social confrontations and, like scientists, test out the most promising ones. In the section on biological perspectives we shall also see that the antisocial personality's failure to profit from punishment may be connected with another cognitive factor: the *meaning* of the aversive stimulus.

Biological Perspectives

Little is known about possible biological involvements in most personality disorders. Although many theorists see personality disorders as the expression of maladaptive personality traits, the potential biological facets of such traits also remain for the most part unknown.

In this section we explore genetic and other factors that provide information about the biological aspects of personality disorders.

■ **Genetic Factors** One approach to discovering whether or not there are biological aspects of abnormal behaviors is based on genetics; that is, the incidence of abnormal behaviors is investigated in the biological relatives of people who display them. The DSM–III–R, however, suggests that there is little or no information concerning familial patterns for paranoid, schizoid, borderline, narcissistic, avoidant, dependent, and passive-aggressive personality disorders. While there is little to report about most of these disorders, a recent twin study failed to show any evidence of borderline personality in the identical twins of borderline personality cases (Torgersen, 1984). We should note, however, that the number of borderline cases in this study were small (ten in all). Schizotypal, antisocial, and obsessive-compulsive personality disorders, however, do show somewhat revealing familial patterns, according to the DSM–III–R and researchers. Schizotypal personality disorder, as noted earlier, is more common among the close biological relatives of schizophrenic adoptees than non-schizophrenic adoptees, suggestive of a possible genetic continuity with schizophrenia. Obsessive-compulsive and antisocial personality disorders are both found more commonly among the close biological relatives of people who have the disorder than among the general population. The greatest amount of research has been done on the genetic and other biological aspects of antisocial personality disorder. For that reason, the remainder of this section will focus on findings related to that social problem.

Adoption studies suggest that there may be a genetic predisposition toward criminal behavior. Studies of Danish people who were adopted in infancy have shown that their biological parents place them at greater risk for criminal behavior than do their adoptive parents, despite the fact that their adoptive families had the opportunity to influence them for so many years (Hutchings & Mednick, 1974; Mednick et al., 1984). For example, Danish adoptees whose biological fathers were criminals were more likely to become criminals themselves than were those with adoptive fathers who were criminals (Hutchings & Mednick, 1977). However, the apparent conclusion that genetic factors are better predictors of criminal behavior than a shared family environment must be tempered by several considerations. First, only about one in five adoptees whose biological fathers were known to be criminals, but whose adoptive fathers were not, later became criminals themselves (Hutchings & Mednick, 1977). Genetics alone cannot account for the larger portion of criminal behavior; environmental influences must also be considered. Consistent with the view that heredity and environment are both involved is the finding that the highest rate (36.2%) of criminal behavior was displayed by adopted sons whose biological *and* adoptive fathers were both criminals (Hutchings & Mednick, 1977). The investigators also caution that the results of these studies may be unique to adoptees. Finally, keep in mind that criminals do not necessarily show antisocial personalities, and antisocial personalities are not necessarily criminals; thus, we need to consider research that focuses more directly on the antisocial personality.

Fortunately, Danish records of biological and adoptive relatives of adopted infants who later became sociopaths (antisocial personalities) have also been analyzed. The findings mirror those of the Danish criminality studies. Schulsinger (1972) found a four- to five-fold greater incidence of sociopathy among the biological relatives of adoptees who later became sociopaths than among the adoptive relatives. But the size of the genetic contribution was relatively small, so environmental influences also appear to be important in the development of antisocial behavior.

■ **Chromosomal Abnormalities** A chromosomal theory that briefly captured the attention of researchers was rooted in the possibility that male aggressive criminals carry two male or Y sex chromosomes and one X sex chromosome, giving them an XYY sex-chromosomal structure rather than the normal XY pattern.

In the 1960s, several men were identified who shared some interesting features: tallness, heavier-than-average beards, mild mental retardation, a history of violent behavior, *and* the XYY pattern (Jacobs et al., 1965). XYY males came to be called **supermales,** because of the apparent exaggeration of masculine characteristics caused by the extra Y sex chromosome. It was soon widely speculated that overly aggressive and violent behavior in general might be linked to the XYY pattern. The flurry of interest in possible chromosomal abnormalities was further stirred by the discovery that a serial killer, Richard Speck, who had been convicted of murdering eight student nurses, also had XYY sex-chromosomal structure (Montague, 1968). Other research findings of the period also suggested that an abnormally large number of men who were convicted of violent crimes fit the XYY pattern (Hunter, 1968; Nielsen, 1968).

Optimism that the XYY pattern would predict potential for violence was short-lived, however. Evidence began to accumulate that the great majority of violent male offenders did not carry the extra male chromosome (Smith, 1978) and that most of the criminals who did had been convicted of nonviolent crimes (Witkin et al., 1976). Only about 2 percent or less of male delinquents and criminals tested show the XYY structure (Rosenthal, 1970; Jarvik et al., 1973). Moreover, most "supermales" do not engage in crime or violence.

■ Lack of Emotional Responsiveness

One of the cardinal features of antisocial personality is the freedom from the emotions of guilt and remorse, despite injuring others. According to Cleckley (1976), sociopaths (antisocial personalities) can maintain their composure in stressful situations that would induce anxiety in most people. Lack of anxiety in response to threatening situations may point to another feature of antisocial personality disorder: the failure of punishment to motivate people with antisocial personalities to adopt more prosocial behavior. For most of us, fears of getting caught and of being punished are sufficient to inhibit antisocial impulses. But punishment seems to have little or no deterrent effect on antisocial people. Antisocial personalities may not learn to inhibit their antagonistic behavior because they experience little or no anticipatory anxiety about being apprehended and punished.

The failure of antisocial personalities to learn to avoid cues that anticipate punishment has been studied in avoidance-learning experiments in which subjects must learn to engage in certain responses in order to avoid aversive stimulation, such as electric shock. In an early classic study, Lykken (1957) showed that sociopathic prison inmates performed more poorly than normal controls on a shock-learning task, although their general learning ability did not differ from the normals. Lykken reasoned that the sociopaths were impaired in avoidance learning ability because of unusually low levels of anticipatory anxiety.

Schachter and Latané (1964) found that sociopathic prisoners performed significantly better on the Lykken avoidance learning task when they received prior injections of epinephrine, a hormone that increases heart rate and generalized arousal. Their performance improved apparently because anticipatory anxiety had been heightened by the epinephrine. Other researchers (Chesno & Kilmann, 1975) showed similar results using a method of raising arousal by means of bursts of aversive noise rather than by injections of epinephrine.

Cognitive theorists can point to research showing that the effects of aversive stimuli on sociopaths may depend on the *meaning* or *value* of the stimuli. Anticipation of aversive stimulation in the form of electric shock may not foster avoidance learning in antisocial personalities, but threat of punishment in the form of loss of money may do so. Schmauk (1970), for example, had subjects perform a maze-learning task under three different forms of punishment for incorrect responses: electric shock, loss of money (losing a quarter for each error from an initial "bankroll" of 40 quarters), and

social disapproval (the experimenter said "Wrong" following each incorrect response). Under the shock and social punishment conditions, sociopaths performed more poorly than did normal controls. But the sociopaths actually outperformed normal controls when they were threatened with forfeiture of money. Although sociopaths may not be deterred from misconduct by the threat of physical punishment, they may be keenly sensitive to the loss of money. Perhaps sociopaths learn quite well from their mistakes when the punishment is meaningful to them.

■ Autonomic Nervous System Reactivity

Sociopaths, as noted, perform relatively poorly on tasks that require learning to avoid physical punishment, perhaps because of relatively low levels of anticipatory anxiety. Some theorists have suggested that the autonomic nervous systems (ANSs) of sociopaths may be generally underresponsive to stressful stimuli, which could explain their "immunity" to guilt and their failure to profit from punishment.

Electrical conductivity of the skin is a measure of ANS reactivity, as noted in Chapter 3. When most people anticipate pain, they show sweaty palms due to overactivity of the palmar sweat glands—the so-called **galvanic skin response** (GSR). In an early study, Hare (1965) found that sociopaths did in fact show lower GSR levels in anticipation of painful stimuli than did normal controls. In a later study, Hare and his colleagues (1978) warned two groups of prisoners, sociopaths and nonsociopaths, to expect a blast of noise following a 12-second countdown. Nonsociopathic prisoners showed high levels of skin conductance 3 seconds into the countdown, suggestive of fear, but sociopathic prisoners failed to react until just before the blast, and then they showed a relatively weak GSR response.

■ The Craving-for-Stimulation Model

Other investigators have attempted to explain the sociopath's lack of emotional response in terms of sociopath–normal differences in the levels of stimulation necessary to maintain an **optimum level of arousal.** Our optimum levels of arousal are the degrees of arousal at which we feel best and function most efficiently.

Quay (1965), for one, proposed that sociopaths require a higher-than-normal threshold of stimulation to maintain an optimum state of arousal. Sociopaths, that is, need more stimulation to operate at peak efficiency and are more quickly satiated by changes in stimulation than normal people are. As a result, sociopaths require higher levels of stimulation to maintain their interest, and they are quickly bored by common activities that most people find stimulating, such as reading, watching TV, or relaxing with friends. Sociopaths crave stimulating activities or sensation in the form of intoxicants like drugs or alcohol, motorcycling, sky-diving, high-stakes gambling, or sexual adventures. A higher-than-normal threshold for stimulation would not directly cause antisocial or criminal behavior; after all, part of the "right stuff" of the nation's respected astronauts includes sensation-seeking. However, threat of boredom and inability to tolerate monotony may influence some sensation-seekers to drift into crime (Smith, 1978) or dangerous behaviors.

In support of Quay's theory, sociopaths do score more highly than normal people on measures of sensation-seeking (Emmons & Webb, 1974). Sociopathic delinquents have been found to register lower levels of physiological reactivity, as measured by GSR, in response to auditory tones than do nonsociopathic delinquents (Borkovec, 1970). When sociopaths were shown more arousing stimuli, however—in the form of nude female figures—their GSRs increased to normal levels. So sociopaths may not react as strongly as normal people to lower levels of stimulation, but highly arousing stimuli may evoke similar responses.

■ **Differences in Brain Wave Patterns**   The electroencephalograph (EEG) has also been used in the attempt to define biological differences between sociopaths and normal people. Early studies of brain waves were suggested of brain abnormalities in between 31 percent and 58 percent of sociopaths studied. Most often the differences involved an unusually high frequency of slow brain waves that tend to occur principally among younger children (Ellington, 1954). These findings, which were generally confirmed in reviews of more recent research (Hare, 1970; Syndulko, 1978), have led to the suggestion that the **cerebral cortex,** the outer layer of the brain that is most directly involved in thought and learning, may mature relatively more slowly in sociopaths (Reid, 1986). As a result, sociopaths might not be as prone as other people to inhibit primitive sexual and aggressive impulses.

Hare (1970) has speculated that abnormal brain wave patterns in sociopaths may originate from defects in the **limbic system,** which is believed to be involved

---

QUESTIONNAIRE
Are You a Sensation-Seeker?

Do you crave stimulation or seek sensation? Are you satisfied by reading or watching TV, or must you ride the big wave or bounce your motorbike over desert dunes? Marvin Zuckerman and his colleagues (1978) have found that four factors are related to sensation-seeking: (1) pursuit of thrill and adventure, (2) disinhibition (that is, proclivity to express impulses), (3) pursuit of experience, and (4) susceptibility to boredom. Sensation-seekers are more likely than other people to abuse drugs, show public drunkenness, seek sexual encounters, and volunteer to participate in experiments and high-risk activities (Kohn et al., 1979; Malatesta et al., 1981; Zuckerman, 1974). *However, many sensation-seekers never find themselves in conflict with the law, so sensation-seeking should not be interpreted as criminal or antisocial in itself.*

Zuckerman (1979) has developed several sensation-seeking scales that assess the levels of stimulation people seek to feel at their best and function efficiently. A brief form of one of them follows. To assess your own sensation-seeking tendencies, pick the choice, A or B, that best depicts you. Then compare your responses to those in the key at the end of the chapter.

1. A. I would like a job that requires a lot of traveling.
   B. I would prefer a job in one location.
2. A. I am invigorated by a brisk, cold day.
   B. I can't wait to get indoors on a cold day.
3. A. I get bored seeing the same old faces.
   B. I like the comfortable familiarity of everyday friends.
4. A. I would prefer living in an ideal society in which everyone is safe, secure, and happy.
   B. I would have preferred living in the unsettled days of our history.
5. A. I sometimes like to do things that are a little frightening.
   B. A sensible person avoids activities that are dangerous.
6. A. I would not like to be hypnotized.
   B. I would like to have the experience of being hypnotized.
7. A. The most important goal in life is to live it to the fullest and experience as much as possible.
   B. The most important goal in life is to find peace and happiness.
8. A. I would like to try parachute-jumping.
   B. I would never want to try jumping out of a plane, with or without a parachute.
9. A. I enter cold water gradually, giving myself time to get used to it.
   B. I like to dive or jump right into the ocean or a cold pool.
10. A. When I go on a vacation, I prefer the change of camping out.
    B. When I go on a vacation, I prefer the comfort of a good room and bed.
11. A. I prefer people who are emotionally expressive even if they are a bit unstable.
    B. I prefer people who are calm and even-tempered.
12. A. A good painting should shock or jolt the senses.
    B. A good painting should give one a feeling of peace and security.
13. A. People who ride motorcycles must have some kind of unconscious need to hurt themselves.
    B. I would like to drive or ride a motorcycle.

in the regulation of basic emotions like fear and anxiety. Defects in the parts of the brain that normally produce anticipatory anxiety could explain why sociopaths fail to profit from punishment and inhibit their maladaptive behaviors (Hare, 1970). It should be recognized, however, that not all sociopaths show abnormal brain wave patterns; nor do we know how sociopaths with abnormal brain wave patterns differ from those with normal patterns (Syndulko, 1978). It has also been suggested that dysfunction in the frontal lobe area of the cerebral cortex may also be connected with antisocial personality (Gorenstein, 1982), although this hypothesis has been brought into doubt by more recent research evidence (Hoffman et al., 1987).

Hence, the biological perspective has spurred research on personality disorders, especially antisocial personality disorder, in several directions and has yielded some promising findings. Some evidence from studies in Denmark have connected genetic factors to antisocial personality characteristics and to criminality. There is also some evidence that shows antisocial personalities lack emotional responsiveness to physically threatening stimuli and display reduced levels of autonomic reactivity. They also seem to require higher levels of stimulation to function optimally. Some, but not all, antisocial personalities show evidence of differences from normals in brain wave patterns, which may indicate greater difficulties in controlling primitive impulses.

Sociocultural Views

The sociocultural perspective focuses on the social conditions that contribute to personality disorders. For example, because antisocial personality disorder is believed to be more common among the lower socioeconomic classes, we might examine the particular stresses encountered by disadvantaged families. Many inner-city neighborhoods are beset by social problems such as alcohol and drug abuse, teenage pregnancy, and disorganized and disintegrating families, so it is no wonder that children often fail to receive consistent and nurturant rearing. Children in such families often receive little love but copious harsh punishments. As a result, their self-esteem may be reduced and they may develop feelings of anger and resentment. Neglect and abuse become translated into lack of warm feelings for others or callous disregard for their welfare.

Children reared in poverty are also more likely to be exposed to deviant role models, such as drug dealers. Maladjustment in school may lead to alienation and frustration with the larger society (Siegel, 1989). Antisocial adolescents often lash out against the larger society, committing violent crimes or wanton vandalism. From the sociocultural perspective, "treatment" of sociopathy requires correction of social injustice and amelioration of deprivation.

From the sociocultural viewpoint, antisocial behavior in the poor can be explained as the effects of the stresses that disadvantaged families are likely to encounter. These include exposure to drug abuse and deviant role models, disorganized or disintegrating family structures, and lack of opportunity.

TREATMENT

We began the chapter with a quote from the eminent psychologist William James, who suggested that people's personalities seem to be "set in plaster" by a certain age. So it may seem for many personality disorders, which appear highly resistant to change.

People with personality disorders usually see their behaviors, even maladaptive, self-defeating behaviors, as inherent parts of themselves. Although they may be quite unhappy and suffer personal distress, they are unlikely to perceive their own behavior as causative. Like Marcella, whom we described as showing a histrionic personality disorder, they may condemn others for their problems and believe that *they*, not themselves, need to change. Thus, they usually do not seek help on their own, or they begrudgingly acquiesce to treatment at the urging of others, only to drop out or fail to cooperate with the therapist. Or they may go for help when they feel overwhelmed by anxiety or depression and terminate treatment as soon as they find some relief rather than probe deeply into the personality patterns that contribute to their problems.

Psychodynamic Approaches

Psychodynamic approaches are used to help people with personality disorders become more aware of the roots of their self-defeating behavior patterns and learn more adaptive ways of relating to others. But progress in therapy may be hampered by difficulties in working therapeutically with people with personality disorders, especially clients with borderline personalities. Psychodynamic therapists often report that people with borderline personalities tend to have turbulent relationships with therapists, sometimes idealizing them and sometimes denouncing them as uncaring. Case studies suggest that therapists feel manipulated and exploited by

317

borderline clients' needs to test their approval, such as calling them at all hours or threatening suicide. Such clients can be exhausting and frustrating, although some successes have been reported among therapists who can handle clients' demands.

Some workers have expressed the belief that sociopaths are beyond the reach of psychotherapy (see Cleckley, 1976). Although this view might be too broad to be accurate, it seems that sociopaths have not responded well to psychodynamic treatment, apparently for several reasons (Smith, 1978). One is that sociopaths, like other clients with personality disorders, rarely seek treatment voluntarily and are not usually motivated to change their behavior. Another is that sociopaths usually lack trust in others, including therapists, making it difficult to establish effective therapeutic relationships. Resistance to therapy also hampers therapists of other persuasions, such as behavior therapists.

Behavioral Approaches

Behavior therapists see their task as changing clients' behaviors rather than their personality structures. Many behavioral theorists do not think in terms of clients' "personalities" at all, but rather in terms of acquired maladaptive behaviors that are maintained by reinforcement contingencies. Behavior therapists therefore focus on attempting to replace maladaptive behaviors with adaptive behaviors through techniques such as extinction, modeling, and reinforcement. If clients are taught more adaptive behaviors that are likely to be reinforced by other people, these new behaviors are likely to be maintained.

For example, behavioral marital therapists may encourage clients not to reinforce their spouses' histrionic behaviors. Therapists may use assertiveness training to help people with dependent or passive-aggressive personalities learn to express their needs and feelings more directly. Treatment of avoidant personality disorder may include social skills training to help clients function in social situations, such as dating and meeting new people. Cognitive methods may be incorporated to help socially avoidant people offset catastrophizing beliefs, such as exaggerated fears of the consequences of being "shot down" or rejected by dates.

Some antisocial adolescents have been immersed in residential and foster-care programs that contain numerous behavioral elements, often by court order (Reid & Balis, 1987). These programs or settings have concrete rules and clear rewards for obeying them (Barkley et al., 1976; Henggeler et al., 1986; Phillips et al., 1976; Stumphauzer, 1981). Achievement Place, founded in Kansas in the 1960s and reproduced in other cities, reinforced prosocial behaviors, such as completing homework, and extinguished antisocial behaviors, such as using profanity (Phillips et al., 1976). Some residential programs rely on **token economies,** in which prosocial behaviors are rewarded with tokens such as plastic chips that can be exchanged for privileges.

Consider another training program for delinquents that was developed in Washington, D.C. (Cohen & Filipczak, 1971). The adolescents enrolled in courses such as remedial math, history, and electronics and earned money for their achievements. Extra cash flowed for earning A's. The adolescents acquired study skills that they subsequently put to use in the public schools. They also got into fewer scrapes with the law than did controls during a two-year follow-up period. But disappointing outcomes have also been reported. Achievement Place, for example, proved successful in reducing antisocial behaviors while adolescents were in residence but was no more effective than comparison programs in reducing conflicts with the law once the residents were discharged to their home environments (Jones, 1978). It is also not known whether such programs reduce the risk of antisocial behavior in adolescence from developing into antisocial behavior patterns in adulthood.

Problems with managing or controlling anger are often implicated in various personality disorders. The indirect expression of anger, in the form of obstructionistic or negativistic behavior, is a primary characteristic of passive-aggressive personality disorder. People with narcissistic personality disorder may react angrily or become enraged at the slightest hint of criticism or when others fail to meet their needs for attention and support. Borderline personalities often present histories of inappropriate and excessive anger or lack of control of anger, leading to frequent temper outbursts or outright aggressive behavior. Antisocial personalities, too, may channel feelings of resentment and anger into violent or aggressive behavior. But anger management is not only a problem for people with personality disorders. Many of us have problems managing or controlling our anger, which can lead to maladaptive behavior when we say things or do things that we later regret. As we saw in Chapter 5, problems related to anger and hostility have also been implicated in hypertension and other cardiovascular disorders. Cognitive-behavior therapists have made important inroads in helping people with anger-management problems, which is the subject of the accompanying box.

Biological Approaches

Chemotherapy does not directly treat personality disorders; however, drugs such as antidepressants or anti-anxiety agents are sometimes used to treat the distress (depression or anxiety) that people with personality disorders may encounter. However, these drugs do not treat the long-standing patterns of maladaptive behavior that may give rise to the distress.

Much remains to be learned about working with

A CLOSER LOOK
Cognitive-Behavioral Approaches to Anger-Management

Albert Ellis (1977b), the founder of **rational-emotive therapy,** looks at anger and other emotions in terms of how automatic, irrational thoughts and beliefs determine people's emotional reactions. Ellis believes that beliefs about events determine emotional reactions, not events themselves, no matter how frustrating, disappointing, or tragic they may be. It is not irrational to react with annoyance when frustrating or perturbing events occur. But people who tend to react angrily to mild annoyances and upsetting events tend to hold irrational beliefs such as the following:

1. *Exaggerating the importance of acts of unfairness and injustice by treating them as if they were* truly *horrible and terrible.* Exaggerating the importance of events that are unjust or unfair may encourage people to "fly off the handle." They may explode when a car repair bill exceeds their expectations since they hold the belief that being treated unfairly is a terrible event, not merely an inconvenience or unfortunate event.

2. *Believing that one cannot tolerate injustice or misconduct.* Inability to tolerate even minor affronts or personal slights can prompt anger outbursts, as with "tough" adolescents who interpret another male's smirk or maintenance of direct eye contact as a challenge to their "honor."

3. *Believing that people shouldn't, mustn't act in ways that are unjust or unfair.* The irrational belief that other people should and must act fairly and justly at all times triggers and maintains anger when others fail to live up to absolutist standards of decency and justice.

4. *Extending perception of other people's badness from their behavior to a blanket indictment of their whole personalities.* When treated unfairly, people may think or say something like, "Since what you've done to me is unfair and unjust, you're an awful, terrible person who deserves nothing more out of life than to be punished for acting toward me so unfairly."

Cognitive behavioral therapists sometimes help people with anger-management problems get in touch with fleeting thoughts that spark anger and aggressive behavior through the technique of "running a movie" (Meichenbaum & Turk, 1976). Clients run movies about events by reliving them in "slow motion" in their imaginations and scrutinizing the fleeting thoughts that might otherwise be overlooked. As an illustration, picture yourself guiding a cart down an aisle in a supermarket. Someone shoves into you, so violently that it seems deliberate, and then says, "What's wrong with you? Watch where you're going!"

What thoughts would cross your mind? Would you think, "This son of a _____ can't do this to me! I can't let him get away with acting like that!" If so, you would be making the cognitive errors of personalizing the stranger's rudeness and demanding that other people live up

"Lucky for you you can't hear my interior monologue."
Drawing by Wm. Hamilton; © 1983 The New Yorker Magazine, Inc.

to your standards. Irrational beliefs and cognitive errors magnify annoyances and induce maladaptive behavior. In this case they may prod you to violence that you might later regret.

Novaco (1974, 1977) has used *stress-inoculation training* (see Chapter 4) to assist people with anger-management problems in managing the frustrations of everyday life. He has also trained police officers to curb tendencies to respond aggressively to social provocations. Stress-inoculation training exposes clients to imaginary stressors to encourage them to plan and rehearse adaptive responses.

Novaco's approach includes three phases: education, planning, and application training. In phase 1, clients are shown how irrational beliefs such as expectations of flawless behavior from others and interpretations of insults as threats to one's self-esteem give rise to ire and aggression. In phase 2, clients are taught relaxation skills (muscle relaxation and deep breathing) and rational alternatives to their anger-inducing beliefs. In phase 3, clients imagine common social provocations and rehearse rational self-statements and relaxation so that their behavior is adaptive and nonviolent. Subjects in Novaco's studies have made dramatic gains in managing provocations in socially acceptable ways. Many subjects also attribute their gains to rethinking provocations as problems to be solved rather than threats demanding a violent response.

"Problem-solving training" also helps violent people manage feelings of anger. In this method, clients scrutinize sample provocations and generate multiple adaptive responses. They select the most promising ones, try them out, and evaluate their effectiveness. In one study of problem-solving training, subjects showed significantly less violence and also tended to respond to provocations with socially skillful behavior (Moon & Eisler, 1983).

people who have personality disorders. The major challenges involve recruiting people who do not see themselves as being disordered into treatment and prompting them to develop insight into their self-defeating or injurious behaviors. Current efforts to help such people are too often reminiscent of the old couplet:

> *He that complies against his will,*
> *Is of his own opinion still.*
>
> Samuel Butler, *Hudibras*

IMPULSE DISORDERS

Be candid. Have you ever blown your budget on a "sale" item? Have you ever made a bet that you could not afford? Have you ever "lost it" and screamed at someone, even though you knew you should be "maintaining your cool"?

Most of us keep most of our impulses under control most of the time. We usually restrain ourselves from blurting out obscenities when riled and prevent ourselves from exploding in anger. Although we may sometimes surrender to temptation and gorge ourselves on a dessert that we have lusted after in our hearts, or occasionally yell at obnoxious people, we generally hold most impulses in check. Some of us, however, suffer from what the DSM–III–R diagnoses as **impulse control disorders.** These disorders are characterized by failure to rein in impulses, temptations, or drives that lead to harmful consequences to oneself or others (see Table 9.4).

We focus on two types of impulse disorders: pathological gambling and kleptomania (compulsive stealing).

TABLE 9.4 Diagnostic Features of Impulse Control Disorders

1. Failure to resist the impulse, drive, or temptation to engage in an act that is harmful to the person or to others. The act may or may not be planned in advance and the person may or may not have attempted consciously to resist the impulse.
2. A sense of mounting arousal or tension is experienced before the act is committed.
3. The person experiences a sense of pleasure, release, or gratification when committing the act. The act is experienced as ego-syntonic, meaning that the act is consistent with the person's conscious wishes at the particular moment that it is committed. Afterwards, the person may or may not feel guilty or have a sense of regret.

Source: *Adapted from DSM–III–R, p. 321.*

Pathological Gambling

Gambling may never have been more popular in the United States than it is today. Legalized gambling is spreading in the form of state lotteries, off-track betting (OTB) parlors, "casino nights" sponsored by religious and fraternal organizations, and legalized gambling meccas, like Atlantic City and Las Vegas. Lottery "fever" is also spreading. Perhaps 23 percent of Americans buy lottery tickets every week. Today, with legalized gambling available at OTB parlors and in the form of state lotteries, women and teenagers constitute more of the gambling population than ever before (Barron, 1989). Illegal betting on sporting events is also growing. Changes in technology are making gambling ever-more convenient—and seductive: Video slot machines captivate younger players and credit cards are used in lieu of cash in many casinos.

Most people who gamble maintain their self-control and can stop whenever they wish. Others, like the man in the following case, fall into a pattern of **pathological gambling.**

■ Twenty-eight years after his first two-bit bet at the race track, the double life of lies and deception caught up with an insurance executive whose gambling debts had climbed into the hundreds of thousands of dollars. The business he had built went bankrupt. His marriage ended in bitter divorce. Often, he considered killing himself.

The former executive does not look like an addict, a liar, a manipulator or someone who would ignore his two young daughters, but he admits to having been all of these.

"Gambling," he said, dragging hard on a cigarette, "took me from a good man, which I basically am, to a person I didn't know. I was only happy when I was in action and I felt most at home when I was in action. The more I won, the more I gambled. The more I lost, the more I gambled. It was a no-win situation.

Gately, 1989, p. 31. Copyright © 1989 by The New York Times Company. Reprinted by permission. ■

By the time he sought treatment, the former executive had lost more than $1 million. Many pathological (also called compulsive) gamblers only seek treatment during a financial or emotional crisis, such as bankruptcy or divorce. Pathological gambling can take many forms, from excessive wagering on horse races, or in card games and in casinos, to extravagant betting on sporting events or stock market fluctuations. Compulsive or pathological gamblers often report they had experienced a big win, or a series of winnings, early in their gambling careers, but eventually their losses began to mount, and they felt driven to bet with increasing desperation to reverse their luck and recoup their losses (Peck, 1986). Sometimes losses began with the first bet, and pathological gamblers became trapped in a negative spiral of betting more frequently to recover losses even as their losses—and their debts—multiplied.

Compulsive or pathological gambling was labeled a "mental disorder" with the 1980 publication of the DSM–III and is believed to be more common among men than women. According to the DSM–III–R, pathological gambling involves repeated failure to resist the urge to gamble resulting in a disruptive pattern of gambling that impairs ability to function in personal, family, or occupational roles (see Table 9.5). Pathological gambling is a progressive problem that, when uncorrected, leads to rising debts, deepening work and family problems, and, sometimes, suicide. Compulsive or pathological gamblers tend to hit "rock bottom," a state of despair characterized by financial ruin, suicidal attempts, and/or shattered family relationships, in as little as one year or as many as 20 years of compulsive or pathological gambling (Peck, 1986).

TABLE 9.5 Diagnostic Features of Pathological Gambling

Pathological gambling is shown by four or more of the following:

1. Preoccupation with gambling or with obtaining money to gamble
2. Frequent gambling of larger amounts or for a longer period of time than intended
3. Need to increase the size or frequency of bets to achieve the desired excitement
4. Restlessness or irritability when unable to gamble
5. Repeated loss of money by gambling and returning another day ("chasing") to win back losses
6. Repeated efforts to reduce or stop gambling
7. Frequent gambling when expected to meet social or occupational obligations
8. Sacrifice of some important social, occupational, or recreational activity in order to gamble
9. Continuation of gambling despite inability to pay mounting debts, or despite other significant social, occupational, or legal problems that the person knows to be exacerbated by gambling

Source: *Adapted from DSM–III–R, p. 325.*

Gambling is big business in America. Most people can stop gambling when they want to, but pathological or compulsive gamblers are unable to resist the urge. Many compulsive gamblers seek help only when their losses mount to the point where they experience a financial or emotional crisis, such as bankruptcy or a divorce.

Pathological gamblers are preoccupied with gambling. Their lives often revolve around pursuing money for stakes. Unlike casual bettors or lottery players, pathological gamblers often risk all their resources (Gately, 1989). Family relationships are strained by both the time and the resources that are spent on gambling. Often, there is little left of family resources for vacations, school tuition, or monthly bills (Gately, 1989). Pathological gamblers often borrow from friends and family. When these sources dry up, they may turn to finance companies or illegal and potentially dangerous sources such as loan sharks and bookies. Pathological gamblers may attempt to reduce the stress of mounting debts by gambling even more frequently, hoping for the ''big score'' that will put them ''into the black.'' Pathological gamblers are sometimes bouncing with energy and overconfidence; at other times they show signs of acute depression, anxiety, or stress.

Curiously, it is not the pursuit of money that seems to motivate many compulsive gamblers, but rather the excitement or thrill of gambling itself (Barron, 1989), as suggested by Steve B., a 46-year-old compulsive gambler from New York City who bets $150 a day on horses:

■ I don't dream of winning a million dollars. . . . I want to have a bet on every thoroughbred race run. My idea of gambling heaven is to sit in a horse parlor in Las Vegas and bet on every horse from 8 A.M. until 2 A.M.

[Steve had held 75 to 80 jobs in 25 years due to problems with gambling.]

Because I've gambled all my adult life, . . . I've never been able to hold a job. I'd louse up on the job because my mind was on the gambling, or I couldn't go to the racetrack. I used to devise incredibly ingenious ways to get there.

Barron, 1989, p. 24. Copyright © 1989 by The New York Times Company. Reprinted by permission. ■

Many compulsive gamblers suffer from low self-esteem and were rejected or abused as children by their parents. Gambling often becomes a means of boosting self-esteem, of showing them that they are winners in life. Unfortunately, far too often the opposite proves true. Losing at gambling only strengthens their negative self-image, which can lead to depression and suicide.

■ **Prevalence of Pathological Gambling**   A government commission estimated that there were more than 1.1 million pathological gamblers in the United States by 1974 (Commission on the Review of the National Policy toward Gambling, 1976). According to the National Council of Compulsive Gambling and other authorities, there may actually be four times as many

today (Gately, 1989; Nadler, 1985). Whatever the actual numbers of gamblers, pathological gambling also affects family members and others whose well-being hinges on the performance of the gamblers, such as friends and employers.

The results of a New York State survey, based on a telephone sampling method, estimated the prevalence of pathological gambling at about 230,000 of New York's 13 million adults, or about 2 percent of the adult population of the state (Volberg & Steadman, 1988). An additional half million to three-quarters of a million reported lesser gambling problems. The typical pathological gambler was a nonwhite male, under the age of 30, who had not graduated from high school and earned $25,000 or less a year. He was also more likely than nongamblers to be out of work. Earlier research on pathological gambling, by contrast, had depicted the typical pathological gambler as a middle- or upper-class white male in his 40s or 50s. Earlier findings, however, were generally based on samples that were obtained from sources like Gambler's Anonymous, college populations, or psychiatric populations and may not have represented the general population of pathological gamblers. Earlier research also frequently portrayed the pathological gambler as having a stable family and occupational life until gambling got out of hand. The New York survey, however, connected pathological gambling with nonfamily men with marginal educational and occupational backgrounds. Thus treatment efforts may need to be expanded in minority communities and to target young, poorly educated, unemployed problem gamblers. A large percentage of women were also found in the 1988 survey (36%), which suggests a need for treatment programs that target female gamblers.

■ **Characteristics of Pathological Gamblers**   Pathological or compulsive gambling has been linked to a history of depression (McCormick et al., 1987) and to early childhood histories of traumatic life events, among other factors. Ramirez and his colleagues (1983) consider pathological gambling to be a form of addictive behavior in that the personality characteristics of the pathological gambler have much in common with other addictive groups, such as alcoholics and substance abusers (McCormick & Russo, 1987). For example, studies show that pathological gamblers and substance abusers both tend to be self-centered, anxious, frustrated, impulsive, and manipulative (Graham, 1978; McCormick et al., 1987). The approach to treatment of pathological gambling in programs such as Gamblers Anonymous is also modeled after programs like Alcoholics Anonymous in which the addictive aspects of the problem are highlighted. But there may be personality differences between pathological gamblers and substance abusers, such as alcoholics. A recent study compared the personality profiles of 70 pathological gamblers and 70 alcoholics, based on the California Psychological Inventory, a widely used personality scale. The gamblers showed relatively greater failure to adhere to social norms, impulsivity, and inability to delay gratification (McCormick et al., 1987)—problems that heighten the difficulties encountered by therapists who work with them.

■ **Stages in the Gambling "Career"**   Lesieur and Custer (1984) describe pathological gambling as frequently following a three-phase course of development: winning, losing, and desperation. In the adventurous or **winning phase,** budding gamblers see wagering as a pleasurable pastime. They enjoy the thrill of the "action." Early winnings also boost self-esteem; big wins make gamblers feel like "big shots." Nearly half of pathological gamblers report a "big win" during this stage, sometimes one that equals their annual salaries. In this stage, gamblers take credit for having a winning system for making bets or handicapping. Losses are dismissed and attributed to external forces like "bad luck," cheating (by others), or untimely accidents (such as the football hitting a goal post on a field-goal attempt). Even during this early stage, however, gamblers frequently begin to borrow repeatedly from friends to recoup losses.

In the middle or **losing phase,** gamblers begin to lose, steadily. They borrow larger amounts of money in the attempt to get even. They take out loans with finance companies, borrow from credit card accounts or credit unions, and hide transactions from their families. Married gamblers run into domestic blow-ups when financial pressures mount and their losses and loans are discovered. In the attempt to break even, gamblers spend more and more time gambling and forsake their work and other responsibilities. They are introduced by gambling "buddies" to other types of gambling that may bring better "luck." Gamblers may lose their jobs due to absences or switch to lines of work that provide more time for gambling. Gamblers may borrow from bookies and stall for time in repaying their debts as they seek the big score.

During the **desperation phase,** gamblers become yet more obsessed with winning in order to break even and pay off debts. Periodic rescues may occur in the form of bail-outs from relatives, but gamblers soon return to the pattern of gambling, losing, and borrowing again. Lies and deceptions are used to conceal gambling activities and secret loans. Spouses become disgusted and feel that their efforts to help are in vain. Problems on the job mount as gamblers focus on personal problems and gambling. If the opportunity is present, they

may embezzle funds from their employers; they seek whatever means are available, legal or otherwise, to obtain money. Eventually, a state of panic ensues, which leads to irrational gambling and greater risk-taking. Optimism that the big win is only a bet away begins to fade, and gamblers grow restless, irritable, and fatigued. They sleep poorly and eat erratically. Periods of deep depression, despair, suicidal thoughts (and some attempts) usually follow. At this stage, they may run away (typically to Las Vegas or another gambling center), end their lives in suicide, become imprisoned for gambling-related offenses or for stealing money to be used in gambling, or more hopefully, seek help.

■ **Treatment of Pathological Gamblers**   Various programs offer treatment for pathological gamblers. Many gamblers attend nonprofessional support groups, like Gamblers Anonymous, or seek professional counseling; some do both (Lesieur & Custer, 1984). Gamblers Anonymous is similar in approach to Alcoholics Anonymous. The organization stresses personal responsibility for one's behavior. It ensures the anonymity of group members so as to spur participation and the sharing of experiences, and it helps members gain insight into their self-destructive behavior. Members make public commitments to stop gambling and help one another resist the urge to gamble.

In addition, hospital-based or residential programs help pathological gamblers break their habits by sequestering them from their regular routines for six weeks or so. While they are in residence, gamblers may be introduced to Gamblers Anonymous or other support groups to help them make the transition back to the community.

Few reports attest to the success of these strategies. For one thing, pathological gambling was first included in the DSM–III–R in 1980, and clinical trials of treatment strategies take time to develop. Moreover, in order to ensure the anonymity of participants, lay organizations like Gamblers Anonymous do not keep detailed records. Even if records were kept at Gamblers Anonymous, the drop-out rate would probably be too high to be encouraging (Lesieur & Custer, 1984).

 Gamblers Anonymous groups have indeed been set up to help pathological gamblers. However, questions remain concerning the effectiveness of these groups.

Some promising results have been shown for a comprehensive treatment program in a veteran's hospital setting (Taber et al., 1987), with success rates, as defined by total abstinence, reported for 56 percent

(32 of 57) gamblers. The program consisted of a highly structured, 28-day hospitalization for gamblers—all male veterans—who had not responded to nonresidential approaches. Upon discharge, participants who attended Gamblers Anonymous meetings fared better than those who dropped out. However, the lack of a control group and the lack of long-term follow-up evaluations limit the validity of the results.

With pathological gambling, as with personality disorders, mental-health professionals are essentially dealing with people who make maladaptive choices and show little insight into the causes of their problems. Such clients are typically the most resistive of attempts to help them.

Kleptomania

Kleptomania derives from the Greek *kleptes*, meaning "thief," and refers to a compulsive pattern of stealing. These stolen objects are typically of little value or use to kleptomaniacs, and they usually give them away, return them secretly, discard them, or keep them hidden at home. In most cases, kleptomaniacs can easily afford the items, and even wealthy people have been known to engage in compulsive shoplifting.

 It is not true that kleptomania is motivated by poverty. Kleptomania is somewhat puzzling because many kleptomaniacs are quite wealthy.

As with other forms of compulsive behavior, kleptomaniacs generally experience a rise in tension immediately preceding the theft and a sense of relief afterward. The thefts are usually crimes of the moment, poorly planned, and sometimes result in arrest. However, kleptomaniacs are usually inhibited by the obvious presence of guards or police officers. The thefts are apparently unmotivated by anger or vengeance.

Kleptomania is regarded as quite rare and, according to the DSM–III–R, accounts for fewer than 5 percent of arrested shoplifters. Shoplifting, including kleptomania-related shoplifting, is more common among women than men, although overall sex differences in the prevalence of kleptomania are uncertain.

Early psychodynamic formulations viewed kleptomania as a defense against feelings of penis envy in women and castration anxiety in men. In effect, kleptomaniacs were believed to be motivated to steal phallic objects (ones that symbolized the penis) as a way of protecting themselves against their own apparent loss (in females) or a threatened loss (in males) of the penis

(Fenichel, 1945). However, testing such formulations of unconscious processes has remained elusive, and kleptomania remains a puzzling disorder to researchers and clinicians.

The following case illustrates a behavioral treatment of kleptomania:

■ The client was a 56-year-old woman who had shoplifted every day of the preceding 14 years. Her compulsive urges to steal fit the clinical criteria which may distinguish kleptomania from other types of shoplifting, although her booty had no apparent meaning to her. Typical loot consisted of a pair of baby shoes, although there was no baby in her family to whom she could give the shoes. The compulsion to steal was so strong that she felt powerless to resist it. She told her therapist that she wished she could be "chained to a wall" (p. 213) in order to prevent her from acting out. She expressed anger that it was so easy to steal from a supermarket, in effect blaming the store for her own misconduct.

Her treatment, **covert sensitization,** involved the imaginal pairing of aversive stimuli with the undesired behavior. In her case, the therapist directed her to imagine feeling nauseous and vomiting while stealing. For example, she pictures herself in the supermarket, approaching an object she intended to steal, and becoming nauseated and vomiting as she removed it, thereby drawing the attention of other shoppers. She was then directed to imagine herself replacing the object and consequently feeling relief from the nausea.

In a subsequent session, she imagines the nausea starting as she approached the object, but the nausea disappeared when she turned away from it rather than removing it. She was also asked to practice the imaginal scenes on her own throughout the week, as homework assignments. She reported a decline in her urges to steal, and a reduction in stealing behavior during the treatment program. She reported only one instance of shoplifting between the completion of treatment and a 19-month follow-up evaluation.

Adapted from Glover, 1985 ■

Although Glover's findings are promising, the report has the limitations of uncontrolled case studies. For example, we cannot know whether the treatment itself or other factors, such as the client's motivation to change her life, were responsible for her changes in behavior. Covert sensitization is discussed further in Chapter 15.

In this chapter we have considered a number of maladaptive behavior patterns in which people often fail to recognize how their behaviors are disrupting their lives. In the following chapter we explore other maladaptive behaviors that are frequently connected with lack of self-insight: behaviors involving substance abuse.

SUMMARY

Types of Personality Disorders

Maladaptive or rigid behavior patterns or personality traits that are associated with states of personal distress or that impair the person's ability to function in social or occupational roles are called personality disorders. People with personality disorders don't generally recognize a need to change themselves. Their personality traits are considered by psychodynamic theorists to be ego-syntonic. The DSM–III–R recognizes eleven types of personality disorders, organized into three clusters, as summarized in the following paragraphs.

Personality Disorders Characterized by Odd or Eccentric Behavior

People with paranoid personality disorder are unduly suspicious and mistrustful of others, to the point that their relationships suffer. But they do not hold the more flagrant paranoid delusions typical of schizophrenia. Schizoid personality disorder describes people who have little if any interest in social relationships, show a restricted range of emotional expression, and appear distant and aloof. Schizotypal personalities appear odd or eccentric in their thoughts, mannerisms and behavior, but not to the degree found in schizophrenia.

Personality Disorders Characterized by Dramatic, Emotional, or Erratic Behavior

Antisocial personality disorder describes people who persistently engage in behavior that violates social norms and the rights of others and who tend to show no remorse for their misdeeds. Other terms such as sociopathy and psychopathy have been used at various times to refer to this type of behavior pattern. Antisocial personality disorder is often, but not always, linked to criminality. Borderline personality disorder is defined in terms of instability in self-image, relationships, and mood. Borderline personalities often engage in impulsive acts, which are frequently self-destructive. These people are often difficult to work with in psychotherapy. Histrionic personalities tend to be highly dramatic and emotional in their behavior. They crave attention, approval, and reassurance from others and tend to be egocentric in their relationships. They appear to lack self-esteem and strive to impress others as a way of boosting feelings of self-worth. Narcissistic personalities have inflated or grandiose senses of themselves and, like histrionic personalities, demand to be the center of attention. They can become enraged or deeply wounded by the slightest criticism.

Personality Disorders Characterized by Anxious or Fearful Behavior

Avoidant personality disorder describes people who are so terrified of rejection and criticism that they are generally unwilling to enter relationships without unusually strong reassurances of acceptance. As a result, they tend to have few close relationships outside their immediate families. People with dependent personality disorder are overly dependent on others and have extreme difficulty acting independently or making even the smallest decisions on their own. People with obsessive-compulsive personality disorder have various traits such as orderliness, perfectionism, rigidity and overattention to detail, but are without the true obsessions and compulsions associated with obsessive-compulsive (anxiety) disorder. However, some people may have both types of disorders. Passive-aggressive personalities express resentment and anger through passive, indirect means, such as procrastination, dawdling, sulking, work slowdowns, intentional errors, and so on.

Proposed Personality Disorders "Needing Further Study"

DSM–III–R includes two categories of proposed personality disorders that require further study before they can be included in the diagnostic manual. People with sadistic personality disorder are intentionally cruel and enjoy making others suffer. People with self-defeating personality disorder engage in a recurrent pattern of self-defeating behavior, such as being drawn to others who mistreat them. Both diagnoses have elicited controversy. Some have charged that criminals may claim to have the mental disorder of sadistic personality disorder as a means of averting responsibility for their criminal actions. Self-defeating personality disorder has been criticized on the basis that it appears to blame victims for their victimization by labeling them as mentally disordered. Researchers argue that women who remain in abusive relationships may be better perceived as survivors of trauma than as driven by unconscious needs to punish themselves.

Problems with Classification of Personality Disorders

Various controversies and problems attend the classification of personality disorders, including lack of demonstrated reliability and validity, too much overlap among the categories, difficulty in distinguishing between variations in normal behavior and abnormal behavior, underlying sexist biases in certain categories, and confusion of labels with explanations.

Theoretical Perspectives

Traditional Freudian theory focused on unresolved Oedipal conflicts in explaining normal and abnormal personality development. More recent psychodynamic theorists have focused on the pre-Oedipal period in explaining the development of such personality disorders as narcissistic and borderline personality. Kohut's self-theory, for example, focused on the processes by which ''healthy narcissism'' in childhood gives way to more realistic self-appraisals and subsequent ego development. But lack of parental empathy and support may set the stage for pathological narcissism in adulthood. Kernberg viewed borderline personality disorder in terms of pre-Oedipal failure to develop a sense of constancy and unity in one's image of the self and others. As a result, borderline personalities in adulthood experience rapidly shifting attitudes toward themselves and others. Mahler and her colleagues viewed the borderline personality in terms of failure to master the early developmental challenge of separation-individuation—the process of achieving psychological identity apart from the mother.

Learning theorists view personality disorders in terms of maladaptive patterns of behavior, rather than enduring personality traits. Learning theorists seek to identify the early learning experiences and present reinforcers that may explain the development and maintenance of the abnormal behavior patterns associated with personality disorders in adulthood.

Many theorists have argued that disturbed family relationships between parent and child play an important role in the development of antisocial personality disorder, especially such factors as parental loss, rejection or neglect, and parental modeling of antisocial behavior.

Cognitive researchers have found that certain cognitive factors, such as private self-consciousness, may help to explain behavioral consistencies. Cognitive research has also focused on the role of encoding strategies in explaining tendencies of antisocial adolescents to presume that others mean them ill.

Research on biological perspectives has shown familial links in various personality disorders that are consistent with, but do not prove, genetic means of transmission. Adoptee studies conducted in Denmark suggest that genetic factors may play a role in antisocial personality, but environment also needs to be considered. There is some research evidence that shows antisocial personalities not only lack emotional responsiveness to physically threatening stimuli but also have reduced levels of autonomic reactivity. Antisocial personalities may also require higher levels of stimulation to maintain optimal levels of arousal. Research evidence has also shown evidence of abnormal brain wave patterns in some, but not all, antisocial personalities.

Sociocultural theorists focus on the adverse social conditions that may contribute to the development of personality disorders, especially antisocial personality. The effects of poverty, urban blight, and drug abuse can lead to family disorganization and disintegration, making it less likely that children will receive the nurturance and support to help them develop more socially adaptive behavior patterns.

Treatment

People with personality disorders often see their behavior patterns, even their self-defeating behaviors, as inherent parts of themselves. As a result they may be less likely to seek help to change their behavior and may blame others for their problems. Or they may seek help when troubled by anxiety or depression, but discontinue treatment when they experience some relief rather than probe more deeply into the personality patterns that may be contributing to their problems. Nonetheless, therapists from different schools of therapy try to assist people with personality disorders to gain better awareness of their self-defeating behavior patterns and learn more adaptive ways of relating to others. But evidence of effectiveness has been lacking, largely as a result of the difficulties encountered in working therapeutically with people who are resistant to change.

Problems relating to anger management are implicated in various personality disorders. Cognitive-behavioral approaches to anger management focus on helping to identify the irrational beliefs that underlie problems with anger control and the anger-arousing thoughts that may occur automatically in response to provocations. Cognitive-behavioral techniques have been developed to help people with anger-management problems.

Impulse Disorders

Impulse disorders involve failures to resist impulses, temptations, or drives that lead to harmful consequences to oneself or others. The person with an impulse disorder usually experiences a rising level of tension or arousal just preceding the act, and then a sense of relief or release when the act is committed.

Pathological gambling involves a pattern of repeated failure to resist the urge to gamble that results in impaired functioning in personal, family, or occupational roles. Some researchers view pathological gambling as a type of nonchemical addiction and have noted similarities (and some differences) in personality profiles between pathological gamblers and substance abusers. Pathological gamblers may progress through certain stages, such as the phases of winning, losing, and desperation, that often typify a "gambling career." Pathological gambling has been treated by various approaches, including hospital-based and residential programs, professional counseling, and nonprofessional support groups like Gamblers Anonymous, but research evidence of the effectiveness of these approaches remains sparse.

Kleptomania involves a compulsion to steal, usually involving items of little value to the person. It remains a puzzling disorder.

KEY FOR SENSATION-SEEKING SCALE

Since this is a shortened version of the questionnaire, there are no norms that are applicable. However, answers that agree with the following key are suggestive of sensation-seeking:

1. A	6. B	11. A
2. A	7. A	12. A
3. A	8. A	13. B
4. B	9. B	
5. A	10. A	

10 Substance Abuse and Dependence

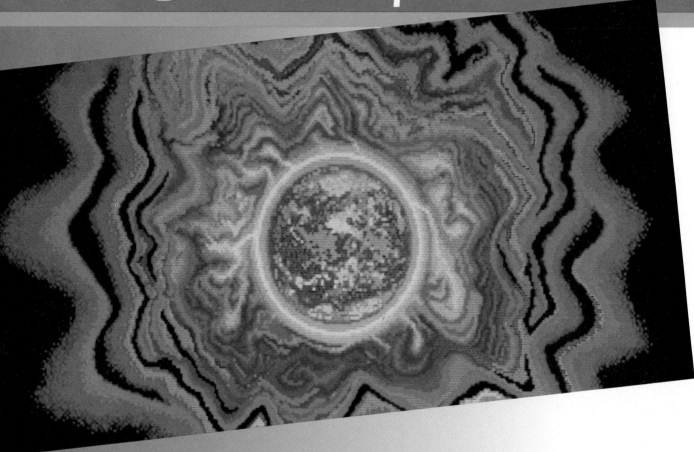

■ ____ Legal substances cause more deaths through sickness and accidents than all illicit drugs combined.

■ ____ Cigarette smoking is a mental disorder.

■ ____ Cocaine is the most widely abused substance in the United States today.

■ ____ Alcohol heightens sexual response.

■ ____ People can drown their sorrows in alcohol.

■ ____ Heroin was developed during a search for a drug that would relieve pain as effectively as morphine, but without causing physical addiction.

■ ____ Cocaine is addictive.

■ ____ Marijuana saps motivation.

■ ____ A recovering alcoholic must abstain from alcohol because just one drink will lead to a binge.

LEARNING OBJECTIVES

When you have completed your study of Chapter 10, you should be able to:

PSYCHOACTIVE SUBSTANCE ABUSE AND DEPENDENCE (pp. 329–335)
1. Define substance abuse and substance dependence.
2. Distinguish between psychological and physiological dependence.

SUBSTANCE ABUSE AND ORGANIC MENTAL DISORDERS (p. 335)
3. Describe organic mental disorders that are induced by use of psychoactive substances.

ALCOHOL (pp. 335–341)
4. Describe U.S. drinking patterns and prevalances of alcoholism
5. Discuss risk factors for alcoholism.
6. Discuss the effects of alcohol.

BARBITURATES (SEDATIVES) AND MINOR TRANQUILIZERS (p. 341)
7. Discuss the effects of barbiturates and minor tranquilizers.

OPIATES (pp. 341–343)
8. Discuss the origins and effects of opiates.

STIMULANTS (pp. 343–350)
9. Discuss the effects of amphetamines.
10. Discuss the effects of cocaine.
11. Discuss the effects of nicotine and tobacco smoke.

PSYCHEDELICS (pp. 350–352)
12. Discuss the effects of LSD.
13. Discuss the effects of PCP.
14. Discuss the effects of marijuana.

THEORETICAL PERSPECTIVES (pp. 352–361)
15. Discuss biological, psychodynamic, learning, cognitive, and sociocultural approaches to substance abuse and dependence.
16. Discuss the disease model of substance abuse and dependence.
17. Discuss genetic factors in alcoholism.

TREATMENT (pp. 361–368)
18. Discuss chemotherapeutic approaches to treatment of substance abuse and dependence.
19. Discuss nonprofessional support groups, such as AA, and residential treatment programs.
20. Discuss psychodynamic and behavioral approaches to treatment.
21. Discuss the controversies concerning controlled drinking.
22. Discuss the need for, methods of, and evaluation of relapse-prevention training.
23. Describe some of the characteristics that are believed to be associated with more successful substance abuse programs for adolescents.

As our society entered the 1990s, the leader of a Central American nation was forcibly deposed by the U.S. military and brought before American justice to stand trial on drug charges. The mayor of Washington, D.C., the nation's capital, was nabbed in a "sting" operation and charged with possession of crack, a smokable form of the drug cocaine. But the real story of crack and other drugs in the 1990s unfolds in the streets of our cities and towns. Let us consider a few nights and days in what the media has called "crack America":

In Detroit, teenage prostitutes sell their bodies for a few dollars worth of crack. In Atlanta, a businessman from New Jersey checks himself into a drug treatment center. He had built up a small chain of women's clothing stores, married, had a son, and then a friend introduced him to cocaine. A few months later his life was spinning out of control. He just wanted to stay by himself and smoke crack. In half a year, his business had collapsed and he moved downward from job to job, ending up as a night manager for a convenience store so that he could steal money from the cash register to buy drugs. Finally, losing that job, he checked himself into a treatment program. But he thinks of himself as lucky, as compared to others. He hadn't hit rock bottom. The money was all gone. But he still had his wife and kid.

In a rundown neighborhood in Houston, a restaurant remains open 24 hours a day, the owner standing guard to keep the drug addicts from robbing him blind. But business is bad and he may be forced to close the place by the end of the year. The people in the neighborhood seldom venture outside their homes anymore, fearful of the street crime that inexorably follows the drug trade.

In Newark, a social worker receives an anonymous tip that an 11-month-old boy was left alone for several hours in a rooming house. His parents are crack users. The child is brought to the hospital for evaluation. His clothing is filthy and he appears dehydrated. He fails to grab a finger and goes limp at the waist when he is hugged around the middle, showing the characteristic lack of response to others of a neglected infant. But he reaches for a bottle of formula and ravenously consumes it. It's an all too familiar but sad pattern. How can parents whose lives revolve around the pursuit of crack be expected to feed and take care of their babies? (Adapted from *Newsweek*, November 28, 1988, pp. 65–74)

The planet is a supermarket of **psychoactive** chemicals or substances, or what are more commonly called drugs. Our society is inundated with substances that alter the mood and twist perceptions—substances that lift you up, calm you down, and turn you upside down. Many people use these substances because their friends do. Adolescents often use them because their parents and authority figures tell them not to. Some users are seeking pleasure. Others are searching for inner truth.

Much of the public attention on the problems of drug abuse in recent years has focused on cocaine, especially crack cocaine. There is good reason for public concern. The number of cocaine-related medical emergencies rose by 900 percent in the period between 1976 and 1985, while the numbers of cocaine-related deaths rose more than 11-fold (Weiss & Mirin, 1987). Cocaine use has spawned a huge illegal network of manufacturers, dealers, and distributers. As this book goes to press, the cocaine-producing Medellin cartel is engaged in a war with the government of Colombia for control of the country. Cocaine abuse is estimated to cost the United States at least $10 billion a year in lost productivity, increased health-care benefits, and job-related accidents (Weiss & Mirin, 1987). The personal costs to users and their families is inestimable.

In this chapter we focus on the relationship between the use of psychoactive drugs and abnormal behavior. There are many forms of drugs and various ways of introducing drugs into our bodies. The category of psychoactive chemicals, or drugs, is not limited to the so-called street drugs—cocaine, heroin, and marijuana, among others. Alcohol, too, is a drug because it is a chemical substance that produces both psychological and physiological effects when it is ingested. So, too, is nicotine, a stimulant found in tobacco smoke and other tobacco products. Ironically, psychoactive substances that are legally sold over the counter and are most widely available—cigarettes and alcohol—have caused more deaths through sickness and accidents than all illicit drugs combined. In fact, alcohol is the most commonly abused drug on the market, although it is so widely used that we tend not to think of it as a drug. But many people who smoke cigarettes and drink alcoholic beverages don't consider their behavior abnormal. How might we distinguish between normal and abnormal patterns of drug use? Or is any regular use of a psychoactive drug considered abnormal?

 It is true that legal substances—alcohol and cigarettes—have caused more deaths through sickness and accidents in the United States than all illicit drugs combined.

In Chapter 1 we said that there are various ways of defining abnormal behavior. Under certain conditions, the use of substances that affect mood and behavior is normal enough, when normal is defined in terms of statistical frequency. It is normal, in this sense, to start the day with caffeine in the form of coffee or tea, to take wine or coffee with meals, to meet friends for a drink after work, and to end the day with a "nightcap." Many of us take prescription drugs that calm us down or ease our pain. Flooding the bloodstream with nicotine by smoking is normal in the sense that nearly 30 percent of us do it regularly. The majority of college students have used marijuana at least once, and a solid minority smoke it regularly. Many Americans rely on depressants to get to sleep at night and on stimulants to get started in the morning.

What, then, defines abnormal patterns of drug use? As we'll see, other criteria than statistical deviance may be used to define abnormality. Drug use may be considered abnormal when it is associated with significant personal distress or becomes self-defeating or mal-adaptive. The person who suffers physical, psychological, occupational, or social problems as the result of the use of a drug but persists in using the drug despite this knowledge may be considered a substance abuser, according to the DSM–III–R. It is not the use of any particular psychoactive substance, or drug, that is considered abnormal, but rather a pattern of abuse. As we'll see, such patterns of abuse may apply not only to such illicit drugs as cocaine or heroin, but also to substances that are legal but whose use or sale is controlled, such as alcohol, cigarettes (nicotine), and certain prescription drugs, such as minor tranquilizers and amphetamines.

In this chapter we focus on a broad array of drugs, including alcohol and other depressants; opiates, such as morphine and heroin; barbiturates or sedatives; stimulants, such as amphetamines, cocaine and nicotine; and psychedelics, such as phencyclidine (PCP), LSD, and marijuana.

PATTERNS OF SUBSTANCE ABUSE AND DEPENDENCE

Where does substance use end and abuse begin? From a legal standpoint, the answer is simple. For example, it is illegal—or legally abusive—in most states for people under the age of 21 to drink alcohol. But when does legal *use* of, say, alcohol cross the line and wax into *abuse*? The DSM–III–R considers use of a psychoactive substance abusive when it persists for at least one month despite the knowledge that it is causing or contributing to a persistent or recurrent social, occupational, psychological, or physical problem. The behavior of people who repeatedly miss school or work because they are drunk, or "sleeping it off," falls within the definition of **substance abuse.** But one incident of drinking to excess at a friend's wedding would not qualify. Nor would regular consumption of alcohol in moderate amounts be considered abusive if it were not associated with any signs of impaired functioning. It is not the amount or the type of the drug ingested that is the central issue in determining substance abuse. Rather, it is whether one continues to use the drug despite the knowledge that repeated use hinders functioning in other areas of life. Substance abuse may also be defined in terms of repeated use in situations in which it would be dangerous or physically hazardous to use such a substance, such as driving while intoxicated. Substance abuse is usually diagnosed in people with substance abuse problems who have never met the stricter criteria for a substance dependence disorder. The following case illustrates how a pattern of abuse of alcohol can hinder social functioning:

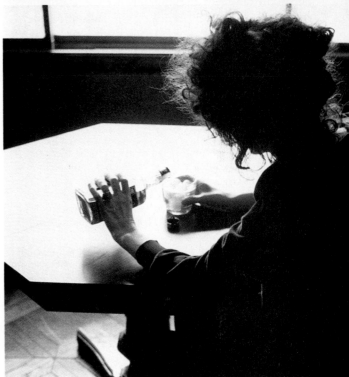

Alcohol is our most widely used—and abused—drug. We use alcohol to celebrate our achievements and facilitate social interactions, as in the top photo. Unfortunately, we sometimes use alcohol to drown our sorrows, as in the bottom photo. Where does substance use end and substance abuse begin? According to the DSM-III-R, use becomes abuse when it persists for at least one month despite the individual's knowledge that it is causing or contributing to social, occupational, psychological, or physical problems.

■ A 38-year-old woman and mother of four consulted a clinician upon recommendation of her priest, to whom she had confided experiencing "fits of rage" in which she struck her children and threw objects at her husband. Her children would run in terror and lock themselves in their rooms when they heard her ranting "Did you do your homework?" or "Just look at this messy house!" After these incidents, she felt guilty and ashamed. Upon interview, she admitted that these incidents were preceded by sneaking a couple of swallows of bourbon from a bottle hidden in the car. Since extreme reactions like this are not typical of a swallow or two of bourbon, the woman might be drinking more than she admits. The rage and violent behavior associated with her drinking would indicate a maladaptive pattern of use of alcohol consistent with a diagnosis of Alcohol Abuse.

Adapted from Spitzer et al., 1989, p. 252 ∎

Substance dependence involves behavior patterns that suggest impaired control over the use of the psychoactive substance and continued or even increased use despite awareness that the substance is disrupting one's life. Substance dependence is also identified by persistent desire or previous unsuccessful attempts to cut down or control the use of the substance, and by orienting one's life toward procuring and using the substance (See Table 10.1). Some features of substance dependence suggest a strong physiological component,

---

TABLE 10.1 Diagnostic Criteria for Psychoactive Substance Dependence

At least three of the following criteria must be met for a person to be diagnosed as dependent on a substance:

1. Taking larger amounts of the substance, or for longer periods of time than the individual intended (for example, person had desired to take only one drink, but after taking the first, continues drinking until severely intoxicated).

2. Persistent desire to cut down or control intake of substance, or lack of success in trying to exercise self-control.

3. Spending a greater amount of time in activities directed toward obtaining the substance (for example, theft), in actually ingesting the substance, or in recovering from its use. In severe cases, the individual's daily life revolves around substance use.

4. Performance of major role obligations is frequently impaired by intoxication or withdrawal symptoms (for example, missing days at work or school due to getting high or because of hangovers).

5. Has reduced or given up important social, occupational, recreational activities due to substance use (for example, person withdraws from family events in order to indulge in drug use).

6. Has continued to use substance despite evidence of persistent or recurrent psychological, social, or physical problems either caused or exacerbated by its use (repeated arrests for driving while intoxicated, for example).

7. Marked tolerance, as shown by need for increased amounts (increase of 50% or more) of the substance to achieve the desired effect or intoxication, or marked reduction in the effects of continuing to ingest the same amounts.

8. Experiences the abstinence syndrome associated with the substance.*

9. Has often taken the substance to relieve or to prevent withdrawal symptoms.*

Source: Adapted from DSM–III–R, pp. 167–168.
* These may not apply to hallucinogenic drugs such as LSD, marijuana, and phencyclidine (PCP).

---

such as tolerance and characteristic withdrawal patterns (Table 10.1). **Tolerance** is physical habituation to a drug so that with frequent usage, higher doses are needed to attain similar effects. People who are dependent on substances frequently show characteristic withdrawal symptoms—referred to as an **abstinence syndrome**—when the degree of use suddenly drops off.

For example, the abstinence syndrome for alcohol includes anxiety, shaking, agitation, weakness, rapid pulse, and elevated blood pressure. People who experience an abstinence syndrome frequently resume their use of the drug to relieve the withdrawal symptoms. However, a substance dependence disorder may be present even in the absence of these physiological features, if the person meets at least three of the other diagnostic criteria listed in Table 10.1. Drugs associated with both substance abuse and dependence disorders include alcohol, opiates (heroin or morphine), stimulants such as amphetamines (''speed'') or cocaine, sedatives or barbiturates, prescription tranquilizers such as diazepam (Valium), and various psychedelic drugs such as phencyclidine (PCP), LSD, and marijuana (cannabis). Nicotine ingestion through the smoking or chewing of tobacco may lead to a substance dependence disorder. But it is not associated with a substance abuse disorder since it is virtually unknown for someone to abuse nicotine (that is, continued use which aggravates an existing physical disorder) without having been dependent on it.

 Cigarette smoking per se is not a mental disorder, but it can lead to a dependence on the stimulant found in cigarette smoke, nicotine. Nicotine dependence is classified as a substance dependence disorder according to the DSM–III–R.

Many people abuse more than one psychoactive substance and are considered polydrug abusers. Heroin abusers, for example, may also abuse alcohol, cocaine, stimulants, or other drugs—simultaneously or successively. Polydrug abusers encounter special problems. Ingestion of multiple drugs increases the potential for harmful overdoses, and ''successful'' treatment of one form of abuse may not affect, or may exacerbate, abuse of other drugs. Some persons dependent on heroin, for example, are maintained on methadone, a synthetic narcotic that blocks the craving for heroin but does not produce a ''high.'' In order to get high, some of them turn to cocaine.

Psychological vs. Physiological Dependence

We noted that the DSM–III–R categorizes substance abuse problems in terms of patterns of abuse and dependence. While the DSM–III–R does not label people with

Physiological dependence on a substance means that the body changes because of regular usage, as shown by development of tolerance and/or a characteristic cluster of withdrawal symptoms referred to as an abstinence syndrome. Here we see a substance abuser undergoing severe withdrawal symptoms.

these disorders as "addicted" to the drugs they abuse, people commonly associate the term "addiction" with these types of problems. But what is meant by addiction?

People define addiction in different ways. For our purposes, we define addiction as the habitual use of a drug that is accompanied by signs of *physiological dependence*. Physiological dependence means that one's body has changed as a result of regular usage of a substance, as shown by the development of tolerance for the substance, by an abstinence syndrome, or both. By contrast, *psychological dependence* involves impaired control over the use of a drug without the physiological signs of dependence.

People can show psychological dependence in the absence of physiological dependence. For example, people can find it difficult to control use of cannabis (marijuana) even though they do not develop tolerance or show an abstinence syndrome when they stop using it. Some drugs are associated with psychological dependence but have not been conclusively shown to produce physiological dependence. These include PCP, cannabis, and, perhaps, cocaine.

A person can also become physiologically dependent on a substance yet not become psychologically dependent. For example, people recuperating from surgery are often given narcotics derived from opium as painkillers. These patients may develop tolerance for the drugs and show withdrawal symptoms when they stop using them, yet not show evidence of habitual use or lack of control over them.

In recent years, the concept of addiction has been extended beyond the abuse of chemical substances to apply to many forms of abnormal behavior involving patterns of habitual maladaptive behavior, such as compulsive gambling. Some have also characterized problems of persistent overeating to the point of extreme obesity as a form of "addiction" to food. In the vernacular, we also hear people speaking of being "addicted" to love, freedom, and clean air, but these are not the equivalent of physiological dependence. We shall limit our usage of *addiction* to the habitual use of substances that produce a state of physiological dependence.

Pathways to Drug Dependence

Although the progression to substance dependence varies, Weiss and Mirin (1987) suggest that there are some common pathways, as outlined in a number of stages.

1. *Experimentation*. During the stage of experimentation, or occasional use, the drug temporarily makes users feel good, even euphoric. Users feel in control and believe that they can stop at any time.

2. *Routine use*. During the next stage, a period of routine use, people begin to structure their lives around the pursuit and use of drugs. Denial plays a major role at this stage, as users mask the negative consequences of their behavior to themselves and others. Values change. What had formerly been important, such as family and work, come to matter less than the drugs.

The following clinical interview illustrates how denial can mask reality. The drug user, a 48-year-old executive, was brought for a consultation by his wife. She complained that his once successful business was jeopardized by his erratic behavior, that he was grouchy and moody, and that he had spent $7,000 in the previous month on cocaine.

CLINICIAN: Have you missed many days of work recently?

EXECUTIVE: Yes, but I can afford to, since I own the business. Nobody checks up on me.

CLINICIAN: It sounds like that's precisely the problem. When you don't go to work, the company stays open, but it doesn't do very well.

EXECUTIVE: My employees are well trained. They can run the company without me.

CLINICIAN: But that's not happening.

EXECUTIVE: Then there's something wrong with them. I'll have to look into it.

CLINICIAN: It sounds as if there's something wrong with you, but you don't want to look into it.

Cocaine is abused by people at all social strata. It is common for substance abusers to deny that they have problems controlling their drug intake. Here a business professional takes a break to snort cocaine.

EXECUTIVE: Now you're on my case. I don't know why you listen to everything my wife says.

CLINICIAN: How many days of work did you miss in the last two months?

EXECUTIVE: A couple.

CLINICIAN: Are you saying that you missed only two days of work?

EXECUTIVE: Maybe a few.

CLINICIAN: Only three or four days?

EXECUTIVE: Maybe a little more.

CLINICIAN: Ten? Fifteen?

EXECUTIVE: Fifteen.

CLINICIAN: All because of cocaine?

EXECUTIVE: No.

CLINICIAN: How many were because of cocaine?

EXECUTIVE: Less than fifteen.

CLINICIAN: Fourteen? Thirteen?

EXECUTIVE: Maybe thirteen.

CLINICIAN: So you missed thirteen days of work in the last two months because of cocaine. That's almost two days a week.

EXECUTIVE: That sounds like a lot but it's no big deal. Like I say, the company can run itself.

CLINICIAN: How long have you been using cocaine?

EXECUTIVE: About three years.

CLINICIAN: Did you ever use drugs or alcohol before that in any kind of quantity?

EXECUTIVE: No.

CLINICIAN: Then let's think back five years. Five years ago, if you had imagined yourself missing over a third of your workdays because of a drug, and if you had imagined yourself spending the equivalent of $84,000 a year on that same drug, and if you saw your once-successful business collapsing all around you, wouldn't you have thought that that was indicative of a pretty serious problem?

EXECUTIVE: Yes, I would have.

CLINICIAN: So what's different now?

EXECUTIVE: I guess I just don't want to think about it.

Source: Weiss & Mirin, 1987, pp. 79–80.

As routine drug use continues, problems begin to mount. Users devote their resources to their drugs. Family bank accounts are ravaged, "temporary" loans are sought from friends and family for trumped-up reasons, family heirlooms and jewelry are sold to pawnbrokers for a fraction of their value. Lying and manipulation become a way of life to cover up the drug use. The husband sells the television set to a pawnbroker and forces the front door open to make it look like a burglary. The wife claims to have been robbed at knifepoint to explain the disappearance of a gold chain, or worse, an engagement ring. Family relationships become strained as the mask of deniability shatters and the consequences of drug abuse become apparent: days lost from work, unexplained absences from home, rapid mood shifts, depletion of family finances, failure to pay bills, stealing from family members, and failure to meet family responsibilities, such as missing family gatherings or children's birthday parties.

3. *Addiction or dependence.* Routine use becomes addiction or dependence when users feel powerless to resist drugs, either to experience their effects or to avoid the consequences of withdrawal. Little or nothing else matters at this stage, as seen in the case of Eugene, a 41-year-old architect, who related the following conversation with his wife:

She had just caught me with cocaine again after I had managed to convince her that I hadn't used it in over a month. Of course I had been tooting (snorting) almost every day, but I had managed to cover my tracks a little better than usual. So she said to me that I was going to have to make a choice—either cocaine or her. Before she finished the sentence, I knew what was coming, so I told her to think carefully about what she was going to say. It was clear to me that there wasn't a choice. I love my wife, but I'm not going to choose *anything* over cocaine. It's sick, but that's what things have come to. Nothing and nobody comes before my coke. (Weiss & Mirin, 1987, p. 55)

SUBSTANCE ABUSE AND ORGANIC MENTAL DISORDERS

Psychoactive substances have direct, sometimes harmful, effects on the brain, in addition to their effects on other parts of the body and their connection with maladaptive behavior. Two of the principal types of organic mental disorders are defined by intoxication by the substances and by withdrawal from them.

Intoxication—also referred to as drunkenness or being high—largely reflects the chemical actions of the psychoactive substances. The pattern of change depends on which drug is ingested, the dose, the user's biological reactivity (Erwin et al., 1984), and—to some degree—the user's expectations (Brown et al., 1980, 1985; Christiansen et al., 1982). Signs of intoxication often include confusion, belligerence, impaired judgment, inattention, and impaired motor and spatial skills. Extreme intoxication by substances such as alcohol, cocaine, opiates, and phencyclidine (PCP) can result in death, either because of the substance's direct effects or because of behavior patterns—such as suicide—that are connected with psychological pain or impaired judgment.

When substances cause physiological dependence, there are characteristic abstinence syndromes upon reduction in use. An alcohol withdrawal symptom may be marked by features of dryness in the mouth, nausea or vomiting, weakness, **tachycardia,** anxiety and depression, headaches, insomnia, and fleeting **hallucinations.** In some cases, withdrawal produces a state of **delirium tremens** or "DTs." The DTs are usually limited to people who dramatically lower their intake of alcohol after many years of heavy drinking. The DTs involve intense autonomic hyperactivity (profuse sweating and tachycardia) and **delirium,** a state of mental confusion characterized by incoherent speech, **disorientation,** and extreme restlessness. Terrifying hallucinations—frequently of creepy, crawling animals—may also be present. The DTs are discussed further in Chapter 13.

Other psychoactive substances, such as opiates, barbiturates, and antianxiety agents (minor tranquilizers) may also produce both intoxication and withdrawal symptoms. Drugs such as marijuana, LSD, phencyclidine (PCP), and caffeine (yes, caffeine) may produce intoxication but have not been connected with abstinence syndromes. Nicotine, the active drug in cigarette smoke, can produce an abstinence syndrome but only rarely induces a state of intoxication.

Now we turn to a discussion of the psychoactive substances themselves. We shall focus much of our attention on alcohol, and for two reasons: (1) alcohol is the most widely abused of the substances, and (2) more research has been done on alcohol—its effects, the causes of dependence, and treatment—than on any other substance.

ALCOHOL

Perhaps no psychoactive substance has been so many things to so many people as alcohol, a drug that is classified as a **depressant.** Alcohol, which is found in such beverages as wine, beer, and "hard" liquors or "spirits" like scotch and rye, is used in many ways. It is our mealtime relaxant, our party social facilitator, our bedtime sedative. We observe holy days, laud our achievements, and express joyful wishes with alcohol. Adolescents assert their maturity with alcohol. The elderly use it to quicken circulation in peripheral parts of the body. Pediatricians have even swabbed the painful gums of teething babes with alcohol. Alcohol even deals the deathblow to germs on surface wounds.

Alcohol is the most widely abused substance in the United States. Perhaps 18 million Americans have serious drinking problems (Desmond, 1987). By contrast, half a million use heroin regularly, and one-third to one-half a million abuse sedatives. Between 2 million and 5 million people use cocaine regularly (Altman, 1988; Kolata, 1989).

 Alcohol, not cocaine, is the most widely abused substance in the United States.

It has been estimated that the personal and social costs of alcoholism exceed those of all illicit drugs combined. The economic costs of alcoholism have been estimated at over $116 billion a year, based on days lost from work, health problems associated with alcoholism, and motor vehicle accidents (National Council on Alcoholism, 1986). Alcohol abuse is connected with lower productivity, loss of jobs, and downward movement in socioeconomic status (Baum-Baicker, 1984; Mider, 1984; Vaillant & Milofsky, 1982). Perhaps half

TABLE 10.2 Prevalences of Alcohol and Drug Abuse and Dependence Across Three U.S. Cities

Lifetime Prevalence (in %)	New Haven, CT N = 3,058	Baltimore, MD N = 3,481	St. Louis, MO N = 3,004
Alcohol abuse or dependence	11.5	13.7	15.7
Drug abuse or dependence	5.8	5.6	5.5
(Current) Prevalence During Past 6 Months (in %)			
Alcohol abuse or dependence	4.8	5.7	4.5
Drug abuse or dependence	1.8	2.2	2.0

Source: Lifetime prevalences (Robins et al., 1984); 6-month prevalences (Myers et al., 1984).

the homeless population in the country consists of alcoholics (Desmond, 1987). Alcohol was also implicated in some 30 percent of the 30,000 suicides recorded in 1986.

Most American adults are not problem drinkers. As noted in the DSM–III–R, about 35 percent of adults abstain from alcohol and another 55 percent have fewer than three alcoholic beverages a week. Only about 11 percent imbibe an average of an ounce or more a day. Still, community studies have shown that between 11 and 16 percent of adult Americans meet diagnostic criteria for either an alcohol abuse or dependence disorder at some point in their lives (see Table 10.2)

There is no universally accepted definition of **alcoholism.** Nor does the DSM–III–R explicitly use the term alcoholism for purposes of classification. Classification is based on patterns of abuse and dependence, and no one pattern is exclusively associated with alcoholism. Three of the principal patterns of chronic abuse and dependence are the following:

1. Regular daily drinking of large amounts of alcohol
2. Regular heavy drinking that is limited to weekends
3. Long periods of abstention that alternate with periods of binge drinking that persist for weeks or months.

Male alcoholics tend to alternate between periods of heavy drinking and periods of abstinence (Hill, 1980). Women alcoholics—apparently more stable than their male counterparts—are more likely to drink steadily and less likely to binge (Hill, 1980).

Estimates of the current and lifetime prevalences of alcohol and drug abuse and dependence for both sexes combined in three U.S. metropolitan areas are shown in Table 10.2. The current prevalences of alcoholism (combined alcohol abuse and dependence) is about 5 percent of the population. At least 19 percent of the men surveyed showed evidence of alcoholism at some point in their lives. Alcoholism, in fact, was the most commonly occurring mental disorder in men up to the age of 65. Even among men over 65, alcoholism ranked third in prevalence. Alcoholism was among

the most common disorders affecting women in the 18–24 age range (Myers et al., 1984). Alcoholism may thus become more prevalent among women in the future (Helzer, 1987)—in part because alcoholism is affecting large numbers of young women, in part because the age group currently most extensively affected is entering older age categories.

Risk Factors for Alcoholism

Investigators have identified a number of factors that place people at risk for developing alcoholism and alcohol-related problems. These include:

1. *Sex.* Men are more prone to develop alcoholism, perhaps because of the tighter social constraints imposed on women drinking to excess. But women who drink heavily may be as apt to develop alcoholism as men who drink heavily (Cloninger et al., 1978).

2. *Age.* The onset of alcoholism among men is generally during their late teens or 20s, although they may not become aware of their dependence until their 30s. Features of alcohol abuse or dependence in men seldom begin after age 45. The course of alcoholism among women appears to be more variable and often begins at a later age than among men. (DSM–III–R, p. 174).

3. *Social class.* Alcoholism is found at all socioeconomic levels. Persons of low socioeconomic status are most likely to suffer the social correlates of excessive drinking, such as family instability and incarceration. More affluent people, however, may be more likely to imbibe large quantities of alcohol (Halldin, 1985) and suffer alcohol-related medical problems like cirrhosis of the liver (Bjurulf et al., 1971). Neither race nor rural vs. urban residence clearly places people at risk for alcoholism (Helzer, 1987).

4. *Ethnic factors.* Some ethnic factors are connected with alcohol abuse. Native Americans and Irish-Americans have the highest rates of alcoholism in the United States (Ewing et al., 1974; Lex, 1987). Although cultural attitudes are connected with patterns of drinking, biological factors may also play a role. For example,

QUESTIONNAIRE
How Do You Know Whether You Are Hooked?

Are you dependent on alcohol? If you shake and shiver and undergo the tortures of the darned (Our editor insisted on changing this word to maintain the decorum of a textbook) when you go without a drink for a while, the answer is clear enough. Sometimes the clues are more subtle, however.

The following items, adapted from the National Council on Alcoholism's self-test, can shed some light on the question. Simply place a check mark in the yes or no column for each item. Then check the key at the end of the chapter.

		YES	NO
1.	Do you sometimes go on drinking binges?	____	____
2.	Does it seem that more and more people are treating you unfairly?	____	____
3.	Do you tend to keep away from your family or friends when you are drinking?	____	____

		YES	NO
4.	Do you become irritated when your family or friends talk about your drinking?	____	____
5.	Do you feel guilty now and then about your drinking?	____	____
6.	Do you often regret the things you have said or done when you have been drinking?	____	____
7.	Do you find that you fail to keep the promises you make about controlling or cutting down on your drinking?	____	____
8.	Do you eat irregularly or not at all when you are drinking?	____	____
9.	Do you feel low after drinking?	____	____
10.	Do you sometimes miss work or appointments because of drinking?	____	____
11.	Do you use more and more to get drunk or high?	____	____

Source: Adapted from *Newsweek*, February 20, 1989, p. 52.

many Asians are more sensitive to alcohol than most Caucasians, as demonstrated by flushing of the skin and nausea. Such sensitivity may inhibit immoderate drinking (Helzer, 1987).

5. *Antisocial personality or behavior.* Antisocial behavior in adolescence or adulthood poses a risk for alcoholism among adults (Helzer, 1987). The features of adolescent antisocial behavior that predict adult alcoholism include independence, rebelliousness, rejection of social rules and legal codes, poor impulse control, low tolerance for frustration, and adoption of lax moral standards (Graham & Strenger, 1988; Jessor & Jessor, 1977; Nathan, 1988; Vaillant, 1983). On the other hand, many alcoholics showed no antisocial tendencies in adolescence, and many antisocial adolescents do not become substance abusers as adults (Nathan, 1988).

6. *Other problems with abnormal behavior.* Other disorders, especially mood disorders, appear to pose a risk for alcoholism among adults (DSM–III–R, p. 174; Helzer, 1987). Research has consistently found that alcoholics as a group are more depressed than nonalcoholics (Nathan, 1988). The causal connection is unclear, however. For example, do depressed people try to medicate themselves with alcohol? Do alcoholics disrupt their lives in depressing ways? Do alcoholics become depressed because of the biochemical properties of ethanol?

7. *Alcoholism in the family.* The best predictor of problem drinking in adulthood appears to be a family history of alcohol abuse (Goodwin, 1985; Tarter & Edwards, 1986). Family members who drink may act as models

("set a poor example"), and the biological relatives of alcoholics may inherit predispositions that favor drinking, such as an inborn tolerance that allows them to drink larger amounts at any one time (DSM–III–R, p. 174).

Effects of Alcohol

The effects of drugs vary from person to person (Erwin et al., 1984). By and large they reflect the interaction of (1) the physiological effects of the substances and (2) our interpretations of those effects. What do most people expect from alcohol? Adolescent and adult samples generally report beliefs that alcohol reduces tension, diverts people from worrying, enhances their pleasure and social ability, and transforms experience in beneficial ways (Brown et al., 1980, 1985; Christiansen et al., 1982; Rohsenow, 1983). These are stereotypical expectations. But what *does* alcohol do?

When we drink, we grow less responsive to personal and social codes and expectations, and also less cognizant of our departure from them. For these reasons, we are less apt to encounter self-censure and feelings of guilt and shame for conduct that we would reject when sober. It becomes tempting to adopt drinking as a way of handling our feelings about behavior that would otherwise be unacceptable.

Research studies show something of a discrepancy between our beliefs about alcohol and our actual responses. These studies are made possible by the fact that most people cannot discern the taste of vodka when it is mixed with tonic water. For this reason, it is possible to deceive experimental subjects as to what they have actually imbibed. Subjects who have had only tonic water may be misled to believe that they have drunk a highball with vodka, and vice versa. In this way, it is possible to control for the effects of expectations about alcohol.

Using this technique, studies of reaction to sexually explicit films suggest that men who *believe* they have drunk alcohol (when they have had tonic water only) show increases in sexual arousal, as measured objectively by the size of erection and subjectively by self-reported feelings of arousal. Men who have *actually* imbibed alcohol, however, but who believe that they have drunk tonic water only, show decreased sexual response (Briddell & Wilson, 1976). Research shows that alcohol also lessens women's sexual response to sexually explicit films (Wilson & Lawson, 1978). Thus, beliefs about the effects of alcohol may differ distinctly from its actual biochemical effects. The "sexy" feelings we may encounter after some drinks may arise from general feelings of euphoria, lessened sympathetic activity, and our anticipations—not from the alcohol itself.

> **?** Chemically speaking, alcohol actually depresses sexual response, although people may be more readily aroused after a drink or two if they *believe* that alcohol facilitates sexual response.

Drinkers may also do things they would not do when sober (Lang et al., 1980; Lansky & Wilson, 1981), like lingering over pornographic pictures as researchers monitor their behavior. One potential reason for the "liberating" effects of alcohol is that it impairs the information-processing that usually inhibits impulses (Hull et al., 1983; Steele & Southwick, 1985). That is, when inebriated, people may be less capable of envisioning the repercussions of misbehavior and less likely to dwell on social and personal standards of conduct. Perhaps the elation and euphoria brought on by alcohol help wash away misgivings. Remember, too, that alcohol is associated with a liberated social role in our culture. That is, it provides an external excuse for questionable behavior. People, after all, can claim, "It was the alcohol, not me."

Alcohol, similarly, has been connected with aggressive behavior. Department of Justice surveys have estimated that as many as one-third of prison inmates across the country had been drinking heavily immediately preceding the commission of their crimes (Desmond, 1987). Carefully controlled experiments with vodka and tonic water suggest, however, that alcohol does not directly cause aggression any more than it increases sexual response (Lang et al., 1975; Marlatt, 1981).

Depressants, like alcohol, generally act by curbing the activity of the central nervous system. All depressants reduce feelings of tension and anxiety, retard motor reactivity, and slow cognitive processes. In high doses, depressants arrest vital functions and can cause death. There are other effects specific to each kind of depressant, however, such as providing a "rush" of pleasure. Opiates, barbiturates, methaqualone, and other kinds of tranquilizers are also depressants.

Biochemically speaking, the primary effect of alcohol is akin to that of the benzodiazepines, a class of minor tranquilizers that includes diazepam (trade name Valium) and chlordiazepoxide (trade name Librium) (Carlson, 1988). Alcohol is our chief over-the-counter tranquilizer. Like the benzodiazepines, alcohol apparently heightens the sensitivity of **GABA** receptor sites (Suzdak et al., 1986). Since GABA is an inhibitory neurotransmitter, increasing the action of GABA serves to diminish overall nervous system activity.

As people drink, their senses become clouded, and balance and coordination suffer. Still higher doses act on the medulla and spinal cord, which regulate involuntary vital functions such as heart rate, respiration rate, and body temperature (Niaura et al., 1988). The slowing of these functions largely accounts for alcohol's classification as a depressant. According to the DSM–III–R, "Alcohol usually exerts its fatal effect by a direct depression of respiration" (p. 127).

One of the lures of alcohol is that it may have short-term effects of elevating mood and inducing feelings of euphoria and elation that can drown self-doubts and self-criticism. Frequent use over a year or more may deepen feelings of depression, however (Aneshensel & Huba, 1983). As an intoxicant, alcohol also impairs intellectual functioning, interferes with judgment, hampers coordination, and slurs the speech. Alcohol is implicated in about 50 percent of the nation's fatal auto accidents, about 25 percent of fatal falls, and 30 to 50 percent of suicides and homocides, respectively (see Figure 10.1). (*Alcohol and Health*, 1987; Desmond, 1987).

Alcohol and Health

It is also ironic that alcohol is fattening, yet habitual drinkers may be malnourished. Although it is high in calories, alcohol lacks vital nutrients like vitamins and proteins. Alcohol also impedes the body's absorption of various vitamins, including thiamine, a B vitamin. Thus chronic drinking can result in disorders that have been related to protein and vitamin deficiencies, including **cirrhosis of the liver** (linked to protein deficiency) and **alcohol amnestic disorder** (connected with vitamin B_1 deficiency) (Eckhardt et al., 1981). In cirrhosis

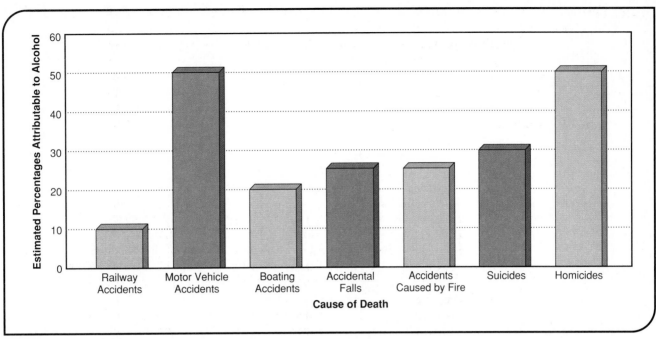

FIGURE 10.1 Estimated percentages of deaths associated with alcohol in the United States, 1980.

Source: Adapted from Ravenholt (1984)

of the liver, which causes about 14,000 deaths annually (Desmond, 1987), connective fibers supplant active liver cells, obstructing circulation of the blood. Alcohol amnestic disorder (also known as Korsakoff's syndrome, which is discussed further in Chapter 13) is an organic mental disorder that is characterized by glaring confusion and disorientation, memory loss for recent events (that is, problems in the formation of new memories), and abnormalities in eye movements.

When alcohol is metabolized, there are increases in levels of lactic and uric acids. Uric acid can give rise to gout. Chronic drinking is also connected with coronary heart disease and elevated blood pressure (Eckhardt et al., 1981).

Heavy alcohol abuse is also connected with cancer of the pancreas (Heuch et al., 1983) and stomach (Gordon & Kannel, 1984; Popham et al., 1984), although light to moderate drinking is not known to increase the risk of stomach cancer. The question has been raised as to whether or not alcohol is connected with breast cancer. Women who have one or two drinks a day may raise their risk of breast cancer from about 7 to 11 percent (Stipp, 1987). But other studies find no connection between alcohol and breast cancer (Kolata, 1988). Heavy maternal drinking of alcohol has been associated with infant deaths, birth deformities, and later growth deficiencies (Streissguth et al., 1980). It is estimated that 40 percent or more of children whose mothers drank heavily during pregnancy develop **fetal alcohol syndrome** (FAS), a cluster of symptoms char-

acterized by developmental delays and characteristic facial features, such as widely spaced eyes, an underdeveloped upper jaw, and a flattened nose. Mental retardation and limb deformities also may occur (Adickes & Shuman, 1981). But FAS and other developmental problems may occur among children whose mothers drank but one or two ounces of alcohol a day during the first month or so of pregnancy when the head of

Women who drink during pregnancy risk giving birth to children with fetal alcohol syndrome. This syndrome is characterized by deficiencies in cognitive functioning and by facial features such as widely spaced eyes and a narrow upper lip.

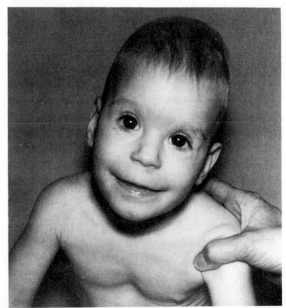

A CLOSER LOOK
Can You Drown Your Sorrows in Alcohol?
The Answer May Depend on Who Is with You

An old saying and a true one, "Much drinking, little thinking."

Jonathan Swift, Journal to Stella

Picture some people about to drown their sorrows in alcohol. Some go to bars. Of these, a few strike up friendships with new companions while they drink. Others have a few too many and start arguing about sports and politics. And some others stay at home. They sit at the table and ponder their problems while they stare at the bottle. You have probably guessed that those who go out to drink and become involved with others usually do a better job of drowning their sorrows in old John Barleycorn. Why?

Many people drink because of its anxiety-relieving and mood-elevating properties. But the alcohol–mood connection is not so clear-cut (Wilson, 1988). One cognitive model, for example, proposes that alcohol may either increase or decrease anxiety, depending on the nature of the cues in the drinking situation—especially on whether or not drinkers are also engaged in diverting activities (Steele et al., 1986).

One cognitive effect of alcohol is to narrow the attention, enabling drinkers to block out disturbing thoughts or stressors. Thus, drinkers may feel less anxious if their attention is centered on a pleasant diversion. But if no diversion is available, drinkers may only hone in on their problems and increase their levels of anxiety.

A recent study showed that alcohol intoxication reduced anxiety among individuals who were given the task of preparing a public speech (the anxiety-evoking responsibility)—but only when they were also given a diverting task (rating art slides) while they awaited the speech (see Figure 10.2) (Steele & Josephs, 1988). The subjects given alcohol but no diverting task actually showed more anticipatory anxiety than did subjects who awaited their speeches without alcohol. Since alcohol narrows the attention, perhaps those who went without drink were more able to divert themselves.

Ironically, using alcohol to cope with a stressor may actually heighten stress, unless one also does something

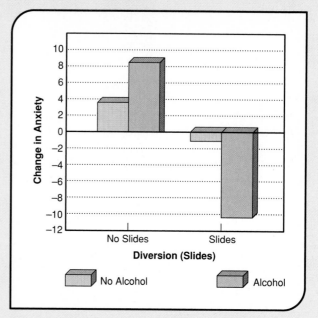

FIGURE 10.2 Can you drown your sorrows in alcohol? *The effects of alcohol on anxiety may depend on the presence of a diversion or distraction. In a study by Steele & Josephs, alcohol decreased anxiety when a diverting task was available, but increased anxiety in the absence of a diversion.* Source: Adapted from Steele & Josephs (1988)

diverting while under the influence. The anxiety-relieving effects of alcohol may have as much to do with the things we do when we are intoxicated than with the pharmacological properties of alcohol.

 People can apparently drown their sorrows in alcohol only when they are focusing on something else. Otherwise, alcohol appears to intensify negative emotions.

the fetus is beginning to take shape (Barr et al., 1984; Hanson et al., 1978; Harlap & Shiono, 1979; Streissguth et al., 1984). Women may not even realize at that early point that they are in fact pregnant. So the safest course for women who either are pregnant or believe they might be pregnant is to abstain from alcohol completely (Rathus, 1988).

Alcohol also has effects on brain cells, can trigger bleeding, can cause deterioration of the heart muscle, depress the functioning of the immune system, and cause hormonal changes that can put a damper on the sex drive in men and disrupt the menstrual cycles

of women. Despite this list of adverse effects, there is some evidence that suggests that light drinking may actually be healthy. Consider the following, for example:

Longitudinal epidemiological studies have observed residents of Hayward, California (Klatsky et al., 1981); Alameda County, California (Berkman et al., 1983); Framingham, Massachusetts (Friedman & Kimball, 1986); and Albany County, New York (Gordon & Doyle, 1987). They have generally shown that men who drink lightly to moderately incur fewer heart attacks and strokes and lower mortality rates than heavy drinkers *and* teetotalers. A nationwide study of 87,526 nurses found that women who imbibed 3 to 15 drinks a week had fewer strokes *caused by obstructed blood vessels in the brain* and fewer heart attacks than heavier drinkers and, again, teetotalers (Stampfer & Hennekens, 1988). However, the women were more prone toward the kind of stroke that is precipitated by excessive bleeding in the brain—a less common type of stroke.

Why may light drinking have health benefits? Some investigators (for example, Stampfer & Hennekens, 1988) propose that light drinking elevates the amount of HDL (high-density lipoproteins, or "good cholesterol") in the blood. HDL, in turn, helps free blood vessels of blockage by LDL (low-density lipoproteins, or "bad cholesterol"). But we must advise caution; the data to support these beliefs are inconsistent (Bennett, 1988).

Moreover, the epidemiological studies are correlational, not experimental. Perhaps the factors that encourage light or moderate drinking also enhance health. Perhaps light to moderate drinkers are more relaxed than abstainers. And perhaps light to moderate drinkers—people who exercise control over their drinking—are generally in greater control of their lives than are heavy drinkers.

Researchers who participated in the epidemiological studies do not recommend that teetotalers take up light to moderate drinking to reap its potential benefits. William Castelli, an investigator in the Framingham study, notes that people "can get the benefit [of light to moderate drinking] in other ways, such as by stopping smoking, lowering [their] cholesterol or . . . blood pressure, and [not] run the risk of becoming an alcoholic" (Castelli, 1988).

We next turn to other categories of drugs that have the potential to induce psychological dependence and, for some, physiological dependence or addiction. These drug categories include barbiturates and minor tranquilizers, opiates, stimulants, and psychedelics.

BARBITURATES (SEDATIVES) AND MINOR TRANQUILIZERS

Barbiturates such as amobarbital, pentobarbital, phenobarbital, and secobarbital are depressants or **sedatives** with several medical uses, including alleviation of anxiety and tension, short-term treatment of insomnia, and treatment of epilepsy and high blood pressure. Barbiturates rapidly create physiological and psychological dependence.

Psychologists generally counsel against using barbiturates for tension, anxiety, and insomnia. They lead quickly to dependence and do nothing to teach users how to modify self-defeating behavior. In contrast to the profiles of young narcotics abusers, most barbiturate addicts are middle-aged people who used barbiturates initially to combat insomnia. As use persisted, however, tolerance built-up so that barbiturates ultimately aggravated insomnia rather than corrected it; and, in the process, many users became physiologically dependent. Most physicians have grown concerned about barbiturate abuse and prefer to prescribe minor tranquilizers such as Valium and Librium for temporary relief of anxiety and tension and other similar drugs for treatment of insomnia. The minor tranquilizers are often referred to as antianxiety agents, since they focus on quelling anxiety without inducing sedation. However, as we shall see in Chapter 15, it is now recognized that minor tranquilizers can also create physiological dependence. Moreover, their prescription still fails to help people alter the sources of stress in their lives.

Barbiturates are also popular street drugs because they are relaxing and produce a mild state of euphoria. High doses of barbiturates, like alcohol, produce drowsiness, slurred speech, motor impairment, irritability, and poor judgment. The effects of barbiturates last from 3 to 6 hours.

Physiologically dependent people need to be withdrawn carefully from barbiturates, under medical supervision; if they are withdrawn abruptly, they may undergo convulsions and die. Because of synergistic effects, a mixture of barbiturates and alcohol is about four times as powerful as either drug used by itself (Combs et al., 1980). Barbiturates and alcohol taken together are regarded as causing the deaths of the entertainers Marilyn Monroe and Judy Garland.

OPIATES

Opiates are **narcotics,** principally morphine, heroin, and codeine, that are extracted from the opium poppy. It was the ancient Sumerians who named the poppy opium, which means "plant of joy." The major medical application of opiates and synthetic drugs that have morphine-like effects is the relief of pain or **analgesia.**

Opiates appear to stimulate brain centers that regulate sensations of pleasure and pain (Goeders & Smith, 1984; Ling et al., 1984). Two revealing discoveries were made in the 1970s. One was that neurons in the brain had receptor sites into which opiates fit—like a lock in a key. The second was that people produce substances that are similar to opiates in chemical structure and that dock at the same receptor sites (Goldstein, 1976). Some of them are labeled **endorphins,** which is short for "endogenous morphine"—that is, morphine coming from within, as mentioned in Chapter 4. Endorphins are apparently involved in the experience of pleasure and the control of pain. Endorphins may also help explain how people's expectations about drugs—including placebos—can enhance their effects: In a benign circle, people expect that drugs will relieve pain, which stimulates the brain to raise production of endorphins, which subsequently does relieve pain.

Morphine

Morphine—which receives its name form Morpheus, the Greek god of dreams—was introduced into the United States around the time of the Civil War. Morphine, one of the most powerful ingredients derived from opium, was used to deaden pain from wounds. Physiological dependence on morphine was called "soldier's disease" and there was little stigma attached to people who became addicted to morphine until the time that its use became restricted.

Heroin

Joletha Simmons is a 34-year-old heroin abuser. Flashbulbs pop as she blends heroin with water on a soda can, cooks the concoction with a flame, and sucks it into her syringe. Then, staring into a mirror, she balloons her cheek to make a vein rise in her neck and plunges the syringe in. She pauses to brush the tears from her eyes, then lowers her head, as if to pray, as the drug takes effect. (Adapted from *The New York Times*, April 4, 1989, p. A26)

Many heroin abusers inject the substance directly into their veins. Abusers who share hypodermic syringes that are contaminated with the AIDS virus risk contracting the infection themselves. Note the "tracks"—that is, marks of previous injections—in the crook of this heroin abuser's elbow.

Photographs of Joletha appeared in the *Washington Post*. Normally fearing arrest, a person would not want evidence of her habit to appear in the papers. Joletha, however, took the risk because she wanted to kick her habit and hoped that the publicity would gain her admission to a drug treatment program.

Ironically *heroin* was so-named because it was hailed as a "hero" when it was first derived. It was believed that it would cure morphine dependence. Heroin was developed in 1875 during a search for a drug that would relieve pain as effectively as morphine, but without causing addiction. Heinrich Dreser transformed morphine into a new and stronger "miracle" drug, heroin, by means of a minor chemical change. He believed, erroneously, that heroin did not create physiological dependence.

> **?** Heroin was in fact developed during a search for a drug that would relieve pain as effectively as morphine, but without causing physical addiction.

Like other opiates, heroin is a powerful depressant that can produce a euphoric rush. Heroin users claim that it is so pleasurable it can eliminate any interest in other pleasures, such as eating or sexual stimulation. Heroin was used to treat so many problems when it was first introduced that it was called G.O.M. ("God's own medicine").

Heroin is usually taken by injection, either directly beneath the skin ("skin popping") or into a vein ("mainlining"). The positive effects are immediate. There is a powerful "rush" that lasts from 5 to 15 minutes and a state of satisfaction, euphoria, and well-being that lasts from 3 to 5 hours. In this state, all positive drives seem satisfied, all negative feelings of guilt, tension, and anxiety disappear. With prolonged use, addiction can develop.

The abstinence syndrome associated with dependence on opiates such as morphine and heroin can be severe, beginning 4 to 6 hours after the last injection. Flu-like symptoms progress in 3 to 5 days to rapid pulse, high blood pressure, cramps, tremors, hot and cold flashes, vomiting, insomnia, diarrhea, and—of course—craving for the drug. However, the abstinence syndrome is variable. Although these symptoms can be uncomfortable, they are usually not devastating, especially when other drugs are prescribed to relieve them. Moreover, unlike withdrawal from alcohol or barbiturates, the abstinence syndrome rarely results in death. Many American soldiers who used heroin regularly in Vietnam are reported to have suspended usage with relatively little trouble when they returned to the United

States (Bourne, 1974). Also, people given opiates in a hospital rarely become addicted afterwards.

While heroin addicts may turn to crime to support their habits, such as by selling drugs (dealing) or stolen property, or by prostitution, heroin is a chemical depressant and does not directly stimulate criminal or violent behavior. The numbers of new heroin users increased through 1975 but have remained level since then. The spread of crack cocaine in recent years may have dampened the demand for heroin, especially among the young. Not surprisingly, heroin users of the 1990s are older than those in the 1960s or 1970s. Moreover, since 1972, new white users have outnumbered blacks. Recent initiates use the drug less frequently than did initiates in the 1960s and 1970s (Kozal et al., 1985).

Although regular users develop tolerance for heroin, high doses can cause drowsiness, stupor, altered time perception, and impaired judgment. A number of dependent people die from so-called overdoses, but "overdose victims" often show no evidence of having taken more than the usual dose. Coroners often list the cause of death as heroin overdose if the victim is known to be a user and if death by natural causes, suicide, or violence has been ruled out.

One of the dangers of heroin use lies in the contamination of the drug with other substances. Since 1939, when many New York City users contracted malaria from an epidemic of contaminated needles, heroin has often been "cut" (diluted) with quinine, a medicine used to treat malaria. But quinine can kill by flooding the lungs with fluid, a finding disclosed by autopsies of some "overdose victims." Users must now also be concerned about contracting the AIDS virus through the sharing of "dirty" (contaminated) needles.

STIMULANTS

Stimulants are psychoactive substances that increase nervous system activity. Some stimulants also appear to produce feelings of euphoria and increased self-confidence.

Stimulants such as amphetamines and cocaine expedite the release of the neurotransmitters norepinephrine and dopamine and also inhibit their re-uptake (their reabsorption by vesicles on presynaptic neurons). High levels of these neurotransmitters therefore remain available to the nervous system, intensifying neural activity and causing a continuous state of high arousal. Caffeine—the stimulant found in coffee, tea, many soft drinks, and chocolate—inhibits the reabsorption of these neurotransmitters by blocking the action of the enzymes that degrade them.

Amphetamines

The **amphetamines** represent a class of stimulants that were initially used by soldiers during World War II to help them stay vigilant through the night. Truck drivers have used amphetamines to remain awake at the wheel. Amphetamines have become even more widely known through students who have used them to "pull all-nighters." Amphetamines suppress the appetite and have been used widely by dieters to accelerate their metabolic rates and reduce pangs of hunger. They also enhance motor coordination and confidence, so athletes sometimes use them before meets and games. In Chapter 14 we shall see that a type of stimulant, methylphenidate (Ritalin), decreases disruptive behaviors in **hyperactive** children, perhaps because it stimulates parts of the cerebral cortex to exercise greater control over more primitive brain centers located in the lower brain.

Common street names for stimulants include uppers, speed, bennies (for Benzedrine), and dexies (for Dexedrine). In high doses, amphetamines produce a euphoric rush. While amphetamines are usually taken in pill form, some users inject liquid methamphetamine (Methedrine), the most potent form, directly into their veins. While some users inject methamphetamine for days on end to maintain an extended high, eventually the high comes to an end. People who have been on extended highs sometimes "crash" or fall into a state of deep sleep or even depression. Some people commit suicide on the way down.

Psychological dependence on amphetamines can develop quickly, especially among people who take them as a way of coping with depression. Tolerance also develops quickly, but it is unclear whether amphetamines cause physiological dependence in the form of a characteristic withdrawal syndrome. High doses can cause restlessness, irritability, hallucinations, paranoid delusions, loss of appetite, and insomnia. The hallucinations and delusions of the **amphetamine psychosis** mimic the features of paranoid schizophrenia, which has encouraged researchers to study the biochemical changes in the brain produced by amphetamines as possible causes of schizophrenia (see Chapter 12).

Cocaine

Do you remember the Coca-Cola commercials proclaiming that "Coke adds life"? Because of its sugar and caffeine content, Coca-Cola should grant quite a boost. But "Coke"—Coca-Cola, that is—has not been

(a) H.G. Wells

(b) Jules Verne

(c) Thomas Edison

During the nineteenth century, many public figures experimented with cocaine as a means of bolstering self-confidence and energy levels. Among the well-known people who endorsed the use of a cocaine-laced tonic were authors H.G. Wells and Jules Verne, and the inventor of the light bulb, the record player, and the motion picture, Thomas Edison. What famous psychological theorist used cocaine at about the same time?

"the real thing" since 1906. In that year the company withdrew **cocaine** from its secret formula. Coca-Cola was first brewed in 1886 by a pharmacist, John Styth Pemberton, who described his product as a "brain tonic and intellectual beverage," in part because of its cocaine content. Cocaine is a natural stimulant that is extracted from the leaves of the coca plant—the plant from which the soft drink obtained its name. Coca-Cola is still flavored with an extract from the coca plant, but one that is not known to be psychoactive (May, 1988).

Ingestion of coca leaves has a long history among the peoples of the coca-growing regions of South America. The Inca Indians used coca to help them endure physical labor without sleep or food (Weiss & Mirin, 1987). Europeans began to experiment with cocaine following the extraction of the drug from coca leaves in the mid-nineteenth century. One of the prominent advocates of cocaine, at least initially, was Sigmund Freud, who reported his personal experiences and those of others. As did the Incas, he found that cocaine enabled people to work longer without sleep or food. Freud also found that cocaine helped relieve pain and had positive psychoactive effects:

> The psychic effect of cocaine consists of exhilaration and lasting euphoria, which does not differ in any way from the normal euphoria of a healthy person. . . . One senses an increase of self-control and feels more vigorous and more capable of work. . . . Long-lasting intensive mental or physical work can be performed without fatigue; it is as though the need for food and sleep, which otherwise makes itself felt peremptorily at certain times of the day, were completely banished. (Freud, "On Coca," 1884)

In addition to enhancing performance, cocaine heightens vigilance and bolsters confidence—properties that have made it popular among professional athletes.

Freud's recognition of cocaine's analgesic qualities blazed the path to its use as the first local anesthetic. Freud changed his views on cocaine when he learned that it was powerfully habit forming. Other notables of the late nineteenth and early twentieth centuries who also endorsed cocaine included H. G. Wells, Thomas Edison, and Jules Verne, as well as kings, queens, and even two popes (Weiss & Mirin, 1987). Societal attitudes, like Freud's views, began to shift against cocaine use, based on increasing awareness of its habit-forming properties.

The effects of cocaine, as noted, may result from its stimulation of the release of the neurotransmitters norepinephrine and dopamine and from the blocking of their reuptake. These actions apparently increase the firing of neurons in certain areas of the brain, especially in areas involved in regulating states of wakefulness, alertness, and arousal (Weiss & Mirin, 1987). Cocaine also induces pleasure, perhaps as a result of stimulation of brain systems regulating the sense of pleasure. Dopamine may be involved in mediating this pleasure or reward mechanism. We know that laboratory rats will work for injections of cocaine by repetitively pressing a lever. They will continue to work for cocaine injections even if the neural pathways that use norepinephrine are destroyed. But their work effort is significantly reduced if the neural pathways for dopamine are destroyed. Perhaps cocaine and other drugs, particularly opiates, produce pleasure effects by activating the neurons that rely on dopamine for transmission of nerve signals (Weiss & Mirin, 1987).

Despite the attention of media and government on cocaine addiction, questions remain as to whether or not cocaine produces physiological dependence. Tolerance may not develop, and there is apparently no specific abstinence syndrome for cocaine (Van Dyke & Byck, 1982). Although cocaine does not produce the physiological symptoms of withdrawal following regular use that are associated with withdrawal from drugs like alcohol and heroin, suspension of use is connected with changes in mood and reduction in ability to experience pleasure (Gawin et al., 1989). These effects may induce cravings, *psychological* dependence, and habitual use (Gawin & Ellinwood, 1988).

> **?** There is no question that cocaine is habit-forming; however, despite the widespread public perception, it has not yet been demonstrated that cocaine is addictive in the sense of creating physiological dependence.

Cocaine is brewed from coca leaves as a "tea," breathed in ("snorted") in powder form, and injected ("shot up") in liquid form. The rise in the use of crack, a hardened form of cocaine suitable for smoking, which may contain more than 75 percent pure cocaine, has made cocaine— once the toy of the well-to-do—available to adolescents. Crack "rocks"—so-called because they resemble white pebbles—are available in small, ready-to-smoke amounts that are priced at about $10 to $15 a dose and considered to be the most habit-forming street drug available (Weiss & Mirin, 1987). Crack produces a prompt and potent rush that wears off in a few minutes. The rush from snorting is milder and takes a while to develop, but it tends to linger longer than the rush of crack.

Freebasing also intensifies the effects of cocaine. Cocaine in powder form is heated with ether, freeing the psychoactive chemical base of the drug, and then smoked. Ether, however, is highly flammable; comedian Richard Pryor received extensive burns while reportedly freebasing cocaine.

While the use of many drugs has fallen off since the 1970s (Kerr, 1988), cocaine has grown in popularity (see Figure 10.3). One survey of young adults (aged about 25) found that 37 percent of males and 24 percent of females had tried cocaine (Kandel et al., 1986). Between 2 million and 5 million people use it regularly (Altman, 1988; Kolata, 1989). Cocaine abuse tends to be characterized by periodic binges that may last 12 to 36 hours, which are then followed by 2 to 5 days of abstinence, during which time the abuser may experience cravings that prompt another binge (Gawin et al., 1989).

Physically, cocaine stimulates abrupt rises in blood pressure, constriction of blood vessels (with associated reduction of the oxygen supply to the heart), and acceleration of the heart rate (Altman, 1988). There are sporadic reports of respiratory and cardiovascular collapse, as with the publicized deaths of athletes Len Bias, Dave Croudip, and Don Rogers. Overdoses can give rise to restlessness, insomnia, headaches, nausea, convulsions, tremors, hallucinations, and delusions. It has been estimated that one out of every six drug-related deaths in 1984 was attributed to overdose of cocaine. While intravenous use of cocaine carries the greatest risk of a lethal overdose, other forms of use can also cause fatal overdoses. Table 10.3 summarizes a number of the health risks of cocaine use.

Repeated and high-dose use of cocaine can also give rise to depression and anxiety. Depression may be severe enough to prompt suicidal behavior. Both initial and routine users report experiences of "crashing" or depression following cessation of cocaine use, although crashing is more common among long-term, high-dose users. Psychotic behaviors have been induced by cocaine as by amphetamines. Cocaine psychosis is usually preceded by a period of heightened suspiciousness, depressed mood, compulsive behavior, fault-finding, irritability, and increasing paranoia (Weiss & Mirin, 1987). The psychosis may include visual and auditory hallucinations and delusions of persecution, as described in the following case:

■ After a while, I was convinced that there were people trying to break into my house. I didn't know who they were, but I was sure that people were after me. There was probably some reality to it too, since I really was scared that the police would come in and bust me. The only way that I felt that I could protect myself was by getting a knife. So I started sleeping with a butcher knife next to me. That didn't work for long, though, because I still felt insecure. So I felt that I had to get a gun. Every night, I went to bed with a gun on one side of me and a butcher knife on the other side. I was just waiting for

A crack vial. Crack "rocks" resemble small, white pebbles. Crack produces a powerful, prompt rush when smoked. Small, ready-to-smoke doses are available for about $10 to $15, a price tag that has made crack available to adolescents.

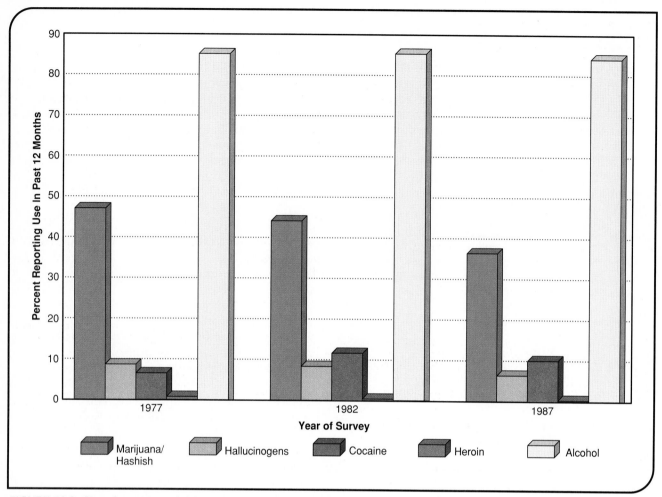

FIGURE 10.3 *Changing patterns in drug use among high school students.*
The prevalence of cocaine use increased slightly from the late 1970s to the 1980s, while the use of other drugs remained fairly steady or declined.

Source: Adapted from Kerr (1988); data based on surveys conducted by the University of Michigan Institute for Social Research.

someone to come in the house so that I could blow his brains out. God knows what I was going to do with the knife. I swear, I was a maniac. It wouldn't have mattered who had come to the door. If someone had come to my door at the wrong time to borrow a cup of sugar, I can tell you with 100 percent certainty, he would have been dead.

Weiss and Mirin, 1987, p. 39. ■

Violence may occur as self-defense against delusional persecutors. Tactile hallucinations, as of bugs crawling under the skin, may cause the user to pick at the skin until scabs form. The risk of cocaine-induced psychosis increases with chronicity and dosage levels.

Although cocaine has been unavailable to the general public since the Harrison Narcotic Act of 1914, it is still commonly the anesthetic of choice for surgery on the nose and throat. Cocaine, by the way, remains a stimulant, not a narcotic. Its classification as a narcotic

was a legality that brought the drug under the prohibitions of the narcotics act.

Nicotine

It is no secret that cigarette smoking is dangerous. Cigarette packs sold in the United States have for years displayed notices such as: "Warning: The Surgeon General Has Determined That Cigarette Smoking Is Dangerous to Your Health." Cigarette advertising is banned on radio and television. In 1988, Surgeon General C. Everett Koop proclaimed that cigarette smoking is the "chief preventable cause of death."

Largely because of health concerns, the percentage of American adults who smoke has declined from the 40 to 50 percent range in the mid-1960s to about 30 percent by the late 1980s (Berke, 1989; Mansnerus, 1988). Many more smokers have tried or would like

TABLE 10.3 Health Risks of Cocaine Use

PHYSICAL EFFECTS AND RISKS OF COCAINE USE

Physical Effects	Risks
1. Increased heart rate	Accelerated heart rate may give rise to heart irregularities that can be fatal, such as ventricular tachycardia (extremely rapid contractions) or ventricular fibrillation (irregular, weakened contractions).
2. Increased blood pressure	Rapid or large changes in blood pressure may place too much stress on a weak-walled blood vessel in the brain, which can cause it to burst, producing cerebral hemorrage or stroke.
3. Increased body temperature	Can be dangerous to some individuals.
4. Possible grand-mal seizures (epileptic convulsions)	Some grand-mal seizures are fatal, particularly when they occur in rapid succession or while driving a car.
5. Respiratory effects	Overdoses can produce gasping or shallow, irregular breathing that can lead to respiratory arrest.
6. Dangerous effects in special populations	Various special populations are at greater risk from cocaine use or overdose. People with coronary heart disease have died because their heart muscles were taxed beyond the capacity of their arteries to supply oxygen.

MEDICAL AND PSYCHOLOGICAL COMPLICATIONS OF COCAINE USE

Nasal problems	When cocaine is administered intranasally (snorted), it constricts the blood vessels serving the nose, decreasing the supply of oxygen to these tissues, leading to irritation and inflammation of the mucous membranes, ulcers in the nostrils, frequent nosebleeds, and chronic sneezing and nasal congestion. Chronic use may lead to tissue death of the nasal septu, the part of the nose that separates the nostrils, requiring plastic surgery.
Lung Problems	Freebase smoking may lead to serious lung dysfunction within three months of initial use.
Malnutrition	Cocaine suppresses the appetite so that weight loss, malnutrition, and vitamin deficiencies may accompany regular use.
Seizures	Grand-mal seizures, typical of epileptics, may occur due to irregularities in the electrical activity of the brain. Repeated use may lower the seizure threshold, described as a type of "kindling" effect.
Sexual Problems	Despite the popular belief that cocaine is an aphrodisiac, frequent use can lead to sexual dysfunctions, such as erectile dysfunction and failure to ejaculate among males, and decreased sexual interest in both sexes. While some people report initial increased sexual pleasure with cocaine use, they may become dependent on cocaine for sexual arousal or lose the ability to enjoy sex for extended periods following long-term use.
Other Effects	Cocaine use may increase the risk of miscarriage among pregnant women. Sharing of infected needles is associated with transmission of hepatitis, endocarditis (infection of the heart valve), and AIDS. Repeated injections often lead to skin infections as bacteria are introduced into the deeper levels of the skin.

Source: Adapted from Weiss & Mirin, 1987.

to quit (Glasgow & Lichtenstein, 1987). A profile of smokers is found in Figure 10.4. Both the federal government and local governments have mounted an offensive against public smoking. Concerned with the possible harmful effects of inhaling other people's smoke—that is, "secondary smoking"—municipalities across the country have enacted restrictions on smoking in public places like elevators, government buildings, doctors' offices, and restaurants. The federal government has banned smoking on domestic airline flights.

Nevertheless, about 350,000 people die from smoking-related illnesses each year. This is seven times greater than the number of people who are killed in motor-vehicle accidents (Cowley, 1988). Cigarette smoking is implicated as a cause of such diseases as cancer of the lungs, throat, and mouth, and it may contribute to cancer of the pancreas, bladder, and kidneys. Smoking has also been linked to heart disease (Epstein & Perkins, 1988), chronic respiratory and lung diseases, and other illnesses. Maternal smoking during pregnancy increases the risk of miscarriage, premature birth, and birth defects.

Once it was believed that the health risks of smoking primarily affected men, but today it is known that women who smoke are 30 percent more likely to die from cancer than women who don't smoke. All in all,

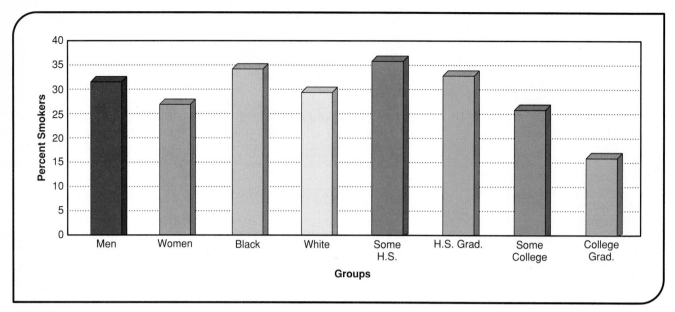

FIGURE 10.4 Cigarette smokers in the United States by sex, race, and education.

Source: Based on data in the Surgeon General's Report (1987); Center for Disease Control

the average life reduction for smokers, depending on level and duration of smoking, is estimated to be from about 5 to 8 years (Fielding, 1985).

Today peer pressure favors *not* smoking. Many people now see smoking as "deviant" behavior and are openly hostile toward people who assail them with "second-hand" smoke (Mansnerus, 1988). Interestingly, a 4-year prospective study of 654 late adolescents in Los Angeles county found that cigarette smoking in adolescence predicted health, personal, and social problems in young adulthood as strongly as the use of marijuana, narcotics, and cocaine did (Newcomb & Bentler, 1988). Because the data are correlational, we cannot conclude that adolescent cigarette use causes problems in adulthood. It is also possible that teenagers who choose to smoke—or who fail to fend off social influences to smoke—are more likely than better self-controlled teenagers to develop problems later on. Since it is no secret that cigarettes are killers, many teenagers who choose to smoke may be more interested in short-sighted pleasure than the long-term view.

■ **Components of Tobacco Smoke**   Tobacco smoke contains *carbon monoxide*, *hydrocarbons* (or "tars"), and *nicotine*.

Oxygen is transported through the bloodstream by **hemoglobin.** When carbon monoxide combines with hemoglobin, however, it lessens the blood's capacity to supply oxygen to the body. One outcome is shortness of breath. **Hydrocarbons** have been demonstrated to cause cancer in laboratory animals.

Nicotine is the stimulant found in tobacco. Nicotine gives rise to cold, clammy skin, faintness and dizziness, nausea and vomiting, and diarrhea—all of which account for the discomforts of novice smokers. Nicotine also stimulates the body by causing a discharge of the hormone epinephrine (adrenalin). Epinephrine generates a burst of autonomic activity, including rapid heart beat and release of sugar into the blood. It also furnishes a mental "kick." Nicotine accounts for the stimulating properties of cigarette smoke, but its effects are short-lived. In the long term it can contribute to fatigue.

■ **Nicotine Dependence**   The addictive properties of nicotine dependence have become widely accepted (Koop, 1988; Pomerleau et al., 1986). Nicotine dependence, which usually develops from cigarette smoking* is characterized by some degree of tolerance and a characteristic abstinence syndrome (Pomerleau et al., 1986). As tolerance for nicotine increases, the smoking rate increases until it levels off—at perhaps one, two, or more packs a day. Common withdrawal symptoms from cigarette smoking include nervousness, irritability, drowsiness, energy loss, difficulty concentrating, impaired physical performance, headaches, fatigue, irregular bowels, lightheadedness, insomnia, dizziness, cramps, palpitations, tremors, sweating, and cravings for cigarettes (Pomerleau et al., 1986).

---

* Other uses of tobacco, such as pipe or cigar smoking, or use of chewing tobacco, may also produce nicotine dependence. But cigarette smoking is the most common form of nicotine ingestion leading to dependence.

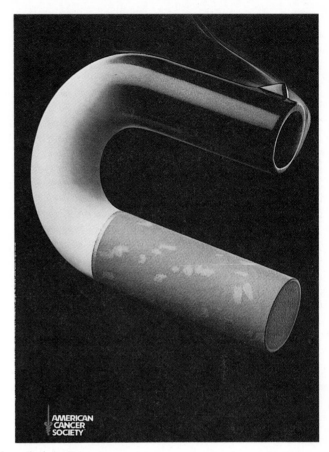

Only a couple of generations ago, cigarette advertisements featured medical doctors recommending the beneficial effects of certain brands. Today, of course, the powerful links between smoking, cancer, and other physical ills are widely known, as shown by the American Cancer Society poster. Camels used to advertise, "I'd walk a mile for a Camel." Many heavy smokers, sad to say, wish they felt well enough to walk a mile.

Further research evidence in support of the addictive aspects of cigarette smoking shows that smokers regulate their smoking patterns to maintain a fairly even level of nicotine in their bloodstreams. Smokers raise their cigarette consumption, take more puffs, or inhale harder as compensatory measures when high-nicotine cigarettes are replaced with low-nicotine brands (Schneider, 1987). Regular smokers also increase their nicotine intake if given certain drugs that speed the rate of elimination of nicotine from the body in the excretion of urine (Benowitz & Jacob, 1985). In one study, for example, subjects elevated their cigarette consumption when they were given vitamin C. Vitamin C lowers nicotine levels by elevating the excretion of nicotine, so again subjects compensated for loss of nicotine by smoking more. Stress, like vitamin C, boosts the excretion of nicotine. Stress increases the amount of acid in the urine, and nicotine is excreted more rapidly when the urine is highly acidic. So smokers may need to smoke more when under stress to maintain the same blood nicotine level, even though they may *think* that smoking is helping them cope with stress. Cigarette smoking is an efficient vehicle for delivering nicotine to the body. The nicotine in cigarette smoke readily reaches the brain in 7 to 10 seconds following each puff, which is less time than it takes heroin to reach the brain following injection into the bloodstream (Schneider, 1987). Blood levels of nicotine are elevated within minutes.

Based on the evidence of physiological dependence, the DSM–III–R categorizes nicotine dependence as a mental disorder, not cigarette smoking per se. But, as noted, the most common form of nicotine dependence is associated with cigarette smoking. However, it is unknown how many smokers meet the strict criteria for a dependence disorder (Hughes et al., 1987). It may be important to know whether or not a smoker is physiologically dependent on nicotine because various treatment techniques can be employed to help would-be quitters manage the dependency aspects of smoking. For example, nicotine-replacement therapy in the form of nicotine chewing gum is available to help dependent smokers quit.

Unlike many other drugs, nicotine does not hinder performance of mental and physical tasks, so smokers are not usually impaired in their social or occupational functioning. Unlike alcohol, nicotine only rarely produces intoxication (DSM–III–R, p. 182).

PSYCHEDELICS

Psychedelics, also known as **hallucinogenics,** are drugs that produce sensory distortions or hallucinations. There are major alterations in color perception and hearing. Various hallucinogenics may also have additional effects, such as relaxation and euphoria or, in some cases, panic.

The hallucinogenics include such drugs as lysergic acid diethylamide (LSD), psilocybin, and mescaline. Other psychoactive substances that are similar in their effects to the hallucinogenics are marijuana (cannabis) and phencyclidine (PCP). There is little or no evidence that these drugs give rise to physiological dependence, although there is no question that people can become psychologically dependent on them—as they can on practically anything. Mescaline is derived from the peyote cactus and has been used for centuries by Indians in the American Southwest, in Mexico, and in Central America in religious ceremonies, as has psilocybin, which is derived from certain mushrooms. But LSD, PCP, and marijuana are more commonly used in North America.

LSD

LSD is the acronym for lysergic acid diethylamide, a synthetic hallucinogenic drug that was discovered by the Swiss chemist Albert Hoffman in 1938. Hoffman penned his initial experience with LSD as follows:

> I was forced to stop my work in the laboratory . . . and to go home, as I was seized by a particular restlessness associated with the sensation of mild dizziness. On arriving home, I lay down and sank into a kind of drunkenness which was not unpleasant and which was characterized by extreme activity of imagination. As I lay in a dazed condition with my eyes closed (I experienced daylight as disagreeably bright) there surged upon me an uninterrupted stream of fantastic images of extraordinary plasticity and vividness and accompanied by an intense, kaleidoscope-like play of colours. This condition gradually passed off after about two hours. (Hoffman, 1971, p. 23)

An LSD "trip." LSD is an hallucinogenic drug that gives rise to a vivid parade of colors and visual distortions. Some users have claimed to have achieved great insights while "tripping," but when the drug wears off, they usually cannot summon up or implement these "insights."

In addition to the vivid parade of colors and visual distortions produced by LSD, users have claimed that it "expands consciousness" and opens new worlds— as if they were looking into some reality beyond the usual reality. Sometimes they believe they have achieved great insights during the LSD "trip," but when it wears off they usually cannot implement or even summon up these discoveries. LSD has been used by about 6 percent of the high school population and by smaller percentages of adults (Johnston, 1988).

LSD apparently decreases the action of serotonin, a neurotransmitter that inhibits neural firing, and LSD may also influence the utilization of dopamine. Thus, by curbing the action of an inhibiting neurotransmitter and increasing dopamine activity, brain activity escalates, in this case giving rise to a flurry of colorful sensations or hallucinations.

LSD trips are somewhat unpredictable. Many frequent users have nothing but good trips. Others have had one bad trip and sworn off. Barber's review of the literature (1970) suggests that the rare psychotic reactions that occur are usually confined to users with a history of abnormal behaviors.

Some users have **flashbacks**—distorted perceptions or hallucinations that occur days, weeks, or longer

350

after usage but mirror the LSD trip. Such flashbacks may stem from chemical changes in the brain produced by LSD, but Heaton and Victor (1976) and Matefy (1980) submit a psychological explanation.

Heaton and Victor (1976) found that LSD users who undergo flashbacks are more oriented toward fantasy, more willing to let their thoughts wander, and more prone toward focusing on internal sensations. If users should encounter sensations similar to a trip, they may construe them as flashbacks and let themselves focus on them indefinitely, encouraging a replay of the experience in which people may psychologically fill in the gaps.

Matefy (1980) found that trippers who report flashbacks also show greater capacity to become engrossed in role-playing, and they hypothesized that flashbacks may amount to nothing more than enacting a trip. This does not mean that people who claim to have flashbacks are lying. They may be more willing to surrender control over internal sensations to try to alter their states of consciousness and seek peak experiences. Users who do not report flashbacks prefer to be more in charge of their thoughts and are more concerned about meeting the demands of daily life.

Phencyclidine (PCP)

Phencyclidine, or PCP—referred to as "angel dust" on the streets—was developed as an anesthetic in the 1950s but was discontinued as such when its hallucinatory side effects were discovered. It became popular as a street drug because it is readily manufactured and relatively inexpensive.

The effects of PCP, as of most drugs, are dose-related. It sometimes causes hallucinations, as well as accelerating the heart rate and blood pressure and causing sweating, flushing, and numbness. It also has dissociating effects—causing users to feel as if there is some sort of invisible barrier or wall between themselves and their environments. Dissociation can be experienced as pleasant, engrossing, or frightening, depending upon the user's expectations, mood, setting, and so on. Overdoses can give rise to drowsiness, convulsions, and, now and then, coma or even death from various causes, such as heart failure or cerebral hemorrhage. PCP can also have unpredictable effects and induce paranoia, violent or aggressive behavior, and accidents that result from perceptual distortions.

Marijuana

Marijuana is derived from the *cannabis sativa* plant. Some people use marijuana to relax; others to elevate their mood. Marijuana can sometimes produce mild hallucinations, so marijuana is regarded as a minor hallucinogenic. The major psychoactive substance in marijuana is **delta-9-tetrahydrocannabinol,** or THC, which is found in the plant's branches and leaves but is most highly concentrated in the resin that comes from the female plant. **Hashish,** or "hash," is the psychoactive substance that is derived from this sticky resin. Although more potent than marijuana, hashish has similar effects.

Perhaps one-third of all Americans have tried marijuana (NIDA, 1983). Marijuana use burgeoned throughout the so-called Swinging Sixties and the 1970s but declined after 1980. In the late 1980s marijuana was used by about 36 percent of high school students, which represents a decline from a peak of 51 percent in 1979 (Kerr, 1988). Marijuana remains the nation's most popular illicit drug, although its prevalence does not compare with that of alcohol.

■ **Psychoactive Effects of Marijuana** The effects of marijuana vary with the level of intoxication. The early stages of intoxication are often characterized by restlessness, which is then supplanted by feelings of serenity. Moderate to strong intoxication gives rise to reports of heightened perceptions and gains in self-insight, creative thinking, and empathy for others. Some users report that marijuana helps them socialize, but the friendliness that typifies early intoxication may give way to self-absorption and social withdrawal as the smoker becomes increasingly intoxicated or "high" (Fabian & Fishkin, 1981). Strongly intoxicated people perceive time as passing more slowly. A song of a few minutes may seem to last an hour. The smoker may experience an increased awareness of physical sensations, such as heart beat. Stronger intoxication may produce subjective feelings of heightened sexual sensations. Visual hallucinations may also occur.

Strong intoxication can cause smokers to become disoriented. If their moods are euphoric, disorientation may be construed as harmony with the universe. Yet some smokers find strong intoxication disturbing. The accelerated heart rate and sharpened awareness of bodily sensations cause some smokers to fear that their hearts will "run away" with them. Some smokers are frightened by disorientation and fear that they will not "come back." High levels of intoxication now and then induce nausea and vomiting.

Regular use of marijuana does not appear to produce physiological dependence. There is no clear withdrawal syndrome associated with marijuana use, nor does tolerance tend to develop. In fact, regular use may lead to **reverse tolerance.** That is, regular users of marijuana may need progressively *less* of the substance to achieve similar effects. Perhaps some of the substances in marijuana smoke require a long time to be metabolized. The effects of smoking would then be added to those of the chemicals tarrying in the body. But regular users also have certain expectations that may interact with even mild bodily cues to produce results formerly achieved through higher doses.

While not physiologically addicting, regular marijuana use can lead to psychological dependence. Concern has also been expressed that marijuana may give rise to **amotivational syndrome,** which saps achievement motivation, melts ambition, and impairs concentration. This fear has been fueled by correlational evidence that heavy collegiate smokers do not struggle to succeed with the intensity of nonsmokers or occasional smokers. But we cannot ignore the selection factor in correlational studies. Other research suggests that people who choose to smoke heavily may differ in basic ways from people who do not (Maugh, 1982). For example, heavy smokers may be more committed to fantasy and emotional experience than to self-regulation and academic excellence. Their general approach to life could underlie their relative lack of ambition and their ingestion of marijuana. Still other investigations find no long-term cognitive effects from heavy use of marijuana over a 7-year period (Schaeffer et al., 1981).

Whatever the final outcome of research on its psychological effects, there are other reasons to be concerned about marijuana use. The Institute of Medicine of the National Academy of Sciences notes that marijuana impairs perception and motor coordination and thus makes driving and the operation of other machines dangerous. It impairs short-term memory and slows

It is unclear as to whether or not marijuana saps motivation (leads to "amotivational syndrome"). The research problem involves a selection factor: people who choose to rely heavily on marijuana may already be less ambitious and achievement-oriented than those who do not.

learning. Although marijuana induces positive mood changes in many users, some people report anxiety and confusion; there are also occasional reports of psychotic reactions. Marijuana elevates the heart rate to about 140 to 150 beats per minute and, in some people, raises the blood pressure. These changes are particularly taxing to people with hypertension and heart disease. Finally, marijuana contains even higher amounts of carcinogenic hydrocarbons than does tobacco.

THEORETICAL PERSPECTIVES

People use psychoactive drugs for different reasons. Some begin using drugs in adolescence because of peer pressure or beliefs that it makes them seem more sophisticated or adult. The use of illicit drugs by some adolescents is an expression of rebellion against the dictates of their parents and the general society. Regardless of the reasons for initial usage, people are more likely to continue using a drug if it makes them feel good (Mizner et al., 1970). Even for most adolescents, alcohol is used to "get high," not to establish that they are adults (Carman et al., 1983). Many people smoke cigarettes for the pleasure they provide. Others smoke to help them

Routine marijuana use is suspected to give rise to so-called amotivational syndrome, which saps achievement motivation, melts ambition, and impairs concentration. Evidence is correlational, however, so it may be that less ambitious individuals are more prone to making marijuana a central feature of their lifestyles.

in part, by where we live, whom we worship with, and by the social norms that regulate our behavior. Cultural attitudes can encourage or discourage problem drinking.

Adolescents (and preadolescents) are exposed to peers who use drugs. In a survey of 563 eleventh and twelfth graders from two southwestern communities, association with peers who used drugs was the single greatest predictor of drug usage (Swaim et al., 1989). Although the demographic composition of the communities is not typical for the nation as a whole, their self-reported patterns of drug use parallel national patterns (as outlined by Johnston et al., 1986), so the findings are instructive.

Children are particularly susceptible to peer pressure from about age 8 to 14 (Rathus, 1988). Children in this age group who are closely connected with groups that use proscribed substances may succumb to pressure to use them. Substance abuse is not just an inner-city problem. Every American city and suburb has groups and subcultures that abuse drugs.

Psychodynamic Perspectives

According to traditional psychodynamic theory, alcoholism reflects certain features of the oral-dependent personality. Alcoholism is, by definition, an "oral" activity. Psychodynamic theory connects immoderate drinking with other "oral traits," such as dependence and depression, and traces this cluster of traits and behaviors to fixation in the oral stage of psychosexual development. Excessive drinking in adulthood symbolizes efforts to attain oral gratification.

Psychodynamic theorists also view smoking as an oral fixation, although they have not been able to predict who will or will not smoke. As mentioned in Chapter 2, Sigmund Freud's cigar smoking could be taken as a sign of an oral fixation. He smoked upwards of 20 cigars a day despite several vain attempts to desist. Although he contracted cancer and had to have his jaw replaced, he would still not surrender his "oral fixation." He eventually succumbed to cancer of the mouth in 1939 at the age of 83, after years of agony.

Research support for these psychodynamic concepts is mixed. Some research suggests, for example, that alcoholics are more likely to be dependent than the general population (McCord et al., 1960). It is unclear, however, whether dependence contributes to or stems from problem drinking (Vaillant & Milofsky, 1982). Chronic drinking, for example, is connected with loss of employment and downward movement in social status, both of which would render drinkers more reliant on others for support. Moreover, the empirical connection between dependence and alcoholism does not establish that alcoholism represents an oral fixation due to unconscious childhood conflict. There are also some

contrary findings regarding personality variables. The National Academy of Sciences (1983) reported that substance abusers are more likely than nonabusers to be sensation-seekers and manifest antisocial personalities; more likely to feel alienated from society and disregard social codes. This should not be surprising since drugs with the exception of alcohol and nicotine (cigarettes) are illegal, and alcohol and cigarettes are illegal for minors. Antisocial personality is likely to take the form of *independence* as expressed through rebelliousness, rejection of social and legal codes, and lax moral standards (Graham & Strenger, 1988; Vaillant, 1983). It appears that there may be different personality subtypes among substance abusers and it would be unfair to characterize them all as dependent or antisocial.

Consistent with psychodynamic theory, alcoholism is also frequently connected with depression (Nathan, 1988). However, as noted earlier, depression can be a long-term effect of immoderate drinking as well as a trigger of drinking.

In sum, there are many perspectives on substance abuse and dependence. It appears that in some cases genetic factors and the early home environment give rise to predispositions to abuse and dependence. In adolescence and adulthood, expectations—many of which are formed by cultural stereotypes, conditioning and observational learning, and cognitive factors—all seem to exert a certain degree of influence in determining patterns of substance abuse and dependence. There is a growing recognition that substance abuse and dependence cannot be explained from a single model or perspective. These behavior patterns apparently reflect complex interactions among biological, psychological, and social factors (Nathan & Niaura, 1985) that may be better understood by research that takes these interactions into account.

TREATMENT

There have been and remain a vast variety of nonprofessional, biological, and psychological approaches to substance abuse and dependence. However, treatment has been a frustrating endeavor. In many, perhaps most cases, substance-dependent people really do not want to discontinue the substances they are abusing—they would much prefer to find ways of simply averting their harmful effects. Helping people through abstinence syndromes is usually straightforward enough, as we shall see. However, helping them to envision a life devoid of their preferred substances is more problematic. We should also note that treatment takes place in a setting—such as the therapist's office, a support group, a residential center, or a hospital—in which abstinence is valued and encouraged. Then the individual returns to the work, family, or street settings in which abuse and dependence were instigated and maintained. So the problem of returning to abuse and dependence following treatment—that is, of *relapse*—can be more troublesome than the problems involved in initial treatment. For this reason, recent treatment efforts have focused on relapse prevention.

Biological Approaches

Various biological approaches have been introduced in the treatment of substance abuse and dependence disorders. For people with chemical dependencies, biological approaches to treatment often begin with **detoxification**—that is, helping physiologically dependent people safely through the abstinence syndrome. Continued treatment is then provided in the form of psychological counseling or peer support groups. Biological researchers are also actively searching for chemicals—drugs—that will block the cravings for cocaine and other problem drugs without incurring risks of abuse or dependence themselves.

■ **Detoxification**   Detoxification is often carried out in a hospital setting to provide the chemically dependent person with as much support as possible and, in the case of alcohol and barbiturates, to allow medical personnel to monitor and treat potentially dangerous withdrawal symptoms, such as convulsions. Dependent people are sometimes given tranquilizers, such as Librium and Valium, to help mute withdrawal symptoms. Detoxification to alcohol takes about one week (Rada & Kellner, 1979). Tranquilizers should be eventually withdrawn to prevent the substitution of one drug dependency for another.

■ **Disulfiram**   A chemotherapeutic approach to the treatment of alcohol abuse is found in the drug disulfiram (brand name Antabuse). When alcohol is ingested within 12 hours of taking disulfiram, a strong aversion reaction including nausea, sweating, flushing, rapid

This young woman is being admitted to a drug rehabilitation center, in which the first step will be helping her safely withdraw from chemical dependence. She will then be faced with the on-going challenge of developing a lifestyle that is devoid of drugs.

heart rate, reduced blood pressure, and vomiting is induced (Murray, 1989a). Disulfiram is intended to discourage use of alcohol by engendering an anticipatory fear reaction, but well-designed studies have not documented its effectiveness (Murray, 1989a). For one thing, people who want to continue to drink can simply stop taking the drug.

■ **Antidepressants**   Antidepressants have shown some promise in stemming cravings for cocaine in some abusers shortly after they discontinue the drug, according to some preliminary research findings, but they are no panacea (Kolata, 1989). In a recent double-blind controlled study (Gawin et al., 1989), cocaine abusers given an antidepressant drug were two to three times as likely to remain abstinent for several weeks during a six-week treatment program as were abusers given a placebo drug or another medication, lithium carbonate. Fifty-nine percent of those given the antidepressant (desipramine; trade name Norpramin) maintained abstinence for at least three to four consecutive weeks, as compared to an average of 21 percent in the other conditions. Desipramine may help activate neural processes that underlie feelings of pleasure in everyday experiences. If substance abusers are more capable of deriving pleasure from nondrug-related activities, they may be less likely to return to cocaine to induce pleasurable feelings. However, the study only addressed a six-week period following initial abstinence. Long-term effects of desipramine need to be studied further.

■ **Nicotine Chewing Gum**   One promising development in the pharmacological treatment of cigarette smoking is a prescription gum that contains nicotine (brand name Nicorette). Some smokers, perhaps most, are nicotine-dependent. Nicotine gum averts withdrawal symptoms when smokers discontinue cigarettes. Once the smoking habit is suspended, ex-smokers can gradually wean themselves from the gum.

A review of placebo-controlled studies of nicotine-chewing-gum treatment supports its usefulness in quitting smoking (Fagerstrom, 1988). Nicotine gum is apparently better at reducing some withdrawal symptoms, such as irritability, than others. (Its success at reducing craving is spottier [Pomerleau, et al., 1986; Fagerstrom, 1988].) Nicotine chewing-gum has been shown to be significantly more effective than placebo or no-gum control treatments in helping smokers quit and at least as effective as more labor- and time-intensive approaches (Fagerstrom, 1988). However, nicotine gum in the absence of other treatment, such as behavior therapy, has not been found to be effective (Feldman, 1985; Schneider et al., 1983; Jamrozik et al., 1984; Sutton & Hallett, 1988). So physicians who merely prescribe the gum treatment to their patients seeking to quit smoking, without additional counseling or support, may not achieve much success. Finally, a combination of nicotine chewing gum and behavior therapy may apparently be more effective than either approach alone—especially for heavier, more nicotine-dependent smokers (Glasgow & Lichtenstein, 1987).

■ *Methadone-Maintenance Programs* **Methadone** is an **opioid**—similar to an opium derivative in chemical structure, but synthesized in the laboratory. Methadone is used to treat physiological dependence on heroin in the same way that heroin was used to treat physiological dependence on morphine. Methadone is slower-acting than heroin and does not provide the thrilling rush. Methadone programs are usually publicly financed and hence relieve heroin-dependent people of the need to engage in illicit activity to support their habits. It can be taken indefinitely. On the other hand, people treated with methadone can be conceptualized as swapping dependence on one drug for dependence on another.

Methadone is taken orally in single doses in the clinic setting. Ironically, methadone has also become desirable as a street drug because users have found that if they inject it rather than take it orally, it can provide sensations similar to those of heroin.

One study compared a combination of paraprofessional drug counseling, professional psychotherapy, and methadone maintenance to paraprofessional drug counseling and methadone maintenance alone among 93 male veterans. The addition of professional psychotherapy produced significantly better results on a battery of tests of abnormal behaviors (Woody et al., 1987). Perhaps skillful therapy better helps people manage stress and develop adaptive behaviors than chemicals alone or chemicals and paraprofessional or lay counseling.

■ *Naloxone* Another drug, **naloxone,** prevents users from becoming high if they subsequently take heroin. Some people are placed on naloxone after being withdrawn from heroin. However, the basic limitation of naloxone is identical to that of disulfiram: People can choose not to use it. Drugs like naloxone also do not provide the positive reinforcement yielded by heroin, so it does not motivate heroin users to undertake a heroin-free lifestyle.

Drugs like disulfiram and methadone are apparently more useful when they are combined with counseling, job training, and stress management—processes that provide substance abusers the skills they need to embark on a life in the mainstream culture.

Nonprofessional Support Groups

Despite the complexity of the factors contributing to substance abuse and dependence, these problems are

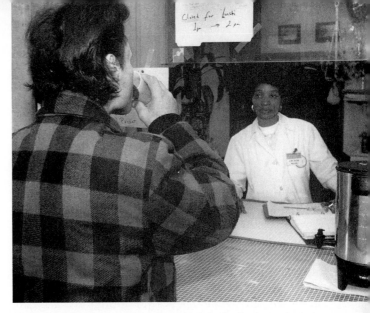

Many people who have become physiologically dependent on heroin are switched to methadone, a synthetic drug that is chemically similar to heroin but is longer acting and does not provide the same thrilling rush. Methadone is meted out in controlled doses at clinics to prevent dependent people from abusing it. While methadone treatment may help break a dependence on heroin, it may also be seen as a game of "musical drugs" in which one form of addiction is substituted for another.

frequently handled by lay people or nonprofessionals— frequently people who have had or have the problems themselves. For example, self-help group meetings are sponsored by organizations like Alcoholics Anonymous (AA), Narcotics Anonymous, and Cocaine Anonymous. These groups promote complete abstinence from substances and provide members with an opportunity to express their feelings and experiences in a supportive group setting. More experienced group members (sponsors) provide direct support to the newer members during periods of crisis or potential relapse. The meetings are without charge.

■ Alcoholics Anonymous

It's the first drink that gets you drunk.

One day at a time.

AA Slogans

Many lay people and professionals consider AA to provide the most effective treatment for problem drinkers. Alcoholics Anonymous was begun in the 1930s and although it is run by lay people, it is based on the disease model of alcoholism. The organization assumes that alcoholics are never cured, regardless of how long they abstain from alcohol or how well they control their drinking. Instead of being "cured," alcoholics are seen as "recovering." It is also assumed that people need help in order to stop drinking. AA is so deeply embedded in the consciousness of helping professionals that many of them automatically refer newly detoxified people to AA as the follow-up agency.

The AA experience is part religious, part group-supportive. Participants in AA meetings are encouraged to recognize their powerlessness over alcohol and seek the help of a "higher power," which discourages some potential members, including agnostics and atheists who prefer not to seek divine support. Prayer and meditation are urged upon members to help them get in touch with the higher power. The meetings themselves provide group support. So does the buddy system, which encourages members to call each other for support when they feel tempted to drink.

Alcoholics Anonymous claims to have a high success rate, one in the neighborhood of 75 percent (Wallace, 1985). Critics note that percentages this high are based on personal testimony, or self-reports, rather than on careful surveys or experiments. Moreover, such estimates include only persons who attend meetings for extended periods. As many as 90 percent of those who try AA drop out after a handful of meetings (Miller, 1982). The organization fails to keep records of many clients in order to protect their anonymity (Brownell et al., 1986). AA also fails to use control groups in assessing the effectiveness of treatment (O'Connor & Daly, 1985). Therefore, we cannot rule out a selection factor as possibly being responsible for any benefits attributed to AA; perhaps some people who apparently benefit from AA actually improve because they have decided to change their lives.

Al-Anon, begun in 1951, is a spin-off of AA that supports the family members of alcoholics—particularly the children, who may number as many as *30 million*. There are now some 26,000 Al-Anon groups nationwide (Desmond, 1987).

■ **Narcotics Anonymous and Cocaine Anonymous**
Narcotics Anonymous and Cocaine Anonymous also urge members to admit their powerlessness, to place their faith in a higher power, and to use a buddy system. The problems of evaluating the effectiveness of these programs parallel the problems of evaluating AA.

In the following case of a cocaine abuser, individual therapy was combined with support group meetings sponsored by Narcotics Anonymous:

■ Paul A., a 31-year-old accountant, entered psychotherapy after his wife told him to either seek treatment for his cocaine abuse or leave the house. He had been treating his wife and son cruelly, was neglecting responsibilities at work, and had experienced numerous bouts of depression. The major focus of his first two months of psychotherapy was stopping his cocaine use. His therapist encouraged Paul to attend Narcotics Anonymous meetings, and they discussed the feelings, events, and places that stimulated his desire for cocaine. Paul's therapist also taught him techniques that could help him avoid drug use even when his craving for cocaine was high.

As Paul's preoccupation with cocaine diminished with a lengthening period of abstinence, the focus of his psychotherapy began to shift toward the initial precipitants for his drug use: anxiety about becoming a father (he began heavy cocaine use during his wife's pregnancy), and his own unresolved relationships with his abusive alcoholic father. As he began to learn more about these issues, he gained a greater sense of mastery over his emotions, and his desire to escape from uncomfortable feelings decreased.

Weiss & Mirin, 1987, p. 126. ■

Residential Approaches

In residential approaches, substance abusers live at their treatment centers, such as hospitals and therapeutic communities.

Hospitalization may be recommended when substance abusers cannot exercise self-control in their usual environments, when dependent users cannot tolerate withdrawal symptoms, and when abusers' behavior is self-destructive or dangerous to others (Weiss & Mirin, 1987). Outpatient treatment is less costly and is often indicated when withdrawal symptoms are less severe, clients are committed to changing their behavior, and environmental support systems, such as families, strive to help clients make the transition to a drug-free lifestyle.

When alcoholism was given "disease" status by the American Medical Association in 1966, only a few medically based treatment programs existed, such as the renowned Hazelden program in Minnesota (Desmond, 1987). Since then, many thousands have come into being; 7,000 new treatment programs sprung up between 1981 and 1987 alone (Desmond, 1987). Some of these programs, like the Betty Ford Clinic, have received a great deal of attention in the popular press.

Most inpatient programs use an extended 28-day detoxification or "drying-out" period, an approach initiated at Hazelden in 1949. Clients are helped through their withdrawal symptoms in the first few days. Then the emphasis shifts to counseling about the destructive effects of alcohol and combating distorted ideas or rationalizations. Within the disease model, the goal of total abstinence is urged (Desmond, 1987).

It must be said that it has not been demonstrated that alcoholics necessarily require hospitalization. A review of studies comparing outpatient and inpatient programs revealed no overall differences in relapse rates (Miller & Hester, 1986). However, medical insurance may not cover outpatient treatment, which may encourage many problem drinkers to admit themselves for inpatient care. Some may need hospital care to monitor severe withdrawal effects.

A number of residential therapeutic communities are also in use. Some of them have part- or full-time

Daytop Village is an example of a residential therapeutic community in which participants are expected to assume responsibility for themselves and lapses are confronted in group sessions. Members are also confronted about their excuses for failing to take responsibility and about their denial of the harm that is done by their substance abuse.

professional staffs; others are run completely by lay people. One of the earliest communities was Synanon, which followed the disease-model belief that substance abusers differed from other people in basic ways and must strive for complete abstinence. Participants were required to assume progressive responsibilities, beginning with maintaining their personal hygiene, beds, and rooms and, eventually, working to contribute to community life. Lapses were confronted harshly in regular and spontaneous group sessions. Members were also confronted about their excuses for failing to take responsibility for themselves and about their denial of the damage being done by their abuse. Members shared their life experiences to help each other develop productive ways of handing stress. Synanon has long since closed its doors, but its communal approach has served as a model for other communities such as Daytop Village and Phoenix House.

Unfortunately, these therapeutic communities, like AA, suffer from an absence of controlled studies attesting to their effectiveness. Like AA, therapeutic communities tend to suffer from high numbers of early dropouts. In addition, many former members who were able to remain substance-free while they remained in residence and helped treat others relapsed when they tried to return to their own communities.

Psychodynamic Approaches

Psychoanalysts view substance abuse and dependence as symptomatic of underlying conflicts that are rooted in childhood experiences. Focusing on substance abuse or dependence per se is seen to offer, at most, a superfi-

cial type of therapy. It is assumed that if the underlying conflicts are resolved, the pattern of abuse is likely to subside on its own as more mature forms of gratification take its place. On the other hand, traditional psychoanalysts also assume that programs directed at abusive behavior will be of limited benefit because they do not address the underlying psychological causes of abuse.

There are many reports of successful psychodynamic case studies with substance abusers, particularly with problem drinkers. However, there is a dearth of controlled and replicable studies, so the effectiveness of psychodynamic methods for substance abuse problems remains unclear.

Behavioral Approaches

Behavioral approaches to problem drinking focus on modifying drinking behavior. The issue to many behaviorally oriented therapists is not whether substance abuse and dependence are "diseases" but whether or not abusers can learn to change problem habits that lead to substance-abuse problems.

■ **Self-Control Strategies** Self-control training focuses on helping abusers develop skills they can use to change their abusive behavior. Behavior therapists focus on three components of substance abuse:

1. The *antecedent* cues or stimuli (A's) that prompt or trigger abuse,
2. The abusive *behaviors* (B's) themselves, and
3. The reinforcing or punishing *consequences* (C's) that maintain or discourage abuse.

As an example, behavior therapists may assist problem drinkers with changing the A's or antecedent cues associated with drinking by asking them to remove all alcoholic beverages, beer mugs, carafes, and so on from their home, by changing their routes around town to avoid passing bars or liquor stores, and by avoiding situations linked to abuse—taverns, the street, bowling alleys, etc. Smokers who are seeking to quit may be instructed to change the behaviors or B's associated with smoking through the use of competing responses to smoking urges, such as taking a long walk or hot bath, calling a friend for support, or practicing meditation or relaxation, or engaging in vigorous exercise. The consequences or C's associated with smoking can be manipulated by the use of self-rewards (personal gifts) for meeting substance-reduction or cessation goals and self-punishment (monetary penalties) for failing to meet these goals.

■ **Aversive Conditioning**   In **aversive conditioning,** painful or aversive stimuli are paired with substance abuse or abuse-related stimuli to make abuse less appealing. In the case of problem drinking, tastes of different alcoholic beverages are usually paired with drug-induced nausea and vomiting or with electric shock (Wilson et al., 1975). As a consequence, alcohol may come to elicit an aversive conditioned response, such as fear or nausea, that inhibits drinking. Avoidance of alcohol is then negatively reinforced by relief from these aversive responses.

In one large-scale study of aversive conditioning in the treatment of alcoholism, 63 percent of the 685 people treated remained abstinent for one year afterward, and about a third remained abstinent for at least three years (Wiens & Menustik, 1983). All in all, however, aversive conditioning has not proved reliable (Lawson, 1983). It seems that aversive conditioned responses are readily extinguished because exposure to alcohol in real-life settings may not be paired with immediate aversive effects.

Aversive conditioning for smoking aims at making once pleasurable smoke aversive through some form of overexposure. In **rapid smoking,** for example, smokers inhale more frequently than usual, about once every six seconds, so they begin to feel nauseated. Nausea acts as an unconditioned stimulus that becomes paired with smoking-related conditioned stimuli such as the taste and aroma of cigarette smoke, the feel of the cigarette in the hand, and so on. After repeated pairings, cigarette smoke becomes aversive and smokers are motivated to avert it by quitting. Rapid smoking led to impressive 6-month abstinence rates of about 60 percent in early studies (Schmahl et al., 1972; Lichtenstein et al., 1973); however, recent studies have revealed more modest abstinence rates in the 20 to 25 percent range (Sateia, 1987). Generally speaking, the long-term results of aversive conditioning in maintaining smoking abstinence have been from poor to modestly successful (Brandon et al., 1987; Glasgow & Lichtenstein, 1987; Schwartz, 1987; Sateia, 1987). A combination of rapid smoking and other behavioral techniques may increase long-term abstinence rates, however (Schwartz, 1987).

Behavior therapists have also used **covert sensitization**—a form of aversive conditioning that employs imaginal rather than actual aversive stimuli. For example, clients are instructed to imagine becoming nauseated and vomiting when taking a drink or puffing a cigarette. The scenes typically end with rejection of the substance and feelings of relief. Evidence from controlled studies of the efficacy of covert sensitization in treating substance abuse is lacking, however.

■ **Skills Training**   Skills training approaches have been used to help people develop more effective interpersonal responses in social situations that prompt substance abuse. Assertiveness training, for example, may be used to teach alcoholic clients how to fend off social pressures to drink (Lawson, 1983). Behavioral marital therapy has been used to improve marital communication and problem-solving skills to relieve marital stresses that can trigger abuse. Couples may use written behavioral contracts. One might stipulate that the substance abuser agrees to abstain, say, from drinking or to take Antabuse, while his or her spouse agrees to refrain from comments about past drinking and the probability of future lapses.

Relapse Prevention Training

The word **relapse** is derived from Latin roots meaning "to slide back." From 50 to 90 percent of those who quit alcohol and other habit-forming substances will return to them, or relapse (Brownell et al., 1986a, 1986b). Perhaps only 12 to 25 percent of alcoholics maintain abstinence for three years following treatment (Desmond, 1987). It is estimated that about three out of four relapses to alcohol abuse occur in response to negative emotional states such as depression or anxiety, to interpersonal conflict, or to social pressures to resume drinking (Lawson, 1983). Problem drinkers who relapse are more likely to have experienced environmental stressors, such as loss of a loved one or economic problems, and are more likely to rely upon avoidance methods of coping, such as denial, than are alcoholics who maintain sobriety. Successful abstainers tend to have more social and family resources and support to draw upon in handling stress (Billings & Moos, 1981).

A CLOSER LOOK
The Controversy about Controlled Social Drinking

The prominent disease model of alcoholism contends that alcoholics who have just one drink will lose control and go on a binge. Some professionals, however, like Linda and Mark Sobell, have argued that behavior modification self-control techniques can teach alcoholics to engage in **controlled social drinking**—to have a drink or two without necessarily falling off the wagon. To support their contention, the Sobells published the results of an experiment with 20 alcoholics who were taught to control their drinking at California's Patton State Hospital in San Bernardino. The Sobells (1973, 1976, 1984) reported that 85 percent of their subjects remained in control of their drinking at a 2-year follow-up.

However, a research group critical of the Sobells (Pendery et al., 1982) published its own follow-up of the Sobells' subjects. The group claimed that only one person had remained successful at controlled social drinking. Most had returned to uncontrolled drinking on many occasions, and four of the group had died from alcohol-related causes.

Yet other investigators also claim that controlled social drinking is possible, at least for younger drinkers on the road to chronic alcoholism (Miller & Muñoz, 1983; Sanchez-Craig et al., 1984; Pomerleau et al., 1977; Strickler et al., 1976; Vogler et al., 1975). The research group headed by M. Sanchez-Craig, for example, assigned 35 early-stage problem drinkers to controlled social drinking. They reported that "Six months after treatment, drinking had been reduced from an average of about 51 drinks per week to 13, and this reduction was maintained throughout the second year" (1984, p. 390). It should be noted, nonetheless, that some critics (see Vaillant, 1983) argue that follow-ups of many years, even decades, are needed to sort out the effects of treatments for problem drinking.

In sum, controlled social drinking *may* be effective with younger problem drinkers, but there is no evidence that it is helpful with chronic alcoholics (Nathan & Skinstad, 1987). Moreover, the proponents of the disease model of alcoholism, who have wielded considerable political strength, stand strongly opposed to attempts to teach controlled social drinking.

Many investigators remain interested in teaching controlled-drinking skills to young problem drinkers to prevent them from progressing to alcohol dependence. Controlled drinking programs may be best suited for alcohol abusers who reject the goal of total abstinence, who have failed in programs requiring abstinence, who have a relatively short history of problem drinking, and who do not show severe withdrawal symptoms (Lawson, 1983). On the other hand, controlled social drinking may not be appropriate for individuals who can abstain from alcohol, who are taking medications that may negatively interact with alcohol, who incur health risks from drinking even small amounts of alcohol, who have histories of severe intoxication ("alcohol binges") or withdrawal symptoms, or who have failed in previous controlled drinking programs (Lawson, 1983).

Research suggests that virtually any behavioral treatment significantly reduces smoking in the short run (Bernstein & McAlister, 1976; Hunt & Bespalec, 1974; Hunt & Matarazzo, 1973; Lichtenstein & Danaher, 1976; McFall & Hammen, 1971). As many as 50 to 80 percent of smokers are able to quit—at least temporarily (Sateia, 1987). Another picture emerges when we consider relapse rates, however. Six-month to 1-year follow-up abstinence rates deteriorate to 20 to 25 percent for behavioral interventions (Sateia, 1987). Even the better-designed behavioral interventions produce abstinence rates at 1-year follow-up of only about 40 percent (Glasgow & Lichtenstein, 1987). Clearly, more effective treatments are needed to assist the 60 percent of smokers or more who either initially fail to break the habit or relapse within a year.

Because of the prevalence of relapse, cognitive behavioral therapists have developed a number of methods referred to as **relapse-prevention training** to help substance abusers cope with temptations and high-risk situations to prevent *lapses*—that is, slips—and moreover, to prevent any lapses that may occur from becoming full-blown relapses (Marlatt & Gordon, 1980, 1985). High-risk situations include negative mood states, such as depression, anger, or anxiety; interpersonal conflict (marital problems or conflicts with employers); and socially conducive situations such as "the guys getting together." Trainees learn to cope with these situations, for example, by practicing relaxation responses and saying no to social pressures. Trainees are taught to avoid practices that might prompt a relapse, such as keeping alcohol in the house for friends.

Although it contains many behavioral strategies, relapse-prevention training is a cognitive-behavioral technique in that it also focuses on substance abusers' *interpretations* of any lapses or slips that may occur, such as smoking a first cigarette or taking a first drink following quitting. Clients are taught how to avoid the so-called **abstinence violation effect** (AVE)—the tendency to overreact to a lapse—by learning to reorient their thinking about lapses and slips. People who have a slip may be more likely to relapse if they attribute their lapse to self-perceived weaknesses and experience guilt and self-blame (Curry et al., 1987). For example, consider a skater who slips on the ice (Marlatt & Gordon, 1985). Whether or not the skater gets up and continues to perform depends largely upon whether the skater perceives the slip as an isolated—and correctable—mistake or as a sign of total failure.

In contrast to the disease model, which contends that alcoholics automatically lose control if they take a single drink, the relapse-prevention model assumes that whether or not a lapse becomes a relapse depends on the individual's reaction to the lapse (Marlatt & Gordon, 1985). Self-defeating attributions such as "What's the use? I'm just doomed to fail" trigger depression, resignation, and subsequent resumption of problem drinking. Participants in relapse-prevention training are encouraged to view lapses as temporary setbacks or mistakes that one can profit from by learning to identify situations that prompt them and learning coping skills to avoid them in the future. If they can learn to think, "Okay, I had a slip. That doesn't mean that all my efforts are out the window unless I believe that they are. I can get right back on track from here," they are less likely to catastrophize their slips and return to uncontrolled smoking or drinking. Participants are trained to challenge dysfunctional thinking about lapses and substitute more adaptive coping thoughts.

Despite their promise, results of relapse-prevention training for smoking cessation have been mixed (Brown et al., 1984; Hill et al., 1986; Lando & McGovern, 1985; Davis & Glaros, 1986; Marlatt et al., 1986). It appears that relapse-prevention is more effective with lighter smokers than with heavier smokers (Glasgow & Lichtenstein, 1987; Hall et al., 1984). Some promising findings have come from a study that showed that hospitalized alcoholics who received social skills training that focused on relapse prevention in high-risk situations continued to improve by a 1-year follow-up, and experienced less severe and prolonged relapses than did an untrained control group (Chaney et al., 1978). But more research is needed to fully evaluate the benefits of relapse prevention training.

All in all, efforts to help people discontinue substance abuse and dependence have been mixed at best. Many substance abusers really do not want to discontinue use of these substances but prefer, if possible, to avert their negative consequences. But negative outcomes frequently take some time to develop—perhaps decades in the cases of alcohol and cigarettes—whereas the pleasures of the next drink, puff, or fix are immediate.

In many cases, particularly with self-help support groups and residential programs, treatment outcomes have not been adequately evaluated, so that most claims of success are suspect. Moreover, because of lack of funds, many thousands of substance abusers who would like treatment find it unavailable. Even the apparently well-controlled experiments conducted by some investigators frequently employ a repertoire of behavioral and cognitive techniques so that it is unclear which ones—if any—are helpful. In addition, we have seen that it is one thing to help abusers and dependent people initially discontinue usage of the substances that entice them; it is another to help them prevent relapse.

In the case of inner-city youth who have become trapped with street drugs and hopelessness, additional services, such as job training, are apparently needed if we wish to help them assume more productive social roles. In support of this contention, Friedman and Glickman (1986) have identified characteristics of apparently more successful substance-abuse programs for adolescents: special schools for school dropouts, therapists with at least two years' experience working with adolescents, vocational counseling, recreational services, birth-control services, and a variety of treatment approaches, including crisis intervention, music/art therapy, and group confrontation. Multicomponent approaches may be most helpful with most substance abusers (Grabowski et al., 1984), although we are still left with the question as to which components are effective. The challenge is clear: to develop cost-effective ways of helping people recognize the negative effects of substances and forego the powerful and immediate reinforcements they provide.

SUMMARY

Psychoactive Substance Abuse and Dependence

The DSM–III–R defines psychoactive substance abuse disorders in terms of patterns of use of one month or longer involving either (a) the continued use of a psychoactive substance (drug) despite the person's knowledge that it causes or aggravates a persistent or recurrent physical, psychological, occupational or social problem, or (b) repeated use in situations in which its use is dangerous, like driving while intoxicated. Substance-dependence disorder refers to a pattern of impaired control over the use of a substance and continued use despite knowledge of adverse effects, often involving signs of physiological dependence, such as tolerance and an abstinence syndrome.

Physiological dependence involves physiological changes that occur as the result of repeated use of a particular substance, as shown by development of tolerance for the substance, an abstinence syndrome following withdrawal, or both. Psychological dependence involves the impaired control over the use of a substance without the physiological signs of dependence. Drug addiction refers to the habitual use of a chemical substance that produces physiological dependence. The road to substance dependence may vary from person to person, but often it involves such common stages as experimentation, routine use, and addiction or dependency.

Substance Abuse and Organic Mental Disorders

Drugs have direct and often harmful effects on the central nervous system. Two major types of organic mental disorders that are induced by psychoactive substances are intoxication and abstinence syndromes. Abrupt withdrawal from long-term abuse of alcohol may produce an abstinence syndrome called the "DTs," characterized by delirium and autonomic hyperactivity, and often involving frightening hallucinations ("bugs crawling").

Alcohol

Alcohol is the most widely abused drug in the United States. While alcoholism is more prevalent among men than women, researchers expect the percentages of women with alcoholism to increase in the future. Other risk factors in alcoholism include age (younger age of onset among men), socioeconomic class (types of alcohol-related problems may vary with socioeconomic status), ethnic factors (some cultural or ethnic groups have higher prevalences of alcoholism), antisocial behavior patterns, other abnormal behavior patterns such as mood disorders, and familial history of alcoholism.

Alcohol has many psychological effects, including reduced self-censure and feelings of guilt, decreased sexual arousal (despite expectations to the contrary), impaired information-processing ability, and increased aggressiveness—apparently due to expectancies about alcohol rather than its chemical effects. As a depressant, alcohol has such physical effects as dampening the activity of the central nervous system, even to the point of death in sufficient amounts. Other effects of alcohol, as an intoxicant, include impaired judgment, coordination, and intellectual functioning, and slurred speech. Chronic alcohol abuse can lead to many serious organic mental and physical disorders, such as alcohol amnestic disorder (Korsakoff's syndrome) and cirrhosis of the liver, for example. Alcohol use or abuse by pregnant women has been linked to various developmental problems or birth deformities of the fetus, including fetal-alcohol syndrome.

Barbiturates (Sedatives) and Minor Tranquilizers

Barbiturates are depressants or sedatives that have been used medically for relief of anxiety and short-term insomnia, among other uses. However, because of the potential risk that these drugs pose in the way of psychological and physiological dependence, many physicians prefer to treat problems of anxiety and insomnia with minor tranquilizers that carry a lower risk of dependence. Even so, it is recognized today that minor tranquilizers also carry a risk of physiological dependence.

Opiates

Opiates, such as morphine and heroin, are derived from the opium poppy. Used medically for relief of pain, they are strongly addictive. Endorphins are naturally occurring substances that lock into the same receptor sites in the brain as the opiates and appear to be involved in the experience of pleasure and relief from pain.

Stimulants

Stimulants increase the activity of the nervous system. While the effects differ somewhat from drug to drug, they may produce feelings of euphoria and self-confidence. Amphetamines and cocaine increase the availability of neurotransmitters in the brain, heightening states of arousal. While psychological dependence on amphetamines may develop, it is unclear whether they produce physiological dependence. High doses can produce an amphetamine psychosis, which mimics features of paranoid schizophrenia, suggesting that schizophrenia may involve the types of changes in the brain induced by amphetamines.

Cocaine is a natural stimulant derived from the coca plant. Cocaine tends to enhance alertness and performance, bolster confidence, and induce states of pleasure. It also possesses certain analgesic effects. Cocaine, too, can produce psychological dependence, but may not produce physiological dependence. Crack, a hardened, smokable form of cocaine, is quickly habit-forming. Use of cocaine is associated with various health risks that can lead to sudden death or to the development of chronic health problems. Long-term use, especially of high doses, can also lead to depression and anxiety, and even psychosis or suicidal behavior.

Nicotine is a stimulant found in cigarette smoke and other tobacco products. Repeated use of nicotine, usually in the form of cigarette smoking, can lead to a physiological dependence. Smoking can cause several forms of cancer and has been implicated as a causal factor in many other diseases. Cigarette smoking produces both tolerance (increased smoking over time) and withdrawal symptoms that are typical of addictive substances in general.

Psychedelics

The hallucinogenics include LSD, psilocybin, and mescaline. Other drugs with similar effects are cannabis (marijuana) and phencyclidine (PCP). There is little evidence that these drugs induce physiological dependence, although psychological dependence may occur.

LSD is a synthetic drug that can induce hallucinations, which can recur at later times in the form of flashbacks. PCP—"angel dust"—can induce feelings of dissociation and hallucinations. Accidents can occur from perceptual distortions, as well as violent behavior. Marijuana, which contains the psychoactive drug THC, may have been used by as many as one-third of all Americans, although its use appears to have declined in recent years. Effects vary with dosage level and from person to person. It remains unclear whether it produces an amotivational syndrome or other long-term cognitive effects. But its short-term negative effects on motor performance and on memory and learning, its ability to elevate the heart rate and perhaps blood pressure, and its carcinogenic potential all raise serious concerns about its use.

Theoretical Perspectives

Biological perspectives focus on uncovering the biological pathways that may explain mechanisms of physiological dependence. The disease model represents a biological perspective that treats problems of substance abuse and dependence as disease processes. The disease models posits that alcoholism, in particular, is an irreversible, permanent condition. But studies by cognitive-behavioral researchers have raised doubts about a central tenet of the disease model, namely the belief that alcoholics have an irresistible physical craving that leads them to "fall off the wagon" if they take even a single drink. These researchers highlight the role of expectancy effects in creating a self-fulfilling prophecy that turns a lapse into a relapse. The disease model finds some support from studies of genetic factors in alcoholism,

but the role of environment also appears to be important.

Learning theorists view substance-abuse disorders as maladaptive behavior patterns that are largely acquired by means of operant and classical conditioning, and by observation. Other social-learning variables, such as outcome and self-efficacy expectancies, also may play a role in determining substance-abuse problems.

Cognitive perspectives have focused on roles of attitudes, beliefs, and expectancies. Some research suggests that the "one-drink" effect may be explained in terms of a self-fulfilling prophecy.

Sociocultural perspectives have focused on the adoption of culturally sanctioned prohibitions against excessive drinking in explaining differences among various ethnic and religious groups in rates of alcoholism. Social factors, such as peer pressure, also influence the development of substance-abuse problems.

Psychodynamic theorists view problems of substance abuse, such as excessive drinking and habitual smoking, as signs of oral fixation. Psychodynamic theory links these traits with other characteristic oral traits, such as dependence and proneness to depression.

Treatment

Biological approaches to substance-abuse disorders include detoxification, the process of helping abusers withdraw safely from chemical substances on which they are dependent. Biological approaches toward maintenance of abstinence include the use of disulfiram (Antabuse), a drug that produces nausea when combined with alcohol ingestion. But discontinuation of the drug defeats its usefulness. Research has shown some promising initial findings in the use of antidepressant medications to curb the cravings for cocaine that follow withdrawal. Nicotine chewing gum appears to be helpful to smokers trying to break the cigarette habit, especially the more heavily dependent smokers, but only when combined with other approaches, such as behavior therapy. Methadone is effective in blocking the cravings for heroin, but it too can be abused. Nalozone, which blocks the high associated with heroin, may be helpful but can also be defeated, like Antabuse, by inconsistent use.

Residential treatment approaches include hospitals and therapeutic communities. Most inpatient programs use a modification of a 28-day detoxification program. Therapeutic communities provide an opportunity for substance abusers to share experiences and confront the destructive nature of their behavior.

leaving their spouses or general social rejection, are reluctant to commit themselves to homosexuality. Many bisexuals disagree and believe that they are capable of maintaining erotic interests in both sexes.

Adjustment of Homosexuals

Despite the social ostracism, prejudice, and discrimination faced by many homosexuals in our society, homosexuals appear to be about as well adjusted as heterosexuals. Saghir and Robins (1973) were unable to distinguish gay males from heterosexual males in terms of such problems as anxiety, depression, and such psychosomatic complaints as headaches and ulcers. A study of professionally employed lesbians failed to differentiate them from heterosexual women on adjustment criteria, with the exception that the lesbian women appeared to be somewhat more socially isolated (Adelman, 1977). Generally speaking, the similarities between lesbians and heterosexual women outweigh the differences (Siegelman, 1978, 1979).

Homosexuals are found at all socioeconomic and occupational levels and live a variety of lifestyles. A study of homosexuals in the San Francisco area found that adjustment was closely linked to lifestyle (Bell & Weinberg, 1978). Homosexuals who lived with stable partners in close, marital-like relationships appeared about as well-adjusted as married heterosexuals. But older homosexuals who lived by themselves and had few if any sexual contacts tended to be more poorly adjusted. So, too, are many heterosexuals who lead similar lifestyles.

Although there are individual differences, gay males as a group have been more likely than lesbians to engage in casual sex with numerous partners (Bell

Researchers have found that homosexual couples who live in close, stable relationships appear to be about as well-adjusted as married heterosexual couples.

& Weinberg, 1978). Lesbians, by contrast, are more likely to seek sexual activity within the bounds of a committed affectionate relationship.

In recent years, however, sexual behavior has changed in the gay male community, largely as the result of the AIDS epidemic. The AIDS virus is found at high levels in semen. Anal intercourse can tear rectal tissue, allowing the virus directly to enter the bloodstream. The AIDS virus can also directly infect cells of the rectum, even without tearing. Because of concern about AIDS, many gay males have changed their sexual practices in various ways to reduce the risk of infection, such as by avoiding anal intercourse, using condoms during oral sex, and limiting sexual contacts to one partner or to a few partners who are well known to them, and by relying more on masturbation as a sexual outlet (Lourea et al., 1986; Schechter et al., 1984).

Theoretical Perspectives

Theoretical understandings of homosexuality have been mainly approached from the psychodynamic, learning-based, and biological perspectives. While there are many theoretical accounts of homosexuality, there is no present consensus concerning its origins.

■ **Psychodynamic Perspectives**   One psychodynamic view is that the penis unconsciously represents the mother's breast. Men (and women) fixated in the oral stage, therefore, might experience impulses to engage in fellatio (Bergler, 1957; Klein et al., 1952). Fixation in the anal stage might similarly trigger impulses to engage in anal intercourse. Most psychodynamic views, however, stress roles for castration anxiety and penis envy, and suggest that homosexuals are fixated in the phallic stage (Meissner, 1980).

Freudian theory suggests that children enter the world open to all forms of sexual stimulation; that is, before they internalize social inhibitions, children are **polymorphously perverse.** Through normal resolution of the Oedipus complex, boys identify with their fathers and seek the (presumably) heterosexual stimulation that sexually arouses their fathers. Girls, through a similar process, which is often termed the *Electra complex,* identify with their mothers and also seek heteroerotic stimulation. A boy who does not resolve the Oedipus complex properly may sexually identify with his mother and even "transform himself into her" (Freud, 1922/1959, p. 40). Castration anxiety may also persist in later life as the residue of an unresolved male Oedipus complex. When sexually mature, the man cannot tolerate having sex with women, whose lack of a penis arouses latent fears of castration within himself. The vaginal cavity itself looms as a threat of possible injury or loss of his penis. He consequently turns to other men for sexual satisfaction, for they too possess a penis and do not unconsciously arouse the fear of the potential loss of his own. A girl who does not resolve her penis envy in childhood may "manifest homosexuality, . . . exhibit markedly masculine traits in the conduct of her later life, choose a masculine vocation, and so on" (Freud, 1922/1959, p. 50). The residue of this unresolved complex is continued penis envy, the striving to become a man by acting like a man and, in the exreme, seeking sexual satisfaction with women.

Over the years psychoanalyst Irving Bieber (1962, 1976) has investigated the origins of homosexuality by means of the case study. In 1962 he reported the results of questionnaires filled out by 77 psychiatrists on 106 homosexual clients. In 1976 he reported the results of similar surveys with homosexual clients. Bieber claimed to find a "classic pattern" among gay males of a dominant, "smothering" mother and a passive father. The mothers were overprotective, seductive, and jealous concerning their sons. The fathers were generally aloof, unaffectionate, and hostile toward them. The parents were often unhappy, and the mother substituted a "close-binding" relationship with her son for the failed relationship with her husband.

Bieber's view is that the "classic pattern" leads boys to fear heterosexual contacts. A female partner unconsciously represents the male's mother. Desire for her stirs unconscious fear of retaliation by the father—that is, castration anxiety. As we noted, the vagina may seem an unsafe place. The gay male lover's penis provides reassurance against the unconscious fears of castration.

Major problems arise with Bieber's research. The subjects, first of all, were all in analytic treatment, and many wanted to become heterosexual. Thus, we may not be able to generalize the findings to well-adjusted homosexuals. Second, the analysts may have chosen cases that confirmed their psychodynamic perspectives. Third, many homosexuals do not fear female genitalia and repeatedly engage in successful coitus. Fourth, many males whose families fit the "classic pattern" are heterosexual. Many gay males, moreover, were closer to their fathers than to their mothers (Bell et al., 1981; Siegelman, 1974).

■ **Learning Perspectives** Many learning theorists agree with psychoanalysts that children come into the world capable of learning to respond to any form of pleasurable sexual stimulation. Then the approaches diverge. Psychoanalysts focus on theoretical unconscious processes. Learning theorists focus largely on the principles of conditioning.

According to principles of classical conditioning, children may become sexually aroused by stimuli associated with past sexual pleasures. Enjoyable early homosexual encounters might condition sexual arousal to same-sex partners. Alternatively, pain, fear, or the threat of social disapproval associated with homosexual activity might lead children to respond to homoerotic stimulation with anxiety.

According to principles of operant conditioning, as set forth by Kinsey and his colleagues, reinforcement of early sexual experiences (as by achieving orgasms through sexual play with children of one's own sex) can influence one's developing sexual orientation. If sexual motivation is high and the only available partners are of the same sex, as is the case for many adolescents, people may experiment with homosexual behavior. If the experiments are reinforced by pleasure, they may become habitual (van Wyk, 1984). Males who had early punitive experiences with females, including their mothers, might tend to avoid females. If they also experience sexual satisfaction with males, they may develop a homosexual orientation.

Like Bieber, learning theorists also point to certain developmental experiences. Many gay males recall their mothers as cold and demanding of attention. Their mothers preferred them (the sons) to their fathers, interfered in their relations with girls, and encouraged feminine sex-role behavior patterns (Evans, 1969). The sons also spent little time with their fathers and reported negative attitudes toward and fear of them. But there are problems with learning perspectives. Many gay males and lesbians become aware of their sexual orientations even *before* they have overt sexual contacts (Bell et al., 1981). Thus, we cannot account for their sexual orientation on the basis of early reinforcement in childhood sexual experiences with members of their own sex. And remember the Sambian males: Repeated homosexual experiences do not sway Sambian youth from eventual exclusive heterosexuality.

We should also recognize that in a society such as ours that denigrates homosexuality, it is unlikely that children will emulate homosexual models. Nor does observational learning from homosexual parents lead to a homosexual orientation. Richard Green (1978) studied 37 children reared in sexually atypical households. Most of them had lesbian mothers. All but one child developed sex-appropriate preferences in toys, games, and ways of relating to other people. Children of lesbian mothers could not be distinguished from children of heterosexual mothers in their sexual orientations and general adjustment (Green et al., 1986).

■ *Biological Perspectives* Biological models have focused on the possible role of genetic and hormonal factors. Kallmann (1952) reported a 100 percent **concordance** rate for homosexuality among 40 monozygotic (identical) twins, compared to only 15 percent among dizygotic (fraternal) twins. More recent studies, however, have reported much lower concordance rates (Eckert et al., 1986; Ellis & Ames, 1987; McConaghy & Blaszczynski, 1980). While genetic factors may partly determine sexual orientation, it doesn't appear that genetic influences directly govern sexual orientation (Money, 1987).

What of a role for sex hormones, such as testosterone in males and estrogen in females? Since sex hormones strongly influence the mating behavior of lower animals (Crew & Moore, 1986), researchers have considered possible hormonal differences between heterosexual and homosexuals. Research evidence, however, has failed to link homosexuality with any reliable differences in current (adult) levels of female or male sex hormones (Feder, 1984). Another possibility concerns the possible prenatal effects of sex hormones. Prenatal sex hormones appear to "masculinize" or "feminize" the brains of lower animals in terms of the development of brain structures along gender-specific lines. One possibility is that the brains of some homosexuals may have been sensitized by prenatal sex hormones in ways that predisposed them to the later development of a homosexual orientation. Even if this theory is upheld in future research, it has been argued that such prenatal influences among humans would not automatically produce a certain sexual orientation in adulthood in a "robot-like" fashion. Socialization (early learning experiences) is also likely to play an important role (Money, 1987).

 Homosexuality is not caused by *current* hormonal imbalances. However, prenatal hormonal factors may well play a role in sexual orientation.

In sum, the causes of human homosexuality remain mysterious and complex—as mysterious and complex as the causes of heterosexuality. An appraisal of the current research suggests, but does not prove, interactive causes are involved. It is possible that genetic factors might influence the levels of secretion of prenatal hormones, which, combined with early socialization experiences, might lead to the development of a homosexual orientation. But the complex ways in which these factors interact have thus far evaded the efforts of researchers to ascertain.

Treatment of Homosexuality

Freud himself recognized that psychoanalysis had limited success in changing sexual orientation. In a letter to a concerned mother of a homosexual son, Freud wrote,

> What analysis can do for your son runs in a different line [*than changing sexual orientation*]. If he is unhappy, neurotic, torn by conflicts, inhibited in his social life, analysis may bring him harmony, peace of mind, full efficiency, whether he remains a homosexual or gets changed. (cited in Jones, 1953, p. 534, italics added)

Numerous learning-based, behavioral treatments

have been devised to induce heteroerotic responses among homosexuals. In one approach, *aversive conditioning*, homosexuals have received electric shock while watching slides of homosexual activity. The slide is then removed, or replaced with a picture of heterosexual activity, and the shock is simultaneously suspended. The viewer thus comes to associate relief from anxiety with heterosexual activity. In the technique of *orgasmic reconditioning*, homosexuals masturbate while viewing slides of homosexual activity. Before reaching orgasm, pictures of the heterosexual activity are introduced, so that orgasm becomes associated with heteroerotic stimuli. Social skills training (which relies on coaching, modeling, and role-playing) has also been used to enhance the abilities of homosexuals to develop relationships with members of the opposite sex. Reliable evidence that such learning-based methods can produce changes in sexual orientation remains lacking.

William Masters and Virginia Johnson (1979) used methods employed in treating sexual dysfunctions to "reverse" clients' homosexual orientations. We shall elaborate on the applications of these methods to heterosexual couples later in the chapter. First, let us note that the treatment involved gay males in pleasurable activities with women, such as massage and genital stimulation, at a relaxed pace. At a five-year follow-up, Masters claimed that more than 70 percent of the clients continued to engage in heterosexual activity (Schwartz & Masters, 1984). Critics note that Masters and Johnson's clients included many bisexuals and heterosexuals with sexual problems. Some were married. Others sought treatment because they were in love with women. These clients appear to be unrepresentative of the homosexual population at large,

It should be noted that some therapists refuse to try to reverse a homosexual orientation. If homosexuality is not a disorder, why try to cure it? Gerald Davison (1976, 1978) contends that even willingness to "treat" homosexuality endorses the notion that homosexuality is a sickness and reinforces societal censure. Today, many therapists of diverse theoretical persuasions closely examine the reasons that clients request a change in sexual orientation and express a willingness to help them improve their lives as homosexuals rather than change their orientation.

GENDER IDENTITY DISORDERS

Our **gender identity** is our sense of being male or being female. Gender identity is normally based on anatomic sex. In the normal run of things, our gender identity is consistent with our anatomic sex. In what the DSM–III–R refers to as **gender identity disorders,** however, there is a conflict between one's anatomic sex and one's gender identity.

Gender Identity Disorder of Childhood

The DSM–III–R diagnosis of gender identity disorder of childhood refers to children who find their anatomic sexes a source of persistent and intense distress. The diagnosis is not used simply to label "tomboyish" girls and "sissyish" boys. It may be applied, however, to children who persistently repudiate their anatomic traits (girls might insist on urinating standing up or assert that they do not want to grow breasts; boys may find their penis and testes revolting) or who are preoccupied with clothing or activities that are stereotypic of the opposite sex. The diagnosis only applies if the child has not yet reached puberty.

According to the DSM–III–R, the disorder is uncommon. More boys than girls receive the diagnosis. The disorder takes many paths. It can come to an end or abate markedly by adolescence, with the child becoming more accepting of his or her gender identity. It may persist as a gender identity disorder of adolescence or adulthood. Or, the child may develop a homosexual orientation at about the time of adolescence. Sometimes the disorder may progress to transsexualism.

Transsexualism

In 1953 headlines were made by an ex-GI who journeyed to Denmark for a "sex-change operation" and became known as Christine (formerly George) Jorgensen. Some 2,500 American transsexuals have subsequently undergone such sex-reassignment surgery. Among the better-known is the tennis player Dr. Renée Richards, formerly Dr. Richard Raskin. Sex-reassign-

ment surgery does not change one's gender by implanting the reproductive organs (gonads) of the opposite sex. Instead, it generates the likeness of external genitals typical of the opposite sex. This can be done more precisely with male-to-female than female-to-male transsexuals. After such operations, people can participate in sexual activity and even attain orgasm, but they cannot conceive or bear children.

Gender identity disorders in adolescence or adulthood may or may not involve transsexualism. Persons with gender disorders of adolescence or adulthood of the nontranssexual type experience persistent or recurrent feelings of discomfort, or a sense of inappropriateness, about their anatomical gender and frequently cross-dress in reality or in their imagination. However, they do not seek to rid themselves of their anatomical sex characteristics or acquire the sex characteristics of the opposite sex. DSM–III–R uses the diagnosis of **transsexualism** for persons who

1. have reached the age of puberty,
2. harbor persistent discomfort and a sense that their anatomic sex is inappropriate, and
3. are preoccupied for at least two years with transforming their sex characteristics to those of the opposite sex.

In other words, transsexuals wish to be rid of their own primary sex characteristics (their external genitals and internal sex organs) and to live fully as members of the opposite sex. Unlike homosexuality, transsexualism is very rare. The DSM–III–R estimates the prevalence of transsexualism at one in 30,000 males and one in 100,000 females. Sexual attractions them-

(a)   (b)

Transsexual Dr. Renée Richards before the sex-change operation as Dr. Richard Raskin (a) and afterwards (b). Richards once served as a coach of Martina Navratlova.

selves do not appear to be central in importance. For example, some transsexuals are subtyped as "asexual" by the DSM–III–R. This subtype reports never having had strong sexual feelings. The subtype termed "homosexual" includes people who are attracted to members of their own anatomic sex. But such transsexuals are not likely to think of themselves as homosexuals. Nature's assignment is a mistake in their eyes. From their perspective, they are "trapped" inside the wrong body. The "heterosexual" subtype includes transsexuals who are attracted to members of the opposite sex. Nonetheless, they want to be rid of their own sex organs and to live as members of the opposite sex.

■ **Sex Reassignment** Surgery is only one part of a protracted process of sex reassignment. The first step is evaluation to determine that the person seeking reassignment appears competent to make such a decision. If the person were seeking change because of paranoid delusions, for example, surgeons would refuse the request. Next, a lifetime of hormone treatments are begun. Male-to-female transsexuals receive estrogen, which fosters the development of female secondary sex characteristics. It causes fatty deposits to develop in the breasts and hips, softens the skin, and inhibits growth of the beard. Female-to-male transsexuals receive androgens, which promote male secondary sex characteristics. The voice deepens, hair becomes distributed according to the male pattern, muscles enlarge, and the fatty deposits in the breasts and hips are lost. The clitoris may become more prominent also. But medical science cannot construct internal sexual organs or **gonads.** Before surgery, the transsexual is also usually required to live for a year or so as a member of the opposite sex. Cross-living allows the transsexual and the treatment team to make some prediction of postoperative adjustment.

In male-to-female transsexuals, the penis and testicles are removed. Tissue from the penis is placed in an artificial vagina so that sensitive nerve endings will provide sexual sensations. A penis-shaped form of plastic or balsa wood is kept in the constructed vagina for some months to prevent it from closing during healing.

In female-to-male transsexuals, the internal sex organs (ovaries, fallopian tubes, uterus) are removed along with the remaining fatty tissue in the breasts. An artificial penis and scrotum are constructed through a series of operations. In either case, the patient can urinate while standing, which appears to be a source of psychological gratification. A variety of methods, such as rigid implants, can be used to allow the artificial penis to approximate erection.

■ **Postoperative Adjustment** In the 1960s, shortly after sex reassignment became available in the United States, most reports of the postoperative adjustment of transsexuals were favorable (Pauly, 1968). However, an influential study by Meyer and Reter (1979) at the prestigious Gender Identity Clinic at Johns Hopkins University was very negative. The researchers used a control group and found more positive results among transsexuals who did not receive sex reassignment than among those who did. The Meyer and Reter study led to the abandonment of sex-reassignment surgery at Johns Hopkins and cast a pall over sex-reassignment surgery nationwide. In retrospect, however, the termination of the Johns Hopkins program may have reflected political pressures from the community as well as these research findings (Lothstein, cited in Abramowitz, 1986). Other researchers have also charged that Meyer and Reter used unscientific measures of adjustment (Abramowitz, 1986; Fleming et al., 1981). Moreover, the positive adjustment of transsexuals who are not sex reassigned does not mean that reassignment is not useful for some transsexuals (Pauly, 1981).

Several reviews have found more positive outcomes for those undergoing sex reassignment (see Pauly, 1981), especially when safeguards are taken to restrict surgical treatment to the most appropriate cases (Lothstein, 1982). One study of 42 male-to-female transsexuals who were interviewed postoperatively found that all but one would elect to repeat the surgery. Moreover, the great majority reported that sexual activity was more pleasurable as a "woman" (Bentler, 1976). Abramowitz (1986) reported that about two out of three cases of transsexuals who underwent sex-reassignment surgery showed at least some postoperative improvement in sexual and psychological functioning. This is not to say that transsexuals are ecstatic about their lives postoperatively; it often means that they are less unhappy. Most transsexuals are socially maladjusted prior to sex reassignment, and many remain lonely and isolated afterward (Lindermalm et al., 1986).

Men seeking sex reassignment outnumber women applicants by three or four to one, but outcomes are generally more favorable for female-to-male cases. One reason may be society's greater acceptance of women who desire to become men than vice-versa (Abramowitz, 1986). Despite the surgical difficulties involved in constructing male-like sexual organs, a group of 22 female-to-male transsexuals were generally satisfied postoperatively with their new bodies (Fleming et al., 1982). Nearly 10 percent of male-to-female cases, as compared to 4 to 5 percent of female-to-male cases, have been linked to grave outcomes, like psychosis, hospitalization, requests for reversal surgery, or suicide (Abramowitz, 1986).

? It is not true that people have become members of the opposite sex through surgery. Instead, their external genitals are fashioned to the appearance of those of the opposite sex. They may experience sexual feelings in their genitals, and even achieve orgasm, but they cannot function in reproductive roles. Whether people think of themselves as being male or female is another matter.

A recent large-scale study at the Gender Identity Clinic at the Clarke Institute of Psychiatry in Toronto reported on the outcomes of 116 transsexuals one year following sexual reorientation surgery. Most were found to have good psychosocial adjustment and were generally satisfied with the results of their surgery (Blanchard et al., 1985). Both male-to-female transsexuals and female-to-male transsexuals showed lower reported levels of anxiety, depression, and other psychological complaints one year following surgery than beforehand. Postoperative transsexuals reported about the same level of symptomatology as the general population, and 93.7 percent reported that they definitely would make the same decision to undergo surgery had they to do it all over again. However promising these results may be, we should recognize that they are limited by the absence of a nonsurgical control group.

■ **Theoretical Perspectives** Views on the origins of transsexualism to some degree parallel those on the origins of homosexuality. Psychodynamic theorists point to extremely close mother–son relationships, parents with empty relationships, and fathers who are absent or detached (Stoller, 1969). These family circumstances may foster identification with the mother in young males. Girls with weak, ineffectual mothers and strong, masculine fathers may identify with their fathers.

Learning theorists similarly point to father-absence in the case of boys and to the unavailability of a strong male role model. Socialization patterns might also have played a part among transsexuals whose parents had wanted children of the opposite sex and who had thus encouraged or rewarded them to cross-dress and engage in play activities associated with the opposite sex.

According to the DSM–III–R, most transsexuals report having had gender identity problems in childhood. In any event, transsexuals often showed cross-sex preferences in toys, games, and clothing very early in childhood. If there are critical early learning experiences in transsexualism, they may occur at preschool ages. But transsexuals may also be influenced by prenatal hormonal imbalances. As noted earlier, it is possible that the brain could be "masculinized" or "feminized" by the influence of prenatal sex hormones. The brain could be influenced to develop in one direction, even as the genitals develop in the other direction (Money, 1987).

Scholars of transsexualism admit that they are less than satisfied with their own hypotheses and much remains to be learned.

PORNOGRAPHY

Many people in our society are troubled by the proliferation of explicit sexual materials or **pornography.** Some feminists and others have argued that pornography degrades women and supports stereotypes of women as submissive to the needs of men (Blakely, 1985). They have charged that materials that depict sexual and other types of violence against women encourage male viewers to abuse women. Others assail pornography from a moral standpoint. The question of the morality of pornography goes beyond the scope of this book. Our concern is about the psychological effects of pornography, particularly whether pornography induces abnormal behavior. Does pornography impair psychological functioning or provoke antisocial behavior?

The Effects of Pornography

A Presidential Commission on Obscenity and Pornography was established in the 1960s to report on the effects of pornography. The commission concluded that while exposure to pornography increased sexual arousal in both sexes, it did not lead people to engage in deviant behaviors (Abelson et al., 1970). Similar results have been reported in more recent studies, which have been based on college students as well as middle-aged couples (Brown et al., 1976; Hatfield et al., 1978; Heiby & Becker, 1980; Herrell, 1975; Schmidt et al., 1973). In general, people who were exposed to pornography became sexually aroused and may have been more motivated to engage in masturbation or in sexual activity with their regular partners. But they did not engage in disturbed behavior or lose self-control.

But experiments appear to support a link, in men, between exposure to violent pornography and aggression against women. In one study (Donnerstein, 1980), 120 college men interacted with a male or female confederate of the experimenter, who treated the participants in either a hostile or neutral manner. The subjects then observed either a neutral, erotic, or an aggressive-erotic film depicting a rape scene. The subjects were then provided with an opportunity to aggress against the female or male confederate with whom they had interacted earlier by means of selecting a higher shock level to "assist" the confederate (learner) on a shock-learning task. Unbeknownst to the subjects, the apparatus was actually a fake and no actual shock was delivered to the confederate. Not surprisingly, the results showed that men who had been provoked selected higher shock levels. But even men who had not been provoked earlier showed greater aggression against female confederates following their exposure to the aggressive-erotic film. The men who selected the highest shock levels were those who had both been provoked and shown aggressive-erotic films. Other research with college men has shown that reported sexual arousal while watching a film depicting a rape was increased when the female victim was depicted as experiencing both pain and orgasm (Malamuth et al., 1980). The researchers suggested that the orgasm legitimized the violence in the viewer's mind, reinforcing the cultural myth that some women need to be dominated and are sexually aroused by an overpowering man. It has been suggested that exposure to aggressive-erotic films may increase violence toward women, even among normal college men (Donnerstein & Linz, 1984).

■ **The Attorney General's Commission Report** In 1986, the Attorney General's Commission on Pornography reviewed the available research and concluded that sexually explicit materials do indeed cause violence against women. The Surgeon General at the time, C. Everett Koop (1987), summarized three main points about the relationship between pornography and sexual *aggression*:

1. Pornography that portrays sexual aggression as pleasurable to the victim increases the acceptance of the use of coercion in sexual relations . . ."

2. "Acceptance of coercive sexuality appears to be related to sexual aggression . . ."

3. "In laboratory studies measuring short-term effects, exposure to violent pornography increases punitive behavior toward women." (Koop, 1987, p. 945).

Donnerstein and Linz (1987) contend that the Attorney General's Report (1986) failed to separate the effects of *explicit sexual materials from those of sexually violent materials*. There remains no evidence that explicit sexual materials that do not contain violence spur antisocial behavior. Donnerstein and Linz note that, "It is not sex, but violence, that is an obscenity in our society" (1987, p. 56). Nor did Surgeon General Koop distinguish in his comments between pornography and violent pornography.

> **?** There is no evidence that pornography in itself causes crimes of violence. However, *aggressive* pornography may contribute to or serve to legitimize violence against women.

It is interesting to note that a minority of Americans support legislation that would make explicit sexual materials illegal, but three out of four favor making violent pornography illegal (Harris, 1988). But legislation that would curtail pornographic materials may conflict with the First Amendment and therefore be judged unconstitutional (Blakely, 1985). There is even a split among feminists on the issue of banning pornography. The feminist writer Kate Millett, for example, argued that "We're better off hanging tight to the First Amendment so that we have freedom of speech" (Press et al., 1985). Questions regarding pornography are likely to remain controversial. As the debate continues, it is useful to separate moral judgments from scientific findings.

What have we learned from researchers about the relationship between exposure to explicit sexual materials and aggression toward women? Is there a difference between violent and nonviolent pornography in terms of their effects on male viewers' tendencies to aggress against females?

RAPE

While rape is not classified as a mental disorder within the DSM system, it is a sexually deviant criminal act with such grievous effects on the victims that it warrants discussion in this chapter. **Forcible rape** refers to the use of force, violence, or threats of violence to coerce the victim into sexual intercourse. **Statutory rape** is defined as intercourse with a person who is under the age of consent, which in most states is 18, even though the person may express willingness.

There are 75,000 to 90,000 reported cases of forcible rape in the United States each year (Allgeier & Allgeier, 1984; Becker et al., 1983). Since fewer than one in five rapes are believed to be reported to authori-

Forcible rape involves the use of force, violence, or threats of violence to coerce the victim into sexual activity. Rapists' motives may have more to do with desires to abuse, control, or punish women than with sexual gratification.

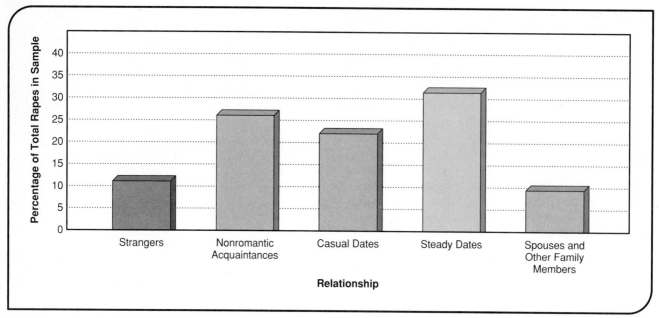

FIGURE 11.1 Relationship of rapist and victim.
Nearly nine of ten rapes reported by college women in a large national survey were committed by an acquaintance of the victim. More than half (53%) of these rapes could be classified as date rapes committed either by casual dates (22%) or steady dates (31%).
Source: Adapted from Koss (1988).

ties, it may be that 375,000 or more rapes each year actually take place. Up to two million instances of coerced sex may also occur within marriage each year, although the victimized women in these cases may be less likely to define coerced sex by their husbands as rape.

In a recent large-scale survey of 3,187 women and 2,972 men attending 32 colleges across the nation, a disturbingly high percentage (27.5%) of the women reported that they had been victims of rape (15.4%) or attempted rape (12.1%) (Koss et al., 1987). In nearly ninety percent of the reported rapes in this survey, the victim was acquainted with the rapist (Koss et al., 1988) (see Figure 11.1). Acquaintance rapes are particularly likely to be underreported to police, for the victims may not perceive them as crimes. About one in thirteen men (7.7%) surveyed admitted to committing or attempting rape (Koss et al., 1987). A further analysis of the data showed that nearly 4 percent of the women reported that they were victims of rape or attempted rape in the six-month period preceding the survey, with most of these rapes occurring on campus.

 Actually, a shockingly large proportion of college men in a recent survey, about one in thirteen, admitted to committing or attempting rape. It is also likely that many others committed such acts but failed to report them.

Theoretical Perspectives

There is no single type of rape or rapist. Some rapists report feeling inadequate around women and say that they cannot find willing partners. They lack social skills for interacting with the opposite sex (Overholser & Beck, 1986). Others, who are basically antisocial, tend to act on their impulses regardless of the cost to the victim. Many antisocial rapists have long histories of violent behavior (Amir, 1971). For some rapists, violence appears to increase sexual arousal; thus, they seek to combine sex with violent behavior (Quinsey et al., 1984). But regardless of motive, rape is a violent crime, not a sexual disorder.

 It is true that some people are sexually aroused by violence. For example, violence appears to enhance sexual arousal in some rapists.

Other rapists, who were abused as children, may humiliate women as a way of expressing anger and power over women, and of taking revenge (Groth & Birnbaum, 1979).

■ **Motives of Rapists** Nicholas Groth and William Hobson (1983) argue that the seeking of sexual gratification has little to do with rape. On the basis of clinical experience with more than 1,000 rapists, Groth and

Hobson hypothesize the existence of three basic kinds of rape: anger rape, power rape, and sadistic rape.

The anger rape is a savage, unpremeditated attack triggered by feelings of hatred and resentment. Anger rapists usually use more force than necessary to gain compliance. They frequently coerce women into degrading acts, fellatio, or anal intercourse. Anger rapists typically report that they were taking revenge for humiliations they had suffered at the hands of women.

The power rapist is basically motivated by the desire to control another person. The wish for sexual gratification is subordinate to the desire to dominate the victim. Groth and Hobson (1983) suggest that power rapists use rape to try "to resolve disturbing doubts about [their] masculine identity and worth, [or] to combat deep-seated feelings of insecurity and vulnerability" (p. 165). Power rapes are premeditated and the rapist uses only enough force to subdue the victim.

Sadistic rapes are premeditated ritualistic assaults. Frequently they employ torture and **bondage,** merging sex and aggression. Sadistic rapists are most likely to mutilate their victims. Groth and Birnbaum (1983) report that many sadistic rapists are preoccupied with violent pornography. Nonviolent pornography holds little interest for them.

■ Socialization Influences   Many rapists cannot be distinguished from nonrapists by means of interviews and psychological tests. Many show no impairment in general functioning or in reality testing (Dean & de Bruyn-Kops, 1982).

The apparent "normality" of rapists suggests that socialization factors may play an important role. Many social critics have argued that our culture socializes men into taking sexually dominant roles that may in the extreme take the form of rape (Burt, 1980). Males are often reinforced in our culture for competitive and aggressive behavior. Cultural influences may also socialize women to assume the victim role. The stereotypical feminine role is traditionally associated with such characteristics as passivity, cooperation, and acceptance. Women may be socialized into roles that encourage submission, rather than resistance. Rape victims in one study were found to be less assertive and dominant than were nonvictims (Myers et al., 1984). Women, too, who appear more vulnerable may be more likely than others to be attacked (Myers et al., 1984). But this should not be taken as blaming the victim for her victimization. The responsibility for crimes of sexual violence always lies with the perpetrator, not with the victim. But victims of rape frequently harbor misplaced guilt, as we shall see.

■ Cognitive Factors   Cognitively oriented psychologists also focus on the ways in which our thoughts and beliefs influence our behavior. Some rapists, particularly men who rape their dates, tend to misread women's expressed wishes (see Lipton et al., 1987). They assume that dates who say no really mean yes and are playing male-female games.

Consider the comments of a 20-year-old date rapist:

I guess that I probably forced five or six women into having sex with me on dates. While I was doing it, I never saw it as rape. It was just the game that males and females play, and I was the winner. When Sara reported me to the campus cops, I laughed about it at first. After all, how could she say that I raped her after the way she'd been flirting with me in the library? How could she prove anything, you know? But now I realize that what I did was wrong, even though it didn't feel wrong to me then. It just made me feel strong and powerful. I never really thought about how the girls felt, though. I guess I sort of thought it was a game for them, too.

(Masters et al., 1988, p. 471)

Myths about Rape

Many of us, including many professionals, harbor various myths about rape. These rape myths tend to minimize the effects of rape and direct blame toward the victim rather than the attacker. Rape myths contribute to a social climate that is too often lenient toward rapists and unsympathetic toward victims. Complete the questionnaire on page 388 if you want to learn whether you harbor some of the more common myths.

Victims of Rape

Not only do rape victims suffer rape itself but they also suffer from society's tendencies to blame victims for what happened to them. The stigma that is attached to the rape-victim role is one reason that so many women fail to report assaults to the authorities. Burgess and Holmstrom (1974) coined the term **rape trauma syndrome** to describe a number of the effects of sexual assault.

■ Rape Trauma Syndrome   Rape trauma syndrome consists of two phases. The first or acute phase follows the rape and usually lasts for several days. Many victims are disorganized during the acute phase and profit from counseling from trained rape-trauma personnel. Victims may cry uncontrollably or show an unrealistic composure, which often gives way to venting of feelings later on. Feelings of anger, fear, nervousness, guilt, shame, powerlessness, and self-blame are common (Roehl & Gray, 1984). Physical symptoms are stress-related and local. There may be headaches, nausea, and insomnia,

QUESTIONNAIRE
Cultural Myths That Create a Climate That Supports Rape

Martha Burt (1980) has constructed a scale that measures cultural myths concerning rape. Indicate whether you believe that each of the following statements is true or false by circling T or F, respectively, for each item. Then consult the key at the end of the chapter to learn more about your answers.

T F 1. A woman who goes to the home or apartment of a man on their first date implies that she is willing to have sex.

T F 2. Any female can get raped.

T F 3. One reason that women falsely report a rape is that they frequently have a need to call attention to themselves.

T F 4. Any healthy woman can successfully resist a rapist if she really wants to.

T F 5. When women go around braless or wearing short skirts and tight tops, they are just asking for trouble.

T F 6. In the majority of rapes, the victim is promiscuous or has a bad reputation.

T F 7. If a girl engages in necking or petting and she lets things get out of hand, it is her own fault if her partner forces sex on her.

T F 8. Women who get raped while hitchhiking get what they deserve.

T F 9. A woman who is stuck-up and thinks she is too good to talk to guys on the street deserves to be taught a lesson.

T F 10. Many women have an unconscious wish to be raped, and may then unconsciously set up a situation in which they are likely to be attacked.

T F 11. If a woman gets drunk at a party and has intercourse with a man she's just met there, she should be considered "fair game" to other males at the party who want to have sex with her too, whether she wants to or not.

T F 12. Many women who report a rape are lying because they are angry and want to get back at the man they accuse.

T F 13. Many, if not most, rapes are merely invented by women who discovered they were pregnant and wanted to protect their reputation.

along with local injuries that require medical attention and a period of healing.

The second phase, a long-term reorganization phase, may last for years (Sales et al., 1984). Feelings of anxiety, anger, depression, embarrassment, fear, and guilt can persist for a year or more, although they tend to diminish with time (Ageton, 1983). Continued nervousness and fear during this period may cause the woman to move to apparently safer surroundings. If

Rape-crisis centers help rape victims cope with the trauma of rape. They provide victims with emotional support and help them obtain medical and legal services. But the psychological effects of rape can be enduring. Many victims have anxiety, depression, fears, and other psychological problems for years afterward.

she has reported the assault, she may also fear retaliation by the rapist. Sexual appetite usually suffers. Eighty-eight percent of a sample of 222 rape victims reported lack of sexual desire and some fear of sex (Becker et al., 1984). Women raped from 2 to 46 years ago were found to be more anxious, fearful, and depressed than were nonvictims, underscoring the potentially enduring aspects of rape trauma (Santiago et al., 1985). Moreover, girls who were sexually assaulted during childhood often showed sexual dysfunctions in adulthood (Becker et al., 1986; Tsai et al., 1979).

A recent population survey of households in the Los Angeles area (Burnam et al., 1988) compared the frequencies of diagnosable mental disorders in victims of sexual assaults and nonvictims (see Figure 11.2). Sexual assault was defined as pressured or forced sexual contact in childhood or adulthood, including acts of rape, molestation, and childhood sexual abuse in which the child was psychologically or physically pressured to engage in sexual acts. Assault victims were two to four times as likely to show evidence of major depression, anxiety disorders, and substance abuse disorders in adulthood than were individuals without a history of assault (Burnam et al., 1988). Men with a history of sexual assault in childhood were as likely as women to develop these disorders, except that men developed alcohol or drug problems at a later age. Childhood assault was more closely linked to adult psychopathology than was assault in adulthood.

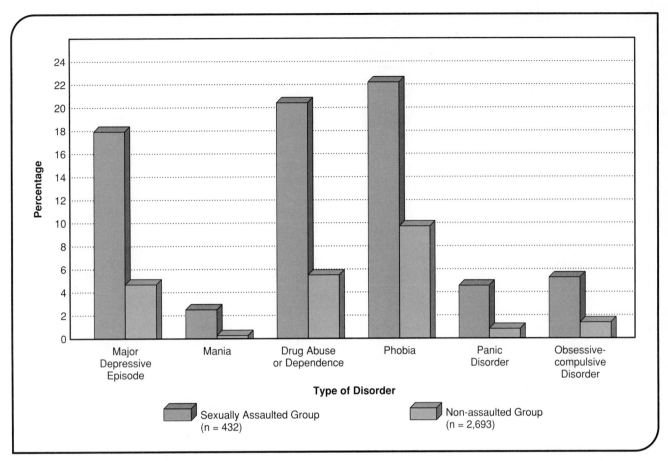

FIGURE 11.2 Mental disorders diagnosed among victims of sexual assault.
Source: Adapted from Burnam et al. (1988).

Treatment of Rapists

Treatment of the rape victim means supporting her through the crisis period and helping foster long-term adjustment. But "treatment" of the rapist can refer to measures that help him adjust to feelings of inadequacy and other deficiencies that may be implicated in his crime—*and* to treatments that are intended to protect society from him.

■ **Psychotherapy and Behavior Therapy** Psychodynamic therapies generally assume that rapists are motivated by internal conflicts and aim to help offenders change their behavior by becoming aware of and resolving these conflicts. But evidence of the effectiveness of psychodynamic approaches in changing the behavior of rapists has been lacking (Groth & Birnbaum, 1979). Cognitively oriented therapies are used to confront rapists with their distorted beliefs—for example, to help them recognize that rape is not simply an extension of typical male-female game playing, but is a terrifying, humiliating experience for a woman. Behavioral methods foster social skills in rapists who have problems making normal heterosexual contacts and attempt to

recondition sexual arousal so that rapists are excited by loving contacts and not by aggression. But these approaches, too, have not yet demonstrated significant beneficial impact on the behavior of rapists following release from incarceration.

■ **Biological Approaches** Some biological approaches to "treatment" of rapists have involved more extreme—and controversial—measures. For example, a number of European rapists who claimed to be unable to control overpowering sex drives have been castrated (Heim & Hursch, 1979). Although castrated rapists no longer produce testosterone, they may retain sexual interests and the ability to produce erections for many years, and occasionally repeat their crimes (Heim, 1981).

Experimental surgery that destroys sections of the hypothalamus linked to sex and aggression has been carried out with small numbers of rapists, but data concerning the utility of this approach are lacking (Rieber & Sigusch, 1979; Schmidt & Schorsch, 1981).

Antiandrogen drugs, like Depo-Provera, lower the testosterone level and perform a sort of chemical, reversible "castration." John Money and Richard Bennett

(1981) describe the effects of Depo-Provera in combination with psychotherapy as being helpful in keeping *"some patients* [italics ours] . . . off a treadmill of imprisonment" (p. 132). On the other hand, once the drug was discontinued, nearly all of the men in the program committed additional rapes (Masters et al., 1988).

PARAPHILIAS

The word *paraphilia* was coined from the Greek roots *para*, meaning "to the side of," and *philos*, meaning "loving." In the **paraphilias** (also called sexual deviations), people show sexual arousal ("loving") in response to stimuli that are unusual or bizarre ("to the side of" normally arousing stimuli). According to the DSM–III–R, paraphilias involve recurrent, powerful sexual urges and sexually arousing fantasies focused on either (1) nonhuman objects (underwear, shoes, leather, silk, etc.); (2) humiliation or experience of pain

in oneself or one's partner; or (3) children or other persons who do not grant consent.

The diagnosis is not made unless the person has acted on the urges or is distinctly distressed by them. *Note that the diagnosis can be made purely on the basis of the person's reported fantasies and distress. Overt paraphilic behavior is not required for a diagnosis.*

Some persons who receive the diagnosis can function sexually in the absence of paraphilic stimuli or fantasies. Others resort to paraphilic stimuli under stress. Still others cannot become sexually aroused unless these stimuli are used, in actuality or in fantasy. For some persons, the paraphilia is their exclusive means of attaining sexual gratification.

Some paraphilias are relatively harmless and victimless. Among these are fetishism and transvestic fetishism. Others—exhibitionism, masochism, pedophilia, and sadism—have victims. A most harmful paraphilia is sexual sadism, when acted out with a nonconsenting partner. Voyeurism falls somewhere in between, since the "victim" does not typically know that he or she is being watched. As noted earlier in the chapter, some of the most brutal rapes are essentially sadistic. Rape is not discussed as a paraphilia because it is treated as a crime that involves sex as an instrument of violence.

The DSM–III–R notes that persons with paraphilias usually do not consider themselves mentally disordered. They are generally seen by the mental-health system only when they get into conflict with their partners or with society. With the exceptions of sexual masochism and some isolated cases of other disorders, paraphilias are almost never diagnosed in women.

Paraphilias are scaled in the DSM–III–R according to level of severity:

MILD: The person experiences recurrent urges that cause personal distress but has never acted on them.
MODERATE: The person occasionally acts out on urges.
SEVERE: The person repeatedly acts out on paraphilic urges.

Now let us consider a number of the paraphilias

Exhibitionism

Exhibitionism is defined as the recurrent, powerful urge, of at least six months' duration, to expose one's genitals to an unsuspecting stranger in order to surprise, shock, or sexually arouse the victim. Exhibitionists either act on or are markedly distressed by these urges and associated fantasies. The exhibitionist may masturbate while fantasizing about or actually exposing oneself. The disorder appears to be limited to males and the victims are almost always females.

Exhibitionists are usually not interested in actual sexual contact with the victim and are therefore not generally considered dangerous. Nevertheless, victims may believe themselves in great danger and may be traumatized by the act. Victims are probably best advised to show no reaction to exhibitionists, if possible. It would be unwise to insult an exhibitionist, lest it provoke a violent reaction. Although most exhibitionists are not violent, one in ten has considered or attempted rape (Gebhard et al., 1965). Nor do we recommend an exaggerated show of shock or fear; it only reinforces the exhibitionist.

The courts tend to be hard on exhibitionists, in part because about 10 percent of rapists and child molesters begin their so-called sexual careers by exposing themselves to unsuspecting victims (Abel et al., 1984). The archetypal exhibitionist is young, sexually repressed, and unhappily married (Mohr et al., 1964). His victim's revulsion or fear heightens his sexual arousal, and he may ejaculate very readily. Many exhibitionists harbor puritanical beliefs about sex. Some doubt their masculinity and hold feelings of inferiority (Blair & Lanyon, 1981).

Consider the case of Michael:

■ Michael was a 26-year-old, handsome, boyish-looking married male with a 3-year-old daughter. He had spent about one-quarter of his life in reform schools and in prison. As an adolescent he had been a fire-setter. As a young adult, he had begun to expose himself. He came to the clinic without his wife's knowledge because he was exposing himself more and more often—up to three times a day.

Michael said he liked sex with his wife, but it wasn't as exciting as exposing himself. He felt he couldn't prevent his exhibitionism but was afraid of being arrested and imprisoned again. He loved his daughter more than anything and couldn't stand the thought of being separated from her.

Michael's method of operation was as follows: He would look for slender adolescent females, usually near the junior high school and the senior high school. He would take his penis out of his pants and play with it while he drove up to a girl or a small group of girls. He would lower the car window, continuing to play with himself, and ask them for directions. Sometimes the girls didn't see his penis. That was okay. Sometimes they saw it and didn't react. That was okay, too. When they saw it and became flustered and afraid, that was best of all. He would start to masturbate harder, and now and then he managed to ejaculate before the girls had departed.

Michael's history was unsettled. His father had left home before he was born, and his mother had drunk heavily. He was in and out of foster homes throughout his childhood. Before he was 10 years old he was involved in homosexual activities with neighborhood boys. Now and then the boys also forced neighborhood girls into

petting, and Michael had mixed feelings when the girls got upset. He felt bad for them, but he also enjoyed it. A couple of times girls seemed horrified at the sight of his penis, and it made him "really feel like a man. To see that look, you know, with a girl, not a woman, but a girl—a slender girl, that's what I'm after."

The Authors' Files ■

Professional stripteasers and swimmers in revealing bathing suits are not usually exhibitionists. Both groups may seek to arouse observers sexually but generally not to shock them.

> It is not true that people who wear revealing bathing suits are exhibitonists. Exhibitionists are almost always men and are motivated by the wish to shock and dismay the people they expose themselves to, not to show off the "attractiveness" of their bodies.

The chief motive of the stripteaser, of course, may simply be to earn a living.

Fetishism

The French *fétiche* is thought to derive from the Portuguese *feitico*, referring to a "magic charm." In this case, the "magic" lies in the object's ability to arouse sexually. According to the DSM–III–R, the chief feature of **fetishism** is recurrent, powerful sexual urges and arousing fantasies, of at least six months' duration, involving inanimate objects, such as an article of clothing (bra, panties, hosiery, boots, shoes, leather, silk, and the like). However, some fetishes, referred to as *partialists*, are also responsive to a bodily part, such as the foot. It may be normal for lovers to like the sight, feel, or even the smell of their lovers' undergarments and of their anatomic features, such as their feet. The fetishist, however, prefers the object or the part to the whole person and may not be able to become sexually aroused without it.

Fetishists often find sexual gratification by masturbating while fondling the object, rubbing it, or smelling it; or by having their partners wear it during sexual activity.

Consider the classic nineteenth-century case of a boy who developed a fetish for shoes. The treatment suggested by Dr. Hammond is a remarkable innovation, which could be said anticipated the later development of related behavioral techniques, such as orgasmic reconditioning:

■ A 7-year-old boy was taught to masturbate by a servant girl. He was sexually aroused when she inadvertently touched his penis with her shoe. His masturbation fantasies subsequently focused on shoes, and he often ran into trouble in school for grabbing at his teacher's shoes. During his teens he was disgusted at the thought of sexual intercourse. At age 18 he opened a shoe store so that he could fit shoes on female customers. One day he experienced epileptic seizures that he attributed to his fetish. He decided he must overcome the fetish and settle into normal married life. He married an attractive woman, but the prospect of intercourse remained distasteful. A Dr. Hammond imaginatively suggested that he might overcome his revulsion toward sexual intercourse by hanging a shoe above the marital bed where he could see it during love-making. He could also imagine that his wife was a shoe! It worked. He became progressively less aroused by shoes and grew attracted to his wife.

Adapted from von Krafft-Ebing, 1886 ■

Transvestic Fetishism

The chief feature of **transvestic fetishism** is recurrent, powerful sexual urges and related fantasies, of at least six months' duration, involving cross-dressing. Other fetishists can be satisfied by handling objects such as women's clothing while they masturbate; transvestites want to wear them and are sexually excited by the act of cross-dressing. Transvestites keep women's clothing around and usually masturbate while imagining that other men are attracted to them in their finery. According to the DSM–III–R, transvestite fetishism has

True transvestites cross-dress for purposes of sexual gratification. Female impersonators or (stage performers who cross-dress for theatrical purposes) are not necessarily true transvestites. Transvestites often cross-dress in private, but may also enjoy masquerading as women in public.

only been described in heterosexual males, although such men may have occasionally had homosexual experiences. Homosexual men may cross-dress for the sake of attracting other men or because it is fashionable in their social circles to masquerade as women. Male transsexuals cross-dress because of gender discomfort associated with wearing masculine clothing. But cross-dressing among male homosexuals and transsexuals does not cause sexual arousal and so is not considered a form of transvestic fetishism. Nor are female impersonators who cross-dress for theatrical purposes considered transvestites, unless they also do so to experience sexual arousal.

Most transvestites are married and engage in sexual activity with their wives, but they seek additional sexual gratification through dressing as women, as in the case of Archie:

■ Archie was a 55-year-old plumber who had been cross-dressing for many years. There was a time when he would go out in public as a woman, but as his prominence in the community grew, he became more afraid of being discovered in public. His wife, Myrna, knew of his "peccadillo," especially since he borrowed many of her clothes, and she also urged him to stay at home, offering to help him with his "weirdness." For many years his paraphilia had been restricted to the home.

The couple came to the clinic at the urging of the wife. Myrna described how Archie had imposed his will on her for 20 years. Archie would wear her undergarments and masturbate while she told him how disgusting he was. (The couple also regularly engaged in "normal" sexual intercourse, which Myrna enjoyed.) The cross-dressing situation had come to a head because a teenaged daughter had almost walked into the couple's bedroom while they were acting out Archie's fantasies.

With Myrna out of the consulting room, Archie explained how he grew up in a family with several older sisters. He described how underwear had been perpetually hanging all around the one bathroom to dry. As an adolescent Archie experimented with rubbing against articles of underwear, then with trying them on. On one occasion a sister walked in while he was modeling panties before the mirror. She told him he was a "dredge to society" and he straightaway experienced unparalleled sexual excitement. He masturbated when she left the room, and his orgasm was the strongest of his young life.

Archie did not think that there was anything wrong with wearing women's undergarments and masturbating. He was not about to give it up, regardless of whether his marriage was destroyed as a result. Myrna's main concern was finally separating herself from Archie's "sickness." She didn't care what he did any more, so long as he did it by himself. "Enough is enough," she said.

That was the compromise the couple worked out in marital therapy. Archie would engage in his fantasies by himself. He would choose times when Myrna was not at home, and she would not be informed of his activities. He would also be very, very careful to choose times when the children would not be around.

Six months later the couple were together and content. Archie had replaced Myrna's input into his fantasies with transvestic-sadomasochistic magazines. Myrna said "I see no evil, hear no evil, smell no evil." They continued to have sexual intercourse. After a while, Myrna even forgot to check to see which underwear had been used.

The Authors' Files ■

Voyeurism

The chief feature of **voyeurism** is either acting upon or being strongly distressed by recurrent, powerful sexual urges and related fantasies, of at least six months' duration, involving watching unsuspecting people, generally strangers, who are undressed, disrobing, or engaging in sexual activity. The purpose of watching, or "peeping," is to attain sexual excitement. The voyeur does not usually seek sexual activity with the person being observed.

Are people who enjoy watching their mates undress in their presence or attending pornographic films voyeurs? The answer is no. The people who are observed know that they are being observed by their mates or will be observed by film audiences. We should also note that feelings of sexual arousal while watching our mates undress or by observing sex scenes in R- and X-rated films fall within the normal spectrum of human sexuality.

 People who like to watch their spouses undress are *not* voyeurs. Enjoying seeing others undress is completely normal. Voyeurs choose unsuspecting victims, and they generally prefer watching to doing.

The voyeur usually masturbates while watching, or while fantasizing about watching. For some voyeurs, peeping is the exclusive sexual outlet. Voyeurs are known to place themselves in risky situations. The prospect of being found out or injured apparently heightens the excitement.

Frotteurism

The French *frottage* refers to the artistic technique of making a drawing by rubbing against a raised object. The chief feature of the paraphilia of **frotteurism** is recurrent, powerful sexual urges and related fantasies, of at least six months' duration, involving rubbing against or touching a nonconsenting person. Frotteurism generally occurs in crowded places, such as subway cars, buses, or elevators. It is the rubbing or touching, not the coercive aspect of the act, that is sexually arousing to the man. During the act he may imagine himself enjoying an exclusive, affectionate sexual relationship with the victim.

Pedophilia

Pedophilia derives from the Greek *paidos*, meaning "child." The chief feature of pedophilia is recurrent, powerful sexual urges and related fantasies, of at least six months' duration, that involve sexual activity with prepubescent children. According to DSM–III–R criteria, the pedophile must be a person of at least 16 years of age who is at least five years older than the victim. In pedophilia, exclusive type, the individual is only attracted to children. In pedophilia, nonexclusive type, the person is also attracted to adults.

Some pedophiles restrict their sexual interest in children to looking at or undressing them. Others fondle children and masturbate in their presence. Children are not worldly wise, and pedophiles frequently inform the youngsters that they are "educating" them, "showing them something," or doing something they will "like." Still others entice or coerce children into oral sex or vaginal or anal intercourse. Some pedophiles are incestuous and limit their activity to family members; others to children outside the family. The pedophile may treat the child with generous attention and consideration of his or her other needs in the interests of gaining the child's affection and preventing the youngster from disclosing the sexual activity to others. Sometimes, however, the pedophile may threaten the child or the child's family with physical harm to prevent disclosure. Children rarely report sexual abuse for fear that they will be blamed for it. Adults may become suspicious if children develop school problems, fears, or eating or sleeping disorders (Finkelhor, 1979). Sometimes a pediatrician discovers physical evidence of sexual abuse.

It is difficult to say how many children are victims of sexual abuse, for studies that have been conducted have been based primarily on identified victims and their families. This may represent the "tip of the iceberg" owing to the fact that many instances are not reported and remain unknown to professionals. Whatever the actual number of cases, sexual abuse of children cuts across all racial, ethnic, and economic boundaries (Alter-Reid et al., 1986). Child sexual abuse, like rape, is underreported, with perhaps only one in three or one in four cases reported to authorities (Alter-Reid et al., 1986). Reported cases numbered about 45,000 in a one-year period (Finkelhor & Hotaling, 1984), but estimates are that there may be as many as 150,000 to 200,000 new cases annually (Alter-Reid et al., 1986). Perhaps 10 to 15 percent of children have been victimized by an adult on at least one occasion (Lanyon, 1986). According to the DSM–III–R, girls are twice as likely as boys to be victimized, especially girls between the ages of 8 and 10. Many pedophiles are attracted to both girls and boys.

Despite the stereotype, most pedophiles are not "dirty old men" hanging around schoolyards in raincoats. They are usually law-abiding, respected citizens

"Anatomically-correct" dolls are used by investigators and therapists to help child victims of sexual abuse describe their experiences. The dolls have movable tongues and fingers that can assist children in describing oral molestation and masturbation.

in their thirties or forties. Most are married or divorced and have children of their own. Pedophiles are usually well-acquainted with their victims, either relatives or friends of the family. Many cases of pedophilia are not isolated incidents. They may be a series of acts that begin when the child victim is very young and continue for many years until the acts are discovered or the relationship is broken off (Finkelhor, 1979).

The origins of pedophilia are complex and varied. Some pedophiles are socially immature. They prefer to relate to children, because children are less critical and demanding than other adults. Among this group are pedophiles who are unable to establish satisfactory sexual relationships with adult partners and who use children as substitutes (Overholser & Beck, 1986). In other cases, it may be that childhood sexual experiences with other children were so enjoyable that the pedophile, as an adult, is attempting to recapture the excitement of earlier years. De Young (1982) hypothesizes that some pedophiles who were sexually abused themselves when they were children may now be reversing the situation in an effort to establish feelings of mastery.

■ **Incest**   The term *incest* derives from the Latin roots *in*, meaning "not," and *castus*, meaning chaste. Sagarin defines incest as "marriage and/or sexual intercourse between persons [consanguineously] of so close a relationship that the act is proscribed and punished by virtue of the closeness of that kinship tie" (1977, p. 128). True incest refers only to people who are related by blood, but the law may also proscribe relationships between, say, stepfathers and stepdaughters.

Brother–sister and father–daughter marriages were practiced during a number of ancient Egyptian dynasties. Although some were intended to maintain the purity and assumed divinity of the royal line, others were reported among commoners. Preservation of the purity of the royal line also motivated incestuous marriages among the Incas and the kings of Hawaii. Incest also kept wealth within the family. Yet the incest taboo is widespread. Not one of nearly 200 preliterate societies studied by Ford and Beach (1951) allowed brother–sister or parent–child incest.

The DSM–III–R does not have a special diagnostic category for incest. Instead, diagnosticians making the diagnosis of pedophilia specify if the offense is limited to incest.

Only 3 percent of the subjects interviewed by Kinsey and his colleagues (1948, 1953) reported experience with incestuous relationships. Fourteen percent of the men and 8 percent of the women in Hunt's national telephone survey reported some kind of sexual contact with relatives. A more recent survey of 800 undergraduates at a New England college found that 15 percent of the women and 10 percent of the men had had some sort of sexual encounter with a sibling. Genital fondling and display were most common (Finkelhor, 1980). A survey of 930 adult women found that 16 percent reported incestuous relationships by the age of 18 (Russell, 1983). Most often the molester lived

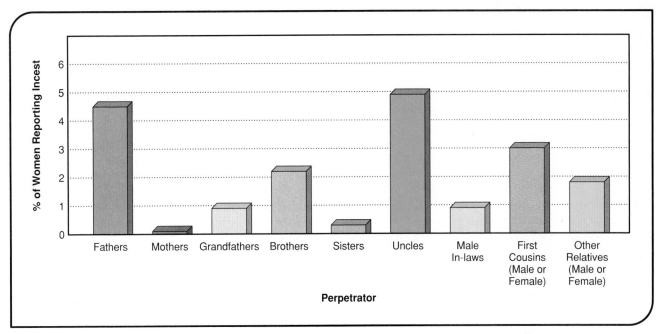

FIGURE 11.3 Relationship of female victims of incest to perpetrators.
These data were drawn from a sample of 930 college women reporting an incestuous relationship occurring by age 18. Uncles were the most frequent perpetrators, followed by fathers, cousins, and brothers.
Source: Adapted from Russell (1983).

in the same household as the victim and was at least 20 years older than the victim. Molestation by uncles was most common, followed, with decreasing incidence, by molestation by fathers, cousins, and brothers (see Figure 11.3). Stepfathers were implicated as offenders about six times as often as biological fathers.

Family Factors Relating to Incest Brother–sister and father–daughter incest may be encouraged by the crowding and open sexuality that is found in some economically disadvantaged families. Incest often occurs in the context of other signs of family disruption, as in families where the father or both parents are alcoholic or physically abusive, and in which the marriage itself is dysfunctional (Alter-Reid et al., 1986; also Molnar & Cameron, 1975).

Gebhard and his colleagues (1965) found that many fathers who committed incest with their daughters were religiously devout, fundamentalistic, and moralistic. Such men, when sexually frustrated, may be less likely to find extramarital and extrafamilial sexual outlets. In many cases, the father is under stress but does not find adequate emotional and sexual support from his wife (Gagnon, 1977). He turns to a daughter as a wife surrogate. The girl is often mature enough to have assumed household chores. Perhaps, in the father's fantasies, she has become the "woman of the house." These men's wives often seem surprised by revelations of incest, despite obvious clues and even

daughters' repeated complaints. Sometimes the wife seems involved in a tacit conspiracy to allow the abuse to continue to preserve the family.

■ **Effects of Sexual Abuse** Among the women victims of childhood incest and sexual abuse will be found low self-esteem, self-blame, self-loathing, anger, emotional coldness, lack of trust, and impaired social and sexual relationships (Alter-Reid et al., 1986; Justice & Justice, 1979; Russell, 1986). Victimized girls sometimes run away or attempt suicide. Sexual promiscuity and pseudomaturity (acting like a grown-up without having mastered prior developmental tasks) are other frequently occurring outcomes (Alter-Reid et al., 1986; Browning & Boatman, 1977).

Incest has immediate and long-term negative consequences, especially when the molester is the father. In families unable to come to grips with the problem of incest, the child's only way to seek help may be to develop symptoms (Alter-Reid et al., 1986) or to express distress through running away.

Children, especially boys, who were sexually abused between the ages of 2 and 6 show more clearly sexualized behaviors than do comparison groups of neglected children and control (nonabused or neglected) children (White et al., 1988). Mothers report that sexually abused boys were more likely to show self-destructive behaviors, such as playing with matches. The abused boys were also more likely to be withdrawn and lonely than were other boys, while there were no such differences between abused girls and other girls. Abused and neglected girls, however, more often had problems with enuresis (lack of urinary control) and encopresis (soiling) than did other girls, although these problems were no more likely to occur among abused boys than among nonabused boys. Because the effects of sexual abuse may be expressed differently for boys and girls, clinicians need to be aware of the sex-specific signs of sexual abuse in investigating cases of suspected abuse.

Much research on the developmental effects of childhood sexual abuse is retrospective. Adults are asked to recollect traumatic events from memory. These recollections may be biased by general inaccuracies as well as cognitive distortion or denial of painful events. To understand better the causal connections between abuse and development would require prospective research in which large random samples of chidren are tracked over the years. In this way, differences could be observed between those who were eventually abused and those who were not (Burnam et al., 1988).

■ **Treatment**   Because most cases of childhood sexual abuse are not reported, psychotherapy in adulthood may represent the first opportunity for survivors of abuse to disclose their traumas and cope with feelings

---

A CLOSER LOOK
Signs of Childhood Sexual Abuse

Because most childhood victims of sexual abuse do not report the abuse to others, nonabusing parents (Alter-Reid et al., 1986), teachers, and helping professionals need to be alert to possible signs of abuse (Russell, 1983). Various signs have been noted in the literature (Miller-Perrin & Wurtele, 1988), including physical ones like suspicious staining or blood in the child's underwear, complaints of pain in the anal or genital area, and presence of sexually transmitted diseases. Various behavioral signs have also been identified: nightmares, anxiety, depression, sleep disturbances, precocious sexual behavior or knowledge, behavior problems, and unusual reactions to stress. However, as many of these signs may be attributable to other causes, more careful questioning and examination needs to be done in cases of suspected abuse. No single behavioral pattern has yet been identified that is reliably associated with childhood sexual abuse (Miller-Perrin & Wurtele, 1988).

Another problem in identifying cases of sexual abuse is that the symptoms of abuse may be "masked" (Miller-Perrin & Wurtele, 1988). Children who have been abused often come to the attention of helping professionals for reasons other than the abuse itself, such as school problems or depression.

---

of anger, pain, and perhaps, misplaced guilt (Alter-Reid et al., 1986). Disclosure within a supportive therapeutic relationship may help to prevent the cycle of abuse from repeating itself from one generation to another. Psychotherapy may also help victims improve their self-images and their abilities to trust others and establish more meaningful intimate relationships (Alter-Reid et al., 1986).

For victimized children, a comprehensive medical and psychological assessment must be conducted. In cases of suspected incest, the children and their families need to be interviewed, including the suspected offender. There should be close monitoring of family interactions. The victim should be interviewed alone to circumvent distortion of events owing to threats or contradictions (Sgroi, 1978).

Sexual Masochism

Sexual masochism derives its name from the nineteenth-century German novelist Leopold von Sacher-Masoch (1836–1895), who wrote stories and novels about men who needed to have women inflict pain on them, often in the form of flagellation (being beaten or whipped). Some writers have attributed the desire to be flagellated to the practice of disciplining children with the rod, which was widely practiced in the nineteenth century. But if such an origin was sufficient explanation, Reay Tannahill, author of *Sex in History* (1980) notes that the wish to be flagellated would have become "an international pandemic" (p. 382). It did not.

The DSM–III–R reserves the diagnosis of **sexual masochism** for people who either act upon or are distressed about recurrent, powerful sexual urges and related fantasies, of at least six months' duration, that involve being humiliated, bound, flogged, or made to suffer in other ways. Sexual masochists usually cannot attain sexual gratification in the absence of pain or humiliation.

Some masochists are distressed by their disorder; it afflicts them in terms of intrusive fantasies but they do not act upon them. Others bind or mutilate themselves. Some engage partners, who may be prostitutes, to restrain them (bondage), blindfold them (sensory bondage), paddle, or whip them. Some want to be urinated or defecated upon or subjected to verbal abuse.

One more dangerous expression of masochism is **hypoxyphilia,** in which a person becomes sexually aroused by being deprived of oxygen—for example, by using a noose, plastic bag, chemical, or pressure on the chest. The oxygen deprivation is usually accompanied by fantasies of asphyxiating or being asphyxiated by a lover. Hypoxyphiliacs generally discontinue their activity before they lose consciousness, but occasional deaths result from tragic miscalculations.

Sexual Sadism

The practice of *sadism* is named after the infamous Marquis de Sade, the eighteenth-century Frenchman who wrote stories about the pleasures of achieving sexual gratification by inflicting pain or humiliation on others. The Marquis's first novel, *Justine*, is also his best-known. The virtuous Justine is bound and spread-eagled so that bloodhounds can savage her. She seeks refuge with a surgeon who tries to vivisect her. Then she falls into the clutches of a saber-wielding mass murderer. After tiring of Justine's purity, Nature releases her by hurling a timely thunderbolt. The Marquis justified his tales by arguing that the men in his stories were only carrying out Nature's bloody, barbarous laws. To the Marquis, the universe was basically evil. Evil acts, then, were consistent with natural law. In virtue lay misery and ruin. Vice was the path to prosperity and fulfillment.

The DSM–III–R reserves the diagnosis of **sexual sadism** for recurrent, powerful urges and related fantasies, of at least six months' duration, involving acts in which the sadist is sexually aroused by the physical suffering or humiliation of a victim, through such acts as whipping, spanking, restraining, beating, or even torturing. The sadist either acts out his fantasies or is distinctly disturbed by them. Some sadists recruit consenting partners into their routines, who may be lovers or wives with a masochistic streak, or prostitutes. **Sadomasochism** describes a mutually gratifying interaction between a sadist and a masochist. Still others stalk and assault nonconsenting victims. The sadistic rapist discussed earlier falls into this last group. According to the DSM–III–R, however, most rapists do not seek to become sexually aroused by inflicting pain on their victims and may even lose sexual interest when observing their victims in pain. It is estimated that fewer than one in ten rapists meets the clinical definition of sexual sadism.

Many people experience occasional sadistic or masochistic fantasies or engage in sexual play involving simulated forms of sadomasochism with their partners. The clinical definition of these disorders is brought to bear upon people who are either distressed by their fantasies or act them out in ways that cause actual pain or humiliation to themselves or others.

Other Paraphilias

The DSM–III–R contains a category for paraphilias otherwise not specified. These include making obscene phone calls ("telephone scatologia"), necrophilia (sex with corpses), partialism (a kind of fetish in which the fetishist focuses exclusively on some part of the lover's body, such as a foot, to achieve sexual excitement), zoophilia (sex with animals—also referred to as *bestiality*), coprophilia (feces), klismaphilia (enemas), and urophilia (urine).

Some examples of the clothing and devices used by sadists and masochists.

Theoretical Perspectives

Psychodynamic theorists see many paraphilias as defenses against castration anxiety. They generally link sexual deviations to unresolved Oedipal problems. The thought of the penis disappearing within the vagina is unconsciously equated with castration. The deviant therefore averts castration anxiety by displacing sexual arousal into safer activities—for example, undergarments, sex with children, or watching others perform sexually.

In Chapter 2 we noted that little boys are hypothesized, in traditional psychodynamic theory, to believe that girls lost their penises through castration. Transvestic fetishism, then, symbolizes denial that women do not have penises. The transvestite, that is, sequesters his sex organ beneath women's clothing, unconsciously providing evidence of women's (and his own) safety. The shock and dismay shown by the exhibitionist's victim reassures him that he does, after all, have a penis. The sadist unconsciously identifies with his father—the "aggressor" of his Oedipal fantasies—and relieves anxiety by enacting the role of the castrater. Some psychodynamic theorists see masochism as a way of coping with conflicting feelings about sex: From this perspective, masochists basically feel guilty about sex, but they can enjoy it as long as they believe they are being appropriately punished for it. Others view masochism as the redirection to the self of aggressive impulses originally aimed at the powerful, threatening father. Like the child who is relieved when his inevitable punishment is over, the masochist gladly accepts bondage and flagellation in the place of castration.

Behaviorists explain paraphilias in terms of classical and operant conditioning. Some object or activity becomes inadvertently associated with sexual arousal. The object or activity then gains the capacity to elicit sexual arousal, and orgasm in the actual or fantasized presence of the object or activity reinforces the connection. As an experimental test of this model, Rachman

(1966) repeatedly alternated slides of a woman's boots with slides of nude women for male subjects, and after a while many of the subjects began to show some sexual response to the boots alone. The results were weak and short-lived, but one could argue that such effects might become more persistent if pairings of such stimuli had repeatedly occurred during childhood. The social learning theorist Albert Bandura (1969) points to a role for modeling of deviant sexual behavior by adults in explaining the development of paraphilias.

Treatment of Paraphilias

Psychodynamic therapy aims at helping bring unconscious sexual conflicts into awareness where they might be worked through in the context of the adult personality. While favorable results from individual case studies have appeared from time to time in the clinical literature, there has been an absence of controlled investigations supporting the effectiveness of psychodynamic approaches in treating these problems.

Various treatment techniques have been spawned by the behavioral and cognitive perspectives. Consider systematic desensitization. The premise is that deep muscle relaxation is incompatible with the tensions of sexual arousal, so exposure to a series of progressively more arousing stimuli while remaining relaxed would be expected to disconnect arousal from deviant stimuli. In one case study, a transvestic fetishist who had become attracted to his mother's lingerie at the age of 13 was taught to relax and presented with audiotaped transvestic and fetishistic themes (Fensterheim & Kantor, 1980). He played the tapes daily while remaining relaxed and reported no fetishistic activity at follow-ups. An uncontrolled case study, however, limits interpretations about cause and effect.

In aversive conditioning, the stimulus that elicits sexual arousal (for example, panties) is paired repeatedly with an aversive stimulus (for example, electric shock) in the belief that the stimulus will acquire aversive properties. For example, electric shock was used with a socially inhibited fetishist who masturbated while wearing or fantasizing about women's panties (Kushner, 1977). He was shocked while imagining, viewing photos of, or holding panties. After 41 sessions distributed over 14 weeks, he reported absence of fetishistic fantasies. He was then desensitized to fear of opposite-sex contacts and afterward enjoyed heterosexual relationships.

Covert sensitization is a variation of aversive conditioning in which a stimulus that elicits sexual arousal is paired with the aversive stimulus in imagination, rather than in reality. In an unusual, broad-scale application, 38 pedophiles and 62 exhibitionists, more than half of whom were court-referred, were instructed to fantasize pedophilic or exhibitionist scenes. Then

> At a point . . . when sexual pleasure is aroused, aversive images are presented. . . . Examples might include a pedophiliac fellating a child, but discovering a festering sore on the boy's penis; an exhibitionist exposing to a woman but then suddenly being discovered by his wife or the police; or a pedophiliac laying a young boy down in a field, only to lie next to him in a pile of dog feces. (Maletzky, 1980, p. 308)

Maletzky used this treatment weekly for six months, then followed it with "booster sessions" every three months over a three-year period. The procedure resulted in at least a 75 percent reduction of the deviant activities and fantasies for over 80 percent of the subjects at follow-up periods of up to 36 months. Treatment was equally effective for both self-referred and court-referred clients.

In orgasmic reconditioning, the person becomes sexually aroused in any way he can, but refocuses on normal images or fantasies during orgasm. Davison (1977) reports reducing sadistic fantasies in an otherwise inhibited 21-year-old college man by reinforcing nonsadistic fantasies. The client was instructed to attain erection any way that he could, but then to masturbate while looking at photos of *Playboy* models. Orgasm was thus paired with normal imagery, which eventually attained the capacity to elicit sexual arousal. The client also received social skills training to help him develop heterosexual relationships.

Another behavioral treatment is stimulus satiation. When stimuli are prolonged, we tend to become habituated or desensitized to them. Pedophiles have been overexposed to pictures of young girls and instructed to repeatedly masturbate to them or to fantasies encompassing them. In many cases, the pedophiles become bored with the deviant stimuli or even found them aversive (LoPiccolo, 1985).

Although there have been many reports of the successful use of behavioral techniques in treating various paraphilias, evidence of the effectiveness of these techniques, as for psychodynamic therapies, is drawn from uncontrolled case studies. The lack of experimental controls leaves open other interpretations of cause and effect. For example, clients may have been highly motivated to change and may have used any systematic approach to modify their own behavior.

SEXUAL DYSFUNCTIONS

We now turn to a very different class of sexual disorders, called *sexual dysfunctions*, that involve a lessening or inhibition of sexual interest, pleasure, or response. Sexual dysfunctions, unlike paraphilias, do not involve so-

Many couples encounter sexual difficulties. Sexual dysfunctions are a source of personal distress to oneself or one's partner and can often lead to friction between the partners. Problems in communication can give rise to or exacerbate sexual dysfunctions.

cially deviant or bizarre sexual urges, fantasies, or behavior patterns. Nor do they cause harm to others, as in the case of sexual sadism or pedophilia. Nor might they be considered abnormal from a statistical perspective, since they are quite commonplace. Psychologists focus on sexual dysfunctions because they are a cause of personal distress to an individual and/or the individual's partner. To give us a better perspective on the sexual dysfunctions, we first describe patterns of sexual response. Then we explore the various types of sexual dysfunctions and the methods of treatment that are used to help couples overcome them.

The Sexual Response Cycle

According to the DSM–III–R, sexual dysfunctions interfere with the initiation or the completion of the sexual response cycle. Much of our understanding of the sexual response cycle is based on the pioneering research in the 1960s of sex researchers William Masters and Virginia Johnson. The DSM–III–R describes the sexual response cycle as consisting of the following four phases:

1.   *Appetitive Phase.* This phase corresponds to the presence of sexual fantasies and desires to engage in sexual activity.

2.   *Excitement Phase.* This phase involves the physical changes and feelings of pleasure that occur during the process of sexual arousal. In response to sexual stimulation, the heart rate, respiration rate, and blood pressure increase. The process of sexual excitement involves two primary sexual reflexes—erection in the man and vaginal lubrication in the woman. In men, erection occurs as blood vessels in chambers of loose tissue within the

penis dilate to permit blood to flow in. In women, the breasts become swollen and the nipples erect. Vaginal lubrication appears within ten seconds to half a minute. Blood engorges the genitals, causing the clitoris to expand. The vagina becomes so swollen that the diameter of the outer part is actually reduced by about one-third. The inner vagina lengthens and dilates.

3.   *Orgasm Phase.* Sexual tension peaks and is released through involuntary rhythmic contractions of the pelvic muscles in both males and females. Orgasm, too, is a reflex. In men, muscles at the bottom of the penis reflexively contract, causing semen to be expelled through the penis. In women, muscles surrounding the outer third of the vagina contract reflexively. In men and women, the first contractions are strongest and spaced at 0.8-second intervals (5 contractions in 4 seconds). Ensuing contractions are weaker and further apart.

?   It is true that orgasm is a reflex. People cannot will or force an orgasm. Nor can they will or force other sexual reflexes, such as erection in the man and vaginal lubrication in the woman. People can only set the stage for these sexual responses and let them happen.

Individuals can set the stage for orgasm by ensuring appropriate sexual stimulation and an accepting attitude toward sexual pleasure. People cannot force or will an orgasm, however. Attempts to compel an orgasm are often counterproductive, as we shall see later.

4.   *Resolution Phase.* A sense of relaxation, well-being, and muscle relaxation occurs. During this phase, men are physiologically incapable of reachieving erection and orgasm for a period of time. But women may be able to respond to additional stimulation with hardly any delay. Masters and Johnson found that women can undergo numerous or multiple orgasms in swift succession with continued stimulation. During the sex-

Pioneering sex researchers and therapists William Masters and Virginia Johnson.

ual liberation of the 1960s and 1970s, awareness of this capacity caused some women to think that they ought not be satisfied with just one orgasm. This is the flip side of the old saw that sexual enjoyment is intended just for men. In sex, like other areas of life, oughts and shoulds are often arbitrary demands that elicit anxiety and a sense of inadequacy.

Types of Sexual Dysfunctions

The DSM–III–R groups most dysfunctions within these categories:

1.   Sexual desire disorders
2.   Sexual arousal disorders
3.   Orgasm disorders
4.   Sexual pain disorders

■ **Sexual Desire Disorders**   The DSM–III–R includes two disorders of sexual desire or appetite: sexual aversion disorder and hypoactive sexual desire disorder. People with **sexual aversion disorder** have a persistent or recurrent aversion to genital sexual contact and avoid all or nearly all genital contact with a partner. They may, however, desire and enjoy affectionate contact or nongenital sexual contact. Their feelings of disgust or repulsion regarding sexual intercourse are often a by-product of past traumatic experiences, such as rape, childhood sexual abuse, or incest. In other cases, a deep-seated sense of guilt or shame about sex impairs sexual functioning.

People with **hypoactive sexual desire disorder** have no aversion to sex but rather a recurrent or persistent deficiency in, or the absence of, sexual desire and fantasies. One problem with the diagnosis is that there is no universally agreed-upon normal level of sexual desire. The clinician must weigh various factors in reaching a diagnostic impression, such as the client's lifestyle, the relationship between the client and the partner, and the client's age and sex. Sex researcher Harold Lief notes that college students who are instructed to press a wrist counter each time they experience a sexual thought, feeling, or fantasy may tally more than 300 a day, while other people may never or only rarely have a sexual desire (cited in Goleman, 1988b). Couples usually seek help when one or both partners recognize that the level of sexual activity in the relationship is deficient or has waned to the point that little desire or interest remains. Sometimes the lack of desire seems limited to one partner. In other cases, anger and conflict concerning other issues have inhibited sexual desire in both partners.

Although problems in sexual desire were only first included in the DSM in 1980, they have become the most common presenting complaint seen by sex therapists. The DSM–III–R estimates that about 20 percent of the total population have hypoactive sexual

desire disorder. As reported in a survey of sex therapists, nearly a third (31%) of couples treated for sexual problems complain of differences in sexual desire between the partners (Goleman, 1988b). Some concerns categorized as problems in arousal or orgasm may actually reflect underlying lack of desire. Sex therapists usually advocate that couples who want different frequencies of sexual activity arrive at a compromise. They do not invariably encourage the less-interested partner to meet all the needs of the other (Goleman, 1988b).

■ **Sexual Arousal Disorders**   Disorders of sexual arousal involve either a lack of sexual pleasure or excitement during sex, or difficulty achieving or sustaining the physiological changes—lubrication and erection—that allow completion of sexual activity.

In women, as noted, sexual arousal is characterized by lubrication of the vaginal walls that makes entry by the penis possible. In men, sexual arousal is characterized by erection. Almost all women now and then have difficulty becoming or remaining lubricated. Almost all men have occasional difficulty attaining or maintaining an erection through intercourse. The diagnoses of **female sexual arousal disorder** and **male erectile disorder** (also called sexual impotence) are reserved for persistent or recurrent arousal problems.

■ **Orgasm Disorders**   There are three orgasm disorders, **inhibited female orgasm, inhibited male orgasm,** and **premature ejaculation.**

Inhibited orgasm is diagnosed when there is persistent or recurrent delay in reaching orgasm following what the clinician judges to be an "adequate" amount of sexual stimulation. Some women require manual clitoral stimulation to reach orgasm during coitus. Years ago, psychodynamically oriented theorists made a distinction between so-called clitoral and vaginal orgasms. Clitoral orgasms were achieved through masturbation and were emblematic of fixation in the phallic stage. Vaginal orgasms were achieved through coitus and considered emblematic of mature, genital sexuality. Masters and Johnson (1966) found only one kind of orgasm, physiologically speaking, regardless of whether the main source of stimulation was clitoral or vaginal. In addition, the distinctions are further blurred because the thrusting of the penis during intercourse indirectly stimulates the clitoris by drawing the clitoral hood back and forth against the clitoris. Thus, clitoral stimulation contributes to the woman's orgasmic response during intercourse as well as masturbation. Some authorities, such as the psychologist Joseph LoPiccolo (1977), argue that a woman who achieves orgasm during intercourse through a combination of penile thrusting and direct stimulation to the clitoris by her own or her partner's hand should not consider herself sexually dysfunctional. The DSM–III–R takes a more equivocal view. According to the DSM–III–R, most cases in which the woman requires additional clitoral stimulation during coitus

TABLE 11.1 Common Features of Sexual Dysfunctions

Fear of failure	Fears relating to failure to achieve or maintain erection, or failure to reach orgasm
Assuming a spectator role, rather than playing a performer role	Monitoring and evaluating your body's reactions during sex.
Diminished self-esteem	Thinking less of yourself for failure to meet your standard of normality
Emotional effects	Guilt, shame, frustration, depression, anxiety
Avoidance behavior	Avoiding sexual contacts for fear of failure to perform adequately; making excuses to your partner

Source: Adapted from DSM–III–R, pp. 291–292.

and is able to achieve orgasm during noncoital stimulation fall within a normal spectrum of female sexuality. But the DSM–III–R allows the clinician to exercise a clinical judgment that in some of the cases the woman's orgasmic response is inhibited by psychological factors and can be considered dysfunctional. The diagnostic manual recognizes that this may be a difficult judgment and suggests that a thorough sexual evaluation, and even a trial treatment, may help the clinician form a diagnostic impression.

In males, a recurrent or persistent difficulty in achieving orgasm following a normal pattern of sexual excitement (that is, erection and heightening of sexual tension) is referred to as *inhibited male orgasm*. Inhibited orgasm is much less common in men than in women and is usually limited in men to coitus. That is, men with this problem can generally achieve orgasm through other means of stimulation, such as by masturbation. Because of its infrequency, there are only a few isolated case studies on the problem (Dow, 1981; Rathus, 1978; Schull & Spenkle, 1980).

Premature ejaculation is defined as recurrent or persistent ejaculation with minimal sexual stimulation or that occurs either prior to, upon, or shortly after penetration, but before the man desires it. Note the subjective elements. In making the diagnosis, the clinician weighs the man's age, the novelty of the partner, and the frequency of sexual activity. Occasional experiences of rapid ejaculation, such as when the man is with a new partner or is very highly aroused, fall within the normal spectrum. But more persistent premature ejaculation would occasion a diagnosis of the disorder. The disorder is actually quite common, affecting perhaps 30 percent of the male population at one time or another according to the DSM–III–R. Men in new sexual relationships and younger men in general tend to be most often troubled by premature ejaculation.

■ **Sexual Pain Disorders** In **dyspareunia,** sexual intercourse is associated with recurrent pain in the genital region. **Vaginismus** involves an involuntary spasm or reflex of the muscles surrounding the vagina, making sexual intercourse painful or impossible.

Theoretical Perspectives

Sexual dysfunctions stem from a variety of causes, both psychological and physical.

■ **Psychodynamic Perspectives** Psychodynamic hypotheses generally revolve around presumed conflicts of the phallic stage (Fenichel, 1945). Mature, genital sexuality is believed to require successful resolution of the Oedipus and Electra complexes. Dysfunctional men may suffer from unconscious castration anxiety. Sexual intercourse elicits fear of retaliation by the father, rendering the vagina unsafe. Erectile dysfunction "saves" the man from having to enter the vagina. In the Freudian view, premature ejaculation represents unconscious hatred of women (Kaplan, 1974). Rapid ejaculation serves the unconscious purpose of expressing this hatred through soiling the woman while also depriving her of pleasure. Inhibited orgasm prevents him from completing the act and unconsciously minimizes his guilt and the fears of castration that are associated with ejaculation. In women, enduring penis envy engenders hostility. The woman fixated in the phallic stage punishes her partner for bearing a penis and does not permit the organ to bring her pleasure, as in female sexual arousal disorder. Vaginismus expresses an unconscious wish to castrate her partner (Kaplan, 1974). In inhibited orgasm, she has failed to overcome penis envy and transfer erotic feelings from the clitoris to the vagina, preventing orgasm from occurring during intercourse. It is difficult to test the validity of these psychoanalytic concepts since they involve unconscious mechanisms, like castration anxiety and penis envy, that cannot be directly observed. Evidence for these views relies on case studies that involve interpretation of patients' histories. But case-study accounts may be open to other interpretations, however.

Modern psychodynamic theorists, like Helen Singer Kaplan (1974), suggest that there are other sources of anger, envy, and fear that women may hold toward men, rather than envy of the penis, that may be involved in sexual dysfunctions. Women in our culture may be socialized to sacrifice their own assertive strivings in submission to the needs of their husbands. Rebellion against this dependency role may be expressed in the form of anger, depression, marital conflict, and sexual dysfunction.

■ **Learning Perspectives** Behaviorists largely focus on the role of conditioned anxiety in explaining sexual dysfunctions. Physically or psychologically painful sexual experiences in the past may cause the person to respond to sexual activity with anxiety that is strong enough to counteract any sexual pleasure. Recall that persons with an aversion to sex may harbor feelings of disgust and revulsion that are linked to a history of rape, childhood sexual abuse, or incest. Such experiences can also occasion other sexual dysfunctions such as vaginismus or inhibited orgasm.

In *Human Sexual Inadequacy*, Masters and Johnson (1970) report cases of men with erectile disorder who had had anxiety-arousing encounters with prostitutes. The prostitutes had pressured them to rush to completion or had belittled them for failing to achieve adequate erections. Premature ejaculation was also reported to have developed among men who had initial sexual experiences with prostitutes who had hurried them to complete the act, or with girlfriends in secretive and hurried liaisons in the back seats of cars or in pay-by-the-hour hotels. Masters and Johnson believe that such experiences may have instilled in such men a learned pattern of rapid ejaculation and concern with self-centered satisfaction rather than attention to the female partner's sexual needs.

■ Sexual Competencies and Skills

Sexual competencies, like other competencies, are built on knowledge and skill. Knowledge and skills are acquired through conditioning and observational learning. We learn what makes us and others feel good through trial and error, by reading and talking about sex, and, perhaps, by viewing sex films or videotapes. Some men with problems of premature ejaculation, especially younger men with less sexual experience, may not have had sufficient opportunity to learn to recognize their threshold of arousal at which point ejaculation becomes inevitable (the "point of no return") and to maintain their sexual stimulation below the triggering level. Some people with sexual dysfunctions were reared in environments in which discussions of sex were shunned and early sexual experimentation was severely inhibited. They may be at a disadvantage for acquiring sexual competencies and may hold attitudes that inhibit their sexual response. Such attitudes bring us to cognitive factors.

■ Cognitive Perspectives

At the turn of the century, Englishwomen were told to "close their eyes and think of England" when they were obligated to engage in sexual activity to satisfy their husband's cravings. There have always been exceptions to every rule, but this old-fashioned stereotype suggests that sexual pleasure was once considered a predominantly male preserve— that sex, for women, was primarily a duty. Mothers usually informed their daughters of the conjugal duties before the wedding, and girls encoded sex as just one of the ways in which women serviced the needs of others. Women who share such sex-negative attitudes are unlikely to become aware of their sexual potentials. In addition, sexual anxieties may transform negative expectations into self-fulfilling prophecies. Sexual dysfunction in men, too, may be linked to severely restrictive cultural beliefs about sex.

Albert Ellis (1977) points out that other kinds of irrational beliefs and attitudes also contribute to sexual dysfunctions. As noted in Chapter 2, several of the foremost irrational beliefs that Ellis cites are that we must have the approval of those who are important to us and that we must be thoroughly competent at what we do. If we cannot abide the occasional disappointment of others, we may catastrophize the significance of a few frustrating sexual episodes. If we insist that every sexual rendezvous be perfect, we set the stage for inevitable failure.

Helen Singer Kaplan (1974) notes problems that can occur with our self-regulatory systems. Premature ejaculators, for example, may be poor at gauging their degrees of sexual arousal. As a consequence, they would not call upon self-control strategies to limit their arousal in time to delay ejaculation.

■ Problems in Relationships

Sexual relations are usually no better than other facets of relationships or marriages (Perlman & Abramson, 1982). Couples who harbor resentments toward each other may choose the sexual arena for combat. Communication problems, moreover, are linked to general marital dissatisfaction. Couples who find it difficult to communicate their sexual desires may lack the means to teach their partners how to provide pleasure.

We can see in the following case how a sexual arousal disorder may occur against a backdrop of relationship problems:

■ After living together for six months, Paul and Petula are contemplating marriage. But a problem has brought them to a sex therapy clinic. As Petula puts it, "For the last two months he hasn't been able to keep his erection after he enters me." Paul is 26, a lawyer; Petula, 24, is a buyer for a large department store. They both grew up in middle-class, suburban families, were introduced through mutual friends and began having intercourse, without difficulty, a few months into their relationship. At Petula's urging, Paul moved into her apartment, although he wasn't sure he was ready for such a step. A week later he began to have difficulty maintaining his erection during intercourse, although he felt strong desires for his partner. When his erection waned, he would try again, but would lose his desire and be unable to achieve another erection. After a few times like this, Petula would become so angry that she began striking Paul in the chest and screaming at him. Paul, who at 200 pounds weighed more than twice as much as Petula, would just walk away, which angered Petula even more.

It became clear that sex was not the only trouble spot in their relationship. Petula complained that he preferred to be with his friends and go to baseball games than to spend time with her. When they were together at home, he would become absorbed in watching sports events on television, and showed no interest in activities she enjoyed—attending the theater, visiting museums, etc. Since there was no evidence that the sexual difficulty was due to either organic problems or depression, a diagnosis of male erectile disorder was given. Neither

A CLOSER LOOK
Biological Treatments of Erectile Dysfunction

When men do not attain erection for organic rather than psychological reasons, biological treatments may be of help.

Biological approaches include surgical implants, hormonal treatment, and vascular surgery (LoPiccolo & Stock, 1986). There are several types of surgical implants. One is a prosthetic device made of two rods of silicone rubber. They remain in a semirigid position that permits intercourse and otherwise allows the penis to be bent closer to the body. The operation can be performed under local anesthesia. Another implant requires more extensive surgery. It consists of cylinders that are attached to a small reservoir of fluid and a tiny pump. When the man wants an erection, he squeezes the pump. Fluid enters the cylinders, creating an erection.

Men with implants and their partners report general satisfaction with the results (Anderson & Wold, 1986; Beutler et al., 1984; Schlamowitz et al., 1983). However, long-term follow-ups have identified a number of poor outcomes (LoPiccolo & Stock, 1986). The inflatable implants are usually preferred to the semirigid kind (Beutler et al., 1984, 1985), perhaps because the actions of the former resemble natural sexual processes.

Hormone treatments are often helpful for men with abnormally low levels of male sex hormones but not for men whose hormone levels are within normal limits (Bancroft, 1984; Krane et al., 1983; LoPiccolo & Stock, 1986). Since hormone treatments can have side effects, such as liver damage, they are not undertaken lightly (LoPiccolo & Stock, 1986). Vascular surgery may be effective in rare cases in which blockage in the blood vessels impedes blood congestion of the penis, or in which the penis is structurally defective (LoPiccolo & Stock, 1986).

In either case, Masters and Johnson work with the couple and use sensate-focus exercises to lessen performance anxiety, to open channels of communication, and to help the couple acquire sexual skills. During genital massage and then during intercourse, the woman directs her partner in the caresses and maneuvers that stimulate her. By taking charge the woman is also psychologically freed from the stereotype of the passive, submissive female. Many clinicians and researchers find that directed practice in masturbation is most effective for preorgasmic women (Andersen, 1981; Heiman & LoPiccolo, 1987; LoPiccolo & Stock, 1986; McMullen & Rosen, 1979; Riley & Riley, 1978). Even Masters and Johnson (1966), who prefer a couples approach, reported that masturbation was the most efficient way for women and men to reach orgasm. Masturbation provides men and women with a chance to learn about their own bodies and to give themselves pleasure without reliance on a partner. Masturbation programs educate women about their sexual anatomy and encourage them to experiment with self-caresses at their own pace. They are not distracted by external pressures to please a partner. Pleasure helps counter sexual anxiety, and women learn gradually to bring themselves to orgasm. Once women can masturbate to orgasm, additional treatment can facilitate but does not guarantee transference to orgasm with a partner (LoPiccolo & Stock, 1986; Heiman & LoPiccolo, 1987).

Systematic desensitization has also been used to help women with inhibited orgasm handle underlying fears of sexual relations (Husted, 1975; Jones & Park, 1972; Obler, 1973). Desensitization of sexual fears and anxieties has also been combined with other behavioral techniques, such as assertiveness training, modeling, and behavioral rehearsal in multicomponent treatment programs (LoPiccolo & Stock, 1986). Treatment of inhibited male orgasm generally focuses on increasing sexual stimulation and reducing performance anxiety (LoPiccolo & Stock, 1986).

Masters and Johnson also use sensate-focus exercises in treating premature ejaculation so that couples learn to give and take pleasure under nondemanding conditions. When the couple is ready to undertake sexual activity, they use the so-called *squeeze* technique, in which the tip of the penis is squeezed by his partner when the man is about to ejaculate and then released. The squeeze technique, which should be learned only through personal instruction, temporarily prevents ejaculation from occurring. The man gradually learns to extend coitus without ejaculating.

In 1956, urologist James Semans suggested the so-called *stop-and-go* technique for premature ejaculation. The man suspends sexual activity when he is about to ejaculate and allows his sensations to subside before resuming. Repeated practice of the "stop and go" procedure enables him to regulate ejaculation by sensitizing him to the cues that precede his point of ejaculatory inevitability (or "point of no return").

■ **Vaginismus** Vaginismus is a psychosomatic reaction to a fear of penetration (LoPiccolo & Stock, 1986). Vaginismus is distinct from dyspareunia, in which a physical condition produces pain during sex. Whereas dyspareunia is generally treated medically, treatment for vaginismus involves a combination of relaxation techniques and the use of vaginal dilators of increasing size to relax the vaginal entrance. The woman herself regulates the insertion of the dilators and proceeds at her own pace so as to avert discomfort (LoPiccolo & Stock, 1986). The method is generally successful as long as it is unhurried. Since women with vaginismus often have histories of sexual molestation or rape, psychotherapy for the psychological effects of traumatic experiences may be part of the treatment program (LoPiccolo & Stock, 1986).

■ **Evaluation of Sex Therapy** The influence of Masters and Johnson in the development of treatment approaches for sexual dysfunction has been extraordinary

(Barlow, 1986). Ever since publication of *Human Sexual Inadequacy* in 1970, innovations have largely centered on variations of the Masters-and-Johnson approach (Barlow, 1986).

Masters and Johnson claimed an overall success rate of 80 percent in treating sexual dysfunctions at their clinic with their intensive two-week therapy approach. Although Masters and Johnson's techniques were innovative, their evaluation of their own success has been criticized on numerous grounds. For example, they did not operationally define degrees of improvement, nor did they adequately follow up clients to evaluate long-term results (Adams, 1980; Zilbergeld & Evans, 1980). Nor did they use control groups to rule out other possible explanations of treatment results.

Other investigators have reported more modest success rates in treating certain types of sexual dysfunctions, especially male erectile disorder. Current estimates place the success rate in treating erectile dysfunction, for example, at approximately 30 percent, with many treated individuals showing unstable performance over time (Barlow, 1986; Crown & D'Ardenne, 1982; Levine & Agle, 1978). But treatment of premature ejaculation has yielded more consistent success. Success rates of over 90 percent have been reported for the squeeze and stop-and-go techniques (Kilmann & Auerbach, 1979). Although initial success rates are impressive, there remains a dearth of long-term follow-up data on premature ejaculation (LoPiccolo & Stock, 1986).

Using masturbation as the primary technique,

LoPiccolo & Stock (1986) report an overall success rate of 95 percent for a sample of 150 preorgasmic women. Most of the women (about 85%) were also able to achieve orgasm through manual stimulation applied by their partners. By contrast, only about 40 percent were able to achieve orgasm during intercourse. Couples who desire to focus on achieving female orgasm during intercourse are encouraged to provide clitoral stimulation in addition to penile thrusting to heighten the female partner's level of sexual arousal to a point at which orgasm is possible (LoPiccolo & Stock, 1986).

Therapists have departed from a number of methods recommended by Masters and Johnson, apparently without lowering their success rates. Although Masters and Johnson use a male-female therapist team, a single therapist is apparently as effective, whether or not the therapist is the same sex as the client (Arentewicz & Schmidt, 1983; Libman et al., 1985). Nor does it seem to matter whether therapy sessions are massed, as with Masters and Johnson, or distributed over time (Libman et al., 1985). Also note that sex-therapy programs tend to combine behavioral methods, cognitive methods, and marital counseling of one kind or another. But we do not always know which treatment components are most helpful (LoPiccolo & Stock, 1986). Then, too, couples are more likely to benefit from sex therapy when their relationships are solid in other areas and they are highly motivated (Hawton & Catalan, 1986). The motivation factor should not come as any surprise. Aren't we generally more successful at those endeavors to which we apply ourselves fully?

SUMMARY

Normal and Abnormal in American Sexual Behavior

Sexual behavior is largely influenced by learning and cultural factors. What is considered normal in one culture may be considered abnormal in another. Sexual customs may also vary from generation to generation within a particular culture. We have seen sexual patterns in the United States shift from repression to revolution to reaction in the latter half of the twentieth century. Some of the major changes that have taken place in American sexual practices include increased incidence of premarital intercourse among young women and more varied sexual practices among married couples. Such behaviors as masturbation, premarital sex, and oral-genital sex are now considered to fall within the normal spectrum of sexual variation.

Homosexuality

Homosexuality involves an erotic attraction to members of one's own sex. Homosexuality is no longer consid-

ered a mental disorder, but people who are confused or distressed about their sexual orientation may be considered to have a psychological disorder. Homosexuals in general do not appear to be more psychologically disturbed than heterosexuals. While theories of homosexuality abound, there is no present consensus on the origins of homosexuality. Traditional psychodynamic theory focused on unresolved Oedipal (and Electra)-conflicts as playing a major role in the development of homosexuality, whereas learning-theorists focused on early learning influences. Biological researchers have explored the role of genetics and hormonal factors. The origins of homosexuality are complex and may involve multiple, interactive causes incorporating both biological and psychosocial factors. Therapies aimed at converting homosexuals to heterosexuals are controversial; their effectiveness have not been reliably established.

Gender Identity Disorders

Gender identity of childhood identifies children who find their anatomic sex to be a source of persistent and intense distress. The disorder may persist into adolescence or adulthood and may take the form of transsexualism. Transsexuals seek to rid themselves of their anatomic sex organs and many have undergone sex-reassignment surgery. Sex-reassignment surgery has had varied outcomes, but most recent research has found the outcomes to be generally favorable, especially in cases of female-to-male transsexuals. But this form of surgery remains controversial. The causes of transsexualism are obscure, but they are likely to involve some combination of biological factors and critical early learning experiences.

Pornography

Studies of the effects of pornography show that exposure tends to increase sexual arousal in both sexes, but does not lead to disturbed behavior. However, exposure to violent pornography may increase the tendency of males, even normal males, to act aggressively against females. Depicting the female victim as experiencing pleasure in the violent act may also legitimize the acceptability of sexual violence in the minds of the male viewers. But nonviolent pornography has not been linked to such outcomes.

Rape

It is estimated that there may be some 375,000 or more forcible rapes in the United States each year. Rape is a violent crime, not a sexual disorder. There are many different types of rapists, including such basic types as the anger rapist, the power rapist, and the sadistic rapist. Socialization influences and cognitive factors may play a role in predisposing certain men to rape. The acceptance of certain cultural myths may engender a social climate of rape. Rape victims suffer both acute and long-lasting effects, described in terms of a rape trauma syndrome. Attempts to "treat" rapists have been controversial and not well established in their utility.

Paraphilias

Paraphilias are sexual deviations involving patterns of arousal to stimuli such as nonhuman objects (for example, shoes or clothes), humiliation or the experience of pain in oneself or one's partner, or children or other nonconsenting persons. The category of paraphilias include exhibitionism, fetishism, transvestic fetishism, voyeurism, frotteurism, pedophilia, sexual masochism, and sexual sadism, among others. While some paraphilias are essentially harmless (such as fetishism), others, such as pedophilia and sexual sadism, can inflict grave

psychological and physical harm on nonconsenting victims.

Psychodynamic theorists interpret paraphilias as defenses against castration anxieties that reflect unresolved Oedipal conflicts. Learning theorists attempt to explain the development of paraphilias on the basis of conditioning and observational learning. Various treatment techniques have been introduced, especially within the behavioral framework, but controlled investigations of their effectiveness are lacking.

Sexual Dysfunctions

Sexual dysfunctions are disorders that involve a lessening or inhibition of sexual interest, pleasure, or response. Sexual dysfunctions interfere with the initiation or the completion of the sexual response cycle, which includes the phases of appetite, excitement, orgasm, and resolution. Various types of sexual dysfunctions exist, including the following: (1) sexual desire disorders (hypoactive sexual desire disorder and sexual aversion disorder); (2) sexual arousal disorder (female sexual arousal disorder and male erectile disorder); (3) orgasm disorders (inhibited female or male orgasm and premature ejaculation); and (4) sexual pain disorders (dyspareunia and vaginismus). Traditional psychodynamic theorists trace sexual dysfunctions to unresolved conflicts from the phallic stage, namely the Oedipus and Electra complexes. But modern psychodynamic theorists believe that negative emotions that may impair sexual response in women could reflect socialization pressures, not unresolved penis envy. Learning theorists focus on the role of conditioned anxiety in impairing sexual response and performance. Cognitive factors, relationship problems, sexual underactivity, lack of effective skills or competencies, performance anxiety, and various biological factors also appear to be involved in sexual dysfunctions. Sex therapy was pioneered by Masters and Johnson and generally involves a relatively brief form of treatment that focuses directly on resolving the sexual problem through the use of specific behavior-change techniques.

SCORING KEY FOR RAPE MYTHS SCALE

All of the items are false, with the exception of item 2, which is true. But our concern with your answers goes beyond their accuracy. The important concern is whether you endorse cultural beliefs that contribute to a social climate that legitimizes rape. As an example, if you believe that women unconsciously desire to be raped, you may also believe that rape victims are responsible for their victimization. Such attitudes tend to excuse the perpetrator and blame the victim.

TRUTH OR FICTION

■ ____ Many schizophrenic people show no emotional response to tragic events.

■ ____ Schizophrenics occupy one hospital bed in four in the United States.

■ ____ Some people show schizophrenic-type behaviors, including flagrant delusions and hallucinations, but they cannot be diagnosed as schizophrenic until half a year later.

■ ____ All people hallucinate in one way or another.

■ ____ Some schizophrenics sustain unusual, uncomfortable positions for hours and will not respond to questions or comments during these periods.

■ ____ A 54-year-old female hospitalized schizophrenic was conditioned to cling to a broom by being given cigarettes as reinforcers.

■ ____ A child with two schizophrenic parents will develop schizophrenia about 90 percent of the time.

■ ____ An excess number of births of schizophrenics occur during the winter months.

■ ____ Schizophrenics have cold, overprotective mothers.

■ ____ Antipsychotic medications cure many cases of schizophrenia.

■ ____ Teaching families how to relate to schizophrenic members and solve family problems reduces the incidence of recurrent acute episodes.

■ ____ Some people are deluded that they are loved by a famous person.

LEARNING OBJECTIVES

When you have completed your study of Chapter 12, you should be able to:

HISTORY OF THE CONCEPT OF SCHIZOPHRENIA (pp. 414–416)

1. Discuss the contributions of Emil Kraepelin, Eugen Bleuler, and Kurt Schneider to the concept of schizophrenia.
2. Discuss the changes in the definition of schizophrenia that have occurred from the time of Kraepelin to the present day.

PREVALENCE OF SCHIZOPHRENIA (pp. 416–417)

3. Discuss the prevalence of schizophrenia in the general population.

PHASES OF SCHIZOPHRENIA (pp. 417–418)

4. Describe various patterns of the course of schizophrenia, referring to the concepts of *acute episode*, *prodromal phase*, and *residual phase*.

BRIEFER FORMS OF PSYCHOSIS (p. 418)

5. Distinguish among schizophrenia, brief reactive psychosis, and schizophreniform disorder.

SCHIZOPHRENIA-SPECTRUM DISORDERS (pp. 418–419)

6. Discuss the concept of schizophrenia-spectrum disorders and distinguish among schizophrenia, schizotypal personality disorder, and schizoaffective disorder.

FEATURES OF SCHIZOPHRENIA (pp. 419–424)

7. Discuss the disturbances in thought and speech that characterize schizophrenia.
8. Discuss deficits in attention, referring to recent psychophysiological research.
9. Discuss perceptual disturbances in schizophrenia.
10. Discuss emotional disturbances in schizophrenia.
11. Discuss the disturbances in self-identity, volition, interpersonal behavior, and psychomotor behavior in schizophrenia.

TYPES OF SCHIZOPHRENIA (pp. 424–426)

12. Discuss the historical changes in the classification of types of schizophrenia.
13. Distinguish among the disorganized, catatonic, paranoid, undifferentiated, and residual types of schizophrenia.

DIMENSIONS OF SCHIZOPHRENIA (pp. 426–427)

14. Discuss the process–reactive dimension of schizophrenia, the positive and negative "symptoms" of schizophrenia, and Type I and Type II schizophrenia.

THEORETICAL PERSPECTIVES (pp. 427–443)

15. Discuss psychodynamic, learning, biological, family, and sociocultural perspectives on schizophrenia.
16. Describe and evaluate research on genetic factors, biochemical factors, viral infections, and brain damage.
17. Discuss evidence for the diathesis–stress model of schizophrenia.

TREATMENT (pp. 443–450)

18. Discuss biological, psychodynamic, learning-based, psychosocial-rehabilitation, and family-intervention treatments of schizophrenia.
19. Discuss research concerning the effects and side effects of antipsychotic medication.

DELUSIONAL (PARANOID) DISORDER (pp. 450–451)

20. Discuss the features of delusional (paranoid) disorder and differentiate the disorder from paranoid schizophrenia and paranoid personality disorder.

Schizophrenia is perhaps the most puzzling and disabling of the mental disorders. It is the clinical syndrome that best corresponds to popular conceptions of "madness" or "lunacy." Psychiatrist William Carpenter (1987), a leading researcher in the field, notes that schizophrenia too often elicits fear, misunderstanding, and even condemnation in others, rather than sympathy and concern. Schizophrenia strikes at the heart of the person. It strips the mind of the intimate connections between thoughts and emotion and fills it with distorted perceptions, false ideas, and illogical conceptions, as in the case of Angela:

■ Angela was 19 years old. Her boyfriend, Jaime, insisted that she come to the emergency room because she had cut her wrists. When she was questioned, her attention wandered. She seemed transfixed by creatures in the air, or by something she might be hearing. It seemed as though she had an invisible earphone.

Angela explained that she had slit her wrists at the command of the "hellsmen." Then she became terrified. Later she related that the hellsmen had cautioned her not to disclose their existence. Angela had been fearful that the hellsmen would punish her for her indiscretion.

Jaime related that Angela and he had been living together for nearly a year. They had initially shared a modest apartment in town. But Angela did not like being around other people and persuaded Jaime to rent a cottage in the country. There Angela spent much of her days making fantastic sketches of goblins and monsters. She occasionally became agitated and behaved as though invisible beings were issuing directions. Her words would begin to become jumbled.

Jaime would try to persuade her to go for help, but she would resist. Then the wrist-cutting began. Jaime believed that he had made the bungalow secure by removing all knives and blades. But Angela always found a sharp object.

Then he would bring Angela to the hospital against her protests. Stitches would be put in, she would be held under observation for a while, and she would be medicated. She would recount that she cut her wrists because the hellsmen had informed her that she was bad and had to die. After a few days in the hospital, she would disavow hearing the hellsmen and insist on discharge.

Jaime would take her home. The pattern would repeat itself.

The Authors' Files ■

When the emergency room team examined Angela's wrists and learned that she thought that she had been following the dictates of "hellsmen," they began to surmise that she was afflicted with schizophrenia. Schizophrenia touches every facet of victims' lives. During acute episodes, schizophrenia is characterized by **delusions, hallucinations,** illogical thinking, incoherent speech, and bizarre behavior. Between acute episodes, schizophrenics may still be unable to think clearly and may lack an appropriate emotional response to the people and events in their lives. They may generally speak in a flat tone and show little if any facial expressiveness.

Although researchers are immersed in probing the psychological and biological foundations of schizophrenia, the disorder remains in many ways a mystery. In this chapter, we examine how modern research has illuminated our understanding of schizophrenia, while taking note of how much remains to be learned.

HISTORY OF THE CONCEPT OF SCHIZOPHRENIA

Although various forms of "madness" have afflicted humans throughout their history, no one knows how long the behavior pattern we now label schizophrenia existed before it was first described as a medical syndrome in 1893 by Emil Kraepelin (Boffey, 1986). Modern conceptualizations of schizophrenia have been largely shaped by the contributions of Kraepelin, Eugen Bleuler, and Kurt Schneider.

Kraepelin (1856–1926), one of the fathers of modern psychiatry, called the disorder **dementia praecox,** from the Latin *dementis,* literally meaning "out" (*de-*) of one's "mind" (*mens*), and the same roots that form the word *precocious,* meaning "before" one's level of "maturity." So *dementia praecox* refers to premature loss or impairment of one's mental abilities. Kraepelin believed that dementia praecox was a disease process that was caused by a specific, though unknown, pathology in the body (Hoenig, 1983). Even today, we may not be much closer to understanding the causal processes in schizophrenia than was Kraepelin himself nearly a century ago (Hoenig, 1983).

Kraepelin wrote that dementia praecox involved the "loss of the inner unity of thought, feeling, and acting." It began early in life and was marked by a deteriorating course that eventually resulted in complete "disintegration of the personality" (Kraepelin, 1909–1913, Vol. 2, p. 943). Kraepelin's description of dementia praecox included behavior patterns such as delusions, hallucinations, and odd or bizarre motor behaviors—the behavior patterns that typically characterize the disorder today.

Emil Kraepelin

Eugen Bleuler

In 1911, the Swiss psychiatrist Eugen Bleuler (1857–1939) renamed dementia praecox *schizophrenia,* from the Greek *schistos,* meaning "cut" or "split," and *phren,* meaning "brain." In doing so, Bleuler was focusing attention on the major characteristic of the behavior pattern, the splitting apart of the brain functions that give rise to cognition, feelings or affective responses, and behavior. For example, the schizophrenic might giggle inappropriately when discussing an upsetting event, or might show no emotional expressiveness in the face of tragedy.

 It is true that many schizophrenic people show no emotional response to tragic events. Their affect is said to be flat or blunted.

Although the Greek roots of *schizophrenia* mean "split brain," schizophrenia should not be confused with the rarer dissociative disorder of multiple personality, which is frequently referred to as "split personality" by lay people. In multiple or "split" personality, as noted in Chapter 7, the personality apparently divides into two or more personalities, but each of them usually shows more integrated functioning on cognitive, affec-

Eugen Bleuler

tive, and behavioral levels than is the case with schizophrenia. In schizophrenia, the splitting cleaves cognition, affect, and behavior, so that there may be little agreement between the thoughts and the emotions, or between the individual's perception of reality and what is truly happening.

Although Bleuler accepted Kraepelin's description of the disorder in general terms, he did not accept Kraepelin's views that it necessarily began early in life and inevitably followed a deteriorating course. Bleuler proposed that schizophrenia followed a more variable course. In some cases, acute episodes would occur intermittently; in others, there might be limited improvement rather than persistent deterioration.

Bleuler believed that schizophrenia could be recognized on the basis of four primary features or, in medical jargon, "primary symptoms." Today, we refer to them as the **four A's:**

1. **Associations.** Associations or relationships among thoughts become disturbed. We now call this type of disturbance "thought disorder" or "looseness of associations." "Looseness of associations" means that ideas shift from one topic to another with little or no relationship between topics and with no apparent awareness on the speaker's part of a lack of connection between topics. Overtly, the individual's speech becomes rambling and confused.

2. **Affect.** The affect or emotional response becomes flattened or inappropriate. The individual may show a lack of response to upsetting events, or even burst into laughter at hearing the news that a family member or friend has died.

3. **Ambivalence.** The schizophrenic holds ambivalent or opposing feelings toward others, both loving and hating the same person or people at the same time.

4. **Autism.** Autism refers to withdrawal into a private fantasy world of one's own creation that is not bound by the principles of logic.

In Bleuler's medical view, hallucinations and delusions represent secondary symptoms that develop along with the primary symptoms. In more recent years, however, other theorists (see Schneider, 1957) have proposed that hallucinations and delusions are to be considered among the key, or primary, features of schizophrenia. Bleuler was also strongly influenced by psychodynamic theory. He came to believe that the content of hallucinations and delusions could be explained by the schizophrenic's attempt to replace the external world, from which the schizophrenic had withdrawn, with a world of fantasy.

Bleuler's contributions led to the adoption of a broader definition of schizophrenia and brought the diagnostic category into more common use, even in cases where only some of the criteria were met. Bleuler's ideas were especially influential in the United States. American-trained psychiatrists began to use the diagnosis more freely than their counterparts in Europe, who were more influenced by the narrower definition of the disorder proposed by Kraepelin. The diagnosis of schizophrenia was even broadened in the United States beyond Bleuler's criteria to include people who showed combined features of schizophrenic and mood disorders. These cases are now generally classified separately from schizophrenia under the category of **schizoaffective disorders.**

Kurt Schneider

Another influential developer of modern concepts of schizophrenia was the German psychiatrist Kurt Schneider (1887–1967). Schneider believed that Bleuler's criteria (his "four A's") were too vague for diagnostic purposes and that they failed to distinguish adequately between schizophrenia and other disorders, such as bipolar disorder.

Schneider's (1957) most notable contribution was to discriminate between the features of schizophrenia, which he believed were central to the diagnosis of the disorder, called **first-rank symptoms,** and those called **second-rank symptoms,** which he believed were found in schizophrenia, other types of psychoses, and still other nonpsychotic maladies such as personality disorders. In Schneider's view, if first-rank symptoms were present and could not be accounted for by organic factors, then a diagnosis of schizophrenia could be established. Hallucinations and delusions were prominent first-rank symptoms. Disturbances in mood and confused thinking were considered second-rank symptoms. Although Schneider's ranking of behaviors helped distinguish schizophrenia from other disorders, we now know that first-rank symptoms are sometimes found among persons with other disorders, especially manic disorders (Mellor, 1982). One study, for example, found that 13 percent of diagnosed manics showed evidence of first-rank symptoms of schizophrenia (Wing & Nixon, 1975), such as hallucinations and delusions. Although first-rank symptoms are clearly associated with schizophrenia, they are not uniquely so (Mellor, 1982).

Contemporary Diagnostic Practices

One of the nagging problems with the conceptualization of schizophrenia has been lack of consistency in diagnostic practices. Although most mental-health professionals accept the view that schizophrenia is an identifiable behavior pattern, widespread disagreement continues over the best way to define the pattern. During the 1950s and 1960s, Bleuler's broad view of schizophrenia was widely accepted in the United States and was used to apply to both mild and severe forms of the disorder (Andreasen, 1987b). By the 1960s, British psychiatrists had adopted the more stringent criteria for defining schizophrenia, based on the specific first-rank symptoms identified by Kurt Schneider. The broadening of the definition of schizophrenia in the United States led to relatively more cases of schizophrenia being diagnosed in America than in Europe. In one study, nearly twice as many patients in a Brooklyn, New York, mental hospital were diagnosed as schizophrenic as were those in a mental hospital outside London, England, although a reevaluation of the diagnoses in both hospitals by stricter criteria showed no significant differences in the incidence of the disorder (Leff, 1977).

By the 1980s, however, the U.S. concept of schizophrenia became even tighter than that of the British, following the introduction of the DSM–III diagnostic system, which narrowed the criteria for defining the disorder. In sum, the same person might or might not have been diagnosed as schizophrenic depending on the country in which he or she was seen and the period of time in which the evaluation was conducted. The tightening of diagnostic criteria with the DSM–III in 1980 and the DSM–III–R in 1987 has helped improve the consistency or reliability of the diagnosis of schizophrenia (Strachan, 1986).

The contributions of Kraepelin, Bleuler, and Schneider are expressed in modified form in the present diagnostic system, the DSM–III–R. Although the diagnostic code incorporates many of the features of schizophrenia identified by these early contributors, it is not limited, as Kraepelin had proposed, to cases in which there is a progressive course of deterioration. The narrower criteria for diagnosing schizophrenia with the DSM–III and DSM–III–R have sorted into other diagnostic categories persons with mood disorders complicated by psychotic behavior (for example, schizoaffective disorders) and those with schizophrenic-like thinking but without overt psychotic behavior (schizotypal personality disorder). In addition, the DSM–III–R criteria for schizophrenia require that psychotic behaviors be present at some point during the course of the disorder and that signs of the disorder be present for at least six months. As we shall see, persons with briefer forms of psychosis are placed in other diagnostic categories that may have more favorable outcomes.

PREVALENCE OF SCHIZOPHRENIA

Schizophrenia is a problem of enormous proportions. Between 1 and 2 percent of the general population have a schizophrenic episode at some point in their lives (Robins et al., 1984). As noted in the DSM–III–R, schizophrenia appears to affect both sexes equally. In 1986, clinical facilities treated some 900,000 people with schizophrenia; this amounted to about 15 percent of the total number of people receiving treatment for any type of behavioral problem (Rosenstein et al., 1989).

The National Academy of Sciences has estimated the cost of schizophrenia at about $48 billion annually. There are costs for treatment and social services, and there are costs in the lost productivity of people disabled by schizophrenia (Boffey, 1986). Schizophrenics occupy more than half of the hospital beds in this country in facilities for the mentally disordered and retarded, and one-quarter of all hospital beds (Boffey, 1986).

 It is true that schizophrenics occupy one hospital bed in four in the United States.

PHASES OF SCHIZOPHRENIA

Schizophrenia typically develops in late adolescence or early adulthood, at the very time that people are making their way from the family into the world outside. People with developing schizophrenia become increasingly disengaged from society. They fail to function in the expected roles of student, worker, or spouse, and their families and communities grow intolerant of their deviant behavior. Table 12.1 describes the diagnostic criteria for schizophrenia set forth in the DSM–III–R.

In some cases, the onset of the disorder is acute. It occurs suddenly, within a few weeks or months. The individual may have been well adjusted and shown few if any signs of a behavioral disturbance beforehand. Then there is a rapid transformation in personality and behavior that leads to an acute psychotic episode.

In other cases, there is a slower, more gradual

TABLE 12.1 DSM–III–R Diagnostic Criteria for Schizophrenia

A. Occurrence of psychotic symptoms in one or more of the following categories during the active phase of the disorder for a period of at least one week, or perhaps less if the symptoms are treated successfully:
   1. Two or more of the following must be present:
      a. delusions
      b. prominent hallucinations (more than a few brief hallucinations, lasting either throughout the day for several days, or occurring several times a week for several weeks)
      c. speech which is either incoherent or characterized by marked loosening of associations
      d. catatonic behavior
      e. flattened or grossly inappropriate affect
   2. Presence of bizarre delusions which would be considered totally implausible within the individual's culture, such as believing that one is controlled by a dead person.
   3. Presence of prominent hallucinations, consistent with (1) (b) above, involving hearing a voice with content that is apparently unrelated to states of depression or elation, or a voice maintaining a running commentary about the individual's behavior or thoughts, or of two or more voices talking to each other.
B. Functioning in such areas as social relations, work, or self-care during the course of the disorder is markedly below the level achieved prior to the onset of the disorder. If the onset develops during childhood or adolescence, there is a failure to achieve the expected level of social development.
C. Major depression or manic syndrome, when present during the active phase of the disorder (period in which symptoms in [A] above are present), is relatively brief in total duration compared to the overall length of the disorder.
D. Signs of the disorder have occurred continuously for a period of at least six months. This six-month period must include an active phase lasting at least one week in duration, or less if symptoms have been treated successfully, in which psychotic symptoms (listed in A) that are characteristic of schizophrenia occur. A prodromal and residual phase (defined below) may or may not occur:
   Prodromal Phase: A period of time before the active phase in which a clear deterioration of functioning occurs, represented by at least two of the symptoms listed below, and which is not due to either a psychoactive substance abuse disorder or a mood disorder.
   Residual Phase: A period of time following the active phase of the disorder, in which at least two of the following are present, with neither being due to either a mood disorder or psychoactive substance disorder.
   Prodromal or residual symptoms:
   1. marked social withdrawal or isolation
   2. markedly impaired role functioning in such roles as wage earner, homemaker, or student
   3. markedly peculiar behavior, such as hoarding food or collecting garbage, or talking to oneself in public within earshot of others
   4. markedly impaired personal hygiene and grooming
   5. blunted or inappropriate affect
   6. speech which is rambling, vague, overly elaborate, circumstantial, or poverty of speech or content of speech
   7. odd beliefs or magical thoughts that affect behavior and are inconsistent with cultural norms, such as believing in clairvoyance, telepathy, having a "sixth sense," believing that others can "feel my feelings" or having ideas of reference
   8. unusual perceptual experiences, such as sensing the presence of someone or some force that is not actually present
   9. marked lack of interest, initiative, or energy
E. No organic factor can be identified that could account for the disturbance.
F. When there is a history of autistic disorder, prominent hallucinations or delusions must also be present for an additional diagnosis of schizophrenia to be made.

Source: *Adapted from DSM–III–R, pp. 194–195.*

decline in functioning. It may take years before actual psychotic behaviors emerge, although early signs of deterioration may be observed. This period of deterioration is called the **prodromal phase** and is characterized by waning interest in social activities and increasing difficulty in meeting the responsibilities of daily living. At first, such people seem to take less care of their appearance. They fail to bathe regularly or repeatedly wear the same clothes. Over time, their behavior may become increasingly odd or eccentric. There are lapses in job performance and in concentrating on schoolwork. Their speech may become increasingly vague and rambling and lack coherence. At first these changes in personality may be so gradual that they raise little concern among friends and families, or they are attributed to "a phase" that the individual is passing through. But as behavior becomes more bizarre—as in hoarding food, collecting garbage, or talking to oneself on the street—the *acute phase* of the disorder begins. Frankly psychotic behaviors develop, such as wild hallucinations, delusions, and increasingly bizarre behavior.

Following acute episodes, schizophrenics may enter the **residual phase,** in which their behavior returns to the level that was characteristic of the prodromal phase. Although schizophrenics are free of active psychotic behaviors during the residual phase, they may continue to be impaired by a deep sense of apathy, by difficulties in thinking or speaking clearly, and by the harboring of certain unusual ideas, such as beliefs in telepathy or clairvoyance. Such patterns of behavior make it difficult for people to assume independent roles in society as wage earners, marital partners, or students.

Although it is uncommon, a full return to normal behavior may occur. But for many, a chronic pattern develops that is characterized by occasional recurrences or—in medical terms—relapses and continued impairment between acute episodes.

BRIEFER FORMS OF PSYCHOSIS

Although we tend to link psychotic behavior with schizophrenia, there are some cases of brief psychosis that do not progress to a more disabling condition like schizophrenia. A **brief reactive psychosis** is defined as a psychotic episode that occurs in response to a major stressful event or events, such as the loss of a loved one or exposure to brutal traumas in wartime. According to the DSM–III–R, a brief reactive psychosis may last for a few hours to no longer than a month's duration. The psychosis is characterized by emotional turmoil, rapidly shifting emotions, states of confusion, and, sometimes, by bizarre behaviors (for example, adoption of peculiar postures or dress, screaming, or muteness), fleeting hallucinations and delusions, inap-

propriate affect, incoherent or gibberish speech, suicidal or aggressive behavior, disorientation, and memory loss. Although some depression or loss of self-esteem may linger beyond a month, individuals with this disorder eventually return to their former selves.

Schizophreniform disorder consists of abnormal behaviors identical to those in schizophrenia, but which have persisted for less than six month's duration and so do not yet justify the diagnosis of schizophrenia. While some cases have good outcomes, in others the disorder persists beyond six months and is relabeled as schizophrenia. The relationship of schizophreniform disorder to schizophrenia remains somewhat clouded, so they are categorized separately from schizophrenia in the DSM–III–R.

It is true that people who show bizarre, schizophrenic-type behaviors are not to be diagnosed as schizophrenic until half a year later. This is because schizophrenia is conceptualized as a persistent disorder. Briefer disorders that resemble schizophrenia are labeled *brief reactive psychosis* and *schizophreniform disorder* according to the DSM–III–R.

SCHIZOPHRENIA-SPECTRUM DISORDERS

Some people have persistent patterns of unusual thinking or emotional responses that seem to lie within a broader schizophrenia-spectrum of problems but do not fit the stringent definition of schizophrenia described in the DSM–III–R. This schizophrenia spectrum may include a range of related disorders that vary in severity from milder personality disorders (schizoid, paranoid, and schizotypal types) to schizophrenia itself (Andreasen, 1987b).

The schizophrenia spectrum may also include **schizoaffective disorder,** which includes prominent psychotic behaviors and disturbances in mood, such as mania or depression. Schizoaffective disorder has been seen by some as a form of mood disorder and by others as a syndrome that lies between mood disorders and schizophrenia (Andreasen, 1987b). At present, schizoaffective disorder has been described as a "mixed bag"—meaning that it refers to a mixed group of psychotic and mood-disordered behaviors (Andreasen, 1987b). In terms of outcome, people with schizoaffective disorder appear to do somewhat better than schizophrenics but not as well as people with pure mood disorders (Coryell, 1986).

The following case of a young woman diagnosed as having schizoaffective disorder shows the intermingling of psychotic and mood disturbances that typifies the disorder:

■ The young woman was 23 and had worked as an assistant editor on a magazine since her college graduation. Her behavior had become increasingly bizarre and it was upon the recommendation of her co-workers that she sought a psychiatric consultation. She reported to the interviewer that she was a member of a foreign race from another planet and complained that her bones felt like they were turning to jelly. It was reported that her behavior at home had become increasingly erratic, that she slept days and walked about the house at night, hearing her grandmother's voice in her ears chastising her for sexual indiscretions. She began telling others that she could cure cancer and eliminate evil from the world. At the urging of her parents, she was hospitalized, where she was treated with antipsychotic medications and psychotherapy for a period of ten months. She was able to resume work on a half-time basis after her release, while continuing in outpatient treatment. But a year or so later, she experienced several manic episodes, characterized by pressured speech, hyperactivity, euphoria, early morning awakenings, an inflated or grandiose self-image, and eventually delusions of influence—believing that she could read other people's minds and that others could read her mind. Her grandiosity, or self-perceived importance, led her to reject her therapist's recommendations and to belittle her treatment. While her original diagnosis had been schizophrenia, paranoid type, the evidence of recurrent manic episodes, a mood disorder, led to a revised diagnosis of schizoaffective disorder (manic type) with paranoid features.

Adapted from Stone (1980), pp. 379–380 ■

Some investigators believe that schizophrenia-spectrum disorders share a common genetic link. There appears to be a greater than average incidence of schizoaffective disorders among the relatives of schizophrenics, for example (Kendler et al., 1985). We noted in Chapter 9 that researchers also suspect a possible genetic link between schizotypal personality disorder and schizophrenia.

FEATURES OF SCHIZOPHRENIA

Schizophrenia is a pervasive disorder that affects a wide range of psychological processes involving cognition, affect, and behavior. In the sections below, we take a closer look at the behaviors that characterize schizophrenia, using the DSM–III–R definition of schizophrenia as our guide (see Table 12.1). Many people diagnosed as schizophrenic show only a few of these behavior patterns. The DSM–III–R takes the position that schizophrenics at some time or another show delusions, problems with associative thinking, and hallucinations, but not necessarily all at once. There are also different kinds or types of schizophrenia, characterized by different behavior patterns. No one behavior pattern is unique to schizophrenia, nor is any one behavior pattern invariably present among schizophrenics.

Impaired Level of Functioning

In schizophrenia, there is a marked decline in occupational and social functioning. Schizophrenics may have difficulty holding a conversation, forming friendships, keeping a job, or taking care of their personal hygiene.

Disturbances in Thought and Speech

Schizophrenia is characterized by disturbances in thinking and in the conveyance of thoughts through coherent, meaningful speech. Disturbances in thinking may be expressed in terms of the content and the form of thought.

■ **Disturbances in the Content of Thought** The most prominent disturbance in the content of thought involves **delusions,** or false beliefs that remain fixed in the person's mind despite their illogic and lack of evidence. Delusions tend to remain fixed despite disconfirming evidence. Delusions may take many forms, including *delusions of persecution* (for example, "Someone is spying on me"), *delusions of reference* ("People on the bus are talking about me; People on television are making fun of me"), *delusions of being controlled* (believing that one's thoughts, feelings, impulses or actions are controlled by external powers, such as evil forces), and delusions of grandeur (believing oneself to be Jesus or believing that one is on a special mission, or having grand but illogical plans for saving the world).

People with delusions of persecution may think that they are being pursued by the Mafia, FBI, CIA, or some other group. A woman with delusions of reference believed that television news correspondents were broadcasting coded information about her. Other delusions include beliefs that one has committed unpardonable sins, or is rotting away from a horrible disease, or that the world or oneself does not really exist. Other commonly occurring delusions include *thought broadcasting* (believing that one's thoughts are somehow transmitted to the external world, such that others can overhear them), *thought insertion* (believing that one's thoughts have been planted in one's mind from an external source), and *thought withdrawal* (believing that certain thoughts have been removed from one's mind). Mellor (1970) offers the following examples of thought broadcasting, thought insertion, and thought withdrawal:

> *Thought Broadcasting:* A 21-year-old student reported, "As I think, my thoughts leave my head on a type of mental ticker-tape. Everyone around has only to pass the tape through their mind and they know my thoughts" (p. 17).
>
> *Thought Insertion:* A 29-year-old housewife reported that when she looks out of the window, she thinks, "The garden looks nice and the grass looks cool, but the thoughts of [a man's name] come into my mind. There are no other thoughts there, only his. . . . He treats my mind like a screen and flashes his thoughts on it like you flash a picture" (p. 17).
>
> *Thought Withdrawal:* A 22-year-old woman experienced the following: "I am thinking about my mother, and suddenly my thoughts are sucked out of my mind by a phrenological vacuum extractor, and there is nothing in my mind, it is empty" (pp. 16–17).

Schizophrenia is not the only diagnostic category characterized by delusional thinking. As noted in Chapter 8, people in a manic episode may experience delusions of grandeur—believing, for example, that they hold a unique relationship to God or that they have some special mission to fulfill. People with "pure" delusional (paranoid) disorders, as discussed later in this chapter, may hold delusions of jealousy or persecution that appear so convincing that others may accept them at face value. Psychotic behavior may also occur in major depression (see Chapter 8), usually in the form of delusions of guilt (beliefs that one is being persecuted because of some transgression) or somatic delusions (false, persistent beliefs that cancer is eating away at one's body).

■ **Disturbances in the Form of Thought** Unless we are engaged in daydreaming or purposefully letting our thoughts "wander," our thoughts tend to be tightly knit together. The connections (or associations) between our thoughts tend to be logical and coherent. Schizophrenics, however, tend to think in a disorganized, illogical fashion. In schizophrenia, both the form or structure of thought processes and their content are often disturbed. Clinicians label a disturbance in the form or structure of thought a **thought disorder.**

A thought disorder is recognized by the breakdown in the organization, processing, and control of thoughts (Holzman, 1986). Looseness of associations, which we now regard as a cardinal sign of thought disorder, was one of Bleuler's four A's. Schizophrenics' speech is often jumbled, with parts of words combined in an incoherent manner or words strung together to make meaningless rhymes. Their speech may also jump from one topic to another but convey little useful information. Schizophrenics themselves are usually unaware that their thoughts and behavior appear abnormal. In severe cases of loosened associations, the individual's speech may become completely incoherent or incomprehensible. Another common sign of thought disorder is poverty of content of speech (that is, speech that is coherent but lacks informational value because it is too vague, abstract, concrete, stereotypic, or repetitive). Less commonly occurring signs of thought disorder include **neologisms** (a new word that the speaker makes up that has little or no meaning to others), **perseveration** (inappropriate but persistent repetition of the same words or train of thought), **clanging** (stringing together words or sounds on the basis of rhyming without regard to their meaning, such as, "I know who I am but I don't know Sam"), and **blocking** (involuntary, abrupt interruption of speech or thought).

Many but not all schizophrenics manifest a thought disorder (Marengo & Harrow, 1985; Harrow & Marengo, 1986). Some schizophrenics appear to think and speak coherently, but have disordered content of thought as evidenced by the presence of delusional thoughts (Andreasen, 1986). Nor is disordered thought necessarily diagnostic of schizophrenia since it has been found to exist in normal people (Andreasen & Grove, 1986; Andreasen, 1986), especially at times of fatigue or stress, although to a milder degree. Disordered thought is also found among other diagnostic groups, such as manic people (Andreasen & Grove, 1986; Oltmanns et al., 1985). But thought disorders among normal and manic people tend to be short-lived and reversible, whereas schizophrenics tend to show more persistent or recurrent abnormalities in thinking (Andreasen & Grove, 1986; Harrow & Marengo, 1986).

Thought disorder in schizophrenia occurs most often during acute episodes but may linger into residual phases. Thought disorders that persist following acute episodes are predictive of poorer outcomes over the following years (Marengo & Harrow, 1987; Harrow & Marengo, 1986). Schizophrenics whose thought patterns remain disordered following acute episodes—at times when flagrant signs of the disorder like hallucinations and delusions have abated—may have a more severe form of schizophrenia, which might also account for their poorer outcomes (Harrow & Marengo, 1986).

Deficits in Attention

If you are trying to read this book, you need to screen out the background sounds and other stimuli in your environment. The ability to focus one's attention on relevant stimuli is basic to learning and thinking. Kraepelin and Bleuler suggested that schizophrenia involves a breakdown in the processes of attention. Schizophrenics appear to have difficulty filtering out irrelevant distracting stimuli, impairing their ability to focus their attention and organize their thoughts. Theorists (see McGhie & Chapman, 1961; Payne, 1966) posit that dysfunction of a hypothetical brain "filter" floods the brain with excess information, resulting in attentional difficulties and confused and illogical thinking (that is, a thought disorder). The mother of a schizophrenic son described her son's difficulties in filtering out extraneous sounds:

> . . . his hearing is different when he's ill. One of the first things we notice when he's deteriorating is his heightened sense of hearing. He cannot filter out anything. He hears each and every sound around him with equal intensity. He hears the sounds from the street, in the yard, and in the house, and they are all much louder than normal. (Anonymous, 1985, p. 1; cited in Freedman et al., 1987, p. 670)

Schizophrenics appear to be *hypervigilant* or acutely sensitive to extraneous sounds, especially during the early stages of the disorder. During acute episodes, they may become "flooded" by these stimuli, overwhelming their ability to make sense of their environment (Venables, 1964). By measuring the brain's automatic or involuntary brain wave responses to sensory stimuli such as sounds, researchers have found that brains of schizophrenics are less able than those of normal people to inhibit or "screen out" responses to extraneous sounds (Freedman et al., 1987). The neurobiology of these sensory disturbances is not fully clear. Researchers are investigating a possible "gating" mechanism in the brain that may be responsible for shutting out or inhibiting extraneous stimuli, much like closing a gate in a road can stem the flow of traffic (Freedman et al., 1987). It may be that schizophrenics are deficient in the sensory gating function that is typical of normal people. These sensory deficits also appear to run in the families of schizophrenics, which could point to an underlying genetic mechanism (Freedman et al., 1987).

Cognitively oriented researchers have focused on the role of information processing in explaining deficits in attention. Information processing refers to the mechanisms by which the individual receives, stores, and processes information from the outside world. Experimental studies have shown that schizophrenics may have deficits in the early stages of information processing—that is, in transferring the immediate sensory impression that is formed in the brain by external stimuli, such as light or sound, into short-term memory (Braff & Saccuzzo, 1985; Miller, Saccuzzo & Braff, 1979). People who have difficulty processing sensory information are handicapped indeed in their attempts to understand the outer world. Their environments may be perceived as confused and fragmentary.

The belief that schizophrenics suffer from attentional deficiencies is supported by various studies that have focused on psychophysiological aspects of attention, which we next describe.

■ **Deficiencies in Orienting Response**   When you are exposed to a stimulus, such as an auditory tone or a flash of light, you experience a pattern of automatic or involuntary psychophysiological responses, called the **orienting response** (OR), that alerts your brain to the presence of the incoming stimulus. These responses include pupil dilation, brain wave patterns connected with states of attention, and changes in the electrical conductivity of the skin—that is, galvanic skin response (GSR).

Studies conducted in the United States, Britain, and Germany (Bernstein, 1987; Bernstein et al., 1988) have shown that 40 to 50 percent of schizophrenics fail to demonstrate a normal OR, as measured by GSR, to auditory tones. The subgroup of schizophrenics who fail to show an OR to tones also appears to be distinguished by a group of deficits including emotional withdrawal and cognitive impairment (Bernstein et al., 1981; Bernstein, 1987). In medical terminology, these deficits are called the **negative symptoms** of schizophrenia—those involving behavioral deficits. Schizophrenics with normal ORs tend to show behavioral excesses or so-called **positive symptoms** of schizophrenia, such as the more dramatic, excited, overt schizophrenic behaviors like delusions, hallucinations, and bizarre behavior (Straube, 1979; Bernstein et al., 1981). Thus, it is possible that the attentional difficulties in at least some schizophrenics may be related to a failure of the brain mechanisms that normally allocate attention to incoming stimuli.

■ **Eye Movement Dysfunctions**   Another approach to studying the psychophysiological mechanisms of attention focuses on eye movements. Schizophrenics have greater difficulty than normals in visually tracking moving objects and in maintaining focus on stationary targets, both of which require control of eye movements (Spohn & Patterson, 1979; Holzman, 1987). Eye movement dysfunctions seem to occur in schizophrenia but not in other patterns of abnormal behavior, and they do not appear to be under voluntary control—subjects, that is, are not simply refusing to cooperate with the experimental task. Thus, these attentional difficulties appear to involve a defect in the automatic or involuntary processes related to visual attention. But more research is needed to determine the potential significance of these findings.

■ **Event-Related Potentials**   Researchers are also studying the brain wave patterns, called event-related potentials or ERPs, that occur in response to external stimuli. ERPs have been broken down into different components that emerge at various intervals following the presentation of a stimulus, like a flash of light or auditory tone. Early components (brain wave patterns occurring within the first 250 milliseconds of exposure to a stimulus) may be involved in the process of registering the stimulus in the brain. Later components such as the P300 component (a brain wave pattern that typically occurs about 300 ms, or three-tenths of a second, after a stimulus) are thought to be linked with processes involving attention to the stimulus.

Schizophrenics show early (less than 250 ms) ERP components of greater than expected magnitude in response to tactile stimuli (sensed by touch). It is possible that such brain wave patterns may result in abnormally high levels of sensory information reaching higher brain centers, producing a state of *sensory overload*. This finding supports the view that schizophrenics may be deficient in their ability to filter out distracting stimuli (Shagass et al., 1979). Research has also shown lower than expected levels of P300 wave patterns in schizophrenics in response to auditory tones (Baribeau-Bruan et al., 1983), which may suggest that schizophrenics have difficulties extracting meaningful information from sensory stimuli (Holzman, 1987). Thus, schizophrenics may be loaded up with unusually high levels of sensory information and also have greater difficulty extracting useful information from this input. As a result, they may experience states of confusion and difficulties filtering out irrelevant stimuli, like extraneous noises.

In sum, research evidence has shown several levels of impaired attentional processing in schizophrenia. Schizophrenics may be deficient in the automatic brain processes that control attention to sensory input, as seen by deficiencies in the OR response and greater than expected early ERP responses, and by dysfunctions in eye movements. They also appear to be deficient in processes relating to the deployment of attention, as shown by reduced P300 wave amplitudes, which could indicate problems in interpreting sensory input. It appears that impaired brain processes involved in attention make it difficult for schizophrenics to ignore distracting stimuli and to make sense of the stimuli that impinge their senses.

Perceptual Disturbances

■ Every so often during the interview, Sally would look over her right shoulder in the direction of the office door, and smile gently. When asked why she kept looking at the door, she said that the voices were talking about the two of us just outside the door and she wanted to hear what they were saying. "Why the smile?" Sally was asked. "They were saying funny things," she replied, "like maybe you thought I was cute or something."

■ Eugene was flailing his arms wildly in the hall of the psychiatric unit. Sweat seemed to pour from his brow, and his eyes darted about with agitation. He was subdued and injected with haloperidol (brand name Haldol) to reduce his agitation. When he was about to be injected he started shouting, "Father, forgive them for they know not . . . forgive them . . . father . . . ." His words became jumbled. Later, after he had calmed down, he reported that the ward attendants had looked to him like devils or evil angels. They were red and burning, and steam issued from their mouths.

The Authors' Files ■

Hallucinations, the most common form of perceptual disturbances among schizophrenics, are images that are perceived in the absence of external stimulation. For Sally, the voices coming from outside the consulting room were real enough, even though no one was there. Hallucinations may involve any of the five senses—auditory, olfactory, visual, tactile, or gustatory. Auditory hallucinations (hearing voices) are most common. Tactile hallucinations (such as tingling, electrical, or burning sensations) and somatic hallucinations (feeling like snakes are crawling inside one's belly) are also common. Visual hallucinations (seeing things that are not there), gustatory hallucinations (experiencing strange tastes), and olfactory hallucinations (smelling odors that are not present) are much rarer.

Because it is the most common form of hallucination among schizophrenics, much of the research attention has been focused on auditory hallucinations. In

Among the more flagrant features of schizophrenia are hallucinations, which involve sensory perceptions that occur in the absence of external stimulation but cannot be distinguished from real perceptions, as in "hearing voices."

lems than were the children of emotionally disturbed but not schizophrenic mothers. Thus the children of mothers with other forms of emotional disturbances, such as depression or personality disorders, may incur similar risks of developmental problems. But children reared in poor families and minority families were at yet greater risk of developmental problems than were children of mothers who were psychiatrically disturbed. Yet the combination of maternal abnormal behavior and low socioeconomic status produced the worst outcomes in early childhood development. Again, though, these problems in early development have not yet been shown to lead to schizophrenia in adulthood.

At Emory University in Atlanta, researchers have followed the children of schizophrenic, depressed, and normal mothers from birth through 5 years (Goodman, 1987). The children were predominantly blacks from poor, single-parent families. Testing at various age intervals revealed that children of schizophrenic mothers had more problems than did the other groups. The schizophrenics' offspring were less socially competent than the other children and more often had multiple deficits. Schizophrenic mothers were also rated as providing a poorer child-rearing environment. They were less emotionally responsive. They provided fewer learning experiences and fewer toys, games, and other forms of play stimulation. Thus, it seems that high-risk children may not only carry increased genetic risk, but poor parenting from their schizophrenic parents may also contribute to early developmental problems.

■ **Protective and Vulnerability Factors in HR Children**   Some HR children are apparently invulnerable to developing schizophrenia, even when they are reared in stressful environments, although we do not know why (Weintraub, 1987). Perhaps invulnerable children are physiologically protected in some way from developing schizophrenia (Marcus et al., 1987). Or perhaps there are environmental factors, such as the availability of supportive others, that protect them.

Some evidence suggests that healthful styles of parental communication, including parental ability to express positive feelings, contribute to the school adjustment of HR children (Wynne et al., 1987). Children whose schizophrenic parents have intermittent acute episodes also show fewer developmental deficits than do children of schizophrenic parents with more chronic disorders (Wynne et al., 1987). The Emory University study cited above found that the most socially competent HR children had the most positive child-rearing environments—even within poor, single-parent families. These environments often included a secondary caregiver who helped meet the child's needs, such as a boyfriend of the mother, or a relative (Goodman, 1987).

In a review of the literature, Asarnow and Goldstein (1986) identified various factors that appear to increase or decrease the risk of developing schizophrenia among HR children:

1. *Vulnerability factors.* Various factors have been identified that may increase risk among HR children: birth complications, deficits in attention during childhood, and environmental factors such as disturbed patterns of communication within the family or impoverished learning or nurturing experiences.

2. *Stressful environmental stimuli or events.* Environmental factors may increase the risk of development of schizophrenia. For example, there is evidence of increased occurrence of stressful life events in the period of 3 to 5 weeks before the initial onset of a schizophrenic episode (Brown & Birley, 1968; Leff et al., 1973). These life events include major stressors such as the death of a parent. An accumulation of daily hassles and the stresses that characterize the adolescent's social roles as student, child, and sibling may also increase the risk of an initial schizophrenic episode.

3. *Protective factors.* Other factors may reduce the risk of development of a schizophrenic disorder, including intelligence, clear communication patterns in the family, and the availability of social support.

A summary of the factors that seem to place HR children at greater or lesser risk for developing the disorder is shown in Table 12.2.

A limitation of studying HR children as a model of the development of schizophrenia is that it is not clear whether the ''markers'' that seem to increase vulnerability among children of schizophrenic parents will generalize to the majority of schizophrenics who do not have schizophrenic parents (Goldstein, 1987).

A supportive and nurturing environment may reduce the risk of developing schizophrenia among high-risk children.

TABLE 12.2 Possible Risk Factors Associated with Vulnerability to Schizophrenia in Children of Schizophrenics (HR children)

High Risk (Vulnerability) Factors	Low Risk (Protective) Factors
Maternal anxiety during pregnancy[a]	Lesser severity of maternal illness[b]
Psychotic status of mother in the period of 6 months to 2 years following the birth[a]	Older age of mothers[b]
	Higher education and IQ of mother[b]
Severity of maternal mental illness[c]	Prior work experience of mother[b]
Negative attitudes of mother toward pregnancy[a]	Presence of secondary caregiver (spouse, boyfriend, or other relative)[b]
Low social class[c]	
Family conflict, marital discord, and lack of parenting skills[d]	Mother's healthy communication with the child, father's expression of positive emotions in a free-play situation, and balance between child initiated and parent-initiated activities in free-play situation[e]
Chronic mental illness in the mentally disturbed parent[e]	
Deviant (confused) communication style and expression of hostile feelings toward the child[e]	
Attentional deficits and social problems relating to withdrawal and antisocial behavior in males and feelings of social rejection in females[f]	Absence of severe environmental trauma in the form of pregnancy and birth complications[f]
Complications during pregnancy and delivery[g]	Supportive and nurturing rearing environment[g]

[a] Swedish high-risk study (McNeil & Kaij, 1987)
[b] Emory University Project on Children of Disturbed Parents (Goodman, 1987)
[c] Rochester Longitudinal Study (Sameroff et al., 1987)
[d] Stony-Brook High-Risk Project (Weintraub, 1987)
[e] University of Rochester Child and Family Study (Wynne et al., 1987)
[f] Israeli High-Risk study (Marcus et al. 1987)
[g] Danish high-risk study (Mednick et al., 1987)

■ **Biochemical Factors** Biological investigations of schizophrenia in the past several decades have focused on the role of the neurotransmitter dopamine (Meltzer, 1987). The **dopamine theory** posits that schizophrenia involves an overreactivity of dopamine receptors in the brain—the receptor sites on postsynaptic neurons into which molecules of dopamine lock.

Schizophrenics do not appear to produce more dopamine than other people. Instead, they appear to *utilize* more of it. But why? Research suggests that schizophrenics may have a greater-than-normal number of dopamine receptors in their brains or that their receptors may be overly sensitive to dopamine (Lee & Seeman, 1977; Mackay et al., 1982; Snyder, 1984; Black et al., 1988).

The dopamine theory has evolved from observation of the effects of the group of stimulants called **amphetamines** (discussed in Chapter 10). It appears

that amphetamines increase the action of dopamine in the brain by blocking its re-uptake by presynaptic vesicles. Blocking the re-uptake function increases the concentration of dopamine in the synaptic cleft. High doses of amphetamines prompt behavior in normal people that mimics paranoid schizophrenia. Among schizophrenics, even low doses of amphetamines exacerbate schizophrenic behavior (Meltzer & Stahl, 1976; Meltzer, 1979; Snyder, 1980; van Kammen, 1977).

Another source of evidence for the dopamine model is found in the effects of the **phenothiazines**, a class of drugs often effective in the treatment of schizophrenia. The phenothiazines (such as Thorazine and Mellaril, discussed later) apparently block the action of dopamine at the receptor sites on postsynaptic neurons (Creese et al., 1978; Turkington, 1983). As a consequence, phenothiazines inhibit excessive transmission of neural impulses that may give rise to schizophrenic behavior.

Another source of evidence is based on autopsies of deceased schizophrenics. Autopsies done on the brains of schizophrenics show evidence of increased *numbers* of dopamine receptor sites in certain parts of the brain (see Mackay, 1980)—findings consistent with the dopamine hypothesis. However, findings of autopsies may be contaminated by the fact that many subjects had regularly used antipsychotic drugs to treat their disorders, possibly altering their brain chemistry.

All in all, the evidence supporting the dopamine theory remains inconclusive. Researchers have not yet determined that overreactivity of dopamine receptors directly causes schizophrenic behavior. Although most investigators believe that dopamine plays some role in schizophrenia, recent research suggests that the dopamine hypothesis may not apply to all schizophrenics and that dopamine activity may play a larger role in explaining the flagrant behavior patterns (positive symptoms) that arise during the early or acute stages of schizophrenia rather than the residual deficits (negative symptoms) that remain following acute phases (Mackay, 1980; Meltzer, 1987; Meltzer & Stahl, 1976). It also appears that decreased, not increased, dopamine reactivity may be connected with some of the negative symptoms of schizophrenia (Meltzer, 1987). In addition, the failure of antipsychotic drugs to correct all features of schizophrenia, especially the more resistant negative symptoms, suggests that other factors are involved (Freedman et al., 1987). Some forms of schizophrenia that are characterized by negative symptoms may be caused by structural defects in the brain rather than by biochemical abnormalities involving dopamine transmission (Crow, 1980a,b).

Although dopamine has been the focus of study, other neurotransmitters such as norepinephrine, acetylcholine, serotonin, and GABA may also play a role in schizophrenia (Kety, 1980). We need to learn more about how neurotransmitters interact if we are to increase our understanding of the biochemistry of schizophrenia. The working brain can be likened to a symphony concert in which each neurotransmitter, like a particular instrument, interacts with others to produce the rich sounds of a concert-hall effect (Kety, 1980).

■ Viral Infections   Could schizophrenia be caused by a slow-acting virus that attacks the developing brain of the fetus or the newborn child? Prenatal rubella (German measles), a viral infection, is a cause of mental retardation. Could another virus give rise to schizophrenia?

Viral infections are more prevalent in the winter months (Machón et al., 1983). The viral theory (Torrey, 1973; Torrey & Peterson, 1974) could therefore account for findings of an excess number of schizophrenics being born in the winter (Hare & Price, 1968; Hare, 1979). Other factors could also explain seasonal differences in schizophrenic births, however, such as seasonal variations in nutrition during pregnancy (Hare, 1979). The apparent greater incidence of winter births among schizophrenics may also be a statistical artifact of failure to account for the fact that the incidence of schizophrenia increases with age. That is, individuals born in the early (winter) months of the year might be more likely to be diagnosed as schizophrenic than those born later in the same year because they are slightly older (Lewis, 1989).

A Danish study, however, revealed findings that are too powerful to be simply explained by the fact that winter-born children are slightly older than others born in the same year. The Danish study examined the HR children of schizophrenic mothers and found that they were most likely to develop schizophrenia when they were born in urban settings during the winter months (Machón et al., 1983). The winter-urban HR children showed a 23.3 percent incidence of schizophrenia, as compared to about 1 percent in the Danish population in general and 8.9 percent among HR children in total. This evidence seems to support the viral theory because viral infections are also more contagious in congested urban settings, especially during the cold winter months. However, it is not known whether or not the children who developed schizophrenia had *actually* suffered a viral attack as fetuses or neonates.

 An excess number of schizophrenics were born during the winter. However, the reasons for this seasonal variation are unclear.

Note also that in October and early November of 1957, the Finnish capital, Helsinki, was swept by a serious virus epidemic (Mednick et al., 1987). Sarnoff Mednick and his colleagues studied the incidence of

Do some forms of schizophrenia represent the effects of a slow-acting virus that attacks the brain during prenatal development or shortly after birth? The finding of a greater-than-expected number of schizophrenics being born during the winter suggests that viral infections—which figure more prominently during winter months—may explain some cases of schizophrenia. But direct evidence of a viral infection in schizophrenia is lacking.

schizophrenia among people who were fetuses at the time of the epidemic. The results are intriguing. Individuals who were exposed to the epidemic during the second trimester of prenatal development had greater-than-average frequencies of admission to a mental hospital with a diagnosis of schizophrenia than were those born during the same period of the year during the previous six years. They also had more admissions for schizophrenia than people who were exposed to the epidemic during the first or third trimesters of prenatal development (Mednick et al., 1987). Although most of the organ systems are formed during the first trimester, the brain is still undergoing crucial developments during the second trimester (Rathus, 1988). Perhaps it is not merely exposure to a viral infection but the timing of the exposure during pregnancy that is predictive of later schizophrenia.

In the absence of an identified viral agent, however, the evidence for the viral theory of schizophrenia remains indirect. Even if viral agents were discovered, they would probably account for but a small fraction of cases of schizophrenia (Meltzer, 1987). Moreover, their effects would probably interact with other factors, genetic and environmental, to produce schizophrenic behavior.

■ *Brain Damage*   Modern methods of brain imaging have revealed evidence of structural abnormalities in the brains of schizophrenics, strengthening the view that brain defects may contribute to schizophrenia.

Positron emission tomography (the PET scan) provides information about the metabolic processes of the brain—that is, the brain's use of oxygen. The faster the metabolic rate, the higher the level of brain activity. PET scans of the brains of schizophrenics find lower-than-normal metabolic rates in the frontal lobes and basal ganglia (Buchsbaum & Haier, 1987; Buchsbaum et al., 1982a). These areas are involved in the regulation of attention, so these findings coincide with psychological evidence of deficits in attention among schizophrenics. However, the brain metabolism of the scanned schizophrenics may have been affected by their histories of use of antipsychotic medication, even though they were drug-free at the time of the study.

Researchers have also examined differences in blood flow to the brain in schizophrenics and normals as an index of differences in rates of brain activity. The bloodstream carries oxygen to the brain, so blood flow is another indicator of metabolic processes. Studies that examined the rate of blood flow to the whole brain have failed to show overall differences between schizophrenics and normals (Gur et al., 1985; Buchsbaum & Haier, 1987), but differences in regional patterns of blood flow have been discovered. Normal people have relatively greater blood flow in the frontal areas of the cerebral cortex as compared to the posterior

regions, whereas schizophrenics show less marked regional differences. These findings are consistent with the brain metabolism studies that show lower-than-normal metabolic rates in schizophrenics in the frontal lobes.

Brain functions in schizophrenics are also studied by means of computer-assisted EEG (electroencephalography) techniques, such as brain-electrical activity mapping (BEAM) (see Chapter 3) and a similar technique, computer electroencephalographic topography (thankfully, CET for short). In CET, a computer analyzes the input from electrodes placed at 16 or more points on the scalp. The computer then generates a simulated map of electrical activity of the brain. The various regions of the brain are colored in by the computer with areas of relatively greater activity indicated by "warm" colors (yellows and oranges) and areas of relative inactivity indicated by "cool colors" (blues and purples). CET technology has begun to map out differences such as the following in brain activity between schizophrenics and normals:

1.   Schizophrenics produce lower rates of alpha waves than do normals (Bernstein et al., 1981; Itil, 1977). Alpha waves are an idling brain rhythm that usually occurs during times of relaxation or rest, generally with the eyes closed. Alpha activity can be interrupted upon opening the eyes or when the individual is engaged in a cognitive task (Buchsbaum & Haier, 1987). The significance of

PET scans comparing the brains of four normal controls (top row) and four schizophrenics (bottom row). Note the reduced levels of activity in the frontal lobes of the brains of the schizophrenics.

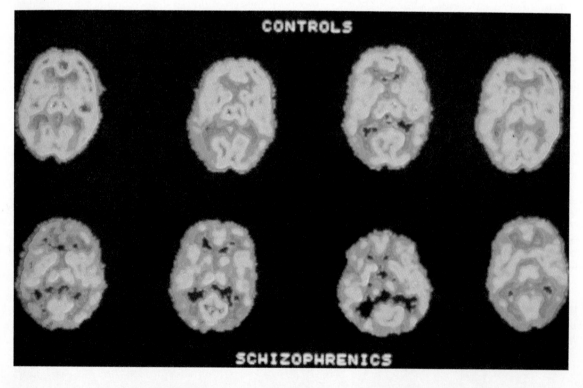

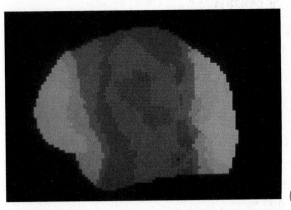 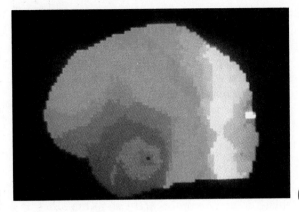

(a)   (b)

Mapping of electrical activity of the brain is one way of investigating brain abnormalities among schizophrenics. Here we see evidence of lower levels of alpha-wave activity in the occipital lobe of the brain of a schizophrenic subject (a) as compared to a composite of 16 normal subjects (b). The lighter colors represent higher levels of the alpha rhythm as measured while the subjects were resting with their eyes closed. The significance of these differences in alpha wave activity remains unclear.

schizophrenic–normal differences in alpha wave production remains unclear, however.

2.   Delta waves may indicate states of drowsiness or lower levels of arousal in the higher (cortical) brain regions (Buchsbaum & Haier, 1987). Schizophrenics have been found to produce higher-than-normal levels of delta waves (Spohn & Patterson, 1979), especially in the frontal lobes (Buchsbaum et al., 1982b; Morihisa, Duffy, & Wyatt, 1983). This production is consistent with PET scan findings of lower metabolic rates in the frontal lobes in schizophrenics. Thus, schizophrenics have abnormally low levels of activity, metabolic and electrical, in their frontal lobes. However, the potential significance of delta wave activity in explaining schizophrenia also remains unclear (Buchsbaum & Haier, 1987).

Computerized axial tomography (the CAT scan) has also revealed brain abnormalities among schizophrenics, such as the enlargement of the brain ventricles (the hollow spaces in the brain) and other measures of brain atrophy (Meltzer, 1987; Pandurangi et al., 1988; Weinberger et al., 1983; Weinberger & Wyatt, 1982). Enlarged brain ventricles are interpreted as a sign of degeneration of brain tissue. Weinberger and Wyatt (1982) found that the ventricles of schizophrenics were twice as large, on the average, as those of normals. However, evidence of brain deterioration in the brains of mature schizophrenics does not tell us whether or not these signs of brain damage preceded the development of the disorder or are themselves a consequence of the disorder or its treatment.

Some research suggests that ventricular enlargements are more common among schizophrenics with poorer premorbid histories, poorer response to antipsychotic drugs, greater evidence of negative symptoms, and more chronic cognitive impairment (Andreasen,

1987; Weinberger et al., 1980). Perhaps these structural abnormalities play a greater part in the development of cases whose clinical profiles correspond to Type II schizophrenia, as described by Crow (1980a). Researchers have speculated that this type of schizophrenia may be caused by structural brain damage (loss of vital brain tissue), rather than by disturbances in the reactivity of dopamine receptors. However, some researchers (Luchins et al., 1983; Pandurangi et al., 1988) have been unable to replicate research that relates negative symptomatology to brain abnormalities such as enlarged ventricles.

Nuclear magnetic resonance or NMR (also called magnetic resonance imaging or MRI) also reveals anatomical structures within the brain. A recent NMR study (Andreasen et al., 1986) found evidence of smaller-than-normal frontal lobes, craniums, and cerebrums in schizophrenics. Others using the technique have found structural differences between the brains of identical twins in which one twin member was schizophrenic and the other was not (Suddath et al., 1990). Specifically, these researchers found that in most all cases, the brains of the schizophrenic twin members had larger ventricles and greater evidence of other structural defects than did the brains of their (nonschizophrenic) co-twins. Studying identical twins offers researchers the advantage of controlling for genetic factors, since identical twins have identical genes. Hence, any observed differences between them reflect other factors than genetics. So while genetic factors may account for a predisposition to schizophrenia, the importance of the study by Richard Suddath and his colleagues was that it showed that there must be other factors besides genetics that are involved in explaining the brain damage associated with schizophrenia. The nature of these causal factors—whether they involve viral infections, birth complications, brain traumas suffered early in life or during prenatal development, or environmental influences in childhood—remains an open question. But we should caution that it remains possible that these structural defects are not actually related to schizophrenia per se, but to other factors that may be associated with schizophrenia, such as prior exposure to stress, histories of hospitalization, and past treatment with antipsychotic drugs (Suddath et al., 1990). It is clear that more research is needed to identify the factors that might account for brain abnormalities associated with schizophrenia.

You should also note that researchers have so far failed to reveal a specific brain abnormality that is unique to schizophrenia. A number of the abnormalities found in the brains of schizophrenics are also found in the brains of individuals with other diagnoses, such as mood disorders (Meltzer, 1987), which clouds our understanding of the specific role they may play in schizophrenia.

In summary, recent advances in genetic research, studies of biochemical systems, and brain imaging have provided strong support for biological factors in schizophrenia. Although the evidence points toward a genetic contribution to schizophrenia, the size of the contribution and the mode of genetic transmission remain unclear (Murray & Reveley, 1986). Research on brain abnormalities has shown evidence of decreased metabolic, blood flow, and electrical activity in areas of the brain that are involved in processes of attention, specifically the frontal lobes. The use of the CAT scan and MRI has shown evidence of structural deterioration in the brain tissue of schizophrenics. However, the significance of these findings of brain abnormalities remains questionable, since they may represent the effects of the disorder itself or its treatment by antipsychotic medication and may not be specific to schizophrenia.

Family Theories

Family theories of schizophrenia examine the contributions of disturbed family relationships to the development and course of schizophrenia.

■ **The Schizophrenogenic Mother**   Early family theories of schizophrenia focused on the role of a "pathogenic" family member, such as the so-called **schizophrenogenic mother** (Fromm-Reichmann, 1948, 1950). The schizophrenogenic mother was described as cold, aloof, domineering, and stripping her children of self-esteem. She was also overprotective, stifling her children's independence, forcing them to become dependent on her. Children reared by such mothers were at special risk for developing schizophrenia if their fathers were passive and failed to counteract the pathogenic influences of the mother. But despite extensive research, it has not been shown that the mothers of schizophrenics fit the archetypical picture of the schizophrenogenic mother (Hirsch & Leff, 1975).

 Despite theoretical assumptions, extensive research has *not* shown that schizophrenics have cold, overprotective, "schizophrenogenic" mothers.

■ **The Double Bind**   In the 1950s, family theorists began to focus on the role of disturbed communications in the family. One of the more prominent theories, put forth by Gregory Bateson and his colleagues (1956), was that **double-bind communications** contributed to the development of schizophrenia. A double-bind communication transmits two mutually incompatible messages without pointing out the discrepancy. In a double-bind communication with a child, a mother might freeze up when the child approaches her and then chide the child for keeping a distance. Whatever the child does, he or she is wrong. With repeated exposure to such double binds, the child's thinking may become disorganized and chaotic. The double-binding mother prevents discussion of her inconsistencies because she cannot admit to herself that she is unable to tolerate closeness. Note this vignette:

> A young man who had fairly well recovered from an acute schizophrenic episode was visited in the hospital by his mother. He was glad to see her and impulsively put his arm around her shoulders whereupon she stiffened. He withdrew his arm and she asked, "Don't you love me anymore?" He then blushed and she said, "Dear, you must not be so easily embarrassed and afraid of your feelings." The patient was able to stay with her only a few minutes more and following her departure he assaulted an aide. (Bateson et al., 1956, p. 251)

Double-bind communications may be one source of family stress that increases the risk of schizophrenia in genetically vulnerable individuals. In more recent years, investigators have broadened the investigation of family factors in schizophrenia by viewing the family in terms of a system of relationships among the members, rather than singling out mother-child or father-child interactions. Two principal sources of family stress that have been studied are patterns of deviant communications and negative emotional expression in the family.

■ **Communication Deviance**   Communication deviance (CD) describes a pattern of parental communication marked by excessive vagueness or blurring of meaning in parental speech and by parental inability to focus in on what the child is saying (Goleman, 1984). Parents who are high in CD tend to attack their children personally rather than offer constructive criticism and may subject them to double-bind communications. They also tend to interrupt the child with intrusive, negative comments. They are prone toward telling the child what he or she "really" thinks rather than allowing the child to formulate his or her own thoughts and feelings (Goleman, 1984).

A longitudinal study at UCLA found that parental

CD predicted the development of schizophrenia or related disorders among a sample of behaviorally troubled adolescents who were not schizophrenic at the time of their initial assessment (Goldstein, 1987a, 1987b). Ten of 20 (50%) of the adolescents whose parents were high in CD were diagnosed 15 years later as suffering from a schizophrenia-spectrum disorder (that is, schizophrenia or a related diagnosis like schizotypal personality disorder or schizoaffective disorder). Only 1 in 12 adolescents from low CD families and 5 of 19 from moderate CD families were similarly diagnosed. Still, we cannot conclude that parental CD was causally related to the later development of such disorders in these adolescents. The parental patterns of communication may have represented a reaction to living with a child who was already disturbed, though not overtly schizophrenic. Or perhaps parents and children shared genetic traits that became expressed through disturbed communications.

Considering the emotional climate in the adolescent's family sharpened the prediction of development of schizophrenia. Adolescents most likely to develop schizophrenia-spectrum disorders were reared by families who interacted in a more negative emotional manner and in which the parents were high in CD. Thus, CD and hostile family interactions represent two sources of family stress that may act, within the diathesis–stress model, to heighten the risk of schizophrenia among genetically vulnerable individuals.

The UCLA study was limited to adolescents who were showing evidence of behavioral disturbance. It remains to be seen whether these factors predict the risk of schizophrenic-type disorders among children who are free of overt behavioral problems. It would also be desirable to study all of the offspring in the family, not just the one at greatest risk, in an effort to determine why some children in disturbed families develop schizophrenic-type disorders and others do not.

■ **Expressed Emotion** Another measure of disturbed family communications is labeled *expressed emotion* (EE), which focuses on the amount of expressed negative emotion that family members direct toward the schizophrenic family member (Leff & Vaughn, 1985; Vaughn & Leff, 1976, 1981). Families high in EE are quick to find fault with the schizophrenic member and express frequent criticism and hostility (Leff & Vaughn, 1985). High EE families also tend to be emotionally overinvolved with the schizophrenic member; for example, they become extremely overprotective and sacrifice their own needs.

Acute episodes among schizophrenics in low EE families have been found to recur less frequently in the first two years following hospitalization than they do in high EE families (Leff & Vaughn, 1981) (see Figure 12.3). Low EE families may actually serve to protect or "buffer" the schizophrenic individual from the adverse impact of outside stressors and help prevent recur-

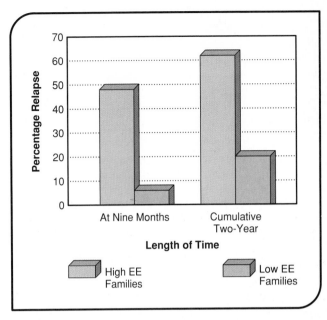

FIGURE 12.3 Relapse rates of schizophrenics in high and low EE families.

Schizophrenics whose families are high in expressed emotion (EE) are at greater risk of relapse than those whose families are low in EE. Whereas low-EE families may help protect the schizophrenic family member from environmental stressors, high-EE families may impose additional stress.
Source: Adapted from Leff & Vaughn (1981)

rent episodes (Strachan, 1986). EE has also been shown to predict recurrence even when the initial level of disturbance of the schizophrenic's behavior is statistically controlled (Brown et al., 1972). EE in the family also appears unrelated to the degree of abnormality in the schizophrenic's behavior at discharge (Vaughn & Leff, 1976). Taken together, these data suggest that high EE may play a causal role in determining the course of schizophrenia (Strachan, 1986) and is not simply a reaction of the family to greater deviance on the schizophrenic's part. However, questions of cause and effect remain unresolved; other behavioral differences between the schizophrenics in high and low EE families may account for differences in outcomes, rather than the differences in their families per se. Moreover, most of the research showing relationships between EE status and recurrence have been conducted on male schizophrenics (Hogarty, 1985), so the relevance of the findings to female schizophrenics remains unknown. We should also note that many schizophrenics are detached from their families and have little if any contact with them (Goldstein, 1987b), so that family factors could not account for recurrent episodes among them.

The EE construct has been criticized by relatives who feel that they are being blamed by mental-health professionals for the disturbed family member's problems (Strachan, 1986). However, research on EE and other family stress factors helps focus attention on the need to help family members change their style of relating to each other, which may reduce the stress imposed on the schizophrenic member (Leff et al., 1982) and improve family harmony.

■ Family Factors in Schizophrenia: Causes or Sources of Stress?

There is little if any evidence that families are responsible for directly causing schizophrenia in their offspring. If rearing factors cause schizophrenia, we would expect that the foster (nonbiologically related) siblings of adoptees who become schizophrenic, and who were reared by the same adoptive parents, would be at greater risk of schizophrenia than the biological siblings of these schizophrenic adoptees who were reared in different families (Kety, 1980). However, evidence from a study in Iceland shows just the opposite results: Biological siblings of eight schizophrenic adoptees showed a greater prevalence of schizophrenia than did their foster siblings (Karlsson, 1966). Similar findings were obtained based on a sample of 12 schizophrenic adoptees in Denmark (Kety, 1980). We do caution that the small numbers of schizophrenic adoptees in these studies limits the significance of these findings, however.

But there is more: We've noted that HR (high-risk) offspring of schizophrenic parents who are reared in some other environment are about as likely to develop schizophrenia as are HR children raised by their own (schizophrenic) parents (see Karlsson, 1966; Heston, 1966; Kety et al., 1968, 1975; Marcus et al., 1987; Rosenthal et al., 1968). We have also noted that children born of normal biological parents but raised by schizophrenic adoptive parents had no greater-than-normal risk of developing schizophrenic-type disorders (Wender et al., 1974). Nor is there empirical support for the view that family factors can account for schizophrenia in children who do not have a genetic vulnerability.

What then is the role of family factors in schizophrenia? Disturbed patterns of emotional interaction and communication in the family may represent a source of stress that may increase the likelihood of the development or recurrence of schizophrenia among individuals with a genetic disposition for the disorder. Some researchers have also suggested that the less contact schizophrenics have with high-stress relatives, the better they are able to function in the community (Vaughn & Leff, 1976). Removing schizophrenics from stressful family environments, at least for some part of the day, through placement in sheltered workshops, gainful employment, and day-treatment programs may lessen the impact of high-stress families and improve the chances of successful community adjustment. Outcomes may also be improved if schizophrenics and their families are taught ways of coping with stress, and if families are taught to be less critical and more supportive of their schizophrenic members. Counseling programs that help family members of chronic schizophrenics learn to express their feelings without attacking or criticizing the schizophrenic member may be helpful in preventing the damaging effects of family conflict on the schizophrenic's adjustment (Spiegel & Wissler, 1986).

Sociocultural Perspectives

The sociocultural model views schizophrenic behavior in the context of the relationship between the individual and society. Researchers suspect that such factors as overcrowding, poor diet and sanitation, and inadequate health care may contribute to increased risk of schizophrenia, at least among people with a genetic vulnerability (Kety, 1980). Some adherents to the sociocultural model believe that more attention should be paid to changing society to eradicate social ills that may give rise to schizophrenic behavior than on changing the person whose behavior is deviant.

Research findings do show that schizophrenia is most common among the lower socioeconomic classes (Kety, 1980). For example, a classic study conducted by Hollingshead and Redlich (1958) in the 1950s in New Haven, Connecticut (see also Chapters 1 and 2), showed that the rate of schizophrenia was twice as high among the lowest socioeconomic class than among the second from the bottom. But low socioeconomic status may be a *consequence* and not an *antecedent* of schizophrenia. Schizophrenics may drift downward in social status because they lack the social skills and cognitive abilities to function at higher levels. Thus, they may wind up in more impoverished areas in disproportionately high numbers.

Evidence for the hypothesis that schizophrenics drift downward in socioeconomic status is mixed. Some evidence is supportive (Turner & Wagonfield, 1967); other evidence is not (Hollingshead & Redlich, 1958; Dunham, 1965). Perhaps both views are partly correct. Although many schizophrenics drift downward occupationally in comparison to their fathers' occupations, many schizophrenics are also reared in families from the lower socioeconomic classes. Thus, the stresses of poverty may also play a role in the development of schizophrenia.

Other sociocultural theorists have attempted to explain schizophrenic behavior in terms of the social role of the mental patient in society. Thomas Scheff (1966), for example, claimed that once mental patients are assigned a diagnostic label, like schizophrenia, they are then selectively reinforced for behavior that is consistent with the stereotype. Mental patients act crazy, in other words, because they are expected to act that way. Scheff's theory may help to explain the **institutionalization syndrome,** a pattern of behavior of institutional residents associated with passivity and dependency. Patients in institutions are frequently rewarded for following orders, for not complaining or making independent decisions. Although role-playing may explain some aspects of schizophrenic behavior, especially in institutional settings, it is difficult to explain disturbances in thinking and perception, such as thought disorder and hallucinations, on the basis of role theory.

The Scottish psychiatrist R. D. Laing straddles the sociocultural and humanistic-existential perspectives. He views the schizophrenic's flight into fantasy as a means of coping with intolerably stressful life conditions. Laing regards schizophrenia as a search for a more authentic identity in a world that squelches individuality and requires individuals to adopt a socially acceptable public self or "mask" that covers up their true inner selves. The stresses of conforming to family and outside pressures can shatter the facade of socially acceptable behavior and cause the individual to retreat into a private fantasy world. In this private world, the schizophrenic undertakes a personal journey of discovery to find his or her true inner self. Laing regards schizophrenia as a valiant act of defiance, not as a kind of illness. To Laing, schizophrenia "is a special sort of strategy that a person invents in order to live in an unlivable situation" (1964, p. 186).

In Laing's view, schizophrenic speech is not meaningless chatter. Laing argues that we should try to understand the meaning that these behaviors hold for the individual in light of the way the individual experiences himself or herself and the world. Schizophrenics are in need of guidance and support to help them resolve the split between their true and false selves and to give their lives new meaning.

Laing and his followers established therapeutic residences or treatment homes built upon his therapeutic model. In such residences, deviant behavior is tolerated more so than in traditional treatment centers, and schizophrenics are encouraged to reach a more authentic identity. However, there is little if any evidence to support the therapeutic value of Laing's approach. But Laing's assertion that schizophrenia reflects family pressures and stress has received some support from research on family factors in schizophrenia.

TREATMENT

While there is no "cure" for schizophrenia, treatment of the disorder is often multifaceted, incorporating chemotherapeutic (or pharmacological), psychological, and rehabilitative approaches. Most schizophrenics in organized mental-health settings are treated with some form of antipsychotic medication, which is intended to control the more flagrant behavior patterns—such as hallucinations and delusions—and to decrease the risk of recurrent episodes among schizophrenics without active (positive) symptoms. We shall see, however, that long-term treatment with antipsychotic medications carries a risk of disabling side effects and holds less promise for treating the negative symptoms of schizophrenia. Psychosocial and rehabilitative ap-proaches are needed to help schizophrenics achieve higher levels of social integration and community functioning.

Biological Approaches

Various biological approaches have been used in the treatment of schizophrenia, including electroconvulsive therapy (ECT), psychosurgery, and chemotherapy. Today, psychosurgery has been all but discontinued, and ECT is used rarely in the treatment of schizophrenia. As noted in Chapter 8, ECT is now primarily used in the treatment of severe depression.

Presently, chemotherapy is the principal modality of treatment when flagrant psychotic behaviors such as hallucinations and delusions occur during an acute episode.

■ Antipsychotic Medication   The advent in the 1950s of antipsychotic drugs—also referred to as major tranquilizers or *neuroleptics*—revolutionized the treatment of schizophrenia and provided the impetus for large-scale releases of mental patients to the community (deinstitutionalization). Medication helps control the more flagrant behavior patterns of schizophrenia, reducing the need for long-term hospitalization and allowing many schizophrenics to return to community life.

Some of the more common classes of antipsychotic drugs include the phenothiazines such as chlorproma-zine (Thorazine), thioridazine (Mellaril), trifluoperazine (Stelaxine), and fluphenazine (Prolixin). Haloperidol (Haldol) is chemically distinct from the phenothiazines but produces similar effects (Crammer et al., 1982). Many kinds of antipsychotic drugs have been developed, but there is a lack of data to suggest that one is more effective than the others (Kane, 1987). The ways in which these drugs lessen psychotic behaviors are not fully known. Evidence is accumulating, however, that their therapeutic action involves the blocking of dopamine receptors in the brain (Marder & May, 1986).

The effectiveness of antipsychotic drugs has been repeatedly demonstrated in placebo-control studies (see May, 1968, for example). However, these drugs are no panacea. A substantial minority of schizophrenics receive little benefit from them, and there are no clear-cut factors that determine who will best respond (Bellack, 1986; Kane, 1987; May & Goldberg, 1978). As a result, alternate approaches need to be developed for schizophrenics who fail to respond to currently available drugs (Carpenter, 1986; Kane, 1987).

Antipsychotic drugs appear to reduce the more florid or positive symptoms that characterize acute episodes, such as hallucinations and delusions, but they do little to alleviate the milder but disabling negative symptoms that persist after the acute episode has been resolved. These negative symptoms include disorga-

Drugs alone are apparently not sufficient to restore the social and occupational functioning of chronic schizophrenics. Antipsychotic drugs have greater effects on the more flagrant features ("positive symptoms") of schizophrenia than on long-standing deficits in cognitive and social functioning ("negative symptoms").

nized thinking, oddities of speech, and social deficits (Bellack, 1986; Johnstone et al., 1978; Mackay, 1980; Spohn et al., 1986). It is also uncertain whether medication helps schizophrenics function socially or keep their jobs (Marder & May, 1986). In sum, treatment with medication alone appears insufficient to meet the multifaceted needs of schizophrenics.

Schizophrenics typically receive maintenance doses of antipsychotic drugs when they leave the hospi-

tal and return to the community. Continued medication reduces the risk of recurrent episodes and rehospitalization (Carpenter, 1986; Kane, 1987) (see Figure 12–4). In one double-blind study, schizophrenics were returned to the community and either continued on their medication or switched to a placebo (Hogarty et al., 1973). Subjects who received the placebo were about twice as likely (68%) to have recurrent episodes during the following year as subjects who continued to receive medication (31%). Although maintenance medication may help reduce the risk of recurrent episodes, we must still note that a third or so of medicated patients do have such episodes in the year following hospitalization (Faloon et al., 1982). Moreover, perhaps one-half to two-thirds (48% reported by Hogarty et al., 1974; 65% reported by Hogarty et al., 1979) have recurrent episodes by a two-year follow-up. Some of those with recurrent episodes fail to take their medication reliably, but half (50%) of schizophrenics who are maintained reliably on long-acting medication also have recurrent episodes (Hogarty, 1979). Hence, problems with recurrent episodes cannot be simply explained away as failure to take the drugs as prescribed (Kane, 1987; Strachan, 1986).

The long-term use of antipsychotics may cause serious side effects, including a possibly irreversible form of brain damage called **tardive dyskinesia** (TD). A movement disorder that affects the face, mouth, neck, trunk, or extremities, TD generally occurs among persons treated with antipsychotic drugs for six months or longer (Marder & May, 1986). It can take different

FIGURE 12.4 Relapse rates at 12-month follow-ups: Maintenance drug vs. placebo.
These data illustrate the greater probability of relapse among schizophrenics who were switched to placebo drugs following discharge from the hospital.

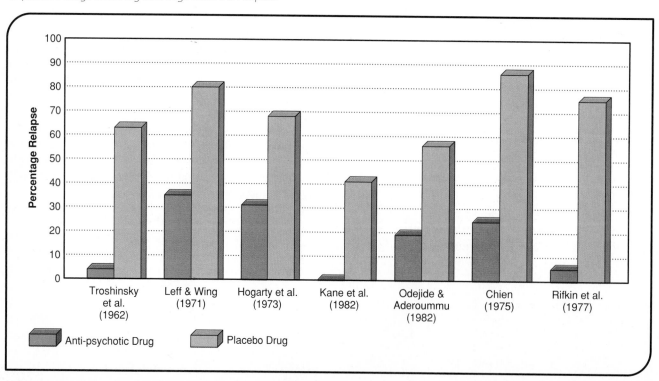

forms, the most common of which is frequent eye blinking (Gardos et al., 1987). Other signs of TD consist of mouth and eye movements, lip smacking and puckering, facial grimacing, and involuntary movements of the limbs and trunk (Marder & May, 1986). The risk of TD seems to increase with age, and TD is especially common among older female patients (Smith & Baldessarini, 1980). Although most TD-related problems are mild, some affected individuals become seriously disabled and have difficulties breathing, talking, or eating (Marder & May, 1986). No treatment for TD has been shown to be both safe and effective, nor have antipsychotic drugs that carry a lower risk of producing TD been brought to market (Kane, 1987). Although some schizophrenics with TD show improvement when antipsychotic drugs are discontinued, many remain permanently and severely disabled.

Tardive dyskinesia occurs with alarming frequency among patients treated for extended periods with antipsychotic drugs (Carpenter, 1986). The rate among those treated for a year or longer has been estimated to be least 10 to 20 percent (Task Force Report, American Psychiatric Association, 1980). Others estimate that about 4 percent of antipsychotic drug users will develop the disorder each year for at least the first five or six years of treatment (Kane et al., 1986). The risk of these potentially disabling side effects require physicians to weigh carefully the risks and benefits of long-term treatment with these drugs (Kane, 1987).

New drug-treatment strategies are being explored to lower their risks, such as the use of lower dosages and of intermittent (noncontinuous) regimens (Carpenter, 1986). Significantly lower incidence of early TD signs are found among patients who receive low doses of medication (Kane, 1985; Kane et al., 1985), but the long-term safety and efficacy of this approach needs to be established. Low-dosage patients who experience recurrent psychotic behaviors can often be restabilized in the community by means of a stepped-up dosage of medication (Kane, 1987). Then dosages may be subsequently lowered again.

Perhaps as many as 20 percent of schizophrenics do not require continuous antipsychotic medication to maintain themselves in the community (Fenton & McGlashan, 1987). It seems that schizophrenics who have acquired social and occupational skills, and those who are recovering from an initial acute episode, may be less likely to need maintenance medication. The social or family environment that the patient faces upon discharge from the hospital may also help determine the schizophrenic's ability to adapt to the community with or without medication.

> **?** Antipsychotic medications *cannot* cure schizophrenia. However, in most cases they can help control the bizarre, flagrant behavior patterns that characterize acute episodes.

Psychodynamic Approaches

Freud did not believe that traditional psychoanalysis was well-suited to treatment of schizophrenia. For one thing, schizophrenics' withdrawal into a fantasy world prevented them from forming a meaningful therapeutic relationship with the psychoanalyst. The techniques of classical psychoanalysis, Freud wrote, must "be replaced by others; and we do not know yet whether we shall succeed in finding a substitute" (cited in Arieti, 1974, p. 532).

Other psychoanalysts such as Harry Stack Sullivan and Frieda Fromm-Reichmann adapted psychodynamic techniques for working specifically with schizophrenics. However, research has failed to demonstrate the effectiveness of psychodynamic or insight-oriented treatments with schizophrenics (Carpenter, 1986; Gunderson et al., 1984; May & Tuma, 1976; Mosher & Keith, 1980; Stanton et al., 1984). In one carefully controlled study (May & Tuma, 1976), for example, psychodynamic treatment proved to be less effective than antipsychotic drugs, nor did psychodynamic treatment increase the effectiveness of drug treatment when the two approaches were combined. In light of such results, some critics have argued that further research on the use of insight-oriented therapies with schizophrenics is no longer warranted (Klerman, 1984). It appears that supportive, psychoeducational approaches that help prepare schizophrenics for societal roles, in combination with drug treatment, may be more helpful than more intensive, psychodynamic approaches (Kane, 1987).

Learning-Based Approaches

Behavioral or learning-based approaches to schizophrenia generally involve the direct modification of schizophrenic behaviors and the development of more adaptive behaviors. Learning-based approaches are problem-oriented and intended to prepare schizophrenics for community roles. Therapy methods include techniques such as (1) selective reinforcement of behavior (as in providing staff attention for appropriate behavior and extinguishing bizarre verbalizations through withdrawal of staff attention); (2) the token economy, in which individuals are rewarded for appropriate behavior with tokens, such as plastic chips, that can be exchanged for tangible reinforcers such as desirable goods or privileges; and (3) social skills training, in which clients are taught conversation skills, eye contact, smiling, and other appropriate social behaviors through coaching, modeling, behavior rehearsal, and feedback.

■ **Social-Learning Programs** Promising results have emerged from studies applying intensive learning-based approaches in hospital settings. A classic study by Paul and Lentz (1977) compared traditional hospital treatment of chronic schizophrenics with two intensive psychosocial programs that were intended to enhance independent functioning. One applied social-learning principles to help schizophrenics acquire more appropriate behaviors. The other, milieu therapy, was based on the model of the **therapeutic community** and involved schizophrenics in group decision making. The subjects in the study were considered "hard-core" schizophrenics who had been generally unresponsive to antipsychotic medication (Paul et al., 1972).

The psychosocial treatments were run on adjoining wards and shared some common features. Subjects in both could progress through a series of steps toward less restrictive treatment settings, earn greater privileges, and assume more responsibilities along the way. Both programs were run around the clock.

The social-learning program employed a token economy. Behaviors reinforced by tokens included attendance at meetings, maintenance of proper grooming, and appropriate verbal communications. Tokens could be exchanged for rewards like food, privacy time, passes, and other privileges. Signs listed the numbers of tokens available for specific behaviors and the numbers of tokens that were necessary to earn particular rewards. Subjects were promoted to higher levels and became eligible to earn greater numbers of tokens and more attractive rewards.

In the milieu program, subjects were divided into small "living groups" that were responsible for delegating responsibilities, such as preparing meals. Groups were encouraged to spend free time together and use peer pressure to promote adaptive behavioral changes. Subjects and staff held group meetings to discuss and vote on issues that affected life on the ward. This exercise in democracy may not seem so radical an idea, but the typical mental hospital at the time of the study tended to treat patients like dependent children, telling them how to behave and offering them little responsibility. The therapeutic community attempts to involve

schizophrenics in the governing process as a way of preparing them for responsible community roles upon discharge.

Both psychosocial treatments yielded significantly better results than the standard hospital regimen, as measured by adaptive behavior in the hospital, need for medication, and community functioning. The social-learning program also produced markedly better results than the milieu treatment (see Figure 12.5). Schizophrenics in the social-learning program reduced the frequency of bizarre behavior to a small fraction of baseline levels—at far less cost than the comparison treatments. The average social-learning program participant improved by more than 1,200 percent in overall measures of interpersonal and communicative skills. Perhaps the most telling statistics involved discharge and community tenure, since the ultimate goal of treating hospitalized patients is to restore them to successful functioning in the community. Nearly all of the social-learning program subjects (97.5%) were able to be discharged and to remain in the community for a minimum of 90 days, as compared to 71 percent of the milieu-therapy participants and 45 percent of the control participants. Social-learning program participants remained in the community longer than participants in the other conditions, ranging from 18 months to 5 years following discharge as of the conclusion of the follow-up period.

From the standpoint of clinical effectiveness and cost of treatment, it is clear that the intensive social-learning program was the treatment of choice (Glynn & Mueser, 1986). However, there are prerequisites that may limit the applicability of this approach, including the need for strong administrative support, skilled treatment leaders, extensive staff training, and ongoing quality control (Glynn & Mueser, 1986).

Ever since publication of the Paul and Lentz study, other researchers have found encouraging results with similar programs (see Fullerton et al., 1978; McCreadie

FIGURE 12.5 Some measures of outcome from the Paul and Lentz study.

The release rates and community tenure (days in the community) of schizophrenics in the three conditions studied by Paul and Lentz: (1) social-learning-based treatment, (2) milieu treatment, and (3) traditional hospital treatment.
Source: Paul, G., and Lentz, R. *Psychosocial Treatment of Chronic Mental Patients: Milieu vs. Social-Learning Programs.* Cambridge, MA: Harvard University Press, 1977. (From Glynn & Mueser, 1986.)

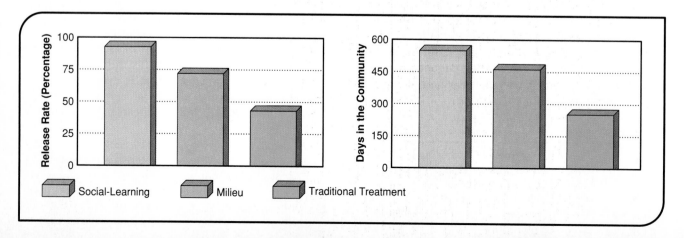

et al., 1978; Turner & Luber, 1980; Wong et al., 1986). Several important issues, however, remain unsettled (Glynn & Mueser, 1986). One of these is identification of the effective components of treatment. It is not clear whether token reinforcement itself (a behavioral variable), the feedback that participants receive about their performance via tokens (a cognitive behavioral variable), or other factors comprise the effective inducers of behavioral change (Glynn & Mueser, 1986). Questions of generalization and maintenance of behavioral changes also remain unsettled. It is not yet known whether token reinforcement programs foster adaptive behavioral changes only during the time the tokens are dispensed or only in the settings, such as the hospital environment, in which the programs are administered.

■ **Social Skills Training** Social skills programs apply principles of social-learning theory to teach participants specific social and vocational skills. Social skills training has been used extensively (Morrison & Bellack, 1984) to help schizophrenics acquire specific social skills such as assertiveness skills or general conversational skills. Such skills facilitate adjustment in the community.

Although different approaches to skills training have been developed, the basic model uses role-playing exercises within a group format. Participants practice skills such as starting or maintaining conversations with new acquaintances and receive feedback and reinforcement from the therapist and other group members (Liberman et al., 1986). The first step might be a "dry run" in which the participant role-plays the targeted behavior, such as asking strangers for bus directions. The therapist and other group members then praise the effort and provide constructive feedback. Role-playing is augmented by techniques such as modeling (observation of the therapist or other group members enacting the desired behavior), direct instruction (specific directions for enacting the desired behavior), shaping (reinforcement for successive approximations to the target behavior), and coaching (therapist use of verbal or nonverbal prompts to elicit a particular desired behavior in the role play). Participants are given homework assignments to practice the behaviors in the settings in which they live, such as on the hospital ward or in the community. The aim is to enhance generalization or transfer of training to other settings. Training sessions may also be run in stores, restaurants, schools, and other **in vivo** settings.

Several controlled studies report success for social skills training as a means of improving interpersonal behavior (Eisler et al., 1978; Bellack et al., 1984; Wallace & Liberman, 1985; Hogarty et al., 1986). But questions remain about the maintenance of these improvements once treatment is completed and about their generalization to social behaviors that were not directly addressed in the program (Kane, 1987). Some critics

also contend that social skills training has not improved the overall quality of life of schizophrenics and that the treatments need to be expanded to include more clinically meaningful behaviors (Wallace et al., 1980).

Psychosocial Rehabilitation

Schizophrenics typically have difficulties functioning in social and occupational roles that limit their ability to adjust to community life even in the absence of overt psychotic behavior. Many older, long-hospitalized schizophrenics who have been resettled in the community are particularly ill-prepared to handle the tasks of daily living, such as cooking, shopping, or traveling around town. Many younger schizophrenics have markedly deficient social skills, even though they have spent only short periods of time in mental hospitals (Anthony & Liberman, 1986).

A number of self-help clubs and more structured psychosocial rehabilitation centers have sprung up to help schizophrenics find places in society. Many centers were launched by nonprofessionals or by schizophrenics themselves, since mental-health agencies often failed to provide comparable services (Anthony & Liberman, 1986). Early examples of self-help clubs were Fountain House and Horizon House, both of which were founded by formerly hospitalized schizophrenics. Each provided clients with social support and assistance. So-called multiservice psychosocial rehabilitation centers also provide clients with housing and occupational opportunities.

These centers often make use of skills training to help clients learn how to handle money, resolve disputes with family members, develop friendships, take buses, cook their own meals, shop, and so on. A review of the research literature shows that even clients with severe abnormal behavior problems can learn useful skills relating to self-care and cognitive and social functioning (Anthony & Margules, 1974; Anthony et al., 1984).

The rehabilitation model teaches that disabled individuals can achieve their potential if they are given the support and structure they need and if the expectations and demands placed upon them are consistent with their capacities. Both the client and the family should be helped to adjust their expectations to attainable levels (Anthony & Liberman, 1986).

Development of community support programs and tax incentives for employers who hire mental patients are additional examples of how society can help provide mental patients with the support they need to lead more productive lives. Consider the following case:

■ A 30-year-old male with a 15-year history of being in and out of private and state psychiatric hospitals decided

A CLOSER LOOK
Helping Schizophrenics Adjust to the Community

Social support programs offer hope that schizophrenics can be reintegrated into the community if they receive proper support and treatment.

In Massachusetts, for example, an innovative program was established to offer help to families who were caring for a schizophrenic member. In times of crisis, the client might be placed in a supervised halfway house (discussed in Chapter 16) rather than the hospital. Or a caseworker might move in with the family to help out for a few days. In addition, specially trained families were available to provide shelter and support through a crisis for up to two months. The aim of the program was to keep the individual in the community, even in a crisis. The key aspect of the Massachusetts program was case management—the assignment of some 30 schizophrenics to a service coordinator or "case manager" whose responsibility was to obtain for clients the services they needed in order to adjust. For example, the case manager would assist clients in finding apartments and help them move in. The case manager would help clients obtain the proper forms for government assistance and help them complete the forms.

Other programs like Fountain House in New York City provide a "clubhouse" environment to help members socialize and make friends. Fountain House also helps its members find temporary paying jobs through a network of businesses that provide entry-level jobs. A staff member accompanies the member on the job and pitches in to perform the job if the member should falter. When members maintain employment for six months they move on to other jobs until they are able to find and maintain full-time work on their own.

Although programs such as these offer hope that schizophrenics may be reintegrated into the community, few states have allocated the funds to support them. Without proper funding, the policy of deinstitutionalization may be no more humane or effective than the practice of "warehousing" patients in the back wards of large mental hospitals. Issues concerning deinstitutionalization are discussed further in Chapter 15.

Community-based rehabilitation centers like Fountain House help schizophrenics to find places for themselves in the community by helping them secure and maintain meaningful employment.

he would like to get a job in the community after being in a psychosocial work adjustment program for 1 year. He did not have a good work history; for example, 6 months was the longest he had ever been able to hold a job. Using the targeted job tax credit legislation as an incentive to the employer, the psychiatric rehabilitation team was able to find the disabled person a job working in a video repair shop, a job consistent with the client's interests and talents. To keep his job at the repair shop, the client needed to learn the skills of taking orders from authority figures (showing understanding of what others say and expressing his own thoughts and feelings to others). The team also made the environment more supportive of the client by educating the employer to the client's needs. The team obtained employer agreement on reducing the initial work load until the disabled person became comfortable with the new environment.

Adapted from Anthony & Liberman, 1986, p. 553 ■

Family Intervention Programs

Family conflict may play a role in the development and course of schizophrenia. Viewed within the diathesis–stress model, family conflicts and tensions can heap stress upon the schizophrenic member, increasing the risk of recurrent episodes. Researchers and clinicians have worked with families of schizophrenics to help them cope with the burdens of care and to assist them in developing more cooperative, less confrontative ways of interrelating.

A recent review of four major investigations of family intervention programs (Goldstein et al., 1978; Leff et al., 1982; Falloon et al., 1982; Hogarty et al., 1986) revealed that each program produced significant reductions in rates of recurrent schizophrenic episodes at 6- to 9-month follow-ups as compared to control groups (Strachan, 1986). All of the schizophrenic subjects in these studies, those treated within a family treatment approach and controls, received continuous medication. Thus the effects of family intervention added to the effects accounted for by medication. Although differences existed in the programs, they all shared certain features, including focus on the practical aspects of everyday living; delivery of information about schizophrenia in a straightforward, educational manner; treatment of the families with respect and dignity; and fostering of effective coping skills.

As an example, a multifaceted family intervention study was conducted by Falloon and his colleagues (1982, 1985) that focused on schizophrenics living with families that were high in conflict or expressed emotion (EE), since these factors are believed to increase the risk of recurrent episodes. The program included an educational component and a behavioral family management component. The educational component focused on increasing the family's understanding of the behaviors that characterize schizophrenia. It also helped the family identify ways of supporting rather than criticizing the schizophrenic member's behavior. The behavioral family management component helped family members communicate—to listen to each other, to make requests specific, and to express feelings clearly. Families were also given training at solving problems: They learned to identify the problem, generate alternate solutions, agree upon a promising solution, try it out, and evaluate the results.

Family intervention was compared to a program in which schizophrenics received individual treatment, consisting of education about schizophrenia and supportive counseling. At a 9-month follow-up, only one of 18 family management clients suffered a recurrent episode of schizophrenic behavior, as compared to 8 of 18 controls in the individual therapy condition. By a 2-year follow-up, only 3 of 18 of the family management clients had significantly worsened, as compared to 15 of 18 in the individual treatment condition. Figure 12.6 shows the ratings across time of schizophrenic features for both treatment conditions. In addition, clients who received individual treatment experienced more frequent and longer hospitalizations during the follow-up period. A cost-benefit analysis revealed that the more effective family management program actually cost 19 percent less than the individual treatment, because individually treated clients required greater use of crisis intervention services and hospitalization (Cardin et al., 1986).

Analysis of the patterns of family communication in the family intervention condition showed that parents made fewer negative or cutting remarks following three months of treatment and that problem-solving efforts came to replace negative emotional interactions (Doane et al., 1985). It could be that improved problem-solving efforts led to these reductions in negative inter-actions, but it is also possible that reduced levels of conflict allowed problem solving to take place. Family intervention programs incorporate multiple treatment components, so it is uncertain which components are therapeutically effective (Strachan, 1986).

Controlled investigations of family intervention programs have consistently demonstrated reductions in the risk of recurrent episodes as compared to pure drug treatment or drug treatment plus individual therapy (Goldstein, 1987b). One question that remains unanswered is whether these approaches prevent recurrent episodes or merely delay them (Goldstein, 1987b). The promising results of family-management-program research offer hope that such techniques will reduce the risks of recurrent episodes at relatively low cost. However, not all schizophrenics live with their families. Perhaps similar psychoeducational programs can be applied to nonfamily environments for schizophrenics, such as foster care homes or board-and-care homes (Strachan, 1986).

In sum, no one treatment approach meets all the needs of schizophrenics. An integrated, comprehensive model of treatment may be most effective in helping psychiatrically disabled people achieve their maximum level of social adjustment (Anthony & Liberman, 1986). This model may consist of drug therapy, hospitalization as needed, hospital-based social-learning programs, family intervention programs, skills training programs,

 Teaching families how to relate to schizophrenic members and solve family problems has been shown to reduce the incidence of recurrent acute episodes.

FIGURE 12.6 Monthly ratings of schizophrenic features.
The mean ratings of schizophrenic ("target") features (for example, hallucinations, delusions, and thought disorder) across a two-year period for participants in the Falloon study.
Source: Falloon et al. (1985), p. 891.

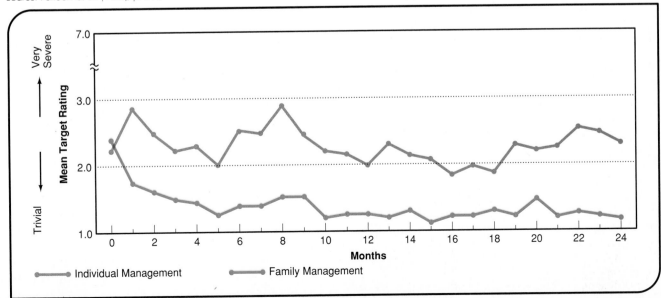

social self-help clubs and rehabilitation programs, and case-management services. Viewed within the diathesis–stress model, the combination of psychosocial, family, and environmental support programs may lower the level of stress below threshold so that recurrent episodes are less likely to occur. With lower stress, the schizophrenic may also not require as much antipsychotic medication (Goldstein, 1987b). Thus the potential for serious side effects will also be reduced.

DELUSIONAL (PARANOID) DISORDER

It may surprise you to learn that some forms of paranoid thinking affect normal people from time to time. Most of us feel suspicious of other people's motives at times or feel that others may have it "in" for us or are talking about us behind our backs. Among normals, however, paranoid thinking is usually short-lived and does not disrupt daily functioning (Haynes, 1986).

People who persistently hold paranoid beliefs that are clearly delusional may be classified as suffering from a delusional disorder. The diagnosis of **delusional (paranoid) disorder** applies to people with persistent delusions that often but not always involve paranoid themes. In delusional disorders, the delusional beliefs concern events that could conceivably occur in real life, such as infidelity of a spouse, persecution by others, or attracting the love of a famous person. The apparent plausibility of these beliefs may lead others to take them seriously and check them out before reaching the conclusion that they are unfounded. Apart from the delusion itself, the individual's behavior may not show evidence of obviously bizarre or odd behavior, as we see in the following case:

■ Mr. Polsen, a married, 42-year-old postal worker, was brought to the hospital by his wife because he had been insisting that there was a contract out on his life. Mr. Polsen told the doctors that the problem had started some four months ago when he was accused by his supervisor of tampering with a package, an offense that could have cost him his job. When he was exonerated at a formal hearing, his supervisor was "furious" and felt publicly humiliated, according to Mr. Polsen. Shortly afterwards, Mr. Polsen reported, his co-workers began avoiding him, turning away from him when he walked by, as if they didn't want to see him. He then began to think that they were talking about him behind his back, although he could never clearly make out what they were saying. He gradually became convinced that his co-workers were avoiding him because his boss had put a contract on his life. Things remained about the same for two months, when Mr. Polsen began to notice several large, white cars cruising up and down the street where he lived. This frightened him and he became convinced there were hit men in these cars. He then refused to leave his home without an escort and would run home in panic when he saw one of these cars approaching. Other than the reports of his belief that his life was in danger, his thinking and behavior appeared entirely normal on interview. He denied experiencing hallucinations and showed no other signs of psychotic behavior, except for the queer beliefs about his life being in danger. The diagnosis of Delusional Disorder, Persecutory type seemed the most appropriate, since there was no evidence that a contract had been taken on his life (hence, a persecutory delusion) and there was an absence of other clear signs of psychosis that might support a diagnosis of a schizophrenic type disorder.
Adapted from Spitzer et al., 1989, pp. 122–123 ■

Mr. Polsen's delusional belief that "hit teams" were pursuing him faded in about three weeks time with hospitalization and treatment with an antipsychotic drug. But his belief that he had been the subject of an attempted "hit" still stuck in his mind. A month following admission, he stated, "I guess my boss has called off the contract. He couldn't get away with it now without publicity" (Spitzer et al., 1989, p. 123).

Although delusions frequently occur in schizophrenia, delusional disorders are believed to be distinct from schizophrenia. Persons with delusional disorders do not exhibit the confused or jumbled thinking that is characteristic of schizophrenia. Hallucinations, when they occur, are not as prominent. Delusions in schizophrenia are embedded within a larger array of disturbed thoughts, perceptions, and behavior. In delusional disorders, the delusion itself may be the only clear sign of abnormality. Also, the paranoid content in paranoid schizophrenia is generally less coherent and more bizarre than in delusional disorders. The schizophrenic, for example, may believe that his or her mind is controlled by external forces that have bombarded the person's brain with messages. The paranoid thinking in delusional disorders often has an apparent plausibility, as noted above. Unlike schizophrenics, persons with delusional disorders are able to function normally in most respects. They are generally able to perform effectively in their work, although their marriages and other relationships may suffer because of their delusional concerns. The curious thing is that they appear quite normal at times when their delusions are not being discussed.

Delusional disorders should also be distinguished from another disorder in which paranoid thinking is present—paranoid personality disorder (discussed in Chapter 9). Recall that people with paranoid personality disorders may hold exaggerated or unwarranted suspicions of others, but not the outright delusions of the type that are found among people with delusional disorders or paranoid schizophrenia. For example, a paranoid personality may believe that he was passed over for a promotion because his boss "had it in for him," but would not maintain the unfounded belief, as in the example of Mr. Polsen, that his boss had actually put a contract on his life.

Various kinds of delusional disorders are described in Table 12.3. According to the DSM–III–R, delusional disorders are relatively uncommon, affecting perhaps about 0.03 percent (3 in 10,000) of the population.

TABLE 12.3 Types of Delusional Disorders

Type	Description
Erotomanic type	Beliefs that someone of higher social status, such as a movie star or political figure, is in love with you.
Grandiose type	Inflated beliefs about your worth, importance, power, knowledge, or identity, or beliefs that you hold a special relationship to a deity or a famous person. Cult leaders who believe they have special mystical powers of enlightenment may have delusional disorders of this type.
Jealous type	Delusions of jealousy in which the person may become convinced, without due cause, that his or her lover is unfaithful. The delusional person may misinterpret certain clues as signs of unfaithfulness, such as spots on the bedsheets.
Persecutory type	The most common type of delusional disorder, persecutory delusions involve themes of being conspired against, followed, cheated, spied upon, poisoned or drugged, or otherwise maligned or mistreated. Persons with such delusions may repeatedly institute court actions, or even commit acts of violence, against those whom they perceive are responsible for their mistreatment.
Somatic type	Delusions involving physical defects, disease, or disorder. Persons with these delusions may believe that foul odors are emanating from their bodies, or that internal parasites are eating away at them, or that certain parts of their body are unusually disfigured or ugly, or not functioning properly despite evidence to the contrary.

Source: *Adapted from DSM–III–R, pp. 199–203.*

Although delusional disorders occur in both sexes, they are slightly more common in females. Most delusional disorders begin between the ages of 40 and 55, although they can occur earlier in life. Once the delusion is established, it may be long-lasting, although the individual's concern about the delusion may wax and wane over time. In other cases, the delusion may disappear entirely for periods of time and then recur. For some, the delusional disorder may permanently disappear.

In this chapter we focused on schizophrenia, perhaps the most severe form of mental disturbance. We saw that research into the origins of schizophrenia highlights roles for both biological and psychosocial factors and their interaction. In the next chapter we turn to mental disorders that are directly caused by known biological abnormalities, such as strokes and brain tumors, or in which biological causes are presumed but have not yet been discovered, such as Alzheimer's disease.

A Closer Look
The Love Delusion

Erotomania, or the love delusion, is a delusional disorder in which the individual believes that he or she is loved by someone of high social status, even though the individual may have only a passing or even a nonexistent relationship with the alleged lover (Goldstein, 1986). Although the love delusion was once thought to be predominantly a female disorder, recent reports suggest that it may not be a rarity among men. It has been suggested, for example, that John Hinckley, Jr., who attempted to assassinate President Reagan, reportedly to impress actress Jody Foster, could be considered a case of erotomania (Stone, 1984). While women with erotomania may have a potential for violence when their attentions are rebuffed, men with this condition may be more likely to threaten or commit acts of violence in the pursuit of the objects of their unrequited desires (Goldstein, 1986). Mental-health professionals need to be aware of the potential for violence in the management of people who possess these delusions of love.

The following cases provide some examples of the love delusion:

- Mr. A., 35, was described as a "love-struck" suitor of a daughter of a former President of the United States. He was arrested for repeatedly harassing the woman in an attempt to win her love, although they were actually perfect strangers. Refusing to adhere to the judge's warnings to stop pestering the woman, he placed numerous phone calls to her from prison and was later transferred to a psychiatric facility, still declaring that they were very much in love.
- Mr. B. was arrested for breaching a court order to stop pestering a famous pop singer. A 44-year-old farmer, Mr. B. had followed his love interest across the country, constantly bombarding her with romantic overtures. He was committed to a psychiatric hospital, but maintained the belief that she'd always wait for him.
- Then there was Mr. C., a 32-year-old businessman, who believed that a well-known woman lawyer had fallen in love with him following a casual meeting. He constantly called and sent flowers and letters, declaring his love. While she repeatedly rejected his advances and eventually filed criminal charges for harassment, he felt that she was only testing his love by placing obstacles in his path. He abandoned his wife and business and his functioning declined. When the woman continued to reject him, he began sending her threatening letters and was committed to a psychiatric facility.

Adapted from Goldstein, 1986, p. 802 ■

 Some people do suffer from the delusion that they are loved by a famous person. They are said to have a delusional (paranoid) disorder, erotomanic type.

SUMMARY

History of the Concept of Schizophrenia

Emil Kraepelin was the first to describe the syndrome we now call schizophrenia. He labeled the disorder *dementia praecox* and believed that it was a disease that developed early in life and followed a progressively deteriorating course. Eugen Bleuler renamed the disorder *schizophrenia* (literally "split brain") and believed that it did not invariably begin in early life or follow a course of persistent deterioration. He also distinguished between primary symptoms (the four A's) and secondary symptoms. Kurt Schneider distinguished between first-rank or core symptoms that defined the disorder and secondary or second-rank symptoms that occurred in both schizophrenia and other disorders. Diagnostic criteria have changed over the years and became much tighter with the introduction of the DSM–III in 1980.

Prevalence of Schizophrenia

Schizophrenia is believed to affect between 1 and 2 percent of the general population at some point in their lives. Schizophrenics occupy one-quarter of all the hospital beds in the United States.

Phases of Schizophrenia

Schizophrenia usually begins to develop in late adolescence or early adulthood. The onset of the disorder may be relatively abrupt or gradual. The period of deterioration preceding the onset of acute symptoms is called the *prodromal phase*. An acute episode involves the emergence of clear psychotic features, such as hallucinations, delusions, and bizarre behavior. The *residual phase* follows acute episodes and is characterized by a level of functioning that was typical of the prodromal phase.

Briefer Forms of Psychosis

Schizophrenia is distinguished from brief reactive psychosis, which is an acute psychosis lasting for less than a month with eventual full return of functioning. Schizophreniform disorder consists of schizophrenic-like behaviors that last less than six months' duration. If it persists beyond six months, the disorder is relabeled as schizophrenia.

Schizophrenia-Spectrum Disorders

Schizophrenia-spectrum disorders refer to schizophrenic-type disorders that range in severity from milder personality disorders, such as schizotypal and schizoid types, to schizophrenia itself. Schizophrenia-spectrum disorders may also include schizoaffective disorder, which involves the intermingling of psychotic features and a mood disturbance. Researchers believe there may be a common genetic link among the schizophrenia-spectrum disorders.

Features of Schizophrenia

Schizophrenia is characterized by disturbances in a wide range of psychological processes, including level of functioning, thinking and speech, attention, perception, emotion, self-identity, volition, interpersonal behavior, and psychomotor behavior. Among the more prominent features are disorders in the content of thought (delusions) and form of thought (thought disorder), as well as the presence of perceptual distortions (hallucinations) and emotional disturbances (flattened or inappropriate affect). Evidence is accumulating that schizophrenics have deficits in the automatic brain processes that control attention to external stimuli.

Types of Schizophrenia

The DSM–III–R recognizes five types of schizophrenia: disorganized, catatonic, paranoid, undifferentiated, and residual types. Another type, simple schizophrenia, is no longer used but describes behavior patterns that would probably be diagnosed today under the category of schizotypal personality disorder. The disorganized (formerly hebephrenic) type describes schizophrenics with grossly disorganized behavior and thought processes. Florid hallucinations are common. The catatonic type describes schizophrenics with grossly impaired motor behaviors, such as those who maintain fixed postures or remain mute for long periods of time. Paranoid type describes those who hold paranoid delusions that tend to be complex and systematized. The undifferentiated type is a catch-all category that applies to schizophrenics with active psychotic behaviors who don't fit any of the other types. The residual type applies to those in a residual phase who do not have prominent psychotic behaviors at the time of evaluation.

Dimensions of Schizophrenia

Researchers have identified various patterns or dimensions of schizophrenia. Process schizophrenia is associated with a gradual decline in functioning prior to the acute phase, whereas reactive schizophrenia is characterized by an acute onset. While process schizophrenia was generally associated with more unfavorable outcomes than reactive schizophrenia in earlier research, the tighter diagnostic criteria for defining schizophrenia by present DSM standards appear to have limited the predictive value of this basis of classification. Researchers have also distinguished between two sets of features or symptoms of schizophrenia—positive symptoms, or behavioral excesses, and negative symptoms, or behavioral deficits. Some researchers believe that these symptom clusters correspond to two basic types of schizophrenia, Type I schizophrenia (positive symptoms, abrupt onset, preserved intelligence, more favorable response to antipsychotic drugs) and Type II schizophrenia (negative symptoms, gradual onset, greater chronicity and intellectual impairment, and poorer response to antipsychotic drugs). But research evidence has not been fully supportive of the distinction between these two types.

Theoretical Perspectives

In the traditional psychoanalytic model, schizophrenia represents a regression to a psychological state corresponding to early infancy in which the proddings of the id produce bizarre, socially deviant behavior and give rise to hallucinations and delusions. Learning theorists propose that schizophrenic behavior may result from a lack of social reinforcement that leads to gradual detachment from the social environment and increased attention to one's private fantasy world. Modeling and selective reinforcement of bizarre behavior may explain some forms of schizophrenic behavior in the hospital setting.

Research has demonstrated strong linkages between biological factors and schizophrenia. Evidence for genetic factors comes from studies of family patterns of schizophrenia, twin studies, and adoption studies. It appears that increased risk of schizophrenia follows biological parentage, not adoptive parentage. The mode of genetic transmission remains unknown, but several models have been proposed. But environmental factors also appear to play a role, and many researchers have adopted the diathesis–stress model to account for the interplay between a genetic predisposition (diathesis) and environmental stress in explaining the development of schizophrenia. The diathesis–stress model has been supported by studies of high-risk (HR) children (children of schizophrenic biological parents) that show that both genetic risk and environmental stress appear to be involved in the development of schizophrenia. Researchers have identified certain characteristics or markers that may increase the vulnerability to schizophrenia of high-risk children, while other factors, called protective factors, may lower risk. Most researchers believe that the neurotransmitter dopamine plays a role in schizophrenia, especially in the more flagrant features of the disorder. Some researchers also believe that at least some cases of schizophrenia may be caused by a slow-acting virus. Evidence of brain dysfunction in schizophrenia is accumulating, leading researchers to speculate that structural damage in the brain may play a causal role, at least in some forms of schizophrenia.

Various family factors have been posited as playing a role in schizophrenia. While research has not demonstrated that family factors directly cause schizophrenia, there is accumulating evidence that such family factors as communication deviance (CD) and expressed emotion (EE) may act as sources of stress that increase the risk of development or recurrence of schizophrenia among people with a genetic predisposition.

The sociocultural perspective focuses on the role that social ills like poverty and overcrowding may play in the development of schizophrenia. While such problems may increase the risk of schizophrenia, at least among people with a genetic predisposition, schizophrenics may also drift into poverty due to a lack of coping behavior. Other sociocultural theorists have attempted to explain schizophrenic behavior as a type of societal role and as a search for identity in a world that squelches individuality and requires conformity.

Treatment

Treatment of schizophrenia tends to be multifaceted, incorporating pharmacological and psychosocial approaches. Antipsychotic medication tends to stem the more flagrant aspects of the disorder, reducing the need for long-term hospitalization and the risk of recurrent episodes. But drugs are not effective in all cases, nor do they effect a cure. Long-term use of antipsychotic drugs may also produce a potentially disabling movement disorder, tardive dyskinesia, so that prescribing physicians need to weigh carefully the relative risks and benefits of long-term treatment with these drugs.

Psychodynamic approaches have not been shown to be effective in treating schizophrenia. Learning-based approaches, such as token economy systems and social skills training, have achieved some success in increasing adaptive functioning and improving interpersonal behavior of schizophrenics. Psychosocial-rehabilitation approaches focus on helping schizophrenics adapt more successfully to occupational and social roles in the community. Family intervention programs help families to cope with the burdens of care, communicate more clearly, and learn more helpful ways of relating to the schizophrenic member.

Delusional (Paranoid) Disorder

People with delusional disorder hold delusional beliefs that are less bizarre than schizophrenic delusions, involving events that could conceivably occur in real life. The delusions are often plausible enough to induce others to check them out. The delusion itself is often the only clear sign of abnormality, whereas schizophrenic delusions are embedded within a more general pattern of disturbed thinking, perceptions, and behavior. People with paranoid personality disorder, by contrast, may hold unwarranted suspicions of others but not outright delusions. There are five types of delusional disorder: erotomanic, grandiose, jealous, persecutory, and somatic.

13 Organic Disorders and Abnormal Behavior

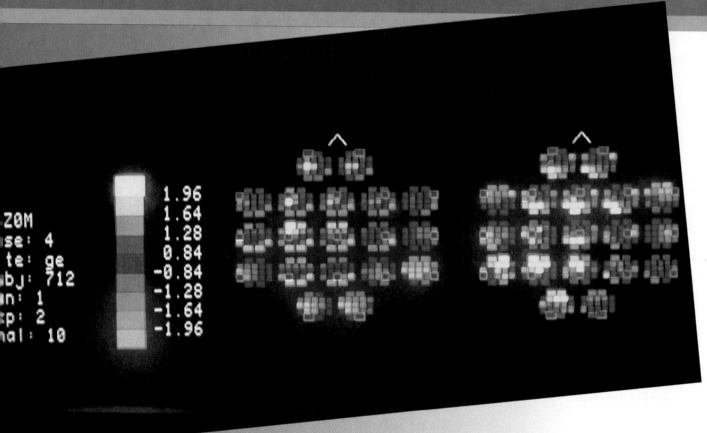

TRUTH OR FICTION?

■ ____ A man with a brain tumor patted the heads of fire hydrants and parking meters in the belief that they were children.

■ ____ The most frequently identified cause of delirium is abrupt withdrawal from alcohol or other drugs.

■ ____ After a motorcycle accident, a medical student failed to recognize the woman whom he had married a few weeks earlier.

■ ____ Dementia is a normal function of the aging process.

■ ____ Alzheimer's disease is found only among the elderly.

■ ____ Alzheimer's disease is caused by aluminum ingestion.

■ ____ When the symptoms of syphilis disappear by themselves, there is nothing to be concerned about.

■ ____ Football players and prizefighters can recover completely from being knocked out without lingering cognitive effects.

■ ____ Julius Caesar and Vincent van Gogh suffered from epilepsy.

LEARNING OBJECTIVES

When you have completed your study of Chapter 13, you should be able to:

ORGANIC MENTAL DISORDERS AND SYNDROMES (pp. 455–459)
1. Describe the features of organic mental disorders.
2. Discuss problems in diagnosing organic mental disorders.
3. Distinguish between organic mental disorders and organic mental syndromes.
4. Describe the features of organic mental syndromes.

DELIRIUM (pp. 459–460)
5. Define *delirium*, and discuss the causes of various kinds of delirium, including the DT's.

AMNESTIC SYNDROME (pp. 460–461)
6. Discuss the features and causes of amnestic syndrome.
7. Discuss the origins and features of Korsakoff's syndrome.

DEMENTIAS (pp. 461–469)
8. Discuss whether or not dementias are a normal feature of aging.
9. Discuss the relationship between depression and memory loss among the elderly and describe cognitive-behavioral approaches to treating depression in the elderly.
10. Discuss the incidence and features of Alzheimer's disease.
11. Discuss the impact of Alzheimer's disease on the family.
12. Discuss theoretical perspectives on Alzheimer's disease.
13. Discuss the features of multi-infarct dementia.
14. Discuss the features of Pick's disease.

DISEASES OF THE BASAL GANGLIA (pp. 469–472)
15. Discuss the features, origins, and treatment of Parkinson's disease.
16. Discuss the features of Huntington's disease.
17. Discuss the genetic transmission of Huntington's disease.

INFECTIONS OF THE BRAIN (pp. 472–473)
18. Discuss the features of encephalitis, meningitis, neuro-syphilis, and AIDS dementia complex.

BRAIN TRAUMAS (pp. 473–474)
19. Discuss the kinds of problems brought about by concussions, contusions, and lacerations of the brain.

CEREBROVASCULAR DISORDERS (pp. 474–475)
20. Discuss the features of strokes and cerebral hemorrhages.

BRAIN TUMORS (p. 475)
21. Discuss the features of brain tumors.

NUTRITIONAL DEFICIENCIES (pp. 475–476)
22. Discuss the features of pellagra and beriberi.

ENDOCRINE DISORDERS (p. 476)
23. Discuss the features of the disorders caused by thyroid and adrenal dysfunctions.

EPILEPSY (pp. 476–479)
24. Discuss the stigma attached to epilepsy.
25. Discuss the various types of epilepsy.
26. Discuss various myths and facts about epilepsy.
27. Discuss the treatment of epilepsy.

I n *The Man Who Mistook His Wife for a Hat*, neurologist Oliver Sacks (1985) tells of Dr. P., a distinguished musician and teacher who had lost the ability to recognize objects visually. For example, Dr. P. failed to recognize the faces of his students at the music school. When a student spoke, however, Dr. P. immediately recognized his or her voice. Not only did the professor fail to discriminate faces visually but sometimes he perceived faces where none existed. He patted the heads of fire hydrants and parking meters, which he took to be children. He warmly addressed the rounded knobs on furniture. These peculiarities were generally dismissed as jokes and laughed off by Dr. P. and his colleagues. After all, Dr. P. was well known for his oddball humor and jests. But Dr. P.'s music remained as accomplished as ever, his general health seemed fine, and so these misperceptions seemed little to be concerned about.

Not until three years later did Dr. P. seek a neurological evaluation. His ophthalmologist had found that although Dr. P.'s eyes were healthy, he had problems interpreting visual stimulation. So he made the referral to Dr. Sacks, a neurologist. When Dr. Sacks engaged Dr. P. in conversation, Dr. P.'s eyes fixated oddly on miscellaneous features of Dr. Sack's face—his nose, then his right ear, then his chin, sensing parts of his face but apparently not connecting them in a meaningful pattern. When Dr. P. sought to put on his shoe after a physical examination, he confused his foot with the shoe. When preparing to leave, Dr. P. looked around for his hat, and then . . .

> [Dr. P.] reached out his hand, and took hold of his wife's head, tried to lift it off, to put it on. He had apparently mistaken his wife for a hat! His wife looked as if she was used to such things. (Sacks, 1985, p. 10)

Dr. P.'s peculiar behavior may seem amusing to some, but his loss of visual perception was tragic. Although Dr. P. could identify abstract forms and shapes—a cube, for example—he no longer recognized the faces of his family, nor his own. Some features of particular faces would strike a chord of recognition. For example, he could recognize a picture of Einstein from the distinctive hair and mustache, and a picture of his own brother from the square jaw and big teeth. But he was responding to isolated features, not grasping the facial patterns as wholes.

Sacks recounts a final test:

> It was still a cold day, in early spring, and I had thrown my coat and gloves on the sofa.
>
> "What is this?" I asked, holding up a glove.
>
> "May I examine it?" he asked, and, taking it from me, he proceeded to examine it as he had examined the geometrical shapes.
>
> "A continuous surface," he announced at last, "infolded on itself. It appears to have"—he hesitated—"five outpouchings, if this is the word."
>
> "Yes," I said cautiously. "You have given me a description. Now tell me what it is."
>
> "A container of some sort?"
>
> "Yes," I said, "and what would it contain?"
>
> "It would contain its contents!" said Dr. P., with a laugh. "There are many possibilities. It could be a change-purse, for example, for coins of five sizes. It could. . . ."
>
> I interrupted the blarney flow. "Does it not look familiar? Do you think it might contain, might fit, a part of your body?"

> No light of recognition dawned on his face.
>
> No child would have the power to see and speak of "a continuous surface . . . infolded on itself," but any child, any infant, would immediately know a glove as a glove, see it as familiar, as going with a hand. Dr. P. didn't. He saw nothing as familiar. Visually, he was lost in a world of lifeless abstractions. (Sacks, 1985, p. 13)

Later, we might add, Dr. P. accidentally put the glove on his hand, exclaiming, "My God, it's a glove!" (Sacks, 1985, p. 13). His brain immediately seized the pattern of **tactile** information, although his visual brain centers were powerless to provide a confirmatory interpretation. Dr. P., that is, showed lack of visual knowledge—a symptom referred to as visual **agnosia,** derived from Greek roots meaning "without knowledge." Still, Dr. P.'s musical abilities and verbal skills remained intact. He was able to function, to dress himself, take a shower and eat his meals by singing various songs to himself—for example, eating songs and dressing songs—that helped him coordinate his actions. However, if his dressing song were interrupted while he was dressing himself, he would lose his train of thought and be unable to recognize not only the clothes that his wife had laid out but also his own body. When the music stopped, so did his ability to make sense of the world. Sacks later learned that Dr. P. had a massive tumor in the area of the brain that processes visual information. Dr. P. was apparently unaware of his deficits, having filled his visually empty world with music in order to function and imbue his life with meaning and purpose.

 It is true that a man with a brain tumor patted the heads of fire hydrants and parking meters in the belief that they were children. The tumor caused dysfunctions in the parts of his brain that processed visual information.

Dr. P.'s case is unusual in the peculiarity of his symptoms, but it illustrates the universal dependence of psychological functioning on an intact brain. The case also shows how some people adjust—sometimes so gradually that the changes are all but imperceptible—to developing physical or organic problems. Mr. P.'s visual problems might have been relatively more debilitating in a person who was less talented or who had less social support to draw upon.

ABNORMAL BEHAVIORS WITH ORGANIC ORIGINS

In this chapter we consider abnormal behaviors with organic origins. In many disorders discussed in earlier chapters, there is *possible* involvement of organic factors, ranging from genetic influences to imbalances in neurotransmitters. Consider the apparent roles of dopamine in schizophrenia and norepinephrine in the mood disorders, for example. In the abnormal behaviors covered in this chapter, however, there is frank or assumed organic causation, as from trauma to the brain, disease, or nutritional imbalances. In disorders with *possible* organic involvement, such as schizophrenia and the mood disorders, the causal connections between specific organic factors (in these cases, neurotransmitters) and abnormal behaviors have not been fully revealed. Put another way: Abnormal behaviors like schizophrenia and bipolar disorder are known to have biological *correlates*, but the significance of these correlates in accounting for the behavioral patterns have not been clearly established. The abnormal behaviors discussed in this chapter, however, either have known biological causes or are presumed to be caused by biological factors that have not yet been uncovered.

The DSM–III–R refers to such behavioral patterns as **organic mental disorders.** The essential feature of "organic mental disorders" is that the disorders are associated with temporary or permanent dysfunctions of the brain (p. 98). Organic mental disorders affect cognitive abilities and daily functioning, such as thought and memory, feeling states, hygiene, and grooming (see Table 13.1).

When the brain is damaged by injury, stroke, or progressive deterioration, there may be rapid or gradual decline in intellectual, social, and occupational functioning. Affected people may become completely dependent on others to meet basic needs in feeding, toileting, and grooming. In some cases, these abnormal behaviors result from intoxication by, or withdrawal from, alcohol or other drugs, or from the ingestion of toxins. Although the disorders discussed in this chapter all involve known

or presumed biological causes, it appears that psychological and environmental factors also play a role in determining symptoms and victims' personal abilities to cope with cognitive and physical defects.

Diagnostic Problems

The diagnosis of abnormal behaviors with organic origins can be a difficult task, for brain damage may result in a variety of symptoms, depending on such factors as the location and extent of the damage, the person's coping ability, and, as in the case of Dr. P., the availability of social support. For example, people may be acutely depressed and frightened by their awareness of a decline in their intellectual functioning, especially when they can no longer meet the daily requirements of their lives or when no one is available to help them.

Damage to the same area of the brain does not invariably result in the same pattern of symptoms, perhaps because of minor shifts in the site of the damage, perhaps because of psychological factors—like histories of learning—that interact with organic factors. Moreover, organic factors sometimes cause abnormal behavior patterns such as depression, disorientation, and suspiciousness. These patterns resemble those occurring in other mental disorders, such as depressive disorders and schizophrenia.

Neurological examinations and neuropsychological testing are used to detect brain damage. Advanced screening techniques, such as the CAT and PET scans (described in Chapters 3 and 12), probe for organic defects that are not revealed by neurological examination. CAT scans generally help clinicians identify structural defects like tumors, whereas PET scans provide insight into apparently structurally intact regions that are made dysfunctional by strokes or other causes. A timely and thorough evaluation can spell the difference

---

TABLE 13.1 Common Features of Organic Mental Disorders

Decline in intellectual functioning or memory. Difficulty in speech, comprehension of language, computation, and loss of general knowledge. Loss of memory for recent rather than remote events is more characteristic of organic impairment.

Disorientation.

Motor impairment, such as difficulties walking or involuntary muscle tremors.

Impaired judgment or difficulty in making proper decisions, such as dressing improperly or choosing to walk home in a snowstorm.

Unstable moods and emotional agitation; for example, rapid changes from laughing to crying, or vice versa.

Personality changes in later life.

Absence of psychosocial factors that might explain abnormal behaviors of decline in intellectual functioning (for example, depression following loss of a loved one).

People whose brains are damaged by injury, stroke, or progressive degeneration may become dependent on others to meet their basic needs. The functional impairment is related to the location and extent of the damage to the brain and to psychosocial factors such as history of learning and availability of social support.

between recovery and impairment—in some cases between life and death—since many organic conditions are treatable or reversible, particularly when they are diagnosed early. And the appropriate treatment for an organic mental disorder may be quite different from that for a similar condition without clear organic causes. For example, disorders caused by brain tumors may be treated successfully with surgery, not with psychotherapy.

The extent and location of brain damage help determine the range and severity of impairment. By and large, the more widespread the damage, the greater and more extensive the impairment in functioning. The location of the damage is also critical, since many brain structures or regions perform specialized functions. Damage to the temporal lobe, for example, is associated with defects in memory and attention, whereas damage to the occipital lobe may result in visual-spatial deficits, such as Dr. P.'s loss of ability to recognize familiar faces.

Organic Mental Disorders versus Organic Mental Syndromes

According to the DSM–III–R, **organic mental syndromes** are clusters of behavioral or psychological symptoms that are believed to be caused by organic disorders that affect the brain. These syndromes involve disruptions in thought, personality, mood, memory, perception, and effects due to intoxication or withdrawal from psychoactive substances such as alcohol and drugs. Each of them may reflect different organic causes. For example, delirium is a syndrome involving a state of mental confusion and difficulty focusing attention, among other features (see Table 13.2), that may be caused by various physical disorders or conditions, such as a blow to the head, a brain infection, or intoxication or withdrawal from various psychoactive substances. When the cause of the syndrome can be related to a specific organic factor, the syndrome is coded on Axis I under the category of *organic mental disorders*. Thus, a state of delirium in a chronic alcoholic who suddenly stops drinking is classified as an organic mental disorder labeled Alcohol Withdrawal Delirium. If the delirium were due to an infection like pneumonia, it too would be classified as an organic mental disorder on Axis I, but its cause, pneumonia, would be coded on Axis III (Physical Disorders and Conditions).

Dementia is an organic mental syndrome involving a general deterioration in mental ability (see Table 13.2) that may be caused by such organic factors as Alzheimer's disease, multiple strokes, or brain infections. A dementia associated with Alzheimer's disease, for example, would be classified as an organic mental disorder labeled Primary Degenerative Dementia of the Alzheimer's Type. Since Alzheimer's disease is a physical illness, it is coded on Axis III.

TABLE 13.2 Features of Organic Mental Syndromes

Organic Mental Syndromes	Features
Delirium	Impaired attention (mind wanders, can't shift attention to new tasks); disorganized thinking marked by rambling or incoherent speech; disorientation, reduced level of consciousness (for example, difficulty staying awake); perceptual disturbances (for example, hallucinations or misinterpretations of sensory stimuli)
Dementia*	Memory deficits in recalling newly learned information, past personal information (for example, one's birthplace), or information of common knowledge (names of past presidents); deficiencies in abstract thinking; impaired judgment; disorders of higher functioning, such as disorders in use of language (aphasia) or ability to carry through a planned series of movements (apraxia); personality changes (for example, a normally active person who becomes lethargic, or a person who no longer seems to be him- or herself to others, or a person who shows accentuation of preexisting traits, such as irritability or compulsivity)
Amnestic Syndrome*	Clear evidence of impairment in both short-term and long-term memory
Organic Delusional Syndrome*	Evidence of prominent delusions, most commonly delusions of persecution
Organic Hallucinosis*	Evidence of prominent or recurrent hallucinations
Organic Mood Syndrome*	Presence of persistent and prominent changes in mood, such as depression or elation
Organic Anxiety Syndrome*	Presence of recurrent, prominent panic attacks or complaints of generalized anxiety
Organic Personality Syndrome*	Disturbance of personality that may be either a lifelong style or represent a change or accentuation of previous personality traits
Intoxication	Maladaptive behavior associated with ingestion of psychoactive substances: for example, belligerence, difficulties meeting work or family responsibilities, or impaired judgment
Withdrawal	Evidence of specific patterns of withdrawal effects associated with cessation or reduction of use of psychoactive substances that the individual had used regularly

* For each of these syndromes, the symptoms are found not to occur exclusively during periods of delirium.
Source: *Adapted from the DSM–III–R, pp. 100–118.*

TABLE 13.3 Features of Delirium

| | Level of Severity | | |
	Mild	Moderate	Severe
Emotion	Apprehension	Fear	Panic
Cognition & Perception	Confusion, racing thoughts	Disorientation, delusions	Meaningless mumbling, vivid hallucinations
Behavior	Tremors	Muscle spasms	Seizures
Autonomic activity	Abnormally fast heartbeat (tachycardia)	Perspiration	Fever

Source: *Adapted from Freemon, 1981, p. 82.*

The most common organic mental syndromes are delirium, dementia, intoxication, and withdrawal, according to the DSM–III–R. We next consider the abnormal behaviors characterized by delirium, amnesia, and dementia. Problems of intoxication and withdrawal were discussed in Chapter 10. We then discuss various physical illnesses and disorders and how they affect psychological functioning and behavior.

DELIRIUM

Delirium derives from the Latin roots *de-*, meaning "from," and *lira*, meaning "line" or "furrow." It means straying from the line, or the norm, in perception, cognition, and behavior. Delirium is characterized by severe difficulty in concentration and by psychological disorganization that is disclosed by rambling, incoherent speech (see Table 13.3). Delirious people find it difficult to tune out irrelevant stimuli or to shift their attention to new tasks. They may speak excitedly, but their speech lacks meaning and coherence (Freemon, 1981). Disorientation as to time and place is common; disorientation to person (the identities of oneself and others) is not. Delirious people may report hallucinations, especially visual hallucinations. Perceptual disturbances may include misinterpretations of sensory stimuli (for example, confusing an alarm clock for a fire bell), or illusions (feeling as if the bed has an electrical charge passing through it). There can be marked retardation of movement into a state resembling catatonia. There can be rapid fluctuations between restlessness and stupor. Restlessness is typified by insomnia; agitated, aimless movements; even bolting out of bed or striking out at nonexistent objects. Or victims may have to struggle to stay awake.

Unlike dementia, which involves a progressive deterioration of mental functioning, delirium may clear up spontaneously or be completely reversed with successful treatment of the underlying organic condition. The course of delirium is relatively brief, usually about a week, rarely longer than a month. If the organic condition persists or deteriorates, however, delirium may progress to coma or death. During the course of delirium, people's mental state will often fluctuate between periods of clarity ("lucid intervals"), which are most common in the morning, and periods of confusion and disorientation. Delirium is generally worse in the dark and following sleepless nights.

Delirium is believed to result from a combination of generalized disturbance of the brain's metabolic processes and imbalances in the levels of neurotransmitters. As a result, the ability to process information is impaired and confusion reigns. The abilities to think and speak clearly, interpret sensory stimuli, and attend to the environment decline. Delirium may occur abruptly, as with seizures or head injuries, or it may gradually develop over hours or days, generally because of infection, fever, or metabolic disorders. The most common causes of delirium are infection, head trauma or seizures, metabolic disturbances caused by diseases of the liver or kidneys, hypoglycemia (low blood sugar), thiamine deficiencies, effects of surgery, and intoxication or withdrawal from psychoactive substances. Often the cause cannot be identified.

The DT's

States of delirium may also result from ingestion of toxic substances. Potentially lethal mushrooms, for example, can produce delirium that is accompanied by vivid hallucinations. But the most frequently identified cause of delirium is abrupt withdrawal from drugs, most commonly alcohol (Freemon, 1981).

 It is true that the most frequently identified cause of delirium is abrupt withdrawal from alcohol or other drugs.

Delirium tremens (the DT's) sometimes follow abrupt withdrawal from alcohol, especially when use has been chronic. Tremors become evident within the first hours of withdrawal (Victor & Adams, 1953). Convulsive seizures may occur after 24 hours, then subside, and the individual may appear normal for the next day or two (Freemon, 1981). Then an acute period of delirium begins in which the patient may be terrorized by wild and frightening hallucinations, as of "bugs crawling down walls" or on the person's skin. The DT's can last for a week or more and are best treated in a hospital setting, where the patient can be carefully monitored and the symptoms treated with tranquilizers and environmental support. The following case illustrates the disorientation, perceptual disturbances, problems in attention, and disorganized thought and speech that characterize the DT's:

> ■ A divorced carpenter, 43 years of age, is brought to a hospital emergency department by his sister. She reports that he has at least a 5-year history of consuming large amounts of alcohol (a fifth of cheap wine) on a daily basis. He has had many blackouts from drinking, and he has lost several jobs due to drinking. He ran out of money three days earlier, at which time he stopped drinking abruptly, and he has been begging for money to buy his meals. On examination, he seems keyed up, talking almost non-stop in an unfocused and rambling manner. He appears confused and believes that the doctor is his brother, calling him by his brother's name. There is evidence of a hand tremor, and he picks at "bugs" that he believes he sees on the hospital bedsheets. He is disoriented as to place and time; he apparently thinks that he is in a parking lot of a supermarket rather than a hospital. He is apprehensive and fears that an impending holocaust is about to end the world. He has difficulty concentrating. His perceptions apparently drift into hallucinations of fiery car crashes that seem to be prompted by sounds of hospital carts crashing against each other in the hallways.
>
> Adapted from Spitzer et al., 1989, pp. 224–226 ■

AMNESTIC SYNDROME

Amnestic syndrome, or amnesia, is characterized by a dramatic decline in memory functioning that is not connected with states of delirium or dementia. Amnesia is characterized by inability to learn new material (short-term memory) and to recall information from the past that was previously known (long-term memory). Problems with short-term memory may be revealed by the inability to remember the names of or even recognize people whom the person met just five or ten minutes earlier. But immediate memory, as measured by ability to repeat back a series of numbers, seems to be unimpaired in the amnestic syndrome. The number series is unlikely to be recalled later, however, no matter how often it is rehearsed.

Amnestic syndrome frequently follows a traumatic event, such as a blow to the head, an electric shock, or an operation. For example, a head injury may prevent people from remembering events that occurred before the accident. The victim of an automobile accident or a football player who is knocked unconscious may be unable to remember events that occurred up to several

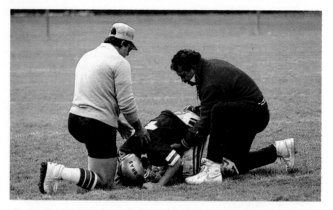

Amnestic syndrome can follow a traumatic injury such as a blow to the head. This football player may not be able to recall events that occurred for several minutes prior to his being tackled on the preceding play, as well as the collision itself.

minutes before the injury. The accident victim may not remember leaving the house. The football player may not remember leaving the locker room. Consider the following case:

> ■ A medical student was rushed to the hospital after he was thrown from a motorcycle. His parents were with him in his hospital room when he awakened. As his parents were explaining what had happened to him, the door suddenly flew open and his flustered wife, whom he had married a few weeks earlier, rushed into the room, leaped onto his bed, and began to caress him and expressed her great relief that he was not seriously injured. After several minutes of expressing her love and reassurance, his wife departed and the flustered student looked at his mother and asked: "Who is she?"
>
> Adapted from Freemon, 1981, p. 96 ■

 It is true that after a motorcycle accident, a medical student failed to recognize the woman whom he had married a few weeks earlier.

The medical student's long-term memory loss not only included memories dating back to the accident itself, but also further back to an earlier time in life before he was married or had even met his wife. But like most victims of post-traumatic amnesia, the medical student recovered completely.

In amnestic syndrome, recall of recently acquired information often suffers greater decrements than memory of distant events. Amnestic people are more likely to remember events from their childhood than last evening's dinner, for example. Amnestic syndrome produces some disorientation, and amnestic people may attempt to fill the gaps in their memories with imaginary events. They tend to lack insight into their loss, however, and they may deny their memory problems to themselves and others. Or they may admit that they have some problem with memory, but appear apathetic about it, showing a kind of emotional blandness, according to the DSM–III–R.

Although amnestic people may have profuse memory losses, their general intelligence tends to remain within a normal range (Butters et al., 1978). Thus, memory loss in pure amnesia may be distinguished from that occurring in progressive dementias like Alzheimer's disease, in which memory functioning and intellectual capacity both deteriorate gradually (Butters et al., 1986). Early detection and diagnosis of the causes of memory problems are vital to many sufferers because between 20 to 30 percent of them have correctable problems (Cohen, 1986).

Other causes of amnesia include secondary effects of surgical procedures on the brain, sudden loss of oxygen to the brain **(hypoxia)**, infection, and **infarction** (blockage) of the blood vessels supplying various parts of the brain.

Alcohol Amnestic Disorder

The most common cause of amnestic syndrome according to the DSM–III–R is thiamine deficiency connected with chronic alcohol abuse. Alcoholics tend to take poor care of their nutritional needs and may not follow a diet that is rich enough in vitamin B_1, or thiamine. Thiamine deficiencies may produce an irreversible form of brain damage called **alcohol amnestic disorder** or **Korsakoff's syndrome.** Korsakoff's syndrome is not limited to alcoholics, however, and it has been reported in other groups who experience thiamine deficiencies, such as prisoners of war (Smith, 1946).

Korsakoff's syndrome produces substantial losses in short-term and long-term memory and inability to acquire new memories. These memory deficits are be-

lieved to result from the destruction of brain tissue due to bleeding (Victor et al., 1971). Despite these memory losses, patients with Korsakoff's syndrome may retain their general level of intelligence (Huppert & Piercy, 1979). They are often described as being superficially friendly but lacking in insight, unable to discriminate between actual events and the implausible or wild stories they invent to fill the gaps in their memories. Korsakoff sufferers sometimes become grossly disoriented and confused and require custodial care.

Korsakoff's syndrome often follows an acute attack of another disorder, **Wernicke's disease,** which is characterized by confusion and disorientation, difficulty maintaining balance while walking **(ataxia),** and paralysis of the muscles that control eye movements. While these symptoms may pass, the individual is often left with Korsakoff's syndrome and enduring memory impairment. If, however, Wernicke's disease is treated promptly with major doses of vitamin B_1, Korsakoff's syndrome may not ensue. Once Korsakoff's syndrome has set in, it usually lasts until death, although slight improvement may be possible, according to the DSM–III–R. Most patients with Korsakoff's syndrome suffer losses of long-term memories going back 20 years or longer (Albert et al., 1979).

DEMENTIAS

Most of us experience mild declines in memory by about the age of 50, followed by modest changes in visual-spatial skills by age 60, and then some slight changes in language skills and the ability to think abstractly by about age 70 (NIMH, 1987). Despite earlier beliefs that people naturally grow senile as they age, the processes of normal aging tend to involve relatively modest

Chronic alcoholics are prone to developing Korsakoff's syndrome, which gives rise to profound deficits in memory and acquisition of new information. Alcoholism is often associated with dietary inadequacies, and Korsakoff's syndrome has been linked to deficient intake of the vitamin thiamine.

A CLOSER LOOK
Organic and Psychological Changes in the Elderly

How old would you be if you didn't know how old you was?

Satchel Paige

Old age isn't so bad when you consider the alternative.
Maurice Chevalier

A number of physical changes accompany our advances toward our later years. Changes in calcium metabolism cause the bones to grow brittle and heighten the risk of breaks from falls. The skin grows less elastic, creating wrinkles and folds. The senses become less keen, so that older people see and hear less acutely. The elderly need more time (called *reaction time*) to respond to stimuli, whether they are driving or taking intelligence tests. For example, elderly drivers require more time to react to traffic signals and other cars. Our immune system functions less effectively with increasing age, so that we become more vulnerable to illness.

Cognitive changes occur as well. The elderly exhibit some drop-off in general cognitive ability as gauged by intelligence tests. The decline is sharpest on timed items, as on the performance scales of the Wechsler Adult Intelligence Scale. We understand little about the causes of these declines in cognitive functioning (Storandt, 1983). Loss of motivation and of sensory acuity play a part. Psychologist B. F. Skinner (1983) contends that much of the decline reflects an "aging environment"—not an aging person. That is, much of the behavior of older people goes unreinforced, especially after retirement. Consider that nursing home residents who are reinforced for retaining recent

events display improved scores on memory tests (Langer et al., 1979; Wolinsky, 1982). Some cognitive changes may reflect psychological problems, like depression, rather than the physical aspects of aging (Albert, 1981). In such cases, the cognitive impairment is not considered to be a feature of an organic mental disorder. If the underlying depression is treated, cognitive performance may also improve. But depression often goes unrecognized among the elderly, as we shall see.

Depression in the Elderly Depression is epidemic among the elderly—the most common emotional problem they face (Butler & Lewis, 1982). Estimates of the prevalence of depression range between 13 and 45 percent of older people (Gurland et al., 1980; Rapp et al., 1988). Suicide, a clear marker of depression, is also most frequent among the elderly (McIntosh, 1985) (see Chapter 8). Infirm older people may be at yet greater risk of depression. One-quarter to one-third of 150 elderly medical inpatients in one Veteran's Administration hospital had diagnosable mental conditions, with the majority of these meeting the criteria for a depressive disorder (Rapp et al., 1988).

The elderly may be especially vulnerable to depression because of the stresses of coping with the life events of the "golden years"—retirement, physical illness or incapacitation, placement in a residential facility or nursing home, and the death of a spouse, siblings, lifetime friends and acquaintances. Retirement, whether voluntary or forced, may sap the sense of meaningfulness in life. Deaths of relatives and friends not only induce grief but remind the elderly of their own advanced years and reduce the

Although there is a decline in some aspects of physical and cognitive functioning, people can remain physically active and engage in rewarding activities in late adulthood, as shown in these photographs. Elderly people whose behavior goes unreinforced, however, may suffer from loss of motivation and feelings of depression.

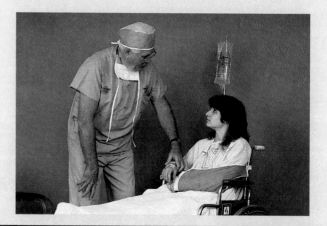

availability of social supports. Elderly adults may feel incapable of forming new friendships or finding new goals in life.

Despite the prevalence of depression in the elderly, hospital physicians often fail to recognize depression among them. In one study of elderly hospitalized medical patients, physicians detected depression in only 8.7 percent of those who were diagnosed as depressed by the researchers (Rapp et al., 1988). Depression may sometimes go undetected because it is masked by physical complaints and sleeping problems (Kazniak & Allender, 1985). Physicians may also be less likely to recognize depression in the elderly than in middle-aged or young people because they tend to focus on physical complaints or fail to interview elderly patients for depression (Rapp et al., 1988).

Memory Functioning and Depression The effects of depression on memory functioning in the elderly appears to be variable. Some studies find memory deficits among elderly depressed people while others do not (Niederehe, 1986). Unlike irreversible dementias such as those attributed to Alzheimer's disease, memory losses and cognitive impairment that accompany depression among the elderly can lift when the depression lifts (Salzman & Gutfreund, 1986). When depression occurs among patients already afflicted with dementia, however, a rapid and dramatic worsening of cognitive functioning may occur.

Depression and memory loss in the elderly may accompany bereavement. But these problems may be resolved as grief resolves and survivors learn to cope on their own, as illustrated in the following case (Salzman & Gutfreund, 1986):

■ Mrs. A. was a 71-year-old retired schoolteacher. Her husband died after a 3-year bout with intestinal cancer. Although his death was expected and prepared for, she was nevertheless overcome by emotion. She had been a highly functioning, scholarly woman who read widely, yet Mrs. A. was suddenly unable to think clearly. She noticed her striking forgetfulness. So did her children, who had come to support her during the period of mourning. Mrs. A. had difficulty recalling where she had placed things. Now and then she forgot the day of the week and the date. She felt incapable of shopping for groceries because it was too arduous to make change. Although she would make lists as a way of reminding herself of her chores, she would misplace the lists and forget about them. She could not concentrate to read or watch television. If she did watch for a while, she did not remember what she had seen. She called her children by the wrong name, and was particularly prone to calling her son by her deceased husband's name. As the weeks elapsed, however, the forgetfulness, disorientation, and diminished capacity for concentration gradually dissipated. After about half a year, Mrs. A returned to her normal level of intellectual functioning and has continued to function adequately.

Adapted from Salzman & Gutfreund, 1986, p. 258 ■

Some depressed older people complain of memory problems even though their memory functioning is average or even above average (Williams et al., 1987). Perhaps perceptions of memory impairment among some depressed elderly people are a kind of cognitive distortion, one that is characteristic of the tendency of depressed persons in general to devalue their abilities. There are also more dysfunctional attitudes, feelings of hopelessness, and negative automatic thoughts among elderly depressed people than among their nondepressed age-mates (Lam et al., 1987).

Treating Depression in Older People Antidepressants and mild tranquilizers like alprazolam (Xanax) have been used with mixed results to treat depressed older people (Feighner, 1982). Psychological approaches appear to provide hopeful alternatives to chemotherapy. For example, a recent study showed that cognitive therapy was effective in reducing depression and improving sleeping patterns among elderly subjects (Beutler et al., 1987). Treatment with alprazolam, by contrast, led to no improvement in subjective feelings of depression or physical complaints.

Zeiss and Lewinsohn (1986) proposed a cognitive-behavioral treatment model that is tailored to the life problems of the elderly. They suggest ways in which therapists can help depressed elderly people cope with stressful life events that affect the elderly, such as coping with loss of loved ones or with physical illness. Therapists also help elderly clients challenge self-defeating attitudes, such as the belief that they are too old to change or to learn new behaviors. Therapists are sensitive to changes in cognitive ability that occur with advancing age, such as a slowing down in the rate of processing information. Therapists must present new material slowly and expect smaller steps in behavioral changes. They also encourage the elderly to draw upon the valuable information they have acquired about coping with life problems, which not only helps them solve problems but also raises their self-esteem.

Elderly people who are in poor health and who lack social support are at greatest risk of depression (Phifer & Murrell, 1986). Clinicians who work with the elderly need to focus on enhancing their clients' social supports, especially following the losses of loved ones and friends.

changes in intellectual abilities. Significant declines in mental or intellectual functioning, or **dementia,** are not considered a normal function of the aging process but rather a sign of a degenerative brain disorder.

 It is *not* true that dementia is considered a normal function of the aging process. Rather, it is considered a sign of a degenerative brain disorder.

Dementia is defined by deterioration in mental abilities such as memory, problem-solving skills, and abstract thinking such that it interferes with social and occupational functioning (Davies, 1988).

Dementias that begin after age 65 are called **senile dementias,** whereas those that begin at age 65 or earlier are called **presenile dementias.** Screening and testing on neurological and neuropsychological tests can help distinguish dementias from normal aging (NIMH, 1987). Generally speaking, the decline in intellectual functioning in dementia is more rapid and more severe.

The causes of dementia include brain diseases such as Alzheimer's disease and Pick's disease, and the lasting effects of chronic intoxication, infections, strokes, and tumors. In many cases the dementia can be halted or reversed, especially in cases of certain tumors and treatable infections, or in depression or alcohol or substance abuse (NIMH, 1987). Most dementias, however, are irreversible, with Alzheimer's disease representing the most common form of irreversible dementia.

Alzheimer's Disease

Alzheimer's disease is a progressive form of mental deterioration that is believed to account for about 75 percent of the cases of dementia in the general population (Gurland & Cross, 1986). As many as 4 million Americans are believed to suffer from Alzheimer's disease (Schmeck, 1989; Gelman et al., 1989). Although Alzheimer's disease (AD) can occur as early as age 40, the risk rises sharply with increasing age. On the basis of an epidemiological study of Boston, Massachusetts (see Figure 13.1), it is estimated that AD affects about 10.3 percent of people over the age of 65 (Evans et al., 1989). However, in the Boston study, only 3 percent of those aged 65 to 74 had probable AD, as compared with 18.7 percent of those aged 75 to 84, and 47.2 percent of those age 85 or older.

 Alzheimer's disease is *not* found only among the elderly. However, its incidence rises with age, and it is most likely to afflict people aged 75 and above.

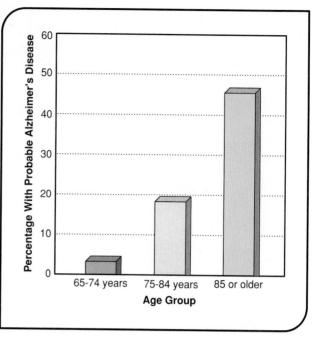

FIGURE 13.1 Prevalence of Alzheimer's disease in relation to age in the Boston community study.
The risk of Alzheimer's disease increases sharply with advanced age.
Source: Evans et al. (1989)

Alzheimer's disease is characterized by progressive deterioration in mental functions including memory, language, and problem solving (Crystal, 1988; Wilson & Kaszniak, 1986). Isolated memory losses are not indicative of AD (Davies, 1988) (for example, forgetting where one put one's glasses) and may occur normally as part of the aging process, but suspicion of AD is raised when cognitive impairment affects the individual's ability to function in daily work and social roles.

There is no cure or effective treatment for AD. The treatment for irreversible dementias like AD usually consists of therapeutic support and tranquilizing medication to help control the emotional agitation and inappropriate behavior that accompanies severe dementias. We generally associate AD with loss of memory and intellectual abilities, but it is also among the leading killers of the elderly, cutting life expectancy among those affected by more than one-half and accounting for perhaps 60,000 deaths per year in the United States (Katzman, 1976).

Alzheimer's disease was first described in 1907 by the German physician Alois Alzheimer (1864–1915). During an autopsy of a 56-year-old woman who had suffered from severe dementia, he noted two brain abnormalities that are now regarded as signs of the disease (Tomlinson et al., 1970): neuritic plaques (portions of degenerative brain tissue) and neurofibrillary tangles (twisted bundles of nerve cells). Perhaps because the patient was younger than 65, many people concluded that AD was a presenile dementia that only affected people below the age of 65. We now know that AD afflicts younger and older people, although the risk of AD increases dramatically among those of advanced ages, as noted.

With the U.S. population increasing in age, the percentage of people aged 65 and older is expected to increase by about 18 percent in the 1990s (U.S. Census, 1976), and people over the age of 75 will constitute at least half of the over-65 age group by the year 2000—the group which is most at risk for the development of AD (Davies, 1988). The public health costs assumed in providing institutional care are likely to mount steadily and strain social and medical resources (Gurland & Cross, 1986).

■ **Diagnosis**   There is no clear-cut test for AD. The diagnosis of AD is based on a process of exclusion, and is given only when other detectable causes of dementia are eliminated (Eisdorfer & Cohen, 1980). Diagnosticians try to rule out other medical conditions that mimic AD (Crystal, 1988), as well as other abnormal behavior patterns, such as severe depression, that might account for the memory loss and impair cognitive functioning. Estimates of misdiagnoses range from under 10 percent to more than 50 percent, even at the hands of specialists such as neurologists (Gurland & Cross, 1986). Although no psychological tests are sensitive to the specific effects of AD (Cohen, 1986), psychological testing helps define patients' general intellectual impairment and deficits in cognitive processes. Further research is needed to develop psychological tests that may be more sensitive to the deficits that result from AD and other dementias (Cohen, 1986).

A confirmatory diagnosis of AD is only made upon inspection of brain tissue by a biopsy or autopsy (Davies, 1988). However, a biopsy is rarely performed because of the risk of hemorrhaging or infection (Crystal, 1988), and an autopsy, of course, occurs too late to be helpful to the patient.

■ **Features of Alzheimer's Disease**   The disease is progressive; cognitive functioning generally declines with the duration of the illness (Teng et al., 1987). In the early stages, effects are generally limited to memory difficulties and subtle personality changes. Alzheimer's patients may have trouble managing their finances; remembering recent events or basic information such as telephone numbers, area codes, Zip codes, and all the names of their grandchildren; and performing numerical computations (Reisberg et al., 1986). A business manager who once handled millions of dollars may become unable to add two numbers (Davies, 1988). There may be subtle personality changes, such as signs of withdrawal in people who had been outgoing or

some irritability in people who had been gentle (Davies, 1988). But in these early stages, according to the DSM–III–R, people with AD generally appear neat and well-groomed and are generally cooperative and socially appropriate.

As AD progresses to a moderate level of severity, people find it harder to manage everyday tasks and require some assistance (Reisberg et al., 1986). They may be unable to select clothes that are right for the season or the occasion. Upon interview, they may be unable to recall their addresses or the names of family members. When they drive, they begin making mistakes, such as failing to stop at stop signs or accelerating when they should be braking, sometimes getting involved in accidents.

Some AD patients are not aware of their deficits; others deny their problems (Dieckmann et al., 1988). At first they may attribute their problems to other causes (Davies, 1988), such as stress or fatigue. Denial may protect AD patients in the early or mild stages of the disease from recognition that they are gradually losing their intellectual abilities (Reisberg et al., 1986). Denial is suspected when there is a clear discrepancy between the realities of patients' conditions and their reported perceptions of their conditions. On the other hand, those who recognize their problems may become depressed by them.

As AD progresses, people become more severely impaired. At the moderately severe level, they encounter difficulties in various aspects of personal functioning, such as toileting and bathing themselves (Reisberg et al., 1986). Large gaps in their memory for recent events and experiences occur. Patients cannot recall their com-

Alzheimer's disease is a progressive form of dementia that may afflict some 4 million Americans. It impairs cognitive functions such as memory, language, and problem solving ability. Alzheimer's patients can become grossly confused and forgetful, so that they may not be able to recall the names of spouses and children, even when they become fully dependent on them.

plete addresses but may remember parts of them. Or they may forget the name of the president but be able to recall his or her last name if given the first name. They may forget the names of their spouses, even though they have become fully dependent on them (Reisberg et al., 1986). Yet they recognize their spouses as being familiar. Memory for remote events is also affected. They are generally unable to recall the names of their schools, parents, or birthplaces. They may no longer be able to speak in full sentences, and verbal responses may be limited to a few words. They may begin walking in shorter, slower steps. Psychomotor coordination is impaired, and they may no longer be able to sign their names, even when assisted by others, and may have difficulty handling a knife and fork. Agitation becomes a prominent feature at this stage, and victims may "act out" in response to the threat of having to contend with an environment that no longer seems controllable. Patients may engage in pacing or fidgeting behavior, or hostile displays of aggressive behavior including yelling, throwing, or hitting. Even patients who had never before engaged in hostile or aggressive behaviors may become unable to control themselves. Patients may wander off because of restlessness or pacing and be unable to find their way back.

Victims at this stage may start talking to themselves, experience visual hallucinations, or suffer from paranoid delusions. For example, they may believe that someone is attempting to harm them or is stealing their possessions, or that their spouses are unfaithful to them. Delusions may develop in which individuals may believe that their spouses are actually other people.

At the most severe stage, cognitive functions decline to the point where sufferers are essentially helpless. They become incontinent, are unable to communicate or walk, and require assistance in toileting and feeding. According to the DSM–III–R, they may be entirely mute and inattentive to the environment.

Several of the principal features of Alzheimer's disease, including disorientation, memory loss, and behavior problems, are illustrated by the following case:

■ A 65-year-old draftsman began to have problems remembering important details at work; at home he began to have difficulty keeping his financial records up-to-date and remembering to pay bills on time. His intellectual abilities progressively declined, forcing him eventually to retire from his job. Behavioral problems began to appear at home, as he grew increasingly stubborn and even verbally and physically abusive toward others when he felt thwarted.

On neurological examination, he displayed disorientation as to place and time, believing that the consultation room was his place of employment and that the year was "1960 or something," when it was actually 1982. He had difficulty with even simple memory tests, failing to remember any of six objects shown to him ten minutes earlier, not recalling the names of his parents

or siblings, or the name of the President of the United States. His speech was vague and filled with meaningless phrases. He couldn't perform simple arithmetical computations, but he could interpret proverbs correctly.

Shortly following the neurological consultation, the man was placed in a hospital since his family was no longer able to control his increasingly disruptive behavior. In the hospital, his mental abilities continued to decline, while his aggressive behavior was largely controlled by major tranquilizers (antipsychotic drugs). He was diagnosed as suffering from a Primary Degenerative Dementia of the Alzheimer's Type. He died at age 74, some 8 years following the onset of his symptoms.

Adapted from Spitzer et al., 1989, pp. 131–132 ■

Victims' difficulties in recalling recent events may stem from breakdown of the biological processes involved in consolidating memories (Hart, 1987). Although intellectual functioning declines progressively in AD, certain cognitive functions appear to remain relatively intact. A study of 141 Alzheimer's patients showed that they performed fairly well at repeating words or phrases that were just spoken to them (Teng et al., 1987). They also were generally able to follow written commands, which suggests that written notes may help them partially to compensate for memory deficits and to better organize their behavior. But AD patients find it difficult to complete more complicated tasks, such as spelling words backwards or copying complex figures or designs. Earlier age of onset of AD was associated with poorer cognitive functioning, when the duration of illness was kept constant. Perhaps the form of AD that strikes patients earlier in life is more severe.

The Global Deterioration Scale or GDS (Reisberg et al., 1982) shows the magnitude or "stage" of cognitive decline associated with normal aging and with various degrees of severity of Alzheimer's disease (see Table 13.4). Keep in mind, however, that forgetfulness among the aged is not necessarily an early sign of Alzheimer's disease; it may fall within the spectrum of normal aging. A study of 40 people who averaged 69 years of age and complained of forgetfulness (GDS Stage 2) were found $3\frac{1}{2}$ years later to be alive and functioning in the community (Reisberg et al., 1986). Only 5 percent of them showed notable cognitive deterioration during the $3\frac{1}{2}$ years. Elderly people (and some of us not quite that advanced in years) complain of not remembering names as well as they used to, or of forgetting names that were once well known to them. Although mild forgetfulness may concern people, it need not have a negative impact on their abilities to function in social or occupational roles (Reisberg et al., 1986).

■ Impact on the Family   Alzheimer's disease touches on people's deepest fears, namely the fear of losing control of one's mind, one's thoughts, one's actions, one's environment. Families who must care for and

TABLE 13.4 The Global Deterioration Scale (GDS) for Assessment of Alzheimer's Disease

GDS Stage	Clinical Phase	Clinical Characteristics	Diagnosis
1 = No cognitive decline	Normal	No subjective complaints of memory deficit. No memory deficit evident on clinical interview.	Normal
2 = Very mild cognitive decline	Forgetfulness	Subjective complaints of memory deficits. No objective deficits in employment or social situations. Appropriate concern with respect to symptomatology.	Normal aged
3 = Mild cognitive decline	Early confusional	Earliest clear-cut deficits. Decreased performance in demanding employment and social settings. Objective evidence of memory deficit obtained only with an intensive interview. Mild to moderate anxiety accompanies symptoms.	Compatible with incipient Alzheimer's disease
4 = Moderate cognitive decline	Late confusional	Clear-cut deficit on careful clinical interview. Inability to perform complex tasks. Denial is dominant defense mechanism. Flattening of affect and withdrawal from challenging situations occur.	Mild Alzheimer's disease
5 = Moderately severe cognitive decline	Early dementia	Patients can no longer survive without some assistance. Patients are unable during interview to recall a major relevant aspect of their current lives. Persons at this stage retain knowledge of many major facts regarding themselves and others. They invariably know their own names and generally know their spouses and children's names. They require no assistance with toileting and eating, but may have some difficulty choosing the proper clothing to wear.	Moderate Alzheimer's disease
6 = Severe cognitive decline	Middle dementia	May occasionally forget the name of the spouse upon whom they are entirely dependent for survival. Will be largely unaware of all recent events and experiences in their lives. Will require some assistance with activities of daily living. Personality and emotional changes occur.	Moderately severe Alzheimer's disease
7 = Very severe cognitive decline	Late dementia	All verbal abilities are lost. Frequently there is no speech at all—only grunting. Incontinent of urine; requires assistance toileting and feeding. Loses basic psychomotor skills (for example, ability to walk).	Severe Alzheimer's disease

Source: *Reisberg et al., 1982. Copyright 1982, The American Psychiatric Association. Reprinted by permission.*

helplessly watch loved ones as they slowly deteriorate have been described as attending a "funeral that never ends" (Aronson, 1988). Living with an advanced AD victim may seem like living with a stranger, as the victim undergoes profound changes.

At least two-thirds of individuals affected by Alzheimer's and related disorders live at home (Gurland & Cross, 1986) and eventually require round-the-clock attention from their family members (Gelman et al., 1989). Alzheimer's is a progressive disease, and victims' functioning deteriorates to the point where they cannot dress themselves, cook, keep house, use the toilet, feed themselves, manage their financial affairs, or even communicate (Gurland & Cross, 1986).

The family's emotional and financial resources to provide home care, and not the degree of dementia or impairment of functioning, generally determine whether or not afflicted people are institutionalized (Aronson, 1988). Spouses usually provide the bulk of care, often with the assistance of their children, principally their daughters or daughters-in-law (Aronson, 1988). The children, usually middle-aged themselves, are caught between the demands of caring for a demented

parent and their own children, marriages, and careers. In addition to the burdens imposed by supporting and supervising the AD family member, caregivers are further stressed by features of the illness like wandering away, aggressiveness, destructiveness, incontinence, screaming, and remaining awake at night on the part of the person afflicted (Gurland & Cross, 1986).

Families who can no longer shoulder the burden of care may seek placement in a nursing home. About 60 percent of nursing home residents suffer from dementia of one type or another (Davies, 1988). Since Medicare, the system of health care for the elderly, does not presently cover longterm custodial care in a nursing home for victims of dementia, the family must either foot the bill themselves or seek subsidized care in the form of Medicaid, if the individual can be certified as indigent (Aronson, 1988).

Self-help support groups have been established to provide families of Alzheimer's patients with opportunities to share the latest information about the disease and to provide emotional support. More than a thousand support groups—composed of individuals who are living through or have lived through the process

Alzehimer's disease can be devastating to the families of patients. Spouses usually provide the bulk of daily care. The man in the photograph has been caring for his wife for several years, and he believes that his hugs and kisses sometimes cause his wife to murmur his name.

of caring for family members with AD—have been started by the Alzheimer's Disease and Related Disorders Association (ADRDA) (Marks, 1988).

■ **Theoretical Perspectives**   The causes of AD remain unknown. Nor are there cures or treatments that can halt the progress of the disease (Schmeck, 1989). However, a number of possible causes have been identified. Some have suggested that Alzheimer's disease is caused by a slow-acting virus. Others have postulated genetic defects or brain traumas as the causes. Aluminum toxicity has also been suggested, based largely on findings of abnormal concentrations of aluminum in the brains of AD victims (Crowley, 1989). However, the evidence for aluminum toxicity is inconclusive.[1]

Metal poisoning may play some role in Alzheimer's disease, but most authorities consider the evidence inconclusive.

Recent research has been focused on the possible role of imbalances in brain neurotransmitters, especially acetylcholine. For example, AD patients show reduced levels of the acetylcholine (ACh) in their brains (Davies, 1988), perhaps because of loss of brain cells in the nucleus basalis of Meynert that manufactures ACh (Coyle et al., 1983; Whitehouse et al., 1982). Perhaps these brain cells are destroyed by a viral infection, but the evidence is sketchy (Davies, 1988).

There is some evidence that ACh deficiencies give rise to AD symptoms. For example, normal young people who take an anticholinergic drug that inhibits the activity of the brain cells that normally respond to ACh undergo memory losses that are similar to those observed among older people with similar losses (Drachman & Leavitt, 1974). These memory losses appear to reflect prevention of transmission of ACh at the synapse, and not drug-induced drowsiness or sedative effects (Drachman, 1977).

If deficiencies in acetylcholine give rise to the cognitive deficits of AD, perhaps increasing the amounts of ACh available to the brain may retard, arrest, or even reverse the process of mental decline. To date, however, only modest levels of improvement have been obtained through drugs that prevent the breakdown of ACh in the brain, and thus increase its availability (Thal, 1988).

Positron emission tomography (the PET scan) provides measures of glucose and oxygen consumption in areas of the brain that might be affected in AD and other dementias. Comparative PET scans of AD patients and normal elderly reference groups show evidence of generally reduced metabolic rates in AD patients of about 33 percent to 37 percent (Ferris et al., 1980). Researchers have also found a negative correlation between metabolic rate and cognitive performance: The greater the cognitive impairment, the lower the metabolic rate (de Leon et al., 1983; Frackowiak et al., 1981). The fact that metabolic changes in the brains of AD patients appear to be widespread suggests that AD may affect multiple areas of the brain (de Leon et al., 1986).

Patients who are suspected of having AD show evidence of reduced blood flow in the brain (see Yamaguchi et al., 1980), but the significance of these findings remains unclear (de Leon et al., 1986). One possibility is that in AD, brain tissue degenerates to the point where it requires fewer nutrients, such as glucose, that are transported by blood—to fuel brain cell activity. Thus, the supply of blood to the brain is reduced (de Leon et al., 1986).

Investigators have also found differences in brain wave patterns, as measured by the electroencephalograph (EEG), between AD and normal subjects. This technique has revealed a relative slowing in brain wave activity among AD patients (Albert et al., 1986). Researchers speculate that the slowing of brain wave activity in Alzheimer's patients may reflect reductions in the activity of neurotransmitters like ACh.

There is also evidence of genetic transmission of AD. The risk of contracting AD has been estimated at about four times greater among first-degree relatives of AD patients—parents, siblings, or offspring—than among the general population (Crystal, 1988; Mohs et al., 1987). It's been estimated that between 10 and 30 percent of AD cases may be transmitted genetically (Cowley, 1989). Also note that the incidence of AD in the spouses of AD patients is apparently no greater

---

[1] Still, Michael A. Weiner (1989), president of the Alzheimer's Research Institute in Tiburon, California, argues that "There is now enough evidence implicating aluminum . . . to curtail its intake from all sources. . . . [A]luminum reduction is one of the most sensible health investments we can make."

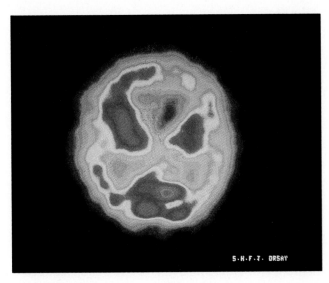

A PET scan of the brain of an Alzheimer's patient, showing a reduced level of metabolic activity in the frontal and parietal lobes (the reduced areas of red at the top right).

of the brain that are affected may cease to function, and the victim may suffer a range of disabilities including problems with motor, speech, and cognitive functions. Death may also occur. Single strokes may produce gross impairments in specific functions, such as **aphasia** or the loss of the ability to speak or to comprehend speech, but single strokes do not typically cause the more generalized declines in cognitive functioning that define dementia. Multi-infarct dementia generally results from multiple strokes that occur at different times, resulting in a wide range of effects on mental functioning.

Multi-infarct dementias are similar in symptomology to Alzheimer's disease (AD), including loss of memory and language ability, emotional agitation and instability, and loss of ability to care for one's own basic needs. But unlike AD, which is characterized by insidious onset and worsening of symptoms, MID tends to occur abruptly and to follow a stepwise deterioration of rapid changes in cognitive functioning, with such declines believed to reflect the effects of additional strokes (Brinkman et al., 1986). According to the DSM–III–R, certain cognitive functions may remain relatively intact in the early course of the disorder, leading to a ''patchy'' deterioration in which ''islands'' of mental competence remain, while other abilities are grossly impaired, depending on the areas of the brain that have been damaged.

than that for the general population. This suggests that any increased familial risk for the disease is caused by genetic rather than environmental modes of transmission (Mohs et al., 1987).

■ **Treatment**   There is, as noted, no cure or established treatment for Alzheimer's disease (Davies, 1988). As noted, only modest levels of improvement have been obtained through the use of drugs that prevent the breakdown of ACh in the brain (Thal, 1988). Although there is no specific treatment, early diagnosis allows the families of AD victims an opportunity to make appropriate business or retirement decisions, or changes in residence to ensure adequate care for the patient and to set aside funds for future use (Crystal, 1988). It is also important for people who are suspected of having AD to be evaluated quickly because other conditions that may be treatable or reversible, such as stroke or depression, can produce AD-like symptoms (Dieckmann et al., 1988). The depression that is frequently connected with AD may be treatable by psychotherapy or antidepressant medication (Dieckmann et al., 1988). Behavioral problems associated with AD may also be treated by behavioral and chemotherapeutic approaches. Clearly, much remains to be learned about the cause and treatment of this devastating disease.

Multi-Infarct Dementia

Multi-infarct dementia (MID) refers to dementias that are caused by repeated strokes or other forms of brain damage. A stroke occurs when a blood clot cuts off the supply of blood to a part of the brain. The areas

Pick's Disease

Pick's disease gives rise to another type of dementia that involves a pattern of progressive deterioration and symptomatology akin to that of AD (Davies, 1988). Symptoms include memory loss and social inappropriateness, such as loss of modesty or flagrant sexual behavior (Davies, 1988). Diagnosis is confirmed only upon autopsy by the absence of the neurofibrillary tangles and placques that are found in Alzheimer's disease and by the presence of certain other abnormal structures—Pick's bodies—in nerve cells (Heston et al., 1987). Pick's disease is believed to account for perhaps 5 percent of dementias. It occurs most frequently between the ages of 60 and 70, and the risk declines with advancing age after 70 (Heston & Mastry, 1982). Men are more likely than women to incur Pick's disease (Heston et al., 1987).

Pick's disease appears to run in families, and a genetic component is suspected in the etiology of the disease (Heston et al., 1987). It has been estimated that family members of victims of Pick's disease have an overall risk of 17 percent of contracting the disease by age 75 (Heston et al., 1987).

Let us now consider a number of physical illnesses and conditions—including Parkinson's disease, infectious diseases, and brain traumas, among others—that are associated with patterns of abnormal behavior.

DISEASES OF THE BASAL GANGLIA

The **basal ganglia** are a collection of neural cell bodies that lie beneath the cerebral cortex and are involved in motor behavior. Thus, diseases of the basal ganglia, like Parkinson's disease and Huntington's disease, have an impact on the regulation of movement as well as on psychological functioning.

Parkinson's Disease

Parkinson's disease was first identified by the physician James Parkinson in 1817. Parkinson treated several patients who suffered from a degenerative process that was characterized by shaking or tremors, rigidity, disturbances in posture (leaning forward), and lack of control over body movements. The incidence of **Parkinson's disease** has been estimated at from 20 to 70 per 100,000 people (Knight et al., 1988; Rajput et al., 1984). It affects men and women about equally and most often strikes between the ages of 50 and 69 (Knight et al., 1988).

Parkinson's patients may be able to exercise control over the shaking or tremors, but only briefly. Some victims cannot walk at all; others walk laboriously, in a crouch. Parkinson's patients execute voluntary body movements with difficulty, have poor control over fine motor movements, such as finger control, and have sluggish reflexes. Parkinson's patients look expressionless, as if they are wearing masks, a symptom that apparently reflects the degeneration of brain tissue that controls facial muscles. It is particularly difficult for them to engage in sequences of complex movements, such as those required to sign their names. Patients with the disease may be unable to coordinate two movements at the same time, as seen in this description of a patient who had difficulty walking and reaching for his wallet at the same time:

> ■ A 58-year-old man was walking across the hotel lobby in order to pay his bill. He reached into his inside jacket pocket for his wallet. He stopped walking instantly as he did so and stood immobile in the lobby in front of strangers. He became aware of his suspended locomotion and resumed his stroll to the cashier; however, his hand remained rooted inside his pocket, as though he were carrying a weapon he might display once he arrived at the cashier.
>
> Adapted from Knight et al., 1988 ■

Parkinson's disease involves the destruction of neurons in the basal ganglia of the brain, specifically in a region called the *substantia nigra* ("black substance"), which lies below the cerebral cortex and is involved in controlling body movements. In about 7 percent of cases, the damage or destruction is considered drug-induced (Rajput et al., 1984). Major tranquilizers like Thorazine or Stelazine are known to induce Parkinsonian-type side effects, for example. Other possible causes, such as viruses, environmental toxins, and arteriosclerosis, have also been noted (Knight et al., 1988; Rajput et al., 1984). In most cases, however, the cause remains unknown.

Since the cells that are affected in Parkinson's disease are involved in the manufacture and storage of the neurotransmitter dopamine, it may be that the disease is related to deficiencies in the amount of dopamine available to the brain. The drug L-dopa, first used in the 1970s, brought hope to Parkinson's patients by increasing the levels of dopamine (Rajput et al., 1984). About 80 percent of Parkinson's patients showed significant improvements in their tremors and motor symptoms following treatment with L-dopa (Helme, 1982). L-dopa helps control the symptoms and slows the progress of the disease, but it does not cure it. The majority of patients treated with L-dopa continue to show gradual deterioration (Yahr, 1976).

Parkinson himself believed that intelligence was unaffected by the disorder, but modern evidence suggests that some Parkinson's victims do suffer cognitive impairments. These intellectual deficits tend to be more subtle than those evinced by Alzheimer's patients (Knight et al., 1988). Intellectual functions appear to remain intact in most Parkinson's patients in the early stages of the disease, despite marked motor disability. But patients in the later stages seem to experience greater deficits in memory, language, and perceptual skills. Parkinson's patients often become socially withdrawn and are at greater than average risk for depression, perhaps because of difficulty in coping with the helplessness instilled by a chronic and irreversible disease.

Parkinson's disease is characterized by tremors, rigidity, disturbances in posture, and lack of control over body movements. There is also some evidence of cognitive and perceptual impairment, especially during the later stages of the disease. Here a physician examines a Parkinson's patient for signs of motor impairment.

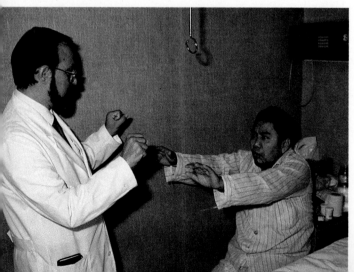

Huntington's Disease

Huntington's disease, or Huntington's chorea, was first recognized by the neurologist George Huntington in 1872. Huntington's disease involves a progressive deterioration of the basal ganglia, especially of the *caudate nucleus* and the *putamen*, which primarily affects neurons that produce ACh and **GABA.**

The symptoms may appear in childhood but usually begin in the prime of adulthood, between the ages of 30 and 50. The most prominent physical symptoms of the disease are involuntary, jerky movements of the face (grimaces), neck, limbs, and trunk—in contrast to the poverty of movement that typifies Parkinson's disease. These twitches are termed *choreiform*, which is derived from the Greek word *choreia*, meaning "dance." The psychological effects of the disease, which precede the development of the choreiform movements, involve progressive dementia with severe memory loss (Caine et al., 1977). Unstable and changeable moods, alternating with apathy and depression, are common. As the disorder progresses, paranoia may develop and patients may become suicidally depressed. Eventually, there is loss of control of bodily functions, leading to death, which generally occurs within 15 years after the onset.

Huntington's disease is transmitted genetically from either parent to children of either sex. The disease has been traced to a mutation on a single gene (Konner, 1988). Anyone who inherits the defective gene gets the disease. People who have a parent with Huntington's disease stand a 50 percent chance of contracting the disease themselves. Researchers are trying to find the precise location on the particular chromosome (believed to be chromosome no. 4) where the defective gene is located (Konner, 1988). Finding the gene and the protein that it produces may hold the key to effective treatment, since the protein is believed to be responsible for the disease.

Until recently, children of Huntington's disease

A CLOSER LOOK
From Parent to Child: The Sad Legacy of Huntington's Disease

Woody Guthrie was the folksinger and songwriter who gave us the beloved song, "This Land Is Your Land." He died of Huntington's disease in 1967, after 22 years of battling the malady. Guthrie had been misdiagnosed as an alcoholic and had been placed in a number of mental hospitals for several years before the correct diagnosis was made. When the symptoms first appeared, he said it felt as though he were drunk. He would become clumsy and fly into fits of despair and rage. Slowly, the disease progressed. He could no longer play the guitar. Eventually, he could not speak. Doctors could do nothing to prevent his decline and death.

Woody's son, Arlo, is also a folksinger. He wrote the classic song about littering and the Vietnam War, "Alice's Restaurant." Arlo Guthrie stands a 50 percent chance of contracting Huntington's disease. One day in 1967, Arlo played "Alice's Restaurant" to his father. Three months later, Woody died. Today, Arlo is healthy and still singing. He has not wanted to take the genetic test that might indicate whether he carries the Huntington's gene. Arlo told an interviewer for the science program *Nova* in 1989 that he'd lead his life exactly the same way whether or not he knew he had the Huntington's gene (*NOVA*, March 28, 1989).

As this book goes to press, Arlo remains healthy and is carrying on the song-writing tradition that was passed from father to son. It remains to be seen whether or not a darker legacy was also transmitted from father to son.

Folksingers Woody Guthrie (left) and his son Arlo. Huntington's chorea involves a progressive deterioration of the basal ganglia, resulting in motor impairment, deterioration in cognitive functioning, and eventual death. The disease is transmitted genetically, and the onset generally occurs between the ages of 30 and 50. Woody Guthrie died from the disorder, and Arlo Guthrie stands a 50 percent chance of developing the disease.

victims had no way of knowing whether or not they would be stricken with the disease until the symptoms developed, usually in mid-life. A genetic diagnostic test has now been developed that can detect carriers of the defective gene—those who will eventually develop the disease should they live long enough. Eventually, perhaps, genetic engineering may provide a means of modifying the defective gene or its effects. But since there is no present cure for the disease, some potential carriers, like folksinger Arlo Guthrie (see the accompanying box), prefer not to know whether they will come down with this incurable degenerative disease.

INFECTIONS OF THE BRAIN

Various infections of the brain may damage or destroy neural tissue and have profound mental and physical effects. We consider several major types of brain infection, including encephalitis, meningitis, neurosyphilis, and AIDS dementia complex.

Encephalitis

Encephalitis is derived from Greek roots meaning "inflammation" (*-itis*) in "the head" (*kephale*) and is a general term that is used to refer to any kind of inflammation of the brain. For example, the brain may become inflamed by microbes that infect brain tissues or by inanimate objects, such as a piece of shrapnel or a bullet that not only causes structural damage but also carries microbes or leaves an orifice that allows microbes to enter. In some cases, infections from other parts of the body spread to the brain. Most infections are caused by viruses carried by mosquitoes, ticks, and other insects.

An epidemic of encephalitis, suspected of being caused by an influenza virus carried by mosquitoes, spread through Europe and the United States around the time of World War I. It was called "sleeping sickness" because it induced prolonged periods of lethargy and sleepiness, which were followed by periods of irritability and excitability. Epidemics of encephalitis are practically unknown today in developed nations, but outbreaks of encephalitis—along with infestations of insects—continue to plague parts of the Third World.

Delirium can occur during the acute phase of encephalitis, and some patients suffer convulsions or coma. Changes in personality also occur, especially in young children, and survivors may be left with psychological symptoms like irritability, restlessness, depression, even dementia. Although there is usually an apparently complete physical recovery, there may be some lingering effects, such as tremors, paralysis in the arms or legs, speech and hearing problems, and, in the case of afflicted infants, mental retardation.

Meningitis

Another type of infection that afflicts the central nervous system, **meningitis,** involves acute inflammation of the membranes or meninges (from the Greek *meningos,* meaning "membrane") that cover the spinal cord and brain. Various microbes, such as viruses, bacteria, and protozoa, may cause meningitis, but the most frequent cause is the meningococcus (from the Greek *kokkos,* meaning "kernel" or "berry") bacterium, which is also responsible for most epidemics. If treated early with antibiotics, this form of meningitis can generally be cured. If left untreated, however, it may lead to coma and death. Victims typically experience a high fever, convulsions, severe headache, muscle stiffness and pain, vomiting, drowsiness, impaired concentration, irritability, and problems with memory. When contracted in infancy, meningitis like encephalitis may cause mental retardation because of its effects on developing brain tissue. And because meningitis is highly contagious, victims are usually quarantined.

Neurosyphilis

General paresis (from the Greek *parienai,* meaning "to relax") is a form of mental deterioration—or "relaxation," in its most negative connotation—that is caused by a syphilitic infection of the brain. The disease is of historical significance to abnormal psychology. The late-nineteenth-century discovery of the connection between this form of dementia and a concrete physical illness seemed to promise that organic causes would be found for other abnormal behaviors. As a consequence, the medical model was buttressed.

Syphilis is a sexually transmitted disease that is caused by the bacterium *Treponema pallidum.* Syphilis is almost always transmitted through genital, oral, or anal contact with an infected person, but it may also be transmitted from mother to child through the placenta. If left untreated, syphilis undergoes several stages of development, beginning with the appearance of a painless chancre (a round, hard sore with raised edges) at the site of the infection about two to four weeks following contact. Although the chancre disappears spontaneously within a few weeks, the infection continues to fester. During the secondary stage, beginning a few weeks to a few months later, a skin rash appears, which consists of reddish, raised bumps. This rash also eventually disappears, and the infection enters a latency stage, which may last from 1 to 40 years, in which the infection appears dormant. But during this interval the bacteria multiply and invade sites throughout the body, sometimes destroying nerve cells in the spinal cord that control motor responses, sometimes attacking brain tissue. In the late stage of the infection, the damage caused by the bacteria produces a wide range of symp-

"Treatment" of syphilis of a Spanish sailor who contracted the disease in the New World during one of Christopher Columbus's voyages. If syphilis is left untreated, it can lead to a form of dementia called general paresis.

toms, including—when the brain is attacked directly—general paresis.

? It is *not* true that there is nothing to be concerned about if the symptoms of syphilis disappear by themselves. Syphilis may apparently lie dormant for many years, yet then strike the central nervous system, producing the symptoms of general paresis.

General paresis is associated with physical symptoms like tremors, slurred speech, impaired motor coordination, and, eventually, paralysis—all of which are suggestive of *relaxed* control over the body. Psychological signs include shifts in mood states, lack of emotional responsiveness to joyous or upsetting events, and irritability; delusions; changes in personal habits, such as suspension of personal grooming and hygiene; and progressive intellectual deterioration, including severe memory loss and impaired judgment and comprehension. Some paretic patients grow euphoric and entertain delusions of grandiosity concerning their power and importance. Others become lethargic and depressed. Eventually, paretic patients lapse into a state of apathy and confusion, characterized by the inability to care for themselves or to speak intelligibly. Death eventually ensues, either because of renewed infection or because of the damage caused by the existing infection.

Late-stage syphilis once accounted for 10 to 30 percent of admissions to psychiatric hospitals. However, advances in detection and the development of antibiotics has sharply reduced the incidences of late-stage syphilis and general paresis. The effectiveness of treatment depends upon the stage of the infection when antibiotics are introduced and the extent of central-nervous-system damage. In cases where extensive tissue damage has been done, antibiotics can stem the infec-tion and prevent further damage, thereby producing some improvement in intellectual performance; however, they cannot restore patients to their premorbid levels of functioning.

AIDS Dementia Complex

The AIDS virus, like *Treponema pallidum*, can attack the central nervous system (Levy et al., 1985), causing **AIDS dementia complex** (ADC), which is characterized by a progressive decline in mental and motor functioning (Tross & Hirsch, 1988). More than half of those who contract AIDS eventually experience some form of mental impairment or dementia, involving difficulties in language skills, memory, and thinking ability (Faulstich, 1987). AIDS patients who show ADC tend to deteriorate and die more rapidly than AIDS patients without ADC (Levy et al., 1984); however, ADC rarely affects people who test positive for the virus but have not yet developed AIDS (Altman, 1989).

The first signs of ADC may mimic depression, including impaired concentration, apathy, social withdrawal, difficulty recalling recent events, and lack of emotional responsiveness (blunted or flat affect) (Faulstich, 1987). Early neurological signs include problems in walking, muscle coordination (ataxia), and reflexes. Cognitive functioning declines rapidly within two months of the appearance of symptoms (Tross & Hirsch, 1988). AIDS patients are often aware of their deteriorating cognitive abilities, and may respond with depression and anger (Tross & Hirsch, 1988). As the disease progresses, dementia grows more severe, taking the form of delusions, disorientation, and marked impairments in memory and thought. In its later stages, ADC may resemble the profound deficiencies found among Alzheimer's victims. Eventually patients may experience seizures, mutism, and coma, leading to death (Faulstich, 1987).

BRAIN TRAUMAS

Brain trauma involves injury to the brain that is caused by jarring, banging, or cutting brain tissue, usually because of accident or assault. There are several types of brain traumas, including concussions, contusions, and lacerations.

Concussion

One type of brain trauma is the **concussion**—epidemic among football players and boxers—which involves the momentary loss of consciousness resulting from a violent blow to, or jarring of, the head. The loss of consciousness may last from a second or two to a few minutes. Recovery is usually complete, without lingering effects.

 It is apparently true that football players and prizefighters can recover completely from being knocked out without lingering cognitive effects.

In severe cases, however, concussions can produce delirium and agitation, and victims have amnesia for the events directly preceding the injury. In some cases, a post-traumatic syndrome may persist for weeks or months following the injury. Such syndromes are characterized by headaches, anxiety, insomnia, depression, and memory deficits. Notable permanent brain damage is rare.

Contusion

A more serious type of brain trauma, the **contusion,** is produced by jarring the brain with sufficient force that the soft brain tissue is bruised by pounding against the hard bone of the skull. A coma typically results and may last for hours or days. Hemorrhaging may require surgery to repair the damage or stop the bleeding. Upon awakening, victims may have problems with cognitive functions and speech, but functioning is usually regained in about a week. Repeated concussions and contusions, however, such as those incurred by professional boxers, can cause brain damage and give rise to permanent cognitive impairment and emotional instability. Boxers who suffer from this condition, called the "punch-drunk syndrome" or *traumatic encephalopathy*[2] experience cognitive and physical symptoms like slurring of speech, shaky or unsteady gait, emotional problems, memory deficits, dizziness, and tremors.

Laceration

The most serious type of brain trauma, a **laceration,** refers to an injury that is caused by a foreign object that pierces the skull and damages brain tissue. The extent of the damage is related to the location and extent of the injury. Although a severe laceration can cause immediate death, survivors often suffer permanent brain damage that results in major impairments in mental and physical functioning. Sometimes, however, the victim "luckily" experiences only minor damage or no permanent effects.

[2] Despite the term's apparent complexity, the Greek roots of *encephalopathy* mean simply "something wrong in the head."

CEREBROVASCULAR DISORDERS

The brain, like other living tissues, depends upon the bloodstream to supply it with oxygen and glucose and to cart away its metabolic wastes. When the blood supply to the brain is cut off by a clot in a blood vessel, the parts of the brain that are normally supplied by that vessel may be damaged or even destroyed, causing a cerebrovascular accident, or CVA, or what more commonly is called a "stroke." In a cerebral hemorrhage, the rupture of a blood vessel in the brain causes the leakage of blood that destroys or damages sensitive brain tissue.

Strokes

In one type of stroke, a *cerebral thrombosis*, a clot is formed at a point in a blood vessel that is constricted to such a degree that a blockage or *occlusion* occurs, cutting off circulation. The constriction of the blood vessel, or *atherosclerosis*, results from the buildup of fatty deposits along the interior walls of the vessel, which makes the vessel more susceptible to the formation of blood clots. In another type of stroke, a *cerebral embolism*, a blood clot or another substance, such as an air bubble or fatty globule, travels from another part of the body and becomes lodged at a site in the constricted blood vessel, cutting off the flow of blood.

The effects of a stroke depend on the extent of the brain damage and can be severe—fatal, in fact. Some trivial ("silent") strokes do not affect key brain regions and produce only minor effects, but most stroke victims must learn to adjust to some degree of permanent impairment. Survivors may experience paralysis or loss of sensation on one side of the body, loss of speech (aphasia), and impaired memory. Some cannot walk on their own. Many victims find it difficult to adjust to their loss of functioning and, as a consequence, may have unstable moods that fluctuate between depression and rage.

Aphasia, the partial or total loss of the ability to speak, is a common effect of stroke. There are sensory or receptive aphasias and motor or expressive aphasias. In sensory aphasias, people have difficulty comprehending speech or written matter but retain the ability to communicate in speech. In motor aphasias, a person's ability to express one's thoughts in speech or writing is impaired, but the person can understand speech and writing. Motor aphasics may not be able to summon up the names of familiar objects when they try to speak or may scramble the normal order of words.

One of the more famous self-descriptions of aphasia is by a nineteenth-century medical scientist, Jacques Lordat:

When I wanted to speak I could not find the right expression. . . . My thoughts were ready, but the sounds that should convey them to my informant were no longer at my disposal. . . . I was no longer able to grasp the ideas of others, for the [aphasia] that prevented me from speaking made me incapable of understanding the sounds I heard quickly enough to grasp their meaning.

(Quoted in Freemon, 1981, p 156).

Cerebral Hemorrhage

In a *cerebral hemorrhage*, a blood vessel in the brain ruptures, causing blood to leak into brain tissue, damaging or destroying it. The causes of cerebral hemorrhages have not been fully explicated; however, the weakness in the vessel wall that permits it to rupture may be a congenital defect or a result of hypertension, which may gradually weaken the walls of blood vessels.

The effects of a cerebral hemorrhage depend upon the size of the ruptured vessel and the area of the brain that is affected. Typically, a victim of a cerebral hemorrhage experiences a sudden loss of consciousness and lapses into a coma, which may be accompanied by convulsions. When the hemorrhage is extensive, death may occur within a week or two. Survivors may experience symptoms like those suffered by stroke victims, including motor problems such as paralysis, aphasias, and disturbances in memory and judgment.

BRAIN TUMORS

Benign and malignant (cancerous) brain tumors can cause serious organic mental syndromes in addition to their physical threat. The skull prevents the brain from expanding, so even a benign tumor can place detrimental pressure on the surrounding tissue. Malignant brain tumors can either be primary, in which case they originate in the brain, or secondary, in which case they metastasize to the brain from other cancerous sites in the body. In either case, they are made up of cells that proliferate rapidly and destroy adjacent healthy cells.

The symptoms produced by a brain tumor depends upon the tumor's size and location. Memory problems sometimes represent the first signs of a tumor. Recurrent headaches are another sign. But these early signs also occur in many other disorders, so the possibility of a brain tumor is often overlooked. As the tumor grows, the symptoms worsen, giving rise to persistent, severe headaches, seizures, disorientation and problems with memory, vomiting, changes in vision, impaired motor coordination, and, in some cases, hallucinations. The

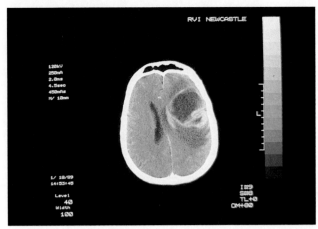

A CAT scan of the brain of a 67-year-old man, showing a tumor on the left side of the brain (the right side of the photograph). The tumor is the dark, roughly circular region.

personality may also be affected. Depression and confusion are some of the personality changes observed among patients with brain tumors. Some patients become slovenly in their dress or careless in their work. Some tumors are operable and can be removed by surgery, so early detection and treatment is critical. Inoperable malignancies sometimes respond to radiation treatment.

NUTRITIONAL DEFICIENCIES: KORSAKOFF'S SYNDROME, PELLAGRA, AND BERIBERI

Various nutritional imbalances or deficiencies may also affect mental functioning. Chronic alcoholics, as noted, may neglect their diets and incur Korsakoff's syndrome as a consequence.

Deficiencies in vitamin B, or niacin, cause **pellagra,** which derives from the Latin *pellis*, meaning "skin," and the Greek *agra*, meaning "seizure." Pellagra gives rise to physical symptoms like diarrhea and skin eruptions (hence the name), and to psychological symptoms such as anxiety, depression, loss of memory for recent events, and problems in concentration. If left untreated, hallucinations and delirium may result, and eventually death. Because of greater attention to diet and an improved standard of living, pellagra is now uncommon in the United States, but it is not unusual in developing countries where diets are nutritionally unbalanced and consist mainly of cornmeal. Except in the most advanced cases, treatment with a diet rich in niacin and other key vitamins is highly effective.

Beriberi (a reduplication of the Sinhalese word meaning "weakness") is another disease caused by thiamine deficiency, like Korsakoff's syndrome. Thus, it is found among alcoholics and others whose diet is lacking in thiamine, sometimes occurring together with pellagra. Beriberi is characterized by nerve disorders that produce difficulties with memory and concentration, irritability, extreme lethargy, lack of appetite, insomnia, problems with memory and concentration, irritability, and general feelings of listlessness and fatigue.

ENDOCRINE DISORDERS

Overactivity or underactivity of endocrine glands can affect psychological as well as physical functions since hormones are released directly into the bloodstream and travel throughout the body, affecting virtually every cell, including brain tissue. We shall consider some thyroid and adrenal problems.

As described in Chapter 2, the thyroid gland secretes **thyroxin,** which is involved in the regulation of the metabolic rate. Hyperthyroidism (also called *Grave's disease*) is caused by oversecretion of thyroxin, which accelerates the metabolism and produces weight loss, "bug eyes," and psychological effects such as excitability, insomnia, anxiety, restlessness, even transient delusions or hallucinations. First Lady Barbara Bush has been treated for Grave's disease.

Hypothyroidism, which results from abnormally low levels of thyroxin, may cause **cretinism** in childhood, a condition characterized by stunted growth and mental retardation. In adulthood, hypothyroidism, also called *myxedema*, slows the metabolism and is associated with physical changes such as dry skin and weight gain, and psychological changes such as sluggishness and fatigue, difficulties in concentration and memory, and depression. The widespread use of iodized salt, which prevents thyroid deficiencies, has greatly reduced the occurrence of hypothyroidism in the United States.

The adrenal glands, which are located above the kidneys, consist of an outer layer, or cortex, and an internal core, or medulla. The adrenal cortex secretes steroids, which enhance resistance to stress and regulate metabolism of carbohydrates. Cortical underactivity may result in **Addison's disease** (after the English physician Thomas Addison), which is characterized by weight loss, low blood pressure, fatigue, irritability, lack of motivation, social withdrawal, and depression. Cortical overactivity, or **Cushing's syndrome** (after the American physician Harvey Cushing), is a relatively rare disease generally affecting young women. Cushing's syndrome is characterized by physical symptoms such as weight gain, fatigue, and muscle weakness, and psychological indications such as negative mood states that may fluctuate between depression and anxiety.

EPILEPSY

CASSIUS: What, did Caesar swound[3]?
CASCA: He fell down in the market place and foamed at the mouth and was speechless.
BRUTUS: 'Tis very like—he hath the falling sickness.
                            Shakespeare, *Julius Caesar*, I,ii

Epilepsy—which Shakespeare referred to as "the falling sickness"—has struck not only Julius Caesar, but other notables such as Peter the Great, Lord Byron, Feodor Dostoevsky, and Vincent van Gogh. Perhaps 2 million Americans today suffer from epilepsy (Blakeslee, 1988b).

> Julius Caesar and Vincent van Gogh did in fact suffer from epilepsy.

---

[3] Swoon, or faint.

A number of noted historic figures have suffered from epilepsy, including Julius Caesar who, in the Shakespearian play given his name, was said to suffer from "the falling sickness." Others with epilepsy include the Russian ruler Peter the Great, as shown in the painting to the left by Louis Caravaque, and the French postimpressionist painter Vincent van Gogh, as shown in the self-portrait to the right.

Consider the stigma the epileptic has had to endure. Traditionally, victims of epilepsy have been feared and shunned. Their wild gyrations during seizures have been taken as signs of possession or insanity. They have been made to feel that they are different, that they should keep their distance and not expect to lead a full life, marry, or rear children. They have been humiliated in ways that were never imposed on victims of most other diseases, causing feelings of inadequacy, shame, and embarrassment. In many cases, the emotional toll of epilepsy has placed a greater burden on sufferers than the physical effects. Because of these attitudes, many epileptics hide their disorders and many physicians avoid using the term, preferring to label epilepsy a seizure disorder (Lechtenberg, 1984).

Epilepsy is not a disease in itself, but rather a manifestation of as many as 500 underlying disorders, such as a brain tumor, high fever during infancy, or a head injury (Blakeslee, 1988b). Epilepsy is characterized by disturbances in the electrical rhythms of the brain, which take the form of seizures and produce changes in states of consciousness (see Table 13.5). The seizures may begin several years after the initial trauma. Sometimes the seizures disappear during adolescence; in other cases, they continue for a lifetime. Some forms of epilepsy may be inherited, but most are not.

Epilepsy that can be attributed to definite causes, such as tumors or brain trauma, is called *acquired* or *symptomatic epilepsy*; cases of unknown origins are called *idiopathic epilepsy*. People with idiopathic epilepsy are believed to have subtle brain abnormalities that are not identifiable by current techniques for studying the functioning of the brain (Lechtenberg, 1984).

Various factors may precipitate an epileptic attack. Even in patients whose seizures are generally well controlled by medication, sleeplessness, infection, trauma, abuse of alcohol or drugs, even flashing lights can trigger attacks (Lechtenberg, 1984). In some epileptics, one night of sleeplessness may be sufficient to evoke an attack; others apparently suffering from the same type of epilepsy may be able to go for days without sleep before an attack occurs. The most common cause of recurrent seizures is haphazard use of prescribed medication. Hormonal changes may induce seizures at about the time of menstruation in female epileptics.

TABLE 13.5 Early Signs of Epilepsy

Wandering
Staring spells
Memory gaps
Bedwetting
Violent muscle spasms in sleep
Nocturnal tongue-biting

Source: *Lechtenberg, 1984.*

Epileptics often experience warning signs of the impending attack, called an **aura.** The aura embodies peculiar sensations or involuntary movements that are actually part of the seizure but experienced as separate (Lechtenberg, 1984). Auras can vary from person to person. Some people experience automatic behaviors like lip-smacking, grimacing, or spitting; or they feel compelled to turn their heads to the side. Others have sensations like unpleasant odors or tastes, feelings of depersonalization, fright, nausea, of a sense of *déjà vu*—that they have previously experienced the events that have just occurred. Some auras are experienced as generalized feelings of strangeness or peculiarity ("funny feelings"). Auras can usually be described vividly as they occur and recalled in detail after the seizure, but there is typically no memory of the convulsions themselves. Auras may help the sufferer prepare for the seizure by reducing the risk of injury.

Types of Epilepsy

There are actually many kinds of epilepsy, so it might be more appropriate to speak of *epilepsies*.

Tonic-clonic epilepsy is the most severe type of seizure. It entails a generalized convulsive or *grand mal seizure* involving abnormal activity in both hemispheres of the brain that causes a sudden loss of consciousness and is followed by convulsive, jerking movements of the body. The seizure often occurs without warning, although it may be preceded by an aura, typically consisting of a few seconds of sickness or lightheadedness. The attack itself may last from a few seconds to a few minutes. There are two phases of muscle activity, a *tonic phase* and a *clonic phase*. In the tonic phase, the muscles in the torso and limbs are rigidified. The legs are extended, the fists clenched, and the arms may be outstretched and forced tight against the body. This is followed by the *clonic stage*, involving strong muscle contractions that follow a rhythmic or clonic pattern and produce violent spasms alternating with moments of relaxation. During grand mal seizures, victims may lose bladder or bowel control and bite their tongues. Grand mal seizures can be frightening experiences to witness. Seeing someone fall to the ground and thrash about wildly can cause some bystanders to turn away or flee in fear. Informed bystanders, however, can help prevent tongue biting or breaking of teeth by placing an object like a folded handkerchief between the back teeth of the victim on one side of the mouth (Miller, 1978). The object should be too large to swallow. Care should be taken during insertion so that the good samaritan's fingers are not bitten. If you want to help, do not try to force the mouth open; wait until it momentarily relaxes.

When consciousness is regained, victims may experience confusion and fatigue, even falling into a deep sleep. Upon awakening, victims may have no memory of the seizure, although evidence of urination or soreness of the tongue may be recognized as signs of a seizure. Sufferers of grand mal seizures do not generally outgrow the disorder with age, but they may go for years or decades without a recurrence. Anticonvulsive medications are generally effective in suppressing recurrence of seizures when taken reliably (Lechtenberg, 1984).

In *petit mal epilepsy* (absence-type epilepsy) the individual experiences *absence attacks* or *petit mal seizures*, involving momentary lapses in consciousness that occur suddenly without a warning aura and usually last for a few seconds. Petit mal seizures are not accompanied by the violent spasms or falling that characterize grand mal seizures. The disorder is most common in children between the ages of 6 and 12. Seizures typically disappear during adolescence, but they may change to another type in adulthood, such as grand mal or psychomotor seizures (Lechtenberg, 1984). Petit mal seizures are characterized by transient loss of consciousness and lack of responsiveness to the environment. The victim may seem to be "staring into space." Attacks may occur repeatedly throughout the day. During such seizures, victims may seem as though they are frozen in place, as if someone had pushed the pause button on a VCR and frozen the action for a few seconds. Afterwards, they pick up where they had left off, often unaware of the intervening lapse and without the confusion and fatigue that usually attend a grand mal seizure. Petit mal seizures can go unrecognized because victims may simply appear to be momentarily lost in thought, distracted, daydreaming, or staring into space.

Victims of *psychomotor* or *temporal lobe* epilepsy retain motor control but experience a loss of contact with reality that may last up to a few minutes. Sufferers of psychomotor seizures may look lost in a trance but can continue to carry out mechanical or routine tasks such as walking down the street or doing repetitive household chores. Psychomotor epilepsy usually begins after puberty and is thought to account for 20 to 30 percent of cases (Lechtenberg, 1984). Psychomotor seizures generally begin in the temporal lobe of the brain, although some do not; other types of epilepsy may also involve temporal lobe disturbance. Some psychomotor seizures are characterized by abrupt, unusual, and apparently aimless behaviors such as running away,

TABLE 13.6 Myths and Facts about Epilepsy

Myth	Fact
All seizures involve convulsions.	Seizures involve disturbances in the brain's electrical activity and may or may not include convulsions.
During a seizure, an epileptic blanks out.	Some seizures involve complete loss of awareness; others involve minimal changes in the state of consciousness.
Epileptics typically experience different types of seizures.	Most epileptics experience only one type of seizure.
Having a seizure means that one is epileptic.	An isolated seizure may be a passing phenomenon—such as a response to a head trauma or brain infection. Following recovery, the individual may have no greater risk of recurrent seizures than the average person.
If one or both of my parents has epilepsy, then I'm bound to get it too.	Epilepsy is not inherited, although the neurological disorders that cause seizures may be. Children of an epileptic parent have less than a 3 percent chance of developing recurrent epilepsy. Epilepsy attributable to a head trauma is not inherited.
Epileptics are intellectually impaired because their brains have been damaged by their seizures.	Most people with idiopathic epilepsy (epilepsy with no known cause) show no sign of mental impairment.
Epileptics have disturbed personalities.	Epileptics can have perfectly normal personalities. Some have psychological problems that stem from coping with stigma. Learning to take precautions to avoid precipitants of seizures (for example, alcohol, exhaustion) and to take medication reliably are also stressful demands that can affect adjustment.
Men with epilepsy may commit rape during their seizures.	Some seizures may include unusual sexual behaviors that appear purposeless and not characteristic of the individual's usual behavior, such as public undressing or masturbation; however, men do not commit rapes, or make purposeful sexual advances, during seizures.
Family members should come to accept the epileptic as totally dependent upon them.	Adequately controlled epilepsy is more of an inconvenience than a calamity. Even when control of seizures requires restrictions, epileptics can look forward to social and financial independence.

Source: *Adapted from Lechtenberg (1984).*

LEARNING OBJECTIVES

When you have completed your study of Chapter 14, you should be able to:

1. Discuss ways of determining what is normal and abnormal in childhood and adolescence.

RISK FACTORS FOR DISORDERS OF CHILDHOOD AND ADOLESCENCE (pp. 484–485)

2. Discuss risk factors for disorders of childhood and adolescence.

AUTISM (pp. 485–491)

3. Discuss theoretical perspectives on autism.
4. Differentiate between autism and childhood schizophrenia.
5. Discuss treatment of autism.

MENTAL RETARDATION (pp. 491–497)

6. Describe how mental retardation is assessed.
7. Describe the levels of severity of mental retardation and review the capabilities and deficits associated with each level.
8. Discuss the causes of mental retardation.
9. Discuss the different methods of testing for genetic defects.
10. Discuss intervention approaches to mental retardation.
11. Discuss the savant syndrome.

LEARNING DISABILITIES (pp. 497–501)

12. Discuss the different types of learning disabilities.
13. Discuss theoretical perspectives on learning disabilities.
14. Discuss approaches to remediating learning disabilities.

DISRUPTIVE BEHAVIOR (pp. 502–506)

15. Discuss theoretical perspectives on attention-deficit hyperactivity disorder (ADHD).
16. Discuss treatment and outcome of ADHD.
17. Discuss theoretical perspectives on conduct disorders and approaches to treatment.

ANXIETY DISORDERS OF CHILDHOOD (pp. 506–509)

18. Describe various anxiety disorders of childhood and approaches to treatment.

DEPRESSION IN CHILDHOOD AND ADOLESCENCE (pp. 509–513)

19. Describe the features of depression in childhood and adolescence and approaches to treatment.
20. Discuss risk factors for suicide in adolescence.

EATING DISORDERS (pp. 513–520)

21. Describe anorexia nervosa and bulimia nervosa.
22. Discuss theoretical perspectives on anorexia nervosa and bulimia nervosa.
23. Discuss treatment of anorexia nervosa and bulimia nervosa.

ELIMINATION DISORDERS (pp. 520–521)

24. Discuss theoretical perspectives on functional enuresis and functional encopresis.
25. Discuss treatment of these disorders.

Insanity is hereditary. You can get it from your children.
(Sam Levenson)

At the age of 5 years 6 months, your first author's daughter, Jordan, would do the following in the course of a given day:

> Repeat verbatim several scenes from the movies *Spaceballs* and *Young Frankenstein*
> Change her clothing five or six times
> Drink orange juice from a baby bottle
> Play "Heart and Soul" on the piano a dozen times
> Punch her 7-year-old sister and her father
> Awaken several times during the night screaming
> Curse like a marine (or like a Mel Brooks film character)
> Curl up on a couch and play with her toes

Demand that one of her parents help wipe her after she makes "poo"

Lisp

Attain (prekindergarten) achievement test scores in the 99th percentile

After the monster goes wild, Igor, Dr. Frankenstein's assistant in *Young Frankenstein*, confesses to the good doctor that he had found the brain of "Abby Someone" for the experiment in rejuvenation. "Abby who?" asks Dr. Frankenstein. "Abby Normal," admits Igor.

Many times Jordan's parents asked themselves whether her behavior was normal or, well, "abby-normal." To determine what is normal and abnormal among children and adolescents, not only do we consider the criteria outlined in Chapter 1 but we also weigh what is to be expected given the child's age, gender, family and cultural background, and the sundry developmental transformations that are taking place (Garber, 1984; Sroufe & Rutter, 1984). Many problems are first identified when the child enters school. They may have existed earlier but been tolerated, or unrecognized as problematic, in the home. Sometimes the stress of starting school contributes to their onset.

There are diverse criteria for defining abnormal behavior in children, just as there are in adults. Some children exhibit bizarre behavior patterns. Others engage in self-defeating behavior, such as refusing to eat or going on a binge and then making themselves vomit. Others have deficiencies in intellectual growth, such as in mental retardation. Some act in ways that are socially inappropriate, as in conduct disorders. Other behavior disorders, such as those that involve anxiety and depression, are mainly characterized by distress in the child. But keep in mind that what is socially acceptable at one age, such as intense fear of strangers at about 18 months, may be socially unacceptable at more advanced ages.

> **?** Many behavior patterns that would be considered abnormal among adults—such as intense fear of strangers and lack of bladder control—are perfectly normal for children at certain ages.

Disorders of childhood and adolescence are classified on either Axis I or Axis II in the DSM–III–R system, depending on the particular disorder. Disorders involving deficits in the development of cognitive, social, and motor skills, such as mental retardation, autism, and learning disabilities, are classified on Axis II. These disorders tend to be chronic and to persist in some stable form into adulthood. Other developmental disorders, which are characterized by problem behaviors or distress, are classified as clinical syndromes on Axis I, such as anxiety disorders of childhood, eating disorders, and problems in controlling urination and defecation. Problems in childhood and adolescence often have a special poignancy. Many of them occur at ages when children have little capacity to cope. Many of them prevent children from fulfilling their developmental potentials.

Psychotherapy with children has been approached from various perspectives and differs in important respects from therapy with adults. Children may not have the verbal skills to be able to express their feelings through speech or even the ability to sit attentively in a chair or lie on a couch throughout a therapy session. So therapy methods must be tailored to the level of the child's cognitive, social, and emotional development. For example, psychodynamic therapists have developed techniques of **play therapy** in which children enact family conflicts symbolically through play activities, such as by "play-acting" with dolls or puppets. Or they might be given drawing materials and asked to sketch pictures, in the belief that their drawings would reflect the problems they are experiencing.

"Pop, am I experiencing a normal childhood?"

Drawing by Lorenz; © 1984. The New Yorker Magazine, Inc.

RISK FACTORS FOR DISORDERS OF CHILDHOOD AND ADOLESCENCE

The problems encountered in childhood and adolescence are quite varied, yet there are a number of risk factors that apply to most of them. Some of the factors that place children at risk are biological. Others involve cognitive or social factors, stresses due to undesirable life changes or family conflict, and parental neglect and abuse. One of the primary risk factors, however, is gender. Boys tend to be at greater risk for developing childhood problems that range from autism to hyperactivity to elimination disorders. Problems of anxiety and depression also affect boys more often than girls, by a ratio of about three to one (Achenbach, 1982). In adolescence, however, anxiety and mood disorders become more common among girls and remain so throughout adulthood. The eating disorders of anorexia and buing of information (Greenspan & Porges, 1984). Evidence is found in the rather specific pattern of cognitive dysfunctioning that characterizes autistic children (Hoffmann & Prior, 1982). It is unlikely that any particular pattern of child rearing could account for the highly similar patterns of bizarre behavior shown by autistic children around the world. The features of autism also resemble patterns that sometimes follow brain diseases such as encephalitis and congenital syphilis.

Many theorists suspect neurological damage because of the sundry impairments in mental functioning, including mental retardation, language deficits, bizarre motor behavior, even seizures. Certain neurological signs like drooling and lack of coordination are also found in most autistic children (Hoffmann & Prior, 1983). Damage in the cerebral cortex might account for seizures, failure to integrate perceptual information, and language problems. Some have placed the site of cerebral dysfunction in the left, or dominant, hemisphere, which tends to govern language and analytic functions—two areas of major deficiency in autistic children. So-called right-brain functions, like visual-motor skills, are relatively more normal among autistic children (Prior, 1979). Many autistic children also show abnormalities in brain waves, as measured by the electroencephalograph (EEG), especially a pattern of brain wave activity that is associated with persistent states of heightened arousal. It has been hypothesized that dysfunction of brain structures involved in regulating levels of arousal, such as the reticular formation, may fail to maintain states of arousal at a proper level (Rimland, 1984). But "hard" evidence of the specific sites of brain pathology that might account for autism has remained elusive.

Research findings conflict concerning the involvement of neurotransmitters in autism (Yuwiler & Freedman, 1987). However, most autistic children have higher-than-normal levels of serotonin and dopamine. Moreover, stimulants like amphetamines, which heighten levels of dopamine, exacerbate the symptoms of autistic children—as they exacerbate the symptoms of adult schizophrenics.

If there is brain dysfunction in autistic children, where does it originate? Some theorists argue in favor of genetic factors. For example, in one study of twins, 4 of 11 monozygotic (identical) twins of autistic children showed the disorder, as compared with none of 10 dizygotic (fraternal) twins of autistic children (Folstein & Rutter, 1978). Moreover, another four of the identical twins shared one or more signs of autism, such as lagging language development or pronoun reversal. But the lack of 100 percent concordance among the identical twins shows that environmental factors are likely to play a role in the disorder. Genetic factors appear to play a relatively stronger role among autistic children who are also severely mentally retarded (Baird & August, 1985).

Other theorists attribute brain dysfunction to congenital disorders and birth complications. For example, whereas autism strikes about 0.2 percent of the general population, it is found among 8 to 10 percent of children with congenital rubella (German measles)—a notable discrepancy (Chess et al., 1971). Yet another hypothesis grows out of the finding that mothers of autistic children are more likely to suffer spontaneous abortions and threatened miscarriages. It has been speculated that these complications, and autism, may result from prenatal damage at the hands of the mothers' immune systems (Stubbs et al., 1985). In a sense, the mother's immune system may attack the unborn child as it would an invading organism.

Treatment Approaches

Psychodynamically oriented treatments for autism have included psychotherapy, play therapy, and placement of children in residential facilities largely governed by Bruno Bettelheim's ideas. The residences aim to provide children the warmth presumed to be lacking in the home. Undeviating support is intended to help autistic children form secure attachments to other people who then become introjected as positive self-images (Sanders, 1974). Children are also given the chance to influence their environments. Their demands are met as long as they are not self-injurious.

Bettelheim claimed that some 42 percent of the children in residence at his Orthogenetic School in Chicago have benefitted from treatment (1967). However, the criteria for improvement have been inconsistent, and Bettelheim's observations may have been colored by his expectations. Other reports suggest that residential treatment and psychodynamically oriented psychotherapy are less effective than behavioral approaches (Rimland, 1977).

Although most behaviorists do not contend that autism is caused by faulty learning, they suggest that principles of learning may be effective in the treatment of autistic behavior. There are reports that operant conditioning methods (that is, systematic use of rewards and punishments) have encouraged autistic children to pay attention to therapists (Lovaas, 1977), to play with other children (Romanczyk et al., 1975), and to stop self-mutilative behavior. Techniques like extinction (withholding reinforcement following a response) are sometimes effective for behaviors like head banging, but a great many unreinforced trials (trials that are ignored) may be required to eliminate the response. In one case, 1,800 head bangs over eight days were required before the response was eliminated (Simmons & Lovaas, 1969). The problem seems to be that many repetitive behavior patterns—like rocking and self-injurious behaviors—are internally reinforced by providing increased stimulation. Therefore, withdrawal of social reinforcers may have little if any effect.

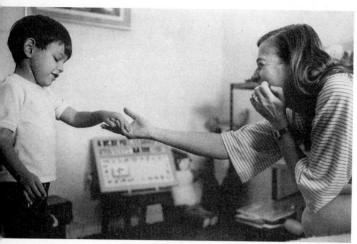

One of the principal therapeutic tasks in working with autistic children is the establishment of interpersonal contact. Psychodynamic therapists emphasize the importance of continual support to help the autistic child form secure attachments. Behavioral therapists use reinforcers to increase adaptive social behaviors, such as paying attention to the therapist and playing with other children. Behavioral therapists may also use punishments to stop self-mutilative behavior.

Use of aversive stimulation such as spanking and, in extreme cases, electric shock produces more rapid effects than extinction. Lovaas reported that painful but apparently noninjurious electric shock can eliminate self-mutilation within a minute of application (Lovaas, 1971). Using electric shock with children raises moral, ethical, and legal concerns, of course. Lovaas has countered that failure to eliminate self-injurious behavior places the child at greater risk of serious physical harm and denies children the opportunity to participate in other kinds of therapy. Lovaas also suggests that the use of aversive stimulation should be combined with positive reinforcement for acceptable alternate behaviors (Simmons & Lovaas, 1969).

Because autistic children show behavioral deficits, a central focus of behavior modification is the development of new behavior. New behaviors are maintained by reinforcements, so it is important to teach autistic children, who often respond to people as they would to a piece of furniture, to accept people as reinforcers. People can be established as reinforcers by pairing praise with primary positive reinforcers like food (Lovaas et al., 1965). Then social reinforcement (praise) and primary reinforcers (food) can be used in shaping and modeling toileting behaviors, speech, and social play (Lovaas et al., 1966). The involvement of families and residential treatment personnel in these behavioral programs prompts the maintenance and generalization of behavioral changes (Anderson et al., 1986; Harris, 1986; Romanczyk, 1986).

The results of a recent long-term study showed significant benefits of intensive behavioral treatment (Lovaas, 1987). In this study, autistic children received 40 hours of one-to-one behavior modification each week for at least two years. Significant intellectual and educational gains were reported for 9 of the 19 children (47%) in the program. These improved children achieved normal IQ scores and were able to succeed in the first grade. Only 2 percent of a control group that did not receive the intensive treatment achieved similar gains. While these are among the most promising results to date in the treatment of autistic children, longer-term follow-ups remain to be reported.

Biological approaches have had some limited impact in the treatment of autism. It is understood that amphetamines excacerbate autistic and schizophrenic behavior patterns, apparently by heightening the action of dopamine in each case. In contrast, phenothiazines, which lessen dopamine activity, have been found to diminish many aspects of autistic behavior, including self-mutilation and rocking movements (Campbell et al., 1982; Clark & Witherspoon, 1984; Geller et al., 1982). However, there is little evidence that drugs foster the cognitive and language development of autistic children.

■ **The Long-Term View** Over the years only a small minority of autistic children—perhaps 5 percent—have developed into self-sufficient and independent adults (DeMyer et al., 1981; Kernberg, 1979; Rutter, 1983). For example, a follow-up study run at a Canadian regional research center showed that more than half of the treated children remained institutionalized, and 90 percent remained intellectually deficient. Only a few held jobs or lived independently (Wolf & Goldberg, 1986). Almost half (46%) lacked meaningful speech (see Figure 14.1).

The long-term prospects may differ for autistic children who are retarded and those who are not (Prior, 1984). Language skills, which correlate with overall intellectual development, are also predictive of future adjustment. It remains to be seen whether efforts to promote language development will lead to long-term improvements.

Autism versus Childhood Schizophrenia

The diagnostic manual no longer includes a separate category of childhood schizophrenia, preferring to use the label of schizophrenia for the relatively rare instances in which a schizophrenic disorder first develops in childhood. **Childhood schizophrenia,** like adult schizophrenia, is marked by confusion and disorientation, social withdrawal, incoherent speech, odd motor behaviors, loose associations, delusions, and hallucinations. Children who have received the diagnosis often report bizarre imaginary events, which suggests that their ways of perceiving the world are severely distorted. The onset of childhood schizophrenia is usually after

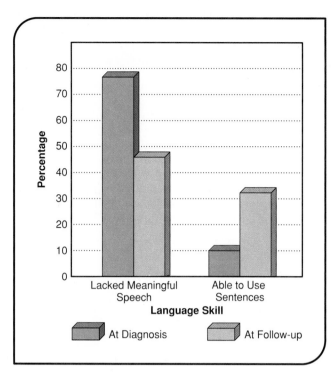

FIGURE 14–1 *Language skills of young adults diagnosed as autistic in childhood.*

Autistic children continue to show widespread deficits in cognitive, social, and emotional development into adulthood. Here we see the percentages of autistics who lacked meaningful speech and were unable to use sentences at the time of initial diagnosis and at a follow-up evaluation occurring some 17 years later when they averaged 20 years of age.

Source: Adapted from Wolf & Goldberg (1986)

30 months of age (autism usually comes on earlier), and it affects boys and girls equally. Autistic children generally show indifference to other people, although they may become attached to inanimate objects. But schizophrenic children, by contrast, appear to become excessively attached to their parents. They may cling to them and shriek at minor separations. Children labeled as childhood schizophrenics also do not show the intellectual and language deficiencies displayed by autistic children. Kernberg (1979) claims that phenothiazines are reasonably effective in treating childhood schizophrenia as they are in the adult version of the disorder. But it is still unclear whether schizophrenia in childhood is the same disorder as schizophrenia in adulthood.

MENTAL RETARDATION

Mental retardation involves a general delay in the development of intellectual and adaptive abilities that affect most areas of social, cognitive, and language functioning. The course of development of mentally retarded children is variable. Many improve over time, especially if they are exposed to stimulating environments that provide support and guidance from others and enriched educational opportunities. Others who are exposed to more impoverished environments may fail to improve or may deteriorate further.

Mental retardation is generally assessed by a combination of testing on formal tests of intelligence and by observation of the child's adaptive functioning. To be considered mentally retarded, the person must meet three diagnosable criteria according to DSM–III–R: (1) receive an IQ score of 70 or below on a test like the Wechsler Intelligence Scale for Children–Revised edition, or the Stanford Binet; (2) show concurrent evidence of impaired functioning in adaptive behavior; and (3) show evidence of onset of the disorder before age 18. Persons whose behavior is impaired fail to meet the standards of behavior that are expected of someone of the same age in a given cultural group, in terms of developing social and communication skills, caring for oneself, and becoming independent and self-sufficient. For infants, qualitative judgments of significant subaverage intellectual functioning are used in place of IQ scores, since tests of infant intelligence do not generally yield numerical IQ scores.

Mental retardation varies in degree of severity, as shown in Table 14.2 A description of the deficits and abilities associated with the degree of severity of mental retardation is shown in Table 14.3. Most mentally retarded children (about 85%) fall in the mildly retarded range. These youngsters are generally capable of meeting the demands of school and can eventually function on their own in adulthood, although they may require additional guidance and support in times of stress. Moderately retarded children can learn to talk and take care of themselves, although they require additional supervision. Eventually they may learn to adapt to useful work roles under supportive conditions, such as in sheltered workshops. According to DSM–III–R, they don't usually progress beyond the second-grade level in acquiring academic skills, such as skills of reading and arithmetic. They tend to adjust successfully to community living, usually within a supervised group home. Most people in the severe range of mental retar-

TABLE 14.2 *Levels of Mental Retardation*

Degree of Severity	Approximate IQ Range	Percentage of Mentally Retarded
Mild mental retardation	50–70	Approx. 85
Moderate mental retardation	35–49	10
Severe mental retardation	20–34	3–4
Profound mental retardation	Below 20	1–2

Source: *Adapted from DSM–III–R, pp. 32–33.*

TABLE 14.3 Levels of Retardation, Typical Ranges of IQ Scores, and Types of Adaptive Behaviors Shown

Approximate IQ Score Range	Preschool Age 0–5 Maturation and Development	School Age 6–21 Training and Education	Adult 21 and Over Social and Vocational Adequacy
Mild 50–70	Often not noticed as retarded by casual observer, but is slower to walk, feed self, and talk than most children.	Can acquire practical skills and useful reading and arithmetic to a 3rd to 6th grade level with special education. Can be guided toward social conformity.	Can usually achieve social and vocational skills adequate to self-maintenance; may need occasional guidance and support when under unusual social or economic stress.
Moderate 35–49	Noticeable delays in motor development, especially in speech; responds to training in various self-help activities.	Can learn simple communication, elementary health and safety habits, and simple manual skills; does not progress in functional reading or arithmetic.	Can perform simple tasks under sheltered conditions; participates in simple recreation; travels alone in familiar places.
Severe 20–34	Marked delay in motor development; little or no communication skill; may respond to training in elementary self-help—for example, self-feeding.	Usually walks, barring specific disability; has some understanding of speech and some response; can profit from systematic habit training.	Can conform to daily routines and repetitive activities; needs continuing direction and supervision in protective environment.
Profound Below 20	Gross retardation; minimal capacity for functioning in sensorimotor areas; needs nursing care.	Obvious delays in all areas of development; shows basic emotional responses; may respond to skillful training in use of legs, hands, and jaws; needs close supervision.	May walk, may need nursing care, may have primitive speech; will usually benefit from regular physical activity; incapable of self-maintenance.

Source: *Adapted from L. E. Bourne, Jr., & B. R. Ekstrand*, Psychology: Its Principles and Meaning, *4th ed. (New York: Holt, Rinehart & Winston, 1982), p. 209. Reprinted from S. A. Rathus,* Understanding Child Development *(New York: Holt, Rinehart & Winston, 1988), p. 374.*

dation are also able to adapt to living in the community when they receive appropriate support, but they are more limited in the skills they can perform. The more profoundly mentally retarded may still be trained to perform simple tasks under close supervision and many are capable of living in the community in structured settings or group homes.

The great majority of mentally retarded people fall in the mild range of severity. They are generally capable of independent functioning, although they may require some guidance and support.

Causes of Retardation

In many cases, mental retardation can be traced to biological causes, including chromosomal and genetic disorders, infectious diseases, and brain damage. In cases where there is no evidence of biological defects, impoverishment in the child's home environment is suspected as a cause or at least a contributor to retardation.

■ **Chromosomal Abnormalities** The most common chromosomal abnormality linked to mental retardation

is **Down syndrome** (formerly called Down's syndrome), which is characterized by an extra or third chromosome on the 21st pair of chromosomes, resulting in 47 chromosomes rather than the normal complement of 46. Down syndrome occurs in about one in 800 births. It usually occurs when the 21st pair of chromosomes in either the egg or the sperm fails to divide normally, resulting in an extra chromosome. The abnormality increases in likelihood with the age of the parents, so that expectant couples in their thirties or older often undergo prenatal genetic tests (see box following) to detect Down syndrome and other genetic abnormalities. While the abnormality is often traced to a defect in the mother's chromosomes, we should note that about 25 percent of cases can be attributed to defects in the father's sperm. People with Down syndrome are recognizable by certain physical features, such as a round face, broad, flat nose, and small, downward-sloping folds of skin at the inside corners of the eyes, which gives the impression of slanted eyes. These physical features create a superficial resemblance to Asian people, which was reflected in the former use of the term *mongolism* to refer to these children. The term was recognized as racist and has since been discarded.

Children with Down syndrome are also characterized by a protruding tongue, small, squarish hands and

A CLOSER LOOK
Genetic Counseling and Prenatal Testing

Genetic counseling has become widely used as a method of helping parents avert genetic tragedies. The genetic counselor takes information about the couple's ages and genetic background characteristics in order to determine the probabilities of genetic or chromosomal defects in their offspring. Couples with high risk potential for these defects may elect adoption rather than incur the risks of bearing children.

Various genetic tests for pregnant women have been developed to help detect the presence of genetic and chromosomal abnormalities in their fetuses, such as Down syndrome and Tay-Sachs disease. In *amniocentesis*, which is usually conducted about 14 to 15 weeks following conception, a sample of amniotic fluid is drawn from the amniotic sac, which contains the fetus. Cells from the fetus can then be separated from the fluid, allowed to grow in a culture, and examined for the presence of biochemical and chromosomal abnormalities. In *chorionic villus sampling* or CVS, small pieces of the hairlike material or villi on the amniotic sac are snipped for analysis. CVS can be performed at 9 to 12 weeks after conception.

Since these tests carry some risk of miscarriage and infection, they are usually performed only on women at greater genetic risk, such as those above the age of 35 or who have other children who are genetically damaged. Because amniocentesis and CVS carry about an equal risk of infection and miscarriage (Kolata, 1988), CVS may increase in popularity over the next several years since it provides results several weeks earlier than amniocentesis. Down syndrome may also be detected on the basis of a blood test, the alpha-fetoprotein test. But since the results of this test are not considered conclusive, a positive finding may be followed up by amniocentesis. Blood tests are also used to detect carriers of Tay-Sachs disease.

Amniocentesis involves the extraction of a sample of amniotic fluid to test for biochemical and chromosomal abnormalities. With sophisticated ultrasound equipment, as shown here, the physician can fix the location of the fetus to help prevent accidental injury to the fetus while inserting the syringe.

In the future, it may be possible to correct the damaging effects of defective genes during prenatal development, sparing the child from predictable consequences of genetic abnormalities. But for the present time, expectant couples who are informed that their unborn children are genetically defective grapple with the often agonizing decision about whether or not to follow through with an abortion. The question of abortion in such cases raises painful moral and personal dilemmas not only for the affected families but also for the larger society.

short fingers, a curved fifth finger, and disproportionately small arms and legs in relation to their bodies. Nearly all these children are mentally retarded and many suffer from physical problems, such as malformations of the heart and respiratory difficulties. Sadly, most die by middle age. In their later years, they tend to suffer memory losses and experience childish emotions that represent a form of senility (Kolata, 1985). While the birth of a Down-syndrome child is often traumatic for the family, with time most of these children become accepted within the family and, like other children, come to provide the family with joy and pleasure (Gath, 1985).

Children with Down syndrome suffer various deficits in learning and development. They tend to be uncoordinated and to lack proper muscle tone, which makes it difficult for them to carry out physical tasks and engage in play activities like other children. Down-syndrome children suffer memory deficits, especially

Although persons with Down syndrome suffer from deficits in learning and development, most can learn to function productively with the right encouragement and training.

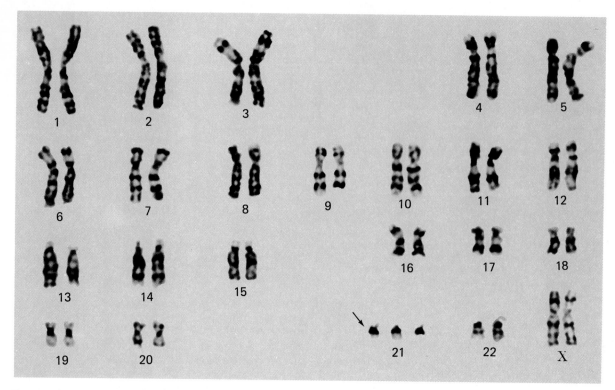

Down syndrome is a genetic disorder which is linked in more than 95% of cases to an extra (third) chromosome on the 21st pair, resulting in 47 chromosomes rather than the normal complement of 46. Here the extra chromosome on the 21st pair is indicated by an arrow. In a few cases of Down syndrome, there are only 46 chromosomes, but one of the chromosomes on the 21st pair is defective.

for information presented verbally, which makes it difficult for them to learn in school. They also have difficulty following instructions from teachers and expressing their thoughts or needs clearly in speech. Despite their disabilities, most can learn to read, write, and perform simple arithmetic, if they receive appropriate schooling and the right encouragement.

Although less common than Down syndrome, chromosomal abnormalities of the sex chromosome may also result in mental retardation, such as in Klinefelter's syndrome and Turner's syndrome. Klinefelter's syndrome, which only occurs among males, is characterized by the presence of an extra X sex chromosome, resulting in an XXY rather than XY pattern. Men with this XXY pattern fail to develop appropriate secondary sex characteristics, resulting in enlarged breasts, poor muscular development, and infertility. Mild retardation occurs frequently among these men.

Found only among females is Turner's syndrome, characterized by the presence of a single X sex chromosome instead of the normal two. While such girls develop normal external genitals, their ovaries remain poorly developed, producing reduced amounts of estrogen. These women tend to be shorter than average and are infertile. They also tend to show evidence of mild retardation, especially in skills relating to math and science.

■ **Recessive-Gene Disorders**   **Phenylketonuria** (PKU), a genetic abnormality transmitted by a recessive gene, prevents the child from metabolizing the amino acid *phenylalanine*, which is found in many foods. Consequently, phenylalanine and its derivative, phenylpyruvic acid, accumulate in the body, causing damage to the central nervous system, which results in mental retardation and emotional disturbance. The presence of PKU can be detected among newborns by analyzing blood or urine samples. While there is no cure for PKU, children with the disorder may suffer less damage or even develop normally if they are placed on a diet low in phenylalanine within three to six weeks after birth. These children also receive protein supplements that compensate for their nutritional loss.

Tay-Sachs disease is also caused by recessive genes. Tay-Sachs disease, which mostly afflicts Jews of Eastern European ancestry, is a fatal degenerative disease of the central nervous system. About one in 25 American Jews is a carrier of the recessive gene responsible for the disorder, so the chances that both members of a Jewish couple carry the gene are about one in 625. Children afflicted with Tay-Sachs disease suffer gradual loss of muscle control, deafness and blindness, retardation and paralysis, and eventually die before the age of 5.

■ **Prenatal Factors**   Some cases of mental retardation are caused by maternal infection or alcohol or drug use during pregnancy. Rubella (German measles) in the mother, for example, can be passed along to the unborn child, causing brain damage that results in later retardation, and it may play a role in autism, as noted earlier. While the mother may experience only mild or even no symptoms, the effects on the fetus she carries can be tragic. Other maternal diseases that carry a risk of mental retardation to the unborn child include **syphilis** and **herpes simplex.**

Widespread programs to immunize women against rubella and to test for syphilis by analysis of maternal blood samples before pregnancy have greatly reduced the risk of transmission of these infections to unborn children. Most children who contract herpes from their mothers do so by contact with the virus in the birth canal during delivery. Caesarean sections can be used when an outbreak in the mother is suspected to help prevent this contact and thereby reduce the risk of transmitting the infection to the child.

Various drugs that the mother ingests during pregnancy can pass through the placenta to the child. Some can cause severe birth deformities and mental retardation, like the tranquilizer thalidomide, which was prescribed in the 1960s to control "morning sickness" in pregnant women until it became known that children whose mothers had been prescribed the drug were born with undeveloped limbs and mental retardation. Children whose mothers abused alcohol during pregnancy are often born with **fetal alcohol syndrome,** which is often characterized by mental retardation and by various physical abnormalities, as discussed earlier in Chapter 10.

Other physical causes of mental retardation occur during or following birth. Birth complications, such as oxygen deprivation or head injuries, place children at risk for development of mental retardation and other neurological disorders. Infants who are born prematurely are also at greater risk of later retardation and other developmental problems. Following birth, infections or traumas to the brain during infancy and early childhood can cause mental retardation and other health problems. Children who ingest environmental toxins, such as paint chips containing lead, may also suffer brain damage that produces mental retardation.

■ **Cultural-Familial Causes**   We have noted that most cases (perhaps 85%) of mental retardation fall in the mild range of severity. For many of these children, there is no apparent biological cause or distinguishing physical feature that sets them apart from other children. It is widely believed that psychosocial factors, such as an impoverished social environment, either cause or contribute to the development of mental retardation in these youngsters. It is also possible that this form of retardation involves complex interactions between heredity and environment.

In these cases, called **cultural-familial retardation,** the child fails to develop age-appropriate behaviors at a normal pace. Children of poverty may be most at risk for development of cultural-familial retardation since they are often raised in impoverished conditions that lack the social and intellectual stimulation to foster cognitive development. For example, children of poverty may lack stimulating books and interactive toys that might otherwise enrich their intellectual development. Their parents may be too stressed from the demands of meeting economic necessities to have the quality time available to stimulate their children's intellectual growth by reading to them, talking to them at length, and by exposing them to creative play activities or trips to museums and parks. Consequently, the children may spend most of their days glued to the TV set. The parents, most of whom were also raised in poverty, may be too deficient themselves in reading or communication skills to help shape the development of these skills in their children. Sadly, a vicious circle of poverty and impoverished intellectual development may be repeated from generation to generation.

Children with this form of retardation may respond dramatically when provided with enriched learning experiences, especially at the earlier ages. Social programs like Head Start, for example, have helped children at risk of cultural-familial retardation to function within the normal range of ability.

Intervention

The services that mentally retarded children require to meet the developmental challenges they face depend in part on the level of severity of retardation. With appropriate training, children with mild retardation may approach a sixth-grade level of competence, and can acquire vocational skills that allow them to support themselves minimally through meaningful work. Many of these children can be "mainstreamed" in regular classes. At the other extreme, the profoundly mentally retarded may need institutional care or placement in a residential care facility in the community, like a group home. Placement in an institution is often based on the need to control destructive or aggressive behavior, not because it is required by the severity of the individual's intellectual impairment, as we see in this case example of a child with moderate retardation:

■ The mother pleaded with the emergency room physician to admit her 15-year-old son, claiming that she couldn't take it anymore. Her son, a Down syndrome patient with an IQ of 45, had alternated since the age of eight between living in institutions and at home. Each visiting day he pleaded with his mother to take him home, and after about a year at each placement, she would bring him home but find herself unable to control his behavior. During temper tantrums, he would break dishes and destroy furniture and had recently become physically assaultive toward his mother, hitting her on the arm and shoulder during a recent scuffle when she attempted to stop him from repeatedly banging a broom on the floor.

Adapted from Spitzer et al., 1989, pp. 338–340 ■

In 1975, Congress passed the Education for All Handicapped Children Act, Public Law 94–142, which required public schools to provide handicapped children with free public education that is appropriate to their needs. This law was an impetus for a massive increase in special education programs for children with mental retardation and other handicapping conditions like physical disability. To ensure the appropriateness of the educational experience for each handicapped child, school officials must adapt the educational program to the needs of the particular student. This often involves a multidisciplinary approach, in which professionals from different disciplines evaluate the child and write specific recommendations for the types of services and training experiences that would be best suited to the child's special needs. Some communities, however, have been slow to act in conforming with the law. This is because Congress has not appropriated the additional funds needed to ensure compliance, and local governments are often unwilling to raise taxes to pay for special education programs in their communities. There also remain some legal questions about the range

In 1975, Congress enacted legislation that required public schools to provide handicapped children with education that meets their individual needs. Here a teacher demonstrates wood-sanding techniques to a severely mentally retarded adolescent.

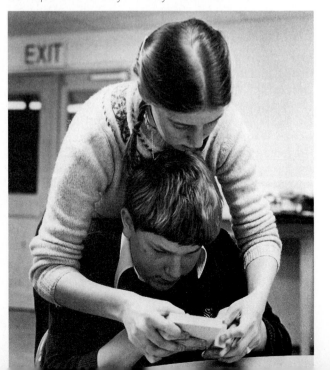

of services to handicapped children that local governments are mandated to provide.

The question of whether mentally retarded children should be "mainstreamed" in regular classes or placed in special education classes remains a matter of controversy. Some mildly retarded children may achieve better when they are mainstreamed in regular classes (Robinson & Robinson, 1976). But others may not do so well in regular classes, for they may find them to be overwhelming, causing them to withdraw from their schoolmates (Linton & Juul, 1980).

There has also been a trend toward deinstitutionalization of the more severely mentally retarded. The Developmentally Disabled Assistance and Bill of Rights Act, which Congress passed in 1975, provided that persons with mental retardation have the right to receive appropriate treatment in the least restrictive treatment setting. Mentally retarded people who are capable of functioning in the community have the right to receive less restrictive care than that provided in large institutions. Many moderately or severely retarded adolescents and adults are capable of living outside the institution and have been placed in supervised group homes, which house perhaps 10 to 15 residents. Residents typically share the household responsibilities and are encouraged by staff members to participate in meaningful daily activities, such as attending specialized training programs or sheltered workshops. Others live with their families while attending structured day programs. Mildly retarded adults often work in outside jobs and live in their own apartments or share apartments with other mildly retarded persons.

Mentally retarded children and adults may need psychological counseling to help them cope with the emotional challenges they face in adjusting to life in the community. Many have difficulty making friends and may become socially isolated. Problems with self-esteem are also common, especially since individuals with mental retardation are often subjected to demeaning comments and ridicule from others. Supportive counseling may be supplemented with more structured behavioral techniques that are focused on helping retarded persons acquire various life skills, such as self-care, vocational, and social skills.

Social skills training is used to help participants learn more appropriate social skills, such as conversational and job interviewing skills (see Kelly et al., 1980). Other behavioral approaches have also been used to teach adaptive behaviors which more severely retarded persons may be lacking, such as self-care skills like brushing one's teeth, dressing oneself, and combing one's hair. In the example of toothbrushing, the therapist might first define the component parts of the targeted behavior (picking up the toothbrush, wetting the toothbrush, taking the cap off the tube, putting the paste on the brush, etc.) (Kissel et al., 1983). The therapist might then shape the desired behavior by using such techniques as *verbal instruction* (for example, "Jim, pick up the toothbrush"), *physical guidance* (physically guiding the client's hand in performing the desired response), and *reward* (use of positive verbal reinforcement) for successful completion of the desired response ("That's really good, Jim"). The use of these behavioral-shaping techniques has even been shown to be effective in teaching a simple but remunerative vocational skill (for example, stamping return addresses on envelopes) to a group of severely retarded adult women who were so handicapped that they were essentially nonverbal (Schepis et al., 1987). Such techniques may help people who are more severely retarded develop adaptive capacities that can enable them to perform more productive roles.

LEARNING DISABILITIES

Nelson Rockefeller served as governor of New York State and as vice president of the United States. He was brilliant and well educated. However, despite the best of tutors, he always struggled to read. Rockefeller suffered from **dyslexia,** which derives from the Greek roots *dys-*, meaning "bad," and *lexikon*, meaning "of words." Dyslexia is a kind of **learning disability.** While mental retardation involves a general delay in intellectual development, people with learning disabilities may be generally intelligent, or even gifted, but show inadequate development in specific arithmetic, writing, reading, language, or speech skills associated with impaired performance in school or in activities of daily living.

The term *learning disability* was coined in the 1960s (Kirk, 1963) to highlight a number of academic and related problems. The exact numbers of the learning disabled are unknown, but it has been estimated that as many as 10 percent of the general population suffer from dyslexia to some degree (Meier, 1971). Boys are more than two to four times as likely as girls to incur problems in reading, writing, language, and speech. Learning disabilities tend to run a chronic course. The more severe the problem is in childhood, the more likely it is that it will affect adult development (Spreen, 1988). Learning-disabled children tend to perform generally poorly in school. They are often viewed as failures by their teachers and their families. It is not surprising that most of them have developed low expectations and problems in self-esteem by the age of 9. Moreover, their academic and personal problems tend to intensify as time passes (Wenar, 1983).

Authorities do not universally agree on ways of defining learning disabilities. One approach considers children to be learning disabled in a particular academic skill if they perform at two grade levels or more below their age levels or grade levels (Morris, 1988). However, children advance more rapidly at younger ages, so a second grader performing at a kindergarten level is relatively more deficient than an eighth grader performing at a sixth-grade level. A specific cut-off point, like the two-year discrepancy, seems arbitrary. A second approach focuses on the gap between the children's achievement test scores and what children of comparable intelligence achieve. The intelligence–achievement gap is the criterion suggested in the DSM–III–R. Some authorities limit the diagnosis of learning disability to children who are "at least average" in intelligence. However, there is no universally accepted standard for determining what is meant by "at least average" (Morris, 1988). Sometimes an IQ score of 90 is used as the lower boundary of average intelligence. In other cases, IQ scores as low as 70 are considered low average as opposed to mentally retarded. Other authorities suggest that even children whose IQ scores fall within the retarded range may be considered learning disabled if their achievement does not keep pace with that of children of comparable potential.

The Education for All Handicapped Children Act, which Congress passed in 1975, drew a distinction between learning disabilities and learning problems that stem from certain causes, such as mental retardation, emotional disorders, visual, hearing or motor handicaps, and cultural, economic, or environmental disadvantage. The exclusion of learning problems that might be attributable to such environmental causes as cultural or economic disadvantage from the purview of learning disabilities has drawn fire on political and scientific grounds. It has been suggested, for example, that attributing the disproportionately high incidence of academic failures among poor children to impoverished environments is tantamount to expecting them to fail (Morris, 1988). The underlying message to the child—and the child's school system—seems to be: Why bother to make special efforts to help them succeed in school? Refusal to accept failure from poor children, on the other hand, might encourage them—and their teachers—to do everything they can to remediate specific deficits in learning.

Types of Learning Disorders

Learning disabilities are referred to as *academic skills disorders* and *language and speech disorders* in the DSM–III–R. The specific disorders are listed in Table 14.4 and are considered in more detail below.

■ **Academic Skills Disorders** *Developmental arithmetic disorder* describes children with deficiencies in arithmetic skills, like problems in understanding basic math-

TABLE 14.4 Subtypes of Academic Skills Disorders and Language and Speech Disorders

Academic Skills Disorders	Developmental Arithmetic Disorder
	Developmental Expressive Writing Disorder
	Developmental Reading Disorder
Language and Speech Disorders	Developmental Articulation Disorder
	Developmental Expressive Language Disorder
	Developmental Receptive Language Disorder

Source: *Adapted from DSM–III–R, pp. 41–48.*

ematical terms or operations, such as addition or subtraction; in decoding mathematical symbols (+, =, etc.); or in learning multiplication tables. The problem may become apparent as early as the first grade (age 6) but is not generally recognized until about the third grade (age 8).

Developmental expressive writing disorder refers to children with grossly deficient writing skills. The impairment in writing ability may be characterized by errors in spelling, grammar, or punctuation, or by difficulty in composing sentences and paragraphs. Severe writing difficulties generally become apparent by age 7 (second grade), although milder cases may not be recognized until the age of 10 (fifth grade) or later.

A CLOSER LOOK
The Savant Syndrome

Got a minute? Try the following:

1. Without referring to a calendar, calculate the day of the week that March 15, 2079, will fall on.

2. List the prime numbers between 1 and 1 billion. (*Hint*: The list starts 1, 2, 3, 5, 7, 11, 13, 17 . . .)

3. Repeat verbatim the newspaper stories you read over coffee this morning.

4. Sing accurately every note played by the first violin in Beethoven's Ninth Symphony.

These tasks are impossible for all but a very few of us. Ironically, those of us who are most likely to be able to accomplish these feats—*idiot savants*—are autistic, retarded, or both.

The idiot savant (derived from the French *savoir*, meaning "to know") has been described as possessing "islands of mental ability in a sea of mental handicap and disability" (Treffert, 1988, p. 563). Idiot (pronounced *id-ee-oh*) savants have severe mental deficiencies but nonetheless possess some remarkable mental abilities. The prevalence of the savant syndrome within the retarded population is estimated at about 1 case in 2,000 (Hill, 1977). Prevalence rates are reported to be higher among autistic populations. Most idiot savants, like most autistic people, are male (Treffert, 1988). Among a sample of 5,400 autistic people, 531 cases (9.8%) were reported by parents to have the savant syndrome (Rimland, 1978). Parents tend to think of their children as special and might overreport the incidence of the savant syndrome, however.

Several hundred savants have been described in this century. They are reported to have shown remarkable but circumscribed mental skills, such as calendar calculating, and rare musical talent, both of which stand in contrast to their limited general intellectual abilities. Idiot savants also have outstanding memories. Just as we learn about health by studying illness, we may be able to learn more about normal mechanisms of memory by studying people

in whom memory stands apart from other aspects of mental functioning (Treffert, 1988).

The label *savant syndrome* is probably preferable to the more common, but pejorative term *idiot savant*. The phenomenon occurs more frequently in males by a ratio of about 6 to 1. The special skills of the savant tend to appear out of the blue and may disappear as suddenly. Some savants engage in lightning calculations. The nineteenth-century Virginia slave Thomas Fuller "was able to calculate the number of seconds in 70 years, 17 days and 12 hours in a minute and one half, taking into account the 17 leap years that would have occurred in the period" (Smith, 1983). So-called calendar calculators, like Fuller, may not actually calculate. Perhaps they rely on camera-sharp memories and are able to scan an endless scroll of calendars in their minds to arrive at the answer. There are also cases of blind savants who could play back any musical piece, no matter how complex, or repeat long passages of foreign languages without losing a syllable. Some savants make exact estimates of elapsed time. One could reportedly repeat verbatim the contents of a newspaper he had just heard; another could repeat backwards what he had just read (Tradgold, 1914, cited in Treffert, 1988).

 Ability to recall news stories verbatim is shown by some individuals with the "savant syndrome."

Sacks (1985) describes the case of savant twins, who were apparently incapable of simple computations and seemed to lack any knowledge of division and multiplication. Yet they immediately "perceived" relationships among numbers. Upon seeing a bunch of matches that had fallen to the floor, they called out "111," the correct number, too quickly to have counted. Then one twin exclaimed "37," having factored 111 into three equal parts, apparently automatically. It was as if the number had

Developmental reading disorder, or **dyslexia,** characterizes children who have poorly developed skills in recognizing words and comprehending written text. Reading-disabled children may read laboriously and distort, omit, or substitute words when reading aloud. Dyslexic children have trouble decoding letters. They may perceive letters upside-down (*w* for *m*) or in reversed images (*b* for *d*). Dyslexia is usually apparent by the age of 7, coinciding with the second grade, although it is sometimes recognized in 6-year-olds.

■ **Language and Speech Disorders**   *Developmental articulation disorder* involves difficulties in articulating the sounds of speech in the absence of defects in the oral speech mechanism or neurological impairment. Children with the disorder may omit, substitute, or mispronounce certain sounds—especially *ch, f, l, r, sh,* and *th* sounds, which are usually articulated properly by the early school years. It may sound as if they are uttering "baby talk." In more severe cases, there are problems articulating sounds usually mastered during the preschool years: *b, m, t, d, n,* and *h.* Speech therapy is often helpful, and milder cases often resolve themselves by the age of 8. About 10 percent of children under the age of 8 and 5 percent 8 years or older are affected by problems in articulation, according to the DSM–III–R.

Developmental expressive language disorder involves

sundered itself into three. The twins were also capable of recognizing prime numbers—integers that can be divided by no other whole numbers but themselves and the number one—although they could not derive prime numbers logically. Linguists like Noam Chomsky theorize that people are neurologically "prewired" to grasp the deep structure that underlies all human languages. Perhaps, Sacks speculates, the brain circuits of savants like the twins are wired with a "deep arithmetic"—an innate structure for perceiving mathematical relationships that is analogous to the prewiring that allows people to perceive and produce language.

Various theories have been presented to explain the savant syndrome (Treffert, 1988). Some believe that savants have unusually well-developed memories that allow them to record and scan vast amounts of information. It has been suggested that savants may inherit two sets of hereditary factors, one for retardation and the other for special abilities. Perhaps it is coincidental that their special abilities and their mental handicaps were inherited in common. Other theorists suggest that the left and right hemispheres of savants' cerebral cortexes are organized in an unusual way. This latter belief is supported by research that suggests that the special abilities of savants often involve skills associated with right-hemisphere functioning. Still other theorists suggest that savants learn special skills to compensate for their lack of more general skills, perhaps as a means of coping with their environment, or perhaps as a means to earn social reinforcements. And some attribute savant syndrome to prolonged periods of sensory deprivation. A barren social environment could have prompted the savant to concentrate on "trivial" pursuits like memorizing obscure facts or learning calendar calculating. In blind or deaf savants, sensory deprivation takes a literal meaning. Among autistics, attending to minute details may derive from inability to focus on stimuli beyond an extremely narrow range. Yet many savants are not blind, deaf, or socially deprived; they have been reared in stimulus-rich environments.

In the recent film *Rainman,* Dustin Hoffman played an autistic savant with a remarkable capacity for numerical calculation. Hoffman is shown here with actor Tom Cruise, who played his brother in the film. Hoffman was able to capture the sense of emotional detachment and isolation of his autistic character.

Recent research has pointed to possible sex-linked, left-hemisphere damage that occurs prenatally or congenitally. Compensatory right-hemisphere development may take place, establishing specialized brain circuitry that processes concrete and narrowly defined kinds of information (Treffert, 1988). An environment that reinforces savant abilities and provides opportunities for practice and concentration could possibly give further impetus to the development of these unusual abilities. Such possibilities remain to be studied in future research. At present, the savant syndrome remains a fascinating but poorly understood phenomenon.

impairments in the spoken language, such as slow vocabulary development, frequent errors in usage, and problems with grammar. Affected children may also have an articulation disorder, compounding their speech problems.

Developmental receptive language disorder refers to children who have difficulties understanding the spoken language. Estimates place the number of affected children at between 3 and 10 percent of the school-age population, according to the DSM–III–R. In mild cases, children have difficulty understanding certain word types (such as words expressing differences in quantity—*large, big,* or *huge*) or certain sentence types (such as sentences that begin with the word *Unlike*). More severe cases are marked by difficulties understanding simple words or sentences. The disorder is usually apparent by the age of 4, although more severe cases may be detected earlier. Children with more subtle forms of the disorder may not be identified until the second grade (age 7) or later.

Theoretical Perspectives

Current hypotheses of learning disabilities tend to focus on cognitive-perceptual problems and possible underlying neurological factors. Many learning-disabled children have problems in visual or auditory perception. They may lack the capacity to copy words or to distinguish between geometric shapes (Lerner, 1976). Other children have short attention spans or hyperactivity.

Learning disabilities also appear to run in families (see Figure 14.2). Sons of dyslexic fathers and mothers have been found to run 39 percent and 34 percent risks, respectively, of developing dyslexia, which is from five to seven times the risk among sons of nondyslexic parents (Vogler et al., 1985). Daughters of dyslexic parents of either sex run a 17 to 18 percent chance of developing dyslexia themselves, which is 10 to 12 times greater than the risk among girls whose parents are not dyslexic. Once again, we must caution that increased occurrence of familial transmission in itself is not proof of genetic transmission. Parents transmit more than their genes to their children.

Twin studies also provide support for a genetic component in dyslexia (Pennington & Smith, 1988). One twin study found 64 identical (MZ) twin pairs and 55 fraternal (DZ) twin pairs in which at least one twin was dyslexic (DeFries et al., 1987). The concordance rate for dyslexia was significantly higher among the MZ twin pairs who, of course, fully share their genetic pools.

Treatment

There are various contemporary approaches to intervention for learning disorders, including the following (Lyon & Moats, 1988):

1.   *The psychoeducational model.* Psychoeducational approaches emphasize the child's strengths and prefer-

FIGURE 14–2 Familial risk of reading disability (dyslexia).
Boys are at increased risk than girls, and children of either sex incur greater risk if their parents are reading disabled. While these data are consistent with a genetic explanation of reading disability, reading disabled parents may also fail to provide the environmental stimulation and modeling influences that would foster reading skills in children.
Source: Adapted from Vogler et al. (1985)

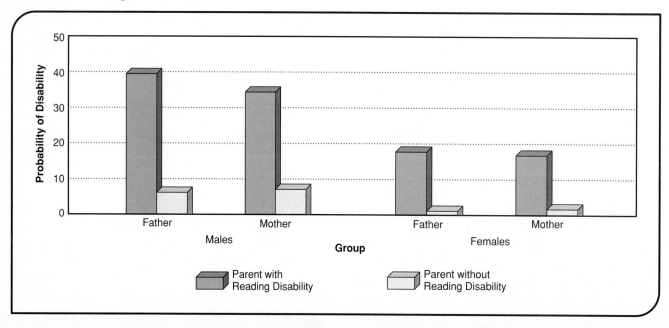

Dyslexic children have difficulty decoding words. Note the reversal of the letters w *and* l *in the word* owl *in this picture of a dyslexic girl completing a writing exercise.*

ences, rather than attempts at correcting assumed underlying cognitive deficiencies. For example, a child who retains auditory information better than visual information might be taught verbally, as by means of tape recordings, rather than by means of written materials.

2.   *The behavioral model.* The behavioral model assumes that academic learning is a complex form of behavior that is built on a hierarchy of basic skills or "enabling behaviors." In order to read effectively, one must first learn to recognize letters, then attach sounds to letters, then combine letters and sounds into words, and so on. The child's learning competencies are assessed to determine where deficiencies lie in the hierarchies of necessary skills. An individualized program, based on learning theory, of instruction and reinforcement, is then designed to help the child acquire the skills necessary to the performance of more complex academic tasks.

3.   *The medical model.* This model assumes that learning disabilities are symptoms of biologically based deficiencies in cognitive processing. Proponents suggest that remediation should be directed at the underlying pathology rather than the learning disability itself. If the child has a visual defect that makes it difficult to follow a line of text, treatment should aim to remediate the visual deficit, perhaps through visual-tracking exercises. Improvement in reading ability would be expected to follow.

4.   *The neuropsychological model.* This approach borrows from the psychoeducational and medical models. It assumes that learning disabilities reflect underlying deficits in processing information, probably involving the cerebral cortex (medical model). It also assumes that remediation should be academic (psychoeducational), involving presentation of instructional material to the more efficient or intact neural systems or cerebral hemispheres. In this way, inefficient or damaged brain regions are bypassed.

5.   *The linguistic model.* Language deficiencies may lead to difficulties in reading, spelling, and finding the words to express meanings. Dyslexic children may have difficulties in recognizing how sounds and words are strung together to create meaning. So adherents to the linguistic approach focus on the child's language deficiencies. Language skills are taught sequentially, helping the student to grasp the structure and use of words (Wagner & Torgesen, 1987).

6.   *The cognitive model.* This model focuses on how children organize their thoughts when they learn academic material. Within this perspective, children are helped to learn by (a) recognizing the nature of the learning task; (b) applying effective problem-solving strategies to complete tasks; and (c) monitoring the success of their strategies.

For example, children with arithmetic problems might be guided to break down an arithmetic problem into its component tasks, think through the steps necessary to complete each task, and evaluate performance at each step so that appropriate adjustments can be made. Children are shown a systematic approach to problem solving that can be applied to diverse academic tasks.

■ **Evaluation**   At present, the medical model is limited by lack of evidence that underlying deficiencies are correctable or that such improvements actually foster development of academic skills (Lyon & Moats, 1988; Wong, 1986). The psychoeducational approach suffers from lack of evidence that educational programs geared toward the child's strengths (for example, auditory, visual, or kinesthetic) increase the child's ability to learn (Brady, 1986; Lyon & Moats, 1988). The neuropsychological approach has not yet been fully tested. In contrast, the behavioral model has produced impressive results in improving the skills of children with problems in reading and arithmetic (Koorland, 1986). It remains to be seen whether or not these gains will generalize beyond the training environment (Trieber & Leahy, 1983). The linguistic approach has received some support, but not enough to support widespread use in treating children with reading and spelling deficiencies (Lyon & Moats, 1988). The cognitive model, too, has received some support, but many learning-disabled children have not developed enough basic knowledge in their problem areas to use it to think through problems (Lyon & Moats, 1988).

At present it seems appropriate to view these approaches as potential tools that teachers can use to help learning-disabled children maximize their potentials. Perhaps no single approach is best suited for all learning-disabled children.

DISRUPTIVE BEHAVIOR

The DSM–III–R contains a category for **disruptive behavior disorders** (coded on Axis I) that are socially disruptive and usually more upsetting to other people than to those who have the disorders. The category contains disorders that are very different in quality, as we shall see: *attention-deficit hyperactivity disorder*, *conduct disorder*, and *oppositional defiant disorder*.

Attention-Deficit Hyperactivity Disorder

Many parents believe that their children are not attentive toward them—that they run around on whim and do things their own way. Some inattention, especially in early childhood, is normal enough. But in **attention-deficit hyperactivity disorder** (ADHD), as diagnosed by the DSM–III–R, the child shows features of impulsivity, inattention, and **hyperactivity** that are considered inappropriate to the child's developmental level.

In order to receive a DSM–III–R diagnosis of ADHD, the disorder must begin by the age of 7 and must have persisted for at least six months. The DSM–III–R provides a "menu" of 14 characteristic behaviors that define the disorder and requires that at least 8 of them be observed in children who are so diagnosed.

ADHD is far from rare. It occurs in about 3 percent of children and is the most common cause of childhood referrals to mental-health agencies (Trites & Caprade, 1983). It occurs in boys six to nine times more often than in girls. While inattention appears to be the basic problem (McGee et al., 1985), there are various associated problems, such as bullying, temper tantrums, stubbornness, and failure to respond to punishment (Hechtman & Weiss, 1983). Table 14.5 contains a more complete listing of problems.

Over the years it has been unclear whether inattention and hyperactivity occur separately or are intertwined. In the previous edition of the DSM, categories of attention-deficit disorder *with* or *without* hyperactivity were employed. The DSM–III–R does permit a diagnosis of attention-deficit disorder without hyperactivity under the diagnostic label of "undifferentiated attention-deficit disorder," but the general assumption is that inattention and hyperactivity usually go hand in hand in most cases.

Activity and restlessness impair ADHD children's ability to function in school. They seem incapable of sitting still. They fidget and squirm in their seats, butt into other children's games, have outbursts of temper, and may engage in dangerous behavior, such as running into the street without looking (Campbell, 1985; Douglas, 1983; Whalen & Henker, 1985). All in all, they can drive parents and teachers to despair.

TABLE 14.5 Features of Attention-Deficit Hyperactivity Disorder (ADHD)

Kind of Problem	Specific Behavior Pattern
Lack of Attention	Frequent failure to finish projects Doesn't appear to pay attention Becomes readily distracted Cannot maintain concentration on schoolwork or related tasks Failure to sustain interest in play activities
Impulsivity	Often acts without thinking Shifts frequently from activity to activity Has difficulty organizing tasks or work Frequently requires constant supervision Frequently "calls out" in class Fails to wait his or her turn in line, games, etc.
Hyperactivity	Is constantly running around or climbing on things Constantly fidgets in seat and cannot sit still for long Exhibits excessive motor activity during sleep Seems to be constantly on the go

ADHD children display many of the behaviors listed in this table. Their academic functioning and sometimes their social functioning suffer as a result. Source: *Adapted from DSM–III–R, pp. 50–53.*

ADHD impairs children's academic progress. Affected children fail to follow instructions, complete assignments, or, often, remember what they were supposed to do. They disrupt classes and other children, so that they get into fights and are frequently unpopular. Motor activity declines by adolescence, but attentional problems may persist into adulthood. ADHD-related problems, such as underachievement, a poor self-image, and impaired social relationships, can persist for a lifetime.

Where does "normal" age-appropriate overactivity end and "hyperactivity" begin? Assessment of the degree of hyperactive behavior is crucial, since many normal children are called "hyper" from time to time. Some critics of the ADHD diagnosis argue that it merely labels children who are difficult to control as mentally disordered or sick. Most normal children, especially boys, are highly active during the early school years. Proponents of the diagnosis counter that there is a difference in quality between normal overactivity and ADHD. Normally overactive children are usually goal-directed and can exert voluntary control over their own behavior. ADHD children appear hyperactive without reason and do not seem to be able to conform their own behavior to the demands of teachers and parents. Put another way: Normal children can sit still and concentrate for a while when they want to do so; hyperactive children seemingly cannot.

Attention-deficit hyperactivity disorder (ADHD), which is six to nine times more common in boys, is characterized by attentional difficulties, restlessness, impulsivity, excessive motor behavior (continual running around or climbing), and temper tantrums.

■ **Theoretical Perspectives** Theorists focus on environmental and biological influences in explaining hyperactivity. For example, hyperactive children are more likely than other children to have mothers who abused alcohol or other drugs during pregnancy. Their family lives were generally less stable, as characterized by marital breakups and frequent moves (Lambert, 1988).

Several lines of evidence support the role of biological factors. ADHD runs in families (American Psychiatric Association, 1987; Gross & Wilson, 1974; Morrison & Stewart, 1973), which is suggestive but not conclusive of genetic influences. The mothers of hyperactive children often had difficult pregnancies. As infants, hyperactive children were more prone to neurological disorders, such as encephalitis and seizures. But most do not show frank signs of neurological damage. Whether or not there is brain damage in ADHD children, it is possible that their nervous systems are less mature than those of unaffected children. This hypothesis receives some support from the observed sex ratio of affected children, because the nervous systems of boys mature more slowly than those of girls. The effects of stimulants on ADHD children also offer some support to the hypothesis of organic causes, as we shall see below. As we shall see in the accompanying box, researchers have also explored whether hyperactivity is caused by dietary factors, in particular the consumption of sugar.

■ **Treatment** The most common treatment for ADHD is pharmacological—the use of stimulants like Ritalin (methylphenidate) and amphetamines. It may seem ironic that stimulants are used to treat children who are overactive. The rationale is that hyperactivity reflects inability of the (possibly immature) cerebral cortex to inhibit more primitive parts of the brain. The drugs, in theory, facilitate **cortical** control over more primitive brain centers in the lower brain.

A CLOSER LOOK
Hold that Twinkie! Does Sugar Cause Hyperactivity?

It is a popular belief that children's intake of sugar is related to various problem behaviors, such as poor attention span, hyperactivity, and irritability. Approximately half (45%) of pediatricians and family physicians surveyed report recommending low sugar diets in at least some cases of childhood hyperactivity (Rosen, 1988). Parents and teachers may assume that sugar heightens children's activity levels because sugar provides a quick source of energy.

Despite these commonly held assumptions, a review of the literature does not support a consistent relationship between sugar and hyperactivity. As many studies reported that sugar actually enhanced behavior as worsened it (Milich et al., 1986). Nor does the sugar substitute aspartame (Nutra-Sweet) appear to have disruptive effects on behavior (Kruesi et al., 1987).

 Actually, it has not been demonstrated that sugar contributes to hyperactivity.

Despite lack of experimental evidence that sugar contributes to hyperactivity, some questions remain. It may be that some children are more adversely affected by sugar intake than others (Milich et al., 1986). Thus, individual differences among children need to be considered in future research. Future studies should also address the question as to whether there are long-term effects of continuous exposure to high doses of sugar. In the meantime, there is no evidence that sugar causes or exacerbates hyperactivity or other forms of disruptive behavior. Still, the clear relationships of sugar to tooth decay, poor nutrition, and obesity argue against excessive consumption (Milich et al., 1986).

Stimulants do calm many hyperactive children, apparently by fostering cortical control over more primitive structures of the brain.

The most commonly prescribed and researched stimulant, methylphenidate, causes the release of dopamine from presynaptic neurons and decreases the re-uptake of dopamine (Dulcan, 1986). Stimulants have the paradoxical effect of decreasing motor activity in ADHD children, as measured, for example, by time spent out of one's seat and by foot movements in the classroom (Dulcan, 1986). But normal (voluntary) high activity levels shown in physical education classes and on weekends are not disrupted. Stimulants also reduce annoying, disruptive, and aggressive behaviors among hyperactive children (Abikoff & Gittelman, 1985; Whalen et al., 1987; Klorman et al., 1988). While psychostimulants do lead to improved cognitive abilities on laboratory tasks that measure distractability, impulsivity, and attention, there is a lack of evidence demonstrating improvements on more general measures of academic achievement (Dulcan, 1986). This lack of consistency is a puzzling finding to many researchers but suggests that medication alone cannot make up for educational deficiencies.

Use of stimulants with ADHD children has been controversial. While short-term side effects are generally resolved in two to three weeks or following dosage reduction, the long-term effects of stimulant medication use are not as well known (Dulcan, 1986). Initial weight loss may occur, which is due to the appetite-suppressing effects of stimulants. But it remains unclear whether stimulant use can retard gains in height, and we do not know which children are at greatest risk for retardation of growth. Supporters of stimulant treatment counter that the suppression of growth appears to be related to the dosage and the specific drug chosen (Mattes & Gittelman, 1983; Rapport, 1984). It is generally agreed that the long-term effects of stimulants on systems such as the cardiovascular system remain unknown.

Treatment of hyperactive children with methylphenidate first became popular in the 1950s. At that time a wide range of children were medicated, including aggressive children and those now considered to have conduct disorders. In the 1970s, however, there was a professional backlash. Many teachers and physicians were accused of overly medicating or drugging children—especially poor children—to render them compliant (Dulcan, 1986). Partly because of this backlash, research was conducted to help determine which children truly benefit from stimulants. These studies led to the present limitation of usage to ADHD children (Dulcan, 1986).

Nine-year-old Eddie provides a case of a child who was treated with stimulant medication:

■ Eddie is a problem in class. His teacher complains that he is so restless and fidgety that the rest of the class cannot concentrate on their work. He hardly ever sits still. He is in constant motion, roaming the classroom, talking to other children while they are working. He has been suspended repeatedly for outrageous behavior, most recently swinging from a fluorescent light fixture and unable to get himself down. His mother reports that Eddie has been a problem since he was a toddler. By the age of 3 he had become unbearably restless and demanding. He has never needed much sleep and always awakened before anyone else in the family, making his way downstairs and wrecking things in the living room and kitchen. Once, at the age of 4, he unlocked the front door and wandered into traffic, but was rescued by a passer-by.

Psychological testing shows Eddie to be average in academic ability, but to have a "virtually nonexistent" attention span. He shows no interest in television or in games or toys that require some concentration. He is unpopular with peers and prefers to ride his bike alone or to play with his dog. He has become disobedient at home and at school and has stolen small amounts of money from his parents and classmates.

Eddie has been treated with methylphenidate (Ritalin), but it was discontinued because it had no effect on his disobedience and stealing. However, it did seem to reduce his restlessness and increase his attention span at school.

Adapted from Spitzer et al., 1989, pp. 315–317 ■

Most behavioral programs for ADHD are based on principles of operant conditioning. For example, teachers have been trained to dispense social reinforcers such as praise systematically for appropriate behavior in the classroom. Operant conditioning methods have shown some success in decreasing hyperactivity and in increasing the time spent on academic work (O'Leary et al., 1976). Cognitive techniques have been developed to teach children strategies for exercising self-control and solving problems (Douglas et al., 1976; Kendall & Braswell, 1985). But behavioral treatments have been criticized on methodological grounds that they rely on too small numbers of subjects, have inadequate follow-up evaluations, and lack evidence of long-term effects (Mash & Dalby, 1979).

Many studies have been undertaken to compare the effectiveness of stimulants with psychological approaches and with approaches that combine pharmacological and psychological methods. The outcomes of these studies are somewhat in conflict. Some suggest that behavioral and cognitive techniques do not augment the effectiveness of stimulants (see Abikoff & Gittleman, 1985; Brown et al., 1985). Ironically, others suggest that stimulants do not augment the effectiveness of behavioral interventions that are focused on promoting academic gains (Gadow, 1985). Some researchers believe that a combination of cognitive behavioral approaches and stimulant medication will ultimately prove to be the most effective treatment for ADHD (Hinshaw et al., 1984; Pelham et al., 1980). At this time, however, we need carefully controlled studies to discern the effective elements in the various treatment programs that have been devised.

We should also mention a nutritional approach to treating hyperactivity described by pediatrician Ben Feingold in his book *Why Your Child Is Hyperactive*. The so-called Feingold diet eliminates junk foods, artificial food coloring, preservatives, salicylates, and other chemicals. However, only 5 to 10 percent of the children given the Feingold diet who have been studied show behavioral improvements (Barkley, 1981; Dulcan, 1986; Henker & Whalen, 1980). Moreover, the changes observed in those who improve are not as dramatic as those changes induced by methylphenidate. Nor have other nutrition-related factors, such as food allergies, vitamin deficiencies, or sugar, been empirically related to hyperactivity (Barkley, 1981; Dulcan, 1986).

■ **ADHD Children and the Future**   ADHD declines by adolescence in most cases, granting further support to the hypothesis that hyperactivity may reflect immaturity of the nervous system. In fact, some hyperactive children show no evidence of continued impairment as adolescents or young adults (Cantwell, 1986; Lambert et al., 1987; Manuzza et al., 1988). This suggests that hyperactivity in childhood is not inevitably linked to problematic behavior in adolescence or early adult life (Manuzza et al., 1988). However, 30 to 80 percent continue to show some persistent problems, such as difficulties getting along with others, poor academic performance, a negative self-concept, antisocial behavior, and poor work histories (Cantwell, 1986; Weiss, 1985). Hyperactive children are also more likely than others to become delinquents, be suspended from school, and to require continued interventions in adolescence (see Figure 14.3) (Lambert et al., 1987). Still, most formerly hyperactive children have attained jobs and are satisfied with their lives by the time they reach young adulthood, despite some enduring problems (Weiss et al., 1971).

Conduct Disorder

Although they are both classified as disruptive behavior disorders in the DSM–III–R, **conduct disorder** differs a great deal from ADHD (Hinshaw, 1987). Whereas ADHD children seem literally incapable of controlling their behavior, children with conduct disorders adopt patterns of intentional antisocial behavior that violate social norms and the rights of others. Whereas ADHD children throw temper tantrums, children diagnosed

FIGURE 14–3 Adolescents diagnosed as hyperactive in childhood.
Adolescents with childhood hyperactivity were more likely than nonhyperactive controls in one study to receive various interventions into adolescence, especially stimulant medication. While many hyperactive children continue to have academic, behavioral, or mental health problems in adolescence and adulthood, some show no evidence of continued impairment.
Source: Adapted from Lambert et al. (1987)

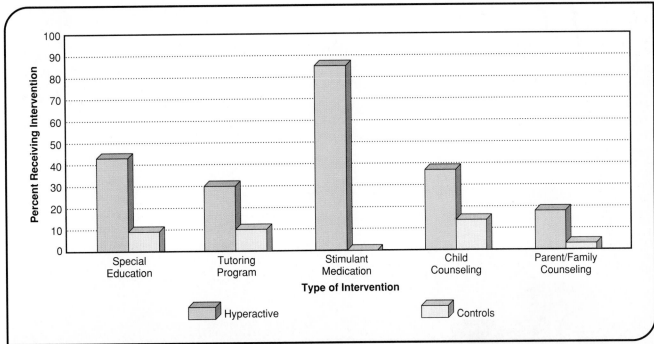

as conduct disordered are intentionally aggressive and cruel. They may steal or destroy property. In adolescence they may commit rape, armed robbery, even homicide. They may cheat in school—when they bother to attend—and may lie to cover their tracks. They frequently engage in substance abuse and sexual activity. Like antisocial adults, many conduct-disordered children are callous and do not experience guilt or remorse for their misdeeds. Conduct-disordered children frequently have academic problems, such as poor reading, math, and expressive language skills, but their disorders do not prevent them from attending in the classroom. Having noted differences between ADHD and conduct disorder, some children with conduct disorder also have short attention spans and hyperactivity that may justify the additional ADHD diagnosis.

As listed in Table 3.1 in Chapter 3 of this text (p. 81), the DSM–III–R applies the diagnosis of conduct disorder when the "disturbance of conduct" has persisted for 6 months or more and 3 of the following behavior patterns are present: stealing with or without confronting the victim; running away from home on at least two occasions; frequent lying; setting fires; repeated truancy; breaking and entering; destruction of property; physical cruelty to people or animals; forcing someone into sexual activity with him or herself; use of a weapon in a fight on more than one occasion; often starting fights; and engaging in acts of physical cruelty towards others. Conduct disorders are much more common among boys than girls (Herbert, 1978). Conduct disorders usually begin just before or during puberty.

Conduct disorders tend to be stable. A longitudinal study found that children in kindergarten through third grade who showed evidence of conduct disorders had a greater than expected frequency of contacts with the police during adolescence (Spivack et al., 1986). Antisocial behavior in the form of delinquent acts (stealing, truancy, vandalism, fighting or threatening others, etc.) during early adolescence (ages 14–15) was found to predict alcohol and drug use four years later during ages 18–19, especially among males (Windle, 1990).

The DSM–III–R distinguishes between conduct disorder and **oppositional defiant disorder.** In the latter disorder, children show negativistic and defiant behavior, but without the serious violations of the rights of others and aggression that characterizes conduct disorders. Since oppositional defiant disorder has received much less attention in the research literature than conduct disorder, we focus much of our discussion on the problem of conduct disorder.

■ **Types of Conduct Disorders**   The DSM–III–R specifies three subtypes of conduct disorder: group type, solitary aggressive type, and undifferentiated type.

Group types usually form normal emotional attachments to family members and friends. But they often belong to a gang and commit their crimes as a feature of gang activity. They seem to have been socialized into a deviant system of values. But they tend to be loyal to gang members, whereas solitary aggressive types are quick to inform on their companions and may try to shift the blame for misdeeds onto them. Most conduct-disordered girls fall into the group category, and their deviance is characterized largely by substance abuse and under-age sexual activity. The solitary aggressive type, by contrast, lacks emotional attachments and is highly aggressive, similar to the adult antisocial personality. Aggressive types are callous and tend to have no genuine friends. As with adult antisocial personalities, their parents are often neglectful, inconsistent in discipline, and antisocial themselves. Many of these children undertake criminal careers that last for many decades. The undifferentiated type combines features of the other types.

■ **Theoretical Perspectives**   Genetic factors may play a role in conduct disorders. Adoptee studies show that antisocial behavior is more likely to be found among the biological parents than the adoptive parents of antisocial adopted children (Mednick, 1985). However, the presence of sociopathic (antisocial) models in the family and inconsistent styles of discipline can also contribute to the development of antisocial behavior (Bond & McMahon, 1984; Griest et al., 1980; Margolin, 1981; Olweus, 1980; Rutter & Garmezy, 1983). Conduct disorders in children sometimes appear to reflect marital conflict (Christensen et al., 1983; Emery, 1982; Forehand et al., 1986). Disruptive behavior is intertwined with emotional distress in parents in complex ways. For example, depressed mothers tend to perceive their children as more disruptive than the way others view them and also to engage in parenting behaviors—such as vague and interrupted commands—that tend to foster disruptive behavior in their children (Forehand et al., 1988).

Recent investigations have focused on the ways in which such children process information. It turns out that aggressive children are biased in their processing of social information: They assume that others intend them ill when they do not (Dodge & Frame, 1982; Jurkovic, 1980). They usually blame others for the scrapes they get into. They believe that they are misperceived and treated unfairly.

■ **Treatment**   The treatment for conduct disorders has been less than satisfactory in its results and remains a challenge to mental-health professionals. Psychotherapy has not generally been shown to be effective in helping these children change their troublesome behavior. Placing children with conduct disorders in programs or treatment settings with explicit rules and clear rewards for obeying them may offer greater promise (Barkley et al., 1976; Cohen & Filipczak, 1971; Henggeler et al., 1986; Phillips et al., 1971; Stumphauzer, 1981). Such programs usually rely on operant conditioning procedures involving systematic use of rewards and punishments.

Other approaches include programs that train aggressive children to use alternative ways of coping with anger that do not violate other people's rights. One of the methods that has shown some promise is problem-solving therapy, in which aggressive boys are taught to reconceptualize confrontations with others as problems to be solved, rather than provocations to violence (Lochman et al., 1984). The boys were trained to generate nonviolent solutions to conflict situations and to try out the most promising ones. The treatment led to significant decreases in disruptive and aggressive behavior at school, and decreased aggression at home. In a later study, aggressive boys who received the treatment also showed increased attention to classroom tasks (Lochman & Curry, 1986). Other researchers have shown that problem-solving skills training was more effective than alternative or control treatments in reducing aggressive behavior and improving behavior at home and school of conduct-disordered children aged 7 to 13 who had been hospitalized for their disruptive behavior (Kazdin et al., 1987). Despite their relative improvement, however, a majority of the children receiving problem-solving skills training in this study generally remained poorly adjusted, highlighting the intractability of antisocial behavior.

Sometimes the child's parents are brought into the treatment process (Baumrind, 1983). Henggeler and his colleagues (Brunk et al., 1987; Henggeler, 1982; Henggeler & Cohen, 1984; Henggeler et al., 1986) have developed a "family-ecological" approach based on Urie Bronfenbrenner's (1979) ecological theory. Like Bronfenbrenner, Henggeler sees the child as embedded within various social systems—family, school, criminal-justice, community, and so on. He focuses on how the juvenile offender affects, and is affected by, the systems with which he or she interacts. The techniques themselves are not unique. Rather, the family-ecological approach tries to change the child's relationship with as many systems as possible with which he or she interacts in order to break disruptive interactions.

Billy's case illustrates involvement of the parents in the behavioral treatment of oppositional defiant disorder:

■ Billy was a 7-year-old second grader referred by his parents. The family was relocated frequently because the father was in the navy. Billy usually behaved when his father was taking care of him, but he was noncompliant with his mother and yelled at her when she gave him instructions. His mother was incurring great stress in the effort to control Billy, especially when her husband was at sea.

Billy had become a problem at home and in school during the first grade. He ignored and violated rules in both settings. Billy failed to carry out his chores and frequently yelled at and hit his younger brother. When he acted up, his parents would restrict him to his room or the yard, take away privileges and toys, and spank him. But all of these measures were used inconsistently. He also played on the railroad tracks near his home and twice the police had brought him home after he had thrown rocks at cars.

A home observation showed that Billy's mother often gave him inappropriate commands. She interacted with him as little as possible and showed no verbal praise, physical closeness, smiles, or positive facial expressions or gestures. She paid attention to him only when he misbehaved. When Billy was noncompliant, she would yell back at him and then try to catch him to force him to comply. Billy would then laugh and run from her.

Billy's parents were informed that the child's behavior was a product of inappropriate cuing techniques (poor directions), a lack of reinforcement for appropriate behavior, and lack of consistent sanctions for misbehavior. They were taught the concepts of reinforcement, punishment, and **time-out.** The parents then charted Billy's problem behaviors to gain a clearer idea of what triggered and maintained them. They were shown how to reinforce acceptable behavior and use time-out as a contingency for misbehavior. Billy's mother was also taught relaxation training to help desensitize her to Billy's disruptions. Biofeedback was used to enhance the relaxation response.

During a 15-day baseline period, Billy behaved in a noncompliant manner about four times per day. When treatment was begun, Billy showed an immediate drop to about one instance of noncompliance every two days. Follow-up data showed that instances of noncompliance were maintained at a bearable level of about one per day. Fewer behavioral problems in school were also reported, even though they had not been addressed directly.

Adapted from Kaplan, 1986, pp. 227–230 ■

ANXIETY DISORDERS OF CHILDHOOD

Anxieties and fears are a normal feature of childhood, just as they are a normal feature of adult life. Children face many fears and anxieties that are deemed normal, because they are so commonplace and seem to reflect natural cognitive-developmental processes. For example, during the second half of the first year, it is normal for children to develop separation anxiety from attachment figures and fear of strangers. Other common childhood anxieties concern supernatural and imaginary creatures, being left alone or in the dark, attack by animals, noise, pain, and injury. Certain fears tend to decline during the first six years, such as fears of noises, of strange people and objects, and of pain. But other fears tend to increase, such as fears of animals, of ridicule, of the dark, and of genuine sources of danger. These trends are quite normal.

However, in anxiety disorders of childhood or adolescence, anxiety is considered excessive and interferes with normal academic or social functioning. Anxiety disorders of childhood do not generally mirror the types found in adulthood (and discussed in Chapter 6). They include, instead, *separation anxiety disorder*, *avoidant disorder*, and *overanxious disorder*.

Separation Anxiety Disorder

It is normal for children to show anxiety when they are separated from their caregivers. As noted by Mary Ainsworth (1989), who has chronicled the development of attachment behaviors, so-called separation anxiety is a normal feature of the child–caregiver relationship and begins during the first year. But Ainsworth also explains that the sense of security normally provided by bonds of attachment apparently encourages children to explore their environments and move progressively further away from their caregivers.

Separation anxiety disorder is diagnosed when separation anxiety is excessive or inappropriate for the child's developmental level and persists for at least two weeks. That is, 3-year-olds ought to be able to attend preschool without nausea and vomiting brought on by anxiety. Six-year-olds ought to be able to attend first grade without persistent dread that they or their parents will come to harm. Children with this disorder tend to cling to their parents and follow them around the house. They may voice concerns about death

In separation anxiety disorder, a child shows persistent anxiety when separated from his/her parents that is inconsistent with his or her developmental level. Such children tend to cling to their parents and resist even brief separations.

and dying and insist that someone stay with them while they are falling asleep. Other features of the disorder include nightmares; stomachaches, nausea and vomiting when separation is anticipated (as on school days); and pleading with parents not to leave or throwing tantrums when parents are about to leave. They may refuse to attend school for fear that something will happen to their parents while they are away. The disorder appears to affect boys and girls in equal numbers.

> **?** Some children with separation anxiety disorder do refuse to go to school because they believe that terrible things may happen to their parents while they are away.

In previous years, separation anxiety disorder was usually referred to as *school phobia*. Separation anxiety disorder may occur at preschool ages, however. Today most cases of "school refusal" (DSM–III–R, p. 58) are also viewed as stemming from separation anxiety, at least among younger children. In adolescence, however, some cases of school refusal stem from academic and social concerns, so the label of separation anxiety disorder would not apply.

According to the DSM–III–R, separation anxiety disorder develops in most cases after a life stress, such as illness, the death of a relative or pet, or a change of schools or homes. Alison's problems followed the death of her grandmother:

■ Alison's grandmother died when Alison was 7 years old. Her parents decided to permit her request to view her grandmother in the open coffin. Alison took a tentative glance from her father's arms across the room, then asked to be taken out of the room. Her 5-year-old sister took a leisurely close-up look, with no apparent distress.

Alison had been concerned about death for two or three years by this time, but her grandmother's passing brought on a new flurry of questions: "Will I die?," "Does everybody die?," and so on. Her parents tried to reassure her by saying, "Grandma was very, very old, and she also had a heart condition. You are very young and in perfect health. You have many, many years before you have to start thinking about death."

Alison also could not be alone in any room in her house. She pulled one of her parents or her sister along with her everywhere she went. She also reported nightmares about her grandmother and, within a couple of days, insisted on sleeping in the same room with her parents. Fortunately, Alison's fears did not extend to school. Her teacher reported that Alison spent some time talking about her grandmother, but her academic performance was apparently unimpaired.

Alison's parents decided to allow Alison time to "get over" the loss. Alison gradually talked less and less about death, and by the time three months had passed, she was able to go into any room in her house by herself. She wanted to continue to sleep in her parents' bedroom, however. So her parents "made a deal" with her. They would put off the return to her own bedroom until the school year had ended (a month away), if Alison would agree to return to her own bed at that time. As a further incentive, a parent would remain with her until she fell asleep for the first month. Alison overcame the anxiety problem in this fashion with no additional delays.

The Authors' Files ■

Avoidant Disorder

Development of fear of strangers during the first year is also a normal aspect of the attachment process (Bowlby, 1982), although it is by no means universal. Infants tend to develop fear of strangers by about 7 months, and it usually wanes at about 15 months.

Children diagnosed as having **avoidant disorder** show excessive avoidance of contact with strangers that persists for at least six months in duration. But they have normal needs for affection and acceptance and develop warm relationships with their parents and families. However, their avoidance of others outside the family interferes with their development of normal peer relationships. They tend to be shy and withdrawn. They usually avoid playgrounds and other children in the neighborhood. Their distress at being around other children at school can impede their academic progress.

Avoidant disorders tend to develop after the normal fear of strangers disappears, at 2½ years or afterward. The disorder may be complicated by feelings of depres-

In avoidant disorder, a child shows avoidance of contact with strangers that persists for six months or longer. Avoidant children tend to be excessively shy and socially withdrawn. They have difficulty interacting with other children.

sion and isolation, since children with the disorder typically fail to establish social relationships outside the immediate family. In some cases, children avoid other children because of lack of experience in relating to them, although they are able to relate relatively well to adults (Scarlett, 1980).

Children who are shy and socially withdrawn, two characteristics commonly associated with avoidant behaviors, have been helped by operant conditioning and modeling techniques. For example, withdrawn children have been "drawn out" by caregivers and teachers who reinforced them for increased socialization and ignored their withdrawn behavior (Hart et al., 1968). Withdrawn children have also been encouraged to socialize with peers by observing films featuring models of withdrawn children who were able gradually to extend their social relationships with peers (O'Connor, 1969).

Overanxious Disorder

Children with **overanxious disorder,** like adults with generalized anxiety, are generally apprehensive and fretful. Simple and social phobias may also be found in these children, but their worries are not limited to overreactions to one or two specific objects or events. Their anxieties extend to future events like visits to the doctor and tests, and to past events, such as whether or not they said the right thing to a peer or responded to a test item correctly. They are also concerned about their overall competence in social relationships, school, and sports. Overanxious children often report the anxiety-related physical symptoms of headaches and stomachaches.

The causes of anxiety in children to some degree parallel those in adults. Psychoanalytic theorists suggest that childhood fears, like their adult counterparts, symbolize unconscious conflicts, as in the case of Little Hans that we discussed in Chapter 6. Cognitive theorists suggest that anxious children, like anxious adults, can make perfectionistic self-demands that set themselves up for failure. Negative outcome expectancies and low self-efficacy expectancies encourage avoidance of feared activities—with friends, in school, and elsewhere. Negative expectations may also heighten feelings of anxiety to the point where they impede performance. Learning theorists suggest that widespread anxiety may touch upon broad themes, such as fears of rejection or failure. Perhaps underlying fears generalize to most areas of social interaction and achievement situations.

Whatever the causes, overanxious children may profit from many of the anxiety-control techniques discussed in Chapter 6. For example, relaxation training and recognizing and challenging irrational expectations have been shown to have some utility with fearful or overanxious children (Kendall & Williams, 1981).

DEPRESSION IN CHILDHOOD AND ADOLESCENCE

The stereotype is that childhood is the happiest time of life. Most children enjoy the protection afforded by their parents and are unencumbered by adult responsibilities. From the perspective of aging adults, their young bodies seem made of rubber and free of aches. They have apparently boundless energy.

Despite the stereotype, depression is actually common among children and adolescents. About 10 percent of the 10-year-olds in one survey described themselves as being tearful, unhappy, or distressed (Rutter et al., 1981). Perhaps one-quarter to one-half of children with mental disorders meet the criteria for depressive disorders (Asarnow & Carlson, 1985). Though rare, major depression has been found even among preschoolers (Kashany et al., 1986). The features of major depression among children are similar to those that characterize the disorder in adults (Ryan et al., 1987). A study of 30 children who were hospitalized for depression found cognitive patterns also associated with adult depressive disorders: a sense of hopelessness, low self-esteem, and low self-efficacy expectancies concerning the abilities to solve their problems (see Figure 14.4) (Asarnow et al., 1987; McCauley et al., 1988). Depressed children also report crying, feeling sad, loss of interest in usually favored activities, and feelings of being alone (Carey et al., 1987). They also complain of insomnia, fatigue, and poor appetite. However, children of various ages show relatively poor appetites, so we need to be aware of developmental norms before we draw conclusions about children's behavior. Many depressed children and adolescents have suicidal thoughts; some even attempt suicide (Asarnow & Carlson, 1985).

Many depressed children neither report nor are aware of feelings of depression, however. Depressed children may not report feeling sad even though they appear tearful and sad (Carlson & Garber, 1986). Part of the problem is cognitive-developmental. Children are not usually capable of recognizing their internal feeling states until about the age of 7. The capacity for **concrete operations** by about that age apparently contributes to the development of self-perception of internal feeling states (Glasberg & Aboud, 1982). But it may not be until adolescence that children develop the ability to identify negative feeling states like depression in themselves (Larson et al., 1990). While children, especially younger children, may not report depressed feelings, depression may be inferred from their behavior. Like adult depressives, depressed children in middle childhood show less social activity and less emotional expression (less often smiling, for example) than do nondepressed peers (Kazdin et al., 1985). In some cases, however, depression in childhood is "masked" by behaviors that do not appear directly related to depression. Conduct disorders, academic problems, physical complaints, and even hyperactivity may stem, now and then, from unrecognized depression. Among adolescents, aggressive and sexual *acting out* may be signs of underlying depression (Achenbach & Edelbrock, 1981; Carlson, 1980).

In some ways, feelings of depression are expressed differently among children. For example, depressed children may refuse to attend school, express fears of their parents' dying, and either cling to their parents or retreat to their rooms. Some children use physical aggression as a means of coping with stressful situations.

As with adults, some of the correlates of childhood depression are situational. One study found that stressful life events were associated with the development of depression among preschoolers who averaged about four years of age (Kashany et al., 1986). Depression and suicidal behavior in childhood are frequently related to family problems and conflicts (Kaslow & Rehm, 1985).

Although we tend to think of childhood as the happiest and most carefree time of life, depression is actually quite common among children and adolescents. Depressed children may report feelings of sadness and lack of interest in previously enjoyable activities. Many, however, do not report or are aware of feelings of depression, even though they may look depressed to observers. Depression may also be "masked" by other problems, such as conduct or school-related problems, physical complaints, and overactivity.

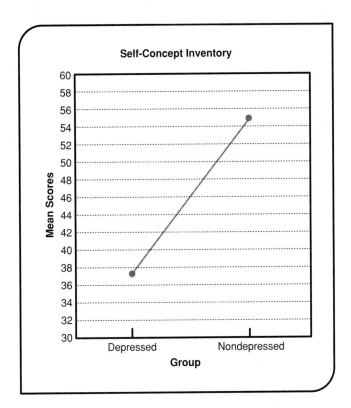

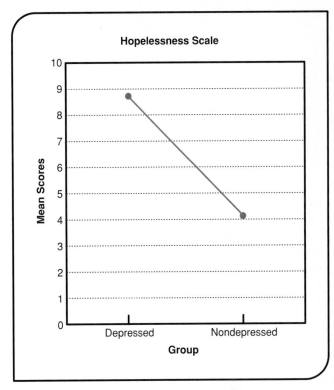

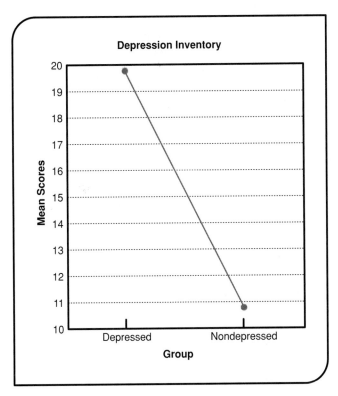

FIGURE 14–4 Differences between depressed and nondepressed children.

Many of the features of depression in adulthood are found in childhood depression. Depressed children have poorer self concepts, greater feelings of hopelessness, and more of the general features of depression than their nondepressed peers.

Source: Adapted from McCauley et al. (1988)

Depressed children, like depressed adults, tend to show distorted cognitions such as the following (Leitenberg et al., 1986; McCauley et al., 1988):

1.   Broad negative expectations for the future (pessimism)

2.   Catastrophizing the consequences of negative events

3.   Assuming personal responsibility for negative outcomes, even when it is unwarranted

4.   Selectively attending to the negative features of an event.

Depressed children and adolescents, like depressed adults, adopt a cognitive style that is characterized by negative attitudes toward themselves and the future. Self-perceptions of incompetence have been linked to low self-esteem, helplessness, and depression in children and adolescents (McCranie & Bass, 1984; Weisz et al., 1987). What remains to be determined is whether children become depressed because they think depressing thoughts, whether depression causes changes in cognitive style, or whether depression and cognitive styles interact in more complex ways.

While the traditional approach to treating childhood depression has been psychodynamic therapy, cognitive-behavioral approaches have been gaining in prominence. As with adults, cognitive behavioral therapy for childhood depression may focus on helping the child acquire more effective social skills to increase the likelihood of obtaining social reinforcement from others. Children are also trained to practice thinking and talking to themselves in more rational ways. Family therapy is often used to resolve family conflicts and reorganize family relationships in ways that members can be more supportive of each other.

Some evidence exists that supports the role of genetics in childhood depression. Children of depressed parents are more likely to become depressed than are children of nondepressed parents (Beardslee et al., 1983). This does not prove the case for genetic transmission, however, since parents may influence their children through their interactions with them as well as by passing along their genes. Low utilization of the neurotransmitters serotonin and norepinephrine may be implicated in both childhood depression and adult depression. Antidepressant drugs that increase utilization of these transmitters have shown some usefulness with depressed children (Petti & Connors, 1983).

Suicide among Children and Adolescents

Though rare, children do occasionally commit suicide. Adolescents do so more often. The suicide rate for adolescents aged 15 to 19 is about 8 per 100,000 per year (Shafi, 1986) and has tripled in the past 30 years (Neiger, 1988). Most children and adolescents who talk about or threaten suicide do not attempt it. Nevertheless, clinicians are usually advised to err on the side of caution and treat suicidal threats by children and adolescent with the utmost seriousness (Shafi, 1986).

Family conflicts may contribute to suicidal thinking in children. Depressed children who attempted suicide perceived their family environments as higher in conflict, less cohesive, and less well controlled than did depressed children who did not attempt suicide (Asarnow et al., 1987). Several risk factors have been identified for adolescent suicide (Neiger, 1988; Shafi, 1986):

1. *Sex.* Girls, like women, are three times more likely than boys to attempt suicide, but boys, like men, are more likely to "succeed," perhaps because boys, like men, are apt to use more lethal means, such as guns.

2. *Age.* Young people in late adolescence or early adulthood (ages 15 to 24) are at greater risk than are younger adolescents.

3. *Geography.* Adolescents in less populated areas are more likely to commit suicide. Adolescents in the more rural western regions of the United States have the highest suicide rate.

4. *Race.* American Indians have the highest rate of completed suicides. White and black adolescents are about equal in number of attempted suicides.

5. *Depression.* Depression, especially when combined with low self-esteem, is a major risk factor for suicide among adolescents.

6. *Previous Suicidal Behavior.* One quarter of adolescents who attempt suicide are repeaters. More than 80 percent of adolescents who take their lives have talked about it before doing so. Suicidal teenagers may carry lethal weapons, talk about death, make suicide plans, or engage in risky or dangerous behavior.

7. *Strained Family Relationships.* Family problems are present in about 75 percent of the cases of adolescent suicide attempters. These involve family instability and conflict, parental abuse, neglect, or rejection, or inconsistency in discipline, sometimes overcontrolling, other times overly lax or uncaring.

8. *Stress.* Stressful life events may trigger suicidal thinking, such as unwanted pregnancy, academic problems, family crises, anticipation of rejection or discipline by a parent or another important person, or a major loss.

9. *Substance Abuse.* Either in the adolescent's family or by the adolescent.

10. *Social Contagion.* Suicide is not contagious in the sense that a disease is contagious, but the term is used to reflect the fact that suicides often occur in clusters. There are often suicides or attempts among the siblings, friends, parents, or adult relatives of suicidal adolescents. Adolescent suicides may occur in bunches in a particular community, especially in communities where they come under high academic pressure. Perhaps the suicide of a family member or schoolmate renders suicide a more "real" option for managing stress or punishing others. Perhaps the other person's suicide gives the adolescent the impression that he or she is "doomed" to commit suicide. Note the case of Pam:

■ Pam was an exceptionally pretty 17-year-old who was hospitalized after cutting her wrists. "Before we moved to [an upper-middle-class town in Westchester County,

New York]," she told the psychologist, "I was the brightest girl in the class. Teachers loved me. If we had had a yearbook, I'd have been the most likely to succeed. Then we moved, and suddenly I was hit with it. Everybody was bright, or tried to be. Suddenly I was just another ordinary student planning to go to college.

"Teachers were good to me, but I was no longer special, and that hurt. Then we all applied to college. Do you know that 90 percent of the kids in the high school go on to college? I mean four-year colleges? And we all knew—or suspected—that the good schools had quotas on kids from here. I mean you can't have 30 kids from our senior class going to Yale or Princeton or Wellesley, can you? You're better off applying from Utah."

"Then Kim got her early-acceptance rejection from Brown. Kim was number one in the class. Nobody could believe it. Her father had gone to Brown and Kim had almost 1500 SATs. Kim was out of commission for a few days—I mean she didn't come to school or anything—and then, boom, she was gone. She offed herself, kaput, no more, the end. Then Brian was rejected from Cornell. A few days later, he was gone, too. And I'm like, 'These kids were better than me.' I mean their grades and their SATs were higher than mine, and I was going to apply to Brown and Cornell. I'm like, 'What chance do I have? Why bother?' "

The Authors' Files ∎

The reader can identify how catastrophizing cognitions can play a role in such tragic cases. Consistent with the literature on suicide among adults, suicidal children make less use of active problem-solving strategies in handling stressful situations. They may see no other way of dealing with their perceived failures or life stresses than by ending it all. As with adults, one approach to working with suicidal children involves helping them challenge distorted thinking and generate alternate strategies for reducing stress or resolving conflict.

EATING DISORDERS

It is normal enough for young children to be fussy eaters. Even the (partial) hunger strikes of 2-year-olds occur quite often. The eating habits of some children and adolescents, however, are immoderate enough to impair their health and social relationships. Children, like adults, can become obese, and much of the time obese children develop into obese adults. In this section we discuss two major types of eating disorders that usually begin in adolescence: anorexia nervosa and bulimia nervosa. Anorexia nervosa and bulimia nervosa are also related because they affect many more girls than boys, involve preoccupations with weight control, and maladaptive ways of keeping weight down.

Anorexia Nervosa

∎ Karen was the 22-year-old daughter of a renowned English professor. She had begun her college career full of promise at the age of 17, but two years ago, after "social problems" occurred, she had returned to live at home and taken progressively lighter course loads at a local college. Karen had never been overweight, but about a year ago her mother noticed that she seemed to be gradually "turning into a skeleton."

Karen spent literally hours every day shopping at the supermarket, butcher, and bakeries, and in conjuring up gourmet treats for her parents and younger siblings. Arguments over her lifestyle and eating habits had divided the family into two camps. The camp led by her father called for patience; that headed by her mother demanded confrontation. Her mother feared that Karen's father would "protect her right into her grave" and wanted Karen placed in residential treatment "for her own good." The parents finally compromised on an outpatient evaluation.

The suicide rate among adolescents is reported to have tripled in the past 30 years. Suicidal children and adolescents may see no other way of handling their perceived failures and life problems. But the availability of counseling and support services may help prevent suicide by assisting them to learn alternative strategies for reducing stress and resolving conflicts.

At an even 5 feet, Karen looked like a prepubescent 11-year-old. Her nose and cheekbones protruded crisply, like those of an elegant young fashion model. Her lips were full, but the redness of the lipstick was unnatural, as if too much paint had been daubed on a corpse for the funeral. Karen weighed only 78 pounds, but she had dressed in a stylish silk blouse, scarf, and baggy pants so that not one inch of her body was revealed.

Karen vehemently denied that she had a problem. Her figure was "just about where I want it to be" and she engaged in aerobic exercise daily. A deal was struck in which outpatient treatment would be tried as long as Karen lost no more weight and showed steady gains back to at least 90 pounds. Treatment included a day hospital with group therapy and two meals a day. But word came back that Karen was artfully toying with her food—cutting it up, sort of licking it, and moving it about her plate—rather than eating it. After three weeks Karen had lost another pound. At that point, her parents were able to persuade her to enter a residential treatment program, where her eating behavior could be more carefully monitored.

The Authors' Files ■

Anorexia derives from the Greek roots *an-*, meaning "without," and *orexis*, meaning "a desire for." *Anorexia* thus means "without desire for [food]," which can be something of a misnomer because some anorexic people report hunger. However, food may impress them as repugnant, and they may refuse to eat more than is absolutely necessary to maintain a minimal weight for their ages and heights. Often they do not eat enough to maintain their health.

 Perhaps you cannot be too rich, but you can be dangerously thin, as in the case of anorexia nervosa.

Anorexia nervosa, which can become a life-threatening problem, is characterized by maintenance of weight at least 15 percent below normal levels; an intense fear of being overweight; a distorted body image (perceiving one's body or parts of one's body as fat, even if one is dangerously thin); and, in females, **amenorrhea.**

By and large, anorexia comes on in early to late adolescence, between the ages of 12 and 18, although earlier and later onsets are sometimes encountered. Ninety-five percent of the cases are females, according to the DSM–III–R. Anorexia nervosa and bulimia nervosa were once considered very rare, but they are becoming increasingly common in the United States and other developed countries (Kagan & Squires, 1984; Killen et al., 1986; Mitchell & Eckert, 1987; Pope et al., 1984; Pyle et al., 1986). Perhaps as many as one of every 100 female adolescents could be considered anorexic, according to DSM–III–R criteria (see Table 14.6).

TABLE 14.6 *DSM–III–R Diagnostic Criteria for Anorexia Nervosa*

A.	Refusal to maintain weight beyond the minimal normal weight for one's age and height; for example, a weight at least 15 percent below normal.
B.	Strong fear of putting on weight or becoming fat, despite being thin.
C.	A distorted body image in which one's body—or part of one's body—is perceived as fat, although others perceive the person as thin.
D.	In females, absence of three or more consecutive menstrual periods.

Source: *Adapted from DSM–III–R, p. 67.*

The typical pattern of anorexia begins after menarche when the girl notices added weight and insists that it must come off. Extreme dieting and, often, excessive exercise continue unabated after the initial weight-loss goal is achieved, however—even after family members and others express concern. Anorexic girls almost always deny that they are losing too much weight or wasting away. They may proffer their stressful exercise regimens as evidence. Although others may see them as "skin and bones," they see themselves as headed in the right direction, as with Karen. They may spend hours before the mirror, focusing on nonexistent but perceived "lingering" pockets of fat.

Although the thought of eating is repugnant to anorexic girls, some experience strong hunger. Loss of appetite is rare. They may be constantly around food. Also, like Karen, they may absorb themselves in cookbooks, assume family shopping chores, and prepare fancy dinners for others.

The typical anorexic or bulimic person is a young white female from a family of higher socioeconomic status, although anorexia is also becoming more prevalent among other social groups and older age categories (Mitchell & Eckert, 1987). Anorexia and bulimia are relatively less common among blacks and Asian Americans (Nevo, 1985; Jones, et al., 1980).

■ *Medical Complications of Anorexia* Anorexics can incur serious medical complications (Kaplan & Woodside, 1987). They may lose as much as 35 percent of their previous weight and develop anemia. Anorexic females also encounter dermatological problems like dry, cracking skin; fine, downy hair; even a yellowish discoloration that may persist for years after weight is regained. Cardiovascular complications include heart irregularities, hypotension (low blood pressure) and associated dizziness upon standing, sometimes causing blackouts. Decreased food ingestion can cause gastrointestinal problems like constipation, abdominal pain, and obstruction or paralysis of the bowels or intestines. Menstrual irregularities are common, and amenorrhea,

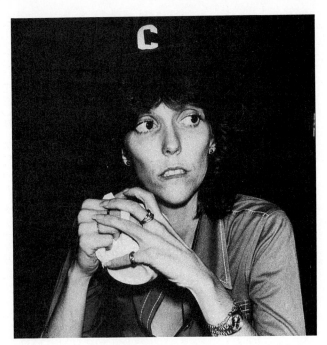

Karen Carpenter was a popular recording star who died from a heart attack in her early thirties. It is believed that her long struggle with anorexia nervosa contributed to her death. She weighed but 80 pounds at one point toward the end of her life.

as noted, is part of the definition of anorexia in females. Muscular weakness and abnormal growth of bones may occur, causing loss of height and **osteoporosis.**

A review of 33 studies on anorexic females found reported mortality rates ranging from 0 to 22 percent. The consensus, however, seems to place the overall mortality rate at about 4 percent or slightly less (Herzog et al., 1988). About half of those who die do so from direct complications of anorexia, such as inanition (a state of weakness from eating or drinking too little) and severe imbalances in **electrolytes.** About one in four commit suicide (Herzog et al., 1988; Hsu, 1980, 1987). The remaining deaths are attributed to various causes, including accidents, lung disease, and unspecified factors.

Bulimia Nervosa

■ Nicole has only opened her eyes, but already she wishes it was time for bed. She dreads going through the day, which threatens to turn out like so many other days of her recent past. Each morning she wonders, Is this the day that she will be able to get by without being obsessed by thoughts of food? Or will she "blow it again" and spend the day gorging herself? Today is the day she will get off to a new start, she promises herself. Today she will begin to live like a normal person. Yet she is not convinced that it is really up to her.

Nicole starts the day with eggs and toast. Then she goes to work on cookies; doughnuts; bagels smothered with butter, cream cheese, and jelly; granola; candy bars; and bowls of cereal and milk—all within 45 minutes. Then she cannot take in any more food and turns her attention to purging what she has eaten. She goes to the bathroom, ties back her hair, turns on the shower to mask any noise she will make, drinks a glass of water, and makes herself vomit. Afterward she vows, "Starting tomorrow, I'm going to change." But she suspects that tomorrow may be just another chapter of the same story.

Adapted from Boskind-White & White, 1983, p. 29 ■

Nicole has **bulimia nervosa.** *Bulimia* derives from the Greek roots *bous,* meaning "ox" or "cow," and *limos,* meaning "hunger." The unpretty picture inspired by the origin of the term is of continuous eating, as a cow chews its cud. Bulimia nervosa is an eating disorder characterized by recurrent episodes of gorging on large quanities of food followed by purging, as by self-induced vomiting, in order to maintain a normal weight (Russell, 1979). The DSM–III–R diagnoses bulimia according to the criteria shown in Table 14.7. Whereas anorexics are extremely thin, bulimic individuals are usually of normal weight. However, they share excessive concern about their body shapes and weight.

Most bulimics gag themselves to induce vomiting following bingeing episodes; some vomit after every meal. Most bulimics attempt to conceal their behavior. Although less common, some use laxatives or compulsive exercise to control their weight. Bulimics live in fear of gaining weight. In one study, 15 female bulimics aged 18 to 25 were matched with 15 nondisordered women according to age, sex, and body shape. Subjects were asked to imagine a weight gain of 5 pounds (Cutts & Barrios, 1986). Bulimics were more highly aroused by the weight-gain imagery, as assessed by subjective report and physiological measures. Although bulimics share with anorexics an overconcern with body shape and weight, bulimics do not pursue extreme thinness. Their ideal weights are similar to those of normal women (Fairburn et al., 1986).

The average age for onset of bulimia is the late teenage years, when concerns about dieting and expres-

TABLE 14.7 DSM–III–R Diagnostic Criteria for Bulimia Nervosa

A. Recurrent episodes of binge eating (gorging).
B. A sense of lack of control over binge eating.
C. Regular purging as by means of self-induced vomiting, laxatives or diuretics, fasting, or vigorous exercise, to prevent gains in weight.
D. A minimum average of two episodes of binge eating a week over a period of at least three months.
E. Persistent overconcern with the shape and weight of one's body.

Source: *Adapted from DSM–III–R, pp. 68–69.*

The bulimic engages in repeated episodes of binge eating which are often followed by purging, such as by self-induced vomiting. When bingeing, the bulimic may gobble down large amounts of fattening or "forbidden" foods directly from the refrigerator. Some bulimics consume food indiscriminately when bingeing, even scooping margarine out of its container with a finger.

sion of body dissatisfaction are at their greatest (Agras & Kirkley, 1986). Bulimics tend to be slightly overweight preceding the development of bulimia, and the binge-purge cycle usually follows a period of highly restrictive dieting. Binge eating tends to alternate with dietary restraint and is often precipitated by emotional distress or unpleasant events (Fairburn et al., 1986). The binge itself usually occurs in secret and involves consumption of usually forbidden, fattening foods with little regard for taste or texture. Bingers may consume 5,000 to 10,000 calories in one episode. The episode continues until the bulimic is spent or exhausted, suffers painful stomach distention, induces vomiting, or runs out of food. Drowsiness, guilt, and depression usually ensue, but bingeing is initially pleasant because of release from constraints. In between binges, bulimics may maintain rigid controls over eating (Fairburn et al., 1986).

Bulimia, like anorexia, predominantly affects females, the majority of whom are in their twenties. Most come from the middle or upper socioeconomic classes. About one-quarter are married (Fairburn et al., 1986). The incidence of bulimia is much higher than that of anorexia, and concern about the disorder has generated much publicity and controversy. The DSM–III–R is not much help on the issue, noting vaguely that "A recent study of college freshmen indicated that 4.5% of the females and 0.4% of the males had a history of bulimia" (p. 68). Actually, many studies have been done, on and off campus. Although some researchers see bulimia as reaching alarming proportions on campus (Halmi,

1981; Pyle et al., 1986), others consider such notions of alarm to be overstated (Kolata, 1988b).

One problem in estimating the incidence of bulimia is found in how the problem is defined. Bingeing itself is quite common, with one to three women in four and two to three men in five reporting binge-eating episodes (Mitchell & Eckert, 1987). However, bingeing alone does not constitute bulimia, according to the DSM–III–R definition. A study done at the University of Pennsylvania found that about 1.3 to 5 percent of the women and 0.1 percent of the men enrolled at the university met DSM–III–R criteria for bulimic disorder, but the incidences of occasional bulimic behaviors were higher (Schott & Stunkard, 1987). A national survey of collegians reported that 1 percent of college women and 0.2 percent of college men met the DSM–III–R criteria for bulimia (Kolata, 1988b).

 ? Some college women do keep their weight down by making themselves vomit after they go on eating binges. A recurrent pattern of binge eating and purging defines the disorder of bulimia nervosa.

■ **Medical Complications of Bulimia**   Bulimia is also associated with many medical complications (Kaplan & Woodside, 1987). Many of these stem from repeated vomiting. There may be irritations of the skin around the mouth due to frequent contact with stomach acid, blockage of salivary ducts, decay of tooth enamel, and dental cavities. The acid from the vomit may damage taste receptors on the palate, which might make the bulimic less sensitive to the taste of vomit with repeated purgings (Rodin et al., 1990). Decreased sensitivity to the aversive taste of vomit may play a role in maintaining the purging behavior (Rodin et al., 1990). Cycles of bingeing and vomiting may cause abdominal pain, hiatus hernia, and other abdominal complaints. Stress on the pancreas may produce pancreatitis (inflammation), a medical emergency (Kaplan & Woodside, 1987). Excessive use of laxatives may cause bloody diarrhea and laxative dependency, so that the person cannot have normal bowel movements without laxatives. In the extreme, the bowel can lose its reflexive eliminatory response to pressure from waste material. Bingeing on large quantities of salty food may cause convulsions and swelling. Repeated vomiting or abuse of laxatives can lead to potassium deficiency, producing muscular weakness, cardiac irregularities, even sudden death—especially among bulimics who use diuretics. As with anorexics, menstruation may come to a halt.

Theoretical Perspectives on Eating Disorders

The link between anorexia and menarche has led psychodynamic theorists to suggest that anorexia may rep-

QUESTIONNAIRE
The Fear of Fat Scale

Fear of body fat underlies eating disorders like anorexia and bulimia. The Goldfarb Fear of Fat scale (Goldfarb et al., 1985) measures the degree to which people fear becoming fat. The scale may help identify individuals who stand a greater risk of developing eating disorders. It differentiates between anorexics and normal women, and between bulimics and nonbulimics. Dieters, however, also score higher on the scale than do nondieters.

To fill out the Fear of Fat scale, read each of the following statements and write in the number that best represents your own feelings and beliefs. Then check the key at the end of the chapter.

1 = very untrue
2 = somewhat untrue
3 = somewhat true
4 = very true

_____ 1. My biggest fear is of becoming fat.
_____ 2. I am afraid to gain even a little weight.
_____ 3. I believe there is a real risk that I will become overweight someday.
_____ 4. I don't understand how overweight people can live with themselves.
_____ 5. Becoming fat would be the worst thing that could happen to me.
_____ 6. If I stopped concentrating on controlling my weight, chances are I would become very fat.
_____ 7. There is nothing that I can do to make the thought of gaining weight less painful and frightening.
_____ 8. I feel like all my energy goes into controlling my weight.
_____ 9. If I eat even a little, I may lose control and not stop eating.
_____ 10. Staying hungry is the only way I can guard against losing control and becoming fat.

Source: *Goldfarb et al., 1985.*

themselves as being separate from their parents and families than were nonanorexics (Strauss & Ryan, 1987).

Some learning theorists view anorexia as a type of "weight phobia" (see Crisp, 1967). Excessive, irrational fears of putting on weight may reflect the tendencies in our culture to idealize the slender female form. Learning theorists also see purging among bulimics as a means of reducing the anxiety and fear that binge eating engenders in individuals who fear gaining weight (Rosen & Leitenberg, 1982). Purging reduces fear of weight gain following bingeing, so that fear reduction negatively reinforces the preceding binge/purge pattern. Purging may be seen as a compulsive ritual which is reinforced by anxiety reduction, just as compulsive hand-washing and checking in obsessive-compulsives (see Chapter 6) are believed to be reinforced by relief from the anxiety induced by obsessive thoughts (Leitenberg et al., 1988).

Regardless of the factors that initiate eating disorders, various social reinforcers may maintain such problem behaviors. Children with eating disorders may quickly become the focus of attention of their families and receive attention from their parents that might otherwise be lacking.

■ Family Factors and Systems

Anorexia, as noted, has a brutal effect on parents. Self-starvation may sometimes be used as a weapon by children when family relationships are disturbed (Bemis, 1978). The binge–purge cycle of the bulimic has been seen as a metaphor for the excesses and deficits that characterize her family (Humphrey, 1986). Bulimic females and their families crave mutual support, nurturance, and empathy in the same way that bulimics crave food. Families of bulimics then purge their mutual frustrations and aggressions through unfocused and unconstructive shows of emotion.

Some recent research is supportive of the presence of disturbed relationships in families of bulimics. Bulimics, in contrast with normal women, perceive their families as less expressive and cohesive but more often in conflict (Johnson & Flach, 1985; Ordman & Kirschenbaum, 1986). Families of bulimics perceive their family relationships as more conflicted and detached, less mutually supportive, and less structured than do families of normal subjects (Humphrey, 1986). Similar findings characterize the family patterns of bulimic anorexics—females who binge and purge but, in contrast to bulimics, do not maintain normal weight levels (Humphrey, 1987). Parents of bulimic anorexics tend to place their daughters in double binds by communicating mixed messages: They pay lip service to encouraging autonomy but at the same time wrest control from their daughters. The daughters, in turn, show ambivalence toward their parents. They alternate between being submissive though resentful and being self-assertive.

resent the girl's effort to remain a prepubescent child. By maintaining the veneer of childhood, the pubescent girl may avoid dealing with such "grown-up" issues as increased independence and separation from her family, sexual maturation, and assumption of adult responsibilities. Because of the loss of fatty deposits, their breasts and hips flatten. Menstrual periods cease. In their fantasies, perhaps, they remain children, sexually undifferentiated.

Conflicts relating to autonomy have been implicated in the development of anorexia nervosa and bulimia (Strauss & Ryan, 1987). Psychodynamically oriented writers note that anorexic girls have difficulties separating from their families and consolidating separate, individuated identities (Bruch, 1973; Minuchin et al., 1978). The results of a recent study showed that anorexic girls were less well defined in how they saw

All in all, the families of females with eating disorders are more often conflicted and disengaged but less cohesive and nurturant than those of reference groups. They seem less capable of promoting independence in their children (Strober & Humphrey, 1987). Note, however, that the preponderance of this research is retrospective—relying on accounts of family patterns in individuals already identified as eating disordered. Therefore, it is unclear as to whether the identified family patterns contribute to the initiation of eating disorders, or whether eating disorders disrupt family life. The truth probably lies in an interaction between the two.

From the **systems perspective,** families are systems that regulate themselves in ways that minimize the open expression of conflict and reduce the immediate need for overt change. Within this perspective, anorexic girls may be seen as helping to maintain the shaky balances and harmonies that are found in dysfunctional families by displacing attention from marital tensions onto themselves (Minuchin et al., 1978). The anorexic girl may become the *identified patient,* although the family unit is actually dysfunctional.

■ **Biological Factors**   Over the years, most theorists have attributed anorexia nervosa and bulimia nervosa to psychological origins. However, recent research has also implicated biological factors. For example, it has been proposed that some cases may reflect problems in the hypothalamus. The neurotransmitters norepinephrine and dopamine stimulate animals to eat when they act on parts of the hypothalamus, and these animals, like bulimic bingers, show preference for carbohydrates (Kaplan & Woodside, 1987; Mitchell & Eckert, 1987; Wurtman & Wurtman, 1984). The neurotransmitter serotonin, by contrast, seems to induce satiation, thereby suppressing appetite and especially the desire for carbohydrates (Halmi et al., 1986; Kaplan & Woodside, 1987). So biological conditions that increase the action of serotonin could inhibit the desire to eat, as in some cases of anorexia. Perhaps conditions that suppress the action of serotonin, which normally inhibits appetite for carbohydrates, can cause episodic carbohydrate bingeing, as found in many cases of bulimia.

These hypotheses receive some support from observed relationships between affective and eating disorders. As noted in Chapter 8, norepinephrine and serotonin are also implicated in mood disorders. Many bulimic females are depressed or present some depressive features (Fairburn & Cooper, 1984; Fairburn et al., 1986; Hudson et al., 1984; Piran et al., 1985). Bulimic females also sometimes respond favorably to antidepressant drugs (Pope et al., 1983; Pope & Hudson, 1982, Walsh et al., 1984; Rosebush, 1986). Another source of evidence is that immediate (first-degree) relatives of bulimics tend to have mood disorders in about the same proportion as the relatives of people with bipolar disorders (Hudson et al., 1983). Perhaps some bulimics binge in an attempt to lift their moods (Johnson & Larson, 1982). But only a minority of persons with eating disorders show evidence of diagnosable depression (Fairburn et al., 1986).

Although eating disorders tend to run in families, it is unlikely that genetic factors fully explain them. Perhaps biological factors involving genetics and neurotransmitters provide a diathesis or predisposition for eating disorders, but their actual development may depend upon the interaction of genetic factors with family, social, cultural, and environmental pressures (Strober & Humphrey, 1987).

Treatment of Anorexia Nervosa and Bulimia Nervosa

Eating disorders are difficult to treat. Anorexic patients are frequently hospitalized. Then they may be given drugs to heighten hunger and inhibit vomiting. Behavioral treatment is also commonly used, with reinforcements made contingent on appropriate eating and weight gain. Commonly used reinforcers include ward privileges and social opportunities (Agras et al., 1974; Hsu, 1980). Behavior therapy is often combined with psychodynamic therapy to probe for deeper psychological conflicts (Bruch, 1973) or with family therapy to resolve underlying family conflicts (Minuchin et al., 1980). In one encouraging study of anorexics (Rosman et al., 1976), more than four out of five young women whose families had received family therapy retained weight gains in follow-up evaluations that ranged from several months to several years. However, the results of another study showed that while most anorexics had maintained or increased their weight gains two years following a treatment program, most also continued to perceive themselves as overweight, even though they averaged 8 percent below the level corresponding to their ideal weight (Nussbaum et al., 1985). These persistent distortions in body image suggest that the longer-term outlook for anorexics who are "successfully" treated may not be as promising.

Research has begun to accumulate that supports the effectiveness of cognitive-behavior therapy approaches to bulimia (Fairburn et al., 1986b). Bulimics are often treated successfully in outpatient programs that focus on developing appropriate eating habits, preventing binge eating and vomiting, and replacing distorted beliefs about food and dieting with more adaptive beliefs. Hospitalization is reserved for those who require more intensive medical interventions or who appear suicidal (Mitchell & Eckert, 1987).

To eliminate self-induced vomiting in these individuals, many therapists use the behavioral technique of exposure coupled with response prevention (Leitenberg et al., 1984). In this technique, the bulimic is

A CLOSER LOOK
Body Image and the Idealization of Thinness

Perhaps many males have claimed that they were leafing through *Playboy* magazine merely to study cultural standards for beauty. Garner and his colleagues (1980) actually lived up to this claim, however. Their aim was to document the increasing pressures on women to be slender. Their method was to compare pictures of *Playboy* centerfolds, Miss America contestants, and models from women's magazine over the past few decades. Sure enough, they found that the idealized models of the feminine form have become progressively thinner and more boyish over the years. In contrast to the large-breasted ideals of the 1950s, busts and hips have become smaller in proportion to the models' waistlines.

As the cultural ideal grows slimmer, women with average or heavier-than-average figures come under more pressure to control their weight. Agras and Kirkley (1986) documented the interest in losing weight by counting the number of diet articles printed in three women's magazines since the year 1900: *Ladies' Home Journal, Good Housekeeping,* and *Harper's Bazaar.* Diet articles were absent until the 1930s. During the 1930s and 1940s, only about one article appeared in every 10 issues. During the 1950s and 1960s, the number of diet articles jumped to about one in every other issue. During the 1980s, however, the number mushroomed to about 1.3 articles per issue. In recent years, that is, there has been an average of *more than one diet article per issue!*

It is no secret that today's college-age and adult women widely believe that their figures are heavier than the ideal (Fallon & Rozin, 1985; Rozin & Fallon, 1988). Today, however, even children express dissatisfaction with their body images. One study surveyed the body-figure preferences of 670 children between the ages of $10\frac{1}{2}$ and 15 (Cohn et al., 1987). *Both* sexes were generally dissatisfied with their bodies. Boys wanted to be heavier than they were, and girls wanted to be thinner. As in the Fallon and Rozin studies, when girls were asked to describe the ideal female figure, they chose a figure that was thinner than they and also thinner than the figure preferred by boys. Boys, on the other hand, had an ideal body shape that was heavier than they were themselves and heavier than the figure they believed that girls would prefer.

Boys will naturally grow heavier as they mature and gain muscle mass. As a result, their bodies will conform more closely to their perceived ideal. Girls, unfortunately, are likely to experience a greater discrepancy between their own body shape and their ideal figure as their busts fill out and their hips grow rounder. The discrepancy between the girls' perceived and ideal figures was in fact greater among the older girls in the study (Cohn et al.,

The idealization of the slender feminine form in our society can place young women under pressures to conform to an unrealistic, idealized concept of thinness. These cultural pressures can place them at risk of developing an eating disorder.

1987). Even as they enter adolescence, present-day females have already developed an unrealistic desire for thinness that can lead to unhappiness and perceptions of "failure."

Society must come to grips with the idealized models that it presents its young women. As suggested by Boskind-White and White (1986).

> . . . *if the toxic chain reaction of the terror of fat, fad diets, and eating disorders is to be broken, it is essential for the public to be properly informed regarding the dangers inherent in severe caloric deprivations. The media and fashion industry must take responsiblity and introduce models who are womanly and fit rather than emaciated and unhealthy. Only then will women, young and old, begin to value themselves enough to reject inappropriate roles and implement more effective coping strategies with respect to food (pp. 363–364).*

exposed to eating forbidden foods while the therapist stands by to prevent vomiting until the urge to purge passes. In this way bulimics learn to tolerate violations of their dietary rules without restorting to purging. In one study, 20 of 34 (nearly 60%) of bulimic females treated by means of 11 exposure-and-response-preven-

tion sessions reduced their binge-purge episodes by 80 percent or more. Fourteen demonstrated complete cessation of vomiting and resumed normal eating (Giles et al., 1985).

Many therapists are also using cognitive restructuring to modify some of the irrational beliefs that main-

Functional enuresis is considered *primary* in the DSM–III–R when the child has never shown satisfactory bladder control. However, when the child has previously exercised bladder control for a year or more, the problem is considered *secondary*.

■ **Theoretical Perspectives**   Numerous psychological explanations of functional enuresis have been advanced. Psychodynamic theory suggests that enuresis may represent the child's expression of hostility toward the parents (because of harsh toilet training) or it may be a sign of regression in response to the birth of a sibling or some other psychosocial stressor or life change, such as starting school or suffering the death of a parent or relative. Learning theorists point out that enuresis occurs most commonly in children whose parents attempted to train them early. Early failures may have connected anxiety with efforts to control the bladder. Conditioned anxiety, then, induces rather than curbs urination.

Genetics may also be involved; the DSM–III–R reports that the concordance rate for functional enuresis is higher among MZ twins than among DZ twins. Genetic factors may regulate the rate of development of cortical control over eliminatory reflexes.

Bed-wetting, the most common type of functional enuresis, usually occurs during the deepest stage of sleep and may reflect immaturity of the nervous system. In most cases, bed-wetting resolves itself by adolescence, and usually by the age of 8. But about 1 percent of cases of functional enuresis persist into adulthood, according to the DSM–III–R.

■ **Treatment**   While enuresis is resolved naturally with time in most cases, it can occasion significant distress in both the family and child. Behavioral methods that condition the child to wake up when the bladder is full have shown some success in treating nighttime enuresis. One reasonably dependable example is Mowrer's bell-and-pad method (Doleys, 1977).

The problem in bed-wetting is that the child sleeps through bladder tension that awakens most other children and thus the child reflexively urinates in bed. Psychologist O. Hobart Mowrer pioneered the bell-and-pad method in which a special pad is placed beneath the sleeping child. When the pad is wet, an electrical circuit closes, causing a bell to ring and the sleeping child to waken. After several repetitions, most children learn to wake up in response to bladder tension—*before* they wet the pad. The technique is usually explained through principles of classical conditioning. In the bell-and-pad method, *tension in children's bladders* is paired repeatedly with a stimulus (a bell) that wakes them up. The bladder tension (conditioned stimulus, or CS) comes to elicit the same response (waking up) that is elicited by the bell (the unconditioned stimulus, or US).

Functional Encopresis

Encopresis derives from the Greek roots *en-* and *kopros,* meaning "feces." **Functional encopresis** is lack of control over bowel movements not due to a physical disorder that occurs in a child with a mental and chronological age of 4 or older. Soiling, like enuresis, is more common among boys. The overall incidence of soiling is lower than that of enuresis, however. Between 1 and 2 percent of children at the ages of 7 and 8 have problems with soiling. Encopresis rarely occurs among adolescents by the middle teens (Schaefer, 1979), except among the profoundly or severely retarded.

Soiling, unlike enuresis, is more likely to happen during the day. Thus it can be keenly embarrassing to the youngster. Classmates often avoid or ridicule soilers. Because feces have a strong odor, teachers may find it hard to act as though nothing of consequence has happened. Parents, too, are eventually galled by recurrent soiling and may increase their demands for self-control and employ powerful punishments for failure. Because of all this, the child may start to hide soiled underwear (Ross, 1981). Such children may distance themselves from classmates, or feign sickness to stay at home. Their levels of anxiety concerning soiling increases. Because anxiety (arousal of the sympathetic branch of the autonomic nervous system) promotes bowel movements, control may become more elusive.

When soiling is involuntary it is often associated with constipation, impaction, or retention that results in subsequent overflow, according to the DSM–III–R. The constipation may be related to psychological fears, such as fears associated with defecating in a particular place or with a more general pattern of negativistic or oppositional behavior. Or the constipation might be related to physiological factors, such as complications from an illness or from medication. Much less frequently, encopresis is deliberate or intentional.

Soiling often appears to follow harsh punishment of an accident or two, particularly in children who are already highly stressed or anxious. Harsh punishment may rivet the children's attention on soiling. They may then ruminate about soiling, raising their level of anxiety to a point that may impair their control.

Operant conditioning methods may be helpful in dealing with soiling. These methods employ rewards (by praise and other means) for successful attempts at self-control and mild punishments for continued accidents, such as gentle reminders to the child to attend more closely to bowel tension and to clean his or her own underwear. But a thorough medical and psychological evaluation is important to determine the possible causes and treatments if the problem is persistent.

SUMMARY

In determining abnormality in children and adolescents we take into account the child's age, sex, family and cultural background, and developmental level.

Risk Factors for Disorders of Childhood and Adolescence

There are various risk factors that researchers have identified, including gender; biological risk factors, such as genetics, prenatal factors, birth complications, premature birth, low birth weights, and childhood illnesses; and psychosocial factors, such as stress, family conflict, cognitive factors, lack of acceptance, and parental neglect and abuse.

Autism

Autism, one of the most severe behavioral problems of childhood, is a pervasive developmental disorder affecting emotional, cognitive, speech, social, and motor development. Autistic children tend to shun affectionate behavior, engage in stereotyped behavior, make demands for sameness in their environment, and have peculiar speech habits, such as echolalia, pronoun reversals, and idiosyncratic speech. Their intellectual development lags far behind the norm. The causes of autism remain unknown. While early psychological views focused on the pathological role of the family, more recent viewpoints stress biological causes, although the specific sites of brain pathology that may be involved have not been revealed. Treatments tend to be focused on supportive therapeutic residences or on more structured operant-conditioning programs in which rewards and punishments are systematically manipulated. Autism should be distinguished from childhood schizophrenia, a much rarer condition that resembles adult schizophrenia.

Mental Retardation

Mental retardation involves a general delay in the development of intellectual and adaptive abilities that affects most areas of social, cognitive, and language functioning. Mental retardation is assessed on the basis of a low IQ, evidence of impaired functioning, and onset before age 18. Mental retardation varies in severity, with most cases falling in the mildly retarded range. In many cases, clear biological causes are involved, such as chromosomal abnormalities, recessive gene disorders, and prenatal factors. In other cases, called cultural-familial retardation, there is no clear biological cause and a combination of cultural, familial, and perhaps genetic factors may be involved. With appropriate intervention and training, most mentally retarded people can become functional enough to support themselves minimally through meaningful work, although the profoundly retarded may need continuing institutional care or a structured living environment. The savant syndrome describes people with autism or mental retardation who possess remarkable mental abilities, such as calendar calculation.

Learning Disabilities

Learning disabilities involve specific deficits in the development of computational, writing, reading, language, or speech skills. The origins of learning disabilities may relate to cognitive-perceptual problems and underlying neurological factors. Approaches to intervention reflect diverse theoretical models, but most involve efforts to remediate the specific skill deficits.

Disruptive Behavior

Disruptive behavior disorders include attention-deficit hyperactivity disorder, conduct disorder, and oppositional defiant disorder. Attention-deficit hyperactivity disorder (ADHD) is characterized by impulsivity, inattention, and hyperactivity to a degree that is inconsistent with developmental level. Much more common in boys, understanding of the disorder has been approached from biological and environmental perspectives. Stimulant medication is the most common intervention, and while it is generally effective in reducing hyperactivity, its use has not yielded general academic gains. While some children outgrow hyperactivity by adolescence or adulthood, many have continuing problems in adjustment.

Children with conduct disorder problems intentionally engage in antisocial behavior that violates the rights of others, such as stealing, destroying property, or even committing violent crimes against others. Several subtypes of conduct disorder have been distinguished: group type, solitary aggressive type, and undifferentiated types. Management of conduct disorder problems often involves operant conditioning methods, problem-solving techniques, and family therapy approaches.

Anxiety Disorders of Childhood

Anxiety disorders in childhood take several forms. Children with separation anxiety show an inappropriate or excessive level of anxiety when separated from their parents, which is inconsistent with the child's developmental level. Children with avoidant disorder show persistent and excessive avoidance of contact with

actualization. When others are selective in their approval of our feelings and behavior during childhood, we may come to disown the parts of ourselves that meet with disapproval. To earn social approval, we may don a social mask or facade. We learn "to be seen and not heard" and may become deaf to even our own inner voices. Over time, we may grow to develop a distorted self-concept that is in keeping with the view that others have of us but is not truly one of our own making and design. As a result, we may become poorly adjusted, unhappy, and confused about who and what we are.

> **?** Some psychotherapists, such as person-centered therapists, do believe that the goal of psychotherapy is to teach clients to be themselves.

The well-adjusted person makes choices and takes actions that are consistent with his or her personal values and needs. Rogers' humanistic approach to therapy, *person-centered therapy*, helps clients become more aware and accepting of their true selves by creating conditions of acceptance and worth in the therapeutic relationship. Rogers was a major shaper of contemporary psychotherapy, and he was rated the most influential psychotherapist in a recent survey of therapists (Smith, 1982). Rogers did not believe that therapists should impose their own goals or values on their clients. The focus of therapy, as the name implies, is centered on the person. The therapy is *nondirective*; the client, not the therapist, takes the lead and directs the course of therapy. The therapist mirrors or reflects the client's expressed feelings to help him or her get in touch with deeper feelings and parts of the self that had become disowned because of social condemnation. The therapist reflects back or paraphrases the client's disclosures without interpretation or passing judgment on them. Here we see how a therapist reflects back a client's disclosures to help her clarify and further explore her feelings:

■ CLIENT: Now—one of the things that . . . had worried me was . . . living at the dorm; it's hard—not to just sort of fall in with a group of people, ah, that aren't interesting, but just around. Well, I . . . found that I had been spending a lot more time with a group of people that I didn't find interesting—. All of them are pleasant people . . . but well, there were a lot of things that I didn't have in common. . . . So, now I find that I'm . . . getting away from that group a little bit. And ah, being with people who are a little bit more stimulating, and people that I really find I have more interests in common with.

COUNSELOR: That is, you've really chosen to draw away from the group you're just thrown with by chance, and you pick people whom you want more to associate with. Is that it?

CLIENT: That's the idea. . . . I haven't taken any great steps by leaps and bounds. But, well, one of the girls lives on my floor and she would come and knock on the door and say, ah, that she wanted to eat lunch . . . or all of us are going down to eat at twelve. Well, it used to be hard for me to say, "Well, no. I would like to eat at twelve-thirty, ah, so I can eat lunch and go to my one-thirty class." And so I'd stop whatever I was doing and drag down at twelve with the group. Well, now I say, occasionally, "Well, that isn't convenient for me. . . . "I'd rather eat earlier." . . . And then another thing is that, ah, with the group of kids that I was eating with, I felt that I had just sort of been dragged into the group, almost. They . . . had sort of pulled me in with a group of their friends that I wouldn't have picked, myself, especially. And ah, so that I found that all my time was being taken up with these people, and now I'm beginning to seek out people that I prefer myself . . . rather than being drawn in with the bunch.

COUNSELOR: You find it a little more possible, I gather, to express your real attitudes in a social situation, like wanting to go to lunch or not wanting to go to lunch, and also to, ah, to make your own choice of friends, and people that you want to mix with. . . .

CLIENT: I mean at first, ah, I tried to see if I was just withdrawing from this bunch of kids I'd been spending my time with, and I'm sincere in thinking that, ah, it's not a withdrawal, but it's more of an assertion of my real interests.

COUNSELOR: M-hm. In other words, you've tried to be self-critical in order to see if you're just running away from the situation, but you feel really, it's an expression of your positive attitudes.

CLIENT: I—I think it is.

Rogers, 1951, pp. 154–155 ■

Rogers stressed the importance of creating a warm, therapeutic relationship that would encourage the client in this process of self-exploration and self-expression. The effective person-centered therapist should possess four basic qualities or attributes: *unconditional positive regard, empathetic understanding, genuineness,* and *congruence.* First, the therapist must be able to express **unconditional positive regard** for clients. In contrast to the conditional approval that the client may have received from parents and others in the past, the therapist must be unconditionally accepting of the client as a person, even if the therapist sometimes objects to the client's choices or behaviors. Unconditional positive regard provides clients with a sense of security that encourages them to explore their feelings without fear of disapproval. As clients feel accepted or prized for themselves, so they are encouraged to accept themselves in turn. To Rogers, every human being has intrinsic worth and value. Traditional psychodynamic theory holds that people are basically motivated by primitive forces, such as sexual and aggressive impulses. Rogers believed, however, that people are basically good and are motivated to pursue *pro* social goals.

Therapists with **empathetic understanding** are able to reflect or mirror accurately their clients' experiences and feelings. Therapists try to see the world through their clients' eyes or frames of reference. They listen actively to clients and set aside their own judgments and interpretations of events. Empathetic understanding encourages clients to get in touch with feelings of which they are only dimly aware.

Genuineness is the ability to be open about one's feelings. Rogers admitted that he had negative feelings at times during therapy sessions, typically boredom, but that he attempted to express these feelings openly rather than hide them (Bennett, 1985).

Congruence refers to the fit between one's thoughts, feelings, and behavior. The congruent person is one whose behavior, thoughts, and feelings are integrated and consistent. Congruent therapists serve as models of integrity to their clients.

Gestalt Therapy

Another type of humanistic therapy, **Gestalt therapy,** was developed by Fritz Perls (1893–1970). Perls was trained as a traditional psychoanalyst but developed an approach to therapy that reflected the humanistic-existential emphasis on the client's subjective experiences in the present, the here and now. Perls adopted the German term *gestalt*, meaning "shape" or "form," to reflect his interest in helping clients blend conflicting parts of their personalities into an integrated form. Perls retained the Freudian belief that psychological disorders reflect internal conflicts, but he also believed that clients must focus on how conflicts affect their experience of themselves and their relationships today rather than dwell on their origins. Gestalt therapists use structured exercises to help expand clients' awareness of their feelings and self-defeating ways of relating to others. While person-centered therapists are warm and accepting toward their clients and nondirective, Perls's approach is directive and confrontational, even hostile. He attempts to break through clients' defenses and help them recognize their underlying conflicts.

Fritz Perls

One Gestalt exercise that is intended to increase awareness of internal conflicts is the **dialogue.** In this technique, clients verbally confront the opposing elements in their personalities. One example is the conflict between two parts of personality that Perls labeled the "top dog" and the "underdog." Your top dog might conservatively command you, "Don't stick your neck out. Play it safe. You might lose everything if you take chances." But the opposing element in your personality, your underdog, might become frustrated and rise up to assert, "You'll never get out of this rut if you don't take on new challenges." Becoming aware of these disparate elements in the personality can lead to an integration that may involve a compromise between both opposing parts.

In other exercises, clients might be encouraged to recognize feelings they may have been denying by arguing in support of ideas that are opposite to their expressed beliefs. Or they might role-play with their therapists encounters with people in their lives toward whom they have conflicted relationships so as to bring out the strong feelings that these conflicts evoke.

Like traditional psychoanalysts, Perls focused on clients' dreams. But he believed that the elements of dreams represented the disowned parts of the personality. To help clients get in touch with these parts, Perls would ask them to role-play the elements in their dreams. In one case, for example, a client (Jim) reported a recurring dream in which he sees a wheel coming toward him, growing to immense size as it bears down on him. Perls asks the client, "If you were this wheel, . . . what would you do with Jim?" Jim replies, "I am just about to roll over Jim" (Perls, 1971, p. 127). Perls encouraged Jim to assume the role of the wheel so as to help him recognize that "the wheel" represented his fears about taking decisive action. Through such exercises, Jim is helped to become more aware of the energy he has been wasting by worrying and can begin to take greater control of his life.

Existential Therapies

Existential therapists share in common with the humanistic therapists an emphasis on helping clients become more aware of their conscious experiences and to make personal choices that give their lives meaning and a sense of fulfillment. They also emphasize the uniqueness of the individual. Some of the more prominent existential therapists include the Swiss psychiatrists Ludwig Binswanger and Medard Boss, and the American psychologist Rollo May. Another existential therapist, as noted in Chapter 2, was the Viennese psychiatrist Victor Frankl, who developed **logotherapy,** a form of therapy that helps clients find meaning in their lives. Existential therapists owe much of their intellectual heritage to the European existential philosophers, in particular the Danish philosopher Sören Kierkegaard, the German philosophers Martin Heidegger and Edmund Husserl, and the French philosopher Jean-Paul Sartre.

Many existential therapists, especially those who trained or practiced in Europe, also incorporate psychodynamic concepts in their approach to therapy, such as the analysis of defenses that people use to distort their feelings and experiences. Whereas Rogerian therapists emphasize acceptance and empathetic understanding of the client, existential therapists stress the importance of coming to terms with the fundamental questions of existence, of recognizing the finality of life and of one's personal responsibility for making choices that give life meaning and purpose.

Rollo May

COGNITIVE THERAPIES

> There is nothing either good or bad, but thinking makes it so.
>
> Shakespeare, *Hamlet*

In these words, Shakespeare did not mean to imply that misfortunes or ailments are painless or easy to manage. His point, rather, appears to be that the ways in which we evaluate upsetting events can heighten our discomfort and impair our ability to cope. Several hundred years later, cognitive therapists would adopt this simple but elegant expression as a kind of motto for their approach to therapy.

Like humanistic-existential therapists, cognitive therapists believe that people can make genuine choices that can help them develop their potentials. Cognitive therapists share with Carl Rogers and Fritz Perls the belief that therapy should address the present, the "here-and-now." But whereas Rogers and Perls helped clients probe deeper feelings, cognitive therapists focus on the clients' beliefs, automatic types of thinking, and self-defeating attitudes that create or compound their emotional problems. Like psychodynamic therapists, cognitive therapists also focus on fostering insight, but they aim to increase their clients' awareness of current cognitions, not of distant sources of unconscious conflict. Cognitive therapies aim to help clients *change* the maladaptive cognitions that are believed to underlie psychological problems and to gain a more accurate picture of themselves and others.

Let us focus on two major cognitive therapies, Albert Ellis's rational-emotive therapy, and Aaron Beck's cognitive therapy.

Rational-Emotive Therapy

We noted in Chapter 2 how Ellis (1977, 1985, 1987) believes that the adoption of irrational, self-defeating beliefs gives rise to psychological problems and negative feelings. One of the most prominent of these irrational beliefs is the belief that you must almost always have the love and approval of the people who are important to you. Ellis finds it understandable to want other people's approval and love, but he argues that it is irrational for us to believe that we cannot survive without it. It is also unrealistic to believe that we must be thoroughly competent and achieving in everything we seek to accomplish. We are usually doomed to fall short of irrational expectations. Therefore, these expectations engender negative emotional consequences, such as depression and lowered self-esteem. Psychological disorders, like anxiety or depression, are not directly caused by negative events, but rather by viewing them through the dark-colored glasses of irrational beliefs. Thinking irrationally converts annoyances or disappointments into lingering depression. Thinking irrationally transforms challenging events, like forthcoming examinations, into looming disasters. Ellis's rational-emotive therapy seeks to free people of such irrational beliefs, and the consequences they incur, through a process in which the therapist actively *disputes* the logical bases of these beliefs and assists the client in developing more adaptive beliefs.

 Some therapists do actively dispute their clients most cherished beliefs. Rational-emotive therapists are one example.

Rational-emotive therapy (RET) is active and directive. The rational-emotive therapist takes an active role in pinpointing the client's irrational beliefs, showing how these beliefs lead to personal misery, challenging their validity, and helping clients find workable alternative beliefs.

Ellis and Dryden (1987) describe the case of a 27-year-old woman, Jane, who was generally socially inhibited and particularly shy with attractive men. Through RET, Jane identified some of her underlying irrational beliefs, such as "I must speak well to people I find attractive," and, "When I don't speak well and impress people as I should, I'm a stupid, inadequate person!" (p. 68). RET helped Jane discriminate between these irrational beliefs and her rational preferences, such as, "If people do reject me for showing them how anxious I am, that will be most unfortunate, but I can stand it" (p. 68). RET helped Jane recognize that she had the option of choosing to think either these irrational beliefs or their rational alternatives. Part of the therapy involved Jane in a process of debating or disputing the irrational beliefs by having her pose challenging questions to herself, such as (1) *Why* must I speak well to people I find attractive?" and (2) "When I don't speak well and impress people, how does that make me a *stupid and inadequate person*?" (p. 69) Jane learned to answer these disputative questions with rational responses, such as (1) "There is no reason I must speak well to people I find attractive, but it would be desirable if I do so, so I shall make an effort—but not kill myself—to do so," and (2) "When I speak poorly and fail to impress people, that only makes me a *person who* spoke unimpressively this time—not a *totally stupid or inadequate person*." (p. 69).

Jane also rehearsed rational self-statements (that is, self-verbalizations or self-talk) several times a day. Examples included, "I would like to speak well, but I never *have to*," and, "When people I favor reject me, it often reveals more about them and their tastes than about me" (pp. 69–70). After nine months of RET, Jane was able to talk comfortably to men she found attractive and was preparing to take a job as a teacher, a position she always had avoided because of fear of facing a classroom of children.

Ellis recognizes that irrational beliefs may be formed on the basis of early childhood experiences. Changing them requires finding rational alternatives in the present—the "here and now." Rational-emotive therapists also help clients substitute more effective interpersonal behavior for self-defeating or maladaptive behavior. Ellis often gives clients specific tasks or homework assignments, like expressing disagreement to an overbearing relative or asking someone for a date. He also helps assist them in practicing or rehearsing more effective behaviors. In these ways, rational-emotive therapy can be considered a cognitive-behavioral form of therapy.

Beck's Cognitive Therapy

As formulated by psychiatrist Aaron Beck and his colleagues (Beck, 1976; Beck et al., 1979; Beck & Emery, 1985), cognitive therapy also focuses on clients' maladaptive cognitions. Cognitive therapists encourage clients to recognize how errors in thinking ("cognitive distortions") affect their moods and impair their behavior. Beck and his colleagues believe that cognitive distortions, such as those listed in Chapter 2 (p. 57) and in Chapter 8 (pp. 263–266), underlie a range of psychological problems, including depression and anxiety disorders.

Cognitive distortions tend to be fleeting and difficult to detect. Cognitive therapists help clients identify and correct cognitive distortions in their thought patterns. To help clients see the relationship between their thoughts and feelings, cognitive therapists utilize homework assignments that require them to record the thoughts that are prompted by upsetting events and to connect them with their emotional responses (Burns & Beck, 1978).

Beck and his colleagues also make use of behavioral homework assignments, such as encouraging depressed clients to fill in their free time with structured activities, like shopping or completing work around the house. Carrying out such tasks serves to counteract the apathy and loss of motivation that tend to characterize depression and may also provide concrete evidence of competence to combat self-perceptions of helplessness and inadequacy (Beck et al., 1979). Like rational-emotive therapy, Beck's cognitive therapy might also be considered a form of cognitive-behavioral therapy.

Another type of homework assignment involves reality testing; clients are asked to test out their negative beliefs in the light of reality. For example, a depressed client who feels unwanted by anyone might be asked to call two or three friends on the phone to gather data about the friends' reactions to the calls. The therapist might then ask the client to report on the assignment: "Did they immediately hang-up the phone? Or did they seem pleased that you called? Did they express any interest in talking to you again or getting together sometime? Does the evidence support the conclusion that *no one* has any interest in you?" Such exercises help clients replace distorted cognitions with rational alternatives.

Consider this case example in which a depressed man was encouraged to test his belief that he was about to be fired from his job. Note also how the case illustrates several cognitive distortions or errors in thinking, such as selectively perceiving only those parts of oneself that reflect upon one's flaws (in this case, self-perceptions of laziness) and expecting the worst (expectations of being fired).

■ A 35 year old man, a frozen foods distributor, had suffered from chronic depression since his divorce six years earlier. During the past year the depression had worsened and he found it increasingly difficult to call upon customers or go to the office. Each day that he avoided working made it more difficult for him to go to the office and face his boss. He was convinced that he was in imminent danger of being fired since he had not made any sales calls for more than a month. He was convinced that his basic problem was laziness, not depression. His therapist pointed out the illogic in his thinking. First of all, there was no real evidence that his boss was about to fire him. His boss had actually encouraged him to get help and was paying for part of the treatment. His therapist also pointed out that judging himself as lazy was unfair because it overlooked the fact that he had been an industrious, successful salesman before he became depressed. While not fully persuaded, the client agreed to a homework assignment in which he was to call his boss and also make a sales call to one of his former customers. His boss expressed support and reassured him that his job was secure. The customer ribbed him about "being on vacation" during the preceding six weeks but placed a small order. The client discovered that the small unpleasantness he experienced in facing the customer and being teased paled in comparison to the intense depression he felt at home while he was avoiding work. Within the next several weeks he gradually worked himself back to a normal routine, calling upon customers and making future plans. This process of viewing himself and the world from a fresh perspective led to a general improvement in his mood and behavior.

Adapted from Burns & Beck, 1978, pp. 124–126 ■

RET and cognitive therapy have much in common, especially the focus on helping clients replace self-defeating thoughts and beliefs with more rational ones. While there may be subtle differences in emphases, perhaps the major differences between the two approaches is one of therapeutic style. RET therapists tend to be more confrontational and forceful in their approach to disputing client's irrational beliefs (Dryden, 1984; Ellis et al., 1989; Marzillier, 1980). Cognitive therapists tend to adopt a more gentle, collaborative

approach in helping clients to discover the distortions in their thinking.

A major, multisite government-sponsored study of the treatment of depression recently compared cognitive therapy with another brief form of psychotherapy, interpersonal psychotherapy, and with anti-depressant medication (imipramine) and a placebo control condition (Elkin et al., 1989). Interpersonal psychotherapy represents a psychodynamic approach to helping people develop a better understanding of the interpersonal problems that may play a role in depression and learn more adaptive ways of relating to others (Klerman et al., 1984). The short-term results following the 16-week treatment period showed both psychological treatment approaches, cognitive therapy and interpersonal therapy, to be about equally effective to each other and to anti-depressant medication in alleviating depression. The results were complicated by the finding that cognitive therapy did not outperform the placebo control condition, in which subjects received a placebo drug combined with supportive counseling from an experienced psychiatrist. Some limited evidence favored interpersonal psychotherapy and the active drug treatment (imipramine) in comparison to the placebo control condition, however. But the long-term follow-ups of the people treated in the study remain to be reported. The results of the multisite study are likely to spark a spirited debate among researchers and therapists for some time to come.

Behavior Therapy

Behavior therapy, which is sometimes called *behavior modification,* involves the systematic application of techniques drawn from the principles of learning (conditioning and social learning theory) to help people make adaptive behavioral changes. Behavior therapists focus on helping clients make overt behavioral changes, but they also frequently use cognitive techniques to modify clients' cognitive distortions and self-defeating beliefs as well (Wilson, 1982). In fact, many common behavioral techniques, such as systematic desensitization and covert sensitization, make use of cognitive processes like visual imagery. But behavior therapists insist that therapeutic outcomes be assessed in terms of behavioral changes that can be observed and measured, such as the ability to approach a phobic stimulus that the person had previously avoided owing to fear.

Like the humanistic-existential and cognitive schools of therapy, behavior therapists focus on the "here-and-now." They also seek to foster insight in the sense of helping clients gain a better awareness of the circumstances in which their problem behaviors occur and the early learning experiences that may have led to their development. But the focus of behavior therapy is on the present, not the past—on making changes in problem behaviors, such as phobias, depressive behaviors, and ineffective ways of relating to others that cause distress and impair functioning. Because the focus is on changing behavior—not on personality change or probing deeply into the past—behavior therapy is relatively brief, with programs lasting anywhere from a day to a few months. Behavior therapists, like other therapists, seek to develop warm, therapeutic relationships with clients, but they believe that the special efficacy of behavior therapy derives from the learning-based techniques themselves (Wolpe, 1985), rather than from the character of the therapeutic relationship.

Throughout this text we have focused on specific behavior-therapy techniques for treating such problems as phobias, obsessive-compulsive behaviors, depression, childhood disorders and sexual dysfunction. Let us now review several of these behavior-therapy techniques.

Methods of Fear Reduction

Behavior therapy first gained acclaim for the innovation of a number of methods for reducing fears and phobias—problems that had proved resistant to insight-oriented therapies. Among these are systematic desensitization, gradual exposure, and modeling.

■ Systematic Desensitization **Systematic desensitization** reduces fears and phobias by combining muscle relaxation with imaginal exposure to a graduated sequence of increasingly phobic stimuli. The client first becomes deeply relaxed, generally through the use of progressive relaxation (see Chapter 4). He or she is then asked to imagine progressively more anxiety-arousing scenes while maintaining the relaxed state. If fear is evoked, the person switches back to restoring relaxation and the process is repeated until the scene can be tolerated without anxiety. When the person is able to remain fully relaxed by imagining a particular scene, or when viewing slides depicting the scene, he or she then progresses to the next scene in the *fear-stimulus hierarchy*. The procedure is continued until the person can remain relaxed while imagining the most distressing scene in the hierarchy.

■ Gradual Exposure In **gradual exposure** (also called *in vivo* ["in life"] exposure), phobic clients expose themselves to actual anxiety-evoking stimuli in a stepwise fashion while they try to maintain a relaxed state. Exposure begins with the least distressing level of contact and then progresses to each next step in the fear-stimulus hierarchy when the individual is able to maintain a calm state at the preceding level. In Chapter 6

we reported the case of Kevin, an elevator phobic who overcome his fears through gradual exposure. Gradual exposure is often combined with cognitive techniques, such as replacing disruptive thoughts with calming, rational ones.

■ Modeling **Modeling** is a form of observational learning in which clients observe and then imitate others who approach or interact with situations or objects they fear. After observing the model, the client may be assisted or guided by the therapist or the model in performing the target behavior. The client receives ample reinforcement from the therapist for making approach attempts. Modeling approaches have been pioneered by Bandura and his colleagues, who have shown remarkable success in using modeling techniques to treat various phobias, especially fears of animals, such as snakes and dogs (Bandura et al., 1967, 1969, 1974).

■ The Symptom-Substitution Controversy Psychoanalysts consider phobias to be symbolic representations of unconscious conflicts. They have argued that treating the "symptom" or phobia through behavioral methods without dealing with the underlying conflict may only lead to the emergence of another symptom—that is, to **symptom substitution.** Behavior therapists contend, however, that maladaptive behavior itself is the problem, not just a symptom of a "deeper" problem. Research has favored the behaviorist position. System-

Modeling techniques are often used to help people overcome phobic behaviors. Here an older child models approaching and petting a dog to a younger, phobic child. As the phobic child observes the older one harmlessly engage in the desired behavior, he is more likely to imitate the behavior.

atic desensitization, for example, has been found effective in treating phobias (Marks, 1982; Smith & Glass, 1977), and symptom substitution has apparently not emerged as a problem (Deffenbacher & Suinn, 1988). Moreover, people who overcome problem behaviors like phobias are more likely to experience other benefits, such as greater self-confidence and increased ability to participate in a wider range of activities, rather than secondary problems.

 People may be able to overcome many kinds of problems whether or not they have insight into their origins. It has not been shown, for example, that brief, behavioral methods lead to symptom substitution.

Aversive Conditioning

Whereas fear-reduction methods attempt to *disconnect* fears from target stimuli, **aversive conditioning** aims to *connect* fear with problem behaviors. Whereas fear-reduction methods instill *approach* behaviors, aversive conditioning inspires *avoidance* behaviors.

Aversive conditioning involves the pairing of painful or aversive stimuli with unwanted responses, such as cigarette smoking, problem drinking, or deviant sexual responses. For example, to help problem drinkers control their intake of alcohol, the tastes of alcoholic beverages can be paired with electric shock, or with drugs that induce nausea or vomiting (Wilson et al., 1975). Smokers have been treated with some success with a form of aversive conditioning, called *rapid-smoking*, in which the rate of puffing is increased to the point that smoking becomes a noxious event (Lichtenstein, 1982). Some success has also been reported with the use of aversive conditioning for such diverse problems as sexual paraphilias (Rathus, 1983), self-injurious behaviors in autistic children (Bucher & Lovaas, 1968), and alcoholism (Wiens & Menustik, 1983). It may seem paradoxical that aversive stimulation in the form of electric shock can sometimes stop such self-punishing behaviors as repeated head-banging in autistic children. Perhaps the head-banging is reinforced by the stimulation it provides, or by attention from others, and not because of the physical pain it induces. But long-term results of aversive conditioning are frequently disappointing, especially with sexual deviations and problems of smoking or alcohol abuse. Unless alternative behaviors are learned that become reinforcing in themselves, the problem behavior often returns when the person is no longer faced with the immediate aversive consequences.

Covert sensitization is a technique for pairing the unwanted behavior (for example, smoking, problem drinking) with aversive stimulation in imagination. The problem drinker, for example, may imagine becoming nauseated shortly after taking a drink at an office party, even to the point of imagining throwing up on the carpet in full view of all of his or her employer and co-workers. While are some case reports of success in using covert sensitization (Cautela, 1966, 1967), there is an absence of controlled research demonstrating its effectiveness.

Operant Conditioning

Operant conditioning involves the use of reinforcement principles to foster learning of adaptive responses and to extinguish maladaptive responses. Operant-conditioning techniques have a wide range of applications. For example, parents may be trained to systematically reinforce their children for appropriate behavior and to extinguish inappropriate behavior by withdrawing attention for problem behaviors. In institutional settings, **token-economy** systems allow patients to earn tokens for performing adaptive behaviors, such as self-grooming or making their beds, which they can exchange at a later time for desired rewards or preferred activities. We saw in Chapter 12 how token-economy systems have been used to help hospitalized schizophrenics develop more cooperative, prosocial behaviors (Paul & Lentz, 1977). Token systems have also been used successfully in treating children with conduct-disorder problems. In one application, conduct-disordered children received tokens for engaging in helpful behaviors, like volunteering, and gave up tokens when they engaged in such behaviors as inattention and arguing (Schneider & Byrne, 1987). In the following case example, a token-reinforcement program was used to improve a child's academic functioning in a classroom setting:

■ The child was a third-grade student who was inattentive to her teacher's instructions and refused to complete school assignments or participate with her classmates in school projects. Most of her time at school was spent dawdling or daydreaming. Her parents reported that she had a few friends and lacked social skills. A token reinforcement program was designed that rewarded her for "on-task" behavior at school—following her teacher's instructions, completing assignments, and participating with her fellow students in class projects. The measure of outcome was the number of reading units the child completed. During a baseline period, the child completed zero reading units. Beans were then used as tokens that the child could earn for "on-task" behavior and later exchange for special privileges. For example, the behavior of "reading first in a reading group" earned 3 beans; staying after school to work on special projects with the teacher earned 9 beans. The number of reading units climbed to 12 during the first three months of treatment and then to 36 during the last three treatment months.

The child also showed increased social participation with friends and greater acceptance by her peers.

Adapted from Walker et al., 1981, pp. 147–148 ■

Social Skills Training

Social skills training is often used to help clients develop more effective social skills and counter social anxieties. Skills training approaches have wide applications. They have helped aggressive people express themselves in a nonthreatening manner. They have helped chronic schizophrenics cope more effectively with the demands of community living. A variety of social skills training called **assertiveness training** helps unassertive people speak up for their rights and communicate their feelings, needs, and interests, such as by learning how to say no to unreasonable demands of others.

Although differences exist in individual approaches, social skills training usually includes such techniques as self-monitoring, modeling, and practice or behavior rehearsal. In *self-monitoring*, clients are instructed to keep a running diary of upsetting social interactions in order to identify examples of social avoidance and awkward behavior. The therapist then *models* more effective social behavior, which is followed by practice or *behavior rehearsal* of the modeled behaviors as the therapist provides constructive *feedback*. The therapist is attentive not only to what the client says and does in the practice opportunities, but also to the client's posture, tone of voice, and facial expressions.

Assertive training is often conducted in a group treatment setting. Group members role-play the parts of important people in each other's lives, such as parents, spouses, employers, or potential dates. Homework assignments are used to provide clients with opportunities to practice the newly acquired assertive behaviors in real-life settings.

Self-Control Techniques

Whereas insight-oriented therapists have traditionally encouraged clients to uncover the "meanings" of problem habits such as smoking or excessive drinking, behavior therapists directly train people in self-management skills to control these problem behaviors. Self-control training can be used for a wide range of problem behaviors, including nail-biting, inadequate study habits, and overeating, to name a few.

Self-control strategies involve changing the A's or stimulus antecedents that trigger the problem behavior, the B's or problem behaviors themselves, and the C's or reinforcement consequences that follow. Smokers, for example, may be instructed to reduce their contact with smoking-related cues (the A's), stretch the chain of behaviors that leads to smoking a cigarette (the B's), and reward or punish themselves (the C's) for meeting or exceeding their smoking reduction goals.

Self-control training often begins with a **functional analysis** of the problem behavior—that is, a systematic study of the antecedent stimuli or cues that trigger it and the reinforcers that maintain it. For example, smokers may be asked to track each cigarette smoked, jotting down the time of day it was smoked, the presence of any cues that may have triggered the urge, including internal cues (negative emotions, hunger sensations, etc.) and external cues (seeing someone else smoking, for example), and the reinforcement consequences—such as feelings of pleasure, relief from anxiety, and relaxation. A functional analysis can reveal stimulus and reinforcement patterns that can be modified to foster self-control. For example, a smoker may find that smoking occurs most often in response to feelings of boredom or loneliness and is maintained by the stimulation that it provides. By filling in unstructured time with stimulating activities, preferably in nonsmoking environments, the smoker may be able to reduce substantially the number of cigarettes smoked.

Other Methods

There are many other forms of behavior therapy that were considered in our discussions of specific disorders. **Biofeedback training,** for example, is often used as

Biofeedback training is often used in the treatment of such stress-related problems as headaches and hypertension. Here clients at a pain clinic use a biofeedback device to learn to relax by focusing on their galvanic-skin response (GSR), a sign of bodily arousal that is associated with states of anxiety or tension.

a relaxation technique or for treatment of stress-related physical disorders, such as headaches or hypertension (Chapter 5). Relaxation techniques, such as progressive relaxation, are used not only in the context of systematic desensitization, but also for treatment of generalized anxiety (Chapter 6) and for stress-related physical disorders like headaches and hypertension (Chapter 5).

Cognitive-Behavior Therapy

The parallel interest in the development of cognitive psychology and information processing in the 1970s and 1980s focused attention on the role of cognitions in psychopathology and the treatment of psychological disorders. Cognitive-behavior therapy developed from the attempt to integrate therapeutic techniques that focus not only on overt behavior but also on dysfunctional thoughts and cognitions (Wilson, 1978). Cognitive-behavior therapy draws upon a basic assumption that cognitions and information processing play an important role in the genesis and maintenance of maladaptive behavior and that the impact of external events is mediated by cognitive processes (Beidel & Turner, 1986). Despite the recency of its development, cognitive-behavior therapy has become the most widely emphasized therapeutic orientation in doctoral training programs in clinical psychology in the United States (see Figure 15.1) (Nevid et al., 1986, 1987).

There is no unified approach among cognitive-behavior therapists but rather an assortment of approaches that combine behavioral and cognitive techniques. For example, a cognitive-behavior therapist might treat a person with a depressive disorder with a combination of techniques drawn from Beck's cognitive therapy approach and from more traditional behavioral approaches that focus on increasing the availability of reinforcement. The following case illustration of cognitive-behavior therapy shows how behavioral (exposure) and cognitive (cognitive restructuring) techniques were used in the treatment of agoraphobia:

■ Mrs. X was a 41-year-old woman with a 12-year history of agoraphobia. She feared venturing into public places alone and required her husband or children to accompany her from place to place. In vivo (actual) exposure sessions were arranged in a series of progressively more fearful encounters—a fear-stimulus hierarchy. The first step in the hierarchy, for example, involved taking a shopping trip while accompanied by the therapist. After accomplishing this task, she gradually moved upwards in the hierarchy. By the third week of treatment, she was able to complete the last step in her hierarchy—shopping by herself in a crowded supermarket. Cognitive restructuring was conducted along with the exposure training. Mrs. X was asked to imagine herself in various fearful situations and to report the self-statements she experienced. The therapist helped her identify disruptive self-statements, such as "I am going to make a fool of

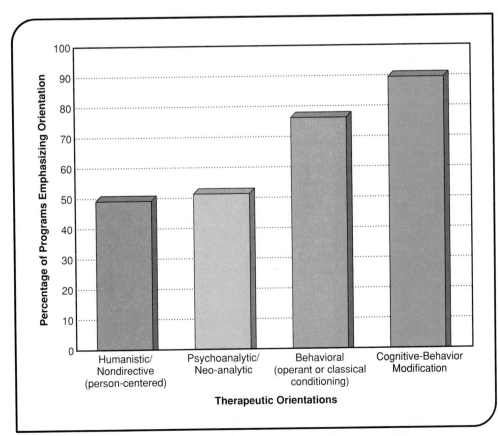

FIGURE 15–1 Therapeutic orientations in clinical psychology (Ph.D.) training programs.

Data are based on a survey of 96 program directors of doctoral training programs in clinical psychology in the United States. The graph shows the percentages of training programs that were judged by their directors to place at least a moderate level of emphasis in training (a rating of at least "3" on a five-point scale of importance) on various therapeutic orientations. Cognitive-behavior modification (also called cognitive-behavior therapy) was emphasized in more than nine of ten programs. But each of the approaches represented in the survey was emphasized by at least half of the programs, which suggests that each of these therapeutic models remains widely represented in training programs.
Source: Original data based on a survey by Colletti et al. (1983). Data analysis based on results reported by Nevid et al. (1986, 1987).

myself." This particular self-statement was challenged by questioning whether it was realistic to believe that she would actually lose control, and, secondly, by disputing the belief that the consequences of losing control, were it to happen, would truly be disastrous. She progressed rapidly with treatment and became capable of functioning more independently. But she still harbored concerns about relapsing in the future. The therapist focused at this point on deeper cognitive structures involving her fears of abandonment by the people she loved if she were to relapse and be unable to attend to their needs. In challenging these beliefs, the therapist helped her realize that she was not as helpless as she perceived herself to be and that she was loved for other reasons than her ability to serve others. She also explored the question, "Who am I improving for?" She realized that she needed to find reasons to overcome her phobia that were related to meeting her own personal needs, not simply the needs of her loved ones. At a follow-up interview nine months after treatment, she was functioning independently, which allowed her to pursue her own interests, such as taking night courses and seeking a job.

Adapted from Biran, 1988, pp. 173–176 ■

While cognitive-behavior therapy appears to be a promising therapeutic approach for treating a variety of problem behaviors, there remains an insufficient research base to conclude that the addition of cognitive components of treatment increases the effectiveness of traditional behavioral therapies, such as gradual exposure or systematic desensitization (Beidel & Turner, 1986). On the other hand, it could be said that any behavioral method that involves mental imagery, such as systematic desensitization or covert desensitization, is in a sense bridging behavioral and cognitive domains. Recall that the cognitive therapies such as Ellis' rational-emotive therapy and Beck's cognitive therapy might also be classified within the framework of cognitive-behavioral therapy since they too incorporate both cognitive and behavioral components in treatment. This only goes to show that the dividing lines between the psychotherapies may not be as clearly drawn for classification purposes as authors of textbooks might desire. Not only are traditional boundaries between the cognitive and behavioral therapies becoming blurry, but many therapists today, as we see next, adopt an **eclectic** approach in which they incorporate principles and techniques from various therapeutic perspectives.

ECLECTICISM IN PSYCHOTHERAPY

A growing movement toward eclecticism in psychotherapy has occurred in recent years. During the 1940s and 1950s, psychotherapy was virtually synonymous with psychodynamic therapy. Few other psychotherapy approaches had much impact on psychotherapists or on public awareness (Garfield, 1981, 1982). But today,

the largest single group of psychologists and psychotherapists identify themselves as eclectic in orientation, according to recent surveys (DeMaria, 1988; Norcross & Prochaska, 1982a, 1982b; Sammons & Gravitz, 1990; Smith, 1982). The percentages of respondents in these surveys who identified themselves as psychodynamic or psychoanalytic ranged from 12 to 30 percent, while the percentages describing themselves as eclectic ranged from 31 to 58 percent. Eclectic therapists incorporate principles and techniques from different therapeutic orientations that they believe will enhance their therapeutic effectiveness (Wolf & Goldfried, 1988). For example, an eclectic therapist might utilize behavior-therapy techniques to help a client change specific maladaptive behaviors, as well as using psychodynamic techniques to assist the client to gain insight into the roots of the problem.

A recent meeting sponsored by the National Institute of Mental Health on issues relating to integrating diverse therapeutic models in clinical practice stressed the role of the therapeutic relationship as an essential aspect of the practice of psychotherapy that cuts across most orientations (Wolf & Goldfried, 1988). But research has yet to be undertaken to assess how different psychotherapies may be integrated to best advantage toward increasing therapeutic effectiveness. Research is also needed to identify the basic principles of change that various therapeutic orientations may share in common and to investigate the specific factors or therapeutic ingredients that each particular approach has to offer.

We now turn our attention to forms of therapy in which the focus of therapy extends beyond the individual to incorporate groups of people, families, and marital couples.

GROUP THERAPY

Group therapy has several advantages over individual treatment. For one, group therapy is less costly since several clients are treated at the same time. For another, many clinicians believe that group therapy may be more effective in treating groups of clients who have similar problems, such as complaints relating to anxiety, depression, lack of social skills, or adjustment to divorce or other life stresses. The group format provides clients with the opportunity to learn how other people with similar problems cope with their difficulties and provides them with social support from other group members as well as from the therapist. The particular approach to treatment reflects the theoretical orientation of the therapist or group leader. In psychoanalytic groups, for example, an emphasis may be placed on interpretations and working through transferences that emerge between members of the group or between individual group members and the therapist. Person-centered groups seek to create an accepting atmosphere for clients to explore their deeper feelings without fears of social criticism. In behavior-therapy groups, people who share similar problems may be brought together to participate in a group administration of a particular technique, such as systematic desensitization. Some behavior-therapy groups focus on helping their members improve their social skills through such procedures as modeling and rehearsal of specific social skills, such as asking someone out on a date or starting conversations with new acquaintances.

In addition to the generally lower cost of group therapy, group therapy has other advantages in relation to individual treatment:

1. *Group therapy allows greater access to limited therapist resources.* Good therapists are often quite busy and may not have time to see all the people who request assistance. The group format may increase the number of people the individual therapist is able to treat, perhaps reducing the need for people to be kept on a waiting list.

2. *Group therapy may increase the fund of information and experience that clients can draw upon.* Group members are likely to have a large fund of life experiences that may be helpful to share with others. Group members may learn how to best approach problem situations in their own lives by learning from the adaptive or maladaptive behavior of other group members who dealt with similar problems in their lives.

3. *Availability of group support for appropriate behavior.* Clients may expect therapists to be supportive toward them, but an outpouring of support from one's peers may have greater impact on increasing self-esteem and self-confidence.

4. *Learning that one's problems or failures are not unique.* People who experience psychological difficulties often feel that they are different from other people, and perhaps inferior. Group members often learn that others have had similar problems and self-doubts, have committed similar mistakes, and experienced similar failures in the past. Sharing such common experiences can be reassuring that one is not so different.

5. *Group members who improve provide a source of hope for other members.* Seeing other people progress may bolster hope of improvement in oneself.

6. *Opportunities for learning to deal more effectively with people.* Many people seek help for difficulties in relating to others or for reasons of social inhibition. Group therapy provides members with opportunities to work out their problems in relating to others. For example, the therapist or other members may point out to a particular member when he or she acts in a bossy manner or tends to withdraw when criticized—patterns of behavior that may mirror the behavior the person shows in his or her relationships with others outside the group.

To be effective, such feedback must be constructive and supportive, rather than critical or condemning. Members of therapy groups may also rehearse social skills with one another in a supportive atmosphere that can foster more adaptive social behavior. Members might role-play important people in each other's lives to help sharpen interpersonal skills.

> **?** Not only is group therapy usually less expensive than individual therapy but it is also sometimes preferable because of the availability of group reinforcement and the fund of knowledge that can be tapped in the group setting. A central issue is for therapists to identify clients who are more likely to profit from one type of therapy or another.

Despite these advantages, individual therapy is often preferred by clients, for several reasons. For one, clients might not wish to disclose their problems to others in a group. Some clients prefer the individual attention of the therapist, while others are too socially inhibited to feel comfortable in a group setting—even though they might be the ones who could most profit from a group experience. Because of such concerns, group therapists must take responsibility for insisting that group disclosures be kept strictly confidential, that group members relate to each other supportively and nondestructively, and that each group member receive the attention that he or she needs.

Evidence from controlled studies examining the effectiveness of group therapy remains mixed. While a recent review of the group-therapy literature showed results that favored group therapy over placebo or no-treatment conditions, the studies comprising the analysis tended to be plagued by poor methodologies (Kaul

A group therapy session. Can you describe some of the advantages that may make group therapy preferable to individual therapy? Despite these advantages, many clients prefer individual therapy. Why?

& Bednar, 1986). Moreover, there is a lack of evidence that directly compares group therapy with individual therapy.

There are several specialized forms of group therapy. In **psychodrama,** a technique developed by Jacob Moreno in the 1920s, group members role-play or re-enact emotionally laden scenes from each other's lives in the form of stage plays. For example, a man might reenact a conflict with his father by having other group members play the roles of the father and other important people who played some part in the conflict. To Moreno, psychodrama was a vehicle for expression of painful or hostile feelings in a supportive setting that helped members achieve insight into their own behavior and gain a more realistic understanding of the behavior of others. By coming to terms with these conflicts, members could be freed of the social inhibitions that limited their spontaneity and ability to form meaningful relationships with others.

Encounter groups are specialized forms of group therapy that emerged from the humanistic movement in the 1960s. Encounter groups aim to foster increased self-awareness by focusing on how members relate to each other in a setting in which open expression of feelings is encouraged. Encounter groups are not appropriate for people with serious psychological problems. Rather, they are intended for people who are fairly well-adjusted but seek personal growth and heightened awareness of their own needs and feelings and the ways they relate to others. Encounter groups seek to meet these needs through a process of intense encounters or direct confrontations between strangers. Some groups are held as marathon encounters that may run continuously for 12 or more hours at a time. Reflecting the humanistic approach, encounter groups stress the interactions taking place in the here-and-now. The focus centers on expression of genuine feelings, not on interpretation or on discussions of the past. When a group member is perceived by the others as hiding behind a social mask or facade, the others might descend on the person en masse to try to rip the mask off and thus encourage the person to express his or her true feelings.

Such confrontational tactics can be damaging if they force overly rapid disclosure of intimate feelings that the person is not yet able to handle, or if the person feels attacked or scapegoated by the others in the group. Responsible leaders try to maintain control of the group to prevent such abuses and to keep it moving in a direction that facilitates personal growth and self-awareness.

FAMILY THERAPY

In **family therapy,** it is the family, not the individual, which is the unit of treatment. Family therapy is directed toward helping troubled families resolve their conflicts and problems in ways that not only help the family to function better as a unit but also help individual members cope more effectively by reducing the stresses that family conflicts impose upon them.

Faulty family communications often play a part in creating problems in the family. In family therapy, family members are helped to communicate more effectively and to air their disagreements more constructively in ways that are not hurtful to other members of the family. Family conflicts often emerge at transitional points in the life cycle when family patterns are altered by changes in one or more members. Conflicts between parents and children, for example, often emerge when adolescent children seek greater independence or autonomy. Such conflicts have meaning for the family as a whole, as well as for the individual members. Family members with low self-esteem may be unable to tolerate different attitudes or behaviors from other members of the family, and may resist their efforts to change or grow in more independent directions. Family therapists work with families to resolve these conflicts to help individual members grow toward greater autonomy and independence.

It is also common for families to scapegoat one member of the family as the "identified client" or source of the problem. But family therapists need to be vigilant to prevent individual members of a dysfunctional family from becoming the scapegoat for the family's problems. Disturbed families seem to adopt a sort of myth: Change the identified client, the "bad apple," and the "barrel," or family, will once again become functional. Family therapists see the process differently. Change must come from the family working together to resolve their disputes and conflicts, not from targeting one individual member as the source of trouble.

There are many contemporary forms of family therapy. One widely adopted approach to family therapy, called *conjoint family therapy*, was developed by Virginia Satir (1967). In Satir's approach, the family is conceptualized in terms of a pattern or *system* of communications and interactions that need to be studied and changed to enhance the family unit as well as the growth of individual family members.

Another prominent approach to family therapy is **structural family therapy** (Minuchin, 1974). This approach also adopts a family systems model of abnormal behavior, which conceptualizes problem behaviors of individual members of the family as characteristics of the family system rather than of the individual members. Individual members may develop psychological or physical problems when pressures of adjusting within the family become great or role relationships become distorted and the family system is resistant to change. The family system seeks to preserve its stability by resisting efforts of individual members to change their role relationships. Structural family therapists focus on analyzing the roles that individual members play in the context of the family and helping families organize

In family therapy, the family, not the individual, is the unit of treatment. Family therapists help family members communicate more effectively with one other, for example, to air their disagreements in ways that are not hurtful to individual members. Family therapists also try to prevent one member of the family from becoming the scapegoat for the family's problems.

themselves differently so that members can relate to each other in more supportive ways.

For example, a child may feel in competition with other siblings for a parent's attention and develop enuresis, or bed-wetting, as the only means available of securing attention. The structural family therapist would help the family bring the "hidden messages" contained in the child's behavior out into the open and then assist the family in making changes in their relationships to meet the child's needs more directly. In so doing, the therapist would show the family how the member with the identified problem has been used as a focus for the problems of the family as a whole.

Marital therapy may be considered a subtype of family therapy, in which the family unit is the marital couple. Like other forms of family therapy, marital therapy focuses on improving communication and analyzing role relationships in order to improve the marital relationship. For example, one partner may play a dominant role and resist any attempt to share power with the other. The marital therapist would help bring these role relationships into the open, so that alternative ways of relating to one another could be explored that would lead to a more satisfying relationship.

EVALUATING THE EFFECTIVENESS OF PSYCHOTHERAPY

The scope of psychotherapy incorporates many different theoretical persuasions and different forms of treatment, such as individual and group therapy. But does psychotherapy work? Is it effective? Are some forms of therapy more effective than others? Are some forms of therapy more effective for some types of clients than for others?

In order to address these questions, researchers must carefully specify the conditions of treatment, such

as characteristics of the clients, the therapists, and the type of therapy itself, and measure the results broadly enough to evaluate various dimensions of change. Let us first consider issues relating to the design of psychotherapy research studies. Then we shall review the evidence that has accumulated concerning the effectiveness of psychotherapy.

Specifying the Conditions of Treatment

In a well-designed study, the investigator clearly specifies the type of therapy investigated, as well as the characteristics of the therapists and clients who participate. By specifying these characteristics, some of which are listed in Table 15.1, researchers can better determine the factors that might influence the results of psychotherapy. A particular form of therapy, for example, may

TABLE 15.1 Factors That May Relate to Treatment Effectiveness in Psychotherapy Research

Client Factors	Age, sex, educational level, ethnicity, marital status, prior treatment history, type of problem or diagnostic category, length or duration of problem, severity of problem, age of onset of problem
Therapist Factors	Training and level of experience, therapeutic orientation, age, sex, race, ethnicity
Treatment Factors	Type of treatment or therapeutic approach (behavioral, cognitive, psychoanalytic, etc.), format of treatment (individual, group, couple), setting of treatment (inpatient, outpatient, day hospital, etc.), length of treatment, frequency of treatment sessions, length of treatment sessions

be more effective when practiced by a therapist of the same sex as the client than when practiced by a therapist of the opposite sex. Or certain types of therapy may be more effective for certain types of clinical problems than for others.

Measuring Therapy Outcomes

Psychotherapy researchers measure the effects of therapy from several vantage points to help ensure that their measures encompass various dimensions of change. Perhaps the most straightforward method of assessing the effectiveness of psychotherapy is to measure clients' reports of their behavior or complaints at *pretreatment* and then again immediately following therapy at *post-treatment*. For example, clients might be administered a complaint or symptom inventory requiring them to rate the degree of frequency or severity of various complaints, such as anxiety, depression, and so on. The difference between pretreatment and post-treatment scores on the complaint inventory would be used as a measure of treatment outcome. There might also be a follow-up assessment taken at some later point following treatment, perhaps at a six-month or one-year interval, to evaluate whether the gains during treatment were lasting or not.

Self-reports are considered by most researchers to be an important dimension of change, since only the clients themselves can directly appraise their subjective complaints. Clients may also be the only ones with the knowledge to measure the frequency of occurrence of certain behaviors, such as consumption of alcohol or cigarette smoking, or of certain abnormal behavior patterns, such as the occurrence of panic attacks or hallucinations. But self-reports are prone to response biases or distortions (see Chapter 3). In a therapy program for smoking cessation, for example, treatment outcomes might be based on asking subjects at treatment termination, and then again at follow-up intervals, whether or not they had succeeded in abstaining from smoking during the preceding day or week. But it is possible that some subjects may report that they had quit smoking when in fact they had not in order to please the experimenter or to prevent losing face. To control for such response biases, the experimenter might seek to verify self-reports of smoking abstinence, such as by asking the subject's spouse or partner to corroborate the subject's self-reports, or by using a *breathalyzer* to test for telltale levels of carbon monoxide in the subject's breath that would indicate continued smoking.

Another limitation to self-reports is that it measures but one dimension of change. A phobia, for example, may be inferred from measures of the client's self-reported anxiety when exposed to the phobic situation, as well as from overt behavior (ability to approach the phobic stimulus) and physiological responses (heightened autonomic activity). As noted in Chapter 3, subjects frequently show greater change in one response domain than in another (Lang, 1968; Rachman & Hodgson, 1974). For example, an elevator phobic might succeed in the behavioral goal of taking an elevator ride to the top floor, but still report feeling jumpy and register a physiological response (heightened heart rate) during the ride. The relative independence of these response domains from one another places an even greater importance upon measuring effects in several response domains, especially in the case of fear or anxiety. The measurement of treatment effects across response domains—self-report, behavioral, and physiological—helps researchers determine the range of a therapy's effects.

Moreover, different therapies are connected with different goals. Some forms of therapy, like behavior therapy, focus on goals that can be defined and measured in behavioral terms—like the former elevator phobic who succeeds in riding unassisted to the top floor of the building. But cognitive therapists seek to alter the ways in which individuals interpret the world and to help them replace distorted beliefs with rational alternatives. How are private events, like thoughts and beliefs, to be measured objectively? The answer is that they cannot be directly measured, but rather must be inferred on the basis of the client's verbal or self-reports of these private events. But strict behaviorists might challenge the validity of measures that cannot be directly observed. Psychoanalysts, too, might object to measures based on the individual's self-reports, arguing that conscious experience may not reflect one's true (unconscious) motives and conflicts. And what of the forms of therapy, like psychoanalysis or person-centered therapies, that foster such goals as insight, personality change, and self-actualization? Is it fair to measure their outcomes by the same yardsticks as might apply to behavior therapies or cognitive therapies? And since each person's self-insights, or growth potentials, are unique, it may be impossible to measure just how much insight or growth an individual has experienced compared to others. Perhaps it is best to base judgments of outcomes on the therapist's clinical judgment? Unfortunately, therapists may not be unbiased judges; they have a stake in believing that their clients benefit from therapy.

So the choice of measures also depends on the goals that the particular form of therapy attempts to achieve. Evaluations of cognitive therapy often include measures of irrational beliefs and attitudes, in addition to self-reports of relief from symptom complaints and perhaps changes in behavior as well. Investigations of person-centered therapies might include measures revealing changes in self-concept or self-acceptance as a marker of therapeutic change. Table 15.2 lists examples of outcome measures in psychotherapy research that represent these various domains.

TABLE 15.2 Types of Outcome Measures in Psychotherapy Research

Response Domain	Types of Measures
Self-Report	Symptom complaints
	Disturbing emotions
	Frequencies of specific behaviors (for example, smoking rate, use of alcohol or drugs)
	Holding irrational or dysfunctional beliefs
	Frequency of specific disruptive thoughts
Reports from Others	Spousal reports of smoking abstinence or employment
	Parent reports of childhood behavior problems
	Therapist reports or ratings of symptoms or problem behaviors
	Supervisor reports of work performance
Behavioral	Direct observation or monitoring of specific problem behaviors (for example, hyperactivity, conduct problems)
	Behavioral tasks or homework assignments, such as approaching a phobic object or situation
Physiological	Heart rate
	Brain wave patterns (EEG)
	Skin conductivity (GSR)
	Analysis of blood, saliva, or urine specimens
Personality or Personal Growth	Personality tests (for example, the MMPI or Rorschach)
	Measures relating to values or purposes in life
	Measures relating to self-esteem, self-acceptance, and self-actualization

Analyses of Psychotherapy Effectiveness

In 1952, the psychologist Hans Eysenck published a review of psychotherapy research that sent shock waves through the psychotherapy community (Eysenck, 1952). Eysenck concluded on the basis of the evidence he compiled that the rate of improvement in psychotherapy among neurotic clients was no greater than the rate of spontaneous remission—that whether or not neurotics received therapy, two-thirds reported substantial improvement within a period of two years. But reviews of more recent research in the field paint a more positive picture of the effectiveness of psychotherapy. These reviews are based on the method of **meta-analysis,** which is a statistical technique for averaging the results of large number of studies in order to deter-mine levels of overall effectiveness (Landman & Dawes, 1982).

In the most frequently cited meta-analysis of psychotherapy research, Smith and Glass (1977) analyzed the results of some 375 controlled studies comparing various types of therapies (psychodynamic, behavioral, humanistic, etc.) against control groups. The results of their analyses showed that the average psychotherapy client in these studies was better off than 75 percent of the clients who remained untreated. In 1980, Smith and Glass and their colleague Miller reported the results of a larger analysis based on 475 controlled outcome studies, which showed that the average person who received therapy was better off at the end of treatment than 80 percent of those who did not (Smith et al., 1980; Glass & Kliegl, 1983). The fact that the average client benefited from psychotherapy doesn't mean, of course, that every client benefited. Negative outcomes certainly do occur: Some clients deteriorate while others experience little if any improvement. It's also true that people who receive other types of intervention, such as drug therapy or electroconvulsive therapy (ECT), sometimes fail to respond or experience adverse effects.

Smith and his colleagues presented powerful evidence supporting the effectiveness of psychotherapy, but questions have since been raised about the appropriateness of meta-analysis as a tool for combining results from different studies into an overall average. Some of the criticisms of the technique of meta-analysis include the following:

1. *Inclusion of poorly designed studies.* Computer specialists have a saying, "Garbage in, garbage out." They mean that the end result of any set of calculations (meta-analysis included) is only as good as the input upon which the calculations are based. Thus, the results of a meta-analysis may be flawed if the studies included in the analysis were faulty in design.

2. *The "apples and oranges" problem.* The question of whether or not psychotherapy *in general* is effective tends to overlook the role that client, therapist, and treatment factors may play in determining treatment effectiveness. To compute one overall averaged result that combines many different forms of therapy for many different types of problems may be likened to adding apples and oranges to the same mix, revealing little if any value in determining the effectiveness of particular forms of therapy for particular types of problems or clients.

3. *Publication bias.* Meta-analyses are generally limited to studies appearing in scientific publications and are thus available for analysis. But scientific journals tend to be less likely to publish studies that fail to produce significant findings than those that do (Greenwald, 1975). As a result, meta-analyses may be positively biased toward findings supporting the effectiveness of psychotherapy, since studies that fail to find significant

differences between treatment and control groups may not be as widely reported in the scientific literature.

4.   *Nonrepresentativeness of studies.* Many of the studies included in the Smith and Glass meta-analysis (and other meta-analyses of psychotherapy effectiveness, such as Shapiro & Shapiro [1982]) are not generally based upon actual clients receiving therapy in clinic or private practice settings. Many of these studies took place in university settings and were based on college volunteers who suffered from relatively minor problems (like snake phobia or nonassertiveness), rather than actual clients. Questions may be raised about whether the results of such studies would generalize to clinical practice. Other questions that need to be considered in generalizing research findings to clinical practice include whether the length of therapy and the level of therapist training and experience were representative of what the typical client would experience in actual practice (Brown, 1987). More carefully designed meta-analysis may depend upon the availability of research studies that are more closely honed to actual clinical realities.

Meta-analysis has provided the strongest evidence to date of the effectiveness of psychotherapy. While the technique of meta-analysis is not without criticism, as noted above, the findings supporting the efficacy of psychotherapy have held up remarkably well under closer scrutiny. Consider the criticism about methodological quality ("garbage in, garbage out") and nonrepresentativeness. It turns out that a meta-analysis based on studies of better methodological quality actually produced more positive results in favor of psychotherapy's effectiveness than did one based on more poorly designed studies (Landman & Dawes, 1982). Psychotherapy still came out ahead in meta-analyses which restricted the analysis to those studies that used actual clients rather than student volunteers (Andrews & Harvey, 1981). The "apples and oranges" problem could perhaps be overcome by breaking down the meta-analysis into smaller components, which examine the effects associated with different combinations of treatments, clients, and therapists. Moreover, while it appears that publication biases may inflate the apparent positive effects of psychotherapy (Brown, 1987), it is unlikely that such biases fully account for the superiority of psychotherapy.

Thus, despite the problems in conducting psychotherapy research, evidence of the effectiveness of psychotherapy has been encouraging. It also appears that the greatest gains in psychotherapy are achieved in the first several months of treatment (Howard et al., 1986), and that these gains tend to be lasting (Nicholson & Berman, 1983).

Comparing the Effectiveness of Different Forms of Psychotherapy

There are but a few well-designed treatment studies that directly compare different forms of therapy with each other. One difficulty in mounting such studies is to secure permission from subjects, and clinic administrators, that assignments to the alternate types of treatment are to be randomized. Another problem is ensuring that the therapists representing the competing therapies are equally well trained and experienced and willing to accept clients at random—not selecting those clients with whom they feel most capable of working effectively. Also, measures of results must be fair to the goals of each of the treatments, and durations of treatment must be comparable.

One of the few examples of a comparative treatment study was reported by Sloane and his colleagues (Sloane et al., 1975). Subjects in this study were college students who sought treatment at the Temple University Outpatient Clinic. The subjects were randomly assigned to either psychoanalytic therapy, behavior therapy, or a waiting-list control condition. Both treatment groups received four months of therapy. The psychoanalytic treatment consisted of a short-term, insight-oriented approach, while the behavior-therapy approach included such techniques as assertiveness training and systematic desensitization. All of the participating therapists were experienced clinicians. The measures of outcome included ratings of client improvement by clinicians who were not part of the treatment program, client self-ratings of improvement, and structured interviews to determine work and social adjustment. The results immediately following treatment showed that both behavior therapy and psychoanalytic therapy produced significantly greater improvement than did the waiting-list control condition, but were not significantly different from each other. The independent clinicians rated 80 percent of the behavior-therapy and psychoanalytic-therapy clients improved, compared to 48 percent of the waiting-list controls. These gains were maintained at a follow-up evaluation eight months later, with no significant differences between the two treatment approaches. The results of this study suggest that there may not be significant differences in effectiveness between different types of therapies.

Researchers have also turned to the use of meta-analysis to determine whether different therapies produce different degrees of benefit. Meta-analysis can be used to reveal the average benefit or size of effect associated with therapy in general, or, when broken down further, with particular types of therapy as measured against control groups.

Smith and colleagues (1980) reported that effect

sizes for several of the major schools of therapy, including psychodynamic, humanistic (Gestalt and person-centered), and behavior modification, were quite similar, falling in a range in which the average client treated by these methods was better off than between 70 and 80 percent of untreated controls. Does this mean that these therapeutic approaches were about equally effective? Perhaps but not necessarily so, since there may be differences in the clinical problems treated by these types of therapy, the goals of therapy, the types of measures used to evaluate outcomes, as well as other differences besides the techniques themselves.

So it is not enough to ask, Which therapy works best? We must ask, Which therapy works best for which particular problem? Which clients are better suited for which types of therapy? What are the advantages and limitations of particular therapies? Behavior therapy, for example, has shown impressive results in treating phobias, obsessive-compulsive behaviors, and sexual dysfunctions, and improving the adaptive functioning of schizophrenics and other institutionalized populations. Psychodynamic and humanistic-existential approaches may be more effective in fostering self-insight

and personality growth. Cognitive therapy has been found to be helpful in treating cases of severe depression that are usually considered to be responsive only to biological treatments (Simons et al, 1986). But psychotherapy researchers have not fully met the challenge posed to them by psychologist Gordon Paul in 1967 (Paul, 1967), who asked his fellow researchers to direct their research to determine the following: What treatment, practiced by whom, under what conditions, is most effective for what particular client, experiencing what particular problem? This challenge remains as timely today as when it was first issued.

BIOLOGICAL THERAPIES

There is a growing emphasis in American psychiatry on biological bases of abnormal behavior, or what is more commonly called **biological psychiatry** (Pardes, 1986; van Praag, 1988). Biological psychiatry focuses on investigations of biological defects that might explain abnormal behavior and on the use of biological inter-

---

A CLOSER LOOK
Is the Effectiveness of Psychotherapy Attributable to Nonspecific Factors?

Does psychotherapy work because of the specific techniques that are employed, or because the different psychotherapies share certain features in common that are responsible for their therapeutic effects? We noted earlier the finding of negligible differences in outcomes among the various therapies in comparison to control groups (Smith et al., 1980). The minor differences suggest that the effectiveness of psychotherapy may have more to do with the features they share than with the techniques that set them apart (Stiles et al., 1986). But it is also possible that research studies have not been sufficiently sensitive to differences that may exist between therapies in the treatment of specific clinical problems (Kazdin et al., 1986; Stiles et al., 1986).

The elements that psychotherapies share are called **nonspecific factors** and stem largely from the therapist–client relationship. These factors include the engendering of positive expectancies to combat feelings of helplessness and hopelessness (Klein & Rabkin, 1984; Rounseaville et al., 1987), as well as the support, warmth, and attention that clients receive from their therapists. Although psychodynamic and person-centered therapists emphasize relationship factors in therapy to a greater extent than do behavior therapists, the latter also try to establish warm working relationships with clients (Wolpe, 1985). If it is true that the effects of therapy stem more from the relationship between the therapist and the client than from the specific techniques employed, then perhaps psychothera-

pists should focus more on bolstering these nonspecific factors than on developing specific techniques and interventions.

But research findings are beginning to accumulate that the effectiveness of psychotherapy is not simply a matter of nonspecific factors. Several other meta-analyses have provided evidence that specific forms of therapy, such as behavior therapy and psychodynamic therapy, produce larger effects than do nonspecific treatment approaches in which therapists provide support and attention, and try to instill hope of change, but do not offer the specific therapy (Landman & Dawes, 1982; Shapiro & Shapiro, 1982; Barker et al., 1988). Psychotherapy (mostly behavioral in emphasis) has also been found to be about twice as effective as well-designed nonspecific therapies that instill equal expectancies of improvement (Barker et al., 1988). Findings from a recent study of a brief (12-session) psychodynamic therapy approach for clients suffering a stress-related reaction following a traumatic event or bereavement showed that therapy outcomes were associated with specific techniques that were used in therapy and could not simply be accounted for by nonspecific factors (Jones et al., 1988). All in all, it appears that psychotherapy is a complex process incorporating various features common to helping roles, such as support, attention, and concern, but that also involves the use of specific techniques that foster adaptive change.

> **?** Although there are many problems in evaluating the effectiveness of psychotherapies, the weight of the evidence suggests that psychotherapy is indeed helpful and that its effectiveness is due to a combination of both nonspecific and specific factors.

ventions, such as drugs and ECT, in treating emotional disorders. The trend toward biological psychiatry has been spurred by recent scientific advancements (Pardes, 1986), such as the development of brain-imaging techniques. Knowledge is expanding concerning the role of neurotransmitters in abnormal behaviors. This knowledge may lead to the development of new classes of drugs to correct neurotransmitter imbalances. In experimental work that a few years ago would have seemed like science fiction, researchers are attempting to repair defective brain tissues by means of implanting brain structures. For example, there is hope that implanting brain cells that produce acetylcholine may one day help Alzheimer's patients.

At even a more basic level of neurobiology, that of molecular genetics, research efforts are continuing to map out the specific areas of genes and chromosomes that might be defective in particular mental disorders. Perhaps it is not too farfetched to imagine that defective human genes may one day be repaired or replaced (Pardes, 1986).

Such advances await future research, however. Let us review current biological approaches to the treatment of abnormal behaviors. Biological approaches include drug therapy or **chemotherapy,** electroconvulsive shock therapy (ECT), and psychosurgery. Biological approaches are administered by medical doctors, many of whom have specialized training in psychiatry or **psychopharmacology.** But some family physicians or general practitioners also prescribe psychoactive or **psychotropic drugs** for their patients, even though they may lack specialized training or certification in psychiatry.

Although the biological or medical approaches have had dramatic success in treating some forms of abnormal behavior, they also have their limitations. For one, biological therapies may have unwelcome or even dangerous side effects, such as tardive dyskinesia in response to treatment with antipsychotic drugs, or memory loss following ECT. For another, there is the potential for abuse. One of the most commonly prescribed minor tranquilizers, Valium, has become a major drug of abuse among people who become psychologically and physiologically dependent on it. Psychosurgery has been all but eliminated as a form of treatment because of serious harmful effects of earlier procedures.

Chemotherapy

For many years, the tranquilizer Valium was the most widely prescribed drug in the world. Valium is a member of the benzodiazepine family of minor tranquilizers (anxiolytic drugs) and is often prescribed for treatment of anxiety, insomnia, and tension. Other drugs in the benzodiazepine class include chlordiazepoxide (Librium), oxazepam (Serax), and flurazepam (Dalmane). Valium and these other tranquilizers are believed to depress the level of activity in certain parts of the central nervous system. In turn, the CNS decreases the level of sympathetic nervous system activity, reducing the respiration rate and heart rate, and lessening feelings of anxiety and tension. Minor tranquilizers became more popular as physicians grew concerned about using more potent sedatives, like barbiturates, which had a high addictive potential and could be extremely dangerous if taken in overdose or when mixed with alcohol. But also as noted, the minor tranquilizers can and often do lead to dependence. People who are dependent on Valium may go into convulsions when they abruptly stop taking the drug. And deaths have been reported among people who mixed Valium with alcohol, or had unusual sensitivities to the drug. There are other less severe side effects, such as fatigue, drowsiness, and impaired motor coordination that might nonetheless impair the ability to function, or to operate an automobile. Regular use of the drugs can produce tolerance, requiring higher dosages for continued effectiveness. Quite commonly, patients become involved in tugs-of-war with their physicians, as they demand increased dosages despite their physicians' concerns about the potential for abuse and dependence.

When used on a short-term basis, minor tranquilizers can be safe and effective in the treatment of anxiety complaints. But drugs in themselves cannot teach people more adaptive ways of solving their problems and may encourage them to rely on a chemical agent to cope with the stresses they face rather than develop more active means of coping. Thus chemotherapy is often combined with psychotherapy to help people with anxiety complaints deal with the psychological bases of their problems. However, combining chemotherapy and psychotherapy may present special problems and challenges. For one, the relief from anxiety that the drugs induce may reduce the person's motivation to try to solve his or her problems. For another, the learning that takes place in psychotherapy while the person is medicated, such as acquiring more effective coping skills for handling stress, may not generalize or be retained once the drugs are removed and the person must cope with similar stresses in a nondrug state.

Rebound anxiety is another problem associated

to help prevent rehospitalization. Indigent, jobless, without viable skills or close family or community ties, these people had little hope of ever escaping from poverty and despair and leading more productive lives. Most eventually returned to the state hospitals, which had provided the only stable environment and source of support they had known.

All in all, deinstitutionalization has failed to increase the quality of life and decrease the dependency on mental health services of vast numbers of discharged patients, or even to help them meet their basic needs (Shadish et al., 1989). Many remain in custodial-type nursing homes that resemble the back wards of the institutions from which they were released. Many others are homeless. In Chapter 16 we shall explore further the challenges facing society with respect to the problem of the psychiatric homeless population, the living testament to the unfulfilled promise of deinstitutionalization.

Although the net results of deinstitutionalization may not have lived up to expectations, a number of successful community-oriented programs have been developed (Stein & Tess, 1978; Lamb, 1982; Talbott, 1981). Deinstitutionalization has worked best for those who experience acute episodes of disturbed behavior, are hospitalized briefly, and are then returned to their homes, families, and jobs (Shadish et al., 1989).

One might ask whether it is fair to place the blame for the current failures of deinstitutionalization on the policy itself. Some have argued that deinstitutionalization has not yet had a fair chance to prove itself, since a combination of factors that would be required for it to be successful have not been met, such as provisions for continuing care and decent housing for discharged mental patients (Lamb, 1984). Others have argued that CMHCs have not been given the support they need to prove themselves (James, 1987; Elpers, 1987). Many CMHCs are understaffed and unprepared to meet the needs of the large numbers of discharged patients released to their care (Wines, 1988). If deinstitutionalization is to succeed, discharged patients must be provided with continuing care and afforded opportunities for decent housing, gainful employment, and training in social and vocational skills (Goering et al., 1984; Lurigio & Lewis, 1989). Viewed in this context, the social experiment called deinstitutionalization is not a failed dream, but rather a promise that remains to be fulfilled if society is able and willing to meet the challenge.

The ability of local facilities to help maintain *new* patients in the community appears to be more promising. A review of ten controlled experiments in which severely disturbed people were randomly assigned to receive either hospitalization or outpatient treatment failed to find even one experiment that showed better results for hospitalization (Kiesler, 1982). Outpatient treatment generally outperformed hospitalization in terms of the ability of the person to maintain independent living arrangements, stay in school, and find gainful employment.

There are no current national legislative efforts to reverse the trend toward deinstitutionalization (James, 1987). In addition, the federal government remains committed to providing support to community-based programs, although at a level of funding that was far less than was promised in the early years of the CMHC movement (Elpers, 1987). Some states appear to be moving in the direction of reinstitutionalization, however. In California, for example, which had achieved an 86 percent reduction in its mental hospital census, the legislature, bending to increased public pressure, has developed initiatives to reinstitutionalize many discharged mental patients in state hospitals (Elpers, 1987). In states such as Washington, Texas, and Indiana, laws have been eased to make it easier to commit patients involuntarily to mental hospitals (Wines, 1988).

Underfunded and understaffed, CMHCs nevertheless continue to serve many functions in the effort to treat emotionally disturbed people in their home communities.

The Community Mental Health Center

Community mental health centers (CMHCs) perform many functions in the effort to reduce the need for hospitalization of new patients and rehospitalization of formerly hospitalized patients. A primary function of the CMHC is to help discharged mental patients adjust to the community by providing continuing care and by closely monitoring their progress. Unfortunately, not enough CMHCs have been established to serve the needs of the hundreds of thousands of ex-hospitalized patients and to try to prevent the need for hospitalization

Halfway houses are transitional (community) facilities that provide sheltered opportunities for mental patients to reenter society. Here, former institutionalized patients who live together in a community residence operate a small home renovation business.

of new patients by providing intervention services and alternatives to full hospitalization, such as day-hospital programs. Patients in day hospitals attend structured therapy and vocational rehabilitation programs in a hospital setting during the day but are returned to their families or homes at night. Many CMHCs also administer transitional treatment facilities in the community, such as halfway houses, which provide not only a sheltered living environment to help discharged mental patients gradually adjust to the community but also pro-

vide people in crisis with an alternative to hospitalization. CMHCs also serve in consultative roles to other professionals in the community, such as in training police officers to handle disturbed people. Many of the features of the CMHC focus on prevention, such as crisis intervention, consultation, and halfway houses. In Chapter 16 we will take a closer look at the ways in which mental health professionals seek to meet the challenge of prevention through these and other approaches.

SUMMARY

Psychotherapy

Psychotherapies share features such as the use of systematic, verbal interactions; incorporation of behavioral principles to effect change in behavior, attitudes, and feelings; attentive listening; nonverbal communication; and the instilling of positive expectancies. The common features of psychotherapy are often referred to as nonspecific factors. The three major professional groups that treat emotional disorders are clinical psychologists, psychiatrists, and psychiatric social workers.

Psychodynamic Therapies

Psychodynamic therapies originated with psychoanalysis, the approach to treatment developed by Sigmund Freud. Psychoanalysts use various techniques to help people gain insight into their unconscious conflicts and work them through in the light of their adult personalities. The major techniques include free association, dream analysis, and the analysis and working-through of the transference relationship.

More recent psychodynamic therapies are generally briefer and less intensive. While they share with traditional psychoanalysis a focus on uncovering unconscious conflicts, they tend to involve a more direct exploration of the client's defenses and transference relationships.

Humanistic-Existential Therapies

Humanistic-existential approaches focus more on the client's subjective, conscious experience in the "here-and-now." Carl Rogers' person-centered therapy focuses on helping people increase their awareness and acceptance of inner feelings that had met with social condemnation and had become disowned from their self-concepts. He believed that the effective person-centered therapist should possess the qualities of uncondi-

tional positive regard, empathetic understanding, genuineness, and congruence.

Fritz Perls's Gestalt therapy focuses on helping people integrate disparate elements in their personalities through structured exercises that bring conflicting parts of the personality into present awareness.

Cognitive Therapies

Cognitive therapies focus on helping people replace the maladaptive cognitions that are believed to underlie their emotional problems and self-defeating behavior. Albert Ellis's rational-emotive therapy focuses on disputing the irrational beliefs that occasion emotional distress and substituting more adaptive behaviors in relating to others. Aaron Beck's cognitive therapy focuses on helping clients identify, challenge, and replace distorted cognitions, such as tendencies to magnify negative events and minimize personal accomplishments.

Behavior Therapy

Behavior therapy involves the systematic application of the principles of learning to help people make adaptive behavioral changes. Behavior therapy incorporates a wide range of learning-based techniques, such as systematic desensitization, gradual exposure, modeling, aversive conditioning, operant conditioning approaches, social skills training, self-control techniques, biofeedback training, skills training approaches, and relaxation techniques. Cognitive-behavior therapy involves the integration of behavioral and cognitive approaches in therapy.

Eclecticism in Psychotherapy

There has been a growing interest in therapeutic eclecticism in recent years. Therapists who adopt an eclectic

In the early 1980s, New York began to provide outreach services to homeless people in need of psychological treatment. Here an outreach team offers assistance to a homeless man in the Port Authority Bus Terminal.

ing the rights of the individual with the rights of society. There are those who argue that a just and humane society has both a right and a responsibility to care for people who are perceived to be incapable of caring for themselves, even if it means involuntarily committing them to a psychiatric institution. Some might argue that to stand idly by and allow its citizens to waste away on the sidewalks of its great cities is not the hallmark of a compassionate society. Others have argued that in a free society, people have a fundamental right to self-determination, even if it means engaging in behavior that is socially offensive or potentially dangerous to themselves, as long as they don't break any laws. If these individuals should break the law, this argument holds, then the criminal justice system should intervene, not the mental-health system.

The case of Joyce Brown brings up complex social, moral, and legal issues surrounding society's interactions with people whose behavior seems strange or menacing to others and themselves. It raises questions not only about the civil rights of the homeless but also about the rights of the government to control deviant behavior through involuntary hospitalization and coercive treatment. Actually, only a small percentage of involuntarily committed people are homeless. Most are committed on the basis of petitions filed by their family members who express concern about their bizarre behavior and apparent dangerousness.

In this chapter we shall examine psychiatric commitment and other issues that arise from society's response to abnormal behavior, such as the rights of patients in institutions, the use of the insanity defense in criminal cases, and the responsibility of professionals to warn people who may be put at risk by the dangerous behavior of their clients. We shall see that the standard for psychiatric commitment rests, in part, on a determi-

nation of dangerousness. But can professionals such as psychiatrists and psychologists really predict who will be dangerous? We shall consider the evidence regarding the prediction of dangerousness and discuss some of the factors that make it difficult for clinicians to make accurate predictions. The chapter concludes with a discussion of two major challenges faced by professionals today: meeting the needs of homeless people with mental disorders and seeking ways to prevent or lessen the impact of abnormal behaviors in society.

PSYCHIATRIC COMMITMENT

The legal process of placing people in psychiatric institutions against their will is called **civil commitment.** Through civil commitment, people who are deemed to show abnormal behaviors and to be a threat to themselves or to others may be involuntarily confined to psychiatric institutions to provide them with treatment and help ensure their safety and that of the general society. Civil commitment, which is also called psychiatric commitment, should be distinguished from legal or criminal commitment, which involves the placement of a person in a psychiatric institution for treatment who has been acquitted of a crime by reason of insanity. In **legal commitment,** a criminal's unlawful act is judged by a court of law to be the result of a mental disorder or defect that should be treated by commitment to a psychiatric hospital rather than by sentencing to a penal institution. We shall return to the issue of the insanity verdict later in the chapter. First, let us focus on the legal procedures that provide for civil or psychiatric commitment.

Civil commitment should also be distinguished from the process of voluntary hospitalization, in which a person voluntarily seeks treatment in a psychiatric institution, and can, with sufficient notice, leave the institution when he or she so desires. But even in such cases, the hospital may petition the court to change the legal status of a patient seeking discharge from voluntary to involuntary if the person is perceived as presenting a serious threat to him or herself or to others should the person be released.

The process of involuntarily placing a person in a psychiatric hospital usually involves a petition that is filed either by a relative or a professional. One or more psychiatric examiners may be empowered by the court to assess the person's mental status and behavior within a set period of time, following which a formal hearing is held in which the psychiatric testimony is heard and a decision is reached by a judge whether or not a stay in the hospital is mandated. If the person is committed, the law provides for a process of periodic review by the court of the person's need for continued hospitalization. The legal process is intended to ensure that people are not simply "warehoused" in psychiatric hospitals for indefinite periods of time. The hospital staff must demonstrate the need for continued confinement in order for people to remain hospitalized without their consent.

Various legal safeguards have been established to protect people's civil rights in commitment proceedings, including the right to due process and the right to be represented by an attorney at the commitment proceedings. In situations in which the person is deemed to present a clear and imminent threat of danger to either oneself or others, however, the court may act under its emergency procedures to order an immediate hospitalization until such time that a more formal commitment hearing can be held. These emergency powers are usually limited to a set period, like 72 hours, during which time a formal petition for commitment must be filed with the court or the person is set free.

The standards for psychiatric commitment have been tightened over the past 20 or 30 years, and the rights of people who are subject to commitment proceedings are more strictly protected today than they were in the past. At one time psychiatric abuses were more commonplace—people were often committed without clear evidence that they posed a danger to themselves or others. It was not until 1979, in fact, that the U.S. Supreme Court ruled, in *Addington* v. *Texas*, that persons involuntarily hospitalized must be judged to be both "mentally ill" and a clear and present danger to themselves or others.

While few would argue that the civil commitment laws have been tightened over the years to better protect the individual's rights, some have called for the complete abolition of psychiatric commitment on the grounds that to deprive one of individual liberties in the name of therapy cannot be justified in a free society. One of the most vocal and persistent critics of the civil commitment statutes has been the psychiatrist Thomas Szasz (Szasz, 1970a). Szasz argues that *mental illness* is a label that society invented to transform social deviance into medical illness. In Szasz's view, people should not be deprived of their liberty simply because their behavior is perceived to be different or disturbing to others. Individuals who are accused of violating the law, Szasz maintains, should be prosecuted according to the law, not confined involuntarily in a psychiatric hospital. Although psychiatric commitment may prevent the potential violence of some individuals, Szasz argues, it does violence to many more in the form of depriving them of their basic liberties:

> The mental patient, we say, *may be* dangerous: he may harm himself or someone else. But we, society, *are* dangerous: we rob him of his good name and of his liberty, and subject him to tortures called "treatments." (Szasz, 1970b, p. 279)

Szasz's strident opposition to institutional psychiatry and his condemnation of psychiatric commitment has focused much needed attention on abuses in the mental-health system. It has also brought many professionals to question the legal, ethical, and moral questions raised by coercive psychiatric treatment in the form of involuntary hospitalization and forced medication. But many caring and concerned professionals draw the line at abolishing psychiatric commitment. They argue that people may not be acting in their considered best interests when they threaten suicide or do harm to others or when their behavior becomes so disorganized that they cannot take care of their basic needs.

PREDICTING DANGEROUSNESS

People must be judged to be dangerous in order to be psychiatrically committed. Thus, professionals are responsible for making accurate predictions of dangerousness in determining whether people should be involuntary hospitalized, or if already hospitalized, whether people requesting release can be safely returned to the community. But how accurate are professionals in predicting who will be dangerous? Do professionals have special skills or clinical wisdom that renders their predictions accurate, or are they no better than the average person in predicting dangerousness?

There is actually little research evidence to support the accuracy of predictions of dangerousness by psychiatrists, psychologists, or other professionals. In one study, for example, two psychiatrists examined each of 257 people who were accused of felony crimes but were remanded to a psychiatric hospital because they were judged incompetent to stand trial (Cocozza & Steadman, 1976). The psychiatrists judged 60 percent of the defendants as dangerous and 40 percent as not dangerous. The subjects were then followed through their hospitalizations and for a period of three years after their release to the community. The results showed that the people judged to be dangerous by the psychiatrists were actually slightly *less* likely than those judged nondangerous to be rearrested for violent crimes (14% v. 16%).

Professionals tend to show a consistent bias in favor of *overpredicting* dangerousness—that is, incorrectly labeling many people as potentially dangerous who in fact are not (Monahan, 1981). The American Psychological Association (1978) and the American Psychiatric Association (1974) have both gone on record as stating that neither psychologists nor psychiatrists, respectively, can predict violence among the people they treat. The prediction problem has been cited by some as grounds for the abandonment of dangerousness as a criterion for civil commitment (Siegel, 1973; Rabkin & Zitrin, 1982).

People must be judged to be dangerous in order to be psychiatrically hospitalized. This dramatic photograph of Boston emergency workers pulling a woman away from a third floor ledge after she threatened to jump leaves little doubt about the dangerousness of her behavior. But professionals have not demonstrated that they can reliably predict *future* dangerousness.

Nor is it clear that persons with abnormal behaviors are especially prone to violence toward others. People with abnormal behaviors who have no prior history of violent behavior are no more likely than the general population to exhibit dangerous behavior in the future (Monahan, 1981).

> **?** People with abnormal behaviors who have no prior history of violent behavior are actually no more likely than the general population to exhibit dangerous behavior in the future.

Nor does the research evidence support the stereotype of the schizophrenic as violent or dangerous (Monahan & Steadman, 1983), despite the general public perception to the contrary. In a recent study in Alaska, schizophrenics accounted for 2 percent or fewer of all arrests for violent crimes, supporting the belief that schizophrenics were not responsible to any appreciable extent for the high level of violence in society (Phillips & Wolf, 1988).

Despite the evidence, therapists may be inclined to err on the side of caution by overpredicting the potential for dangerous behavior in the belief that a failure to predict a dangerous act has more serious consequences than falsely predicting dangerousness. However, a likely consequence of overpredicting dangerousness is that many people who are perceived as being dangerous may be committed on the basis of suspicions of dangerousness that turn out to be groundless. The result of consistently overpredicting dangerousness, as Szasz recognized, is to deprive large numbers of people of their basic human right to liberty in order to prevent the few isolated cases of violence that might occur. According to Szasz, the commitment of the many to prevent the violence of the few is a form of preventive detention that violates the basic principles upon which the United States was founded.

A number of factors have been cited to account for the lack of success of professionals in predicting dangerousness:

1. *Recognizing violent tendencies after a violent incident is easier than predicting it beforehand.* It is often said that hindsight is 20/20. Like Monday morning quarterbacking, it is easier to piece together fragments of people's prior behaviors as evidence of their violent tendencies *after* they have committed acts of violence. Predicting a violent act before the fact is a more difficult task, however.

2. *Generalized perceptions of violent tendencies may not predict specific acts of violence.* The great majority of people who have generalized tendencies toward violence may never act out on them. Even classification within a diagnostic category that is often characterized by violent or dangerous behavior, such as antisocial personality disorder, is not sufficient to predict specific violent acts (Bloom & Rogers, 1987).

3. *Lack of agreement in defining violence or dangerousness.* One difficulty in assessing the predictability of dangerousness is the lack of agreement in defining the criteria for labeling violent or dangerous behavior. Most people would agree that crimes such as murder, rape, and assault are acts of violence. But there is less agreement, even among authorities, for labeling other acts as either violent or dangerous, such as driving at excessive speeds, harshly criticizing one's spouse or children, destroying property, selling drugs, or even passing bad checks.

Szasz has argued that value judgments form the basis of deciding which dangerous acts are considered grounds for commitment:

> Drunken drivers are dangerous both to themselves and to others. They injure and kill many more people than, for example, persons with paranoid delusions of persecution. Yet, people labeled ''paranoid'' are readily committable, while drunken drivers are not.

(a)

(b)

(c)

Which of these people is most dangerous? The apparently drunken driver (a)? The institutionalized psychiatric patient (b)? Or the corporate executives (c)? Critics of the mental-health system, such as psychiatrist Thomas Szasz, point out that drunken drivers account for more injuries and deaths than paranoid schizophrenics, although paranoid schizophrenics are more likely to be committed. Others have suggested that those corporate executives who knowingly make decisions that jeopardize the health of employees and consumers to maximize profits are guilty of a type of "corporate violence" that accounts for more deaths and injuries than other types of crime.

Some types of dangerous behavior are even rewarded. Race-car drivers, trapeze artists, and astronauts receive admiration and applause. . . . Thus, it is not dangerousness in general that is at issue, but rather the manner in which one is dangerous. (Szasz, 1963, p. 46)

Some have suggested that the decisions of corporate executives which expose consumers or employees to unreasonable risks to their personal safety may represent a form of "corporate violence" (or *suite* crime as opposed to *street* crime) that has actually accounted for more deaths and injuries than other types of crimes (Monahan et al., 1979). Clearly, the determination of which behaviors are regarded as dangerous involves moral and political judgments (Monahan, 1981).

4. *Base-rate problems.* One of the reasons why predicting dangerousness is a difficult task is that violent acts like murder, assault, or suicide are relatively rare events. They have low base rates of occurrence, and such rare events—like earthquakes—are difficult to predict with accuracy. The relative difficulty of making predictions of rare events is known as the "base-rate problem." Consider the problems in predicting suicide, for example.

If the suicide rate in a given year is less than 1 percent of a clinical population, the likelihood of predicting suicide in this population is not very favorable, given the low base rate. Statistics alone would tell you that you would be right 99 percent of the time if you predicted that any given person from the clinical population would *not* commit suicide in a given year. You would be wrong most of the time if you predicted that three or more people would commit suicide in a given year (even if one of the three did commit suicide). But to predict the nonoccurrence of suicide in every case would mean that you would fail to predict the relatively few cases in which suicide does occur. In making predictions, one must weigh the relative risks of failing to predict the occurrence of a certain behavior against the consequences of predicting the behavior will occur when in fact it does not. Clinicians must weigh their decisions in the balance between these relative risks. Clinicians, as noted, tend to err on the side of caution by overpredicting dangerousness. For example, say that an individual makes veiled threats to harm him or herself. The clinician might decide that the person is a serious suicide risk and needs to be hospitalized, either with or without his or her consent. If the person is then hospitalized and no suicide occurs, the clinician is in a position to claim that the hospitalization may have prevented a possible suicide. On the other hand, had the clinician not sought involuntary commitment and a suicide then occurred, the clinician might be held to account for poor professional judgment. However, erring on the side of caution might lead to the denial of liberty for many individuals whose threats were not seriously intended.

5. *Unlikelihood of direct threats of violence.* Another difficulty faced by professionals in assessing dangerousness is the unlikelihood that people who are truly dangerous would be willing to express their dangerous intent openly to a therapist. The therapy client is not likely to express to a therapist a clear threat of the type, "I'm going to kill _____ next Wednesday morning!" Rather, threats are often vague and nonspecific, and the therapist must weigh the person's hostile gestures and veiled threats as possible indicators of potential violence. Indirect threats are likely to be less reliable indicators of the potential for violence than are direct threats, reducing the accuracy of clinical predictions.

6.   *Predictions based on hospital behavior may not generalize to community settings.* Much of the research examining clinical predictions of dangerousness is based upon the long-term predictions of the future dangerousness of hospitalized patients when they are released to the community. The clinician bases these predictions, in large part, on an appraisal of the person's behavior while in the hospital setting. But violence or dangerous behavior, like other forms of behavior, may be situation-specific. A model patient who is able to adapt to a structured environment like a psychiatric hospital may be unable to cope with the pressures of independent living in the community. Accuracy is improved when predictions of potential violence are based upon the person's past community behavior, such as a history of violent incidents, rather than on the person's behavior in the hospital setting (Klassen & O'Connor, 1988).

In sum, it may be expecting too much of clinicians to make long-term predictions of dangerousness or potential for violence. It is one thing to predict dangerousness of people in emergency situations in which they appear to be "out of control" and may be threatening others verbally or at the point of a gun or a knife. It is another to expect clinicians to predict potential violence in the indeterminate future. The results of a recent study suggest that predictions of imminent dangerousness may yield more accurate findings than studies examining long-term predictability. This study (McNeil & Binder, 1987) examined the predictions of imminent dangerousness that were made at the time of admission following an emergency civil commitment. People who were judged by hospital staff to be dangerous when admitted to the hospital engaged in more acts of violence during the first 72 hours of hospitalization than did involuntarily committed patients who were not considered dangerous at the point of admission. As many as two out of three people who were judged to be violent to others engaged in a violent behavior within the first three days of hospitalization.

Although these results support the predictability of dangerousness within the context of an emergency commitment, the study was not designed to answer the question of whether the people who were judged to be dangerous at admission would have committed more dangerous acts had they not been hospitalized than those who were not considered dangerous. It is possible that those people who were judged to be violent were more likely to act violently only in a confined setting such as a secure psychiatric facility. To answer the question of whether these people would be more violent if they were not involuntarily committed would require a controlled study in which the decision to hospitalize or not hospitalize people who were judged to be violent at the point of admission would be randomly determined (Monahan, 1981). Researchers

might then be able to determine whether their predictions of dangerousness proved to be accurate. Of course, a study such as this would incur ethical problems in releasing people who are judged to be violent and in need of care to the community.

PATIENTS' RIGHTS

Up to this point we have considered the rights of society to use its powers of psychiatric commitment to hospitalize people against their will who are judged to be mentally ill and to pose a threat to themselves or others. But what of the rights of patients in psychiatric hospitals? Do involuntarily committed patients have a right to receive treatment? Or can society just lock them up in psychiatric facilities and fail to offer the treatment which their commitment was intended to provide? Also consider the opposite side of the coin: Do people who are involuntarily committed have a right to refuse treatment? These issues, which fall under the umbrella of patients' rights, have been brought into public focus by landmark court cases that have clarified, if not fully resolved, the rights of patients in psychiatric institutions. The history of abuses in the mental-health system, which has been highlighted in such popular books and movies as *One Flew Over the Cuckoo's Nest*, has led to a tightening of standards of care and adoption of legal guarantees to protect patients' rights. But the legal status of some issues still remains unsettled, such as the right to treatment.

Popular books and films such as *One Flew Over the Cuckoo's Nest* with Jack Nicholson and Louise Fletcher have highlighted many of the abuses of mental hospitals. In recent years, a tightening of standards of care and the adoption of legal safeguards have protected the rights of mental patients.

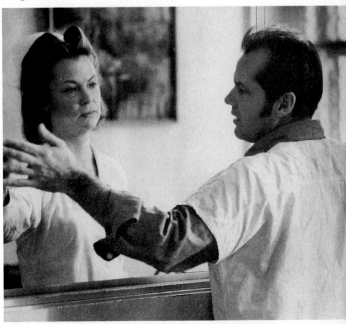

Right to Treatment

It may be natural to assume that institutions that accept people for treatment would be obligated to provide treatment, but it wasn't until a landmark federal court case, *Wyatt* v. *Stickney* (1971), that a federal court in Alabama established a minimum standard of care that hospitals were required to meet. The case involved a class-action suit brought on behalf of Ricky Wyatt, a mentally retarded young man, and other patients at a state hospital and school in Tuscaloosa, Alabama. The suit was brought against Dr. Stickney, who was then the Commissioner of Mental Health for the state of Alabama.

The federal district court in Alabama held that not only did the hospital fail to provide treatment to Ricky and others but that the general living conditions at the hospital were grossly inadequate. The court described the hospital dormitories as being ''barn-like structures'' that afforded no privacy to the residents. The general conditions were described as degrading and dehumanizing. The common bathrooms had no partitions between the toilets, the patients were outfitted with shoddy clothes, the wards were filthy and overcrowded, the kitchens unsanitary and the food substandard. In addition, the staff were poorly trained and their numbers were inadequate to administer treatment. The court held that mental hospitals must, at a minimum, provide the following:

(1)   A humane psychological and physical environment,

(2)   qualified staff in numbers sufficient to administer adequate treatment and

(3)   individualized treatment plans (*Wyatt* v. *Stickney*, 334 Supp., p. 1343 (1971)).

The court ruling established that the state has the obligation to provide adequate treatment for people who are involuntarily confined in its psychiatric hospitals. The court further ruled that to commit people involuntarily to hospitals on the basis that they needed treatment, and then to fail to provide such treatment, was a violation of their basic rights to due process under the law.

The scope of the court's decision was far-reaching. The court ordered the state of Alabama to (1) provide a program of treatment that was individually tailored to each patient's needs, (2) to increase staff-patient ratios to ensure that an adequate staff was available to administer treatment, and (3) to provide patients with humane and decent living conditions. In effect, the court established a minimal level of care that a mental hospital must provide in order to meet its responsibility to provide adequate treatment. Among the specific requirements that it mandated, the court ruled that there must be at least two psychiatrists, 12 nurses, one doctoral-level psychologist, and two master's-level social work-

TABLE 16.1 *Partial Listing of the Patient's Bill of Rights Under* Wyatt v. Stickney

1. Patients have rights to privacy and to be treated with dignity.
2. Patients shall be treated under the least restrictive conditions that can be provided to meet the purposes that commitment was intended to serve.
3. Patients shall have rights to visitation and telephone privileges unless special restrictions apply.
4. Patients have the right to refuse excessive or unnecessary medication. In addition, medication may not be used as a form of punishment.
5. Patients shall not be kept in restraints or isolation except in emergency conditions in which their behavior is likely to pose a threat to themselves or others and less restrictive restraints are not feasible.
6. Patients shall not be subject to experimental research unless their rights to informed consent are protected.
7. Patients have the right to refuse potentially hazardous or unusual treatments, such as lobotomy, electroconvulsive shock, or aversive behavioral treatments.
8. Unless when it is dangerous or inappropriate to the treatment program, patients shall have the right to wear their own clothing and keep possessions.
9. Patients have rights to regular exercise and to opportunities to spend time outdoors.
10. Patients have rights to suitable opportunities to interact with the opposite sex.
11. Patients have rights to humane and decent living conditions.
12. No more than six patients shall be housed in a room, and screen or curtains must be provided to afford a sense of privacy.
13. No more than eight patients shall share one toilet facility, with separate stalls provided for privacy.
14. Patients have a right to nutritionally balanced diets.
15. Patients shall not be required to perform work that is performed for the sake of maintenance of the facility.

ers for every 250 patients. A wide range of physical, recreational, and social conditions were required to be improved, as shown in Table 16.1. While the ruling of the court was limited to the state of Alabama, many other states have followed suit in revising their mental hospital standards to ensure that involuntarily committed patients are not denied their basic rights.

Other court cases have further clarified the rights of patients, including the following:

■ *O'Connor* v. *Donaldson*   Another landmark case in which the issue of patient's rights was raised was that of Kenneth Donaldson, a former patient at a state hospital in Florida who sued two of the hospital doctors on the grounds that he had been involuntarily confined without receiving treatment for a period of 14 years although he posed no serious threat to either himself or others. Donaldson had been originally committed on the basis of a petition filed by his father who had perceived him to be delusional. Despite the fact that Donaldson failed to receive any treatment during his confinement and was denied the opportunities for ground privileges and for occupational training, his repeated attempts to secure his release were denied by the hospital staff. Donaldson was finally released only when he threatened to sue the hospital. Once discharged, Donaldson did sue his doctors and was awarded damages of $38,500 from Dr. O'Connor, the superintendent of the hospital. The case was eventually argued before the United States Supreme Court.

Court testimony established that although the hospital staff had not perceived Donaldson to be dangerous at any time during his hospitalization, they still refused to release him. The hospital doctors argued that his continued hospitalization had been necessary because they had believed that Donaldson was unlikely to be able to adapt successfully to community living. While the hospital doctors had prescribed antipsychotic medications as a course of treatment, Donaldson refused to take the medications because of his Christian Science beliefs. The only treatment he received was custodial care.

In its ruling on the case in 1975, the U.S. Supreme Court held that ''mental illness [alone] cannot justify a State's locking up a person against his will and keeping him indefinitely in simple custodial confinement. . . . There is still no constitutional basis for confining such persons involuntarily if they are dangerous to no one and can live safely in freedom'' (p. 2493). The thrust of this ruling was that the state may not confine a person who is considered mentally ill but nondangerous if that person can be maintained safely in the community.

In its ruling on *O'Connor* v. *Donaldson*, the Supreme Court did not deal with the larger issue of the rights of patients to receive treatment. The ruling does not directly impose an obligation on state institutions to provide treatment for nondangerous people who are committed to its care, since the institutions may elect to release them instead.

The Supreme Court did touch upon the larger issue of society's rights to protect itself from individuals who are perceived as offensive. In delivering the opinion of the court, Justice Potter Stewart wrote,

> May the State fence in the harmless mentally ill solely to save its citizens from exposure to those whose ways are different? One might as well ask if the State, to avoid public unease, could incarcerate all who are physically unattractive or socially eccentric. Mere public intolerance or animosity cannot constitutionally justify the deprivation of a person's physical liberty. (*O'Connor* v. *Donaldson*, 95 S. Ct. 2486, 1975).

■ *Youngberg* v. *Romeo*   In a more recent case, *Youngberg* v. *Romeo* in 1982, the U.S. Supreme Court dealt more directly with the issue of a patient's right to treatment, but seemed to retreat somewhat from the standards established in *Wyatt* v. *Stickney*. Nicholas Romeo, a 33-year-old profoundly retarded man who was judged

Kenneth Donaldson points to the Supreme Court decision which ruled that people considered mentally ill but not dangerous could not be confined against their will if they could be maintained safely in the community.

to have a mental capacity of an 18-month-old child, and who was unable to talk or care for himself, had been institutionalized in a state hospital and school in Pennsylvania. While in the state facility he had a history of injuring himself through his violent behavior and was often kept in restraints. The case was brought by the patient's mother, who alleged that the hospital was negligent in not preventing her son's injuries from occurring and for routinely using physical restraints for prolonged periods while not providing adequate treatment.

The Supreme Court ruled that involuntarily committed patients, like Nicholas, have a right to be confined in less restrictive conditions, such as being freed from physical restraints whenever it is reasonable to do so. The Court's ruling also included a limited recognition of the committed patient's right to treatment. The Court held that institutionalized patients have a right to minimally adequate training to help them function free of physical restraints, but only to the extent that such training can be provided in *reasonable* safety. The determination of reasonableness, the Court held, should be made on the basis of the judgment of the qualified professionals in the facility. The federal courts should not interfere with the internal operations of the facility, the Court ruled, since ''there certainly is no reason to think judges or juries are better qualified than appropriate professionals in making such decisions'' (p. 2462). The courts should not second-guess the judgments of qualified professionals, the Court further held, unless such judgments are determined to depart from professional standards of practice. The High Court did not address the broader issues of the rights of committed patients to receive training that might eventually enable them to function at more independent levels of functioning outside the hospital.

The rights of involuntarily committed mental patients have not been fully determined by the courts. We are left to await future court decisions to determine the breadth of rights that mental patients are entitled to under the Constitution.

Right to Refuse Treatment

Consider the following scenario. A person, John Citizen, is involuntarily committed to a mental hospital for treatment. The hospital staff determines that John suffers from a psychotic disorder, paranoid schizophrenia, and should be treated with antipsychotic medications, such as major tranquilizers. John, however, decides not to cooperate with treatment, claiming that the hospital has no right to treat him against his will. The hospital staff seeks a court order to mandate treatment, arguing that it makes little if any sense to involuntarily commit someone unless the hospital is empowered to provide that person with the treatment believed to be most appropriate.

Does an involuntary patient, like John, have a right to refuse treatment? If so, would such a right make a mockery of a legal standard in which people could be involuntarily committed to mental institutions to receive treatment for mental disorders, but then be afforded the right to refuse the treatments that the hospitalization was intended to provide? One might also wonder whether people who are judged to be in need of involuntary hospitalization are competent enough to make decisions about which treatments are in their best interests. There are many different opinions about this issue.

A psychiatrist, Alan Stone (1975), argues that people who are involuntarily hospitalized, even those who are criminally committed, should have a right to refuse certain treatments that might be considered radical, such as electroconvulsive therapy (ECT), aversion therapy, psychosurgery, or certain forms of chemotherapy involving the use of addictive drugs. But Stone draws the line at the more conventional treatments, arguing that treatments which carry a lesser risk, such as psychotropic medications, should fall within the discretion of the professional staff to provide, with involuntary patients having little if any say in the matter. It might be argued, however, that even such lower-risk treatments, such as anti-psychotic drugs like Prolixin or Thorazine, may produce serious or disabling neurological side effects, like tardive dyskinesia. If one accepts the argument that hospitalized patients, regardless of their commitment status, should have a basic right to protect themselves from risky treatments, should not this right be extended to all treatments that carry definable risks, not simply the more radical treatments? Court rulings have established that hospitalized patients do have a right to refuse medications. However, the right is not unlimited; it may be overruled by a court of law or by an independent review panel.

The rights of committed patients to refuse psychotropic medications was tested in the case of *Rogers* v. *Okin* in 1979, in which a federal district court in Massachusetts imposed an injunction on a state hospital in Boston that prohibited the forced medication of patients except in emergency situations. The court ruled that committed patients could not be forcibly medicated, except in emergency situations in which the patient's behavior posed a significant risk of physical harm occurring to the patient or to others. The district court recognized that the patient may be wrong in his or her judgment in refusing medication, but that a person, whether behaviorally disordered or not, has a right to be wrong or unwise, as long as the effects of the "error" did not impose "a danger of physical harm to himself, fellow patients, or hospital staff" (p. 1367).

Many professionals were outraged by this court ruling. As one psychiatrist put it, patients who refused medications would literally find themselves "rotting with their rights on" (Gutheil, 1980). Others, however, viewed the court decision in more favorable terms, seeing it as a means of ensuring that hospitalized patients would be treated with greater dignity and would be more likely to receive proper treatment (Cole, 1982).

We should point out that voluntarily admitted patients have always had the right to refuse treatment. They may also sign themselves out of the hospital, even if their doctors believe that they should remain. As noted previously, however, the hospital may petition the court to change the commitment status from voluntary to involuntary if it believes that the person is dangerous and in need of continued treatment.

The results of a nationwide study in 1983 revealed that a patient's right to refuse medication, and to have such refusals reviewed by the court, was recognized in half the states in the Union (Callahan & Longmire, 1983). While statutes and regulations vary from state to state, cases in which hospitalized patients refuse medications are often first brought before an independent review panel. If the panel rules against the patient, the case may then be brought before a judge, who makes the final decision about whether or not the patient is to be forcibly medicated.

Most recent studies have found that the number of refusals of medication is generally low, about 10 percent overall (Appelbaum & Hoges, 1986). Between 70 and 90 percent of refusals that reach the review process are eventually overridden (Appelbaum & Hoges, 1986). In practice, then, the number of patients who refuse their medications and have their refusals upheld has turned out to be small.

It is now recognized by many of those who initially challenged the rights of involuntarily hospitalized mental patients to refuse treatment that some type of independent review must be incorporated into hospital procedures to ensure that the type of treatment received is appropriate. The adoption of carefully conducted review procedures may help reduce the potential for unfortunate or unskillful use of medications (Appelbaum, 1988). Some psychiatrists, like Paul Appelbaum, have gone further in suggesting that all involuntarily hospitalized patients should have their medication subject to an independent review process, whether they refuse them or not, so that those patients who are more compliant or who don't protest their treatment openly would not be subject to inappropriate treatment.

The incorporation of independent review panels into customary hospital practices is a laudable goal. But it raises the question of who is to be charged with handling this review process. In Appelbaum's view, the review panels should be controlled by psychiatrists, because they are the professionals best prepared by virtue of their training and experience to evaluate both the need, and the skillful use, of medications and other biological treatments, such as ECT. While it is common practice for psychiatrists to handle these responsibilities in many hospital settings, it might be argued that putting the psychiatrists in charge of monitoring the use of medications sounds a little like putting the fox in charge of guarding the chicken coop. Psychiatrists may be unlikely to second-guess the professional judgments of their colleagues. Appelbaum has recognized that when psychiatrists are called upon to review a patient's refusal to accept medication, they generally tend to overrule the patient in favor of the prescribing physician, or as he puts it, "When physicians act like judges, they still tend to think like physicians" (Appelbaum, 1988, p. 417). An independent review panel that incorporates the opinions of both psychiatrists and nonpsychiatrists might provide a better opportunity for divergent opinions to be heard and discussed when reaching decisions about the most appropriate care that a patient should receive.

Our discussion of legal issues and abnormal behavior now turns to the controversy concerning the **insanity defense.**

THE INSANITY DEFENSE

Leaving from a side entrance of the Washington Hilton in the nation's capital on March 31, 1981, the President of the United States was approaching his waiting limousine when gunshots rang out. Reflexively, he turned in the direction of the line of fire, as Secret Service agents pulled out their weapons and leaped into position to form a human shield around President Ronald Reagan. In an instant, the President was shoved by a Secret Service agent into the limousine, which then quickly sped away. At first, President Reagan didn't know that he had been wounded. He said later that it sounded like firecrackers. Agents seized the gunman, later identified as John Hinckley, Jr., a 25-year-old who

John W. Hinckley, Jr., shown here, (center), attempted to assassinate President Ronald Reagan in 1981 but was found not guilty by reason of insanity. The public outrage over the Hinckley verdict led to a reexamination of the insanity plea in many states.

had worked at odd jobs but was unemployed at the time of the shooting. President Reagan had been wounded, as had James Brady, his press secretary, who was hit by a stray bullet that pierced his skull, causing brain damage and leaving him partially paralyzed.

A letter Hinckley had written and left behind in his hotel room revealed that he had hoped that his assassination of the President would impress a young actress, Jodie Foster, on whom he had a crush but had never met. While there was never any question at the trial that Hinckley had fired the shots that wounded President Reagan and his press secretary, the burden was placed on the prosecutor to demonstrate beyond a reasonable doubt that Hinckley had had the mental capacity, at the time of the assassination attempt, to appreciate that what he was doing was wrong and that he had the capability of controlling his behavior. The defense presented testimony that portrayed Hinckley as a schizophrenic who suffered under the delusionary belief that he would achieve a "magic union" with Ms. Foster as a result of accomplishing the deed of killing the President. But the prosecutor portrayed Hinckley as having made a conscious and willful choice to kill the President, and that whatever mental disorder he might have suffered from did not prevent him from controlling his behavior.

The jury sided with the defense, finding Hinckley not guilty by reason of insanity. The verdict led to a public outcry across the country, with many calling for the abolition of the insanity defense. Public opinion polls taken several days after the Hinckley verdict was

Actress Jody Foster, as she appeared in the film *Taxi Driver*. John Hinckley, Jr. reportedly attempted to assassinate the President in order to impress Ms. Foster, whom he had seen in the film but never met. In the film, Robert DeNiro rescued Foster's character from a life of prostitution. Hinckley's attorneys claimed that their client experienced similar rescue fantasies.

? It is true that a man was seen by millions of television viewers attempting to assassinate the President of the United States, but he was found not guilty by a court of law. He was found "not guilty by reason of insanity."

returned showed that the public had little confidence in the psychiatric testimony that had been offered at the trial (Slater & Hans, 1984). One objection focused on the fact that in the federal courts, which had jurisdiction in the Hinckley trial, the prosecutor had the responsibility of proving beyond a reasonable doubt that the defendant was sane, once the defense presented evidence to support a plea of insanity. Some jurors in the Hinckley case claimed afterwards that the prosecution had been unable *beyond a reasonable doubt* to prove that Hinckley had sufficient mental capacity to control his actions.

In the aftermath of the Hinckley verdict, the federal government and some states changed their statutes to shift the burden of proof to the defense to prove insanity, relieving the prosecution of an unfair burden to prove sanity beyond a reasonable doubt. In some states, such as Idaho and Montana, the insanity defense had been abolished long before the Hinckley case. Even the American Psychiatric Association (*Psychiatric News*, February 4, 1983) went on record as stating that psychiatric expert

witnesses should not be called upon to render opinions about whether or not a person is able to control his or her actions. In the opinion of the psychiatric association, these were not medical judgments that a psychiatrist is trained to provide.

Despite the few celebrated cases, like the Hinckley affair, in which the insanity defense was put in the public spotlight, successful insanity defenses have been found to occur in fewer than 1 percent of cases in which they were pleaded (Pasewark, 1981; Rogers, et al., 1983; Phillips & Wolf, 1988; Weiner, 1985). In a study in Alaska (Phillips & Wolf, 1988), for example, the insanity defense was successfully applied in but 0.1 percent or fewer of *all* criminal cases between 1977 and 1981. Nor is the common perception that psychiatric experts who give testimony in court often disagree with each other supported by the available evidence. The Alaska study, for example, showed that psychiatrists who were called as expert witnesses agreed with each other in giving testimony 79 percent of the time in a variety of cases. Conflicting psychiatric testimony was presented in only 1.5 percent of all criminal cases in the Alaskan study in which psychiatric testimony was presented, and in seven of ten of these cases the defendant was found guilty. However uncommon, battles between opposing witnesses were unlikely to lead to acquittals. The net result of these findings is that while changes in the insanity defense, or its outright abolition, may prevent some few flagrant cases of abuse, it's not likely to afford any great protection to the public.

Perceptions of the use of the insanity defense tend to stray far from the facts. A study in Wyoming asked state legislators to estimate the percentage of cases that had resulted in an insanity verdict among 21,012 felony cases that were tried in the state. The legislators, presumably knowledgable about the law in their own state, estimated, on the average, that the insanity plea had been offered in 21 percent of these cases and that successful defenses occurred in about 8.5 percent of felony cases (Pasewark & Pantle, 1979). Laymen who were also interviewed provided estimates that were about double those given by the state legislators. In fact, the actual frequency of insanity pleas was 102 (less than 0.5% of the total cases) and only one person was successfully acquitted.

While the public outrage over the Hinckley and other celebrated insanity verdicts has led to a reexamination of the insanity defense (see nearby "A Closer Look" section), society has long held to the doctrine of free will as a basis for determining responsibility for wrongdoing. The doctrine of free will, as applied to criminal responsibility, requires that people can be held guilty of a crime only if they are judged to have been in control of their actions at the time of commission of the crime. Not only must it be determined by a court of law that a defendant had committed a crime beyond

Halfway houses for formerly institutionalized patients represent a type of tertiary prevention effort which helps residents adjust to community living. How might halfway houses also serve a secondary prevention function?

achieve higher levels of independent functioning (Fairweather et al., 1969; Fairweather, 1980; Lamb & Goertzel, 1971).

There is a nationwide shortage of well-run halfway houses. A major problem in establishing additional halfway houses is community resistance. Community residents often object to the presence of mental patients in their midst and may wrongly perceive the residents as dangerous or object to the sight of people whose behavior seems bizarre or strange.

A Final Word on Prevention

Psychologists, like other helping professionals, tend to focus on providing care to those who have identifiable problems or are clearly in need. They tend to react to needs for treatment when they arise, rather than focusing their efforts on spearheading social reforms that might eventually reduce the prevalence of abnormal behaviors or eradicate them entirely. To take a more active stance in promoting social and environmental changes that might enhance psychological functioning and reduce abnormal behaviors, psychologists need to extend their traditional role of providing direct services in several directions. As a profession, psychology can contribute its resources and knowledge in providing increased consultation to other professionals and community members who have more frequent contact with high-risk populations that are not yet impaired to the point that they require clinical treatment. It may be penny wise and pound foolish, as the expression goes, to concentrate resources on clinical services but not provide support for community consultation that might reduce the frequency or intensity of abnormal behaviors through early detection and intervention.

Psychologists need to apply their clinical skills to develop preventive programs for high-risk populations, like the program for early-stage problem drinkers described previously. Psychologists need to continue the effort, along with other professionals, to expand the body of knowledge about cause and effect in abnormal behaviors. This effort should incorporate research that examines abnormal behaviors in terms of the interrelationships among biological, psychosocial, and environmental factors. Once these factors are identified, psychologists and others must bring this knowledge into the public forum to enable society to direct resources toward eradicating the underlying causes of abnormal behaviors. Sweeping social changes may be necessary, such as the expansion of government assistance programs to improve housing conditions, provide childhood enrichment programs, and improve nutrition and health care for populations in the high-risk categories. It may require innovative thinking to develop new approaches to providing a more enriching and supportive environment in which children can develop to their potential.

As we look toward the turning of a new century, we can hope that the challenge of prevention will be met through research, consultation, innovation, and implementation.

SUMMARY

Psychiatric Commitment

The legal process by which people are placed in psychiatric institutions against their will is called psychiatric or civil commitment. Psychiatric commitment is intended to provide treatment to people whose abnormal behavior is believed to pose a threat to themselves or to others. Legal or criminal commitment, by comparison, involves the placement of a person in a psychiatric institution for treatment who has been acquitted of a crime by reason of insanity. In voluntary hospitalization, people voluntarily seek treatment in a psychiatric facility, and can leave of their own accord, unless a court rules otherwise. Psychiatric commitment usually begins with a petition filed by a family member or professional, which is then subject to review by the court. The U.S. Supreme Court ruled in 1979 that people involuntarily hospitalized must be judged to be both "mentally ill" and a clear and present danger to themselves or others. This helped protect people against arbitrary commitment practices. But some critics, such as Thomas Szasz, argue for the abolition of involuntary hospitalization, claiming that people should not be deprived of their liberty because of disturbing but otherwise lawful behavior.

Predicting Dangerousness

While people must be judged dangerous to be placed involuntarily in a psychiatric facility, mental-health professionals have not demonstrated any special ability to predict dangerousness accurately. Professionals tend to overpredict dangerousness, but research evidence shows that mental patients without prior histories of dangerous behavior are no more likely than the general population to commit violent acts against others in the future. Some of the factors that may account for the failure to predict dangerousness include (1) recognizing violent tendencies after a violent incident is easier than predicting it beforehand; (2) generalized perceptions of violent tendencies may not predict specific acts of violence; (3) lack of agreement in defining violence or dangerousness; (4) base-rate problems; (5) unlikelihood of direct threats of violence; and (6) predictions based on hospital behavior may not generalize to community settings. But predictions of imminent danger may be more accurate.

Patients' Rights

Several landmark court cases have clarified, though not fully resolved, issues of patients' rights in psychiatric facilities. In *Wyatt* v. *Stickney*, a court in Alabama imposed a minimum standard of care that hospitals were obliged to provide. In *O'Connor,* v. *Donaldson,* the U.S. Supreme Court ruled that nondangerous mentally ill people could not be held in psychiatric facilities against their will if such people can be maintained safely in the community. In *Youngberg* v. *Romeo*, the U.S. Supreme Court ruled that involuntarily confined patients have a right to less restrictive types of treatment and to receive minimally adequate training to help them function free of physical restraints, but only if such measures can be taken in reasonable safety. Court rulings, such as that of *Rogers* v. *Okin* in Massachusetts, have also established that patients have a right to refuse medication, except under emergency conditions in which the patient's behavior posed a significant risk of physical harm to himself or herself or to others. But few patients actually refuse medications, and the large majority of these refusals are overturned upon review.

The Insanity Defense

The verdict of "not guilty by reason of insanity" in the Hinckley case focused public attention on the insanity defense. But despite the popular perception, the insanity defense is invoked successfully in very few cases. Three major court cases established legal precedents for the insanity defense. In 1834 a court in Ohio applied a principle of irresistible impulse as the basis of an insanity defense. The M'Naghten rule, based on a case in England in 1843, treated the failure to appreciate the wrongfulness of one's action as the basis of legal insanity. The *Durham* ruling was based on a case in the United States in 1954 in which it was held that persons did not bear criminal responsibility if their criminal behavior was the product of "mental disease or mental defect." But problems with applying the *Durham* rule in practice led to its failure in many jurisdictions and to the adoption of a set of guidelines from the American Law Institute for determining the legal basis for the insanity defense. But juries must still struggle with the complex questions of determining criminal responsibility, not merely criminal actions, in cases in which the insanity defense is used. People who are criminally committed may be hospitalized for an indefinite period of time, according to a U.S. Supreme Court ruling in *Jones* v. *United States*.

Competency to Stand Trial

People who are accused of crimes but are incapable of understanding the charges against them or assisting in their own defense can be found incompetent to stand trial and remanded to a psychiatric facility. In the case of *Jackson* v. *Indiana*, the U.S. Supreme Court placed restrictions on the length of time a person judged incompetent to stand trial could be held on such a basis in a psychiatric facility.

The Duty to Warn

While information disclosed by a client to a therapist generally carries a right to confidentiality, the right is not absolute. The *Tarasoff* ruling, brought in a California case in which a rejected suitor threatened his love interest and later killed her, held that therapists have a duty or obligation to warn third parties of threats made against them by the therapists' clients. Some have questioned whether *Tarasoff* might inadvertently increase the risk of violence to others by discouraging violent clients from confiding in their therapists or even from entering therapy.

Facing the Challenges of Homelessness and Prevention

Many, but certainly not all, homeless people are ex-hospitalized mental patients or people who might have been hospitalized involuntarily under laxer standards for commitment in earlier times. It will take multifaceted efforts of mental-health agencies and other community support services to meet the needs of the psychiatric homeless population.

There are three major types of prevention: primary prevention, secondary prevention, and tertiary prevention. Primary prevention involves efforts to prevent the development of illness and abnormal behaviors. Secondary prevention involves efforts at early intervention to forestall the development of more severe problems. Tertiary prevention involves efforts that focus on reducing the impact of existing problems or need for rehospitalization.

The systems-level approach to primary prevention focuses on making changes in society, not the individual, to help prevent illness and abnormal behavior. By contrast, person-centered approaches focus on helping individuals cope more effectively with their life stressors. Two types of person-centered approaches are discussed, situation-focused approaches and competence-enhancement approaches. In situation-focused approaches, services are provided to people to help them cope with specific stressors, such as divorce or other losses. In competence-enhancement approaches, people are trained in specific skills that they can use to manage stress more effectively.

There are various forms of secondary prevention in mental health, including crisis intervention, self-help groups, telephone hot lines, community consultation, and early intervention. Tertiary prevention in mental health is primarily focused on providing aftercare services to ex-hospitalized mental patients. By helping these people to adjust better to community living, it is hoped that the need for rehospitalization will be reduced. Such efforts take many forms, including day hospital programs, rehabilitation and structured workshop services, outpatient treatment, halfway houses, and community support services. Halfway houses, for example, provide a structured living environment in the community to people who do not require more restrictive treatment settings. Halfway houses can serve both secondary and tertiary prevention purposes.

Glossary

Abnormal psychology. The branch of psychology that deals with the description, causes, and treatment of abnormal behavior patterns.

Abstinence syndrome. The characteristic cluster of withdrawal symptoms following the sudden reduction or abrupt cessation of use of a psychoactive substance to which a physiological dependence has developed.

Abstinence violation effect. The tendency in people who are trying to abstain from a substance, such as alcohol or cigarettes, to overreact to a slight lapse with feelings of guilt and a sense of resignation that may then trigger a full-blown relapse.

Acetylcholine. A type of neurotransmitter involved in the control of muscle contractions. Abbreviated *ACh*.

Acrophobia. Fear of heights.

Addison's disease. A disease caused by underactivity of the adrenal cortex.

Adjustment disorder. A maladaptive reaction to an identified stressor or stressors that occurs shortly following exposure to the stressor(s) and results in impaired functioning or signs of emotional distress that exceed what would normally be expected in the situation. The reaction may be resolved if the stressor is removed or the individual learns to adapt to it successfully.

Adrenalin. A hormone produced by the adrenal medulla that is involved in stimulating the sympathetic division of the autonomic nervous system. Also called *epinephrine*.

Adult antisocial behavior. Adult antisocial behavior that is not believed to result from a diagnosable mental disorder. Classified under a "V Code" by DSM–III–R, examples include the behavior of professional thieves, drug dealers, or racketeers.

Aerobic. Pertaining to exercises or activities, such as running or swimming, that condition the lungs and hearts by requiring sustained increases in the consumption of oxygen by the body.

Affect. Emotion or feeling state that is attached to objects, ideas, or life experiences.

Agnosia. A disturbance of sensory perception.

Agoraphobic. Pertaining to fear of open places.

AIDS dementia complex. A form of dementia that is believed to result from an infection of the brain caused by the AIDS virus.

Al-Anon. An organization sponsoring support groups for family members of alcoholics.

Alarm reaction. The first stage of the general adaptation syndrome following response to a stressor; it is characterized by heightened sympathetic activity.

Alcohol amnestic disorder. See *Korsakoff's syndrome*.

Alcoholism. Physiological dependence on alcohol that results in impaired personal, social, or physical functioning.

Alzheimer's disease. A progressive brain disease characterized by gradual loss of memory and intellectual functioning, personality changes, and eventual loss of ability to care for oneself.

Ambivalence. Holding conflicting feelings toward another person or goal, such as both loving and hating the same person.

Ambivalent. Pertaining to ambivalence, as in holding ambivalent attitudes toward a particular person.

Ambulatory. Able to walk about on one's own.

Amenorrhea. Absence of menstruation.

Amnestic syndrome. Disturbance of memory associated with inability to learn new material and recall past events.

Amotivational syndrome. A loss of ambition or motivation to achieve.

Amphetamine psychosis. A psychotic state induced by ingestion of amphetamines.

Amphetamines. Types of stimulants, such as Dexedrine and Benzedrine. Abuse can trigger an ampethamine psychosis that mimics acute episodes of schizophrenia.

Anaerobic exercises. Exercises not demanding sustained increase in consumption of oxygen, such as weight lifting.

Anal-expulsive. In psychodynamic theory, a personality type characterized by excessive self-expression, such as extreme sloppiness or messiness.

Anal fixations. In psychodynamic theory, attachment to objects and behaviors that characterize the anal stage.

Anal retentive. In psychodynamic theory, a personality type characterized by excessive needs for self-control, such as extreme neatness and punctuality.

Anal stage. The second stage of psychosexual development in Freud's theory, in which gratification is achieved through anal activities, such as by the elimination of bodily wastes.

Analgesia. A state of relief from pain without loss of consciousness.

Analgesic. A substance that produces analgesia, or relief from pain.

Analogue study. A method of research that involves the simulation of naturally occurring conditions in a controlled setting.

Analogues. Something that resembles something else in many respects.

Analytical psychology. Jung's psychodynamic theory, which emphasizes such concepts as the collective unconscious, the existence of archetypes, and the notion of the self as a unifying force of personality.

Anorexia nervosa. An eating disorder, primarily affecting young women, characterized by maintenance of an abnormally low body weight, distortions of body image, intense fears of gaining weight, and, in females, amenorrhea.

Antibodies. Substances produced by white blood cells that identify and destroy antigens.

Antidepressants. Types of drugs that act to relieve depression. Tricyclics and MAO-inhibitors are two major classes of antidepressants.

Antigens. A substance that triggers an immune-system response to it. (The contraction for *anti*body *gen*erator.)

Antisocial personality disorder. A type of personality disorder characterized by a chronic pattern of antisocial and irresponsible behavior. Also referred to as *psychopathy* or *sociopathy*.

Anxiety. An emotional state characterized by physiological arousal, unpleasant feelings of tension, and a sense of apprehension, foreboding, and dread about the future.

Anxiety disorder. A type of mental disorder in which anxiety is the prominent feature. Formerly called *neurosis*.

Aphasia. Impaired ability to understand or express oneself through speech.

Approach-approach conflict. A type of conflict involving two positive but mutually exclusive goals.

Approach-avoidance conflict. A type of conflict involving a goal that has both positive and negative features.

Archetypes. Jung's concept of primitive images or concepts that reside in the collective unconscious.

Arteriosclerosis. A disease involving the thickening and hardening of the arteries.

Assertiveness training. A set of techniques in behavior therapy, generally consisting of modeling, behavior rehearsal, and feedback that is intended to train clients to become more self-expressive and to stand up for their rights.

Associations. Relationships among thoughts. In thought disorder, there is a breakdown in the cohesiveness of associations, a disturbance which is referred to as "looseness of associations."

Asylums. Formerly, institutions that cared for the mentally ill. Also, a safe place or refuge.

Ataxia. Loss of muscle coordination.

Atherosclerosis. A disease process consisting of arteriosclerosis with the deposition of fatty substances along the walls of the arteries.

Attention-deficit hyperactivity disorder. A behavior disorder of childhood characterized by excessive motor activity and inability to maintain attention.

Attributional style. A personal style for explaining cause-and-effect relationships between events.

Aura. A warning sign or cluster of symptoms preceding the occurrence of a migraine headache or epileptic seizure.

Authentic. In the humanistic-existential model, a term describing choices and actions that reflect upon our true feelings and needs.

Autism. (1) Absorption in daydreaming and fantasy. (2) A disorder in childhood characterized by failure to relate to others, lack of speech, disturbed motor behaviors, intellectual impairment, and demands for sameness in the environment. (3) Also one of Bleuler's Four A's, describing one of the primary symptoms of schizophrenia.

Automatic thoughts. Thoughts that seem to just "pop" into one's mind. In Aaron Beck's theory, automatic thoughts that reflect cognitive distortions induce negative feelings like anxiety or depression.

Autonomic nervous system. The division of the peripheral nervous system that regulates the activities of glands and involuntary functions such as respiration, heartbeat, and digestion. Abbreviated *ANS*. Also see *sympathetic* and *parasympathetic* branches of the ANS.

Aversive conditioning. A behavior therapy technique in which a maladaptive response is paired with exposure to an aversive stimulus, such as electric shock or nausea, so that a conditioned aversion develops toward the stimuli associated with the maladaptive response.

Avoidance-avoidance conflict. A type of conflict involving two negative goals in which the avoidance of one goal requires the approach of the other.

Avoidant disorder of childhood or adolescence. A childhood behavior disorder characterized by excessive fear and avoidance of strangers.

Avoidant personality disorder. A type of personality disorder characterized by avoidance of social relationships due to fear of rejection.

Axon. The long, thin part of the neuron along which nervous impulses travel.

Barbiturates. Types of depressants that are sometimes used to relieve anxiety or induce sleep, but which are highly addictive.

Basal ganglia. Ganglia located between the thalamus and the cerebrum in the brain that are involved in processes controlling motor coordination.

Baseline. A period of time preceding the implementation of a treatment. Used to gather data regarding the rate of occurrence of the target behavior before treatment is introduced.

Behavior genetics. The study of the role of genetics in explaining behavior.

Behavior modification. The application of learning principles to effect behavior change in desired directions.

Behavioral rating scale. A method of behavioral assessment involving the use of a scale to record the frequency of occurrence of target behaviors.

Behavior therapy. The application of learning principles to modify problem behavior directly. Also see *behavior modification*.

Behavioral assessment. The approach to clinical assessment that focuses on the objective recording or description of the problem behavior rather than inferences about personality traits.

Behavioral interview. An approach to clinical interviewing that focuses on relating the problem behavior to antecedent stimuli and reinforcement consequences.

Behaviorism. The school of psychology that defines psychology as the study of observable or overt behavior; it focuses on investigating the relationships between stimuli and responses.

Behaviorist. One who adheres to the school of behaviorism.

Benzodiazepines. The class of minor tranquilizers that includes Valium and Librium.

Bereavement. The experience of suffering following the loss of a loved one.

Beriberi. A nutritional disorder caused by thiamine deficiency.

Biofeedback training. A method of feeding back to the individual information about bodily functions so that the person is able to gain better control over these functions. Abbreviated *BFT*.

Biological markers. Biological characteristics that identify people who have greater vulnerability to particular disorders.

Biological psychiatry. The movement within modern psychiatry that focuses on biological explanations and treatments of mental disorders.

Bipolar disorder. A disorder characterized by mood swings between states of extreme elation and severe depression. Formerly called *manic-depression.*

Bisexuals. People who are sexually aroused by members of both sexes.

Blind. In the experimental context, a state of being unaware of whether or not one has received a treatment.

Blocking. (1) A disruption of self-expression of threatening or emotionally laden material. (2) In schizophrenics, a condition of suddenly becoming silent with loss of memory for what they have just discussed.

Bondage. A form of sadomasochism involving the binding of the arms or legs of one of the partners during sexual activity.

Borderline personality disorder. A type of personality disorder characterized by abrupt shifts in mood, lack of coherent sense of self, and unpredictable, impulsive behavior.

Brain electrical activity mapping. A method of brain imaging involving the computer analysis of data from multiple electrodes placed on the scalp so as to reveal areas of the brain with relatively higher or lower levels of electrical activity.

Brief reactive psychosis. A psychotic episode of generally less than two weeks' duration that follows a particular stressful event.

Bulimia nervosa. An eating disorder characterized by a recurrent pattern of binge eating followed by self-induced purging and accompanied by persistent overconcern with body weight and shape.

Cardiovascular disorders. Diseases of the cardiovascular system, such as coronary heart disease, hypertension, and arteriosclerosis.

Case studies. Carefully sketched biographies that are generally constructed on the basis of clinical interviews, observations, psychological tests, and, in some cases, historical records.

Cases. In the context of abnormal psychology, individuals identified as having particular disorders or receiving treatment.

Castration anxiety. In psychodynamic theory, a young male's unconscious fear that he will be castrated as a form of punishment for having incestuous wishes for his mother.

Catastrophizing. The tendency to exaggerate or magnify the negative consequences of events; to "blow things out of proportion."

Catatonic type. The subtype of schizophrenia characterized by gross disturbances in motor activity, such as catatonic stupor.

Catecholamine hypothesis. The belief that decreased availability of norepinephrine produces depression, while increased levels produce mania.

Catecholamines. A group of chemically related substances that function as neurotransmitters in the brain (dopamine and norepinephrine) and as hormones (epinephrine and norepinephrine).

Catharsis. (1) The discharge of states of tension associated with repression of threatening impulses or material; (2) the free expression or purging of feelings. Also called *abreaction.*

Causal relationship. A relationship between two factors or events in which one is held to be a cause of the other; also called a *cause-and-effect* relationship.

Central nervous system. The brain and spinal cord.

Cerebellum. A part of the hindbrain involved in control of muscle coordination and balance.

Cerebral cortex. The wrinkled surface area of the cerebrum; often called "gray matter" because of the appearance produced by the high density of cell bodies.

Cerebrum. The large mass of the forebrain, consisting of two hemispheres.

Chemotherapy. The use of psychoactive drugs to treat abnormal behavior patterns.

Childhood schizophrenia. The development of a schizophrenic disorder in childhood; considered a relatively rare occurrence.

Choleric. Bad temper.

Chromosomes. The structures found in the nuclei of all the body's cells that carry the genetic elements, or genes.

Cirrhosis of the liver. A disease of the liver caused by chronic protein deficiency, often associated with prolonged alcohol abuse (because alcoholics drink to excess in place of eating regular meals).

Civil commitment. The legal process involved in placing an individual in a mental institution, even against his or her will. Also called *psychiatric commitment.*

Clanging. In schizophrenics, the tendency to string words together because they rhyme or sound alike.

Classical conditioning. In behavioral terms, a form of learning in which a previously neutral stimulus (the conditioned stimulus) comes to elicit a response (the conditioned response) that is similar to or the same as the response (the unconditioned response) usually elicited by a second stimulus (called the unconditioned stimulus), by being repeatedly paired with the second stimulus. Also called *Pavlovian conditioning.*

Claustrophobia. Fear of tight, small places.

Client-centered therapy. Another name for Carl Rogers' *person-centered therapy.*

Closed-ended questions. Questionnaire or test items that have a limited range of response options.

Cocaine. A stimulant derived from coca leaves. The hardened, smokable form of cocaine is called *crack.*

Coefficient alpha. A measure of internal consistency or reliability that represents the average intercorrelation among the items composing a particular scale or test.

Cognition. Mental processes such as sensation and perception, memory, intelligence, language, thought, and problem solving.

Cognitive-behavior therapy. A form of therapy characterized by the integration of cognitive and behavioral approaches to treatment. Also called *cognitive-behavior modification*.

Cognitive restructuring. A method of cognitive therapy that involves replacing irrational or self-defeating cognitions or self-statements with rational alternatives.

Cognitive-specificity hypothesis. In Aaron Beck's theory, the belief that different feeling states like depression and anxiety are linked to particular kinds of automatic thoughts.

Cognitive therapy. Aaron Beck's form of psychotherapy that focuses on how thought processes and belief systems lead to states of emotional distress and may be changed to relieve distress and foster adaptive behavior.

Cognitive triad of depression. In Aaron Beck's theory, the belief that depression derives from the adoption of a mental set or schema consisting of negative views of oneself, the environment, and the future.

Coitus interruptus. The practice in sexual intercourse of withdrawing the penis before ejaculation.

Collective unconscious. In Carl Jung's theory, the hypothesized storehouse of archetypes and racial memories.

Comatose. In a coma; a state of deep and prolonged unconsciousness.

Community psychology. The branch of psychology that focuses its efforts on making changes in social systems in the community in the interest of preventing and remedying maladaptive behavior patterns.

Competencies. In social-learning theory terms, a type of person variable involving the acquisition of knowledge and skills.

Competency to stand trial. The legal status of being able to comprehend the charges against oneself and having the ability to assist in one's own defense during a court proceeding.

Compulsion. A persistent and apparently irresistible urge to repeat a certain act or ritualistic behavior, such as compulsive hand-washing.

Compulsion to utter. In psychodynamic theory, the urge to express repressed material verbally.

Computerized axial tomography. The generation of a computer-enhanced image of the internal structures of the brain by means of passing a narrow X-ray beam through the head at different angles. Abbreviated *CAT scan*.

Concordance. Agreement.

Concrete operations. The stage of cognitive development in Jean Piaget's theory that corresponds to the development of logical thought processes involving the relationships among objects.

Concurrent validity. A type of test validity that is determined on the basis of the statistical relationship or correlation between the test and a criterion measure taken at the same point in time.

Concussion. A blow to, or jarring of, the head that results in momentary loss of consciousness or disruption of brain functioning.

Conditional positive regard. In Carl Rogers' theory, valuing other people on the basis of whether their behavior meets with your approval.

Conditioned response. (1) In classical conditioning, a learned or acquired response to a previously neutral stimulus. (2) A response to a conditioned stimulus. Abbreviated *CR*.

Conditioned stimulus. A previously neutral stimulus that comes to evoke a conditioned response following repeated pairings with a stimulus (unconditioned stimulus) that had already evoked that response. Abbreviated *CS*.

Conditions of worth. Standards by which one judges the worth or value of oneself or others.

Conduct disorder. A pattern of abnormal behavior in childhood characterized by disruptive, antisocial behavior.

Conflict. (1) A state of being pulled in different directions by opposing feelings or forces. (2) The feelings produced by being in a state of conflict.

Congruence. In Carl Rogers' theory, the fit between one's self-concept and one's thoughts, behaviors, and feelings. One of the principal characteristics of effective person-centered therapists.

Conscious. In psychodynamic theory, the part of the mind that corresponds to present awareness.

Construct validity. (1) The degree to which a test or instrument measures the hypothetical construct that it purports to measure. (2) In experiments, the degree to which treatment effects can be accounted for by the theoretical mechanisms or constructs represented by the independent variables.

Content validity. (1) The degree to which the content of a test or measure represents the content domain of the construct it purports to measure. (2) The degree to which the content of a test or measure covers a representative sample of the behaviors associated with the construct dimension or trait in question.

Continuous amnesia. A form of psychogenic amnesia in which the person loses the memory of all events occurring since the problem began.

Contrasted groups approach. A method of concurrent validity in which group membership is used as the criterion by which the validity of a test is measured. The ability of the test to differentiate between two or more comparison groups (for example, schizophrenics vs. normals) is taken as evidence of concurrent validity.

Control subjects. Subjects who do not receive the experimental treatment or manipulation.

Controlled social drinking. A controversial approach to treating problem drinkers in which the goal of treatment is the maintenance of controlled social drinking in moderate amounts, rather than total abstinence.

Contusion. Brain trauma caused by jarring the brain with sufficient force so that the brain is shifted and pressed against the skull, causing structural damage to the soft brain tissue.

Conversion disorder. A type of somatoform disorder characterized by loss or impairment of physical function in the absence of any organic causes that might account for the changes. Formerly called *hysteria* or *hysterical neurosis*.

Corpus callosum. The thick bundle of fibers connecting the two hemispheres of the brain.

Correlation. A relationship or association between two variables. A correlation between two variables may suggest, but does not prove, that a causal relationship exists between the two.

Correlation coefficient. A statistic that expresses the

strength and direction (whether positive or negative) of the relationship between two variables.

Cortical. Referring to the cortex or covering layer, as in the cerebral cortex or adrenal cortex.

Corticosteroids. Steroids manufactured by the adrenal cortex that are involved in regulating the metabolism of carbohydrates and that increase resistance to stress by stemming inflammation and allergic reactions. Also called *cortical steroids.*

Countertransference. In psychoanalysis, the transfer onto the client of feelings that the analyst holds toward other persons in his or her own life.

Co-varies. A verb form of *co-variation,* referring to the association between two variables such that when one changes the other also changes.

Covert sensitization. A technique of aversive conditioning in which the client associates the undesired response or behavior with imaginal aversive stimuli.

Creative self. In Alfred Adler's theory, the self-aware part of the personality that strives to achieve its potential.

Cretinism. A disorder caused by thyroid deficiency in childhood that is characterized by stunted growth and mental retardation.

Criterion validity. The degree to which a test or instrument correlates with an independent, external criterion (standard) representing the construct or trait that the test or instrument is intended to measure. The two general types of criterion validity are concurrent validity and predictive validity.

Cross-fostering study. A method of determining heritability of a trait or disorder by examining differences in prevalence among adoptees reared by either adoptive parents or biological parents who possessed the trait or disorder in question. Evidence that the disorder followed biological, rather than adoptive, parentage favors the heritability of the trait or disorder.

Cultural-familial retardation. A milder form of mental retardation that is believed to result, or at least be influenced by, impoverishment in the child's home environment.

Cushing's syndrome. A relatively rare disease primarily affecting young women, it is caused by overactivity of the adrenal cortex and involves both physical and psychological changes.

Cyclothymia. A mood disorder characterized by a chronic pattern of mild mood swings between depression and mania that are not of sufficient severity to be classified as bipolar disorder.

Daily hassles. The occurrence of various stressful experiences that occur from day to day and that may be harmful over the long run to a person's general well-being.

Defense mechanisms. In psychodynamic theory, the reality-distorting strategies used by the ego to shield itself from conscious awareness of anxiety-evoking or troubling thoughts, emotions, etc.

Deinstitutionalization. The practice of discharging large numbers of hospitalized mental patients to the community and of reducing the need for new admissions through the development of alternative treatment approaches such as halfway houses and crisis intervention services. The practice of deinstitutionalization has been criticized for failing to provide discharged mental patients with continuing care and adequate housing.

Delirium. A state of mental confusion, disorientation, and extreme difficulty in focusing one's attention.

Delirium tremens. A withdrawal syndrome that often occurs following a sudden decrease or cessation of drinking in chronic alcoholics; characterized by extreme restlessness, sweating, disorientation, and hallucinations. Abbreviated *DT's.*

Delta-9-tetrahydrocannabinol. The major active ingredient in marijuana. Abbreviated *THC.*

Delusional (paranoid) disorder. A type of psychosis characterized by the presence of persistent delusions, often of a paranoid nature, that do not have the bizarre quality of the type often found in paranoid schizophrenia. Other than the delusion itself, the person's behavior may appear entirely normal.

Delusions. Firmly held but false beliefs that persist despite clear evidence that the beliefs have no basis in reality.

Dementia. A state of deterioration of mental functioning, involving impairment of memory, thinking, judgment, use of language, and ability to carry through purposeful movements, and eventually resulting in personality changes.

Dementia praecox. The term given by Emil Kraepelin to the disorder we now call schizophrenia.

Demonological model. Earlier superstitious model that attempted to explain abnormal behaviors on the basis of supernatural elements, such as possession by evil forces or demons.

Dendrites. The rootlike structures at the end of the neuron that receive nerve impulses from other neurons.

Dependent personality disorder. A type of personality disorder characterized by difficulties making independent decisions and by overly dependent behaviors.

Dependent variable. A measure of outcome in a scientific study that is assumed to be dependent on the effects of the independent variable.

Depersonalization. Feelings of unreality or detachment from one's self or one's body, as if one were a robot or functioning on automatic pilot, or observing oneself from outside.

Depersonalization disorder. A disorder characterized by persistent or recurrent episodes of depersonalization.

Depressant. A drug that lowers the level of activity of the central nervous system.

Derealization. Loss of the sense of reality of one's surroundings, experienced in terms of strange changes in one's environment (for example, people or objects changing size or shape) or in the sense of the passage of time.

Description. In science, the clear representation of observations without interpretation or drawing conclusions as to their nature or meaning. Description can be contrasted with *inference,* which is the process of drawing conclusions based on observations.

Desperation phase. The latter stage of pathological gambling in which the gambler hits "rock bottom."

Determinants. Factors believed to determine responses to the Rorschach inkblot test; these include various properties of the blot such as form, shading, texture, or color, and features of the percept that the respondent imposes upon, or reads into, the blot, such as movement.

Detoxification. The process of ridding the system of alcohol or drugs under supervised conditions in which withdrawal symptoms can be monitored.

Deviation IQ. An intelligence quotient that is derived by determining the deviation between the individual's score and the norm (mean).

Dialogue. A technique of Gestalt therapy in which one enacts a confrontation between two opposing parts of one's personality, such as between one's "top dog" and "underdog."

Diathesis–stress. A model of abnormal behavior that posits that abnormal behavior patterns, such as schizophrenia, involve the interaction of genetic and environmental influences. In this model, a genetic predisposition, or diathesis, increases the individual's vulnerability to develop the disorder in response to stressful life circumstances.

Disorganized type. The subtype of schizophrenia that is characterized by disorganized behavior, bizarre delusions, and vivid hallucinations. Formerly called *hebephrenic schizophrenia.*

Disorientation. A state of mental confusion or lack of awareness with respect to time, place, or the identity of oneself or others.

Displacement. In psychodynamic theory, a type of defense mechanism that involves the transferring of impulses toward threatening or unacceptable objects onto more acceptable or safer objects.

Displacing. The verb form of *displacement.*

Disruptive behavior disorders. A category of behavior disorders in childhood involving socially disruptive behavior patterns, including attention-deficit hyperactivity disorder, conduct disorder, and oppositional defiant disorder.

Dissociative disorder. A category of mental disorders involving sudden changes in consciousness or self-identity, including psychogenic amnesia, psychogenic fugue, and multiple personality.

Distinct heterogeneity model. A model of genetic transmission of schizophrenia that proposes that schizophrenia represents a number of different disorders, each having its own distinct causes that may involve genetic defects traceable to particular genes or environmental factors.

Dizygotic twins. Twins who develop from separate fertilized eggs. Also called *fraternal twins.* Abbreviated *DZ twins.* Often contrasted with *monozygotic twins* in studies of heritability of particular traits or disorders.

Dopamine. A type of neurotransmitter of the catecholamine class that is involved in Parkinson's disease and is posited to play a role in schizophrenia (see *dopamine theory*).

Dopamine theory. The biochemical theory of schizophrenia that proposes that schizophrenia involves an overreactivity of dopamine receptors in the brain.

Double-bind communications. A pattern of communication involving the transmission of contradictory or mixed messages without acknowledgment of the inherent conflict; posited by some theorists to play a role in the development of schizophrenia.

Double depression. Persons diagnosed with both major depression and dysthymia.

Down syndrome. A condition caused by a chromosomal abnormality; characterized by mental retardation and various physical abnormalities. Formerly called *Down's syndrome* or *mongolism.*

Drive for superiority. In Adler's theory, a term describing the desire to compensate for feelings of inferiority.

Duty to warn. An obligation imposed on therapists to warn third parties of threats made against them by the therapists' clients. The *Tarasoff* case established the legal basis for the duty-to-warn obligation.

Dyslexia. A type of learning disability characterized by impaired reading ability.

Dyspareunia. Persistent or recurrent pain experienced during or following sexual intercourse.

Dysthymia. A mild but chronic type of depressive disorder.

Eclectic. The adoption of principles or techniques from various systems or theories.

Ego. In psychodynamic theory, the psychic structure corresponding to the concept of "self." The ego is governed by the reality principle and is responsible for finding socially acceptable outlets for the urgings of the id. The ego is characterized by the capacity to tolerate frustration and delay gratification.

Ego analyst. Psychodynamically-oriented therapists who are influenced by ego psychology.

Ego-dystonic. Behavior or feelings perceived to be foreign or alien to one's self-identity.

Ego-dystonic homosexual. A homosexual whose homosexuality is perceived as inconsistent with his or her self-concept and therefore becomes a source of personal distress.

Ego ideal. In Freud's view, the configuration of higher social values and moral ideals embodied in the superego.

Ego identity. In Erik Erikson's view, the sense of personal identity; the achievement of a firm sense of who one is and what one stands for.

Ego psychology. The approach of modern psychodynamic theorists that posits that the ego has energy and strivings of its own apart from the id. Ego psychologists focus more on the conscious strivings of the ego than on the hypothesized unconscious functioning of the id.

Ego syntonic. Behavior or feelings perceived as natural parts of the self.

Electra complex. In psychodynamic theory, the term sometimes used to describe the conflict in young females during the phallic stage of development involving their longings for their fathers and their resentment of their mothers.

Electroconvulsive therapy. The induction of a convulsive seizure by means of passing an electric current through the head; used primarily in the treatment of severe depression. Abbreviated *ECT.*

Electrodermal response. Changes in the electrical conductivity of the skin following exposure to a stimulus.

Electroencephalogram. A record of the electrical activity of the brain (brain waves). Abbreviated *EEG.*

Electrolytes. Nonmetallic substances that serve as electrical conductors. In the body, electrolytes, such as dissolved salt, play vital roles in cell functioning, such as the maintenance of appropriate fluid balance in cells.

Electromyograph. An instrument for measuring muscle

tension that is often used in biofeedback training. Abbreviated *EMG*.

Electromyographic (EMG). Relating to the use of the electromyograph.

Emotion-focused coping. A style of coping with stress that involves attempts to minimize emotional responsiveness rather than deal with the source of stress directly (for example, the use of denial to avoid thinking about the stress, or the use of tranquilizers to quell feelings of anxiety).

Empathetic understanding. In Carl Rogers' theory, the ability to understand a client's experiences and feelings from the client's frame of reference. It is considered one of the principal characteristics of effective person-centered therapists.

Encephalitis. Inflammation of the brain.

Encoding. The stage of information processing that involves the modification of information for placement in memory.

Encounter group. A specialized form of group therapy or group process that focuses on increased self-awareness in a setting that encourages open expression of feelings.

Endocrine system. The system of ductless glands in the body that secrete hormones directly into the bloodstream.

Endogenous. Meaning "from within"; often used to describe abnormal behavior patterns that appear to arise from biochemical processes.

Endorphins. Natural substances that function as neurotransmitters in the brain and are similar in their effects to morphine.

Epidemiological method. A method of research involved in tracking the rates of occurrence of particular disorders among different groups.

Epilepsy. Temporary, sudden changes in the electrical activity of the brain, resulting in convulsive seizures or changes in the level of consciousness or motor activity.

Erogenous zone. A part of the body that is sensitive to sexual stimulation.

Eros. Freud's concept of the basic life instinct, which seeks to preserve and perpetuate life.

Erotomania. A form of delusional (paranoid) disorder characterized by delusional beliefs that one is loved by someone of high social status, even though one may have only a passing or even a nonexistent relationship with the alleged lover. Also called the *love delusion*.

Estrogen. A female sex hormone involved in promoting growth of female sexual characteristics and regulating the menstrual cycle.

Etiological. Relating to the cause of something, or the study of causes.

Exhaustion stage. The third stage of the general adaptation syndrome that is characterized by a lowering of resistance, increased parasympathetic activity, and possible physical deterioration.

Exhibitionism. A type of paraphilia apparently occurring only in males, in which the man experiences persistent and recurrent sexual urges and sexually arousing fantasies involving the exposure of his genitals to a stranger. This individual has either acted upon these urges or feels strongly distressed by them.

Exorcism. A ritual intended to expel demons or evil spirits from a person believed to be possessed.

Expectancies. In social-learning theory, a person variable describing the personal predictions that people make about the outcomes of particular behaviors—"if-then" statements.

Experimental method. A scientific method that aims to discover cause-and-effect relationships by means of manipulating the independent variable(s) and observing their effect(s) on the dependent variable(s).

Experimental subject. (1) In an experiment, a subject receiving a treatment or intervention, in contrast to a *control subject*. (2) More generally, one who participates in an experiment.

External eater. A person who eats primarily in response to external stimuli, such as the smell or aroma of food, the time of day, or the presence of others who are eating. Contrasted with *internal eater*.

External factors. In the reformulated helplessness theory, a type of attribution involving the belief that the cause of an event involved factors outside the self. Contrasted with *internal factors*.

External validity. A type of experimental validity involving the degree to which the experimental results can be generalized to other settings and populations.

Extinguish. (1) Weaken a conditioned response by presenting the conditioned stimulus in the absence of the unconditioned stimulus. (2) Weaken a previously reinforced response by withholding or withdrawing reinforcement.

Extraversion. A personality trait describing someone whose interests and attention are directed to people and things outside the self. Extraverted people tend to be sociable, outgoing, and self-expressive. Opposite of *introversion*.

Face validity. An aspect of content validity, this represents the degree to which the content of a test or measure bears an apparent relationship to the constructs or traits it is purported to measure.

Factitious disorder. A type of mental disorder characterized by the intentional fabrication of psychological or physical symptoms for no apparent gain.

Factor analysis. A statistical technique for determining relationships that exist among items, such as those that appear on psychological tests or personality scales.

False negatives. An appraisal that people are free of a particular disorder when in fact they are not.

Family therapy. A form of therapy in which the family unit is treated as the client.

Fat cells. Cells that store fat. Also called *adipose tissue*.

Fear. An unpleasant, negative emotion characterized by the perception of a specific threat, sympathetic nervous system activity, and tendencies to avoid the feared object.

Fear-stimulus hierarchy. A ordered series of increasingly more fearful stimuli. Used in the behavioral techniques of *systematic desensitization* and *gradual exposure*.

Feedback. Information relating to one's own behavior.

Female sexual arousal disorder. A type of sexual dysfunction in women involving difficulties becoming sexually aroused, as defined by a lack of vaginal lubrication or failure to maintain sufficient lubrication to complete the sexual act, or lack of sexual excitement or pleasure during sexual activity.

Fetal alcohol syndrome. A cluster of symptoms appearing in children whose mothers drank alcohol during certain

Myocardial infarction. A breakdown of the tissue of the heart due to an obstruction of the blood vessels that supply blood to the affected area—a heart attack.

Naloxone. A drug that prevents or reverses the effects of heroin and other opioids.

Narcissistic personality disorder. A type of personality disorder characterized by the adoption of an inflated self-image, demands for constant attention and admiration, and extreme sensitivity to criticism, among other features.

Narcotics. Drugs, such as opiates, that are used for pain relief and treatment of insomnia, but which have strong addictive potential.

Naturalistic-observation method. A method of scientific research in which the behavior of subjects is carefully and unobtrusively observed and measured in their natural environments.

Negative correlation. A statistical relationship between two variables such that increases in one variable are associated with decreases in the other.

Negative reinforcer. A reinforcer whose removal increases the frequency of an operant behavior. Anxiety, pain, and some forms of social disapproval (for example, nagging) often function as negative reinforcers in the sense that their removal tends to increase the rate of the immediately preceding behavior. Contrast with *positive reinforcer.*

Negative symptoms. The deficits or behavioral deficiencies associated with schizophrenia, such as social skills deficits, social withdrawal, flattened affect, poverty of speech and thought, psychomotor retardation, and failure to experience pleasure in pleasant activities.

Neo-Freudians. A term used to describe the "second generation" of theorists who followed in the Freudian tradition. On the whole, neo-Freudians (such as Jung, Adler, Horney, Sullivan) placed greater emphasis on the importance of cultural and social influences on behavior and lesser importance on sexual impulses and the functioning of the id.

Neologisms. A type of disturbed thinking associated with schizophrenia involving the coining of new words.

Neuroleptics. A group of antipsychotic drugs used in the treatment of schizophrenia; these include the phenothiazines (Thorazine, Mellaril, etc.) and others like Haldol.

Neurons. Nerve cells.

Neuropsychological. Having to do with the relationship between the brain and behavior.

Neuropsychologist. (1) A psychologist specializing in the study of relationships between the brain and behavior. (2) A psychologist specializing in the measurement of intellectual and behavioral deficits associated with brain damage.

Neurosis or Neuroses. The type or types, respectively, of nonpsychotic behavioral disturbances characterized chiefly by the use of defensive behaviors to control anxiety, in which the person is generally able to function but is impaired in some aspect(s) of functioning. The term "neurosis" is no longer used as a basis of classification in the DSM system.

Neurotic anxiety. In psychodynamic theory, the feelings of anxiety that stem from the unconscious perception of threat that unacceptable impulses may rise to the level of consciousness or become expressed in overt behavior.

Neuroticism. A trait describing a general neurotic quality involving such characteristics as anxious, worrisome behavior, apprehension about the future, and avoidance behavior.

Neurotransmitter. A chemical substance that serves as a type of messenger by transmitting neural impulses from one neuron to another.

Nicotine. A stimulant found principally in tobacco.

Nonspecific factors. Characteristics that are not specific to any one form of psychotherapy, but tend to be shared in common among the psychotherapies, such as the attention a client receives from a therapist and the therapist's encouragement of the client's sense of hope and positive expectancies.

Norepinephrine. A type of neurotransmitter of the catecholamine class.

Nuclear magnetic resonance. A means of displaying an image of the brain on the basis of measuring the signals that brain structures emit when the head is surrounded by a strong magnetic field. Also called *magnetic resonance imaging (MRI).*

Obesity. Excessive body weight or plumpness.

Object-relations. An individual's relationships to the internalized objects or representations of other people's personalities that have been introjected within the individual's ego structure. See *object-relations theory.*

Object-relations theory. In psychodynamic theory, the viewpoint that focuses on the influences of the introjected objects within the person's ego structure representing the personalities of parents and other figures of strong attachment.

Objective tests. Tests that allow a limited, specified range of response options or answers so that they can be scored objectively.

Obsession. A recurring or nagging thought or image that seems beyond the individual's ability to control.

Obsessive-compulsive disorder. A type of anxiety disorder characterized by the occurrence of obsessional thoughts and/or compulsions to perform certain actions.

Obsessive-compulsive personality disorder. A type of personality disorder characterized by rigid ways of relating to others, perfectionistic tendencies, lack of spontaneity, and excessive attention to details.

Oedipus complex. In psychodynamic theory, the conflict that occurs during the phallic stage of development in which the son incestuously desires his mother and perceives his father as a rival for his mother's love and attention.

Open-ended question. A type of question that provides an unlimited range of response options.

Operant conditioning. A form of learning in which the organism acquires new behaviors on the basis of reinforcement.

Opiate. A type of depressant drug with strong addictive properties that is derived from the opium poppy and provides relief from pain and feelings of euphoria.

Opioid. A natural or synthetic (artificial) substance with opiate-like properties and effects.

Oppositional defiant disorder. A disorder in childhood or adolescence characterized by excessive oppositionality or tendencies to refuse requests from parents and others.

Optimal arousal. The level of arousal corresponding to the optimum level of arousal. See *optimum level of arousal.*

Optimum level of arousal. The level of arousal associated with peak performance and maximum feelings of well-being.

Oral stage. In psychodynamic theory, the first of Freud's stages of psychosexual development, during which pleasure is primarily sought through such oral activities as sucking and biting.

Organic mental disorders. An organic mental syndrome in which the organic cause can be specified or presumed.

Organic mental syndromes. A cluster of psychological and behavioral features arising from an organic defect of unspecified origin.

Orienting response. An unlearned pattern of responses to an incoming stimulus, including pupil dilation, particular brain wave patterns associated with states of attention, and changes in the electrical conductivity of the skin (GSR).

Osteoporosis. A physical disorder caused by calcium deficiency that is characterized by extreme brittleness of the bones.

Overanxious disorder. A disorder in childhood or adolescence characterized by excessive anxiety or worrisome behavior.

Panic disorder. A type of anxiety disorder characterized by the occurrence of episodes or attacks of severe panic.

Paranoid. Relating to irrational suspicions.

Paranoid personality disorder. A type of personality disorder characterized by persistent suspiciousness of the motives of others, but not to the point of holding clear-cut delusions.

Paranoid type. A subtype of schizophrenia characterized by hallucinations and systematized delusions, commonly involving themes of persecution.

Paraphilias. Sexual deviations or types of sexual disorders in which the person experiences recurrent sexual urges and sexually arousing fantasies involving nonhuman objects (such as articles of clothing), inappropriate or nonconsenting partners (for example, children), or situations producing humiliation or pain to oneself or one's partner. The paraphiliac has either acted upon such urges or is strongly distressed by them.

Parasympathetic. Relating to the activity of the parasympathetic branch of the autonomic nervous system.

Parkinson's disease. A progressive disease of the basal ganglia characterized by muscle tremor and shakiness, rigidity, difficulty walking, poor control over fine body movements, lack of facial muscle tonus, and cognitive impairment in some cases, especially in later stages of the disorder.

Passive-aggressive personality disorder. A type of personality disorder involving a recurrent pattern in which hostility is expressed through passive or indirect means, such as by intentionally delaying the completion of work.

Pathogens. An organism such as a bacterium or virus that can cause disease.

Pathological gambling. A type of impulse disorder involving a compulsive pattern of gambling characterized by impaired control over the urge to gamble.

Pathological gambler. A person who gambles habitually despite consistent losses. A compulsive gambler.

Peak experience. In humanistic theory, a brief moment of rapture stemming from the realization that one is on the path toward self-actualization.

Pellagra. A disease caused by deficiency of niacin (vitamin B) characterized by skin eruptions and various behavioral features.

Penile strain gauge. A device for measuring the size of penile erection.

Performance anxiety. Fear relating to the threat of failing to perform adequately.

Peripheral nervous system. That part of the nervous system consisting of the somatic nervous system and the autonomic nervous system.

Perseveration. The persistent repetition of the same thought or response.

Person-centered therapy. Carl Rogers' method of psychotherapy, emphasizing the establishment of a warm, accepting therapeutic relationship that frees clients to engage in a process of self-exploration and self-acceptance.

Person-variables. In social-learning theory, the influences on behavior of characteristics relating to the person, including encoding strategies, competencies, expectancies, subjective values, and self-regulatory systems and plans.

Personal constructs. In George Kelly's theory, the personal dimensions of judgment by which individuals evaluate events, such as strong-weak, good-bad, etc.

Personality. The composite attributes that distinguish the person's individuality and manner of adapting to life's demands.

Personality disorders. Types of abnormal behavior patterns involving excessively rigid patterns of behaviors, or ways of relating to others, that ultimately become self-defeating because their rigidity prevents adjustment to external demands.

Pervasive developmental disorder. Gross impairment in the development of a broad array of skills relating to social, cognitive, and language functioning. Autistic disorder is the only recognized subtype in the present DSM system.

Phallic stage. In psychodynamic theory, Freud's third stage of psychosexual development, characterized by sexual interest focused on the phallic region and the development of incestuous desires for the parent of the opposite sex and rivalry with the parent of the same sex (the Oedipus complex).

Phencyclidine. A psychedelic drug, also known as "angel dust."

Phenothiazines. A group of antipsychotic drugs or "major tranquilizers" used in the treatment of schizophrenia.

Phenotypes. The representations of the total arrays of traits, as influenced by environment and heredity.

Phenylketonuria. A genetic disorder that prevents the metabolization of phenylpyruvic acid, leading to mental retardation. Abbreviated *PKU.*

Phlegmatic. Slow and stolid.

Phobia. An excessive, irrational fear that is out of proportion to the degree of actual danger.

Phrenologists. Practitioners of the study of the bumps on a person's head as indications of the individual's underlying traits or characteristics.

Pick's disease. A form of dementia, similar in its features to Alzheimer's disease, but characterized by the presence of specific abnormalities (Pick's bodies) in nerve cells and the absence of the neurofibrillary tangles and placques found in Alzheimer's disease.

Placebo. An inert medication or form of bogus treatment that is intended to control for the effects of expectancies. Sometimes referred to as a "sugar pill."

Play therapy. A form of psychodynamic therapy with children in which play activities and objects are used as a means of helping youngsters symbolically enact family conflicts or express underlying feelings or personal problems.

Pleasure principle. In psychodynamic theory, the governing principle of the id, involving the demands for immediate gratification of instinctive needs.

Polygenic. Traits or characteristics that are determined by more than one gene.

Polymorphously perverse. In psychodynamic theory, the belief that humans are born with the capacity of achieving sexual gratification through various ways, such as heterosexual, homosexual, and autoerotic (pleasure from one's body organs) activities.

Pons. A brain structure, located in the hindbrain, which is involved in respiration.

Population. A total grouping of people, other organisms, or events.

Pornography. Portrayals of explicit sexual activity intended to arouse the observer sexually.

Positive correlation. A statistical relationship between two variables such that increases in one variable are associated with increases in the other.

Positive reinforcer. Types of reinforcers that increase the frequency of behavior when they are presented. Food and social approval are generally, but not always, positive reinforcers. Contrast with *negative reinforcer*.

Positive symptoms. The more flagrant features of schizophrenia associated with behavioral excesses, such as hallucinations, delusions, bizarre behavior, and thought disorder.

Positron-emission tomography. A brain-imaging technique in which a computer-generated image of the neural activity of regions of the brain is formed by tracing the amounts of glucose used in the various regions. Abbreviated *PET scan*.

Possession. A type of superstitious belief in which abnormal behavior is taken as a sign that the individual has become possessed by demons or the Devil.

Postpartum depression. Persistent and severe mood changes that occur following childbirth.

Postpartum psychosis. A psychotic condition that occurs following childbirth.

Post-traumatic stress disorder. A type of disorder involving impaired functioning following exposure to a traumatic experience, such as combat, physical assault or rape, natural or technological disasters, etc., in which the person experiences such problems as reliving or reexperiencing the trauma, intense fear, avoidance of event-related stimuli, generalized "numbing" of emotional responsiveness, and heightened autonomic arousal.

Preconscious. In psychodynamic theory, the part of the mind that contains material that lies outside of present awareness but which can be brought into awareness by focusing attention. See also *conscious* and *unconscious*.

Predictive validity. The degree to which a test response or score is predictive of some criterion behavior (such as school performance) in the future.

Prefrontal lobotomy. A form of psychosurgery in which certain neural pathways in the brain are severed in the attempt to control disturbed behavior. The operation has been essentially eliminated because of serious side effects and the introduction of other therapeutic means to control agitated or disruptive behavior, such as the use of phenothiazines.

Pregenital. In psychodynamic theory, characteristics typical of stages of psychosexual development that precede the genital stage.

Premature ejaculation. A type of sexual dysfunction involving a persistent or recurrent pattern of ejaculation occurring during sexual activity at a point before the male desires it.

Premenstrual syndrome (PMS). Symptoms that many women experience before menstruation. These may include feelings of irritability, tension, depressed mood, and fatigue.

Prepared conditioning. The belief that humans are genetically prepared to acquire fear responses to certain classes of stimuli, such as fears of large animals, snakes, heights, or even strangers. While the development of such phobias may have had survival value to our human ancestors, such behavior patterns may be less functional today.

Presenile dementias. Dementias that begin at age 65 or earlier.

Presenting problem. The complaint that prompts initial contact with a helping professional.

Pressured speech. An outpouring of speech in which words seem to surge urgently for expression, as in a manic state.

Primary gains. In psychodynamic theory, the relief from anxiety obtained through the development of a neurotic symptom.

Primary prevention. Efforts placed on preventing the development of psychological or medical problems before they start.

Primary process thinking. In psychodynamic theory, the mental process in infancy by which the id seeks gratification of primitive impulses by means of imaging that it possesses what it desires. Thinking that is illogical, magical, and fails to discriminate between reality and fantasy.

Primary reinforcers. Natural reinforcers or stimuli that have reinforcement value without learning. Water, food, warmth, and relief from pain are examples of primary reinforcers. Contrast with *secondary reinforcer*.

Primary sex characteristics. The distinguishing characteristics between the sexes that are directly involved in reproduction, such as the sex organs. Contrast with *secondary sex characteristics*.

Private self-consciousness. The cognitive process by which individuals take note of their own behavior, even those behaviors unobserved by others.

Problem-focused coping. A form of coping with stress characterized by efforts to directly confront the source of the stress.

Problem-solving therapy. A form of therapy focusing on helping people develop more effective problem-solving skills.

Process schizophrenia. A type of schizophrenia characterized by gradual onset, poor premorbid functioning, and poor outcomes. Contrast with *reactive schizophrenia.*

Prodromal phase. (1) A stage in which the early features or signs of a disorder become apparent. (2) In schizophrenia, the period of decline in functioning that precedes the development of the first acute psychotic episode.

Progesterone. A female sex hormone involved in promoting the growth and development of the sex organs and helping to maintain pregnancy.

Prognosis. A prediction of the probable course or outcome of a disorder.

Projection. In psychodynamic theory, a defense mechanism in which one's own impulses are attributed to another person.

Projective test. A psychological test that presents ambiguous or vague stimuli onto which the examinee is believed to project his or her own personality and unconscious motives in making a response. The Rorschach and TAT (Thematic Apperception Test) are examples of projective tests.

Prophylactive. Relating to a device, drug, or remedy designed to preserve health or prevent disease.

Prostaglandins. Chemical substances produced in the body from fatty acids that are involved in such processes as transmission of pain messages to the brain, inflammation, and menstrual cramping.

Psychedelic. Relating to the experience of altered sensory perceptions or expansion of consciousness, often in the form of hallucinations.

Psychiatric commitment. See *civil commitment.*

Psychiatrist. A physician who specializes in the diagnosis and treatment of emotional disorders.

Psychic. (1) Relating to mental phenomena. (2) A person who is sensitive to supernatural forces.

Psychic determinism. The belief that emotions and behavior are caused by the interplay of internal mental processes.

Psychoactive. Describing chemical substances or drugs that have psychological effects.

Psychoanalysis. Both the theoretical model and method of psychotherapy developed by Sigmund Freud.

Psychoanalytic theory. The theoretical model developed by Freud. Also called *psychoanalysis.*

Psychodrama. The method of group therapy developed by Moreno in which people express emotional responses and enact conflicts with significant others in their lives through dramatized role-enactments.

Psychodynamic model. The theoretical model of Freud and his followers in which behavior is viewed as the product of clashing forces within the personality.

Psychogenic amnesia. A type of dissociative disorder in which a person experiences memory losses in the absence of any identifiable organic cause. But general knowledge and skills are usually retained.

Psychogenic fugue. A type of dissociative disorder in which one suddenly flees from one's life situation, travels to a new location, assumes a new identity, and has amnesia for past experiences. The person usually retains skills and other abilities and may appear to others in the new environment to be leading a normal life.

Psychological hardiness. A cluster of stress-buffering traits characterized by commitment, challenge, and control.

Psychologist. A person with advanced graduate training (usually a Ph.D. or Psy.D. degree) in psychology. A clinical psychologist is a type of psychologist who specializes in the assessment and treatment of emotional disorders.

Psychometric approach. A method of psychological assessment that seeks to use psychological tests to identify and measure the reasonably stable traits in an individual's personality that are believed largely to determine the person's behavior.

Psychomotor retardation. A general slowing down of motor behavior and psychological functioning.

Psychoneuroimmunology. The field of scientific investigation that studies relationships between psychological factors, such as coping styles, attitudes, and behavior patterns, and immunological functioning.

Psychopharmacology. The field of study that examines the effects of drugs on behavior and psychological functioning and that explores the use of psychoactive drugs in the treatment of emotional disorders.

Psychoses. Disorders in which people show impaired ability to interpret reality and difficulties in meeting the demands of daily life. Schizophrenia is a prominent example of a psychotic disorder.

Psychosexual. Descriptive of the stages of human development in Freud's theory in which sexual energy (libido) becomes expressed through different erogenous zones of the body during different developmental stages.

Psychosocial. Relating to interpersonal relationships and social interactions that influence behavior and development.

Psychosocial development. Erikson's theory of personality development that extends through multiple stages of development from infancy through old age.

Psychotherapy. A method of treatment involving a systematic interaction between a therapist and a client that uses psychological principles to bear on influencing the client's thoughts, feelings, or behaviors in order to help that client overcome abnormal behavior or adjust to problems in living.

Psychotic. Relating to psychosis.

Psychotropic. See *psychotropic drugs.*

Psychotropic drugs. Drugs that are used in the treatment of emotional disorders whose main effects are psychological or behavioral.

Punishments. Unpleasant stimuli that suppress the frequency of the behaviors they follow.

Quasi-experiments. A method of research that is "similar to" the experimental method, except that experimental and control subjects are not assigned to their respective groups by random assignment. Hence, a selection factor may operate to distort results. See *selection factor.*

Random sample. A sample that is drawn in such a way that every member of a population has an equal probability of being selected.

Rape trauma syndrome. A cluster of symptoms that victims often experience in the aftermath of rape.

Rapid flight of ideas. A characteristic of manic behavior involving rapid speech and changes of topics.

Rapid smoking. A method of aversive conditioning in which cigarettes are inhaled at a much faster than usual rate, making smoking an aversive experience.

Rapport. In psychotherapy, the interpersonal relationship between a therapist and a client; characterized by harmony, trust, and cooperation.

Rational-emotive therapy. Albert Ellis' method of therapy, which focuses on helping clients challenge and correct irrational beliefs that are believed to produce emotional and behavioral difficulties.

Rationalization. In psychodynamic theory, a type of defense mechanism involving a process of self-deception in the form of finding justifications for unacceptable impulses, ideas, or behaviors.

Reactive schizophrenia. A type of schizophrenia characterized by relatively abrupt onset that is believed to be precipitated by stressful or traumatic events. Contrast with *process schizophrenia.*

Reality anxiety. The concept in psychodynamic theory relating to reality-based fear.

Reality principle. In psychodynamic theory, the governing principle of the ego that involves consideration of what is socially acceptable and practical in gratifying needs.

Reality testing. The ability to perceive the world accurately and to distinguish reality from fantasy.

Rebound anxiety. The occurrence of strong anxiety following withdrawal from a tranquilizer.

Receptor site. A part of a dendrite on the receiving neuron that is structured to receive a neurotransmitter.

Rehearsal. In behavior therapy, a practice opportunity by which a person enacts a desired response and receives feedback from others.

Reinforcement. A stimulus that increases the frequency of the response that it follows. See *positive* and *negative,* and *primary* and *secondary* reinforcers.

Relapse. A recurrence of a problem behavior or disorder.

Relapse-prevention training. A cognitive-behavioral technique used in the treatment of addictive behaviors and involving the use of behavioral and cognitive strategies to resist temptations and prevent lapses from becoming relapses.

Relaxation training. A technique for acquiring skills of self-relaxation, such as progressive muscle relaxation.

Reliability. In psychological assessment, the consistency of a measurement instrument, such as a psychological test or rating scale. Various ways exist to measure reliability, such as test-retest reliability, internal consistency, and inter-rater reliability. Also see *validity.*

Reliable. Relating to tests or measurement instruments that are consistent.

Repression. In psychodynamic theory, a type of defense mechanism involving the ejection from awareness of anxiety-provoking ideas, images, or impulses, without the conscious awareness that one has done so.

Residual phase. In schizophrenia, the phase of the disorder that follows an acute phase, characterized by a return to a level of functioning that was typical of the prodromal phase.

Resistance. During psychoanalysis, the blocking of thoughts or feelings that would evoke anxiety if they were consciously experienced. Resistance may also take the form of missed sessions by the client or the client's verbal confrontation with the analyst as threatening material is about to be uncovered.

Resistance stage. In Selye's view, the second stage of the general adaptation syndrome, involving the attempt to withstand prolonged stress and preserve bodily resources. Also called the *adaptation stage.*

Response. A reaction to a stimulus.

Reticular activating system. A part of the brain involved in processes of attention, sleep, and arousal. Abbreviated *RAS.*

Reverse tolerance. The acquisition of decreased tolerance for a psychoactive drug such that lesser amounts of the substance become capable, over time, of producing the same effects as greater amounts.

Reward. A pleasant stimulus or event that increases the frequency of the behavior it follows.

Role diffusion. In Erikson's theory, a state of confusion, aimlessness, insecurity, and heightened susceptibility to the suggestions of others that is associated with the failure to acquire a firm sense of ego identity during adolescence.

Sadistic personality disorder. A proposed type of personality disorder characterized by a persistent pattern of intentionally cruel behavior toward others in which the individual seems to enjoy causing the suffering of others in the form of physical violence or humiliation.

Sadomasochism. Sexual activities between partners involving the attainment of gratification by means of inflicting and receiving pain and humiliation.

Sample. A part of a population.

Sanguine. A cheerful disposition.

Schizoaffective disorder. A type of psychotic disorder in which individuals experience both severe mood disturbance and features associated with schizophrenia.

Schizoid personality disorder. A type of personality disorder characterized by a persistent lack of interest in social relationships, flattened affect, and social withdrawal.

Schizophrenia. A psychosis lasting at least six months in duration that involves failure to maintain integrated personality functioning, impaired reality testing, and disturbances in thinking. Common features of schizophrenia include delusions, hallucinations, flattened or inappropriate affect, and bizarre behavior. Also see *schizophreniform disorder, schizotypal personality disorder,* and *brief reactive psychosis.*

Schizophreniform disorder. A psychotic disorder lasting under six months in duration with schizophrenic-like features.

Schizophrenogenic mother. The type of mother, described as cold but also overprotective, that was believed to be capable of causing schizophrenia in her children. Research has failed to support the validity of this concept.

Schizotypal personality disorder. A type of personality disorder characterized by eccentricities or oddities of thought and behavior but without clearly psychotic features. Many persons formerly called *simple schizophrenics* might be given this diagnosis today.

Second-rank symptoms. In Goldstein's view, symptoms associated with schizophrenia that also occur in other mental disorders.

Secondary gains. Side-benefits associated with neuroses or other disorders, such as expressions of sympathy and increased attention from others, and release from ordinary responsibilities.

Secondary prevention. An approach to prevention that focuses on the early detection and treatment of physical or psychological problems.

Secondary process thinking. In psychodynamic theory, the reality-based thinking processes and problem-solving activities of the ego.

Secondary reinforcer. Stimuli that gain reinforcement value through their association with established reinforcers. Money and social approval are typically secondary reinforcers. Contrast with *primary reinforcers.*

Secondary sex characteristics. The physical traits that differentiate men from women.

Sedatives. Types of depressant drugs that reduce states of tension and restlessness and induce sleep.

Selection factor. A kind of confound or bias in experimental or quasi-experimental studies in which differences between experimental and control groups are due to differences in the types of subjects comprising the groups, rather than to the independent variable.

Selective abstraction. In Beck's theory, a type of cognitive distortion involving the tendency to focus selectively only on the parts of one's experiences that reflect upon one's flaws and to ignore those aspects that reveal one's strengths or competencies.

Selective amnesia. A type of psychogenic amnesia involving the loss of memory for disturbing events that occurred during a certain time period.

Self. The center of a person's consciousness that organizes one's sensory impressions and governs one's perceptions of the world. The sum total of an individual's thoughts, sensory impressions, and feelings.

Self-actualization. In humanistic psychology, the tendency to strive to become all that one is capable of being. The motive that drives one to reach one's full potential and to express one's unique capabilities.

Self-defeating personality disorder. A proposed type of personality disorder involving a persistent pattern of self-defeating behavior. The term masochistic personality was formerly used to describe this disorder, but it has since been dropped to avoid the implication that people with this behavior pattern derive pleasure from suffering.

Self-efficacy expectations. Our beliefs that we can accomplish certain tasks or bring about desired results through our own efforts.

Self-esteem. One's sense of worth or value as a human being.

Self-ideals. The mental image or representation of what we expect ourselves to be.

Self-insight. Awareness of the relationships between one's behavior and one's motivations, needs, and wants.

Self-monitoring. In behavioral assessment, the process of recording or observing one's own behavior, thoughts, or emotions.

Self psychology. Hans Kohut's theory that describes processes that normally lead to the achievement of a cohesive sense of self, or in narcissistic personality disorder, to a grandiose, but fragile sense of self.

Self-spectatoring. The tendency to observe one's behavior as if one were a spectator of oneself. People with sexual dysfunctions often become self-spectators in the sense of focusing their attention during sex on the response of their sexual organs rather than on their sexual activity.

Senile dementias. Forms of dementia that begin after the age of 65.

Sensate focus exercises. In sex therapy, the mutual pleasuring activities between partners that is focused on the participants taking turns giving and receiving physical pleasure.

Sensorium. A person's entire sensory apparatus. It is used by clinicians to refer to the client's focusing of attention, capacity for concentration, and level of awareness of the world.

Sensory cortex. The part of the cerebral cortex, located in the parietal lobe, that receives sensory stimulation.

Separation anxiety disorder. A childhood disorder characterized by extreme fears of separation from parents or others upon whom the child is dependent.

Separation-individuation. In Margaret Mahler's theory, the process by which young children come to separate psychologically from their mothers and to perceive themselves as separate and distinct individuals.

Serotonin. A type of neurotransmitter, imbalances of which have been linked to mood disorders and anxiety.

Serum cholesterol. A fatty substance (cholesterol) in the blood serum that has been implicated in cardiovascular disease.

Set point. A value that regulatory mechanisms in the body attempt to maintain. For example, regulatory mechanisms in the brain may try to maintain a certain body weight by adjusting the rate of metabolism.

Sex role. A constellation of traits and behaviors associated with traditional concepts of masculinity and femininity.

Sexual aversion disorder. A type of sexual dysfunction characterized by aversion to, and avoidance of, genital sexual contact.

Sexual masochism. A type of paraphilia characterized by sexual urges and sexually arousing fantasies involving receiving humiliation or physical pain and in which the person has either acted upon these urges or is strongly distressed by them.

Sexual sadism. A type of paraphilia or sexual deviation characterized by recurrent sexual urges and sexually arousing fantasies that involve inflicting humiliation or physical pain on sex partners and in which the person has either acted upon these urges or is strongly distressed by them.

Significant. The magnitude of difference that is taken as meaningful or as indicating meaningful differences between groups because of the low probability that such a difference could have occurred by chance.

Simple phobias. A persistent but excessive fear of a specific object or situation, such as a fear of heights or of small animals.

Simple schizophrenia. See *schizotypal personality disorder.*

Single-case experimental designs. A type of case study in which the subject (case) is used as his or her own control by varying the conditions to which the subject is exposed (by use of a *reversal* phase) or by means of a *multiple-baseline* design.

Situation variables. In social-learning theory, the external influences on behavior, such as rewards and punishments.

Social comparison. A process by which one looks to others for cues as to how to behave in certain situations.

Social-learning theory. A learning-based theory that emphasizes observational learning and incorporates roles for both situation and person variables in determining behavior.

Social phobia. An excessive fear of engaging in behaviors that involve public scrutiny.

Social skills training. In behavior therapy, a technique for helping people acquire or improve their social skills. Assertiveness training can be considered a form of social skills training.

Sociocultural perspective. A model of abnormal behavior that emphasizes the social and cultural influences that lead to deviant behavior, rather than the pathological influences within the person. More broadly, the model that interprets behavior within a larger social and cultural context.

Sodium lactate. A salt of inactive lactic acid that has been found to induce panic in some people, especially in people with panic disorder.

Soma. A cell body.

Somatic nervous system. The division of the peripheral nervous system that relays information from the sense organs to the brain and transmits messages from the brain to the skeletal muscles, resulting in body movements.

Somatization disorder. A type of somatoform disorder involving recurrent multiple complaints that cannot be explained by any clear physical causes. Has also been called *Briquet's syndrome.*

Somatoform disorders. Disorders in which people complain of physical (somatic) problems, although no physical abnormality can be found that accounts for their complaints. See *conversion disorder, hypochondriasis,* and *somatization disorder.*

Specific factors. In the reformulated helplessness theory, a type of attribution involving the belief that the cause of an event involved specific, rather than generalized, factors. Contrast with *global factors.*

Splitting. A term describing the inability of some people (especially borderline personalities) to reconcile the positive and negative aspects of themselves or others into a cohesive integration, resulting in sudden and radical shifts between strongly positive and strongly negative feelings.

Spontaneous recovery. The recurrence of an extinguished response as a function of the passage of time.

Stable factors. In the reformulated helplessness theory, a type of attribution involving the belief that the cause of an event involved stable, rather than changeable, factors. Contrast with *unstable factors.*

Standard scores. Scores that indicate the relative standing of raw scores in relation to the distribution of normative scores. For example, raw scores on the MMPI scales are converted into standard scores that indicate the degree to which each of the individual raw scores deviates from the mean.

Standardized interview. A highly structured form of clinical interviewing that makes use of a series of specific questions to help the clinician reach the most appropriate diagnosis.

Statutory rape. A legal term referring to sexual intercourse with a minor, even with the minor's consent.

Steroids. A group of hormones including testosterone, estrogen, progesterone, and corticosteroids.

Stimulus. (1) An aspect of the environment that produces a change in an organism's behavior (a response). (2) A form of physical energy, such as sound or light, that impinges on the senses.

Stratified random sample. A random sample that was drawn in such a way that certain identified subgroups within the population were represented in the sample in relation to their numbers in the population.

Stress-inoculation therapy. A form of cognitive-behavior therapy that focuses on helping people acquire more adaptive coping responses for handling stress. Participants are exposed in their imaginations to manageable "doses" of identified stressors so that they can practice using behavioral and cognitive coping strategies that they can then use when faced with the actual stressors.

Structural family therapy. A form of family therapy that analyzes the structure of the family unit in terms of the role relationships and communications that exist within the family.

Structural hypothesis. In Freud's theory, the belief that the clashing forces within the personality can be divided into three psychic structures: the id, the ego, and the superego.

Structured interview. A means by which an interviewer obtains clinical information from a client by asking a fairly standard series of questions concerning such issues as the client's presenting complaints or problems, mental state, life circumstances, and psychosocial or developmental history.

Stupor. A state of relative or complete unconsciousness in which the person is not generally aware of, or responsive to, the environment, as in a *catatonic stupor.*

Subjective values. The values that individuals place on objects or events.

Substance abuse. The continued use of a psychoactive drug for a period of a month or more despite the knowledge that it is causing or contributing to a persistent or recurrent social, occupational, psychological, or physical problem.

Substance dependence. Impaired control over the use of a psychoactive drug; often characterized by physiological dependence.

Superego. In psychodynamic theory, the psychic structure that represents the incorporation of the moral values of the parents and important others and that floods the ego with guilt and shame when the ego falls short of meeting those standards. The superego is governed by the moral principle and consists of two parts, the conscience and the ego-ideal.

Supermales. Males who possess the XYY chromosomal structure, which has been associated with exaggerated male characteristics such as heavier beards, and which was linked in some earlier research to violent tendencies in some cases.

Survey method. A method of scientific research in which large samples of people are questioned by use of a survey instrument.

Survivor guilt. The feelings of guilt often experienced by survivors of calamities.

Symbiotic. (1) In biology, the living together of two different but interdependent organisms. (2) In Mahler's object-relations theory, the term used to describe the state of oneness that normally exists between mother and infant in which the infant's identity is fused with the mother's.

Sympathetic. Pertaining to the sympathetic branch of the autonomic nervous system that becomes active in meeting the demands of stress, such as adjusting to cold temperatures, or in expending bodily reserves of energy through physical exertion or through emotional reactions, such as anxiety or fear.

Symptom substitution. The appearance of a new symptom as a substitute for one which has been removed or suppressed. In psychodynamic terms, a symptom, such as a phobia, represents an indirect expression of an unconscious conflict. In this view, the removal of a symptom without the resolution of the underlying conflict would be expected to lead to the emergence of another symptom that would represent the continuing conflict.

Synapse. A junction or small gap between the terminal knob of one neuron and the dendrite or soma of another through which the nerve impulses pass.

Syndromes. Clusters of symptoms that are characteristic of particular disorders.

Syphilis. A type of sexually transmitted disease, implicated in its final stages of causing a mental disorder termed *general paresis*.

Systematic desensitization. A behavior therapy technique for overcoming phobias by means of exposure (in imagination or by means of slides) to progressively more fearful stimuli while one remains deeply relaxed.

Systems perspective. The view that problems reflect the systems (whether family, social, school, ecological systems, etc.) in which they are embedded.

Tachycardia. Abnormally rapid heartbeat.

Tactile. Pertaining to the sense of touch.

Tardive dyskinesia. A movement disorder characterized by involuntary movements of the face, mouth, neck, trunk, or extremities that is caused by long-term use of antipsychotic medications.

Tay-Sachs disease. A disease of lipid metabolism that is genetically transmitted and generally results in death in early childhood.

Temporal stability. The consistency of test responses across time, as measured by test-retest reliability.

Terminals. The small branching structures found at the tips of axons.

Tertiary prevention. An approach to prevention that focuses on reducing the level of impairment of distressed individuals. (See *primary* and *secondary prevention*.)

Test–retest reliability. A method for measuring the reliability of a test by means of comparing (correlating) the scores of the same examinees on separate occasions.

Testosterone. A male sex hormone (steroid), produced by the testes, that is involved in promoting growth of male sexual characteristics and sperm.

Thalamus. A structure in the brain that is involved in relaying sensory information to the cortex and in processes relating to sleep and attention.

Theories. (1) Plausible or scientifically defensible explanations of events. (2) Formulations of the relationships underlying observed events. Theories are helpful to scientists because they provide a means of organizing observations and lead to predictions about future events.

Therapeutic community. A treatment setting, such as in a special ward in a hospital or in a community residence, in which the interactions among the residents and staff are structured to serve a therapeutic purpose.

Thermistor. A small device that is strapped to the skin for registering body temperature, as used in biofeedback training.

Thought disorder. Disturbances in thinking characterized by various features, especially the breakdown in logical associations between thoughts.

Thought insertion. A type of delusion in which people believe that their thoughts have been planted in their minds from external sources.

Thyroxin. A hormone produced by the thyroid gland that increases the metabolic rate.

Time-out. A behavioral technique in which an individual who emits an undesired behavior is removed from an environment in which reinforcers are available and placed in an unreinforcing environment for a period of time as a form of punishment. Time-out is frequently used in behavioral programs for modifying behavior problems in children, in combination with positive reinforcement for desirable behavior.

Token economies. Behavioral treatment programs in institutional settings in which a controlled environment is constructed such that people are reinforced for desired behaviors by receiving tokens (such as poker chips) that may be exchanged for desired rewards or privileges.

Tolerance. Physical habituation to a drug so that with frequent usage, higher doses are needed to attain similar effects.

Transcendental meditation. A popular form of meditation introduced into the United States by the Maharishi Mahesh Yogi; focuses on the repeating of a mantra to induce a meditative state. Abbreviated *TM*.

Transference relationship. In psychoanalysis, the client's transfer or generalization to the analyst of feelings and attitudes the client holds toward important figures in his or her life.

Transsexualism. A type of gender identity disorder characterized by feelings of being trapped inside a body of the wrong sex.

Transvestic fetishism. A type of paraphilia in heterosexual males characterized by recurrent sexual urges and sexually arousing fantasies involving dressing in female clothing and in which the person has either acted upon these urges or is strongly distressed by them.

Trephining. A harsh, prehistoric practice of cutting a hole in a person's skull, possibly as an ancient form of surgery for brain trauma, or possibly as a means of releasing the demons that prehistoric people may have believed caused abnormal behavior in afflicted individuals.

Trichotillomania. According to the DSM–III–R, a type of impulse control disorder involving persistent failure to resist urges to pull out one's own hair, thus producing noticeable hair loss.

Tricyclics. A group of antidepressant drugs that increase the activity of norepinephrine and serotonin in the brain by interfering with the re-uptake of these neurotransmitters by transmitting neurons. Also called TCAs (tricyclic antidepressants).

Tumescence. A swelling or a swollen part, as in penile tumescence (erection).

Two-factor model. O. Hobart Mowrer's belief that both operant and classical conditioning are involved in the acquisition of phobic responses. Basically, the fear component of phobia is acquired by means of classical conditioning (pairing of a previously neutral stimulus with an aversive stimulus), while the avoidance component is acquired by means of operant conditioning (relief from anxiety negatively reinforces avoidance behavior).

Ulcers. Open sores, as in the stomach lining.

Unconditional positive regard. In Carl Rogers' view, the expression of unconditional acceptance of another individual's basic worth as a person, regardless of whether one approves of all of the behavior of that person. The ability to express unconditional positive regard is considered a quality of an effective person-centered therapist.

Unconditioned response. An unlearned response or a response to an unconditioned stimulus. Abbreviated *UR.*

Unconditioned stimulus. A stimulus that elicits an instinctive or unlearned response from an organism. Abbreviated *US.*

Unconscious. (1) In psychodynamic theory, pertaining to impulses or ideas that are not readily available to awareness, in many instances because they are kept from awareness by means of *repression.* (2) Also in psychodynamic theory, the part of the mind that contains repressed material and primitive urges of the id. (3) More generally, a state of unawareness or loss of consciousness.

Unipolar. Pertaining to a single pole or direction, as in unipolar (depressive) disorders. Contrast with *bipolar disorder.*

Unobtrusive. Not interfering.

Unstable factors. In the reformulated helplessness theory, a type of attribution involving the belief that the cause of an event involved changeable, rather than stable, factors. Contrast with *stable factors.*

Vacillate. To move back and forth.

Vaginal plethysmograph. A device for measuring sexual arousal in females as a function of the amount of blood congestion in the vaginal cavity.

Vaginismus. A type of sexual dysfunction characterized by a recurrent or persistent contraction of the muscles surrounding the vaginal entrance, making penile entry while attempting intercourse difficult or impossible.

Validity. (1) With respect to tests, the degree to which a test measures the traits or constructs that it purports to measure. (2) With respect to experiments, the degree to which an experiment yields scientifically accurate and defensible results.

Validity scales. Groups of test items that serve to detect whether the results of a particular test are valid or whether a person responded in a random manner or in a way that was intended to create a favorable or unfavorable impression.

Variables. Conditions that are measured (dependent variables) or manipulated (independent variables) in scientific studies.

Voyeurism. A type of paraphilia characterized by recurrent sexual urges and sexually arousing fantasies involving the act of watching unsuspecting others who are naked, in the act of undressing, or engaging in sexual activity, in which the person has either acted upon these urges or is strongly distressed by them.

Vulnerability mode. In Beck's view, a pattern of distorted thinking involving processing information in terms of perceived weaknesses rather than strengths.

Waxy flexibility. A feature of catatonic schizophrenia in which a person's limbs are moved into a certain posture or position, which the person then rigidly maintains for an extended period of time.

Weaning. The process of getting a child to eat solid food, rather than continuing to seek nourishment through breast feeding or sucking a baby bottle.

Wernicke's disease. A brain disorder associated with chronic alcoholism that is characterized by confusion, disorientation, and difficulties maintaining balance while walking (ataxia). If left untreated, it may lead to *Korsakoff's syndrome.*

Winning phase. The first stage in a ''gambling career,'' marked by perceptions of gambling as a pleasant pastime, in which early winnings boost self-esteem. But pathological gamblers eventually progress to *losing* and *desperation* phases.

World view. The prevailing view of the times.

References

Abel, G., Becker, J., & Cunningham-Rather, J. (1984). Complications, consent, and cognitions in sex between children and adults. *International Journal of Law and Psychiatry*, 7, 89–103.

Abelson, H., Cohen, R., Heaton, E., & Slider, C. (1970). Public attitudes toward and experience with erotic materials. In *Technical reports of the Commission on Obscenity and Pornography*, Vol. 6. Washington, DC: U.S. Government Printing Office.

Abend, S. M., Porder, M. S., & Willick, M. S. (1983). *Borderline patients: Psychoanalytic perspectives*. New York: International Universities Press.

Aber, J. L., & Allen, J. (1987). Effects of maltreatment on young children's socioemotional development: An attachment theory perspective. *Developmental Psychology*, 23, 406–414.

Abikoff, H. (1985). Efficacy of cognitive training interventions in hyperactive children: A critical review. *Clinical Psychology Review*, 5, 479–512.

Abikoff, H., & Gittleman, R. (1985). Hyperactive children treated with stimulants: Is cognitive training a useful adjunct? *Archives of General Psychiatry*, 72, 953–961.

Abraham, K. (1948). The first pregenital stage of the libido (1916). In D. Bryan & A. Strachey (Eds.), *Selected papers of Karl Abraham, M. D.* London: The Hogarth Press.

Abrahamson, D. J., and others (1985). The effects of attentional focus and partner responsiveness on sexual responding: Replication and extension. *Archives of Sexual Behavior*, 14, 361–371.

Abrahamson, D. J., et al. (1985). Effects of distraction on sexual responding in functional and dysfunctional men. *Behavior Therapy*, 16, 503–515.

Abramowitz, S. (1986). Psychosocial outcomes of sex reassignment surgery. *Journal of Consulting and Clinical Psychology*, 54, 183–189.

Abrams, D. B., Monti, P. M., Pinto, R. P., Elder, J. P., Brown, R. S., & Jacobus, S. I. (1987). Psychosocial stress and coping in smokers who relapse or quit. *Health Psychology*, 6, 289–303.

Abrams, R., & Fink, M. (1984). The present status of unilateral ECT: Some recommendations. *Journal of Affective Disorders*, 7, 245–247.

Abrams, R., and others (1983). Bilateral versus unilateral electroconvulsive therapy-efficacy in melancholia. *American Journal of Psychiatry*, 140, 463–465.

Abramson, L. T., Seligman, M. E. P., & Teasdale, J. D. (1978). Learned helplessness in humans: Critique and reformulation. *Journal of Abnormal Psychology*, 87, 49–74.

Abramson, L. Y., Garber, J., & Seligman, M. E. P. (1980). Learned helplessness in humans: An attributional hypothesis. In G. Garber & M. E. P. Seligman (Eds.), *Human helplessness: Theory and application* (pp. 3–34). New York: Academic Press.

Abramson, P. R., & Mosher, D. L. (1975). Development of a measure of negative attitudes toward masturbation. *Journal of Consulting and Clinical Psychology*, 43, 485–490.

Achenbach, T. M. (1978). The Child Behavior Profile: I. Boys aged 6 through 11. *Journal of Consulting and Clinical Psychology*, 46, 478–488.

Achenbach, T. M. (1982). *Developmental psychopathology* (2nd ed.). New York: Wiley.

Achenbach, T. M., & Edelbrock, C. S. (1979). The Child Behavior Profile: I. Boys aged 12–16 and girls aged 6–11 and 12–16. *Journal of Consulting and Clinical Psychology*, 47, 223–233.

Achenbach, T. M., & Edelbrock, C. S. (1981). Behavioral problems and competencies reported by parents of normal and disturbed children aged 4 to 16. *Monographs of the Society for Research in Child Development*, 46 (Whole No. 188).

Ackerman, S. H., Manaker, S., & Cohen, M. I. (1981). Recent separation and the onset of peptic ulcer disease in older children and adolescents. *Psychosomatic Medicine*, 43, 305–310.

Adams, H. E., & Chiodo, J. (1983). Sexual deviations. In H. E. Adams & P. B. Sutker (Eds.), *Comprehensive handbook of psychopathology*. New York: Plenum.

Adams, K. M. (1984). Luria left in the lurch: Unfulfilled promises are not valid tests. *Journal of Clinical Neuropsychology*, 6, 455–458.

Adams, V. (1980, August). Sex therapists in perspective. *Psychology Today*, pp. 35–36.

Adelman, M. R. (1977). A comparison of professionally employed lesbians and heterosexual women on the MMPI. *Archives of Sexual Behavior*, 6, 193–202.

Affleck, G., Tennen, H., Croog, S., & Levine, S. (1987). Causal attribution, perceived benefits, and morbidity after a heart attack: An 8–year study. *Journal of Consulting and Clinical Psychology*, 55, 29–35.

Ageton, S. (1983). *Sexual assault among adolescents*. Lexington, MA: D. C. Heath.

Agras, W. S., Barlow, D. H., Chapin, H. N., & Abel, G. (1974). Behavior modification of anorexia nervosa. *Archives of General Psychiatry*, 30, 279–286.

Agras, W. S., & Kirkley, B. G. (1986). Bulimia: Theories of etiology. In K. D. Brownell & J. P. Foreyt (Eds.), *Handbook of eating disorders* (pp. 367–378). New York: Basic Books.

AIDS policy: Confidentiality and disclosure (1988). Official Actions. *American Journal of Psychiatry*, 145, 541.

Ainsworth, M. D. S. (1989). Attachments beyond infancy. *American Psychologist*, 44, 709–716.

Akhtar, A. (1987). Schizoid personality disorder: A synthesis of developmental, dynamic, and descriptive features. *American Journal of Psychotherapy*, 41, 499–517.

Akiskal, H. S. (1983). Dysthymic disorder: Psychopathology of proposed chronic depressive subtypes. *American Journal of Psychiatry*, 140, 11–20.

Alain, R. P. (1986). The sleepy patient: Evaluation and management. *Clinical Psychology Review*, 6, 51–66.

Albert, M. S. (1981). Geriatric neuropsychology. *Journal of Consulting and Clinical Psychology*, 49, 835–850.

Albert, M. S., Butters, N., & Levin, J. (1979). Temporal gradients in the retrograde amnesia of patients with alcoholic Korsakoff's disease. *Archives of Neurology*, 36, 211–216.

Albert, M. S., Naeser, M. A., Duffy, F. H., & Mc-

Anulty, G. (1986). CT and EEG validators for Alzheimer's disease. In L. W. Poon (Ed.), *Handbook for clinical memory assessment of older adults* (pp. 383–392). Washington, DC: American Psychological Association.

Alcohol and Health (1987). Rockville, MD: National Institute of Alcohol Abuse and Alcoholism.

Alden, L. E. (1988). Behavioral self-management controlled-drinking strategies in a context of secondary prevention. *Journal of Consulting and Clinical Psychology*, 56, 280–286.

Alexander, A. B. (1981). Asthma. In S. N. Haynes & L. Gannon (Eds.), *Psychosomatic disorders: A psychophysiological approach to etiology and treatment*. New York: Praeger.

Alexander, F. (1939). Emotional factors in essential hypertension. *Psychosomatic Medicine*, 1, 153–216.

Alexander, F. (1950). *Psychosomatic medicine*. New York: W. W. Norton & Co., Inc.

Allbutt, T. C. (1910). Neuroses of the stomach and of other parts of the abdomen. In T. C. Allbutt & H. D. Rolleston (Eds.), *A system of medicine*, Vol. 3. London: Macmillan.

Allderidge, P. (1979). Hospitals, madhouses and asylums: Cycles in the care of the insane. *British Journal of Psychiatry*, 134, 1476–1478.

Allen, M. G. (1976). Twin studies of affective illness. *Archives of General Psychiatry*, 33, 1476–1478.

Allgeier, E. R., & Allgeier, A. A. (1984). *Sexual interactions*. Lexington, MA: D. C. Heath.

Alloy, L. B., & Abramson, L. Y. (1979). Judgment of contingency in depressed and nondepressed students: Sadder but wiser? *Journal of Experimental Psychology: General*, 108, 441–485.

Allport, G. W., & Odbert, H. S. (1936). Trait-names: A psycholexical study. *Psychological Monographs: General and Applied*, 47 (Whole, No. 211).

Alter-Reid, K., Gibbs, M. S., Lachenmeyer, J. R., Sigal, J., & Mossoth, N. A. (1986). Sexual abuse of children: A review of the empirical findings. *Clinical Psychology Review*, 6, 249–266.

Altman, L. K. (1988, January 26). Cocaine's many dangers: The evidence mounts. *The New York Times*, p. C3.

Altman, L. K. (1989, April 24). Experts on AIDS, citing new data, push for testing. *The New York Times*, pp. 1, B8.

Aman, M. (1984). Hyperactive: Nature of the syndrome and its natural history. *Journal of Autism and Developmental Disorders*, 14, 13–56.

American College of Obstetricians and Gynecologists (1985, January). *Dysmenorrhea*.

American Humane Association (1984). *Highlights of official child neglect and abuse reporting, 1982*. Denver: Author.

American Psychiatric Association (1974). *Clinical aspects of the violent individual*. Washington, DC: Author.

American Psychiatric Association (1978a). *Electroconvulsive Therapy, Task Force Report 14*. Washington, DC: Author.

American Psychiatric Association (1987) *Diagnostic and statistical manual of mental disorders* (3rd ed., rev.). Washington, DC: Author.

American Psychiatric Association. (1987b). Dexamethasone suppression test: An overview of its current status in psychiatry. Washington, DC: Author.

American Psychiatric Association (1988). AIDS Policy: Confidentiality and disclosure. *American Journal of Psychiatry*, 145, 541.

American Psychological Association (1978). Report of the Task Force on the Role of Psychology in the Criminal Justice System. *American Psychologist*, 33, 1099–1113.

Amir, M. (1971). *Patterns in forcible rape*. Chicago: University of Chicago Press.

Ammerman, R. T., Cassisi, J. E., Herson, M., & Van Hasselt, V. B. (1986). Consequences of physical abuse and neglect in children. *Clinical Psychology Review*, 6, 291–310.

Anastasi, A. (1983). Evolving trait concepts. *American Psychologist*, 38, 175–184.

Anderson, S. R., Christian, W. P., & Luce, S. C. (1986). Transitional residential programming for autistic individuals. *The Behavior Therapist*, 9, 205–211.

Anderson, B. J., & Wold, F. M. (1986). Chronic physical illness and sexual behavior. *Journal of Consulting and Clinical Psychology*, 54, 168–175.

Anderson, B. L. (1981). A comparison of systemic desensitization and directed masturbation in the treatment of primary orgasmic dysfunction in females. *Journal of Consulting and Clinical Psychology*, 49, 568–570.

Andreasen, N. C. (1979). Thought, language, and communication disorders: II. Diagnostic significance. *Archives of General Psychiatry*, 36, 1325–1331.

Andreasen, N. C. (1982). Negative vs. positive schizophrenia: Definition and validation. *Archives of General Psychiatry*, 39, 789–794.

Andreasen, N. C. (1986). Scale for the Assessment of Thought, Language, and Communication (TLC). *Schizophrenia Bulletin*, 12, 473–482.

Andreasen, N. C. (1987a). Creativity and mental illness: Prevalence rates in writers and their first-degree relatives. *American Journal of Psychiatry*, 144, 1288–1292.

Andreasen, N. C. (1987b). The diagnosis of schizophrenia. *Schizophrenia Bulletin*, 13, 1–8.

Andreasen, N. C., & Grove, W. M. (1986). Thought, language, and communication in schizophrenia: Diagnosis and prognosis. *Schizophrenia Bulletin*, 12, 348–359.

Andreasen, N., Nasrallah, H. A., Dunn, V., Olson, S. C., Grove W. M., Ehrhardt, J. C., Coffman, J. A., & Crossett, J. H. W. (1986). Structural abnormalities in the frontal system in schizophrenia. *Archives of General Psychiatry*, 43, 136–144.

Andreasen, N. C., Rice, J., Endicott, J. Coryell, W., & Reich, T. (1987). Familial rates of affective disorder: A report from the National Institute of Mental Health Collaborative Study. *Archives of General Psychiatry*, 44, 461–469.

Andrews, G., & Harvey, R. (1981). Does psychotherapy benefit neurotic patients? *Archives of General Psychiatry*, 38, 1203–1208.

Aneshensel, C. S., & Huba, G. J. (1983). Depression, alcohol use, and smoking over one year: A four-wave longitudinal causal model. *Journal of Abnormal Psychology*, 134–150.

Angier, N. (1990, March 29). New antidepressant is acclaimed but not perfect. *The New York Times*, B9.

Angle, H. V., Johnson T., Grebenkemper, N. S., & Ellinwood, E. H. (1979). Computer interview support for clinicians. *Professional Psychology*, 10, 49–57.

Angrist, B., Rotrosen, J., & Gershon, S. (1980). Differential effects of amphetamine and neuroleptics on negative vs. positive symptoms in schizophrenia. *Psychopharmacology*, 72, 17–19.

Anonymous (1985, June 13). Schizophrenia—A mother's agony over her son's pain. *Chicago Tribune*, Section 5, pp. 1–3.

Anthony, E. J. (1977). Depression and children.

In G. D. Burrow (Ed.), *Handbook of studies of depression*. Amsterdam: Excerpta Medica.

Anthony, J. C., and others (1985). Comparison of a lay Diagnostic Interview Schedule and a standardized psychiatric diagnosis: Experience in Eastern Baltimore. *Archives of General Psychiatry*, 42, 667–675.

Anthony, W. A., Cohen, M. R., & Cohen, B. (1984). Psychiatric rehabilitation. In J. Talbott (Ed.), *The chronic mental patient: Five years later* (pp. 213–252). New York: Grune & Stratton.

Anthony, W. A., & Liberman, R. P. (1986). The practice of psychiatric rehabilitation: Historical, conceptual, and research base. *Schizophrenia Bulletin*, 12, 542–559.

Anthony, W. A., & Margules, A. (1974). Toward improving the efficacy of psychiatric rehabilitation: A skills training approach. *Rehabilitation Psychology*, 21, 101–105.

Antoni, M., Levine, J., Tischer, P., Green, C., & Millon, T. (1986). Refining personality assessments by combining MCMI high-point profiles and MMPI codes: IV. MMPI 89/98. *Journal of Personality Assessment*, 50, 65–72.

Antoni M., Tischer, P., Levine, J., Green, C., & Millon, T. (1985). Refining personality assessments by combining MCMI high-point profiles and MMPI codes, Part I: MMPI code 28/82. *Journal of Personality Assessment*, 49, 392–398.

APA Task Force on Laboratory Tests in Psychiatry (1987). *American Journal of Psychiatry*, 144, 1253–1262.

Aplin, D. Y., & Kane, J. M. (1985). Variables affecting pure tone and speech audiometry in experimentally simulated hearing loss. *British Journal of Audiology*, 19, 219–228.

Appelbaum, P. S. (1988). The right to refuse treatment with antipsychotic medications: Retrospect and prospect. *American Journal of Psychiatry*, 145, 413–419.

Appelbaum, P. S., & Hoges, K. (1986). The right to refuse treatment: What the research reveals. *Behavioral Sciences and the Law*, 4, 279–292.

Appelbaum, S. (1963). The problem-solving aspects of suicide. *Journal of Projective Technology*, 27, 259.

Arana, G. W., Baldessarini, R. J., & Ornstein, M. (1985). The dexamethasone suppression test for diagnosis and prognosis in psychiatry: Commentary and review. *Archives of General Psychiatry*, 42, 1193–1204.

Arce, A. A., Tadlock, M., Vergare. M. J., & Shapiro, S. H. (1983). A psychiatric profile of street people admitted to an emergency shelter. *Hospital and Community Psychiatry*, 34, 812–817.

Arentewicz, G., & Schmidt, G. (1983). *The treatment of sexual disorder*. New York: Karger.

Arieti, S. (1974). *Interpretation of schizophrenia* (2nd ed.). New York: Basic Books.

Arkin, R. M., Detchon, C. S., & Maruyama, G. M. (1982). Roles of attribution, affect, and cognitive interference in test anxiety. *Journal of Personality and Social Psychology*, 43, 1111–1124.

Armor, D. J., Polich, J. M., & Stambul, H. B. (1978). *Alcoholism and treatment*. New York: Wiley.

Aronson, M. K. (1988). Patients and families: Impact and long-term management implications. In M. K. Aronson (Ed.), *Understanding Alzheimer's Disease* (pp. 74–78). New York: Scribner's.

Aronson, T. A. (1987). A naturalistic study of imipramine in panic disorder and agoraphobia. *American Journal of Psychiatry*, 144, 1014–1019.

Asaad, G., & Shapiro, B. (1986). Hallucinations: Theoretical and clinical overview. *American Journal of Psychiatry*, 143, 1088–1097.

Asarnow, J. R., & Carlson, G. A. (1985). Depression self-rating scale: Utility with child psychiatric inpatients. *Journal of Consulting and Clinical Psychology*, 53, 491–499.

Asarnow, J. R., Carlson, G. A., & Guthrie, D. (1987). Coping strategies, self-perceptions, hopelessness, and perceived family environments in depressed and suicidal children. *Journal of Consulting and Clinical Psychology*, 55, 361–366.

Asarnow, J. R., & Goldstein, M. J. (1986). Schizophrenia during adolescence and early adulthood: A developmental perspective on risk research. *Clinical Psychology Review*, 6, 211–235.

Asarnow, J. R., Lewis, J. M., Doane J. A., Goldstein, M. J., & Rodnick, E. H. (1982). Family interaction and the course of adolescent psychopathology: An analysis of adolescent and parent defects. *Journal of Abnormal Child Psychology*, 10, 427–442.

Athanasiou, R., Shaver, P., & Tavris, C. (1970, July). Sex. *Psychology Today*, pp. 39–52.

Attorney General's Commission on Pornography (1986, July). *Final report*. Washington DC: U.S. Department of Justice.

Ax, A. F. (1953). The physiological differentiation between fear and anger in humans. *Psychosomatic Medicine*, 15, 433–442.

Ayllon, T., & Haughton, E. (1962). Control of the behavior of schizophrenic patients by food. *Journal of the Experimental Analysis of Behavior*, 5, 343–352.

Azrin, N. H., & Peterson, A. L. (1989). Reduction of an eye tic by controlled blinking. *Behavior Therapy*, 20, 467–473.

Bachrach, L. L. (1989). Deinstitutionalization: A semantic analysis. *Journal of Social Issues*, 45, 161–171.

Backman, E. L. (1952). *Religious dances in the Christian church and in popular medicine*. London: Allen & Unwin.

Baird, T. D., & August, G. J. (1985). Familial heterogeneity in infantile autism. *Journal of Autism and Developmental Disorders*, 15, 315–321.

Baldessarini, R. J. (1985). Clinical and epidemiological aspects of tardive dyskinesia. *Journal of Clinical Psychiatry*, 46, 8–13.

Baldessarini, R. J., & Cohen, B. M. (1987). Drs. Baldessarini and Cohen Reply. *American Journal of Psychiatry*, 144, 262.

Bancroft, J. (1984). Testosterone therapy for low sexual interest and erectile dysfunctions in men: A controlled study. *British Journal of Psychiatry*, 14, 146–151.

Bandura, A. (1973). *Aggression: A social learning analysis*. Englewood Cliffs, NJ: Prentice Hall.

Bandura, A. (1977). Self-efficacy: Toward a unifying theory of behavioral change. *Psychological Review*, 84, 191–215.

Bandura, A. (1982). Self-efficacy mechanism in human agency. *American Psychologist*, 37, 122–147.

Bandura, A. (1986). *Social foundations of thought and action: A social-cognitive theory*. Englewood Cliffs, NJ: Prentice Hall.

Bandura, A. (1989). Human agency in social cognitive theory. *American Psychologist*, 44, 1175–1184.

Bandura, A., Barr-Taylor, C., Williams, S. L., Mefford, I. N., & Barchas, J. D. (1985). Catecholamine secretion as a function of perceived coping self-efficacy. *Journal of Consulting and Clinical Psychology*, 53, 406–414.

Bandura, A., Blanchard, E. B., & Ritter, B. (1969). The relative efficacy of desensitization and modeling approaches for inducing behavioral, affective, and cognitive changes. *Journal of Personality and Social Psychology*, 13, 173–199.

Bandura, A. J., Grusen, J. E., & Menlove, F. L. (1967). Relative efficacy of desensitization and modeling approaches for inducing behavioral, affective, and attitudinal changes. *Journal of Personality and Social Psychology*, 5, 16–23.

Bandura, A., Jeffery, R. W., & Wright, C. L. (1974). Efficacy of participant modeling as a function of response induction aids. *Journal of Abnormal Psychology*, 83, 56–64.

Bandura, A., & Rosenthal, T. L. (1966). Vicarious classical conditioning as a function of fear arousal. *Journal of Personality and Social Psychology*, 3, 54–62.

Bandura, A., Ross, S. A., & Ross, D. (1963). Imitation of film-mediated aggressive models. *Journal of Abnormal and Social Psychology*, 66, 3–11.

Barber, T. X. (1970). *LSD, marijuana, yoga, and hypnosis*. Chicago: Aldine.

Barber, T. X. (1982). Hypnosuggestive procedures in the treatment of clinical pain: Implications for theories of hypnosis and suggestive therapy. In T. Millon, C. J. Green, & R. B. Meagher, Jr. (Eds.), *Handbook of clinical health psychology*. New York: Plenum.

Bardwick, J. (1971). *Psychology of women: A study of biocultural conflicts*. New York: Harper & Row.

Baribeau-Brown, J., Picton, T. W., & Gosselin, J. Y. (1983). Schizophrenia: A neurophysiological evaluation of abnormal information processing. *Science, 219*, 874–876.

Barker, S. L., Funk, S. C., & Houston, B. K. (1988). Psychological treatment versus nonspecific factors: A meta-analysis of conditions that engender comparable expectations for improvement. *Clinical Psychology Review, 8*, 579–594.

Barkin, R., Braun, B. G., & Kluft, R. P. (1986). The dilemma of drug therapy for multiple personality disorder. In B. G. Braun (Ed.), *Treatment of multiple personality disorder*. Washington, DC: American Psychiatric Press.

Barkley, R. A. (1981). *Hyperactive children: A handbook for diagnosis and treatment*. New York: Guilford Press.

Barkley, R. A., Hasting, J. E., Tousel, R. E., & Tousel, S. E. (1976). Evaluation of a token system for juvenile delinquents in a residential setting. *Journal of Behavior Therapy and Experimental Psychiatry, 7*, 227–230.

Barkley, R. A., Karlsson, J., Strzelecki, E., & Murphy, J. V. (1984). Effects of age and Ritalin dosage on the mother–child interactions of hyperactive children. *Journal of Consulting and Clinical Psychology, 52*, 750–758.

Barlow, D. H. (1986). Causes of sexual dysfunction: The role of anxiety and cognitive interference. *Journal of Consulting and Clinical Psychology, 54*, 140–148.

Barlow, D. H., Blanchard, E. B., Vermilyea, J. A., Vermilyea, B. B., & DiNardo, P. A. (1986). Generalized anxiety and generalized anxiety disorder: Description and reconceptualization. *American Journal of Psychiatry, 143*, 40–44.

Barlow, D. H., and others (1984). Panic and generalized anxiety disorders: Nature and treatment. *Behavior Therapy, 15*, 431–449.

Barlow, D. H., Sakheim, D. K., & Beck, J. G. (1983). Anxiety increases sexual arousal. *Journal of Abnormal Psychology, 92*, 49–54.

Barlow, D. H., Vermilyea, Y., Blanchard, E. B., Vermilyea, B. B., DiNardo, P. A., & Cerny, J. A. (1985). The phenomenon of panic. *Journal of Abnormal Psychology, 94*, 320–328.

Barnett, P. A. & Gotlib, I. (1988). Psychosocial functioning and depression: Distinguishing among antecedents, concomitants, and consequences. *Psychological Bulletin, 104*, 97–126.

Baron, M., Gruen, R., Asnis, L, & Lord, S. (1985). Familial transmission of schizotypal and borderline personality disorder. *Journal of Clinical Psychology, 142*, 927–934.

Barron, J. (1989, May 28). States sell chances for gold as rush turns to stampede. *The New York Times*, p. 24.

Basham, R. B. (1986). Scientific and practical advantages of comparative design in psychotherapy outcome research. *Journal of Consulting and Clinical Psychology, 54*, 88–94.

Bateson, G. D., Jackson, D., Haley, J., & Weakland, J. (1956). Toward a theory of schizophrenia. *Behavioral Science, 1*, 251–264.

Bauer, R. B., Stevens, J., Reveno, W. S., & Rosenbaum, H. (1982). L-Dopa treatment of Parkinson's disease: A ten-year follow-up study. *Journal of the American Geriatric Society, 42*, 187–195.

Baum, A., Deckel, A. W., & Gatchel, R. J. (1982). Environmental stress and health: Is there a relationship? In G. S. Sanders & J. Suls (Eds.), *Social psychology of health and illness*. Hillsdale, NJ: Erlbaum.

Baum, A., Gatchel, R. J., & Schaeffer, M. A. (1983). Emotional, behavioral, and physiological effects of chronic stress at Three Mile Island. *Journal of Consulting and Clinical Psychology, 43*, 565–572.

Baum, A., & Nesselhof, S. E. A. (1988). Psychological research and the prevention, etiology, and treatment of AIDS. *American Psychologist, 43*, 900–906.

Baumrind, D. (1983). Rejoinder to Lewis's reinterpretation of parental firm control effects: Are authoritative families really harmonious? *Psychological Bulletin, 94*, 132–142.

Beardslee, W. R., Bemporad, J., Keller, M. B., & Klerman, G. L. (1983). Children of parents with major affective disorder: A review. *American Journal of Psychiatry, 140*, 825–832.

Beaser, R. S., Vander Hoek, C., Jacobson, A. M., Flood, T. M., & Desautels, R. E. (1982). Experience with penile protheses in the treatment of impotence of diabetic men. *Journal of the American Medical Association, 248*, 943–948.

Beatrice, J. (1985). A psychological comparison of heterosexuals, transvestites, preoperative transsexuals, and postoperative transsexuals. *The Journal of Nervous and Mental Disease, 173*, 358–365.

Beck, A. T. (1976). *Cognitive therapy and the emotional disorders*. New York: International Universities Press.

Beck, A. T. (1985). Theoretical perspectives on clinical anxiety. In A. H. Tuma & J. D. Maser (Eds.), *Anxiety and the anxiety disorders*, Hillsdale, NJ: Erlbaum.

Beck, A. T., Brown, G., Steer, R. A., Eidelson, J. I., & Riskind, J. H. (1987). Differentiating anxiety and depression: A test of the cognitive content-specificity hypothesis. *Journal of Abnormal Psychology, 96*, 179–183.

Beck, A. T., Emery, G., & Greenberg, R. L. (1985). *Anxiety disorders and phobias: A cognitive perspective*. New York: Basic Books.

Beck, A. T., Epstein, N., Brown, G., & Steer, R. A. (1988). An inventory for measuring clinical anxiety: Psychometric properties. *Journal of Consulting and Clinical Psychology, 56*, 893–897.

Beck, A. T., Laude, R., & Bohnert, M. (1974). Ideational components of anxiety neurosis. *Archives of General Psychiatry, 31*, 319–325.

Beck, A. T., Rush, A. J., Shaw, B. F., & Emery, G. (1979). *Cognitive therapy of depression*. New York: Guilford Press.

Beck, A. T., Ward, C. H., Mendelson, M., Mock, J., & Erbaugh, J. (1961). An inventory for measuring depression. *Archives of General Psychiatry, 4*, 561–571

Beck, A. T., & Young, J. E. (1985). Depression. In D. H. Barlow (Ed.), *Clinical handbook of psychological disorders* (pp. 206–244). New York: Guilford Press.

Beck, J. G. (1984). *The effect of performance demand and attentional focus on sexual responding in functional and dysfunctional men*. Unpublished doctoral dissertation, State University of New York at Albany.

Beck, J. G., & Barlow, D. H. (1986). The effects of anxiety and attentional focus on sexual responding: II. Cognitive and affective patterns in erectile dysfunction. *Behaviour Research and Therapy, 24*, 19–26.

Becker, J. A. V., Skinner, L. J., & Abel, G. G. (1983). Sequelae of sexual assault: The survivor's perspective. In J. G. Greer & I. R. Stuart (Eds.), *The sexual aggressor* (pp. 240–266). New York: Van Nostrand Reinhold.

Becker, J. V., Skinner, L. J., Abel, G. G., & Cichon, J. (1984). Time-limited therapy with sexually dysfunctional sexually assaulted women. *Journal of Social Work and Human Sexuality, 3*, 97–115.

Becker, J. V., Skinner, L. J., Abel, G. G., & Cichon, J. (1986). Level of postassault sexual functioning in rape and incest victims. *Archives of Sexual Behavior, 15*, 37–49.

Beckham, E. E., & Leber, W. R. (1985). The comparative efficacy of psychotherapy and pharmacotherapy for depression. In E. E. Beckham & W. R. Leber (Eds.), *Handbook of depression: Treatment, assessment, and research*. Homewood, IL: Dorsey Press.

Beckham, E. E., Leber, W. R., Watkins, J. T., Boyer, J. L., & Cook, J. B. (1986). Development of an instrument to measure Beck's cognitive triad: The Cognitive Triad Inventory. *Journal of Consulting and Clinical Psychology, 54*, 566–567.

Begleiter, H., Parjesz, B., Bihari, B., & Kissin, B. (1984). Event-related brain potentials in boys at risk for alcoholism. *Science, 225*, 1493–1496.

Beidel, D. C., & Turner, S. M. (1986). A critique of the theoretical bases of cognitive-behavioral theories and therapy. *Clinical Psychology Review, 6*, 177–199.

Beis, E. (1983). State involuntary commitment statutes. *Mental Disability Law Recorder, 7*, 358–369.

Beitman, B. D. (1987). Panic attacks and their treatment: An introduction. *Journal of Integrative and Eclectic Psychotherapy, 6*, 412–420.

Bell, A. P., & Weinberg, M. S. (1978). *Homosexualities: A study of diversity among men and women*. New York: Simon & Schuster.

Bell, A. P., Weinberg, M. S., & Hammersmith, S. K. (1981). *Sexual preference: Its development in men and women*. Bloomington: University of Indiana Press.

Bellack, A. S. (1986). Schizophrenia: Behavior therapy's forgotten child. *Behavior Therapy, 17*, 199–214.

Bellack, A. S., & Hersen, M. (1978). Chronic psychiatric patients: Social skills training. In M. Hersen & A. S. Bellack (Eds.), *Behavior therapy in the psychiatric setting*. Baltimore: Williams & Wilkins.

Bellack, A. S., Turner, S. M., Hersen, M., & Luber, R. F. (1984). An examination of social skills training for chronic schizophrenic patients. *Hospitals and Community Psychiatry, 35*, 1023–1028

Belsher, G., & Costello, C. G. (1988). Relapse after recovery from unipolar depression: A critical review. *Psychological Bulletin, 104*, 84–96.

Bemis, K. M. (1978). Current approaches to the etiology and treatment of anorexia nervosa. *Psychological Bulletin, 85*, 593–617.

Bender, L. (1938). A visual motor gestalt test and its clinical use. *Research Monograph of the American Orthopsychiatric Association, 3*, XI, 176.

Bender, L. (1947). Childhood schizophrenia: Clinical study of one hundred schizophrenic children. *American Journal of Orthopsychiatry, 17*, 40–56.

Bender L. (1956). Schizophrenia in childhood—its recognition, description and treatment. *American Journal of Orthopsychiatry, 26*, 499–506.

Bennett, D. (1985). Rogers: More intuition in therapy. *APA Monitor, 16*, 3.

Bennett, G. (1986). Behavior therapy for obesity: A quantitative review of the effects of selected treatment characteristics on outcome. *Behavior Therapy, 17*, 554–562.

Bennett, W. (1988, January 10). The drink-a-day lore. *The New York Times Magazine*, pp. 55–56.

Benowitz, N. L., & Jacob, P., III. (1985). Nicotine renal excretion rate influences nicotine intake during cigarette smoking. *Journal of Pharmacological and Experimental Therapeutics, 234*, 153–155.

Benson, C. S., & Heller, K. (1987). Factors in the current adjustment of young adult daughters of alcoholic and problem drinking fathers. *Journal of Abnormal Psychology, 96*, 305–312.

Benson, H. (1975). *The relaxation response*. New York: Morrow.

Benson, H., Manzetta, B. R., & Rosner, B. (1973). Decreased systolic blood pressure in hypertensive subjects who practiced meditation. *Journal of Clinical Investigation, 52*, 8.

Bentler, M. (1976). A typology of transsexualism:

A behavior and your heart. New York: Fawcett Crest.

Friedman, S. R., and others (1987). AIDS and self-organization among intravenous drug users. *International Journal of Addictions, 22,* 201–220.

Friedrich, W. N., & Boriskin, J. A. (1976). The role of the child in abuse: A review of the literature. *American Journal of Orthopsychiatry, 46,* 580–589.

Frieze, I. (1979). Perception of battered wives. In I. H. Frieze, D. Bar-Tal, & J. S. Carroll (Eds.), *New approaches to social problems: Applications of attribution theory.* San Francisco: Jossey-Bass.

Frodi, A. M. (1981). Contribution of infant characteristics to child abuse. *American Journal of Mental Deficiency, 85,* 341–349.

Frodi, A. M. (1985). When empathy fails: Infant crying and child abuse. In B. M. Lester & C. F. Z. Boukydis (Eds.) *Infant crying.* New York: Plenum Press.

Fromm-Reichmann, F. (1948). Notes on the development of treatment of schizophrenics by psychoanalytic psychotherapy. *Psychiatry, 11,* 263–273.

Fromm-Reichmann, F. (1950). *Principles of intensive psychotherapy.* Chicago: University of Chicago Press.

Frye, J. S., & Stockton, R. A. (1982). Discriminant analysis of posttraumatic stress disorder among a group of Vietnam veterans. *American Journal of Psychiatry, 139,* 52–56.

Fuchs, C. Z., & Rehm, L. P. (1977). A self-control behavior therapy program for depression. *Journal of Consulting and Clinical Psychology, 45,* 206–215.

Fulero, S. M. (1988). Tarasoff: 10 Years Later. *Professional Psychology: Research and Practice, 19,* 184–190.

Fullerton, D. I., Cayner, J. J., & McLaughlin-Reidel, T. (1978). Results of a token economy. *Archives of General Psychiatry, 35,* 1451–1453.

Funkenstein, D. (1955, May). The physiology of fear and anger. *Scientific American,* pp. 74–80.

Fustero, S. (1984, February). Home on the street. *Psychology Today,* pp. 56–63.

Gadow, K. D. (1985). Relative efficacy of pharmacological, behavioral, and combination treatment for enhancing academic performance. *Clinical Psychology Review, 5,* 513–533.

Gagnon, J. H. (1977). *Human Sexualities.* Glenview, IL: Scott, Foresman.

Galassi, J. P. (1988). Four cognitive-behavioral approaches: Additional considerations. *The Counseling Psychologist, 16*(1), 102–105.

Gallant, S. J. & Hamilton, J. A. (1988). On a premenstrual psychiatric diagnosis: What's in a name? *Professional Psychology Research and Practice, 19,* 271–278.

Ganellen, R. J., & Blaney, P. H. (1984). Hardiness and social support as moderators of the effects of life stress. *Journal of Personality and Social Psychology, 47,* 156–163.

Garcia, J. (1981). The logic and limits of mental aptitude testing. *American Psychologist, 36,* 1172–1180.

Gardos, G., & Cole, J. O. (1976). Maintenance antipsychotic therapy: Is the cure worse than the disease? *American Journal of Psychiatry, 133,* 32–36.

Gardos, G., Cole, J. O, Salomon, M., & Schniebolk, S. (1987). Clinical forms of severe tardive dyskinesia. *American Journal of Psychiatry, 144,* 895–902.

Garfield, S. L. (1981). Psychotherapy: A 40-year appraisal. *American Psychologist, 36,* 174–183.

Garfield, S. L. (1982). Eclecticism and integration in psychotherapy. *Behavior Therapy, 13,* 610–623.

Garner, D. M. (1985). Individual psychotherapy for anorexia nervosa. *Journal of Psychiatric Research, 19,* 423–433.

Garner, D. M., Garfinkel, P. E., Schwartz, D. M., & Thompson, M. G. (1980). Cultural expecta-

tions of thinness in women. *Psychological Reports, 47,* 483–491.

Garner, D. M., Olmstead, M. P., & Polivy, J. (1983). Development and validation of a multidimensional eating disorder inventory for anorexia and bulimia. *International Journal of Eating Disorders, 2,* 15–34.

Garrow, J. S., Durant, M. L., Mann, S., Stalley, S. F., & Warwick, P. M. (1978). Factors determining weight loss in obese patients in a metabolic ward. *International Journal of Obesity, 2,* 441–447.

Gately, G. (1989, January 22). Hospital leads patients to where all bets are off. *The New York Times,* p. 31.

Gath, A. (1985). Down's syndrome in the first nine years. In A. R. Nicol (Ed.), *Longitudinal studies in child psychology and psychiatry.* New York: Wiley.

Gawin, F. H., & Ellinwood, E. H. (1988). Cocaine and other stimulants: Actions, abuse, and treatment. *New England Journal of Medicine, 318,* 1173–1182.

Gawin, F. H., & Ellinwood, E. H. (1989). Cocaine dependence. *Annual Review of Medicine, 40,* 149–161.

Gawin, F. H., Kleber, H. D., Byck, R., Rounsaville, B. J., Kosten, T. R., Jatlow, P. I., & Morgan, C. (1989). Desipramine facilitation of initial cocaine abstinence. *Archives of General Psychiatry, 46,* 117–121.

Gebhard, P. H. (1976). The institute. In M. S. Weinberg (Ed.), *Sex research: Studies from the Kinsey Institute.* New York: Oxford University Press.

Gebhard, P. H., Gagnon, J. H., Pomeroy, W. B., & Christenson, C. V. (1965). *Sex offenders: An analysis of types.* New York: Harper & Row.

Geer, J., Morokoff, P., & Greenwood, P. (1974). Sexual arousal in women: The development of a measurement device for vaginal blood volume. *Archives of Sexual Behavior, 3,* 559–564.

Gelberg, L., Linn, L. S., & Leake, B. D. (1988). Mental health, alcohol and drug use, and criminal history among homeless adults. *American Journal of Psychiatry, 144,* 191–196.

Geller, E., Ritvo, E. F., Freeman, B. J., & Yuwiler, A. (1982). Preliminary observations on the effect of fenfluramine on blood serotonin and symptoms in three autistic boys. *New England Journal of Medicine, 307,* 3.

Gelman, D. (1988, August 29). Treating war's psychic wounds: Stress disorder among Vietnam vets may be rising. *Newsweek,* pp. 62–64.

Gelman, D., Hager, M., & Quade, V. (1989, December 18). The brain killer. *Newsweek,* pp. 54–56.

Gentry, W. D., Chesney, A. P., Hall, R. P., & Harburg, E. (1982). Habitual anger-coping styles: I. Effect of mean blood pressure and risk for essential hypertension. *Psychosomatic Medicine, 44,* 195–202.

Georgotas, A., & McCue, R. E. (1986). Benefits and limitations of major pharmacological treatment for depression. *American Journal of Psychotherapy, 40,* 370–376.

Gerrard, G. (1986). Are men and women really different? In K. Kelley (Ed.), *Females, males, and sexuality.* Albany: State University of New York at Albany Press.

Gershon, E. S., Bunney, W. E., Leckman, J. F., Van Eerdewegh, M., & Debaughce, B. A. (1976). The inheritance of affective disorders: A review of data and hypotheses. *Behaviour Genetics, 6,* 227–261.

Ghose, K., & Coppen, A. (1977). Noradrenaline, depressive illness, and the action of amitriptyline. *Psychopharmacology, 54,* 57–60.

Giles, T. R., Young, R. R., & Young, D. E. (1985). Behavioral treatment of severe bulimia. *Behavior Therapy, 16,* 393–405.

Gill, J. S., and others (1986). Stroke and alcohol consumption. *New England Journal of Medicine, 315,* 1041–1046.

Girardi, J. A., Keese, R. M., Traver, L. B., & Cooksey,

D. R. (1988). Psychotherapist responsibility in notifying individuals at risk for exposure to HIV. *Journal of Sex Research, 25,* 1–27.

Gitlin, B., and others (1985). Behavior therapy for panic disorder. *Journal of Nervous and Mental Disease, 173,* 742–743.

Gitlin, M. J., & Pasnau, R. O. (1989). Psychiatric syndromes linked to reproductive function in women: A review of current knowledge. *American Journal of Psychiatry, 146,* 1413–1422.

Gittleman-Klein, R., & Klein, D. F. (1969). Premorbid asocial adjustment and prognosis in schizophrenia. *Journal of Psychiatric Research, 7,* 35–53.

Glasberg, R., & Aboud, F. (1982). Keeping one's distance from sadness: Children's self-reports of emotional experience. *Developmental Psychology, 18,* 287–293.

Glaser, R., and others (1985). Stress-related impairments in cellular immunity. *Psychiatry Research, 16,* 233–239.

Glaser, R., & Kiecolt-Glaser, J. K. (1987). Stress-associated depression in cellular immunity: Implications for acquired immune deficiency syndrome (AIDS). *Brain, Behavior, and Immunity, 1,* 107–112.

Glaser, R., and others (1987). Stress-related immune suppression: Health implications. *Brain, Behavior, and Immunity, 1,* 7–20.

Glaser, R., and others (1986). Stress depresses interferon production by leukocytes concomitant with a decrease in natural killer cell activity. *Behavioral Neuroscience, 100,* 675–678.

Glasgow, R. E. (1986). Smoking. In K. Holroyd & T. Creer (Eds.), *Self-management of chronic disease and handbook of clinical interventions and research* (pp. 99–126). Orlando, FL: Academic Press.

Glasgow, R. E., Klesges, R. C., Godding, P. R., & Gegelman, R. (1983). Controlled smoking, with or without carbon monoxide feedback, as an alternative for chronic smokers. *Behavior Therapy, 14,* 396–397.

Glasgow, R. E., Klesges, R. C., Godding, P. R., Vasey, M. W., & O'Neill, H. K. (1984). Evaluation of a worksite-controlled smoking program. *Journal of Consulting and Clinical Psychology, 52,* 137–138.

Glasgow, R. E., Klesges, R. C., Klesges, L. M., Vasey, M. W., & Gunnarson, D. F. (1985). Long-term effects of a controlled smoking program: A two and one-half year follow-up. *Behavior Therapy, 16,* 303–307.

Glasgow, R. E., & Lichtenstein, E. (1987). Long-term effects of behavioral smoking cessation interventions. *Behavior Therapy, 18,* 297–324.

Glasgow, R. E., & Terborg, J. R. (1988). Occupational health promotion programs to reduce cardiovascular risk. *Journal of Consulting and Clinical Psychology, 56,* 365–373.

Glasner, P. D., & Kaslow, R. A. (1990) The epidemiology of human immunodeficiency virus infection. *Journal of Consulting and Clinical Psychology, 58,* 13–21.

Glass, D. C., & Singer, J. E. (1972). *Urban stress: Experiments on noise and social stressors.* New York: Academic Press.

Glass, G. V., & Kliegl, R. M. (1983). An apology for research intergration in the study of psychotherapy. *Journal of Consulting and Clinical Psychology, 51,* 28–41.

Glasscote, R. (1978). What programs work and what programs do not work for chronic mental patients? In J. A. Talbott (Ed.), *The chronic mental patient: Problems, solutions and recommendations for a public policy.* Washington, DC: American Psychiatric Press.

Gleser, G., Green, B., & Winget, C. (1981). *Prolonged psychosocial effects of disaster: A study of Buffalo Creek.* New York: Academic Press.

Glover, J. H. (1985). A case of kleptomania treated by covert sensitization. *British Journal of Clinical Psychology, 24,* 213–214.

Glueck, S., & Glueck, E. (1950). *Unraveling juvenile*

delinquency. New York: The Commonwealth Fund.

Glynn, S., & Mueser, K. T. (1986). Social learning for chronic mental inpatients. *Schizophrenia Bulletin, 12*, 648–668.

Goddard, H. H. (1917). Mental tests and the immigrant. *The Journal of Delinquency, 2*, 243–277.

Godfrey, H. P., & Knight, R. G. (1987). Interventions for amnesics: A review. *British Journal of Clinical Psychology, 26*, 83–91.

Goeders, N. E., & Smith, J. E. (1983). Cortical dopaminergic involvement in cocaine reinforcement. *Science, 221*, 773–775.

Goldberg, E., & Bilder, R. M. (1986). Neuropsychological perspectives: Retrograde amnesia and executive deficits. In L. W. Poon (Ed.), *Handbook for clinical memory assessment of older adults* (pp. 55–68). Washington, DC: American Psychological Association.

Golden, C. J., Hammeke, T. A., & Purisch, A. D. (1980). *The Luria-Nebraska Neuropsychological Battery: Manual*. Los Angeles: Western Psychological Services.

Goldfarb, L. A., Dykens, E. M., & Gerrard, M. (1985). The Goldfarb Fear of Fat Scale. *Journal of Personality Assessment, 49*, 329–332.

Goldfried, M., & Zax, M. (1965). The stimulus value of the TAT. *Journal of Projective Techniques, 29*, 46–57.

Goldfried, M. R. (1988). Application of rational restructuring to anxiety disorders. *The Counseling Psychologist, 16*, 50–68.

Goldfried, M. R., & Davison, G. C. (1976). *Clinical behavior therapy*. New York: Holt, Rinehart & Winston.

Goldfried, M. R., Linehan, M. M., & Smith, J. L. (1978). Reduction of test anxiety through cognitive restructuring. *Journal of Consulting and Clinical Psychology, 46*, 32–39.

Goldfried, M. R., & Kent, R. N. (1972). Traditional versus behavioral assessment: A comparison of methodological and theoretical assumptions. *Psychological Bulletin, 77*, 409–420.

Goldman, H. H., Taub, C. A., & Regier, D. A. (1983). The multiple functions of the state mental hospital. *American Journal of Psychiatry, 140*, 296–300.

Goldsmith, H. H. (1983). Genetic influences on personality from infancy to adulthood. *Child Development, 54*, 331–355.

Goldstein, A. (1976). Opioid peptides (endorphines) in pituitary and brain. *Science, 193*, 1081–1086.

Goldstein, J. M. (1988). Gender differences in the course of schizophrenia. *American Journal of Psychiatry, 145*, 684–689.

Goldstein, M. J. (1987a). The UCLA high-risk project. *Schizophrenia Bulletin, 13*, 505–514.

Goldstein, M. J. (1987b). Psychosocial issues. *Schizophrenia Bulletin, 13*, 157–171.

Goldstein, M. J., Rodnick, E. H., Evans, J. R., May, P. R. A., & Steinberg, M. R. (1978). Drug and family therapy in the aftercare of acute schizophrenics. *Archives of General Psychiatry, 35*, 1169–1177.

Goldstein, M. J., & Tuma, A. H. (1987). High-risk research: Editors' introduction. *Schizophrenia Bulletin, 13*, 369–371.

Goldstein, R. L. (1986). Erotomania. *American Journal of Psychiatry, 143*, 802.

Goleman, D. (1984, December 11). Schizophrenia: Early signs found. *The New York Times*, pp. C1, C16.

Goleman, D. J. (1985, January 15). Pressure mounts for analysts to prove theory is scientific. *The New York Times*, pp. C1, C9.

Goleman, D. (1986a, March 19). Focus on day-to-day support offers hope to schizophrenics. *The New York Times*, p. B12.

Goleman, D. (1986b, November 4). To expert eyes, city streets are open mental wards. *The New York Times*, pp. C1, C3.

Goleman, D. (1988, December 13). Obsessive disorder: Secret toll is found. *The New York Times*, pp. C1, C11.

Goleman, D. (1988a, November 1). Narcissism looming larger as root of personality woes. *The New York Times: Science Times*, pp. C1, C16.

Goleman, D. (1988b, October 18). Chemistry of sexual desire yields its elusive secrets. *The New York Times*, pp. C1, C15.

Gomberg, E. S. (1980). Risk factors related to alcohol problems among women. In *Alcoholism and alcohol abuse among women* (Research Monograph No. 1, pp. 83–106). Rockville, MD: National Institute on Alcohol Abuse and Alcoholism.

Gonzales, L. R., Lewinsohn, P. M., & Clarke, G. N. (1985). Longitudinal follow-up of unipolar depressives: An investigation of predictors of relapse. *Journal of Consulting and Clinical Psychology, 53*, 461–469.

Goodman, A. B., Siegel, C., Craig, T., Wanderling, J., & Haugland, G. (1981). Inpatient alcoholism treatment rates in a suburban county, by sex, age and social class. *Journal of Studies on Alcohol, 42*, 414–420.

Goodman, S. H. (1987). Emory University project on children of disturbed parents. *Schizophrenia Bulletin, 13*, 411–423.

Goodwin, D. W. (1979). Alcoholism and heredity: A review and hypothesis. *Archives of General Psychiatry, 36*, 57–61.

Goodwin, D. W. (1985). Alcoholism and genetics. *Archives of General Psychiatry, 42*, 171–174.

Goodwin, D. W., Schulsinger, F., Hermansen, L., Guze, S. B., & Winokur, G. (1973). Alcohol problems in adoptees raised apart from alcoholic biological parents. *Archives of General Psychiatry, 28*, 238–243.

Goodwin, D. W., Schulsinger, F., Knop, J., Mednick, S., & Guze, S. B. (1977). Alcoholism and depression in adopted-out daughters of alcoholics. *Archives of General Psychiatry, 34*, 751–755.

Goodwin, D. W., Schulsinger, F., Moller, N., Hermansen, L., Winokur, G., & Guze, S. B. (1974). Drinking problems in adopted and nonadopted sons of alcoholics. *Archives of General Psychiatry, 31*, 164–169.

Goodwin, F. K., & Jamision, K. R. (1987). Bipolar disorders. In R. E. Hales & A. J. Frances (Eds.), *American Psychiatric Association Annual Review* (Vol. 6). Washington, DC: American Psychiatric Press.

Gordon, T., & Doyle, J. T. (1987). Drinking and mortality: The Albany Study. *American Journal of Epidemiology, 125*, 263–270.

Gorenstein, E. (1982). Frontal lobe function in psychopaths. *Journal of Abnormal Psychology, 91*, 368–379.

Gormally, J., Sipps, G., Raphael, R., Edwin, D., & Varvil-Weld, D. (1981). The relationship between maladaptive cognitions and social anxiety. *Journal of Consulting and Clinical Psychology, 49*, 300–301.

Gorman, J. M., and others (1985). Lactate infusions in obsessive-compulsive disorder. *American Journal of Psychiatry, 142*, 864–866.

Gotlib, I. H. (1982). Self-reinforcement and depression in interpersonal interaction: The role of performance level. *Journal of Abnormal Psychology, 91*, 3–13.

Gotlib, I. H. (1984). Depression and general psychopathology in university students. *Journal of Abnormal Psychology, 93*, 19–30.

Gottesman, I. I., McGuffin, P., & Farmer, A. E. (1987). Clinical genetics as clues to the "real" genetics of schizophrenia. *Schizophrenia Bulletin, 13*, 23–47.

Gottesman, I. I., & Shields, J. (1972). *Schizophrenia and genetics: A twin study vantage point*. New York: Academic Press.

Gottesman, I. I., & Shields, J. (1982). *Schizophrenia: The epigenetic puzzle* (pp. xiii and 258). Cambridge, England: Cambridge University Press.

Gottesman, I. I., & Shields, J. (1976). A critical review of recent adoption, twin, and family studies of schizophrenia: Behavioral genetics perspectives. *Schizophrenia Bulletin, 2*, 360–401.

Gottlieb, A. M., Killen, J. D., Marlatt, G. A., & Barr-Taylor C. (1987). Psychological and pharmacological influences in cigarette smoking withdrawal: Effects of nicotine gum and expectancy on smoking withdrawal symptoms and relapse. *Journal of Consulting and Clinical Psychology, 55*, 606–608.

Gould, R., Miller, B. L., Goldberg, M. A., & Benson, D. F. (1986). The validity of hysterical signs and symptoms. *The Journal of Nervous and Mental Disease, 174*, 593–597.

Goy, R. W., & Goldfoot, D. A. (1976). Neuroendocrinology: Animal models and problems of human sexuality. In E. A. Rubenstein and others (Eds.), *New directions in sex research*. New York: Plenum.

Goy, R. W., & McEwen, B. S. (1982). *Sexual differentiation of the brain*. Cambridge, MA: MIT Press.

Grabowski, J. (1984) (Ed.). *Cocaine: Pharmacology, effects, and treatment of abuse*. Rockville, MD: National Institute on Drug Abuse.

Graham, J. R. (1990). *MMPI-2: Assessing personality and psychopathology*. New York: Oxford University Press.

Graham, J. R., & Strenger, V. E. (1988). MMPI characteristics of alcoholics: A review. *Journal of Consulting and Clinical Psychology, 56*, 197–205.

Grant, I., & Heaton, R. K. (1990). Human immunodeficiency virus-type 1 (HIV-1) and the brain. *Journal of Consulting and Clinical Psychology, 58*, 22–30.

Greaves, G. B. (1980). Multiple personality: 165 years after Mary Reynolds. *Journal of Nervous and Mental Diseases, 168*, 577–596.

Green, A. H. (1978). Self-destructive behavior in battered children. *American Journal of Psychiatry, 135*, 579–582.

Green, A. R., & Goodwin, G. M. (1986). Antidepressants and monoamines: Actions and interactions. In J. W. W. Deakin (Ed.), *The biology of depression. Proceedings of a meeting of the Biological Group of the Royal College of psychiatrists held at Manchester University, 1985* (pp. 174–189). Washington, DC: American Psychiatric Press.

Green, B. L., Grace, M. C., Lindy, J. D., Titchener, J. L., & Lindy, J. G. (1983). Levels of functional impairment following a civilian disaster: The Beverly Hills Supper Club fire. *Journal of Consulting and Clinical Psychology, 51*, 573–580.

Green, J. A., Jones, L. E., & Gustafson, G. E. (1987). Perception of cries by parents and nonparents: Relation to cry acoustics. *Developmental Psychology, 23*, 370–382.

Green, R. (1978). Sexual identity of 37 children raised by homosexual or transsexual parents. *American Journal of Psychiatry, 135*, 692–697.

Green, R. (1987). *The "sissy boy syndrome" and the development of homosexuality*. New Haven, CT: Yale University Press.

Green, R., Mandel, J., Hotvedt, M., Gray, J., & Smith, L. (1986). Lesbian mothers and their children: A comparison with solo parent heterosexual mothers and their children. *Archives of Sexual Behavior, 15*, 167–184.

Greenberg, R. P., & Bornstein, R. F. (1988a). The dependent personality: I. Risk for physical disorders. *Journal of Personality Disorders, 2*, 126–135.

Greenberg, R. P., & Bornstein, R. F. (1988b). The dependent personality: II. Risk for psychological disorders. *Journal of Personality Disorders, 2*, 136–143.

Greene, J. G., Stevens, P. A., & Primavera, L. H. (1982). Predicting successful smoking cessation. *Journal of Social Psychology, 118*, 235–241.

Greenspan, S. I., & Porges, S. W. (1984). Psychopathology in infancy and early childhood: Clinical perspectives on the organization of sensory and affective-thematic experience. *Child Development, 55*, 49–70.

Greenwald, A. G. (1975). Consequences of prejudice against the null hypothesis. *Psychological Bulletin, 82*, 1–20.

Greer, S. (1964). Study of parental loss in neurotics

and sociopaths. *Archives of General Psychiatry, 11*, 177–180.

Greist, J. H. (1984). Exercise in the treatment of depression. *Coping with mental stress: The potential and limits of exercise intervention.* Washington, DC: National Institute of Mental Health.

Griest, D., Forehand, R., Wells, K., & McMahon, R. J. (1980). An examination of differences between non-clinic and behavior problem clinic-referred children and their mothers. *Journal of Abnormal Psychology, 89*, 497–500.

Grinspoon, L. (1987, July 28). Cancer patients should get marijuana. *The New York Times*, pp. A23.

Grob, G. N. (1983). *Mental illness and American Society, 1875–1940.* Princeton, NJ: Princeton University Press.

Gross, J., Rosen, J. C., Leitenberg, H., & Willmuth, M. E. (1986). Validity of the Eating Attitudes Test and the Eating Disorders Inventory in bulimia nervosa. *Journal of Consulting and Clinical Psychology, 54*, 875–876.

Gross, M. B., & Wilson, W. C. (1974). *Minimal brain dysfunction.* New York: Brunner/Mazel.

Groth, A. N., & Birnbaum, J. J. (1979). *Men who rape.* New York: Plenum.

Groth, A., & Hobson, W. (1983). The dynamics of sexual assault. In L. Schlesinger & E. Revitch (Eds.), *Sexual dynamics of antisocial behavior.* Springfield, IL: Chas. C Thomas.

Gruber, V. A., & Wildman, B. G. (1987). The impact of dysmenhorrea on daily activities. *Behavior Research and Therapy, 25*, 123–128.

Grünbaum, A. (1985). Cited in Goleman, D. J. (1985).

Gubman, G. D., Tessler, R. C., & Willis, G. (1987). Living with the mentally ill: Factors affecting household complaints. *Schizophrenia Bulletin, 13*, 727–736.

Guilford, J. P. (1959). *Personality.* New York: McGraw-Hill.

Gunderson, J. G., Frank, A. F., Katz, H. M., Vannicelli, M. L., Frosch, J. P., & Knapp, P. H. (1984). Effects of psychotherapy in schizophrenia: II. Comparative outcome of two forms of treatment. *Schizophrenia Bulletin, 10*, 564–598.

Gunderson, J. G., & Singer, M. T. (1986). Defining borderline patients: An overview. In M. H. Stone (Ed.), *Essential papers on borderline disorders* (pp. 453–474). New York: New York University Press.

Gur, R. E., Gur, R. C., Skolnick, B. E., Caroff, S., Obrist, W. D., Resnick, M. (1985). Brain function in psychiatric disorders. *Archives of General Psychiatry, 42*, 329–334.

Gur, R. E., and others (1987). Regional brain function in schizophrenia. *Archives of General Psychiatry, 44*, 119–125.

Gurevitz, H. (1977). Tarasoff: Protective privilege versus public peril. *American Journal of Psychiatry, 134*, 289–292.

Gurland, B., Dean, L., Cross, P., & Golder, R. (1980). The epidemiology of depression and dementia in the elderly: The use of multiple indicators of these conditions. In J. O. Cole & J. E. Barrett (Eds.), *Psychopathology in the aged* (pp. 37–62). New York: Raven Press.

Gurland, B. J., & Cross, P. S. (1986). Public health perspectives on clinical memory testing of Alzheimer's disease and related disorders. In L. W. Poon (Ed.), *Handbook for clinical memory assessment of older adults* (pp. 11–20). Washington, DC: American Psychological Association.

Gurling, H. M., Oppenheim, B. E., & Murray, R. M. (1984). Depression, criminality and psychopathology associated with alcoholism: Evidence from a twin study. *Acta Geneticae Medicae et Gemellologiae: Twin Research, 33*, 333–339.

Gutheil, T. G. (1980). In search of true freedom: Drug refusal, involuntary medication, and "rotting with your rights on." *American Journal of Psychiatry, 137*, 327–328.

Guttmacher, L. V., Murphy, D. L., & Infell, T. R.

(1983). Pharmacological models of anxiety. *Psychiatry, 24*, 312–326.

Gwinup, G. (1975). Effects of exercise alone on the weight of obese women. *Archives of Internal Medicine, 135*, 676–680.

Haaga, D. A. (1987). Treatment of the Type A behavior pattern. *Clinical Psychology Review, 7*, 557–574.

Haas, G. L., Clarkin, J. F., & Glick, I. D. (1985). Marital and family treatment of depression. In E. E. Beckham & W. R. Leber (Eds.), *Handbook of depression: Treatment, assessment and research* (pp. 151–183). Homewood, IL: Dorsey Press.

Hackett, T. P., & Cassem, N. H. (1974). Development of a quantitative rating scale to assess denial. *Journal of Psychosomatic Research, 18*, 93–100.

Hackett, T. P., Cassem, H. H., & Wishnie, H. (1968). The coronary-care unit: An appraisal of its psychologic hazards. *New England Journal of Medicine, 279*, 1365–1370.

Hall, G. S. (1904). *Adolescence: Its psychology and its relations to physiology, anthropology, sociology, sex, crime, religion, and education.* New York: D. Appleton.

Hall, N. R. S. (1988). The virology of AIDS. *American Psychologist, 43*, 907–913.

Hall, S. M., Rugg, D., Tunstall, C., & Jones, R. T. (1984). Preventing relapse to cigarette smoking by behavioral skill training. *Journal of Consulting and Clinical Psychology, 52*, 372–382.

Hall, V. C., & Kaye, D. B. (1980). Early patterns of cognitive development. *Monographs of the Society for Research in Child Development, 45*(2), Serial No. 184.

Halldin, M. (1985). Alcohol consumption and alcoholism in an urban population in central Sweden. *Acta Psychiatrica Scandinavica, 71*, 128–140.

Halleck, S. (1980). *Law in the practice of psychiatry: A handbook for clinicians.* New York: Plenum.

Halmi, K. A., Eckert, E., LaDu, T. J., & Cohen, J. (1986). Treatment efficacy of cyproheptadine and amitriptyline. *Archives of General Psychiatry, 43*, 177–181.

Halmi, K. A., Falk, J. R., & Schwartz, E. (1981). Binge-eating and vomiting: A survey of a college population. *Psychological Medicine, 11*, 697–706.

Hamilton, E. W., & Abramson, L. Y. (1983). Cognitive patterns and major depressive disorders: A longitudinal study in a hospital setting. *Journal of Abnormal Psychology, 92*, 173–184.

Hammen, C., Marks, T., Mayol, A., & deMayo, R. (1985). Depressive self-schemas, life stress, and vulnerability to depression. *Journal of Abnormal Psychology, 94*, 308–319.

Hammen, C., & de Mayo, R. (1982). Cognitive correlates of teacher stress and depressive symptoms: Implications for attributional models of depression. *Journal of Abnormal Psychology, 91*, 96–101.

Harackiewicz, J. M., Sansone, C., Blair, L. W., Epstein, J. A., & Manderlink, G. (1987). Attributional processes in behavior change and maintenance: Smoking cessation and continued abstinence. *Journal of Consulting and Clinical Psychology, 55*, 372–378.

Haracz, J. L. (1982). The dopamine hypothesis: An overview of studies with schizophrenic patients. *Schizophrenia Bulletin, 8*, 438–469.

Harburg, E., and others (1973). Socioecological stress, suppressed hostility, skin color, and black-white male blood pressure: Detroit. *Psychosomatic Medicine, 35*, 276–296.

Harding, J. J. (1989). Postpartum psychiatric disorders: A review. *Comprehensive Psychiatry, 30*, 109–112.

Hare, E. (1979). Schizophrenia as an infectious disease. *British Journal of Psychiatry, 135*, 468–470.

Hare, E. H., & Price, J. S. (1968). Mental disorder and season of birth: Comparison of psychoses with neurosis. *British Journal of Psychiatry, 115*, 533–540.

Hare, R. (1970). *Psychopathy: Theory and research.* New York: Wiley.

Hare, R. (1984). Performance of psychopaths on cognitive tasks related to frontal lobe function. *Journal of Abnormal Psychology, 93*, 133–140.

Hare, R. D. (1965). Temporal gradient of fear arousal in psychopaths. *Journal of Abnormal Psychology, 70*, 442–445.

Hare, R. D. (1984). Performance of psychopaths on cognitive tasks related to frontal lobe function. *Journal of Abnormal Psychology, 93*, 133–140.

Hare, R. D. (1986). Criminal psychopaths. In J. C. Yuille (Ed.), *Police selection and training: The role of psychology* (pp. 187–206). Dordrecht, Netherlands: Martinos Nijhoff.

Hare, R. D. (in press). Psychopathy and physiological activity during anticipation of an aversive stimulus in a distraction paradigm. *Psychophysiology.*

Hare, R. D., Frazelle, J., & Cox, D. N. (1978). Psychopathy and physiological responses to threat of an aversive stimulus. *Psychophysiology, 15*, 165–172.

Hare, R. D., McPherson, L. M., & Forth, A. E. (1988). Male psychopaths and their criminal careers. *Journal of Consulting and Clinical Psychology, 56*, 710–714.

Harrell, T. H., & Ryon, N. B. (1983). Cognitive-behavioral assessment of depression: Clinical validation of the Automatic Thoughts Questionnaire. *Journal of Consulting and Clinical Psychology, 51*, 721–725.

Harris, L. (1988). *Inside America.* New York: Vintage Books.

Harris, F. C., & Phelps, C. S. (1987). Anorexia and bulimia. In M. Hersen & V. B. Van Hasselt (Eds.), *Behavior therapy with children and adolescents: A clinical approach.* New York: Wiley.

Harris, G. W., & Levine, S. (1965). Sexual differentiation of the brain and its experimental control. *Journal of Physiology, 181*, 379–400.

Harris, J. G., Jr. (1984). Prognosis in schizophrenia. In A. S. Bellack (Ed.), *Schizophrenia: Treatment, management and rehabilitation* (pp. 79–112). Orlando, FL: Grune & Stratton.

Harris, S. L. (1986). Families of children with autism: Issues for the behavior therapist. *The Behavior Therapist, 9*, 175–177.

Harrow, M., & Marengo, J. T. (1986). Schizophrenic thought disorder at follow-up: Its persistence and prognostic significance. *Schizophrenia Bulletin, 12*, 373–393.

Harrow, M., & Quinlan, D. (1977). Is disordered thinking unique to schizophrenia? *Archives of General Psychiatry, 34*, 15–21.

Harrow, M., & Westermeyer, J. F. (1987). Process-reactive dimension and outcome for narrow concepts of schizophrenia. *Schizophrenia Bulletin, 13*, 361–368.

Harrow, M., Westermeyer, J. F., Silverstein, M., Strauss, B. S., & Cohler, B. J. (1986). Prediction of outcome in schizophrenia: The process-reactive dimension. *Schizophrenia Bulletin, 12*, 195–207.

Hart, B. M., Reynolds, N. J., Baer, D. M., Brawley, E. R. & Harris, F. R. (1968). Effect of contingent and non-contingent social reinforcement on the cooperative play of a preschool child. *Journal of Applied Behavior Analysis, 1*, 73–76.

Hart, K. J., & Ollendick, T. H. (1985). Prevalence of bulimia in working and university women. *American Journal of Psychiatry, 142*, 851–854.

Hart, R. P. (1987). Rate of forgetting in dementia and depression. *Journal of Consulting and Clinical Psychology, 55*, 101–105.

Harvey, P., Weintraub, S., & Neale, J. (1982). Speech competence of children vulnerable to psychopathology. *Journal of Abnormal Child Psychology, 10*, 373–388.

Hatfield, E., Sprecher, S., & Traupman, J. (1978). Men's and women's reactions to sexually explicit films: A serendipitous finding. *Archives of Sexual Behavior, 6*, 583–592.

Haughton, E., & Ayllon, T. (1965). Production and elimination of symptomatic behavior. In L. P. Ullmann & L. Krasner (Eds.), *Case studies in behavior modification*. New York: Holt, Rinehart & Winston.

Hauri, (1982). *The sleep disorders* (2nd Ed.). Kalamazoo, MI: Upjohn Company.

Hawkrigg, J. J. (1975). Agoraphobia. *Nursing Times, 71*, 1280–1282.

Hawton, K., & Catalan, J. (1986). Prognostic factors in sex therapy. *Behaviour Research and Therapy, 34*, 377–385.

Hawton, K., Catalan, J., Martin, P., & Fagg, J. (1986). Long–term outcome of sex therapy. *Behavior Research and Therapy, 24*, 665–675.

Hay, W. M., & Nathan, P. E. (Eds.). (1982). *Clinical case studies in the behavioral treatment of alcoholism*. New York: Plenum.

Haynes, S. G., & Feinleib, M. (1980). Women, work, and coronary heart disease: Prospective findings from the Framingham heart study. *American Journal of Public Health, 70*, 133–141.

Haynes, S. N. (1986). A behavioral model of paranoid behaviors. *Behavior Therapy, 17*, 266–287.

Hays, P. (1964). *New horizons in psychiatry*. Baltimore: Penguin Books.

Healy, D., & Williams, J. M. (1988). Dysrhythmia, dysphoria, and depression: The interaction of learned helplessness and circadian dysrhythmia in the pathogenesis of depression. *Psychological Bulletin, 103*, 163–178.

Heather, N., Rollnick, S., & Winton, M. (1983). A comparison of objective and subjective measures of alcohol dependence as predictors of relapse following treatment. *British Journal of Clinical Psychology, 22*, 11–17.

Heaton, R. K., & Victor, R. G. (1976). Personality characteristics associated with psychedelic flashbacks in natural and experimental settings. *Journal of Abnormal Psychology, 85*, 83–90.

Hechtman, L., & Weiss, G. (1983). Long-term outcome of hyperactive children. *American Journal of Orthopsychiatry, 53*, 522–541.

Heiby, E., & Becker, J. D. (1980). Effect of filmed modeling on the self-reported frequency of masturbation. *Archives of Sexual Behavior, 9*, 115–122.

Heiby, E. M., Campos, P. E., Remick, R. A., & Keller, F. D. (1987). Dexamethasone suppression and self-reinforcement correlates of clinical depression. *Journal of Abnormal Psychology, 96*, 70–72.

Heim, N. (1981). Sexual behavior of castrated sex offenders. *Archives of Sexual Behavior, 10*, 11–20.

Heim, N., & Hursch, C. J. (1979). Castration for sex offenders: Treatment or punishment: A review and critique of recent European literature. *Archives of Sexual Behavior, 8*, 281–304.

Heiman, J. R. (1978). Uses of psychophysiology in the assessment and treatment of sexual dysfunction. In J. LoPiccolo & L. LoPiccolo (Eds.), *Handbook of sex therapy* (pp. 123–135). New York: Plenum.

Heiman, J. R., & LoPiccolo, J. (1987). *Becoming orgasmic* (2nd ed.). Englewood Cliffs, NJ: Prentice Hall.

Heiman, J. R., LoPiccolo, L., & LoPiccolo, J. (1976). *Becoming orgasmic: A sexual growth program for women*. Englewood Cliffs, NJ: Prentice Hall.

Heiman, J. R., & Rowland, D. L. (1983). Affective and physiological sexual patterns: The effects of instructions on sexually functional and dysfunctional men. *Journal of Psychosomatic Research, 27*, 105–116.

Heimberg, R. G. (1989). Cognitive and behavioral treatments for social phobia: A critical analysis. *Clinical Psychology Review, 9*, 107–128.

Heimberg, R. G., and others (1987). Attributional style, depression, and anxiety: An evaluation of the specificity of depressive attributions. *Cognitive Therapy and Research, 11*, 537–550.

Heinrich, A. G. (1976, October). The effect of group and self-directed behavioral-educational treatment of primary orgasmic dysfunction in fe-

males treated without their partners. *Dissertation Abstracts International, 37*, 1902B.

Heinrichs, D. W., & Buchanan, R. W. (1988). Significance and meaning of neurological signs in schizophrenia. *American Journal of Psychiatry, 145*, 11–18.

Heisel, J. S., Locke, S. E., Kraus, L. J., & Williams, R. M. (1986). Natural killer cell activity and MMPI scores of a cohort of college students. *American Journal of Psychiatry, 143*, 1382–1386.

Hellerstein, D., Frosch, W., & Koenigsberg, H. W. (1987). The clinical significance of command hallucinations. *American Journal of Psychiatry, 144*, 219–221.

Helzer, J. E. (1987). Epidemiology of alcoholism. *Journal of Consulting and Clinical Psychology, 55*, 284–292.

Helzer, J. E., and others (1985). A comparison of clinical and diagnostic interview schedule diagnoses. *Archives of General Psychiatry, 42*, 657–666.

Henggeler, S. W. (Ed.) (1982). *Delinquency and adolescent psychopathology: A family-ecological systems approach*. Littleton, MA: Wright-PSG.

Henggeler, S. W., & Cohen, R. (1984). The role of cognitive development in the family-ecological systems approach to childhood psychopathology. In B. Gholson & T. L. Rosenthal (Eds.), *Applications of cognitive developmental theory*. New York: Academic Press.

Henggeler, S. W., Rodick, J. D., Borduin, C. M., Hanson, C. L., Watson, S. M., & Urey, J. R. (1986). Multisystemic treatment of juvenile offenders: Effects on adolescent behavior and family interaction. *Developmental Psychology, 22*, 132–141.

Henker, B., & Whalen, C. K. (1980). The changing faces of hyperactivity: Retrospect and prospect. In C. K. Whalen & B. Henker (Eds.), *Hyperactive children* (pp. 321–363). New York: Academic Press.

Herbert, M. (1978). *Conduct disorders of childhood and adolescence*. New York: Wiley.

Herman, C. P., & Polivy, J. (1980). Restrained eating. In A. J. Stunkard (Ed.), *Obesity* (pp. 208–225). Philadelphia: Saunders.

Herman, C. P., Polivy, J., Lank, C. N., & Heatherton, T. F. (1987). Anxiety, hunger, and eating behavior. *Journal of Abnormal Psychology, 96*, 264–269.

Herrell, J. M. (1975). Sex differences in emotional response to "erotic literature." *Journal of Consulting and Clinical Psychology, 43*, 921.

Herron, W. G. (1987). Evaluating the process-reactive dimension. *Schizophrenia Bulletin, 13*, 357–359.

Hersen, M., Bellack, A. S., Himmelhoch, J. M., & Thase, M. E. (1984). Effect of social skill training, amitriptyline, and psychotherapy in unipolar depressed women. *Behavior Therapy, 15*, 21–40.

Hertz, M. R. (1986). Rorschach bound: A 50-year memoir. *Journal of Personality Assessment, 50*, 396–416.

Herzog, D. B., Keller, M. B., & Lavori, P. W. (1988). Outcome in anorexia and bulimia nervosa: A review of the literature. *The Journal of Nervous and Mental Disease, 176*, 131–143.

Heston, L. L. (1966). Psychiatric disorders in foster home reared children of schizophrenic mothers. *British Journal of Psychiatry, 112*, 819–825.

Heston, L. L., Mastri, A. R., Anderson, V. E., & White, J. (1981). Dementia of the Alzheimer type: Clinical genetics, natural history, and associated conditions. *Archives of General Psychiatry, 38*, 1085–1090.

Heston, L. L., & Mastry, A. R. (1982). Age at onset of Pick's and Alzheimer's dementia: Implications for diagnosis and research. *Journal of Gerontology, 37*, 422–424.

Heston, L. L., White, J. A., & Mastri, A. R. (1987). Pick's disease: Clinical genetics and natural history. *Archives of General Psychiatry, 44*, 409–411.

Heuch, I., and others (1983). Use of alcohol, tobacco

and coffee, and risk of pancreatic cancer. *British Journal of Cancer, 48*, 637–643.

Heyman, A., and others (1983). Alzheimer's disease: Genetic aspects and associated clinical disorders. *Annals of Neurology, 14*, 507–515.

Hibbert, G. A. (1984). Ideational components of anxiety. *British Journal of Psychiatry, 144*, 618–624.

Higgins, J. (1966). Effects of child rearing by schizophrenic mothers. *Journal of Psychiatric Research, 4*, 153–167.

Hilberman, E. (1980). Overview: "The wife-beater's wife" reconsidered. *American Journal of Psychiatry, 137*, 1336–1347.

Hilgard, E. R. (1978). Hypnosis and pain. In R. A. Sternbach (Ed.), *The psychology of pain*. New York: Raven Press.

Hill, A. L. (1977). Idiot savants: The rate of incidence. *Perceptual and Motor Skills, 44*, 161–162.

Hill, R. D., Johnson, D., & Maccoby, N. (1986). *Prescribing relapse to enhance nonsmoking treatment gains*. Manuscript submitted for publication.

Hill, S. Y. (1980). The biological consequences of alcohol for women. In *Alcoholism and alcohol abuse among women* (Research Monograph No. 1, pp. 45–62). Rockville, MD: National Institute on Alcohol Abuse and Alcoholism.

Hinshaw, S. (1987). On the distinction between attentional deficits/hyperactivity and conduct problems/aggression in child psychopathology. *Psychological Bulletin, 101*, 443–463.

Hinz, L. D., & Williamson, D. A. (1987). Bulimia and depression: A review of the affective variant hypothesis. *Psychological Bulletin, 102*, 150–158.

Hirsch, S. R., & Leff, J. P. (1975). *Abnormalities in parents of schizophrenics*. Oxford, England: Oxford University Press.

Hirschfeld, R. M. A., & Cross, C. (1982). Epidemiology of affective disorders. *Archives of General Psychiatry, 39*, 35–46.

Hoelscher, T. J., Lichstein, K. L., Fischer, S., & Hegarty, T. B. (1987). Relaxation treatment of hypertension: Do home relaxation tapes enhance treatment outcome? *Behavior Therapy, 18*, 33–37.

Hoenig, J. (1983). The concept of schizophrenia: Kraepelin-Bleuler-Schneider. *British Journal of Psychiatry, 142*, 547–556.

Hoffman, A. (1971). LSD discoverer disputes "chance" factor in finding. *Psychiatric News, 6*, 23–26.

Hoffman, J. J., Hall, R. W., & Bartsch, T. W. (1987). On the relative importance of "psychopathic" personality and alcoholism on neuropsychological measures of frontal lobe dysfunction. *Journal of Abnormal Psychology, 96*, 158–160.

Hoffman, K. (1981). Phototherapy periodism in vertebrates. In J. Ascher (Ed.), *Handbook of behavioral neurobiology* (Vol. 4). New York: Plenum.

Hoffman, L. (1981). *Foundations of family therapy: A conceptual framework for systems change*. New York: Basic Books.

Hoffman-Plotkin, D., & Twentyman, C. T. (1984). A multimodal assessment of behavioral and cognitive deficits in abused and neglected preschoolers. *Child Development, 55*, 794–802.

Hoffmann, W., & Prior, M. (1982). Neuropsychological dimensions of autism in children: A test of the hemispheric dysfunction hypothesis. *Journal of Clinical Neuropsychology, 4*, 27–42.

Hogarty, G. E. (1985). Expressed emotion and schizophrenic relapse: Implications from the Pittsburgh study. In M. Alpert (Ed.), *Controversies in schizophrenia* (pp. 354–365). New York: Guilford Press.

Hogarty, G. E., Anderson, C. M., Reiss, D. J., Kornblith, S. J., Greenwald, D. P., Javna, C. D., & Madonia, M. J. (1986). Family psychoeducation, social skills training, and maintenance chemotherapy in the aftercare of schizophrenia. *Archives of General Psychiatry, 43*, 633–642.

Hogarty, G. E., Goldberg, S. C., & the Collaborative Study Group (1973). Drug and sociotherapy in the aftercare of schizophrenic patients: One-year relapse rates. *Archives of General Psychiatry, 28*, 54–64.

Hogarty, G. E., and others (1974). Drug and sociotherapy in the aftercare of schizophrenic patients. II: Two-year relapse rates. *Archives of General Psychiatry, 31*, 603–608.

Hogarty, G. E., Schroeder, N. R., Ulrich, R., Mussare, N., Peregino, F., & Herron, E. (1979). Fluphenazine and social therapy in the aftercare of schizophrenic patients. *Archives of General Psychiatry, 36*, 1283–1294.

Holahan, C. J., & Moos, R. H. (1985). Life stress and health: Personality, coping, and family support in stress resistance. *Journal of Personality and Social Psychology, 49*, 739–747.

Holahan, C. J., & Moos, R. H. (1987). Risk, resistance, and psychological distress: A longitudinal analysis with adults and children. *Journal of Abnormal Psychology, 96*, 3–13.

Holden, A. E., Jr., & Barlow, D. H. (1986). Heart rate and heart rate variability recorded in vivo in agoraphobics and nonphobics. *Behavior Therapy, 17*, 26–42.

Holden, C. (1986). Researchers grapple with problems of updating classic psychological test. *Science*, 1249–1251.

Hollingshead, A. B., & Redlich, F. C. (1958). *Social class and mental illness: A community study*. New York: Wiley.

Hollon, S. D., & Beck, A. T. (1979). Cognitive therapy for depression. In P. C. Kendall & S. D. Hollon (Eds.), *Cognitive-behavioral interventions: Theory, research and procedures* (pp. 153–196). Orlando, FL: Academic Press.

Hollon, S. D., & Kendall, P. C. (1980). Cognitive self-statements in depression: Development of an automatic thoughts questionnaire. *Cognitive Therapy and Research, 4*, 383–395.

Holloway, W., & McNally, R. J. (1987). Effects of anxiety sensitivity on the response to hyperventilation. *Journal of Abnormal Psychology, 96*, 330–334.

Holmes, D. S. (1984). Meditation and somatic arousal reduction: A review of the experimental evidence. *American Psychologist, 39*, 1–10.

Holmes, D. S. (1985). To meditate or to simply rest, that is the question: A response to the comments of Shapiro. *American Psychologist, 40*, 722–725.

Holmes, D. S., Solomon, S., Cappo, B. M., & Greenberg, J. L. (1983). Effects of transcendental meditation versus resting on physiological and subjective arousal. *Journal of Personality and Social Psychology, 44*, 1244–1252.

Holmes, T. H., & Rahe, R. H. (1967). The social readjustment rating scale. *Journal of Psychosomatic Research, 11*, 213–218.

Holroyd, K. A., and others (1988). Recurrent vascular headache: Home-based behavioral treatment versus abortive pharmacological treatment. *Journal of Consulting and Clinical Psychology, 56*, 218–223.

Holroyd, K. A., & Penzien, D. B. (1986). Behavioral treatment of tension headache: Meta-analytic review. *Journal of Behavioral Medicine, 9*, 515–536.

Holroyd, K. A., Westbrook, T., Wolf, M., & Badhorn, E. (1978). Performance, cognition, and physiological responding in test anxiety. *Journal of Abnormal Psychology, 87*, 442–451.

Holtzman, S. C. (1974). Behavioral effects of separate and combined administration of naloxone and d-amphetamine. *Journal of Pharmacology and Experimental Therapy, 189*, 51–60.

Holzman, P. S. (1986). Thought disorder in schizophrenia: Editor's introduction. *Schizophrenia Bulletin, 12*, 342–347.

Holzman, P. S. (1987). Recent studies of psychophysiology in schizophrenia. *Schizophrenia Bulletin, 13*, 49–75.

Holzman, P. S., Shenton, M. E., & Solovay, M. R. (1986). Quality of thought disorder in differential diagnosis. *Schizophrenia Bulletin, 12*, 360–372.

Hooley, J. M., Richters, J. E., Weintraub, S., & Neal, J. M. (1987). Psychopathology and marital distress: The positive side of positive symptoms. *Journal of Abnormal Psychology, 96*, 27–33.

Hoon, P., Wincze, J., & Hoon, E. (1977). A test of reciprocal inhibition: Are anxiety and sexual arousal in women mutually inhibitory? *Journal of Abnormal Psychology, 86*, 65–74.

Hopkins, J., Campbell, S. B., & Marcus, M. (1987). Role of infant-related stressors in postpartum depression. *Journal of Abnormal Psychology, 96*, 237–241.

Horan, J. J., Hacket, G., Nicholas, W. C., Linberg, S. E., Stone, C. I., & Lukaski, H. C. (1977). Rapid-smoking, a cautionary note. *Journal of Consulting and Clinical Psychology, 45*, 341–343.

Horn, D. (1979). *Why do you smoke?* Department of Health, Education and Welfare, U. S. Public Health Service (National Institutes of Health Publication No. 79–1822). Washington, DC: U. S. Government Printing Office.

Horn, E., & Fuchs, D. (1987). Using adaptive behavior in assessment and intervention: An overview. *The Journal of Special Education, 21*, 11–26.

Hoshmand, L. T., & Austin, G. W. (1987). Validation studies of a multifactor cognitive-behavioral Anger Control Inventory. *Journal of Personality Assessment, 51*, 417–432.

House, J. S. (1981). *Work stress and social support*. Reading, MA: Addison-Wesley.

House, J. S. (1984). Barriers to work stress: I. Social support. In W. D. Gentry, H. Benson, & C. deWolff (Eds.), *Behavioral medicine: Work, stress, and health*. The Hague: Nijhoff.

House, J. S., Robbins, C., & Metzner, H. L. (1982). The association of social relationships and activities with mortality: Prospective evidence from the Tecumseh Community Health Study. *American Journal of Epidemiology, 116*, 123–140.

Houts, P. S., Miller, R. W., Tokuhata, G. K., & Ham, K. S. (1980, April). *Health-related behavioral impact of the Three Mile Island nuclear incident*. Report submitted to the TMI Advisory Panel on Health Research Studies of the Pennsylvania Department of Health, Part I.

Howard, K. I., Kopta, S. M., Krause, M. S., & Orlinksy, D. E. (1986). The dose-effect relationship in psychotherapy. *American Psychologist, 41*, 159–164.

Hrncir, E. J., Speller, G. M., & West, M. (1985). What are we testing? *Developmental Psychology, 21*, 226–232.

Hrubec, Z., & Omenn, G. S. (1981). Evidence of genetic predisposition to alcohol cirrhosis and psychosis: Twin concordances for alcoholism and its biological end points by zygosity among male veterans. *Alcoholism: Clinical and Experimental Research, 5*, 207–212.

Hsu, L. K. G. (1980). Outcome of anorexia nervosa: A review of the literature (1954 to 1978). *Archives of General Psychiatry, 37*, 1041–1046.

Hsu, L. K. G. (1986). The treatment of anorexia nervosa. *American Journal of Psychiatry, 143*, 573–581.

Hsu, L. K. G. (1987). Treatment of anorexia nervosa: Dr. Hsu replies. *American Journal of Psychiatry, 144*, 260–261.

Huber, G., Gross, G., & Chuettler, R. (1980). Longitudinal studies of schizophrenic patients. *Schizophrenia Bulletin, 6*, 592–605.

Hubert, H. B., Feinleib, M., McNamara, P. M., & Castelli, W. P. (1983). Obesity as an independent risk factor for cardiovascular disease: A 26-year follow-up of participants in the Framingham Heart Study. *Circulation, 67*, 968–977.

Hudson, J. I., Pope, H. G., & Jonas, J. M. (1984). Treatment of bulimia with antidepressants: Theoretical considerations and clinical findings. In A. J. Stunkard & E. Stellar (Eds.), *Eating and its disorders* (pp. 259–273). New York: Raven Press.

Hudson, J. I., Pope, H. G., Jr., Jonas, J. M., & Yurgelun-Todd, D. (1983). Family history study of anorexia nervosa and bulimia. *British Journal of Psychiatry, 142*, 133–138, 428–429.

Hugdahl, K., & Ohman, A. (1977). Effects of instruction on acquisition and extinction of electrodermal response to fear-relevant stimuli. *Journal of Experimental Psychology: Human Learning and Memory, 3*, 608–618.

Hughes, J. R., Gust, S. W., & Pechacek, T. F. (1987). Prevalence of tobacco dependence and withdrawal. *American Journal of Psychiatry, 144*, 205–208.

Hughes, J. R., & Hatsukami, D. K. (1987). Criteria of a pharmacologic withdrawal syndrome: Reply. *Archives of General Psychiatry, 44*, 392.

Hughes, P. L., Wells, L. A., Cunningham, C. J., & Ilstrup, D. M. (1986). Treating bulimia with desipramine. *Archives of General Psychiatry, 43*, 182–186.

Hull, J. G. (1987). Self-awareness model. In H. T. Blane & K. E. Leonard (Eds.), *Psychological theories of drinking and alcoholism* (pp. 272–304). New York: Guilford Press.

Hull, J. G., Van Treuren, R. R., & Virnelli, S. (1987). Hardiness and health: A critique and alternative approach. *Journal of Personality and Social Psychology, 53*, 518–530.

Hull, J. G., & Young, R. D. (1983). Self-consciousness, self-esteem, and success-failure as determinants of alcohol consumption in male social drinkers. *Journal of Personality and Social Psychology, 44*, 1097–1109.

Hull, J. G., Young, R. D., & Jouriles, E. (1986). Applications of the self-awareness model of alcohol consumption: Predicting patterns of use and abuse. *Journal of Personality and Social Psychology, 51*, 790–796.

Humphrey, L. L. (1986). Family relations in bulimic-anorexic and non-distressed families. *International Journal of Eating Disorders, 5*, 223–232

Humphrey, L. L. (1987). A comparison of bulimic-anorexic and non-distressed families using structural analysis of social behavior. *Journal of the American Academy of Child Psychiatry, 26*, 248–255.

Humphrey, L. L. (in press). Family-wide distress in bulimia. In D. Cannon & T. Baker (Eds.), *Addictive disorders: Psychological assessment and treatment*. New York: Praeger.

Hunsley, J. (1987). Internal dialogue during academic examination. *Cognitive Therapy and Research, 11*, 653–664.

Hunt, M. (1974). *Sexual behavior in the 1970s*. Chicago: Playboy Press.

Hunt, W. A., & Bespalec, D. A. (1974). An evaluation of current methods of modifying smoking behavior. *Journal of Clinical Psychology, 30*, 431–438.

Hunt, W. A., & Matarazzo, J. D. (1973). Three years later: Recent Developments in the experimental modification of smoking behavior. *Journal of Abnormal Psychology, 81*, 107–114.

Huppert, F. A., & Piercy, M. (1979). Normal and abnormal forgetting in organic amnesia: Effect of locus of lesion. *Cortex, 15*, 385–390.

Husted, J. R. (1975). Desensitization procedures in dealing with female sexual dysfunction. In J. LoPiccolo & L. LoPiccolo (Eds.), *Handbook of sex therapy* (pp. 195–208). New York: Plenum.

Hutchings, B., & Mednick, S. A. (1974). Registered criminality in the adoptive and biological parents of registered male adoptees. In S. A. Mednick, F. Schulsinger, J. Higgins, & B. Bell (Eds.), *Genetics, environment and psychopathology*. New York: Elsevier.

Hutchings, B., & Mednick, S. A. (1977). Criminality in adoptees and their adoptive and biological parents: A pilot study. In S. A. Mednick & K. O. Christensen (Eds.), *Biosocial bases of criminal behavior*. New York: Gardner Press.

Iacono, W., Lykken, D., Peloquin, L., Lumry, A., Valentine, R., & Tuason, V. (1983). Electrodermal activity in euthymic unipolar and bipolar affective disorders. *Archives of General Psychiatry, 40,* 557–568.

Ingram, R. E., & Wisnicki, K. S. (1988). Assessment of positive automatic cognition. *Journal of Consulting and Clinical Psychology, 56,* 898–902.

Irwin, M., Daniels, M., Bloom, E. T., Smith, T. L., & Weiner, H. (1987). Life events, depressive symptoms, and immune function. *American Journal of Psychiatry, 144,* 437–441.

Itel, T. (1977). Qualitative and quantitative EEG findings in schizophrenia. *Schizophrenia Bulletin, 3,* 61–79.

Ivey, M. E., & Bardwick, J. M. (1968). Patterns of affective fluctuation in the menstrual cycle. *Psychosomatic Medicine, 30,* 336–345.

Jackson v. Indiana, 406 U.S. 715, 92 S. Ct. 1845, 32 L. Ed. 2d 435 (1972).

Jacob, R. G., Wing, R. R., & Shapiro, A. P. (1987). The behavioral treatment of hypertension: Long-term effects. *Behavior Therapy, 18,* 325–352.

Jacobovits, C., Holstead, P., Kelley, L., Roe, D. A., & Young, C. M. (1977). Eating habits and nutrient intakes of college women over a thirty-year period. *Journal of the American Dietetic Association, 71,* 405–411.

Jacobs, P. A., Brunton, M., Melville, M., M., Brittain, R. P., & McClemont, W. F. (1965). Aggressive behavior, mental subnormality, and the XYY male. *Nature, 208,* 1351–1352.

Jacobsen, F. M., Wehr, T. A., Skewer, R. A., Sack, D. A., & Rosenthal, N. E. (1987). Morning versus midday phototherapy of seasonal affective disorder. *American Journal of Psychiatry, 144,* 1301–1305.

Jacobson, E. (1938). *Progressive Relaxation.* Chicago: University of Chicago Press.

James, J. F. (1987). Does the community mental health movement have the momentum to survive? *American Journal of Orthopsychiatry, 57,* 446–451.

Jamison, K. K., & Akiskal, H. S. (1983). Medication compliance in patients with bipolar disorder. *Psychiatric Clinics of North America, 6,* 175–192.

Jamrozik, K., Fowler, G., Vessey, M., & Wald, N. (1984). Placebo controlled trial of nicotine chewing gum in general practice. *British Medical Journal, 289,* 794–797.

Janet, P. (1889). *L'automatisme psychologique.* Paris: Alcan.

Janicak, P. G., Davis, J. M., Gibbons, R. D., Ericksen, S., Chang, S., & Gallagher, P. (1985). Efficacy of ECT: A meta-analysis. *American Journal of Psychiatry, 142,* 297–302.

Janoff-Bulman, R., & Frieze, I. (1983). A theoretical perspective for understanding reactions to victimization. *Journal of Social Issues, 39,* 1–17.

Jarvik, L. F., Klodin, V., & Matsuyama, S. S. (1973). Human aggression and the extra Y chromosome: Fact or fiction? *American Psychologist, 28,* 674–676.

Jarvik, L. F., & Trader, D. W. (1988). Treatment of behavioral and mood changes. In M. K. Aronson, (Ed.), *Understanding Alzheimer's disease* (pp. 128–145). New York: Scribner's.

Jay, S. M., Ozolins, M., Elliott, C. H., & Caldwell, S. (1983). Assessment of children's distress during painful medical procedures. *Health Psychology, 2,* 133–147.

Jeffery, R. W. (1988). Dietary risk factors and their modification in cardiovascular disease. *Journal of Consulting and Clinical Psychology, 56,* 350–357.

Jellinek, E. M. (1960). *The disease concept of alcoholism.* New Haven, CT: Hillhouse Press.

Jemmott, J. B., and others (1983). Academic stress, power motivation, and decrease in secretion rate of salivary secretory immunoglobin A. *Lancet, 1,* 1400–1402.

Jenkins, C. D. (1988). Epidemiology of cardiovascular diseases. *Journal of Consulting and Clinical Psychology, 56,* 324–332.

Jenni, M., & Wollersheim, J. (1979). Cognitive ther-

apy, stress management training, and the Type A behavior pattern. *Cognitive Therapy and Research, 3,* 61–73.

Jernigan, T. L. (1986). Anatomical validators: Issues in the use of computed tomography. In L. W. Poon (Ed.), *Handbook for clinical memory assessment of older adults* (pp. 353–358). Washington, DC: American Psychological Association.

Jessor, R., & Jessor, S. (1977). *Problem behavior and psychosocial development: A longitudinal study.* New York: Academic Press.

Johnson, C., & Flach, A. (1985). Family characteristics of 105 patients with bulimia. *American Journal of Psychiatry, 142,* 1321–1324.

Johnson, C., & Larson, R. (1982). Bulimia: An analysis of mood and behavior. *Psychosomatic Medicine, 44,* 341–351.

Johnson, C. L., Lewis, G., Love S., Stuckey, M., & Lewis, L. (1983). A descriptive survey of dieting and bulimic behavior in a female high school population. In *Understanding anorexia nervosa and bulimia* (pp. 14–18). Columbus, OH: Ross Laboratories.

Johnson, D. L. (1989). Schizophrenia as a brain disease: Implications for psychologists and families. *American Psychologist, 44,* 553–555.

Johnson, F. N. (1975). (Ed.) *Lithium research and therapy.* New York: Academic Press.

Johnson, J. D. (1984). A mechanism to inhibit input activation and its dysfunction in schizophrenia. *British Journal of Psychiatry, 146,* 429–435.

Johnston, L. D., O'Malley, P. M., & Bachman, J. G. (1990, February 9). *Annual survey of drug use.* Ann Arbor, MI: News and Information Services, University of Michigan Institute for Social Research. (Also 1986).

Johnstone, E. C., Crow, T. J., Frith, C. D., Carney, M. W. P., & Price, J. S. (1978). Mechanisms of the antipsychotic effect in the treatment of acute schizophrenia. *Lancet, i,* 848–851.

Joint Commission on Mental Illness and Health (1961). *Action for mental health: Final report of the Joint Commission on Mental Illness and Health.* New York: Basic Books.

Jones, D. J., Fox, M. M., Babigan, H. M., & Hutton, H. E. (1980). Epidemiology of anorexia nervosa in Monroe County, New York, 1960–1976. *Psychosomatic Medicine, 42,* 551–558.

Jones, E. (1953). *The life and work of Sigmund Freud.* New York: Basic Books.

Jones, E. E., Cumming, J. D., & Horowitz, M. J. (1988). Another look at the nonspecific hypothesis of therapeutic effectiveness. *Journal of Consulting and Clinical Psychology, 56,* 48–55.

Jones v. United States, 103 S. Ct. 3043 (1983).

Jones, W., & Park, P. M. (1972, March). Treatment of single-partner sexual dysfunction by systematic desensitization. *Obstetrics and Gynecology, 39,* 411–417.

Jurkovic, G. J. (1980). The juvenile delinquent as a moral philosopher: A structural-developmental perspective. *Psychological Bulletin, 88,* 709–727.

Justice, B., & Justice, R. (1979). *The broken taboo.* New York: Human Services Press.

Jutai, J. W., & Hare, R. D. (1983). Psychopathy and selective attention during performance of a complex perceptual-motor task. *Psychophysiology, 20,* 140–151.

Kagan, D. M., & Squires, R. L. (1984). Eating disorders among adolescents: Patterns and prevalence. *Adolescence, 19,* 15–29.

Kagan, J. (1984). *The nature of the child.* New York: Basic Books.

Kahn, J. P., Drusin, R. E., & Klein, D. F. (1987). Idiopathic cardiomyopathy and panic disorder. *American Journal of Psychiatry, 144,* 1327–1330.

Kahn, M. W., Hannah, M., Hinkin, C., Montgomery, C., & Pitz, D. (1987). Psychopathology on the streets: Psychological assessment of the homeless. *Professional Psychology: Research and Practice, 18,* 580–586.

Kaiij, L. (1960). *Alcoholism in twins.* Stockholm: Almqvist & Wiksell.

Kallmann, F. J. (1952). Comparative twin study on the genetic aspects of male homosexuality. *Journal of Nervous and Mental Disease, 115,* 283–298.

Kamin, L. J. (1982). Mental testing and immigration. *American Psychologist, 37,* 97–98.

Kandel, D. B., and others (1986). The consequences in young adulthood of adolescent drug involvement. *Archives of General Psychiatry, 43,* 746–754.

Kane, J. M. (1985). Antipsychotic drug side-effects: Their relationship to dose. *Journal of Clinical Psychiatry, 46,* 16–20.

Kane, J. M. (1987). Treatment of schizophrenia. *Schizophrenia Bulletin, 13,* 133–156.

Kane, J. M., and others (1985). High-dose versus low-dose strategies in the treatment of schizophrenia. *Psychopharmacology Bulletin, 21,* 533–537.

Kane, J. M., Woerner, M., S., Borenstein, M., Wegner, J., & Lieberman, J. (1986). Integrating incidence and prevalence of tardive dyskinesia. *Psychopharmacology Bulletin, 22,* 254–258.

Kanfer, F., & Goldfoot, D. (1966). Self-control and tolerance of noxious stimulation. *Psychological Reports, 18,* 79–85.

Kanin, E. J., & Parcell, S. R. (1977). Sexual aggression: A second look at the offended female. *Archives of Sexual Behavior, 6,* 67–76.

Kannel, W. B., McGee, D. L., & Castelli, W. P. (1984). Latest perspectives on cigarette smoking and cardiovascular disease: The Framingham Study. *Journal of Cardiac Rehabilitation, 4,* 267–277.

Kanner, A. D., Coyne, J. C., Schaefer, C., & Lazarus, R. S. (1981). Comparison of two modes of stress measurement: Daily hassles and uplifts versus major life events. *Journal of Behavioral Medicine, 4,* 1–39.

Kanner, L. (1943). Autistic disturbances of effective content. *Nervous Child, 2,* 217–240.

Kanner, L., & Eisenberg, L. (1955). Notes on the follow-up studies of autistic children. In P. Hoch & J. Zubin (Eds.), *Psychopathology of Childhood.* New York: Grune & Stratton.

Kaplan, A. S., & Woodside, D. B. (1987). Biological aspects of anorexia nervosa and bulimia nervosa. *Journal of Consulting and Clinical Psychology 55,* 645–653.

Kaplan, H. S. (1974). *The new sex therapy: Active treatment of sexual dysfunctions.* New York: Brunner/Mazel.

Kaplan, H. S. (1983). *The evaluation of sexual disorders.* New York: Brunner/Mazel.

Kaplan, R. M. (1988). Health-related quality of life in cardiovascular disease. *Journal of Consulting and Clinical Psychology, 56,* 382–392.

Kaplan, S. J. (1986). *The private practice of behavior therapy: A guide for behavioral practitioners.* New York: Plenum.

Karacan, I. (1982). Nocturnal penile tumescence as a biologic marker assessing erectile dysfunction. *Psychosomatics, 23,* 349, 351–353, 356–357, 359–360.

Karasek, R. A., Baker, D., Marxer, F., Ahlbom, A., & Theorell, T. (1981). Job decision latitude, job demands, and cardiovascular disease: A prospective study of Swedish men. *American Journal of Public Health, 71,* 694–705.

Karasek, R. A., Theorell, T. G., Schwartz, J., Pieper, C., & Alfredsson, L. (1982). Job, psychological factors and coronary heart disease: Swedish prospective findings and U.S. prevalence findings using a new occupational inference method. *Advances in Cardiology, 29,* 62–67.

Kardiner, A. (1947). *War stress and neurotic illness.* New York: Paul D. Hoeber.

Karlin, R. A., McFarland, D., Aiello, J. R., & Epstein, Y. M. (1976). Normative mediation of reactions to crowding. *Environmental Psychology and Non-Verbal Behavior, 1,* 30–40.

Karlsson, J. L. (1966). *The biological basis of schizophrenia.* Springfield, IL: Chas. C Thomas.

Karlsson, J. L. (1982). Family transmission of

schizophrenia: A review and synthesis. *British Journal of Psychiatry, 140*, 600–606.

Katona, C. L. E., and others (1986). Platelet binding and neuroendocrine responses in depression. In J. W. W. Deakin (Ed.), *The biology of depression. Proceedings of a meeting of the Biological Group of the Royal College of Psychiatrists held at Manchester University, 1985* (pp. 121–136). Washington, DC: American Psychiatric Press.

Katz, R. C., & Singh, N. N. (1986). Reflections on the ex-smoker: Some findings on successful quitters. *Journal of Behavioral Medicine, 9*, 191–202.

Katzman, R. (1976). The prevalence and malignancy of Alzheimer's disease: A major killer. *Archives of Neurology, 33*, 217–218.

Kaufman, E., & Pattison, E. M. (1981). Differential methods of family therapy in the treatment of alcoholism. *Journal of Studies on Alcohol, 42*, 951–971.

Kaufman, J., & Zigler, E. (1987). Do abused children become abusive parents? *American Journal of Orthopsychiatry, 57*, 186–192.

Kaul, T. J., & Bednar, R. L. (1986). Experiential group research: Results, questions, and suggestions. In S. L. Garfield & A. E. Bergin (Eds.), *Handbook of psychotherapy and behavior change: An evaluative analysis* (3rd ed.). New York: Wiley.

Kavale, K. (1982). The efficacy of stimulant drug treatment for hyperactivity: A meta-analysis. *Journal of Learning Disabilities, 15*, 280–289.

Kaya, N., Moore, C., & Karacan, I. (1979). Nocturnal penile tumescence and its role in impotence. *Psychiatric Annals, 9*, 426–431.

Kazdin, A. E. (1977). Artifact, bias, and complexity of assessment: The ABCs of reliability. *Journal of Applied Behavior Analysis, 10*, 141–150.

Kazdin, A. E. (1984). *Behavior modification in applied settings*. Homewood, NJ: Dorsey Press.

Kazdin, A. E. (1986). Comparative outcome studies of psychotherapy: Methodological issues and strategies. *Journal of Consulting and Clinical Psychology, 54*, 95–105.

Kazdin, A. E., Esveldt-Dawson, K., French, N. H., & Unis, A. S. (1987). Problem-solving skills training and relationship therapy in the treatment of antisocial child behavior. *Journal of Consulting and Clinical Psychology, 55*, 76–85.

Kazdin, A. E., Esveldt-Dawson, K., Sherick, R. B., & Colbus, D. (1985). Assessment of overt behavior and childhood depression among psychiatrically disturbed children. *Journal of Consulting and Clinical Psychology, 53*, 201–210.

Kazdin, A. E., Moser, J., Colbus, D., & Bell, R. (1985). Depressive symptoms among physically abused and psychiatrically disturbed children. *Journal of Abnormal Psychology, 94*, 298–307.

Kazniak, A. W., & Allender, J. R. (1985). Psychological assessment of depression in older adults. In G. M. Chaisson-Stewart (Ed.), *Depression in the elderly: An interdisciplinary approach* (pp. 107–160). New York: Wiley.

Kedia, K. (1983). Ejaculation and emission: Normal physiology, dysfunction, and therapy. In R. J. Krane, M. B. Siroky, & I. Goldstein (Eds.), *Male sexual dysfunction* (pp. 37–54). Boston: Little, Brown.

Keefe, F. J., and others (1987). Pain-coping strategies in osteoarthritis patients. *Journal of Consulting and Clinical Psychology, 55*, 208–212.

Keesey, R. E. (1980). A set-point analysis of the regulation of body weight. In A. J. Stunkard (Ed.), *Obesity*. Philadelphia: Saunders.

Kegeles, S. M., Alan, M. E., Irwin, C. (1988). Sexually active adolescents and condoms: Changes over one year in knowledge, attitudes, and use. *Americal Journal of Public Health, 78*, 460–461.

Keisler, C. A., & Sibulkin, A. E. (1987). *Mental hospitalization: Myths and facts about a national crisis*. Beverly Hills, CA: Sage Publications, Inc.

Keller, M. B., Levoia, P. W., Endicott, J., Coryell, W., & Klerman, G. L. (1983). "Double depres-

sion'': Two-year follow-up. *American Journal of Psychiatry, 140*, 689–694.

Kellner, R., Abbot, P., Winslow, W. W., & Pathak, D. (1987). Fears, beliefs, and attitudes in DSM-III hypochondriasis. *Journal of Nervous and Mental Disease, 175*, 20–25.

Kelly, G. A. (1955). *The psychology of personal constructs* (Vols. 1 & 2.). New York: W. W. Norton & Co., Inc.

Kelly, G. A. (1958). Man's construction of his alternatives. In G. Lindzey (Ed.), *Assessment of human motives*. New York: Holt, Rinehart & Winston.

Kelly, J. A., & St. Lawrence, J. S. (1988). AIDS prevention and treatment: Psychology's role in the health crisis. *Clinical Psychology Review, 8*, 255–284.

Kelly, J. A., Wildman, B. G., & Berler, E. S. (1980). Small group behavioral training to improve the job interview skills repertoire of mildly retarded adolescents. *Journal of Applied Behavior Analysis, 13*, 461–471.

Kelsoe, J. R., and others (1989). Re-evaluation of the linkage relationship between chromosome 11p loci and the gene for bipolar affective disorder in the Old Order Amish. *Nature, 342*, 238–243.

Kempe, C. H., Silverman, F. N., Steele, Droegemueller, W. E., & Silver, H. K. (1982). The battered child syndrome. *Journal of American Medical Association, 181*, 17–24.

Kendall, P. A., & Reber, M. (1987). Letters to the editor: Cognitive training in treatment of hyperactivity in children. *Archives of General Psychiatry, 44*, 296.

Kendall, P. C., & Braswell, L. (1985). *Cognitive-behavioral therapy for impulsive children*. New York: Guilford Press.

Kendall, P. C., & Hollon, S. D. (Eds.) (1981). *Assessment strategies for cognitive-behavioral interventions*. New York: Academic Press.

Kendall, P. C., & Williams, C. L. (1981). Behavioral and cognitive behavioral approaches to outpatient treatment with children. In W. E. Craighead, A. E. Kazdin, & M. J. Mahoney, *Behavior modification: Principles, issues, and applications* (2d ed). Boston: Houghton Mifflin.

Kendell, R. E. (1983). Hysteria. In G. F. M. Russell & L. A. Hersov (Eds.), *Handbook of psychiatry* (Vol. 4): *The neuroses and personality disorders* (pp. 232–246). Cambridge, England: Cambridge University Press.

Kendler, K. S., & Gruenberg, A. M. (1984). An independent analysis of the Danish Adoption Study of Schizophrenia. *Archives of General Psychiatry, 41*, 555–564.

Kendler, K. S., Gruenberg, A. M., & Tsuang, M. T. (1985). Psychiatric illness in first-degree relatives of schizophrenic and surgical control patients: A family study using DSM-III criteria. *Archives of General Psychiatry, 42*, 770–779.

Kendler, K. S., Masterson, C., Ungaro, R., & Davis, K. (1984). A family history study of schizophrenia-related personality disorders. *American Journal of Psychiatry, 141*, 424–427.

Kendler, K. S., & Robinette, C. D. (1983). Schizophrenia in the National Academy of Sciences National Research Council Twin Registry: A 16-year update. *American Journal of Psychiatry, 140*, 1551–1563.

Kernberg, O. F. (1975). *Borderline conditions and pathological narcissism*. New York: Jason Aronson.

Kernberg, P. F. (1979). Childhood schizophrenia and autism: A selective review. In L. Bellak (Ed.), *Disorders of the schizophrenic syndrome*. New York: Basic Books.

Kerr, P. (1988, July, 10). The American drug problem takes on two faces. *The New York Times*, S4, p. 5.

Kety, S. (1980). The syndrome of schizophrenia: Unresolved questions and opportunities for research. *British Journal of Psychiatry, 136*, 421–436.

Kety, S. S., Rosenthal, D., Wender, P. H., & Schul-

singer, F. (1968). The types of prevalence of mental illness in the biological and adoptive families of adopted schizophrenics. In D. Rosenthal & S. S. Kety (Eds.), *The transmission of schizophrenia*. Oxford, England: Pergamon Press.

Kety, S. S., Rosenthal, D., Wender, P. H., Schulsinger, F., & Jacobsen, B. (1975). Mental illness in the biological and adoptive families of adoptive individuals who have become schizophrenic: A preliminary report based on psychiatric interviews. In R. R. Fieve, D. Rosenthal & H. Brill (Eds.), *Genetic research in psychiatry*. Baltimore: Johns Hopkins University Press.

Kety, S. S., Rosenthal, D., Wender, P. H., Schulsinger, F., & Jacobsen, B. (1978). The biological and adoptive families of adopted individuals who become schizophrenic. In C. Wynne, R. L. Cromwell, & S. Mathysse (Eds.), *The nature of schizophrenia* (pp. 25–37). New York: Wiley.

Keyes, D. (1982). *The minds of Billy Milligan*. New York: Bantam.

Kiecolt-Glaser, J. K., Fisher, L., Ogrocki, P., Stout, J. C., Speicher, C. E., & Glaser, R. (1987). Marital quality, marital disruption, and immune function. *Psychosomatic Medicine, 49*, 13–34.

Kiecolt-Glaser, J. K., Garner, W., Speicher, C. E., Penn, G., & Glaser, R. (1984). Psychosocial modifiers of immunocompetence in medical students. *Psychosomatic Medicine, 46*, 7–14.

Kiecolt-Glaser, J. K., & Glaser, R. (1988). Psychological influences on immunity: Implications for AIDS. *American Psychologist, 43*, 892–898.

Kiecolt-Glaser, J. K., and others (1985). Psychosocial enhancement of immunocompetence in a geriatric population. *Health Psychology, 4*, 25–41.

Kiecolt-Glaser, J. K., Kennedy, S., Malkoff, S., Fisher, L., Speicher, C. E., & Glaser, R. (1988). Marital discord and immunity in males. *Psychosomatic Medicine, 50*, 213–229.

Kiecolt-Glaser, J. K., Speicher, C. E., Holliday, J. E., & Glaser, R. (1984). Stress and the transformation of lymphocytes in Epstein-Barr virus. *Journal of Behavioral Medicine, 7*, 1–12.

Kiesler, C. A. (1982). Mental hospitalization and alternative care. *American Psychologist, 37*, 349–360.

Kiesler, C. A., & Sibulkin, A. E. (1987). *Mental hospitalization: Myths and facts about a national crisis*. Newbury Park, CA: Sage.

Killen, J. D., Fortmann, S. P., Newman, B., & Varady, A. (1990). Evaluation of a treatment approach combining nicotine gum with self-guided behavioral treatments for smoking relapse prevention. *Journal of Consulting and Clinical Psychology, 58*, 85–92.

Killen, J. D., Taylor, B., Telch, M. J., Saylor, K. E., Maron, D. J., & Robinson, T. N. (1986). Self-induced vomiting and laxative and diuretic use among teenagers. *Journal of the American Medical Association, 225*, 1417–1449.

Kilmann, P. R., & Auerbach, R. (1979). Treatments of premature ejaculation and psychogenic impotence: A critical review of the literature. *Archives of Sexual Behavior, 8*, 81–100.

Kimble, D. P. (1988). *Biological psychology*. New York: Holt, Rinehart & Winston.

Kimble, G. A. (1989). Psychology from the standpoint of a generalist. *American Psychologist, 44*, 491–499.

Kinney, D. K., & Jacobsen, B. (1978). Environmental factors in schizophrenia: New adoption study evidence and its implications for genetic and environmental research. In L. C. Wynne, R. L. Cromwell, & S. Matthysse (Eds.), *The nature of schizophrenia*. New York: Wiley.

Kinsey, A. C., Pomeroy, W. B., & Martin, C. E. (1948). *Sexual behavior in the human male*. Philadelphia: Saunders.

Kinsey, A. C., Pomeroy, W. B., Martin, C. E., & Gebhard, P. H. (1953). *Sexual behavior in the human female*. Philadelphia: Saunders.

Kirk, S. A. (1963, April 6). Behavioral prognosis

and remediation of learning disabilities. *Proceedings, Conference on Exploration into the Problems of the Perceptually Handicapped Child, First Annual Meeting*. Vol. 1. Chicago.

Kissel, R. C., Whitman, T. L., & Reid, D. H. (1983). An institutional staff training and self-management program for developing multiple self-care skills in severely-profoundly retarded individuals. *Journal of Applied Behavior Analysis, 16,* 395–415.

Klassen, D., & O'Connor, W. A. (1988). Predicting violence in schizophrenic and non-schizophrenic patients: A prospective study. *Journal of Community Psychology, 16,* 217–227.

Klatsky, A. L., Freidman, G. D., & Siegelaub, A. B. (1981). Alcohol and mortality: A ten-year Kaiser-Permanente experience. *Annals of Internal Medicine, 95,* 139–145.

Kleiman, D. (1988, November 7). A day in a mental hospital, a dream of life outside. *The New York Times* pp. B1, B2.

Klein, D. F. (1980). Anxiety reconceptualized. *Comprehensive Psychiatry, 21,* 411–427.

Klein, D. F. (1981). Anxiety reconceptualized. In D. F. Klein & J. Rabkin (Eds.), *Anxiety: New research and changing concepts*. New York: Raven Press.

Klein, D. F., & Rabkin, J. G. (1984). Specificity and strategy in psychotherapy research and practice. In R. L. Spitzer & J. R. W. Williams (Eds.), *Psychotherapy research: Where are we and where should we go?* New York: Guilford Press.

Klein, D. F., Ross, D. C., & Cohen, P. (1987). Panic and avoidance in agoraphobia: Application of path analysis to treatment studies. *Archives of General Psychiatry, 44,* 377–385.

Klein, D. N., & Depue, R. A. (1985). Obsessional personality traits and risk for bipolar affective disorder: An offspring study. *Journal of Abnormal Psychology, 94,* 291–297.

Klein, D. N., Depue, R. A., & Slater, J. F. (1985). Cyclothymia in the adolescent offspring of parents with bipolar affective disorder. *Journal of Abnormal Psychology, 94,* 115–127.

Klein, D. N., Taylor, E. B., Dickstein, S., & Harding, K. (1988). Primary early-onset dysthymia: Comparison with primary nonbipolar nonchronic major depression on demographic, clinical, familial, personality, and socioenvironmental characteristics and short-term outcome. *Journal of Abnormal Psychology, 97,* 387–398.

Klein, M. (1981). On Mahler's autistic and symbiotic phases: An exposition and evaluation. *Psychoanalysis and Contemporary Thought, 4,* 69–105.

Klein, M. H., and others (1985). A comparative outcome study of group psychotherapy versus exercise treatments for depression. *International Journal of Mental Health, 13,* 148–175.

Kleiner, L., & Marshall, W. L. (1985). Relationship difficulties and agoraphobia. *Clinical Psychology Review, 5,* 581–595.

Kleinmuntz, B. (1982). *Personality and psychological assessment*. New York: St. Martin's Press.

Kleinmuntz, B., & Szucko, J. J. (1984). Lie detection in ancient and modern times: A call for contemporary scientific study. *American Psychologist, 394,* 766–776.

Klerman, G. L. (1984). Ideology and science in the individual psychotherapy of schizophrenia. *Schizophrenia Bulletin, 10,* 608–612.

Klerman, G. L., and others (1989). Increasing rates of depression. *Journal of the American Medical Association, 261,* 2229–2235.

Klerman, G. L., Weissman, M. M., Rounsaville, B. J., & Chevron, E. S. (1984). *Interpersonal psychotherapy of depression* New York: Basic Books.

Klopfer, B., & Davidson, H., H. (1962). *The Rorschach technique: An introductory manual*. New York: Harcourt, Brace & World.

Klorman, R., and others (1988). Effects of methylphenidate on attention-deficit hyperactivity disorder with and without aggressive/noncompli-

ant features. *Journal of Abnormal Psychology, 97,* 413–422.

Klosko, J. S., Barlow, D. H., Tassinari, R., & Cerny, J. A. (1990). A comparison of alprazolam and behavior therapy in treatment of panic disorder. *Journal of Consulting and Clinical Psychology, 58,* 77–84.

Kluft, R. P. (1984). An introduction to multiple personality disorder. *Psychiatric Annals, 14,* 19–24.

Kluft, R. P. (1986). Three high functioning multiples. *Journal of Nervous and Mental Disease, 174,* 722–726.

Kluft, R. P. (1987). First-rank symptoms as a diagnostic clue to multiple personality disorder. *American Journal of Psychiatry, 144,* 293–298.

Kluznik, J. C., Speed, N., VanValkenburg, C., & Magraw, R. (1986). Forty-year follow-up of United States prisoners of war. *American Journal of Psychiatry, 143,* 1443–1446.

Knapp, S., & Vandercreek, L. (1982). Tarasoff: Five years later. *Professional Psychology, 13,* 511–516.

Knight, R. G., Godfrey, H. P. D., & Shelton, E. J. (1988). The psychological deficits associated with Parkinson's disease. *Clinical Psychology Review, 8,* 391–410.

Knorring, A., von, Cloninger, C. R., Bohman, M., & Sigvardsson, S. (1983). An adoption study of depressive disorders and substance abuse. *Archives of General Psychiatry, 40,* 943–950.

Kobasa, S. C. (1979). Stressful life events, personality, and health: An inquiry into hardiness. *Journal of Personality and Social Psychology, 374,* 1–11.

Kobasa, S. C. (1985). Personality and health: Specifying and strengthening the conceptual links. In P. Shaver (Ed.), *Self, situations, and social behavior*. Beverly Hills, CA: Sage Publications, Inc.

Kobasa, S. C., Maddi, S. R., & Kahn, S. (1982). Hardiness and health: A prospective study. *Journal of Personality and Social Psychology, 42,* 168–177.

Kobasa, S. C., Maddi, S. R., & Zola, M. A. (1983). Type A and hardiness. *Journal of Behavioral Medicine, 6,* 41–51.

Kobasa, S. C., & Puccetti, M. C. (1983). Personality and social resources in stress resistance. *Journal of Personality and Social Psychology, 45,* 839–850.

Kockott, G., Feil, W., Ferstl, R., Aldenhoff, J., & Besinger, U. (1980). Psychophysiological aspects of male sexual inadequacy: Results of an experimental study. *Archives of Sexual Behavior, 9,* 477–493.

Kocsis, J. H., & Franes, A. J. (1987). A critical discussion of DSM-III dysthymic disorder. *American Journal of Psychiatry, 144,* 1534–1542.

Kocsis, J. H., Frances, A. J., Voss, C. B., Mann, J., Mason, B. J., & Sweeney, J. (1988). Imipramine treatment for chronic depression. *Archives of General Psychiatry, 45,* 253–257.

Kohlenberg, R. J. (1973). Behavioristic approach to multiple personality. *Behavior Therapy, 4,* 137–140.

Kohlenberg, R. J. (1974). Directed masturbation and the treatment of primary orgasmic dysfunction. *Archives of Sexual Behavior, 3,* 349.

Kohn, M. L. (1976). The interaction of social class and other factors in the etiology of schizophrenia. *American Journal of Psychiatry, 133,* 177–180.

Kohn, P. M., Barnes, G. E., & Hoffman, F. M. (1979). Drug-use history and experience seeking among adult male correctional inmates. *Journal of Consulting and Clinical Psychology, 47,* 708–715.

Kohut, H. (1966). Forms and transformations of narcissism. *Journal of the American Psychoanalytic Association, 14,* 243–272.

Kolata, G. (1985). Down-Syndrome-Alzheimer's linked. *Science, 230,* 1152–1153.

Kolata, G. (1987, November 10). Alcoholism: Genetic links grow clearer. *The New York Times,* pp. C1, C2.

Kolata, G. (1988a, May 5). Prenatal test for defects

termed safe in U.S. study. *The New York Times,* p. B19.

Kolata, G. (1988b, August 25). Epidemic of dangerous eating disorder may be false alarm. *The New York Times,* p. B16.

Kolata, G. (1989, March 7). Some addicts find medication can ease craving for cocaine. *The New York Times,* p. C4.

Kolko, D. J. (1988). Educational programs to promote awareness and prevention of child sexual victimization: A review and methodological critique. *Clinical Psychology Review, 8,* 195–209.

Kolko, D. J., & Rickard-Figueroa, J. L. (1985). Effects of video games on the adverse corollaries of chemotherapy in pediatric oncology patients: A single-case analysis. *Journal of Consulting and Clinical Psychology, 53,* 223–228.

Konner, M. (1988, July 7). New keys to the mind. *The New York Times Magazine,* pp. 49–50.

Koop, C. E. (1987). Report of the surgeon general's workshop on pornography and public health. *American Psychologist, 42,* 944–945.

Koop, C. E. (1988). *Understanding AIDS* (HHS Publication No. [CDC] HHS-88-8404). Washington, DC: U.S. Government Printing Office.

Koorland, M. A. (1986). Applied behavior analysis and the correction of learning disabilities. In J. K. Torgesen & B. Y. L. Wong (Eds.), *Psychological and educational perspectives on learning disabilities* (pp. 297–328). Orlando, FL: Academic Press.

Korlath, E., & Munson, K. (1978). Six battered women. *Victimology: An International Journal, 2,* 460–476.

Korlath, M. J. (1979). Alcoholism in battered women: A report of advocacy services to clients in a detoxification facility. *Victimology: An International Journal, 4,* 292–299.

Kornberg, M. S., & Kaplan, G. (1980). Risk factors and preventive intervention in child psychopathology: A review. *Journal of Prevention, 1,* 71–133.

Koss, M. P. (1988). Stranger and acquaintance rape: Are there differences in the victim's experience? *Psychology of Women Quarterly, 12,* 1–24.

Koss, M. P., Butcher, J. L., & Strupp, H. H. (1986). Brief psychotherapy methods in clinical research. *Journal of Consulting and Clinical Psychology, 54,* 60–67.

Koss, M. P., Gidycz, C. A., & Wisniewski, N. (1987). The scope of rape: Incidence and prevalance of sexual aggression and victimization in a national sample of higher education students. *Journal of Consulting and Clinical Psychology, 55,* 162–170.

Kottke, T. E., Battista, R. N., DeFriese, G. H., & Brekke, M. L. (1988). Attributes of successful smoking cessation interventions in medical practice: A meta-analysis of 39 controlled trials. *Journal of the American Medical Association, 259,* 2883–2889.

Kovacs, M. (1985). The Children's Depression Inventory. *Psychopharmacological Bulletin, 21,* 995–998.

Kovacs, M., & Beck, A. T. (1978). Maladaptive cognitive structure in depression. *American Journal of Psychiatry, 135,* 525–533.

Kovacs, M., Feinberg, T. L., Crause-Novak, M., Paulauskas, S. L., & Finkelstein, R. (1984). Depressive disorders in childhood: I. A longitudinal prospective study of characteristics and recovery. *Archives of General Psychiatry, 41,* 229–237.

Kovacs, M,. Rush, A. J., Beck, A. T., & Hollon, S. D. (1981). Depressed outpatients treated with cognitive therapy or pharmacotherapy: A one-year follow up. *Archives of General Psychiatry, 38,* 33–39.

Kraepelin, E. (1893). *Psychiatrie* (4th Ed.). Leipzig: J. A. Barth.

Kraepelin, E. (1909–1913). *Psychiatrie* (8th Ed.). Leipzig: J. A. Barth.

Krafft-Ebing, R., von (1886). *Psychopathia Sexualis*. New York: Putnam's. (Reprinted in 1965)

Kramsch, D. M., and others (1981). Reduction of

coronary atherosclerosis by moderate conditioning exercise in monkeys on an atherogenic diet. *New England Journal of Medicine, 306,* 1483–1489.

Krane, R. J., Siroky, M. B., & Goldstein, I. (1983). *Male sexual dysfunction* Boston: Little, Brown.

Krantz, D. S. (1980). Cognitive processes and recovery from heart attack: A review and theoretical analysis. *Journal of Human Stress, 6,* 27–38.

Krantz, D. S., Contrada, R. J., Hills, D. R., & Friedler, E. (1988). Environmental stress and biobehavioral antecedents of coronary heart disease. *Journal of Consulting and Clinical Psychology, 56,* 333–341.

Krantz, D. S., Grunberg, N. E., & Baum, A. (1985). Health psychology. *Annual Review of Psychology, 36,* 349–383.

Krantz, D. S., Schaeffer, M. A., Davis, J. E., Dembroski, T. M., MacDougall, J. M., & Shaffer, R. T. (1981). Extent of coronary atherosclerosis, Type A behavior, and cardiovascular response to social interaction. *Psychophysiology, 18,* 654–664.

Krantz, S. (1985). When depressive cognitions reflect negative realities. *Cognitive Therapy and Research, 9,* 595–610.

Krantz, S. E., & Moos, R. H. (1988). Risk factors at intake predict nonremission among depressed patients. *Journal of Consulting and Clinical Psychology, 56,* 863–869.

Krauss, D. (1983). The physiologic basis of male sexual dysfunction. *Hospital Practice, 2,* 193–222.

Krauss, P., & Brown, G. M. (1988). Drugs and the DST: Need for a reappraisal. *American Journal of Psychiatry, 145,* 666–674.

Kripke, D. F., Simons, A. N., Garfinkel, L., & Hammond, E. C. (1979). Short and long sleep and sleeping pills: Is increased mortality associated? *Archives of General Psychiatry, 36,* 103–116.

Kruesi, M. J. P., and others (1987). Effects of sugar and aspartame on aggression and activity in children. *American Journal of Psychiatry, 144,* 1487–1490.

Kushner, M. (1977). The reduction of a longstanding fetish by means of aversive conditioning. In J. Fischer & H. Gochios (Eds.), *Handbook of behavior therapy with sexual problems.* New York: Pergamon Press.

LaCroix, A. Z., & Haynes, S. G. (1987). Gender differences in the stressfulness of workplace roles: A focus on work and health. In R. Barnett, G. Baruch, & L. Biener (Eds.), *Gender and stress* (pp. 96–121). New York: Free Press.

Lacks, P. E., Bertelson, A. D., Ganz, L., & Kunkel, J. (1983). The effectiveness of three behavioral treatments for different degrees of sleep-onset insomnia. *Behavior Therapy, 14,* 593–605.

Laing, R. D. (1964). Is schizophrenia a disease? *International Journal of Social Psychiatry, 10,* 184–193.

Laing, R. D. (1976, July 20). Round the bend. *New Statesman.*

Lam, D. H., Brewin, C. R., Woods, R. T., & Bebbington, P. E. (1987). Cognition and social adversity in the depressed elderly. *Journal of Abnormal Psychology, 96,* 23–26.

Lamb, H. R. (1982). *Treating the long-term mentally ill: Beyond deinstitutionalization.* San Francisco: Jossey-Bass.

Lamb, H. R. (1984). Deinstitutionalization and the homeless mentally ill. In H. R. Lamb (Ed.), *The homeless mentally ill: A Task Force Report of the American Psychiatric Association* (pp. 55–74). Washington, DC: American Psychiatric Press.

Lamb, H. R., & Goertzel, V. (1971). Discharge of mental patients: Are they really in the community? *Archives of General Psychiatry, 24,* 29–34.

Lambert, B. (1987, December 13). New York City maps deadly pattern of AIDS. *The New York Times,* pp. 1, 58.

Lambert, M. J., Shapiro, D. A., & Bergin, A. E. (1986). The effectivensss of psychotherapy. In S. L. Garfield & A. E. Bergin (Eds.), *Handbook of psychotherapy and behavior change* (3d ed.). New York: Wiley.

Lambert, N. M., Hartsough, C. S., Sassone, D., & Sandoval, J. (1987). Persistence of hyperactivity symptoms from childhood to adolescence and associated outcomes. *American Journal of Orthopsychiatry, 57,* 22–32.

Landers, S. (1989). In U.S., mental disorders afect 15 percent of adults. *APA Monitor, 20,* 16.

Landman, J. T., & Dawes, R. M. (1982). Psychotherapy outcome: Smith and Glass' conclusions stand up under scrutiny. *American Psychologist, 38,* 504–516.

Lando, H. A., & McGovern, P. G. (1985). Nicotine fading as a nonaversive alternative in a broad-spectrum treatment for eliminating smoking. *Addictive Behaviors, 10,* 153–161.

Lang, A. R., Goeckner, D. J., Adesso, V. J., & Marlatt, G. A. (1975). Effects of alcohol on aggression in male social drinkers. *Journal of Abnormal Psychology, 84,* 508–518.

Lang, A. R., Searles, J., Lauerman, R., & Adesso, V. J. (1980). Expectancy, alcohol, and sex guilt as determinants of interest in and reaction to sexual stimuli. *Journal of Abnormal Psychology, 89,* 644–653.

Lang, P. J. (1968). Fear reduction and fear behavior: Problems in treating a construct. In J. M. Schlein (Ed.), *Research in Psychotherapy,* Vol. III (pp. 90–102). Washington, DC: American Psychological Association.

Lang, P. J. (1985). The cognitive psychophysiology of emotion: Fear and anxiety. In A. H. Tuma & J. D. Maser (Eds.), *Anxiety and the anxiety disorders* (pp. 131–170). Hillsdale, NJ: Erlbaum.

Lang, P. J., & Lazovik, A. D. (1963). Experimental desensitization of a phobia. *Journal of Abnormal and Social Psychology, 66,* 519–525.

Lang, P. J., & Melamed, B. B. (1969). Case report: Avoidance conditioning therapy of an infant with chronic ruminative vomiting. *Journal of Abnormal Psychology, 74,* 1–8.

Langer, E. J., Rodin, J., Beck, P., Weinan, C., & Spitzer, L. (1979). Environmental determinants of memory improvement in late adulthood. *Journal of Personality and Social Psychology, 37,* 2003–2013.

Langford, H. G., and others (1985). Dietary therapy slows the return of hypertension after stopping prolonged medication. *Journal of the American Medical Association, 253,* 657–664.

Lansky, D., & Wilson, G. T. (1981). Alcohol, expectations, and sexual arousal. *Journal of Abnormal Psychology, 90,* 35–45.

Lanyon, R. I. (1986). Theory and treatment in child molestation. *Journal of Consulting and Clinical Psychology, 54* 176–182.

Lapan, R., & Patton, M. J. (1986). Self-psychology and the adolescent process: Measures of pseudoautonomy and peer-group dependence. *Journal of Counseling Psychology, 33,* 136–142.

LaPouse, R., & Monk, M. (1959). Fears and worries in a representative sample of children. *American Journal of Orthopsychiatry, 29,* 803–818.

Larson, R. W., Raffaelli, M., Richards, M. H., Ham, M., & Jewell, L. (1990). Ecology of depression in late childhood and early adolescence: A profile of daily states and activities. *Journal of Abnormal Psychology, 99,* 92–102.

Latimer, P. R., & Sweet, A. A. (1984). Cognitive vs. behavioral procedures in cognitive-behavior therapy: A critical review of the evidence. *Journal of Behavior Therapy and Experimental Psychiatry, 15,* 9–22.

Laudenslager, M. L., and others (1983). Coping and immunosuppression: Inescapable but not escapable shock suppresses lymphocyte proliferation. *Science, 221,* 568–570.

Lawson, D. M. (1983). Alcoholism. In M. Hersen (Ed.), *Outpatient behavior therapy: A clinical guide* (pp. 143–172). New York: Grune & Stratton.

Lazarus, R. S. (1984). Puzzles in the study of daily hassles. *Journal of Behavioral Medicine, 7,* 375–389.

Lazarus, R. S., DeLongis, A., Folkman, S., & Gruen, R. (1985). Stress and adaptational outcomes: The problem of confounded measures. *American Psychologist, 40,* 770–779.

Lazarus, R. S., & Folkman, S. (1984). *Stress, appraisal, and coping.* New York: Springer-Verlag.

Le Shan, L. (1966). An emotional life-history pattern associated with neoplastic disease. *Annals of New York Academy of Sciences, 125,* 780–792.

Lear, M. W. (1988, July 3). Mad malady. *The New York Times Magazine,* pp. 21–22.

Lechtenberg, R. (1984). *Epilepsy and the family.* Cambridge, MA: Harvard University Press.

Lee, T., & Seeman, P. (1977). Dopamine receptors in normal and schizophrenic human brains. *Proceedings of the Society of Neurosciences, 3,* 443.

Lefcourt, H. M., & Martin, R. A. (1986). *Humor and life stress: Antidote to adversity.* New York: Springer-Verlag.

Lefcourt, H. M., Miller, R. S., Ware, E. E., & Sherk, D. (1981). Locus of control as a modifier of the relationship between stressors and moods. *Journal of Personality and Social Psychology, 41,* 357–369.

Leff, J. (1977). International variations in the diagnosis of schizophrenia. *British Journal of Psychiatry, 131,* 329–338.

Leff, J., Kuipers, L., Berkowitz, R., Eberlein-Vries, R., & Sturgeon, D. (1982). A controlled trial of social intervention in the families of schizophrenic patients. *British Journal of Psychiatry, 141,* 121–134.

Leff, J., & Vaughn, C. (1981). The role of maintenance therapy and relatives' expressed emotion in relapse of schizophrenia: A two-year follow-up. *British Journal of Psychiatry, 139,* 102–104.

Leff, J., & Vaughn, C. (1985). *Expressed emotion in families.* New York: Guilford Press.

Leff, J. P. (1976). Schizophrenia and sensitivity to the family environment. *Schizophrenia Bulletin, 2,* 566–574.

Leff, J. P., Hirsch, S. R., Gaind, R., Rohde, P. D., & Stevens, B. S. (1973). Life events and maintenance therapy in schizophrenic relapse. *British Journal of Psychiatry, 123,* 659–660.

Leff, J. P., & Wing, J. K. (1971). Trial of maintenance therapy in schizophrenia. *British Medical Journal, 11,* 599–604.

Leibowitz, S. F. (1986). Brain monoamines and peptides: Role in the control of eating behavior. *Federation Proceedings, 45,* 1396–1403.

Leibowitz, S. F. (1986). Brain monoamines and peptides: Role in the control of eating behavior. *Federation Proceedings, 45,* 599–615.

Leishman, K. (1987, February). Heterosexuals and AIDS. *The Atlantic Monthly,* 39–58.

Leitenberg, H., Gross, J., Peterson, J., & Rosen, J. C. (1984). Analysis of an anxiety model and the process of change during exposure plus response prevention treatment of bulimia nervosa. *Behavior Therapy, 15,* 3–20.

Leitenberg, H., Rosen, J. C., Gross, J., Nudelman, S., & Vara, L. S. (1988). Exposure plus response-prevention treatment of bulimia nervosa. *Journal of Consulting and Clinical Psychology, 56,* 535–541.

Leitenberg, H., Yost, L. W., & Carroll-Wilson, M. (1986). Negative cognitive errors in children: Questionnaire development, normative data, and comparisons between children with and without self-reported symptoms of depression, low self-esteem, and evaluation anxiety. *Journal of Consulting and Clinical Psychology, 54,* 528–536.

Lelliott, P. T., and others (1987). Agoraphobics 5 years after imipramine and exposure: Outcome and predictors. *Journal of Nervous and Mental Disease, 175,* 599–605.

Leon, G. R., Finn, S. E., Murray, D., & Bailey, J. M. (1988). Inability to predict cardiovascular disease from hostility scores or MMPI items related to Type A behavior. *Journal of Consulting and Clinical Psychology, 56,* 597–600.

Leonard, C. V. (1977). The MMPI as a suicide predictor. *Journal of Consulting and Clinical Psychology*, *45*, 367–377.

Lerner, H. (1986). Research perspectives on borderlines. *Psychotherapy*, *23*, 57–69.

Lerner, P. (1985). Current psychoanalytic perspectives on the borderline and narcissistic concepts. *Clinical Psychology Review*, *5*, 199–214.

Lerner, R. M. (1976). *Concepts and theories of human development*. Reading, MA: Addison-Wesley.

Lesieur, H. R., Blume, S. B., & Zoppa, R. M. (1986). Alcoholism, drug abuse, and gambling. *Alcoholism: Clinical and Experimental Research*, *10*, 33–38.

Lesieur, H. R., & Custer, R. L. (1984, July). Pathological gambling: Roots, phases, and treatment. *Annals, AAPSS*, *474*, 146–156.

Levenkron, J. C., Cohen, J. D., Mueller, H. S., & Fisher, E. B. (1983). Modifying the Type A coronary-prone behavior pattern. *Journal of Consulting and Clinical Psychology*, *51*, 192–204.

Leventhal, H., & Cleary, P. D. (1980). The smoking problem: A review of the research and theory in behavioral risk modification. *Psychological Bulletin*, *88*, 370–405.

Levin, A. P., Schneier, F. R., & Liebowitz, M. R. (1989). Social phobia: Biology and pharmacology. *Clinical Psychology Review*, *9*, 129–140.

Levine, J., and others (1987). The role of denial in recovery from coronary heart disease. *Psychosomatic Medicine*, *49*, 109–117.

Levine, J. B., Green, C. J., & Millon, T. (1986). The separation-individuation test of adolescence. *Journal of Personality Assessment*, *50*, 123–137.

Levine, S. B., & Agle, D. (1978). The effectiveness of sex therapy for chronic secondary psychological impotence. *Journal of Sex and Marital Therapy*, *4*, 235–258.

Levy, J. A., Shimabukoro, J., Hollander, H., Mills, J., & Kaminsky, L. (1985). Isolation of AIDS-associated retrovirus from cerebrospinal fluid and brains of patients with neurological symptoms. *Lancet*, *2*, 586–588.

Levy, R. M., Pons, V. G., & Rosenblum, M. L. (1984). Central nervous system mass lesions in the acquired immune deficiency syndrome (AIDS). *Journal of Neurosurgery*, *61*, 9–16.

Levy, S. M. (1985). *Behavior and cancer: Life-style and psychosocial factors in the initiation and progression of cancer*. San Francisco: Jossey-Bass.

Levy, S. M., Herberman, R. B., Maluish, A. M., Schlien, B., & Lippman, M. (1985). Prognostic risk assessment in the primary breast cancer by behavioral and immunological parameters. *Health Psychology*, *4*, 99–113.

Lewinsohn, P. M. (1974). A behavioral approach to depression. In R. J. Friedman & M. M. Katz (Eds.), *The psychology of depression*: Contemporary theory and research. Washington, DC: Winston-Wiley.

Lewinsohn, P. M., & Amenson, C. S. (1978). Some relations between pleasant and unpleasant mood-related events and depression. *Journal of Abnormal Psychology*, *87*, 644–654.

Lewinsohn, P. M., Antonuccio, D., Steinmetz, J., & Terry, L. (1984). *The coping with depression course: A psychoeducational intervention for unipolar depression*. Eugene, OR: Castalia.

Lewinsohn, P. M., Duncan, E. M., Stanton, A. K., & Hautzinger, M. (1986). Age at first onset for nonpolar depression. *Journal of Abnormal Psychology*, *95*, 378–383.

Lewinsohn, P. H., & Libet, J. M. (1972). Pleasant events, activity schedules and depression. *Journal of Abnormal Psychology*, *79*, 291–295.

Lewinsohn, P., Steinmetz, J., Larson, D., & Franklin, J. (1981). Depression–related cognitions: Antecedent or consequence? *Journal of Abnormal Psychology*, *90*, 213–219.

Lewinsohn, P. M., Teri, L., & Wasserman, D. (1983). Depression. In M. Hersen (Ed.), *Outpatient behavior therapy: A practical guide* (pp. 81–108). New York: Grune & Stratton.

Lewis, D. O., Balla, D. A., & Shanok, S. S. (1979).

Some evidence of race bias in the diagnosis and treatment of the juvenile offender. *American Journal of Orthopsychiatry*, *49*, 53–61.

Lewis, M. S. (1989). Age incidence and schizophrenia: Part I. The season of birth controversy. *Schizophrenia Bulletin*, *15*, 59–73.

Lewis, R. J., Dlugokinski, E. L., Caputo, L. M., & Griffin, R. B. (1988). Children at risk for emotional disorders: Risk and resource dimensions. *Clinical Psychology Review*, *8*, 417–440.

Lewy, A. J. (1987). The psychopharmacological effect of light in seasonal effective disorder. *Psychopharmacology Bulletin*, *23*, 347–348.

Lex, B. W. (1987). Review of alcohol problems in ethnic minority groups. *Journal of Consulting and Clinical Psychology*, *55*, 293–300.

Ley, R. (1985). Blood, breath, and fears: A hyperventilation theory of panic attacks and agoraphobia. *Clinical Psychology Review*, *5*, 271–285.

Libman, E., Fichten, C. S., & Brender, W. (1985). The role of therapeutic format in the treatment of sexual dysfunction: A review. *Clinical Psychology Review*, *5*, 103–117.

Liberman, R. P., Mueser, K. T., Wallace, C. J., Jacobs, H. E., Eckman, T., & Massel, H. K. (1986). Training skills in the psychiatrically disabled: Learning, coping and competence. *Schizophrenia Bulletin*, *12*, 631–647.

Lichtenstein, E. (1982). The smoking problem: A behavioral perspective. *Journal of Consulting and Clinical Psychology*, *50*, 804–819.

Lichtenstein, E., & Brown, R. A. (1982). Current trends in the modification of cigarette dependence. In A. S. Bellack, M. Hersen, & A. E. Kazdin (Eds.), *International handbook of behavior modification and therapy* (pp. 575–611). New York: Plenum.

Lichtenstein, E., & Danaher, B. G. (1976). Modification of smoking behavior: A critical analysis of theory, research, and practice. In M. Hersen, R. M. Eisler, and P. M. Miller (Eds.), *Progress in behavior modification* (Vol. 3). New York: Academic Press.

Lichtenstein, E., Glasgow, R. E., & Abrams, D. B. (1986). Social support in smoking cessation: In search of effective interventions. *Behavior Therapy*, *17*, 607–619.

Lichtenstein, E., Harris, D., Birchler, G., Wahl, J., & Schmahl, D. (1973). Comparison of rapid smoking, warm, smoky air, and attention placebo in the modification of smoking behavior. *Journal of Consulting and Clinical Psychology*, *40*, 92–98.

Lick, J. R., & Heffler, D. (1977). Relaxation training and attention placebo in the treatment of severe insomnia. *Journal of Consulting and Clinical Psychology*, *45*, 153–161.

Lieberman, M. A., Yalom, I. D., & Miles, M. (1973). *Encounter groups: First facts*. New York: Basic Books.

Liebowitz, M. R., and others (1984). Lactate provocation of panic attacks. I. Clinical and behavioral findings. *Archives of General Psychiatry*, *41*, 764–770.

Liebowitz, M. R., Gorman, J. M., Fyer, A. J., & Klein, D. F. (1985). Social phobia: Review of a neglected anxiety disorder. *Archives of General Psychiatry*, *42*, 729–736.

Lied, E. R., & Marlatt, G. A. (1979). Modeling as a determinant of alcohol consumption: Effect of subject sex and prior drinking history. *Addictive Behaviors*, *4*, 47–54.

Lindemalm, G., Korlin, D., & Uddenberg, N. (1986). Long-term follow-up of "sex change" in 134 male to female transsexuals. *Archives of Sexual Behavior*, *15*, 187–210.

Linehan, M. M., Campter, P., Chiles, J. A., Strosahl, K., & Shearin, E. (1987). Interpersonal problem solving and parasuicide. *Cognitive Therapy and Research*, *11*, 1–12.

Ling, G. S. F., and others (1984). Separation of morphine analgesia from physical dependence. *Science*, *226*, 462–464.

Lingswiler, V. M., Crowther, J. H., & Stephens,

M. A. (1987). Emotional reactivity and eating in binge eating and obestiy. *Journal of Behavioral Medicine*, *10*, 287–299.

Linton, T. E., & Juul, K. D. (1980). Mainstreaming: Time for reassessment. *Educational Leadership*, *37*, 433–437.

Linz, D., Donnerstein, E., & Penrod, S. (1987). The findings and recommendations of the Attorney General's Commission on Pornography: Do the psychological facts fit the political fury? *American Psychologist*, *42*, 946–953.

Lipinski, D. P., Black, J. L., Nelson, R. O., & Ciminero, A. R. (1975). Influence of motivational variables on the reactivity and reliability of self-recording. *Journal of Consulting and Clinical Psychology*, *43*, 637–646.

Lipinsky, M., Kassinove, H., & Miller, N. (1980). Effects of rational-emotive therapy, rational role reversal, and rational-emotive imagery on the emotional adjustment of community mental-health-center patients. *Journal of Consulting and Clinical Psychology*, *48*, 366–374.

Lipton, D. N., McDonel, E. C., & McFall, R. M. (1987). Heterosocial perception in rapists. *Journal of Consulting and Clinical Psychology*, *55*, 17–21.

Litman, G., & Topman, A. (1983). Outcome studies on techniques in alcoholism treatment. In M. Galanter (Ed.), *Recent developments in alcoholism* (Vol. 1). New York: Plenum.

Livesley, W. J. (1985). The classification of personality disorder: II. The problem of criteria. *Canadian Journal of Psychiatry*, *30*, 359–362.

Livesley, W. J., West, M., & Tanney, A. (1985). Historical comment on DSM-III schizoid and avoidant personality disorders. *American Journal of Psychiatry*, *142*, 1344–1347.

Livesley, W. J., West, M., & Tanney, A. (1986). Doctor Livesley and associates reply. *American Journal of Psychiatry*, *143*, 1062–1063.

Lloyd, C., Alexander, A. A., Rice, D. G., & Greenfield, N. S. (1980). Life events as predictors of academic performance. *Journal of Human Stress*, *6*, 15–25.

Lochman, J. E. (1987). Self- and peer perceptions and attributional biases of aggressive and nonaggressive boys in dyadic interactions. *Journal of Consulting and Clinical Psychology*, *55*, 404–410.

Lochman, J. E., Burch, P. R., Curry, J. F., & Lampron, L. B. (1984). Treatment and generalization effects of cognitive behavioral and goal setting interventions with aggressive boys. *Journal of Consulting and Clinical Psychology*, *52*, 915–916.

Lochman, J. E., & Curry, J. F. (1986). Effects of social problem-solving training and self-instruction training with aggressive boys. *Journal of Clinical Child Psychology*, *15*, 159–164.

Loehlin, J. C., Willerman, L., & Horn, J. M. (1982). Personality resemblances between unwed mothers and their adopted-away offspring. *Journal of Personality and Social Psychology*, *42*, 1089–1099.

Logue, J. N., Hansen, F., & Struening, E. (1979). Emotional and physical distress following Hurricane Agnes in the Wyoming Valley of Pennsylvania. *Public Health Reports*, *94*, 495–502.

Lombroso, C. T., & Duffy, F. H. (1982). Brain electrical activity mapping as an adjunct to CT scanning. In R. Canger, F. Angeleri, & J. K. Penry (Eds.), *Advances in epileptology: 11th Epilepsy International Symposium*. New York: Raven Press, 83–88.

Lopez, S., & Hernandez, P. (1986). How culture is considered in evaluations of psychopathology. *The Journal of Nervous and Mental Diseases*, *176*, 598–606.

Lopez, S., & Nunez, J. A. (1987). Cultural factors considered in selected diagnostic criteria and interview schedules. *Journal of Abnormal Psychology*, *96*, 270–272.

LoPiccolo, J. (1977). Direct treatment of sexual dysfunction in the couple. In J. Money & H. Museph (Eds.), *Handbook of sexology*. Amsterdam: Excerpta Medica.

LoPiccolo, J. (1985, September). *Advances in diagnosis and treatment of sexual dysfunction*. Paper presented at the 28th annual meeting of the Society for the Scientific Study of Sex, San Diego, CA.

LoPiccolo, J., Heiman, J. R., Hogan, D. R., & Roberts, C. W. (1985). Effectiveness of single therapists versus cotherapy teams in sex therapy. *Journal of Consulting and Clinical Psychology, 53,* 287–294.

LoPiccolo, J., & Lobitz, W. C. (1972). The role of masturbation in the treatment of orgasmic dysfunction. *Archives of Sexual Behavior, 2,* 163.

LoPiccolo, J., & Stock, W. E. (1986). Treatment of sexual dysfunction. *Journal of Consulting and Clinical Psychology, 54,* 158–167.

Lothstein, L. M. (1982). Sex reassignment surgery: Historical, bioethical, and theoretical issues. *American Journal of Psychiatry, 139,* 417–426.

Lourea, D., Rila, M., & Taylor, C. (1986). *Sex in the age of AIDS*. Paper presented to the Western Region Conference of the Society for the Scientific Study of Sex, Scottsdale, AZ.

Lovaas, O. I. (1971). Considerations in the development of a behavioral treatment program for psychotic children. In D. W. Churchill, G. D. Alpern, & M. DeMyer (Eds.), *Infantile autism*. Springfield, IL: Chas C Thomas.

Lovaas, O. I. (1977). *The autistic child: Language development through behavior modification*. New York: Halsted Press.

Lovaas, O. I. (1987). Behavioral treatment and normal educational and intellectual functioning in young autistic children. *Journal of Consulting and Clinical Psychology, 55,* 3–9.

Lovaas, O. I., Freitag, G., Gold, V. J., & Kassorla, I. C. (1965). Experimental studies in childhood schizophrenia: Analysis of self-destructive behavior. *Journal of Experimental Child Psychology, 2,* 67–84.

Lovaas, O. I. Freitag, G., Kinder, M. I., Rubenstein, B. D., Schaeffer, B., & Simmons, J. Q. (1966). Establishment of social reinforcers in two schizophrenic children on the basis of food. *Journal of Experimental Child Psychology, 4,* 109–125.

Lovaas, O. I., Koegel, R. L., & Schreibman, L. (1979). Stimulus overselectivity in autism: A review of research. *Psychological Bulletin, 86,* 1236–1254.

Lovejoy, M. (1982). Expectations and the recovery process. *Schizophrenia Bulletin, 8,* 605–609.

Lubin, B., Larsen, R. M., & Matarazzo, J. D. (1984). Patterns of psychological test usage in the United States: 1935–1982. *American Psychologist, 39,* 451–454.

Lubin, B., Larsen, R. M., Matarazzo, J. D., & Seever, M. (1985). Psychological test usage patterns in five professional settings. *American Psychologist, 40,* 857–861.

Luborsky, L., & DeRubeis, R. J. (1984). The use of psychotherapy treatment manuals: A small revolution in psychotherapy research style. *Clinical Psychology Review, 4,* 5–15.

Luborsky, L., and others (1985). A verification of Freud's grandest clinical hypothesis: The transference. *Clinical Psychology Review, 5,* 231–246.

Luborsky, L., & Spence, D. P. (1971). Quantitative research on psychoanalytic therapy. In A. E. Bergin & S. L. Garfield (Eds.), *Handbook of psychotherapy and behavior change: An empirical analysis*. New York: Wiley

Luchins, D. J., Levine, R. R., & Meltzer, H. Y. (1983). Lateral ventricular size, psychopathology and medication response in the psychoses. *Biological Psychiatry, 19,* 29–44.

Ludolph, P. S. (1985). How prevalent is multiple personality? *American Journal of Psychiatry, 142,* 1526–1527.

Lui, K., Darrow, W., & Rutherford, G. W. (1988). A model-based estimate of the mean incubation period for AIDS in homosexual men. *Science, 240,* 1333–1335.

Lurigio, A. J., & Lewis, D. A. (1989). Worlds that fail: A longitudinal study of urban mental patients. *Journal of Social Issues, 45,* 79–90.

Lykken, D. T. (1957). A study of anxiety in the sociopathic personality. *Journal of Abnormal and Social Psychology, 55,* 6–10.

Lykken, D. T. (1981). *A tremor in the blood: Uses and abuses of the lie detector*. New York: McGraw-Hill.

Lykken, D. T. (1982, September). Fearlessness: Its carefree charm and deadly risks. *Psychology Today,* pp. 20–28.

Lynn, R. (1977). The intelligence of the Japanese. *Bulletin of the British Psychological Society, 30,* 69–72.

Lynn, R. (1982). IQ in Japan and in the United States shows a growing disparity. *Nature, 297,* 222–223.

Lyon, F. R., & Moats, L. K. (1988). Critical issues in the instruction of the learning disabled. *Journal of Consulting and Clinical Psychology, 56,* 830–835.

Lyons, J. S., Rosen, A. J., & Dysken, M. W. (1985). Behavioral effects of tricyclic drugs in depressed patients. *Journal of Consulting and Clinical Psychology, 53,* 17–24.

MacDougall, J. M., Dembroski, T. M., Dimsdale, J. E., & Hackett, T. D. (1985). Components of Type A, hostility and anger-in: Further relationships to angiographic findings. *Health Psychology, 4,* 137–152.

Machón, R. A., Mednick, S. A., & Schulsinger, F. (1983). The interaction of seasonality, place of birth, genetic risk and subsequent schizophrenia in a high-risk sample. *British Journal of Psychiatry, 143,* 383–388.

Mackay, A. V. P. (1980). Positive and negative symptoms and the role of dopamine. *British Journal of Psychiatry, 137,* 379–383.

Mackay, A. V. P., and others (1982). Increased brain dopamine and dopamine receptors in schizophrenia. *Archives of General Psychiatry, 39,* 991–997.

MacPhillamy, D. J., & Lewinsohn, P. M. (1974). Depression as a function of levels of desired and obtained pleasure. *Journal of Abnormal Psychology, 83,* 651–657.

MacPhillamy, D. J., & Lewinsohn, P. M. (1982). The Pleasant Events Schedule: Studies on reliability, validity, and scale intercorrelations. *Journal of Consulting and Clinical Psychology, 50,* 363–380.

Maddi, S. R., & Kobasa, S. C. (1984). *The hardy executive: Health under stress*. Homewood, IL: Dow Jones-Irwin.

Madigan, R. J., & Bollenbach, A. K. (1986). The effects of induced mood on irrational thoughts and views of the world. *Cognitive Therapy and Research, 10,* 547–562.

Maeder, T. (1985). *Crime and madness: The origins and evolution of the insanity defense*. New York: Harper & Row.

Maher, W. B., & Maher, B. A. (1985). Psychopathology: I. From ancient times to the eighteenth century. In G. A. Kimble & K. Schlesinger (Eds.), *Topics in the history of psychology* (Vol. 2). Hillsdale, NJ: Erlbaum, 1985.

Mahler, M. (1968). *On human symbiosis and the vicissitudes of individuation*. New York: International Universities Press.

Mahler, M., & Kaplan, L. (1977). Developmental aspects in the assessment of narcissistic and so-called borderline personalities. In P. Hartocollis (Ed.), *Borderline personality disorders: The concept, the syndrome, the patient* (pp. 71–85). New York: International Universities Press.

Mahler, M. S., Pine, F., & Bergman, A. (1975). The borderline syndrome: The role of the mother in the genesis and psychic structure of the borderline personality. *International Journal of Psychoanalysis, 56,* 163–177.

Maier, S. F., & Seligman, M. E. P. (1976). Learned helplessness: Theory and evidence. *Journal of Experimental Psychology: General, 105,* 3–46.

Malamuth, N. M. (1981). Rape fantasies as a function of exposure to violent sexual stimuli. *Archives of Sexual Behavior, 10,* 33–48.

Malamuth, N. M., Heim, N., & Feshbach, S. (1980). Sexual responsiveness of college students to rape depictions: Inhibitory or disinhibitory effects. *Journal of Personality and Social Psychology, 38,* 399–408.

Malatesta, V. J., Sutker, P. B., & Treiber, F. A. (1981). Sensation seeking and chronic public drunkenness. *Journal of Consulting and Clinical Psychology, 49,* 282–294.

Maletsky, B. M. (1974). "Assisted" covert sensitization in the treatment of exhibitionism. *Journal of Consulting and Clinical Psychology, 42,* 34–40.

Maletsky, B. M. (1980). Self-referred vs. court-referred sexually deviant patients: Success with assisted covert sensitization. *Behavior Therapy, 11,* 306–314.

Malloy, P. F., Fairbank, J. A., & Keane, T. M. (1983). Validation of a multimethod assessment of posttraumatic stress disorder in Vietnam veterans. *Journal of Consulting and Clinical Psychology, 51,* 488–494.

Malmo, R. B., & Shagass, C. (1949). Physiological study of symptom mechanism in psychiatric patients under stress. *Psychosomatic Medicine, 11,* 25–29.

Maloney, M. P., & Ward, M. P. (1976). *Psychological assessment: A conceptual approach*. New York: Oxford University Press.

Malouff, J. M., & Schutte, N. S. (1986). Development and validation of a measure of irrational belief. *Journal of Consulting and Clinical Psychology, 54,* 860–862.

Mann, H. R., Weinberger, L. E., & Gross, B. H. (1988). Court-mandated community outpatient treatment for persons found not guilty by reason of insanity: A five-year follow-up. *American Journal of Psychiatry, 145,* 450–456.

Manning, M. M., & Wright, T. L. (1983). Self-efficacy expectancies, outcome expectancies, and the persistence of pain control in childbirth. *Journal of Personality and Social Psychology, 45,* 421–431.

Mannuzza, S., Gittelman-Klein, R., Bonagura, N., Horowitz-Konig, P. H., & Shenker, R. (1988). Hyperactive boys almost grown up: II. Status of subjects without a mental disorder. *Archives of General Psychiatry, 45,* 13–18.

Mansnerus, L. (1988, October 12). The darker side of the "baby blues." *The New York Times,* pp. C1, C8.

Marchione, K. E., Michelson, L., Greenwald, M., & Dancu, C. (1987). Cognitive behavioral treatment of agoraphobia. *Behaviour Research and Therapy, 25,* 319–328.

Marcus, J., Hans, S. L., Nagler, S., Auerbach, J. G., Mirsky, A. F., & Aubrey, A. (1987). Review of the NIMH Israeli Kibbutz-City study and the Jerusalem infant development study. *Schizophrenia Bulletin, 13,* 425–438.

Marder, S. R., & May, P. R. A. (1986). Benefits and limitations of neuroleptics and other forms of treatment in schizophrenia. *American Journal of Psychotherapy, 40,* 357–369.

Marengo, J., & Harrow, M. (1985). Thought disorder: A function of schizophrenia, mania, or psychosis? *Journal of Nervous and Mental Disease, 173,* 35–41.

Marengo, J., & Harrow, M. (1987). Schizophrenic thought disorder at follow-up: A persistent or episodic course? *Archives of General Psychiatry, 44,* 651–659.

Margolin, G. (1981). The reciprocal relationship between marital and child problems. In J. P. Vincent (Ed.), *Advances in family intervention, assessment and theory: An annual compilation of research*. Greenwich, CT: JAI Press.

Margraf, J., Ehlers, A., & Roth, W. T. (1986). Biological models of panic disorder and agoraphobia: A review. *Behaviour Research and Therapy, 24,* 553–567.

Markman, H. J. (1981). Prediction of marital distress: A 5-year follow-up. *Journal of Consulting and Clinical Psychology, 49,* 760–762.

Markman, H. J., Floyd, F. J., Stanley, S. M., & Staraasli, R. D. (1988). Prevention of marital distress: A longitudinal investigation. *Journal of Consulting and Clinical Psychology, 56,* 210–217.

Marks, I. M. (1970). Agoraphobic syndrome (Phobic anxiety state). *Archives of General Psychiatry, 23,* 538–553.

Marks, I. M. (1982). Toward an empirical clinical science: Behavioral psychotherapy in the 1980s. *Behavior Therapy, 13,* 63–81.

Marks, I. M. (1985). Behavioral treatment of social phobia. *Psychopharmacology Bulletin, 21,* 615–618.

Marks, I. M. (1987). Behavioral aspects of panic disorder. *American Journal of Psychiatry, 144,* 1160–1165.

Marks, I. M., and others (1980). Clomipramine and exposure for obsessive-compulsive rituals: I. *British Journal of Psychiatry, 136,* 1–25.

Marks, I. M., Gray, S., Cohen, D., Hill, R., Mawson, D., Ramm, E., & Stern, R. S. (1983). Imipramine and brief therapist-aided exposure in agoraphobics having self-exposure homework. *Archives of General Psychiatry, 40,* 153–162.

Marks, J. (1978). *The benzodiazepines: Use, overuse, misuse, abuse.* Baltimore: University Park Press.

Marks, J. (1988). Alzheimer support groups: A framework for survival. In M. K. Aronson (Ed.), *Understanding Alzheimer's disease* ((pp. 188–197). New York: Scribner's.

Marlatt, G. A. (1978). Craving for alcohol, loss of control, and relapse: A cognitive-behavioral analysis. In P. E. Nathan, G. A. Marlatt, & T. Loberg (Eds.), *Alcoholism: New directions in behavioral research and treatment* (pp. 271–314). New York: Plenum.

Marlatt, G. A. (1985). Controlled drinking: The controversy rages on. *American Psychologist, 40,* 374–375.

Marlatt, G. A., Curry, S. G., & Gordon, J. R. (1986). *Treatment for smoking cessation: The relative effectiveness of different programs and formats.* Manuscript in preparation, University of Washington.

Marlatt, G. A., Demming, B., & Reid, J. B. (1973). Loss of control drinking in alcoholics: An experimental analogue. *Journal of Abnormal Psychology, 81,* 233–241.

Marlatt, G. A., & Gordon, J. R. (1980). Determinants of relapse: Implications for the maintenance of behavior change. In P. O. Davidson & S. M. Davidson (Eds.), *Behavioral medicine: Changing health lifestyles.* New York: Brunner/Mazel.

Marlatt, G. A., & Gordon, J. R. (1985). *Relapse prevention: Maintenance strategies in the treatment of addictive behaviors.* New York: Guilford Press.

Marlatt, G. A., & Rohsenow, D. J. (1981, December). The think-drink effect. *Psychology Today,* pp. 60–69.

Marshall, D. (1971). Sexual behavior on Mangaia. In D. Marshall & R. Suggs (Eds.), *Human sexual behavior: Variations in the ethnographic spectrum.* Englewood Cliffs, NJ: Prentice Hall.

Martelli, M. F., Auerbach, S. M., Alexander, J., & Mercuri, L. G. (1987). Stress management in the health care setting: Matching interventions with patient coping styles. *Journal of Consulting and Clinical Psychology, 55,* 201–207.

Martin, D. (1989, January 25). Autism: Illness that can steal a child's sparkle. *The New York Times,* p. B1.

Martin, J. L. (1988). Psychological consequences of AIDS-related bereavement among gay men. *Journal of Consulting and Clinical Psychology, 56,* 856–862.

Martin, N. G., & Jardine, R. (1986). Eysenck's contributions to behavior genetics. In S. Modgil & C. Modgil (Eds.), *Hans Eysenck: Consensus and controversy.* Philadelphia: Falmer.

Martin, R. A., & Lefcourt, H. M. (1983). Sense of humor as a moderator of the relation between

stressors and moods. *Journal of Personality and Social Psychology, 45,* 1313–1324.

Martin, R. L., and others (1985). Mortality in a follow-up of 500 psychiatric outpatients: I. Total mortality. *Archives of General Psychiatry, 42,* 47–54.

Marzillier, J. S. (1980). Cognitive therapy and behavioural practice. *Behaviour Research and Therapy, 18,* 249–258.

Mash, E. J., & Dalby, J. T. (1979). Behavioral interventions in hyperactivity. In R. L. Trites (Ed.), *Hyperactivity in children: Etiology, measurement, and treatment implications.* Baltimore: University Park Press.

Maslow, A. H. (1963). The need to know and the fear of knowing. *Journal of General Psychology, 68,* 111–124.

Masters, W. H., & Johnson, V. E. (1966). *Human sexual response.* Boston: Little, Brown.

Masters, W. H., & Johnson, V. E. (1970). *Human sexual inadequacy.* Boston: Little, Brown.

Masters, W. H., & Johnson, V. E. (1979). *Homosexuality in perspective.* Boston: Little, Brown.

Masters, W. H., Johnson, V. E., & Kolodny, R. C. (1988). *Human sexuality* (3rd ed.). Boston: Little, Brown.

Matefy, R. (1980). Role-playing theory of psychedelic flashbacks. *Journal of Consulting and Clinical Psychology, 48,* 551–553.

Mathews, A. M. (1985). Anxiety states: A cognitive-behavioural approach. In B. P. Bradley & C. Thompson (Eds.), *Psychological applications in psychiatry* (pp. 41–59). New York: Wiley.

Mathews, A. M., Johnston, D. W., Lancashire, M., Munby, M., Shaw, P. M., & Gelder, M. G. (1976). Imaginal flooding and exposure to real phobic situations: Treatment outcome with agoraphobic patients. *British Journal of Psychiatry, 129,* 362–371.

Mattes, J. A., & Gittelman, R. (1983). Growth of hyperactive children on maintenance regimen of methylphenidate. *Archives of General Psychiatry, 40,* 317–321.

Matthews, K. A., Glass, D. C., Rosenman, R. H., & Bortner, R. W. (1977). Competitive drive, pattern A and coronary heart disease: A further analysis of some data from the Western Collaborative Group Study. *Journal of Chronic Diseases, 30,* 489–498.

Matthews, K. A., & Haynes, S. G. (1986). Type A behavior pattern and coronary disease risk: Update and critical evaluation. *American Journal of Epidemiology, 123,* 923–960.

Matthews, K. A., Krantz, D. S., Dembroski, T. M., & MacDougall, J. M. (1982). Unique and common variance in structured interview and Jenkins Activity Survey measures of the Type A behavior pattern. *Journal of Personality and Social Psychology, 42,* 303–313.

Mattick, R. P., & Peteres, L. (1988). Treatment of severe social phobia: Effects of guided exposure with and without cognitive restructuring. *Journal of Consulting and Clinical Psychology, 56,* 251–260.

Maugh, T. H. (1982). Marijuana "justifies serious concern." *Science, 215,* 1488–1489.

Mavissakalian, M. (1987). Initial depression and response to imipramine in agoraphobia. *Journal of Nervous and Mental Disease, 175,* 358–361.

Mavissakalian, M., & Michelson, L. (1986). Two-year follow-up of exposure and imipramine treatment of agoraphobia. *American Journal of Psychiatry, 143,* 1106–1112.

Mavissakalian, M., Michelson, L., Greenwald, D., Kornblith, S., & Greenwald, M. (1983). Cognitive-behavioral treatment of agoraphobia: Paradoxical intention vs. self-statement training. *Behaviour Research and Therapy, 21,* 75–86.

Mavissakalian, M., & Perel, J. (1985). Imipramine in the treatment of agoraphobia: Dose-response relationships. *American Journal of Psychiatry, 142,* 1032–1036.

May, C. D. (1988, July 1). How Coca-Cola obtains its coca. *The New York Times,* pp. D1, 5.

May, P. R. (1975). A follow-up study of treatment of schizophrenia. In R. L. Spitzer & D. F. Klein (Eds.), *Evaluation of psychological therapies.* Baltimore: Johns Hopkins University Press.

May, P. R. A., & Goldberg, S. C. (1978). Prediction of schizophrenic patient's response to pharmacotherapy. In M. A. Lipton, A. DiMascio, & K. F. Killam (Eds.), *Psychopharmacology: A generation of progress* (pp. 1139–1153). New York: Raven Press.

May, P. R. A., & Tuma, A. H. (1976). The Paul H. Hoch Award Lecture: A follow-up study of the results of treatment of schizophrenia. In R. L. Spitzer & D. F. Klein (Eds.), *Evaluation of psychological therapies* (pp. 256–284). Baltimore: Johns Hopkins University Press.

May, R. (1953). *Man's search for himself.* New York: W. W Norton & Co., Inc.

May, R. (1958). Contributions of existential psychotherapy. In R. May, E. Angel, & H. F. Ellenberger, *Existence* (pp. 37–91). New York: Simon & Schuster.

May, R. (1968). *Treatment of schizophrenia.* New York: Science House.

Mays, V. M., & Cochran, S. D. (1988). Issues in the perception of AIDS risk and risk reduction activities by black and Hispanic/Latina women. *American Psychologist, 43,* 949–957.

McCall, R. B. (1975). *Intelligence and heredity.* Homewood, IL: Learning Systems Company.

McCaul, K. D., & Haugvedt, C. (1982). Attention, distraction, and cold-pressor pain. *Journal of Personality and Social Psychology, 43,* 154–162.

McCauley, E., Mitchell, J. R., Burke, P., & Moss, S. (1988). Cognitive attributes of depression in children and adolescents. *Journal of Consulting and Clinical Psychology, 56,* 903–908.

McClelland, D. C. (1958). Methods of measuring human motivation. In J. W. Atkinson (Ed.), *Motives in fantasy, action, and society.* Princeton, NJ: Van Nostrand.

McClelland, D. C. (1989). Motivational factors in health and disease. *American Psychologist, 44,* 675–683.

McClelland, D. C., Alexander, C., & Marks, E. (1982). The need for power, stress, immune functions, and illness among male prisoners. *Journal of Abnormal Psychology, 91,* 61–70.

McClelland, D. C., Davidson, R. J., Floor, E., & Saron, C. (1980). Stressed power motivation, sympathetic activation, immune function and illness. *Journal of Human Stress, 6*(2), 11–19.

McClelland, D. C., & Jemmott, J. B., III (1980). Power motivation, stress and physical illness. *Journal of Human Stress, 6*(4), 6–15.

McClelland, D. C., & Kirshnit, C. (1988). The effect of motivational arousal through films on salivary immunoglobulin A. *Psychology and Health, 2,* 31–52.

McConaghy, M. C., Armstrong, M. F., Balszczynski, A., & Allcock, C. (1983). Controlled comparison of aversive therapy and imaginal desensitization in compulsive gambling. *British Journal of Psychiatry, 142,* 366–372.

McConaghy, N., & Blaszczynski, A. (1980). A pair of monozygotic twins discordant for homosexuality: Sex-dimorphic behavior and penile volume responses. *Archives of Sexual Behavior, 9,* 123–124.

McCord, J. (1983). A 40-year prospective on effects of child abuse and neglect. *Child Abuse and Neglect, 7,* 265–270.

McCord, W., & McCord, J. (1964). *The psychopath: An essay on the criminal mind.* New York: D. Van Nostrand Company.

McCord, W., McCord, J., & Gudeman, J. (1960). *Origins of alcoholism.* Stanford, CA: Stanford University Press.

McCormick, R. A., Russo, A. M., Ramirez, L. F., & Taber, J. I. (1984). Affective disorders among pathological gamblers seeking treatment. *American Journal of Psychiatry, 141,* 215–218.

McCormick, R. A., Taber, J., Kruedelbach, N., Russo, A. (1987). Personality profiles of hospitalized pathological gamblers: The California Personality Inventory. *Journal of Clinical Psychology, 43*, 521–527.

McCranie, E. W., & Bass, J. D. (1984). Childhood family antecedents of dependency and self-criticism: Implications for depression. *Journal of Abnormal Psychology, 93*, 3–8.

McCranie, E. W., Watkins, L. O, Brandsma, J. M., & Sisson, B. D. (1986). Hostility, coronary heart disease (CHD) incidence, and total mortality: Lack of association in a 25-year follow-up study of 478 physicians. *Journal of Behavioral Medicine, 9*, 119–126.

McCreadie, R. G., Main, C. J., & Dunlap, R. A. (1978). Token economy, pimozide and chronic schizophrenia. *British Journal of Psychiatry, 133*, 179–181.

McCullough, L., & Farrell, A. D. (1983). *The Computerized Assessment System for Psychotherapy Evaluation and Research* (computer program). New York: Beth Israel Medical Center, Department of Psychiatry.

McCullough, L., Farrell, A. D., & Longabaugh, R. (1986). The development of a microcomputer-based mental health information system: A potential tool for bridging the scientist-practitioner gap. *American Psychologist, 41*, 207–214.

McCutchan, J. A. (1990). Virology, immunology, and clinical course of HIV infection. *Journal of Consulting and Clinical Psychology, 58*, 5–12.

McFall, R. M., & Hammen, C. L. (1971). Motivation, structure, and self-monitoring: Role of nonspecific factors in smoking reduction. *Journal of Consulting and Clinical Psychology, 37*, 80–86.

McGee, R., Williams, S., & Silva, P. A. (1985). Factor structure and correlates of ratings of inattention, hyperactivity, and antisocial behavior in a large sample of 9-year-old children from the general population. *Journal of Consulting and Clinical Psychology, 53*, 480–490.

McGhie, A., & Chapman, J. (1961). Disorders of attention and perception in early schizophrenia. *British Journal of Medical Psychology, 34*, 102–116.

McGill, D. C. (1988, November 26). Tobacco industry counterattacks. *The New York Times*, pp. 31, 41.

McGlashan, T. H. (1983). The borderline syndrome. *Archives of General Psychiatry, 40*, 1319–1323.

McGlashan, T. H. (1984). The Chestnut Lodge follow-up study: 2. Long-term outcome of schizophrenia and the affective disorders. *Archives of General Psychiatry, 41*, 586–601.

McGovern, F. J., & Nevid, J. S. (1986). Evaluation apprehension on psychological inventories in a prison-based setting. *Journal of Consulting and Clinical Psychology, 54*, 576–578.

McGuffin, P., & Katz, R. (1986). Nature, nurture and affective disorder. In J. W. W. Deakin (Ed.), *The biology of depression. Proceedings of a meeting of the Biological Group of the Royal College of Psychiatrists held at Manchester University, 1985* (pp. 26–52). Washington, DC: American Psychiatric Press.

McIntosh, J. L. (1985). Suicide among the elderly: Levels and trends. *American Journal of Orthopsychiatry, 55*, 288–293.

McIntyre, K. O., Lichtenstein, E., & Mermelstein, R. J. (1983). Self-efficacy and relapse in smoking cessation: A replication and extension. *Journal of Consulting and Clinical Psychology, 51*, 632–633.

McIntyre-Kingsolver, K., Lichtenstein, E., & Mermelstein, R. J. (1986). Spouse training in a multicomponent smoking-cessation program. *Behavior Therapy, 17*, 67–74.

McMillan, M. J., & Pihl, R. O. (1987). Premenstrual depression: A distinct entity. *Journal of Abnormal Psychology, 96*, 149–154.

McMullen, S., & Rosen, R. C. (1979). Self-administered masturbation training in the treatment of primary orgasmic dysfunction. *Journal of Consulting and Clinical Psychology, 47*, 912–918.

McNally, R. (1987). Preparedness and phobias: A review. *Psychological Bulletin, 101*, 283–303.

McNally, R. J., & Foa, E. B. (1987). Cognition and agoraphobia: Bias in the interpretation of threat. *Cognitive Therapy and Research, 11*, 567–581.

McNeil, D. E., Arkowitz, H. S., & Pritchard, B. E. (1987). The response of others to face-to-face interaction with depressed patients. *Journal of Abnormal Psychology, 96*, 341–344.

McNeil, D. E., & Binder, R. L. (1987). Predictive validity of judgements of dangerousness in emergency civil commitment. *American Journal of Psychiatry, 144*, 197–200.

McNeil, T. F., & Kaiij, L. (1978). Obstetrical factors in the development of schizophrenia: Complications in the births of preschizophrenics and in reproduction by schizophrenic parents. In L. C. Wynne, R. L. Cromwell, & S. Matthysse (Eds.), *The nature of schizophrenia: New approaches to research and treatment*. New York: Wiley.

McPherson, F. M., Brougham, L., & McLaren, S. (1980). Maintenance of improvement in agoraphobia patients treated by behavioral methods: A four-year follow-up. *Behaviour Research and Therapy, 18*, 150–152.

Mead, M. (1935). *Sex and temperament in three primitive societies*. New York: Morrow.

Mednick, S. A. (1970). Breakdown in individuals at high risk for schizophrenia: Possible predispositional perinatal factors. *Mental Hygiene, 54*, 50–63.

Mednick, S. A. (1985, March). Crime in the family tree. *Psychology Today*, pp. 58–61.

Mednick, S. A., Gabrielli, W. F., & Hutchings, B. (1984). Genetic influences in criminal convictions: Evidence from an adoption cohort. *Science, 244*, 891–894.

Mednick, S. A., Machón, R., Huttunen, M. O., & Bonett, D. (in press). Fetal viral infection and adult schizophrenia. *Archives of General Psychiatry*.

Mednick, S. A., Moffitt, T. E., & Stack, S. (1987). *The causes of crime: New biological approaches*. New York: Cambridge University Press.

Mednick, S. A., Parnas, J., & Schulsinger, F. (1987). The Copenhagen High-Risk project, 1962–86. *Schizophrenia Bulletin, 13*, 485–495.

Mednick, S. A., & Schulsinger, F. (1965). A longitudinal study of children with a high risk for schizophrenia: A preliminary report. In S. Vandenberg (Ed.), *Methods and goals in human behavior genetics* (pp. 255–296). New York: Academic Press.

Mednick, S. A., & Schulsinger, F. (1968). Some pre-morbid characteristics related to breakdown in children with schizophrenic mothers. In D. Rosenthal & S. S. Kety (Eds.), *The transmission of schizophrenia* (pp. 267–291). New York: Pergamon Press.

Meehl, P. E. (1962). Schizotaxia, schizotypy, schizophrenia. *American Psychologist, 17*, 827–838.

Meehl, P. E. (1972). A critical afterword. In I. I. Gottesman & J. Shields (Eds.), *Schizophrenia and genetics: A twin study vantage point* (pp. 367–415). New York: Academic Press.

Mehrabian, A., & Weinstein, L. (1985). Temperament characteristics of suicide attempters. *Journal of Consulting and Clinical Psychology, 53*, 544–546.

Meichenbaum, D. (1977). *Cognitive behavior modification: An integrative approach*. New York: Plenum.

Meichenbaum, D., & Cameron, R. (1983). Stress inoculation training: Toward a general paradigm for training coping skills, In D. Meichenbaum & M. E. Jaremko (Eds.), *Stress reduction and prevention* (pp. 115–154). New York: Plenum.

Meichenbaum, D., & Deffenbacher, J. L. (1988). Stress inoculation training. *The Counseling Psychologist, 16*(1), 69–90.

Meichenbaum, D., & Goodman, J. (1971). Training impulsive children to talk to themselves: A means of developing self-control. *Journal of Abnormal Psychology, 77*, 115–126.

Meichenbaum, D., & Jaremko, M. E. (Eds.). (1983). *Stress reduction and prevention*. New York: Plenum.

Meichenbaum, D., & Turk, S. (1976). The cognitive-behavioral management of anxiety, anger, and pain. In P. O. Davidson (Ed.), *The behavioral management of anxiety, depression, and pain*. New York: Brunner/Mazel.

Meier, J. H. (1971). Prevalence and characteristics of learning disabilities in second grade children. *Journal of Learning Disabilities, 4*, 1–16.

Meissner, W. W. (1980). Psychoanalysis and sexual disorders. In B. J. Wolman & J. Money (Eds.), *Handbook of human sexuality*. Englewood Cliffs, NJ: Prentice Hall.

Meissner, W. W. (1981). The schizophrenic and the paranoid process. *Schizophrenia Bulletin, 7*, 611–631.

Mellinger, G. D., Balter, M. B., & Uhlenhuth, E. H. (1985). Insomnia and its treatment: Prevalence and correlates. *Archives of General Psychiatry, 42*, 225–232.

Mellor, C. S. (1970). First rank symptoms of schizophrenia. *British Journal of Psychiatry, 177*, 15–23.

Mellor, C. S. (1982). The present status of first rank symptoms. *British Journal of Psychiatry, 140*, 423–424.

Melton, G. B. (1988). Ethical and legal issues in AIDS-related practice. *American Psychologist, 43*, 941–947.

Meltzer, H. Y. (1985). Dopamine and negative symptoms in schizophrenia: Critique of the Type I–Type II hypothesis. In M. Alpert (Ed.), *Controversies in schizophrenia: Changes and constancies* (pp. 110–136). New York: Guilford Press.

Meltzer, H. Y. (1987). Biological studies in schizophrenia. *Schizophrenia Bulletin, 13*, 77–111.

Meltzer, H. Y., & Stahl, S. M. (1976). The dopamine hypothesis of schizophrenia: A review. *Schizophrenia Bulletin, 2*, 19–76.

Menaghan, E. G., & Lieberman, M. A. (1986). Changes in depression following divorce: A panel study. *Journal of Marriage and the Family, 17*, 319–328.

Mendelson, J. H., & Mello, N. K. (1979). Biological concomitants of alcoholism. *New England Journal of Medicine, 301*, 912–921.

Mendelson, J. H., Miller, K. D., Mello, N. K., Pratt, H., & Schmitz, R. (1982). Hospital treatment of alcoholism: A profile of middle income Americans. *Alcoholism: Clinical and Experimental Research, 6*, 377–383.

Mendlewicz, J., & Rainer, J. D. (1977). Adoption study supporting genetic transmission in manic depressive illness. *Nature, 268*, 326–329.

Menninger, K. (1983). *The vital balance*. New York: Viking.

Messenger, J. (1971). Sex and repression in an Irish folk community. In D. Marshall & R. Suggs (Eds.), *Human sexual behavior: Variations in the ethnographic spectrum*. Englewood Cliffs, NJ: Prentice Hall.

Metalsky, G. I., Abramson, L. Y., Seligman, M. E. P., Semmel, A., & Peterson, C. (1982). Attributional styles and life events in the classroom: Vulnerability and invulnerability to depressive mood reactions. *Journal of Abnormal Psychology, 43*, 612–617.

Metcalfe, M., & Goldman, E. (1965). Validation of an inventory for measuring depression. *British Journal of Psychiatry, 111*, 240–242.

Meyer, J. K., & Reter, D. J. (1979). Sex reassignment: Follow-up. *Archives of General Psychiatry, 36*, 1010–1015.

Meyers, J. K., and others (1984). Six-month prevalence of psychiatric disorders in three communities. *Archives of General Psychiatry, 41*, 959–967.

Michael, C. C., & Funabiki, D. (1985). Depression,

distortion and life stress: Extended findings. *Cognitive Therapy and Research, 9,* 659–666.

Mider, P. A. (1984). Failures in alcoholism and drug dependence prevention and learning from the past. *American Psychologist, 39,* 183.

Milich, R., Wolraich, M., & Lindgren, S. (1986). Sugar and hyperactivity: A critical review of empirical findings. *Clinical Psychology Review, 6,* 493–513.

Miller, B. J. (1978). *The complete medical guide* (4th ed.). New York: Simon & Schuster.

Miller, B. L., Benson, D. F., Goldberg, M. A., and others (in press). The misdiagnosis of hysteria. *American Family Physician.*

Miller, E. (1987). Hysteria: Its nature and explanation. *British Journal of Clinical Psychology, 26,* 163–173.

Miller, I. W., Klee, S. H., & Norman, W. H. (1982). Depressed and nondepressed inpatients' cognitions of hypothetical events, experimental tasks, and stressful life events. *Journal of Abnormal Psychology, 91,* 78–81.

Miller, I. W., & Norman, W. H. (1986). Persistence of depressive cognitions within a sub-group of depressed patients. *Cognitive Therapy and Research, 10,* 211–224.

Miller, R. D. (1985). Commitment to outpatient treatment: A national survey. *Hospital and Community Psychiatry, 36,* 265–267.

Miller, R. E. (1987). Method to study anhedonia in hospitalized psychiatric patients. *Journal of Abnormal Psychology, 96,* 41–45.

Miller, S., Saccuzzo, D., & Braff, D. (1979). Information processing deficits in remitted schizophrenics. *Journal of Abnormal Psychology, 88,* 446–449.

Miller, S. M. (1980). Why having control reduces stress: If I can stop the roller coaster I don't want to get off. In J. Garber & M. E. P. Seligman (Eds.), *Human helplessness: Theory and research.* New York: Academic Press.

Miller, S. M., Lack, E. R., & Asroff, S. (1985). Preference for control and the coronary-prone behavior pattern. *Journal of Personality and Social Psychology, 49,* 492–499.

Miller, W. R. (1982). Treating problem drinkers: What works? *The Behavior Therapist, 5,* 15–18.

Miller, W. R., & Hester, R. K. (1986). Inpatient alcoholism treatment: Who benefits? *American Psychologist, 41,* 794–805.

Miller, W. R., & Lief, H. I. (1976). Masturbatory attitudes, knowledge, and experience. Data from the Sex Knowledge and Attitude Test (SKAT). *Archives of Sexual Behavior, 5,* 447–468.

Miller, W. R., & Muñoz, R. F. (1983). *How to control your drinking* (2nd ed.). Albuquerque: University of New Mexico Press.

Miller-Perrin, C. L., & Wurtele, S. K. (1988). The child sexual abuse prevention movement: A critical analysis of primary and secondary approaches. *Clinical Psychology Review, 8,* 313–329.

Millon, T. (1981). *Disorders of personality DSM-III: Axis II.* New York: Wiley.

Millon, T. (1982). *Millon Clinical Multiaxial Inventory Manual* (3rd ed.). Minneapolis: National Computer Systems.

Milner, B. R. (1966). Amnesia following operation on temporal lobes. In C. W. M. Whitty & O. L. Zangwill (Eds.), *Amnesia.* London: Butterworth.

Minkoff, K. (1978). A map of the chronic mental patient. In J. A. Talbott (Ed.), *The chronic mental patient: Problems, solutions, and recommendations for public policy.* Washington, DC: American Psychiatric Press.

Minuchin, S. (1974). *Families and family therapy.* Cambridge, MA: Harvard University Press.

Minuchin, S., Rosman, B. L., & Baker, L. (1978). *Psychosomatic Families: Anorexia nervosa in context.* Cambridge, MA: Harvard University Press.

Mirsky, A. F., & Orzack, M. H. (1980). Two retrospective studies of psychosurgery. In E. S. Valenstein (Ed.), *The psychosurgery debate.* San Francisco: W. H. Freeman & Company Publishers.

Mischel, W. (1977). On the future of personality measurement. *American Psychologist, 32,* 246–254.

Mischel, W. (1979). On the interface of cognition and personality: Beyond the person-situation debate. *American Psychologist, 34,* 740–754.

Mischel, W. (1986). *Introduction to personality* (4th ed.). New York: Holt, Rinehart & Winston.

Mitchell, J. E., & Eckert, E. D. (1987). Scope and significance of eating disorders. *Journal of Consulting and Clinical Psychology, 55,* 628–634.

Mitchelson, L., & Ascher, M. (1984). Paradoxical intention: Theory, research, and clinical application for anxiety disorders. *Journal of Behavior Therapy and Experimental Psychiatry, 15,* 215–220.

Mittelmark, M. B., and others (1986). Community-wide prevention of cardiovascular disease: Education strategies of the Minnesota Heart Health Program. *Preventive Medicine, 15,* 1–17.

Mittelmark, M. B., and others (1987). Predicting experimentation with cigarettes: The Childhood Antecedents of Smoking Study. *American Journal of Public Health, 77,* 206–208.

Mizes, J. S., Landolf-Fritsche, B., & Grossman-McKee, D. (1987). Patterns of distorted cognitions in phobic disorders: An investigation of clinically severe simple phobics, social phobics, and agoraphobics. *Cognitive Therapy and Research, 11,* 583–592.

M'Naghten, 10 Cl & F, 200, 8 Eng. Rep. 718 (H & L) 1843.

Mohr, J. W., Turner, R. E., & Jerry, M. B. (1964). *Pedophilia and exhibitionism.* Toronto: University of Toronto Press.

Mohs, R. C., Breitner, J. C., Silverman, J. M., & Davis, K. L. (1987). Alzheimer's disease: Morbid risk among first-degree relatives approximates 50% by 90 years of age. *Archives of General Psychiatry, 44,* 405–408.

Moller, H. J., von Zerssen, D., Werner-Eilert, K., & Wuschner-Stockheim, M. (1982). Outcome in schizophrenic and similar paranoid psychoses. *Schizophrenia Bulletin, 8,* 99–108.

Molnar, G., & Cameron, P. (1975). Incest syndromes: Observations in a general psychiatric unit. *Canadian Psychiatric Journal, 20,* 373–377.

Monahan, J. (1981). *A clinical prediction of violent behavior* (DHHS Publication No. ADM. 81–921). Rockville, MD: National Institute of Mental Health.

Monahan, J., Novaco, R., & Geis, G. (1979). Corporate violence: Research strategies for community psychology. In T. Sarbin (Ed.), *Challenges to the criminal justice system.* New York: Human Sciences.

Monahan, J., & Steadman, H. J. (1983). Crime and mental disorder: An epidemiological approach. In A. Morris & M. Tomroy (Eds.), *Crime and justice: An annual review of research.* Chicago: University of Chicago Press.

Money, J. (1987). Sin, sickness, or status? Homosexual gender identity and psychoneuroendocrinology. *American Psychologist, 42,* 384–399.

Money, J., & Bennett, R. (1981). Postadolescent paraphilic sex offenders: Antiandrogenic and counseling therapy follow-up. *International Journal of Mental Health, 10,* 122–133.

Money, J., & Ehrhardt, A. (1972). *Man and woman, boy and girl.* Baltimore, MD: Johns Hopkins University Press.

Monroe, S. M. (1982). Life events and disorder: Event-symptom associations and the course of disorder. *Journal of Abnormal Psychology, 91,* 14–24.

Monroe, S. M. (1983). Major and minor life events as predictors of psychological distress: Further issues and findings. *Journal of Behavioral Medicine, 6,* 189–205.

Monroe, S. M., Bromet, E. J., Connell, M. M., & Stener, S. C. (1986). Social support, life events, and depressive symptoms: A 1-year prospective study. *Journal of Consulting and Clinical Psychology, 54,* 423–431.

Montague, A. (1968, May). Chromosomes and crime. *Psychology Today,* pp. 43–49.

Monti, P. M., and others (1987). Reactivity of alcoholics and nonalcoholics to drinking cues. *Journal of Abnormal Psychology, 96,* 122–126.

Moon, J. R., & Eisler, R. M. (1983). Anger control: An experimental comparison of three behavioral treatments. *Behavior Therapy, 14,* 493–505.

Moore, J. E., & Chaney, E. F. (1985). Outpatient group treatment of chronic pain: Effects of spouse involvement. *Journal of Consulting and Clinical Psychology, 53,* 325–334.

Moos, R. H., & Billings, A. G. (1982). Children of alcoholics during the recovery process: Alcoholic and matched control families. *Addictive Behaviors, 7,* 155–163.

Morey, L. C. (1988). Personality disorders in DSM-III and DSM-III-R: Convergence, coverage, and internal consistency. *American Journal of Psychiatry, 145,* 573–577.

Morey, L. C., Roberts, W. R., & Penk, W. (1987). MMPI alcoholic subtypes: Replicability and validity of the 2–8–7–4 subtype. *Journal of Abnormal Psychology, 96,* 164–166.

Morey, L. C., Skinner, H. A., & Blashfield, R. K. (1984). A typology of alcohol abusers: Correlates and implications. *Journal of Abnormal Psychology, 93,* 408–417.

Morgan, T. (1988, October 31). Learning disabilities and crime: Struggle to snap the link. *The New York Times,* pp. B1, B7.

Morganthau, T., and others (1986, January 6). Abandoned: The chronic mentally ill. *Newsweek,* pp. 14–19.

Morihisa, J. M., Duffy, F. H., & Wyatt, R. J. (1983). Brain electrical activity mapping (BEAM) in schizophrenic patients. *Archives of General Psychiatry, 40,* 719–728.

Morin, C. M., & Azrin, N. H. (1988). Behavioral and cognitive treatments of geriatric insomnia. *Journal of Consulting and Clinical Psychology, 56,* 748–753.

Morin, S. F. (1988). AIDS: The challenge to psychology. *American Psychologist, 43,* 838–842.

Morokoff, P. J., & Heiman, J. R. (1980). Effects of erotic stimuli on sexually functional and dysfunctional women: Multiple measures before and after sex therapy. *Behaviour Research and Therapy, 18,* 127–137.

Morris, J. B., & Beck, A. T. (1974). The efficacy of antidepressant drugs. A review of research (1958–1972). *Archives of General Psychiatry, 30,* 667–674.

Morris, R. D. (1988). Classification of learning disabilities: Old problems and new approaches. *Journal of Consulting and Clinical Psychology, 56,* 789–794.

Morrison, J. R., & Stewart, M. A. (1973). The psychiatric status of the legal families of adopted hyperactive children. *Archives of General Psychiatry, 28,* 888–891.

Morrison, R. L., & Bellack, A. S. (1984). Social skills training. In A. S. Bellack (Ed.), *Schizophrenia: Treatment, management and rehabilitation* (pp. 247–279). Orlando, FL: Grune & Stratton.

Morrison, R. L., & Bellack, A. S. (1987). Social functioning of schizophrenic patients: Clinical and research issues. *Schizophrenia Bulletin, 13,* 715–725.

Mosher, L. R., & Keith, S. J. (1980). Psychosocial treatment: Individual, group, family, and community support approaches. *Schizophrenia Bulletin, 6,* 10–41.

Mowrer, O. H. (1960). *Learning theory and the symbolic processes.* New York: Wiley.

Moynihan, D. P. (1989, May 22). Promise to the mentally ill has not been kept. *The New York Times,* p. A16.

Mullen, B., & Suls, J. (1982). The effectiveness of attention and rejection as coping styles: A meta-analysis of temporal differences. *Journal of Psychosomatic Research, 26,* 43–49.

Munby, M., & Johnston, D. W. (1981). Agoraphobia: The long-term follow-up of behavioural treatment. *British Journal of Psychiatry, 137,* 418–427.

Munich, R. L. (1987). Conceptual trends and issues in the psychotherapy of schizophrenia. *American Journal of Psychotherapy, 41,* 23–37.

Murray, A. D. (1985). Aversiveness is in the mind of the beholder. In B. M. Lester & C. F. Z. Boukydis (Eds.), *Infant crying.* New York: Plenum Press.

Murray, D. M., Richards, P. S., Luepker, R. V., & Johnson, C. A. (1987). The prevention of cigarette smoking in children: Two- and three-year follow-up comparisons of four prevention strategies. *Journal of Behavioral Medicine, 10,* 595–611.

Murray, H. A. (1943). *Thematic Apperception Test: Pictures and manual.* Cambridge, MA: Harvard University Press.

Murray, J. B. (1989a). Alcoholism: Etiologies proposed and therapeutic approaches tried. *Genetic, Social, and General Psychology Monographs, 115,* 81–121.

Murray, J. B. (1989b). Geophysical variables and behavior: VIII. Seasonal affective disorder and phototherapy. *Psychological Reports, 64,* 787–801.

Murray, R. M., Clifford, C., Gurling, H. M. D., Topham, A., Clow, A., & Bernadt, M. (1983). Current genetic and biological approaches to alcoholism. *Psychiatric Developments, 2,* 179–192.

Murray, R. M., & Reveley, A. M. (1986). Genetic aspects of schizophrenia: Overview. In A. Kerr & P. Snaith (Eds.), *Contemporary issues in schizophrenia* (pp. 261–267). Avon, England: The Bath Press.

Myers, J. K., and others (1984). Six-month prevalence of psychiatric disorders in three communities. *Archives of General Psychiatry, 41,* 959–967.

Myers, M. B., Templer, D. I., & Brown, R. (1984). Coping ability of women who become victims of rape. *Journal of Consulting and Clinical Psychology, 52,* 73–78.

Myers, M. B., Templer, D. I., & Brown, R. (1985). Reply to Wieder on rape victims: Vulnerability does not imply responsibility. *Journal of Consulting and Clinical Psychology, 53,* 431.

Nader, L. B. (1985). The epidemiology of pathological gambling: Critique of existing research and alternative strategies. *Journal of Gambling Behavior, 1,* 35–50.

Nadi, N. S., Nurnberger, J. I., & Gershon, E. S. (1984). Muscarinic cholinergic receptors on skin fibroblasts in familiar affective disorder. *New England Journal of Medicine, 311,* 225–230.

Naditch, M. P. (1986). STAYWELL: Evolution of a behavioral medicine program in industry. In M. F. Cataldo & T. J. Coates (Eds.), *Health and industry: A behavioral medicine perspective* (pp. 323–337). New York: Wiley.

Nadler, L. B. (1985). The epidemiology of pathological gambling: Critique of existing research and alternative strategies. *Journal of Gambling Behavior, 1,* 35–50.

Nathan, P. E. (1988). The addictive personality is the behavior of the addict. *Journal of Consulting and Clinical Psychology, 56,* 183–188.

Nathan, P. E., & Skinstad, A. H. (1987). Outcomes of treatment for alcohol problems: Current methods, problems, and results. *Journal of Consulting and Clinical Psychology, 55,* 332–340.

National Center for Health Statistics (1967). *Suicide in the United States, 1950–1964.* Washington, DC.: U.S. Department of Health, Education, and Welfare.

National Center on Child Abuse and Neglect (1979). *Child sexual abuse: Incest, assault, and sexual exploitation* (DHEW Publication No. 79–30166). Washington, DC: U.S. Government Printing Office.

National Center on Child Abuse and Neglect Report (1982, January–February). *Children Today,* pp. 27–28.

National Committee for the Prevention of Child Abuse (1985). *The size of the child abuse problem.* Chicago: Author.

National Council on Alcoholism (1986). *Facts on alcoholism.* New York: Author.

National Institutes of Health (1987). *Differential diagnosis of dementing diseases* (NIH Consensus Development Conference Statement, Vol. 6, No. 11). Bethesda, MD: Author.

National Institute of Mental Health (1985). *Electroconvulsive therapy: Consensus development conference statement.* Bethesda, MD: Office of Medical Applications of Research.

National Institute on Drug Abuse (NIDA) (1983). *Population projections, based on the national survey on drug abuse, 1982.* Rockville, MD: Author.

National Opinion Research Center. General Social Surveys (1977, 1978, 1982, 1983). Chicago: Author.

Neale, J. M., Cox, D. S., Valdimarsdottir, H., & Stone, A. A. (1988). The relation between immunity and health: Comment on Pennebaker, Kiecolt, Glaser, and Glaser. *Journal of Consulting and Clinical Psychology, 56,* 636–637.

Neale, J. M., & Oltmanns, T. F. (1980). *Schizophrenia.* New York: Wiley.

Neiger, B. L. (1988). Adolescent suicide: Character traits of high-risk teenagers. *Adolescence, 23,* 469–475.

Nemiah, J. C. (1978). Psychoneurotic disorders. In A. M. Nicholi (Ed.), *Harvard guide to modern psychiatry.* Cambridge, MA: Harvard University Press.

Neugebauer, R. (1978). Treatment of the mentally ill in medieval and early modern England: A reappraisal. *Journal of the History of the Behavioral Sciences, 14,* 158–169.

Neugebauer, R. (1979). Medieval and early modern theories of mental illness. *Archives of General Psychiatry, 36,* 477–484.

Neuringer, C. (1982). Affect configurations and changes in women who threaten suicide following a crisis. *Journal of Consulting and Clinical Psychology, 50,* 182–186.

Nevid, J. S., Capurso, R., & Morrison, J. K. (1980). Patient's adjustment to family-care as related to their perceptions of real–ideal differences in treatment environments. *American Journal of Community Psychology, 8,* 117–120.

Nevid, J. S., Lavi, B., & Primavera, L. H. (1986). Cluster analysis of training orientations in clinical psychology. *Professional Psychology: Research and Practice, 17,* 367–370.

Nevid, J. S., Lavi, B., & Primavera, L. H. (1987). Principal components analysis of therapeutic orientations of doctoral programs in clinical psychology. *Journal of Clinical Psychology, 43,* 723–729.

Newcomb, M. D., & Bentler, P. M. (1988). Impact of adolescent drug use and social support on problems of young adults: A longitudinal study. *Journal of Abnormal Psychology, 97,* 64–75.

Newman, J. P., Patterson, C. M., & Kosson, D. S. (1987). Response perseveration in psychopaths. *Journal of Abnormal Psychology, 96,* 145–148.

Newmark, C. S., Frerking, R. A., Cook, L., & Newmark, L. (1973). Endorsement of Ellis's irrational beliefs as a function of psychopathology. *Journal of Clinical Psychology, 29,* 300–302.

Nezu, A. M., & Carnevale, G. J. (1987). Interpersonal problem solving and coping reactions of Vietnam veterans with posttraumatic stress disorder. *Journal of Abnormal Psychology, 96,* 155–157.

Nezu, A. M., & Ronan, G. F. (1985). Life stress, current problems, problem solving, and depressive symptoms: An integrative model. *Journal of Consulting and Clinical Psychology, 53,* 693–697.

Niaura, R. S., and others (1988). Relevance of cue reactivity to understanding alcohol and smoking relapse. *Journal of Abnormal Psychology, 97,* 133–152.

Nicholson, R. A. (1986). Correlates of commitment status in psychiatric patients. *Psychological Bulletin, 100,* 241–250.

Nicholson, R. A., & Berman, J. S. (1983). Is follow-up necessary in evaluating psychotherapy? *Psychological Bulletin, 93,* 261–278.

Niederehe, G. (1986). Depression and memory impairment in the aged. In L. W. Poon (Ed.), *Handbook for clinical memory assessment of older adults* (pp. 226–237). Washington, DC: American Psychological Association.

Nielsen, J. (1968). The XYY syndrome in a mental hospital. *British Journal of Criminology, 8,* 186–203.

Nolen-Hoeksema, S. (1987). Sex differences in unipolar depression: Evidence and theory. *Psychological Bulletin, 101,* 259–282.

Norcross, J. C., & Prochaska, J. O. (1982a). A national survey of clinical psychologists: Characteristics and activities. *The Clinical Psychologist, 35*(2), 1, 5–8.

Norcross, J. C., & Prochaska, J. O. (1982b). A national survey of clinical psychologists: Affiliations and orientations. *The Clinical Psychologist, 35*(3), 1, 4–6.

Norcross, J. C., & Prochaska, J. O. (1983). Clinicians' theoretical orientations: Selection, utilization, and efficacy. *Professional Psychology: Research and Practice, 14,* 197–208.

Norton, G. R., Harrison, B., Hauch, J., & Rhodes, L. (1985). Characteristics of people with infrequent panic attacks. *Journal of Abnormal Psychology, 94,* 216–221.

Norton, G. R., & Rhodes, L. (1983). *Characteristics of people with infrequent panic attacks: A preliminary analysis.* Unpublished manuscript, University of Winnipeg.

NOVA, *Confronting the killer gene.* (Telecast). (1989, March 28) (T. Hunt & J. Weber, Producers). Boston: WGBH Educational Foundation.

Novaco, R. (1974). *A treatment program for the management of anger through cognitive and relaxation control.* Doctoral Dissertation, Indiana University.

Novaco, R. (1977). A stress inoculation approach to anger management in the training of law enforcement officers. *American Journal of Community Psychology, 5,* 327–346.

Noyes, R., Clancy, J., Crowe, R., Hoenk, P. R., & Slymen, D. J. (1978). The familial prevalence of anxiety neurosis. *Archives of General Psychiatry, 35,* 1057–1059.

Noyes, R., Crowe, R., Harris, E. L., Hamra, B. J., McChesney, C. M., & Chaudhry, D. R. (1986). Relationship between panic disorder and agoraphobia: A family study. *Archives of General Psychiatry, 43,* 227–232.

Nussbaum, M., and others (1985). Follow-up investigation of patients with anorexia nervosa. *The Journal of Pediatrics, 106,* 835–840.

Obler, M. (1973). Systematic desensitization in sexual disorders. *Journal of Behavior Therapy and Experimental Psychiatry, 4,* 93–101.

Ochberg, F. M. (1980). Victims of terrorism. *Journal of Clinical Psychiatry, 41,* 73–74.

O'Connell, K. A., & Martin, E. J. (1987). Highly tempting situations associated with abstinence, temporary lapse, and relapse among participants in smoking cessation programs. *Journal of Consulting and Clinical Psychology, 55,* 367–371.

O'Connor, A., & Daly, J. (1985). Alcoholics: A twenty-year follow-up study. *British Journal of Psychiatry, 146,* 645–647.

O'Connor, J. C., & Koch, E. I. (1989). *His eminence and hizzoner.* New York: Morrow.

O'Connor, R. D. (1969). Modification of social withdrawal through symbolic modeling. *Journal of Applied Behavior Analysis, 2,* 15–22.

O'Connor v. Donaldson, 95 S. Ct. 2486 (1975).

Ohman, A., Fredrikson, M., Hugdahl, K., & Rimmo, P. (1976). The premise of equipotentiality in human classical conditioning: Conditioned electrodermal responses to potentially phobic stimuli. *Journal of Experimental Psychology: General, 104,* 313–337.

O'Leary, K. D., Pelham, W. E., Rosenbaum, A., & Price, G. H. (1976). Behavioral treatment of hyperkinetic children: An experimental evolution of its usefulness. *Clinical Pediatrics, 15,* 510–515.

Olinger, J. L., Kuiper, N. A., & Shaw, B. F. (1987). Dysfunctional attitudes and stressful life events: An interactive model of depression. *Cognitive Therapy and Research, 11,* 25–40.

Ollendick, T. H. (1981). Self-monitoring and self-administered overcorrection: The modification of nervous tics in children. *Behavior Modification, 5,* 75–84.

Olmsted, M. P., & Garner, D. M. (1986). The significance of self-induced vomiting as a weight-control method among non-clinical samples. *International Journal of Eating Disorders, 5,* 683–700.

Oltmanns, T. F., Murphy, R., Berenbaum, H., & Dunlop, S. R. (1985). Rating verbal communication impairment in schizophrenia and affective disorders. *Schizophrenia Bulletin, 11,* 292–299.

Olweus, D. (1980). Familial and temperamental determinants of aggressive behavior in adolescent boys: A causal analysis. *Developmental Psychology, 16,* 644–660.

O'Malley, S. S., and others (1988). Therapist competence and patient outcome in interpersonal psychotherapy of depression. *Journal of Consulting and Clinical Psychology, 56,* 496–501.

Ordman, A. M., & Kirschenbaum, D. S. (1985). Cognitive-behavioral therapy for bulimia: An initial outcome study. *Journal of Consulting and Clinical Psychology, 53,* 305–313.

Ordman, A. M., & Kirschenbaum, D. S. (1986). Bulimia: Assessment of eating, psychological adjustment, and familial characteristics. *International Journal of Eating Disorders, 5,* 865–876.

Ornitz, E. M. (1974). The modulation of sensory input and motor output in autistic children. *Journal of Autism and Childhood Schizophrenia, 4,* 197–215.

Ortega, D. F., & Pipal, J. E. (1984). Challenge seeking and the Type A coronary-prone behavior pattern. *Journal of Personality and Social Psychology, 46,* 1328–1334.

Ost, L. G. (1987). Age of onset in different phobias. *Journal of Abnormal Psychology, 96,* 223–229.

Overholser, J. C., & Beck, S. (1986). Multimethod assessment of rapists, child molesters, and three control groups on behavioral and psychological measures. *Journal of Consulting and Clinical Psychology, 54,* 682–687.

Overmier, J. B. L., & Seligman, M. E. P. (1967). Effect of inescapable shock upon subsequent escape and avoidance learning. *Journal of Comparative and Physiological Psychology, 63,* 28–33.

Paffenbarger, R. S., Jr., and others (1984). A natural history of athleticism and cardiovascular health. *Journal of the American Medical Association, 252,* 491–495.

Paffenbarger, R. S., Jr., and others (1986). Physical activity, all-cause mortality, and longevity of college alumni. *New England Journal of Medicine, 314,* 605–613.

Pagel, M., & Becker, J. (1987). Depressive thinking and depression: Relations with personality and social resources. *Journal of Personality and Social Psychology, 52,* 1043–1052.

Paige, K. E. (1971). Effects of oral contraceptives on affective fluctuations associated with the menstrual cycle. *Psychosomatic Medicine, 33,* 515–537.

Paige, K. E. (1973, July). Women learn to sing the menstrual blues. *Psychology Today,* p. 41.

Paige, K. E. (1977). Sexual pollution: Reproductive sex taboos in American society. *Journal of Social Issues, 33,* 144.

Paige, K. E. (1978, July). The declining taboo against menstrual sex. *Psychology Today,* pp. 50–51.

Pandurangi, A. K., Bilder, R. M., Rieder, R. O.,

Mukherjee, S., & Hamer, R. M. (1988). Schizophrenic symptoms and deterioration: Relation to computed tomographic findings. *The Journal of Nervous and Mental Disease, 176,* 200–206.

Paniagua, C. (1987). Can clinical psychoanalysis be scientific? *American Journal of Psychotherapy, 41,* 104–116.

Pardes, H. (1986). Neuroscience and psychiatry: Marriage or coexistence? *American Journal of Psychiatry, 143,* 1205–1212.

Parker, K. C. H., Hanson, R. K., & Hinsley, J. (1988). MMPI, Rorschach, and WAIS: A meta-analytic comparison of reliability, stability, and validity. *Psychological Bulletin, 103,* 367–373.

Parloff, M. B. (1986). Placebo controls in psychotherapy research: A sine qua non or a placebo for research problems? *Journal of Consulting and Clinical Psychology, 54,* 79–87.

Parloff, M. B., Waskow, I. E., & Wolfe, B. E. (1978). Research on therapist variables in relation to process and outcome. In S. L. Garfield & A. E. Bergin (Eds.), *Handbook of psychotherapy and behavior change* (2nd ed.). New York: Wiley.

Parnas, D. J., Schulsinger, F., Schulsinger, H., Teasdale, T. W., & Mednick, S. A. (1982a). Behavioral precursors of the schizophrenia spectrum: A prospective study. *Archives of General Psychiatry, 39,* 658–664.

Parnas, D. J., Schulsinger, F., Teasdale, T. W., Schulsinger, H., Feldman, P. M., & Mednick, S. A. (1982b). Perinatal complications and clinical outcome within the schizophrenia spectrum. *British Journal of Psychiatry, 140,* 416–420.

Partanen, J., Bruun, K., & Markkanen, T. (1966). *Inheritance of drinking behavior.* New Brunswick, NJ: Rutgers Center for Alcohol Studies.

Pasewark, R. A. (1981). Insanity plea: A review of the research literature. *Journal of Psychiatry and Law, 9,* 357–401.

Pasewark, R. A., & Pantle, M. L. (1979). Insanity plea: Legislator's view. *American Journal of Psychiatry, 136,* 222–223.

Patterson, T., Spohn, H. E., Bogia, D. P., & Hayes, K. (1986). Thought disorder in schizophrenia: Cognitive and neuroscience approaches. *Schizophrenia Bulletin, 12,* 460–472.

Paul, G. L. (1967). Strategy of outcome research in psychotherapy. *Journal of Consulting Psychology, 31,* 109–118.

Paul, G. L. (1969). Outcome of systematic desensitization: II. Controlled investigations of individual treatment, technique variations, and current status. In C. M. Franks (Ed.), *Behavior therapy: Appraisal and status.* New York: McGraw-Hill.

Paul, G. L., & Lentz, R. J. (1977). *Psychosocial treatment of chronic mental patients: Milieu versus social-learning programs.* Cambridge, MA: Harvard University Press.

Paul, G. L., Tobias, L. T., & Holly, B. L. (1972). Maintenance psychotropic drugs in the presence of active treatment programs. A triple blind withdrawal study with long-term mental patients. *Archives of General Psychiatry, 27,* 106–115.

Pauly, I. B. (1981). Outcome of sex reassignment surgery for transsexuals. *Australian & New Zealand Journal of Psychiatry, 15,* 45–51.

Pavlov, I. (1927). *Conditioned reflexes.* London: Oxford University Press.

Paykel, E. S. (1979). Recent life events in the development of the depressive disorders. In R. A. Depue (Ed.), *The psychobiology of the depressive disorders: Implications for the effects of stress* (pp. 245–262). New York: Academic Press.

Paykel, E. S. (1982). Life events and early environments. In E. S. Paykel (Ed.), *Handbook of affective disorders.* New York: Guilford Press.

Paykel, E. S., & Hale, A. S. (1986). Recent advances in the treatment of depression. In J. W. W. Deakin (Ed.), *The biology of depression. Proceedings of a meeting of the Biological Group of the Royal College of Psychiatrists held at Manchester University, 1985* (pp. 153–173). Washington, DC: American Psychiatric Press.

Payne, R. W. (1966). The measurement and significance of overinclusive thinking and retardation in schizophrenic patients. In P. Hoch & J. Zubin (Eds.), *Psychopathology of schizophrenia.* New York: Grune & Stratton.

Pearlman, K., Schmidt, F. L., & Hunter, J. E. (1980). Test of a new model of validity generalization: Results for job proficiency and training criteria in clerical occupations. *Journal of Applied Psychology, 65,* 373–406.

Peck, C. P. (1986). A public mental health issue: Risk-taking behavior and compulsive gambling. *American Psychologist, 41,* 461–465.

Peck v. Counseling Service of Addison County, 499 A.2d 422, Vermont Supreme Court Docket 83–062 (June 14, 1985).

Pederen, N. L., Plomin, R., McClearn, G. E., & Friberg, L. (1988). Neuroticism, extraversion, and related traits in adult twins reared apart and reared together. *Journal of Personality and Social Psychology, 55,* 950–957.

Pelham, W. E., Milich, R., & Walker, J. L. (1986). Effects of continuous and partial reinforcement and methylphenidate on learning in children with attention deficit disorder. *Journal of Abnormal Psychology, 95,* 319–325.

Pendery, M. L., Maltzman, I. M., & West, L. J. (1982). Controlled drinking by alcoholics? New findings and a re-evaluation of a major affirmative study. *Science, 217,* 169–174.

Pennebaker, J. W., Kiecolt-Glaser, J. K., & Glaser, R. (1988). Disclosure of traumas and immune function: Health implications for psychotherapy. *Journal of Consulting and Clinical Psychology, 56,* 239–245.

Pennebaker, J. W., & Skelton, J. A. (1981). Selective monitoring of physical sensations. *Journal of Personality and Social Psychology, 41,* 213–223.

Pennington, B. F., & Smith, S. D. (1988). Genetic influences on learning disabilities: An update. *Journal of Consulting and Clinical Psychology, 56,* 817–823.

Perkins, D. (1982). The assessment of stress using life events scales. In L. Goldberger & S. Brenitz (Eds.), *Handbook of stress: Theoretical and clinical aspects.* New York: Free Press.

Perlman, J. D., & Abramson, P. R. (1982). Sexual satisfaction among married and cohabitating individuals. *Journal of Consulting and Clinical Psychology, 50,* 458–460.

Perls, F. S. (1971). *Gestalt therapy verbatim.* New York: Bantam.

Perri, M. G., McAdoo, W. G., McAllister, D. A., Laver, J. B., Jordan, R. C., Yancey, D. Z., & Nezu, A. M. (1987). Effects of peer support and therapist contact on long-term weight loss. *Journal of Consulting and Clinical Psychology, 55,* 615–617

Perri, M. G., and others (1988). Effects of four maintenance programs on long-term management of obesity. *Journal of Consulting and Clinical Psychology, 56,* 529–534.

Perry, C. L., and others (1987). Promoting healthy eating and physical activity patterns among adolescents: Slice of life. *Health Education Research: Theory and Practice, 2,* 93–104.

Perry, C. L., Klepp, K., & Shultz, J. M. (1988). Primary prevention of cardiovascular disease: Community-wide strategies for youth. *Journal of Consulting and Clinical Psychology, 56,* 358–364.

Peterson, C., & Raps, C. S. (1984). Helplessness and hospitalization: More remarks. *Journal of Personality and Social Psychology, 46,* 82–83.

Peterson, C., Schwartz, S. M., & Seligman, M. E. P. (1981). Self-blame and depressive symptoms. *Journal of Personality and Social Psychology, 41,* 253–259.

Peterson, C., & Villanova, P. (1988). An expanded Attributional Style Questionnaire. *Journal of Abnormal Psychology, 97,* 87–89.

Peterson, C., Villanova, P., & Raps, C. S. (1985). Depression and attributions: Factors responsible for inconsistent results in the published literature. *Journal of Abnormal Psychology, 94,* 165–168.

Peterson, J. L., & Marin, G. (1988). Issues in the prevention of AIDS among black and Hispanic men. *American Psychologist, 43,* 871–877.

Petersen, S. E., and others (1988). Positron emission tomographic studies of the cortical anatomy of single-word processing. *Nature, 331,* 585–589.

Petri, E. (1934). Studies on the onset of menarche. *Journal of Morphological Anthropology, 33,* 43–48.

Petti, T. A., & Connors, C. K. (1983). Changes in behavioral ratings of depressed children treated with imipramine. *Journal of the American Academy of Child Psychiatry, 22,* 355–360.

Pettinati, H. M., Franks, V., Wade, J. H., & Kogan, L. G. (1987). Distinguishing the role of eating disturbance from depression in the sex role self-perceptions of anorexic and bulimic inpatients. *Journal of Abnormal Psychology, 96,* 280–282.

Pettiti, D. B., & Friedman, G. D. (1985). Cardiovascular and other diseases in smokers of low-yield cigarettes. *Journal of Chronic Diseases, 38,* 582–588.

Phifer, J. F., & Murrell, S. A. (1986). Etiologic factors in the onset of depressive symptoms in older adults. *Journal of Abnormal Psychology, 93,* 282–291.

Phillips, D. P., & Cartensen, L. S. (1986). Clustering of teenage suicide after television news stories about suicide. *New England Journal of Medicine, 315,* 685–689.

Phillips, E. L., Phillips, E. A., Fixsen, D. L., & Wolf, M. M. (1971). Achievement place: Modifications of the behaviors of pre-delinquent boys within a token economy. *Journal of Applied Behavior Analysis, 4,* 45–59.

Phillips, L. W. (1981). Roots and branches of behavioral and cognitive practice. *Journal of Behavior Therapy and Experimental Psychiatry, 12,* 5–17.

Phillips, M. R., & Wolf, A. S. (1988). Psychiatry and the criminal justice system: Testing and myths. *American Journal of Psychiatry, 145,* 605–610.

Piran, N., Kennedy, S., Garfinkel, P. E., & Owens, M. (1985). Affective disturbance in eating disorders. *Journal of Nervous and Mental Disease, 173,* 395–400.

Pitts, F. N., Jr., & McClure, J. N., Jr. (1967). Lactate metabolism in anxiety neurosis. *New England Journal of Medicine, 277,* 1328–1336.

Plomin, R. (1989). Environment and genes: Determinants of behavior. *American Psychologist, 44,* 105–111.

Polivy, J., & Herman, C. P. (1983). *Breaking the diet habit.* New York: Basic Books.

Polivy, J., & Herman, C. P. (1985). Dieting and binging: A causal analysis. *American Psychologist, 40,* 193–201.

Polivy, J., & Herman, C. P. (1987). Diagnosis and treatment of normal eating. *Journal of Consulting and Clinical Psychology, 55,* 635–644.

Pomerleau, O. F., Adkins, D., & Pertschuk, M. (1978). Predictors of outcome and recidivism in smoking-cessation treatment. *Additive Behaviors, 3,* 65–70.

Pomerleau, O. F., and others (1986). Task Force 4: Nicotine and smoking relapse. National Working Conference on Smoking Relapse. *Health Psychology, 5*(Suppl.), 41–51.

Pomerleau, O. F., Pertschuk, M., Adkins, D., & Brady, J. P. (1977). A comparison of behavioral and traditional treatment for middle-income problem drinkers. *Journal of Behavioral Medicine, 1,* 187–200.

Pope, H. G., Hudson, J. I., Jonas, J. M., & Yurgelun-Todd, M. S. (1983). Bulimia treatment with imiprimine: A placebo-controlled, double-blind study. *American Journal of Psychiatry, 140,* 554–558.

Pope, H. G., Hudson, J. I., Yurgelun-Todd, D., & Hudson, M. S. (1984). Prevalence of anorexia nervosa and bulimia in three student popula-tions. *International Journal of Eating Disorders, 3,* 45–51.

Pope, H. G., Jr., Jones, J. M., Hudson, J., Cohen, B. M., & Gunderson, J. G. (1983). The validity of DSM-III borderline personality disorder. *Archives of General Psychiatry, 40,* 23–30.

Popham, R. E., Schmidt, W., & Israelstam, S. (1984). Heavy alcohol consumption and physical health problems: A review of the epidemiologic evidence. In R. G. Smart and others (Eds.), *Research advances in alcohol and drug problems* (Vol. 8). New York: Plenum.

Popper, K. (1985). Cited in Goleman (1985).

Post, R. M., & Uhde, T. W. (1983). Treatment of mood disorders with antiepileptic medication: Clinical and theoretical implications. *Epilepsia, 24*(Suppl. 2), 97–108.

Powell, B. J., Penick, E. C., Read, M. R., & Ludwig, A. M. (1985). Comparison of three outpatient treatment interventions: A twelve-month follow-up of men alcoholics. *Journal of Studies on Alcohol, 46,* 309–312.

Powell, L. H., Friedman, M., Thoresen, C. E., Gill, J. J., & Ulmer, D. K. (1984). Can the Type A behavior pattern be altered after myocardial infarction? A second-year report from the Recurrent Coronary Prevention Project. *Psychosomatic Medicine, 46,* 293–313.

Powers, P. S., Schulman, R. G., Gleghorn, A. A., & Prange, M. E. (1987). Perceptual and cognitive abnormalities in bulimia. *American Journal of Psychiatry, 144,* 1456–1460.

Press, A., and others (1985, March 18). The war against pornography. *Newsweek,* pp. 58–66.

Prichard, J. C. (1835). *Treatise on insanity.* London: Gilbert & Piper.

Prince, M. (1906). *The Dissociation of a personality: A biographical study in abnormal psychology.* New York: Longmans, Green.

Prior, M. R. (1979). Cognitive abilities and disabilities in infantile autism: A review. *Journal of Abnormal Child Psychology, 7,* 357–380.

Prior, M. R. (1984). Developing concepts of childhood autism: The influence of experimental cognitive research. *Journal of Consulting and Clinical Psychology, 52,* 4–16.

Prior, M. R., Gajzago, C., & Knox, D. (1976). An epidemiological study of autistic and psychotic children in the four eastern states of Australia. *Australian and New Zealand Journal of Psychiatry, 10,* 173–184.

Psychiatric Times (1988, November). The treatment of panic disorder. *The Psychiatric Times.*

Putnam, F. W., Guroff, J. J., Silberman, E. K., Barban, L., & Post, R. M. (1986). The clinical phenomenology of multiple personality disorder: Review of 100 recent cases. *Journal of Clinical Psychiatry, 47,* 285–293.

Pyle, R. L., Halvorson, P. A., & Goff, G. M. (1986). The increasing prevalence of bulimia in freshman college students. *International Journal of Eating Disorders, 5,* 631–647.

Pyszczynski, T., & Greenberg J. (1985). Depression and preference for self-focusing stimuli after success and failure. *Journal of Personality and Social Psychology, 49,* 1066–1075.

Pyszczynski, T., & Greenberg, J. (1986). Evidence for a depressive self-focusing style. *Journal of Research in Personality, 20,* 95–106.

Pyszczynski, T., & Greenberg, J. (1987). Self-regulatory perseveration and the depressive self-focusing style: A self-awareness theory of reactive depression. *Psychological Bulletin, 102,* 122–138.

Pyszczynski, T., Holt, K., & Greenberg, J. (1987). Depression, self-focused attention, and expectancies for positive and negative future life events for self and others. *Journal of Personality and Social Psychology, 52,* 994–1001.

Quay, H. C. (1965). Psychopathic personality as pathological stimulation seeking. *American Journal of Psychiatry, 122,* 180–183.

Quinn, S. (1987). *A mind of her own: The life of Karen Horney.* New York: Summit Books.

Quinsey, V. L., Chaplin, T. C., & Upfold, D. (1984). Sexual arousal to nonsexual violence and sado-masochistic themes among rapists and non-sex-offenders. *Journal of Consulting and Clinical Psychology, 52,* 651–657.

Rabkin, J. G. (1979). Criminal behavior of discharged mental patients: A critical appraisal of the research. *Psychological Bulletin, 86,* 1–27.

Rabkin, J. G. (1980). Stressful life events and schizophrenia: A review of the literature. *Psychological Bulletin, 87,* 408–425.

Rabkin, J. G., & Zitrin, A. (1982). Antisocial behavior of discharged mental patients: Research findings and policy implications. In B. L. Bloom & S. J. Asher (Eds.), *Psychiatric patient's rights and patient advocacy.* New York: Human Sciences.

Rachman, S. (1966). Sexual fetishism: An experimental analogue. *Psychological Record, 16,* 293–296.

Rachman, S. (1983). Fear and fearlessness among trainee parachutists. *Advances in Behaviour Research and Theory, 4,* 153–160.

Rachman, S., & Bichard, S. (1988). The overprediction of fear. *Clinical Psychology Review, 8,* 303–312.

Rachman, S., & Levitt, K. (1985). Panics and their consequences. *Behaviour Research and Theory, 23,* 600.

Rachman, S., Levitt, K., & Lopatka, C. (1988). Experimental analyses of panic: III. Claustrophobic subjects. *Behaviour Research and Theory, 26,* 41–52.

Rachman, S. & Lopatka, C. (1986). Match and mismatch in the prediction of fear: I. *Behaviour Research and Theory, 24,* 387–393.

Rachman, S., Lopatka, C., & Levitt, K. (1988). Experimental analyses of panic: II. Panic patients. *Behaviour Research and Theory, 26,* 33–40.

Rachman, S. J., & Hodgson, R. (1974). Synchrony and desynchrony in fear and avoidance. *Behaviour Research and Theory, 12,* 311–318.

Rachman, S. J., & Hodgson, R. J. (1980). *Obsessions and compulsions.* Englewood Cliffs, NJ: Prentice Hall.

Rada, R. T., & Kellner, R. (1979). Drug treatment in alcoholism. In J. David & D. J. Greenblatt (Eds.), *Recent developments in psychopharmacology.* New York: Grune & Stratton.

Ragland, D. R., & Brand, R. J. (1988). Type A behavior and mortality from coronary heart disease. *New England Journal of Medicine, 318,* 65–69.

Raine, A., Andrews, H., Sheard, C., Walder, C., & Manders, D. (1989). Interhemispheric transfer in schizophrenics, depressives, and normals with schizoid tendencies. *Journal of Abnormal Psychology, 98,* 35–41.

Rajput, A. H., Offord, K. P., Beard, C. M., & Kurland, L. T. (1984). Epidemiology of Parkinsonism: Incidence, classification, and mortality. *Annals of Neurology, 16,* 278–282.

Ramirez, L. F., McCormick, R. A., Russo, A. M., & Taber, J. I. (1983). Patterns of substance abuse in pathological gamblers undergoing treatment. *Addictive Behaviors, 8,* 425–428.

Rapee, R. (1985). Distinction between panic disorder and generalized anxiety disorder: Clinical presentation. *Australian and New Zealand Journal of Psychiatry, 19,* 227–232.

Rapee, R. (1986). Differential response to hyperventilation in panic disorder and generalized anxiety disorder. *Journal of Abnormal Psychology, 95,* 24–28.

Rapee, R. (1987). The psychological treatment of panic attacks: Theoretical conceptualization and review of evidence. *Clinical Psychology Review, 7,* 427–438.

Rapoport, K., & Burkhart, B. R. (1984). Personality and attitudinal characteristics of sexually coercive males. *Journal of Abnormal Psychology, 93,* 216–221.

Rapp, S. R., Parisi, S. A., & Walsh, D. A. (1988). Psychological dysfunction and physical health among elderly medical inpatients. *Journal of Consulting and Clinical Psychology, 56,* 851–855.

Rappaport, N. B., McAnulty, D. P., & Brantley,

P. J. (1988). Exploration of the type A behavior pattern in chronic headache sufferers. *Journal of Consulting and Clinical Psychology, 56,* 621–623.

Rapport, M. D. (1984). Hyperactivity and stimulant treatment. *The Behavior Therapist, 7,* 133–134.

Raps, C. S., Peterson, C., Reinhard, K. E., Abramson, L. Y., & Seligman, M. E. P. (1982). Attributional style among depressed patients. *Journal of Abnormal Psychology, 91,* 102–108.

Rasmussen, T., & Milner, B. (1975). Clinical and surgical studies of the cerebral speech areas in man. In K. J. Zulch, O. Creutzfeldt, & G. C. Galbraith (Eds.), *Cerebral localization.* Berlin: Springer-Verlag.

Rathus, S. A. (1973). Motoric, autonomic, and cognitive reciprocal inhibition of a case of hysterical bronchial asthma. *Adolescence, 8,* 29–32.

Rathus, S. A. (1978). Treatment of recalcitrant ejaculatory incompetence. *Behavior Therapy, 9,* 962.

Rathus, S. A. (1983). *Human sexuality.* New York: Holt, Rinehart & Winston.

Rathus, S. A. (1988). *Understanding child development.* New York: Holt, Rinehart & Winston.

Rathus, S. A., & Nevid, J. S. (1977). *Behavior therapy.* Garden City, NY: Doubleday.

Rathus, S. A., Senna, J., & Siegel, L. (1974). Delinquent behavior and academic investment among suburban youth. *Adolescence, 9,* 481–494.

Ravenholt, R. T. (1984). Addiction mortality in the United States, 1980: Tobacco, alcohol, and other substances. *Population and Development Review, 10* 697–724.

Ravussin, E., Lillioja, S., Knowler, W. C., Christin, L., Freymond, D., Abbott, W. G. H., Boyce, V., Howard, B. V., & Bogardus, C. (1988). Reduced rate of energy expenditure as a risk factor for body-weight gain. *New England Journal of Medicine, 318,* 467–472.

Razin, A. M., Swencionis, C., & Zohman, L. R. (1986). Reduction of physiological, behavioral, and self-report responses in Type A behavior: A preliminary report. *International Journal of Psychiatry in Medicine, 16,* 31–47.

Redd, W. H., Jacobsen, P. B., Die-Trill, M., Dermatis, H., McEvoy, M., & Holland, J. C. (1987). Cognitive/attentional distraction in the control of conditioned nausea in pediatric cancer patients receiving chemotherapy. *Journal of Consulting and Clinical Psychology, 55,* 391–395.

Regier, D. A., and others (1988). One-month prevalance of mental disorders in the United States. *Archives of General Psychiatry, 45,* 977–986.

Regier, D. A., and others (1984). The NIMH Epidemiologic Catchment Area Program. *Archives of General Psychiatry, 41,* 934–941.

Reich, J. (1986). Prevalence of DSM-III-R self-defeating (masochistic) personality disorder in normal and outpatient populations. *Journal of Nervous and Mental Diseases, 175,* 52–54.

Reich, J., & Noyes, R. (1986). Differentiating schizoid and avoidant personality disorders [Letter to the editor]. *American Journal of Psychiatry, 143,* 1061–1063.

Reich, J., & Yates, W. (1988). A pilot study of treatment of social phobia with alprazolam. *American Journal of Psychiatry, 145,* 590–594.

Reid, W. H., & Balis, G. U. (1987). Evaluation of the violent patient. In R. E. Hales & A. J. Frances (Eds.), *American Psychiatric Association Annual Review* (Vol. 6) Washington, DC: American Psychiatric Press.

Reid, W. J. (1986). Antisocial personality. In R. Michels & J. O. Cavenar, Jr., (Eds.), *Psychiatry* (Vol. 1). New York: Basic Books.

Reinisch, J. M., Sanders, S. A., & Ziemba-Davis, M. (1988). The study of sexual behavior in relation to the transmission of human immunodeficiency virus: Caveats and recommendations. *American Psychologist, 43,* 921–927.

Reisberg, B., Ferris, S. H., Borenstein, J., Sinaiko,

E., de Leon, M. J., & Buttinger, C. (1986). Assessment of presenting symptoms. In L. W. Poon (Ed.), *Handbook for clinical memory assessment of older adults* (pp. 108–128). Washington, DC: American Psychological Association.

Reisberg, B., Ferris, S. H., DeLeon, M. J., & Crook, T. (1982). The Global Deterioration Scale for Assessment of Primary Degenerative Dementia. *American Journal of Psychiatry, 139,* 1136–1139.

Reiss, S. (1987). Theoretical perspectives on the fear of anxiety. *Clinical Psychology Review, 7,* 585–596.

Reiss, S., Peterson, R. A., Gursky, D. M., & McNally, R. J. (1986). Anxiety sensitivity, anxiety frequency and the predictions of fearfulness. *Behaviour Research and Theory, 24,* 1–8.

Review Panel (1981). Coronary-prone behavior and coronary heart disease: A critical review. *Circulation, 63,* 1199–1215.

Rey, J. M., Stuart, G. W., Platt, J. M., Bashir, M. R., & Richards, I. M. (1988). DSM-III Axis IV revisited. *American Journal of Psychiatry, 145,* 286–292.

Reynolds, E. (1977). Psychological treatment models and outcome results for erectile dysfunction. *Psychological Bulletin, 84,* 1218–1238.

Rhodewalt, F., & Agustsdottir, S. (1984). On the relationship of hardiness to the Type A behavior pattern: Perception of life events versus coping with life events. *Journal of Research in Personality, 18,* 212–223.

Rich, C. L., Ricketts, J. E., Thaler, R. C., & Young, D. (1988). Some differences between men and women who commit suicide. *American Journal of Psychiatry, 145,* 718–722.

Rieber, I., & Sigusch, V. (1979). Psychosurgery on sex offenders and sexual "deviants" in West Germany [Guest editorial]. *Archives of Sexual Behavior, 8,* 523–528.

Riese, W. (1954). Auto-observation of aphasia: Reported by an eminent 19th century medical scientist. *Bulletin of the History of Medicine, 28,* 237–242.

Riley, A. J., & Riley, E. J. (1978). A controlled study to evaluate directed masturbation in the management of primary orgasmic failure in women. *British Journal of Psychiatry, 133,* 404–409.

Riley, V. (1981). Psychoneuroendocrine influences on immunocompetence and neoplasia. *Science, 212,* 1100–1109.

Rimland, B. (1977). Comparative effects of treatment on child's behavior (drugs, therapies, schooling, and several non-treatment events.). *Institute for Child Behavior Research,* Publication 34.

Rimland, B. (1978). The savant capabilities of autistic children and their cognitive implications. In G. Serban (Ed.), *Cognitive defects in the development of mental illness.* New York: Brunner/Mazel.

Riskind, J. H., Beck, A. T., Berchick, R. J., Brown, G., & Steer, R. A. (1987). Reliability of DSM-III diagnoses for major depression and generalized anxiety disorder using the structured clinical interview for DSM-III. *Archives of General Psychiatry, 44,* 817–820.

Rist, F., & Watzl, H. (1983). Self-assessment of relapse risk and assertiveness in relation to treatment outcome of female alcoholics. *Addictive Behaviors, 8,* 121–127.

Ritvo, E. R. (1976). Autism: From adjective to noun. In E. R. Ritvo (Ed.), *Autism: Diagnosis, current research and management* (pp. 3–6). New York: Spectrum Publications.

Rizley, R. (1978). Depression and distortion in the attribution of causality. *Journal of Abnormal Psychology, 87,* 32–48.

Roberts, M. A., & Caird, F. I. (1982). Computerized tomography and intellectual decline in the elderly. *Journal of Neurology, Neurosurgery, and Psychiatry, 45,* 50–54.

Roberts, S. V. (1988, June 2). Reagan says he was moved by contacts with Russians. *The New York Times,* p. C16.

Robey, A. (1978). Guilty but mentally ill. *Bulletin of the American Academy of Psychiatry and the Law, 6,* 376.

Robins, L. (1966). *Deviant children grow up: A sociological and psychiatric study of sociopathic personality.* Baltimore: Williams & Wilkins.

Robins, L. (1978). Sturdy childhood predictors of adult antisocial behavior: Replication from longitudinal studies. *Psychological Medicine, 8,* 611–622.

Robins, L. N., Helzer, J. E., Croughan, J., & Ratcliff, K. S. (1981). National Institute of Mental Health: Diagnostic Interview Schedule. *Archives of General Psychiatry, 41,* 949–958.

Robins, L. N., and others (1984). Lifetime prevalence of specific psychiatric disorders in three sites. *Archives of General Psychiatry, 41,* 949–958.

Rodin, J. (1980). Current status of the internal-external hypothesis of obesity: What went wrong? *American Psychologist, 36,* 361–372.

Rodin, J., Bartoshuk, L., Peterson, C., & Schank, D. (1990). Bulimia and taste: Possible interactions. *Journal of Abnormal Psychology, 99,* 32–39.

Rodin, J., & Slochower, J. (1976). Externality in the nonobese: The effects of environmental responsiveness on weight. *Journal of Personality and Social Psychology, 33,* 338–344.

Roehl, J. E., & Gray, D. (1984). The crisis of rape: A guide to counseling victims of rape. *Crisis Intervention, 13,* 67–77.

Roehling, P. V., & Robin, A. L. (1986). Development and validation of the Family Beliefs Inventory: A measure of unrealistic beliefs among parents and adolescents. *Journal of Consulting and Clinical Psychology, 54,* 693–697.

Rogentine, G. N., and others (1979). Psychological factors in the prognosis of malignant melanoma: A prospective study. *Psychosomatic Medicine, 41,* 647–655.

Rogers v. Okin, 478 F. Supp. 1342 (D Mass. 1979).

Rogers v. Okin, 634 F. 2d. 650 (1980).

Rogers, C. R. (1951). *Client-centered therapy.* Boston: Houghton Mifflin.

Rogers, C. R. (1959). A theory of therapy, personality and interpersonal relationships, as developed in the client-centered framework. In S. Koch (Ed.), *Psychology: A study of science,* Vol. 3. New York: McGraw Hill.

Rogers, C. R. (1963). The actualizing tendency in relationship to "motives" and to consciousness. In M. R. Jones (Ed.), *Nebraska symposium on motivation,* Lincoln: University of Nebraska Press.

Rogers, C. R. (1974). In retrospect: 46 years. *American Psychologist, 29,* 115–123.

Rogers, J. L., Bloom, J. D., Manson, S. I., and others (1983). Oregon's insanity defense system: A review of the first five years. *Bulletin of the American Academy of Psychiatry and Law, 12,* 383–402.

Rohan, W. P. (1982). The concept of alcoholism: Assumptions and issues. In E. M. Pattison & E. Kaufman (Eds.), *Encyclopedic handbook of alcoholism* (pp. 31–39). New York: Gardner Press.

Rohsenow, D. J. (1983). Drinking habits and expectancies about alcohol's effects for self versus others. *Journal of Consulting and Clinical Psychology, 51,* 752–756.

Romanczyk, R. G. (1986). Some thoughts on future trends in the education of individuals with autism. *The Behavior Therapist, 8,* 162–164.

Romanczyk, R. G., Diament, C., Goren, E. R., Trunell, G., & Harris, S. L. (1975). Increasing isolate and social play in severely disturbed children: Intervention and postintervention effectiveness. *Journal of Autism and Childhood Schizophrenia, 5,* 730–739.

Rook, K. S., & Dooley, D. (1985). Applying social support research: Theoretical problems and future directions. *Journal of Social Issues, 41,* 5–28.

Rosebush, P. (1986). Double-blind, placebo-controlled studies of bulimic patients. *American Journal of Psychiatry, 144,* 1197–1198.

Rosen, B., Englehart, D. M., Freedman, N., Margolis, R., & Klein, D. F. (1971). The Hospitalization Proneness Scale as a predictor of response to phenothiazine treatment: II: Delay of psychiatric hospitalization. *Journal of Nervous and Mental Disease, 152*, 405–411.

Rosen, J. C., Gross, J., & Vara, L. (1987). Psychological adjustment of adolescents attempting to lose or gain weight. *Journal of Consulting and Clinical Psychology, 55*, 742–747.

Rosen, J. C., & Leitenberg, H. (1982). Bulimia nervosa: Treatment with exposure and response prevention. *Behavior Therapy, 13*, 117–124.

Rosen, L. A., Booth, S. R., Bender, M. E., McGrath, M. L., Sorrell, S., & Drabham, R. S. (1988). Effects of sugar (sucrose) on children's behavior. *Journal of Consulting and Clinical Psychology, 56*, 583–589.

Rosen, W. G., and others (1984). Positive and negative symptoms in schizophrenia. *Psychiatry Research, 13*, 277–284.

Rosenbaum, G., Shore, D. L., & Chapin, K. (1988). Attention deficit in schizophrenia and schizotypy: Marker versus symptom variables. *Journal of Abnormal Psychology, 97*, 41–47.

Rosenbaum, M., & Hadari, D. (1985). Personal efficacy, external locus of control, and perceived contingency of parental reinforcement among depressed, paranoid, and normal subjects. *Journal of Personality and Social Psychology, 49*, 539–547.

Rosenhan, D. L. (1973). On being sane in insane places. *Science, 179*, 250–258.

Rosenman, R. H., Brand, R. J., Jenkins, C. D., Friedman, M., Straus, R., & Wurm, M. (1975). Coronary heart disease in the Western Collaborative Group Study: Final follow-up experience of 8½ years. *Journal of the American Medical Association, 233*, 872–877.

Rosenstein, M. J., Milazzo-Sayre, L. J., & Manderscheid, R. W. (1989). Care of persons with schizophrenia: A statistical profile. *Schizophrenia Bulletin, 15*, 45–58.

Rosenthal, D. (1970). *Genetic theory and abnormal behavior.* New York: McGraw-Hill.

Rosenthal, D., Wender, P. H., Kety, S. S., Schulsinger, F., Welner, J., & Ostergaard, L. (1968). Schizophrenics' offspring in adoptive homes. In D. Rosenthal & S. S. Kety (Eds.), *The transmission of schizophrenia.* Oxford, England: Pergamon Press.

Rosenthal, D., Wender, P. H., Kety S. S., Schulsinger, F., Welner, J., & Reider, R. (1975). Parent-child relationships and psychopathological disorder in the child. *Archives of General Psychiatry, 32*, 466–476.

Rosenthal, N. E., and others (1984). Seasonal affective disorder: A description of the syndrome and preliminary findings with light therapy. *Archives of General Psychiatry, 41*, 72–80.

Rosenthal, N. E., and others (1985). Seasonal affective disorder and phototherapy. *Annals of the New York Academy of Sciences, 453*, 260–269.

Rosenthal, R. (1983). Improving meta-analytic procedures for assessing the effects of psychotherapy vs. placebo. *The Behavioral and Brain Sciences, 8*, 298–299.

Roskies, E. (1983). Stress management for Type A individuals. In D. Meichenbaum & M. E. Jaremko (Eds.), *Stress reduction and prevention* (pp. 261–268). New York: Plenum.

Roskies, E., Kearney, H., Spevack, M., Surkis, A., Cohen, C., & Gilman, S. (1979). Generalizability and durability of treatment effects in an intervention program for coronary-prone (Type A) managers. *Journal of Behavioral Medicine, 2*, 195–207.

Roskies, E., and others (1986) The Montreal Type A intervention project: Major findings. *Health Psychology, 5*, 45–69.

Rossman, B. L., Minuchin, S., & Liebman, R. (1976). Input and outcome of family therapy of anorexia nervosa. In J. L. Claghorn (Ed.), *Successful psychotherapy.* New York: Brunner/Mazel.

Ross, A. D. (1981). *Psychological disorders of childhood: A behavioral approach to theory, research, & practice* (2d ed.). New York: McGraw Hill.

Roth, L., & Meisel, A. (1977). Dangerousness, confidentiality, and the duty to warn. *American Journal of Psychiatry, 134*, 508–511.

Rotter, J. B. (1972). Beliefs, social attitudes, and behavior: A social learning analysis. In J. B. Rotter, J. E. Chance, & E. J. Phares (Eds.), *Applications of a social learning theory of personality.* New York: Holt, Rinehart & Winston.

Roueche, B. (1980). *The medical detectives.* New York: Truman Talley.

Rounsaville, B. J., and others (1987). The relation between specific and general dimensions of the psychotherapy process in interpersonal psychotherapy of depression. *Journal of Consulting and Clinical Psychology, 55*, 379–384.

Rourke, B. P. (Ed.) (1985). *Neuropsychology of learning disabilities: Essentials of subtype analysis.* New York: Guilford Press.

Roy-Byrne, P. P., Geraci, M., & Uhde, T. W. (1986). Life events and the onset of panic disorder. *American Journal of Psychiatry, 143*, 1424–1427.

Rozin, P., & Fallon, A. (1988). Body image, attitudes to weight, and misperceptions of figure preferences of the opposite sex: A comparison of men and women in two generations. *Journal of Abnormal Psychology, 97*, 342–345.

Rubinow, D. R., & Roy-Byrne, P. (1984). Premenstrual syndromes: Overview from a methodologic perspective. *American Journal of Psychiatry, 141*, 163–172.

Ruderman, A. J., Belzer, L. J., & Halperin, A. (1985). Restraint, anticipated consumption, and overeating. *Journal of Abnormal Psychology, 94*, 547–555.

Ruehlman, L. L. (1985). Depression and affective meaning for current concerns. *Cognitive Therapy and Research, 9*, 553–560.

Ruff, G. A., & St. Lawrence, J. S. (1985). Premature ejaculation: Past research progress, future directions. *Clinical Psychology Review, 5*, 627–639.

Rundell, J. R., Wise, M. G., & Ursano, R. J. (1986). Three cases of AIDS-related psychiatric disorders. *American Journal of Psychiatry, 143*, 777–778.

Rundell, J. R., Wise, M. G., & Ursano, R. J. (1987). Dr. Rundell and associates reply. *American Journal of Psychiatry, 144*, 537–538.

Rush, A. J., Beck, A. T., Kovacs, M., & Hollon, S. (1977). Comparative efficacy of cognitive therapy and pharmacotherapy in the treatment of depressed outpatients. *Cognitive Therapy and Research, 1*, 17–37.

Rush, A. J., Beck, A. T., Kovacs, M., Weissenberger, J., & Hollon, S. D. (1982). Comparison of the effects of cognitive therapy and pharmacotherapy on hopelessness and self-concept. *American Journal of Psychiatry, 139*, 862–866.

Rush, A. J., Khatami, M., & Beck, A. T. (1975). Cognitive and behavior therapy in chronic depression. *Behavior Therapy, 6*, 398–404.

Rush, A. J., & Weissenberger, J. (1986). Do thinking patterns predict depressive symptoms? *Cognitive Therapy and Research, 10*, 225–236.

Russell, D. (1983). The incidence and prevalence of intrafamilial and extrafamilial sexual abuse of female children. *Child Abuse and Neglect, 7*, 133–146.

Russell, D. (1986). *The secret trauma: Incest in the lives of girls and women.* New York: Basic Books.

Russell, G. (1979). Bulimia nervosa: An ominous variant of anorexia nervosa. *Psychological Medicine, 9*, 419–448.

Rutter, M. (1983). Cognitive deficits in the pathogenesis of autism. *Journal of Child Psychology & Psychiatry, 24*, 513–531.

Rutter, M., Garmezy, N. (1983). Developmental psychopathology. In P. H. Mussen (Ed.), *Handbook of child psychology*: Vol. 4, *Socialization, Personality, and Social Development* (pp. 776–911). New York: Wiley.

Rutter, M., Tizard, J., & Whitmore, K. (Eds.) (1981). *Education, health and behavior.* Huntington, N.Y.: Krieger.

Ryan, N. D., and others (1987). The clinical picture of major depression in children and adolescents. *Archives of General Psychiatry, 44*, 854–861.

Saccuzzo, D. P., & Braff, D. L. (1981). Early information processing deficits in schizophrenia: New findings using schizophrenic subgroups and manic controls. *Archives of General Psychiatry, 38*, 175–179.

Sachs, E. P. L., Hall, R. G., & Hall, S. M. (1978). Effects of rapid smoking: Physiologic evaluation of a smoking-cessation therapy. *Annals of Internal Medicine, 88*, 639–641.

Sackeim, H. A. (1985, June). The case for ECT. *Psychology today.* pp. 36–40.

Sackeim, H. A., Decina, P., Kanzler, M., Kerr, B., & Malitz, S. (1987) ECT. *American Journal of Psychiatry, 144*, 1449–1455.

Sackeim, H. A., and others (1985). Cognitive consequences of low dosage ECT. In S. Malitz & H. A. Sackeim (Eds.), *Electroconvulsive therapy: Clinical and basic research issues.* New York: Annals of the New York Academy of Science.

Sacks, C. H., & Bugental, D. B. (1987). Attributions as moderators of affective and behavioral responses to social failure. *Journal of Personality and Social Psychology, 53*, 939–947.

Sacks, O. (1985). *The man who mistook his wife for a hat and other clinical tales.* New York: Summit Books.

Sadker, M., & Sadker, D. (1985, March). Sexism in the schoolroom of the 1980s. *Psychology Today,* pp. 54–57.

Sagarin, E. (1977). Incest: Problems of definition and frequency. *Journal of Sex Research, 13*, 126–135.

Saghir, M. T., & Robins, E. (1973). *Male and female homosexuality: A comprehensive investigation.* Baltimore: Williams & Wilkins.

Sakheim, D. K. (1984). *Waking assessment of erectile potential: The validation of a laboratory procedure to aid in the differential diagnosis of psychogenic and organic impotence.* Unpublished doctoral dissertation, State University of New York at Albany.

Sakheim, D. K. (1987). Distinguishing between organogenic and psychogenic erectile dysfunction. *Behaviour Research and Therapy, 25*, 379–390.

Sales, E., Baum, M., & Shore, B. (1984). Victim readjustment following assault. *Journal of Social Issues, 40*, 117–136.

Salkovskis, P. M., & Warwick, H. M. (1986). Morbid preoccupations, health anxiety, and reassurance: A cognitive-behavioral approach to hypochondriasis. *Behaviour Research and Theory, 24*, 597–602.

Salkovskis, P. M., Warwick, H. M. C., Clark, D. M., & Wessels, D. J. (1986). A demonstration of acute hyperventilation during naturally occurring panic attacks. *Behaviour Research and Theory, 24*, 91–94.

Salzman, C., & Gutfreund, M. J. (1986). Clinical techniques and research strategies for studying depression and memory. In L. W. Poon (Ed.), *Handbook for clinical memory assessment of older adults* (pp. 257–267). Washington, DC: American Psychological Association.

Sameroff, A., Seifer, R., Zax, M., & Barocas, R. (1987). Early indicators of developmental risk: Rochester Longitudinal Study. *Schizophrenia Bulletin, 13*, 383–394.

Sammons, M. T., & Gravitz, M. A. (1990). Theoretical orientations of professional psychologists and their former professors. *Professional Psychology: Research and Practice, 21*, 131–134.

Sanchez, B. C., Lewinsohn, P. M., & Larson, D. (1980). Assertion training: Effectiveness in the treatment of depression. *Journal of Clinical Psychology, 36*, 526–529.

Sanchez-Craig, M., Annis, H. M., Bornet, A. R., & MacDonald, K. R. (1984). Random assignment to abstinence or controlled drinking: Evaluation of a cognitive-behavioral program for problem drinkers: *Journal of Consulting and Clinical Psychology, 52,* 390–403.

Sanders, J. (1974, September). *An autistic child in residential treatment.* Paper presented at American Psychological Association meeting, New Orleans.

Santiago, J. M., McCall-Perez, F., Gorcery, M., & Beigel, A. (1985). Long-term psychological effects of rape in 35 rape victims. *American Journal of Psychiatry, 142,* 1338–1340.

Sass, L. (1982, August 22). The borderline personality. *The New York Times Magazine,* pp. 12–15, 66–67.

Sateia, M. J. (1987). Behavioral modification in the treatment of smoking. *Psychiatric Medicine, 5,* 375–387.

Satir, V. (1967). *Conjoint family therapy* (rev. ed). Palo Alto, CA: Science and Behavior Books.

Saypol, D. C., Petersen, G. A., Howards, S. S., & Yanzel, J. J. (1983). Impotence: Are the newer diagnostic methods a necessity? *Journal of Urology, 130,* 260–262.

Scarlett, W. A. (1980). Social isolation from agemates among nursery school children. *Journal of Child Psychology and Psychiatry, 21,* 231–240.

Scarr, S. (1981). Testing *for* children: Assessment and the many determinants of intellectual competence. *American Psychologist, 36,* 1159–1166.

Scarr, S., & Kidd, K. K. (1983). Developmental behavior genetics. In M. Haith & J. J. Campos (Eds.), *Handbook of child psychology.* New York: Wiley.

Scarr, S., Webber, P. L., Weinberg, R. A., & Wittig, M. A. (1981). Personality resemblance among adolescents and their parents in biologically related and adoptive families. *Journal of Personality and Social Psychology, 41,* 885–898.

Schachter, S. (1977). Nicotine regulation in heavy and light smokers. *Journal of Experimental Psychology: General, 106,* 5–12.

Schachter, S., Kozlowski, L. T., & Silverstein, B. (1977). Effects of urinary pH on cigarette smoking. *Journal of Experimental Psychology: General, 106,* 13–19.

Schachter, S., & Latané, B. (1964). Crime, cognition, and the autonomic nervous system. In D. Levine (Ed.), *Nebraska symposium on motivation* (Vol. 12) (pp. 221–273). Lincoln: University of Nebraska Press.

Schaefer, C. E. (1979). *Childhood encopresis and enuresis.* New York: Van Nostrand.

Schaeffer, J., Andrysiak, T., & Ungerleider, J. T. (1981). Cognition and long-term use of ganja (cannabis). *Science, 213,* 465–466.

Schaeffer, M., & Baum, A. (1982, August). *Consistency of stress response at Three Mile Island.* Paper presented at the meeting of the American Psychological Association, Washington, DC.

Schafer, D. W. (1986). Recognizing multiple personality patients. *American Journal of Psychotherapy, 40,* 500–510.

Scharf, M. B., & Brown, S. L. (1986). Hypnotic drugs: Use and abuse. *Clinical Psychology Review, 6,* 39–50.

Schechter, M., and others (1984). Changes in sexual behavior and fear of AIDS. *Lancet,* 1293.

Scheff, T. J. (1966). *Being mentally ill: A sociological theory.* Chicago: Aldine.

Schepis, M. R., Reid, D. H., & Fitzgerald, J. R. (1987). Group instruction with profoundly retarded persons: Acquisition, generalization, and maintenance of a remunerative work skill. *Journal of Applied Behavior Analysis, 20,* 97–105.

Schifter, D. E., & Ajzen, I. (1985). Intention, perceived control, and weight loss: An application of the theory of planned behavior. *Journal of Personality and Social Psychology, 49,* 843–851.

Schildkraut, J. J. (1965). The catecholamine hypothesis of affective disorders: A review of the supporting evidence. *American Journal of Psychiatry, 122,* 509–522.

Schindler, B. A. (1965). Stress, affective disorders, and immune function. *Medical Clinics of North America, 69,* 585–597.

Schlamowitz, K. E., Beutler, L. E., Scott, F. B., Karacan, I., & Ware, C. (1983). Reactions to the implantation of an inflatable penile prothesis among psychogenetically and organically impotent men. *Journal of Urology, 129,* 295–298.

Schleifer, S. J., Keller, S. E., Camerino, M., Thornton, J. C., & Stein, M. (1983). Suppression of lymphocyte stimulation following bereavement. *Journal of the American Medical Association, 250,* 374–377.

Schmahl, D. P., Lichtenstein, E., & Harris, D. E. (1972). Successful treatment of habitual smokers with warm, smoky air and rapid smoking. *Journal of Consulting and Clinical Psychology, 38,* 105–111.

Schmauk, F. J. (1970). Punishment, arousal, and avoidance learning in sociopaths. *Journal of Abnormal Psychology, 76,* 443–453.

Schmeck, H., Jr. (1988, November 15). Depression and anxiety seen as cause of much addiction. *The New York Times,* p. C3.

Schmeck, H., Jr. (1989, April 11). New findings offer clues to the process of Alzheimer's disease. *The New York Times,* p. C3.

Schmidt, F. L., Hunter, J. E., & Pearlman, K. (1981). Task differences as moderators of aptitude test validity in selection: A red herring. *Journal of Applied Psychology, 66,* 161–185.

Schmidt, G., & Schoisch, E. (1981). Psychosurgery of sexually deviant patients: Review of and analysis of new empirical findings. *Archives of Sexual Behavior, 10,* 301–323.

Schmidt, G., & Sigusch, V. (1973). Women's sexual arousal. In J. Zubin & J. Money (Eds.), *Contemporary sexual behavior: Critical issues in the 1970's.* Baltimore: Johns Hopkins University Press.

Schneider, B. H., & Byrne, B. M. (1987). Individualizing social skills training for behavior-disordered children. *Journal of Consulting and Clinical Psychology, 55,* 444–445.

Schneider, K. (1957). Prima(:)re und sekunda(:)re symptome bei der schizophrenia. *Fortschritte der Neurologie-Psychiatrie, 25,* 487–490.

Schneider, N. G. (1987). Nicotine gum in smoking cessation: Rationale, efficacy, and proper use. *Comprehensive Therapy, 13,* 32–37.

Schneider, N. G., Jarvik, M. E., Forsythe, A. B., Read, L. L., Elliott, M. L., & Schweiger, A. (1983). Nicotine gum in smoking cessation: A placebo-controlled, double-blind trial. *Addictive Behaviors, 8,* 253–261.

Schneidman, B., & McGuire, L. (1976). Group therapy for nonorgasmic women: Two age levels. *Archives of Sexual Behavior, 5,* 239–248.

Schoenfeld, H., Margolin, J., & Baum, S. (1987). Münchausen syndrome as a suicide equivalent: Abolition of syndrome by psychotherapy. *American Journal of Psychotherapy, 41,* 604–612.

Schoenman, T. J. (1984). The mentally ill witch in textbooks of abnormal psychology: Current status and implications of a fallacy. *Professional Psychology, 15,* 299–314.

Schopler, E., & Mesibov, G. B. (Eds.) (1984). *The effects of autism of the family.* New York: Plenum Press.

Schott, E. D. E., & Stunkard, A. J. (1987). Bulimia vs. bulimic behaviors on a college campus. *Journal of the American Medical Association, 258,* 1213–1215.

Schotte, D. E., & Clum, G. A. (1982). Suicide ideation in a college population: A test of a model. *Journal of Consulting and Clinical Psychology, 50,* 690–696.

Schotte, D. E., & Clum, G. A. (1987). Problem-solving skills in suicidal psychiatric patients. *Journal of Consulting and Clinical Psychology, 55,* 49–54.

Schretlen, D. J. (1988). The use of psychological tests to identify malingered symptoms of mental disorder. *Clinical Psychology Review, 8,* 451–476.

Schuckit, M. A. (1973). Alcoholism and sociopathy—diagnostic confusion. *Journal of Studies on Alcohol, 34,* 157–164.

Schuckit, M. A. (1984). Subjective responses to alcohol in sons of alcoholics and control. *Archives of General Psychiatry, 41,* 879–884.

Schuckit, M. A. (1985). Ethanol-induced changes in body sway in men at high alcoholism risk. *Archives of General Psychiatry, 42,* 375–379.

Schuckit, M. A. (1986). Alcoholism and affective disorders: Genetic and clinical implications. *Journal of Psychiatry, 143,* 140–147.

Schuckit, M. A. (1987). Biological vulnerability to alcoholism. *Journal of Consulting and Clinical Psychology, 55,* 301–309.

Schuckit, M. A., Goodwin, D. W., & Winokur, G. A. (1972). A study of alcoholism in half siblings. *American Journal of Psychiatry, 128,* 122–126.

Schuckit, M. A., & Rayses, U. (1979). Ethanol ingestion: Differences in blood acetaldehyde concentrations in relatives of alcoholics and controls. *Science, 203,* 54–55.

Schulsinger, F. (1972). Psychopathy: Heredity and environment. *International Journal of Mental Health, 1,* 190–206.

Schulsinger, H. (1976). A ten-year follow-up of children of schizophrenic mothers: A clinical assessment. *Acta Psychiatrica Scandinavica, 53,* 371–386.

Schwab, J. J., Bialow, M. R., & Holzer, C. E. (1967). A comparison of two rating scales for depression. *Journal of Clinical Psychology, 23,* 94–96.

Schwab, R. S., Chafetz, M. E., & Walkers, S. (1954). Control of two simultaneous voluntary motor acts in normals and in Parkinsonism. *Archives of Neurology and Psychiatry, 72,* 591–598.

Schwartz, J. L. (1987). *Review and evaluation of smoking cessation methods: The United States and Canada, 1978–1985.* Published by the Division of Cancer Prevention and Control, National Cancer Institute, U.S. Department of Health and Human Services, Public Health Service, National Institutes of Health (NIH Publication No. 87–2940). Washington DC: U.S. Government Printing Office.

Schwartz, M. F., & Masters, W. H. (1984). The Masters and Johnson treatment program for dissatisfied homosexual men. *American Journal of Psychiatry, 141,* 173–181.

Schwartz, M., & Masters, W. (1988). Inhibited sexual desire: The Masters and Johnson Institute treatment model. In S. Lieblum & R. Rosen (Eds.), *Sexual desire disorders.* New York: Guilford Press.

Schwartz, R. M. (1986). The internal dialogue: On the asymmetry between positive and negative thoughts. *Cognitive Therapy and Research, 10,* 591–605.

Schwartz, R. M., & Michelson, L. (1987). States-of-mind model: Cognitive balance in the treatment of agoraphobia. *Journal of Consulting and Clinical Psychology, 55,* 557–565.

Schwill, W., & Sprenkle, T. (1980). Retarded ejaculation. *Journal of Sex and Marital Therapy, 6,* 234–246.

Schwitzgebel, R. L., & Schwitzgebel, R. K. (1980). *Law and psychological practice.* New York: Wiley.

Scovern, A. W., & Kilmann, P. R. (1980). Status of electroconvulsive therapy: Review of the outcome literature. *Psychological Bulletin, 87,* 260–303.

Searles, J. S. (1988). The role of genetics in the pathogenesis of alcoholism. *Journal of Abnormal Psychology, 97,* 153–167.

Sears, R. R., Maccoby, E. E., & Levin, H. (1957). *Patterns of child rearing.* New York: Harper & Row.

Seer, P. (1979). Psychological control of essential hypertension: Review of the literature and methodological critique. *Psychological Bulletin, 86,* 1015–1043.

Seligman, M. E. P. (1973, June). Fall into helplessness. *Psychology Today*, pp. 43–48.

Seligman, M. E. P. (1975). *Helplessness On depression, development, and death*. San Francisco: W. H. Freeman & Company Publishers.

Seligman, M. E. P., Abramson, L. Y., Semmel, A., & von Baeyer, C. (1979). Depressive attributional style. *Journal of Abnormal Psychology, 88*, 242–247.

Seligman, M. E. P., and others (1988). Explanatory style change during cognitive therapy for unipolar depression. *Journal of Abnormal Psychology, 97*, 13–18.

Seligman, M. E. P., and others (1984). Attributional style and depressive symptoms among children. *Journal of Abnormal Psychology, 93*, 235–238.

Seligman, M. E. P., & Maier, S. F. (1967). Failure to escape traumatic shock. *Journal of Experimental Psychology, 74*, 1–9.

Seligman, M. E. P., & Rosenhan, D. L. (1984). *Abnormal Psychology*. New York: W. W. Norton & Co., Inc.

Selye, H. (1976). *The stress of life* (rev. ed.) New York: McGraw-Hill.

Selye, H. (1980). The stress concept today. In I. L. Kutash and others (Eds.), *Handbook on stress and anxiety*. San Francisco: Jossey-Bass.

Selzer, M. L. (1980). Alcoholism and alcoholic psychoses (3rd ed.). In H. J. Kaplan, A. M. Freedman, & B. J. Sadock (Eds.), *Comprehensive textbook of psychiatry* (Vol. 2) (pp. 1629–1645). Baltimore: Williams & Wilkins.

Semans, J. (1956). Premature ejaculation: A new approach. *Southern Medical Journal, 49*, 353–358.

Sgroi, S. M. (1978). Comprehensive examination for child sexual assault: Diagnostic, therapeutic, and child protection issues. In A. W. Burgess, A. N. Groth, L. L. Holstrom, & S. M. Sgroi (Eds.), *Sexual assault of children and adolescents* (pp. 143–157). Lexington, MA: D.C. Heath.

Shadish, W. R., Jr., Lurigio, A. J., & Lewis, D. A. (1989). After deinstitutionalization: The present and future of mental health long-term care policy. *Journal of Social Issues, 45*, 1–15.

Shafi, I. (1986). Dr. Shafi replies. *American Journal of Psychiatry, 143*, 1193–1194.

Shafi, M., Carrigan, S., Whittinghill, J. R., & Derrick, A. (1985). Psychological autopsy of completed suicide in children and adolescents. *American Journal of Psychiatry, 142*, 1061–1064.

Shagass, C., Straumanis, J. J., Roemer, R. A., & Amadeo, M. (1979). Temporal variability of somatosensory, visual, and auditory evoked potentials in schizophrenia. *Archives of General Psychiatry, 36*, 1341–1351.

Shah, S. A. (1981). Dangerousness: Conceptual, prediction, and public policy issues. In J. R. Hays, T. K. Roberts, & K. S. Solway (Eds.), *Violence and the violent individual*. New York: SP Medical and Scientific Books.

Shapiro, D., & Goldstein, I. B. (1982). Behavioral perspectives on hypertension. *Journal of Consulting and Clinical Psychology, 50*, 841–859.

Shapiro, D. A. (1985). Recent applications of meta-analysis in clinical research. *Clinical Psychology Review, 5*, 13–34.

Shapiro, D. A., & Shapiro, D. (1982). Meta-analysis of comparative therapy outcome studies: A replication and refinement. *Psychological Bulletin, 92*, 581–594.

Shapiro, S., Weinblatt, E., Frank, C., & Sager, R. V. (1969). Incidence of coronary heart disease in a population insured for medical care (HIP). *American Journal of Health, 59*, 1–101.

Shaw, E. D., Stokes, P. E., Mann, J. J., & Manevitz, A. Z. A. (1987). Effects of lithium carbonate on the memory and motor speed of bipolar patients. *Journal of Abnormal Psychology, 96*, 64–69.

Shaw, R., Cohen, F., Doyle, B., & Palesky, J. (1985). The impact of denial and repressive style on information gain and rehabilitation outcomes in myocardial infarction patients. *Psychosomatic Medicine, 47*, 262–273.

Sheehan, D. V. (1982). Panic attacks and phobias. *New England Journal of Medicine, 307*, 156–158.

Sheikh, J. I., & Yesavage, J. A. (1986). Geriatric Depression Scale (GDS): Recent evidence and development of a shorter version. In T. L. Brink (Ed.), *Clinical gerontology: A guide to assessment and intervention* (pp. 165–173). New York: Haworth Press.

Sheingold, K., & Tenney, Y. J. (1982). Memory for a salient childhood event. In U. Niesser (Eds.), *Memory observed: Remembering in natural contexts*. San Francisco: W. H. Freeman & Company Publishers.

Shekelle, R. B., and others (1985). The MRFIT behavior pattern study: II. Type A behavior and incidence of coronary heart disease. *American Journal of Epidemiology, 122*, 559–570.

Shekelle, R. B., Gale, M., & Norusis, M. (1985). Type A score (Jenkins Activity Survey) and risk of recurrent coronary heart disease in the Aspirin Myocardial Infarction Study. *American Journal of Cardiology, 56*, 221–225.

Shekelle, R. B., Gale, M., Ostfeld, A., & Paul, O. (1983). Hostility, risk of coronary heart disease, and mortality. *Psychosomatic Medicine, 45*, 109–114.

Sheldon, W. H. (1949). *Varieties of delinquent youth*. New York: Harper.

Shelton, R. C., & Weinberger, D. R. (1986). X-ray computed tomography studies in schizophrenia: A review and synthesis. In H. A. Nasrallah & D. R. Weinberger (Eds.), *The neurology of schizophrenia* (pp. 207–250). Amsterdam: Elsevier Science Publishers.

Sherif, C. W. (1980). A social psychological perspective on the menstrual cycle. In J. E. Parsons (Eds.), *The psychobiology of sex differences and sex roles*. New York: Hemisphere/McGraw-Hill.

Sherrington, R., and others (1988). Localization of a susceptibility locus for schizophrenia on chromosome 5. *Nature, 336*, 164–167.

Sherwin, B., Gelfand, M., & Brender, W. (1985). Androgen enhances sexual motivation in females: A prospective crossover study of sex steroid administration in the surgical menopause. *Psychosomatic Medicine, 47*, 339–351.

Shipley, R. H. (1981). Maintenance of smoking cessation: Effect of follow-up letters, smoking motivation, muscle tension, and health locus of control. *Journal of Consulting and Clinical Psychology, 49*, 982–984.

Shipley, R. H., Butt, J. H., Horwitz, B., & Farbry, J. E. (1978). Preparation for a stressful medical procedure: Effect of amount of stimulus preexposure and coping style. *Journal of Consulting and Clinical Psychology, 46*, 499–507.

Shisslak, C. M., Crago, M., Neal, M. E., & Swain, B. (1987). Primary prevention of eating disorders. *Journal of Consulting and Clinical Psychology, 55*, 660–667.

Shneidman, E. S. (1985). *Definition of suicide*. New York: Wiley.

Shneidman, E. S. (1987). A psychological approach to suicide. In G. R. VanderBos & B. K. Bryant (Eds.), *Cataclysms, cries, and catastrophes: Psychology in action* (Master Lecture Series, Vol. 6, pp. 151–183). Washington DC: U.S. American Psychological Association.

Shneidman, E. S., Farberow, N. L., & Litman, R. E. (Eds) (1970). *The psychology of suicide*. New York: Science House.

Shuddath, R. L., Christison, G. W., Torrey, E. F., Casanova, M. F., & Weinberger, D. R. (1990). Anatomical abnormalities in the brains of monozygotic twins discordant for schizophrenia. *New England Journal of Medicine, 322*, 789–794.

Shuller, D. Y., & McNamara, J. R. (1976). Expectancy factors in behavioral observation. *Behavior Therapy, 7*, 519–527.

Siegel, D. (1973). *The rights of mental patients*. New York: Avon.

Siegel, L. J. (1989). *Criminology* (3rd ed.). St. Paul, MN: West Publishing.

Siegelman, M. (1974). Parental background of male homosexuals and heterosexuals. *Archives of Sexual Behavior, 3*, 3–18.

Siegelman, M. (1978). Psychological adjustment of homosexual and heterosexual men: A cross-national replication. *Archives of Sexual Behavior, 7*, 1–11.

Siegelman, M. (1979). Adjustment of homosexual and heterosexual women: A cross-national replication. *Archives of Sexual Behavior, 8*, 121–126.

Silver, R. L., & Wortman, C. B. (1980). Coping with undesirable life events. In J. Garber & M. E. P. Seligman (Eds.), *Human helplessness: Theory and applications*. New York: Academic Press.

Silver, W. F. (1986). Medication refusal by involuntary psychiatric patients: Legal and clinical issues. *Clinical Psychology Review, 6*, 115–132.

Silverman, L. H. (1984). Beyond insight: An additional necessary step in redressing intrapsychic conflict. *Psychoanalytic Psychology, 1*, 215–234.

Silverstein, B. (1982). Cigarette smoking, nicotine addiction, and relaxation. *Journal of Personality and Social Psychology, 42*, 946–950.

Silverstein, B., Koslowski, L. T., & Schachter, S. (1977). Social life, cigarette smoking, and urinary pH. *Journal of Experimental Psychology: General, 106*, 20–23.

Silverton, L., Finell, K. M., Mednick, S. A., & Schulsinger, F. (1985). Low birth weight and ventricular enlargement in a high-risk sample. *Journal of Abnormal Psychology, 94*, 405–409.

Simmons, J. Q., & Lovaas, O. I. (1969). Use of pain and punishment as treatment techniques with childhood schizophrenics. *American Journal of Psychotherapy, 23*, 23–36.

Simons, A. D., McGowan, C. R., Epstein, L. H., Kupfer, D. J., & Robertson, R. J. (1985). Exercise as a treatment for depression: An update. *Clinical Psychology Review, 5*, 553–568.

Simons, A. D., Murphy, G. E., Levine, J. L., & Wetzel, R. D. (1986). Cognitive therapy and pharmacotherapy for depression: Sustained improvement over one year. *Archives of General Psychiatry, 43*, 43–48.

Sintchak, J., & Geer, J. (1975). A vaginal plethysmograph system. *Psychophysiology, 12*, 113–115.

Skinner, B. F. (1938). *The behavior of organisms: An experimental analysis*. New York: Appleton.

Skinner, B. F. (1983). Intellectual self-management in old age. *American Psychologist, 38*, 239–244.

Skinner, B. F. (1987). Whatever happened to psychology as the science of behavior? *American Psychologist, 42*, 780–786.

Skodol, A. E., & Spitzer, R. I. (1983). An indexed bibliography of DSM-III: An international perspective on DSM-III. In R. I. Spitzer, J. B. W. Williams, & A. E. Skodol. *International Perspectives on DSM-III*. Washington, DC: American Psychiatric Press.

Slater, D., & Hans, V. P. (1984) Public opinion of forensic psychiatry following the Hinckley verdict. *American Journal of Psychiatry, 141*, 675–679.

Slater, E. (1965). Diagnosis of hysteria. *British Medical Journal, 1*, 1395–1399.

Slater, E. T. O., & Glithero, E. (1965). A follow-up of patients diagnosed as suffering from "hysteria." *Journal of Psychosomatic Research, 9*, 9–13.

Slater, J., & Depue, R. A. (1981). The contribution of environmental events and social support to serious suicide attempts in primary depressive disorder. *Journal of Abnormal Psychology, 90*, 275–285.

Sloane, R. B., Staples, F. R., Yorkston, N. J., Whipple, K., & Cristol, A. H. (1975). *Short-term analytically oriented psychotherapy versus behavior therapy*. Cambridge, MA: Harvard University Press.

Smith, A. C. (1986). General and historical concepts in schizophrenia: Overview. In A. Kerr & P. Snaith (Eds.), *Contemporary issues in schizophre-*

nia (pp. 3–17). Avon, England: The Bath Press.

Smith, D. (1982). Trends in counseling and psychotherapy. *American Psychologist, 37,* 802–809.

Smith, D. A. (1946). Nutritional neuropathies in the civilian interment camp, Hong Kong. January, 1942 to August, 1945. *Brain, 69,* 209–222.

Smith, G. A., & Hall, J. A. (1982). Evaluating Michigan's Guilty but Mentally Ill verdict: An empirical study. *University of Michigan Journal of Law Reform, 16,* 77.

Smith, J. N., & Baldessarini, R. J. (1980). Changes in prevalence, severity, and recovery in tardive dyskinesia with age. *Archives of General Psychiatry, 37,* 1368–1373.

Smith, J. W. (1988). Long-term outcome of clients treated in a commercial stop smoking program. *Journal of Substance Abuse Treatment, 5,* 33–36.

Smith, M. E., & Fremouw, W. J. (1987). A realistic approach to treating obesity. *Clinical Psychology Review, 7,* 449–465.

Smith, M. L., & Glass, G. V. (1977). Meta-analysis of psychotherapy outcome studies. *American Psychologist, 32,* 752–760.

Smith, M. L., Glass, G. V., & Miller, T. I. (1980). *The benefits of psychotherapy.* Baltimore: Johns Hopkins University Press.

Smith, R. E. (1979). The movement of women into the labor force. In R. E. Smith (Ed.), *The subtle revolution: Women at work.* Washington, DC: The Urban Institute.

Smith, R. E., & Winokur, G. (1983). Affective disorders. In R. E. Tarter (Ed.), *The child at psychiatric risk.* New York: Oxford University Press.

Smith, R. J. (1978). *The psychopath in society,* New York: Academic Press.

Smith, S. C. (1983). *The great mental calculators.* New York: Columbia University Press.

Smith, S. M., & Hanson, R. (1974). One hundred and thirty-four battered children: A medical and psychological study. *British Medical Journal, 14,* 666–670.

Smith, T. W. (1983). Change in irrational beliefs and the outcome of rational-emotive psychotherapy. *Journal of Consulting and Clinical Psychology, 51,* 156–157.

Smith, T. W., Snyder, C. R., & Perkins, S. C. (1983). The self-serving function of hypochondriacal complaints: Physical symptoms as self-handicapping strategies. *Journal of Personality and Social Psychology, 44,* 787–797.

Snyder, A., LoPiccolo, L., & LoPiccolo, J. (1975). Secondary orgasmic dysfunction: II. Case study. *Archives of Sexual Behavior, 4,* 239–247.

Snyder, C. R. (1958). Alcohol and the Jews: A cultural study of drinking and sobriety. New Brunswick, NJ: Rutgers Center for Alcoholism Studies.

Snyder, S. H. (1977). Opiate receptors and internal opiates. *Scientific American, 236,* 44–56.

Snyder, S. H. (1980). *Biological aspects of mental disorder.* New York: Oxford University Press.

Snyder, S. H. (1984). Drug and neurotransmitter receptors in the brain. *Science, 224,* 22–31.

Snyder, S. H., Banerjee, S. P., Yamamura, H. I., & Greenberg, D. (1974). Drugs, neurotransmitters and schizophrenia. *Science, 814,* 1243–1253.

Snyderman, M., & Rothman, S. (1987). Survey of expert opinion on intelligence and aptitude testing. *American Psychologist, 42,* 137–144.

Sobell, M. B., & Sobell, L. C. (1973). Alcoholics treated by individualized behavior therapy: One-year treatment outcome. *Behaviour Research and Therapy, 11,* 599–618.

Sobell, M. B., & Sobell, L. C. (1976). Second-year treatment outcome of alcoholics treated by individualzied behavior therapy: Results. *Behaviour Research and Therapy, 14,* 195–215.

Sobell, M. B., & Sobell, L. C. (1984). The aftermath of heresy: A response to Pendery et al.'s critique of "Individualized behavior therapy for alcoholics." *Behaviour Research and Therapy, 22,* 413–440.

Solomon, Z., Weisenberg, M., Schwarzwald, J., & Mikulincer, M. (1987). Posttraumatic stress disorder among frontline soldiers with combat stress reaction: The 1982 Israeli experience. *American Journal of Psychiatry, 144,* 448–454.

Somers, A. R. (1979). Marital status, health and use of health services. *Journal of the American Medical Association, 241,* 1818–1822.

Sommers, I. (1988). The influence of environmental factors on the community adjustment of the mentally ill. *Journal of Nervous and Mental Disease, 176,* 221–226.

Sorensen, G., & Pechacek, T. F. (1987). Attitudes toward smoking cessation among men and women. *Journal of Behavioral Medicine, 10,* 129–137.

Spanos, N. P. (1978). Witchcraft in histories of psychiatry: A critical analysis and an alternative conceptualization. *Psychological Bulletin, 85,* 417–439.

Spanos, N. P., McNeil, C., Gwynn, M. I., & Stam, H. J. (1984). Effects of suggestion and distraction on reported pain in subjects high and low on hypnotic suggestibility. *Journal of Abnormal Psychology, 93,* 277–284.

Spanos, N. P., Weekes, J. R., & Bertrand, L. D. (1985). Multiple personality: A social psychological perspective. *Journal of Abnormal Psychology, 94,* 362–376.

Sparadeo, F. R., Zwick, W. R., Ruggierio, S. D., Meek, D. A., Carloni, J. A., & Simone, S. S. (1982). Evaluation of a social-setting detoxification program. *Journal of Studies on Alcohol, 43,* 1124–1136.

Speiss, W. F., Geer, J. H., & O'Donohue, W. T. (1984). Premature ejaculation: Investigation of factors in ejaculatory latency. *Journal of Applied Psychology, 93,* 242–245.

Spiegel, D. S., & Wissler, T. (1986). Family environment as a predictor of psychiatric rehospitalization. *American Journal of Psychiatry, 143,* 56–60.

Spielberger, C. D., and others (1985). In M. A. Chesney & R. H. Rosenman (Eds.), *Anger and hostility in cardiovascular and behavioral disorders.* New York: Hemisphere/McGraw-Hill.

Spiker, D., & Ricks, M. (1984). Visual self-recognition in autistic children: Developmental relationships. *Child Development, 55,* 214–225.

Spitzer, R. L. (1976). More on pseudoscience in science and the case for psychiatric diagnosis: A critique of D. L. Rosenhan's "On Being Sane in Insane Places" and "The Contextual Nature of Psychiatric Diagnosis. *Archives of General Psychiatry, 33,* 459–470.

Spitzer, R. L., & Forman, J. B. (1979). DSM-III field trials: II. Initial experience with the multiaxial system. *American Journal of Psychiatry, 136,* 818–820.

Spitzer, R. L., Forman, J. B., & Nee, J. (1979). DSM-III field trials: I. Initial inter-rater diagnostic reliability. *American Journal of Psychiatry, 136,* 815–817.

Spitzer, R. L., Gibbon, M., Skodol, A. E., Williams, J. B. W., & First, M. B. (1989). *DSM-III-R casebook.* Washington, DC: American Psychiatric Press.

Spitzer, R. L., & Williams, J. B. W. (1984). *Structured clinical interview for DSM-III.* New York: New York State Psychiatric Institute, Biometrics Research Division.

Spivack, G., Marcus, J., & Swift, M. (1986). Early classroom behaviors and later misconduct. *Developmental Psychology, 22,* 124–131.

Spivack, G., Platt, J. J., & Shure, M. B. (1976). *The problem-solving approach to adjustment.* San Francisco: Jossey-Bass.

Spohn, H. E., Coyne, L., Larson, J., Mittleman, F., Spray, J., & Hayes, K. (1986). Episodic and residual thought pathology in chronic schizophrenics: Effects of neuroleptics. *Schizophrenia Bulletin, 12,* 394–407.

Spohn, H. E., & Patterson, T. (1979). Recent studies of psychophysiology in schizophrenia. *Schizophrenia Bulletin, 5,* 581–611.

Spreen, O. (1988). Prognosis of learning disability.

Journal of Consulting and Clinical Psychology, 56, 836–842.

Squire, L. R. (1977). ECT and memory loss. *American Journal of Psychiatry, 134,* 997–1001.

Squire, L. R. (1982). Neuropsychological effects of ECT. In W. B. Essman & R. Abrams (Eds.), *Electroconvulsive Therapy.* New York: SP Medical and Scientific Books.

Squire, L. R., & Slater, P. C. (1978). Bilateral and unilateral ECT: Effects on verbal and nonverbal memory. *American Journal of Psychiatry, 135,* 1316–1320.

Squire, L. R., & Slater, P. C. (1983). Electroconvulsive therapy and complaints of memory dysfunction—A prospective 3-year follow-up study. *British Journal of Psychiatry, 142,* 1–8.

Squire, L. R., & Zouzounis, J. A. (1986). ECT and memory: Brief pulse versus sine wave. *American Journal of Psychiatry, 143,* 595–601.

Stall, R. D., Coates, T. J., & Hoff, C. (1988). Behavioral risk reduction for HIV infection among gay and bisexual men: A review of results from the United States. *American Psychologist, 43,* 878–885.

Stalonas, P. M., & Kirschenbaum, D. S. (1985). Behavioral treatments for obesity: Eating habits revisited. *Behavior Therapy, 16,* 1–14.

Stambrook, M. (1983). The Luria-Nebraska Neuropsychological Battery: A promise that may be partly fulfilled. *American Journal of Neuropsychology, 5,* 247–269.

Stamler, J. (1985a). Coronary heart disease: Doing the "right things." *New England Journal of Medicine, 312,* 1053–1055.

Stamler, J. (1985b). The marked decline in coronary heart disease mortality rates in the United States, 1968–1981: Summary of findings and possible explanations. *Cardiology, 72,* 11–12.

Stamler, J. and others (1986). Is the relationship between serum cholesterol and risk of premature death from coronary heart disease continuous and graded? Findings in 356,222 primary screenees of the Multiple Risk Factor Intervention Trial (MRFIT). *Journal of the American Medical Association, 256,* 2823–2828.

Stampfer, M., & Hennekens, C. (1988). Alcohol consumption and cardiovascular disease in women. *New England Journal of Medicine, 319,* 267–273.

Stanton, A. H., Gunderson, J. G., Knapp, P. H., Frank, A. F., Vannicelle, M. L., Schnitzer, R., & Rosenthal, R. (1984). Effects of psychotherapy in schizophrenia: I. Design and implementation of a controlled study. *Schizophrenia Bulletin, 10,* 520–563.

Staub, E., Tursky, B., & Schwartz, G. (1971). Self-control and predictability: Their effects on reactions to aversive stimulation. *Journal of Personality and Social Psychology, 18,* 157–162.

Steadman, H. J. (1979). *Beating a rap: Defendants found incompetent to stand trial.* Chicago: University of Chicago Press.

Steele, C. M., & Josephs, R. A. (1988). Drinking your troubles away: II. An attention-allocation model of alcohol's effect on psychological stress. *Journal of Abnormal Psychology, 97,* 196–205.

Steele, C. M., & Southwick, L. (1985). Alcohol and social behavior: I. The psychology of drunken excess. *Journal of Personality and Social Psychology, 48,* 18–34.

Steele, C. M., Southwick, L., & Pagano, R. (1986). Drinking your troubles away: The role of activity in mediating alcohol's reduction of psychological stress. *Journal of Abnormal Psychology, 95,* 173–180.

Steer, R. A., Beck, A. T., Brown, G., & Berchick, R. J. (1987). Self-reported depressive symptoms that differentiate recurrent episode major depression from dysthymic disorders. *Journal of Clinical Psychology, 43,* 246–250.

Stefanek, M. E., Ollendick, T. H., Baldock, W. P., Francis, G., & Yaeger, N. J. (1987). Self-statements in aggressive, withdrawn, and popular children. *Cognitive Therapy and Research, 11,* 229–239.

Stein, L. I., & Tess, A. A. (Eds.) (1978). *Alternatives to mental hospital treatment.* New York: Plenum.

Steinmetz, J. L., Lewinsohn, P. M., & Antonuccio, D. O. (1983). Prediction of individual outcome in a group intervention for depression. *Journal of Consulting and Clinical Psychology, 51,* 331–337.

Steinmetz, S. K. (1978). Violence between family members. *Marriage and Family Review, 1,* 1–16.

Steketee, G., & Foa, E. B. (1985). Obsessive-compulsive disorder. In D. H. Barlow (Ed.), *Clinical handbook of psychological disorders* (pp. 69–144). New York: Guilford Press.

Stephenson, L. A., Denney, D. R., & Aberger, W. (1983). Factor structure of the menstrual symptom questionnaire: Relationship to oral contraceptives, neuroticism and life stress. *Behaviour Research and Therapy, 21,* 129–135.

Steptoe, A., Melville, D., & Ross, A. (1984). Behavioral response demands, cardiovascular reactivity, and essential hypertension. *Psychosomatic Medicine, 46,* 33–48.

Stern, J. S., & Lowney, P. (1986). Obesity: The role of physical activity. In K. Brownell & J. Fereyt (Eds.), Handbook of eating disorders. New York: Basic Books.

Stevenson, H. W., and others (1985). Cognitive performance and academic achievement of Japanese, Chinese, and American children. *Child Development, 56,* 718–734.

Stevenson, H. W., Lee, S. Y., & Stigler, J. W. (1986). Mathematics achievement of Chinese, Japanese, and American children. *Science, 231,* 693–699.

Stiles, W. B., Shapiro, D. A., & Elliott, R. (1986). "Are all psychotherapies equivalent?" *American Psychologist, 41,* 165–180.

Stinson, D. J., Smith, W. G., Amidjaya, I., & Kaplan. J. M. (1979). Systems of care and treatment outcomes for alcoholic patients. *Archives of General Psychiatry, 36,* 535–539.

Stipp, D. (1987, May 7). Breast-cancer risk may increase 40% with moderate alcohol use, studies say. *The Wall Street Journal,* p. 34.

Stoller, R. J. (1969). Parental influences in male transexualism. In R. Green & J. Money (eds.), *Transexualism and Sex Reassignment.* Baltimore: Johns Hopkins University Press.

Stone, A. (1975). *Mental health and the law: A system in transition* (National Institute of Mental Health Publication No. ADM 76–176). Washington, DC: U.S. Government Printing Office.

Stone, A. (1976). The *Tarasoff* decisions: Suing psychotherapists to safeguard society. *Harvard Law Review, 90,* 358–378.

Stone, A. (1984). *Law, psychiatry and morality.* Washington, DC: American Psychiatric Press.

Stone, A. (1986). Vermont adopts *Tarasoff*: A real barn-burner. *American Journal of Psychiatry, 143,* 352–355.

Stone, A., & Neale, J. M. (1984). Effects of severe daily events on mood. *Journal of Personality and Social Psychology, 46,* 137–144.

Stone, M. H. (1980). *The borderline syndromes: Constitution, personality, and adaptation.* New York: McGraw-Hill.

Storandt, M. (1983). Psychology's response to the graying of America. *American Psychologist, 38,* 323–326.

Strachan, A. M. (1986). Family intervention for the rehabilitation of schizophrenia: Toward protection and coping. *Schizophrenia Bulletin, 12,* 678–698.

Straube, E. (1979). On the meaning of electrodermal nonresponding in schizophrenia. *Journal of Nervous and Mental Disease, 167,* 601–611.

Straus, M. A. (1978). Wife-battering: How common and why? *Victimology:* An International Journal, *2,* 443–458.

Strauss, J., & Ryan, R. M. (1987). Autonomy disturbances in subtypes of anorexia nervosa. *Journal of Abnormal Psychology, 96,* 254–258.

Strauss, J. S., Carpenter, W. T., & Bartko, J. J. (1974). The diagnosis and understanding of schizophrenia: Part III. Speculation on the processes that underlie schizophrenia symptoms and signs. *Schizophrenia Bulletin, 1,* 61–69.

Strauss, J. S., Carpenter, W. T., & Bartko, J. J. (1985). Speculations on the processes that underlie schizophrenic symptoms and signs. *Schizophrenia Bulletin, 11,* 61–75.

Strauss, J. S., Kokes, R. F., Klorman, R., & Sacksteder, J. J. (1977). Premorbid adjustment in schizophrenia: Concepts, measures, and implications. *Schizophrenia Bulletin, 3,* 184–244.

Streissguth, A. P., and others (1984). Interuterine alcohol and nicotine exposure: Attention and reaction time in 4-year-old children. *Developmental Psychology, 20,* 533–541.

Streissguth, A. P., Barr, H. M., Sampson, P. D., Darby, B. L., & Martin, D. C. (1989). IQ at age 4 in relation to maternal alcohol use and smoking during pregnancy. *Developmental Psychology, 25,* 3–11.

Stretch, R. H. (1985). Posttraumatic stress disorder among U.S. Army Reserve Vietnam and Vietnam-era veterans. *Journal of Consulting and Clinical Psychology, 53,* 935–936.

Stretch, R. H. (1986). Posttraumatic stress disorder among Vietnam and Vietnam-era veterans. In C. R. Figley (Ed.), *Trauma and its wake: Vol. 2. Traumatic stress theory, research, and intervention.* New York: Brunner/Mazel.

Stretch, R. H. (1987). Posttraumatic stress disorder among U.S. Army reservists: Reply to Nezu and Carnevale. *Journal of Consulting and Clinical Psychology, 55,* 272–273.

Strickler, D. P., Bigelow, G., Lawrence, C., & Liebson, I. (1976). Moderate drinking as an alternative to alcohol abuse: A nonaversive procedure. *Behaviour Research and Therapy, 14,* 279–288.

Strober, M. (1986). Psychopathology of adolescence revisited. *Clinical Psychology Review, 6,* 199–209

Strober, M., & Carlson, G. (1982). Bipolar illness in adolescents: Clinical, genetic and pharmacologic predictors in a three-to-four-year prospective follow-up. *Archives of General Psychiatry, 39,* 549–555.

Strober, M., & Humphrey, L. L. (1987). Familial contributions to the etiology and course of anorexia nervosa and bulimia. *Journal of Consulting and Clinical Psychology, 55,* 654–659.

Strube, M. J. (1988). The decision to leave an abusive relationship: Empirical evidence and theoretical issues. *Psychological Bulletin, 104,* 236–250.

Strunk, R. C., Mrazek, D. A., Fuhrman, A. S. W., & LaBrecque, J. F. (1985). Physiologic and psychological characteristics associated with deaths due to asthma in childhood: A case-controlled study. *Journal of the American Medical Association, 254,* 1193–1198.

Stubbs, E. G., Ritvo, E. R., & Mason-Brothers, A. (1985). Autsim and shared parental HLA antigens. *Journal of Child Psychiatry, 24,* 182–185.

Stumphauzer, J. S. (1981). Behavior modification with delinquents and criminals. In W. E. Craighead, A. E., Kazdin, & M. J. Mahoney (Eds.), *Behavior modification: Principles, issues, and applications* (2d ed.). Boston: Houghton Mifflin.

Stunkard, A. J., & Brownell, K. D. (1979). Behavior therapy and self-help programs for obesity. In J. F. Munro (Ed.), *The treatment of obesity* (pp. 190–230). London: MTP Press.

Stunkard, A. J., Sorensen, T. I. A., Hanis, C., Teasdale, R. W., Chakraborty, R., Schall, W. J., & Schulsinger, F. (1986). An adoption study of human obesity. *New England Journal of Medicine, 314,* 193–198.

Suinn, R. (1975). *Fundamentals of behavior pathology.* New York: Wiley.

Suinn, R. (1976, December). How to break the vicious cycle of stress. *Psychology Today,* pp. 59–60.

Suinn, R. (1982). Intervention with Type A behaviors. *Journal of Consulting and Clinical Psychology, 50,* 933–949.

Sullivan, H. S. (1962). *Schizophrenia as a human process.* New York: W. W. Norton & Co., Inc.

Summit, R. (1983). The child sexual abuse accommodation syndrome. *Child Abuse and Neglect, 7,* 177–193.

Surgeon General's Report (1989) *Reducing the health consequences of smoking: 25 years of progress.* Atlanta: Centers for Disease Control.

Susser, E., Struenig, E. L., & Conover, S. (1987). Childhood experiences of homeless men. *American Journal of Psychiatry, 144,* 1599–1601.

Sussman, N., Borod, J. C., Cancelmo, J. A., & Braun, D. (1987). Münchausen's syndrome: A reconceptualization of the disorder. *Journal of Nervous and Mental Disease, 175,* 692–695.

Sutker, P. B., & Allain, A. N., Jr. (1988). Issues in personality conceptualizations of addictive behaviors. *Journal of Consulting and Clinical Psychology, 56,* 172–182.

Sutton, S., & Hallett, R. (1988). Smoking intervention in the workplace using videotapes and nicotine chewing gum. *Preventive Medicine, 17,* 48–59.

Suzdak, P. D., Glowa, J. R., Crawley, J. N., & Schwartz, R. D. (1986). A selective imidazobenzodiazepine antagonist of ethanol in the rat. *Science, 225,* 1243–1247.

Swaim, R. C., Oetting E. R., Edwards, R. W., & Beauvais, F. (1989). Links from emotional distress to adolescent drug use: A path model. *Journal of Consulting and Clinical Psychology, 57,* 227–231.

Swan, G. E., & Denk, C. E. (1987). Dynamic models for the maintenance of smoking cessation: Event history analysis of late relapse. *Journal of Behavioral Medicine, 10,* 527–554.

Sweeney, P. D., Anderson, K., & Bailey, S. (1986). Attributional style in depression: A meta-analytic review. *Journal of Personality and Social Psychology, 50,* 974–991.

Swift, W. J., Andrews, D., & Barklage, N. E. (1986). The relationship between affective disorder and eating disorders: A review of the literature. *American Journal of Psychiatry, 143,* 290–299.

Symonds, A. (1974). Victims of violence: Psychological effects and after-effects. *American Journal of Psychoanalysis, 35,* 19–26.

Syndulko, K. (1978). Electrocortical investigations of sociopathy. In R. D. Hare & D. Schalling (Eds.), *Psychopathic behavior: Approaches to research* (pp. 145–156). Chichester, England: Wiley.

Szasz, T. S. (1961). *The myth of mental illness.* New York: Harper & Row.

Szasz, T. S. (1963). *Law, liberty and psychiatry.* New York: Macmillan.

Szasz, T. S. (1970a). *Ideology and insanity: Essays on the psychiatric dehumanization of man.* New York: Doubleday/Anchor.

Szasz, T. S. (1970b). *The manufacture of madness: A comparative study of the inquisition and the mental health movement.* New York: Harper & Row.

Szasz, T. S. (1976). *Schizophrenia: The sacred symbol of psychiatry.* New York: Basic Books.

Szasz, T. S. (1984). *The therapeutic state: Psychiatry in the mirror of current events.* Buffalo, NY: Prometheus.

Szmukler, G. I., & Russell, G. F. M. (1986). Outcome and prognosis of anorexia nervosa. In K. D. Brownell & J. P. Foreyt (Eds.), *Handbook of eating disorders.* New York: Basic Books.

Taber, G. I., McCormick, R. A., Russo, A. N., Adkins, B. J., & Ramirez, L. F. (1987). Follow-up of pathological gamblers after treatment. *American Journal of Psychiatry, 144,* 757–761.

Talbott, E., and others (1985). Occupational noise exposure, noise-induced hearing loss, and the epidemiology of high blood pressure. *American Journal of Epidemiology, 121,* 501–514.

Talbott, J. A. (1981). *The chronic mentally ill: Treatment, programs, systems.* New York: Human Sciences.

Tannahill, R. (1980). *Sex in history.* Briarcliff Manor, NY: Stein & Day.

Tarasoff v. Regents of the University of California, 131 Cal Rptr. 14, 551 P. 2d 344 (1976).

Tarter, R. (1988). Are there inherited behavioral traits that predipose to substance abuse? *Journal of Consulting and Clinical Psychology, 56,* 189–196.

Tarter, R., & Edwards, K. (1986). Antecedents to alcoholism: Implications for prevention and treatment. *Behavior Therapy, 7,* 346–361.

Tarter, R., Hegedus, A. M., Winsten, N. E., & Alterman, A. I. (1984). Neuropsychological, personality, and family characteristics of physically abused delinquents. *Journal of the American Academy of Child Psychiatry, 23,* 668–674.

Task Force Report, American Psychiatric Association (1980). Effects of antipsychotic drugs: Tardive dyskinesia. *American Journal of Psychiatry, 37,* 1163–1171.

Tavris, C., & Sadd, S. (1977). *The Redbook report on female sexuality.* New York: Delacorte.

Taylor, W. N. (1985, May). Super athletes made to order. *Psychology Today,* pp. 62–66.

Teders, S. J., Blanchard, E. B., Andrasik, F., Jurish, S. E., Neff, D. F., & Arena, J. G. (1984). Relaxation training for tension headache: Comparative efficacy and cost-effectiveness of a minimal-therapist-contact versus a therapist-delivered procedure. *Behavior Therapy, 15,* 59–70.

Telch, C. F., & Telch, M. J. (1986). Group coping skills instruction and supportive group therapy for cancer patients: A comparison of strategies. *Journal of Consulting and Clinical Psychology, 54,* 802–808.

Telfer, M., Clark, G., Baker, D. V., & Richardson, C. (1968). Incidence of gross chromosomal errors among tall, criminal American males. *Science, 159,* 1249–1250.

Tellegen, A., Lykken, D. T., Bouchard, T. J., Wilcox, K., Segal, N., & Rich, S. (1988). Personality similarity in twins reared apart and together. *Journal of Personality and Social Psychology, 54,* 1031–1039.

Teng, E. L., Chui, H. C., Schneider, L. S., & Metzger, L. E. (1987). Alzheimer's dementia: Performance on the Mini-Mental State Examination. *Journal of Consulting and Clinical Psychology, 55,* 96–100.

Tennant, F. S., Jr. (1979). Ambulatory alcohol withdrawal. *Journal of Family Practice, 8,* 621–623.

Teri, L., & Lewinsohn, P. M. (1986). Individual and group treatment of unipolar depression: Comparison of treatment outcome and identification of predictors of successful treatment outcome. *Behavior Therapy, 17,* 215–228.

Thal, L. G. (1988). Treatment strategies: Present and future. In M. K. Aronson (Ed.), *Understanding Alzheimer's disease.* New York: Scribner's.

Theander, S. (1985). Outcome and prognosis in anorexia nervosa and bulimia: Some results of previous investigations, compared with those of a Swedish long-term study. *Journal of Psychiatric Research, 19,* 493–508.

Thigpen, C. H., & Cleckley, H. M. (1984). On the incidence of multiple personality disorder. *International Journal of Clinical and Experimental Hypnosis, 32,* 63–66.

Thoits, P. A. (1983). Dimensions of life events as influences upon the genesis of psychological distress and associated conditions: An evaluation and synthesis of the literature. In H. B. Kaplan (Ed.), *Psychosocial stress: Trends in theory and research.* New York: Academic Press.

Thomas, C. S. (1987). The AIDS virus and the CNS. *American Journal of Psychiatry, 144,* 537.

Thompson, J. W., & Blaine, J. D. (1987). Use of ECT in the United States in 1975 and 1980. *American Journal of Psychiatric, 144,* 557–562.

Thoreson, C. E., & Mahoney, M. J. (1974). *Behavioral self-control.* New York: Holt, Rinehart & Winston.

Thurman, C. W. (1985a). Effectiveness of cognitive-behavioral treatments in reducing Type A behavior among university faculty. *Journal of Counseling Psychology, 32,* 74–83.

Thurman, C. W. (1985b). Effectiveness of cognitive-behavioral treatments in reducing type A behavior among university faculty—one year later. *Journal of Counseling Psychology, 32,* 445–448.

Tienari, P., and others (1987). Genetic and psychosocial factors in schizophrenia: The Finnish Adoptive Family Study. *Schizophrenia Bulletin, 13,* 477–484.

Tober, J. I., McCormick, R. A., & Ramirey, L. F. (in press). The prevalence and impact of major stressors among pathological gamblers. *International Journal of the Addictions.*

Tolchin, M. (1989, July 19). When long life is too much: Suicide rises among elderly. *The New York Times,* pp. A1, A15.

Tomlinson, B. E., Blessed, G., & Roth, M. (1970). Observations on the brains of demented old people. *Journal of the Neurological Sciences, 11,* 205–242.

Torgersen, S. (1983). Genetic factors in anxiety disorders. *Archives of General Psychiatry, 40,* 1085–1089.

Torgersen, S. (1984). Genetic and nosological aspects of schizotypal and borderline personality disorders: A twin study. *Archives of General Psychiatry, 41,* 546–554.

Torgersen, S. (1986). Genetic factors in moderately severe and mild affective disorder. *Archives of General Psychiatry, 43,* 222–226.

Torrey, E. F. (1973). Is schizophrenia universal? An open question. *Schizophrenia Bulletin, 7,* 53–59.

Torrey, E. F., & Peterson, M. R. (1974). Schizophrenia and the limbic system. *Lancet, ii,* 942–946.

Toubiana, Y. H., Milgram, N. A., Strich, Y., & Edelstein, A. (1988). Crisis intervention in a school-community disaster: Principles and practice. *Journal of Community Psychology, 16,* 228–240.

Tradgold, A. F. (1914). *Mental deficiency.* New York: Wainwood.

Treffert, D. A. (1988). The idiot savant: A review of the syndrome. *American Journal of Psychiatry, 145,* 563–572.

Treiber, F. A., & Lahey, B. B. (1983). Toward a behavioral model of academic remediation with learning disabled children. *Journal of Learning Disabilities, 16,* 111–116.

Trites, R. L., & Caprade, K. (1983). Evidence for an independent syndrome of hyperactivity. *Journal of Child Psychology and Psychiatry, 24,* 573–586.

Tross, S., & Hirsch, D. A. (1988). Psychological distress and neuropsychological complications of HIV infection and AIDS. *American Psychologist, 43,* 929–934.

Tross, S., Price, R. W., Thaler, H. T., Gold, J. V., Hirsch, D. A., & Sidtis, J. J. (1988). Neuropsychological characterization of the AIDS dementia complex: A preliminary report. *AIDS, 2,* 81–88.

Trunnell, E. P., Tuner, C. W., & Keye, W. R. (1988). A comparison of the psychological and hormonal factors in women with and without premenstrual syndrome. *Journal of Abnormal Psychology, 97,* 429–436.

Tsai, M., Feldman-Summers, S., & Edgar, M. (1979). Childhood molestation variables related to differential impact of psychosexual functioning in adult women. *Journal of Abnormal Psychology, 88,* 407–417.

Tucker, J. A., Vuchinich, R. E., & Sobell, M. B. (1981). Alcohol consumption as a self-handicapping strategy. *Journal of Abnormal Psychology, 90,* 220–230.

Turk, D., Meichenbaum, D., & Genest, M. (1983). *Pain and behavioral medicine: A cognitive behavioral perspective.* New York: Guilford Press.

Turk, D., & Thomas, R. (1986). Assessment of cognitive factors in chronic pain: A worthwhile enterprise? *Journal of Clinical Psychology, 54,* 760–768.

Turner, J. A., & Chapman, C. R. (1982a). Psychological interventions for chronic pain: A critical review: I. Relaxation training and biofeedback. *Pain, 12,* 1–21.

Turner, J. A., & Chapman, C. R. (1982b). Psychological interventions for chronic pain: A critical review: II. Operant conditioning, hypnosis, and cognitive-behavior therapy. *Pain, 12,* 23–46.

Turner, R. J., & Wagonfield, M. O. (1967). Occupational mobility and schizophrenia. *American Sociological Review, 32,* 104–113.

Turner, S. A., Daniels, J. L., & Hollandsworth, J. G. (1985). The effects of a multicomponent smoking cessation program with chronic obstructive pulmonary disease outpatients. *Addictive Behaviors, 10,* 87–90.

Turner, S. M., & Beidel, D. C. (1989). Social phobia: Clinical syndrome, diagnosis, and comorbidity. *Clinical Psychology Review, 9,* 3–18.

Turner, S. M., Beidel, D. C., & Costello, A. (1987). Psychopathology in the offspring of anxiety disorder patients. *Journal of Consulting and Clinical Psychology, 55,* 229–235.

Turner, S. M., Beidel, D. C., Dancu, C. V., & Keys, D. J. (1986). Psychopathology of social phobia and comparison to avoidant personality disorder. *Journal of Abnormal Psychology, 95,* 389–394.

Turner, S. M., & Luber, R. F. (1980). The token economy in day hospital settings: Contingency management or information feedback. *Journal of Behavior Therapy and Experimental Psychiatry, 11,* 89–94.

Turner, S. M., McCann, B. S., Beidel, D. C., & Mezzich, J. E. (1986). DSM-III classification of the anxiety disorders: A psychometric study. *Journal of Abnormal Psychology, 95,* 169–172.

Turns, D. M. (1985). Epidemiology of phobic and obsessive-compulsive disorders among adults. *American Journal of Psychotherapy, 39,* 360–370.

Uebersax, J. S. (1987). ECT results and meta-analysis. *American Journal of Psychiatry, 144,* 255–256.

Ullmann, L. P., & Krasner, L. (1969). *A psychological approach to abnormal behavior.* Englewood Cliffs, NJ: Prentice Hall.

Ullmann, L. P., & Krasner, L. (1975). *A psychological approach to abnormal behavior* (2nd ed.). Englewood Cliffs, NJ: Prentice Hall.

Underwood, B., & Moore, B. S. (1981). Sources of behavioral consistency. *Journal of Personality and Social Psychology, 40,* 780–785.

United States Bureau of the Census (1976). *Demographic aspects of aging and the older population in the United States* (Current Population Reports, Series P-23, No. 59). Washington, DC: U.S. Government Printing Office.

United States Bureau of the Census (1986). *Statistical Abstract of the United States: 1986.* Washington, DC: U.S. Government Printing Office.

United States Bureau of the Census (1989). *Statistical Abstract of the United States: 1989* (109th ed.). Washington, DC: U.S. Government Printing Office.

United States Department of Health and Human Services (1982). *The health consequences of smoking: A report of the Surgeon General.* Washington, DC: U.S. Public Health Service, Office on Smoking and Health.

United States Department of Health and Human Services (1985). *The health consequences of smoking: Cancer and chronic lung disease in the workplace: A report of the Surgeon General* (DHHS Publication No. PHS 85–50207). Washington, DC: U.S. Government Printing Office.

United States Department of Health and Human Services (1986). *Surgeon General's Report on AIDS.* Washington, DC: U.S. Government Printing Office.

United States Department of Health, Education, and Welfare (1979). *Smoking and Health: A report of the Surgeon General* (Department of Health, Education, and Welfare, Public Health Service, Office on Smoking and Health; DHEW Publication No. PHS 79–50066). Washington, DC: U.S. Government Printing Office.

Vaillant, G. E. (1983). *The natural history of alcoholism*. Cambridge, MA: Harvard University Press.

Vaillant, G. E., & Milofsky, E. S. (1982). The etiology of alcoholism. *American Psychologist, 37,* 494–503.

Valenstein, E. S. (1978, July). Science-fiction fantasy and the brain. *Psychology Today,* pp. 28–39.

Vallis, M., McCabe, S. B., & Shaw, B. F. (1986, June). *The relationships between therapist skill in cognitive therapy and general therapy skill.* Paper presented to the Society for Psychotherapy Research, Wellesley, MA.

Van Den Hout, M., Emmelkamp, P., Kraaykamp, H., & Griez, E. (1988). Behavioral treatment of obsessive-compulsives: Inpatient vs. outpatient. *Behaviour Research and Therapy, 26,* 331–332.

Van Den Hout, M. A., van Der Molen, M., Griez, E., Lousberg, H., & Nansen, A. (1987). Reduction of CO_2-induced anxiety in panic attacks after repeated CO_2 exposure. *American Journal of Psychiatry, 144,* 788–791.

van Der Molen, G. M., Van Den Hout, M. A., Vroemen, J., Loustberg, H., and others (1986). Cognitive determinants of lactate-induced anxiety. *Behaviour Research and Therapy, 24,* 677–680.

Van Dyke, C., & Byck, R. (1982). Cocaine. *Scientific American, 44*(3), 128–141.

Van Kammen, D. P. (1977). γ-Aminobutyric acid (GABA) and the dopamine hypothesis of schizophrenia. *American Journal of Psychiatry, 134,* 138–143.

Van Kammen, D. P., Van Kammen, W. B., Mann, L. L., Seppala, T., & Linnoila, M. (1986). Dopamine metabolism in the cerebrospinal fluid of drug-free schizophrenic patients with and without cortical atrophy. *Archives of General Psychiatry, 43,* 978–983.

Van Praag, H. M. (1988). Editorial: Biological psychiatry audited. *Journal of Nervous and Mental Disease, 176,* 196–199.

Vandenberg, S. G., Singer, S. M., & Pauls, D. L. (1986). *The heredity of behavior disorders in adults and children.* New York: Plenum.

Vaughn, C. E., & Leff, J. P. (1976). The influence of family and social factors on the course of psychiatric illness: A comparison of schizophrenic and depressed neurotic patients. *British Journal of Psychiatry, 129,* 125–137.

Vaughn, C. E., & Leff, J. P. (1981). Patterns of emotional response in relatives of schizophrenic patients. *Schizophrenia Bulletin, 7,* 43–44.

Vaughn, C. E., Snyder, K. S., Jones, S., Freeman, W. B., & Falloon, I. R. H. (1984). Family factors in schizophrenic relapse: A California replication of the British research on expressed emotion. *Archives of General Psychiatry, 41,* 1169–1177.

Venables, P. H. (1964). Input dysfunction in schizophrenia. In B. A. Maher (Ed.), *Progress in experimental personality research, Vol. 1* (pp. 1–47). New York: Academic Press.

Venables, P. H. (1984). Cerebral mechanisms, autonomic responsiveness, and attention in schizophrenia. In W. D. Spaulding & J. K. Cole (Eds.), *Nebraska symposium on motivation, 1983: Theories of schizophrenia and psychosis* (pp. 47–91). Lincoln: University of Nebraska Press.

Vestre, N. D. (1984). Irrational beliefs and self-reported depressed mood. *Journal of Abnormal Psychology, 93,* 239–241.

Victor, M., & Adams, R. (1953). The effect of alcohol on the nervous system. *Association of Nervous and Mental Disease, 32,* 526–573.

Victor, M., Adams, R., & Collins, G. (1971). *The Wernicke-Korsakoff syndrome.* Philadelphia: F. A. Davis.

Visintainer, M. A., Volpicelli, J. R., & Seligman, M. E. P. (1982). Tumor rejection in rats after inescapable or escapable shock. *Science, 216,* 437–439.

Vogler, G. P., DeFries, J. C., & Decker, S. N. (1985). Family history as an indicator of risk for reading disability. *Journal of Learning Disabilities, 18,* 419–421.

Vogler, R. E., Compton, J. V., & Weissbach, T. A. (1975). Integrated behavior change techniques for alcoholics. *Journal of Consulting and Clinical Psychology, 43,* 233–243.

Volberg, R. A., & Steadman, H. J. (1988). Refining prevalence estimates of pathological gambling. *American Journal of Psychiatry, 145,* 502–505.

Voors, A. W., Srinivasan, S. R., Hunter, S. M., Webber, L. S., Sklov, M. C., & Berenson, G. S. (1982). Smoking, oral contraceptives, and serum lipid and lipoprotein levels in youths. *Preventive Medicine, 11,* 1–12.

Vuchinich, R. E., & Tucker, J. A. (1988). Contributions from behavioral theories of choice to an analysis of alcohol abuse. *Journal of Abnormal Psychology, 97,* 181–195.

Vuchinich, R. E., Tucker, J. A., & Rudd, E. J. (1987). Preference for alcohol consumption as a function of amount and delay of alternative reward. *Journal of Abnormal Psychology, 96,* 259–263.

Wachtel, P. L. (1982). What can dynamic therapies contribute to behavior therapy? *Behavior Therapy, 13,* 594–609.

Wadden, T. A., & Stunkard, A. J. (1988). Controlled trial of very low calorie diet, behavior therapy, and their combination in the treatment of obesity. *Journal of Consulting and Clinical Psychology, 54,* 482–488.

Wadden, T. A., Stunkard, & Liebschutz, J. (1988). Three-year follow-up of the treatment of obesity by very low calorie diet, behavior therapy, and their combination. *Journal of Consulting and Clinical Psychology, 56,* 925–928.

Wagner, R. K., & Torgesen, J. K. (1987). The nature of phonological processing and its causal role in the acquisition of reading skills. *Psychological Bulletin, 101,* 192–212.

Waldinger, R. J., & Gunderson, J. G. (1984). Complete psychotherapies with borderline patients. *American Journal of Psychotherapy, 38,* 190–202.

Waldron, I. (1976). Why do women live longer than men? Part I. *Journal of Human Stress, 2,* 2–13.

Walen, S. R., DiGiuseppe, R., & Wessler, R. L. (1980). *A practitioner's guide to rational-emotive therapy.* New York: Oxford University Press.

Walker, B. B. (1983). Treating stomach disorders: Can we reinstate regulatory processes? In W. E. Whitehead & R. Holzl (Eds.), *Psychophysiology of the gastrointestinal tract.* New York: Plenum.

Walker, C. E., Hedberg, A., Clement, P. W., & Wright, L. (1981). *Clinical procedures for behavior therapy.* Englewood Cliffs, NJ: Prentice Hall.

Walker, E., & Emery, E. (1983). Infants at risk for psychopathology: Offspring or schizophrenic parents. *Child Development, 54,* 1269–1285.

Walker, W. B., & Franzini, L. R. (1985). Low-risk aversive group treatments, physiological feedback, and booster treatments for smoking cessation. *Behavior Therapy, 16,* 263–274.

Wallace, C. J., & Liberman, R. P. (1985). Social skills training for patients with schizophrenia: A controlled clinical trial. *Psychiatry Research, 15,* 239–247.

Wallace, C. J., and others (1980). A review of skills training with schizophrenic patients. *Schizophrenia Bulletin, 6,* 42–63.

Wallace, J. (1985). The alcoholism controversy. *American Psychologist, 40,* 372–373.

Walsh, B. T., and others (1984). Treatment of bulimia with phenelzine: A double-blind, placebo-controlled study. *Archives of General Psychiatry, 41,* 1105–1109.

Walsh, R. N., and others (1981). The menstrual cycle, sex and academic performance. *Archives of General Psychiatry, 38,* 219–221.

Wardle, J., & Beales, S. (1988). Control and loss of control over eating: An experimental investigation. *Journal of Abnormal Psychology, 97,* 35–40.

Warner, R. (1989). Deinstitutionalization: How did we get where we are? *Journal of Social Issues, 45,* 17–30.

Waterhouse, L., & Fein, D. (1984). Developmental trends in cognitive skills for children diagnosed as autistic and schizophrenic. *Child Development, 55,* 236–248.

Watson, J. B. (1924). *Behaviorism.* New York: W. W. Norton & Co., Inc.

Watson, J. B., & Rayner, R. (1920). Conditioned emotional reactions. *Journal of Experimental Psychology, 3,* 1–14.

Watson, J. D., & Crick, F. H. C. (1953). Molecular structure of nucleic acids: A structure for deoxyribose nucleic acid. *Nature, 171,* 737–738.

Watson, S. J., and others (1978). Effects of naloxone on schizophrenia: Reductions in hallucinations in a subpopulation of subjects. *Science, 201,* 73–76.

Watt, D. C. (1982). The search for genetic linkage in schizophrenia. *British Journal of Psychiatry, 140,* 532–537.

Watt, N. F., Grubb, T. W., & Erlenmeyer-Kimling, L. (1982). Social, emotional, and intellectual behavior among children at high risk for schizophrenia. *Journal of Consulting and Clinical Psychology, 50,* 171–181.

Wechsler, D. (1945). A standardized memory scale for clinical use. *Journal of Psychology, 19,* 87–95.

Wechsler, D. (1975). Intelligence defined and undefined: A relativistic appraisal. *American Psychologist, 30,* 135–139.

Wehr, T. A., Skwewrrer, R. G., Jacobsen, F. M., Sack, D. A., & Rosenthal, N. E. (1987). Eye versus skin phototherapy of seasonal affective disorder. *American Journal of Psychiatry, 144,* 753–757.

Weinberg, J., & Levine, S. (1980). Psychobiology of coping in animals: The effects of predictability. In S. Levine & H. Ursin (Eds.), *Coping and health.* New York: Plenum.

Weinberg, R. S., Yukelson, S., & Jackson, A. (1980). Effect of public and private efficacy expectations on competitive performance. *Journal of Sports Psychology, 2,* 340–349.

Weinberger, D. R. (1984). CAT-scan findings in schizophrenia: Speculation on the meaning of it all. *Journal of Psychiatric Research, 18,* 477–490.

Weinberger, D. R. (1987). Implications of normal brain development for the pathogenesis of schizophrenia. *Archives of General Psychiatry, 44,* 660–669.

Weinberger, D. R., Bigelow, L. B., Kleinman, J. E., Klein, S. T., Rosenblatt, J. E., & Wyatt, R. J. (1980). Cerebral ventricular enlargement in chronic schizophrenia: An association with poor response to treatment. *Archives of General Psychiatry, 37,* 11–13.

Weinberger, D. R., Wagner, R. L., & Wyatt, R. J. (1983). Neuropathological studies of schizophrenia. A selective review. *Schizophrenia Bulletin, 9,* 193–212.

Weinberger, D. R., & Wyatt, R. J. (1982). Cerebral ventricular size: A biological marker for subtyping chronic schizophrenia. In E. Usdin & I. T. Hanin (Eds.), *Biological markers in psychiatry and neurology* (pp. 505–512). New York: Pergamon Press.

Weiner, B. A. (1985). The insanity defense: Historical development and present status. *Behavioral Sciences and the Law, 3,* 3–35.

Weiner, M. (1989, November 26). Evidence points to aluminum's link with Alzheimer's disease. *The New York Times,* p. C12.

Weiner, M. (1988). A crisis as a challenge. In M. K. Aronson (Ed.), *Understanding Alzheimer's disease.* New York: Scribner's.

Weiner, R. D. (1984). Convulsive therapy: 50 years later. *American Journal of Psychiatry, 141,* 1078–1079.

Weiner, R. D., and others (1984). ECT stimulus parameters and electrode placement: Relevance to therapeutic and adverse effects. In B. Lerer,

R. D. Weiner, & R. H. Belmaker (Eds.), *ECT: Basic mechanisms*. London: John Libby.

Weintraub, S. (1987). Risk factors in schizophrenia: The Stony Brook High-Risk Project. *Schizophrenia Bulletin, 13*, 439–450.

Weintraub, S., & Neale, J. M. (1984). Social behavior of children at risk for schizophrenia. In N. Watt, E. J. Anthony, L. C. Wynne, & J. E. Rolf (Eds.), *Children at risk for schizophrenia: A longitudinal perspective* (pp. 279–285). New York: Cambridge University Press.

Weisman, A., & Worden, W. (1976). The existential plight in cancer: Significance of the first 100 days. *International Journal of Psychiatry and Medicine, 7*, 1–15.

Weisman, A. D. (1979). *Coping with Cancer*. New York: McGraw-Hill.

Weiss, G. (1985). Follow-up studies on outcome of hyperactive children. *Psychopharmacology Bulletin, 21*, 169–177.

Weiss, G., Minde, K., Werry, J. S., Douglas, V., & Nemeth, E. (1971). Studies on the hyperactive child: V. Five-year follow-up. *Archives of General Psychiatry, 24*, 409–414.

Weiss, J. M. (1972). Psychological factors in stress and disease. *Scientific American, 226*, 104–113.

Weiss, J. M. (1982, August). *A model for the neurochemical study of depression*. Paper presented to the American Psychological Association, Washington, DC.

Weiss, J. M., Glazer, H. I., & Pohorecky, L. A. (1976). Coping behavior and neurochemical changes: An alternative explanation for the original "learned helplessness" experiments. In G. Serban & A. Kling (Eds.), *Animal models of human psychobiology*. New York: Plenum.

Weiss, M., & Richter-Heinrich, E. (1985). Type A behavior in a population of Berlin, GDR. Its relation to personality and sociological variables, and association to coronary heart disease. *Activitas Nervosa Superior (Prague), 27*, 7–9.

Weiss, R. D., & Mirin, S. M. (1987). *Cocaine*. Washington, DC: American Psychiatric Press.

Weissman, A. N., & Beck, A. T. (1978, November). *Development and validation of the Dysfunctional Attitudes Scale: A preliminary investigation*. Paper presented at the meeting of the American Educational Research Association, Toronto, Canada.

Weissman, M. (1987). Epidemiology of depression: Frequency, risk groups and risk factors. In *Perspectives on depressive disorders*. Rockville, MD: National Institute of Mental Health.

Weissman, M., and others (1981). Depressed outpatients. Results one year after treatment with drugs and/or interpersonal psychotherapy. *Archives of General Psychology, 18*, 51–55.

Weisz, J. R., Weiss, B., Alicke, M. D., & Klotz, M. L. (1987). Effectiveness of psychotherapy with children and adolescents: A meta-analysis for clinicians. *Journal of Consulting and Clinical Psychology, 55*, 542–549.

Wells, K. C., Hersen, M., Bellack, A. S., & Himmelhoch, J. H. (1979). Social skills training in unipolar nonpsychotic depression. *American Journal of Psychiatry, 136*, 131–132.

Wenar, C. (1983). *Psychopathology from infancy through adolescence: A developmental approach*. New York: Random House.

Wender, P. H., & Klein, D. F. (1981). *Mind, mood, and medicine: A guide to the new biopsychiatry*. New York: Farrar, Straus & Giroux.

Wender, P. H., Rosenthal, D., Kety, S. S., Schulsinger, F., & Welner, J. (1974). Cross-fostering: A research strategy for clarifying the role of genetic and experiential factors in the etiology of schizophrenia. *Archives of General Psychiatry, 30*, 121–128.

Wenzlaff, R. M., & Grozier, S. A. (1988). Depression and the magnification of failure. *Journal of Abnormal Psychology, 97*, 90–93.

Werry, J. S. (1979). The childhood psychoses. In H. C. Quay & J. S. Werry (Eds.), *Psychopathologi-

cal disorders of childhood* (2d ed.). New York: Wiley.

Werry, J. S. (1986). Handling suicide threats in children and adolescents. *American Journal of Psychiatry, 143*, 1193–1194.

Wertlieb, D., Weigel, C., & Feldstein, M. (1987). Stress, social support, and behavior symptoms in middle childhood. *Journal of Clinical Child Psychology, 16*, 204–211.

West, D. W., Graham, S., Swanson, M., & Wilkinson, G. (1977). Five year follow-up of a smoking withdrawal clinic population. *American Journal of Public Health, 67*, 536–544.

West, M. A. (1985). Meditation and somatic arousal reduction. *American Psychologist, 40*, 717–719.

West, M. O., & Prinz, R. J. (1987). Parental alcoholism and childhood psychopathology. *Psychological Bulletin, 102*, 204–218.

Westermeyer, J. (1987). Cross-cultural factors in clinical assessment. *Journal of Consulting and Clinical Psychology, 55*, 471–478.

Whalen, C. K., Collins, B. E., Henker, B., Alkus, S. R., Adams, D., & Stapp, J. (1978). Behavior observations of hyperactive children and methylphenidate (Ritalin) effects in systematically structured classroom environments: Now you see them, now you don't. *Journal of Pediatric Psychology, 3*, 177–187.

Whalen, C. K., & Henker, B. (1985). The social worlds of hyperactive (ADDH) children. *Clinical Psychology Review, 5*, 447–478.

Whalen, C. K., Kenker, B., Swanson, J. M., Granger, D., Kliewer, W., & Spencer, J. (1987). Natural social behaviors in hyperactive children: Dose effects of methylphenidate. *Journal of Consulting and Clinical Psychology, 55*, 187–193.

Whiffen, V. E. (1988). Vulnerability to postpartum depression: A prospective multivariate study. *Journal of Abnormal Psychology, 97*, 467–474.

White, S., Halpin, B. M., Strom, G. A., & Santilli, G. (1988). Behavioral comparisons of young sexually abused, neglected, and nonreferred children. *Journal of Clinical Child Psychology, 17*, 53–61.

Whitehead, A., Mathews, A., & Ramage, M. (1987). The treatment of sexually unresponsive women: A comparative evaluation. *Behaviour Research and Therapy, 25*, 195–205.

Whitehead, W. E., & Bosmajian, L. S. (1982). Behavioral medicine approaches to gastrointestinal disorders. *Journal of Consulting and Clinical Psychology, 50*, 972–983.

Whitehouse, P. J., Price, D. L., Struble, R. G., Clark, A. W., Coyle, J. T., & DeLong, M. R. (1982). Alzheimer's disease and senile dementia: Loss of neurons in the basal forebrain. *Science, 215*, 1237–1239.

Whitlock, F. A. (1967). The aetiology of hysteria. *Acta Psychiatric Scandinavia, 43*, 144–162.

Whybrow, P. C., & Prange, A. J. (1981). A hypothesis of thyroid-catecholamine-receptor interaction. *Archives of General Psychiatry, 38*, 106–113.

Wiens, A. N., & Menustik, C. E. (1983). Treatment outcome and patient characteristics in an aversion therapy program for alcoholism. *American Psychologist, 38*, 1089–1096.

Wilbur, C. B. (1986). Psychoanalysis and multiple personality disorder. In B. G. Braun (Ed.), *Treatment of multiple personality disorder*. Washington, DC: American Psychiatric Press.

Wilbur, C. S., Hartwell, T. D., & Piserchia, P. V. (1986). The Johnson & Johnson Live for Life Program: Its organization and evaluation plan. In M. F. Cataldo & T. J. Coates (Eds.), *Health promotion and industry: A behavioral medicine perspective* (pp. 338–350). New York: Wiley.

Wildman, B. G., & White, P. A. (1986). Assessment of dysmenorrhea using the Menstrual Symptom Questionnaire: Factor structure and validity. *Behavior Research and Therapy, 24*, 547–551.

Williams, J. B. W. (1985). The Multiaxial system of DSM III: Where did it come from and where

should it go? Its origins and critics. *Archives of General Psychiatry, 42*, 175–180.

Williams, J. M. (1984). *The psychological treatment of depression: A guide to the theory and practice of cognitive-behavior therapy*. New York: Free Press.

Williams, J. M., Little, M. M., Scates, S., & Blockman, N. (1987). Memory complaints and abilities among depressed older adults. *Journal of Consulting and Clinical Psychology, 55*, 595–598.

Williams, L. (1989, November 22). Psychotherapy gaining favor among blacks. *The New York Times*, pp. A1, C7.

Williams, R. (1974, May). Scientific racism and IQ: The silent mugging of the black community. *Psychology Today*, p. 8.

Williams, R., Goldman, M. S., & Williams, D. L. (1981). Expectancy and pharmacological effects of alcohol on human cognitive and motor performance: The compensation for alcohol effect. *Journal of Abnormal Psychology, 90*, 267–270.

Williamson, D. A., Davis, C. J., Goreczny, A. J., & Blouin, D. C. (1989). Body-image disturbances in bulimia nervosa: Influences of actual body size. *Journal of Abnormal Psychology, 98*, 97–99.

Wills, T. A. (1986). Stress and coping in adolescence: Relationships to substance use in urban school samples. *Health Psychology, 5*, 503–530.

Wilson, C. C. (1987). Physiological responses of college students to a pet. *Journal of Nervous and Mental Disease, 175*, 606–612.

Wilson, G. T. (1978). Cognitive-behavior therapy: Paradigm shift or passing phase. In J. P. Foreyt & D. P. Rathjen (Eds.), *Cognitive-behavior therapy: Research and application* (pp. 7–33). New York: Plenum.

Wilson, G. T. (1982). Psychotherapy process and procedure: The behavioral mandate. *Behavior Therapy, 13*, 291–312.

Wilson, G. T. (1986). Cognitive-behavioral and pharmacological therapies for bulimia. In K. D. Brownell & J. P. Foeyt (Eds.), *Handbook of eating disorders* (pp. 450–475). New York: Basic Books.

Wilson, G. T. (1987). Cognitive studies in alcoholism. *Journal of Consulting and Clinical Psychology, 55*, 325–331.

Wilson, G. T. (1988). Alcohol and anxiety. *Behaviour Research and Therapy, 26*, 369–381.

Wilson, G. T., & Abrams, D. B. (1977). Effects of alcohol on social anxiety and physiological arousal: Cognitive versus pharmacological processes. *Cognitive Therapy and Research, 5*, 251–264.

Wilson, G. T., & Lawson, D. M. (1978). Expectancies, alcohol, and sexual arousal in women. *Journal of Abnormal Psychology, 87*, 609–616.

Wilson, G. T., Lawson, D. M., & Abrams, D. B. (1978). Effects of alcohol on sexual arousal in male alcoholics. *Journal of Abnormal Psychology, 87*, 609–616.

Wilson, G. T., Leaf, R. C., & Nathan, P. E. (1975). The aversive control of excessive alcohol consumption by chronic alcoholics in the laboratory setting. *Journal of Applied Behavior Analysis, 8*, 13–26.

Wilson, G. T., & O'Leary, K. D. (1980). *Principles of behavior therapy*. Englewood Cliffs, NJ: Prentice Hall.

Wilson, G. T., Rossiter, E., Kleifield, E. I., & Lindholm, L. (1986). Cognitive-behavioral treatment of bulimia nervosa: A controlled evaluation. *Behaviour Research and Therapy, 24*, 277–288.

Wilson, J. P. (1977). *Ideology and Crisis: The Vietnam veteran in transition: Part II. Final report to the Disabled Veterans Association*. Cleveland: Cleveland State University.

Wilson, R. S., & Kaszniak, A. W. (1986). Longitudinal changes: Progressive idiopathic dementia. In L. W. Poon (Ed.), *Handbook for clinical memory* assessment of older adults (pp. 285–294). Washington, DC: American Psychological Association.

Windle, M. (1990). A longitudinal study of antisocial behaviors in early adolescence as predictors of later adolescent substance use: Gender and ethnic group differences. Journal of Abnormal Psychology, 99, 86–91.

Wines, M. (1988, September 4). Mental institutions may be as empty as they'll ever be. The New York Times, p. E.6.

Wing, J., & Bebbington, P. (1985). Epidemiology of depression. In E. E. Beckham & W. R. Leber (Eds.), Handbook of depression: Treatment, assessment, and research (pp. 765–794). Homewood, IL: Dorsey Press.

Wing, J., & Nixon, J. (1975). Discriminating symptoms in schizophrenia. Archives of General Psychiatry, 32, 853–859.

Wing, L. (1972). Autistic children: A guide for parents and professionals. New York: Brunner/Mazel.

Wirtz, P. W., & Harrell, A. V. (1987a). Effects of postassault exposure to attack-similar stimuli on long-term recovery of victims. Journal of Consulting and Clinical Psychology, 55, 10–16.

Wirtz, P. W., & Harrell, A. V. (1987b). Victim and crime characteristics, coping responses, and short- and long-term recovery from victimization. Journal of Consulting and Clinical Psychology, 55, 866–871.

Wise, E. H., & Barnes, D. R. (1986). The relationship among life events, dysfunctional attitudes, and depression. Cognitive Therapy and Research, 10, 257–266.

Wise, R. A. (1988). The neurobiology of craving. Journal of Abnormal Psychology, 97, 117–132.

Wise, T. P. (1978). Where the public peril begins: A survey of psychotherapists to determine the effects of Tarasoff. Stanford Law Review, 135, 165–190.

Withers, L. E., & Kaplan, D. W. (1987). Adolescents who attempt suicide: A retrospective clinical chart review of hospitalized patients. Professional Psychology: Research and Practice, 18, 391–393.

Witkin, H. A., and others (1976). XYY and XXY men: Criminality and aggression. Science, 193, 547–555.

Wojcik, J. V. (1988). Social learning predictors of the avoidance of smoking relapse. Addictive Behaviors, 13, 177–180.

Wolchick, S. A., Beggs, V., Wincze, J. P., Sakheim, D. K., Barlow, D. H., & Mavissakalian, M. (1980). The effects of emotional arousal on subsequent sexual arousal in men. Journal of Abnormal Psychology, 89, 595–598.

Wolf, E. (1980). Learning theory and psychoanalysis. In J. Marmor & S. M. Woods (Eds.), The interface between the psychodynamic and behavioral therapies. New York: Plenum.

Wolf, L., & Goldberg, B. (1986). Autistic children group: An 8- to 24-year follow-up study. Canadian Journal of Psychiatry, 31, 550–556.

Wolfe, B. E., & Goldfried, M. R. (1988). Research on psychotherapy integration: Recommendations and conclusions from an NIMH workshop. Journal of Consulting and Clinical Psychology, 56, 448–451.

Wolfe, L. (1981). The Cosmo report. New York: Arbor House.

Wolinsky, J. (1982). Responsibility can delay aging. APA Monitor, 13, 14, 41.

Wolpe, J. (1958). Psychotherapy by reciprocal inhibition. Stanford, CA: Stanford University Press.

Wolpe, J. (1973). The practice of behavior therapy. New York: Pergamon Press.

Wolpe, J. (1985). Existential problems and behavior therapy. The Behavior Therapist, 8, 126–127.

Wolpe, J., & Lazarus, A. A. (1966). Behavior therapy techniques. New York: Pergamon Press.

Wolpe, J., & Rachman, S. (1960). Psychoanalytic "evidence": A critique based on Freud's case of Little Hans. Journal of Nervous and Mental Disease, 131, 135–147.

Wolraich, N. L., Milich, R., Stumbo, P., & Schultz, F. (1985). Effects of sucrose ingestion on the behavior of hyperactive boys. Journal of Pediatrics, 106, 675–681.

Wong, B. Y. L. (1986). Problems and issues in the definition of learning disabilities. In J. K. Torgeson & B. Y. L. Wong (Eds.), Psychological and educational perspectives on learning disabilities (pp. 3–26). Orlando, FL: Academic Press.

Wong, S. E., Massel, H. K., Mosk, M. D., & Liberman, R. P. (1986). Behavioral approaches to the treatment of schizophrenia. In G. D. Burrows, T. R. Norman, & G. Rubenstein (Eds.), Handbook of studies on schizophrenia (pp. 79–100). New York: Elsevier.

Wood, J. M., & Bootzin, R. R. (1990). The prevalence of nightmares and their independence from anxiety. Journal of Abnormal Psychology, 99, 64–68.

Wood, K. (1986). 5HT transport and the mediation of actional antidepressants. Do antidepressant treatments facilitate 5HT transport? In J. F. W. Deakin (Ed.), The biology of depression (pp. 100–120). Oxford, England: Alden Press.

Woodruff, R. A., Clayton, P. J., & Guze, S. B. (1975). Is everyone depressed? American Journal of Psychiatry, 132, 627–628.

Woods, S. W., Charney, D. S., McPherson, C. A., Gradman, A. H., & Heninger, G. R. (1987). Situational panic attacks: Behavioral, physiologic, and biochemical characterization. Archives of General Psychiatry, 44, 365–375.

Woody, G. E., McLellan, A. T., Luborsky, L., & O'Brien, C. P. (1987). Twelve-month follow-up of psychotherapy for opiate dependence. American Psychologist, 144, 590–596.

World Health Organization (1982). Trends of mortality from ischaemic heart disease and other cardiovascular diseases in 27 countries from 1968 to 1977. World Health Statistics Quarterly, 35, 11–47.

Wright, L. (1988). The Type A behavior pattern and coronary artery disease: Quest for the active ingredients and the elusive mechanism. American Psychologist, 43, 2–14.

Wurtman, R. J., & Wurtman, J. J. (1984). Nutrients, neurotransmitter synthesis, and the control of food intake. In J. A. Stunkard & E. Stellar (Eds.), Eating and its disorders (pp. 77–86). New York: Raven Press.

Wyatt v. Stickney, 334 F. Supp. 1341 (1971).

Wynne, L. C., Cole, R. E., & Perkins, P. (1987). University of Rochester Child and Family Study: Risk research in progress. Schizophrenia Bulletin, 13, 463–476.

Wynne, L. C., Singer, M. T., Bartko, J. J., & Tookey, M. L. (1977). Schizophrenics and their families: Research on parental communication. In J. M. Tanner (Ed.), Developments in psychiatric research (pp. 254–286). London: Hoder & Stoughton.

Yahr, M. D. (1976). Evaluation of long-term therapy in Parkinson's disease: Mortality and therapeutic efficacy. In M. Birkmayer & L. Hirnykiewicz (Eds.), Advances in Parkinsonism (pp. 443–445). Basel: Roche.

Yalom, I. D., Lunde, D. T., Moos, R. H., & Hamburg, D. A. (1968). "Postpartum blues" syndrome. Archives of General Psychiatry, 18, 16–27.

Yamaguchi, F., Meyer, J. S., Yamamoto, M., Sakai, F., & Shaw, T. (1980). Noninvasive regional cerebral blood flow measurements in dementia. Archives of Neurology, 37, 410–418.

Youngberg v. Romeo, 102 S. Ct. 2452, 2463 (1982).

Yuwiler, A., & Freedman, D. X. (1987). Neurotransmitter research in autism. In E. Schloper & G. B. Mesibov (Eds.), Neurobiological Issues in Autism. New York: Plenum.

Zaiden, J. (1982). Psychodynamic therapy: Clinical applications. In A. J. Rush (Ed.), Short-term psychotherapies for depression. New York: Guilford Press.

Zarski, J. J. (1984). Hassles and health: A replication. Health Psychology, 3, 243–251.

Zatz, S., & Chassin, L. (1985). Cognitions of test-anxious children under naturalistic test-taking conditions. Journal of Consulting and Clinical Psychology, 53, 393–401.

Zautra, A. J., Guenther, R. T., & Chartier, G. M. (1985). Attributions of real and hypothetical events: Their relation to self-esteem and depression. Journal of Abnormal Psychology, 94, 530–540.

Zeiss, A. M., & Lewinsohn, P. M. (1986). Adapting behavioral treatment for depression to meet the needs of the elderly. The Clinical Psychologist, 98–100.

Zellner, D. A., Harner, D. E., & Adler, R. L. (1989). Effects of eating abnormalities and gender on perceptions of desirable body shape. Journal of Abnormal Psychology, 98, 93–96.

Zilbergeld, B., & Evans, M. (1980, August). The inadequacy of Masters & Johnson. Psychology Today, pp. 29–34, 47–53.

Zillmann, D., & Bryant, J. (1983). Effects of massive exposure to pornography. In N. M. Malamuth & E. Donnerstein (Eds.), Pornography and sexual aggression. New York: Academic Press.

Zimmerman, M., & Coryell, W. (1986). Dysfunctional attitudes in endogenous and nonendogenous depressed inpatients. Cognitive Therapy and Research, 10, 339–346.

Zubin, J., & Spring, B. (1977). Vulnerability—New view of schizophrenia. Journal of Abnormal Psychology, 86, 103–126.

Zuckerman, D. M., Colby, A., Waren, N. C., & Lazerson, J. S. (1986). The prevalence of bulimia among college students. American Journal of Public Health, 76, 1135–1137.

Zuckerman, M. (1974). The sensation-seeking motive. In B. Maher (Ed.), Progress in experimental personality research, 7. New York: Academic Press.

Zuckerman, M. (1979). Sensation Seeking: Beyond the optimal level of arousal. Hillsdale, NJ: Erlbaum.

Zuckerman, M. (1980). Sensation seeking. In H. London & J. Exner (Eds.), Dimensions of personality. New York: Wiley.

Zyzanski, S. J., Jenkins, C. D., Ryan, T. J., Flessas, A., & Everist, M. (1976). Psychological correlates of coronary angiographic findings. Archives of Internal Medicine, 136, 1234–1237.

Photo Acknowledgments

CHAPTER 1 Page 1, M. de Camp/The Image Bank; p. 2 top, Bob Daemmrich/Stock, Boston; p. 2 bottom, John Griffin/The Image Works; p. 3, Jack Fields/Photo Researchers; p. 4, Dean A. Bramson/Stock, Boston; p. 6, American Museum of Natural History; p. 7, The Granger Collection; p. 8, The Granger Collection; p. 9, The Granger Collection; p. 10 left, The Granger Collection; p. 10 right, National Library of Medicine; p. 11, The Bettmann Archive; p. 14 left, The Granger Collection; p. 14 right, The Granger Collection; p. 15, The Granger Collection; p. 16 top, Historical American Psychology Archives/University of Akron, Ohio; p. 16 bottom left, The Bettmann Archive; p. 16 bottom right, Courtesy of Brooks/Cole Publishing Company, Pacific Grove, California; p. 20, Rogers/Monkmeyer Press.

CHAPTER 2 Page 34, Image Factory-Explorer/Photo Researchers; William H. Mullins/Photo Researchers; p. 40, Elizabeth Crews/The Image Works; p. 41, Fredrik D. Bodin/Stock, Boston; p. 42, The Bettmann Archive; p. 43, The Bettmann Archive; p. 46, The Granger Collection; p. 49, Ken Heyman; p. 50 left, © Joel Gordon 1990; p. 50 right, Frank Siteman/Stock, Boston; p. 52 left, Allsport U.S.A.; p. 52 right, Michael Grecco/Stock, Boston; p. 55, Courtesy, Brandeis University; p. 56, Harriet Gans/The Image Works; p. 57, Aaron T. Beck; p. 59, Austrian Information Service, New York; p. 60, Susan Lapides/Design Conception; p. 62, Gabor Demjen/Stock, Boston; p. 64, Peter Southwick/Stock, Boston; p. 73, Bob Daemmrich/Stock, Boston.

CHAPTER 3 Page 78, Pete Turner/The Image Bank; p. 82, Judy Canty/Stock, Boston; p. 87, The Bettmann Archive; p. 88, Frank Siteman/Jeroboam, Inc.; p. 94, Honeywell Inc.; p. 105, Lacks (1984), p. 34, copyright 1984 by John Wiley & Sons, reprinted by permission; p. 108, Susan Rosenberg/Photo Researchers; p. 109, Cary Wolinski/Stock, Boston; p. 112 left, Dan McCoy/Rainbow; p. 112 right, Stacy Pick/Stock, Boston; p. 313 top left, Brookhaven National Laboratory; p. 313 top right, G. Zimbel/Monkmeyer Press (Mtl. Neurological Inst.); p. 313 bottom right, Archive of General Psychiatry; p. 313 bottom left, Alexander Tsiaras/Science Source/Photo Researchers.

CHAPTER 4 Page 118, Geoffrey Gove/The Image Bank; p. 121, Pete Seaward/Tony Stone Worldwide; p. 124 top, Dan Chidester/The Image Works; p. 124 bottom, Leslie Deeb; p. 125, Dion Ogust/The Image Works; p. 128, Reuters/Bettmann Newsphotos; p. 132, © Joel Gordon; p. 135, Mike Kagan/Monkmeyer Press; p. 139, Carolyn A. McKeone/Photo Researchers; p. 141, Mike Mazzaschi/Stock, Boston; p. 143, Robert Ellison/Black Star; p. 146, Thomas S. England/Photo Researchers.

CHAPTER 5 Page 150, Ellen Schuster/The Image Bank; p. 153, Lester V. Bergman & Associates, Inc.; p. 155 top, © Joel Gordon; p. 155 bottom, © Joel Gordon; p. 157, Dan McCoy/Rainbow; p. 159, Frank Pedrick/The Image Works; p. 160, Jan Lukas/Photo Researchers; p. 162, W. Marc Bernsau/The Image Works; p. 164, Gabe Palmer/The Stock Market; p. 165, Freda Leinwand/Monkmeyer Press; p. 167 top, Tom Bean/The Stock Market; p. 171, Blair Seitz/Photo Researchers; p. 177, © Joel Gordon; p. 179, © Joel Gordon; p. 181, Charles Gatewood/The Image Works.

CHAPTER 6 Page 190, Kristofik Productions/The Image Bank; p. 194, David E. Dempster; p. 196, Suzanne Szasz/Photo Researchers; p. 197 top, David E. Dempster; p. 197 middle, Billy E. Barnes/Stock, Boston; p. 197, bottom, David E. Dempster; p. 202, Wally Eberhart, TSW-Click/Chicago; p. 204, John Vassos Papers, Arents Research Library for Special Collections at Syracuse University; p. 206, Photofest; p. 208, Focus on Sports; p. 216, Van Bucher/Photo Researchers; p. 217, James Wilson/Woodfin Camp & Associates.

CHAPTER 7 Page 224, Geoffrey Gove/The Image Bank; p. 226, AP/Wide World Photos; p. 227 left, Photofest; p. 227 middle, Photofest; p. 227 right, Movie Star News; p. 232, Peter Arnold, Inc.; p. 235, Michael Weisbrot/Stock, Boston; p. 236, AP/Wide World Photos; p. 240, Ray Ellis/Science Source/Photo Researchers; p. 242, UPI/Bettmann Newsphotos; p. 244, The Granger Collection; p. 245, Laima Druskis.

CHAPTER 8 Page 248, Pete Saloutos/The Stock Market; p. 250, © Joel Gordon; p. 252, John Coletti/Stock, Boston; p. 254, Charles Gatewood/Stock, Boston; p. 255, Douglas Goodman/Monkmeyer Press; p. 256, Bob Kalman/The Image Works; p. 260, Mieke Maas/The Image Bank; p. 261, C. Seghers/Photo Researchers; p. 265 top left, Grant DeLuc/Monkmeyer Press; p. 265 top right, Susan Lapides/Design Conceptions; p. 265 bottom, Hugh Rogers/Monkmeyer Press; p. 267, The Seattle Post Intelligencer; p. 272, Willie L. Hill, Jr./Stock, Boston; p. 280, James D. Wilson/Woodfin Camp & Associates; p. 285, Sybil Shackman/Monkmeyer Press.

CHAPTER 9 Page 290, Jeremy Gardiner; p. 293, Tony Savino/The Image Works; p. 296 left, UPI/Bettmann Newsphotos; p. 296 right, Andy Schwartz/Photofest; p. 298 left, AP/Wide World Photos; p. 298 right, The Granger Collection; p. 301 left, The Bettmann Archive; p. 301 right, © Joel Gordon; p. 302, Erika Stone; p. 304, Laima Druskis; p. 308, Mark Antman/Stock, Boston; p. 317, C. Vergara/Photo Researchers; p. 321, Jan Halaska/Photo Researchers.

CHAPTER 10 Page 328, Ilene Astrahan/The Image Bank; p. 331 top, Arlene Collins/Monkmeyer Press; p. 331 bottom, Ken Kaminsky/The Picture Cube; p. 333, © Joel Gordon; p. 334, Carol Lee/Boston/The Picture Cube; p. 339, James W. Hanson, M.D./University of Iowa; p. 342, John Isaac/United Nations Photo; p. 344 left, © Harris & Ewing; p. 344 middle, The Granger Collection; p. 345, © Joel Gordon; p. 349 left, R. J. Reynolds Tobacco Company, Winston-Salem, N.C.; p. 349 right, American Cancer Society; p. 350, Anne Marie Rousseau/The Image Works; p. 352, Charles Gatewood; p. 358 top, Ray Ellis/Photo Researchers; p. 358 bottom, Alan Carey/The Image Works; p. 362, Jay Wiley/Monkmeyer Press; p. 363, Reuters/Bettmann; p. 365, Mark Antman/The Image Works.

CHAPTER 11 Page 372, Geoffrey Gove/The Image Bank; p. 375 left, The Bettmann Archive; p. 375 middle, Paul Fusco, Magnum Photos; p. 375 right, Bob Daemmrich/Stock, Boston; p. 376 top, The Bettmann Archive; p. 376 bottom, UPI/Bettmann; p. 378, Stephen Capra; p. 379, © Joel Gordon; p. 382 left, AP/Wide World Photos; p. 382 right, AP/Wide World Photos; p. 385 top, © Joel Gordon; p. 385 bottom, Laima Druskis; p. 388, Rhoda Sidney; p. 392, Thomas Craig/The Picture Cube; p. 394, from Real People Dolls, Hylands Anatomical Dolls, Inc., 4455 Torrance Blvd., Suite 310, Torrance, Ca 90503; p. 397, Robert V. Eckert, Jr./Stock, Boston; p. 399 top, Frank Siteman/Stock, Boston; p. 399 bottom, UPI/Bettmann; p. 406 top, Didier De Fays/Tony Stone Worldwide; p. 406 bottom, Courtesy Dr. Helen Singer Kaplan.

CHAPTER 12 Page 412, Alfred Gescheidt/The Image Bank; p. 414, The Granger Collection; p. 415, The Granger Collection; p. 422, Peter Ginter/The Image Bank; p. 423, UPI/Bettmann; p. 425 left, Benyas Kaufman/Black Star; p. 425 right, Grunnitus/Monkmeyer Press; p. 426, Mitchell Funk/The Image Bank; p. 429, UPI/Bettmann; p. 437, G. G. Zimbel/Monkmeyer Press; p. 438, Courtesy of Dr. Monte S. Buchsbaum; p. 439 left, Courtesy of Dr. Monte S. Buchsbaum; p. 439 right, Courtesy of Dr. Monte S. Buchsbaum; p. 444, Michael Weisbrot/Stock, Boston; p. 448, Freda Leinwand/Monkmeyer Press.

CHAPTER 13 Page 454, Comstock; p. 457, © Joel Gordon; p. 460, Jeff Persons/Stock, Boston; p. 461, Budd Gray/Stock, Boston; p. 462 left, Lew Merrim/Monkmeyer Press; p. 462 right, Mark Antman/The Image Works; p. 465, SIU/Photo Researchers; p. 468, AP/Wide World Photos; p. 469, CEA-ORSAY/CNRI/Science Photo Library/Photo Researchers; p. 470, David Leah/Science Photo Library/Photo Researchers; p. 471 left, UPI/Bettmann Newsphotos; p. 471 right, UPI/Bettmann Newsphotos; p. 473, The Granger Collection; p. 475, Simon Fraser/Science Photo Library/Photo Researchers; p. 476 left, The Granger Collection; p. 476 right, The Granger Collection.

CHAPTER 14 Page 482, Richard Hutchings/Photo Researchers; p. 488, Erika Stone; p. 490, Mimi Forsyth/Monkmeyer Press; p. 493 top, Alexander Tsiaras/Science Source/Photo Researchers; p. 493 bottom, MacPherson/Monkmeyer Press; p. 496, Susan Lapides/Design Conceptions; p. 499, AP/Wide World Photos; p. 501, Will & Deni McIntyre/Photo Researchers; p. 503, Michael Weisbrot and Family; p. 508, Charles Harbutt/Actuality Inc.; p. 509, Bob Daemmrich/The Image Works; p. 510, Jean Claude Lejeune/Stock, Boston; p. 513, Mieke Maas/The Image Bank; p. 515, Bonnie Schiffman/Onyx; p. 516, Rhoda Sidney/Monkmeyer Press; p. 519, Levi Strauss & Company.

CHAPTER 15 Page 524, Mitchell Funk/The Image Bank; p. 528, Edmund Engelman; p. 529, Erich Hartmann/Magnum Photos; p. 532, Deke Simon/The Real People Press; p. 533, R. Rowan/Photo Researchers; p. 536, Susan Rosenberg/Photo Researchers; p. 538, Dan McCoy/Rainbow; p. 541, Jim Pickerell/TSW-Click/Chicago Ltd.; p. 543, Susan Lapides/Design Conceptions; p. 549, Louis Fernandez/Black Star; p. 550, Photo C. Andy Freeberg; p. 555, Chester Higgins, NYT Pictures; p. 556, Ellis Herwig/Stock, Boston; p. 557, Lionel J. M. Delevingne/Stock, Boston.

CHAPTER 16 Page 560, Mitchell Funk/The Image Bank; p. 562, AP/Wide World Photos; p. 563, David M. Grossman; p. 565, AP/Wide World Photos; p. 566 left, Mark Reinstein/TSW-Click/Chicago Ltd.; p. 566 middle, Peter Southwick/Stock, Boston, p. 566 right, Tom McCarthy/The Picture Cube; p. 567, Photofest; p. 569, AP/World Wide Photos; p. 571, UPI/Bettman News photos; p. 572, Movie Star News; p. 577, AP/Wide World Photos; p. 581, Jerry Howard/Stock, Boston; p. 583 left, Elizabeth Crews/The Image Works; p. 583 middle, Lawrence Migdale/Stock, Boston; p. 583 right, Bob Daemmrich/Stock, Boston; p. 585, Mark Antman/The Image Works; p. 587, Alan Carey/The Image Works.

Index

SUBJECT